A retired U   of General George
biography o
S. Patton. His works of military history are highly regarded on both sides of the
Atlantic: *Decision in Normandy, Bitter Victory: The Battle for Sicily, 1943, World War
II in the Mediterranean, 1942–1945* and *Fatal Decision: Anzio and the Battle for Rome.*

EISENHOWER

ALLIED SUPREME COMMANDER

CARLO D'ESTE

CASSELL

Cassell Military Paperbacks

Cassell
Wellington House, 125 Strand
London WC2R 0BB

First published in the United States in 2002
By Henry Holt and Company, LLC
First published in Great Britain in 2003
By Weidenfeld & Nicolson
This Cassell Military Paperbacks edition 2004

Design by Fritz Metsch
Maps by Paul Pugliese
Frontispiece photograph of Dwight Eisenhower, June 6, 1944
courtesy of the Library of Congress

British Library Cataloguing-in-Publication Data.
A catalogue record for this book is available
from the British Library.

ISBN 0 304 36658 7

Printed and bound in Great Britain by Clays Ltd, St Ives plc

For

SHIRLEY ANN

with love

For

M. S. "BUZ" WYETH, JR.

one of the great editors of our time

In memory of my friend

DAVID S. TERRY,

World War II citizen-soldier, esteemed educator, talented musician, and one who made this world a better place

and

In memory of the victims of the outrage of September 11, 2001

Contents

EISENHOWER

Prologue:
"An Astonishing Man"

Dwight D. Eisenhower endured many dramatic, tension-filled days, but nothing ever exceeded the events leading up to his courageous decision to launch the greatest military invasion in the history of warfare on June 6, 1944. The outcome of the war hinged on its success. Failure was unthinkable but nevertheless entirely possible, as Eisenhower knew only too well.

More than 150,000 Allied troops, nearly six thousand ships of every description, and masses of military hardware were crammed on ships and landing craft, and on airfields, awaiting Eisenhower's "Go" order to commence what he would later term "the great crusade," the cross-Channel operation that was the necessary overture to victory in Europe.

At the last minute the forces of nature intervened when a full-blown gale swept in from the Atlantic Ocean, and on June 4 Eisenhower was forced to postpone D-Day, originally scheduled for June 5, for at least twenty-four hours while the weathermen consulted their charts and received new data before the next weather update. At 4:15 A.M. on the morning of June 5, 1944, the Allied commanders in chief met to learn if the invasion could take place or would have to be postponed indefinitely. When the meteorologists predicted a break in the weather just sufficient to mount the invasion, Eisenhower made a historic decision that set into motion the most vital Allied operation of World War II—the operation that would decide the victor and the vanquished. To go or not to go based on this small window of acceptable weather became the basis for a decision only Eisenhower himself could make. And make it he did, deciding that the invasion must be launched on June 6.

In public Eisenhower exuded confidence; in private, however, he was a seething bundle of nervous energy. "Ike could not have been more anxiety ridden," noted his British chauffeur and confidante, Kay Summersby. His smoking had increased to four packs a day, and he was rarely seen without a cigarette in his hand. "There were smoldering cigarettes in every ashtray. He would light one, put it down, forget it, and light another."[1] On this day, June 5, he drank one pot of coffee after another and was once heard to mutter, "I hope to God I know what I'm doing." Time dragged interminably, each hour seeming as long as a day.

Early that evening, with only his British aide, Lt. Col. Jimmy Gault, for company, he had Kay Summersby drive him to Newbury, Wiltshire, where the U.S. 101st Airborne Division was staging for its parachute and glider landings in Normandy's Cotentin Peninsula that night to help protect the landings on Utah Beach. Beginning that afternoon, the division had marched to its loading sites to the strains of "A Hell of a Way to Die"—also known as "He Ain't Gonna Jump No More," the song was actually "The Battle Hymn of the Republic" with lyrics appropriate to paratroopers—played by the division band. Arriving unannounced, he ordered the four-star plate on the front of his automobile covered, and permitted only a single division officer to accompany him on a random stroll through the ranks of the paratroopers, their faces blackened, full combat packs weighing an average of 125 to 150 pounds littering the ground around them, as they awaited darkness and the signal to begin the laborious process of loading. Although Eisenhower never spoke or wrote much about the experience, he cannot have forgotten the ominous warnings of his air commander in chief, Air Chief Marshal Sir Trafford Leigh-Mallory, that he fully expected casualties among the men of the elite airborne to be prohibitively high.

In total informality Eisenhower wandered from group to group, as men crowded around him, anxious to meet the general known as Ike. As he moved among the ranks he would ask repeatedly, "Where are you from, soldier?" "What did you do in civilian life?" Back came replies from young men from virtually every state in the Union. Some joked with Eisenhower, others remained somber. One invited him to Texas to herd cattle at his ranch after the war. "They went crazy, yelling and cheering because 'Ike' had come to see them off."

Possibly the most famous photograph of Eisenhower taken during the war depicts him surrounded by "Screaming Eagles" (the 101st's nickname), as he questioned one of the jumpmasters, Lt. Wallace Strobel, who assured him that he and his men were ready to do the job they had been trained for. Strobel would later say of his brief encounter with the supreme Allied commander, "I honestly think it was his morale that was improved by being with us." Others interjected remarks such as, "Don't worry, General, we'll take care of this thing for you." As twilight settled over southern England, the men of the 101st began the tedious process of loading aboard their C-47s and gliders. Eisenhower went to the runway to see them off, wishing them good luck. Some saluted and had their salute returned. One paratrooper was heard to announce, "Look out, Hitler. Here we come!"[2]

In some respects the scene was surreal: brave young men, many of whom would be wounded and perish in the coming hours and days, camouflaging their natural fears with bravado; and their commander in chief, deeply cognizant of what he had wrought, concealing his apprehension with smiles and small talk. "It's very hard to look a soldier in the eye when you fear that you are sending him to his death," Eisenhower later related to Kay Summersby. Yet those who had seen or spoken with him that fateful night carried into battle a conviction that their top soldier cared personally about each of them.

By nightfall Eisenhower had visited three airfields, at each of which the cheering was repeated. "I found the men in fine fettle," he said, "many of them joshingly admonishing me that I had no cause for worry, since the 101st was on the job and everything would be taken care of in fine shape."³ The last man to embark was the division commander, Maj. Gen. Maxwell D. Taylor, who would shortly parachute into a Normandy cow pasture. Eisenhower saluted Taylor's aircraft as it moved off to join the enormous queue awaiting takeoff.

The noise was deafening. Eisenhower and the members of his party climbed onto the roof of the division headquarters to watch in silence as hundreds of planes and gliders lumbered into the rapidly darkening sky, again saluting as each aircraft passed by. For Eisenhower, a man unused to expressing his emotions publicly, it was a painfully moving yet exhilarating experience, and the closest he would come to being one of them. NBC correspondent Merrill Mueller stood nearby and noted that Eisenhower, his hands deep in his pockets, had tears in his eyes.⁴

Eisenhower remained after the last aircraft had taken off and their sounds had faded away in the night. Watching him stroll back to his staff car, deep in thought, his shoulders sagging as they did whenever he was troubled, Kay Summersby thought him the loneliest man in the world at that moment. The knot of apprehension in his gut can only be imagined, but the expression on his face revealed more than words. "Well, it's on," he said somberly, again looking up at the night sky. "No one can stop it now."⁵

His birth name was David Dwight Eisenhower, but he was best known simply by his nickname, "Ike." Well before he became president of the United States, Dwight Eisenhower was already a national hero and one of the most universally respected Americans of his time. As his son, noted historian John S. D. Eisenhower, would later write of Gen. Winfield Scott, Dwight Eisenhower was "an astonishing man, one of the most astonishing in American history."⁶

His life was an amazing saga of the American dream come true. He came from humble, undistinguished midwestern roots, yet rose to a position undreamed of during the most destructive war in the history of mankind. The son of pacifists, he became a soldier whose life and career were shaped by the very wars his parents despised; yet he decried war as "the most stupid and tragic of human ventures."⁷ Had he followed the destiny predicted for him when he graduated from high school in Abilene, Kansas, in 1909, Eisenhower would have taught history instead of making it.

In 1941, as the United States was being drawn into a world war with

Japan, Italy, and Nazi Germany, Eisenhower's aspirations were modest. An earlier biographer has observed that the first fifty-two years of Eisenhower's life were not only unexceptional, but in complete contradiction of the notion that a heroic life is one filled with dramatic and noteworthy feats.[8] He would have considered himself successful to have served as a mere colonel in an armored division under the command of his longtime friend, the flamboyant Gen. George S. Patton, Jr.

Instead he rose to the highest command accorded any soldier in the Western Alliance of World War II. The fate of the war against Germany fell on his shoulders in June 1944, a responsibility of awesome and terrifying potential for failure—one faced by few military commanders in history.

By the time Germany surrendered in May 1945 Eisenhower's name was known and acclaimed throughout the world. "He came home with the cheers of millions from London, Paris, New York, and Kansas City ringing in his ears, heavily laden with medals, citations, decorations and honors such as had been bestowed on no other American in history."[9] Yet, at a huge welcome ceremony, he said humbly to the citizens of his beloved hometown, "The proudest thing I can say today is that I am from Abilene."[10]

How much do we really know about Eisenhower? A great deal has been written about him, but surprisingly little of it reflects the anguish of high command or of the two decades of behind-the-scenes toil, study, and apprenticeship that helped to prepare him. Or of his debilitating health problems, any one of which might have ended his career. One of the questions this book seeks to answer is what it was like to have been the supreme Allied commander; to face problems that would have crushed a lesser man; to deal with the likes of Winston Churchill, George C. Marshall, Franklin Delano Roosevelt, and a host of British military men, more experienced than he was, including three field marshals—Harold Alexander, Alan Brooke, and the controversial Bernard Law Montgomery.

More than a half century later, it is still difficult to grasp fully the enormity of his responsibilities, and the pressures placed upon him, first in the Mediterranean and then later in England, where he faced the greatest test of all, the invasion of Normandy in June 1944. As the story of his life through 1945 is unveiled, it will become evident that no amount of training or experience could fully have prepared Dwight Eisenhower for his role in World War II. That he was equal to the task is now virtually taken for granted; however, during those desperate and bloody years nothing was certain. Indeed, on the basis of Eisenhower's first experiences in North Africa, many expected him to fail.

He may not have fitted the mold of the warrior hero or of a battlefield general in the tradition of Robert E. Lee, J. E. B. Stuart, Stonewall Jackson, or George S. Patton, yet he was every inch a soldier. His legacy is based on his molding an alliance of two prickly, independent-minded allies with fundamentally disparate philosophies of waging war. Many have been misled by Eisenhower's easygoing manner and charming smile, a disarming facade behind which lay a ruthless, ambitious officer who thirsted to advance his chosen career by answering the call to war, which eventually led him to the pinnacle of his profession as a soldier. Eisenhower's well-concealed but towering ambition, his lifetime of study and drive to succeed was, like Patton's, one of the best-kept secrets of his extraordinary success. His infectious grin may have been "worth an army corps in any campaign," as his wartime British subordinate Lt. Gen. Sir Frederick Morgan has said, "but mostly," notes historian Eric Larrabee, "it was a quality that Eisenhower himself went to some lengths to conceal from the public: intelligence, an intelligence as icy as has ever risen to the higher reaches of American life."[11]

The path from the poverty of turn-of-the-century Abilene, Kansas, to supreme Allied commander was as improbable as it was spectacular. Certainly the advent of the new millennium is an auspicious occasion to introduce Dwight Eisenhower to new generations of Americans who know too little of this remarkable man. In chronicling his life through World War II, I am mindful of the observation by Gen. Claire Chennault's biographer, Martha Byrd: "To write an individual's biography is a joy, a privilege and a sobering responsibility."[12]

Part I

THE EISENHOWERS, 1741–1909

History is lived forwards but it is written in retrospect. We know the end before we consider the beginning and we can never wholly recapture what it was to know the beginning only.

— C. V. WEDGWOOD
William the Silent

1.

"Say Eisenhauer for Ironcutter."

They were believers in the doctrine of Menno Simons, who preached no authority outside the Bible.

Dwight D. Eisenhower's first ancestor in America was Hans Nicholas Eisenhauer, who emigrated from Germany's Rhineland to Pennsylvania in 1741. As the name was then spelled, it meant "iron hewer" or "iron cutter."

According to family lore, some of the earliest Eisenhauers may have been medieval warriors, dating possibly to the time of Charlemagne, who lived in Bavaria's Odenwald farming region. Over time the Eisenhauers evolved from warriors into pacifists. Many German Protestants at the time were followers of the doctrine of Menno Simons, the Swiss founder of the Mennonite movement, who preached in 1528 that no authority, either religious or political, existed other than the Bible and personal conscience. Simons advocated pacifism and urged his followers to reject the evils of materialism, proclaiming that "the true Christian should make no compromise with the world . . . [but] follow the dictates of his own conscience, inspired and guided by the Word of God."

Among the disciples of the Mennonite movement were Dwight Eisenhower's ancestors, who were undoubtedly among those victimized during the Thirty Years' War (1618–48) for their beliefs. The movements of the Eisenhauers during this time are unclear, but the family is thought to have fled to Switzerland for sanctuary at some point. By the eighteenth century, religious persecution, lawlessness, plagues, and pestilence had become the stimulus for a great many Europeans to seek a better life in the British New World colonies. Many were persuaded to emigrate by William Penn, the founder and first governor of the Quaker colony called Pennsylvania, which had also become a haven for all other persecuted religious sects. Although Penn's new colony had a great deal to offer, it was populated mainly by craftsmen and merchants and seriously lacked the skills of farmers to till the land and produce the food needed for survival. In the 1740s this void led Penn to Germany's Rhineland, where he gave speeches encouraging German Protestant farmers to emigrate to Pennsylvania with glowing tales of its spiritual riches and its arable lands.

"The result was a flood of emigration from Germany to Pennsylvania, of which the Eisenhauers were to become a part."[1]

The earliest identifiable ancestor was Hans Peter Eisenhauer of Elterbach in the Rhineland. His youngest son was Hans Nicholas Eisenhauer, who left Rotterdam aboard the sailing ship *Europa*, arriving in Philadelphia on November 20, 1741. After swearing the required oath of allegiance to both the British Crown and the Commonwealth of Pennsylvania, the Eisenhauer family settled in Bethel Township, near Harrisburg. On January 20, 1753, Hans Nicholas purchased a 168-acre farm, which "was recorded under the name of Nicholas Ironcutter. The clerk wrote on the draft: 'Say Eisenhauer for Ironcutter.' "[2] It would be two hundred years later to the day that Hans Nicholas's great-great-great grandson was inaugurated as the thirty-fourth president of the United States.

Upon his death, Hans Nicholas deeded the farm to his eldest son, John Peter Eisenhauer, also known as Peter Ironcutter, who became a successful farmer and merchant in nearby Fredericksburg, Pennsylvania. John Peter Eisenhauer died in 1802 at the age of seventy-eight, the same year Frederick, the youngest of his seventeen children, was born. The second of Eisenhauer's sons to be named Frederick, he was the great grandfather of Dwight D. Eisenhower.

Frederick was both a farmer and a weaver, and breaking with the tradition of large families, he and his wife, Barbara Miller, produced a mere six children. Before Frederick, little is known of the religious practices of the first Eisenhowers in America other than that they were predominantly Lutheran. Barbara Miller, who brought a generous dowry to their marriage, belonged to the church of the River Brethren, which Frederick joined in 1816.

The River Brethren, officially organized in 1862 as the Brethren in Christ, were a fundamentalist sect of the Mennonites, who had broken with their order as a result of religious quarrels.[3]

One of Frederick's sons, the Reverend Jacob Eisenhower, was Dwight Eisenhower's grandfather, and the most dynamic and admired of his ancestors. A devoutly religious farmer, Jacob purchased one hundred acres of prime land outside Elizabethville, in the lush Lykens Valley, some twenty-five miles northwest of Harrisburg in an area that was home to many of the River Brethren.

Practicing what they preached, the Eisenhowers graciously opened their spacious, nine-room manor house to travelers, vagrants, and anyone in need of food and shelter. The large living room also doubled as a place of worship and communion for members of the Reverend Mr. Eisenhower's flock. It was here that Eisenhower, an acclaimed orator who sported a beard around his chin but had his upper lip clean-shaven in the manner of the Puritans and the Pennsylvania Amish community, delivered his sermons in German, which was still the mother tongue of most of Elizabethville's citizenry. Years later, his grandson, Edgar Eisenhower, would remember how Jacob spoke "with a broken Pennsylvania Dutch brogue."[4]

Several Eisenhower relatives are known to have served the Union during the Civil War, but Jacob Eisenhower himself took no part. The war posed a troubling dilemma for Jacob, who neither condemned nor endorsed the Union but so greatly admired President Lincoln that he named one of his sons Abraham.

Before Kansas became a state, most maps showed the region west of the town of Manhattan as uncharted territory. On some maps it was marked the "Great American Desert."[5] In 1877, some of the River Brethren, no doubt lured by advertisements that promised bountiful crops and newspaper articles praising the richness of the land and its open spaces, ventured to Kansas to see for themselves. They arrived at the peak of the harvest season and found an area of rich soil capable of producing large crops, orchards, grass for cattle, unspoiled rivers, and stands of adequate timber along the creeks and rivers. Their reports of life in Kansas were so encouraging that within the River Brethren community there was discussion of relocating the entire sect to Dickinson County, considered the best of the sites investigated. This led to a momentous group decision by many of the Brethren voluntarily to give up their homes and farms in Pennsylvania and move en masse to a promised but largely unknown land in Middle America.

The westward expansion of the United States was spurred by the explosive growth of the railroads. Between 1865 and 1880, the American railway system grew from thirty-five to ninety-three thousand miles, and in 1869, the transcontinental railway was completed in Utah with the symbolic ceremony of the golden spike.

The lure of the great American West was bolstered by Lincoln's major land reform, the Homestead Act of 1862, which granted 160 acres of land to each new settler and hastened the demise of the traditional Indian lands. Inexorably the tribes were forced into reservations as white ranchers took over the fertile land and erected fences, while farmers began to make use of new farming machinery pioneered by John Deere.[6] The subjugation of the western Indian tribes may have been inevitable, but their shameful mistreatment was also one of the great tragedies of American history.

With the age of the railroad in Texas still some years away, the only means Texas cattlemen had of reaching a market was via the trail drive along the dusty Chisholm Trail into Kansas, across what is now Oklahoma but in the 1860s was still called Indian Territory.[7]

Between 1867 and 1885 Kansas became the ideal location to which the Texas herds could be driven and sold to livestock brokers. Among the first to realize the profit potential of buying and selling cattle to the lucrative eastern markets was a young Springfield, Illinois, livestock entrepreneur named Joseph G. McCoy, who sought a suitable location in Kansas "undisturbed by mobs or swindling thieves."[8] McCoy chose the tiny village of Abilene, where an extension of the Chisholm Trail terminated, as did the Kansas Pacific Railroad, which reached the town in March 1867.[9]

When McCoy established residence in 1867 he described Abilene as a "small, dead place consisting of about one dozen log huts" with dirt roofs, and a single saloon keeper who maintained a colony of prairie dogs with which he supplemented his income by selling them as curiosities to eastern tourists. Nevertheless McCoy deemed Abilene an ideal site, not only for its location but also for its grasslands and excellent water supply. Determined to turn Abilene into a thriving railhead cattle town, in a mere sixty days McCoy built stockyards large enough to hold a thousand head of cattle. Soon cattlemen began diverting their herds to Abilene.

Abilene quickly numbered some three thousand inhabitants as the trappings of a busy trading post sprang up almost overnight, bringing to the burgeoning town traders, merchants, gamblers, cardsharps, outlaws, assorted riffraff, and most of all, cowboys anxious, after the hardships of the trail, to enjoy home cooking and to patronize the saloons, dance halls, and whorehouses.[10] Most of Abilene's commerce was situated on Texas Street, which ran parallel to the Kansas Pacific tracks. Later, the action shifted to sin-filled districts called by various names, such as "Hell's Half-Acre," "Texas Town," and the "Devil's Addition," where about one hundred prostitutes plied their trade. One Abilene resident described the garishness of the "Devil's Addition" as "rightly named, for Hell reigned there. . . . in that damned Valley of Perdition." In July 1868 a Topeka newspaper observed, "Hell is now in session in Abilene."[11]

The term "Wild West" was coined in Kansas, and there was no cattle town wilder than Abilene in its heyday. In its infancy Abilene was a thoroughly inhospitable place: dusty and hellishly hot in summer and forbiddingly cold in winter, its streets a sea of mud whenever it rained. From the time that Joseph McCoy had put Abilene on the map, the town had endured a reign of terror by unruly roughnecks who jeeringly defied the town's attempts to control them. Its first lawmen either quit or were hounded out of town. No one paid the slightest attention to a new city ordinance banning guns, and as soon as a jail was constructed, it was torn down by a group of carousing cowboys. Killings and violence became so commonplace that even by the town's pinnacle in 1871 the founder of Abilene's first newspaper characterized the place as having more desperadoes than any other town of comparable size in the United States.[12]

In 1870, in an attempt to bring Abilene's lawlessness under control, the mayor hired a soft-spoken, fearless marshal named Thomas J. "Bear River Tom" Smith, a former New York City cop turned frontier lawman. Smith quickly lived up to his lofty reputation and during his brief tenure there were no more killings in Abilene. What made Tom Smith so unique was that he used his fists rather than guns to tame the town. In November 1870, Smith was brutally executed near Abilene while attempting to arrest two farmers. Tom Smith was followed for a short time by the notorious Wild Bill Hickok, who kept the peace in Abilene and killed his share of lawbreakers who dared to challenge his authority.[13]

In the post–Civil War period Abilene represented the best and worst of a growing and expanding America. Both Billy the Kid and Wyatt Earp are known to have passed through Abilene (without incident) during its brief reign as the West's wildest town. "Abilene was corruption personified," wrote one historian. "Life was hectic, raw, lurid, awful."[14]

In September 1867 the first cattle were shipped from Abilene to Chicago and put Abilene on the map.[15] During Abilene's heyday, between 1876 and 1879, 1,046,732 head of cattle were shipped east. In the end, however, McCoy lost money in Abilene, and moved on. The ultimate irony was that the strongly religious McCoy utterly detested the violence and wickedness he had helped create in Abilene.

Abilene's tenuous monopoly as a cattle town and sin city lasted barely four years, and by 1872 it had fallen victim to the westward extension of the railroads, and the opposition of its now largely farming citizenry, who declared that "the inhabitants of Dickinson [County] . . . will no longer submit to the evils of the [cattle] trade."[16] Other sites, such as Wichita, Salina, and Ellsworth, soon flourished as cattle towns, their proliferation fueled by the emergence of a powerful rival to the Kansas Pacific: the Atchison, Topeka & Santa Fe Railway. By 1875 Dodge City had superseded Abilene in notoriety thanks to such colorful Western characters as Wyatt Earp, Billy Tilghman, Bat Masterson, Buffalo Bill Cody, John Wesley Hardin, and Doc Holliday.[17]

In the aftermath of its glory days, Abilene had, by the early 1880s, evolved into a typical Kansas agricultural town that catered to farmers and ranchers. Dickinson County began attracting land speculators; they bought up parcels of unimproved land, divided them into lots, and advertised in eastern newspapers to attract settlers anxious to find new lives in the West. An 1887 brochure luridly proclaimed that "Abilene is to be a city of ten thousands in a few years," with "factories, fine business blocks, beautiful homes," and even a streetcar line. Another advertised that Abilene "has all the right stuff."[18] Dwight Eisenhower would later write, "Civic pride, in many American towns of that period, was the most flourishing local industry."[19] Although Abilene ultimately turned out to be a bad investment for the speculators (who outnumbered buyers by the late 1880s), it brought settlers keen to take advantage of the Homestead Act. So rapid was Abilene's evolution from Wild West town to agrarian center that the River Brethren, undeterred by its violent reputation, began to settle in Dickinson County less than a decade after Joseph McCoy had turned Abilene into "America's first great cowtown."[20]

2.

The Promised Land

They were good people.
—MILTON S. EISENHOWER

In the year 1878, Jacob Eisenhower and his family were part of a migration to Dickinson County, Kansas, that numbered several hundred Pennsylvania River Brethren. The Eisenhowers arrived in Abilene in April in the first group and settled some twelve miles southeast of Abilene, where he purchased 160 acres of prime farmland. For nearly a year the Eisenhowers lived in a covered wagon while Jacob built a spacious new home for his family.[1]

It did not take long for the River Brethren to validate the wisdom of their decision to leave Pennsylvania. Even during the depression years of the late 1880s and the 1890s, they prospered in Kansas. Corn, hay, wheat, barley, and oats were staples, and their large herds of cows almost always produced a surplus of milk. Their cooperative religious spirit also extended to economic matters, in which the River Brethren proved to be shrewd businessmen.

In 1886 the sect established the Belle Springs Creamery near Jacob Eisenhower's farm.[2] The creamery skimmed butterfat from milk and paid dividends based on each farmer's contribution. It proved to be an enormously important addition to the economic well-being of the farmers of Dickinson County. In 1890 the creamery was moved to Abilene, where it became a major factor in the lives of the Eisenhowers and a vital economic component of the Abilene community, both for its output and as a significant source of employment.[3]

In a profession fraught with risk and failure, Jacob Eisenhower was even more successful in Kansas than he had been in Pennsylvania. The family's lives revolved around crops and religion. They worked six days a week tilling the land; on the seventh day Jacob preached to the assembled River Brethren in his grand new home. Within a few years he was sufficiently affluent to invest in a team of fast ponies, a small county bank, and to purchase real estate in Hope, Kansas, then a tiny village near the family homestead in Belle Springs. The success that Jacob enjoyed in Kansas also promised a similarly good life for his children. Although strict and demanding, Jacob was also exceedingly generous. When his children married each received two thousand dollars in cash and a quarter section of farmland (160 acres).

Farming did not appeal to Jacob's eldest surviving son, dark-haired, brooding David Jacob Eisenhower, who was born in 1863.[4] His father's success at farming and modest wealth notwithstanding, David Eisenhower was at a rebellious and restless age, and filled with dreams, few of which seemed rooted in reality. He despised farming and had for some time been steadfastly determined not to carry on the family tradition, which he found tedious and unrewarding. David's only known aspirations were to become an engineer and a successful businessman. Although he delighted in using his hands, especially to repair farm machinery, David was scholarly, contemplative, and possessed of an inquiring and restless mind. He learned to read Greek for his own enjoyment, and his sons later recalled him reading the Bible in Greek, which was the only version he seemed to trust. He has been described as having unusually large hands, a thick shock of black hair, and was "tall and muscular, with the broad shoulders that characterized all Eisenhower men."[5] David also possessed in abundance the Eisenhower trait of stubbornness.

The United Brethren in Christ were another of the evangelical fundamentalist sects that abounded in Kansas, and their religious doctrine was more Methodist than Baptist. Although Lane emphasized religious education, the university offered both liberal arts and vocational training.[6] The entire school consisted of ten instructors and a small student body of approximately two hundred.[7]

David studied Greek, rhetoric, mechanics, and mathematics, and soon met his future wife, a vivacious young woman named Ida Elizabeth Stover, whose ancestors had emigrated from Europe two hundred years earlier for the same reasons as the Eisenhowers. Ida was born May 1, 1862, in Mount Sidney, Virginia, a tiny township in the Shenandoah Valley near Staunton, the next to youngest and the only girl of the eight children of Simon P. and Elizabeth Link Stover. Originally christened in the Lutheran Church as Elizabeth Ida, she later reversed her names, just as she would one day do for her famous son.[8]

Ida Stover—who was fondly remembered as a young girl of great charm and brightness—grew up with strong religious convictions and a pacifism powerfully influenced by painful memories of slavery and war. After the death of her mother in 1867, her father was unable to cope with raising so many children, and in 1869 sent seven-year-old Ida to live with her maternal grandfather, William Link. After Simon Stover died in 1873, William Link became Ida's guardian. She chafed at her grandfather's disdain for higher learning by women, something he—like most men of his time—regarded as unnecessary and unladylike. The adventuresome Ida refused to be deterred from her burning ambition to achieve a proper education, with or without permission. At age eighteen she left home to attend high school in Staunton and earned money for her keep by baking pies and cooking in private homes, a skill she had been perfecting since the age of seven. Ida's studies included the Bible, and she once memorized 1,365 biblical verses, any of which she could freely quote.[9] During her last two years in Virginia, Ida taught in a one-room schoolhouse near Mount Sidney.

At age twenty-one Ida received a one-thousand-dollar inheritance left by her late father and decided to join several of her brothers, who were part of the great Kansas migration. In June 1883 Ida settled in Lecompton with her elder brother William, a preacher.[10]

Ida's greatest passion was music, so much so that she spent six hundred dollars of her precious dowry for an ebony piano, which, to the end of her life, would remain her most cherished possession. Now free to make her own decisions, Ida enrolled in nearby Lane University in the autumn of 1883 to take advantage of its courses in music and the liberal arts.[11]

Early photographs depict a self-assured, attractive young woman. There were few women at Lane, and the golden-blond-haired Ida quickly became an extremely popular student, as well as the object of attention from young men anxious to win her approval. Ida did not meet David Eisenhower until the autumn of 1884, David's first year at Lane. At first David showed interest in several other female students, each of whom rebuffed his advances. Before long, however, David and Ida began attending various school functions together. If there is truth in the adage that opposites attract, it certainly applied to David Eisenhower and Ida Elizabeth Stover.

Young Ida Stover's personality and traits were everything David's were not: She was witty, popular, vivacious, and outgoing. David was considered by his peers at Lane to be as disagreeable as Ida was well-liked. A fellow student has painted an unflattering portrait of David, noting that when he enrolled at Lane he was cocky, very smart, with an extremely large ego and an inflated opinion of himself. "He *never* quit loving himself . . . but after awhile he settled down and found he was as common as an old shoe." One evening David was so rude to Ida at a student social that he was firmly rebuked by a number of his classmates, giving him to understand "that they would not tolerate his ugly attitude toward Ida . . . after that he seemed to try to please her and be somewhat human."[12]

David's behavior may occasionally have been insensitive, but it did not deter Ida from becoming deeply attracted to the handsome young man whose intellect far outweighed his introverted nature. What had begun as an instant attraction rapidly evolved into a serious courtship. David became a frequent visitor to the Link household. Ida's cousin Nettie Stover recalled how, at ten P.M. one night, William's second wife, Annie, bluntly announced, "It's time all decent folks were home in bed." David regarded the rebuke as a personal affront and vowed "to fix it so nobody was telling him when he had to leave."[13]

(One of David's traits was indecisiveness, at least until he made up his mind; then he became single-minded and beyond persuasion. Neither trait would necessarily serve him well.)

According to Nettie Stover the incident merely served to intensify David's courtship of Ida, although he never again returned to Will Stover's home until the day of his wedding to Ida, on his twenty-second birthday, September 23, 1885. Significantly the ceremony was performed not by Jacob Eisenhower or Will Stover, but by a River Brethren minister, E. B. Slade, in the presence of twenty guests.[14]

Whether David and Ida were true River Brethren remains in considerable doubt, however. According to David's nephew, the Reverend Ray Witter, neither David nor Ida ever became full-fledged members of the sect, even though they supported its basic tenets, sent their sons to its Sunday school, and attended its religious services until 1895. Another family friend confirms that he "never knew any of the family to attend the River Brethren Church." Both were perhaps too independent-minded to have sustained a permanent affiliation. Dwight Eisenhower would later describe his parents as "somewhat rebellious" in their approach to religion, and "not easily satisfied with any church."[15]

To support a wife, David had decided that his future lay in the mercantile and grocery business. He approached his father, offering to trade his inheritance for a start-up loan to open a store in Hope. The price of opening the store required that David bargain away his farm. Having rejected farming for business, the young couple were obliged to quit Lane University. David withdrew, probably in early 1885, followed by Ida at the end of the 1884–85 school year.

The year before Jacob had given two thousand dollars and a farm to David's older sister Amanda when she wed Christian O. Musser, a young member of the River Brethren who had migrated to Kansas from Pennsylvania in March 1884. Chris Musser regularly attended Jacob Eisenhower's Sunday services, where he met and courted Amanda, whom he married six months later. Chris Musser used Amanda's dowry wisely, and in later years the couple became two of Abilene's most prominent citizens, farming families, and business successes.

When David asked his father for a loan, Jacob agreed to mortgage the farm he intended to deed to his son. According to Musser, Jacob approached him to ask "if I could get some money from Pennsylvania for [David] to go into the mercantile and grocery business." Chris Musser's uncle bought the mortgage for two thousand dollars, and Jacob used the proceeds to construct a two-story store on a vacant lot he owned in Hope.

David lacked business acumen and, very likely at the urging of his father, elected to take in a partner named Milton D. Good, a highly regarded, congenial salesman in an Abilene clothing store, once described in the *Hope*

Dispatch as "one of the best merchants who ever measured off a piece of bacon or weighed a yard of calico."

Milton Good and David Eisenhower thus became equal partners in the fledging business that opened its doors as the Good & Eisenhower Store in March 1885. The store had two apartments upstairs—one for David and his new bride, and the other for his newly acquired partner.

Young David and Ida Eisenhower could hardly have been more mismatched in personality and temperament. David was introspective, reclusive, a dreamer, and utterly lacking a sense of humor. He also possessed a violent temper and was given to fits of rage over the commission of sins (real or imagined) by others, including members of his own family. His admirable traits of decency notwithstanding, throughout his life David remained the same incommunicative person who was described so unflatteringly by his Lane University classmates.

Ida promptly learned how to overcome David's bullheadedness. Shortly after settling into their first home above the store in Hope, Ida said David would have to help her fix a balky window shade. "I don't have to do anything," he replied, ignoring her request. Instead of expressing anger, Ida calmly outwitted her husband. The next time she announced, "Dave, I wonder if you could do this: I can't seem to get it done." At once David leaped to do her bidding. It was a lesson she later used to great effect raising her sons, whom she taught that there was more than one way to overcome a problem.[16] However, when it came to the family finances, Ida willingly deferred that right and responsibility to her husband.

Like other women of the Kansas River Brethren, Ida adapted the traditional garb, which consisted of a long black dress with a matching black cape and apron, called a "frock and yock." On her head she wore a white cap called a "prayer covering," which was only removed for sleeping or combing. No jewelry or other adornments were permitted. After a time Ida asserted her independence by becoming only the second woman in the Belle Springs sect permanently to discard the traditional headgear.[17]

The new business prospered at first, far better than relations between the two partners. The accepted but apocryphal version passed down by David Eisenhower and his sons is that the store failed in 1887 or 1888, and Milton Good and his wife absconded with all the store's cash and were never seen again, leaving David Eisenhower a ruined man, responsible for its debts, which he turned over to a lawyer who Ida later believed had also cheated them.

This tale never had a factual basis and is founded solely on Eisenhower family lore. The fiction of Good's alleged treachery was passed down to David and Ida's sons, who accepted it as fact. The truth of what actually occurred was not revealed until 1990, when Thomas Branigar, a historian-archivist at the Eisenhower Presidential Library in Abilene, published an illuminating investigative article about David Eisenhower and Milton Good.[18]

The Good & Eisenhower Store did not fail, it was dissolved by mutual consent. The only failure was the incompatibility of the two partners after just eighteen months in business together. David mortgaged the entire stock of the store to his father for $3,500 and used the money to buy out Milton Good's share of the partnership on November 4, 1886. The official notice posted by David in the next day's edition of the *Hope Dispatch* stated that Milton Good was released "from all responsibilities of the late firm."[19] Three days later Jacob Eisenhower forgave David his obligation to repay the debt.

The heroic portrayal of David Eisenhower's alleged travails with Milton Good and how he spent years repaying his debts was a fantasy perpetuated and later embellished by his famous third son, Dwight, in his best-selling memoir, *At Ease: Stories I Tell to Friends.*

Not only was there no bankruptcy, but the store was reorganized and renamed "Eisenhower Brothers" when David's younger brother, Abraham, a River Brethren preacher and self-taught veterinarian, became his new partner. Abe Eisenhower was a character as outgoing as David was introverted. He loved horses and people with equal passion, and despite a lack of formal training and professional skills, made up for them with, as his grandson remembered well, "boundless energy and showmanship." To encourage the local farmers to seek his services, Abe would dash madly around the countryside in a two-wheeled buggy as if responding to a veterinary emergency. The ruse worked, and Abe was praised in the local paper for having "extraordinary luck with his veterinary practice."[20]

David's final two years in the business were marked by the same traits of unhappiness and barely concealed resentments that had characterized his short, unfortunate partnership with Milton Good. David clashed with a tenant who briefly operated a bakery in the Eisenhower building. Like so many other small businessmen of that era, the tenant, E. A. Gehrig, found himself in financial straits in early 1888. Soon rumors began spreading in Hope that Gehrig had been forced into bankruptcy by his creditors. The source was a vindictive David Eisenhower, who was still angry at Gehrig for moving his bakery. To defend himself Gehrig felt obliged to place a public notice in the April 7, 1887, edition of the *Hope Herald:* "The report that I have been closed was given circulation by David Eisenhower, whose malice toward me, because I recently moved from his building, is a matter of general knowledge."[21]

Contrary, too, to the family myth, Milton Good did not flee Dickinson County with the firm's cash. Instead, Good returned to Abilene in 1886, where he was active in town affairs. He opened a dry-goods store in 1892 at the worst of economic times.

•   •   •

A restless David Eisenhower quit his job at the Eisenhower Brothers general store in October 1888, just as his rapidly growing family was about to include its second child. In light of his family responsibilities, his decision is utterly incomprehensible, but it was not impulsive. To the contrary, David had long since lost interest in running the store.[22]

Now that he was jobless, it became imperative that David find work. Broke and clearly discouraged, David elected to leave Hope. One of his son's first biographers notes, "In self-violation, in violation of the frontier tradition of courage and self-reliance . . . he sought only to escape from the scene of his humiliation."[23] David may well have felt mortified, but it had nothing whatsoever to do with his alleged business failure or his debts. It is more likely that David Eisenhower was simply unable to cope with his own sense of failure. Neither parent ever revealed the truth to their sons, who went to their own graves believing that their father had been the victim of Milton Good's treachery. In so doing, Ida became her husband's accomplice, repeating the tale, Dwight remembers, "many times" to the Eisenhower children.[24] What is indisputable is that David Eisenhower left Ida and their firstborn son, Arthur, in the care of his brother Abe while he traveled to Texas in search of work.

Scarcely three years into their marriage, Ida was compelled to cope with the baby; a second pregnancy, then in its sixth month; and the unhappiness of being forsaken by her husband. In January 1889 Ida delivered a second son, Edgar, named in honor of Edgar Allan Poe. Years later, when her sons reminded her that Poe had been an alcoholic, she replied, "I don't care. I still like his poems."[25]

In February 1889 Jacob Eisenhower decided to move his family to Abilene, and soon afterward the store was sold to the owners of an Abilene hardware store after Abe too elected to leave Hope and follow his parents to Abilene after disposing of his veterinary business.[26] Their decision was undoubtedly buttressed by David's flight to Texas.

The southern terminus of the Missouri, Kansas & Texas Railway was the bustling railroad town of Denison, Texas.[27] Known colloquially as the Katy Railroad, then simply as the Katy, at its zenith it was linked to five other railway systems. The most significant date in Denison's history was an equally important one in that of the United States. On March 10, 1873, the first train arrived in Denison, which—the city's historian notes—"was more significant than the event in Utah . . . all of the United States—North, South, East and West—were linked for the first time by the steel bands of the railroad."[28]

It was the emergence of the Katy that lured David Eisenhower to Denison in October 1888, where he was hired as a lowly engine wiper for the grand sum of ten dollars per week. David rented a room in a nearby boardinghouse and lived frugally and alone. Perhaps to assuage his loneliness, David turned to religious mysticism for spiritual guidance and solace. He designed an enormous wall chart of the Egyptian pyramids, complete with lines, angles, and captions to which he assigned symbolic meanings. The chart was an amazingly original, if incomprehensible, work that endlessly fascinated his sons.[29] Throughout his life the reserved David remained a man of few words. Dwight Eisenhower's son, John, thought that "Granddad was something else," recalling the occasion when his father received a postcard from David that said simply, "Hot."[30]

In 1888 David Eisenhower was twenty-five years old and utterly miserable. The Denison years of his self-imposed exile, between October 1888 and March 1892, were undoubtedly the most dismal period of his life. He labored for minimal wages and in total obscurity "somewhere near the bottom of the American heap, without any discernible future."[31]

When Abe Eisenhower left Hope to join his father, Jacob, in Abilene in April 1889, Ida, Arthur, and the newborn Edgar were reunited with David, who rented a modest, run-down wood-frame house on the wrong side of the tracks in a working-class section of Denison, a few blocks from the Katy railroad yards. Soot from passing trains coated the tiny house, which the Eisenhowers shared with a boarder, James Redmon, a Katy engineer who lived upstairs. The railroad tracks were dangerously close to the home and no place for young children to play. So grave was their poverty in Denison that it was a luxury when Ida occasionally bought hot tamales, which were sold six for five cents by a local peddler.[32]

When his mother, Rebecca, died in June 1890 at the age of seventy-five, David left Ida (then five months pregnant with their third child) and Edgar in Denison and returned to Abilene for her funeral, bringing with him young Arthur Eisenhower. David's mournful trip merely reinforced his sense of loneliness at being far from his family.

Despite their obvious discontent, the Eisenhowers had scant time for reflection as the birth of their next child drew near. The imminent arrival of yet another mouth to feed on his miserable salary only deepened David's gloom. Moreover, with two boys already, the Eisenhowers understandably hoped that their next child would be a girl. It was not to be.

Named in honor of his father, David Dwight, the third Eisenhower son, was born under the sign of Libra on the night of October 14, 1890, during a violent Texas thunderstorm. When Ida went into labor, James Redmon, who happened to be home, was sent to summon a physician. Before he arrived, the child was born with the assistance of neighbors, who had crowded into the tiny house in the spirit of communal cooperation. Brother Edgar later jokingly noted that Dwight was the only member of the family born outside Kansas. "There he was, a renegade Texan in a family of Kansans."[33]

Ida abhorred the notion that her third son would undoubtedly be referred to as David Eisenhower, Jr., or nicknamed "Dave," and soon reversed his names ("Dwight" was given in honor of a leading evangelist of the time, Dwight Moody.) No birth certificate was ever officially recorded for Eisenhower, and the transposition of his two first names was strictly at his mother's whim. Nonetheless, his name appears in the family Bible as "David Dwight Eisenhower."[34]

Dwight Eisenhower had no recollection and only scant knowledge of his birthplace until June 1945, when a delegation from Denison traveled to Abilene to present him with a framed photograph of the house where he was born. The following year he made the first of two visits to Denison, but overall Eisenhower never evinced more than polite interest in his birthplace. As far as he was concerned, Abilene was his only home and Denison little more than a bad memory in his parents' lives.

Yet another of the myths about Eisenhower is that he always believed he had been born in the East Texas town of Tyler, where his father was alleged to have worked briefly before moving to Denison. David, however, never worked in Tyler, and when Dwight entered West Point in 1911 he correctly entered "Denison, Texas," as his birthplace on the admissions form.[35]

Arthur would later recall the profound sense of gloom that pervaded the Eisenhower home whenever the subject of Kansas arose, which was apparently often. "God himself is the only one who knows how our parents managed to feed five mouths on dad's salary," wrote Edgar.[36]

The Texas years had not only mellowed David but infused him with a genuine awareness of just how deeply he and his family missed Kansas. After the death of his wife, Jacob Eisenhower was himself increasingly lonely. In the spring of 1891 he visited Denison and returned home visibly shaken by the unhappiness of David and his family. Hints continued from Abilene that the family should return, but without the certainty of a job, David hesitated until Chris Musser, now the foreman at the Belle Springs Creamery, let it be known that a job awaited him.[37]

In March 1892, nearly three and a half years after David Eisenhower had left Hope, the exile ended when the family returned to Abilene and were reunited with Jacob and Uncle Abe. On the day they arrived, David Eisenhower's sole assets amounted to the $24.15 in his pocket.[38] Two blocks south of the Union Pacific tracks, David rented a tiny house that was barely one step above a shanty. It was all he could afford on his meager salary. For the next six years it would be home to his rapidly expanding family.[39]

For Ida it meant more than a homecoming. During her three years in Texas her cherished ebony piano had been left in the care of a friend in Abilene. Now she would have it back. David, Ida (once again pregnant with what would be their fourth son, Roy), Arthur, Edgar, and baby Dwight David had returned to the Kansas town that would forever be linked with the Eisenhower name.

3.

"A Good Place for Boys to Grow into Men"

Our lives as youngsters were full and purposeful.
——EDGAR EISENHOWER

Dwight Eisenhower's childhood resembled the quintessential depictions of rural American youth in the paintings of Norman Rockwell. Milton recalls that his older brother was "just about the most normal boy" imaginable.[1] Baseball was Dwight's true love, and his boyhood sports hero was the great Pittsburgh Pirates Hall of Fame shortstop, Honus Wagner. "Edgar, Roy and I, we could make a third of a team ourselves and we'd get over here in the schoolground and we would play every minute that we could possibly get . . . the life of all us boys together was more of fun and frolic than it was just drudgery. . . . We felt that we had a pretty good thing going here."[2]

Whenever he was not in school or working, young Eisenhower could be found sipping a sundae at Case's Department Store, riding precariously on the handlebars of a friend's bicycle, wading or fishing in nearby Mud Creek, shooting rabbits, general horseplay, engaging in fisticuffs, or competing in all manner of sports. There was little his boyhood in Abilene had to offer that Dwight Eisenhower did not take part in during an untroubled youth. The Eisenhowers could not afford toys, but with David's encouragement his sons became adept at manufacturing their own from whatever materials were handy. Camping and boating were all part of a life filled with activities, as were acrobatics and balancing acts in the family barn—often futile attempts to defy the laws of gravity that usually cost little more than numerous bumps, bruises, cuts, and scrapes. Whenever there was a water fight, young Eisenhower was certain to be an eager participant. Whether the fight was with relatives or friends, entire buckets of cold water were employed, usually flung directly into the face of the chosen victim. The boys had no bathing suits but swam anyway, as one friend recalled, "in nature's clothes," often paying for it later with a serious case of sunburn.[3]

Dwight sometimes rode his father's solid-tire bicycle or a horse, which was the primary means of travel in Abilene. With six active sons, Ida hastily developed impressive first-aid skills to treat their never-ending succession of minor injuries. She also developed an array of home remedies for virtually any occasion. Easily the most unpopular was a vile concoction of molasses and sulfur that Ida insisted on administering every spring. To enhance their iron levels, she also made her sons ingest gunpowder, which was highly unpopular. A never-opened bottle of whiskey was kept in the cupboard for medicinal purposes.[4]

Like the rest of the nation, the Eisenhower sons were captivated by the sinking of the battleship *Maine* in Havana harbor in 1898 and the heroic charge of Teddy Roosevelt's Rough Riders during the subsequent Spanish-American War. "Remember the *Maine*" and the Rough Riders became part of numerous imaginative childhood games played by the Eisenhowers. "A tiny knoll became San Juan Hill," where they "gallantly charged, fighting and dying gloriously. The mother, in one of her rare moments of interference with their play, strongly disapproved. For the first time they encountered her extreme pacifism as she lectured them on the wickedness of war. Thereafter the game of war was faintly flavored for them with the spice of sin."[5]

The sons of David and Ida Eisenhower grew up with an impressive array of skills that included forecasting the weather, telling time from the position of the sun, catching frogs, curing warts, making apple cider, wrestling, and, whenever (albeit rarely) possible, avoiding both work and soap and water. Loose teeth were dealt with by pulling out the offending tooth either with their own fingers or by means of a string tied to a doorknob, and fillings were the ingredients in pies, not teeth. What they lacked in material wealth they more than made up for in amusements and pranks. Edgar and Dwight were often the center of mischief, such as the occasions when they poured beer into a neighbor's hen to see its reaction or stripped someone's farm wagon and rebuilt it on the roof of their barn.

Dwight Eisenhower grew up with an affinity for his hometown that he never lost. His two enduring childhood fantasies were of being the engineer of a locomotive racing across the plains and arriving in Abilene with its bell clanging, or of being a fearless pitcher striking out the side with the bases loaded in the bottom of the ninth inning of a baseball game to the cheers of a great crowd of five hundred spectators.[6] The Abilene he knew at the turn of the century bore scant resemblance to the onetime Wild West town. One of young Eisenhower's boyhood heroes was Marshal Tom Smith. Not only in his youth did Eisenhower hear local tales of Smith's courage, but throughout his life he voraciously read stirring Western pulp novels. A favorite childhood game played by Dwight and Edgar was Wild West, in which they each played the role of Bat Masterson, Wild Bill Hickok, Jesse James, or perhaps Billy the Kid and had imaginary shoot-outs with equally make-believe six-shooters.

During World War II his enlisted orderly would regularly write to Mamie Eisenhower requesting Western novels, "preferably with a lot of shooting in them. It was sort of funny, considering the amount of shooting we were getting most nights, that he still wanted stories full of six-shooters and bar-room brawls." With the advent of motion pictures, it was no coincidence that one of Eisenhower's all-time favorites was *High Noon*.[7]

Eisenhower frequently visited Smith's gravesite in Abilene, including three occasions during his presidency, taking inspiration from the words carved into the headstone:

> THOMAS J. SMITH
> Marshal of Abilene, 1870
> Dead, a Martyr to Duty, Nov. 2, 1870.
> A Fearless Hero of Frontier Days
> Who in Cowboy Chaos
> Established the Supremacy of Law.[8]

Eisenhower's first living boyhood hero was an Abilene resident named Bob Davis, whom he first met about 1898. Davis was a jack of all trades who earned his living as a fisherman, guide, and trapper. For the next eight years Davis was both the mentor and the father figure he never had in his own stolid parent. A bachelor, Bob Davis was in his fifties when he and young Dwight Eisenhower became fast friends. In Eisenhower the older man had a willing pupil who was eager to absorb his knowledge. Davis imbued Eisenhower with his knowledge of fishing, trapping, poling a flatboat with a single oar, duck shooting, and how to cook over a campfire. Besides a teacher and an inspiration, Eisenhower exuberantly found in Bob Davis a living link to the glory days of Abilene. It was no coincidence that Dwight Eisenhower was considered the best shot in the family. While in high school he inherited a 16-gauge, pump-action Winchester shotgun from older brother Edgar, with which he hunted wolves, coyotes, and jackrabbits. So great was his love of hunting that he organized hunting trips to a favorite retreat twenty miles south of Abilene, called Lyon's Creek. Thanks to his growing prowess as a cook, no one went hungry.[9]

Bob Davis's most enduring legacy is undoubtedly what he taught Dwight Eisenhower about the game of poker. Although illiterate, Davis showed Eisenhower how to play poker successfully, if conservatively. During camping trips Davis drilled into Eisenhower a card sense based on percentages and odds. With his natural skill at mathematics and the lessons imparted by the worldly Davis, Eisenhower eventually developed into a master player who years later would supplement his meager army pay at the poker table. There were few secrets in the Eisenhower household, but Dwight's poker education was one that he kept to himself.[10]

· · ·

When the Eisenhowers moved from Denison, Texas, to Abilene in 1892, the town was still primitive, with no sewers, no paved roads (until 1910), and a water supply that served only the elite north side. The sidewalks were wood planks, and stones were placed at street corners to facilitate crossings in bad weather. A mule-drawn streetcar line provided transportation. Milk was available only from those owning cows or from street peddlers, who sold it from open containers. The fire department used horse-drawn equipment until 1915, and its volunteer firemen were summoned by means of a loud whistle at the Belle Springs Creamery. There was a one-man (later two) police force, whose chief function was to collect "the [annual] two-dollar poll tax levied on all adult males and chasing truant youngsters" and to check that the local merchants had locked their doors.[11] The adult citizens of Abilene were all frontier pioneers who had brought with them the virtues of plain speaking, their strong religious beliefs, and a trust that hard work and success went hand in hand.

Strong social divisions prevailed in Abilene between the haves and the have-nots. The dividing line was the Union Pacific railroad tracks, which bisected the town. The contrast between the two was obvious: To the north were the fine Victorian homes of the well-to-do situated along affluent Buckeye and Third Streets; to the south working-class families like the Eisenhowers resided in smaller wood-frame houses. Many lived well below the poverty line. The religious and social life of the town was centered in Abilene's numerous churches, where its citizens came together to pray and to partake in group picnics. One of the many carnivals of that era was based in Abilene. The carnival families all lived in Abilene's south side, and their children attended elementary school with the Eisenhowers. Ike's boyhood friend John E. Long remembered "an unusual number of bad boys," who offered ample opportunities for fighting—of which Dwight Eisenhower took his fair share.[12]

David Eisenhower went to work at the Belle Springs Creamery as a maintenance engineer in March 1892. By the early 1900s the business would grow to become one of the largest and most successful independent creameries in the entire Midwest.[13] The creamery account book for 1892 reveals that on March 12, the owner, a member of the River Brethren named J. E. Nissley, hired D. J. Eisenhower at an annual salary of $350.[14] The title "engineer" was a euphemism. His work at the creamery involved twelve-hour days and hard manual labor maintaining the machinery and steam equipment. It wasn't much, but Eisenhower never complained: The family's obvious delight at being back in the company of family and friends outweighed the paucity of David's salary and the humble nature of his work. Even so, the family thrived through its own self-sufficiency. Except for a break in service due to illness in 1912, David Eisenhower worked for the Belle Springs Creamery for twenty-four years, before leaving in 1916 for a similar position at the local gas plant, where he was soon promoted to general manager, a position he held until his retirement in 1931. During his thirty-nine years of toil in Abilene David Eisenhower never earned more than $150 per month.[15]

Dwight Eisenhower's first and perhaps most lasting recollection of his childhood occurred shortly before his fifth birthday, when his aunt escorted him by rail, then by horse and buggy, to a family gathering on a farm near Topeka, where most of Ida's relatives resided. His recollections were typical of what children experience when thrust into a strange environment for the first time. "It was peculiar to be surrounded by so many strangers. It seemed to me that there were dozens or hundreds of people—all grown-ups—in the house. Even though they were, somehow, my family, I felt lonesome and lost among them."[16]

Eisenhower fled the house for the sanctuary of the barnyard, which he began exploring until he encountered a particularly bad-tempered, aggressive male goose that deemed the youngster's presence a territorial affront. Frightened but determined not to be intimidated by this surly creature, Eisenhower wept tears of frustration after he was repeatedly driven from the barnyard. Taking pity, his uncle Luther (Stover) stripped an old broom of its straw, showed the child how to employ it as a weapon, and then left him to fend for himself. More afraid of the disapprobation of his uncle and his relatives than of the surly goose, a trembling Eisenhower advanced, yelling, and gave the goose "a satisfying smack on the fanny." Though still belligerent, the goose never again bothered Eisenhower. The self-esteem of a five-year-old boy was restored and, more important, the lesson imparted in his uncle's farmyard that day was not lost on young Eisenhower, who later recalled: "I learned never to negotiate with an adversary except from a position of strength."[17]

Eisenhower's favorite relative was his vibrant Uncle Abe, who found his true calling as an itinerant preacher. Part preacher, part carnival barker, and part happy-go-lucky gypsy, Abe traveled into western Kansas and the Oklahoma territory in a large, unwieldy, covered, horse-drawn vehicle he nicknamed the "gospel wagon." Abe knew how to attract a crowd of strangers with cries of "This way to heaven!," then mesmerize them with rousing sermons. In 1901, Abe and his wife founded a missionary home for orphans in Guthrie, Oklahoma, before eventually moving to California. Years later, when Abe's nephew had become world famous, Dwight Eisenhower would tell friends that he was "damned if I've ever been able to figure out" the message of his uncle's sermons. "I know the old man was mighty proud of himself, the way he could raise an audience out of dust."[18]

When Abe left Abilene in 1898, David and Ida were given possession of his house, located a few blocks away at 201 Southeast Fourth Street. Situated on three acres of land that included a large barn, the two-story white frame home was surrounded by maple trees and seemed like a mansion after six years in the tiny, cramped house on Second Street. It can only be imagined what David and Ida's reaction might have been had they known that their permanent home (now the location of the Eisenhower Center) once adjoined the site of the wild and wicked whorehouses of the "Devil's Addition" during Abilene's heyday.[19]

Still, with eight people living in it, the Eisenhowers' new home was hardly spacious. The rooms were small by modern standards. Daily life revolved around organization, cooperation, and a vast array of duties, alternated weekly among the brothers, from which no one was exempt. Merely feeding six growing boys with enormous appetites was itself an exceptional logistical feat. As brother Earl remembers, "That house was all things to us, football field, boxing arena, chapel, assembly line, study room, emergency hospital, cooking school and hobby center. It was, in short, 'home,' a good place for boys to grow into men."[20]

Dwight's first household duties consisted of collecting kindling for the stove and shaving it into pieces. Often he would start bawling to attract attention, in the vain hope that parental sympathy would relieve him of this chore. "I was a great bawler when I was very young . . . I remember a neighbor lady coming in one day and saying, 'Ida, what are you doing to that child?' She said, 'Oh, he'll be all right as soon as he brings his kindling in.' And, of course, I was."[21] Attempts at intimidation never worked either. Edgar once threatened to run away from home. His father suggested various routes he might take, while his mother offered to prepare a lunch for him to take along.

In summer each son tended his own garden plot in addition to working in the nearby cornfield and the rest of the family plot. Dwight became an adept gardener and a shrewd young businessman who grew and peddled the vegetables most in demand, usually cucumbers and sweet corn. David permitted his sons to earn their own spending money. Dwight's usually went to purchase athletic equipment. In his memoirs Eisenhower recounts the valuable lessons he learned about money.[22] The many duties performed by the Eisenhower boys were part of Ida's domain and included cooking; dishwashing; laundry; milking the family cow; feeding the chickens; putting hay in their large barn; weeding, pruning, and maintaining the gardens and cornfield; and harvesting and storing the fruit. Their large garden was so carefully cultivated that it yielded an abundance of fruit and vegetables. Rounding out the family menagerie were two cows, numerous chickens, several pigs, and Belgian hares. During the growing season, the only chores universally despised were those inside the house. "To help meet household expenses," remembered Edgar, "mother often sent Dwight and me over to the north side of town with our little red wagon loaded with sweet corn, peas, beans, tomatoes and eggs." Although it never visibly bothered Dwight, Edgar never got over his deep resentment at the haughtiness of some of their snooty customers, who he sensed regarded them as little better than panhandlers.[23]

The most odious chores of all were cleaning out the chicken coop and washing the family clothes, a complicated process involving copious gallons of water that had to be boiled to heat the washing machine. Washing the smelly diapers of the youngest Eisenhowers was a duty no one wanted.

Another duty performed by the older boys was to take turns pushing Milton or Earl in a baby buggy. Either through lethargy or perhaps a determination to do things his own way, Dwight would lie on the floor or, if outside, on the grass, and with his feet or a rope tied to the buggy, push it back and forth to the complete satisfaction of its occupant. It also became a means of indulging his passion for reading while ostensibly performing a family duty. For a time Dwight was also responsible for putting Earl to bed at night and dressing him in the morning, a task he despised.[24]

The Eisenhower boys also shared the cooking duties. When it was their turn on a Sunday, Dwight and Edgar returned home after Sunday school at the nearby River Brethren church to prepare dinner while the rest of the family attended the service. On one occasion the two decided it would be fun to make a pie. They rolled up the dough and began playing catch with it. Although the dough was dropped on the floor several times, the brothers baked a somewhat discolored but nevertheless delicious pie. As with everything he ever took seriously, Eisenhower worked assiduously to become a first-class cook, which, his high jinks aside, became a valuable skill that would prove immensely useful in the years ahead.[25]

The main staple of the family diet was potatoes, which were served at virtually every meal. The prodigious amounts of potatoes consumed by the Eisenhower boys eventually spawned a ditty they repeated:

> Oh, the 'taters they grew small,
> And we ate them skin and all,
> Out in Kansas. . . .[26]

For the rest of his life Dwight Eisenhower viewed everything through the prism of the "waste not, want not" virtue instilled in him as a youth. He thought any excess deplorable, and once at a banquet in Chicago after World War II, Chris Musser claims to have seen him cut a large steak in half and send the other half back to the kitchen with a pronouncement that as long as people were starving elsewhere in the world, food should not be wasted.[27]

The family had no alarm clock, nor did they need one. "Dad was the alarm clock," and at 5:30 A.M. he would come to the bottom of the stairs and call out, "Boys!," which was their signal to begin a new day. Dwight was the hardest of the sons to awaken and often had to be cajoled or threatened from his bed. During cold weather they dressed under the covers; in summer the house became nearly unbearable, with the heat often exceeding one hundred degrees.

For many years there was neither running water nor indoor plumbing. In the bitter cold of winter, when temperatures often dropped below zero, a trip to the outhouse was an adventure not soon forgotten. Except in summer, when the water was heated outside by the sun, bathing involved filling a large tub in the kitchen using water heated on the stove. Usually the bathwater was used by more than one boy, and since bathing was on a first-come basis there was always intense competition to be the first. For many years none of the boys even knew what a bathtub was.[28]

It was a rule in the Eisenhower household that no one was permitted to leave the dinner table until after Ida said, "Amen." Dwight usually sat on a stool, champing at the bit to be freed of this symbol of family togetherness. His anxiety was evident by his habit of stealthily turning on the stool to face outward, as if to obtain a head start. When his mother finally pronounced the magic word, "he was off and gone like a shot." For a time Ida even worried that her impetuous young son somehow might not turn out very well.[29]

A significant part of their lives revolved around baseball and football. The boys lost no opportunity to play their favorite games, even in the kitchen where Dwight would wash plates, then throw them to Ed on first base, who tossed them to Art or Milton covering home. It is a tribute to their athletic skills that there were no broken dishes, which would surely have ended their kitchen sport.[30]

David Eisenhower's exile in Texas had failed to mellow his enmity toward Milton Good. During their youth the Eisenhower sons all learned David's version of the affair. No bill could ever be carried over, even if it meant the family had to do without.[31] Dwight Eisenhower and his brothers were left with an enduring and bitter conviction that their father had been grievously wronged by Milton Good.[32]

Although it had been 150 years since the first Eisenhower had arrived in America, German was still the mother tongue of his Abilene descendants. Jacob's years of generosity to his family had left him financially strapped in his old age, and in the final years before his death he lived with David and Ida. David and Jacob conversed almost exclusively in German, but with Jacob's death in 1906, the custom ended. Thereafter David refused to speak German to Ida or his sons, in the belief that they were better off being like other children in Abilene who spoke only English.[33]

Once settled in Abilene, the Eisenhower family continued to grow at a rapid rate. As each new birth took place, David and Ida's yearning for a girl was again dashed. Roy was born in 1892, followed by Paul in 1894. Almost nothing is known of baby Paul, who was apparently sickly from birth and was only ten months old at the time of his death from diphtheria in 1895.

David and Ida managed to keep their deeply felt grief private and thus never conveyed a lasting impression to any of their six surviving sons.

The Eisenhowers had no more children until 1898, when Earl was born. The baby brother of the family, Milton, arrived in 1899. By now the parents, particularly David, openly longed for a baby girl and were sorely disappointed at the birth of yet another son.[34]

Arthur, Roy, and Milton were dark-haired and resembled their father, but, like his mother, Dwight's eyes were blue and his hair was so light blond that he was often referred to as "Swede." Earl, whose reddish-blond hair made him a genetic throwback to his grandfather, lost the sight in his left eye from a tragic mishap at the age of four that would obsess Dwight Eisenhower for the rest of his life. The incident took place in the family toolshed, where Dwight was busily making a toy while Earl played nearby. A butcher knife he had just used was carefully placed on a nearby windowsill to keep it away from his brother. Dwight failed to notice that the inquisitive Earl had managed to climb on a chair, where he attempted to grasp the knife, which fell and struck him in the left eye. Earl's eye was permanently damaged, and several years later he lost his sight in the eye entirely while roughhousing with Milton. At Ida's insistence that no one should be blamed, the accident was never again spoken of by the Eisenhowers. Although Ida was attempting to instill in her sons the notion that life is risky and that while accidents happen, lingering resentments were self-destructive, her admonition had the opposite effect on Dwight, who was remorseful for the remainder of his life.[35]

More than any of the other Eisenhower sons, Dwight inherited his father's violent temper. Examples of his rages as a child are legendary. The Eisenhower brothers fought frequently, often with bloody results. Dwight, Edgar, and Earl had the hottest tempers, but it was Edgar and Dwight who had the greatest rivalry and the most fights. "You were always vastly my superior," Dwight acknowledged in 1944. "You could run faster, hit better, field better, tote the foot-ball better, and do everything except beat me at shotgun shooting. . . . I was just the tail to your kite."[36] None of which deterred Dwight from continually taking on Edgar in frustration and an unfulfilled determination to best his older brother. Whether it was sporting competition, who had first rights to the *Saturday Evening Post*, or for the most trivial reason, rivalries abounded in the Eisenhower household. Nevertheless Dwight's son, John Sheldon Doud Eisenhower, is justifiably suspicious that their claims of combat were grossly exaggerated. "I doubt that anyone could fight as much as they say they did," he has said, noting that the tale of Dwight losing a wrestling match with his father "probably lost nothing in the telling."[37] Still, Eisenhower's steely resolve, whether in coping with the responsibilities of high command or staring down Russian premier Nikita Khrushchev was a reflection of the lessons learned at the hands of a stern, uncompromising father.[38]

"Hate" was a nonexistent word in the Eisenhower family vocabulary, but David and his son Dwight both possessed long memories for those unfortunate enough to have aroused their anger. David so rarely spoke that he left the perception that inside the man lay a heart of darkness rarely lit. Even his own sons believed that he was far too solemn, and there is no known photograph in which David Eisenhower is seen to be smiling. Certainly he contributed little to prepare his sons for adulthood and "managed to be absent even when he was present." His life revolved around his work. "He never came home for lunch . . . reappeared at six in the evening, to say grace at the start of supper, eat silently through it, then hole up in a room with a book."[39]

A forceful example of both Dwight Eisenhower's sense of family and his explosive temper was expressed in 1947 on the occasion of a visit to Abilene. When he found that a sign had been erected in front of the family home announcing that it was the boyhood home of General Eisenhower, his face flushed red and his famous temper erupted: "That sign is not right. This is the boyhood home of the Eisenhower family. I want it changed immediately." The next day it was.[40]

The most important lesson the Eisenhowers taught their sons was that they must think and shift for themselves. Edgar notes: "There was bred into us a certain independence and a determination to rise above our humble beginnings and try to some day amount to something."[41] It became an absolute article of faith in the minds of their sons that being poor was no disgrace and no less honorable than being born rich. What counted was one's faith and old-fashioned hard work.

David and Ida's sons had no inclination to disparage their poverty. They were always neatly dressed in clean clothes handed down from one brother to the next. Clothes and shoes were altered, mended, and—however threadbare—eventually passed down the family ladder to the youngest sons, Earl and Milton. Nothing was ever wasted. Having their own shoes was prized, but during warm weather the boys often attended school barefoot. Mending became such a burdensome task that Ida taught each of the boys how to darn his own socks. The result was that they developed a healthy respect for the value of money and possessions.[42]

Nevertheless, memories of Dwight Eisenhower's childhood poverty still clung, even in his old age. On one occasion after his second presidential term, he and Mamie visited a clothing store in Ayr, Scotland. Eisenhower's eyes lit up at the sight of such fine clothing. The clerk who made a large sale to the Eisenhowers was overheard to opine that the former president "acted like a lad from the hills," which Eisenhower thought "may well be one of the better compliments paid me in recent years." He also recalled that the compliment he received from the Scottish clerk would never have happened in Abilene. When it came to forking over money, "the canny Scots of Ayr could not hold a candle to us in our painstakingly critical scrutiny of goods and prices. . . .

The Indian on our penny would have screamed if we could have possibly have held it tighter."[43]

The Eisenhower family's return to stability in Abilene also brought about a change in David and Ida's approach to religion. The six Eisenhower brothers all attended the River Brethren Sunday school, where Dwight and his brothers "never seemed to pay any attention or take any interest in the lesson."[44] Although the River Brethren were still the centerpiece of their spiritual lives, David and Ida began searching for new meanings and became interested in a fundamentalist sect then known as the Bible Students.[45] According to Edgar, "The meetings were held at our house, and everyone made his own interpretation of the Scripture lessons. Mother played the piano, and they sang hymns before and after each meeting. . . . They talked to God, read Scriptures, and everyone got a chance to state his relationship with Him. . . . I have never forgotten those Scripture lessons, nor the influence they have had on my life. Simple people taking a simple approach to God. We couldn't have forgotten because mother impressed those creeds deep in our memories."[46] During the services Dwight and his brothers were permitted to remain outside, where they played such games as blindman's bluff and hide-and-seek.

When the River Brethren failed to provide the solace they sought in the wake of baby Paul's death in 1895, Ida became a convert to the Bible Student movement, which in 1931 adopted the name "Jehovah's Witnesses." David is thought to have involved himself reluctantly to placate Ida until about 1915, when he ceased any religious involvement.

Those closest to the Eisenhower family remember it as a happy house, free of friction. And Milton recalled of his parents, "I never heard a cross word pass between them."[47] The sons not only listened to David and Ida read the Bible during a daily ritual but were often permitted to read from it themselves. Bible readings were deemed an honor, but there was one explicit house rule: The privilege ended whenever the reader made a mistake and was caught by another of the boys. Eisenhower believed that these family Bible readings greatly simplified the requirement to read aloud in front of his teachers and classmates.

By the age of twelve Eisenhower had read the entire Bible, and by the time he left Abilene in 1911, he had read it for a second time. He remembered most of what he read, and during World War II would frequently astonish his aides by his ability to quote from memory a suitable passage for any occasion.

Until the time of his presidency, Dwight Eisenhower never attended church, and, as adults, none of the Eisenhower sons followed the religious beliefs of their parents, but all were deeply affected by their religious upbringing. "Clearly the dominant religious influence in the Eisenhower home from the time the boys were young was Watchtower theology and beliefs."[48] Nevertheless their mother's religious affiliation appears to have been a source of considerable embarrassment. Ida had subscribed to the official Witnesses' publication, the *Watchtower*, but after her death in 1946, Milton quietly disposed of his mother's fifty-year-old collection lest there be undue publicity. Although Dwight briefly acknowledged his mother's association with the Witnesses in his memoir, his brothers rarely spoke of Ida's religious beliefs and then only in vague terms. Milton, in particular, would concede only that "we were raised as a fundamentalist family."[49] Throughout his life, Dwight Eisenhower would reaffirm his religious upbringing in various ways. During World War II it was often simply to ask for "God's guidance in making the right decision."[50] Ida was fond of playing solitaire, and from this pastime emerged one of her many homilies that became a guiding principle of his life: "The Lord deals the cards; you play them."[51]

In 1906 Jacob Eisenhower died at the age of eighty after a long and successful life. As a child, Dwight remembered him for his black dress, his underbeard, and particularly for his horse and buggy, riding in which became a sought-after luxury. Only as an adult would Eisenhower fully recognize the unique qualities of his pioneer-farmer grandfather. His worth "rests far more on his own deeds, on the family he raised and the spiritual heritage he left them, than on one grandson," he wrote.[52]

Ida was understanding and tolerant, but there were occasions when Dwight exceeded her dictum: "He who conquers his temper is greater than he who taketh the city."[53] Although she was not above slapping an errant hand, the real discipline fell to David, whose explosive temper was on full display the day Edgar was severely whipped for having quit school without permission to earn money working for a local doctor. Dwight was twelve years old and witnessed Edgar being severely beaten with a leather harness and began shouting at his father to stop. Ignored, he began to cry, partly in the hope his mother would come to the rescue. When he attempted to grab his father's arms only to be asked if he wanted some of the same, Dwight hotly replied, "I don't think anyone ought to be whipped like that, not even a dog." Both brothers rationalized their father's rage as a severe but necessary means of teaching Edgar not to jeopardize his future.[54] On other disciplinary occasions, as often as not, the recipient was the rebellious young Dwight Eisenhower.

Dwight credits his mother with teaching him to control his temper. One Halloween when he was about ten years old, his two older brothers were given permission to venture out with a group of local youths. Dwight was deemed too young and became so agitated that, in a blind rage, he began beating the apple tree in front of the house with his fists. "For some reason, I guess, I thought the apple tree was to blame and I was there crying as hard as I could and beating this apple tree with my fists, and they were all bleeding and messy."[55] His tantrum earned Dwight a severe thrashing from his father, who ordered him to his bed.

A short time later Ida arrived with a washcloth and salve to clean and wrap Dwight's bleeding hands. Using some Bible verses by way of explanation, she calmly demonstrated to her mercurial son why he was only harming himself by such irrational displays of behavior. "I think that was one of the most important moments of my life," recalled Eisenhower, "because since then . . . I've gotten angry many times, but I certainly have tried to keep from showing it."[56] Nevertheless Eisenhower never fully gained control of his temper.

The Eisenhower sons recognized David's contributions to their upbringing, but they were in awe of Ida, the glue that held the family together during the good times and the bad. Her influence upon her sons was incalculable, none more so than on Dwight Eisenhower, who venerated her. Throughout World War II, when the heavy responsibility of the Western Alliance rested on his shoulders, Eisenhower thought often and fondly of Ida, wishing that somehow he could see her and be calmed and reassured by her presence and her wisdom. "I think my mother is the finest person I've ever known," he wrote in a note to himself in March 1942.[57] No wonder Eisenhower would later say of his beloved mother, "For her sons, privileged to spend a boyhood in her company, the memories are indelible. . . . Mother was by far the greatest personal influence on our lives."[58]

Her niece, Nettie Stover Jackson, recalled how Ida once said, "I studied each of my boys to know how to deal with them," each as a unique individual, and to respond accordingly.[59] She urged them to behave not out of fear of the consequences of disobedience but "because it was the right thing to do."[60] To her death, she treated all her sons as equals. When a reporter once asked Ida what she thought of her most famous son, she replied, "Which son do you mean?"[61]

Each of the Eisenhower sons had a distinctive character. As the eldest, Arthur accepted the role with equanimity and little fanfare. Although quick tempered like all the Eisenhower brothers, Arthur is remembered by Dwight as the son who gave his parents the least trouble and was the best behaved. Unlike the others Arthur cared little for either athletics or fisticuffs, although he indulged in his fair share of the latter when provoked. Starting at the bottom of the ladder, Arthur became a successful banker in Kansas City.

Edgar matched Dwight's fiery temperament in every way. A man of boundless energy and intemperate and impulsive behavior, Edgar was the most sentimental of the brothers, a trait unshared by Dwight. Financially Edgar was the most successful of the Eisenhowers, but although he became a millionaire, he too never forgot the privations of his childhood. His reputation as one of the south side's toughest youths was well earned, but his energy as a grown man was channeled into a successful and highly lucrative law practice in Tacoma, Washington, while his famous brother lived much more modestly for most of his life.

Dwight never bested Edgar, but their lifelong sibling rivalry left him determined eventually to prevail over his older brother. His "don't get mad, get even" attitude carried over into his West Point years, and in 1913 Eisenhower challenged his brother, then a law student at the University of Michigan, to any competition he would accept, whether boxing, wrestling, or bare knuckles. A far more mature Edgar politely declined, but even in his old age Dwight remembered being "robbed of sweet revenge."[62] As their paths crossed less and less as grown men, the closeness they once shared seemed to wane, leaving in its place some lingering resentments from childhood, at least on Dwight's part. Whenever the subject of his youthful rivalry with Dwight arose, Edgar, even at the age of sixty-six, would assert, "I still can lick him anytime."[63] The rivalry and occasional bad feeling between Dwight and Edgar ended only with their respective deaths.

Roy became a pharmacist in nearby Junction City and seems to have had the clearest vision of his future profession. Some thought Roy most resembled his father, but he lacked David's brooding nature, was unpretentious and full of life, and loved sports and a good joke. He was perhaps the most social of the six brothers. Dwight, however, thought him "a bit of a lone wolf."[64]

The least known was Earl, a modest man who shunned the limelight in his chosen field as an electrical engineer for a utility company in Pennsylvania. Later he changed professions and became the general manager of a biweekly rural newspaper in Illinois. Earl preferred small-town life and possessed the distinction of being the only Eisenhower son to escape the curse of baldness.

To compensate for his physical ailments as a child, Dwight's kid brother, Milton, became the family scholar and a gifted educator and statesman. The eight-year age difference between Dwight and Milton was significant when they were children, but as grown men the two would eventually bond with an intimacy that did not exist between any of the other brothers.

Dwight was the most volatile and perhaps the most stubborn of David and Ida's sons. He was too young to compete with his two older brothers in sports or fighting, and too old to connect in a meaningful way with his younger brothers.

The one distinction that all six brothers had in common was their burning desire to obtain a one-way ticket out of Abilene in order to escape the fate that had befallen their father. Although Abilene has become legendary for its connection to the Eisenhowers, the sons of David and Ida Eisenhower fully understood that their respective destinies lay elsewhere. "They were all good guys," remembers John. "The six brothers were very different in many ways, but they were alike in all being driven men . . . they saw a highly educated, intelligent father live his life in near poverty and frustration and each concluded, 'This isn't going to happen to me.' "[65]

However, the long-perpetuated notion that the Eisenhower sons never knew they were poor is part of the myth created as early as 1942, when the print media hastened to investigate and publicize in the most heroic manner this heretofore unknown American and his family. To the contrary, their poverty was unavoidably obvious to each of the Eisenhower sons. Their fights, said John Eisenhower, "stemmed from the fact that, though Dwight Eisenhower claimed that the Eisenhowers never knew they were poor, they were definitely from the wrong side of the tracks (literally). But they were proud, and that fact brought on combats with the snobbish elements in town."[66] Biographer Peter Lyon accurately notes, "There is no question that poverty steeled young Dwight's ambition and his determination to excel, to succeed."[67]

For the most part, horseplay and fighting were a harmless means of letting off excess energy. Although their parents disapproved of fighting or even any form of quarreling, Dwight learned to his surprise that there were times when it was justified in his father's eyes. One day, for example, David returned home just as Dwight was being chased into their front yard by another child. When his father inquired why he tolerated being pushed around, Dwight replied, "Because if I fight him, you'll give me a whipping, whether I win or lose!" Instead David ordered him to chase the fellow away, and his son responded by throwing his tormentor to the ground and, although it was mostly bluff, "voiced threats of violence." The incident taught another childhood lesson that Eisenhower never forgot, namely that to feign domination of others is often just as effective as physical force.[68] Ida generally turned a blind eye to her sons' altercations, and when Dwight once came home with his face swollen, she merely asked if it had been a fair fight.

In May 1903 Kansas was ravaged by the worst flood in the state's history. In Abilene, both Mud Creek and the Smoky Hill River flooded south Abilene. Edgar and Dwight treated the disaster as a marvelous opportunity for a great adventure. The two decided it would be exciting to ride the floodwaters down Buckeye Street, on a broken piece of wooden sidewalk that made a serviceable raft upon which they imagined themselves as pirates, loudly singing "Marching Through Georgia." Their merriment left both oblivious to the fact that they were in danger of being swept into the raging Smoky Hill River and drowning. The soaking-wet boys were jarred from their reverie by a man on horseback who sternly ordered them to return to Abilene through waters that by then were waist high. Only then did it dawn on the two adventurers that they had completely forgotten their only reason for being outside that day—to deliver their father's lunch to the creamery. For once an irate Ida did not spare the rod. Still bemused many years later, Edgar recalled that "the thrashing taught us a most important rule of boyhood; namely, don't forget your father's lunch."[69]

4.

A Young Man's Education

My hand was made less for the use of the pen than of the ax—or possibly a pistol.

Eisenhower entered Lincoln Elementary School in 1896 at the age of six. Virtually all who enter the alien world of primary school for the first time have vivid, often unwelcome memories of the occasion. Although used to a regimented existence at home, Eisenhower well remembered that day as a cataclysmic experience.[1] Situated near the family home on Abilene's south side, the school lacked lighting or indoor plumbing and was dark and forbidding in winter. For the first few years, slates were used for writing, with paper furnished only from about the sixth grade. Learning was by the traditional method of repetition and offered little incentive to hold a child's interest. Eisenhower's boredom was only assuaged by an infrequent spelling bee or the "suppression of a disorderly boy."

Although education in Eisenhower's time was intended to produce informed citizens, there was little endorsement in places like Abilene for education unless it had some demonstrably practical value. As Eisenhower notes, "It was a male-run society and schools were preponderately feminine," by about two to one.[2] A college education was simply a fantasy for most at a time when few young people even completed high school. Of the two hundred students who entered the first grade at Abilene's two elementary schools in 1897, a mere sixty-seven entered the town's high school.

Although dismal and unrewarding, school was not all work. Recess was a time to let off steam as only young boys can. Their usual recreation was a game called shinny, a "ground version of ice hockey with rules made up on the spot and promptly ignored. They used sticks or whatever they could find for clubs and the puck was a battered tin can. Dwight excelled at this dangerous game and could always be found where the action was the roughest." A corner of the school grounds overlooked his future home, then Uncle Abe's house. One of their favorite pastimes was to line up and watch him treat animals on an improvised table and sling in the yard until the clanging of a triangle signaled the end of recess.[3]

Eisenhower's favorite subjects in grammar school were spelling and arithmetic, which to his logical mind meant that there was never any ambiguity whatsoever in what one did. His interest in proper usage of words turned into a near obsession, and their misapplication he deemed inexcusable. The pragmatic side of Eisenhower can be seen in his love of mathematics. "Practical problems have always been my equivalent of crossword puzzles."[4] Although he practiced it regularly, Eisenhower's penmanship was dreadful, and he never bothered to learn the elaborate Victorian style of the times. "My hand was made less for the use of the pen than of the ax—or possibly a pistol," he later said.[5] Deciphering Eisenhower's handwriting was invariably a challenge to others but never more so than after he became a general. Eisenhower himself could not always read his own writing, which was as contorted as his father's had been neat and elegant. Kevin McCann, a postwar assistant, likened it to something that was written on a lazy Susan, while his longtime friend and military colleague, Gen. Alfred Gruenther, described it as among the world's worst. A junior high school classmate, Wilbur Jeffcoat, laughingly recalled, "I never became president but I sure as heck can write legibly and Eisenhower can't."[6]

Fight as they might among themselves, the brothers would not tolerate others picking on one of their own. To the contrary, Eisenhower seemed to relish confronting a bully or someone clearly superior in size.[7] In 1902 Eisenhower moved to Garfield Junior High School, where he spent the seventh and eighth grades. Situated on the town's north side, Garfield was a mix of students from both north and south. During recess on Dwight's first day, a much bigger bully chased him around the playground threatening to bite off his ears until Arthur intervened and warned the boy to "have your fun with someone else." Although he later realized it was mostly teasing, until he grew strong enough to fend for himself, young Eisenhower was terrified of bullies and their threats. When that day came he never again backed down from the challenge of another or shied from a fight. One day Eisenhower tackled and subdued a particularly large and unpleasant tormentor who was wielding a dangerous weapon in the form of a large steel nut attached to a cord, daring anyone to touch him. As classmate John Long recalled, "From that time on whenever there was any kind of trouble on the school grounds [the students] always wailed 'Ike, Ike, Ike,'" even if he was not involved.[8]

Dwight and his brothers eventually acquired a well-earned reputation as "those little roughnecks from the wrong side of the railroad tracks."[9] By the time they were enrolled in Garfield, both Edgar and Dwight were regarded as the best bare-knuckle fighters in the tough south side. Long before the word "macho" was ever coined, the young men of Abilene, like the Eisenhowers, could lay claim to having acted out the continuing fantasy of the bad old days when it was a Wild West cowtown. Every year there were one or more significant scraps between the two sides for pride and bragging rights during the school term. "We didn't go around looking for them," said Edgar. "No one knew in advance who the combatants would be. They just happened."[10] A large crowd of spectators would form a circle around the fighters in a vacant lot, and only the winner would walk away. That an Eisenhower would be involved was virtually inevitable, and with Dwight now attending Garfield, it came as no surprise that he would be obliged to uphold what had become something of an Eisenhower tradition, as well as the honor of the south siders.

The most wildly exaggerated tale of Eisenhower's boyhood was his alleged marathon fight with a tough north sider named Wesley Merrifield in October 1903. The year before, Edgar had beaten a larger opponent senseless to claim the honor of south side superiority. Dwight was just thirteen when he was obliged to fight Merrifield in a nearby vacant lot in the presence of a large crowd. Neither boy had any inclination to fight the other, particularly for the amusement of a howling mob. Both, however, were eventually intimidated by irresistible pressure from classmates. "The two of us were practically forced together. Neither of us had the courage to say, 'I won't fight,' " wrote Eisenhower.[11] This much is true.

Abilene lore has it that Eisenhower was given no chance against the stronger, faster, bull-like Merrifield. The first full account of the battle was written by Kenneth Davis and has been widely repeated and exploited to turn a fairly ordinary schoolboy fight into a heroic two-hour test of endurance in which Eisenhower is said to have fearlessly withstood the challenge of a bully. The reality was that there was far more pushing and shoving than fisticuffs. In his memoir, Eisenhower recalled that the two went at each other for about an hour, "with occasional pauses for breath."[12]

Whether the fight lasted twenty minutes or an hour, it was said to have ended in a draw when both became too exhausted to continue. Eisenhower later quoted Merrifield saying, " 'I can't lick you.' I said the same thing, and that was that." Eisenhower sustained a black eye that was too obvious to hide from his parents, who kept him out of school for several days. "I got off with a strong reprimand," he recalled.[13] He had long since proved his resilience and physical courage, but a decade later he willingly conceded that Merrifield had licked him. Other than enhancing Eisenhower's reputation in the Abilene community, the most notable aspect of the fight was that Merrifield would be remembered for having fought a future five-star general and president of the United States.

In the autumn of 1904 Eisenhower entered Abilene High School, which was then situated in makeshift quarters on the second floor of the city hall. One room served as the chapel, and the teachers took turns leading devotional services and giving lectures on the Bible and its various Scriptures.[14] The city jail and the quarters of the town fire marshal occupied the first floor. The male students served in the Abilene volunteer fire department. The town fire bell was situated in a cupola in one of the recitation rooms, and whenever it rang to summon them to a fire, Eisenhower and his classmates would seize the opportunity to skip school by helping out. A friend and classmate, Lelia Picking, recalls, "If Dwight didn't get to the hose cart he was among those who sprinted to the store to buy treats for the girls." One morning the students arrived to find that a prisoner had dynamited a corner of the building during an attempted jailbreak, leading one teacher later to observe wryly that the students received their education "midst the howling of the dogs, the wailing of the prisoners and the odor of the onions being cooked for the marshal's dinner."[15]

In the spring of 1905, when Eisenhower was fourteen and in his first year at Abilene High School, what began as a seemingly minor knee abrasion after a fall led to the creation of another exaggerated tale of Dwight Eisenhower's youth. It was a story of near death and miraculous recovery told within the family and related melodramatically to Eisenhower's first biographer, Kenneth Davis—and subsequently repeated in other biographies. What is certain is that the wound became infected, and after several days, Eisenhower's left knee became swollen and quite painful. Fearing the worst when she noticed a black streak running up his thigh, Ida immediately summoned the Eisenhower family physician, Dr. Tracy R. Conklin, known familiarly as "Doc Conklin," who was well respected throughout the Abilene community.

According to the tale, Conklin is thought to have confirmed Ida's worst fear: that Dwight was in an advanced stage of blood poisoning, and if it infected his abdomen, he would die. Dwight's fever was said to have risen so high that he had sunk into a semicoma. Conklin repeatedly urged the Eisenhowers to permit him to amputate Dwight's poisoned leg in order to save his life. Terrified that if he lost his leg he would never again play sports, Eisenhower supposedly declared he'd rather die. Edgar claimed his younger brother extracted a promise that Conklin would not be permitted to take his leg. In his autobiography Edgar insists that he stationed himself in front of the bedroom door and warned, "Nobody's going to touch Dwight. . . . For two days I kept watch," permitting the doctor to enter the room only to medicate and bandage his brother's leg. A frustrated and helpless Conklin allegedly told the parents it was murder.[16] After some three days, however, the fever miraculously abated and the ominous black line gradually disappeared. That Dwight's life and his leg had been saved was viewed by the family as nothing less than God's will.

According to one of Eisenhower's presidential physicians, who made an extensive study of his health, "it was labelled 'blood poisoning' at the time, but over the years physicians who have evaluated the characteristics of the infection have considered it to have been . . . a streptococcal infection of the skin and soft tissues."[17] Without antibiotics, which had yet to be discovered,

Eisenhower's wound could only have been healed by his immune system. What was thought to have been a coma was almost certainly delirium brought on by the high fever. That he was well conditioned and in the peak of health are the more probable reasons why Eisenhower did not die from the infection.[18] His recovery kept him out of school for the remainder of the school term, which obliged him to repeat his freshman year in 1905–06.[19]

Eisenhower later scoffed at the tales appearing in magazine and newspaper articles of how his distraught parents prayed continuously throughout his ordeal, but Edgar insists that there was indeed a great deal of prayer by everyone. "Doc Conklin admitted that he had once more met the medical man's superior—God Almighty."[20]

Conklin's granddaughter recalls that his wife was furious when Kenneth Davis's account was published in 1945. On more than one occasion she privately proclaimed that her husband's reputation had been besmirched by the Eisenhowers. "It was not the way things happened," she said, noting that her husband had never recommended amputating Dwight Eisenhower's leg.[21]

In 1907 a fine new high school opened farther uptown, finally bringing to an inglorious end the bizarre experiences Eisenhower and his classmates had had in the city hall. Although Edgar should have been several years ahead of Dwight in school, the year he skipped to work and an illness that kept him home for a year resulted in both attending Abilene High together.

During his early schooldays, he was called Dwight, but during his high school years, from 1905 to 1909, he was nicknamed "Little Ike," to distinguish him from Edgar, who was known as "Big Ike." Dwight was also sometimes called "Ugly Ike," an appellation whose origin was never clear. Ida heartily disapproved of the nickname "Ike" even though it was applied to all her sons at one time or another. When asked, she was likely to reply stubbornly, with a straight face, "Ike? Who's Ike?"[22]

Dwight is remembered as an extremely popular student who worked very hard at after-school jobs and thus had little time for socializing or involvement in any of the school clubs. His reputation was that of a tough, self-assured, and bright south-side youth who more than fulfilled his wish to be seen as one of the boys. The girls liked him for his seemingly carefree personality, and the boys appreciated his willingness to stand up to schoolyard bullies. However, girls were not high among Eisenhower's priorities, which began with sports, work, hunting, and even his studies. He was far more interested in impressing his peers with his athleticism or his fists. Other than close friendships with several girls from the south side, among them Ruby Norman, Gladys Harding, and Minnie Stewart, Eisenhower evinced little curiosity about the opposite sex and was shy in the company of young women, regarding himself as "gangly and awkward, with few of the social graces."[23] Once asked why he dated only rarely, Eisenhower replied that he had no money, no clothes, and no time. On the only occasion when he arranged a date with a north-side girl, she stood him up.[24] In reality, Eisenhower's purported indifference to the opposite sex masked an innate shyness that was usually manifested by his unkempt dress and disheveled hair. Nor did it enhance his self-confidence that, by his own admission, he was "a terrible dancer."[25]

He had yet to fall in love, although Ruby Norman, a pretty, vivacious redhead with violet eyes and a talent for the violin, appears to have had a serious crush on him. She was his first girlfriend, and the two dated now and then, usually taking in a film at the local movie house (which cost about five cents each), but mostly they were simply best friends. Eisenhower thought of Ruby as the sister he never had. Minnie Stewart was several years older and taught mathematics in the high school. She was in awe of Eisenhower and thought him "brilliant." Another girl he dated was Gladys Harding, whom he would later nearly marry.

Charles M. Harger, editor of the *Abilene Daily-Reflector* and one of Abilene's most respected citizens, knew Eisenhower well. "Coming to high school age, Dwight was a natural leader. He organized groups and was popular with teachers. He was no miracle child; he was just a strong, healthy boy with a serious mind, who looked upon the world as waiting for him—in what capacity he did not know. My daughter [Lois Bradshaw Harger] was in his class, and when a troop of teenagers came to the house with Dwight in the lead, it was certain not to be a quiet evening at home."[26]

When not around women, Eisenhower was self-assured but never conceited, and had no use for others who acted vainly. Although he was never a disciplinary problem, Eisenhower recalled that his school deportment was less than model and more than once resulted in reports to the superintendent of schools, a no-nonsense gentleman who regarded discipline as important as academics.[27] According to Lelia Picking, whenever he was called on to recite, he invariably did so. "I never heard him say, 'I don't know.' "[28] Eisenhower earned very respectable grades, particularly during his junior and senior years, when he scored high in every subject but Latin, even though he possessed the potential to have done even better academically.[29]

Another classmate remembered Eisenhower as "a happy sort of fellow . . . every time I'd see him, he'd be laughing [and] kidding with the fellows."[30] He seemed intuitively to sense his strengths. Milton believed that his brother's mind most closely resembled that of their father, "because it was completely logical." One who knew him well at Abilene High School remembers a well-built young man ("strong as an ox") who was never afraid of work and did so without complaint. His mind was quick and inquiring as long as the subject interested him. Otherwise he became bored and disinterested.

A sure sign of Eisenhower's short attention span for a subject he disliked or that bored him was repeated scribblings of his name in his Latin book. He had little patience with teachers he deemed incompetent, and would express his disdain by asking pointed questions designed mostly to embarrass or humiliate. Although utterly tactless, these schoolboy displays were the first signs of Eisenhower's most impressive qualities, which set him apart from his classmates and which would prove to be priceless assets in his future career as an army officer: the ability to remember everything he read or that was shown to him, to listen well, and invariably to ask the right questions.[31]

One of Eisenhower's lifelong habits was to write private evaluations of his superiors and, during World War II, of his principal subordinate officers. The practice had its origins in Abilene High School. Several of his schoolbooks survive and are marked by his scrawls in the margins. In his German book, for example, he graded his teachers as either "good" or "cross." One was scorned as "nothing." Another "cross" teacher was Alice Gentry, who taught algebra and recalled Eisenhower as "an earnest, studious boy, interested in baseball."[32] Miss Gentry's standing with her pupil was undoubtedly exacerbated by the fact that although he enjoyed mathematics, Eisenhower thoroughly despised algebra, and his disinterest was reflected in erratic test scores, which ranged from a failing to a very respectable 95.[33]

Plane geometry was one of the subjects taught during his junior and senior years. Eisenhower found himself attracted to its logic and consistently scored nearly perfect marks in what he has described as "an intellectual adventure." He was so good that the principal made an unusual deal with Eisenhower: They would take away his textbook and let him solve the problems on his own. He accepted the challenge with alacrity and in return was promised an A+ grade if the teacher elected to terminate the experiment.[34]

However, it was the study of ancient history that dominated Eisenhower's interest from an early age. An entire chapter of his memoir is devoted to recounting his enduring love affair with history. His friend John Long recalled that from an early age Eisenhower displayed an unusual interest in history. When Japan invaded Russia in 1904, "Dwight and I used to follow the latest reports and comments on the war in the *Literary Digest*, which Dwight brought to school. . . . [He] was very much interested in every move or detail of the Russian-Japanese War."[35]

Eisenhower idolized George Washington for his courage and daring, and for his brilliant speeches. He avidly studied accounts of Princeton, Trenton, and Valley Forge, and was amazed by what he deemed the stupidity of Washington's enemies, who campaigned for his removal as commander in chief of the Revolutionary Army. Eisenhower combined his extraordinary memory with his father's fascination with Greece, and became so conversant with Greek and Roman history that, until old age, he would instantly interrupt and correct anyone who failed to identify correctly a historical date or missed an element of an important battle or campaign.

Among the ancients, Eisenhower's principal hero was Hannibal, not only for his military daring but for his mastery of the logistics of his times. He marveled how Hannibal had managed to survive as a historical icon despite being portrayed badly by a legion of unfriendly historians and biographers. His other "white hats" included Caesar, Socrates, Pericles, and Themistocles. The "black hats" included Darius, Brutus, Xerxes, and the evil Roman emperor Nero.

In 1967 Eisenhower was visited at his Gettysburg farm by former army chief of staff Gen. Harold K. Johnson. During their conversation Johnson said, "Herodotus wrote about the Peloponnesian War that one cannot be an armchair general twenty miles from the front." Afterward one of his former White House speechwriters, who had been present, asked Eisenhower if he knew the precise wording of the quote. He replied, "First, it wasn't Herodotus but Aemilius Paulanus. Second, it was not the Peloponnesian War, but the Punic War with Carthage. And third, he misquoted." Asked why he hadn't corrected General Johnson, Eisenhower replied, "I got where I did by knowing how to hide my ego and hide my intelligence. I knew the actual quote, but why should I embarrass him?"[36]

At first Eisenhower was content merely to absorb the writings of historians. "As a boy, I never played the prophet, . . . I read history for history's sake, for myself alone."[37] Eisenhower read history so voraciously that he began noticeably neglecting his household duties, to the point that Ida felt obliged to lock up his books in a cabinet. She ought to have known that her strong-willed son would not be deterred from his passion. He soon found the key Ida had hidden, and whenever she left the house, he raided the cabinet to retrieve and read a history book.

It would come as no surprise to those who knew him that he would one day retire to a home on the edge of the Gettysburg battlefield. During his youth the Civil War was still too recent to have generated the enormous body of literature it now has. However, as he grew older it became a fountain of interest. Eisenhower especially empathized with the awesome responsibility of the Union commander at Gettysburg, Gen. George Gordon Meade. At the time of his greatest test as a military commander in June 1944, Eisenhower would draw solace from his knowledge of Meade at Gettysburg.[38] Another of Eisenhower's greatest boyhood heroes was Teddy Roosevelt. "To me he seemed to typify integrity, patriotism and moral courage. . . . in my eyes he was a glamorous figure."[39]

During the same period that Eisenhower was developing his affinity for history, a young blond-haired cadet at West Point by the name of George S. Patton, Jr., was similarly engrossed in the study of history and its consequences. Although the two could not have been more disparate in temperament, Patton's own childhood education in Southern California was dominated by a corresponding passion for history that was the centerpiece of his intellectual life. Like Eisenhower, Patton was tutored on the Bible and could recite passages from memory by the hour. The two studied the same commanders of antiquity but drew different conclusions.

In a small black notebook Patton recorded his thoughts, and throughout his colorful military career constantly drew historical parallels to situations he faced. His frequent exhortation to his soldiers was, "To be a successful soldier you must know history," while Eisenhower regarded the study and practice of history as not only an essential means of learning about war but as the study of the triumph of good over evil. Patton rated the commanders of history by what they accomplished with the forces at their disposal. The "black hats" were those who, in Patton's judgment, failed to measure up or who displayed weakness. Eisenhower never had a great deal to say about Alexander the Great, while Patton scorned him because "in a fit of drunkenness [he] took his own life and his empire fell to pieces."[40]

School was meant to be a place of learning, and there was little interest on the part of the school authorities in promoting or supporting athletics. Football was not sanctioned until Eisenhower's senior year. The initiative was left to the students, and there was sometimes a problem finding enough players to make up a team. The baseball team had real uniforms with AHS inscribed on their shirts, but each football player had to supply his own homemade equipment, usually a sweater and duck pants with some padding added. Football was played without helmets and was not a sport for the faint of heart.[41]

During his high school years Eisenhower blossomed as an athlete. His unusually large hands helped his athleticism immensely. In the autumn of 1908 Eisenhower was elected president of the newly revived Athletic Association, which was organized by the students to raise funds to support the baseball and football teams. For the first time he had been selected to carry out a formal responsibility. Eisenhower worked diligently but learned early on that petty politics within the membership undermined its effectiveness. The experience taught him how difficult it could be to meet the challenge of leading a diverse group of individuals, each of whom had his or her own ideas how things ought to be done. His proudest achievement was writing a constitution that he hoped would insure the association's survival.[42]

Eisenhower played baseball and football during his last two years at Abilene High. No matter the sport, he played with abandon and utter disregard for his own safety. During baseball season he usually played center field, and Edgar, the team captain, was the first baseman.[43] During their senior year Edgar was the fullback, and Dwight played right end in an abbreviated, four-game football season. As president of the Athletic Association, Eisenhower wrote the "Athletics" entry in the school yearbook. His great love of sports shined through when he wrote, "After the football season closed, we had to spend the winter dreaming of past victories and future glories."[44]

Since he was one of the school's most influential athletes, his word carried considerable weight. On one occasion, when the football team traveled to another town for a game, his teammates objected to playing because of the presence of a black athlete on the opposing team. In his typically unequivocal manner, Eisenhower lectured his teammates that this was no excuse for failing to play the game and threatened to go home and play no more that season. They listened, and the game was played. Both before and after the game Eisenhower made a point of shaking the black player's hand.[45] Although he was too young to understand fully what he had done, Eisenhower had just demonstrated a flair for leadership.

Graduation week ceremonies at Abilene High School included the senior class play. Both Edgar and Dwight took part in an outlandish spoof of Shakespeare's *The Merchant of Venice*. Edgar was cast as the Duke of Venice, and Dwight appeared in face paint and a comical costume as a bumbling servant, Launcelot Gobbo. For the only time in their high school careers, Dwight overshadowed his brother. A newspaper review called him "the best amateur humorous character seen on the Abilene stage in this generation and gave an impression that many professionals fail to reach."[46] It was the first and only theater production in which Eisenhower ever participated.

Throughout his high school years he appeared in the yearbook as David Dwight Eisenhower. Only when he entered West Point were the two names unofficially transposed. For the remainder of his life he was Dwight David Eisenhower.

When he graduated on May 27, 1909, he was a far different young man from the gangly youth of 1904.[47] Eighteen-year-old Dwight Eisenhower had grown into a rugged, handsome young man standing five feet eleven inches, his 145-pound body toughened by years of sports and strenuous physical labor.

Eisenhower's entry in the school yearbook, the *Helianthus* (Latin for "sunflower"), described him as the "best historian and mathematician." Edgar was written up as "the greatest football player of the class." It was customary to publish class prophecies for each graduate. The author, Agnes Curry, ventured the prediction that Edgar would become a future two-term president of the United States, while she thought Dwight would become a professor of history at Yale.[48]

Although he still had no career goal in life, both Dwight and Edgar were powerfully motivated to attend college. They were encouraged by the words of the commencement speaker, Henry J. Allen, the editor of the *Wichita Beacon* (later a governor of Kansas and a U.S. senator), who extolled the importance of self-reliance and a college education. "I would sooner begin life over again with one arm cut off than attempt to struggle without a college education," he told them. With Edgar and Dwight, Henry Allen was preaching to the converted.

By 1909 Dwight Eisenhower had outgrown his Abilene roots. His future had yet to be determined, but it clearly lay elsewhere. Although Abilene has become virtually synonymous with the Eisenhower name, behind the later praise and public affection for his hometown lay unforgettable memories of hard times. In his old age Eisenhower reflected a certain weariness at the burdens he had carried, once ruminating how he wished he could return to Abilene and "just be a boy again. How nice that would be."[49] Time changes and often dims memories, but in 1909 Eisenhower's ambition was simply to escape the same fate that had befallen their father.

Even though Dwight's overall grades in high school were well above average, no one seems to have sensed that he would ever become anyone special. Yet high school had kindled a powerful belief that education was the handmaiden to future professional success. The more immediate problem of what direction his life would take was now acute. Unless some means of furthering their educations could be found, both Dwight and Edgar appeared doomed to follow in David's footsteps at the Belle Springs Creamery. There was no money to educate even one brother, much less six. During the summer of 1909, "Ed and I had just one idea . . . to get our hands on every cent we could possibly earn."[50] Their futures looked bleak.

Part II

THE ACCIDENTAL SOLDIER, 1910–1916

5.

Abilene to West Point

I think his grin saved Ike a lot of trouble.
— JOSEPH W. HOWE
editor, Dickinson County News

The same year Dwight Eisenhower graduated from Abilene High School, George S. Patton graduated from West Point with a commission in the cavalry and a clear conviction that he would one day become a famous general. Eisenhower had no idea what he would do with his life. What Eisenhower lacked in 1909 was not determination but merely a vision of what occupation he would pursue or how he would go about it. He received encouragement to continue his education from Charlie Harger, who offered him a job on his newspaper. Eisenhower declined, saying: "No, that is a place for Milton; he is a student." Milton possessed an inquiring mind and a formidable intellect but was frail and had none of the physical toughness of his older brothers. "The older boys enjoyed teasing Milton and making him cry, while at the same time they were determined to make him into a tough-guy imitation of themselves." To help toughen him up, Edgar once locked him in a dark attic, inducing instead a dread of darkness that haunted Milton for many years.[1] Because of their eight-year age difference, Dwight and Milton were never particularly close as children. But as adults the two forged a bond that never existed in their relationships with the other four Eisenhower brothers. "Milton has the brains of the Eisenhower family," Dwight once declared.[2]

David and Ida never foisted their ideas or beliefs onto their six sons. They were taught not only to think for themselves but to choose their own paths in life. Their fierce competitiveness notwithstanding, Edgar and Dwight were in full accord in their resolve to attain a higher education as a means of escaping the drudgery of life in Abilene.[3] Each was resolutely determined to help the other somehow achieve a prized college education. The problem was how to pay for it. The two made a pact: As the eldest, Edgar would be afforded the opportunity to pursue his dream while Dwight worked for a year to raise funds to assist him. Then it would be Dwight's turn for a year. The two would alternate work and school until each graduated eight years later. Edgar was committed to becoming a lawyer and set his sights on the University of Michigan, which he believed had the best law school in the country. Initially Dwight intended to follow Edgar to Michigan, although he had no specific goal in mind other than a college education and a chance to continue playing football and baseball.

The only time David ever spoke openly about one of his children's future careers was his attempt to sway Edgar by offering financial help on the condition he study medicine at the University of Kansas. Edgar rebuffed his father's offer just as David had adamantly spurned Jacob's advice twenty-five years earlier. "There I was, on my own, without a dime," recalled Edgar. With no place else to turn, he approached his uncle, Chris Musser, who offered his patronage as a director of the Farmers National Bank, by personally guaranteeing repayment of a two-hundred-dollar loan that sent Edgar on his way to the University of Michigan. Neither bothered to inform David of the arrangement.[4]

Eisenhower later vehemently disavowed biographer Kenneth Davis's assertion that he spent the years 1910–11 in "aimless drifting."[5] Shortly before his death, Eisenhower chided some of his biographers who had suggested he didn't know what he wanted to do with his life, as "the craziest thing I ever heard of. I was going to go to school but I had to get some money. And I stayed out of school two years in order to help my brother [Edgar]."[6]

Eisenhower's after-school and summer jobs included picking apples, working in a lumberyard and coal yard, and as a straw boss in a small plant that manufactured steel grain bins. He also worked harvesting wheat from dawn to dusk for fifty cents a day. After two years Eisenhower was told he was too big for the job and too small for another. He later described the experience as "my first lesson that relations are governed by neither fixed rules nor logic. . . . For years I had been taught that it takes two to start a quarrel. Now, I saw that in any organized effort there may be as many disagreements about policy and practice as there are participants."[7]

By 1910 Eisenhower had given up his various other jobs for a better-paying full-time position at the Belle Springs Creamery, where his principal duty was to operate the ice tank, from which he had to extract three-hundred-pound blocks of ice with steel tongs and send them down a chute into the ice storage room, then help load them into wagons or boxcars. In summer he could usually be found barefoot, with his sleeves rolled up. On a slow night friends might drop by to play penny-ante poker or help raid the company food locker for ice cream or eggs. They also cooked chickens "on a well-scrubbed shovel in the boiler room."[8]

He was soon promoted to fireman. His responsibilities were to stoke the coal-fired boilers and remove and extinguish hot embers; it was hot, dirty, and unrewarding work. Edgar had once held the same job for less pay and never forgot the "terrible heat," exacerbated by outside temperatures of over one hundred degrees in summer, the sweating, the filth, and the physically exhausting exertion required to load an average of three tons of coal per day. "In this small inferno, life lost its charm but the job led to another promotion," remembered Dwight. During his last year there, in 1910–11, Eisenhower was again advanced, this time to second engineer, and during his last three months earned sixty dollars per month, a salary he deemed impressive. Indeed, Eisenhower's salary was nearly double what his father earned when he was first employed at the creamery in 1892.[9] In return, he worked eighty-four hours per week, from six P.M. to six A.M. in the ice plant.[10] True to his word, Dwight sent Edgar two hundred dollars in 1910. (Years later Edgar mentioned to a friend that he still owed his brother for his share of helping finance his education. Asked why he had not repaid the debt, Edgar replied, "Dwight hasn't asked for it.")[11]

In addition to his work at the creamery, Eisenhower played semipro baseball under an assumed name in another nearby town before entering West Point. For reasons he never explained, it was not until 1961 that Eisenhower finally admitted that he had in fact played professional baseball for one season under a pseudonym (possibly Wilson). He refused to go into detail because it was "too complicated," and ordered his staff not to answer questions on the subject.[12]

Eisenhower's future course was aided immensely by his friendship with a younger classmate named John F. "Six" McDonnell, a talented athlete who played for the high school team and eventually became a successful semipro pitcher. Eisenhower got in the habit of visiting the offices of the weekly newspaper, the *Dickinson County News*, where McDonnell worked part-time for editor Joseph W. Howe.

Howe was a member of the school board, a state senator, and a man of some influence who headed the Dickinson County Democratic Party Committee. The windows of Howe's office were plastered with newspapers from places such as New York, Kansas City, and St. Louis. Eisenhower would avidly devour each while waiting for Six McDonnell to get off work. Howe had set aside a room in the back of the newspaper as a recreational place where young men could meet, read, or just shoot the breeze. Sometimes Eisenhower and his friends boxed to let off steam. Howe remembered him as a good boxer. "He was not revengeful. He never went out looking for trouble, but . . . he never ran away from it. I think his grin saved Ike a lot of trouble." Howe greatly admired that Eisenhower displayed a distinct lack of bitterness about his poverty or his hard work at any job he could find.[13]

The greatest benefit from Eisenhower's friendship with Howe was that he was given access to the books in Howe's sizable library. Abilene had no public library, and Howe's books became a prime source for high school research papers and for learning about the world outside Abilene. One of them was

The Life of Hannibal, a book that ignited Eisenhower's great interest in Hannibal's exploits.

Another of the places frequented by McDonnell and Eisenhower was a nearby pool hall. Even in the early days of the century, pool halls had an unsavory reputation. Yet, for young men like Dwight Eisenhower and Six McDonnell, they were a haven in a small, conservative town like Abilene. "The pool hall was my country club and it also was Dwight's," said McDonnell.[14]

Joe Howe was impressed by this intelligent young man who was better educated and poised than he himself knew. Howe became both a friend and mentor and was undoubtedly responsible for encouraging Eisenhower to pursue the possibility of obtaining a free education at West Point or Annapolis. From his association with Howe, Eisenhower learned about the vast world outside Abilene. For a young man who had never been out of Kansas, it came as a revelation that can only have enhanced Eisenhower's desire to seek his destiny elsewhere. The two frequently engaged in political discussions and debates. Eisenhower had the knack of knowing when to speak and when to keep quiet. Recalled Howe, "He liked to debate subjects and had the faculty of asking controversial questions . . . to confuse his opponent. . . . [If] cornered he would come forth with some witticism and put on his best smile. In that way he generally ended the debate by disposing of his opponent's argument."[15]

Although Eisenhower was too young to have any genuine political persuasion, Howe was convinced that his young friend was a Democrat.[16] Undoubtedly at Howe's instigation, Eisenhower was one of three young men invited to speak at the annual banquet of the Dickinson County Young Men's Democratic Club on November 9, 1909. Whether or not he took the speech seriously is not known, but an indication may be the fact that Eisenhower did not write it until the night before in Howe's back room. He titled it "The Student in Politics," and in it Eisenhower "drew the Republican party as the party of privilege, the Democratic party as the party of the people, and concluded that the only course for a young man who was a student of politics was to vote for the Democrats." It was a remarkable performance for a young man with no previous training in public speaking or speech writing.[17]

Howe would later express the conviction that Eisenhower had given a decidedly Democratic speech. "I'm certain," he said, "that the young Dwight I knew in Abilene thought of himself as a Democrat," like his father, David, who was a registered member of the party.[18] When Eisenhower ran for president as a Republican in 1952, Howe wrote bitterly to Six McDonnell that he felt betrayed by Eisenhower's decision.[19] Perhaps his displeasure reached Eisenhower's ears, but in his memoir, *At Ease*, he fails to acknowledge or even mention Joe Howe's important contributions at a key juncture in his life.

Dwight Eisenhower's own recollections suggest that he first began to consider attending the U.S. Naval Academy at Annapolis in 1910 at the urging
of his friend Everett E. "Swede" Hazlett, Jr. Eisenhower had first met Hazlett,
a physician's son, in 1905, when he was a sophomore and Hazlett a freshman
at Abilene High School. Perhaps recollecting his own childhood nickname,
he dubbed the blond youth "Swede," a name that stuck for the rest of his life.
Hazlett was a well-built young man who had no interest in either sports or
fighting. As a north-side boy from a prosperous family, Swede had led a more
sheltered life. Despite his size Swede became the target of school bullies until
Eisenhower intervened to put an end to such shenanigans. The two became
close friends, but after a year their budding friendship was put on hold when
Hazlett left Abilene to attend a military academy in Wisconsin. Eisenhower
did not see him again until the summer of 1910.[20]

From the time he was twelve, Hazlett loved to ride horses and actually
coveted an appointment to West Point and a career in the cavalry, whose
home base was at nearby Fort Riley. Dr. Hazlett had sent Swede to Wisconsin
in an effort to "cure" him of his desire to pursue a career that was then held
in low esteem. The plan backfired after Hazlett became even more enthusiastic, although ultimately unable to obtain an appointment to West Point.
Instead, thanks to his family's influence, he was tendered an appointment to
Annapolis in the spring of 1910 by the local congressman, Rep. Roland R.
Rees. When he returned to Abilene in June, Eisenhower learned that his friend
had failed the mathematics portion of the Annapolis entrance examination,
and was home to retake the test and pursue a reappointment.

During the summer of 1910 Hazlett regaled his friend with tales of life
outside Kansas, and suggested that Eisenhower should pursue an appointment
to Annapolis. Eisenhower was easily convinced. "He got to telling me about
these two academies (West Point and Annapolis) and he got me steamed up
about it." Moreover, Hazlett reminded him, if Eisenhower managed to secure
an appointment to Annapolis, it would mean they would become classmates,
making their ordeal of surviving for four years more tolerable.

Eisenhower wrote to Representative Rees, who replied that he had no
further vacancies but suggested he contact Sen. Joseph L. Bristow, who had
been elected to the U.S. Senate in 1908 and was the only Kansas legislator
who had one vacancy to each school to fill in 1911.[21] Eisenhower immediately
wrote to Bristow on August 20, 1910:

Dear Sir:
I would very much like to enter either the school at Annapolis, or the
one at West Point. In order to do this, I must have an appointment
to one of these places and so I am writing to you in order to secure
the same.

I have graduated from high school and will be nineteen years of age this fall [*sic*].

If you find it possible to appoint me to one of these schools, your kindness will certainly be appreciated by me.

Trusting to hear from you, concerning this matter, at your earliest convenience, I am, respectfully yours,

Dwight Eisenhower.[22]

Although Bristow never replied to his letter, Eisenhower set out to obtain sponsorship for his nomination.[23] As well as securing the support of Democrat Joe Howe, he solicited and received letters of recommendation from both factions of the Abilene Republican party: Charlie Harger, editor of the *Abilene Daily Reflector,* and Phil Heath, editor of the more liberal Republican *Abilene Chronicle,* a remarkable feat for a rather unsophisticated young man. Eisenhower also visited virtually every Abilene business and civic leader, and his efforts paid off with a number of other letters supporting his nomination.

A mere two weeks after his first letter to Bristow, Eisenhower again wrote rather forcefully to ask for the senator's consideration. "Some time ago [*sic*], I wrote to you applying for an appointment to West Point or Annapolis. As yet I have heard nothing definite from you about the matter, but I noticed in the daily papers that you would soon give a competitive examination for these appointments. Now, if you find it impossible to give me an appointment outright, to one of these places, would I have the right to enter this competitive examination?"[24]

Yes, indeed, replied Bristow. The examination was to be held on October 4 and 5 in Topeka, which left Eisenhower a mere three weeks to prepare. Fortunately the night shift at Belle Springs Creamery provided time for Eisenhower to study for the examination. With Swede's help "the two of us began studying together, and we did it by getting the old examinations that these schools had been putting out for years. They had the answers, so we studied and reexamined each other." A decade later at Camp Meade, Maryland, Eisenhower would employ the same technique to study battlefield problems used in the army's Command and General Staff School at Fort Leavenworth with his charismatic new friend, Col. George S. Patton, Jr. He had never before studied as diligently as he did during September 1910. Night after night the two crammed for the examination and tested each other. Years later Swede would remember that Eisenhower's "God-given brain had sped him along" to the point where the pupil had forged ahead of his teacher.[25]

Eisenhower's hard work soon paid off. Eight candidates participated in the two-day examination. He was one of four who kept his options open by indicating he would accept either West Point or Annapolis, while the other four applied only for West Point. When the results were tallied, Eisenhower had finished second overall by only a slim margin with a score of 87.5. The top candidate, George Pulsifer, Jr., scored 89.5 but because Pulsifer had specified only West Point, it meant that Eisenhower had finished as the top candidate for Annapolis.

Senator Bristow decided not to tender Eisenhower an appointment to Annapolis. Instead he wrote on October 24 to announce that Eisenhower was his nominee for the vacancy at West Point in 1911, and his name would be forwarded to the secretary of war. The letter required that Eisenhower furnish "a statement of your exact age, years and months, and a statement as to how long you have been an actual resident of Kansas." In his reply the following day thanking the senator for the appointment, Eisenhower either lied or again misstated his age: "I am just nineteen years [*sic*] and eleven days of age and have been a resident of Kansas for eighteen years," he wrote.[26]

What Eisenhower never knew was that Bristow had sent his friend Phil Heath the applications of all the candidates and asked for his recommendations. Heath had placed Eisenhower's name first for the West Point vacancy, which explains why Bristow passed over Pulsifer in favor of Eisenhower. It turned out to be a stroke of good fortune for Eisenhower. The rules for admission to Annapolis required that a candidate must enter before his twentieth birthday. Thus, had Bristow appointed him to Annapolis, Eisenhower could not legally have accepted, even though he had finished first.

Bristow's decision now meant that Eisenhower had only to pass the West Point entrance and physical exams, without which the appointment would default to Pulsifer. His parents were not overjoyed by the news but kept their silence. Eisenhower attempted to sugarcoat it by observing he had yet to pass an examination others had had far more time to prepare for. He borrowed one of Howe's books, called *Century Book of Facts*, to study for the forthcoming West Point exam, remarking that "he guessed he would have to do some real studying now."[27] Minnie Stewart thought Eisenhower was wasting his talents. "There's just no *future* in the Army," she said. "You're just throwing yourself away." This time it was Eisenhower who kept silent.[28]

To better prepare himself Eisenhower returned to Abilene High School in the autumn of 1910 to take refresher classes in math and physics. With no eligibility rules in those days, it was also a grand opportunity to play another year of football, this time as a tackle. During a game with archrival Salina, Eisenhower is alleged to have ferociously leveled an opponent in retaliation after the Abilene quarterback, Six McDonnell, was accidentally knocked unconscious. It was actually a teammate who had reciprocated, but the tale became another of the fanciful legends about Eisenhower.[29]

The West Point entrance examination was held in January 1911. Eisenhower traveled to Jefferson Barracks, Missouri, an army post on the outskirts of St. Louis, where the test was administered over four days. It marked the farthest he had ever been from Abilene. Both Eisenhower and Pulsifer passed the written and physical examinations. Eisenhower was ordered to report to West Point in June 1911 as a member of the class of 1915.[30]

(In July 1911 a young man from rural Missouri who was likewise too poor to afford a higher education reported to Jefferson Barracks to take the grueling entrance examination as an alternate candidate from his congressional district. He left St. Louis believing he had failed miserably. Three weeks later he was astonished to learn he had not only passed but that the principal candidate had failed some parts of the exam and had been disqualified. As the alternate, he was to report immediately to join the class of 1915 at West Point. His name was Omar Nelson Bradley.)

Eisenhower later gave full credit to Swede Hazlett for alerting him to the opportunities offered by West Point and Annapolis. "As you well know, it was only through you that I ever heard of the Government academies." The truth is that well before the summer of 1910 Eisenhower already knew all about West Point and Annapolis, both through conversations with Joe Howe and, much earlier, with his close boyhood friend, John E. Long. According to Long, "I spent more time with him than I spent with any other boy." The two often spoke of how they might obtain a free education. "We often planned and talked about going to Annapolis to get an [college] education. . . . as we were both too poor." After moving to Lawrence, Long later took the Annapolis entrance exam and failed it badly. He wrote to Eisenhower advising, "Please don't take that examination until you're well prepared."[31]

Ida Eisenhower was dismayed by the news her son would attend West Point. "She didn't like it," said her most mercurial son, "but she never made the fuss about it that some people have tried to [suggest]—she just thought that for one of her boys to go into the Army [and] have something to do with war . . . [was] rather wicked. And I know that she was sad."[32] Dwight's decision went to the heart of her deeply held beliefs, which had less to do with pacifism than they did with Witness theology, which holds that all war is wrong. However, Ida's true reservation was the fact that she was obliged to hide from her six sons "her 'weakened faith' and 'grief' that resulted from Dwight Eisenhower's pursuit of a military career."[33]

The day he left home to board a train at the nearby Abilene terminal to begin the long journey to West Point, Eisenhower remembered bidding a hasty good-bye to his mother "before I started bawling." Milton was the only son present and vividly remembers, "Mother stood there like a stone statue, and I stood right by her until Ike was out of sight. Then she came in and went to her room and bawled like a baby. . . . I cried too."[34]

6.

The Long Gray Line

From the first day at West Point, and any number of times thereafter, I often asked myself: What am I doing here?

Eisenhower's journey by rail to West Point evoked mixed emotions. Although driven to leave Abilene and continue his education, there was the unease and fear that comes with being abruptly wrenched from the security of a close-knit family. Other than his brief trip to St. Louis to take the West Point entrance exam earlier in 1911, Eisenhower had never seen a big city.

During a stopover in Chicago he was reunited with Ruby Norman, who was a student at the Chicago Conservatory of Music. They spent several care-free days exploring the sights of the city and attending films at night. Ruby was the only person outside members of his family whom Eisenhower had ever confided in, and during the next four years she would become not only a pen pal but a sounding board for his triumphs and tribulations.

Eisenhower then detoured to Ann Arbor for a brief reunion with Edgar at the University of Michigan. One evening the two rented a canoe and, with two coeds in tow, paddled leisurely on a nearby river to the accompaniment of popular tunes of the day played on Edgar's portable phonograph. Eisenhower called it the most romantic evening he had ever known, although it left him envious of his brother's status and apprehensive that he might have erred in not following in Edgar's footsteps.[1] The two brothers would not see each other again until 1926.

Eisenhower's inexperience of big cities left him "scared to death" at the thought of stopping in New York. His trepidations were somewhat assuaged by the presence on the train of a number of other new cadets, many of whom displayed their collective uncertainty. The train stopped at the village of Highland Falls, forty-five miles north of New York City on the morning of June 14, 1911. On a typically hot and steamy summer day, Dwight Eisenhower, like so many others before him, made the trek with a heavy suitcase up the steep hill from the railway station to the place where "I really hit a new world." Within the space of several hours his life would be turned upside down.

First established in 1775 as a military fortress, West Point still retained many characteristics from its grim origins dating to the Revolutionary War. Situated astride a sharp bend in the Hudson River, the fort had been a strategically important outpost of the fledgling nation, and the ideal site from which to prevent the British fleet from occupying the Hudson River Valley and possibly suppressing the budding Revolution. West Point's elaborate defenses included guns mounted on the parapets overlooking the river, which at one time had a great chain across it. George Washington once called West Point "the key to the continent."[2] In 1780 its commander was Benedict Arnold—the hero of the historic battles of Fort Ticonderoga, Quebec, and Saratoga—once rated "the most brilliant soldier of the Continental Army," who became the archbetrayer of the American Revolution.

In the century before Eisenhower arrived there as a cadet, West Point had evolved from a school for engineers that had graduated a mere two officers in 1802 to a national institution that supplied the U.S. Army with the majority of its professional officers. The top graduates became engineer and artillery officers, while the middle and bottom ranks of each class found themselves commissioned in the infantry. Thus, when Robert E. Lee finished second in the class of 1829 he became an engineer, while Grant, who finished in the middle of his class, was relegated to the infantry.[3]

During the Civil War the armies of the Union and the Confederacy were dominated by its graduates, which in addition to Grant and Lee included George McClellan, Abner Doubleday, George G. Meade, J. E. B. Stuart, Philip H. Sheridan, William Tecumseh Sherman, Stonewall Jackson, Joe Johnston, Ambrose Burnside, Jefferson Davis, and the "goat" (lowest ranking) of the class of 1861, an intensely ambitious young officer named George Armstrong Custer. Although the Civil War pitted West Point classmates against one another, it failed either to seriously disrupt the academy's mission or to prevent those who fought for the Confederacy from eventually sending their sons there in the post–Civil War years.

During this period the practice of hazing became an integral part of plebe life, and a West Point tradition. Its excesses included strenuous and often harmful physical exercise, liberal doses of Tabasco sauce in a plebe's food, and being forced to participate in elaborate funeral ceremonies for dead rats. Hazing produced a code of silence on the part of the hapless plebes, and it became a matter of dishonor to expose the upperclassmen who perpetrated such mischief. Among those who was hazed unmercifully as a cadet was a 1903 graduate named Douglas MacArthur, an officer who would one day play a pivotal role in the military career of Dwight Eisenhower.[4]

At the start of the twentieth century the U.S. Military Academy was considerably smaller than the present imposing facility. In 1911 Eisenhower and the other incoming members of the class of 1915 entered a world little changed from that of the remote nineteenth-century outpost. There to greet them rudely with shouts, abuse, and instructions were upper-class cadre, some of whom were yearlings (sophomores) newly liberated from their own year of hell as plebes. The arrival of a new class marked the start of what is still inelegantly dubbed "beast barracks," a rite of passage designed to indoctrinate civilians in the West Point way and to identify and weed out those unable or unwilling to function as future officers. The cadet yearbook still referred to plebes as "scum of the earth."

West Point has been aptly described as "a military monastery" whose occupants "were isolated from the outside diseases of commercialism and money-grubbing."[5] MacArthur once likened it to "a provincial reformatory based on fear,"[6] and in fact four years at West Point were their own form of penal servitude, eased only by a two-month leave the summer after the second class year, and a Christmas leave or two for those in high academic standing.

The entire corps of cadets consisted of 650 young men organized as "the Battalion," which consisted of six companies, A through F, commanded by a quartermaster. Of the 287 cadets who constituted the class of 1915 (at the time West Point's largest plebe class), only 162 actually graduated—an attrition rate of 44 percent. Moreover, Eisenhower's class was hardly a representative cross section of young American men. Most were predominantly Protestants of Anglo-Saxon Irish, English, Scottish, or German origin.

Discipline verged on the Draconian and was ruthlessly enforced in the form of demerits for infractions of the rules and regulations. Excessive demerits earned the offender punishment tours marched with military precision twice weekly for two hours, with rifle and pack. Serious offenses required a personal explanation to the commandant of cadets, about 90 percent of which were rejected. "It hardly seems possible," remembered Col. Joseph C. Haw, a graduate of the class of 1915, "that a grown man was actually reported for touching a lady's arm, but it is an undisputable fact. So zealously did the Tactical Department guard our manners and morals that a contemporary of ours was actually 'skinned' [assessed demerits] for assisting his own mother across the street."[7] Other offenses included "strong odor of perfume in room," "displaying indifference at [horseback] riding," and "highly unmilitary conduct . . . allowing a guard tent to be used for the amusement of ladies." Despite its rigidity and provincialism, "we managed to have lots of fun . . . out of the little daily incidents of cadet life," recalled Haw. " 'Kidding' and 'razzing' were almost too incessant and intense, for there was little else to joke about."[8]

The West Point method of turning a civilian into a professional soldier was autocratic. Hazing still occurred but had been made punishable by dismissal, and the treatment of plebes was generally restricted to the more traditional, less harmful harassments. Young men were stripped of their civilian mores and over four years the makings of an officer and a gentleman were created. Yet despite its minor reforms, West Point remained deeply tradition-bound and set in its ways. The cold and forbidding gray granite buildings of West Point were unlike anything most new arrivals had ever seen. The rooms and living conditions were equally bleak, and the amenities few. The winters were frigid, and the summers hellishly hot.

Eisenhower's enduring recollection of his first day at West Point was of "bewilderment and calculated chaos." Cadets were not permitted to have money and were required to turn in whatever funds they possessed to the bursar to pay a monthly charge levied by the government for uniforms. The new plebes were measured for their uniforms, filled out forms, and hustled from place to place to carry out a timeworn practice. Eisenhower described their rude introduction to cadet life as "a series of shouts and barks" by "self-important upperclassmen."

Plebes were assigned to cadet companies based on height. Eisenhower was assigned to F Company, where the tallest cadets were placed. Late that afternoon, the members of the new class of 1915 assembled in full-dress uniform on the fabled Plain of West Point to participate in the traditional first review of the "long gray line." To the accompaniment of guns firing salutes and the band playing martial music, young men who had been civilians only hours earlier marched awkwardly but proudly and then swore the required oath that officially made them the newest members of the corps of cadets. The sight of the American flag and the pomp of his first military parade deeply moved Eisenhower. For the first time in his life it dawned on him what commitment really meant. "Across a half century," he later wrote, it was "a supreme moment . . . I can look back and see a rawboned, gawky Kansas boy from the farm country earnestly repeating the words that would make him a cadet."[9]

For the next three weeks the newcomers were subjected to the rigors of beast barracks in a tent city established at the edge of the Plain. Until September they were taught the rudiments of military drill and ceremonies and participated in an endless routine of drill, guard duty, inspections, and petty intimidations. Nearly a half century later Eisenhower recalled that in the summer of 1911, "no form of animal life [was] more obnoxious and pestiferous than the ubiquitous cadet instructor."[10] Even so, the heat, the shouting, the necessity for instant obedience to the most banal commands, and the constant drills and harassment by the upperclassmen did not unduly trouble Cadet Eisenhower. His boyhood in Abilene had prepared him well for the physical ordeal of West Point. During his few moments of free time he would often reflect on the comic aspects of life as plebe. He reckoned that if he and his classmates had been given time for contemplation, most would have left West Point aboard the next train to pass through Highland Falls. Not for the first time Eisenhower asked himself, "What am I doing here? Like the other young men, I sometimes wondered—where did I come from, by what route and why; by what chance arrangement of fate did I come by this uniform?"[11] Yet, it was a constant source of comfort that no matter how difficult the ordeal, Eisenhower's education was being paid for by the government. His only major obstacle those first weeks was his difficulty in learning to march properly. Until he finally got the hang of it, Eisenhower was consigned to the aptly named Awkward Squad.

The rituals plebes were taught included saluting all officers. The rule was unambiguous: If in doubt, salute. Soon after his arrival Eisenhower's inexperience proved embarrassing. As the academy band came marching down a street, he encountered "the most decorated fellow I had ever seen. I hesitated just a second, then snapped to attention and presented arms but he did not return the salute. I did it again and a third time before realizing he was the drum major."[12]

Plebes were obliged to memorize the name of every classmate and of every upperclassman. Overall, however, the relationship between the upperclassmen and the plebe class was good-natured, remembers Haw. "The 'plebe' system was well calculated to take the conceit out of a man, and a year of it has cured many a swollen head."[13]

The education of West Point's teachers, all of whom were graduates, was generally restricted to what they had learned as cadets, and was "narrow, formalistic, and unimaginative."[14] Teaching was by rote and there was only the approved "school solution" to an academic problem. Independent thinking was not only discouraged but punished. When Douglas MacArthur became superintendent in 1919, he was determined to revise the curriculum and to prepare future officers for what he was certain would be another world war. "How long are we going on preparing for the War of 1812?" he once remarked.[15] Eisenhower soon learned the lesson that "at West Point we were going to do it West Point's way or we were not going to do it at all."

For all its shortcomings West Point, with its creed of "Duty, Honor, Country," instilled in men like MacArthur, Patton, Eisenhower, and Bradley a profound sense of pride, nostalgia, and commitment that endured for the rest of their lives. Other than athletics, the one aspect of cadet life Eisenhower firmly embraced was the West Point honor code. Then, as now, the heart of West Point life is the honor system, under which a cadet will not lie, cheat, steal, or tolerate those who do. Conviction of an honor offense usually meant automatic dismissal. Cadets typically reported themselves, as Eisenhower once did for an infraction as the officer of the guard.

For one of the first times in his life the drawbacks of being the middle child of a large family paid off. The discipline and petty harassments were physically trying but never even remotely overwhelming. Everyone suffered from the effects of the stupefying heat, but it was the rigid discipline that overwhelmed many, including Eisenhower's first roommate, a young man from Kansas who soon quit. "He had come from this little town as the town hero. They'd put him on a train with the band, the mayor made speeches, and when he had this kind of treatment, this just shocked him and he thought everybody was cutting him to pieces. . . . I tried to tell him that, after all, thousands of boys had gone through this same experience ahead of him but he'd put his head down and weep."[16]

Eisenhower's new roommate ("wife" in the West Point vernacular) turned out to be another Kansan, Paul Alfred Hodgson, who hailed from nearby Wichita. The two instantly bonded, roomed together for the full four years, and thereafter remained close friends for life. P.A., as he was known, was a serious student and a distinguished athlete who starred on the great unde-feated football team of 1914. Eisenhower's influence on P.A. was addictive. Normally a studious, sincere young man, Hodgson was not cut from the same devil-may-care cloth as Eisenhower; nevertheless one or the other was in recurring disciplinary trouble. During their four years together, both did time in arrest of quarters for more serious violations and walked punishment tours twice a week, thus joining the ranks of the "area birds." It might have been worse—their shenanigans were as daring as they were numerous. P.A.'s letters to his family began to make flattering references to his new "wife," and Eisen-hower said, "The four years we spent in the same room more than a quarter of a century ago are still some of my most treasured memories."[17]

Nevertheless Hodgson recalled with amusement that when it came to performing required minor duties, his roommate "could be a sly one. . . . We were supposed to take turns opening the windows at night and closing them first thing in the morning. But Ike dressed so fast that he could linger in bed—and I, a slower dresser, always had to get out of my warm bed onto the cold floor and close the windows. I was always very careful about cleaning my part of the room whereas Ike was very nonchalant. But, somehow I always got the demerits."[18]

West Point's authoritarian system failed unduly to concern Eisenhower, who dismissed his mediocre disciplinary record by recalling how he simply ignored or evaded the many details required of a cadet. "I couldn't be both-ered with such things, and so I got lots of demerits." He readily admitted that while he was far from being a careful cadet, "I was far from being a trouble-maker but I didn't think of myself as either a scholar . . . or as a military figure whose professional career might be seriously affected by his academic and disciplinary record."[19]

Eisenhower viewed it as a challenge to violate West Point's strict rules without getting caught. He displayed no fear whatsoever that his conduct might result in dire repercussions, and his escapades ranged from hilarious to downright venturesome. Eisenhower seemed to relish every opportunity to outwit an instructor or upperclassman. An example during his plebe year occurred when he and another cadet were cited for a minor infraction and ordered to appear in a cadet corporal's room in "full-dress coats." The two duly presented themselves clad in only their tunics, under which they were both naked. When ordered to explain himself, Eisenhower replied with a straight face, "Nothing was said about trousers, sir." The prank outraged the corporal and drew the mirth of his roommate. The two plebes were directed to return after taps in full uniform. Their punishment consisted of bracing (a rigid position of attention with one's chin pushed firmly into one's chest) against the wall "until we left our bodily outlines on it in perspiration." Afterward Eisenhower and his fellow plebes had a good but quiet laugh at the corporal's expense.[20]

On another occasion a classmate was hit on the back of his head in the mess hall with a piece of beef. Only Eisenhower's face contained a hint of a smile, and the victim retaliated by heaving a potato at him, "but a poor plebe picked that moment to stand up. He got it right in the eye."[21]

For the most part his transgressions reflected indifference and rebelliousness and ran the gamut of sloppiness, uniform violations, lateness, and other infractions. His laid-back attitude once cost him a hefty five demerits for "smiling in ranks at drill after being corrected."[22] His colorful vocabulary earned him five more for "using profanity at supper." Although Eisenhower's use of profanity did not originate at West Point, it was sufficiently refined during his four-year tenure that it became a permanent part of his persona.

The cadets of F Company were bigger, more athletic, tougher, and inclined to look down on the cadets of the other companies as "runts." Whether it was short-sheeting someone's bed or dumping buckets of water on an unsuspecting cadet, no prank was too small or scheme too audacious that it did not involve Eisenhower.[23] It did not take long for Eisenhower to emerge as one of the most popular cadets in his class. His smile, fun-loving demeanor, and impish disdain for authority were attractive qualities. It was now that the nickname his mother so disliked was first used by his classmates. It stuck for the remainder of his life.

Eisenhower's litany of infractions between 1911 and 1915 fills nearly ten pages. In his senior year alone, he accumulated 100 of his 307 total demerits, thus joining a prestigious group of West Point graduates ranging from J. E. B. Stuart and U. S. Grant ("maltreating a horse—arrested"); Custer ("maltreating new cadet—arrested"); and George McClellan, A. P. Hill, and William T. Sherman ("discharging his musket"), whose names appeared in the commandant's disciplinary register. "My success in compiling a staggering catalogue of demerits," said Eisenhower, "was largely due to a lack of motivation in almost everything other than athletics, except for the simple and stark resolve to get a college education."[24]

Once asked if he ever thought he might not make it through his plebe year, Eisenhower replied, "No, no. I watched my studies and I knew I was going all right. . . . I was very strong and fit physically in those days . . . and when I found I could meet my academic demands, I was all right. I was confident."[25] As he had previously in high school, Eisenhower did not excel academically anywhere near his potential at West Point. Admitting that "I paid no attention" as a cadet, Eisenhower knew he could have done far better. More often than not he would wait until the very last minute to compose papers that were actually remarkably polished pieces of writing. "I'd go to sleep when my roommate would be working. In the morning he'd get up and say, 'Do you know anything about this lesson?' I'd say, 'No, what is it? You tell me.' "[26]

Eisenhower's stubbornness, although sometimes carried to extremes, was also indicative of how important he considered keeping one's word. Classmate James Van Fleet, a future four-star general, remembers how he was razzed by classmates for "bookworming his way to the top" of his English class. Eisenhower responded by pledging not to study an English book outside class for the remainder of the term. "I don't know why he did it," said Van Fleet, but "he finally hit the bottom of the class. But he wouldn't crack a book until the class members released him from his pledge."[27]

One year, several of the hell-raising cadets in Eisenhower's circle were abruptly transferred to other cadet companies by the tactical officers in order "to break up this rabble." Chief among them was Eisenhower. Another self-described "roughneck" was Charles C. Herrick, who recalled that, "One of the worst offenses at the Point was to get caught off the reservation. But somehow it never worried Ike and some of the others. They'd sneak out the lavatory windows, and past the sentry post and off they'd go up the Hudson in a rented boat to Newburgh for coffee and sandwiches. Imagine, they'd travel 30 miles—15 there and 15 back—just for chow. If any of those guys had been caught they'd have been thrown right out of the academy."[28]

Alexander M. "Babe" Weyand, who later earned prominence as an army football player, Olympic wrestler, and noted sports historian, was also a plebe in 1911, and vividly remembers his first encounter with Dwight Eisenhower. One day soon after plebe camp, a cadet entered his room and barked: "Who lives in this house?" Thinking it was an upperclassman, Weyand and his roommate immediately leaped to attention and braced only to find it was a grinning classmate. "In those days, Eisenhower affected a tough breezy western manner. 'At ease,' he barked as he swaggered into the room . . . his smile was so warm and friendly that I had to laugh." Eisenhower and Weyand's roommate "frequently teamed in bizarre enterprises for the sole purpose of annoying the upperclassmen. They were usually caught and disciplined but they had fun while it lasted."[29] Wherever there was mischief, Eisenhower was almost certain to be in the middle. A classmate recalled how, whenever there was a snowball fight, "Ike was always in the thick of it." Cadets would often use the roof of the barracks to gain access to the ground floor after taps. "We would hear a splash of water and everyone knew Ike had caught someone sneaking along the roof below his [third floor] window."[30]

. . .

Eisenhower freely admitted that one of his principal motivations in attending West Point was his expectation that he would be selected to the varsity football and baseball teams. "It would be difficult to overemphasize the importance that I attached to participation in sports," he said. Plebes were eligible for the varsity teams, and with his experience in Abilene he fully expected to be selected. "Ike talked such a grand game," said Weyand, "that we thought he would make the big squad but he was in for a keen disappointment. When the squad was announced Paul Hodgson was on it but Ike was not. To use one of his favorite expressions, he was 'fit to be tied,' as he thought he deserved a place."[31] However, he was deemed too small and light. Instead he played football on the Cullum Hall team, a junior varsity squad that had been created several years earlier by a member of the class of 1904 named Joseph W. Stilwell (the "Vinegar Joe" of future World War II fame). Eisenhower acquitted himself well and helped win the most important game of a short season against a nearby military academy.

Eisenhower did earn a place on the varsity baseball team, but the coach disliked his hitting style and he never played in a single game. He was also selected for the intramural medicine ball team, which comprised the eight cadets judged the fastest. Overall, however, Eisenhower's athletic career at West Point during his plebe year was a major disappointment.

Eisenhower entered West Point in 1911 weighing about 150 pounds, but by the autumn of 1912, between indulging his appetite in the mess hall and engaging in strenuous workouts in the gym, he had bulked up to a very solid 174 pounds in an effort to make the football team. He was still thought to be too light to make the first team, but his hustle, intensity, and "love for hard bodily contact" made a good impression on the coach. The trainer, Sgt. Marty Maher, who spent fifty-five years at West Point, described how "Ike was the first cadet on the field for football practice and the very last to leave. I used to curse him because he would practice so late that I would be collecting footballs he had kicked away in the darkness. He never hit the rubbing table because he would always be out there practicing punts instead of getting a rubdown."[32]

Although he started the 1912 season as a substitute, Eisenhower was soon promoted to the varsity football squad and played in five games as a linebacker on defense and a running back (then called a "plunging back") on offense. Against Colgate he was sent into the game late in the fourth quarter and scored a touchdown, earning praise from the *New York Tribune*, which wrote that "the work of Eisenhower brought joy to the ARMY rooters." Suddenly he was regarded as a talented running back.

His solid play earned him a start as a halfback and linebacker against the Carlisle Indian School, coached by Pop Warner. The star of the Carlisle team was the legendary football great and 1912 decathlon and pentathlon Olympic gold medalist, Jim Thorpe. It usually took at least two defenders to tackle Thorpe, one to hit him high, the other low. On one play he was hammered so hard by Eisenhower and his linebacker partner that Carlisle was obliged to take an injury time-out while Thorpe caught his breath. Eisenhower's happiest memory of playing football was that particular play, when Thorpe "proved as human as any of them." Elation soon turned to dismay, however, when Thorpe niftily averted an attempted gang tackle by Eisenhower and his partner. Instead of tackling Thorpe, the two defenders collided with each other and were so banged up they had to be removed from the game, even though Eisenhower protested that he was well enough to continue. Under the rules neither player could return until the start of the next quarter. Army had scored first, but with its two best linebackers out of action, the game became a rout, which Carlisle won 27–6 in one of the most memorable sporting events in West Point history. After Eisenhower became famous, Babe Weyand asked Jim Thorpe if he recalled the game. "Jim nodded his head vigorously and grunted, 'Good linebacker.' "[33]

Eisenhower's football career came to an abrupt end the following week during a game against Tufts University. He was tackled by the ankle and severely twisted his knee struggling to pick up extra yardage as he was falling. "I could feel something rip although it didn't particularly hurt." After several more plays Eisenhower fell to the ground without being touched. "I couldn't get up, so they took me off the field, and I never got back on as a player again." After he gained prominence, numerous men who claimed to have played that day for Tufts, and to have inflicted Eisenhower's injury, apologized to him at least several dozen times, he laughingly recalled. "I wonder how many men Tufts had on the field when I was hurt?"[34]

The doctors examined his swollen knee but prescribed only rest until the swelling disappeared, leaving Eisenhower convinced he had recovered. Then disaster struck. "The doctors didn't warn me I had a permanently weakened knee. So I went riding" during a voluntary "monkey-drill team" performance, which required dismounting and remounting a horse at the gallop, often facing to the rear. The first time Eisenhower tried it, "I just crashed myself all to pieces."

Eisenhower never challenged biographer Kenneth Davis's version that the injury was precipitated by an allegation of malingering by the riding instructor, and Eisenhower's stubborn refusal to invoke the decision of the doctors that he refrain from participating in riding drills. P. A. Hodgson was said to have attempted to no avail to persuade his defiant roommate not to continue, but Eisenhower was determined to prove the slur wrong. P.A. half-carried, half-dragged him to the infirmary, all the while cursing both "the drillmaster, and Dwight for being a fool . . . when they reached the hospital the doctor cursed too. The knee, red and swollen, was a mess."[35]

Eisenhower spent four agonizing days in the infirmary, where the doctors pronounced the injury permanent. "So I had to give that [athletics] up."[36] His leg was immobilized in a cast, his days as an athlete at an inglorious end; "it was just too hard for me to accept for a while." Head coach Capt. Ernest "Pot" Graves was livid when he learned that Eisenhower had reinjured his knee while riding and would be unavailable to play in the Army-Navy game. "Here I come up with the best line plunger and linebacker I've ever seen at West Point and he busts his knee in the riding hall."[37]

Equitation was the most difficult physical requirement a cadet had to successfully pass and was far more dangerous than football. Most of the horses were former army polo ponies with evil tempers, including one that not only threw its riders but then delighted in kicking them in the face. Once there were three cadets in the infirmary with broken jaws from the same pony. Given the rigors of equitation and the so-called monkey drills, it was hardly surprising that Eisenhower's athletic career ended in 1912.

The senior riding instructor was one of West Point's most eccentric characters, a cavalry major, Julian R. Lindsey, nicknamed "the Squire." Horsemanship was made deliberately difficult: Cadets were obliged to ride with only a saddle pad and a surcingle (a makeshift girth to hold the pad in place). Recalled Joseph Haw, "Some of us fell off our horses so frequently that we could almost tell what part of the riding hall we had fallen by the taste of the tanbark." The following year English saddles were used, but without stirrups. "In those days the cavalry idea was to make riding rough and tough. If a horse refused a jump and catapulted his rider headfirst into the hurdle," the instructor would drawl, " 'You, man, are you trying to break that hurdle?' . . . Not until the middle of our last year were we able to hold the reins when taking a jump."[38]

As the cadets went through the prescribed drills, the Squire would shriek, "That's terrible, [Mr. So-and-so]! Oh, my God, how I suffer! What would the people in Virginia say?" His orderly was a black enlisted man named Hazel, "who was always armed with notebook and pencil. In the midst of his agony at our antics 'the Squire' would yell, 'Report him! Hazel, report that man!' and another 'skin' would go down in Hazel's little black book." The cadets achieved a small measure of retribution by staging a lifelike parody of the two in the annual Hundredth Night Play, a stage revue similar to Eisenhower's high school senior class play. Two impersonators would croon:

> For I'm a nut, a nutty nut,
> A Hazel nut perhaps.
> I'm always fixin' little things
> From reveille till taps.[39]

For a time Eisenhower studied scientific boxing, which he thought would aid him in one day finally besting Edgar. He again reinjured the same knee after twisting it while boxing. This too landed him back in the infirmary, as did an injury playing handball in 1913. "He is afraid it is worse than ever," wrote P.A. to his family. "It finishes his chances for ever again playing football. . . . He had to be carried to the hospital. . . . He was certainly a blue boy."[40]

Eisenhower's knee injury never healed properly and would plague him for the remainder of his life. To his death he blamed the riding instructor for permanently ruining his knee. Psychologically Eisenhower perceived his new handicap as a badge of shame that had cruelly changed the course of his life and negated any chance of his ever again playing sports. "I was like a man with his nose cut off going out into society!" he said.[41] He once tried running as a means of strengthening his knee but was dismayed to learn that it could not withstand the stress. The inevitable result was usually another dislocation. Eisenhower became so discouraged by a future without football and other sports that more than once he considered resigning, until common sense prevailed and he was talked out of it by his classmates. "Life seemed to have no meaning. A need to excel was gone," he lamented.[42] His entry in the 1915 *Howitzer* (the cadet yearbook), written by his roommate, cruelly lampooned that "Ike must content himself with tea, tiddleywinks and talk, at all of which he excels." His misery was evident when he wrote to Ruby Norman a few days after this setback that it seemed like "I am never cheerful anymore. The fellows that used to call me 'sunny jim' call me 'gloomy face' now. . . . I hate to be so worthless and helpless. . . . Anyway I'm getting to be such a confirmed grouch you'd hardly know me. Guess I'll come out of it soon though."[43]

Eisenhower managed to remain close to his beloved football team by becoming the head cheerleader in 1914–15. His experience leading pep rallies the night before games enhanced his ability to act and speak effectively in public. In addition, Coach Graves was so impressed with Eisenhower's grasp of football strategy that he encouraged him to take charge of the Cullum Hall junior varsity football team, which he did with considerable success. The high point of Eisenhower's four years at West Point occurred when he was presented the coveted letter *A* after the 1912 football season. "Ike was very nearly tickled to death," wrote P.A. "He hasn't received his sweater yet, though, and so can't wear it. He borrows mine occasionally so as to enjoy the sensation."[44]

Patton was never as good a football player as Eisenhower but both were relegated to intramural football during their plebe year. In 1905 Patton was likewise injured in a scrimmage against the varsity team, and hospitalized. He doggedly tried out each year for the football team but never earned the coveted *A* that was awarded to Eisenhower, even though he could no longer play. Eisenhower never lost his enthusiasm for the game. When Army beat Navy in 1913 he wrote exuberantly to Ruby Norman, "some game, some game! . . . the joy of the thing is too much—I feel my reason toppling."[45]

The injury had another equally serious consequence. With his morale and self-esteem at an all-time low, Eisenhower began a smoking habit that lasted until 1949. Although pipe and cigar smoking were permitted in cadet rooms, possession of cigarettes was a serious violation of West Point regulations—a fact that failed to dissuade Eisenhower or his classmates who had taken up the habit at the risk of expulsion. With cigarettes unavailable, those who dared to smoke rolled their own. Another bad habit begun at West Point was Eisenhower's practice of wolfing down his food so rapidly it was a wonder he even knew what he was eating. Notes Eisenhower scholar Robert H. Ferrell, "at first he did it for a reason, and later out of habit." To gain sufficient weight to make the football team, "he took up a crash regimen of eating everything in sight in the dining hall and ran his weight up twenty pounds." Both habits would later be of considerable medical concern.[46]

7.

"Popular but Undistinguished"

Poor Dwight merely consents to exist until graduation shall set him free.

— P. A. HODGSON

The impressive brick houses along West Point's faculty row have changed little since the early twentieth century. When once asked if he was ever invited by any of his instructors to their homes, Eisenhower replied derisively, "I didn't know any professors and I didn't want any of them to ask me in[to] their house, I'll tell you that." The cadets regarded both the faculty and the tactical department as the enemy. "We were thoroughly convinced," recalled Joseph Haw, "that the professors lay awake nights thinking up new ways to 'find' cadets deficient in studies and to ensure their departure from the sacred precincts of West Point."[1]

Although the class of 1915 was later dubbed "the class the stars fell on," the daring antics of some of its members made it a matter of astonishment that generals' stars ever fell on them. There was very little to do on weekends and even less for plebes. For diversion during Eisenhower's first year, two enterprising plebes inaugurated what they called "boxing smokers" in their room on alternate Saturday nights, when the upperclassmen were otherwise occupied at cadet hops. Entry required a spectator to "pay" his way in by fighting another cadet. It was inevitable that Eisenhower and Hodgson would be unable to resist the lure, and the two boxed each other as the price of admission. Friendship was momentarily forgotten. Paul was the quicker of the two, but Eisenhower's tactics were to savagely bore in and overwhelm his friend with a knockout punch.[2]

At West Point playing poker was another forbidden pastime that Eisenhower passionately embraced, usually when the tacs (army officers assigned to supervise the cadets) were the least vigilant. No one had money, and the stakes were pride. Having learned poker from a master, Eisenhower more than held his own. In 1913 he learned to play bridge, a game that would become his greatest source of entertainment for the rest of his life. As with everything Eisenhower did at West Point, he tempted disciplinary action by avidly playing after lights out.

Whenever Eisenhower and Hodgson were not otherwise engaged in breaking the rules, they kept their record intact by holding bull sessions after taps. A cadet would be detailed as a lookout to warn the group in the event a tac officer appeared. Eisenhower's penchant for talking elicited an entry in the 1915 yearbook, *Howitzer:*

INQUISITIVE CIVILIAN—Is Mr. Eisenhower good at athletics?
CAYDET—Yes, Mexican athletics.
INQUISITIVE CIVILIAN—What is that?
CAYDET—Slinging the bull.[3]

Dwight Eisenhower's passion for athletics was to have a profound effect on his choice of candidates to fill important roles during World War II. The sports-as-war metaphor was one that stuck with him. When it came to selecting the men who commanded major combat units in the European Theater of Operations, he rated athletes above others. To have excelled on the "friendly fields of strife," as MacArthur has said, was great preparation in Eisenhower's eyes. "I had occasion to be on the lookout for natural leaders. Athletes take a certain amount of kidding, especially from those who think it's always brain vs. brawn. But, I noted . . . how well ex-footballers seemed to have leadership qualifications and it wasn't sentiment that made it seem so."[4]

For the rest of his life he avidly followed the fortunes of the West Point football team. In 1960 President Eisenhower sent for the incoming superintendent, Lt. Gen. William C. Westmoreland. As their visit ended, Eisenhower pulled Westmoreland back into the Oval Office. "I do have one instruction for you, General," he said. "Do something about that damned football team," which had been faring badly of late.[5]

At the end of his plebe year Eisenhower's grades were respectable. His highest marks were in English, history, and military surveying; his worst subject was mathematics, in which he was rated 112th in the class. Neither Hodgson nor Eisenhower expected a promotion. "Dwight doesn't think he has any chance to get a 'corp' but I think he has," wrote P.A. to his mother. "He doesn't get as many demerits as I do, and he is fairly 'military' and thoroughly likeable."[6] Despite many unnecessary demerits and a less than sterling attitude, Eisenhower stood an acceptable thirty-ninth in conduct.[7] His record was good enough to earn him (and P.A.) a promotion to corporal, the highest rank a yearling could attain.

Most new upperclassmen took great pleasure in doling out the harassment they had received as plebes. Eisenhower was an exception and was never comfortable in the role of tormentor. In the summer of 1912 a plebe who happened to be from Kansas inadvertently bowled over Eisenhower, who arose and mocked the man by suggesting he looked like a barber. The plebe replied he had indeed been a barber in civilian life. The incident so embarrassed Eisenhower that he told P.A., "I'm never going to crawl another Plebe as long as I live. . . . I've done something that was stupid and unforgivable. I managed to make a man ashamed of the work he did for a living."[8]

After his third class (sophomore) year ended in June 1913, Eisenhower returned to Abilene as a newly promoted cadet supply sergeant for the ten weeks of his first and only summer furlough. Charlie Harger thought he detected a change in the young man, who seemed "more mature, more sedate. He felt the responsibility placed upon him. However, he was still the same high-spirited and attractive youth who had won the town's admiration in his boyhood days. He never showed the least touch of superiority in social activities."[9] Indeed, Eisenhower was now a small-town celebrity and the object of attention and admiration.

Harger's impressions differed significantly from those of Earl Eisenhower, who observed that in the summer of 1913 his older brother "was treated as the town hero, and he acted the part . . . [and] lost no opportunity to impress us with what he knew and had done." Eisenhower sometimes strutted around Abilene in his dress white summer uniform.[10] On one such occasion Eisenhower encountered Wes Merrifield, who was working in a local bakery. The two reminisced about their famous fight. For the first time Eisenhower publicly admitted that "I had the far worst of it. I'm willing to admit now that you really licked me then." A more mature person might have left it at that, but Eisenhower let his competitive nature get in the way of his common sense when he could not resist taking a parting shot at Merrifield. "But what I want to know," he challenged, "is whether you have any ambitions now." Merrifield had noted how Eisenhower had grown bigger and stronger during the years since their fight, and he judiciously replied, "Ike, I'm the most unambitious man in town."[11]

Unable to participate in summer sports, Eisenhower had to content himself with umpiring friendly baseball games between rival towns for fifteen dollars per game. Thanks to Bob Davis, he had had no trouble qualifying at West Point as a sharpshooter with a Springfield Model 1903 rifle. While killing time before the start of a game he was to umpire in a nearby town, Eisenhower stopped at a shooting gallery in his civilian clothes. Although no one knew him, he overheard a stranger offering to bet his friend ten dollars that Eisenhower would beat him. For the first time in his life he experienced sheer panic and began to tremble, his hands shaking. "Without a word, I laid down the rifle, having already paid for the shells, and left the place without a backward glance. Never before or since have I experienced the same kind of attack."[12]

An unfortunate incident marred an otherwise enjoyable furlough when

Eisenhower reluctantly fought a onetime professional fighter named Dirk Tyler, one of the few black men in mostly white Abilene. Tyler's modest success at fisticuffs had turned a well-regarded man into a local bully, who bragged that he had never been beaten by anyone in town. Eisenhower's reputation as a fighter led to an inevitable confrontation one day as he was getting a haircut in the barbershop where Tyler worked as a porter. Tyler none too subtly announced he was ready and willing to meet Ike "anywhere, anytime." Prodded by others and unable to resist this challenge to his manhood, Eisenhower reluctantly agreed to fight Tyler in the basement of a department store across the street.

Tyler was far superior in size and strength to Eisenhower, who instantly perceived that his only chance to whip his strapping opponent was to outbox him. Tyler's advantage was quickly nullified when he came out flailing punches, none of which troubled Eisenhower. Tyler consistently left his jaw unprotected, and the fight ended almost as soon as it began. Even with his injured knee, Eisenhower was the better boxer. Tyler was promptly flattened by a series of counterblows to the jaw and crumpled to the floor, out cold. "I went out determined to use every bit of skill to protect myself. And then to find that the boy didn't know the first thing about fighting! He telegraphed his punches from a mile away. Poor Dirk. Honestly, I've never been particularly proud of that scrap."[13]

At West Point token attempts were made to instill minimal social graces in the form of dancing classes and cadet hops, which had rigid rules of conduct. Eisenhower claims to have preferred poker to attending cadet hops, but his classmates remember him differently, as a "PSer"—which stood for "parlor snake," a term applied to anyone who loved to dance. The carefree Eisenhower was also often heard singing "Clementine" in the shower at the top of his lungs. His singing voice remained dreadfully off-key, and despite the pleas of his friends, such as cadet Mark Clark, who attempted to dissuade him, Eisenhower went through life blissfully butchering songs.[14]

During one of the occasions when he actually danced, Eisenhower was "skinned" for "improper dancing." "I guess her ankles showed or something," he later grumbled. "Dancing was very sedate at West Point in my days and we weren't very sedate."[15] In fact, Eisenhower was twice reported for the same infraction, the second time in June 1913 during a hop the night before his class departed on furlough. His partner, the daughter of a professor, asked him to dance the turkey trot, which he did with gusto. On his return to West Point in August 1913, he learned that a tactical officer had reported him. Since it was his second offense, Eisenhower was directed to appear before the commandant, who summarily reduced him to private, awarded eight demerits, confined Eisenhower to quarters for one month during off-duty time, and assessed twice-weekly punishment tours.[16]

It may well have been a record for the shortest time in grade before a newly promoted cadet was demoted. Later Eisenhower became one of seven members of the class on whom his classmates conferred the honorary title of "BA"—"busted aristocrat."

Throughout his West Point years Eisenhower remained extremely popular with his classmates, as much for his nonchalance as his sunny disposition. "There were some remarkable conversationalists in the class but the best of them had to talk fast to keep up with Ike. He could and did talk at the drop of a hat about anything, anytime, anywhere," said Haw. Eisenhower's academic indifference extended throughout his four years at West Point and failed "to impress the authorities with his fitness for appointment as a cadet officer. Despite his easy-going manner, no one doubted that his was an unusually strong character." During one of his numerous sojourns in the infirmary, a very sick cadet needed attention. "The soldier attendant made no move to comply with the cadet's urgent request. Standing on his good leg, Eisenhower told the orderly to hurry or he would 'knock hell out of him.' The man took one look at Ike's face and did the errand on the run."[17]

Eisenhower's strong influence on his devoted roommate was reflected during his absences in the infirmary. When he returned from yet another treatment of his ailing knee in 1913, P.A. wrote joyously to his mother, "Dwight came back to me yesterday and things seem much better already. Married life is a great thing for human contentment."[18]

For all his air of indifference, by his final year at West Point Eisenhower was already displaying traits of leadership. A classmate in confinement for taking an officer's horse on an unauthorized midnight ride was also a key member of the football team. Eisenhower was determined that the cadet be free to play against archenemy Navy. When he learned that the cadet was planning to break arrest to attend a hop, Eisenhower "came stalking in and told me that he'd smash a billiard cue over my head if I tried to break confinement. I stayed in quarters."[19]

Each cadet was usually required to recite at least once in each class on that day's assignment. They would first write the question or problem on the blackboard, then explain the answer when called on. Those unprepared were reported, and their only hope of avoiding trouble was to "bugle"— that is, stall in any way possible in the hope that the bugle call sounding the end of the class would come first. A cadet was called on in one of Eisenhower's classes without the foggiest notion of what he was doing. With five minutes left in the class, he was about to be "found" when his friend intervened. "Ike stood up and asked a question, then another, then still another. The instructor was completely taken in and answered each question thoroughly. Then the blessed bugle blew and I was off the hook. No 'bugler' was ever more expertly rescued."[20]

Eisenhower's stiffest challenge occurred during a class in integral calculus during his second year. A complex problem was presented that had to be solved the following day by one of the twelve cadets in the class. With the odds eleven to one that he would not be chosen, Eisenhower failed to prepare. As luck would have it, he was summoned to the blackboard to solve and explain the problem. Eisenhower remembers standing before the blackboard in a state of "mental paralysis" and "a sweat of helplessness." Facing severe disciplinary action and a poor grade if he failed, Eisenhower employed his math skills to devise a simpler, more logical solution. Instead of praising him, the instructor angrily accused him of memorizing the answer and of having written a meaningless series of numbers on the blackboard to deceive the class. Eisenhower stood his ground and vehemently rejected the assertion that he had cheated. "I gave one angry bark and I started a hot tirade."

About this time an associate professor of mathematics, Maj. J. Franklin Bell (affectionately nicknamed "Poopy"), quietly entered the classroom. Such inspections by a senior instructor were equated by the cadets with visitations from God. Ordering the instructor to have Eisenhower repeat his solution, Bell listened and then pronounced, "Mr. Eisenhower's solution is more logical and easier than the one we've been using. I'm surprised that none of us supposedly good mathematicians has stumbled on it. It will be incorporated in our procedures from now on." Eisenhower never forgot the debt he owed to "Poopy" Bell, or the fact that the instructor "was the only man I met at West Point for whom I ever developed any lasting resentment." Fifty-five years later Eisenhower wrote to thank Bell for saving his career that day. His bitterness about the slur upon his honesty was still unmistakable. "My army career could well have ended at that moment except for you. . . . I've always been certain that you saved me from making a spectacle of myself and getting tried for insubordination," he wrote, "for I was practically uncontrollable with anger."[21]

While at West Point, Eisenhower began to take a more active interest in members of the opposite sex. Women were naturally attracted to the handsome, gregarious, fun loving, and vain young man. His arrogance once landed him in a formidable social dilemma, when he tried to convince two young women that he was crazy about each of them. As his amused roommate wrote, "Unknown to him they were very good friends. . . . They then put their heads together and this week he received a pair of letters in which each volunteered to come up for the same dance." Somehow the crisis was averted, and "though [he is] rather wan and pale, his appetite is returning."[22]

During his senior year Eisenhower became intrigued with an attractive twenty-year-old Brooklynite named Dorothy Mills, who had been dating his roommate and was to be P.A.'s date for the graduation hop. His letters to Dorothy in 1914–15 begin to reveal another side to Eisenhower. For the most part the relationship never appeared to have serious overtones, and their correspondence was generally lighthearted. He eventually asked her to be his date for the annual Hundredth Night play. Dorothy was clearly attracted to Eisenhower but often offended by his flippant attitude, which only made him try harder to please her. His letters alternated from self-deprecating to pompously condescending. In reply to a particularly unseemly letter Dorothy once called him "a fresh masher."[23]

Eisenhower's letters to Dorothy Mills were small windows to a man no one ever really knew. In March there was an exchange of letters in which Dorothy wrote of their mutual "wanderlust." Eisenhower confessed: "It's affected me ever since I could walk. More than one night on furlough I spent all by my lonesome, out in the country—along the river bank—or up in the hills—just walking—smoking and . . . as I think of it—this is the first time I've told it. But one morning, I got in town just as a girl I knew was going up to take an early train. . . . She asked me later where I'd been—but I never tried to explain . . . she'd have suspected me of being 'touched'—or at least possessed of a sickly sentimentalism—which is worse."[25]

Sentimentality was a trait Eisenhower eschewed. Throughout his life he rarely displayed his true feelings to his family or his associates. Whatever he felt deeply was mostly a mystery he was loath to permit anyone to unlock. From time to time he permitted the briefest of glimpses before the door slammed shut and he again assumed the role of stern father and ever-efficient career soldier. Like most men of his generation, Eisenhower deemed it unmanly to unburden himself. His son, John, would later write of his father's remoteness, "Dad was a terrifying figure to a small boy."[26]

For all his gregariousness, Eisenhower was a solitary man. When not showing off the side of his personality he wanted the world to see, Eisenhower found solace by himself, often on the steep banks overlooking the Hudson River, in what Kenneth Davis has called "his secret life." Whenever the demands of the strict regimen permitted, Eisenhower liked nothing better than to explore the wilds of the West Point reservation and its steep cliffs above the river. Sometimes he stopped in the ruins of Fort Putnam, which formed the bulwark of the American defense of the Hudson during the Revolutionary War. Here, unburdened and undistracted by cadet duties, he would critique the battles, assess the terrain as a military commander would have, and re-create in his mind how they were fought and what mistakes were made by both sides. "As laboratory studies he considered them a major factor in his education as a cadet."[27]

Another glimpse of the stubborn Eisenhower can be seen in a letter P. A. Hodgson wrote to his parents in March 1912, the year former president Theodore Roosevelt ran in a three-way race for the presidency, against the incumbent Republican, William Howard Taft, and his Democratic challenger, Woodrow Wilson. Roosevelt had bolted the Republican Party to form his own Progressive "Bull Moose" ticket, and his espousal of neutrality toward Europe so angered Eisenhower that Hodgson thought him unreasonably stubborn. For reasons that never made sense to P.A., Eisenhower suddenly developed an intense dislike for his boyhood hero. "I never knew any one with such a strong and at the same time, causeless and unreasonable dislike for another, as he has for Roosevelt," wrote Hodgson. "You'd think that Teddy had done him some irreparable wrong from the way he talks and he hasn't a reason in the world for his attitude. He actually offered to bet me his furlough that Roosevelt wouldn't even be nominated."[28]

For all his casual attitude toward West Point, by early in his third year he would write to Ruby, "Remember that it is good to write once in a while, just to keep in practice—also that West Point, N.Y. looks awfully nice as an address on an envelope."[29] His letters also began to exhibit the first signs of sexual awareness and innuendo. In November 1913, for example, Eisenhower wrote that if Ruby's six-person all-girl orchestra was in New York during his Christmas leave, "we don't know *what might* happen. . . . I'm not going to open up and tell you all I'd really like to this evening. . . . I've changed my views concerning matrimony. I saw in the paper it was 'kisstomary to cuss the bride' so me for it. I'm looking for someone that I can pummel and bruise and pinch and fight and etc etc."[30]

One of Eisenhower's surviving letters was to a young lady named Brush, whom he had met at the 1914 Army-Navy football game, in which P.A. starred for Army in one of their greatest victories over the midshipmen of Annapolis. "It was a great day and a greater game. The only thing I regretted was that I couldn't inflict my presence on that delightful party after the game—but fate, the hussy interfered." His letter continued, "Just a second, my skag [cigarette] went out—All lit up once more. The whole purpose of this letter was to ask you to write me, and since I got up the courage to do it, I reckon I'd better stop . . . what do you think of Hodgson, the man that made that long run at the beginning of the game. Some boy, and he's my 'roomie.' I'm some proud! . . . in case you've forgotten my name, it is, D. D. Eisenhower."[31]

Newspapers and radios were a rarity at West Point, but Eisenhower and P.A. nevertheless managed to track on a map the events transpiring in Europe after World War I erupted in 1914. They put pins in the map to denote the movement of the opposing armies, a practice Eisenhower had begun in Abilene in 1904 during the Russo-Japanese War, and would employ the rest of his military career. During their senior year, Eisenhower and his classmates also traveled to Gettysburg, where they spent three days studying the most important battle of the Civil War.

Near the end of his junior year Eisenhower inscribed a permanent reminder of his presence at West Point by etching "Ike Eisenhower" on the copper sheathing of a corner of the inside roof of the cadet chapel.

In his first class (senior) year in 1914–15, he was promoted to F Company color sergeant. Although he continued to rack up demerits, this time Eisenhower managed to hang on to his sergeant's stripes. His first sergeant was his close friend, a mild-mannered, soft-spoken young man, with a pronounced Missouri accent, Omar N. Bradley. Their friendship was based on their rural Midwest roots and a passionate love of sports. Bradley played baseball and was known as an outfielder with a strong arm and a high batting average. After several earlier tryouts, Bradley also made the varsity football team in 1914, playing in five games, and later reflected that, "No extracurricular endeavor I know of could better prepare a soldier for the battlefield."[32]

Bradley's somber face and hangdog looks resulted in the cruel designation of "ugliest man in his class." Eisenhower, who had long since learned the folly of personal insults, was outraged when a classmate once likened Bradley to an ape. Next to sports, Bradley's other consuming passion was F Company, and he earned considerable prestige for refusing a promotion that would have meant a transfer to another company. "Sir, I would rather be first sergeant of "F" Co. than captain of any other company," he declared.[33]

Whenever football was involved Eisenhower's attitude changed dramatically. As the assistant coach of the Cullum Hall football team in 1914, Eisenhower both impressed and inspired his players by his hard work and dedication, which may well have been one of the first manifestations of his emerging leadership skills. He also joined the West Point chapter of the YMCA, which met every Sunday evening to hear a different speaker. The principal function of the YMCA was Bible study. Its members also helped teach Sunday school to the children of West Point personnel. Eisenhower quietly taught one of the classes.[34]

As graduation approached in the spring of 1915, Eisenhower's unresolved knee injury was deemed sufficiently serious that the army planned to deny him a commission. According to a classmate, a medical board had already decided that Eisenhower was physically unfit. Had it not been for the timely intervention of a white knight in the person of the academy surgeon, Lt. Col. Henry A. Shaw, Cadet Eisenhower would not have been commissioned in June 1915. Fortunately Shaw was a pragmatist who believed that neither Eisenhower nor the army would benefit by such a decision. He lobbied members of the tactical department and the academic board to support Eisenhower. Shaw's efforts paid off when the decision was reversed and the War Department agreed.[35]

Shaw summoned Eisenhower and offered to recommend his commissioning if he would apply for the coast artillery. Eisenhower knew the coast artillery to be a dead-end career in a service that, in his opinion, "provided a numbing series of routine chores and a minimum of excitement" and, to Shaw's annoyance, instantly spurned the proposition. Given that Shaw himself had served in the coast artillery, Eisenhower's disdainful rejection could have proved fatal. The young man who would one day become renowned for his tactfulness as a supreme commander was especially fortunate to have had a forgiving officer like Shaw on his side. Eisenhower shrugged it off, declaring that if he could not serve in the U.S. Army he would pack up, move to Argentina (a place he had learned about in his study of geography), and become a gaucho. He even sent for travel literature before abandoning the idea.

Several days later Eisenhower was summoned again by Shaw. "He said he realized that [a] great part of the injury was [horseback] riding. . . . So he said, 'Mr. Eisenhower, if you will not ask for a mounted service, I will recommend you for commission.' " Eisenhower readily agreed, noting that his preference was the infantry. Shaw, he said, concurred, and according to Eisenhower, the three choices entered on his preference sheet were identical: "Infantry." His official personnel file for 1915, however, records that the commandant of cadets noted his preferences as: (1) infantry, (2) coast artillery, and (3) cavalry. To everyone's relief he was accepted in the infantry.[36]

Eisenhower's recurring four-year affiliation with the post infirmary nearly caused him to miss his own graduation. He was admitted for the last time on June 6, 1915, with acute influenza.[37] By the time he graduated several days later, it had practically verged on the miraculous that Eisenhower somehow managed to avoid being expelled from West Point. Whereas Cadet Patton would agonize over demerits and attempt to deport himself as perfectly as possible in everything he did, Cadet Eisenhower became noted as a fun-loving maverick who would not back down when he believed himself in the right, no matter who in authority demanded it. The parallels between the two at West Point are almost eerily similar. Both young men were obsessive in their desire to succeed in athletics. Patton had to repeat his plebe year after failing a mathematics exam in 1905, and his undiagnosed dyslexia dogged him throughout his five years there.

Each considered quitting. While Eisenhower spoke of going to Argentina to become a gaucho if he was not commissioned, Lt. Patton unsuccessfully attempted to participate in World War I before the United States entered the war. He begged for a leave of absence to accept a commission in the French army but was turned down.[38] The escalating troubles with Mexico in 1913 led both young men to anticipate the coming conflict with relish. In Pattonesque language Eisenhower wrote to Ruby Norman, "The only bright spot is, just now, that trouble with Mexico seems imminent. We may stir up a little excitement yet, let's hope so, at least."[39]

The graduation address was delivered on June 12, 1915, by President Woodrow Wilson's secretary of war, Lindley M. Garrison, whose brief speech contained the usual exhortations to excel and sacrifice, and was immediately forgotten by most. Afterward the new graduates swore to uphold and defend the Constitution and were duly commissioned as second lieutenants in the U.S. Army. That night the men of the class of 1915 attended a gala graduation dinner held at New York's prestigious Astor Hotel, followed by attendance at a hit Broadway musical.

Eisenhower was easily the youngest-looking graduate of the class of 1915 and certainly one of the most popular. Although generally humorous, Eisenhower's entry in the *Howitzer* by P. A. Hodgson was regarded by some classmates as being in poor taste. Although it was traditional to lampoon one another, "Ike" was described as "the terrible Swedish-Jew, as big as life and twice as natural. He claims to have the best authority for the statement that he is the handsomest man in the Corps. . . . Poor Dwight merely consents to exist until graduation shall set him free. . . . [He] won his 'A' by being the most promising back in Eastern football—but the Tufts game broke his knee and the promise."[40]

Bradley's entry in the 1915 *Howitzer* was written by Eisenhower and would prove remarkably prophetic. "His most prominent characteristic," he wrote, " 'is getting there,' and if he keeps up the clip he's started, some of us will one some day be bragging to our grandchildren that 'sure, General Bradley was a classmate of mine.' "

The extent to which Eisenhower took West Point seriously until after his graduation is debatable. Beyond attaining a coveted all-expenses-paid college education (and indulging his passion for sports), he had yet to display any great commitment to becoming an army officer for the next eight years, the time then required for all graduates to serve on active duty. Moreover, not everyone was impressed. Later assessments by two officers who served in the tactical department were wildly dissimilar. One rated him "Born to command," while another said, "We saw in Eisenhower a not uncommon type, a man who would thoroughly enjoy his Army life, giving both to duty and recreation their fair values. We did not see in him a man who would throw himself into his job so completely that nothing else would matter." The commandant of cadets noted in an official evaluation that Eisenhower "should be assigned to an organization under [a] strict commanding officer."[41]

Yet, for all his alleged indifference, Eisenhower had learned far more than his deportment revealed about his preparation to assume the duties and responsibilities of an officer. Academically he did far better than his recollections suggest, graduating 61 of 164. Not surprisingly, however, he stood 125th in discipline. His eagerness to move on was reflected in his disciplinary record in 1914–15, during which he earned 100 demerits, the most of his four-year tenure at West Point.

For most graduates the West Point experience evokes mixed feelings. Not so Dwight Eisenhower. "I enjoyed West Point; I was one of the few that really thought I was having a good time . . . getting an education when you don't have to pay for it when I'd been working for two years to help my brother? Well, I thought this was a wonderful thing. I absorbed West Point and I think no cadet was more jealous of its reputation and its honor system. But I just wasn't bothered about the little things."[42]

His official biographer has noted how Eisenhower had "drifted" through West Point just as he had in Abilene, but correctly surmised that he "took from West Point what was positive and rejected that which was negative."[43] Still, it remained a measure of Eisenhower's immaturity that he so often and so frivolously risked losing the very education and opportunities he had dedicated himself to obtaining.

For all their hardships, both Eisenhower and Douglas MacArthur were typical of so many graduates whose veneration of West Point lasted a lifetime. Joseph Haw may well have spoken for the class of 1915 when he noted that "the historic traditions of West Point were rarely discussed yet somehow the part of the academy had played in the history of our country was unconsciously absorbed by the most thoughtless cadet. . . . There was no flag-waving but there grew up within us a deep pride in our school and our army and a feeling that we must live up to the great tradition we had inherited."[44]

The roster of the class of 1915 would later read like a military who's who of World War II. They ranged from his Missouri friend, the soft-spoken Bradley, to Joseph Swing and future U.S. Air Force general George Stratemeyer. James Van Fleet and Joseph McNarney would attain four-star rank. Seven others would reach the three-star rank of lieutenant general, twenty-four became major generals (fifteen of whom commanded divisions in combat), and twenty-five brigadier generals. All told more than half the 115 graduates who served in World War II became generals. No West Point class before or since has produced so many—two of whom, Bradley and Eisenhower, rose to the five-star rank of general of the army—and one, Dwight Eisenhower, also became the thirty-fourth president of the United States. To this day "the class the stars fell on" remains the most famous in West Point history.

For all his compliments about West Point, Eisenhower's remembrance of his four years was mixed. "I wanted no part of that," he said, after refusing to consider seriously an offer to become commandant of cadets in 1937. Nor was Eisenhower the first to deprecate his West Point experience to conceal his true feelings, which grew deeper with age. One of his oldest friends, Gen. Mark Clark, visited a gravely ill Eisenhower frequently before his death in 1969 in Walter Reed Army Hospital. "But you know, all he wanted to talk about was West Point. Not about being president, not about being supreme commander, about D-Day, none of that. West Point was all, ever."[45]

With tongue in cheek, the editors of the *Howitzer* captioned a photograph of the cadet barracks, "Wherein reside the nation's pampered pets." The last entry in the 1915 *Howitzer* was a photograph of a cadet with the caption "Lights Out." The same could be said for Eisenhower's West Point years. Ahead of him lay the long train journey back to Abilene and the uncertainty of learning a new profession in a minuscule peacetime army as a newly commissioned second lieutenant of infantry.

8.

"1915—the Summer Dwight Came Back from West Point"

I love you Gladys.

When Eisenhower returned to Abilene in June 1915, Ida presented him with a copy of the standard version of the Bible used by the Jehovah's Witnesses.[1] The book became a treasured keepsake on which Eisenhower later swore the oath of office when he was inaugurated as president in January 1953.

Although eligible to draw the pay of a second lieutenant, Eisenhower was in temporary limbo. His commission was not official until formally signed by the president. Typically commissions were signed promptly, but Woodrow Wilson was otherwise absorbed not only with the outbreak of World War I in Europe but with the escalating lawlessness along the Mexican border. Before the commission could be formalized, the adjutant general sent Eisenhower two forms to complete. One asked for his place of birth, to which he inexplicably entered "Tyler, Texas." As late as 1963 the uncertainty over Eisenhower's birthplace was still a subject of misunderstanding. Based on conversations with his father, John Eisenhower wrote to a Dallas newsman that his father "believed his birthplace to be Tyler for many years." However, there was no logical reason for the slightest confusion in Eisenhower's mind. At West Point in 1911, and subsequently on forms that asked for "Candidate's Place of Birth," Eisenhower unfailingly entered "Denison, Texas."[2]

Eisenhower spent the summer of 1915 vowing "to have a good time" during what turned out to be the most bittersweet interlude of his life. Although he was regularly "slugged" (another term coined by cadets for a violation of Academy regulations resulting in dements) at West Point for a variety of uniform violations, when he was home in Abilene, Eisenhower suddenly became utterly fastidious in his dress. During his summer leave in 1913 one of the reasons he had often worn his cadet uniform around town was to impress not only the townsfolk but a young woman on whom he had a secret crush while attending Abilene High School. She was Gladys Harding, the blue-eyed, blond daughter of a successful Abilene businessman, an accomplished pianist, and reputed to have been one of the prettiest girls in town. Although the two had been friends throughout high school, their relationship never passed beyond mutual admiration until the summer of 1913, when Eisenhower finally dared to ask Gladys for a date. She readily accepted, and despite the existence of other would-be beaux (as befitted one of Abilene's prettiest girls), they not only dated frequently but the first signs of a more serious romance took root.

Suddenly Eisenhower began spending most evenings in her company at the nearby Harding home, often wearing his uniform to impress Gladys and her father. The ritual beforehand was excruciating. Ida was recruited to carefully iron his uniform pants, which, her son informed her, "have to be so well pressed that they will stand up by themselves." Milton and Earl did the rest, acting as aides-de-camp. "Dwight lay on the bed while we eased his razor-sharp trousers on, one leg at a time. Then he stood up slowly, so as not to spoil the crease."[3]

Before returning to West Point in 1913, Eisenhower asked Six McDonnell to watch over Gladys while he was gone and "take her to a show once in a while." McDonnell complied but became infatuated with Gladys. He dated her a number of times and once obtained leave from his baseball team, then playing in Nebraska, to pay a surprise visit to Abilene to see Gladys, even hiring a taxi for the final leg of the trip. Six intended to be dropped off at the Harding house until he spied Gladys and Eisenhower in his cadet uniform sitting in chairs on the lawn. Instead he hastily told the taxi driver to " 'Just keep on going.' The next morning I went back to Lincoln. . . . I was embarrassed."[4]

Eisenhower and Gladys were briefly reunited in December 1914, when the traveling Apollo Concert Company, in which she did recitals and pianologues, played in New York City. He savored his classmates' envy that such an attractive woman was his date. Although none of the Eisenhower family attended his graduation from West Point, held in June, his only regret seems to have been his disappointment that Gladys was unable to be present.

In the summer of 1915 their budding romance was revived when Gladys was on summer hiatus. The two became virtually inseparable, with most of their evenings together spent in the Harding home, much to Mr. Harding's growing dismay over his daughter's romance with Eisenhower. Not unreasonably, he was convinced that she had no future married to a soldier with no money and few prospects, and urged Gladys to ditch him. "That Eisenhower kid will never amount to anything," he predicted.[5] As children are wont to do, Gladys ignored her father's exhortations.

Although he and Gladys were soon seeing each other on a daily basis, Eisenhower felt compelled to write her love letters, which he delivered personally. They vividly expressed the amorous feelings of a young man in love for the first time. In one he declared his "need and hunger for you," and deemed himself "far luckier than I ever even dared hope . . . your soldier boy really *loves* you." Eisenhower's words left no doubt of his intentions. He found in Gladys "the purest, sweetest and strongest love he ever gave to a woman except his mother, and loved you as a man does the one woman, whom in his most cherished dreams, he hopes some day to call his wife."

When they were not together, Gladys was noting her own growing feelings. She kept Eisenhower's letters, and in an intimate diary recorded the progress of their romance, which she called, "1915—The Summer Dwight Came Back from West Point." The extent of her love for Eisenhower is quite evident in a cover note she wrote in 1957: "Letters—from Dwight D. Eisenhower—that I rec'd, when we were *young* and *happy*! (Back in 1914–1915)."[6]

On August 5 Gladys wrote in her diary, "D. asked me to marry him." She neither accepted nor rejected Eisenhower's proposal, and although clearly torn, was simply not prepared to commit herself to a marriage that would effectively end her musical career. Nor could her father's attitude have helped, an obstacle likewise encountered by Patton during his courtship of his future wife, Beatrice Ayer. The U.S. Army was widely thought to be a dead-end career that paid slave wages to men otherwise regarded as the misfits of society. Patton's future father-in-law, the self-made millionaire tycoon Frederick Ayer, possessed "the typical New England view of the 'brutal and licentious mercenary.' . . . the Yankee[s] always thought of the army as the refuge for thieves and murderers."[7] No doubt Mr. Harding held a similar view.

With little else to do in Abilene, whenever he was not in Gladys's company, Eisenhower could usually be found hunting, fishing, and occasionally drinking or playing poker. One evening he and several friends had imbibed enough bootleg whiskey to become loud and boisterous when they ambled into a local café. Eisenhower attempted to teach his friends some of his West Point songs in his dreadful singing voice, which, more often than not, resulted in exhortations that he *please* stop. Eisenhower defied several profane requests from the owner to stop or be tossed out, responding by angrily daring him to try; then, to make the point, he thrust his fist through the wall of the café, where it became stuck. A portion of the wall had to be cut away with a kitchen knife to free a very chagrined Dwight Eisenhower. Although he later characterized the incident as "wildly exaggerated," it was nevertheless a vivid illustration that after four years at West Point, Eisenhower was still unable to control his explosive temper.[8] It was a side of his personality that Gladys Harding never glimpsed.

In September, Gladys was set to return to her touring company, and Dwight thought he would soon be leaving for the Philippines. As their time together grew ever shorter, Eisenhower's penchant for keeping a tight rein on his emotions failed him. In the early morning hours of August 17, 1915, he penned the first of the two most impassioned letters of his life. "Dearest Girl," he wrote:

> . . . I think I appreciate you more than ever before. I have a keener realization of your worth and sweetness—and feel how lucky I am that you give me even a thought. . . . More than ever, now, I want to hear you say the three words with "Better than I ever have anyone in the world!" If you can say that to me . . . then I'll know that I've *won*. From that time—if it ever comes—I'll know you're mine—no matter where you go—or what you do. . . . For girl I do love you and want you to KNOW it—to be as certain of it as I am—and to believe in me and trust me as you would your dad. . . .
>
> Sept 1st seems so fearfully close . . . this parting is going to be the hardest so far in my life. . . . I don't know how little or how much you do love me—but I do know that you do not care now like I dare to hope that you will.
>
> Please don't think that I'm presuming to be worthy of even the faintest spark of affection from you. I know that I've made miserable mistakes and botches—but girl I'm *trying*. . . .

Decked out in his white dress uniform, Eisenhower accompanied Gladys to Kansas City, where she boarded a train for New York on September 1. Their final three days together were poignant. In her diary Gladys wrote, "Sad parting. **** Love *." Her only visual memories of Eisenhower were his name card from his graduation hop at West Point, "a faded red rose and the remnants of a four-leaf clover."[9]

After their farewell a heartbroken and by now rather desperate Eisenhower endured a fitful night in a Kansas City hotel where he poured out his pent-up feelings in a letter addressed to "Sweet girl of Mine." "My heart seems to choke me," he wrote. "And yet there is a certain happiness there too. Even while seeing you go—I know that you love me—me! And, oh girl! that knowledge is the great and wondrous influence which will help me through this coming year and bring me to you again—to claim you forever and always and now sweetheart good night. Your devoted Dwight."

Gladys replied at once from New York, prompting yet another declaration of Eisenhower's love. Calling her "his beautiful lady," he wrote that he simply had to "just whisper over and over 'I love you Gladys'—'I love you Gladys' . . . I'll meet you in Dreamland—if you will meet me there. And *there*—as sometime in reality—you *shall* be my dearest and closest friend—my own sweetheart and true blue wife."[10]

Eisenhower's letters may have been mushy, even mawkish, but there is no doubt of his love for Gladys Harding in the summer of 1915. However, unlike so many summer romances, this one, in hindsight, might well have survived had Eisenhower not met his future wife soon after reporting for duty at Fort Sam Houston. Although the two exchanged letters for a time, and both continued to profess their love, their geographical separation began to cool the romance. Subsequent events have revealed that Gladys Harding was very much in love with Dwight Eisenhower and fully expected him to marry her. Six McDonnell likewise thought Eisenhower and Gladys would marry, and was surprised when they did not.[11]

Whatever misgivings either had over their breakup in September 1915 were taken to the grave. Eisenhower never publicly or privately mentioned his first serious romance. Still, the two never forgot each other. They exchanged infrequent, innocuous letters until Gladys's death in 1959, but neither ever again spoke about the summer of 1915. When President Eisenhower visited Abilene in 1953, the most exciting incident of his visit occurred when "a plump woman with blond hair darted out into the street and bore down on his motorcade." The president's Secret Service escorts began reacting to this apparent threat but even after thirty-eight years Dwight Eisenhower recognized his old flame. He ordered the driver to stop, and to the delight of the crowd the two embraced; then Eisenhower "gave her a hearty kiss." His obvious affection for this woman from his past "made Mamie madder than hell," remembered Earl Endacott.[12]

The only other woman close to Eisenhower was Ruby Norman, who always insisted that her relations with Ike were strictly platonic. "I was his friend. Gladys Harding was his *girl*. She was the only girl he ever had in Abilene."[13]

In early August 1915, Eisenhower's commission arrived, and he wrote at once to the adjutant general that, "I accept the commission as Second Lieutenant of Infantry."[14] His preference sheet listed the Philippines, a remote posting that, despite its hardships, offered adventure and possible combat. In the past, duty in the Philippines was considered a rather routine assignment for a newly commissioned officer. And, as the only cadet in his class to request such duty, Eisenhower was so confident of a Philippine assignment that he purchased only tropical uniforms, but none of the other types required for service elsewhere. What he had not counted on was that the problems with Mexico resulted in Regular Army troops being sent to guard the border from California to Brownsville, Texas. Although there was as yet no actual state of war between the Mexico and the United States, border duty was so miserable that the War Department began receiving numerous requests for Philippine duty, which had suddenly became a far more attractive alternative.

At West Point between $14 and $15 had been withheld from his pay every month until graduation, when Eisenhower received what seemed to him a financial windfall. The amount left over from his partial uniform purchases was used to finance his summer vacation in Abilene. Oblivious to the fact that the War Department might not approve his request, Eisenhower was embarrassed to learn he would be traveling only as far as Fort Sam Houston, in San Antonio, Texas. His savings soon ran out, and to continue his courtship of Gladys Harding, Eisenhower was obliged to borrow from his father merely to make it through the summer.[15] He also hocked his watch to Earl for a small loan that was never repaid.

The announcement of his new assignment required Eisenhower to report to Fort Sam Houston in mid-September, with all mandatory uniforms in his possession, for duty with the 19th Infantry Regiment. In desperation he visited a well-known uniform outfitter in Leavenworth and purchased his uniforms on credit. On a second lieutenant's minuscule pay of $141.67 per month, Eisenhower was already well in debt before ever serving a single day on active duty.[16] It was an inauspicious beginning to his military career.

9.

Miss Mamie Doud

I made up my mind, I was going to make myself as good an Army officer as I could.

The young man who graduated from West Point in 1915 was to become as much of an enigma as Patton, who in a few short years would become one of his closest friends. The image Dwight Eisenhower presented to the world was vastly different from the inner man. Eisenhower's future brilliance was masked by the extroverted personality of an underachiever with a perpetual demeanor of casual rebelliousness and nonchalance. Publicly he remained seemingly without a care in the world and determined to sample life's pleasures while in the service of the U.S. Army.

So much for the facade. Behind his genuine love of his hometown and his sunny smile lay Eisenhower's lifelong fear of being regarded as a country bumpkin. As one observer has astutely noted, "All his life, believing it a weakness, he would disguise the great country within him, giving his mother's friendliness to the public world and his father's toughness to the practical problems of command. They were studied roles, both of them, calculated to misdirect. He feared nothing so much as exposure."[1]

Unlike the public person he later became, Eisenhower studiously shunned the limelight whenever possible. In San Antonio he once attended a victory dance at a local hotel to celebrate the triumphant 1915 football season of Saint Louis College, a tiny Catholic school that Eisenhower had coached to its first victories in five years. When he entered the ballroom, "Everybody stopped and started clapping and cheering. I blushed like a baby—Gee! surely was embarrassed [*sic*]. I made a run for a corner, believe me."[2]

Those who mistook Dwight Eisenhower for nothing more than a country boy never saw the depth of intelligence behind the charm and the smile. "No one seems to have understood that he was a brilliant man. He was not an intellectual, and perhaps that fact confused people of intellect who assume intelligence must always breathe an air of the salon."[3] This outgoing persona would be his armor against the slings and arrows of the uncertain world he now entered.

Eisenhower had no illusions about his future in the army, believing it unthinkable that he could ever earn a general's stars in peacetime. He also went to great lengths to assume the role he had decided to carve out for himself: that of a solid, dependable officer who performed his duties efficiently but without drawing undue attention to himself. "I wasn't too concerned about promotion . . . and when my son John wanted to go to West Point I told him never to think about promotion but to do his job well and make every boss sorry when he leaves."[4]

Eisenhower Spartan explanation was part of the deception. Two of the most competitive soldiers in the U.S. Army were Dwight Eisenhower and George S. Patton. Though it was never evident in public, Dwight Eisenhower simply hated to lose or be crossed. As a previous biographer has noted, he was not spiteful but neither was he particularly forgiving, even with lifelong friends whose actions displeased him. John Eisenhower experienced firsthand his father's ultracompetitive nature. "Dad could get over any disagreement very easily, as long as he won."[5] A senior officer always walks on the right, and his subordinates on the left. As a boy, and later an army officer, John learned never to violate this army custom. For those who knew Eisenhower or worked for him, his temper was as notorious as his grin was famous. Whatever David Eisenhower and his son Dwight had in common did not extend to the father's abhorrence of swearing, alcohol in any form, smoking, gambling, or card playing. By the time Dwight graduated from West Point and became an army officer, he had done all of them.[6]

The military establishment of which Eisenhower became a part in 1915 was ingrained with the view that the military as an established institution was apolitical and conservative in outlook. He entered the army at a time when "The new American professional officer had an inbred respect for the integrity of the chain of command," as Samuel P. Huntington wrote in his landmark study, *The Soldier and the State*. The president of the United States was deemed a benevolent figure of respect and admiration to whom each officer owed his unqualified allegiance as commander in chief of the armed forces. "Duty is the Army's highest law . . . ," noted Huntington. "The twenty years prior to World War I were the heyday of the belief that war might be prevented by treaties or institutional devices. Again and again the military warned that Peace Palaces would not bring peace."[7] (This peace principle was the very foundation of Woodrow Wilson's presidency and would prove as fragile as it was misguided.)

In addition to a reverence for the presidency, West Point had also repeatedly instilled in young Eisenhower and his classmates a thorough distrust of politics and politicians. The cadets were inculcated with, and readily came to accept, the premise that politicians in general, and Congress in particular, were a contemptible, dishonest lot. During the 1930s, when Eisenhower spent nearly five years toiling in the War Department, his aversion to politicians would harden. As a body the officer corps avoided politics to the point where fewer than one in five hundred ever bothered to register as a member of a political party or vote in an election. The still-vivid historical example of Grant's disastrous presidency served as a clear affirmation that the military and politics simply did not mix. While it held relatively little importance in the performance of his duties as a junior officer, this belief would later have enormous implications in Eisenhower's performance as supreme commander.

During the summer of 1915 Eisenhower decided the time had come for him to change his blasé attitude. "I made up my mind," he said, that henceforth "I was going to make myself as good an Army officer as I could. Out of whatever I could do, it wasn't going to be a lack of work that kept me from doing it. I worked very hard. Now, I had my fun, and a lot of fun, but I did work very hard."[8] Notes Stephen Ambrose, "It was resolve rather than an ambition, and sprang from a sense of obligation and responsibility rather than from a competitive drive, for he felt that with the end of his sports career, his competitive days were over."[9]

In the summer of 1915 American troubles with Mexico had escalated to the point where Eisenhower's regiment was ordered to border duty in Galveston. Eisenhower arrived in Galveston in mid-September only to learn that the 19th Infantry Regiment had been flooded out of its cantonment and had returned to Fort Sam Houston. He took the next train to San Antonio and reported for duty. He was assigned to Company F, commanded by Capt. George W. Helms, whom Eisenhower would later recall with fondness. "I shall never forget the day I reported to you. . . . Because I had some little reputation as a football player, you were apparently expecting a regular Goliath, and expressed your immediate disappointment that I was a man of medium build and size." Helms's tolerance toward his new lieutenant was reciprocated when he took "charge of my somewhat unruly, harum-scarum personality in time to keep me from getting too far off the track. I owe a lot to you personally; a fact which I never forgot."[10]

The small standing Regular Army of 1915 was poorly paid and its enlisted ranks populated by men of scant education and little ambition. Between 1895—when the figure was less than $52 million—and 1916, the average military budget was barely $150 million, and funds to improve the squalid living conditions in the army's remote outposts were virtually nonexistent.[11] The active army in 1915 totaled 106,754 (4,948 officers and 101,806 enlisted men), most of whom were dispersed in small military garrisons that were rarely larger than battalion size. These tiny outposts were a relic of eighteenth-century frontier America. Unlike that of Wilson, Theodore Roosevelt's administration believed that the U.S. Army must be modernized to fight a future war but had run afoul of politicians determined to retain the status quo and the "fort" mentality.[12] Until U.S. entry into World War I in 1917, Wilson had evinced little interest in the military, and during his first administration the military continued to stagnate.

There was no better example of the boredom of military life than the high desertion rate and the high occupancy rate of the post stockade. Drunkenness remained a serious problem and in many places, particularly the larger cities, enlisted men were regarded with utter contempt. Discipline was swift and harsh, the duty usually mind numbing, and the pay—though better in the U.S. Army than in other armies—wretchedly low. Some enlisted without fully understanding what they were letting themselves in for; literacy was a major problem, and conditions, albeit improved from those of the post–Civil War period, were at best austere. Life was governed by the call of the bugle.

An exception was Fort Sam Houston, one of the crown jewels of the prewar army. With its lovely brick quarters, famous quadrangle, and easygoing ambiance, it was one of the most popular and sought-after assignments for an officer. Except, that is, Dwight Eisenhower, whose hopes of a Philippine assignment had been abruptly dashed.

Peacetime duty at one of the army's prestigious military posts hardly posed a challenge. Fort Sam Houston had been a military post since 1845, the year Texas joined the Union. Originally called the "Post of San Antonio," it was renamed in 1890 in honor of the father of Texas. Opportunities abounded for participation in social life. So many officers were married there that Fort Sam (as it was informally called) eventually earned the nickname the "mother-in-law" of the army. The pace was generally unhurried, with as much time available for sports and socializing as for military duties.

As the newest arrival, Eisenhower automatically earned the dubious distinction of being the most junior second lieutenant in the regiment. He was assigned to regimental duties suitable for a junior officer. The regimental commander, Col. Millard Fillmore Waltz, an 1879 graduate of West Point, had served with distinction on the western frontier and in the Spanish-American War. A tough, bad-tempered, no-nonsense Regular Army infantry officer who suffered neither fools nor second lieutenants gladly, his bull-like demeanor so thoroughly intimidated his junior officers that they made it a point to avoid him whenever possible. Other than formally reporting to his new commanding officer in September, Eisenhower had yet to make the acquaintance of Colonel Waltz.

With little disposable income for recreation, Eisenhower and his fellow bachelor lieutenants were a restless lot and spent a great deal of their free time wandering aimlessly around Fort Sam in search of entertainment. Almost anything would do. One evening, in a most unmilitary fashion, Eisenhower and some other lieutenants were lingering near the fifty-foot-high post flagpole, which was anchored by steel cables. Eisenhower bragged that having done considerable rope climbing at West Point, he could easily scale one of the support cables to the top, using only his hands. His challenge was so utterly disparaged that one officer offered to bet the not insignificant sum of five dollars that Eisenhower would fail.

Sensing quick compensation for a few moments' work that would enrich his paltry pay and enhance his standing in the eyes of his fellow officers, Eisenhower took the dare and the bet duly placed with a third party, a lieutenant named Wade "Ham" Haislip. Eisenhower discarded his uniform blouse and was partway up the cable and already counting his winnings when a gruff voice from below demanded to know who he was and what the hell he was doing hanging on to the cable. "Mr. Eisenhower, Sir," he replied at once, quickly explaining the circumstances. He begged to be allowed to complete his climb, but his irate commanding officer bellowed for Eisenhower to climb down at once. Eisenhower hastily complied and still minus his blouse, saluted his commander. Eisenhower never forgot his first severe chewing out as a U.S. Army officer, as Colonel Waltz enlightened his new lieutenant about his many shortcomings. "Foolhardy," "undignified," "untrustworthy," "undependable," and "ignorant" were among the attributes mentioned.

Eisenhower, however, seemed more concerned about losing his precious five-dollar bet than with the fact that he had just made an appalling first impression on his commanding officer. A loud quarrel ensued when he refused to pay off, arguing that he would easily have won had the colonel not interfered. Tempers flared as the two officers argued, with Eisenhower offering to settle the matter of who won with his fists. Reason prevailed, and the bet was declared a draw. Eisenhower's knee was again bothering him, and he later admitted relief that he had not had to fight a much larger opponent and possibly further injure himself.[13]

Throughout his military career, the one army custom Eisenhower despised above all others was the courtesy call. A newly arrived officer was expected to visit the quarters of his superiors and formally introduce himself. It was acceptable to leave one's calling card at the residence in lieu of the visit if the officer was not at home. Eisenhower thought the practice tedious and, never comfortable engaging in small talk with people for whom he cared not a whit, would deliberately wait until the regimental officers were attending a function to leave his card. As John remembers, "This was a chore that Dad detested and he made little secret of it."[14]

Like any other inexperienced new officer, Eisenhower had a great deal to learn. To absorb and master the duties of a junior officer was one thing, but the most important and clearly the most difficult aspect of his new profession was to earn the respect of his men. Eisenhower set about the task with a determination to perform well without drawing undue attention to himself.

When it came to army politics, he rapidly absorbed the rules of the game and executed them to near perfection. Even though he was known for occasional instances of compassion and forgiveness of military transgressions (for example, condoning the unauthorized wearing of his dress ·shoes by his enlisted orderly), during the first years of his career, Eisenhower was a stern disciplinarian who once punished an errant soldier by ordering him to dig a very large, very deep hole and then to fill it in.

In a profession in which discipline was the cornerstone of daily life, Eisenhower was soon well regarded by his men and his superiors, a laudable achievement for a young officer. Early in his career Eisenhower also demonstrated a special interest in the welfare of his troops, especially the food they ate. One of the additional duties routinely assigned new second lieutenants is that of mess officer, which, for most, is a most unwelcome task. Eisenhower, however, was delighted. The experience gained during his youth in Abilene merely enhanced his love of food and cooking. He attended a course on cooking and managing mess-hall operations. From that time forth, the proper feeding of troops became an important focus, and those who failed to measure up to his standards earned his wrath. From 1915 through his tenure as army chief of staff after World War II, Eisenhower never forgot the maxim that an army travels on its stomach, and woe to the officer who took his mess duties lightly. "I have made things miserable on occasion," he remarked, "for young captains or lieutenants, responsible for messes, who limited their inspection to questioning whether pots and pans were shined brightly enough."[15]

It was at this time, too, that Bob Davis's lessons in the art of poker began to pay off handsomely for a young man of limited means. Eisenhower had no trouble finding eager poker-playing benefactors who generally lost to him. Once he reluctantly joined a game with only two silver dollars in his pocket. He won one hundred dollars and as he began cashing out to keep a date with his new girlfriend, the two big losers demanded that he stay and give them a chance to win their money back. Eisenhower refused and instead offered to bet each fifty dollars that they could not win a single roll of the dice. They declined to call his bluff. Although Eisenhower used his bountiful profit and his back pay from June to reimburse the Leavenworth tailor for his uniforms, he had yet to repay his father's loan.

With so little for the army to do in peacetime, sports, particularly football, rated very high on most commanders' list of priorities. Good coaches were hard to find, and Eisenhower's experience coaching football at West Point was an entry on his résumé that he came to regret shortly after arriving at Fort Sam Houston. Although he loved coaching, he abhorred being assigned to a post solely because he was wanted as the football coach. Eisenhower correctly concluded that having a primary attribute "coach" affixed to his name was hardly a route to higher promotions and top-level assignments.

Yet, he was frequently to become the target of zealous commanders who saw Eisenhower not as competent career-officer material but as a present-day successful football coach. It did not help that being so junior, he was at the mercy of the whims of his superiors.

In the autumn of 1915, Eisenhower was approached by the superintendent of the Peacock Military Academy, a local private school, and asked if he would coach its football team. For his services he would be paid $150, a handsome stipend for one still deeply in debt. Although tempted, Eisenhower decided that coaching was incompatible with his duties and rejected the offer.

General officers are rarely in the habit of seeking out a junior officer to ask for a favor, and even less inclined to buy them drinks at the officers' club. However, not long afterward, Maj. Gen. Frederick Funston, the commanding general of the Southern Department (also located at Fort Sam), appeared there without warning and asked, "Is Mr. Eisenhower in the room?" Eisenhower and several friends were drinking beer, and he immediately stood up and replied, "Sir?" wondering why he had been sought out. The general ordered drinks, then got to the point. The superintendent had been in touch with him about Eisenhower. "It would please me and it would be good for the Army if you would accept this offer," Funston said. Although tactfully phrased, the "request" was a none-too-subtle command for Eisenhower to change his mind. He dutifully said, "Yes, Sir," and complied. If measured solely by his success during his first coaching stint as an army officer, he would have been very highly rated indeed. The team performed well, and Eisenhower's reputation as an excellent football coach soared.

In 1916 he was again recruited, this time to coach Saint Louis College, a small Catholic parochial school in San Antonio that had not won a single football game in five years. Eisenhower's growing reputation as a successful football coach was secured when the team staged a remarkable turnaround and even reached the finals of the San Antonio city competition before losing a close championship game.

As he settled into the routine of duty with a peacetime Regular Army regiment, Eisenhower still retained powerful feelings for Gladys Harding and at first cared little about the social life of the post. One of his letters that has survived (undated, as usual) was a clear indication that he still missed her deeply and was no closer to getting over her than he had been in September.

"I just *had* to write," he penned to Gladys. "Made me feel sad and lonesome. Somehow when I get into a rather rebellious mood, I can't enjoy life at all. I was so happy last summer. And now—seems that you are sort of 'drifting'—as you said you would. . . . With me its [*sic*] the same routine day after day, and I have all my evenings to just *think* of you. I live in memories and in hopes. You are so desirable and lovely—and honey, how I miss you . . . write me a letter and make it *big*—tell me all I *want* to hear . . . girl—you are concerned in everything I do—or think—why you are *all* to me." Under his signature Eisenhower wrote: "I've done been true, my gal, to you."[16]

He did not remain so for long. Eisenhower's first stint as officer of the day on a Sunday in October 1915 changed his life forever. The Fort Sam Houston BOQ were situated along Infantry Row and across the street from the officers' club. On either side were the quarters of married officers. As Eisenhower emerged from his quarters smartly attired, with a pistol strapped to his waist and wearing a campaign hat cocked at a jaunty angle in imitation of those worn by Teddy Roosevelt's Rough Riders, he was hailed by Lulu Ingrum Harris, the wife of Maj. Hunter Harris, an officer assigned to Eisenhower's regiment. A group was lounging on the steps and lawn of the Harrises' quarters enjoying the late-afternoon sunshine, sipping grape juice, and gossiping. Lulu Harris called out, "Come here, Ike. I want to introduce you to some friends."

Her friends consisted of two bachelor officers and a group of civilians, among them several young women. One of the officers was Lt. Leonard T. "Gee" Gerow, a graduate of the Virginia Military Institute, with whom Eisenhower began a lifelong friendship that would take them from the halls of military academe at Fort Leavenworth to the Normandy beachhead and the Battle of the Bulge.

Eisenhower brushed off Lulu Harris by replying that he was on duty and could not spare the time. Then he noticed that one of the group was a very attractive young woman dressed in a white summer frock, and promptly changed his mind. He was introduced to John and Elvira Mathilde Carlson Doud and their three daughters. The Douds were a well-to-do Denver family who wintered each year in an upscale section of San Antonio. John Sheldon Doud, a businessman of English descent, was a doting father to his pampered daughters and was called "Pupah" by his family. His wife, Elvira, who was called Nana by her family, was a child of first-generation Swedish parents.[17]

John Doud was a restless and adventuresome fellow who, by the age of eighteen, had already run away from home three times. When he eventually settled down, Doud rose from rags to riches managing the family meatpacking business in Boone, Iowa, becoming a millionaire at a very young age. When Nana's health began to suffer in the harsh climate of Iowa, John Doud relocated his family to the friendlier climate of Colorado, settling first in Colorado Springs, and later moving to an exclusive Denver neighborhood in deference to their eldest daughter, Eleanor. She was born exceptionally frail, and by an early age had developed a serious heart condition that was exacerbated by the high altitude of Colorado Springs. Her decline was steady, and she died in 1912, aged seventeen, causing untold grief in the Doud family.[18]

John Doud had few intimate friends, was secretive about his private life, and is said to have kept two mistresses under assumed names he created to deceive the two women and his wife. He endured a lifetime of disappointment that Nana was unable to present him with a male heir. As partial compensation, two of his other daughters were given male nicknames. Still, he lavished all the trappings of the good life on his daughters. Papa Doud was especially close to his second child, Mamie Geneva Doud, who was born in Boone on November 14, 1896. He lovingly called Mamie "Little Puddy"; she called him "Pooh-Bah." Of the three surviving Doud girls, Mamie had, by 1915, become the most proficient at inducing him to cater to her every whim.

In San Antonio it was customary for the family to take a Sunday-afternoon drive in John Doud's electric car. By happenstance the Douds were present at the Harris quarters when Lt. Dwight Eisenhower appeared and was introduced to Miss Mamie Geneva Doud. A spirited eighteen-year-old socialite who had recently completed Miss Wolcott's (Finishing) School in Denver, Mamie later admitted to an instant attraction to the twenty-five-year-old officer, whom she thought was "the handsomest man" she had ever met.

Eisenhower thought her vivacious and saucy, with an intriguing air of impertinence. The flirtatious Mamie Doud tried but seems to have failed to disguise her reciprocal interest in Eisenhower, despite a warning from Lulu Harris that he was well known as Fort Sam's "woman-hater."[19] For Mamie the comment was as if Lulu had waved the proverbial red flag. She would later say of the man who became her husband, "Ike has the most engaging grin of anybody I ever met. Though when he turns it off his face is as bleak as the plains of Kansas."[20]

Within moments of their first meeting, Eisenhower impulsively asked Miss Doud if she would care to accompany him as he inspected the guard posts. Eisenhower's invitation was as unconventional as it was daring for an unattached female civilian—even one as fascinating as Mamie Doud—to accompany an officer making his official rounds. To his surprise Mamie accepted, "though I loathed walking." As they passed the troop barracks during their stroll, Eisenhower formally explained that she might see or hear things unsuitable for a young lady and urged her to keep her eyes straight ahead. Mamie, of course, did the exact opposite. Nevertheless their lengthy promenade around the post was agonizing for Mamie, who was wearing fashionable new shoes that were wholly inappropriate for walking. "I never walked so far in my life," she remembered. Eisenhower then asked Mamie for a date. Shocked, she refused, pointing out that her social calendar was already booked for some weeks ahead.

Although described as "an outrageous flirt" in her debutante year, Mamie Doud had actually dated relatively few young men. Her social status notwithstanding, Mamie was then unworldly and, by her own admission, naive.

Compared to the "lounge lizards with patent-leather hair," as she referred to the sons of the Denver social crowd, Mamie found the smooth-talking Eisenhower an alluring combination of brashness and manliness.

The following day Eisenhower telephoned the Doud home only to learn that Mamie had gone fishing with another beau. From then on he would call two or three times daily, only to be informed by the maid that Mamie was not available or by Mamie herself that her datebook was full for the next three weeks. "What did he expect? I was booked solid. It was my debutante year!"[21] When that ploy failed to sway Mamie into reserving a date for him, Eisenhower began showing up unannounced and uninvited at the Doud home. Mamie was frequently out on a date, and he would patiently sit on the porch awaiting her return. He used the time to good advantage by doing his best to impress her parents. Eisenhower's relentless pursuit of Mamie was part of a deliberate plan to make himself her only suitor by discouraging his would-be rivals, who would note his frequent presence at the Doud home as evidence that he had cornered her affections.

Still, for a time the romance went nowhere. Although Mamie had had little experience with men, she had mastered the skill of intentionally stimulating Eisenhower's growing interest by playing hard to get. After several weeks of this game, John Doud scolded Mamie "to stop her flighty nonsense or the 'Army boy' will give up in disgust."[22]

Mamie took the hint, and after a month of amorous denial, the spoiled Denver socialite and the acknowledged "woman-hater" of Fort Sam Houston began an improbable courtship. From then on Eisenhower became a fixture at the Doud household, and before long the two were dating each other exclusively. They went to places Eisenhower could barely afford: a vaudeville show, an occasional dance on the roof of a downtown hotel, and numerous meals at an inexpensive Mexican restaurant.[23] Unable to support himself, court Mamie, and pay off his debts, Eisenhower was usually broke before the end of the month, and lived from hand to mouth until the next payday. Nevertheless at Christmas 1915, possibly paying with poker winnings, Eisenhower managed to present Mamie with an expensive, engraved jewelry box. Even though such a gift violated Doud protocol, Mamie swayed her parents into letting her keep it.

Eisenhower's charm handily won over the Douds, with the lone exception of Mamie's spiteful eight-year-old sister Mabel Frances ("Mike"), who perceived him as a serious threat to the family's equilibrium and did everything in her power to make his visits miserable. "When her parents weren't looking," wrote one of Mamie's biographers, "she bit, kicked and scratched her big sister's caller. Mamie and Ike gave her as wide a berth as possible, but 'Mike,' even in her less violent moods, would thunder up and down the north porch, screeching insults."[24]

For Dwight Eisenhower, raised in the Spartan atmosphere of a home where he never observed his parents embrace each other or exchange a harsh word, life with the Douds was an eye-opening introduction to an utterly different form of family life. Sentimental and demonstrative, they spoke their minds, argued frequently, threw tantrums, cried, and made up. Where John Doud was outgoing and doted on his family, the dour David Eisenhower apparently endured a life of utter joylessness.

John Doud's grandson and namesake, John Sheldon Doud Eisenhower, who spent considerable time with the Douds as a young man, found the family passionate but excessive in their frequent displays of emotion with one another. "I came from the kind of family," said Mamie, "where if one of us was going around the corner we all kissed her goodbye and then went to the window to wave her out of sight."[25]

John Eisenhower thought John Doud "regarded Ike as a son" he never had, and "Nana just doted on him."[26] As time passed it was strikingly evident that Eisenhower greatly preferred the company of the Douds to that of his own family. Nana was captivated by Eisenhower and, "after we were married," remembered Mamie, "I learned quickly not to run to her seeking comfort when my husband and I had a spat. She always sided with Ike. The two had a great liking and respect for each other."[27]

By early 1916 Eisenhower had won over Mamie, yet remained as restless as ever, writing to Ruby Norman: "My life here is, in the main, uninteresting—nothing much doing—and I get tired of the same old grind some times. The girl I'm running around with now is named Miss Doud, from Denver. Winters here. Pretty nice—but awful strong for society—which often bores me. But we get on well together—and I'm at her house whenever I'm off duty." Eisenhower's heartache over Gladys Harding's rejection of his marriage proposal obviously still rankled. Although pleased when Gladys sent him an expensive smoking jacket for Christmas, he concluded his letter to Ruby Norman by remarking, "Sometime, if you are interested, I'll tell you all about the girl I run around with *since* I learned that G. H. cared so terribly for her work."[28]

Unlike his proposal of marriage to Gladys Harding, Eisenhower never formally asked Mamie to marry him. As their courtship deepened both simply *assumed* they would one day marry. On Valentine's Day in 1916, Eisenhower presented Mamie with a miniature replica of his class ring—the traditional custom when a West Pointer becomes engaged. Mamie would have none of it, insisting that she wanted and would accept nothing less than a *full-size* ring. She got one and proudly wore it throughout their marriage. The couple decided to wed in November 1916, on Mamie's twentieth birthday.

Still apprehensive about his continual lack of funds and all too aware that he would have to find some means of properly supporting Mamie when they married, Eisenhower applied for aviation duty with the forerunner of what would become the Army Air Service. Army aviation was then under the aegis of the Signal Corps, and his acceptance would mean a not-inconsequential 50 percent increase in pay. Moreover, flying fascinated him, and the attraction of becoming one of the army's elite pioneer aviators was irresistible. "I'll get a lot more then," he told Ruby Norman, "and maybe I can make ends meet. Ha Ha—you know me—I'll never have a sou."[29]

Though troubled by the notion of her fiancé entering an untested, dangerous vocation, Mamie was surprisingly supportive when Eisenhower was quickly accepted. Eisenhower remembered how he had eagerly anticipated the experience. Mr. Doud had graciously given his permission for their union, even though he and Nana both thought Mamie far too young to be married at age twenty. When Eisenhower arrived at the Doud home he remembers "walking on air" until he told the assembled Douds that he would soon become an aviator. Eisenhower's announcement was greeted with chilling silence and stony disapproval from John Doud.

Aviation was then in its infancy, untested and unsafe. The first active aviation unit operated in Mexico in short-lived support of the so-called punitive expedition. The inexperienced First Aero Squadron was equipped with the dangerously unstable Curtiss JN-2 "Jennies." The gallant men who flew these death traps were all pioneer aviators. Three of them—Carl Spaatz, Millard Harmon, and Ralph Royce—would become prominent commanders in the Army Air Corps during World War II. A number of other young lieutenants and captains assigned to the punitive expedition were also destined for high rank, and for a close future association with Dwight Eisenhower: George S. Patton, Courtney H. Hodges, William H. Simpson, Kenyon A. Joyce (a future commanding officer of both Eisenhower and Patton), Lesley J. McNair, and Brehon B. Somervell.[30]

The six Jennies lasted barely one month before all crashed. Two were lost within the first week of the expedition. Despite their brief participation in the punitive expedition to carry mail and dispatches, the need for aviation in a modern war was affirmed.[31]

His courtship of Mamie Doud had not quenched Eisenhower's thirst for action. Pershing's punitive expedition was the perfect chance, but his request for a transfer was rejected. Despite his obvious affection for Eisenhower, John Doud was deeply troubled at the prospect of his beloved daughter marrying someone about to become part of an untested and inherently hazardous profession. He balked at subjecting his Mamie to such perils, and threatened to withdraw his approval if Eisenhower carried out his irresponsible intention. It was bad enough that Mamie would live under greatly reduced economic and social circumstances, but the notion of her also becoming a widow was too much. Mamie argued in vain with her father that Eisenhower should be permitted to follow his dream. Faced with accepting the aviation assignment or very possibly losing Mamie, Eisenhower hesitated for several days before relenting and announcing to the assembled Douds that he would pass up becoming an aviator. Notwithstanding his later claim to have had no regrets about his decision, Eisenhower never lost his enthusiasm for flying or his desire to qualify as a pilot.

That Eisenhower fell for and married Mamie Doud on the rebound from the unhappy end of his romance with Gladys Harding is unequivocal. Moreover, it is likely that sometime in early 1916 Gladys sent Eisenhower a "Dear John" letter, most likely after she learned of Eisenhower's intention to marry Mamie, when she knew for certain they would have no future together.

Whether out of love or need, Gladys Harding left the music circuit for good in 1916 and returned to Abilene. She later revealed to Ruby Norman's daughter that she had expected to marry Eisenhower and that the news of his engagement to Mamie Doud was crushing. "Gladys *had* to be married before Eisenhower, and she was, sixteen days before"—in June 1916, to an older local man named Cecil Brooks, a widower whose first wife had died the previous year during childbirth. Brooks's previous overtures toward Gladys had been rebuffed until she learned that Dwight Eisenhower was marrying another. In short order she married Cecil Brooks, a man she barely knew, solely "to spite Dwight." Indeed, her impulsive and emotional decision doomed Eisenhower's first love to a joyless marriage that lasted until Cecil Brooks's death in 1944. Afterward, Gladys suffered a nervous breakdown from what Ruby Norman was convinced was overwhelming guilt at never having loved Cecil Brooks.[32]

In the years before it was recognized as a deadly health menace, smoking was considered fashionable. Eisenhower's smoking habit, begun at West Point, continued unabated despite his forthcoming marriage to Mamie. As a concession to his more serious new attitude, Eisenhower proudly but foolishly stopped smoking ready-made cigarettes and reverted to the roll-your-own variety to save money. Eisenhower smoked heavily until 1949, when he was sternly warned by his doctor to stop or face serious consequences. He did so cold turkey, and, although he never again touched a cigarette, it has since become clear that nearly forty years of smoking that ranged from moderate to uncurbed excess eventually took its toll on Eisenhower's already questionable health.[33] Mamie also smoked for many years, probably beginning about the time she met Ike. Whether or not he influenced her decision to start is not known but she was never a heavy smoker like her husband and eventually stopped in her later years.[34]

The Douds returned to Denver soon after the engagement was announced, and the courtship continued by letter. Initially their plans did not take into account the expanding global war in Europe and the beginning of mass mobilization in the United States. Mamie was hardly reassured by the knowledge that her fiancé was intent on sticking his neck out, if not in aviation, then either in Mexico or Europe. Frightened that "[she] might lose him," she privately vowed to marry Ike as soon as possible, regardless of the anticipated objections from her parents.

The initiative actually came from Eisenhower, who telephoned in late June and said, "Let's get married *now*." Mamie still had to overcome the small matter of notifying and obtaining permission from her parents, who were away on a trip to Iowa. They were "speechless" at the news and "raised the roof," recalled Mamie. "They had the old-fashioned notion that quick weddings weren't quite decent." Mamie Doud had to employ all her powers of persuasion to overcome the Douds' serious misgivings that such a brief engagement might wrongly convey an impression that the marriage was a matter of urgency rather than of choice. "But I was stubborn. Finally, Mama gave in and pretty soon she brought Papa around."[35]

Their timing could not have been much worse. The army was on a virtual war footing, and ordinary furloughs were cancelled for the duration. Eisenhower requested a twenty-day leave to marry Mamie and was bewildered when he was summoned to appear before General Funston to explain himself. Such is the discretion of general officers that—although in direct violation of War Department policy—Funston nevertheless granted Lieutenant Eisenhower a ten-day leave. Undoubtedly Funston's generosity was a subtle reward to Eisenhower for having coached football the year before.

With the wedding only a short time off, Eisenhower was again broke and in dire need of a wedding ring for Mamie, as well as funds for travel and a brief honeymoon. He persuaded a jeweler to sell him a ring on credit, and a local bank agreed to cover the overdrafts he expected to incur.

The first two and a half days of his furlough consisted of a frustrating, flood-delayed journey by train from San Antonio to Denver. Eisenhower's marriage to Mamie Geneva Doud was a family-only ceremony performed in the music room of the Doud home at noon on July 1, 1916, the same day the army promoted him to the rank of first lieutenant. In a scene reminiscent of the summer of 1913 in Abilene, Eisenhower stood virtually motionless for two hours before the ceremony to avoid creasing his immaculate white dress uniform. The short notice meant that the family pastor was not available, and the wedding ceremony was instead conducted by an English clergyman whom the family barely knew. The honeymoon was necessarily short, at a nearby resort hotel to which the couple traveled by train.

No correspondence has survived, and his memoir is unhelpful in answering the question of just when Eisenhower notified his parents of his engagement and forthcoming marriage. Their return to San Antonio was via Abilene, to meet his family, and then Kansas City, where they would visit his brother Arthur. The tiresome train journey from Denver to Abilene was hot and uncomfortable, and when they arrived in Abilene about 3:00 A.M., Mamie discovered that, in a parting prank, her two younger sisters had filled her

powder box with rice. They were met by David, whom she found polite and rather shy. Mamie's first impression was that Mr. Eisenhower had defied the accepted social custom of her world by not wearing a coat when outside.

Mamie quickly discerned that the Eisenhowers were unlike any family she had ever encountered, and that she had no more in common with the senior Eisenhowers than she did with her bridegroom. She was appalled at the amount of work Ida performed and surprised at the family's lack of world-liness. They neither drank, smoked, nor played cards and appeared not to enjoy life as she knew it. During later visits to Abilene, in deference to her in-laws Mamie would smoke furtively, leaning out of an upstairs window, "hoping she wouldn't be caught."[36]

While she found Ida friendly and outgoing, Mamie never warmed to David, even though she politely addressed them as "Grandma" and "Grandpa." "Ike's father was a good man but to me he always seemed stern. . . . The boys owed everything to their mother." Nor was she ever truly at ease in the Eisenhower home during their infrequent visits to Abi-lene, particularly in summertime when the brass bedsteads were too hot to touch. "I got out of there in a hurry, I'll tell you, every time I got the chance."

Mamie also became an unwitting participant in the continuing fantasy surrounding David Eisenhower, once relating Milton Good's alleged treachery to an interviewer, concluding, "He [David] had taken engineering by mail, so he went to Texas and took a job as [a] construction engineer."[37]

Not surprisingly Eisenhower seemed increasingly uncomfortable around his parents but completely at ease with the Douds, whose company he far preferred.[38] John Eisenhower's observation is instructive: "The Eisenhowers were so rigidly Pennsylvania Dutch, I don't think Dad communicated on a confidential basis with his father, *ever*."[39]

However, when Mamie met Milton for the first time, she planted a kiss on his cheek and said how much she had always wanted to have a brother. Milton was captivated. "And I've been her willing slave ever since!"[40] Mamie adored Milton, and over the years he became a treasured part of her inner circle of close friends.

Ida had prepared an enormous feast to welcome them. Although the visit lasted a mere eight hours, its impression on Mamie was indelible. The new-lyweds departed for Kansas City with their bellies stuffed with Ida's finest cooking. After a reunion with Arthur they entrained for San Antonio to begin married life, arriving just as Eisenhower's leave expired. Their journey to San Antonio was on the Katy railroad, which passed through Denison, Texas, and within a few yards of his birthplace.[41]

Part III

WORLD WAR I, 1917–1919

Woe to him who sets Europe ablaze.

—FIELD MARSHAL HELMUTH VON MOLTKE

10.

Roses Have Thorns

Mamie, there is one thing you must understand.
My country comes first and always will; you come second.

First Lieutenant and Mrs. Dwight Eisenhower returned to Fort Sam Houston and the congratulations of friends and colleagues, who showered the couple with badly needed presents. They moved into Eisenhower's two-room apartment in the BOQ along Infantry Row. Marriage would toughen Mamie to a world she had no conception even existed: one in which there were no servants and the comforts of an upper-class home were replaced by drab, Lilliputian military quarters designed for spartan utility. She rented a piano for five dollars per month, and Ike installed a wooden icebox in their bathroom. However, Mamie frequently neglected to empty the drainage pan, resulting in a flood in their parlor.

Many years later Mamie candidly admitted that they had had little in common when they married. Indeed, Mamie Geneva Doud and Dwight David Eisenhower were a classic romantic mismatch, with almost nothing in common but love. Their granddaughter, Susan, has aptly described their union as "an attraction of opposites" in which each took the best qualities from the other. One was born into a family of high social status and wanted for nothing, yet was utterly unsophisticated about the world outside her immediate social circle; the other was the product of an impoverished childhood, who was cocksure but uncomfortable in the presence of women.

Mamie had never cooked a meal, happily endorsing her mother's dictum that: "If you don't learn to cook, no one will ask you to do it."[1] Never having been obliged to so much as make her own bed, the overindulged Mamie regarded housekeeping as a duty to be performed by servants. In a reversal of roles, Eisenhower was an expert at cooking and was no stranger to every conceivable household chore. For a time the couple ate all their meals at the officers' club, but the expense eventually grew too great on a salary that inevitably ran out before month's end. Fortunately her husband's love of cooking saved the newlyweds from a daily gastronomical fiasco. Finally "she allowed

Ike to teach her some basic cooking skills, and they started to eat simply at home."[2]

No matter how inadequate or uncomfortable their apartment was, Mamie kept an immaculate house, entertained in accordance with military custom, and helped turn the Eisenhower quarters at Fort Sam (and later at other duty stations), into a social refuge for Ike's military friends, who always received a warm welcome at what was eventually christened "Club Eisenhower."[3] "Ike is the kind," said Mamie, "who would rather give you a fried egg in his own home than take you to the finest night club in the world." They had no radio, and evenings were often spent reading. Eisenhower remained an inveterate reader, continuing to expand his knowledge of military history. "In our home everyone does as he pleases. If Ike wants to read, he reads or takes a nap." In addition to practicing his cooking skills, what pleased him most was good conversation. Mamie judged him a fascinating talker: "At any party there is always a group around Ike." His thirst for information had turned him into a very good listener. "If you were interviewing him, you would find yourself doing all the talking."[4]

She had also entered the provincial world of the Regular Army, which itself was a rude awakening. For the first time Mamie was exposed to the camaraderie of other women, with whom she stoically endured the hardships of frequent moves, miserable quarters, the long hours her husband worked, and a meager income. The most unrewarding aspect of military life, however was the gossip, the pettiness, and backstabbing of some military wives—bored or ambitious women who advanced their own agendas, ranging from promoting their husbands' careers to avenging real or imagined slights. Mamie would have none of it and refused to play this game or to engage in such trivia, which she disavowed.

On the positive side, military families tended to look out for one another. Mamie found other wives who were friendly and supportive. It was customary to welcome new arrivals with a helping hand in the form of food or the loan of household items until the family could settle in. "We all did it, everybody helped out," remembered Mamie. Other young couples became part of the Eisenhowers' social circle, all of them sharing a common bond of being at the bottom of the army's social and military pecking order. Before long Mamie had become very popular with the other wives for her friendliness and endearing manner, traits that were perhaps her strongest contributions to her new husband's budding career.

In addition, Mamie's friends in the San Antonio community provided a welcome outlet from the Fort Sam social routine. Their social life included frequent trips to town to eat or go dancing, as they had during their brief courtship. The arrival of her family for their annual sojourn in San Antonio was also a great source of comfort. When Nana visited in the autumn of 1916, the change in her daughter was noticeable: "Four months of married responsibility had tamed her social butterfly to a serious housewife, one who was perhaps too worried about household matters."[5]

Mamie viewed her role as strictly that of a homemaker whose function was to focus on making her husband content by creating a tranquil home environment. For all her inexperience, she strove mightily to become a good army wife, once saying, "You can't be much help to your husband but you can do a lot to hurt him."[6] Fifty-six years later, as Mamie looked back on her marriage to Eisenhower, she expressed her gratitude. "I'd say to God every day, 'I'm so thankful.' . . . I don't know exactly how to explain it, but everything was a pattern, like it had been planned. But it wasn't planned by us. God planned it."[7]

Unlike his verbal outpouring of love for Gladys Harding, Eisenhower was rarely able to express his love for Mamie. Julie Nixon Eisenhower once remarked that whereas Mamie's emotions were an open book—"every complaint, every thought, petty or important"—Eisenhower "to his dying day, found it difficult to express his feelings." Even on the joyous occasion of the birth of their first child, Eisenhower's love for his wife and newborn son was kept safely locked within.[8]

Mamie thought Ike worked too hard but kept her opinion to herself with the observation that, "No woman can run him."[9] Nothing, however, could have adequately prepared her for a role as the wife of a poorly paid army officer in a profession that was, at best, regarded with indifference in the world outside the military. From the outset she made it a point never to involve herself in her husband's business. His work problems remained in the office, not in the Eisenhower household. During their fifty-two years of marriage, Mamie Eisenhower never wavered in her dedication to her husband and his career. In later years stories about Mamie would trumpet such headlines as HER CAREER IS IKE. In today's more liberated age, Mamie Eisenhower might inaccurately be portrayed as a classic example of a (military) wife in a Victorian age of male chauvinism where the husband was the boss; where *his* views were regarded as gospel; where wives were seen but not heard; and where their role was to cook, raise the kids, and provide a happy and contented home.

Much like her mother-in-law, Mamie exercised her own form of influence. In public she never expressed opinions or openly disagreed with Ike. Unlike the fiery Beatrice Patton, who once swung a sword at her husband's head when he took her for granted, and physically attacked a portly, deskbound Washington colonel who insulted her husband, Mamie was undemonstrative in public. She once told her granddaughter-in-law, Julie Nixon Eisenhower, "There can be only one star in the heaven, Sugar, and there is only one way to live with an Eisenhower. Let him have his own way."[10]

One of Eisenhower's presidential speechwriters once opined, "Ike would have been *Colonel* Dwight D. Eisenhower, if it weren't for Mamie."[11] Over time Mamie's influence would grow, and she would later avow, "Ike took care of the office—I ran the house." This included the family finances, which she ran thriftily and efficiently, thanks to her mother, who had trained Mamie how to budget the family finances, keep meticulous records, and economize.

Perhaps it was a lucky omen that Eisenhower was promoted to first lieutenant on his wedding day, thenceforth to earn a princely extra twenty dollars per month. John Doud announced that he would not subsidize their income; the couple would have to learn to subsist on Ike's pay. He did, however, present them with a four-year-old Pullman automobile and a cash gift, part of which was spent to furnish their quarters. The remainder was jealously hoarded by Mamie in her role of family banker. Although thereafter the Eisenhowers were never without an automobile, courtesy of Pupah, despite Mamie's valiant efforts to "squeeze a dollar until the eagle screamed" by making Ike's pay last through the entire month, it was often a losing battle. "Many a time we were down to our last twenty-five cents when payday dawned."[12] Mamie would later proudly state: "There may have been times when we had only a dollar in the bank, but we have never owed a cent in our lives."[13]

John Doud never fully carried out his plan not to support his daughter and son-in-law, and after the birth of their first child in 1917, he sent Mamie one hundred dollars monthly. During the trying interwar years and the Great Depression, it was this monthly stipend that enabled Eisenhower to remain in the army at a time when he seriously considered resigning for a better-paying civilian job.[14]

If there were already definite signs of change and a growing maturity as a result of his marriage, there would soon be emerging evidence that behaviorally Eisenhower was a classic type A personality. "Such an individual," notes Eisenhower scholar Robert Ferrell, "is careless about health, immoderate in regard to working hours, driven by the need to go at top speed day after day." Brig. Gen. Thomas Mattingly, one of Eisenhower's presidential physicians, thoroughly investigated his entire history of health problems and concluded, "As a youth Eisenhower showed none of the driving ambition and the tension that later became so obvious. Perhaps it was there but no one recorded it." Yet, as Ferrell notes, "The entire Eisenhower family had a history of hypertension, cardiovascular disease . . . and coronary disease."[15]

Between their money woes and Eisenhower's poor health, the marriage was far from easy. In December 1916 he contracted malaria and was confined to his quarters for eight days. Several months later, in March 1917, tonsillitis resulted in another six days at home. In May, the malaria recurred, and Eisenhower was sent home for ten more days until the fever passed.[16] Although the malaria would not return, Eisenhower's military career would be marked by a variety of health problems.

One of Eisenhower's assigned duties was that of provost marshal, the military version of a chief of police. It was a position that kept Eisenhower and the military police hopping. Numerous brawls in San Antonio, usually alcohol related, broke out between national guardsmen and Regular Army soldiers. To help prevent incidents Eisenhower and several MPs would visit the local bars and brothels and arrest those who were being unruly or were found to be AWOL. One night a drunken national guard lieutenant fired two pistol rounds at Eisenhower from a nearby alley, nearly killing him. The incident shook Eisenhower so badly he feared for Mamie's safety on a military post where there were few women. He presented Mamie with a .45 pistol and taught her its proper use in an emergency. However, when he attempted to test her reaction to a simulated break-in, Eisenhower discovered that she had hidden it so well that "she couldn't have gotten it out in a week, much less in a hurry. I decided to concentrate on making the camp safer."[17]

The Douds had always been very formal, and the girls were required to present themselves in proper dress for meals, even breakfast. Mamie's modest economic means notwithstanding, throughout her marriage she always worked strenuously to maintain herself as glamorously as possible for her husband. On the dubious recommendation of her doctor, who claimed it would do wonders for the skin of her face, she often spent one day a week in bed. He seems to have noticed and appreciated Mamie's appearance and fastidious dress. From the time he met Mamie, Eisenhower would become annoyed whenever he encountered women who were improperly or sloppily dressed in public.[18]

Ike's West Point classmates were surprised at his marriage. Although it was customary for an officer who married to notify the academy jeweler, who would then send him a gift from the class, which each officer would help pay for, Eisenhower had not bothered. Thus, when Lt. (later Maj. Gen.) John B. Wogan was passing through San Antonio and decided to visit Eisenhower, "The door was opened by a pretty girl wearing an apron and holding a broom . . . we'd always considered him the true bachelor type—a good bet for the last man in the class to get married. Who was this girl?

"I stood at the open door, embarrassed, and inquired in my best stammer if she knew the whereabouts of Lieutenant Eisenhower. She replied that he was drilling with his company; would I like to come in and wait for him? . . . My confusion obviously amused her. Finally, she rescued me. 'I'm Mrs. Eisenhower,' she said smiling. 'Ike and I were married on the first of July.' "[19]

The instability that had racked Mexico since 1910 had, by 1914, evolved into increasing hostility to the United States, principally over Woodrow

Wilson's interference in Mexican affairs and his inept handling of U.S.-Mexican relations. After longtime dictator Porfirio Díaz was overthrown in 1910, there followed a period of revolution and turmoil in which a short-lived democratic government was itself overthrown by a military coup in 1913. Wilson refused to recognize the new regime, and an incident in Tampico and the occupation of Veracruz in 1914 by an American military force was an attempt by the president to persuade the Mexican people to replace yet another in a long line of despots. The ploy backfired, instead exacerbating the growing anti-Americanism in Mexico. The United States withheld recognition and sent military supplies to the regime's opponent, Venustiano Carranza, a former senator, wealthy landowner, and a ruthless revolutionary.

Among Carranza's early supporters was a charismatic renegade from Durango named Francisco Villa, who was better known to his legion of followers as "Pancho." A notorious bandit leader and folk hero, Villa epitomized the Mexicans' love of *macho* and had become the Latino version of Robin Hood, looting the rich, rustling their cattle, and giving to the poor. Villa's folk-hero stature notwithstanding, he was also a cold-blooded killer who "could shoot down a man point-blank, showing no more emotion than if he were stepping on a bug."[20]

The Veracruz incident brought about the installation of Carranza as president. The ambitious Villa broke with Carranza and began opposing his former cohort. The Mexican economy was in disarray, and instability grew as intrigue and lawlessness swept the nation. Villa had counted on American support to obtain the presidency. Instead, when Wilson recognized the new Carranza government in October 1915, an irate Villa swore revenge on the United States.[21]

By the end of 1915 not only had Villa and his *pistoleros* launched a series of raids along the U.S.-Mexican border, but Carranza's forces were engaged in similar burning and looting. Mexico was swept by violence as Villistas, Carranzistas, and several other factions reduced the nation to a state of virtual anarchy. Wilson, who had once supported Villa, now regarded him as little more than a bandit who threatened the security of the southwestern United States. Fighting appeared imminent as the War Department began deploying troops to Texas and New Mexico.

True to his threat, in early January 1916, Villa began a bloody campaign against the United States. The kidnapping and execution of sixteen American mining engineers left the United States on a virtual war footing. Early on March 9, 1916, Villa and his army of between four and five hundred men raided the small border town of Columbus, New Mexico, and began indiscriminate burning, looting, and killing. The Columbus raid left eighteen Americans dead, and although Mexican losses were very high, Villa had achieved his aim of arousing the United States.[22] A punitive expedition was quickly formed under the command of Brig. Gen. John J. "Black Jack" Pershing, a harsh disciplinarian who was considered the army's premier soldier.

The news excited Eisenhower, who immediately applied for a transfer to the punitive expedition but was summarily turned down. Nonetheless Mamie was devastated when Eisenhower returned home grim-faced one noontime in August to reveal that he had been ordered to temporary duty with the national guard. Already her first taste of army life had left her disheartened by Eisenhower's long workdays. Now, he would be away for an indeterminate time barely a month after their marriage. For an overindulged, temperamental nineteen-year-old, the prospect of her new husband's prolonged absence brought tears and complaints that fell on deaf ears. The U.S. Army, as she had quickly discovered, was a demanding and altogether formidable mistress. Mamie was "utterly accustomed to being the focus of attention," notes Susan Eisenhower, and when she "cried that Ike was leaving her, he put his arm around her and said gently, 'My duty will always come first.' Mamie understood . . . that he meant it."[23] During Eisenhower's military career there would be many more such separations, which, as she matured, Mamie learned to accept as the price of being an army wife, although she never really got over the loneliness.

Units of the national guard were mobilized for border duty, and Fort Sam Houston became the focus of the army's preparations. As one of the Regular Army officers assigned to help train the guard, Eisenhower moved to a nearby training area called Camp Wilson, where he was detailed as an inspector-instructor of the 7th Illinois ("Fighting Irish") Infantry, a unit made up almost exclusively of Chicago Irishmen. The regiment was more of a social entity than a military unit. With ill-equipped, badly trained, and decidedly unruly soldiers, scarcely a night passed when its men failed to put their motto into practice.

Eisenhower's duties included supervising close-order drill and training his charges in trench warfare, which necessitated not only digging an extensive trench system but practicing movements between positions. The regimental commander, Col. Daniel Moriarity, was a gregarious, elderly Irishman who had served under Teddy Roosevelt in the Spanish-American War. Eisenhower described him as "a fine old fellow," neglecting to mention that more often than not he was inebriated, as were numerous others (including the regimental chaplain) whose preference for drink far exceeded their interest in performing military duties. Moriarity distanced himself from training and administrative duties and virtually turned over the running of the 7th Illinois to Lieutenant Eisenhower, who was delighted to accept the de facto responsibility of running his regiment for him.

Eisenhower soon found that he not only related well to enlisted men but that his leadership was reciprocated by the high esteem in which they held him.[24] More important, the experience was an early milestone in his military career. The experience gained at Camp Wilson encouraged Eisenhower to begin taking his profession more seriously. "I began to devote more hours of study and reading to my profession," he wrote in his memoir. Yet he often did so as much from boredom as professional necessity, writing in January 1916 to Ruby Norman, "I surely hate to study. That's no fun."[25]

After one particularly ineffective trench exercise, Eisenhower bluntly asserted, "You know, colonel, if this were actual trench warfare, about half your men would be dead by now because they don't keep their heads down." Before Colonel Moriarity could reply, a quick-witted private quipped, "And you wouldn't be alive standing up there either, lieutenant." During his brief tenure with the Fighting Irish, Eisenhower developed an affinity for his charges that was fully reciprocated. By December 1916 it was abundantly clear that Pancho Villa would never be captured by the punitive expedition. The regiment was recalled from active duty and returned to Illinois, with Eisenhower present to see them off. Not only would his resourceful presence be missed, but many "felt they were losing a close friend and inspiration."[26] It was Eisenhower's first test of leadership and he had made the most of it.

As 1916 drew to a close neither Mamie nor Ike could have anticipated the stresses on their marriage that were to result from America's formal entry into World War I in April 1917. Although Ike rarely discussed his work with Mamie, he did so in December, when he broached the subject of his aspiration to transfer to the Air Corps. However, when Mamie announced she was pregnant with their first child in late December, further discussion of the Air Corps evaporated.

What had begun with a minor event in Sarajevo in June 1914—the assassination of Archduke Franz Ferdinand of Austria—had, by virtue of the complicated European linkage of treaties and alliances, escalated into a war of such dimensions that it engulfed not only Europe but the Middle East as well. By waiting until 1917, the United States avoided bloodbaths such as Gallipoli, Ypres, Arras, Passchendaele, and the Somme—horrific manifestations of the carnage that characterized World War I. On a single day—July 1, 1916—the British Army sustained 57,000 casualties, including more than 19,000 dead, in the Battle of the Somme, while at Gallipoli, British and French forces fought the Turks during an eight-month killing frenzy.[27] As appalling as these battles were, they were dwarfed by the 1916 siege of Verdun, in which the French and German armies racked up nearly 1 million casualties during the bloodiest battle in the history of warfare. By 1917 the Western Front had become a grotesque scar that ran from the North Sea across northern France to the Swiss border, and the war had evolved into a stalemate, a war of attrition in which trench warfare had become the norm in what was being called "the war to end all wars."[28]

The United States was drawn into the conflict even though Wilson and his secretary of state, William Jennings Bryan, subscribed to the belief that "a nation could remain aloof from war by refusing to prepare for it."[29] However, as relations deteriorated and Germany became more belligerent toward the United States, Wilson became more realistic about the inevitable need to employ military force. Although officially still neutral, the United States had been supporting the Allied powers—Britain, France, and Russia—with military hardware and loans that totaled nearly $1 billion, a charade that fooled no one, least of all Germany.

The Central Powers (Germany, Austria, and Turkey) were wary of the United States but undeterred from employing unlimited submarine warfare, which by early 1917 culminated in the indiscriminate sinking of Allied and neutral ships. In the end it was the aggressive acts by German U-boats that, more than anything else, goaded Wilson into seeking a declaration of war from Congress in April.[30]

War fever swiftly gripped the United States. Men rushed to volunteer in droves and posters of "Uncle Sam" appeared, proclaiming, I WANT YOU FOR U.S. ARMY. Patriotism in the form of slogans and songs swept the nation.

The decision to send an American Expeditionary Force (AEF) to France required the ablest commander in chief who could be found, an officer of proven courage and resolution to carry out the exceptionally difficult task ahead. There was only one bona fide candidate for the appointment, Black Jack Pershing, who was given a virtual carte blanche to organize the AEF. To create and train a fighting force from a tiny peacetime army, ill equipped to fight any kind of war—much less one against the formidable German army—was one of the most daunting tasks ever given to an American military commander.

The U.S. Army of 1917 was cursed with staggering shortcomings in men and equipment. The army possessed only 285,000 Springfield rifles, 544 three-inch field guns, and sufficient ammunition for a mere nine-hour bombardment. The shortage of basic weapons was so dire that the troops of one newly formed division were obliged to create mock weapons whittled from wooden sticks, a sorry state of affairs that would be replicated a quarter of a century later. Of the fifty-five planes in the fledgling Army Air Service, 93 percent were obsolete.[31]

The United States faced the daunting prospect of mobilization on a massive scale. In December 1916 the strength of the army was still a paltry 108,399 officers and men, whose fundamental weaknesses had been exposed during the Punitive Expedition. America may have been a slumbering giant, but neither its military establishment, its people, nor its civilian industry were prepared for a major war to be fought in a foreign land more than three thousand miles from its shores. The decision to institute a Selective Service system to draft men aged eighteen to thirty-five (later raised to age forty-five) had, by the end of the war in 1918, resulted in the drafting of 2.75 million men.[32] Thus, as historian Russell F. Weigley notes, "The help that America could offer in 1917 was mostly a promise."[33]

Among the many varied and complex problems to be solved were the production and supply of weapons, uniforms, and vehicles of all sorts; the purchase of more than three hundred thousand horses and mules; the creation of training facilities; and the development and manufacture of modern weapons that would permit the U.S. Army to compete on a level playing field with the German army.[34]

For Dwight Eisenhower and other professional soldiers in the peacetime army, American entry into the war had far-reaching implications, opportunities, and disappointments. The regimental spirit that existed in the army (which has since been all but lost), decreed that an officer spend most of his career in the same regiment with which he became identified. However, to Eisenhower's intense regret, in May 1917 he was abruptly transferred to the newly forming 57th Infantry Regiment, which had no troops, no equipment, and no permanent home. To complicate matters, it was decided that the regimental bivouac and training area would be established at Leon Springs, an outpost twenty miles north of San Antonio. Situated in a dusty hellhole devoid of facilities of any kind, it meant starting from scratch to construct and staff a regimental bivouac.

The newlyweds endured their second separation and could see each other only on Sunday. For Mamie it was another manifestation of the tribulations of being an army wife whose husband was as much married to the army as he was to her. Subjected as he was to "the needs of the service," the experience of the Eisenhowers in 1917 was typical of the hardships the young couple would experience off and on throughout their marriage. The anxiety of the community of army wives who gathered in "Club Eisenhower" was not eased by the constant talk of war by their husbands or how an assignment to the AEF might be obtained. Their days playing cards or socializing with other military wives were of little comfort during the lonely nights. Their husbands never saw the tears or the loneliness. "They were, Mamie admitted afterward, the bleakest of times for her."[35] As one of her biographers has observed, "It might be military glory for the men in khaki to move in the direction of the trenches of France . . . but for their women who must wait—and hope—what could be greater torture?"[36]

The 57th Regiment was initially staffed with only a skeleton cadre from the 19th Infantry. Eisenhower's principal duty—one of the most challenging in the entire regiment—was that of regimental supply officer. On his shoulders fell the unenviable responsibility of outfitting and equipping the 3,500 men who would shortly be arriving for training. Other units were also forming, and the needs of so many new formations severely taxed the limited assets available from the Quartermaster and Ordnance Departments. Eisenhower threw himself into what would become his trademark: hard work and long hours. He solved a legion of problems with the help of an experienced supply sergeant who engaged in the army's unofficial barter system, of one hand washing another. Starting with nothing, Eisenhower and his NCO managed to beg, borrow, or trade for tentage, foodstuffs, and the other necessary essentials.

One of Eisenhower's closest friends was the regimental adjutant, Lt. Walton H. Walker, who later became one of the most aggressive corps commanders in northwestern Europe, earning him the nickname "Bulldog." Their duties brought both officers into frequent contact with the regimental commander, Col. David J. Baker, who "rewarded" them for their efficiency by assigning each a myriad of extra duties. Baker was particularly fussy about the food served in the mess hall and constantly complained that it was not to his satisfaction. Several officers had already tried to please the colonel and been dismissed before Eisenhower was given the unenviable assignment as the new mess officer. After overhearing the colonel mention how much he liked eating game, Eisenhower thought he had found a means of placating his commander. Early one morning he and Walker rode their horses to a nearby field to shoot doves, which were duly dressed and served to the finicky colonel. Unfortunately Baker became so fond of this delicacy that he pestered Eisenhower to serve game at other meals as well. Thus, Eisenhower and Walker were obliged to continue their shooting forays until the day disaster nearly struck.

Walker's regular mount was lame one morning, and he was obliged to ride a replacement horse. When he fired the first cartridge from an automatic five-shot shotgun, the horse panicked and reared uncontrollably. Then, with Walker already unable to restrain the animal, his shotgun began discharging wildly each time the horse bucked. Fearing for their lives, Eisenhower and his orderly hastily dismounted and sought refuge behind their horses. Although it could later be viewed with amusement, at the time it was another of many close calls Eisenhower would experience during his army career. On another occasion he gathered the battalion and company supply officers for a lecture when the tree under which they had sought shelter from the rain was struck by lightning. Eisenhower was knocked unconscious, and Walker, who had been on the telephone in a nearby tent, had his arm turn black and blue after nearly being fried by the electricity in the telephone line.[37]

Peacetime army promotions were so slow that it was not uncommon for it to take fifteen years or more for an officer to attain the grade of captain. In May 1917, with less than two years' service, Eisenhower was promoted to that rank.

Although Mamie had previously driven the Douds' electric car in Denver, she had never driven a gasoline-powered automobile with a standard shift. In fact, she did not even know how to start the machine or how to operate the brakes. However, if she and Ike were to see each other, Mamie made up her mind that she would have to drive the Pullman to Leon Springs. They made a date for a Sunday morning, and, as the appointed hour passed, an agitated Mamie appeared chugging down the road, shouting for Ike to jump on to the running board and *stop* the car. To avoid traffic Mamie had begun her journey near dawn by soliciting an obliging sergeant to crank the starter. Once pointed in the right direction, she somehow managed to make the entire trip to Leon Springs without braking, despite careening into a number of ditches (from which she emerged amazingly unscathed). Eisenhower often wondered how she had done it and prudently arranged for an experienced driver to accompany her whenever possible. "It was difficult to judge who was in more danger," he remarked. "The men on their way to war, or the women on their way to the men."[38] Later, whenever Eisenhower was given a rare weekend off, he hitched rides to Fort Sam on all manner of conveyances. "The trips were always through a tunnel of dust, and he was usually one of the dirtiest men on duty with Uncle Sam's Army by the time he embraced his wife."[39]

Eisenhower's experience as a supply officer left a lasting impression of the inherent perils of being accountable to the U.S. Army for its equipment. Whenever—and it was often—equipment was missing or a request went unfilled, it became Eisenhower's problem to solve. The final shipment that would complete the outfitting of the regiment was an enormous box containing carriers for the entrenching tools, an essential item for trench warfare. The regimental and battalion commanders all gathered to witness this signal event, only to discover that an outdated model had mistakenly been substituted. The box was immediately resealed and returned to the Quartermaster Department. Some months later Eisenhower was shocked to find himself billed $22.04 by the army for nineteen allegedly missing items. Despite presenting affidavits supporting his contention that nothing was taken from the shipment, Eisenhower was nevertheless held responsible for having failed to comply with a regulation requiring a complete inventory. Disgusted, he paid up, and the family budget took the hit.[40] It was his first of many disagreeable experiences with "bureaucratic blundering," and one that left him with the (mistaken) impression that in the eyes of the War Department, "I had been found wanting."[41]

The efficiency report, rendered annually or whenever an officer's principal duty is changed, is one of two powerful indicators of how far his or her career will likely advance. The other is the unofficial necessity to impress a senior officer so he will act as a mentor to help guide and promote his protégé's career. All of the high-ranking officers of World War II would have in common the support of a higher-up in a key position. However, in 1917 Eisenhower was as yet too junior to require a mentor. High praise from rating officers was a rare phenomenon, thus Eisenhower's early efficiency reports were all favorable but not particularly outstanding. For example, the endorsement by Colonel Baker in his 1917 efficiency report for his duty with the 57th Regiment rated him generally excellent in all respects but only "above the average capacity: has executive ability and considerable initiative."[42]

As the war in Europe raged on, it seemed less and less likely Eisenhower would ever be a part of it. In mid-September there was more disheartening news when he was reassigned to Fort Oglethorpe, a bleak outpost in central Georgia, where prospective officers were being trained. Although Baker endeavored to persuade the army to retain Eisenhower by substituting another captain in his place, the request was swiftly rejected. Mamie remained behind at Fort Sam to await the birth of their child, which was due at any time.

Although he later softened his recollections in his memoir, Eisenhower loathed his new duty training officer candidates, the so-called ninety-day wonders, who were needed to fill the great number of vacancies created by mobilization. Most of his days were spent in a field training area that simulated the conditions of trench warfare, including incessant rain and mud. His requests for combat duty were regularly turned down.

Except for an occasional social outing, Mamie seemed imprisoned as she awaited the birth and Ike's eventual return. With not even so much as a radio to help lighten the loneliness, her life revolved around spending many an evening knitting a garment in which the new baby would be christened. On September 24, 1917, Mamie gave birth to their first child, a son she named Doud Dwight Eisenhower. Fortunately Nana, who was recuperating in Denver from surgery, had arrived to assist her daughter. When Mamie went into labor the only transportation available was the post shuttle taxi, a medieval-looking wagon pulled by a mule, on which they hitched a ride to the infirmary. "Fort Sam Houston had no maternity facilities. 'It was no place for a mother of babies,' " Mamie later recalled. "They had to fashion a hopelessly primitive, makeshift delivery room" that was little better than a broom closet.[43] In this tiny room the birth of blond Doud Dwight Eisenhower took place so suddenly and unexpectedly that neither Nana nor the doctor were in the "delivery room" at the time. At once Mamie began calling him "Little Ike," because he bore such a striking resemblance to his father. Later this nickname was inevitably abbreviated to "Ikey" and, later still, to "Ikky."[44]

Eisenhower had barely arrived at Fort Oglethorpe when he received a telegram from his mother-in-law announcing the birth of his son. "Dearest Sweetheart," he immediately wrote to Mamie, "You could have knocked me over with a feather. Why you sweet old girl, somehow it doesn't seem possible. How I wish I could come and see you and 'IT.' . . . I'm wondering exactly what you will call the BOY. I know it will be 'Doud' for the sake of the Folks, and I think it will be fine. I hope you give him a middle name either beginning with D. or J. If it is D. then he can sign his name as D. Eisenhower, Jr., but if it is J. then it will be the same as my Dad's 'D.J.' Anyway, I'll love the name and Him (no matter what you call him), but most of all, I'll love *YOU*. I've sent you 100,483,491,342 kisses since I've been gone." Eisenhower signed it, "Your Lover" and noted in the margin, "*YOU BET*."[45]

Ikky had his father's big hands and feet, and in his next letter Eisenhower wrote, "I'm surely glad the young scoundrel can *howl* . . . as long as it is a boy. . . . Though how in the world mother [Nana] can tell that it 'looks like us both' is more than I can see. Just wait until I get home, I'll start teaching him boxing pronto. . . . The day Mr. Young One arrived in this world his fond father was sloshing up and down the coldest, wettest, 'slipperiest' trenches in the U.S. Gee! It was awful."[46]

To no one's regret, the army abruptly closed Fort Oglethorpe in December 1917.[47] Eisenhower was ordered to Fort Leavenworth, Kansas, to embark on yet another training duty at the Army Service School. He was allowed leave to return to San Antonio to spend Christmas with Mamie and baby Doud Dwight, who became the joy of Dwight Eisenhower's life. Ikky would hang on to his father's finger, which to his proud father meant that he would surely become a football player and enter West Point.[48] For perhaps the only time during his life, Dwight Eisenhower permitted himself fully to bare his emotions. He would coo and act the clown in order to make Ikky giggle gleefully at his antics. The image of Eisenhower on his hands and knees happily uttering gibberish for Ikky's amusement was so far out of character as to be unparalleled. Other than Ida, Ikky was the only blood relative who could bring out Eisenhower's inner joy at the creation of such a beloved child and heir.

While at Fort Sam Houston he learned that a friend from the 19th Regiment was now in command of a machine-gun battalion soon to deploy overseas. Another transfer request went forward with high expectations, only to have Eisenhower's hopes dashed by yet another disapproval. To his disgust the army had clearly placed a higher value on Eisenhower's services as a training officer than in having him serve in combat. Soon after reporting to Fort Leavenworth to commence his new assignment training provisional lieutenants, Eisenhower was summoned by the post commandant and read a letter from the War Department denying his latest request for overseas duty and admonishing him for having the nerve to request it repeatedly. The place of a young officer, he was informed, was to be seen, not heard. Initiative was not only unwelcome but downright harmful to a career (another reason why Eisenhower learned never to reveal his cards in poker or to reveal his full abilities to his superiors' attention).

When the colonel added his own admonishments and suggested he ought to be punished, Eisenhower had had enough. His face turned pale with anger, and "I reverted to the old, red-necked cadet," arguing that since when was appealing for a opportunity to fight for one's country a military offense? If there was to be any punishment meted out, it must be administered by the War Department. To his surprise the colonel agreed and complimented Eisenhower for having stood up for his principles. There was no more talk of punishment.

Eisenhower knew he would probably not get another chance and that he was inexorably bound to the whims of the Washington bureaucrats. This latest incident left Eisenhower so discouraged that he never lost his contempt for deskbound staff officers who had the power to make or break his career.[49] Even in old age, Eisenhower's disgust resonated in *At Ease*, in which he wrote, "A man at a desk a thousand miles away knew better than I what my military capabilities and talents were."[50] For an officer who yearned to command troops and serve in combat, it was a substantial setback.

11.

"I . . . Will Make Up for This."

Our new Captain, Eisenhower by name, is, I believe, one of the most efficient and best army officers in the country. —LT. EDWARD C. THAYER

The winter of 1917–18 was bitterly cold, and Eisenhower was thankful for the extensive physical activity supervising bayonet training and calisthenics that at least helped ward off frostbite. He deeply missed Mamie and baby Ikky, and was utterly miserable at Fort Leavenworth performing duties he abhorred. West Point had trained him for war, but at places like Fort Oglethorpe and Fort Leavenworth, Eisenhower could hardly have been farther away from proving himself in battle. That he had little chance of escaping the repetitive training assignments rankled deeply, as did the knowledge that many of his classmates were already serving in the AEF. Worse, he was embarrassed and reckoned that to even attend a future class reunion without having served in France would be the ultimate humiliation.

Still, his success was a clear indication of his expertise as a trainer of troops. Despite his distress at being denied a chance to go overseas, during his brief tenure at Fort Leavenworth, Eisenhower made a strong impression on his charges, one of whom, Lt. Edward C. Thayer, wrote to his mother that Eisenhower "is a corker and has put more fight into us in three days than we got in all the previous time we were here. . . . He knows his job, is enthusiastic, can tell us what he wants us to do, and is pretty human, though wickedly harsh and abrupt. He has given us wonderful bayonet drills. He gets the fellows' imaginations worked up and hollers and yells and makes us shout and stomp until we go tearing into the air as if we meant business."[1] However, not everyone responded so enthusiastically to Eisenhower's brand of teaching. One of the student officers, a handsome young man named F. Scott Fitzgerald, was far more absorbed in writing his first novel, and occasionally slept through Eisenhower's lectures. Fitzgerald would later write of their mutual hostility.[2]

Eisenhower had no compassion for officers who abused their authority.

On one occasion a first lieutenant loudly berated a student in front of a group outside his office. Eisenhower summoned the lieutenant and sharply reprimanded him. As a West Point classmate who was present remembered, Eisenhower said that "no infraction could conceivably have justified the public humiliation to which this boy had been subjected. Then his voice grew kinder, but no less firm and he lectured the lieutenant on the responsibility which comes with authority. It was hardly a new idea, but Ike expressed it so eloquently yet so simply that I found myself listening as intently as the lieutenant."[3]

At the end of February 1918 his assignment to Fort Leavenworth was suddenly cut short by orders to report to Camp Meade, Maryland, an army post midway between Baltimore and Washington, D.C. Eisenhower learned that he was being assigned to an engineer unit that was organizing troops for overseas service in the newly formed Tank Corps. Excited and heartened that there might after all be a chance to participate in the war, he made a brief detour to San Antonio to see Mamie and Ikky before reporting to Camp Meade.

Early in the war the stalemate in France brought about attempts by the British to create an armored vehicle that could be used to crush the deadly barbed wire, climb up and over trenches, and advance across no-man's-land into the German trenchworks, thereby creating a breach that could be exploited by the infantry. If such a vehicle could be developed it just might turn the tide in favor of the Allies. The idea for an armored vehicle was first brought to the attention of the British War Office in October 1914 by a war correspondent who had learned of an American Holt caterpillar tractor, "which could climb like the devil."

Among the traditionalists in the British army there was scant excitement over any form of original thinking, particularly for a nonexistent mechanical monstrosity. Except, that is, for an independent-minded Englishman named Winston Churchill, the First Lord of the Admiralty. The idea held spontaneous appeal for Churchill's resourceful imagination, and he ordered his staff to get busy.[4]

By 1916 a design breakthrough occurred and a tank called "Mother" (later "Big Willie") became the first operational armored vehicle produced by the British.[5] The machine was equipped with a six-pounder gun inside a small turret, and four machine guns.[6] Although the first armored vehicles were flawed, their employment on the battlefield forever changed the course of modern warfare.[7] Forty-nine "Big Willies" participated in the Battle of the Somme, with mixed results. There was, as yet, no doctrine for their employment, and instead of massing, they were engaged individually across the front. Most broke down or became hopelessly stuck in the mud. Nevertheless several of these ungainly iron monsters were spectacularly successful, and terrorized the Germans. One led the assault on the town of Flers, which was taken without a single loss, to the cheers of the New Zealand infantry who followed them. Another straddled a trenchwork and captured three hundred German prisoners, while still another attacked a German artillery battery before being knocked out. The panic created in the front lines by these first tanks on the battlefield was reported in the German press as, "The devil is coming!"

The British painted their tanks in a variety of rainbow colors and the sight of these incredible machines may have looked comical, but they created very real alarm in the German High Command. "Secret and urgent orders were issued to German troops to hold their ground at all costs and fight to the last man against these new weapons of war."[8]

U.S. Army officer observers were interested spectators of these events, and although their reports to the War Department were disparaging of the future of the tank as a weapon of war, they nevertheless generated considerable interest in Washington and in Pershing. He established an AEF tank board, which concluded that American use of tanks was "destined to become an important element in this war," and recommended the immediate creation of a Tank Department to implement a plan to manufacture and field a force of two hundred heavy and two thousand light tanks, modeled on the British Mark VI and the Renault.[9]

In November 1917 Pershing's protégé Capt. George S. Patton became the first U.S. Army soldier to be assigned to the Tank Corps. His orders directed him to establish a tank school in Lorraine that would equip and train men in the new undertaking. At first the entire AEF Tank Corps consisted solely of Patton and a lieutenant. Yet what began without a single tank or facility would, in a matter of months, evolve into an enormous training center, which by March 1919 consisted of four hundred tanks, and five thousand tank officers and enlisted men.

As the AEF and the War Department grappled with the immense problem of creating, staffing, training, and deploying a tank service that had not only never been tested in battle but which lacked tanks, several tank training centers were rapidly established in the United States to begin training additional troops for future deployment to France and service in the AEF.

The headquarters of the new U.S. Tank Corps evolved from the former engineer unit at Camp Meade and was mainly responsible for training and deploying troops and formations for service in the AEF Tank Corps. Its first director was Lt. Col. Ira C. Welborn, an infantry officer who had won the Medal of Honor during the Spanish-American War. Based in Washington, Welborn was primarily an administrator who coordinated the recruitment of volunteers, rather than a commander.[10] But, as historian Dale Wilson notes in his landmark account of the birth of the Tank Corps, there were no tanks yet available to train in, nor was there even any contact with the AEF Tank

Corps. "It was, in effect, a Tank Corps in name only. Each of the Corps's training centers provided little more than basic soldier training . . . actual combat training would have to wait until units deployed to France."[11]

At Camp Meade, Eisenhower quickly put his training experience to good use and made a strong first impression upon his superiors by helping to organize, train, and equip an all-volunteer unit designated the 301st Tank Battalion. Eisenhower believed that it was only a matter of time before the 301st deployed overseas, and in mid-March he learned that not only was the 301st being sent to France, but that he would be its commander. Ecstatic that his luck had finally turned, Eisenhower rushed to New York to coordinate the sailing of the 301st to France. His attention to the smallest detail and seemingly endless questions annoyed the Port of New York authorities, but Eisenhower was determined that nothing untoward occur to mar the timely sailing of his battalion.

At the last moment, however, Eisenhower's hopes were dashed when he was informed that instead of leading the 301st to France, he was being reassigned to command a temporary military garrison adjacent to the Gettysburg battlefield: Camp Colt. Eisenhower's organizational abilities had convinced his superiors that he was more valuable training troops. The curse of being a successful troop trainer had struck again, and "My mood was black," he said.[12] His new assignment was a perfect example of the military axiom "For the good of the service." Eisenhower's method of coping was to vent his frustrations in private. "Whenever I had convinced myself that my superiors, through bureaucratic oversights . . . had doomed me to run-of-the-mill assignments, I found no better cure than to blow off steam in private and then settle down to the job at hand."[13]

Near the site of Pickett's charge, Eisenhower established and commanded the largest tank-training center in the United States so impressively that he was promoted from captain to lieutenant colonel in seven months.[14] Eisenhower arrived at Camp Colt on March 24, 1918, with a small cadre and hoisted the American flag on the camp flagpole. He replaced an older former NCO named Garner, who had been promoted to captain in 1917. After the brief ceremony, "with tears steaming down his face," Garner related how he had once been court-martialed at Camp Colt and ironically was now the temporary commander at the site of his disgrace. This event left a permanent mark on Eisenhower, who never again saluted a flag without thinking with compassion of the older officer.[15]

Situated inside the Gettysburg National Park, Camp Colt was first occupied in 1917, then enlarged the following year to accommodate four thousand men.[16] The place was crude and lacked even the most basic amenities, including stoves in the tents. In April 1918 a blizzard buried the camp and Eisenhower trudged through the snowdrifts to Gettysburg, where he purchased every available stove he could locate. Such was the state of the U.S. military that even this stopgap measure did not fulfill his requirements. Frequently during his tenure at Camp Colt, Eisenhower was hampered by army red tape that further affirmed his aversion to bureaucrats. Fortunately there were only about five hundred men in Camp Colt at the time, or the results might have been far more serious.

Gettysburg was a place that possessed a special attraction for Eisenhower. He was intimately knowledgeable about every aspect of the desperate battles fought there in July 1863, both from a battlefield tour in 1915 while still at West Point, and from his extensive reading. Of all the campaigns and battles Eisenhower studied in his lifetime, none intrigued him more than Gettysburg. He felt deeply for the men of the Confederacy who were so needlessly slaughtered there and, years later, as Allied supreme commander in Europe, he empathized with and drew strength from the loneliness of command and the trials of the Union commander, Gen. George Meade. As he had at West Point, where he roamed the academy grounds, Eisenhower found solace tramping the battlefield alone whenever he could spare some time for himself. Later on, when Mamie arrived, he would take her to the various battlefield sites and explain the events that had taken place there. Even though it was not a subject that particularly interested her, Mamie was proud that her husband was so knowledgeable that he "knew every rock of that battlefield."

Eisenhower was in his element at Camp Colt. His work was manly, rewarding, and challenging. The ultimate rewards were promotion and, if his luck held, perhaps a chance to test himself in battle. Those who served there soon learned that their new commanding officer was a strict disciplinarian with a terrible temper that, when triggered, often caused its recipients literally to quake in their boots. Soldiers who chafed under Patton's strict observance of high standards and attention to detail would have found no consolation in Eisenhower's command of Camp Colt. He believed that high morale is obtained through exacting standards of discipline, and weathered demands from politicians who attempted to influence him on behalf of a constituent. Eisenhower demanded—and won—unquestioning obedience from his officers and men. The tent city grew explosively as additional units were organized and new recruits flooded in during the summer of 1918. Eventually Camp Colt became both a mobilization and training center. Although its capacity was 4,000, by midsummer 1918, 10,600 troops had been assigned there.

Eisenhower's favorable impression on his superiors brought rapid promotions, first to temporary major in June 1918, and then to temporary lieutenant colonel in mid-October, on his twenty-eighth birthday. For an officer with less than three years' commissioned service, the responsibilities he was given in 1918 were a sure sign of his professional competence.[17]

An essential element of any successful command is to forge a strong first impression. Although Eisenhower was only a very junior captain when he took over, there was never the slightest doubt who was in charge of Camp Colt. He exerted his will in a number of ways that gained the respect of the new tank men, who were reassured that they were serving under an outstanding officer who cared about them as individuals. Those who failed to live up to his standards were shown no mercy. Discipline was severe, and Eisenhower its eager administrator. Violators of army and camp regulations were swiftly punished. Throughout his military career, Eisenhower had no toleration for yes-men and once was heard to berate a lieutenant: "I want you to figure out some things which are wrong with this camp. You make me uncomfortable by always agreeing with me . . . you either don't say what you think, or you are as big a fool as I am!"[18]

After one of his junior officers was caught cheating with a marked deck of playing cards, an unforgiving Eisenhower offered him a simple choice: Resign or face a court-martial. The officer resigned, but his father complained to his congressman. Several days later the father and the politician arrived to attempt to persuade Eisenhower to cancel the resignation and transfer the man to another post. When Eisenhower refused, pointing out that he would not send an unfit officer to another command where he would repeat his bad behavior, the congressman suggested he amend the discharge to read, "For the good of the service." Eisenhower again declined, and the two left empty-handed.[19]

Despite his enthusiasm and organizational abilities, Eisenhower could not overcome the lack of tank doctrine and equipment with which to train his recruits. Reduced to a superficial form of basic training and parade-ground drill and ceremonies, the "Treat 'Em Rough" Boys, as the men of the Tank Corps became known, were soldiers without a mission.

A camp newspaper, created in May 1918, also called *Treat 'Em Rough,* served as a morale builder by offering news of interest. Poetry, which was very popular during the war, also appeared. One of World War I's oddities was the mournful singing by German soldiers and British Tommies across no-man's-land during the spontaneous Christmas truce of 1914. Americans had their own nationalistic songs such as "Over There," but the rebel yells of the Civil War had progressed to songs praising the Doughboy of World War I. Anxious for an identity, the soldiers of the new tank service invented their own limericks and songs, which Eisenhower avidly supported, as much for his love of singing (which he still did quite badly) as for their effect as a morale builder.[20] One of the most original poems was called "We'll All Tank Together Over There." An example:

> It takes the good old tank boys
> To show them the way;
> To win the town to-day.

You talk about your infantry,
Your blooming engineers,
But they'll never beat the tanks
In a hundred thousand years.

. . . It takes the good old tank boys
To beat the dirty Hun;
It takes the good old tank boys
To keep them on the run.
They've got the giant Zeppelin,
The cruel submarine,
But we'll grease their road to hell, boys,
With oleomargarine.

(Refrain)
We'll all tank together over there, boys,
We'll all tank together over there, boys,
Some will go to heaven
Some will go to hell,
But we'll all tank together over there, boys.[21]

The possession or consumption of alcohol was forbidden, and nearby Gettysburg and several other small towns became meccas for thirsty soldiers in search of refreshment while on pass. In spite of the troops' generally favorable acceptance by the local people, a growing number of incidents involving Eisenhower's men brought complaints of bad behavior, drunkenness, and brawling. The other side of the coin was that some civilian establishments preyed on soldiers. Under War Department regulations, local commanders were given the authority to place off-limits any local establishment serving liquor. Rather than encourage a black market in bootleg booze, Eisenhower requested that saloonkeepers regulate themselves by voluntarily refraining from catering to soldiers in uniform. The alternative, he said, was the imposition of an off-limits edict. Most complied, but one Gettysburg hotel, although not technically a saloon, covertly continued to sell liquor until the day Eisenhower ordered his provost marshal to surround the establishment with military police, thus effectively cutting off business not just to his soldiers but to visiting civilians.

After promising to comply, the owner reneged and the MPs returned. The irate owner obtained the assistance of the local congressman, both men expecting that Eisenhower, then a mere major, would be sufficiently intimidated to acquiesce. The congressman's crude threat, "We have means—we can go to the War Department. If you're going to be so stubborn, I'll have to take up the question of replacing you," was met by the full fury of Eisenhower's monumental temper and his refusal to be unnerved by a mere politician. "You do just exactly that," he angrily retorted. "Nothing would please me better than to be taken out of this job. I want to go overseas. If they take me out of here, maybe I can get there."[22] A complaint was duly filed but was strongly rebuffed by the War Department. Rather than be relieved of command, Eisenhower received a letter of commendation from the assistant secretary of war, conveying Secretary of War Newton D. Baker's compliments for his diligence in safekeeping the welfare of his troops.[23] His run-ins with conniving politicians while at Camp Colt merely reinforced what West Point had instilled in him: that politicians were a despicable lot. Yet it would prove to have been good experience for what lay two decades ahead.

The Tank Corps was expected to find and commission officers from within its own ranks, and Eisenhower used this as a motivational tool, writing in a formal letter that one "who shows in his appearance that he has the proper pride in himself, the Tank Corps, and the Army, has a big start toward a commission."[24] The troops assigned to Camp Colt were organized into tank battalions, which eventually grew in number to five tank regiments, twenty-seven tank battalions, and units from four divisions, all of which trained there under Eisenhower's command, and many of which were subsequently deployed to the AEF.[25]

Training raw recruits was a great challenge. Camp Colt and army general orders had to be memorized, then practiced while on guard duty. His tankless units were formed so quickly that some were commanded by junior officers as low in grade as first lieutenant. One of these was 2nd Lt. Floyd Parks, who made such an outstanding impression on his commander that in short order he was given command of a battalion. The two never lost contact with each other after the war, and for the rest of his life Eisenhower counted Parks, who eventually rose to the rank of lieutenant general, as one of his dearest friends.

As volunteers, the men who made up the Tank Corps were generally a cut above the World War I level of recruit, better educated and high spirited. The problem was finding sufficient activities to keep them interested and involved. Although he knew next to nothing about tanks or their employment, Eisenhower wrote in "A Message to the Men," in July 1918, that they were an elite group who would have to learn not only how to employ tanks on a battlefield but work in full cooperation with the three basic branches of the army: the infantry, cavalry, and artillery. "We read on our poster—'Why walk to Berlin when you can ride in a tank?' . . . we have here in Camp Colt one of the finest collections of men and officers anywhere in our army." The memo was typically Eisenhower in its combination of praise and exhortation. "[T]he Tank Corps," he wrote, "although the baby branch of the service, is a baby only in name—perhaps a baby wild cat—and the slogan 'Treat 'Em Rough' will prove to be a very appreciative phrase when the kitten has grown a bit more and sharpened his claws for the Boche."[26] Recruiting posters depicted a vicious-looking black cat with sharp teeth and formidable claws, above which was written TREAT 'EM ROUGH! Below, there appeared underneath a group of tanks the words JOIN THE TANKS, UNITED STATES TANK CORPS.

Like everyone else in the Tank Corps in the United States, including Welborn, Eisenhower was completely unaware of the tank activity in France. His future friend George S. Patton was busily rounding the AEF Tank Corps into a first-class fighting force that would in September and October 1918 distinguish itself during the Saint-Mihiel offensive and the Meuse-Argonne campaign.

Although no one expected there would be any tanks to train with in the United States, in June 1918, a Renault light tank, the same machine used by the AEF Tank Corps and the first anyone in America had ever seen, was delivered to Camp Colt. The troops reacted to this signal event with what Eisenhower called "cheerful cynicism" at finally being able to actually train on a real tank. Eventually Camp Colt received two additional tanks, along with two British tank officer advisers. Unfortunately one of the most important aspects of tank training vanished when it was learned that the Renaults had been sent without their armaments. Once again, as was so often the case during the war, training centers such as Camp Colt were reduced to "simulation," a term that really meant teaching theory and making believe. Although Camp Colt lacked the necessary equipment to fully prepare men for battle in France, it did not lack for initiative and ingenuity, both of which Eisenhower prized. He and his staff resorted to every means they could think of to sustain morale and improve training, including scouring books, magazines, and military manuals for ideas that might have application to tank training.

His frequent letters, speeches, and memos to his troops were a forerunner of the wealth of such missives penned by Eisenhower during World War II. Some, like the intense and melodramatic speech called "Our Flag," which he delivered on the activation of a tank battalion, praised the flag and all it stood for: duty and the "great honor" they had been given of fighting for the United States. "Together with millions of others of America's Best, you have arisen to defiantly shout IT SHALL BE DONE, and now you are offering your lives to prove your words . . . as you go forth to take your part in this greatest war . . . may this flag sustain you."[27] It may have been theatrical but it helped achieve the high morale Eisenhower sought. Even more relevant was the fact that the cynical West Point cadet of 1911–15 had, by 1918, matured into both a patriot and an ambitious and dedicated career army officer.

Mamie's transition from San Antonio to Gettysburg required a difficult and exhausting four-day rail journey. Seven-month-old Ikky was ill with a fever that was a prelude to the chicken pox, when they arrived inauspiciously in the snow and freezing temperatures of the storm of April 1918. The frustrating journey ended on a disagreeable note when Eisenhower failed to turn up at the railroad station. Mamie was met instead by one of his men who explained that Captain Eisenhower was busy dealing with the problem of obtaining heaters for his frozen troops.

Mamie had never made a move to another place army-style, much less by herself. There are few secrets in a tight-knit military community, and word quickly spread that Mamie would shortly be leaving for Gettysburg to join her husband. An older, neighboring army wife appeared at her door and asked Mamie what she planned to do with her furniture and household goods, noting that any experienced army family avoided the hassle of moving by selling them, then buying new items at the next post. Naturally, the woman said, she would be quite willing to take them all off Mamie's hands for a fair price. To her great regret, Mamie fell for this ruse and received only ninety dollars for virtually everything in the family quarters except for a rug, linens, and personal items. The army had prohibited the wearing of civilian clothes off duty, which became Mamie's rationale for getting rid of Ike's two custom-made double-breasted suits, which he loved but she thought were "horrid eyesores." They cost three hundred dollars and were sold to a rag man for ten dollars. Mamie ill-advisedly believed Ike would not miss them until after the war. However, as soon as he began unpacking their trunks in Gettysburg, Eisenhower began searching in vain for his suits, at which point Mamie was obliged to admit what she had done. Eisenhower's monumental temper erupted in brief outrage. Recalled Mamie, "The suit episode was enough to unsettle a saint." Although he quickly dropped the matter, "he told her he hoped she'd grow up and learn a true sense of values, a remark which hurt more than his anger." Left unspoken was the small matter of the pittance she had received for their household items. Her husband never asked, and she never volunteered an explanation. "How could I have been so gullible?" Mamie later wondered. "I know I was young, but not *that* young . . . what I exchanged for nine $10 bills cost originally over $900." Her carefully guarded savings took a severe hit, and it was not until years later that she told Ike the truth.[28]

Military quarters were either nonexistent or difficult to secure. The first of the Eisenhowers' three domiciles in Gettysburg was a dank, evil-smelling, two-story frame house of microscopic size. The only heat came from a coal stove that Eisenhower had to show Mamie how to operate. She remembered, "It *was* a very difficult time for me . . . at home [in Denver] the cook would not allow us in the kitchen, so I never had any kitchen experience at all." During the summer of 1918, they moved into much roomier accommodations in a large fraternity house at Gettysburg College, which lacked a kitchen. "Ike had a chef . . . in his headquarters company. No wonder he'd go and eat at camp—and take me."[29]

Eisenhower was rarely home and thus unable to spend much time with his family. What precious little free time he did have was typically spent playing with or holding his small son. More often, however, he could be found prowling around the camp at all hours, checking up, asking questions, and using his presence to signal the importance of the training. One day Mamie jokingly suggested that perhaps she could have a ride in one of Ike's steel contraptions. He happily acceded, and Mamie got the ride of her life one evening as her husband drove a Renault tank, at bone-jarring speeds, through a ditch, in reverse, and through the equivalent of modern-day "wheelies." The crude roar of the engine ringing in her ears, the eye-watering, pungent odor of gasoline, and clouds of choking dust combined to make her one and only venture into her husband's work arena memorable. Secretly Mamie was proud of her feat, particularly inasmuch as she knew she was likely to be the first woman ever to have ridden in a tank.[30]

In September 1918 Eisenhower's earlier problems were dwarfed by comparison with one of the gravest challenges he ever faced. Camp Colt's population had swelled to more than ten thousand men when Eisenhower suddenly had to employ every skill he possessed to contain a threat far more deadly than the world war then in progress. Dubbed the "Spanish flu," it was a deadly and particularly virulent outbreak of biblical proportions that spread throughout the world and hit the United States like a hurricane. Although the true numbers will never be known, the 1918 virus killed an estimated 548,000 Americans. Nothing like it had been seen before (or has been since). Overnight the profession of undertaking became a growth industry. Worldwide, an estimated 20 to 100 million people died rapid and horrible deaths from this plague that was twenty-five times more deadly than so-called ordinary flu. The U.S. Army was not spared; indeed, the frequent movement of troops from place to place helped spread the virus, which was eventually contracted by more than one-third of its members. Before it ended, the average life expectancy in the United States had dropped by a staggering twelve years.[31]

The camp surgeon, Lt. Col. Thomas Scott, initially misdiagnosed the suddenly growing numbers of sick soldiers before realizing his mistake and quarantining the infected in segregated areas of the camp. All manner of inoculations were tried, and each failed. Men began dying (literally overnight), and a grave problem became, in Eisenhower's words, "a nightmare," which spread to the town of Gettysburg. As lines grew outside the hospital, there was no place to store the dead and no coffins in which to place them. A mounting sense of fear pervaded Camp Colt. (One soldier who was thought to have died was moved to a makeshift morgue and laid out naked with the other dead. Later, as his comrades filed by to pay their last respects, the man awoke and exclaimed, "Get me out of here!" The men were so unnerved by this bizarre incident that they stampeded from the tent and into the site of Pickett's charge, taking with them the troops awaiting inoculations intended to prevent an outbreak of other diseases, such as smallpox and typhoid.) When his medics ran out of space, Eisenhower arranged to have the overflow sent to a parochial school in Gettysburg and to local churches, which were turned into makeshift hospitals.

The medical staff acted aggressively to isolate the sick from the rest of the camp. Inoculations and daily examinations were ordered. Even as he was coping with the epidemic, Eisenhower feared for his family's safety. Dr. Scott concocted two homemade nasal and throat sprays that he tried out on Eisenhower, his staff, and Mamie, one of which was so noxious that Eisenhower thought the top of his head would blow off each time it was administered twice daily. Whether or not the remedy worked is unknown, but no one who used the spray became ill. Although the epidemic was contained in about a week, before the crisis passed there were 150 deaths from the Spanish flu at Camp Colt. Compared with responses at other military facilities, the actions taken by Eisenhower and his medical staff at Camp Colt were so efficient that the War Department ordered him to send thirty of his physicians to other installations to train their medical personnel.

Although mass fatalities were avoided within the U.S. military, the Spanish flu and pneumonia killed more military men (52,019) than were killed in combat (50,475). Eisenhower never forgot the contributions of his chief surgeon, noting in his memoir that Scott was "another of those men to whom I will always feel obligated."[32]

Rumors of a possible armistice in Europe began reaching Gettysburg about the time a telegram from Denver left Mamie thunderstruck. Her beloved younger sister Buster had died suddenly at age seventeen. Buster was the second of Mamie's sisters to die in childhood (and at the same age as Mamie's older sister, Eleanor).[33] After Ike and Mamie bade each other a tearful good-bye in Harrisburg, Eisenhower sent Elvira Doud a poignant condolence letter. "My Own Dearest Mother," he wrote, ". . . we are heartbroken. . . . We can feel *your* grief. . . . I cannot come—duty prevents—but even now I know that the love you bear your children tells you that my heart and my love are with you."[34]

Colonel Welborn had assured Eisenhower that he would be permitted to deploy to France in command of a tank regiment, and, adding to Mamie's anxiety, she left Gettysburg fully expecting that she might not see him again. The death of Buster was difficult enough; now she also had to contend with her husband's imminent departure for France and the unknown terrors that face all families with loved ones placed in harm's way. Even so, Welborn attempted to dissuade Eisenhower from going to France by dangling the promise of an immediate promotion to full colonel, an offer he flatly rejected.

So anxious was Eisenhower to achieve his ambition that he made it known he would, if need be, cheerfully accept a reduction in rank to major, "if the lieutenant colonelcy which I have now stands in the way of my going overseas."[35]

His promotion to lieutenant colonel turned out to be a short-lived source of pride. By the time Mamie and Ikky reached Denver the war had ended, with rejoicing all across the United States. And, while the announcement of the armistice on the Western Front that brought to a conclusion the most terrible war in the history of mankind, on the eleventh hour of the eleventh day of the eleventh month of 1918, brought a sense of relief to Mamie, it thoroughly dismayed her husband.

A frustrated Eisenhower angrily remarked to his classmate Norman Randolph, "I suppose we'll spend the rest of our lives explaining why we didn't get into this war. By God, from now on I am cutting myself a swath and will make up for this."[36]

To have missed such an opportunity was not only dismaying but potentially career killing. His friend and classmate Omar Bradley had likewise seen no overseas duty during the war; instead he was placed in command of a security force sent to guard the Anaconda copper mines in Butte, Montana, against strikers and agitators thought to be anarchists. Bradley's disappointment mirrored Eisenhower's. Proclaiming it "professionally, the most frustrating [event] of my early Army career," Bradley described how "my overwhelming desire at that time was to go to France and prove my mettle in a real war. . . . I tried every possible scheme I could dream up . . . [to join] an outfit bound for France."[37]

So it was that instead of going off to war, Eisenhower was ordered to disband Camp Colt, and by December 1918 the once-sprawling complex once again resembled a graveyard. The dreary period between the armistice and demobilization proved to be the greatest hurdle he had to overcome as camp commander. Nothing he had learned at West Point or during his three years of service had prepared him for the challenge of demobilization on a truly massive scale. Suddenly there was little to do other than unnecessary training ("ridiculous," he called it) or make-work projects that Eisenhower deemed "self-defeating." He was all too aware that, "No human enterprise goes flat so instantly as an Army training camp when war ends."[38] Housekeeping details were tightened, and Eisenhower dangled the lure of imminent discharges in exchange for patience. Most cooperated, in no small part because of his persuasiveness.

Most of those still remaining at Camp Colt were moved in December 1918 to Camp Dix, New Jersey, for discharge from the mobilization that had seen the U.S. Army expand to 2,395,742 officers and men earlier in the same year. The Tank Corps likewise had grown from nothing in early 1918 to 1,275 officers and 18,977 enlisted men by November. By December fewer than 6,000 men remained at Camp Colt. The move itself, logistically complicated, turned out to be Eisenhower's final act as camp commander.

Shortly after the armistice was declared, another classmate, Maj. Philip K. McNair, encountered Eisenhower on a train. "He was greatly upset. He hadn't been sent overseas and now he never would be. He said he had been educated to be a soldier, and when a war came along, he had to sit it out without even getting close to the battle. He was so keenly disappointed. . . . I had the definite impression that he intended on resigning his commission. I was sure he and the Army were through."[39]

For all his frustrations and fears about his professional future, Eisenhower had performed admirably in a very difficult job that won him many admirers. As historian Dale Wilson sums up Ike's Camp Colt experience, "He had excelled in every way, showing great ingenuity in developing a meaningful training program despite the lack of resources. He had also shown a great deal of skill in dealing with politicians and community and business leaders," as well as with the two British liaison officers, with whom he had worked well.[40] For his service at Camp Colt, Welborn recommended Eisenhower for the Distinguished Service Medal, the army's highest peacetime decoration, but the army bounced the recommendation around until 1924, when it was finally approved. Welborn's esteem for his subordinate was also noted on Eisenhower's efficiency report. As a captain Eisenhower had performed duties equivalent to those of a brigadier general. "I regard this officer as one of the most efficient young officers I have known," Welborn wrote.[41]

During the rush to return soldiers to civilian life, an appeal was made to induce enough men to form the nucleus of a postwar Tank Corps to remain on active duty. Several hundred accepted, and both Eisenhower and his volunteers were ordered to report to Fort Benning, Georgia, the home of the infantry. The rail journey to Georgia was hellish. The train was constantly shuttled onto sidings for higher-priority movements. Even low-flying birds, mused Eisenhower, seemed to move faster and have a higher precedence. There was no kitchen, no lights, no heat, and no hot water, though Eisenhower managed to fashion a crude kitchen of sorts in the baggage car, using portable stoves. His own World War I could not have ended on a more ignominious note.[42] For all his success as a trainer and troop commander, Eisenhower's future remained clouded as the United States approached the decade of the Roaring Twenties, during which its armed forces all but vanished.

12.

"A Journey Through Darkest America"

I wanted to go along partly for a lark and partly to learn.

After Buster's funeral Mamie remained in Denver while the army pondered the future of the Tank Corps. Nearly a year would elapse before Ike and Mamie were reunited. The move to Fort Benning was temporary, and, with little to do in the euphoric aftermath of the armistice, Eisenhower had "far too much time on my hands." In March 1919 he was delighted to receive orders to return to Camp Meade, which had been selected as the permanent home of the Tank Corps. When re-formed, the Tank Corps consisted of units from the United States and the AEF, under the command of Brig. Gen. Samuel D. Rockenbach, a cavalry officer and the director of the AEF Tank Corps, who took over from Ira Welborn in August 1919. Rockenbach, an officer "famous for his razor-edged tongue and his martinet ship," was Patton's boss in France. Rockenbach often exasperated him by what Patton perceived as foot dragging in the acquisition of the first tanks for the AEF Tank Corps, once privately calling him "a good hearted wind bag." Despite their differences and the occasional dust-up, Rockenbach stoutly defended Patton and generally avoided interfering. Rockenbach's wife, a noted horsewoman, when once asked why she had married "Rocky," replied, "I married him for his conformation, of course. Did you ever see a finer piece of man-flesh?"[1] Eisenhower was never enamored of Rockenbach, because of his new commander's direct order that he coach the Camp Meade football team. Eisenhower mistakenly thought that, as a senior officer in the Tank Corps, he had advanced to the point where coaching was no longer a career necessity. Rockenbach quickly disabused him of this notion, and Eisenhower had the good sense not to protest the assignment further. With his usual verve and leadership, Eisenhower successfully coached the Tank School football team from 1919 to 1921, for which he received a glowing letter of commendation from Rockenbach for his "splendid efforts."

• • •

In the aftermath of the war, pressure began mounting for Eisenhower to leave the army. One of his junior officers at Camp Colt failed to tempt him to accept employment with his firm in Indiana at a considerably higher salary. Mamie observed, "A lot of his classmates were getting out and they had big positions with this firm and that. The next thing I knew they were working on Ike to get him out of the service." Despite the wretched pay and lack of amenities, however, Eisenhower was simply not prepared to give up his career for the humdrum existence and the uncertainties of civilian life. Tempted as he may have been, he knew that military life suited him well, and even Mamie, who might have been expected to endorse the stability of civilian life, had matured to the point where she advised her husband not to leave the army. "I said to him—it was about only twice that I remember that I really interfered—and this time I said, 'Well, Ike, I don't think you'd be happy. This is your life and you know it and you like it. Now true, there's not any money in it, but we have other personal things that make up for the lack of currency . . . so I talked him into staying."[2]

The decision proved fortuitous. "I knew no matter what I said he was going to make his own decision" as the head of the family. "My father cracked the whip around the house, and I tell you everybody paid attention to Mr. Doud. I never felt like I had to help Ike in any way, except in making as nice a family-life as possible. I thought he was perfectly capable of paddling his own canoe. It just never occurred to me to give him any advice on his business."[3]

The perks of army life and the kinship of the brotherhood of the officer corps proved to be a greater enticement to Eisenhower. Moreover, there would always be a steady paycheck each month from the government, a point underscored when the country sank into the depths of the Great Depression. Despite obvious relief that Ike was out of harm's way, Mamie shared his disappointment at not having gone overseas. "I felt so sorry for him. . . . After all this career that he'd worked so hard for, and he thought so much of, he just didn't think there was going to be any solution," after trying so hard and failing to see action in France.

At Camp Meade, Eisenhower was back on familiar ground working with the Tank Corps, although initially in a paper-shuffling job. In 1919 Meade was a major demobilization point as the army grappled with the problem of reducing its massive troop strength to a peacetime level. Despite a heavy workload, and on their own initiative, Eisenhower and several colleagues managed to find time to organize and teach a night school for aspiring Regular Army officers in such subjects as tactics, math, history, and English.

Also in March 1919 the remnants of the AEF Tank Corps, led by Col. George S. Patton, returned from France to the United States and Camp

Meade, their final destination. Patton retained command of the 304th Tank Brigade, which he had trained and commanded in France. Soon afterward, however, Patton left for detached service in Washington as a member of a Tank Board charged with writing formal army doctrine and the necessary military manuals governing the operation of tank units. The very survival of the Tank Corps was already in question, and its future depended on establishing it as a necessary arm of the army in a future war. While Patton was away Eisenhower was given temporary command of the 304th. The two officers had yet to meet each other. All Patton knew was that an unknown lieutenant colonel named Eisenhower was standing in for him.

In 1919 there was no such thing as a highway system in the United States. Most roads were still dirt, and where they even existed they were poorly constructed, dangerous, and all but impassable in bad weather—facts that were not lost on the War Department, which had experienced serious problems attempting to move units and equipment by road during the war. At the instigation of a bright young officer who perceived the public relations value of such a venture, the War Department decided to create a transcontinental motor expedition, whereby a convoy of eighty-one assorted U.S. Army vehicles would attempt to cross the continental United States, no mean feat in 1919.

"The 1919 transcontinental convoy had a Homeric flavor to it. The internal combustion engine was still in its infancy and was not as dependable as it is today. A transcontinental convoy had never been attempted before and the army, in fact, was not sure that it could be done."[4] A journey by road in 1919, when the railroad was still supreme and some so-called roads were little more than cart tracks or trails carved out of the wilderness, was truly an adventure not to be undertaken lightly.

The section of Camp Meade assigned to the tank men had no married quarters, thus Mamie was still in Denver and not likely to be joining him for the foreseeable future. Eisenhower was bored to tears and thirsting for adventure, anything to escape the humdrum existence of the peacetime army. When he learned of the proposed expedition, Eisenhower immediately volunteered and was accepted as a Tank Corps observer, "partly for a lark and partly to learn."

At his recommendation Eisenhower was joined by a second Tank Corps observer, Maj. Sereno E. Brett, a veteran tank officer who had commanded a battalion with distinction under Patton in the Meuse-Argonne. Next to Patton, Brett was regarded as the most aggressive tank commander in the entire AEF and was an officer Patton held in high esteem. After Patton was severely wounded during the first day of the Meuse-Argonne campaign, Brett assumed command of his 1st Tank Brigade for the remainder of the war, fighting until all that was left were a handful of men and tanks. Patton recommended

Brett for the Distinguished Service Cross and wrote a heartfelt letter, "putting in writing what I have long felt in my heart. . . . As far as I know no officer of the AEF has given more faithful, loyal, and gallant service."[5] Like Eisenhower, Brett had opted to remain in the service after the war and was also assigned to Camp Meade, where he and Eisenhower became friends. Brett was outgoing and great company, and from him Eisenhower learned what he had missed by not having been a participant in the AEF Tank Corps. Both were sufficiently bored with garrison duty to volunteer immediately for the expedition.

The expedition departed Washington, D.C., on July 7, 1919, bound for San Francisco, 3,251 miles away. Their orders arrived too late for Eisenhower and Brett to attend the official send-off in Washington, held at the Zero Milestone marker, situated not far from the White House. In attendance at the typically Washingtonian ceremony were a host of VIPs, including Secretary of War Newton Baker, U.S. Army Chief of Staff Peyton C. March, and a bevy of politicians. There were the usual long-winded speeches, about which Eisenhower later gleefully noted, "My luck was running; we missed the ceremony."[6] The two officers caught up with the convoy in Frederick, Maryland, the first night.

To add realism to the expedition, the convoy operated under simulated wartime conditions as a motor march through enemy territory. The convoy consisted of army vehicles, some with solid rubber tires, others with pneumatic tires. In addition to some sixty trucks (two of which had been turned into makeshift ambulances), there were also motorcycles (some with sidecars), staff cars, a powerful van-mounted searchlight, a tank transported on a flatbed trailer, and various other trailers used as mobile kitchens and repair shops. The expedition was sponsored in part by several of the major automobile manufacturers, including Willys, Packard, Mack, and General Motors. Willys sent several "mystery cars," which were prototype models not yet available to the public. The lead truck was emblazoned with the words WE'RE OFF TO FRISCO!

Overall the expedition consisted of 24 officers, 258 enlisted men, some two dozen War Department observers, and numerous others who tagged along for parts of the journey, as well as reporters and representatives of auto and tire manufacturers. Officially its mission was "to test various military vehicles, many developed too late for use in World War I, and to determine by actual experience the feasibility of moving an army across the continent."[7]

The trip also served as a selling point for the military. At virtually every stop, curious townspeople across the country ventured out to view the expedition and hear speeches about its purpose, and the members of the expedition were royally received. "Almost every town in the vicinity of the route of travel, and the nightly encampments, would provide some social activity as well as food and drink. These events ranged from dances and banquets, to melon feeds, and outdoor movies."[8] The official report of the expedition stated that the meals produced by the mobile mess were dreadful at the start but improved partway through the journey, after the officer in charge was replaced. An experienced army engineer, Master Sgt. Harry C. DeMars, had a different recollection. Shortly after the trip commenced, the mess truck was "left behind, as so many organizations were preparing meals for them when they entered the various towns. When crossing the desert, meals were brought to them. The soldiers stopped at Y.M.C.A.s to take baths." Most of the men slept on cots outside their vehicles, but sleep remained at a premium; "Towns-people would mill through the camp all night."[9] In Sacramento the governor lauded them as akin to the "Immortal Forty-Niners." There were also seemingly endless speeches by VIPs, which severely tested Eisenhower's capacity for enduring pompous rhetoric.

In the tradition of the expeditions that opened the western United States, the motorcycles were ridden by scouts, whose task it was to investigate road conditions and, with road signs generally lacking, determine the convoy's route. To gain an idea of the hardships of crossing the United States, the convoy averaged fifty-eight miles per day at an average speed of six miles per hour.

The realism of this pioneering journey hardly needed the simulation of wartime conditions. Traveling across the United States in 1919 was a major feat in itself. "For the next two months, through rain, mud and searing heat of summer on the western plains and deserts, Eisenhower and Brett learned firsthand why America needed a transcontinental system of highways."[10]

One of the most instrumental members of the expedition was a civilian ordnance technician from Raritan Arsenal, New Jersey, Edwin A. Reis, "who was given high praise for the success of the convoy for he frequently was the only person who could figure out what to do when vehicles broke down or were totally mired."[11] Indeed, Murphy's law was in full force over the course of the expedition. Vehicles broke down with regularity, became stuck in the mud or quicksand, sank when the roads collapsed beneath them, or absorbed enormous quantities of choking dust. A truck sped out of control down a Pennsylvania mountain, tires shredded, ignitions failed, engines died, vehicles slid off the roads into ditches and gullies, and in Utah some broke through the salt flats. Remarkably, however, the expedition lost only a handful of vehicles that could not be repaired.

Wyoming was particularly difficult. Most of the bridges were too light to cross with the expedition's five-ton vehicles and had to be either replaced or jury-rigged. Sometimes both a truck and the tractor attempting to pull it out sank into the mud, necessitating Herculean efforts by the engineers to recover them. Often roads had to be constructed or rebuilt in places. Some days the expedition averaged only a few miles. Overall the engineers rebuilt or modified sixty-two bridges between Washington and San Francisco.

Although Eisenhower thought discipline was far too lax, he and Brett enjoyed a carefree interlude with few responsibilities and ample time for fun. The same prankish Eisenhower who delighted in pouring buckets of water on unsuspecting victims at West Point resurfaced during the expedition. Each perhaps spurred on by the other, both men became first-rate pranksters who relished frightening the citified easterners who made up most of the convoy. As time passed the pranks became more and more comical and bizarre. In Wyoming the two staged an elaborate hoax that the convoy was about to be attacked by rampaging Indians. The official expedition scribe was so taken in by this ruse that he would have reported the matter to the War Department had not Eisenhower and Brett intercepted his telegram at the last moment. Yet another prank took place one night when Brett climbed a bluff behind the bivouac area and howled like a coyote. Scarcely a night went by without one or the other devising some devious scheme to bedevil the city slickers. Eisenhower thought their escapades were "part of an audience for a troupe of traveling clowns."[12]

In North Platte, Nebraska, Eisenhower was reunited with Mamie, Ikky, Pupah, and Nana, who had driven from Denver to meet the convoy. From Nebraska to Laramie, Wyoming, the Eisenhowers spent their first time together in nearly nine months. By the time it ended in San Francisco on Labor Day, 1919, the expedition had been seen firsthand by an estimated 3.25 million people. After gala festivities in Oakland, the participants paraded through the streets of San Francisco to the accompaniment of cheers and whistles blowing from ships in the bay. The mayor presented the keys to the city. "They had a big dance and a show at the St. Francis Hotel. Girls put on burlesque dances which caused the mothers to take their daughters home. The mothers then came back to see the show and dance with the soldiers."[13]

The expedition was officially disbanded in San Francisco, and each participant returned to his own home station. The journey had taken sixty-two days, a mere five days behind the original timetable, a remarkable feat in early-twentieth-century American history. The official report noted that the expedition had suffered 230 road accidents, including breakdowns, delays, mud, and quicksand, most of them minor. The army's image was enhanced, and many valuable lessons were learned that were incorporated into the future design of military vehicles. Awareness of the expedition reached an estimated 33 million Americans and helped to spur several state legislatures to begin enacting bills to build new roads.[14] Thirty-seven years later President Dwight Eisenhower would sign into law one of his highest priorities, the Interstate Highway Act of 1956, which created the Eisenhower Interstate Highway System.

· · ·

Eisenhower was granted a month's leave and accompanied Mamie and Ikky from Denver to San Antonio, where they would remain for several months before moving to Maryland. For a brief time during the summer of 1919 it had been a time of adventure that Eisenhower termed "a journey through darkest America."[15] There would be precious few such free-spirited occasions during his military career.

13.

A Friendship Forged

From the beginning he and I got along famously.

When he returned to Camp Meade in the summer of 1919, Eisenhower finally met Colonel Patton, the officer who was to have such a profound effect on his military career for the next twenty-five years, and who would both "delight and dismay him for the rest of his life."[1] Patton commanded the light tanks of the 304th Brigade, while Eisenhower was second in command of the 305th Brigade, composed of newly manufactured Mark VIII Liberty tanks, which had come off the assembly line too late to be used in France.

There was an instant affinity between the two men, who were nonetheless as different as night and day. Patton was a decorated combat veteran with a Distinguished Service Cross who had single-handedly organized the AEF Tank Corps and been gravely wounded on the first day of the Meuse-Argonne offensive the previous year. Five years older than Eisenhower, he had graduated from West Point in 1909. Patton seemed monumentally egotistical next to the more self-effacing Eisenhower, who was nevertheless particularly impressed by the incongruity of this impatient, self-confident, elegant soldier with his high, squeaky voice. Patton loved horses, riding, and polo, and both men were avid riders, hunters, and pistol shooters, although Eisenhower had no interest in polo. One was wealthy and could afford an extravagant lifestyle; the other was dirt poor and had difficulty making ends meet. For a time the two played poker together twice a week. One could afford to lose; the other continued to supplement his meager pay by his shrewdness at the table. One of Eisenhower's biographers has noted another significant difference: "Everybody thought from the beginning of Georgie's career that there were no limits to the heights he might achieve. For most of his life very few people thought that Eisenhower would achieve anything much."[2] Another has observed, "Tact became a way of life to Ike, whereas Patton (to paraphrase Winston Churchill on John Foster Dulles) was a bull who always carried his own china shop around."[3]

On balance they seemed a genuinely mismatched pair: the brash, outspoken cavalryman and pioneer tank officer, and the fun-loving midwesterner whose roots were in the infantry. Yet the two soon forged an enduring friendship that lasted until shortly before Patton's death in December 1945. As Eisenhower would later write, "From the beginning he and I got along famously. Both of us were students of current military doctrine. Part of our passion was our belief in tanks—a belief derided at the time by others."[4] Their strong conviction that the tank had a greater role in the army of the future than merely as a subordinate arm of the infantry, as it had been during World War I, would eventually land Eisenhower in career-threatening trouble.

Both thirsted for something more exciting than the bland peacetime existence of Camp Meade, where Eisenhower spent his leisure time gardening and perusing a Burpee seed catalog for entertainment. The highway to the main encampment had been plagued by a number of holdups, and their boredom led Eisenhower and Patton to undertake their own version of cops and robbers by bringing the bandits to heel. Armed with half a dozen pistols, they drove very slowly down the road in the hope that they would be attacked. According to John Eisenhower, "Dad always said, 'We wanted to see what a fellow's face looked like when he's looking into the other end of a gun.' They were both going to pull guns in different directions and fix this guy. They thought they were going to be a two-man posse on the blacktop road there, but nobody stopped them. They were both disappointed."[5]

At first there were no married quarters for Tank Corps personnel at Camp Meade, and Eisenhower lived in bachelor quarters until the autumn of 1919 when he was reunited with Mamie. He rented a wretched single room in a Laurel, Maryland, boardinghouse that was too tiny to include Ikky, who was left in Denver in his grandparents' care.

Eisenhower's home life at Camp Meade was a mirror image of his Abilene upbringing, where make-do and secondhand were bywords. The experience was taxing, and Mamie never forgot how "they would turn off the electric lights at 6:00 o'clock in the morning and not turn them on again until 6:00 o'clock at night." With no place to cook, the Eisenhowers ate their meals in a nearby boardinghouse. Ike was often on duty until late at night, while Mamie was left alone in a depressing, often dark room to cope as best she could. "That was a horrible time," she recalled. After several weeks her life had become so intolerable that she returned to Denver and the comfort of her family. "Ike begged me to stay," but Mamie told him, "Ike, I just can't take this any longer."[6]

The hardships of army life had clearly stretched the bonds of their marriage. Still smarting over his inability to serve in the AEF, and deeply hurt by his disastrous reunion and unhappy parting from Mamie, Eisenhower was disconsolate. Even more dismaying, Mamie wrote only infrequently and then rarely mentioned their son or her family. Desperate for information, Eisenhower wrote instead to Nana.

> Dearest Mother:
>
> I hear from Mamie so infrequently that I have no idea how you all are getting along . . . we are very busy, [but with so many tank corps slots left unfilled], we seem to be chasing ourselves in a circle. . . . Would you mind, when you have time, writing me about Ikky & daddy & yourself. . . . I try to be patient & cheerful—but I do like to be with people I love. . . .
>
> Devotedly, your Son.[7]

Mamie did not return to Maryland until May 1920, after the authorities magnanimously permitted some rundown barracks in a sandy corner of Camp Meade to be converted into family living quarters. However, the army declined to assist in any way and left the expense of remodeling and furnishings to be paid for by each occupant. Thus it was that Eisenhower and Patton—now neighbors—added the title of "handyman" to their résumés.

Despite Beatrice Ayer Patton's wealth, a bevy of servants, and an automobile, at times the Pattons too had to make do with whatever was available. George Patton scrounged the only paint available from the quartermaster, blue and yellow—which became the primary motif throughout. Bea Patton solved the problem of what to do with the latrine by "planting wandering jew and trailing ivy in the urinals."[8]

Eisenhower likewise put considerable effort into remodeling the barracks into a suitable home, which included a lawn and a white picket fence. He hired off-duty soldiers, and a great deal of hard labor went into turning their quarters into a reasonable semblance of a home, though he could barely afford the expense, nearly eight hundred dollars, a hefty sum in 1919.[9] His love of gardening and tilling the soil was manifested at Camp Meade, even though the place was mostly sand. The pleasing results were proof positive of Eisenhower's green thumb.

"We didn't have a stick of furniture," remembered Mamie, to whom the task of furnishing the place fell. "I took orange crates and made a dressing table. . . . I got some cretonne and little thumb tacks and covered up the orange crates." In a former Red Cross building classified as a "dump pile," Mamie located a beat-up chaise and a table for the living room. Ike said, "My God, Mamie, you're not going to keep that?" Mamie replied, "Yes, I like it—I got it off the dump heap." Their beds were two army cots covered in cretonne adorned with Japanese prints, which she had purchased by the yard to make drapes. Impoverished as they were, Mamie Eisenhower managed to make a home for her family in what were scarcely better than broken-down old wooden buildings covered with tarpaper, where "you could see the cracks and they were built right, square, bang on the ground."[10]

In 1919 the temperance movement brought about the Eighteenth Amendment and Prohibition. Eisenhower and Patton both avidly joined in the all-American pastime of distilling their own bootleg alcohol. Eisenhower concocted his own gin in an unused bathtub, while Patton brewed beer in a woodshed and stored the bottles in the covered walkway between his quarters and the kitchen shack. One evening there was a sudden noise that sounded like a machine gun. Patton instantly dived to the floor, and the cook began screaming in the kitchen. The beer had exploded. "Georgie got up, rather shamefacedly, and explained that it had sounded so much like hostile fire that he instinctively had taken cover." Bea Patton "laughed and laughed and called him 'her hero,' and he got very red."[11]

Patton's two daughters, Beatrice and Ruth Ellen, were enchanted by Mamie Eisenhower, whom they found "the most glamorous creature that ever appeared in our lives. She insisted, very daringly we thought, that we call her Mamie and not Mrs. Eisenhower, as she said she wasn't that old yet." Although Beatrice Patton disapproved of her children calling any adult by her first name, she could do little when Mamie insisted. "She drank a lot of iced tea, which she stirred by swirling it around in her glass. We thought this the ultimate in sophistication, and tried to do the same with our milk, with bad results."[12] Despite the budding friendship between their husbands, however, Beatrice Patton and Mamie Eisenhower were never close, and seemed to have in common only the trait of frailty.

Mamie and Ike entertained frequently both for visiting dignitaries and in conformance with army custom that decreed the social responsibilities of a senior officer. For a brief period in 1920, their painful separations behind them, the Eisenhowers spent perhaps the most contented months of their married life. Although Eisenhower's competitive fires had been dampened by the end of the war, now that he and Mamie had been reunited, he enjoyed the slower pace of peacetime life at Camp Meade. Both cherished a beautiful, delightful son who enriched their lives.

Whereas the urbane Beatrice Patton was an avid participant in life and a major influence in promoting her husband's career, she and other casual acquaintances never saw the tougher side of Mamie: a woman of wit and charm who, although mostly a quiet spectator, nevertheless believed a military wife played an important role in her husband's career. There were even rare occasions when she would speak out forcefully when someone she thought unworthy was unduly rewarded, once complaining that the wife of a newly promoted brigadier general was "simply awful." Yet despite her growing confidence and maturity, Mamie was nonetheless guilty of the occasional gaffe, such as the time, when asked by Secretary of War Baker what Eisenhower was good at, she replied that he was an excellent poker player. A livid Ike berated Mamie for not telling Baker that he was a fine soldier. Mamie had merely assumed everyone already knew that.[13]

Baby Ikky spent a good deal of his time in the Patton household. The children of Camp Meade loved to fish in a nearby ditch, using bent-pin hooks and grasshoppers for bait. One day Ikky returned to the Patton quarters with a fish he had just caught and asked Beatrice to cook it for him. By then the fish "was pretty run down," recalled Ruth Ellen. "Ma told us to go and play. Pretty soon she came out with Icky's fish on a dish; a piece of buttered toast under it; garnished with a sprig of parsley and a lemon wedge. Icky ate it in ecstasy. Ma told us later that she had opened a can of sardines and dressed one up for the occasion."[14]

When the National Defense Act became law in June 1920, the Regular Army was authorized 300,000 men, but only 200,000 were left from what had once been a gigantic force of 3.7 million. By January 1921 Congress mandated another reduction in enlisted strength to 175,000, and in June a further cutback to 150,000 men. The ax fell again the following year, when Congress decreed that the active army consist of no more than 12,000 commissioned officers and 125,000 enlisted men, a strength it remained at until 1936.[15] The army's principal mission was relegated to that of training national guard and army reserves. Eisenhower and Patton were among those who disagreed but were too junior for their opinions to matter. The entire War Department appropriation was established at about $300 million annually, and with the navy considered the first line of defense, the army's share was woefully inadequate to meet its needs. In 1922 the U.S. Army ranked seventeenth among nations with standing armies, and in 1933, the chief of staff, Gen. Douglas MacArthur, noted that what few tanks the army possessed (except for a dozen or so experimental models) were "completely useless for employment against any modern unit on the battlefield."[16]

Although Woodrow Wilson's personal utopian vision of peace was a fantasy, it was his vision of a postwar world in which peace reigned supreme that gripped the United States in the aftermath of the armistice. Wilson had taken Europe by storm as the living embodiment of a golden age in which war would be relegated to the history books. The creation of the League of Nations was to be Wilson's eternal contribution to the world. However noble its intentions and potential role as the world's peacekeeper, the League instead was relegated to the role of an inconsequential body of diplomats and politicians whose power was limited to the use of persuasion without force. As historian Robert Leckie observes, "Not even Woodrow Wilson could have envisioned . . . the death of the dynasties and the end of empires was to be so quickly succeeded by the day of the dictator."[17] The surviving veterans of the German army were bitter at what they believed was the perfidy of the Jews and the politicians. Many, including a former corporal named Adolf Hitler, vowed one day to avenge their betrayal at Versailles by the Weimar regime.

In the United States the terrible bloodshed in Europe had bred disinterest in future war. The great patriotism of World War I had, by the early 1920s, turned into a national mania of aversion to all things military, and to the symbol of war, the military establishment. A militant pacifism took seriously the notion that America had indeed fought "the war to end all wars." Veterans, who months earlier had been wined and dined as national heroes, suddenly found themselves shunned. As MacArthur's biographer D. Clayton James has written, "Wrenched by fears of radicalism, economic depression, and renewed entanglement in Europe's distresses, the American people yearned for conditions of tranquillity, innocence, and isolation."[18]

Demobilization occurred on such a massive scale that it managed to overshadow the purge of the Union Army after the Civil War. By the end of June 1919, the Regular Army had been reduced to a mere 130,000, including the troops still on occupation duty in Germany.[19] Woodrow Wilson's illusory belief that future wars could be prevented by the new League of Nations left the military little more than an afterthought in the Roaring Twenties. The peacetime army of the interwar years has been aptly described as "an island surrounded by a sea of uncaring, more often contemptuous civilians," who had little regard for men with nothing better to do with their lives than soldier.[20] To all but a handful of officers, their government seemed to care only about reverting the armed forces to their prewar size. The last thing anyone wanted to hear was talk of another war from professional soldiers. Men like Eisenhower and Patton thus became anachronisms, even within their own army.[21]

During congressional hearings in 1919 on a bill to reorganize the army both Secretary of War Baker and the chief of staff, Gen. Peyton C. March, argued for retaining the independence of the Tank Corps.[22] Just when there seemed to be hope, it was dashed a week later when Pershing testified that the Tank Corps "ought to be placed under the Chief of Infantry as an adjunct of that arm."[23] Rockenbach's lame arguments for an independent corps were too conservative and neither passionate nor persuasive at the most critical moment in the history of the tank service. In the end it hardly mattered. Pershing's towering reputation and his opposition sounded the death knell of the Tank Corps. A War Department mandate ensured that the corps would now lose its identity and with it, its raison d'être. For Eisenhower, Patton, Brett, and the other intrepid pioneers of the Tank Corps who comprised the "Treat 'Em Rough" Boys, it was a bitter pill.

The total authorization of the Tank Corps was established in 1919 at 154 officers and 2,508 enlisted men, and the dreaded (but expected) postwar demotions finally caught up with both Patton and Eisenhower in the summer of 1920. Eisenhower was demoted to captain but a month later was promoted to major. Patton too reverted to his permanent Regular Army grade of captain but was likewise fortunate enough to be promoted to major. Both officers were among only a handful to be so propitiously promoted. The army had indeed fallen on hard times.[24]

Just as the army was sliding to its nadir, their brief time at Camp Meade brought together two of the pivotal U.S. leaders of World War II. Both might justifiably have walked away from any responsibility for the future of a spiritless army. Fortunately its soul was held together by the dedication of these men and others like them, who argued that the tank ought to be more than merely an auxiliary arm of the infantry. As Eisenhower has explained, "George and I and a group of young officers thought this was wrong. Tanks could have a more valuable and more spectacular role. We believed . . . that they should attack by surprise and mass. . . . We wanted speed, reliability and firepower."[25]

By themselves they stripped a tank down to its last nut and bolt and managed to put it back together—and make it run. They tinkered with supporting weapons and endlessly debated tank employment and the tactics of surprise. One day they narrowly escaped death when a cable stretched taut between two tanks suddenly snapped and barely missed their heads as, at lightning speed, it cut a lethal path through the nearby brush and saplings, in what both acknowledged was one of the most frightening moments of either man's life. Patton likened it to his near-death wounding in the Meuse-Argonne, while Eisenhower later wrote, "We were too startled at the moment to realize what had happened but then we looked at each other. I'm sure I was just as pale as George. That evening after dinner, he said, 'Ike, were you as scared as I was?' 'I was afraid to bring the subject up,' I said. We were certainly not more than five or six inches from sudden death."[26]

Another time Patton was test firing a .30-caliber machine gun while Eisenhower observed the trajectory of the bullets through field glasses. Without warning the weapon "cooked" and began spewing bullets everywhere. The two future generals raced off in panic but returned to disable the gun with sheepish expressions on their faces. After this second near-disaster both decided they had about exhausted their luck. Nevertheless they kept at it within a small circle of converts, among them Serano Brett, learning lessons, analyzing tactics, and creating scenarios in which tanks were employed under a variety of situations and conditions. As Eisenhower later said of this period in their careers, "These were the beginnings of a comprehensive tank doctrine that in George Patton's case would make him a legend. Naturally, as enthusiasts, we tried to win converts. This wasn't easy but George and I had the enthusiasm of zealots."[27]

In 1920, Eisenhower and Patton each published provocative articles about tanks in the prestigious *Infantry Journal*.[28] Their articles were nothing less than a proposed tank doctrine for the next war. Eisenhower's article was titled "A Tank Discussion," and it stressed the need for a newly designed tank of the future, armed with two machine guns and a six-pounder main gun, able to cross nine-foot trenches and speed cross-country at twelve miles per hour. The clumsy, inefficient machines of Saint-Mihiel and the Meuse-Argonne were now relics of the past, and "in their place we must picture this speedy, reliable and efficient engine of destruction . . . in the future tanks will be called upon to use their ability of swift movement and great fire power . . . against the flanks of attacking forces."[29]

By combining maneuver with the traditional supporting artillery fire, Eisenhower and Patton began to make the case that well-designed tanks could maneuver en masse and either outflank an enemy position or, as Fuller suggested, tear gaping holes in an enemy line and precipitate the collapse of an entire front. The possibilities of such tactics were nothing less than breathtaking. In future wars the infantry would close on the enemy and hold them in place, while tanks enveloped and either destroyed them or set the stage for the infantry to win a decisive victory at a fraction of the cost in blood of the linear battles of the past.

For many years branch chiefs in the War Department administered the engineer, ordnance, medical, and quartermaster functions, but for the first time since the Civil War the National Defense Act reestablished these offices for the combat arms: the infantry, artillery, and cavalry. Each chief was a major general, and collectively the branch chiefs constituted what was known as the special staff of the War Department. These powerful men spoke for their particular service and were a virtual law unto themselves when it came to branch doctrine, research and development, and the control of personnel assignments. The Tank Corps had no independence, few friends in court, and was now at the mercy of the chief of infantry, Maj. Gen. Charles S. Farnsworth, who had no fondness for either tanks or the officers who commanded them.

What each had concluded was heresy to the leaders of the infantry, with its long tradition (and privilege) of being the decisive arm of war and the "Queen of Battle." What these two upstart tank officers were suggesting would alter the whole doctrine of land warfare. Some infantrymen regarded Eisenhower's article as blasphemy, and in the autumn of 1920 he was summoned to Washington for an unpleasant audience with Farnsworth, during which he was warned that his ideas "were not only wrong but dangerous and that henceforth I would keep them to myself. Particularly I was not to publish anything incompatible with solid infantry doctrine. If I did, I would be hauled before a court-martial. . . . George, I think, was given the same message. This was a blow. One effect was to bring George and me even closer."[30]

Eisenhower's verbal censure in 1920 for daring to advocate the study of tanks and the need to enlarge their role was a message that even the dimmest could appreciate.[31] Undeterred, however, Eisenhower and Patton began spending even more time together, riding, studying, stalking the elusive bandits, and cementing a friendship that both prized. Eisenhower noted in his memoirs, "With George's temper and my own capacity for something more than mild irritation, there was surely more steam around the Officers Quarters than at the post laundry."[32]

Of their time together at Camp Meade, Eisenhower would later recall that

George had become convinced . . . as I had—that the Treaty of Versailles had practically guaranteed the outbreak of another great war within something like a quarter-century.

Typically, George was not only a believer, he became a flaming apostle. In idle conversations and in the studies we jointly undertook, he never said "if" war might break out, always it was "when." As we worked, talked and studied together we became close friends. In our outlook on the future we were always partners; in those days it never occurred to either [of us] that we might, in war, become separated from each other.

Yet in all his speculative ramblings he always saw himself as commander of highly mobile troops. Initially he likened himself to Ashby, the brilliant cavalry leader under Stonewall Jackson. But he soon raised his sights. "Ike," he'd say, "This [next] war may happen just about 20 years from now. This is what we'll do. I'll be Jackson, you'll be Lee. I don't want to do the heavy thinking; you do that and I'll get loose among our #%&%$# enemies." This thought was repeated time and time again.[33]

When intra-army rifle competition at Camp Perry, Virginia, was resumed in 1920, and at Camp Meade, Eisenhower and Patton each coached one of the two Tank Corps teams. This was a serious rivalry between two of the most competitive men the army has ever known. Debates and arguments constantly raged, and wagers made between the two until the demise of the Tank Corps in 1921 caused the breakup of the rifle teams.[34]

Anticipating eventual attendance at the prestigious School of the Line (as the future Command and General Staff School at Fort Leavenworth, Kansas, was then called), Patton obtained copies of previous tactical problems used in the school and said to Eisenhower, " 'Let's you and I solve these together' . . . I worked the problems with him . . . and got a lot of fun out of it. We'd go to his house or my house and the two of us would sit down, and while our wives talked for the evening, we would work the problems . . . and grade ourselves."[35] In fact it was a group effort that also involved Brett and other tank officers. Patton thought Leavenworth's authors were too conservative and their solutions, "much too timid." The group reworked each problem by adding tanks to the scenario and were ebullient when their side consistently prevailed. "Such wargaming exercises inevitably led to detailed discussions about how to best employ tanks. These, in turn, helped the participants, especially Patton and Eisenhower, focus their thoughts. . . ."[36] However, it was not all work and no play. They made sure there was ample time set aside for their twice-weekly poker game. However, by the end of 1920 Eisenhower had given up poker, except with friends, in part because of his great skill, which he felt left him with an unfair advantage over colleagues who played badly and could not afford to lose.[37]

For all their compatibility, the two men held widely differing points of view about fundamental philosophical issues, some of which, recalled Eisenhower, were "heated, sometimes almost screaming, argument[s] over matters that more often than not were doctrinal and academic rather than personal or material."[38] As Stephen E. Ambrose writes, "they began an argument that would last until Patton's death. Patton thought that the chief ingredient in modern war was inspired leadership on the battlefield. Eisenhower felt that leadership was just one factor. He believed that Patton was inclined to indulge his romantic nature, neglecting such matters as logistics, a proper world-wide strategy, and getting along with allies."[39] Although they would not serve together again until World War II, their passionate discussions during their Camp Meade days would continue during the interwar years by correspondence and occasionally in person.[40]

However deep their commitment to the future of the tank as an important weapon of war, neither Patton nor Eisenhower was actually willing to stick his neck out publicly as had pioneer aviator Col. Billy Mitchell, who had branded his superiors "incompetent, criminally negligent and almost treasonable." His controversial advocacy of an independent air corps was acknowledged in Britain, where Sir Hugh Trenchard's forcefully articulated doctrine called for the Royal Air Force to become a separate arm of the military. In the United States such heresy earned Mitchell conviction by a general court-martial for insubordination. The court-martial of Billy Mitchell was not only a national cause célèbre but a discouraging sign of the times. By 1921 Eisenhower had privately signaled that he had clearly heeded General Farnsworth's warning. He authored "Tanks with Infantry," an unpublished, densely detailed essay that put forth the notion that, no matter how many advances there might be in design and performance, "it is apparent that tanks can never take over the mission of the infantry, no matter to what degree developed. Advancing infantry will continue to be the deciding factor."[41] Patton likewise concluded that the tank service had become a dead-end career, and in the autumn of 1920 transferred back to the cavalry where the old ways still prevailed, thus forfeiting his best chance of becoming the patriarch of the American armored force of World War II, a role that was supplanted by other visionary officers, such as Adna R. Chaffee.[42]

During their yearlong service together at Camp Meade, Eisenhower and Patton made significant contributions that became evident only during World War II. They studied and prepared for the day when their knowledge and insights might actually be put to use. Ambrose credits both men:

> As World War II would prove, the two young officers had it exactly right, so right in fact that their conclusions seem commonplace today. But in 1920 they were two decades ahead of most military theorists, except for Fuller and Liddell Hart, whom they seem to have been unaware of, and whose works were just beginning to appear in any case. Eisenhower and Patton were true pioneers, original and creative in their thought. But the Army was not pleased. The Great War had been won by infantry, charging in mass. Future wars would be won the same way. The Army's postgraduate schools all taught that basic lesson, all scorned maneuvering and outflanking attempts and concentrated on the problem of how to get the infantry across no-man's land.[43]

Doud Dwight Eisenhower was a delightful, happy child, adored by his father and a favorite of Eisenhower's junior officers, who outfitted him with a replica of a Tank Corps uniform and proclaimed him their official mascot. Eisenhower had just passed his thirtieth birthday, and, as Christmas 1920 approached, their world was shattered. Ikky had become ill and feverish one afternoon, which an army doctor summoned to examine him shrugged off as probably no more than an upset stomach. When his fever rose overnight, Ikky was admitted to the post hospital, where for a time he seemed better. Even though he was the only patient, the hospital staff exhibited little concern and paid scant attention to a child who seemed healthy enough and who possessed sufficient energy to turn the corridors into a playground.

When his condition worsened, a physician from Johns Hopkins Medical School was summoned from Baltimore to assist. Ikky, he pronounced, had scarlet fever. "We have no cure for this. Either they get well or you lose them." The effect of this chilling diagnosis and its bleak forecast can only be imagined. Ikky was quarantined; his parents could only watch helplessly through a glass window and send him kisses. Eventually Eisenhower was permitted into the room to be with his ailing son. Nana rushed to their side to provide what comfort she could, but the scarlet fever turned into meningitis, and within a week Ikky died in the early morning hours of January 2, 1921. He was barely three years old. A small red tricycle Ike and Mamie had bought for Ikky remained forlornly beside their Christmas tree, a visible reminder of the enormous void left by his sudden passing.

The soldiers of the Tank Corps were a tight-knit group, and its members shared in the Eisenhower tragedy through gestures of condolence and by providing an honor guard as Ikky's tiny coffin was borne to the Baltimore train station for the sad journey to Denver. The funeral service was held in the music room of the Doud home, where his parents had been married in 1916. Ikky's final resting place was in the Doud family plot next to his aunts Buster and Eleanor.[44]

Upon their return to Maryland, Mamie wrote to her parents of the gnawing emptiness that ruled their lives. "Ike and I didn't sleep an hour," the first night and several days later noted, "We feel like a couple of lost kids."[45]

The hardest part for Mamie had been the anguish of knowing that Ikky would die. On the day of his death, she was home in bed with a heavy cold that was thought might turn into pneumonia. "I had never seen a person die before, let alone my beloved."[46] Eisenhower later said in the only public comment he ever made about Ikky's death, "We were crushed. For Mamie, the loss was heartbreaking, and her grief in turn would have broken the hardest heart."

Ikky's death left a permanent scar on both parents. Somehow they pretended to cope but fooled no one. Instead of drawing closer together in the wake of Ikky's death, each retreated into a private world of sorrow and suffered in silence, their only common bond their beloved son's death. Eisenhower threw himself relentlessly into his work and was rarely home. Not until 1948 did he privately admit to a friend the extent of his grief. "I was on the ragged edge of a breakdown," he wrote.[47]

On the verge of a nervous breakdown herself, Mamie was left to persevere as best she could in the same quarters where Ikky had brought such joy to their lives.[48] She hid her anguish behind a mask of stoicism that lasted two years before she finally allowed herself to break down and weep over his loss. Mamie was not only desperately sad but worried for the health of her volatile husband. "Ike's grief, as all-consuming as her own, was pitched to frightening intensity . . . causing her to fear for his health. They have never put aside their cross of sorrow."[49] Ike and Mamie rarely spoke of their lost son, but Eisenhower would mark Ikky's birthday each year by sending a bouquet of yellow roses to Mamie as a remembrance of their son and his favorite color. The anniversary of his death, however, passed without comment or observation, and Mamie said she eventually forgot the date, and thereafter rarely spoke of little Ikky's death.[50] Writing of the most traumatic event in their marriage brought back terrible memories that forty-six years had failed to diminish.[51]

Eisenhower never spoke publicly until the publication of his 1967 memoir, in which he wrote that Ikky's death was still "as fresh and terrible as it was in that long dark day." Losing his firstborn remained "the greatest disappointment and disaster of my life, the one I have never been able to forget completely."[52] John Eisenhower believes that his father's feelings were "very severe, very, all his life."[53] There were numerous private occasions throughout his life when his despair would momentarily surface. In 1949, for example, he wrote to the actress Helen Hayes, who had lost her daughter to polio, that, "We were once in that same black pit. . . ." In 1966 Eisenhower had Ikky's remains secretly removed from Denver and just as secretly reburied in the chapel of the Eisenhower Center in Abilene, where he and Mamie would eventually lie. Except for his one admission in *At Ease*, Eisenhower never permitted his lifetime of sorrow to become public.

Julie Nixon Eisenhower (the wife of Ike's grandson, David), later wrote of the tragedy, "Half a century later, Mamie was still unwilling to say much about how Icky's death changed her relationship with Ike. The pain is too deep. But there is no doubt that the loss of their beloved son closed a chapter in the marriage. It could never again be unblemished first love." Indeed, the marriage was further strained at various times by the hardships of living in strange places and in undesirable circumstances. "There were a lot of times when Ike broke my heart," she told Julie Eisenhower shortly before her death. "I wouldn't have stood it for a minute if I didn't respect him. . . . I didn't want to do anything to disappoint him."[54]

In little more than a year since the war ended, Eisenhower had been demoted, threatened with dire consequences by the chief of infantry for advocating the continued existence of the Tank Corps, and his precious young son had died early in the new year of 1921. How much worse could things get?

Part IV

THE INTERWAR YEARS, 1920–1939

14.

"The Man Who Made Eisenhower"

Your admitted ignorance of the law . . . is to your discredit and your failure to take
proper precautions . . . [is] likewise to your discredit.
—ADJUTANT GENERAL, U.S. ARMY, TO MAJ. DWIGHT D. EISENHOWER
  December 16, 1921

In the wake of Ikky's tragic death only a few months earlier, the summer of 1921 brought with it more pain, in the form of serious charges against Eisenhower of financial abuse and defrauding the U.S. government. He was charged with claiming a quarters allowance at Camp Meade for Ikky while the child was residing in the temporary care of Mamie's spinster aunt, Eda Carlson, in Boone, Iowa, from mid-May to September 1920. Before this unseemly incident ended, the army was on the verge of court-martialing Dwight Eisenhower and more than likely ending his budding career.

The investigation was triggered in the summer of 1921 when it was learned that Eisenhower had received $250.67 in reimbursement for light and heating expenses for Ikky while the child was in Iowa. Eisenhower, alleged the army, had falsely and illegally accepted payments for Ikky in clear violation of army regulations. While Eisenhower was perfectly within his rights to draw this monthly allowance for his wife and dependents, the regulation specifically stated that it could only be drawn for one abode, his quarters at Camp Meade. By claiming Ikky as a dependent entitled to the allowance while his son was in Iowa, Eisenhower was in violation of army regulations. What made the offense so grave was that it involved the misuse of public funds.

The inspector general's office (IG) is the army's internal watchdog agency, which inspects and investigates all aspects of army matters, including misconduct. The investigation of Eisenhower came about quite by accident. He had been called as a witness in an investigation of another junior officer, also for drawing a quarters allowance to which he was not entitled. During Eisenhower's testimony he revealed that he too had drawn the same allowance. This admission spurred a lengthy investigation by the Camp Meade inspector general. Offered the chance to refuse, in effect, to testify against himself,

Eisenhower declined and related candidly both orally and in writing the circumstances—as he interpreted them—surrounding his drawing of the allowance. Eisenhower was grilled but stuck to his assertion that any wrongdoing on his part was inadvertent, and that, at the time, he had had every reason to believe he was entitled to the allowance. If he had erred, it was an honest mistake.

The investigator, however, was unforgiving, even referring to Eisenhower as "the accused." Ultimately the IG concluded that Eisenhower had no excuse for failing to recognize that he was not entitled to draw the allowance. His damning report also recommended that Eisenhower should not only be required to repay the allowance but he should also be court-martialed.

Twenty-six separate endorsements to the original investigation kept Eisenhower in limbo, and the matter unresolved, until December 1921. Up and down the chain of command it went, as resolutions and punishments were debated. In the end Eisenhower was barely saved from court-martial and an almost certain ignominious end to his promising army career by a strong recommendation from his commanding officer, Colonel Rockenbach. While Eisenhower's actions were in violation of the regulation, said Rockenbach, "there was no intent to defraud the government or to make a false certificate. . . . I was convinced, however, that the commutation was illegally drawn and directed Major Eisenhower to refund the amounts so drawn." Rockenbach verbally reprimanded Eisenhower and suggested to the army that the matter be closed.

The army inspector general, Brig. Gen. Eli A. Helmick, strongly disagreed, however, charging that "the verbal reprimand administered to him by his Commanding Officer has not met the disciplinary requirements in this case . . . without authorization . . . recommend it be discarded, and Major Eisenhower be appropriately reprimanded by competent authority."[1]

The message from Washington was quite clear: Eisenhower had broken an army regulation and would have to be punished. In the end his honesty may well have been what saved his career. In his defense the fact that others were similarly investigated for the same offense suggests that the regulation was subject to misinterpretation.

Hard times had indeed befallen the Eisenhowers. Nevertheless Ike shouldered this burden with equanimity, just as he would so many others in the years ahead. Given the circumstances, the incident was all the more galling for the pain it inflicted. The fact that Eisenhower had recently suffered the untimely death of his son evoked no sympathy with the unforgiving keepers of army regulations. The amount was duly repaid, and the family finances took a severe hit. To protect her from further travail, it is doubtful if Eisenhower shared his latest troubles with Mamie, at least until he had to cough up $250.67, which could hardly have been glossed over. Eisenhower never again referred to the matter or how close his career had come to derailment.[2]

. . .

A year earlier there had occurred one of the most fateful encounters of Eisenhower's military life. On a Sunday afternoon in the autumn of 1919 he was a dinner guest of the Pattons. Also present was a visiting dignitary, Brig. Gen. Fox Conner, one of the most brilliant staff officers ever produced by the army. Patton and Conner first met during the punitive expedition in 1916, when Conner was a major and Patton a junior first lieutenant and an aide to Pershing. The following year the two renewed their budding friendship during the six months Patton served in Pershing's headquarters in France.

A wealthy, soft-spoken southerner from Mississippi, and a 1898 West Point graduate, Conner was a keen military thinker, teacher, intellectual, and a noteworthy influence on younger officers like Eisenhower. As Pershing's erstwhile chief of plans and operations (G-3), Conner was Pershing's right-hand man and trusted confidant in all matters relating to the employment of the AEF. "Some have called him 'the father of the A.E.F.,' but even if parenthood really belonged to General Pershing, Conner was at least the midwife."[3]

Fox Conner inevitably drew men like Patton and Eisenhower into his circle of friends and admirers. A consummate professional, he was also the top strategist in the army, and it was through his initiative that Pershing launched the first American offensive at Saint-Mihiel in September 1918. Pershing would later say of Conner that "no commander had an abler Chief of Operations. . . . I could have spared any other man in the A.E.F. better than you."[4]

The immense respect in which Conner was held in the army meant that his views carried considerable weight with younger officers like Patton and Eisenhower. Although World War I was barely over, Conner "believed that another war was written into the Treaty of Versailles," remembered Eisenhower; "he was sure that we with the British and French would be pitted against the Germans and probably some allies of others."[5]

The dinner to which Conner and Eisenhower had been invited was typical of the social affairs hosted by George and Beatrice Patton, which they employed to create a congenial setting where good food and drink were the stimuli for meaningful conversation. In an era when the radio was the newest of inventions, such events were the cornerstones of the social life of families like the Pattons and the Eisenhowers. After dinner on this particular day, Patton and Eisenhower spent the remainder of the afternoon touring Camp Meade with Conner, conversing about their ideas for the future of the tank and attempting to answer his myriad questions. It was another indicator of the new era that Fox Conner was one of the few officers who even bothered to express an interest in what they were doing, and the only one ever to provide any encouragement. (Most accounts incorrectly date Eisenhower's fateful introduction to Fox Conner as either the autumn of 1920 or 1921. It actually occurred in September 1919.)[6]

Eisenhower has credited Patton with first introducing him to Fox Conner. During the interwar years Conner became Eisenhower's teacher and a father figure whom he admired above all others. After nearly fifty years of public service during which he met the most famous men of the twentieth century, Eisenhower would still repeat with deep conviction, "Fox Conner was the ablest man I ever knew," and perhaps the greatest reward of his friendship with George S. Patton was meeting Fox Conner that autumn afternoon. "In a lifetime of association with great and good men, he is the one . . . to whom I owe an incalculable debt."[7]

When Fox Conner took command of an infantry brigade in Panama late in 1921, he asked for Eisenhower as his executive officer. Rockenbach flatly refused to release Eisenhower; retaining a top-notch football coach in the 1920s was considered as important as being successful in one's other duties. As much as he loved football, Eisenhower loathed coaching in lieu of soldiering and resented Rockenbach's reluctance to release him. "That just irritated him beyond words," said Mamie. Eisenhower's demotion from a lieutenant colonel commanding thousands of troops to a lowly captain coaching an amateur football team was too much for an ambitious young officer to swallow when he was wanted by one of the army's best officers. Once again it seemed that football was about to force him to miss out on an important assignment. Fox Conner, however, was equally determined, and used his considerable clout with new Army Chief of Staff, John J. Pershing, to personally request Eisenhower's assignment to Panama. It was granted, and the Eisenhowers left Camp Meade for good in December 1922 after a tearful send-off from the Tank Corps.[8]

When the Eisenhowers departed for Panama in January 1922, Mamie was newly pregnant with a child due to be born in August. As the commander of the ship's complement of troops, Eisenhower was given excellent accommodations and looked forward to a pleasant voyage. Before long his quarters were appropriated by several joyriding generals who had no legitimate business being there—which may well have been the spark that led to Eisenhower's lifetime loathing of officers who misused their position.

The Eisenhowers were relegated to a cramped cabin with a tiny couch and a double-decker bunk. Mamie suffered from claustrophobia, "and I wasn't about to get in a bunk, so I'd sleep on that small seat," curled in an uncomfortable position. The ship was buffeted by storms in the Caribbean, and Mamie added seasickness to her daily bout of morning sickness. The trip took ten days, which Eisenhower likened to living in a sardine can.

One of Eisenhower's favorite off-duty recreations at Camp Meade was tinkering with the family Ford. A group of tank men would often assist and, as Mamie has quaintly described it, "they duded that thing up until it was really something." The car was loaded on the deck of what had been a wartime troopship, and accompanied them on the trip from New York to Panama. By the time the ship docked "somebody had stolen everything on that car," recalled Mamie. "You couldn't even move the car off the ship. They had taken the engine and everything [else] out. Stripped it! Completely!"⁹

The army's presence in Panama was to defend and police the Panama Canal Zone, the area ceded to the United States in return for the construction and total control of the canal that connected the Atlantic and Pacific Oceans. Camp Gaillard was an isolated outpost situated on a hilltop overlooking the Pedro Miguel Locks, on the Pacific end of the canal. Its only access from the other side of the canal was by means of a tenuous catwalk across the lock. Everyone then had to negotiate a mud path up a hill to the camp itself. The path was unsafe, virtually impassable by night, and ever in danger of sliding into the canal. The Eisenhowers were assigned old, second-rate, French-built military quarters on stilts and a tin roof that leaked whenever it rained—which was every day. The dwelling had not been used in years, and Mamie discovered that in addition to decay and rot, "It was covered with cockroaches, bedbugs, bats . . . we slept on Army cots. Once a week you'd take your bed and put the legs in cans of kerosene, and . . . take paper and light it and go all over the springs to get the bedbugs . . . the first night we were there a rat gnawed all night long."¹⁰ Snakes, lizards, and insects were a constant danger outside.

Fox Conner's wife, Virginia, was the daughter of a millionaire father who had made his fortune in patent medicine (as had Beatrice Patton's father, Frederick Ayer). "Mrs. Conner thought I was a namby-pamby," ruefully recalled Mamie, "but to have bats crawl in under the door at night and fly around was not my idea of a good time . . . [nor were the] huge cockroaches [that] would jump at you from the top of the door."¹¹ During their failed attempt to build a canal in the 1880s, the French had imported bats in the belief they would consume mosquitos that carried deadly yellow fever. Killing them was illegal, but when a bat began flying around their bedroom, "Mamie recalls peering cautiously from beneath the sheets as her groom, completely ignoring the law, charged after it in pajamas and sword until a desperate lunge completed the crime." In her old age Mamie could laugh at the experience of her husband gallantly waving his sword "just like Douglas Fairbanks," but at the time it was no laughing matter.¹²

Of the many disagreeable places the Eisenhowers lived during their marriage, Camp Gaillard was by far the worst. In 1922, "life in Panama was as alien to Mamie as life on Mars." She had traveled to Panama once before with her father and was under no illusions about what she was getting into. Nothing, however, could have adequately prepared her for the hideous heat and humidity in a place where dysentery and malaria were rife and no one ever drank the water. Mostly Ike and Mamie ate canned goods. Social life barely existed except for weekly dances and bridge games. After some months

Mamie at last "achieved an uneasy peace with her surroundings."[13] She was determined to stick it out and deliver her child in a makeshift maternity clinic she and other volunteers helped to create for the wives of the enlisted men, whose families resided across the canal in utter squalor. Gradually the Eisenhowers toiled and managed, with plenty of help, to turn their decrepit house into a semblance of a livable home.

Although Mamie and Ike managed to overcome the housing predicament, during their first months in Panama they were unsuccessful at resolving what had become a shaky marriage. All was not well, nor had it been since the death of Ikky. While Eisenhower had Fox Conner and his duties (both real and self-created) to occupy most of his time, Mamie had no one except Virginia Conner, to whom she turned to pour out her troubles. "She made no bones about how mad she was that they had been ordered to such a horrid post. She was young and inexperienced, but she was the most honest person I have ever known."[14] Mamie was becoming an unusually self-reliant woman, unaccustomed to leaning on others for counsel except in this rare instance, when she was in urgent need of a sympathetic ear. In Virginia Conner, Mamie found a friend who understood her pain and was able to offer reassurance and practical advice. Having experienced her own hardships as an army wife for some twenty years, Virginia Conner did what she could to ease Mamie's anxieties. "The marriage was clearly in danger . . . it was evident that there was a serious difficulty at the time," she said. "They were two young people who were drifting apart. It was a critical time in their relationship."[15] The crux of their marital problem was that each had turned inward. Eisenhower assiduously hid his pain behind longer and longer work and study hours. His unwillingness to help Mamie (and, in the process, himself) deal with their mutual grief further exacerbated the chill that had fallen over them. Ironically, the son whose birth had cemented their marriage had, in death, nearly brought about the breakdown of their union. Each parent, notes biographer Peter Lyon, "shouldered a self-imposed burden of guilt. . . . Was there nothing more they could have done for him?"[16]

No doubt exacerbated by the loss of his son and by a desperately unhappy wife, Eisenhower's time in Panama also evidenced that his competitive nature was stronger than ever, which often resulted in furious outbursts of temper. To help fill the time Eisenhower took up tennis, a sport he signally failed to master. According to Mamie, "When he found he could not control his tennis strokes he used to beat his head literally against the wall."[17]

Virginia Conner never fathomed what Eisenhower really felt, and in his typically close-mouthed manner, he gave no hint, even to Mamie. What was inescapable was that Mamie Eisenhower was a desperately unhappy woman who "was wearing down a path to my front porch."

When Mamie's parents visited in the spring of 1922 they were so appalled at her primitive living conditions that they insisted she return to Denver for the birth of the baby. Although Mamie rued the various times when she had fled to the sanctuary of her parents' home, she did not resist, and the Eisenhowers were separated for the sixth time in their marriage.

On paper Fox Conner commanded a brigade (that is, several regiments), but in reality it consisted of a single infantry regiment of Puerto Rican enlisted men commanded by North American officers. Their mission was to plan and provide security for the Panama Canal. Duty in Panama was dull, uninspired, and fraught with the unpleasantness of life in the tropics in a crude encampment. The daily rains resulted in frequent mud slides that plunged thick deposits into the canal which then had to be dredged. Some years later a gargantuan mud slide caused the entire camp to disappear into the canal.

The Conners lived next door to Ike and Mamie, and the two men became virtually inseparable both on and off duty. Eisenhower revealed that he had lost most of his interest in history as a result of his experience at West Point, where the subject was badly taught by means of memorization of inane facts such as the name and exact location of every general on both sides at Gettysburg. "If this was military history, I wanted no part of it."[18]

He soon changed his mind. Fox Conner rejuvenated and further sharpened Eisenhower's already significant appetite for reading and studying history. Conner was both a teacher and a philosopher, and under his intense one-on-one tutelage Eisenhower's military education began to take shape. As one account notes, "In Panama, Gen. Conner really took Eisenhower under his wing, acting as a professor with only one man in his class . . . the general taught Ike the real meaning and value of military history. He taught the younger officer the art of reading, thinking and talking of what was read. Eisenhower could not afford to buy books but made full use of Conner's extensive library, and his three years of postgraduate education under Fox Conner in the isolation of Panama were the most formative of Eisenhower's entire military career."[19]

Conner insisted that Eisenhower commit himself to a study of military history, starting him slowly with historical novels before advancing to the dissection of the classic military books of the time, most relating to the Civil War. "Following each reading, Conner would quiz him relentlessly. His pedagogical technique was very Socratic. He would ask Eisenhower, 'Why did Lee invade the North a second time? Why was Meade successful? Why did Lee choose to fight at Gettysburg? What were Lee's alternatives?' The young major always attempted to digest the major themes of each text, knowing sooner or later Conner would ask him about them."[20]

His service with Fox Conner was the greatest education of Eisenhower's life and probably did more to prepare him for World War II than any post he ever held. He called it a graduate school in military history. Among the lessons Conner taught Eisenhower, which he never forgot, was to take your job seriously but never yourself. When, toward the end of his life, Eisenhower was asked to name the most influential military book he had ever read, he unhesitatingly replied that it was Carl von Clausewitz's classic study, *On War*, which Conner obliged him to read three times. To have read and absorbed Clausewitz once is difficult and noteworthy; to have read and actually digested it three times is exceptional. Rather than the rote learning stressed at West Point, for the first time in his military career Eisenhower was compelled to contemplate strategy and tactics on the high level of those who had made history. After studying a text, Eisenhower faced incessant probing questions from Conner, such as, What did each of Clausewitz's maxims really mean? What else should have been done, or "What would you have done?" in a particular military situation.

A screened-in porch became a makeshift study, where Eisenhower could retreat to read and study maps of various wars and campaigns. No aspect of warfare was left untouched. Although Eisenhower was particularly fascinated by the Civil War, at Conner's urging he also immersed himself in the campaigns of Frederick the Great and Napoleon. It was not enough merely to have read a text. Conner insisted that Eisenhower study it thoroughly and discuss with him the various alternatives available to a commander such as Napoleon, Grant, or Robert E. Lee. Virginia Conner later wrote, "I never saw two men more congenial than Ike Eisenhower and my husband. They spent hours discussing wars, past and future. Fox had always felt that the Versailles peace treaty had been the perfect breeder of a new war that would take place in about twenty years. Gradually Ike became convinced that Fox was right."[21]

Conner made certain that Eisenhower was tested in every conceivable way. "Every day, he required his executive officer to write a field order for the operation of the post. As a result Eisenhower became so well acquainted with the techniques of preparing and issuing orders that they became second nature to him."[22] Fox Conner's ratings on Eisenhower's annual efficiency reports were consistently "superior" for "manner of performance" of duty. Not everyone agreed. His endorsing officer for 1922–23 wrote that while he trusted Conner's judgment and sense of fairness, "I believe the rating given is too high."[23]

Much of their free time was spent on horseback, which was the primary means of transport in the wilderness that comprised the Canal Zone in the early 1920s. Eisenhower selected a black, rather stubborn gelding he named Blackie, and began investing considerable time in training the animal. Eisenhower's duties required him to spend as much as eight or more hours a day in the saddle, and his reconnaissance forays with Conner into the wilderness provided ample time for conversation. At night the two would sit at a campfire, where the conversations continued. "O[h], God, we'd get into the hottest arguments. We slept in the same tent. He was a heavy smoker—so was I, then—and we'd get up in the night and light a cigarette and go on talking."[24]

Eisenhower's training of Blackie included not only getting the animal to respond to commands but teaching the horse tricks, such as negotiating steps, which he performed at an equitation event. Horse and rider earned a third-place yellow ribbon and the ire of the head judge, a pompous colonel who complained vocally that Blackie was nothing more than a plowhorse and that Eisenhower was undeserving of his ribbon. Eisenhower "laughed courteously" at the colonel and respectfully disagreed, managing to keep his temper in check. Blackie became so adept at his step routine that it was performed whenever Conner had visitors to Camp Gaillard. Blackie was also a bit of a ham, who responded to applause for his feats. The careful training paid off one day along a jungle trail when horse and rider slipped into a jungle ravine. Had he not managed to jump clear, Eisenhower believed he might have been killed. Blackie was mired in deep mud and began thrashing around in terror, posing a serious danger that he would be buried alive. At Eisenhower's command, Blackie calmed down until rescued with the aid of ropes.[25] Eisenhower later reflected that his experience of training Blackie taught him the lesson that no animal or person is beyond reach if a leader undertakes careful nurturing.

The paradox of Eisenhower's relationship with Fox Conner was that the latter's experience dealing with the French had left him "hoping to God" that in any future war the United States would manage to avoid having to deal with allies such as those of World War I. In lectures and writings, he mentioned repeatedly the pitfalls of coalition warfare. While accepting the inevitability of such necessity in future wars, Conner sounded warnings designed to improve on the unhappy experience of the AEF and the immense pressures put on Pershing to submit American troops to French control. Conner "laid great stress in his instruction to me on what he called 'the art of persuasion.' Since no foreigner could be given outright administrative command of troops of another nation . . . they would have to be coordinated very closely and this needed persuasion. He would even talk about the types of organization he thought would bring this about with the least friction. . . . How do you get allies of different nations to march and think as a nation? There is no question of his molding my thinking on this from the time I was thirty-one."[26]

Eisenhower's adulation of Fox Conner had several caveats, however. He later stopped short of giving Conner full credit for the manner in which he approached supreme command in World War II. "No, I would not say that his views had any specific influence on my conduct of SHAEF but his forcing me to think about these things gave me a preparation that was unusual in the Army at that time."[27] Yet, in correspondence during the years after Panama, the younger officer would solicit the advice of his esteemed mentor. "In sheer ability and character, he was the outstanding soldier of my time," Eisenhower recalled in 1964. "Outside of my parents he had more influence on me and my outlook than any other individual, especially in regard to the military profession." In the narrow world of the interwar military, where budgets rather than military necessity reigned supreme, Conner's was a steady voice of reason, announcing that the future boded ill from a resurgent and aggressive Germany.

Although little has changed in today's modern army, Conner's mentoring of Eisenhower provides a classic example of the unofficial ways in which the military functions. For an officer to enjoy a successful military career (then and now) and attain generalship, it was absolutely necessary to impress at least one senior officer, who would then act as a mentor. Rare are the instances in which an officer rises to high command without the backing of someone in a position to influence his or her career. Even Mamie, whose knowledge of things military was practically nonexistent, scoffed at her husband's claims to success. "Ike used to have a favorite expression that he was a self-made man . . . [but] nobody can make it in this world without the help of somebody else. Ike had a lot of help from different officers."[28] In addition to Fox Conner, Douglas MacArthur, George Van Horn Moseley, Kenyon Joyce, and Walter Krueger would all advance Eisenhower's military education and career in various ways. The final advice given Eisenhower by Fox Conner was that he would do well to hitch his star to an up-and-coming officer named George Catlett Marshall, who had distinguished himself in the AEF.

In August 1922 Mamie gave birth to a son who was christened John Sheldon Doud Eisenhower. Ike was granted leave and was present in Denver when the child was born. Mamie went into labor when her water broke after she laughed hard at several Ring Lardner short stories Ike read to her to help pass the time. Granddaughter Susan recounts, "He was a nervous wreck. . . . He jumped into the car and put his foot hard on the accelerator and nothing happened. Mamie had to start the car, later saying, 'John was literally laughed into this world.' "[29] Mamie and baby John remained in Denver for several months before she brought her new son to Panama in the autumn of 1922 on a freighter transporting fruit. Mamie and baby John were accompanied by a nurse named Katherine Herrick, whose salary and travel expenses were paid by John Doud.[30] Once in Panama, baby John was fed only powdered milk. Virginia Conner began to notice a change in Mamie, who had begun to blossom. "I had the delight of seeing a rather callow young woman turn into the person to whom everyone turned. I have seen her, with her gay laugh and personality, smooth out Ike's occasional irritability."[31]

Yet Mamie's return to Panama with their newborn son did little to ease the marital tribulations of what had become a rather tense relationship. Eisenhower's frequent, often prolonged absences, and his incessant sessions with Fox Conner, all took their toll. For once another man became an object of envy for keeping her husband so occupied that he barely acknowledged her presence. Mamie's health suffered, both emotionally and physically, leaving her so debilitated that she could barely face each day. Sleeplessness and intestinal problems exacerbated matters. "I was down to skin and bones and hollow-eyed. . . . My health and vitality seemed to ebb away. I don't know how I existed," she said.[32] Pacing the porch or lying awake in bed, Mamie was serenaded by the screeching of monkeys, "And I felt like screaming too."[33]

Again she fled to Denver, where she pondered her future. Surely she could not continue fleeing from her husband at the first signs of adversity. Whether it was an epiphany or simply a natural evolution, thereafter Mamie made a commitment that if the marriage was to continue, she would have to make additional accommodations to her husband and his career. "So she made a decision to go back . . . and to tough it out again."[34] Although Mamie's decision was actually a turning point in the Eisenhower marriage, and John's birth was one of the happiest events in their lives, Ikky's death still hung over them like a shroud.

There was a noticeable increase in Eisenhower's health problems after Ikky died. Over the next two years he lost some fifteen pounds and began experiencing gastrointestinal problems in the summer of 1922, not all of which he was convinced had to do with the unhealthy conditions in Panama. A common myth is that Eisenhower, with single-minded determination to ensure that nothing would prevent him from playing a role in a future war, deliberately had his appendix removed. While Eisenhower was in Denver with Mamie and John during a forty-five-day leave in the late summer of 1923, his chronic abdominal pains continued, as did his discontent: "The urgency of his calling was upon him." He continued the habit (begun with Patton) of obtaining the records of previous problems from Leavenworth and "studying them to tatters." Nonetheless perhaps the most bizarre incident of the Eisenhowers' marriage occurred when, without informing Mamie, Eisenhower sought treatment at nearby Fitzsimmons Army Hospital. His complaint of abdominal pain led the army physicians to remove his appendix, even though the organ turned out not to be diseased. Only after the surgery was Mamie even notified that her husband was in the hospital. The official diagnosis listed "appendicitis" in his health records, but Mamie remembers that it was "not definite." In all, Eisenhower spent a total of fifteen days in the hospital before returning to duty in Panama.[35]

Eisenhower's very real physical ailments notwithstanding, the most serious of his problems remained beyond the reach of medicine. The death of Ikky "changed Ike's character," observed his post–World War II military aide and speechwriter Kevin McCann. The son born to Eisenhower in 1922 did not for some years generate the joyous relationship he had experienced with Ikky. Gone were the charming grin and the outgoing personality by which Ike had become known, and in its place up went an emotional wall designed to shield himself from further anguish lest anything bad happen to his second son. The good humor and impishness were replaced by a grim visage, the heartache shutting out through work—as much as possible, all of which proved unfortunate for John. Interviews and his own memoir make clear that the relationship between father and son was far different than it had been with Ikky. "The glimpse John Eisenhower gives into his childhood makes it apparent that Ike was not the playful, tolerant, all-embracing father to his second son that he had been to Icky." The image presented by John Eisenhower is of a distant and authoritarian father. "Dad," remembered John, "was a terrifying figure to a small boy."[36]

The first words of John Eisenhower's memoir relate that "I am certain that I was born standing at attention . . . something like the top sergeant who was not born, but issued. . . . I am inclined to think that I remained in that posture, figuratively . . . until I was nearly forty." His father's great success, "while exhilarating to us all, made me feel that among strangers I was always some sort of curiosity. And it affected the normal relations between a father and son." Only during the final years of Eisenhower's life did father and son finally bond.[37] Until then he was called Johnny, and the son's references to his father were highly impersonal: "the boss" or "the old man."

Mamie's approach for the remainder of her life was to baby John. As a teenager John joined the Boy Scouts, which required a candidate for promotion to first-class scout to hike fourteen miles. The family was vacationing in Mexico with the Douds when John announced his intention to do so. His overprotective mother and grandmother, horrified at the notion of their beloved Johnny wandering around alone in the rattlesnake-infested Mexican wilderness, insisted that he be chaperoned by his father in a fully provisioned automobile. Ike protested, and a full-fledged "hot argument" ensued, which he lost. Unable to pacify the women, Eisenhower did as he was told and followed his son, who completed his journey without incident. Although the event failed to assuage Mamie and Nana's fears that John was not capable of taking care of himself, his father pronounced that his son would do just fine without being constantly babied.[38] Despite constant reminders, Ike was never able to persuade Mamie to cut the apron strings to their son. "Mamie kept mothering John even after he was fifty years old," said a longtime family friend. "He was always like a little boy to her. She would tell him to watch what he ate and to wear the proper clothes when it rained."[39]

The change in Eisenhower's demeanor extended to his military duties. Not everyone at Camp Gaillard was enamored of either Fox Conner or Eisenhower. Indeed, Conner's rigid adherence to doing everything "by the book" led to considerable resentment among the officers and enlisted men. Conner's deputy was a "weak-kneed but amiable" lieutenant colonel who took every opportunity to subvert Conner's orders, leaving Eisenhower to act as his commander's "hatchet man." Some regarded Eisenhower as Conner's pampered pet and a martinet who urged his commander to be tougher on the men. The dislike of Eisenhower ranged from impatience to irritability and always there was the matter of his volatile temper, which would erupt without warning.

Maj. (later Brig. Gen.) Bradford G. Chynoweth was a 1912 West Pointer, who been Plebe Eisenhower's file leader at West Point in 1912. An engineer officer who had served in the Tank Corps at Camp Meade, Chynoweth commanded one of the three infantry battalions at Camp Gaillard. The two men had later become close friends, and it was Eisenhower's recommendation that led to his Panama assignment. Chynoweth, a brilliant, outspoken, often acerbic maverick, was never afraid to criticize his superiors to their faces by telling them the truth as he saw it (rather than what they wanted to hear). In the modern army of the twenty-first century, Chynoweth would never have lasted with such deportment, but in the pre–World War II army there were others like Chynoweth who spoke their minds, a list that included Patton and Vinegar Joe Stilwell.

Although Chynoweth genuinely liked both men personally, he thought both Conner and Eisenhower, "as a team, were the most ineffective training command that I can remember. Our officers, mostly war product, were in great need of instruction. They got none from brigade headquarters. Fox and Ike visited every unit on the training field every morning, looked sour, criticized, and condemned. Then they returned to their office, where Fox gave Ike lectures on military history."[40]

Chynoweth detected disturbing signs that, in his opinion, marked Eisenhower as something of a yes-man. After a tense meeting with Conner over regulations for marksmanship training during which Chynoweth and the other battalion commanders won their point, he and Eisenhower walked home together. Chynoweth angrily challenged Eisenhower's failure to support them. "Ike you are an infantryman. You know that we were right. Yet you never said a word to support us." Eisenhower replied, "Well, Chen, I'll tell you my guiding philosophy. When I go to a new station I look to see who is the strongest and ablest man on the post. I forget my own ideas and do everything in my power to promote what *he* says is right."[41] In his postpresidential memoir, *Mandate for Change*, Eisenhower signaled that he had not forgotten their fiery encounters forty years earlier, noting that he and Chynoweth had engaged in "very fine and hot arguments" in Panama.[42] Nor was he ever apologetic over his maxim that, to be successful, one had to learn from and profit by an association with those wiser, more experienced, and of higher rank.

Toward the end of Eisenhower's tour of duty, Mamie's mood brightened considerably. The monotony of life in Panama was enhanced by visits from

Mamie's sister Mike in the winter of 1923, and by Swede Hazlett, whom they saw frequently on weekends while the submarine he commanded was being repaired at a nearby naval base.

Fox Conner was reassigned to Washington as deputy chief of staff of the army before Eisenhower's tour of duty in Panama ended. In this capacity Conner all but ran the army in the name of the chief of staff, who was frequently absent.[43] Besides lighting a flame in Eisenhower's mind, Fox Conner had helped to resurrect a military career that had nearly ended over a misunderstanding at Camp Meade. A posthumous tribute in 1969 to both men would later describe Fox Conner as "the man who made Eisenhower."[44]

After two and a half years of exile, Eisenhower returned to the United States in September 1924, where, once again, football would take precedence, culminating in yet another strange twist in Eisenhower's military career.

15.

"A Watershed in My Life"

When he went to Leavenworth, he said he was going to come out number one.
—LT. GEN. JOHN T. LEONARD

In September 1924, three months before the scheduled end of his tour of duty in Panama, Eisenhower was ordered back to Camp Meade, Maryland, the very last place he or Mamie had any desire to revisit. Mamie and John preceded him by several weeks, and the family ended up being assigned to the same inferior converted quarters they had left in 1921 under tragic circumstances. When Eisenhower arrived after a six-day voyage aboard a cramped troopship, the reason became all too clear: The III Corps football team needed top-notch coaches, among them Eisenhower, who was tapped to be the backfield coach. His friend and classmate Vernon E. Pritchard was the head coach, and Ralph Sasse, one of Patton's outstanding tank commanders in France, was another assistant coach.

What made Eisenhower's return to Camp Meade all the more grating was that he had been sent there by the army solely to coach football during the 1924 football season, and it was on this criterion that he would later be rated. However doubtful its veracity, a letter sent in July 1924 to Washington by the III Corps HQ asked for Eisenhower by name and noted that "Captain Eisenhower has informally expressed his desire to be sent to this Corps Area at least temporarily during the football season."[1] On behalf of the chief of infantry, the War Department emphatically disapproved the request and announced that Captain Eisenhower "has been chosen by the Chief of Infantry for assignment as Commanding Officer, 15th Tank Battalion . . . [he] will not be available for temporary duty . . . during the coming football season."[2] What remains unanswered is how Eisenhower was ever assigned to Camp Meade over the (initial) objections of his branch and the subsequent nonconcurrence of the adjutant general.

Eisenhower's scathing version is that some bureaucratic "genius" in Washington had dreamed up the notion of an Army–Marine Corps competition from which resulted an alleged need for his services. The army had assembled excellent coaches, but, having created an interservice competition, it had not supported the need to recruit good players. The predictable result was a forgettable season in which the army team usually lost. In November they were matched against a more experienced team of marines in a highly publicized game in Baltimore. At stake were both bragging rights and possession of a bronze trophy awarded to the winner. The sponsoring *Baltimore Evening Sun* proclaimed, "Gob eleven favored to whip Third Corps in stadium battle." Maj. Dwight Eisenhower was pictured and quoted as saying: "I don't make many prophecies, but I know this much: My team will give the Fleet players the battle of their lives."[3] The army team tried hard but was shut out by a vastly superior marine team, thus ending a dismal season. Although he did not know it at the time, Eisenhower's army coaching career was still not behind him.

Eisenhower's third tour of duty at Camp Meade was cut mercifully short. After three months he received fresh orders to report to Fort Benning, where he was to command the 15th (light tank) Battalion—the same assignment he had held briefly in 1919 and for which he had been slated before being diverted to Maryland. Dismayed by the prospect of serving again in a capacity that had brought him serious career troubles, Eisenhower journeyed to Washington to plead his case to the chief of infantry, the same general who had threatened him with court-martial for his unwelcome ideas about tanks. Fox Conner had repeatedly recommended on each of his efficiency reports that he be assigned to a service school, but, according to Eisenhower, his request fell on the deaf ears of General Farnsworth. A disheartened Eisenhower said he left with the clear impression that he was still very much in disfavor within the infantry. With a letter of reprimand and extensive coaching on his résumé, Eisenhower's military career could hardly have sunk lower than when his efficiency report by another major rated him only "average" as a football coach.[4]

Eisenhower particularly wanted to attend the prestigious Command and General Staff School at Fort Leavenworth. Except for the formal tank instruction he received at Camp Meade, Eisenhower had had no other formal advanced schooling during his nine years of service. Nor had he attended a course at the Infantry School. Unless he attended Leavenworth, he simply had no chance of reaching the higher ranks of the army. In August 1924, six months before he was due for reassignment, Eisenhower wrote a letter, warmly endorsed by Fox Conner, to the adjutant general requesting assignment to Fort Leavenworth. The letter ended up in the office of the chief of infantry, where a staff officer appended a handwritten note on behalf of his boss stating that Eisenhower was eligible to attend and his name "has been placed on the tentative list of those officers who will be considered to attend the 1925–26 course at the C&GSS."[5]

There is nothing in the official record to suggest that in 1924–25 Eisenhower was in disfavor or would not be selected to attend Leavenworth. Moreover, he had been selected for battalion command, and however negative or repetitive the assignment may have been viewed by Eisenhower, it made sense. Had the chief of infantry actually held him in disfavor, Eisenhower would surely have been handed one of many undesirable assignments at one of the army's remote outposts.

It seems likely that Eisenhower visited with Fox Conner after his interview with the chief of infantry. Both offices were located in the same building, and Eisenhower would certainly have confided his plight to his mentor. Not long afterward Conner sent his protégé a cryptic telegram that read, "No matter what orders you receive from the War Department, make no protest. Accept them without question." In a prime example of mentorship at work, Conner had used his influential position to circumvent the powerful chief of infantry in order to lay the groundwork for Eisenhower's eventual attendance at Fort Leavenworth. Instead of Fort Benning, Eisenhower received orders transferring him to the Adjutant General Corps, and assigning him to Fort Logan, Colorado, as a recruiting officer. For an ambitious infantry officer, such an unprecedented action amounted to a career-killing demotion from the "Queen of Battle" to an exile in the hinterlands of the woeful U.S. Army of the interwar years. A letter sent to his new commanding general extolling Eisenhower as "an exceptionally efficient officer" did little to assuage his disappointment.

The transfer was a ploy by Fox Conner to secure Eisenhower an appointment to Fort Leavenworth by means of one of the several vacancies accorded the Adjutant General Corps. Unhappy at this turn of events, but implicitly trusting Fox Conner, he complied without protest. After leave in Denver, the Eisenhowers moved to nearby Fort Logan, where Ike became the post recruiting officer, an uninspiring duty whose chief benefit was the free time it created. For Mamie it was the first time in years that she saw her family regularly and a delightful respite after the dismal places she had lived since 1916.

Eisenhower believed that his philosophical and personal disagreements with the chief of infantry would have kept him from attending Leavenworth. When Eisenhower was notified in April 1925 that he had been selected to attend the 1925–26 class at the CGSS, he credited Fox Conner with influencing his selection. As it turned out, Conner's backstage gambit had been unnecessary. In January 1925 the chief of infantry had submitted to the War Department adjutant general a list of names of forty-seven infantry officers eligible and recommended to attend the 1925–26 course. Name number twenty-eight on that list was that of Major Dwight D. Eisenhower. Barring unforeseen circumstances the chief's recommended list was tantamount to an appointment. (The function of the adjutant general in this matter was simply to rubber-stamp approval and carry out the desires of the chief of infantry by issuing the appropriate transfer orders.) Despite his foreboding that he was persona non grata, it is clear that the chief of infantry bore Eisenhower no personal or professional grudge. Neither Conner nor Eisenhower was apparently aware that the transfer had been unnecessary.[6]

His elation ("I was ready to fly—and needed no airplane!") was tempered by deep concern that he had never attended an infantry course and therefore might have trouble passing the Command and General Staff School. His expectations were not boosted when an aide to Farnsworth allegedly sent Eisenhower a note suggesting that he not attend the course as he would surely fail, thus terminating his future usefulness as an infantry officer.[7] Implicit was the prophecy that he could expect to become a career football coach. Fox Conner would not hear of it and wrote to reassure Eisenhower that he was better prepared than most and should have no doubts about his capabilities. "You are far better trained and ready for Leavenworth than anybody I know. . . . You will feel no sense of inferiority."

Well before his selection, and more in hope than reality, Eisenhower resumed the practice he and Patton had begun at Camp Meade of working and reworking problems previously presented during the course. He wrote of his selection to Patton, who had been an honor graduate the year before. In turn Patton sent him one hundred pages of detailed notes and observations on all aspects of the course.[8] Thus armed with newfound confidence, and determined to make up for having missed frontline service in France, Eisenhower reported to Fort Leavenworth in August 1925 to begin the yearlong grind of the Command and General Staff School.

In 1881 Gen. William Tecumseh Sherman established Leavenworth as the site of what eventually became the most important military school for a professional U.S. Army officer. Attendance at Leavenworth was the most challenging year of an officer's peacetime career. When Eisenhower attended, it was called the Command and General Staff School, later redesignated the U.S. Army Command & General Staff College.[9] Those who have risen to the highest positions in the army are all graduates of the school, including Douglas MacArthur and George C. Marshall.[10] To become what Marshall referred to as "a Leavenworth" man was a prestigious mark of success without which no officer could aspire to future high command or compete for the few high positions in the peacetime army.[11]

The CGSS was not unlike West Point. Bradford Chynoweth, who attended the course two years after Eisenhower, noted, "The Instructor Staff were a hierarchy, to whom the School Doctrine was sacred. They were not teaching War. They were teaching Dogma."[12] Even so, the school was "where they separated the sheep from the goats."

The occasional gallows humor aside, the highly competitive, one-year course at Leavenworth was taken very seriously by those fortunate enough to be selected. Careers were made and broken—as were more than a few marriages. Nervous breakdowns were unexceptional; depression and insomnia were as common as colds, and there was even the occasional suicide by officers who failed to make the grade. "My class," joked Chynoweth, "made a joint resolve that if anyone contemplated suicide, he would first kill an instructor." The commandant was not amused to learn of this dark-humored tale and scolded the class to behave themselves.[13]

The typical school day was long, highly structured, and required considerable off-duty study.[14] In addition to turning out qualified staff officers, the course at Leavenworth was designed to test the mettle of its students by placing them under great stress and obliging them to think and react even if exhausted, which is usually the case in war.[15] Using the case-study method, students were obliged to solve a variety of tactical problems for which there was an "approved" or "school" solution.

The students spent considerable time on horseback in the countryside around the fort, performing tactical rides to undisclosed locations in order to solve problems presented to them. "Many hated this with a passion," Eisenhower said of what were for him—after Fox Conner's intense schooling in the jungles of Panama—mostly routine exercises. Ambition and fear of failure were the twin forces that drove the students, and at the conclusion of a day spent in conferences, lectures, or map and field exercises, students studied, often far into the night. Eisenhower claimed that he refused to succumb to the pressure, deciding that a fresh mind each morning was preferable to the usual numb exhaustion of the average student. His claim that he studied only two and a half hours per night and was in bed by 9:30 P.M. seems at best wildly exaggerated, particularly as he was known to make an occasional midnight raid on the refrigerator.

For once lady luck smiled when the Eisenhowers were assigned a spacious four-room apartment in Otis Hall (now the visiting VIP quarters at Fort Leavenworth), instead of in the so-called Beehive, a large building across the street where some one hundred families were quartered in exceedingly cramped conditions. The apartment was centrally heated and contained an electric stove, both of which were alien to Mamie's most recent experiences. When they first moved in there was only one bed, so Mamie went to Abilene and asked Ida if she happened to have an extra bed she could borrow for John. A discarded rope bed was located in the loft of the barn and became one of Mamie's prized possessions, even though a special mattress and box spring had to be made to fit its odd size.[16]

Students were given three options for off-duty studying: in an informal group, with a partner, or by themselves. Although invited to join a study group, Eisenhower thought the committee approach was too wasteful of time and declined the invitation. Instead he invited one of his first friends from

Fort Sam Houston, Maj. Leonard T. "Gee" Gerow, to team up with him. The two were together nightly in a makeshift "command post" study Eisenhower created in the loft of his second-floor apartment. Maps were pinned up everywhere, and books, notes, pens, and pencils were strewn across a makeshift table on which the two officers, complete with green eyeshades, studied war and prepared for upcoming classes and field problems. The study room was off-limits to all, but John remembers creeping up the stairs one night to see for himself—at age three—what his father was doing for so many hours. His most vivid memory was the sight of his father and Gerow "poring intensely over a large table. . . . I was too small to see what was on the table but stared in wonderment at the huge maps tacked on the wall. . . . Dad and Gee welcomed me with a laugh and shoved me out the door in the course of perhaps half a minute."[17] Recalling his year at Leavenworth, Eisenhower noted, "We learned far more in quiet concentration than in the lecture hall."[18] His enthusiasm and driving ambition were discernible in his eagerness to begin his nightly studies, usually not waiting for Gerow to put in an appearance.

Patton's meticulous one-hundred page notebook certainly helped.[19] A classmate later wrote in the *Cavalry Journal* that "among the most helpful aids to study are the old problems used in former years."[20]

Like West Point, the school attempted to instill a rather rigid methodology of how general staff officers should function. Free thinking was not necessarily discouraged but a student who presented a nonconforming reason had better be convincing when it ran counter to the approved school solution. However, its shortcomings notwithstanding, Fort Leavenworth was a far cry from what a Leavenworth historian notes was the "easygoing anti-intellectual atmosphere of the Old Army," where nineteen years earlier George C. Marshall had easily secured an appointment normally reserved by many commanders for "their regimental idiot."[21]

There was no school on Saturdays or Sundays, and it was while at Fort Leavenworth in 1926 that Eisenhower began what became a lifelong love affair with the sport of golf on the newly built post course. It afforded relaxation and a challenge he never quite overcame, although he did graduate from hacker to a reasonably decent golfer after many years. Of his first experience at Leavenworth, Eisenhower joked that, "if my progress in academics had been no greater than in golf I would never have gotten through the course."[22] Not surprisingly Mamie and Gee's wife, Katie Gerow, formed an instant friendship. "She knew her way around the army, and while their husbands worked, Katie did much to teach Mamie the ropes, to show her how one could contentedly survive the nomadic life of the army."[23]

Fox Conner had taught him well, and, determined to prove that his tutelage had not been in vain, Eisenhower entered Leavenworth with a strong sense of purpose and a coldly pragmatic attitude. He never became embroiled in the self-imposed pressures that drove most of his classmates. In fact, the course was tailor-made for the military skills Eisenhower had acquired during his ten years of service. For example, the Battle of Gettysburg was often the subject of exercises that provided Eisenhower with "a rare advantage: he knew the terrain from his Camp Colt days and could orient himself quickly from his first-hand knowledge of the area."[24]

The competition was so intense that the faculty started a betting pool when it had become evident that Eisenhower was one of only two students left in the race to be number one. Through deliberately contrived conversations with faculty members, whom he used as sources of information, as the course drew to a close Eisenhower seems to have been aware that he was at or near the top of the class.

By a close margin Eisenhower was rated number one in his class. His high standing also earned him the distinction of being both the distinguished graduate as well as an honor graduate, the latter an accolade given to the top twenty-five graduates. Just as important, Eisenhower's success was quiet validation that Fox Conner's assessment of his abilities had been correct. Moreover, his first-place finish was no fluke: His organizational skills and attention to detail, combined with his avid determination to succeed, were a winning combination. Privately Eisenhower denied he knew he was number one, but his close friend John Leonard remembers, "When he went to Leavenworth, he said he was going to come out number one."[25] (Shortly after Eisenhower graduated, the Command and General Staff School did away with class standings.)

Then, as now, there were few secrets in a tightly-knit military community. When the class standings were published, word quickly spread across Fort Leavenworth. Mamie received an anonymous telephone call from someone who said, "Eisenhower's first." As a steady stream of well-wishers descended on the Eisenhower quarters, Mamie was giddy with delight, proclaiming, "I knew, every hour of every month at Leavenworth, that Ike would come out Number One. But when he made it, I was so tumbled inside with gladness, it was days before I could eat properly." The celebrations went on into the night as friends came and went. The revelry ended near dawn in complete exhaustion. According to Mamie her husband had reacted with a combination of pure joy and "a newfound seriousness."[26] Eisenhower also thanked her for taking such good care of him during their time at Leavenworth, during which he had, for all practical purposes, been an absentee husband.

Few students ever left Leavenworth without being thoroughly drained by the intensity of the course, and Eisenhower was no exception. The steady grind of study and examinations took their toll. As the time drew near for the final course exams, "Ike was no use to anybody," recalled Mamie. The graduation ceremony was held on the parade ground, but was disrupted by a heavy rain that soaked everyone. The commandant, Brig. Gen. Edward L. King, a popular officer nicknamed "Big-hearted Eddie," told the new graduates that "the foundation has been laid, and the framework of your future life erected."[27]

The night after graduation Eisenhower and Gerow hosted a noisy, memorable celebration at a downtown Kansas City hotel, arranged by Eisenhower's eldest brother, Arthur. After leaving home in 1905, Arthur had risen steadily from messenger to his then position as the vice president of the Commerce Trust Company. "One of Arthur's roommates at a [Kansas City] boarding house had been Harry S. Truman, a bookkeeper for the Union National Bank. . . . Truman was to continue to speak warmly of Arthur long after his break with Ike." Each paid five dollars a week for room and board. " 'Harry and I had only a dollar a week left over for riotous living,' Arthur would recall."[28]

Arthur's successful banking career and an income to match were in stark contrast to Dwight's perpetual financial privation. As usual Eisenhower had no spare funds to pay for the festivities and was obliged to borrow $150 from Arthur. The United States was deep into the era of Prohibition, and the use of alcohol at Fort Leavenworth was expressly forbidden. However, it was no problem for Arthur to arrange for a plentiful supply of bootleg gin and whiskey to be served. The gala celebration lasted into the early morning hours, with Eisenhower singing some of his best-loved songs (as usual, off-key) at the top of his lungs. His favorite was "Abdul the Bulbul Amir" ("to which he can sing about fifty verses," said Mamie).[29] It was a rare respite from the stresses that the course had wrought on Eisenhower and his friends.

Among the flood of congratulations that inundated Eisenhower was a letter of praise from his friend George S. Patton, who wrote how pleased he was "to think my notes helped you," although, "I feel sure that you would have done as well without them."[30] Privately Patton was certain that his notebook was the *sole* reason Eisenhower had been so successful.[31] For his part Eisenhower never revealed to what extent Patton's notes bettered his standing.

Patton and Eisenhower each emerged from Fort Leavenworth with significant philosophical differences that would one day contribute to the rupture of their friendship. Eisenhower was perhaps more of a firm believer in the need for efficacious plans, and Patton more so in the need for their execution. In correspondence during the interwar years, the two continued to debate about how wars ought to be fought. "We talk a hell of a lot about tactics and such and we never get to brass tacks," complained Patton. "Namely what is it that makes the Poor S.O.B. who constitutes the casualtie [*sic*] lists fight and in what formation is he going to fight. The answer to the first is Leadership. . . . I don't try for approved solutions any more but rather to do what I will do in war." Patton also advised his friend to "stop thinking about drafting orders and moving supplies and start thinking about 'some means of making the infantry move under fire.' " Victory in the next war, he said, would hinge more on leadership than plans.[32]

In December 1926 Eisenhower submitted an essay detailing his experiences to the assistant commandant at Fort Leavenworth, Col. H. J. Brees, who liked it and suggested he submit it to the *Infantry Journal,* in which it was published in June 1927. Written anonymously by "A Young Graduate," the article was a practical primer on surviving the CGSS experience. The advice to future students included the admonition that one ought to go along to get along, as well as how to avoid the customary pressures common to each new class. He also suggested absorbing the small talk of the faculty during informal sessions. "The insight into the school, and the understanding of the whole course you will pick up in this manner is remarkable." Eisenhower concluded with this reassuring pronouncement: "Everybody graduates."[33]

George Marshall once defined his Leavenworth experience as where he "learned how to learn."[34] Eisenhower said that his year at Fort Leavenworth was a watershed in his military career.[35] In the long run, one of the most important but intangible advantages of attending Leavenworth was that it brought together promising officers from all branches of the army, men who had every future chance of assuming important positions. "Numerous graduates attributed [their] later success, at least in part, to associations first formed at Leavenworth . . . [which] gave officers an opportunity to demonstrate intellectual and leadership ability. Colleagues remembered these traits later."[36] Chief among them would be Dwight Eisenhower, whose friendships and associations first forged at the CGSS would have an enormous impact on many of the top command selections of World War II.

16.

Fort Benning, Washington, and France, 1926–1929

Very much against his will, we went [to France] . . . he disliked every moment he was over there.
— MAMIE EISENHOWER

After Eisenhower's graduation in June 1926, he, Mamie, and John traveled to Abilene, where the six surviving Eisenhower brothers had assembled for the first full family reunion since each had moved away. Dwight would later observe that "it seemed harder to get all we brothers together at a single place, at a single time, than to arrange the whole invasion of Europe in World War II."[1]

According to Edgar, when he greeted Dwight for the first time in nearly fifteen years, it was clear that his younger brother's competitive juices had not abated since 1911, the last time the two had seen each other. Gleefully if rather immaturely declaring, "Brother, I've been waiting a long time to give you a whipping and this is going to be it," Dwight was still determined to best Edgar in *something*. But by that time thirty-seven-year-old Edgar had come to the realization that his days of winning were probably over, and he tactfully declined Dwight's challenge. A thoroughly frustrated Dwight continued to goad Edgar, to no avail. Instead the brothers prodded David into a wrestling match with his third son. Dwight may have been in his prime as a young and fit soldier, but he was apparently unable to best his father, whose many years of hard physical labor more than compensated for their twenty-three-year age difference.[2]

Throughout the reunion Edgar managed to evade his brother's challenge despite such exchanges as "Well, Edgar, time to give you that whipping." Edgar would reply: "Not now, Dwight, later. . . . He never caught on to why I was dodging him."[3]

Ida was elated to have all her sons back home, but David, as usual, remained as taciturn as ever, rarely speaking except to lead the family in grace at mealtime and revealing nothing of himself or his feelings. On the front porch the six sons posed for a local photographer with their parents. For the occasion Dwight wore his uniform, complete with highly polished boots and his Distinguished Service Medal pinned to his left breast pocket. In what would become the best known of the pictures, Dwight is the only Eisenhower seen to be smiling in an otherwise rather somber family portrait. Family friend Charlie Harger publicized the Eisenhower reunion in the *Abilene Daily-Reflector,* and the article was later reprinted in a number of other cities and towns.[4]

One afternoon there occurred one of the most unusual incidents in Abilene's history, when the six brothers marched arm in arm through the streets of the business district. Some thought it was meant as a challenge to the police chief, with whom various of the brothers had tangled in their youth; others interpreted the act as good-natured show of solidarity in remembrance of their battles with the north siders.[5] This astounding sight drew people in droves from local shops to greet and shake hands with the Eisenhowers. Abilene has not seen its like since. Whether or not any of the six was entirely sober, however, has remained a well-guarded family secret. In Abilene legend it would forever be remembered as the "Big Parade of 1926."

Eisenhower had been ordered back to Fort Benning. Before departing Fort Leavenworth, big-hearted Eddie King solicited Eisenhower to accept a teaching post at the school. The War Department was also searching for a qualified regular officer to fill a position in the Reserve Officer Training Corps (ROTC) unit at a university Eisenhower later declined to name. In addition to teaching, he could earn an additional $3,500 per year for coaching the football team, a hefty supplement to the family's meager finances. Neither assignment came to fruition but as much as he disliked coaching army football teams, doing so for considerable extra pay would have been an entirely different matter.

Before reporting to Fort Benning, Eisenhower was granted a two-month leave, which was spent in Denver with the Douds. In August the nearly bald, thirty-five-year-old major reported for duty as the executive officer of the 24th Infantry Regiment. Thanks to Fox Conner, Eisenhower was once again an infantry officer. He was under no illusions that his class standing would have an immediate impact on his career, and in that respect he was not disappointed. The indisputable reason behind his assignment became all too clear when Eisenhower learned that his services as a head football coach were again required. Interservice football was still a high priority in the interwar era. Eisenhower resisted, pointing out that he had just turned down $3,500 to coach a college team. With great reluctance he agreed to become an assistant coach for the 1926 season, one in which the army team fared little better than the one at Camp Meade in 1921. So much for having been first at CGSS! Whatever benefits were to be derived from Leavenworth were yet to be realized.

Eisenhower's assignment to Fort Benning was fleeting and as inconsequential as his previous duty at Camp Meade. It was notable only for Mamie's health problems. Soon after the Eisenhowers arrived, she developed a serious gastrointestinal condition that necessitated transferring her to Washington, where for several months she was a patient in the army's best-known hospital, Walter Reed. Young John was sent to San Antonio and left in the care of his flighty, fun-loving aunt Mike, whose ascendance to adulthood had done nothing to quench her rebellious and mischievous nature. Nor was she cut out for the traditional role of baby-sitter, and "True to form, she eventually eloped . . . with a wealthy Texas entrepreneur, while John, age three, was the only witness."[6]

Whether he believed it possible or not, Eisenhower was rescued from the clutches of boredom by the chief of infantry. A letter from the War Department to his commanding general stated that Eisenhower was a candidate to attend the 1927–28 course at the War College, then located in downtown Washington, D.C. The letter also expressed concern that Eisenhower did not yet have sufficient command time, without which he was unlikely to be detailed to the War Department General Staff after completion of the nine-month course.[7] In December 1926 Eisenhower received orders, again orchestrated by Fox Conner, assigning him to the American Battle Monuments Commission (ABMC) in Washington, D.C.

The final official business of any change of duty is an efficiency report rendered on the officer's service. Eisenhower's regimental commander at Fort Benning did him a grave disservice by rating him merely "average" in his army duties but "superior" as a football coach. The endorsing officer, Brig. Gen. Edgar T. Collins, took strong exception to the low rating and pointedly wrote that "in both capacities his duties were discharged in a superior manner. He is qualified to a very exceptional degree."[8] Eisenhower never forgot how Collins had stood up for him in 1927.

The Eisenhowers moved to Washington in January 1927, where, in the decades before the proliferation of big government, lawyers, lobbyists, and "beltway bandits" (firms with strong military connections), the city was a kinder and gentler place to reside. Despite their meager income, they managed to rent a three-bedroom apartment in the elegant six-story Wyoming.

An ornate apartment building with a marble-floored lobby, the Wyoming was situated in an exclusive area of northwest Washington off Dupont Circle, near Rock Creek Park. With the Gerows and other friends also residing there, in short order Club Eisenhower reopened for business and was frequently a convivial gathering place for food, drink, and conversation. Other than golf, one of Eisenhower's few lifetime hobbies (and a great luxury during the depression years) was a fondness for colorful Oriental rugs, which adorned Chez Eisenhower wherever they lived. With Prohibition still in effect, booze had to be created the hard way, but, since he had learned well the art of making bathtub gin in his Camp Meade quarters, there was no shortage of liquid refreshment whenever the Eisenhowers entertained.[9]

For the first time two of the Eisenhower brothers lived in the same city. Milton had graduated from Kansas State University in Manhattan and was the assistant to the secretary of agriculture, Kansan William H. Jardine. In Jardine, Milton found a mentor who nurtured his gifted protégé with increasing responsibilities that included writing his speeches and testifying before Congress. As Milton's biographers note, "His work for Jardine quickly threw him into the higher reaches of government . . . he was the first civil-service assistant to a Cabinet officer."[10] His charm and intelligence won him many friends inside the government and out, including a close rapport with the members of the Washington press corps.

In 1927 Milton was commencing what would become an extremely successful and distinguished career in education and government. Though he was a comparative rookie in the political world, it was not long before Milton was seen as someone to watch. Thanks to Jardine, he soon became a regular White House guest of President Calvin Coolidge.

With a nine-year age difference between them, the two brothers had never really bonded in Abilene. The Washington years brought the two close to each other for the first time, and for the remainder of their lives Dwight and Milton were inseparable. They developed an affinity unshared with or by any of the other four Eisenhower brothers. Dwight would regularly seek Milton's advice, which was invariably sound and thoughtful. Milton's intimate understanding of Washington politics proved invaluable. With Milton's guidance, Dwight was better able to avoid the pitfalls facing the unwary. "We were not only intimate, but we found that we liked to talk over our problems together," said Milton.[11]

Both men were intensely ambitious, but Milton's older brother was known to few outside the military, and those who did know him generally regarded Dwight as a lowly army major with no discernible future—either in Washington or in the peacetime army. As Milton's star began rising during the Coolidge presidency, he frequently brought Dwight as his guest to Washington social functions, where he was known primarily as "Milton's brother." Milton worked assiduously but without noticeable success to promote Dwight's image as something more than that of yet another peacetime military pen-pusher, once appealing to a reporter, "Please don't go until you've met my brother; he's a major in the army and I know he is going places."[12] The reporter's reaction was, "If he's going far he had better start soon."[13]

Milton was engaged to a vivacious young woman named Helen Eakin, the daughter of a wealthy Kansas entrepreneur. Immaculately attired in his white dress uniform, complete with ceremonial saber, Dwight served as

Milton's best man at his marriage to Helen at the Mayflower Hotel in Washington in October. At Mamie's instigation, the saber was used by the new Mrs. Milton Eisenhower to cut their wedding cake.[14]

When the two couples were not playing bridge, a pastime Eisenhower enjoyed nearly as much as golf, he and Milton would debate the pros and cons of government and its role in society. Building on beliefs formed at West Point, Eisenhower retained his palpable dislike and distrust of big government and the bureaucracies it spawned. Philosophically Eisenhower was both conservative and pragmatic, but he nevertheless believed that less government was desirable. Milton, however, was more middle-of-the-road and thought bigger government served a useful purpose. The experience broadened Eisenhower's outlook and for the first time in his life he was obliged to consider issues that, heretofore, had been largely theoretical. The two would debate endlessly, and Milton sometimes came away embarrassed at being bested by his brother's skill at producing facts and figures to back up dialogues about a variety of subjects. "Ike knew so much and pounced upon the slightest misstatement of fact," said Milton.[15] The distinction was that "their disagreements were cheerful rather than combative, unlike Ike's arguments with his big brother Edgar."[16]

The two brothers shared a love of practical jokes, and their wives were fair game. A typical prank would involve Milton calling Mamie, pretending to be Dwight, and vice versa. Neither wife could tell the difference.[17] While Dwight and Mamie's social life was focused around Club Eisenhower, family life revolved around John. Mamie worried excessively about her son's welfare to the point where she smothered him with affection. Her protectiveness included bundling him in all manner of winter clothing on cold mornings. John longed to be one of the boys, but could not avoid becoming an object of amusement among his friends when he appeared clad more like an Eskimo than a Washington, D.C., schoolboy. After leaving home and ensuring he was well out of her sight, he would remove the offending items and happily play with his friends.[18] "It took me years, many years, to get over my 'smother love,'" recalled Mamie. "It wasn't until [he] had children of his own that I stopped worrying."[19]

Except for one occasion, Eisenhower never resorted to corporal punishment in disciplining his son, which John believes was unwise inasmuch as his usual methods of discipline were even more frightening. John notes that his father—possibly afraid of his own great strength when angry—"conducted discipline in the West Point manner. I was dressed down smartly on many occasions." The lone exception came about after John ignored several warnings to take his elbows off the table, at which he found himself herded into the bedroom with his father's hand firmly gripping his neck. He remembers thinking, "Well, John, your time has come; you're finished."[20]

As a child John was slight of frame and underweight. He was convinced he could never measure up to his father's raw strength and athletic prowess—golf notwithstanding. Although he tried hard and participated in various schoolboy sports, "Dad could never understand why I was not a star."[21] As a youngster John was unable to shake off his trepidation about disappointing his demanding father. No opportunity was lost to quiz John on his school subjects. In math, for example, John found himself well ahead of his class-mates in learning the multiplication tables. "I was drilled without mercy" each morning in the bathroom father and son shared simultaneously. "And no errors were tolerated." Their regimen did bring the young man and his stern father together for rare but congenial moments of bonding. John loved his parents unreservedly and regarded them as good people who cared deeply for him.

The marriage was not without its disagreements and quarrels, some of them severe. Even so, as John writes, "it seemed that the Old Man's views nearly always prevailed. But one thing the two of them were careful of: they never quarreled in front of me. I have memories of catching the devil from both of them singly or together; but I have no memories of the two of them arguing between themselves."[22]

From 1929 to 1935 John was sent to what he privately dreaded as his annual summer "exile" in Denver with his grandparents. Except for the mis-chievous Mike, for whom he developed a great fondness, John otherwise found the Doud home a somber, disconcerting place and longed to be back in Washington with his friends. The toll on Nana and Pupah—already prone to emotional outbursts—of losing two of their four daughters and a grandson had become profound. Both had lost their joie de vivre, and every Sunday John accompanied them to sorrowful vigils at the gravesites. Although the Douds were "exceedingly good to me," they were, like his mother, over-protective lest they lose yet another precious grandchild. By the end of the summer John was relieved to put the experience behind him for another year.[23]

World War I had made John J. Pershing a household name and a national hero. Wherever he went, Pershing was instantly mobbed by admirers and well-wishers. His less pleasant task as army chief of staff from 1921 to 1924 was to preside over the dismembering of the great American war machine, which was now deemed an unnecessary luxury. Pershing would have been satisfied merely to have kept intact an army that, as his official biographer notes, "need not grow large to be effective. But Congress dawdled. His words, comforting to the army, merely vexed a languid nation—why weren't those old AEF people quieter? Their time had passed."[24]

Although the National Defense Act of 1920 made allowance for a small professional force, neither Congress nor the administrations in power had the will to reverse a disturbing trend. Forrest C. Pogue notes, "From 1921 on, the generation which admired public frugality, hated war, and shunned collective security was easily persuaded to neglect its own defense. Congress found the coincidence of anti-militarism and saving money irresistibly popular."[25]

The U.S. Army of the interwar years was so ineffective that a mere one-quarter of the authorized Regular Army officers and one-half of the enlisted men were available to fill positions in fighting units. Of the nine authorized divisions only three actually existed. The few infantry and cavalry units were scattered among the so-called hitching post forts left over from the Indian wars of the previous century. The sad truth was that the army had come full circle from its frontier days before World War I, and what had been one of the world's most modern armies was again a third-rate force that was only kept afloat by dedicated senior officers like Pershing, MacArthur, Conner, and junior officers such as Marshall, Eisenhower, and Patton, who stuck it out despite atrocious living conditions, reductions in grade to prewar levels, miserable pay that went down instead of up, and no incentives whatsoever to remain soldiers.[26]

Pershing's most enduring legacy was the creation of the Battle Monuments Commission in 1923. The early task of the commission was to mark the World War I battlefields with suitable memorials and to prepare guidebooks to the places where Americans had fought in 1917–18.[27] While still on active duty Pershing chaired the ABMC, and, as the former commission historian, Roger Cirillo, writes, "Pershing did not relish the role of esteemed old soldier. He felt that he had one last task to perform, to repay a debt deeply felt. He wanted to immortalize the achievements of the American Expeditionary Force that had fought in France and Flanders . . . and to make sure that the AEF's dead were rendered the honors that they deserved. . . . 'When the last bugle is sounded, I want to stand up with my soldiers,' he said."[28]

No one was assigned to the ABMC without Pershing's personal approval. In December 1926 Eisenhower's name was one of several submitted by the War Department for Pershing's consideration. When asked if he would accept such an assignment, Eisenhower agreed but was privately ambivalent, conjecturing that it could hardly be worse than his current inconsequential duties at Fort Benning. Eisenhower did not realize that duty at the ABMC was a meaningful posting for a junior officer, and a stepping-stone to higher rank and responsibilities. Pershing's deep personal involvement in the work of the commission meant that only promising officers who passed muster were assigned to the ABMC. Besides the weight of his personal recommendation to Pershing, Fox Conner had also pointed out that Eisenhower was a whiz at organizing and interpreting material.

One of the commission's primary endeavors was the writing of a guide to the U.S. battlefields in France.[29] Some preliminary work had been done toward the guidebook, but the raw material was an uncataloged mess and urgently in need of someone with Eisenhower's organizational skills to assemble and write (with help and advice from Milton). When *A Guide to the American Battlefields in Europe* was published later in 1927, Eisenhower deemed it a routine piece of staff work, but Pershing thought otherwise and subsequently praised him effusively in a letter to the chief of infantry.[30]

Since the death of his wife and three of his four children in a tragic fire at their quarters at the Presidio of San Francisco in 1915, Pershing had become a far different person than in his younger years. In 1916 he met Patton's sister, Anne (called "Nita" by family and friends), to whom he became engaged before leaving for France in 1917 to command the AEF. Pershing eventually spurned Nita for liaisons with other women while in Europe, but to his death he rued the fact that he had let her get away.[31] The Black Jack Pershing whom Dwight Eisenhower knew in the late 1920s was a reserved and lonely man to whom he never quite warmed.

Pershing was a notorious tightwad and ruled the commission with an iron fist. All decisions, including the most puny expenditure, had to be personally approved. Eisenhower's duties brought him into close contact with Pershing, who tasked him to write letters and speeches. The speeches were routinely discarded, although letters drafted for the old general's signature occasionally fared slightly better.

Eisenhower sometimes acted as Pershing's unofficial aide at social events. Black Jack, however, kept erratic hours and often worked until midnight, thus obliging his subordinates to do the same. He was possessed of an annoying habit of being habitually late, even to events given in his honor, thus leaving an embarrassed and irritated Eisenhower to dream up suitable excuses for his tardiness. The long hours, many of them during his off-duty time, that Eisenhower spent attempting to satisfy Pershing's demands was a challenging, useful, but ultimately unrewarding experience.

Although officially assigned to the Battle Monuments Commission, Eisenhower was also detailed to perform the additional duty of commander of the enlisted detachment assigned to the chief of infantry. More a name than a reality, this rather inconsequential duty nonetheless earned him credit for command time, thus adding to his qualifications to attend the prestigious War College.[32] In the spring of 1927 Eisenhower learned he had been chosen to attend the next course at the War College, then located on the Potomac River on the site of what is now Fort Lesley J. McNair. Eisenhower's boss, the commission secretary, Maj. Xenophon Price, attempted to dissuade him, arguing, "Every officer attached to the Commission is going to be known as a man of special merit." Eisenhower wisely would not hear of it; "the [War] Department has given me a choice," he replied. "And for once I'm going to say yes to something I'm anxious to do."[33]

In September 1927 Eisenhower reported for the "gentlemen's" course of instruction where neither examinations nor class standings were part of the curriculum. Whereas Leavenworth focused on creating trained general staff officers, the object of the War College curriculum was to teach potential future generals the "big picture" of war—how armies were organized, mobilized, supplied, and employed. Planning for future wars was a major aspect of the course. Unfortunately, however, the War College curriculum "was structured to reflect the staff organization of the American Expeditionary Force (AEF), as if every future war would be fought in the image of the one just past."[34] However flawed its academic premise, which was wedded to World War I, the experience was enlightening and again brought Eisenhower into contact with men with whom he would one day serve or command. His classmates included Gerow, Haislip, and one of his instructors from Leavenworth, Maj. Everett S. Hughes.

The principal requirement of the course was to research and write a paper on a subject of military relevance. Eisenhower selected an obscure topic: "An Enlisted Reserve for the Regular Army." Prophetically he had chosen a topic that would become the primary focus of his future assignment to the War Department. The paper was professionally written, with Eisenhower's demonstrated talent for organization and lucidity. He concluded that there existed a serious need for an effective reserve force in the event of future mobilization, pointing out that "with the contingent of veterans rapidly disappearing as a military asset, and with the National Guard less than one-half the strength it was expected to reach, the Regular Army had been reduced to about 40% of that considered necessary under the most favorable conditions." In such fiscally conservative times, the crux of Eisenhower's thesis was, "Experience has shown that the cost of maintaining a soldier in the reserve is only a small fraction of that necessary to maintain him in the active force."[35]

The commandant was Maj. Gen. William D. Connor, who has sometimes been mistaken for Fox Conner. The two were not related, and their only similarity was that Eisenhower greatly admired both men. W. D. Connor carefully evaluated his paper and wrote to Eisenhower, "The examination of your individual staff memorandum shows it to be of exceptional merit." Connor also rated Eisenhower superior in eight of ten categories on his efficiency report.[36] Eisenhower's paper was forwarded to the War Department, where it disappeared forever into the maze of the bureaucracy.

After graduation in June 1928, Eisenhower was faced with accepting Pershing's offer that he return to the Battle Monuments Commission—a job he had no particular desire to resume—or to take a post on the War Department General Staff, a prestigious assignment for an ambitious career officer. Returning to the ABMC meant a yearlong tour of duty in France to gather information for a revised guidebook. For only the second time during their marriage, Mamie intervened actively to influence his decision. She pleaded,

"Honey, let's go to Europe. Let's take this assignment. This gives us an opportunity to see the Old World and travel."[37] It was with considerable misgivings that he agreed to Mamie's plea to return to the commission. "Very much against his will, we went."[38] On July 31, 1928, the Eisenhowers sailed from New York for Southampton, England, aboard the liner SS *America*, accompanied by Mamie's parents.

Mamie located a charming three-bedroom apartment on the Right Bank in the Rue d'Auteuil, within walking distance of the commission offices near the Pont Mirabeau, which some of their friends nicknamed "Pont Mamie." John was happily enrolled in a nearby private American school and learned French far better than his parents, both of whom studied the language but neither succeeded in learning more than a few words. Although Eisenhower's French was abysmal, he refused to stop trying to master it, but without much success. As he later told his World War II naval aide, Harry C. Butcher, "his ear simply could not separate the French words and although he could read it well and write it fairly well, he could not speak or understand it."[39]

Paris in the 1920s was a very expensive place in which to live on a major's meager income. Such luxuries as dining out, dancing, or attending the theater were rarely affordable. When they were, Ike and Mamie liked nothing better than "kicking up their heels." Somewhat puzzlingly Mamie loved France but found the French people provincial and irksome. The daily life of the Eisenhowers was further complicated by a pervasive postwar anti-Americanism, exacerbated by the inability of most Americans in the 1920s to speak French. Instead their apartment became a Parisian version of Club Eisenhower, which he once described as "an informal, junior-size American Express."[40] One of Eisenhower's most enjoyable pastimes was to demonstrate his culinary prowess by cooking old-fashioned American food for his guests. After the meal, everyone would accompany Mamie at the piano in songfests. "A homesick lot, their hearts and souls went into the choruses of American ballads and jazz."[41]

Although Eisenhower avowed that he enjoyed touring the French countryside and mingling with friendly locals, Mamie remembered it quite differently. "I think he disliked every moment he was over there. He didn't like his commanding officer, and he had to tramp, and I mean literally walk, over all that part of France, but [in the end] it stood him in such good stead in World War II, for he knew exactly where he was going."[42] His French assignment was also an eye-opener he would put to good use during the next war. "He learned much about the French army and if he ever thought that 'politics' entered into the U.S. Army he thought one should refer to the French!"[43]

Usually accompanied by a driver/interpreter, Eisenhower was away a good deal of the time inspecting not only the battlefields over which American troops had fought, but the entire front from Switzerland to the North Sea, cataloging, mapping, taking notes about every aspect of the battles, and preparing draft revisions to the guidebook. Eisenhower became so intimately knowledgeable with the battlefields of the Argonne, Saint-Mihiel, and Château-Thierry that he became an expert tour guide who could discourse on what had transpired, how many had died, and what the outcome had been.

From the time of the Roman Empire to Napoleon and Bismarck, France has been Europe's primary battleground. In the late 1920s, it still bore the fresh scars of what had been the greatest slaughter in history. Battlefields from Alsace-Lorraine to the North Sea littered the lush landscape with the stark vestiges of war. Military cemeteries contained the graves of 1.7 million Frenchmen. Virtually every city, town, and village in France erected monuments to the sacred dead, every one of which was engraved with the poignantly familiar words, *"Mort pour la France."* Britain's male population had been reduced by more than a million men, who were buried in more than six hundred British cemeteries, a permanent reminder of horrors like Ypres and the Somme (where seventy thousand were forever "missing in action").

Often away from Paris for several days or even a week at a time, Eisenhower brought to this enterprise his usual careful attention to the minutest detail. The regrowth of trees and vegetation on the battlefields complicated his task but failed to deter his investigations, which frequently took him deep into forests and thick undergrowth in search of such evidence as battle markers and trench lines.[44]

Eisenhower's sense of history had been so well honed by Fox Conner that for the first time he easily grasped the full extent of the war he had studied in such depth. In 1913 Patton had explored the backroads and byways of Normandy in the belief that he would someday fight battles there. Although his reasons were different, Eisenhower's experience in France was similar and helped prepare him for high command in World War II. One of his commission colleagues, Capt. George A. Horkan, frequently accompanied Eisenhower and came away impressed by his thoroughness and determination to fulfill his solemn responsibility of accurately recording the events that occurred on each American battlefield. Horkan believed that Eisenhower's experience "gave him a grasp of the military terrain of northern Europe which was just absolutely invaluable."[45]

In the spring of 1929 Eisenhower began to take Mamie and John along on his battlefield trips. For Mamie it was an interesting, if queasiness-inducing, experience that exposed her to the ugliest side of war and of a sordid human existence that had previously been as alien to her as visitors from outer space. Eisenhower took John and Captain Horkan's son, "Bo," on an unforgettable visit to Verdun, where in 1916 an estimated 700,000 men were killed in the single bloodiest battle in history. The vista of row upon row of white crosses became engraved in the mind of six-year-old John, who remembers Verdun as "a forbidding place," as somber as it was ghostly. In 1929 its sheer horror was still unforgettably evident. The aura of death was still evident in memorialized sites such as the Trench of Bayonets (an aura still present when I first visited Verdun in 1968). Outside Fort Douaumont, John and his friend glimpsed the gruesome sight of a grinning skull with a single tooth still intact in its mouth. Much to Eisenhower's annoyance the two children developed a sudden urge to beat a hasty retreat by visiting the public bathroom. John started to kick a pineapple-shaped object that turned out to be a live hand grenade before being alertly restrained by his father's driver, thus thwarting a likely tragedy in the nick of time. "Instances of French farmers being blown to bits by ten-year-old grenades and shells were still common," remembered John.[46]

The Verdun experience seemed to enhance Eisenhower's pessimism, born of Fox Conner's tutelage, that the United States would one day inevitably become involved in another such calamitous war.

His fieldwork completed by June 1929, Eisenhower intended to use his leave to see the sights of Europe. With Eisenhower at the wheel of the family sedan, the three visited the French Riviera and San Remo, Italy, a vacation that ended almost as soon as it began when John contracted whooping cough. That same month Eisenhower entered the American Hospital in Paris for three days, for what was diagnosed as colitis stemming from amoebic dysentery acquired in Panama.[47]

Eisenhower's tour of duty in France was due to end in September 1929. Before returning to Washington, he applied for a second leave. At the end of August, Eisenhower, Mamie, and a commission friend and colleague, Maj. William R. Gruber and his wife, Helen, began a leisurely seventeen-day automobile trip during which they visited Belgium, Germany (the Rhineland, Coblenz, Heidelberg, and the Black Forest), and finally Switzerland. All came away with exceptionally favorable impressions of Germany and its people. Eisenhower far preferred the simplicity of German food and recalled that his ancestors had lived nearby. "We seemed to experience a very definite exhilaration upon leaving Belgium and entering the Fatherland," Eisenhower wrote. "Maybe it's because both Bill and I have our family roots in this country. . . . We like Germany!" Eisenhower wrote.[48]

Despite his original aversion to the assignment, Eisenhower's year in France, particularly the summer of 1929, was by far the most relaxed, idyllic period of Ike and Mamie's lives.[49] The only disagreeable aspect of his assignment was working under Major Price's supervision. Outwardly the two men were cordial and respectful of each other, and though he never publicly alluded to his disagreeable relationship with Price, privately his diary recorded the opinion that Price was "old-maidish," and that "I was not so successful as I should have been in concealing my impatience with some of his impossible ideas and methods."[50] Although his diplomacy later became a trademark, at this stage of his career Eisenhower was inclined to be uncompromisingly blunt. His candid letters and an afteraction report to Price, critical of the methods by which the commission carried out its mission in France, were apparently not welcomed even though in every instance Eisenhower added practical suggestions for improving the operation of the Paris office.[51]

Eisenhower's service with the commission thus ended on an unpleasant note. Inevitably an officer will eventually run afoul of a superior for reasons ranging from personality clashes to professional jealously. Eisenhower was no exception. Price, a 1914 graduate of West Point, felt threatened by Eisenhower's effectiveness. Additionally his refusal to turn down the War College appointment and his later decision to leave the commission were certain to have irked Price. His first evaluation of Eisenhower in 1928–29 rated him "excellent" or "superior" in various categories. However, by the time he submitted Eisenhower's final report, Price had clearly decided that his performance of duty in France had been merely "satisfactory." Although Eisenhower was "an excellent officer of great natural ability," Price thought he was "not especially versitile [sic] in adjusting to changed conditions. Family worries sometime[s] effect [his] efficiency? Had difficulty adjusting to changed conditions existing in France."[52] There was nothing to substantiate Price's allegations, yet such is the military way that vague assertions of the sort leveled against Eisenhower often leave a permanent stain on an officer's record. Fortunately for Eisenhower, Price's poor appraisal would have no discernible effect on his career.[53]

His duties in France completed, the Eisenhowers sailed for the United States in mid-September 1929. Their departure was quite different from their lonely arrival a year earlier. The Eisenhowers had been one of the most popular couples in the American community in Paris, and the members of Club Eisenhower turned out en masse to provide a royal send-off and good wishes at the Gare Saint-Lazare. Aboard ship they were showered with flowers and presents sent from Paris by their friends.[54]

Back in Washington, they moved once more into their old apartment in the Wyoming, which had been sublet during their absence. Offered a choice of remaining with the ABMC or transferring to the War Department General Staff, a posting available to only a select few, and yet another important step up the promotion ladder, Eisenhower unhesitatingly accepted a transfer in November 1929. The next five years would earn him considerable notice inside the heart of the military bureaucracy in Washington.

17.

"Nothing Short of a Genius"

The aristocrat of our time . . . and the most selfless man that has reached public office in the last century in this country. —MAJ. GEN. ELWOOD P. QUESADA

In November 1929 Eisenhower reported for duty as a staff officer in the War Department, which occupied an ornate stone edifice (next door to the White House) then called the State, War, and Navy Department Building (now the Executive Office Building). His close friends Gee Gerow and Ham Haislip were already serving in the same office. "Except for the fact that I do not like to live in a city I am particularly pleased with this detail," he said. Eisenhower's fancy title was assistant executive to Brig. Gen. George Van Horn Moseley, the principal military adviser to the civilian assistant secretary of war, a position that had been created after World War I specifically to address the problems of mobilization and procurement of war matériel that had plagued the United States in 1917–18.

Shortly after assuming his new duties in the winter of 1929–30, Eisenhower received a summons from Pershing. For the past ten years Pershing had been writing his war memoirs, occasionally sending parts of the manuscript for review to men whose opinions he respected. Although few men ever really earned his complete trust, the most notable exceptions were Lt. Col. George Catlett Marshall and, to a less intimate degree, Eisenhower. Although Eisenhower was no longer assigned to the Battle Monuments Commission, Pershing nevertheless sought his opinion about the format in which the two principal American battles of the war, Saint-Mihiel and the Meuse-Argonne, should be presented. "Read the two parts of the book that covers these two periods and let me know what you think." Though Eisenhower left no record of his reaction to taking on this additional workload, in any event, one simply did not say no to Black Jack Pershing.[1]

As Eisenhower saw it, the book was unfit for publication because Pershing insisted on writing it from his war-diary entries, which made his recounting of the AEF battles disjointed and highly confusing. Instead of merely submitting his recommendations, Eisenhower produced two draft chapters for Pershing's consideration. He thought he had convinced Pershing that his opus would better be told in a narrative form, until the day, not long afterward, that Lieutenant Colonel Marshall unexpectedly stopped in to see him during a trip to Washington. He too had been summoned to advise Pershing on the merits of Eisenhower's proposal.

It was the first time Eisenhower had met the officer who Fox Conner had extolled as "nothing short of a genius," and someone he should seek to serve under. Indeed, Conner's greatest compliment was that Eisenhower's methods were "exactly the way Marshall would handle it."[2] Included in Conner's prediction that the United States would again fight a war with allies was the caveat that it would require "very well understood mechanisms and organisms to keep themselves together and not work at cross-purposes. Nobody will be the equal to Marshall in doing this."[3]

Fox Conner had had good reason to recommend Marshall to Eisenhower. As Marshall's direct superior in AEF headquarters, Conner had seen the fruits of his brilliance firsthand. Although he had yet to advance beyond the temporary grade of colonel (held during the war), Marshall, a 1901 graduate of VMI and the first captain of the corps of cadets, had steadily risen to positions of prominence as one of the most competent and admired officers in the entire army. In 1907, after a mere six years' service, and newly promoted to first lieutenant, Marshall finished first in his class at Fort Leavenworth's School of the Line.

As a junior officer Marshall gained notice as someone to watch, particularly during the periodic maneuvers held by the army to test tactics and readiness. As ambitious as Eisenhower and just as adept at concealing it, Marshall was adept at planning large-scale operations that gained him recognition during what were in 1910 the army's largest-ever peacetime maneuvers, held along the Texas-Mexico border. After Marshall trained the Massachusetts national guard, his prowess in an even larger, more successful maneuver in Connecticut in 1912 brought him to the attention of both the army chief of staff, Gen. Leonard Wood, and Secretary of War Henry L. Stimson.

Marshall's grasp of the intricacies of moving and supplying large armies was the product of a brilliant mind and practical experience gained during 1914 war maneuvers held in the Philippines. His first duty during the early months of the AEF in France was as the operations officer of the famed 1st Division (the "Big Red One"), where "At first from afar, later close at hand, Marshall learned of . . . [the] realities of coalition warfare and international politics."[4]

Marshall was a blunt-speaking officer who had once daringly challenged Pershing in France in 1917, during an emotional confrontation after the AEF commander had scathingly blistered the "Big Red One" and its commander for its performance during a training maneuver. At grave risk to his career, Marshall decided to act in the belief that Pershing's criticism was misplaced. Marshall actually grabbed the fiery Pershing by the arm and demanded to be heard. An equally outraged Pershing listened as Marshall "overwhelmed his opponent by a torrent of facts" that left the AEF commander nearly speechless. His biographer Ed Cray notes that "when Marshall was angry, 'his eyes flashed and he talked so rapidly and vehemently no one else could get in a word.' . . . The facts tumbled out." Virtually speechless, Pershing could only huff, "Well, you must appreciate the troubles we have," bringing an instant retort from Marshall: "Yes, General, but we have them every day and many a day, and we have to solve every one of them by night[fall]."[5] Marshall's unheard-of challenge of the most formidable general in the U.S. Army was breathtakingly daring, and although he successfully rebutted Pershing's criticisms of the division, Marshall fully expected to be relieved. Instead Marshall learned that he had earned the respect of a man whom everyone perceived expected unquestioning obedience, not dissent. For his part Pershing had the good sense not to have relieved Marshall after their confrontation. As one historian notes, Marshall's "audacious act of near insubordination . . . could have terminated the career of the junior officer and irrevocably altered the course of events for the United States Army during the second world conflict."[6]

Marshall was one of the very few to discern that Pershing accepted criticism only from subordinates who knew what they were talking about. "Rumor made Pershing a tough, unbending martinet at GHQ," but Marshall scoffed at this judgment; "you could talk to him as if you were discussing somebody in the next country. I never saw another commander I could do that with."[7] What ensued was a curious but lasting friendship between two very dissimilar men. Pershing discerned Marshall's professionalism and used it well; and Marshall staunchly protected his mentor by action and by deed.

When Marshall requested a transfer to frontline duty with troops in December 1917 ("I have been on staff duty since February 1915, and I am tired from the incessant strain of office work"), his new division commander, Maj. Gen. Robert L. Bullard, recommended disapproval. "I cannot approve because I know that Lieut. Col. Marshall's special fitness is for staff work and because I doubt that in this, whether it be teaching or practice, he has an equal in the Army to-day."[8]

Marshall was instead transferred to the AEF, where he was assigned to the Operations Section. His most remarkable accomplishment was to mastermind the most staggering logistical problem ever faced by a military planner: to reposition nearly 1 million tons of ammunition and supplies, 500,000 American troops of the U.S. First Army, and 2,000 pieces of artillery from the Saint-Mihiel sector in complete secrecy some sixty miles to the Meuse-Argonne, where a massive new Allied offensive was to be launched a mere ten days later. Marshall first had to devise a plan to displace 220,000 French troops from the front lines without tipping off the Germans. In the middle of the rainy season the sparse roads were a sea of mud, over which 90,000 horses labored to move equipment and supplies.

Another of Pershing's trusted subordinates, former AEF chief of staff and commander of the 2nd Division, Maj. Gen. James G. Harbord, wrote of Marshall in a 1936 memoir that he was "universally regarded as one of the most outstanding officers America developed in the World War."[9]

Marshall's experiences left him with an abhorrence of war and scars in the form of "a nervous tic that pulled the corner of his mouth into a strained smile when he was under pressure."[10] "There is nothing romantic, dramatic or satisfying in modern conflict. It is all horrible," he said. A widower renowned for his stone face and serious manner, there existed behind Marshall's public mask a fun-loving man possessing a great sense of humor. After he married Katherine Boyce Tupper Brown, herself a widow, in 1931, Marshall's second marriage brought him great contentment.

Marshall's relationship with Pershing served the same end as did Eisenhower's with Fox Conner. Like all senior officers, Pershing surrounded himself with men he implicitly trusted. Having demonstrated why he was one of the army's most promising officers, Marshall accepted an invitation to become Pershing's aide-de-camp, a post in which he served from 1919 to 1924. The two men grew even closer; Marshall was Pershing's most trusted subordinate, confidant, and his chief's eyes and ears. He served as Pershing's representative on various high-level boards and was given other tasks usually reserved for an officer of much higher rank. Marshall was also the go-between in a bitter feud that existed between Pershing and the autocratic Gen. Peyton March, the army chief of staff from 1918 to 1921, of whom Marshall said that he had "a weakness for antagonizing everybody." Marshall admired both men and thought each at fault.[11]

In 1923 Pershing spent six months based in Paris to visit battlefield cemeteries, work on his memoirs, and actively involve himself in the planning of war memorials. "During those months George Marshall [then a lieutenant colonel] held the chief of staff's office together. . . . Marshall knew the chief's mind, and everyone in the office accepted his decisions."[12]

At the time Pershing asked Marshall to review Eisenhower's opus, he was the assistant commandant of the infantry school at Fort Benning, and in charge of the academic program. By virtue of his position and the esteem in which he was held, Marshall exerted a powerful influence over many of the officers who would assume positions of high command and responsibility during World War II. During Marshall's tenure there from 1927 to 1932, more than two hundred future generals were either assigned or trained at the infantry school. He completely revamped the school's training program by reforming its outmoded curriculum, which, like that of interwar Leavenworth, was modeled on the trench warfare and set-piece battles of World War I. Marshall instituted practical training that emphasized fire, maneuver, and simplicity. Wars of movement, not siege warfare, became standard training for infantry officers. "He challenged and stretched the young professionals who came to Fort Benning as never before in their lives."[13] Gen. Omar Bradley served under Marshall as a tactics instructor. "He really established the standards of instruction as we know them today. We were allowed no notes. We had to know our subject so well that notes were unnecessary. . . . He insisted on simplicity and thoroughness. . . . He taught those lessons of World War I that were applicable to latter-day problems . . . and insisted that a maximum of our training take place on the ground, not in the classroom."[14]

Marshall's ultimate aim was nothing less than to professionalize the Regular Army. His experience, notes his official biographer, had taught him that change was necessary for the army to survive the next war. "With strong and revolutionary ideas . . . he had often itched to be just where he now found himself, in position to apply them to the training of young combat officers."[15] His own education "came primarily from constant study of his trade. He learned what made the Army work and then sought to improve the way in which it accomplished its purposes."[16]

Marshall was a deft talent spotter. Officers who impressed him had their names entered in an informal black notebook, along with notations listing their attributes. Among the names included were those of the foremost figures of World War II: Omar N. Bradley, Joseph Stilwell, Matthew B. Ridgway, George S. Patton, J. Lawton Collins, Walter Bedell "Beetle" Smith, Terry de la Mesa Allen, and, soon, that of Major Dwight Eisenhower.

During their first encounter Marshall declined to sit, instead standing throughout their entire conversation. Marshall explained that although he liked what Eisenhower had written, he would recommend against Pershing breaking up the diary format of his memoirs. To no avail Eisenhower briefly remonstrated that he still believed his idea for the two battle narratives was a good one. Pershing's memoir, duly published in 1931, won a Pulitzer Prize but went largely unread, in no small part because it was as dull and confusing as Eisenhower had predicted. Typically, when Eisenhower recounted their first meeting in his memoirs he declared that he still believed he had been right.[17]

Marshall's unfavorable reaction had little to do with the quality of Eisenhower's work and everything to do with protecting Pershing, whose vitriol against his enemies Marshall feared would rekindle unnecessary controversy. In the role of his former chief's "most honest critic," Marshall noted the enormous damage done to reputations in memoirs and reminiscences. "That strange compulsion of ego led droves of World War I figures to historical suicide. Once armed with pen and foolscap generals of judgment became contenders against their comrades for glory. Few, Marshall thought, emerged unsullied."[18] In the end Pershing proved no different, succumbing to the sin of revenge. Although he toned down some of his indignation, the memoir smacked of his unforgiving resentments.

Despite their personal differences over Pershing's book, Marshall was sufficiently impressed by Major Eisenhower to offer him a teaching post at the infantry school. Eisenhower, however, already had orders to the War Department General Staff and could not accept.

There was little in their lengthy initial encounter to indicate the powerful influence Marshall would eventually exert on Eisenhower's military career. It must have been unremarkable inasmuch as Eisenhower has left only the barest first impressions of the man who, like Fox Conner, was to shape his destiny. Although the two men would not meet again until early 1940, Eisenhower's name was one Marshall earmarked for the future.

18.

The Indispensable Staff Officer

. . . one of the coming men of the Army.
—MAJ. GEN. GEORGE VAN HORN MOSELEY

America in the 1930s was the antithesis of the hedonistic Roaring Twenties. Not only were the good times over, but the nation was firmly in the grip of the Great Depression, with no end to America's economic woes in sight. The War Department General Staff during the interwar years was a lean organization consisting of approximately one hundred officers, most hand-picked for their jobs. Eisenhower's boss, Brig. Gen. George Van Horn Moseley, was a disciple of Pershing and had served as the AEF's chief logistician. Eisenhower greatly respected Moseley, and the two officers warmed to each other from the outset. Eisenhower was appreciated for his talents as never before. Moseley was fond of referring to him as "my brainy assistant," and "one of the coming men of the Army."[1] On his first efficiency report Moseley not only rated Eisenhower "superior" but noted that "No limit should be placed on this officer" in peace or war. "A powerful, thick-set fellow with a strong personality, able to put over his ideas very tactfully. He represents the best type of Regular Army officer."[2]

Moseley "has been my most intimate friend . . . a wonderful officer—a splendid gentleman," Eisenhower noted in his diary. "Mentally honest and with great moral courage he is well equipped for any task this govt. can possibly give him."

Moseley's praise notwithstanding, in 1930 Eisenhower had been a major for a decade, and his future prospects were grim. The army had yet to institute a formal system of officer promotions. Seniority ruled, which meant that it was virtually impossible for fresh, younger talent to gain promotion to the top rungs of the peacetime army. In the ranks of colonel and below, promotion was considered automatic, "if one lived that long."[3] Career officers like Eisenhower languished, were aging fast, and had little expectation of ever again plying their trade in battle. Promotions were so dismally slow that it became a standing joke that the obituary columns provided a source of hope whenever a senior officer died. (Patton once informed his wife, "General so-and-so died today and every colonel in Washington is like a wolf bitch in heat, waiting to see who will step up into his slot.")[4]

The whims and prejudices of senior officer promotions were the province of the chief of staff, who had the power to punish or reward a favored few. The "selectionists" were the minority within the army who fervently believed that the selection and promotion of officers ought to be based on merit, not seniority. A fervent selectionist himself, Eisenhower approved of Moseley's practice of reaching out to utilize his subordinates in a manner that did not always follow the traditional and rather rigid staff protocols. It was, Eisenhower gleefully wrote, "a trait that grinds the soul of some of our 'so-called' Gen.[eral] staff people, particularly those whose god is 'ritual.'" When Moseley was promoted to deputy chief of staff in late 1931, he officially commended Eisenhower: "What a great blessing you have been!"[5]

Mobilization became the focus of Eisenhower's assignment. As the newest member of the War Department staff, the issues he dealt with were complex and politically explosive. America's most glaring crisis during World War I had been emergency mobilization. Not only was there a lack of modern weapons and equipment, but there existed an antiquated and chaotic peacetime supply system unable to cope with the requirements of modern war. The resulting civilian industrial mobilization had been the most monumental undertaking in American history, and—in the wake of the Wilsonian vision of world peace through the League of Nations—there was an unheard minority voice in Washington that remembered that World War I was a lesson in unpreparedness that must not be repeated.

One of the strongest proponents of preparedness, Moseley believed that the same problems would inevitably recur in a future war unless the army took matters into its own hands. He assigned Eisenhower a key role in drawing up an industrial mobilization plan for the army. "Eisenhower was thrilled to find he was in at the start of something new and important."[6] His familiarity with the problems of mobilization, learned at the War College, began to pay off. He wrote detailed memorandums, letters, and position papers packed with facts, figures, and a clear rationale for his superiors. Eisenhower became so proficient at his job that he often testified on behalf of the army before congressional committees.

It hardly mattered that Eisenhower knew next to nothing about some of the subjects he was assigned to investigate. In the spring of 1930, for example, he was dispatched on a monthlong trip to California, Texas, and Mexico to investigate the guayule rubber industry. The guayule bush, a plentiful desert shrub native to the deserts of northern Mexico, has a high rubber content. Over the years unsuccessful attempts had been made by the rubber industry to grow the shrub in the southwestern United States, and to extract from it a usable rubber product. The army was interested in its wartime potential and sent Eisenhower and a colleague to investigate. The trip was tiring, physically unpleasant, and ultimately unproductive, when it was determined that guayule was not a viable option. During visits to American and Mexican facilities, Eisenhower generally wore his tattered old suit and paid for it by sweltering in the intense heat and humidity. His report to the War Department was a detailed assessment of a complex issue about which, as John Eisenhower notes, "Dad didn't have the first clue." Anyone reading Eisenhower's report, however, would naturally have concluded that he was an expert on the subject.

Since the National Defense Act of 1920, the army's earnest attempt to develop and maintain war plans was met by roadblocks, most of them within the government itself. No one was interested in what was derided as "militarism." "In the mood of 'never again' which characterized interwar America, there was general public agreement that the next war, if there was a next war, would come only in the event of a direct invasion of the United States. Such a prospect seemed faintly incredible."[7] Army planners were also faced with the reluctance of any interwar administration to provide the strategic guidance necessary for them to develop meaningful plans. "The interwar years saw the apogee of the peculiar American notion that 'political' and 'military' considerations both can and should be divorced. . . . Army leaders often complained about the difficulties involved in framing military plans in a vacuum: State Department leaders . . . feared the taint of 'militarism' and steadfastly refused to participate in joint planning bodies."[8]

In 1930 pacifist sentiments swayed Congress into enacting legislation creating a high-level War Policies Commission, whose mission was not only to create government programs to be implemented in wartime but also to develop guidelines to prevent war profiteering. Chaired by Secretary of War Patrick J. Hurley, the commission consisted of senators, representatives, and cabinet officers. At issue was a controversial proposal by some of its members to deter profiteering by seizing private property for war production. Idealism and the move toward pacifism were also endorsed by some veterans' organizations and civilians who decried war and demanded an end to rampant wartime profiteering. The peace faction, wrote Eisenhower, "insisted that to admit the possibility of war was to make war more likely, and helped to make our people 'war-minded.' "[9]

Eisenhower was assigned to work with the commission. He described his duties as "sort of a 'working' secretary but with no official title or authority." Eisenhower was, in fact, its de facto executive secretary. The officially appointed executive secretary was Robert H. Montgomery, a New York lawyer and former army officer who had served on the General Staff during World

War I. Montgomery was something of a figurehead who was present only part-time. The day-to-day drudge work of the commission was supervised by Eisenhower, who was secretary in all but name.[10]

In November 1930 Gen. Charles P. Summerall ended his contentious stewardship of the army and was replaced as chief of staff by MacArthur.[11] As the army's youngest-ever chief of staff, MacArthur swept into the office like a breath of fresh air after the dour Summerall. MacArthur brought a wealth of sound ideas, genuinely fought for military preparedness, and was open-minded about new innovations even if there were no funds to finance them. One of MacArthur's first acts was to end the petty bickering indulged in by his predecessor.

MacArthur was charged with submitting to the commission the War Department's so-called secret mobilization plan, which had never been written. A plan had to be created, and the task—a difficult and demanding one that required a thorough understanding of how the U.S. economy worked, and how key industries could and should be utilized in wartime—was assigned to Moseley and Eisenhower, who submitted a document that addressed a complex range of subjects including price controls, selective service, and the agencies necessary to control civilian industry.[12] As the principal author, Eisenhower attacked the mobilization study with his usual vigor and presented his superiors with a thorough analysis of the problems and recommended solutions. Those who sought MacArthur's advice were invariably sent to see Eisenhower.

Eisenhower's and the army's challenge was to prepare the country for a future war at the worst possible time. The economy was at rock bottom, businesses were in disarray or bankruptcy, and hardly anyone outside of the War Department cared about military preparedness. The last thing on anyone's mind was pursuing the impossible. Eisenhower's task was made all the more difficult by the poisonous atmosphere within the War Department, which was still rife with internecine squabbles and rivalries, at least one of which threatened to scuttle the study.

Eisenhower traveled throughout the United States to tour manufacturing plants and confer with some of the country's leading industrialists, who included the presidents of the Baltimore & Ohio Railroad and the American Telephone & Telegraph Company. However, Eisenhower's attempts to interest American businessmen in the production, transportation, and control of war matériel in wartime was an exercise in futility. Economic depression, combined with the lethargy Eisenhower encountered in men who simply could not envision a future war, made his task even more difficult. Even so, Eisenhower's experience left him uniquely equipped to spearhead the mobilization plan. Indeed, Eisenhower's work was so effective that it contributed to MacArthur's decision to promote Moseley to deputy chief of staff.

Eisenhower played a key role in the preparation of MacArthur's twenty-four-page policy statement to the War Policies Commission, delivered in May 1931. "I worked for ten days (and nights) getting it ready," he recorded in his diary.[13] Among the report's most pointed observations was, "The [War] Department holds to the belief, so often reiterated by our first President, that *a reasonable preparation for defense is one of the best guarantees of peace. . . . The objective of any warring nation is victory, immediate and complete.*"

The Hoover administration paid mere lip service to the commission's work. Hoover personally disapproved of its work, and the completed commission report never even made it into his in-basket. "It came back from one of his staff," remembered Eisenhower, "saying that the President was far too busy to read such drivel as this—'that the Government is not thinking of a future war and has no intention of doing so.' "[14] In 1932, on behalf of the War Department, Eisenhower drafted a joint resolution of Congress for Sen. Arthur Vandenberg that would outlaw price-fixing and profiteering in wartime.

The acclaim accorded the citizen soldiers who had fought and died in France was by the 1930s a distant memory. The Depression's accompanying national despair diminished the role of the military to new lows in the order of government priorities, as budgetary cutbacks continued to prevent its modernization. Many units existed on paper only or were so woefully understaffed that they were completely ineffective as a fighting force. According to historian Russell F. Weigley, "The Army during the 1920's and 1930's may have been less ready to function as a fighting force than at any time in its history. It lacked even the combat capacity that the Indian campaigns had forced on it during the nineteenth century."[15]

The 1930s were not only the greatest economic catastrophe in American history but also a decade in which the world was becoming increasingly unstable. The Russian Revolution that produced Lenin and Stalin gave rise to a revulsion in the United States to anything that smacked of Communism. Fear of a "Red menace" swept the nation and in the process brought to the forefront bigots and ordinary citizens brainwashed into believing that America was in serious danger. The United States also became fertile ground for Communist labor organizers, who infiltrated the unions but failed to incite working-class Americans more interested in jobs than a revolution.

MacArthur's official biographer points out, "During MacArthur's term as chief of staff [from 1930 to 1935] most of the members of the General Staff probably viewed all outbursts of violence and unrest with red-tinted glasses."[16] Not surprisingly, while the military profession as a whole preached loyalty and the tenets of West Point, within the War Department there were some who saw the alarming spread of Communism as a genuine national threat. Among the chief proponents of this view was Moseley, who advocated army preparedness to deal with a potential Communist uprising. Communism must be stopped in its tracks, he warned. The government, he said, should deal with its radical leaders, preferably by exiling them. Moseley went so far as to propose to MacArthur that criminals and undesirables be exiled to one of the Hawaiian Islands to await deportation. Moseley was not alone in promoting such stern measures, merely the most vocal. "Moseley was an embarrassment to the Army," concludes historian Geoffrey Perret.[17] No matter that Eisenhower must have found Moseley's views personally repugnant; he nevertheless rationalized his superior's virulent anti-Semitism and concluded that Moseley's virtues as an army officer far outweighed his flaws.[18]

As he would later, as a politician during the McCarthy era, Eisenhower kept his thoughts about such controversial subjects to himself, although his own views can clearly be discerned in a 1931 article, "War Policies," published in the *Cavalry Journal*, based on his experience with the War Policies Commission.

Pointedly referring to the dovish element of the commission, Eisenhower wrote (without editorial comment but clearly disapprovingly), "Among those who confined their attention almost exclusively to methods for preventing war were a retired admiral of the Navy, two ministers of the Gospel, a leader of the Socialist party, an ocultist, editors of magazines of so-called 'pacifist' leanings, and officials of various peace associations."[19]

Eisenhower's none-too-subtle opinion was merely a reflection of the men of his profession, virtually all of whom were embittered by the verbal brickbats from business and academic liberals and pacifists, and whose leanings were to the right. The military felt alone in a surreal wilderness and cut off from society, which failed to take into account the rise of fascism in Germany and Italy and the expansionist threat in Asia posed by an increasingly militant Japan.

In the spring of 1930 Eisenhower began working for a new assistant secretary, Frederick H. Payne, a self-made millionaire and a man whom Eisenhower described as "an old-line Republican. Anti-prohibitionist . . . [possessed of] lots of common sense and very shrewd."[20] Eisenhower's reputation as a can-do officer was now well established and earned him valuable recognition even though his duties were both endless and largely thankless. After completing his mobilization study, Eisenhower wrote speeches for Payne and Secretary of War Patrick Hurley, drafted letters and memos, and advised when asked, which was with increasing frequency. Virtually anything of merit was probably written by Eisenhower. By the end of his tour under Payne and

Moseley, Eisenhower had become an expert in every aspect of mobilization. "He learned supply from the factory up, and knew by heart production man-hours on everything from a bomber to a mess kit."[21]

During the Washington years Eisenhower's greatest asset was his pen. He authored anything of substance created by MacArthur or the office of the assistant secretary, be it speeches, letters, reports, or staff studies. Despite the drudgery of such staff work, Eisenhower was at the right place and time to be at the forefront of American military policy in the 1930s, an experience he would assimilate and draw on in World War II. Despite his rather lowly status as a very junior General Staff officer, in an era when the General Staff was markedly unpopular on Capitol Hill, congressmen and senators were in the habit of contacting Eisenhower directly on matters concerning the War Department.

When it came to manipulating and taking advantage of the bureaucracy, Eisenhower had no peer. He developed a political awareness and a thorough understanding of what it took to survive in the higher reaches of the military and political jungle of the 1930s. However, Eisenhower's efficiency as a General Staff officer came at a price. His type A personality, with its explosive temper and relentless intensity in his work took a heavy toll on his health. Photographs taken at the time reflect a man apparently in the peak of health. Yet he was anything but robust. Among the various ailments for which he sought treatment were: bursitis in his left shoulder, acute gastroenteritis, colitis, hemorrhoids, influenza, tonsillitis, an acute intestinal obstruction, constipation, mild arthritis, kidney problems, dental disease, recurrent pain in his damaged knee, and, worst of all, severe back pain. His eyesight was affected by long hours of paperwork, and his prescription was increased.

In 1931 he noted "lots of troubles with my insides lately. Have been bothered for 5–6 years with something that seems to border on dysentery," which baffled his doctors, who could "find nothing wrong with my insides."[22] Although his ailing back disrupted his performance of duty, sometimes seriously, Eisenhower soldiered on, complaining only to the doctors about his medical problems. By 1932 he had begun to experience recurring back pain, which continued to bother him even though the army doctors were unable to arrive at a conclusive diagnosis or ease his pain.[23] That his health continued to plague him during the Washington years is no surprise and can be attributed to the fact that Eisenhower was seriously overworked by superiors eager to take advantage of his impressive staff work, clear thinking, and exceptional writing ability. The prevailing attitude seemed to be "let Eisenhower do it," and the result was excessive hours of toil.

He not only worked six days per week, but even Sunday was rarely a day of relaxation. Whenever Mamie remonstrated that he worked too hard, and reminded him that his fellow officers were not so inclined, Eisenhower would not only ignore her but sometimes forsake his guests during a social gathering to complete his night work in the bedroom.

Mamie remembered Washington in the 1930s as "an overgrown country town" where "carfare was still five cents. . . . I'd watch the senators and all the ambassadors stand and wait for the streetcar. Nobody ever thought of taking a taxi." The Eisenhowers were obliged to socialize with increasing frequency, sometimes as often as four nights a week. Ike and Mamie willingly played by the rules of social etiquette, which required that dinner invitations be promptly reciprocated. On one occasion they felt obliged to repay Patrick Hurley and his wife by hosting them for dinner at the posh Willard Hotel, complete with flowers. The cost of the evening nearly broke the family bank.[24] To save money Eisenhower would wait until Christmas Eve, when prices were cheaper, to purchase a tree. He and John would drag it home and trim it.

After many years of observing the good life enjoyed by other, financially more successful men, Eisenhower had developed more expensive tastes, which, on his pay of $391 per month, were rigidly curbed by Mamie. There was never enough money. "I still don't know how I did it," she recalled. "I gave Ike five dollars a week, and that was supposed to pay for his carfare and his lunches."[25] Eisenhower was pleased if he could scrape up enough cash to purchase cigarettes and razor blades.

Eisenhower family life in the 1930s could best be described as leisurely in the middle of genteel poverty. Military personnel assigned to Washington normally wore civilian clothes and kept a low profile, and after the fiasco in San Antonio, Mamie had taken charge of her husband's wardrobe and bought all his civilian clothes.

One of the brightest aspects of life in Washington was the continued bonding between Milton and Dwight and their wives. The two couples were inseparable, getting together three or four times a week, usually to play bridge. Milton's career had continued to soar in the Department of Agriculture, and within the War Department, Ike's name had begun to command attention.

Although an ideal staff officer, Eisenhower was never content with such assignments. The highest aspiration of a professional officer to is attain command; failing that, troop duty in some capacity. Eisenhower was no exception, but having been identified in the highest councils of the War Department as a comer, he had no chance of fulfilling his dream during the 1930s. Mamie could only sympathize with her husband's frustration. "They were always looking for somebody that was capable. So he became a staff officer, which just irked him frightfully because he wanted to be a fighter."[26] As his prestige grew, his chances for troop duty all but vanished.

Eisenhower generally left his problems at the office. Mamie noted, "When he came home, he was home and we didn't discuss what his big problems were . . . that was the way we managed our lives . . . so many people said to me, 'Didn't General Eisenhower used to talk over some of his problems with you?' And I'd say, 'Well, no.' "[27] After some fifteen years of marriage, their roles were solidly etched into an unfailing routine: Mamie ran the home, and Ike performed his duties at the office.

Throughout their marriage Eisenhower was rarely demonstrative about expressing his feelings for Mamie, and she never pressed him to do so. An exception was their fifteenth anniversary, in 1931, when Eisenhower scrawled a brief note that managed to indicate yet again how difficult it would always be for him to articulate his feelings. "Darling: July 1 is a reminder to me that my good fortune in getting you has borne interest for another twelve months. That you have stood me for fifteen years is only another proof that you are the outstanding woman in the world—and since you love me—you are all the *world* to me."[28] The implicit words "I love you" remained bottled up inside. Mamie's thirty-eighth birthday in November 1934 was a rare and memorable treat. "What a birthday I had," she exulted. "We marched with Ike & I singing and John playing the harmonica."[29]

Dinner-table conversation often revolved around John's academic progress. Eisenhower would quiz him relentlessly about school: "We practically had school at the dinner table." John developed his father's love of history at an early age. "He was a great reader. . . . I can remember when he was studying Roman history, he made shields and helmets . . . out of pasteboard." He was also fascinated by the *Book of Knowledge*, a multivolume encyclopedia that became a mainstay of John's reading.

John was reunited with his boyhood friend Bo Horkan, who was a frequent visitor to the Eisenhower apartment. Once—when one of their concoctions "blew all over the kitchen. Green foam was dripping off the ceiling and it was a mess"—an experiment with John's chemical set produced a minor disaster. Mamie was "fairly unhappy about it," recalled Horkan, but Eisenhower was more amused than angry. "He thought it reflected the creative approach to things. John and I were very pleased with that reaction, because he could be right severe on occasion."[30]

John sometimes visited Abilene in the summer, but mostly he spent his time in Denver, where the Doud home remained as depressing as ever. He had long since wearied of the frequent, maudlin visits to the cemetery and far preferred visiting his paternal grandparents in Abilene, where the atmosphere was congenial and informal. He was entranced by Ida's tales of his father and the other five Eisenhower "hellions."[31] Hints to the Douds about the good times he enjoyed in Abilene fell on deaf ears. "They would say, 'Of course, it is just a hick town.' " Once, when John became ill during a visit to Denver, Mamie demonstrated her growing maturity by calmly reassuring her parents that he was in good hands.[32]

Except for those like Patton, whose wife's wealth permitted him to live a lavish lifestyle, underpaid army officers like Eisenhower usually entertained at home during the worst years of the depression, with an inner circle of close friends with whom they could relax and let their hair down. Young John became a favorite of his father's visiting friends, who adopted him as their mascot.[33] Occasionally he was permitted to join the group for short intervals before being exiled to his bedroom, where, to his delight, Gee Gerow, Ham Haislip, or P. A. Hodgson would sometimes break away from the festivities to chat with him. A great favorite was Major Everett S. Hughes, an ordnance officer and Ike's classmate at the War College. "Uncle" Everett was fond of extolling Eisenhower's attributes to his son. " 'Your father is a man to watch!' he admonished me one evening. I agreed, but in the light of the Old Man's disciplinary policies, I probably interpreted the statement a little differently from the way it was intended."[34]

On the rare occasions he found time to play golf, Eisenhower gave new meaning to the term "hacker." Piles of sand were substituted for tees, and his aggressive swing mimicked his temperament. His ball, said John, "seemed to wind up in the alfalfa an inordinate amount of the time, the air punctuated with certain expletives that I had thought were unknown to adults—only to kids."[35]

Beginning in 1929, Eisenhower had renewed his friendship with George Patton. The Eisenhowers were frequent guests in the Pattons' spacious, six-bedroom mansion in northwest Washington, complete with nine servants. Their rich social agenda served as a glaring reminder to Eisenhower of the significant disparity between being rich and poor. Whereas the Pattons engaged in fox hunting, polo, horseshoes, steeplechasing, sailing on the Potomac, and lavishly entertaining Washington VIPs, the Eisenhowers were limited to the modest activities of Club Eisenhower. As John later remembered:

> I always held the Pattons in considerable awe, because of their obvious wealth and the fact that Patton was a lieutenant colonel while Dad was a major. Silver horsemanship trophies covered a complete wall in the living room of their quarters. Patton was a good-humored man who loved to joke. His language was full of the purple expressions for which he later became famous. I was astonished that he not only swore profusely around ladies but also encouraged all three of his children to do the same. When young George, a fine boy slightly younger than I, would come out with an appropriate piece of blasphemy, Patton would roar with pleasure.[36]

One of the many people Eisenhower met in Washington was Harry Butcher, who would become his close friend of forty-three years and his trusted naval aide and confidant in World War II. Butcher, an Iowan, had previously edited the *Fertilizer Review* before moving to Washington, where he became chief of the Washington bureau of the Columbia Broadcasting

System, thanks to the right introductions from Milton in 1926. Eisenhower and "Butch" often played golf together. Butcher recalled a time when Eisenhower attempted to drive his golf ball over a high stone wall only to have it ricochet right back at his head like a rocket.[37]

The first time they met socially, Eisenhower demonstrated a parlor trick that reflected a side of his personality only his intimates ever saw. "Standing at rigid attention, hands at sides, Ike would fall forward like a wooden soldier. An instant before it looked . . . as though his face would be smashed against the floor, his hands would flash forward to cushion the fall." (It was a trick he still performed on occasion during World War II.)[38]

From the time of their first meeting Butcher recalls being impressed with Eisenhower's rapt concentration and intensity. Even in such horseplay as his parlor trick, "he had complete mental control of his body. When he sang 'Abdul' you would have thought there was nothing in the world he had ever done or wanted to do but sing 'Abdul.' . . . Playing bridge, his favorite . . . sport, he could determine after the first round of bidding with astounding accuracy the number of cards of each suit held by the other three players. . . . By the time the party broke up, we all felt we had known Ike for years."[39]

The Great Depression validated Eisenhower's decision to remain in the army, despite a 10 percent pay cut mandated by the Hoover administration, and later, another cut by the new Roosevelt administration. Such was its toll that when many of the tenants of the Wyoming could no longer afford the rent, the owners became insolvent and sold out. Thanks to John Doud's monthly stipend and the reduced rents charged by the new landlords, the hit on the Eisenhower finances was minimal.

Nevertheless Eisenhower and Patton were hardly alone in wondering why they did not resign their commissions. Eisenhower's reputation as a superb writer came to the attention of publishing magnate William Randolph Hearst, who sensed the war clouds in both the Pacific and Europe, and endeavored to lure Eisenhower into resigning from the army with an offer to become the military correspondent for his newspaper chain. Hearst offered a salary of between fifteen and twenty thousand dollars per year, a princely sum more than triple his army pay, and an opportunity to escape the military life forever. Eisenhower was tempted by the prospect of being financially self-sufficient for the first time in his life, however, after consulting Milton, he summarily turned down the offer, in part because of John Doud's continuing financial support of the family, but primarily out of the conviction that Fox Conner's prophecy of the inevitability of another world war was about to come true.

His decision came at a time when Eisenhower was discouraged to witness the deliberate disregard of America's national interests in favor of a tenuous peace that he believed had no chance of working. With Conner's prediction echoing in his mind, Eisenhower was damned if he would miss another war as he had in 1918. For better or worse he had cast his lot in a dubious career that seemed to promise only overwork, disappointment, and continued penury. Eisenhower's decision was the turning point of his military career. "Moments such as this are the defining acts in a man's life," writes Geoffrey Perret, "and his was the kind of reaction nearly everyone would want to be judged by."[40]

After a leisurely two-month leave in the summer of 1931, Eisenhower resumed his writing duties for the top brass in the War Department. He wrote numerous speeches for Payne, including the 1931 commencement address the secretary delivered at West Point. Eisenhower also authored the annual reports of Payne, Hurley, and MacArthur, and wrote with evident pride in his diary, "All went through as written—and I received from Gen. MacA. a very splendid letter of Commendation. Mamie had it framed!!!"[41] All the while Eisenhower was taking the measure of the men he served. Few passed muster. In June 1932 he wrote the first entry in a diary he kept for the remainder of his service in Washington.

His first entries, penned in 1932 and 1933 were called "Notes on Men."[42] Eisenhower seemed to delight in his contempt for many of the general staff. A mental exercise it may have been, but it was also a reflection of his intolerance of those who did not measure up to his high standards of professional competence.

While some, including generals Moseley, Hugh Drum, W. D. Connor, and Fox Conner, earned Eisenhower's unqualified acclaim, others came in for scathing criticism or condescending recognition. Although he regarded these private thoughts as little more than a useful diversion, they were also deadly serious evaluations.

Public backlash from the crash of 1929 was resounding in the presidential election of 1932. Not only was Hoover ousted by Franklin Delano Roosevelt, but the Democrats also won both houses of Congress. As Roosevelt grappled with restoring economic stability, few paid attention in the early 1930s to the danger signals emanating from a troubled interwar Europe, where a new menace called Nazism was sweeping Germany. As troop reductions and budget cuts continued to plague the American military, the Nazi party, led by an obscure former corporal named Adolf Hitler, came to power in 1933, ushering in the era of the dictator and what one historian has aptly called "the nightmare decade," with "a terrible inevitability about the collapse of the world order after 1930."[43]

MacArthur's most difficult task as chief of staff was merely to hold the army together and stave off repeated attempts to decimate the army budget appropriation in 1934 by $90 million. Eisenhower praised MacArthur for persuading the Roosevelt administration to restore the funds and to add another $40 million, but questioned a proposal to shift procurement to the Treasury Department, a bureaucracy he deemed incapable of functioning effectively in wartime. "My God, but we have a lot of theorists and academicians in the administration," he bemoaned. The army never received the projected increase because the budgetmeisters directed the War Department to spend $91 million less than their approved total.

Eisenhower began to show a political awareness not previously evident. His duties had brought him into contact with many of the country's movers and shakers. He mingled with businessmen, senators, congressmen, industrialists, and financiers. One was influential millionaire Wall Street speculator and sometime presidential adviser Bernard M. Baruch, who headed the War Industries Board during World War I. Eisenhower frequently conferred with Baruch, and the two became lifelong friends. Although Baruch was conservative and anti–New Deal, he and FDR nevertheless used each other to the mutual benefit of the nation. Baruch, who urged the implementation of strict price controls during wartime and was a supporter of the army, exerted considerable influence in Congress.

Like most professional soldiers, Eisenhower was not known to have voted in an election. Outside his family and close friends, he was strictly apolitical in public and kept his opinions to himself. Roosevelt was not particularly well thought of within the military, and not surprisingly Eisenhower once strongly hinted to his son his preference for the reelection of Herbert Hoover over his challenger. Eisenhower remained unimpressed with FDR and after World War II made no secret of his disapproval of Roosevelt's New Deal economic agenda.[44] After one of Roosevelt's famous fireside chats on the radio in 1934, he addressed a woman who had effusively praised the president's speech, saying how she had understood every word by replying, "Well, I'm happy for you, because I didn't understand one word of it myself." On another occasion he opined, "I think Mr. Roosevelt is a mediocre man who has a pleasant-sounding voice on the radio."[45]

However reluctantly, Eisenhower nevertheless privately approved of FDR's election, writing, "While I have no definite leanings toward any political party I believe it is a good thing the Democrats won—and particularly that one party will have such overwhelming superiority in Congress."

In February 1933 he wrote, "But right now, I'm going to make one prediction. Things are not going to take an upturn until more power is centered in one man's hands. . . . For two years I have been called 'Dictator Ike' because I believe virtual dictatorship must be exercised by our President. So now I keep still—but I still believe it!"[46]

Eisenhower got his wish with the inauguration of Roosevelt and the New Deal. He expected that big cuts in government and tighter control of the economy were on the way and applauded their necessity. "My own salary will be cut some more if these things come to pass. I cannot afford it, and will have to ask for relief from this city. Nevertheless he [Roosevelt] *should* do it—and if he doesn't I'll be disappointed in him."

Never one to back away from a confrontation, particularly when it involved his brothers, he engaged in many heated arguments during their occasional visits. During a reunion in Washington in 1934 between Dwight, Milton, Earl, and Edgar, sparks flew when the irascible brothers debated the merits of the New Deal. Edgar was by far the most conservative of the brothers and became so incensed with Earl, an avid Roosevelt supporter, that he ridiculed him for being as politically "red" as his hair. For Earl's new wife, who accompanied him to Washington, it was an eye-opening introduction to the fighting Eisenhower brothers.[47]

His diary continued to reflect his conceptions of the role of government in the economic crisis, and in support of FDR's initiatives. He was amused at what he saw as the contradiction of the New Deal, noting that "the word 'dictator' has always (and properly) been anathema to the Average American. So today, when in some respects we have the strongest possible form of dictatorship—we go to great lengths to congratulate ourselves that *we* have not fallen for the terrible systems in vogue in Italy, Germany, Turkey, Poland, etc. . . . unity of action is essential . . . individual right must be subordinate to public good. . . . We *must* conform to the President's program regardless of consequences. Otherwise dissension, confusion and partisan politics will ruin us."[48]

One of the effects of his service in the War Department was Eisenhower's ever-expanding knowledge of the U.S. economy and a confidence in his private opinions. Before long MacArthur, too, had begun to appreciate the unique talents of Major Eisenhower and started to utilize them. Although he was still assigned to Payne's office, throughout 1932 his duties were more and more as MacArthur's unofficial principal assistant. "Here is a man I should always like to have with me," Payne pleaded somewhat plaintively in Eisenhower's efficiency report in June 1932. If they had had the authority, Payne and Moseley would have promoted Eisenhower from major directly to brigadier general. When Republican Frederick Payne resigned to return to Massachusetts in the wake of Roosevelt's election, MacArthur used the occasion to appropriate Eisenhower's services exclusively for himself.[49]

Eisenhower was shortly due for troop duty, and Mamie was anxious for him to seek a return assignment to Fort Sam Houston in order to be near the Doud winter home. In early 1932 Eisenhower received two offers of new duty, one from William D. Connor to accompany him to West Point and become manager of athletics the following year; the other was an assignment to Fort Leavenworth in the dual capacity of instructor and commander of an infantry battalion. Eisenhower was lukewarm about returning to Leavenworth and had scant interest in an assignment to West Point. He happily noted in his diary that both were disapproved by Moseley and MacArthur.[50]

Even though a return to troop duty was both desirable and essential, Eisenhower was also unenthusiastic about returning to Texas: "I hate the heat." Nonetheless, he asked for Fort Sam "only after a long struggle" with Mamie, who longed to settle in a place where she was emotionally comfortable, and servants cheaper and more plentiful than in Washington. Although he was by now sick of staff duty in Washington and a change of scene seemed a wise career move, Eisenhower decided the lesser of two evils was to remain where he was. "Dad, mother [the Douds], and Mamie have talked about S[an] A[ntonio] until it is apparent they're going to be all down in the mouth with any other selection. So I *asked* for it." What Eisenhower had not told his family was that he secretly hoped his request would be turned down.

Indeed, Moseley and MacArthur had no trouble persuading Eisenhower to remain in Washington. MacArthur disingenuously dangled the prospect of the command of nearby Fort Washington the following year. By eagerly accepting, Eisenhower willingly allowed himself to be hoodwinked by MacArthur, knowing full well that it was inconceivable for him to have been promoted from major to full colonel by 1933. Still, he readily succumbed to MacArthur's praise "without a murmur of protest," and accepted his offer to become his assistant, rationalizing that it made him proud to feel wanted. "Gen. MacA. was very nice to me—and after all I know of no greater compliment the bosses can give you than I want you hanging around."[51]

Eisenhower himself was disingenuous when he alleged that his retention in Washington was a great surprise, blaming it on MacArthur's need for his services. "It is an opportunity that comes rarely," he wrote to Pupah.[52]

The Douds were disappointed, but, as Mamie wrote, army life was unpredictable and, "although it was a shock to us," it was "a marvelous compliment to Ike"; they could be "loads worse off." Moreover, should war erupt in China, as then seemed possible, Ike would be in precisely the right place to become involved. "It would kill him," she wrote, "if another war broke out and he didn't get in it."[53]

In February 1933 Eisenhower formally commenced what would be nearly seven years as a staff officer and principal assistant to MacArthur in Washington and Manila. They would be among the most frustrating years of his military career.

19.

"Shame! Shame!"

I told that dumb son-of-a-bitch he had no business going down there.

As the United States entered the 1930s, the breadline and the soup kitchen had become national symbols of the Great Depression. The inane 1928 Republican Party slogans ("A Chicken in Every Pot" and "Two Cars in Every Garage") had by then been shown to be meaningless rhetoric. In the summer of 1932, with the nation at an economic low, joblessness, unrest, and privation became catalysts for the Bonus March on Washington.

Although still officially assigned to Secretary Payne's office, Eisenhower had long since become MacArthur's de facto military secretary. In July 1932 he found himself involved in the most personally repugnant and controversial incident of his military service under MacArthur.

In 1924 Congress had voted to award to some 3.5 million veterans what were called Adjusted Compensation Certificates—basically bonds masquerading as a thousand-dollar bonus due to mature in 1945 (or on the death of the holder). The veterans believed that their government had betrayed them in their hour of need by failing to pay the promised compensation for their war service. For some it was the only asset they possessed. An unsympathetic Hoover administration turned a blind eye to the plight of the veterans and never even considered paying the bonus, wishing they would simply go away. When the veterans began to mount organized protests, they were stonewalled in the ill-advised belief that to react would inevitably lead to even further unrest.

During the winter of 1931–32 their discontent was widely reported in the press, and various veterans' groups across the United States began supporting a march on Washington to lobby Congress and to demonstrate their solidarity.[1] A bill to pay the bonus, introduced by Rep. Wright Patman of Texas, provided a ray of hope that was eventually shattered. Destitute veterans, many of them homeless, had already begun turning up at Fort Myer, Virginia, where benevolent soldiers paid small sums from their monthly wage to help support the hiring of some to perform menial kitchen and stable duties.

By May 1932 what had begun as a trickle had reached an estimated ten to seventeen thousand men who converged on Washington, some with their families, but virtually all with no place to live and no money for food or accommodations.[2] A few squatted in unoccupied, condemned buildings along Pennsylvania Avenue, not far from the White House. The largest contingent created an enormous shantytown in the Anacostia mudflats, officially called Camp Marks but better known as "the Flats" or "Hooverville." In a strange twist, their squalid settlement became a bizarre tourist attraction.

The Bonus March took place hard on the heels of earlier protests in Washington and elsewhere, which Communists participated in and sometimes dominated. "Thus when the Bonus Army began to arrive in May, swelling in numbers daily, it seemed to many federal officials that the battle of Armageddon was at hand," notes MacArthur's official biographer. "The President and his military leaders saw thousands of Red revolutionaries entrenching themselves within the bounds of the national capitol. Others saw only a pitiful horde of ragged veterans exhausted by futility and near starvation." The two leading officers in the War Department, MacArthur and Moseley, despised Communists and equated pacifists as a similar evil. Both were convinced that the march was part of a seditious plot "to incite revolutionary action."[3]

MacArthur, who had initially rejected Moseley's arguments that the army must prepare for action, then reversed himself and seized on the alleged threat posed by the tiny Communist element, exhorting Hurley to do something about the bonus marchers, for whom he had little sympathy. In Secretary of War Hurley, MacArthur found a sympathetic ear. Perhaps the most callous government official of all, Hurley has been described as "driven by naked ambition for money, fame, and power. Having become a millionaire before he was thirty, he had little or no patience with the bonus marchers, considering them pathetic losers in the struggle of life."[4] Eisenhower had certainly taken Hurley's measure, opining in his diary: "He is not big enough to go higher. Unquestionably he has decided that his one chance of political advancement is as a henchman of Pres. Hoover. Consequently in public utterances he is slavish in his support of the Pres. He is jealous and unstable."[5]

Except for several hundred reactionary veterans (led by two known Communists), the marchers had organized themselves into a paramilitary organization called the Bonus Expeditionary Force (BEF), which was led by Walter W. Waters, a respected combat veteran. The BEF was committed to the attainment of its goals by peaceful means and was policed by its own members, thus becoming an army of sorts.

Veterans haunted Capitol Hill, demonstrating and lobbying Congress, hoping to drum up support. Some congressmen were sympathetic, but as is so often the case, the House and Senate could not agree on compromise legislation. Patman's House bill, which would have fed and sheltered the men of the BEF and paid the bonus, failed. As the weeks passed, tensions grew and Congress dithered and then adjourned in mid-July, having authorized the veterans only to borrow against their certificates for transportation back to their homes. In the scheme of things the congressional summer recess was deemed too sacrosanct for it to be sacrificed to resolve a contentious national issue. About ten thousand marchers remained in Washington, vowing to "stay till 1945 to get the bonus," and chanting, "Bonus or a job." Tensions appeared to ease despite the distribution by the small number of hard-core Communist veterans of handbills condemning the government and demanding action.

The Bonus March might have ended peacefully if the authorities had acted with the same compassion and restraint as the District of Columbia chief of police, Pelham D. Glassford, a former army brigadier general and classmate of MacArthur at West Point. Glassford assisted rather than persecuted the bonus marchers, who might well have departed Washington of their own accord before much longer without intervention.

Inevitably, however, violence broke out between a group of Communist-led marchers and the authorities on the morning of July 28, 1932, when District of Columbia police attempted to eject eleven hundred squatters from their makeshift quarters in the condemned buildings. The Washington commissioners believed that the police could not control the marchers and formally asked Hoover to intervene with federal troops. Hurley and MacArthur went one step further, imploring Hoover to declare martial law, a strategy he flatly rejected.

However, the bonus marchers failed to reckon on the paranoia of the Hoover administration, which completely overreacted. That same afternoon Hoover directed the army to cooperate with the District of Columbia police and to "surround the effected area and clear it without delay." Hurley sent MacArthur a written order to not only disperse the BEF, but to clear the veterans from the condemned buildings in downtown Washington. Hoover's original orders to Hurley had been merely to round up and incarcerate every single bonus marcher, so that each could be identified and the ringleaders tried in court. After consulting MacArthur, Hurley believed that the order was not only impossible to carry out but potentially disastrous, and took it upon himself unilaterally to amend the army's mission to that of clearing the entire city. When MacArthur received Hurley's orders he exclaimed, "We are going to break the back of the BEF."

The 3rd Cavalry, based across the Potomac at nearby Fort Myer (whose executive officer was George S. Patton), was ordered into Washington for riot duty.[6] With Patton at its head, the regiment galloped across the Memorial Bridge and on to the Ellipse. The appearance of two hundred cavalry troopers on horseback along Pennsylvania Avenue, clad in steel helmets, gas masks, and full battle gear and with drawn sabers, was an ominous sight not seen again until 1970, when paratroopers of the 82nd Airborne Division were summoned to guard the Pentagon during the massive Vietnam War protest march on Washington.

Both MacArthur and Eisenhower arrived for work that day dressed in their usual civilian attire. But on that July afternoon MacArthur announced that he intended to direct the operation personally even though Hoover had directed that the matter remain under police control. He sent an aide to fetch his uniform from home, much to the disgust of Eisenhower, who remonstrated that it was unnecessarily provocative. "I thought it had the aspect of a riot rather than a big military movement, and so I told him that I thought this was inadvisable, that the Chief of Staff should not dignify the incident by going out himself."[7] MacArthur not only disagreed but portrayed himself as the savior of the nation's capital from anarchy. To his dismay, Eisenhower, who kept no uniform in his office, was ordered to accompany MacArthur and to present himself in uniform. He rushed home to change. John witnessed a chaotic scene as his father flung clothes about the room, cursing under his breath all the while. When Mamie returned later that afternoon, "there were clothes from [the] front door back . . . boxes, bags and boot trees all over."[8]

One of the best-known photographs of the two men, taken that day, depicts MacArthur with a cigarette dangling from his lips while Eisenhower stands glumly in the background, his displeasure clearly etched in his face. Also present was MacArthur's official aide, Capt. Thomas Jefferson Davis, familiarly known as "T.J." Davis had been MacArthur's aide since 1927, but was also a close friend of Eisenhower, whom he would faithfully serve during World War II.

About 4:00 P.M., the army commanders were ordered to disperse the veterans. The bonus marchers were attacked by infantry and cavalry in downtown Washington. Such was the sorry state of the army that its handful of tanks immediately broke down. Thousands of spectators—some of whom heaved rocks and bricks and were tear-gassed by the infantry—witnessed the clash. Some cursed the troops with "Shame! Shame!" and "You goddamned bums!"[9] Even though they did not resist, the veterans were tear-gassed and forcibly driven into Hooverville by about eight hundred federal troops, among them Patton's cavalry, which advanced with sabers drawn and occasionally used the flats of their blades across the buttocks to disperse anyone who resisted. As distressful as it was for soldiers to be attacking and routing their comrades, their sworn oath to the Constitution and their duty to carry out the lawful orders of the commander in chief left no other option. Responsibility for the tragedy lay in the failure of the president and the War Department to have found a more humane way of dealing with the problem before it got out of hand.

Shortly thereafter Hoover issued a further order that the army was not to pursue the marchers across the Anacostia Bridge into Hooverville, or to evict its inhabitants. With MacArthur unavailable, the order was passed to his deputy, Moseley, who wrote in his memoirs, "I delivered that message to him. He was very much annoyed at having his plans interfered with." The accepted version for more than sixty years was that MacArthur willfully disobeyed the orders of the president. Moseley claims he personally delivered Hoover's order to MacArthur and, later, "I sent Colonel Clement B. Wright, the Secretary of the General Staff, to repeat the message to MacArthur." A later account suggests that Moseley probably lied about having personally conveyed Hoover's order to MacArthur.[10] Even so, MacArthur's biographer D. Clayton James notes, "Hurley twice sent messengers to tell MacArthur . . . that the President did not want the Army to pursue the B.E.F. across the Anacostia River."[11]

Although MacArthur may or may not ever have received the president's order, it was more by design than chance. Eisenhower's recollection never mentions Moseley, only that Wright attempted to deliver an unspecified order and that MacArthur flatly declined to accept it.[12] "I went up to the General [MacArthur] and said, 'There's a man here who has some orders about this.' He said, 'I don't want to hear them and I don't want to see them. Get him away.' He wouldn't listen to these instructions, and so far as I knew he never heard them." Eisenhower also recalled that MacArthur had not officially received the order because he refused to be bothered by "people coming down and pretending to bring orders . . . so the President's message to him just didn't get to him."[13] Although MacArthur thus absolved himself from violating a presidential order by employing the pretext of not having received it, he implicitly violated its spirit. What counted in the end was that Hoover's presidential directive to the army *not* to pursue the BEF across the Anacostia River was never carried out.

MacArthur issued orders at 9:30 P.M. that evening for the troops to cross the bridge and begin clearing the shantytown. Someone set fire to one of the shanties, and as veterans fled into the night, Hooverville was consumed in a conflagration that reduced it to ashes as quickly as the infamous Branch Davidian compound in Waco, Texas, in 1993. It was never established how the fire began or who was responsible. Although he offered to resign, MacArthur fatuously defended his actions by claiming the BEF was a Communist-inspired plot to incite an uprising, and that the fire had been deliberately set by the veterans.[14] Eisenhower thought any public comment by the army inadvisable, and as MacArthur prepared to return to the War Department, he suggested he avoid contact with the press and let the Hoover administration defend the army's actions. Eisenhower was left behind to witness the end of one of the most disgraceful incidents in American history. He returned home at 1:00 A.M. the following morning, his uniform soaked with sweat.

At a late-night press conference, MacArthur was unable to resist gloating at having saved the nation from "incipient revolution" by a mob of "insur-rectionists." Pouring more fuel on the incident, MacArthur proclaimed that he had "never seen greater relief on the part of the distressed populace than I saw today," likening it to the liberation of a nation from tyranny.[15] Led by the *Baltimore Sun*, which called it "Horsefeathers," the press reacted to Mac-Arthur's outburst with almost universal condemnation.[16]

Amid the ambiguities surrounding this incident, the one indisputable fact is that the dispersal of the Bonus Army saw streams of "bedraggled, hungry, [and] shabby" marchers lining the roads leading out of Washington. "The BEF had died in the same confusion in which it was born."[17]

As the most highly regarded staff officer in the War Department, Eisen-hower drafted the official after-action report, which stoutly defended Mac-Arthur and the army. In it the army patted itself on the back, noting that "its allotted tasks were performed rapidly and efficiently but with the maximum consideration for the members of the riotous groups consistent with their compulsory eviction."[18]

Even as an unwilling party to this event, Eisenhower shared in the general disgust at the army being ordered to attack its own veterans, calling it a pitiful scene.[19] Less clear are Eisenhower's personal feelings about the Bonus March itself. About all he ever publicly said regarding the incident was that he had counseled MacArthur concerning the impropriety of becoming directly involved. Yet at times his attitude toward MacArthur and the Bonus March seems rather self-serving, and his few public remarks biographer Piers Bren-don describes as "disingenuous," "bland," and "charitable." Eisenhower, he believes, was "ever ready to sacrifice plain-speaking on the altar of benevo-lence."[20]

Eisenhower espoused the conviction that politics and the military properly did not mix, even though he himself later admitted that the two were ines-capably linked. Although he violated his own maxim from time to time, as in his 1931 article about the War Policies Commission, Eisenhower was con-vinced that MacArthur had gone too far during the Bonus March by defend-ing his actions on the grounds that it was a seditious Communist plot.

Although he had become an ardent diarist, Eisenhower's sole reference was a terse comment he did not write until August 10: "As Gen. MacA's aide took part in Bonus incident of July 28, a lot of furor has been stirred up, but mostly to make political capital. I wrote the General's report which was as accurate as I could make it."[21] In a postpresidential interview, Eisenhower all but dismissed the Bonus March as trivial, noting that "the Government decided they had to go ahead with their contracts for demolishing these [con-demned] buildings. . . . There was a little disorder . . . so they brought in a few troops."[22] Moreover, as willing as he was to challenge authority, even Eisen-hower was unlikely to have criticized MacArthur to his face when he appeared in uniform, complete with medals, one of which was a Philippine decoration earned by his father, Gen. Arthur MacArthur.[23]

At the time Eisenhower loyally defended his boss. He railed in his diary when syndicated columnists Drew Pearson and Robert S. Allen relentlessly attacked MacArthur—unfairly, in his opinion—in their "Washington Merry-Go-Round" column over his behavior during the Bonus March. Eisenhower referred to the two as "newspaper men of the lower order (scandalmongers)," and innate cowards, "giving expression to an inferiority complex by ceaseless attempts to belittle a man recognized as courageous."[24] However, a truer expression of Eisenhower's disdain was revealed in 1954, when he privately expressed the opinion that: "I just can't understand how such a damn fool could have gotten to be a general."[25] He was even more candid later, during an interview with Stephen Ambrose. "I told that dumb son-of-a-bitch he had no business going down there. I told him it was no place for the Chief of Staff."[26]

The long-term damage from the Bonus March was incalculable in an era in which the military was already under fire and facing still more budgetary cutbacks. MacArthur and the army became the public exemplars of an ungrateful nation that rewarded its veterans by gassing, bayoneting, and shooting them. During his long and distinguished military career MacArthur was at the heart of numerous controversies, but none did more to permanently tarnish his reputation, and that of the army he headed, than the Bonus March. Eisenhower properly anticipated trouble and offered sound advice; MacArthur, perhaps blinded by his own self-importance, did not heed it. The lamentable result was an unmitigated public relations fiasco at a moment when the army could ill afford to become even more inconsequential.[27]

20.

Toiling for MacArthur

Dad writhed in frustration in Washington. . . . He worked like a slave.

The often turbulent relationship between Douglas MacArthur and Dwight Eisenhower spanned virtually the entire decade of the 1930s. After Fox Connor, MacArthur was the second of the four men who would exercise a profound influence on Eisenhower's military career.

MacArthur had risen to the army's highest and only four-star position in 1930 after a brilliant career that mirrored the exploits of his famous father, Lt. Gen. Arthur MacArthur, Jr. Both father and son had earned acclaim for their exceptional bravery in battle. As a lieutenant in a Union regiment from Wisconsin, Arthur earned the Medal of Honor on Missionary Ridge, Tennessee, in September 1863.[1] His son, Douglas, obsessed with emulating his father, became first captain of the corps of cadets, graduated first in his class at West Point, and was recommended for but not awarded the Medal of Honor for his exploits during the Veracruz expedition to Mexico in April 1914.

Although his exploits at the Veracruz customhouse lacked reliable witnesses, Douglas MacArthur craved this honor both as a symbol of having lived up to his father's bravery, and to advance his own grand ambitions. MacArthur's valor under fire during World War I was legendary, earning him the distinction of being the most decorated American soldier of that war as a colonel, and later as a brigadier general, in the famed 42nd "Rainbow" Division. As the superintendent of West Point from 1919 to 1922, MacArthur instituted major reforms that finally brought the archaic military academy into the twentieth century. His postwar rise to chief of staff was rapid and, in retrospect, inevitable. The chestful of ribbons that occupied eight rows on the left breast pocket of his uniform made MacArthur "the first among peacocks."[2] Those who knew or served under MacArthur either admired his genius or despised his narcissism. D. Clayton James interacted with MacArthur for twenty years during the research and writing of his superb three-volume biography. Once asked what it was like, James replied: "Hated him on Tuesday! Loved him on Wednesday!"[3] James also observed, "No character in modern American military history, even Patton, has been the subject of as much adulation and condemnation as MacArthur . . . there has been virtually no middle ground; he has been extravagantly praised or severely censured."[4] Eisenhower was one of MacArthur's few subordinates who could objectively judge both his virtues and flaws.

Few men in American military history were greater enigmas than Douglas MacArthur, an officer whose extraordinary brilliance was matched only by his towering ego. Although the MacArthur persona has been thoroughly examined in numerous biographies, his was such a multilayered personality that the full extent of his brilliance cannot be measured merely by his actions. What especially impressed Eisenhower was MacArthur's intellect. Never one to dispense praise easily, Eisenhower reserved his greatest compliments for MacArthur. "He did have a hell of an intellect! My God, but he was smart. He had a *brain.*"[5]

All genius has its price, and for MacArthur it was an inviolate belief in his own infallibility. "MacArthur could never see another sun, or even a moon, for that matter, in the heavens as long as *he* was the sun," Eisenhower said of him.[6] Joshena M. Ingersoll, the *grande dame* of Manila's social life in the 1930s, knew MacArthur well in the Philippines and offers this thoughtful assessment: "There was never any middle ground; people either idolized this man or hated him, while all the time he dwelt on another mental plane, and was probably seldom aware of either the worship or the hate."[7]

Eisenhower was by equal measures awed and repelled by MacArthur. Although impressed by his genius, charm, and especially his flattery toward a junior officer, he deplored MacArthur's posturing and unwillingness to accept advice. On balance, however, "Eisenhower relished the relationship." The two constants were a mutual respect that sometimes appeared to have been lost in the heat of their intense verbal battles, and the common trait of being very heavy smokers thoroughly addicted to nicotine. Eisenhower had been a devoted chain-smoker since West Point, and the air around the two men was filled with the endless pungent smell of cigarette smoke. MacArthur and Eisenhower were ideal candidates for lung cancer, but although neither ever contracted the deadly disease, Eisenhower's years of smoking undoubtedly contributed to his later health problems.[8]

It was inevitable that Eisenhower would eventually be chosen to toil exclusively for MacArthur. His drive, initiative, and seemingly endless capacity for producing well-organized and thoughtful staff work made Eisenhower an invaluable commodity. Eisenhower was not only exceptionally loyal to his bosses but was "able to think from the point of view of his chief, a quality both MacArthur and Marshall often singled out for praise. He had an instinctive sense of when to make a decision himself and when to pass it up to his boss."[9]

MacArthur, notes Samuel Huntington, was a general in the tradition of Winfield Scott: "brilliant, imperious, cold, dramatic officers deriving their values and behavior from an older, aristocratic heritage and finding it difficult to subordinate themselves to civilian authorities." Gen. Harold K. Johnson, U.S. Army chief of staff from 1964 to 1968, a survivor of the Bataan Death March, viewed MacArthur as "a great commander in the tradition of a Caesar. [But] I don't think that he was the human sort of man that Eisenhower was."[10]

By contrast Eisenhower was representative of "the friendly, folksy, easygoing soldier who reflects the ideals of a democratic and industrial civilization and who cooperates easily with his civilian superiors." Whereas MacArthur seemed to relish controversy and often dashed boldly into a fray such as the Bonus March, Eisenhower, "[s]peaking less and smiling more than MacArthur, ... appeared the embodiment of consensus rather than controversy. MacArthur was a beacon, Eisenhower a mirror."[11] Only in fairy tales do two such polar opposites survive each other without conflict.

In February 1933 Eisenhower moved into a tiny alcove no larger than a broom closet, behind a slatted door adjacent to MacArthur's large inner sanctum, to become his principal special assistant and, on occasion, his aide. "My work will apparently be little different from that I have been performing for him for two years but he alone will be my boss."[12]

MacArthur's method of summoning Eisenhower to his presence was "raising his voice." Eisenhower would later write that Douglas MacArthur "spoke and wrote in purple splendor."[13] Most of their discussions were really monologues in which MacArthur pontificated and Eisenhower listened, often bemused by his chief's references to himself in the third person. Whereas Patton and MacArthur believed themselves to be men of destiny, Eisenhower had no such illusions or aspirations. MacArthur was driven to Capitol Hill and around Washington in a fancy, chauffeured limousine. Eisenhower, whose business frequently required him to visit Capitol Hill, took a streetcar or taxi and was humiliated at having to return all small change left over and file a travel voucher for reimbursement. MacArthur "never once offered Eisenhower a ride in or use of the car." Eisenhower never forgot it, and even after his two terms as president the memories still smarted. "No matter what happens later you never forget something like that," he confessed to a reporter shortly before his death.[14]

Life with MacArthur was a vivid reminder of the difference between the haves and the have-nots. More than twenty years after leaving Abilene, Eisenhower was still dirt poor and faced career prospects as bleak as the economy. What little hope the military professionals of the 1930s had was vested in Douglas MacArthur, whose reputation for bravery and the reform of West Point had no equal in the army. Although MacArthur managed to successfully lobby against a 1932 Senate bill to reduce the army by another two thousand officers, try as he might he generally fought a losing battle against budget and manpower cuts that he (correctly) argued brought the army's ability to function into serious question. FDR's New Deal policies, which included massive spending programs to reduce unemployment and right the economy, did not include the armed forces. "For the professional soldier it was not a happy time. Tradition obliged him to stand mute on political issues that gravely disturbed him," or to "wait for retirement to speak his mind."[15]

Despite Eisenhower's admiration for MacArthur, he found himself increasingly dismayed—even appalled—by his superior's massive ego and pompous behavior. When it came to melodrama, complete with exhortations to duty and invocations to the Almighty, punctuated by exaggerated body language, MacArthur had no equal.[16] Eisenhower was exposed to his full array of ploys and thought MacArthur would have been "a *great* actor."[17] MacArthur's most polished performance was to parade back and forth in front of a large mirror across from his desk, dressed in a Japanese silk dressing gown, an ivory cigarette holder clamped in his mouth, admiring his profile while orating. MacArthur's mastery of theatrics was world-class *opéra bouffe* and "the best free show in town."[18] Future Army Air Corps general Louis H. Brereton, who served under both MacArthur and, later, Eisenhower, in Europe, once remarked that MacArthur "cannot talk sitting down."[19]

MacArthur, in turn, valued his subordinate and lavished praise on Eisenhower in letters of commendation and consistently superior efficiency reports, once thanking him "for a magnificent effort on your part. Much better than I could have done myself. I am grateful," [signed] "MacArthur."[20] In 1932 he wrote that Eisenhower was "one of the most outstanding officers of his time and service . . . he has no superior in his grade."[21] In short MacArthur's praise was both as heartfelt as it was genuine.

Eisenhower completed the Army Industrial College in 1931, a newly created school in Washington, which he had helped create to prepare officers for mobilization and its many related problems. Given Eisenhower's extensive background in planning for industrial mobilization, his attendance at the school could be regarded as a case of the pupil knowing more than his teachers.[22] His required course paper drew on his burgeoning knowledge of industrial mobilization and procurement. Eisenhower contended that wartime mobilization was not inconsistent with the War Policies Commission's goal of neutralizing the war profiteers; in fact it was vital to distinguish between the two. Eisenhower's military reputation rests in large part on his ability to find acceptable common ground between competing priorities and people. His 1931 study was an early manifestation of that ability.[23]

In direct contrast to his willingness to stand up to powerful men like MacArthur, by the mid-1930s Eisenhower occasionally lapsed into displays of the same traits as the pen-pushing bureaucrats he had scorned for years. Friends and acquaintances often wrote to him for advice or assistance. In his replies Eisenhower could be elusive and almost impossible to pin down, tending to overqualify his responses whenever he was asked to commit himself, particularly replies to touchy questions. Often Eisenhower's primary concern seemed to have been to avoid having to stick out his neck. Once, for example, an officer facing mandatory retirement after being classified as overage sought Eisenhower's advice. His reply included this convoluted gem:

> I stand ready to do anything that I possibly can but of course any official testimony that I would be called upon to give would have to be limited to that based upon general contact and impression as I have explained above, rather than upon any kind of direct observation and responsibility.[24]

Life with MacArthur had as its price long hours and chronic stress. Years later Ike told John that "I always resented the years I spent as a slave in the War Department."[25] By the summer of 1934 his back problems had become so persistent and painful that he could barely function at work and was unable to walk more than a short distance, bend over, play golf, or dance. He reported to Walter Reed Army Hospital complaining of pain and stiffness in his back and hip during the preceding two and one-half years and was admitted. Over the course of the next five weeks Eisenhower was thoroughly examined and tested "with no definite findings," other than mild arthritis and what his doctors called "sacroiliac disease," a diagnosis that really meant they had no idea what was causing his pain. They concluded he was fit for duty and advised him to undergo massage and sleep on a hard bed.[26] Eisenhower complained mildly that his doctors "didn't take the thing anywhere near as seriously as I did."[27]

More and more frequently Eisenhower relieved his frustrations through his diary and occasional letters to trusted friends. With dismay he witnessed the infighting between the War Department, Congress, and the president over the military budget and several brewing scandals involving munitions profiteering.[28]

On the job Eisenhower was the consummate staff officer, ambitious and all business. Occasionally the mask slipped, and his compassionate side emerged. In word and deed Eisenhower was protective of his West Point classmates. When one of their own suddenly died in 1934, Eisenhower wrote a touching tribute that read in part, "No wonder that a sense of futility overpowers the pen in attempting to express in words the feeling of loss that his passing inspires. . . . And so we blow the trumpets and fire the vollies [*sic*], a soldier's goodbye to our friend and classmate."[29]

In the summer of 1935 the Eisenhowers were devastated by the excruciatingly painful and untimely death of their dear friend Katie Gerow, from what then was thought to have been a mysterious illness contracted while the

Gerows were stationed in the Philippines. More than likely she had died of cancer.[30] Her death was a painful reminder of Ike and Mamie's own losses. They comforted a distraught Gee Gerow as best they could, and in the process Eisenhower grew even closer to his friend. Rather than abandon the heat of Washington for a summer vacation, they remained to offer what comfort and support they could to the Gerow family.[31]

The New Deal zealots who surrounded FDR treated the army with much the same contempt as the patronizing Young Turks of the Clinton administration exhibited toward the Pentagon in the 1990s. FDR's most visible point man was a liberal New York reformer named Harry Hopkins, the newly appointed czar of the Federal Emergency Relief Administration (FERA), which spent billions on national projects through such new agencies as the Works Progress Administration (WPA) and the Public Works Administration (PWA). The new administration created a bevy of alphabet commissions to cope with the depression. One of the best known was the Civilian Conservation Corps (CCC), a quasi-military organization mobilized and administered by the army to carry out massive public works projects across the rural United States through the immediate employment of some 250,000 jobless youths. Roosevelt's pet project, the CCC eventually employed twelve times that number in carrying out the largest conservation and reforestation projects ever undertaken in the United States.[32]

Few in the conservative, army officer corps thought well of Roosevelt's liberal-minded do-gooders or wanted their own reputations tainted by association with "such vulgar, radical fellows as [Harry] Hopkins." Not surprisingly, the best-known exception was George Marshall, who perceived the military importance of Roosevelt's modernization activities.[33] By World War II, Hopkins would become Roosevelt's most trusted and influential adviser and one of the top officials who would work closely with Marshall and a rising officer named Eisenhower.

In part because of the unprecedented success of the CCC, Roosevelt resisted the temptation to fire MacArthur and left him in his post. In the 1930s there was no fixed tenure for the chief of staff, who served at the pleasure of the president. By the autumn of 1934 MacArthur had served for four years, the unofficial term for most chiefs of staff. Roosevelt vacillated, but in December he honored pleas from such luminaries as Pershing that MacArthur be retained. His tenure was extended by an additional year to December 1935, after which a new chief of staff would be appointed.

Spain had ruled the Philippines—its 7,100 islands named for King Phillip II—since 1571, the year Manila was founded. When the Spanish-American War commenced in 1898, the United States dispatched Commodore George Dewey's fleet to the Philippines from Hong Kong, and it destroyed the Spanish fleet in Manila Bay on May 1, 1898. From the time Spain ceded the Philippines to the United States for $20 million in 1899, American officers had served there. The names of those who had served in the Philippines—long considered a plum assignment—included MacArthur, Marshall, Krueger (all whom Eisenhower served under), mechanization pioneer Adna Chaffee, Mark Clark, and many of the future architects of the modern army.

In 1900 Arthur MacArthur was appointed military governor and fought guerrilla insurgents, led by Emilio Aguinaldo, who were bent on creating a free and independent Philippine nation. After a serious rift with MacArthur's handpicked civilian successor, William Howard Taft, Arthur was relieved and returned to the United States in 1901. He was greeted as a national icon, just as his son would be a half century later after being relieved of command by President Harry S. Truman during the Korean War. One of Aguinaldo's aides was an ardent young nationalist named Manuel Quezon, who became a lawyer and, by the 1930s, the most prominent political figure in the Philippines. In 1934 Congress passed the Tydings-McDuffie Act, which bestowed commonwealth status on the Philippines effective in 1935, and promised complete independence in 1946. Its first president was the same Manuel Quezon who had fought MacArthur's father during the short but bloody Philippine rebellion of 1900–01.

During his second tour of duty in the Philippines from 1922 to 1925, Douglas MacArthur became closely acquainted with Quezon, who was then still deeply involved in the Philippine independence movement as the leader of the Nacionalista Party. The MacArthur name was still highly esteemed in the Philippines, which Douglas fondly regarded as his home.[34] During a trip to the United States in 1935, Quezon implored MacArthur to become his military adviser and had no trouble persuading Roosevelt to send him to the Philippines. Roosevelt detailed MacArthur "to survey the military needs of the Philippine commonwealth, in anticipation of the commonwealth's full independence in 1946."[35] Offered the opportunity to return to a place he dearly loved during his previous service, MacArthur accepted at once. It never seems to have dawned on the politically naive MacArthur that it suited both Roosevelt and his many other enemies to have him eleven thousand miles from Washington.[36]

MacArthur resolved that Eisenhower accompany him to Manila and subjected him to the full MacArthur melodramatics. Ultimately, however, Eisenhower's decision had less to do with better pay or an opportunity to satisfy his lifelong yen for duty in the exotic Philippines than it did with the fact that subordinates simply did not say no to Douglas MacArthur. John Eisenhower recalls how, as a teenager, he too was the recipient of MacArthur's charm.

Nor was John the least bit surprised by his father's decision. MacArthur, he wrote, could "mesmerize any individual he wanted, even including my recalcitrant Old Man."[37] MacArthur sweetened the offer by permitting Eisenhower to nominate another officer to accompany them and share in the duties. Without hesitation Eisenhower chose his old friend and West Point classmate James Basevi Ord, who enthusiastically agreed.

If two decades of service had not dampened his zeal, neither had they altered the manner in which his career decisions were made. He made them and expected Mamie's complete acquiescence. Later, as first lady, she was notable for publicly articulating that her marital role was to please her husband and enhance his career. In this instance, however, Eisenhower does not seem to have taken into account (or perhaps even recognized) Mamie's growing independence. Nor had he reckoned how deeply the death of Katie Gerow had affected her.

Mamie was openly dismayed by the news and uncharacteristically negative. She was reluctant to trade the only real stability she had known since marrying Eisenhower for the discomfort and uncertainties of the Philippines. Vivid memories of Panama were still fresh, and Mamie was terrified of contracting the same illness that she believed had killed Katie Gerow, or of placing John in harm's way. With Mamie being torn between her very real fears and her duty to her husband, some emotionally painful times ensued as they argued and debated the matter. Their dilemma was exacerbated by MacArthur's refusal to specify the length of Eisenhower's assignment. In the end Mamie insisted on remaining in Washington and would not be dissuaded. The ostensible reason for this decision was to permit John to complete the 1935–36 school year in Washington. Although stung and gravely disappointed by Mamie's refusal to accompany him, Eisenhower managed to hide his true feelings so well that Mamie became convinced that he really did not care if she came or not, thus further worsening the impasse. To make matters worse, he and John had grown closer, and the prospect of being separated from his son made Mamie's refusal even more disheartening.

The extent of Mamie's distress is unambiguous in a letter to her parents in June 1935: "We have talked and talked things over and have practically decided that John & I will stay on here in Washington till we see how the thing is going to turn out. . . . I don't want to go over there & this *way* at least one of us can have John." To soften the impending separation Mamie begged them, "Do you think you could come and be with me? This job may peter out or Ike might not be able to stand the climate and then we would be in a mess. I hate to let him go alone . . . [but] I don't want to go away so far from u-all and after Katie's experience I'm *scared*. Such a mess this whole thing is . . . so hard to write about these things."[38] Her granddaughter is convinced that Mamie's fears were genuine and that she "was literally incapable of getting on a boat to be with her husband."[39]

Mamie had little use for MacArthur, and her unhappiness was directed as much toward the man for whom her husband had toiled as toward Ike himself. She told their mutual friend Robert L. Eichelberger, "Eich, Ike is ruined. He has gone off to the Philippines with that man MacArthur. In the five years he has known him, he has never broken bread with MacArthur."[40]

Mamie's decision was a source of anguish to both. Eisenhower wrote plaintively to the Douds of their impending separation, "I hate the whole thought and I know that I'm going to be miserable. On the other hand, Mamie's so badly frightened, both for John and herself, at the prospect of going out there that I simply cannot urge her to go. . . . I can only hope for the best, as the idea of being separated from my family has nothing for me but grief."[41]

On October 1, 1935, with a heavy heart, Eisenhower boarded a train in Union Station. Aboard were Jimmy Ord; MacArthur; his eighty-two year-old mother, Mary "Pinky" MacArthur, who was in poor health; and an entourage that included T.J. Davis. The first leg of the monthlong journey to Manila was to take them to San Francisco, where they would embark on the liner SS *President Hoover* for the voyage to Manila to help MacArthur prepare the Philippine army to defend its homeland.

21.

Mission Impossible

I could be the fair-haired boy if I'd only yes, yes, yes!!

After serving an unprecedented five years as army chief of staff, MacArthur thought he had secured Roosevelt's assent to retain his four-star rank and position until December 15, 1935, the final day of his yearlong extension, thus enabling him to arrive in Manila wearing the four stars of a full general. MacArthur had repeatedly skirmished with Roosevelt and mistakenly believed that he had held his own. But when it came to political acumen, MacArthur was a rank amateur in the playing fields of Washington, especially against a wily politician like FDR. MacArthur had no sooner left Washington than Roosevelt named Gen. Malin Craig, a disciple of Pershing, as the new chief of staff. The official version was that for MacArthur to retain his rank until mid-December would effectively cripple Craig's ability to function as chief of staff for some ten weeks. What MacArthur did not know was that he was a victim of a devilishly devious scheme by Roosevelt. Not only did FDR send MacArthur into exile, but he deftly stripped him of his four-star rank only *after* he had departed Washington. When his train stopped in Cheyenne, Wyoming, on October 2, MacArthur received a telegram that Roosevelt had replaced him, effective immediately. Not only was MacArthur no longer chief of staff, but he had already reverted to his permanent rank of major general.

The blow shattered MacArthur's composure. On the station platform Eisenhower and Ord witnessed MacArthur rage aimlessly at anyone whom he believed might have had anything to do with his forced retirement. Eisenhower described it as "an explosive denunciation of politics, bad manners, bad judgment, broken promises, arrogance, unconstitutionality, insensitivity, and the way the world had gone to hell."[1] It was as unpleasant a spectacle as Eisenhower ever witnessed. When his rage abated, MacArthur swallowed his pride and graciously sent telegrams of congratulations to FDR, the secretary of war, and Craig, praising the president's choice.[2] However, MacArthur's antipathy toward Roosevelt never abated. On the day of the president's death

in April 1945, MacArthur said to a confidant, "Well, the old man is gone—
a man who never told the truth if a lie would suffice."[3]

For the ever-ambitious Dwight Eisenhower, acceptance of the Philippine
assignment was fraught with negatives. By becoming closely identified with
MacArthur's falling star, Eisenhower also put his own future squarely on the
line. Eisenhower entertained no illusions that he was destined for anything
more than a modest rank as perhaps a junior general officer in the event of
war. "He was tying his kite to an officer whose career was finished," notes
historian Robert H. Ferrell.[4] Time was running out for Eisenhower, now in
his mid-forties. His qualifications notwithstanding, in his past and present
roles he was a little more than a pawn who toiled in the service of others.
Although its provenance has never been proved, when Eisenhower was elected
president in 1952, MacArthur is said to have declared tartly, "He was the best
clerk who ever served under me."[5]

Hardly anyone in Washington cared about the Philippines, which were
seen as not only indefensible but of no strategic importance. In short the
negatives vastly outweighed the positives. Worse, MacArthur's long-running
feud with the army's influential Pershing-AEF element would not serve him
well in the Philippines. With few backers to look after his interests in Washington, and no power, MacArthur had gone from a high-profile player to an
also-ran. As for Eisenhower, he was now seriously overdue for troop duty,
and the Philippine assignment would ensure that another lengthy period
would ensue before such an assignment was possible. He was still a lowly
major after more than fifteen years, and his prospects were bleak. Stuck in
far-away Manila, any immediate prospects of reversing his outlook grew dim-
mer with each passing year.

As Eisenhower sailed on a twenty-two-day voyage into a Philippine exile,
Germany had begun massive rearmament that flouted the Versailles treaty.
In Italy, Benito Mussolini's fascist armies would invade and brutally subdue
Ethiopia the following year. By the mid-1930s the threat of Japanese expan-
sionism in Asia had become an alarmingly visible reality. Japanese militarism
had already resulted in that nation's seizure of Manchuria in 1931 and the
invasion of China the following year. An equally disturbing harbinger
occurred in 1933 when Japan abruptly quit the League of Nations, setting its
own course free of international restraints. That path led to a renewal of war
in 1937 against Chiang Kai-shek's Nationalist Chinese army, and the capture
of Peking, Shanghai, and the provisional Chinese capital of Nanking, where
some one hundred thousand noncombatants were slaughtered and raped. The
prestige of the isolationist United States would sink to an all-time low in
December 1937, when Japanese aircraft attacked the U.S. gunboat *Panay* in
the Yangtze River. After the *Panay* incident, the British prime minister, Neville

Chamberlain, whose name would several years later become synonymous with the appeasement of Hitler, declared: "It is always best and safest to count on nothing from the Americans but words."

Despite U.S. isolationism, War Department military planners took cognizance of what would have to be done to protect American interests in the Pacific in the event of war. The result—the War Department's strategic blueprint for fighting a naval and amphibious war against Japan in defense of the Pacific Ocean—was called Plan Orange. At its center were the Philippines. Reduced to its simplest terms the plan "envisioned a prolonged, step-by-step return to the Philippines, the path subsequently taken by [Adm. Chester W.] Nimitz's Central Pacific offensive in late 1943."[6] U.S. and Philippine forces would have to hold Manila for at least six months before the arrival of a relief expeditionary force. Surprisingly it was the naval planners, not the army, who argued that "in case of war the navy should mount a serious effort to rescue or recover the Philippines."[7] The larger question remained how Plan Orange could successfully be implemented in a reasonable time frame—or if the plan would ever be implemented.

The Tydings-McDuffie Act included a provision (insisted on by both the War Department and MacArthur) that the United States continue stationing military forces in the Philippine Department of the U.S. Army until independence in 1946. The role of the American military mission was to assist in the creation and training of a Filipino citizen army capable of defending the country after independence. The problems posed by Japan were only partly addressed by Plan Orange. MacArthur and his military mission had to create a Philippine defense force to safeguard a virtually indefensible island nation.

By 1936 the urgency faced by the American mission increased with each new act of Japanese aggression in Asia. What was a vital priority in Manila, however, was treated with indifference and a lack of funding by Washington, and the changing of the guard from MacArthur to Malin Craig brought about changes that lessened War Department defense priorities for the Philippines in order to concentrate on what was thought to be the more viable defense of Alaska, Hawaii, and Panama. Yet without a large, well-trained and -equipped army, supported by powerful American naval forces, any defense of the Philippines was inconceivable. In 1933 the coast artillery general responsible for the harbor defenses of Manila, Stanley D. Embrick, concluded that the Philippines were indefensible and that there existed "a military liability of incalculable magnitude."[8] The strategic bastion of Corregidor, which guarded the entrance to Manila Bay, "would be lost immediately after the opening of hostilities," not unlike France's vaunted but useless Maginot Line, which became irrelevant after the Germans simply bypassed its defenses. In short, the United States faced insurmountable odds in attempting to defend the Philippines.[9]

MacArthur saw a higher purpose, arguing passionately that not only were the Philippines the key to American defense of the Pacific, but that the United

States had a higher moral obligation. "We've been telling the world [that] people can govern themselves democratically. Now we've got to help the Filipinos prove we are right. If the Filipino experiment fails, the prestige of the United States goes down to zero in a world that would like to see us flop anyway. If we let it fail, we'll be the world's worst skunks."[10] MacArthur obstinately maintained the illusion of Philippine readiness. Malin Craig's secretary of the general staff (and Eisenhower's friend), Robert Eichelberger, notes, "From late 1935 to 1938 we had heard many times the MacArthur expression, 'The Japanese would not invade the Philippines, but if they do, in case of war, we shall meet them at the beaches and destroy them.' "[11]

MacArthur's plan for defense of the Philippines was predicated on the presence of an American battle fleet to discourage a would-be Japanese invasion, yet Plan Orange contained no such provision. MacArthur thus became the architect of a noble but ultimately unachievable undertaking.[12]

During his 1935 visit to the United States, Quezon had bluntly asked MacArthur if the islands could be defended solely by a Philippine force. "I know they can," replied MacArthur, although, as Eisenhower wrote in his diary, "at no time has General MacArthur intended that the P.I. could defend themselves against a major assault . . . [by] one of the great powers."[13] Some years later Eisenhower would learn the sad truth of his prediction.

Eisenhower tackled his new duties as a jack-of-all-trades staff officer and MacArthur's chief of staff with the same zeal that had become his trademark. In addition to his office at the U.S. mission, at 1 Calle Victoria, a spacious building constructed atop a large, fortified seventeenth-century wall in downtown Manila, Eisenhower was also given an office in the Malacañan Palace, which he usually visited daily. Although he had no idea that the experience he gained in the Philippines would ever serve him particularly well, in his new position under MacArthur, Eisenhower "learned to build and train an army from practically nothing while being as politically and diplomatically sensitive as possible, negotiating difficult logistical circumstances, and working with hair-trigger personalities."[14]

Eisenhower's work partner, Jimmy Ord, the grandson of a Union general who commanded a corps under Grant at Richmond and Appomattox, was uniquely qualified to help Eisenhower share the duties of assistant to MacArthur. Jovial, roly-poly, intelligent, and brave, Ord was fluent in French and Spanish. He had been recommended for the Medal of Honor during the punitive expedition to Mexico in 1916, and was eventually awarded the army's second-highest decoration for bravery, the Distinguished Service Cross. A born entertainer, Ord livened up a gathering with his wit and charm. Ord had been a close pal of Eisenhower's at West Point, and both men had vivid memories of their antics and of walking punishment tours together. Although he may have looked unsoldierly to some (he was said to resemble "central casting's idea of a small-town bank manager"), Ord, as brilliant as Eisenhower, was esteemed both professionally and socially and was one of the best-liked Americans in the Philippines.[15]

Eisenhower was already well versed in Philippine problems from his service under MacArthur in Washington. However, confronting the real-world problems of forming and training an army from scratch was another matter altogether. The primary problem was money. It became virtually impossible to persuade Washington to increase the minuscule Philippine budget. MacArthur consistently downplayed the amounts needed to finance the annual budget in order to obtain Quezon's approval, leaving Eisenhower and Ord to bear the brunt of trying to find a workable solution to the impossible. Quezon, in turn, constantly complained that his government could not afford to support even MacArthur's understated proposals.[16]

Frustration set in quickly. Eisenhower and Ord learned the same lesson as would American advisers during the Vietnam War: Business in Asia was accomplished in a far different fashion from what prevailed at home. They found themselves attempting to cope with the Byzantine political intrigues and patronage of Filipinos with their own agendas. Agreement was less a sign of compliance than a traditional ploy to save face and avoid commitment, with the result that undertakings the American advisers thought were being implemented were instead being ignored or subverted. To avoid unfavorable reactions from the Philippine president, Eisenhower occasionally deliberately mislead Quezon with more optimistic predictions than either he or MacArthur actually believed possible.

One of MacArthur's conditions for accepting the job was that Quezon promote him to the rank of field marshal. Quezon agreed, and in 1935 the Philippine government enacted a National Defense Act. One of its provisions permitted the appointment of Douglas MacArthur as a field marshal in the Philippine army. MacArthur's willing acceptance of an ersatz field marshal's commission contradicted American military tradition and appalled Eisenhower. It became one of the primary reasons for their later estrangement. MacArthur thought that such an exalted rank was quite necessary to enhance the prestige of his position. He accepted not only the title, but the extra pay of $3,980 per month, making him the highest-paid military officer in the world.[17]

At an opulent ceremony presided over by Quezon at the Malacañan Palace, MacArthur was formally presented with a gold baton as a symbol of his new position, after which he delivered one of his patented, stirring speeches, made without notes. Enemies and colleagues alike regarded MacArthur's self-anointed field-marshalship with derision. Eisenhower nearly gagged with disgust, terming the ceremony "rather fantastic." He thought it "pompous and rather ridiculous" for MacArthur "to be the field marshal of a virtually non-existing army." His staff had been led to believe that Quezon had initiated

MacArthur's field-marshalship, but when Quezon visited Washington in 1942, Eisenhower learned that it had been MacArthur's idea.[18]

Quezon attempted to have both Eisenhower and Ord promoted to brigadier generals in the Philippine army. Eisenhower adamantly refused to accept such a "promotion" and wrote in his diary that he was "unalterably opposed" and had informed MacArthur "that I personally would decline . . . in the event it were tendered to me."[19] Three decades later Eisenhower had lost none of his indignation over what he believed was MacArthur's disloyalty to the army. "You have been a four-star general," he said. " 'This is a *proud* thing. There's only been a few who had it. Why in the *hell* do you want a *banana* country giving you a field-marshalship?' MacArthur not only rejected Eisenhower's pleas but, "Oh, Jesus, he just gave me hell!"[20]

Relations between Quezon and MacArthur, never close to begin with, soured almost from the outset and continued to deteriorate throughout Eisenhower's assignment in the Philippines. MacArthur's advice was expressed more in the form of demands, which rankled the vanity of the Philippine president. Although MacArthur kept an office in the presidential palace, the two rarely met or spoke. MacArthur made arbitrary changes without coordinating with Quezon about the size of the Philippine army or the numbers of men to be trained, and rarely accepted dissenting advice from Eisenhower or Ord. Eisenhower once heard MacArthur refer to Quezon as a "conceited little monkey."[21] MacArthur's relations with Quezon deteriorated to the point where the Philippine president would directly solicit Eisenhower's advice. Eisenhower not only filled the void but, at Quezon's request, every so often even wrote the president's speeches. Thus it was Eisenhower and Ord, not MacArthur, to whom Quezon most often turned for advice. The longer MacArthur remained in Manila, the more estranged he became from Quezon.

How did Eisenhower manage to challenge one of the U.S. Army's most autocratic soldiers with virtual impunity? Few officers of any rank ever dared to defy MacArthur, much less with Eisenhower's vehemence. The reasons had much to do with Eisenhower's increasing confidence in his own professional ability, and with his belief that MacArthur needed him more than he needed MacArthur. Eisenhower's flaming temper and his own considerable ego made him a match for MacArthur's imperiousness. Each man was far too stubborn to give in to the other. John Eisenhower believes that both were at fault. "Faced with plenty of other frustrations in the job they were trying to perform, neither man seems to have made much effort to realize what the other was going through."[22]

Even so, Eisenhower's shouting matches and his defiance verged on outright insubordination. "Probably no one had tougher fights with a senior man than I did with MacArthur. I told him time and time again, 'Why in the *hell* don't you *fire* me? Goddammit, you do things I don't agree with and you know damn well I don't.'" The usual result of such an intemperate pronouncement is to have one's wish speedily granted, at the price of a career-ending bad efficiency report. That MacArthur could have ruined his career at the stroke of a pen does not seem to have bothered Eisenhower, nor, he said, did it occur to him to worry about the possible consequences.[23]

His stormy encounters with MacArthur undoubtedly toughened Eisenhower to the enormous pressures and demands that would be placed on him during World War II. However, so weary did he become of their deteriorating relations that there were times when Eisenhower wished MacArthur had actually sacked him. During MacArthur's forty-eight-year military career no one ever stood up to him more forcefully than Eisenhower. Although Ord and Eisenhower aroused MacArthur's wrath for daring to challenge him, he was too shrewd to relieve the two best staff officers he ever had.

MacArthur's duties in the Philippines were more befitting a noble gentleman of leisure than a military adviser. He rarely came to work before 11:00 A.M. and usually departed for the day after a late lunch with his young son Arthur, and his second wife, Jean (née Faircloth), a vivacious Tennesseean whom he had met and courted during the voyage to the Philippines in 1935. MacArthur's strange work hours put additional pressures on his staff, who could not leave until he did. During World War II, MacArthur followed the same practice. A longtime subordinate remembers that, when informed by a visiting civilian executive "that he was killing his staff with such long hours, General MacArthur simply replied, 'Do you know a better way for them to die?' "[24]

After MacArthur ordered the mobilization of twenty thousand Filipinos in 1937, Eisenhower and Ord pleaded with him that there were no funds to support such an action. "Jim and I undertook to get the general to modify his order. . . . We insisted further than the general thought we should, and he gave us one of his regular shouting tirades. He seemed particularly bitter toward me. . . . I argue these points with more heat and persistency than does Jim—consequently I come in for the more severe criticism."[25]

Eisenhower became mired in a dreary routine of playing mediator between MacArthur and Quezon. The only bright spot occurred when, after serving nearly sixteen years as a major, Eisenhower was promoted to lieutenant colonel on July 1, 1936, his twentieth wedding anniversary. The event, however, did not even merit an entry in his diary.

In September 1936 Eisenhower was under active consideration for the position of commandant of cadets at West Point by his War College mentor, Maj. Gen. William D. Connor, the new superintendent. After MacArthur refused to release him, Connor declined to give up, and in January 1937 again requested Eisenhower. MacArthur again adamantly refused, citing Eisenhower's duties "of the gravest importance. He could not adequately be replaced."[26]

It was Eisenhower's only chance to have escaped MacArthur and the Philippines, but he would not have accepted the post if given the choice. As much as he had enjoyed his West Point experience, he had no interest in duty there, recalling that in his time, "the Commandant was merely the head of the 'skinning' department. . . . I had no ambition to get into that kind of business."[27] If Eisenhower had any regrets, they were never publicly articulated, other than a pointed comment that "I wanted no part of that."

Despite all the social activity in bustling Manila, Eisenhower was a lonely man who attempted to hide it through his work and the pretense that it did not matter that his family was not with him. The separation was more difficult for Ike than Mamie. He was utterly miserable during their year apart, and five years later the memories were still fresh when he wrote to a friend being assigned to the Philippines, "it's h—— to be separated so long from families. I was out there a year alone, and I did *not* like it."[28]

In his friend's absence Gee Gerow acted as a surrogate father to John and a guardian angel to Mamie.[29] As much as she missed Ike, Mamie nevertheless enjoyed herself socially through frequent outings in and around Washington. During the Christmas holidays in 1935 Mamie was hardly ever home at night, and was a regular sight on the social circuit. "Word of her apparent independence and resourcefulness no doubt made its way to Manila," wrote her granddaughter.[30]

Ike wrote Mamie infrequently, and her doubts began to mount. His discontent over her refusal to accompany him was palpable in his somber letters, completely lacking his usual upbeat tone. They were also vague about when or where the family would be reunited. As time passed, Mamie reluctantly began to wonder "if he cared as much as he had when he left."

For a time she thought that perhaps the Philippines might take a toll on his health and thus compel his return to the United States. Although he underwent a tonsillectomy and a painful tooth extraction in the spring of 1936, Eisenhower's previous health problems remained in abeyance. The outlet for her fear and frustration continued to be her parents, to whom she confided that Ike "always acts queer in [the] tropics," and wondered if she and John ought to join him, "altho I don't think he's very keen about it."[31] Finally, in the summer of 1936, Mamie faced up to the reality that he would not be cutting short his Philippine assignment, and that "if she wanted to stay married to Ike," she would have to move to Manila.[32]

Their reunion in Manila in October 1936 was chilly. Looking tanned and fit, Ike met Mamie and John wearing a tropical white linen suit and a jaunty panama hat. When he doffed his hat to embrace Mamie, his head was as shiny and bald as the proverbial billiard ball. He explained he had begun shaving it because of the extreme heat and humidity. Although initially unnerved by the sight, Mamie later joked that her husband had not had a lot of hair to shave off.[33]

Mamie found the heat, humidity, and torrential monsoon rains unpleasant reminders of Panama, but took some comfort that their apartment in the Manila Hotel was rather posh by their previous living standards. However, whereas MacArthur's penthouse suite was air-conditioned, the Eisenhower apartment was not, and they sweltered in the summer heat. When Ike returned to the apartment for lunch the two would often eat in their underwear.[34]

Their reunion reopened old wounds over the Philippine assignment. Eisenhower family lore has it that an undercurrent of anger and resentment boiled over almost immediately when Eisenhower made a tart remark that he supposed he now had grounds for divorce, a none-too-subtle backhanded reference to Mamie's socializing in Washington during his absence. Mamie, in turn, was equally displeased (and jealous) to learn that Ike had been playing golf with an American naval officer's wife.

The only Eisenhower who was truly happy was John, who has only glowing memories of the Philippine years. He spent most of the year at a private Episcopalian mission school in Baguio, a resort city in the mountains of central Luzon, where he discovered girls, played tennis, did well academically, and was growing into an independent young man. Although Ike saw less of his son than he would have liked, their reunions did not always turn out the way John imagined. Once he returned to Manila with a white cockatoo presented to him by a Filipino army officer. The bird, which John named Oswald, was dirty and smelly from the trip, and when his father was shown the bird for the first time, he exploded. "Real outbursts of temper were rare with Dad—and he almost always recovered immediately—but when he did become angry, he was spectacular. This time he outdid himself. 'There's nothing I hate worse than parrots and monkeys!' he roared." John was secretly thankful the only reason he had not brought along a monkey was that he had not located one. There followed what one friend described as "operation flying-feathers and bird seed," with "Ike again voicing damnations." Mamie quietly defused the standoff by finding Oswald a new home.[35]

Eventually Mamie got over her dislike of the Philippines, and began to enjoy herself, once scolding her parents "to stop complaining that she was in the Philippines and would be gone for so long, saying simply, 'I know how many mistakes I've made and it's up to me to rectify them.' "[36] Social life in Manila in the 1930s resembled that of Paris in the 1920s. Sexual diversions and other vices were accessible in abundance in one of the world's most hedonistic cities. Most Americans were typically insular and tended to socialize mostly among themselves. Mamie, however, thought Manila was the "partying-est place" she had ever been. Virtually every day there was some sort of social event, ranging from poker, mah-jongg, and bridge to elaborate polo matches and dinners at the Army-Navy Club. "Oh, the social life was terrific," she remembered.[37]

Ike and Mamie were frequently invited to elaborate formal dinners with Quezon at the Malacañan Palace. As Eisenhower's friendship with Quezon matured, on other occasions the two men fished or played bridge together. Sometimes Eisenhower spent stag weekends aboard the presidential yacht, where he was Quezon's preferred bridge partner. Ike's frequent absences in male company or visiting Philippine training sites left Mamie lonely and "desperately homesick."[38]

In 1936 it was decided that the Philippine army needed to train its own pilots to fly light aircraft. A training field was established outside Manila, and two U.S. Army Air Corps flight instructors were recruited to conduct flight training. To call the endeavor the creation of a Philippine air force is to misstate the truth; its primary function was little more than to provide transportation to isolated training sites that otherwise entailed long journeys along a rather crude road system. Coincidentally the endeavor would actually be more beneficial to the American officers helping train the Philippine army.

Eisenhower viewed the occasion as a great opportunity to engage in a pastime that had intrigued him since 1916. Two U.S. Army Air Corps lieutenants, whose mission was to train pilots, Hugh A. Parker and William L. Lee, both future World War II generals, constituted the Philippine "air force," which consisted of a mere handful of borrowed or scrounged assets. One of the trainers they had acquired was a Boeing/Stearman PT-13, the most common aircraft used for training pilots in the United States in the 1930s. Eisenhower hitched a ride with one of the pilots and was immediately hooked on flying. With Mamie still in Washington and thus unable to dissuade him, Eisenhower began taking flying lessons at the age of forty-six. The experience was not only exhilarating but proved a welcome respite from his office routine. Lee was certain that MacArthur had no inkling of Eisenhower's extracurricular activity. Nor did Mamie until her arrival in Manila, when he revealed his new pursuit. Appalled but resigned to having no chance of deterring him, Mamie silently accepted that her husband would become an aviator whether she agreed or not. Her fears were dramatically escalated when Ike also proclaimed that he and John would be accompanying Lieutenant Lee in a flight to Baguio. On hearing this disturbing news Mamie is said to have fled to the sanctity of her bedroom and prayed for divine guidance.[39] John, who would later become a pilot himself, thought it a great adventure. Mamie never learned that Lee and her husband had nearly been killed taking off from what passed as the Bagiuo airfield. When the plane could not muster sufficient power during takeoff to clear a hill at the end of the runway, Lee announced, "We ain't going to make it." Eisenhower sat in the copilot seat, his arms folded across his stomach, and said nothing. At the last moment Lee managed to clear the hill. The two later debated how close they had come to crashing.

"Lee said they cleared it by several feet but Eisenhower was more inclined to measure the clearance in inches."[40]

The most memorable aspect of Eisenhower's Philippine assignment—and indeed of his life—was the times when he could escape the daily tribulations of home and work for the exhilarating freedom of flying. Much later Eisenhower penned a nostalgic reminiscence of the first time he actually flew an airplane, an experience that he titled "Fledgling at Fifty." He recounted a flight with pilot Bill Lee that tested his airman's mettle for the first time. Although he passed it off as a spur-of-the moment decision, Lee had already decided to test how well Eisenhower had absorbed his instruction by turning over the controls and pretending to take a nap as their plane flew at five thousand feet. "Sheer panic crawled up and down my spine, shook my knees and, worst of all, paralyzed my tongue," wrote Eisenhower. " 'My Lord,' I thought, 'does this fool really believe I can fly this thing?' . . . I was tense as a fiddle string." Desperate to perform adequately for his friend and instructor without crashing, Eisenhower overcame his terror and, with some gentle guidance from Lee, managed to fly the machine despite the inevitable mistakes. "I've got that blankety-blank needle almost to where it belongs, and a few more taps this way, that way, and it's perfect. I'm really picking this business up remarkably fast; I'll bet that if I had started a little younger I could be a crack pilot by this time. . . . Ah, boy, I'm really learning."[41]

As often as he could Eisenhower spent the early morning hours taking flying lessons before reporting for duty at the Calle Victoria. On one occasion after he began soloing, Eisenhower could not land his aircraft because a sandbag had become wedged under the control stick. After several passes over the field, he finally managed to land the plane. It was a close call for an inexperienced pilot like Eisenhower, as was another incident during which his plane narrowly averted flying into a mountain. Others far more experienced have paid for such mistakes with their lives.[42]

No one worked harder at becoming proficient than Eisenhower, who was little better than average and whose farsightedness made landings an adventure. He had trouble determining how close the aircraft was to the runway and was coached by Hugh Parker to use the hanger as a point of reference. Parker was particularly impressed that "he had a memory like an elephant" and readily absorbed everything taught to him.[43]

In May 1937 Lee decided that Eisenhower was ready to solo. "After flying with him for about 20 minutes, I got out and told him to get going. 'You mean you want me to fly it by myself?' asked Ike. 'Hell, yes, you can fly it, so get going.' Off he went, alone, circled and landed several times. He was one happy fellow."[44]

After passing his flight physical, he realized one of his most ardent ambitions when he was certified as a qualified private pilot on July 1, 1939, the magic date that now held added importance in his life. Eisenhower eventually logged about 320 hours, 180 as a pilot and 140 as an observer. For all their inherent dangers, Eisenhower's flying lessons remained one of the memorable highlights of his career.

Mamie was anxious to visit John but unwilling to fly to Baguio. Instead, against Ike's advice, she undertook a difficult automobile ride in April 1937 along a so-called road, the last leg of which was up a near-vertical one-way trail. Ike was not thrilled that his driver, a U.S. Army sergeant, would be driving his wife. He regarded the man as "wild beyond reason," and suggested she delay the trip until he could drive her himself. However, their relationship was still mercurial, and both nursed resentments brought about by their painful separation. On this occasion Mamie demonstrated that she could be as stubborn as her husband and refused to delay the trip. In the mountains near Baguio the driver accidentally struck but did not seriously injure a child. For a time, however, it was thought that the child had been killed. Their automobile had been surrounded by local villagers whose intentions were uncertain, and the trip was delayed for many hours until they were cleared by the police to proceed to Baguio. The incident deeply unsettled Mamie.

A short time later an army friend stationed in Baguio telephoned Eisenhower that Mamie had suffered a ruptured blood vessel in her stomach and had vomited blood before lapsing into a coma in the station hospital there. The cause of the hemorrhage was never precisely determined but may have been induced by a combination of stress, altitude, and the jolting trip. What is certain is that without prompt medical attention she would have died. A somber and deeply worried Eisenhower flew immediately to Baguio and kept a bedside vigil until the doctors declared that she would recover. Mamie returned to Manila weak, seriously underweight at less than one hundred pounds, and bedridden much of the time. More than ever she dreamed of the day she would return to the United States for good.[45]

Mamie's near-death illness seems to have been the catalyst that finally restored equilibrium to their marriage. Eisenhower realized how close he had come to losing his wife, and Mamie accepted that a good deal of their marital problems were of her making. Ever since refusing to accompany Ike to Manila in 1935, she had been beset with guilt. A letter written on Easter Sunday 1938 admitted to her parents that she had "made a terrible mistake in not coming out here with Ike."[46]

Jimmy Ord was sent to Washington in 1937 to beg for the loan of field artillery, patrol boats, and other armaments and war matériel for the Philippines from an indifferent War Department. With Ord away, the full workload fell on Eisenhower, who longed for his friend's return. "The sooner he comes the better for me, I'm tired. Over a year and a half at this slavery in this climate and no leave!"[47]

When the position of U.S. high commissioner of the Philippines was created in 1935, Roosevelt selected a powerful political ally, Frank Murphy. Relations between the commission and MacArthur's headquarters grew frosty. Murphy not only disliked MacArthur but was thought to have been behind an attempt to force the closure of the military mission and MacArthur's recall to the United States. Eisenhower was fed up with the intrigues. Murphy, he wrote in his diary in July 1937, was "supposed to have written letters home to the President and the Secretary of War demanding relief of mission. O.K. by me!! *I'm ready to go*. No one seems to realize how much energy and slavery Jim and I put into this d—— job."

The year 1938 was the most stressful of Eisenhower's service in the Philippines. The pressure on him worsened as he became the butt of MacArthur's frustrations. "I'm worn out," he wrote.

In early January Ord and Eisenhower again clashed with MacArthur, this time over the latter's insistence that a number of Filipino army units be assembled for a national parade through the streets of Manila as a means of invigorating public morale. MacArthur had not discussed, much less cleared, his idea with Quezon, and when informed by Ord and Eisenhower that their budget could not possibly stand such a hit without sacrificing funds needed to carry out more important projects, he summarily overruled them. As the two officers began planning for the event, a distressed Quezon learned of the plan and telephoned Eisenhower to inquire why his chief adviser had not bothered to consult him. Quezon then conveyed his displeasure to MacArthur. Embarrassed by the matter, MacArthur lamely denied he had ever ordered his staff to proceed. The chief scapegoats were Ord and Eisenhower. The parade was duly canceled, but the bad feelings between MacArthur and his two assistants was heightened; "never again were we on the same warm and cordial terms," recalled Eisenhower.[48]

Nevertheless, in early 1938, Eisenhower willingly agreed to a one-year extension in Manila at the urging of both Quezon and MacArthur, a decision made more out of loyalty to the president than allegiance to MacArthur. For all their stormy encounters, MacArthur was determined to retain Eisenhower for a fourth year.

Although she would rather have returned to the United States, Mamie made no attempt to influence Ike's decision. Her stubbornness, she realized, had threatened their marriage and, as she confessed to her parents, Mamie did not relish another year in steamy Manila, "but what can I do?" For a decade Ike had reminded her how much he had disliked duty in France with the Battle Monuments Commission, and after their recent difficulties Mamie had resolved never again to meddle in her husband's career decisions. "You know Ike," she lamented, "I told him the other day that it has taken me 22 years to find out that the only way I can get along with him is to give him his own way *constantly*."[49]

On January 28, 1938, Eisenhower checked into the hospital suffering from an intestinal obstruction so acute that his abdomen was distended like that of a "dying frog." Years later his ailment was diagnosed as ileitis, also known as Crohn's disease. Ileitis occurs from an inability to digest certain foods properly, resulting in scarring of the tissue of the lower part of the small intestine, called the ileum. His doctors described it as a dangerous "stoppage of the bowel" and prepared to operate at once. At some point Eisenhower fainted from the pain and awakened on the operating table as he was about to be anesthetized. "I think I would like to go to the toilet," he announced. The surgery was postponed and later canceled after he was able to expel the rest of the gas, an experience that was made deeply embarrassing for the extremely private Eisenhower by the presence of a nurse assigned to his bedside for the sole purpose of monitoring him. He later recalled the ordeal as one in which he had suffered "the tortures of the damned."[50]

The last straw was the untimely death of his best friend, Jimmy Ord, on January 30, 1938, the result of a freak accident of the sort that nearly killed Eisenhower in 1937. The morning of his death Ord had visited Eisenhower in the hospital. When he mentioned his forthcoming trip to Baguio with a Filipino student pilot, Eisenhower begged him to have Bill Lee or Hugh Parker pilot the aircraft. Ord's decision not to do so cost him his life. Flying over Baguio, Ord decided to drop a rock with a note attached at the house of a friend to notify him of his arrival. The student pilot misjudged his speed, the engine stalled, and the plane crash-landed on a hillside, mortally injuring Ord, who had been leaning out of the aircraft and was crushed.

Ord's death left an enormous void in Eisenhower's life. The news left him thunderstruck and grieving at the loss of a dear friend whom he regarded like a brother.[51] Quezon publicly lamented that he was "grieved beyond measure over the tragic death of Colonel Ord," whom he described as one of the best friends the Philippine Commonwealth had ever had.[52] A large crowd that included Quezon and other government officials attended Ord's funeral. Conspicuous by his absence was MacArthur, who had a lifelong aversion to funerals and would not attend them.[53]

Ord was replaced by Maj. Richard D. Sutherland, a dour infantry officer and a future general, who remained in MacArthur's service throughout World War II, rising to become his chief of staff and principal yes man. Eisenhower was previously acquainted with Sutherland, who had lived in the Wyoming Apartments in Washington. Sutherland was universally disliked both by civilians and military personnel, and has been variously described as "efficient," "ruthless," a "martinet," and by MacArthur's chief World War II airman, Gen. George Kenney, as someone who "always rubbed people the wrong way."[54] One of MacArthur's biographers more bluntly describes Sutherland as "an unpleasant son of a bitch."[55] Ruthlessly ambitious, Sutherland had no intention of sharing access to MacArthur, and schemed to get rid of Eisenhower, who did not seem to recognize the full extent of Sutherland's determination to undermine his standing with MacArthur. The perfect opportunity arose in 1938, when Eisenhower returned to the United States for several months. Sutherland filled in for him, and whereas Eisenhower would challenge Mac-Arthur, Sutherland effectively stroked his ego.

Nothing was ever again the same for Eisenhower after Ord's passing. Three months later he still mourned his friend deeply, writing in his diary, "I cannot fully realize that he is never again to come walking into the office with his cheery 'top of the morning, Comra-a-ade!' "[56] He had not only lost a friend but had gained a cold-blooded rival. Eisenhower managed to conceal his anger and frustration from Mamie and John, who "had no inkling, when the two of us toured Northern Luzon in May 1938, that he was undergoing some of his worst moments in . . . MacArthur's headquarters."[57] Without Jimmy Ord to help relieve the strain, Eisenhower felt hopelessly isolated.

In 1938 Eisenhower received another strange but lucrative offer to return to civilian life. He had heated arguments with Hitler supporters within the Spanish populace in Manila, and even with some American civilians. His anti-Nazi and anti-Hitler views had become well-enough known to Manila's tiny Jewish community that he was approached by a committee of Jewish expatriates who wanted him to establish sanctuaries throughout Asia for escapees from Hitler's anti-Semitic Reich. In return, they guaranteed him the princely sum of sixty thousand dollars annually (more than $1.85 million in 1989 dollars) for a minimum of five years. Eisenhower politely declined.

In late June 1938 the Eisenhowers departed for the United States aboard the S.S. *President Coolidge*. Two of the liner's ports of call were Tokyo and Yokohama. In Yokohama the ship was boarded by Japanese customs officers to clear passengers for trips ashore. However, when Eisenhower handed over his passport, the Japanese seemed to know that he was an army officer. He was treated with outright hostility and subjected to a lengthy interrogation. John remembers, "Finally, Dad lost his temper and said, 'I want nothing here; only to spend a few damned yen in your country!' " The officials relented, but the experience left Eisenhower convinced that their English-speaking tour guides were really Japanese intelligence agents.[58]

The family arrived in San Francisco three weeks later and traveled to Denver and a joyful reunion with the Douds. After the incident in Baguio, Mamie had continued to experience painful gastrointestinal distress, and it was decided that the cure lay in an operation to remove her gallbladder. She remained in Denver until September recuperating, while Ike was in Washington to take up where Ord had left off the previous year. The summer passed like a whirlwind as Eisenhower met repeatedly with War Department officials to plead MacArthur's case for war matériel. He also visited several arms and aircraft manufacturers before sailing from Vancouver, British Columbia, in mid-October.[59]

.   .   .

After his return to Manila in November 1938, Eisenhower was shocked to learn that in his absence MacArthur had stripped him of his role as his principle adviser and chief of staff, replacing him with the scheming Sutherland. Too late Eisenhower learned that Sutherland had used his absence to ingratiate himself with MacArthur, who promoted him to lieutenant colonel and installed him as his new right-hand man. Eisenhower's new job, ostensibly to better utilize his talents, was that of MacArthur's chief planner. Eisenhower thought otherwise, believing it was payback for one quarrel too many with the boss. Moreover, with the year's extension nearly over, Eisenhower was convinced that his usefulness in Manila was at an end. With one or two exceptions he had lost contact with anyone of influence in Washington, and could not even be certain of obtaining a coveted troop assignment in the United States. If Eisenhower had been otherwise tempted to extend his tour of duty to a fifth year, MacArthur's reorganization irrefutably terminated any consideration of remaining in Manila beyond the end of 1939. It was indeed time to return to the United States.

22.

"I'm a Soldier. I'm Going Home."

We're going to go to war and I'm going to be in it.

On September 1, 1939, war erupted in Europe when Hitler's armies invaded Poland, using a bogus pretext to crush a valiant but hopelessly outgunned Polish army in a matter of days. Britain and France responded by declaring war against Germany. For the time being the United States remained neutral. Despite FDR's great empathy with Britain's plight, he was seriously hampered by the pervasive American isolationism of the 1930s.

On September 3 a somber Prime Minister Neville Chamberlain addressed the British nation to announce that Britain had declared war on Germany. In faraway Manila, Ike, Mamie, and John listened raptly to what was "a solemn moment" on a friend's shortwave radio. Eisenhower correctly envisioned that the mobilization of the U.S. armed forces was only a matter of time.

Deeply unsettled by what he had just heard, Eisenhower wrote in his diary, "It's a sad day for Europe and for the whole civilized world. . . . If the war, which now seems to be upon us, is as long, drawn out and disastrous, as bloody and as costly as was the so-called World War, then I believe the remnants of nations emerging from it will be scarcely recognizable . . . it doesn't seem possible that people that proudly refer to themselves as intelligent could let the situation come about."

During their trip to the United States in 1938 John was thought to have appendicitis. (He did not.) "The two of us were standing in the hospital, talking about this Munich agreement that everybody else was so infuriated about. Dad was discouraged, but he said, 'Things are so bad right now, at least *something* might happen. Maybe this son-of-a-bitch (Hitler) will get shot. At least this buys a little time. . . . Dad figured that the time has come, and he wanted to be back for the mobilization of the U.S. Army, if for no other reason."[1] Mamie was convinced that "his mind was made up, as of September [1938], that this was the time to go." Quezon's pleas were to no avail. Said Eisenhower emphatically, "I'm a soldier. I'm going home. We're going to go to war and I'm going to be in it."[2] Three weeks later Eisenhower wrote to Mark Clark that his imminent return to the Regular Army left him feeling "like a boy who has been promised an electric train for Christmas."[3]

MacArthur's staff reorganization was a terrible blow that left Eisenhower not only stripped of his powers but feeling like an outsider kept around merely as window dressing. His bitterness was evident in his first diary entry after returning from the United States. He defended his contacts and high-level friendships within the Philippine government. "Why the man should so patently exhibit a jealousy of a subordinate is beyond me," he wrote. ". . . I'm going at the earliest possible moment." Later Sutherland would proudly state that he had "gotten rid of Eisenhower."[4]

Eisenhower was forty-nine years old and his career was seemingly stuck in reverse gear. If he was to fulfill even part of his ambition before facing an inevitable forced retirement, he had to make something positive happen. His duty in the Philippines brought home that while he still appeared youthful, he had slipped into middle age and possessed few prospects other than more years of toil for a man for whom he had lost respect. As Eisenhower historian Robert Ferrell notes, "The face revealed an easy affability, but behind it was a tension that sometimes came out in irritation or anger and in any event showed a personality desirous of making every minute count . . . the face of the youth of Abilene showed in the changes of aging but the purposefulness was always there."[5] So too was the brusqueness and the lack of patience to suffer fools—a category MacArthur had increasingly come to fit since the disastrous Bonus March. If two descriptions were to characterize Eisenhower's duty in the Philippines, they were anger and frustration. Although his reaction to MacArthur's snub may have seemed at the time to be another example of Eisenhower's habit of blowing off steam to rid his mind of an unpleasant incident, he never forgot that his "reward" for more than six years of toil was a *demotion.*

Eisenhower decided that the time had come to do something constructive to resurrect his career. Since 1927 he had labored at the behest of Pershing, Moseley, and (since 1933) MacArthur. Although his reputation had prospered, his career had not. He turned for help to his colleague Mark W. Clark. Eisenhower and Clark first met and became friends at West Point. Clark was a member of the class of 1917, and as one of the tallest cadets, was assigned to Eisenhower's barracks. Clark's biographer, Martin Blumenson, notes, "Although close relationships between members of different classes were discouraged, Clark and Eisenhower struck it off. They formed the basis of what would be a deep and enduring friendship."[6]

Eisenhower was far more successful in sequestering his own aspirations behind the mask of the good-old-country-boy from Kansas. Clark, whose friends and superiors addressed him by his middle name, Wayne, was intensely and openly ambitious. Like MacArthur, there was hardly a middle

ground of opinion about him. Whereas Clark's supporters perceived professionalism and self-confidence, his detractors saw only conceit and ruthlessness. What was never in dispute, however, was Clark's great physical courage,
which he would demonstrate time and again during World War II.

Commissioned for barely a year, Clark had fleeting World War I experience in France as an acting infantry battalion commander in the 5th Division
in June 1918. He was gravely wounded the first time his unit came under
German artillery fire, dashing his fantasy of becoming a heroic battlefield
figure. Although he recovered from his near-death injuries, Clark was classified as unfit for further combat duty and ended the war as a staff officer.

Clark's World War I experience merely fueled his towering ambition to
climb to the top of his profession. During the interwar years he gained a
reputation as the foremost training expert in the army, and one of its most
highly regarded young officers. In the process he caught the eye of George
Marshall, then army deputy chief of staff, who became both a friend and
mentor.

At the end of the trip to the United States in 1938, where Eisenhower
continued the effort begun by Ord to gain the release of surplus equipment
to the Philippine army, Eisenhower visited his friend Mark Clark at Fort
Lewis. Clark greeted him warmly and took him on a tour of the fort and
expounded his ideas for conducting large-scale training to a responsive Eisenhower. His visit with Clark was all the incentive Eisenhower needed to remind
himself that he was first and foremost a soldier who had been away from his
fundamental infantry duties far too long. He left determined to actively seek
a troop assignment when his tour of duty ended in Manila in 1939. Clark
promised to use his newfound influence to help his friend secure troop duty.[7]

The renewal of their friendship was a turning point in both their careers.
Clark used every opportunity to extol Eisenhower's qualifications. Although
it cannot be argued that Eisenhower would never have been "discovered"
without Clark to boost his cause, what is certain is that Clark's voice was
heard in the right quarters and his advice heeded at precisely the right times.
Eisenhower never had a stronger advocate than Mark Clark, and the results
of this mutual esteem would soon pay off.

In the small professional army of the interwar years, ambitious junior
officers like Eisenhower, Patton, and Clark used virtually any means at their
disposal to gain favor, influence an assignment, or obtain support for a particular cause. Unofficial letters from junior officers to the chief of staff or
other senior officer are virtually unknown in today's army. From the time he
was commissioned a second lieutenant of cavalry in 1909, Patton had proved
a master at what today is termed "bootlicking," but that in his time was
considered neither unusual nor pretentious. Likewise Eisenhower and Mark
Clark had both mastered the fine art of schmoozing a senior officer. When

Gen. Malin Craig was succeeded as chief of staff by George Marshall in September 1939, Eisenhower used the occasion to write a glowing letter praising Craig as a member of a "brilliant group" of army officers: "You occupy in my mind a very special place . . . [for your] unswerving devotion to the Army rather than to self."[8]

Among its many functions the Adjutant General's Department administered the army bureaucracy: transfers, personnel actions, and such other activities. The adjutant general himself was one of the most powerful figures in the War Department, and his function in the 1930s included an advisory role in personnel assignments. Although Eisenhower was still under the control of the infantry branch, a friend in the AG's office could be extremely helpful. Eisenhower, Clark, and T. J. Davis had a mutual friend and benefactor in James Ulio, then the adjutant general's executive officer. Not long after Eisenhower's visit to Fort Lewis, Clark kept his word and sought Ulio's intervention on behalf of Eisenhower. Another of Ulio's friends was his AG colleague, T. J. Davis, who had served MacArthur even longer than Eisenhower. Davis was anxious to escape Manila for a stateside assignment and wrote to Ulio on behalf of himself and Eisenhower.

Thus it was hardly a coincidence that in May 1939 Eisenhower received orders from the War Department assigning him to Fort Lewis. Even so, the fact that Ulio successfully influenced Eisenhower's assignment was no mean feat, given that there was an excess of lieutenant colonels competing for only a handful of command and staff positions in the only three active U.S. Army infantry divisions.[9]

Eisenhower asked to be relieved of his duties in Manila effective in August 1939 and met immediate opposition from both MacArthur and Quezon. However, no amount of persuasion or inducements, including a large amount of cash and other perks from Quezon, who offered him a virtual blank check, would dissuade Eisenhower, who said, "Mr. President . . . no amount of money can make me change my mind." Publicly Eisenhower would later moderate his relationship with MacArthur. "Hostility between us has been exaggerated. After all, there must be a strong tie for two men to work so closely for seven years."[10] Privately Eisenhower was resentful of his many years of being used like Kleenex by MacArthur, and weary of his shameless politicking and his imperiousness in Washington and Manila, which obliged him to play the intermediary. MacArthur attempted to talk Eisenhower out of leaving, but by this time the MacArthur charm had worn too thin. Eisenhower remained adamant about rejoining the Regular Army. Had he elected to, MacArthur could have blocked his reassignment on the grounds that he was vital to the success of the American effort, and for a time Eisenhower worried that he might do so.

Eisenhower resented being overworked for ten thousand dollars per annum while MacArthur was being richly rewarded for doing very little. A group of Filipino congressmen was on the verge of introducing a bill in the Philippine legislature to reward Eisenhower by abolishing MacArthur's job, thus effectively leaving Eisenhower as the senior U.S. military adviser in the American mission. "When Eisenhower heard about it, he went to them and told them that if they ever introduced that bill he would immediately ask to be returned to the United States. Under no circumstances would he be a party to it."[11] Given their growing alienation, all indications point to a desire on Quezon's part to be rid of MacArthur, and he may well have been behind the initiative to promote Eisenhower in his place. The Philippine president was genuinely sad to lose Eisenhower, both for his role as a buffer between himself and MacArthur, but also as a close friend and confidant whose judgment he implicitly trusted.

On Eisenhower's penultimate day in Manila, Quezon hosted a luncheon in his honor where he was decorated with the Philippine Distinguished Service Star. The medal was pinned on his uniform blouse by Mamie; the citation praised Eisenhower's "exceptional talents . . . his breadth of understanding [and] his zeal and magnetic leadership."[12]

In a rare gesture of goodwill, MacArthur and Jean not only saw the Eisenhowers off in mid-December 1939 but the usually reserved MacArthur presented Eisenhower with a bottle of Scotch. Undoubtedly the reality of losing his trusted assistant had finally registered. "We talked of the gloominess of world prospects, but our forebodings turned toward Europe—not Asia."[13] The two would not see each other again until after World War II.

Outwardly both men parted on cordial terms that masked their true feelings. In retrospect their clashes had been inevitable. "Where the practical Eisenhower saw problems, the visionary MacArthur saw possibilities. To Eisenhower, the Philippine General Staff was beset by rank-conscious, backbiting, inefficiency, and corruption. To MacArthur it was composed of loyal, intelligent men who were well on their way to learning how to run an army."[14]

Eisenhower's "betrayal"—leaving his service in 1939—earned MacArthur's enmity, which was destined to reach monumental proportions. Eisenhower never forgave MacArthur for branding him a liar over the parade incident in 1938, which he deemed the ultimate disloyalty. In 1940 Eisenhower related to his friend Robert L. Eichelberger that the incident had been the last straw in their deteriorating relationship.[15] Their disparities notwithstanding, each had profited from the relationship: MacArthur from the services of a brilliant staff officer, and Eisenhower from the experience gained in high-level politics in Washington and Manila, which would shortly serve him well.

What then may be concluded from the seven years these two strong-willed men served together? Despite their diverse personalities, Eisenhower was capable of separating MacArthur's virtues from his shortcomings and making the most of them. Eisenhower's unflattering observations of MacArthur between 1932 and 1940 were more the product of frustration than of animosity. Eisenhower was smart enough to realize how much he had to learn from MacArthur. He related to MacArthur's official biographer that he was "deeply grateful for the administrative experience gained under General MacArthur," which helped prepare him for "the great responsibilities of the war period."[16] Eisenhower's intelligence, seemingly unlimited capacity for sheer hard work, and his superb organizational skills had proven invaluable to MacArthur, albeit in what was ultimately the losing cause of Philippine military preparedness. Yet Eisenhower left Manila with a great sense of relief. Recalling his Philippine experience in 1941, Eisenhower declared, "I don't give a hoot who gets credit for anything in the P.I. I got out *clean*—and that's that!"[17]

For Mamie, who had resisted accompanying Ike to the Philippines, it was a bittersweet occasion. In spite of the heat, and a husband who was rarely home, she had enjoyed herself far more than she had ever thought possible and was actually sorry to be leaving their many good friends. Both were deeply touched by their send-off. It seemed that the entire American population of Manila had come out to bid them farewell. As a band played on the dockside, the transport ship *Cleveland* slipped its moorings and headed out to sea. The ship was escorted from Manila harbor by two aircraft piloted by Army Air Corps friends of Colonel Eisenhower. "It was a swell goodbye."[18]

Part V

THE UNITED STATES PREPARES
FOR WAR, 1940–1942

*The American army's capacity to transform itself
during the next few years was as impressive an
achievement as any in military history.*

RUSSELL F. WEIGLEY

23.

"This Work Is Fun!"

I could not conceive of a better job. . . . I belonged with troops; with them I was always happy.

When Gen. Malin Craig retired at the end of August 1939, Roosevelt appointed Brig. Gen. George C. Marshall over thirty-three more senior generals to become the new army chief of staff. When FDR announced his appointment, Pershing wrote that Marshall "will make a great name for himself and prove a great credit to the American Army and the American people."[1] The army Marshall inherited was woefully unprepared for war. Although generally without either influence or direction from above, the army nevertheless did nothing to help itself by its signal failure to utilize even a fraction of its budget on research and development or to modernize its existing organization during the interwar years.[2]

Marshall was one of Franklin Delano Roosevelt's most inspired appointments. A difficult and demanding officer to work for, Marshall was renowned for his bluntness and his impatience. Those who served under him soon learned they either produced or were cut from his team. Not even the president could intimidate Marshall, who never hesitated to disagree with Roosevelt when he thought his commander in chief was mistaken. It is said only the president and Vinegar Joe Stilwell ever dared to call Marshall "George" to his face, and that Roosevelt did so only once. In the highly politicized atmosphere of Washington the president valued Marshall's willingness to speak truthfully and candidly without fear of the consequences. It was the beginning of what historian Thomas Parrish has so aptly described as "the most triumphantly effective political-military team in American history."[3]

When Germany overran Poland, the United States was arguably a third-rate power with an army that ranked a pathetic seventeenth in the world.[4] It was made up of many phantom fighting units; those that did exist, like the 3rd Division, were understrength. Such was the sorry state of the U.S. Army in 1940 that it would have been ill-prepared to "to repel raids across the Rio Grande by Mexican bandits."[5]

By 1940 Marshall had already begun expediting a complete overhaul of the training of the army's regular, reserve, and national guard units for war. Marshall's blueprint for streamlining the army's organization was made all the more difficult to carry out because of continued U.S. isolationism and the ingrained World War I mentality that still prevailed at too many levels within the army itself, even among good and honorable men. Everything from weapons to tactics and training was hopelessly outdated. However, to establish a modern fighting army required far more than a change of attitude; it meant a commitment from a core of professionals whom Marshall trusted to carry out this task. A number of his senior staff officers were men soon to be pegged for greater rank and responsibility, among them some of the best-known commanders and senior officers of World War II: Omar Bradley, Walter Bedell Smith, J. Lawton Collins, Maxwell Taylor, and Leonard Gerow.

Although conscription was not enacted until the summer of 1940, when Congress created the Selective Service System, Marshall nevertheless had already begun to step up training. One of his first acts after becoming chief of staff was to persuade the usually obstinate navy to cooperate in joint army-navy exercises to train for the inevitable occasions when American fighting units would have to assault enemy-held shores and engage Hitler's powerful panzer divisions. To develop new weapons, tactics, and, indeed, a whole new mind-set was as daunting a challenge as has ever been faced by an American general. What few maneuvers the army had staged during the interwar years were of little consequence. To begin remedying this problem, the War Department ordered every unit in the Fourth Army to assemble in California for training exercises to be held in Monterey and at the sprawling Hunter Liggett Military Reservation near Salinas, commencing in January 1940.

Planning large-scale exercises is a complex, time-consuming venture involving myriad planning activities at every level in the chain of command. Months of preparation are normally required, but time had become an unaffordable luxury. What might have taken nearly a year in peacetime was reduced to a matter of weeks. The exercise called for the navy to transport an element of the 3rd Division from its home station at Fort Lewis to Monterey, where it would stage a mock invasion against a national guard "enemy" division defending the town, in what would be the first amphibious exercise ever mounted by the U.S. Army in peacetime.

None of this was known to Eisenhower aboard the *Cleveland* as it followed its normal route, sailing first to Hong Kong, then Shanghai, where "we got tight (only one of us)," wrote Eisenhower some months later, followed by stops in Kobe ("disgusted") and Yokohama ("more so"). The voyage from Japan to Hawaii and then San Francisco was less than idyllic. In addition to an unsettling trip across the storm-tossed Pacific, Eisenhower was unable to find anyone on board with enough skill to make up a decent bridge game. By the time they arrived in San Francisco on January 5, 1940, Eisenhower's assignment to Fort Lewis had already been temporarily derailed. "We were hustling off the dock when a very military looking sergeant came down the line paging Colonel Eisenhower, in a voice that indicated he thought I was still in Hawaii. Upon acknowledging, unwillingly, my identity (I could smell trouble) I was handed an order" to report for temporary duty in the headquarters of Lt. Gen. John L. DeWitt's Fourth Army, at the nearby Presidio of San Francisco. "That order blew up a sizeable typhoon in the family." When it quickly became obvious that the family's relocation to Fort Lewis would be delayed indefinitely, John was sent ahead to reside with his Uncle Edgar and attend school in nearby Tacoma. Ike and Mamie reluctantly settled into a hotel in San Francisco.[6]

DeWitt, who had commanded the Philippine Department in 1936–37, knew Eisenhower well and admired his skills. Faced with a shortage of experienced planners to help formulate plans for the coming exercise, an event that would draw enormous interest at the highest levels of the army, DeWitt appropriated Eisenhower and assigned him to help plan the maneuver. A dismayed Eisenhower made it clear that he was sick of staff duty and was not there by choice. "At first I thought it was the old, old story, and that once more I was to start a tour of 'staff' duty instead of getting to troops." He appealed to be permitted to report to his regiment for duty as soon as possible, and was assured by DeWitt that the assignment was only temporary "pick and shovel work during the month of January."[7]

Eisenhower was tasked to study the problem of moving numerous troop units to California, and concluded that transportation complications would preclude all units training together as directed by the War Department. His immediate superior rigidly interpreted all orders as gospel and rebuffed Eisenhower's recommendations for a compromise plan. Although Eisenhower was forbidden to inform DeWitt, the general accidentally learned of the problem and questioned Eisenhower as to why he had not reported the matter to him. Eisenhower loyally defended his superior even though he did not agree with him, noting only that the colonel had thought it unnecessary to bother DeWitt. The general, who thought otherwise, had Eisenhower rewrite the plan.[8]

Eisenhower's second encounter with Marshall took place purely by chance on a Monterey, California, beach shortly before the exercise commenced. Accompanied by DeWitt, the chief of staff was present not only to observe but to lend substance to its importance by his presence. Many years earlier Marshall had been exposed to the good life of Manila that enabled even underpaid officers to hire domestic help at a modest cost. Marshall greeted Eisenhower and remarked drily, displaying a humorous side few realized he possessed, "Have you learned to tie your own shoes again since coming back [from the Philippines], Eisenhower?" A grinning Eisenhower replied, "Yes, Sir," he could indeed handle that chore just fine.[9]

True to his word, DeWitt reluctantly released Eisenhower early February 1940 to join the 15th Infantry at Fort Lewis. He had only a week to settle Mamie into post quarters before accompanying the regiment to California, where it was housed at Camp Ord, a new post being created of primitive wood buildings on the sandy heights overlooking Monterey Bay. Camp (later Fort) Ord was named in honor of Jimmy Ord's grandfather, Maj. Gen. E. O. C. Ord, a noted Indian fighter and one of Ulysses S. Grant's corps commanders during the Civil War.[10]

Eisenhower was assigned as the executive officer and immediately detailed as the regiment's chief umpire, earning high marks during training exercises that took place from February to mid-May 1940. After more than three months, Eisenhower had lost none of his enthusiasm, writing to newly promoted Brig. Gen. Courtney Hodges that he was having a "grand time." The 15th Infantry was to redeploy to Fort Lewis shortly, and Eisenhower noted that he expected to be given command of one of its three infantry battalions.

Mark Clark's boss was Maj. Gen. Walter C. Sweeney, the 3rd Division commander. During the divisional exercises, Sweeney, an avid poker player, insisted on a nightly game and tasked Clark to line up the players. Only members of the division staff were allowed to participate. One night, however, several of the regulars were unavailable; Clark proposed admitting an outsider to the poker circle. "Who is he? Can he play poker?" challenged the general. Sweeney was told yes, and that it was newly assigned Lt. Col. Dwight Eisenhower. The two men were longtime acquaintances, and Sweeney was pleased with Eisenhower's assignment to Fort Lewis. "That did it. Ike was welcomed warmly into the staff poker game, even though he was a regimental officer, a sort of 'outsider.' " Eisenhower's return to the poker table lost nothing to his years of abstinence. By the time the game ended Eisenhower's wallet was very much fatter. His victims included both Clark and Sweeney, who glared at Clark and groused, 'What do you mean bringing a ringer into the game?' "[11] Eisenhower is not known to have been invited back.

When the 3rd Division returned to Fort Lewis, Eisenhower was appointed to a highly dual role of regimental executive officer and commander of the 1st Battalion, 15th Infantry, an unusual arrangement made possible through Clark's influence.[12] For a second time Eisenhower owed his friend a substantial debt.

Like virtually every other such unit in 1940, his battalion was at about half strength and consisted of a mix of experienced Regular Army men and raw, untrained volunteer recruits. Eisenhower's arrival was like a dose of cold Pacific air. Little had changed in his approach to command since Camp Colt in 1918. He was stern but fair, insistent on military discipline, and an exacting taskmaster. Nothing escaped his attention. One morning Eisenhower ordered a soldier participating in a weapons-firing exercise to produce his score book, which turned out to be blank. The young man had failed to record a single entry, for which Eisenhower properly blamed his platoon leader, Lt. Burton S. Barr, who was summoned to face his new battalion commander, out of earshot of the men. Barr was subjected to a lambasting that he took to the grave. "I've heard about being eaten out," he said, "and I've seen it, but this was unique. This wasn't being eaten out. This was Eisenhower having a buffet supper, and I was the complete meal." To say that Eisenhower had put the fear of God into his lieutenant (and everyone else) was an understatement. Yet later that day, Eisenhower said to Barr, "I'm going to tell you something, lieutenant, and you'd better listen carefully. This morning you did something wrong, and I bawled you out for it. *That was the end.* We don't carry grudges around here."[13]

Not long after assuming command, Eisenhower wrote to Omar Bradley, with whom he had not served since West Point. Bradley was a lieutenant colonel on the War Department General Staff, and the letter was a gauge of Eisenhower's exhilaration at being back with troops. "Ike Eisenhower, 15th Infantry, speaking," he wrote:

> I am having the time of my life. Like everyone else in the army, we're up to our necks in work and problems, big and little. But this work is fun! . . . I could not conceive of a better job; except, of course, having one's own regiment, which is out of the question because of rank. I'm regimental executive, command the 1st Battalion, and run a [training] school four afternoons per week. I hope the students don't know it, but I learn more than they do.[14]

Eisenhower's thinking and acute sense of urgency mirrored that of Marshall and others, among them Patton. While Eisenhower struggled to impart a sense of urgency to an infantry battalion at Fort Lewis in 1940–41, at Fort Benning, Georgia, Patton was driving his troops unremittingly to prepare them for combat, endlessly preaching that training, discipline, and leadership would win battles and keep them alive. Eisenhower was contemptuous of many of the old army types for their naïve beliefs and an unwillingness to treat the war in Europe as an event that would deeply affect the United States. The period of the so-called Phony War in Europe, between the fall of Poland in September 1939 and the German invasion of France in May 1940, may have reassured many, but Eisenhower was not among them.

At first evolving changes emanating from Washington had little effect on commanders in the army's far-flung outposts, where, as Eisenhower wrote, it was hopeless to "eliminate an apathy that had its roots in comfort, blindness, and wishful thinking."[15] Why were socializing, athletics, and dull military routine taking precedence over building and training an army for war? Where was a sense of urgency?

Determined to jar his men from their peacetime reveries, Eisenhower began to preach some unpleasant truths, namely that the United States would soon be at war in Europe. Some were incredulous: How could there be war when the nation was isolationist and pacifist? Was this man a lunatic? Eisenhower assembled his officers and proclaimed, "If any of you think we are not going to war, I don't want you in my battalion. We're going to war. This country is going to war, and I want people who are prepared to fight that war."[16] His words made a swift impression on his new charges. It was the first time they heard anyone actually speak seriously about war.

It became obvious to all that here was an officer whom one crossed at one's peril. Although some remained incredulous at the notion that the United States would ever become involved in another European war, no one asked for a transfer. To the contrary his officers and men soon developed a healthy respect for their new commander. Others at Fort Lewis, however, began to refer to him as "Alarmist Ike." But at least the message had gone out to his command that peacetime business as usual was history.

Eisenhower's primary scorn was reserved for "the apparent indifference . . . that is displayed by so many of our officers. Training programs are scanned carefully and fearfully to see whether they demand more hours; whether their execution is going to cause some inconvenience! Jesus wept—if ever we are to prove that we're worth the salaries the government has been paying us all these years—now is the time!" Anticipating forthcoming War Department policy, Eisenhower concluded, "The sooner the weaklings in the officers' corps (and I don't mean the physical cripples) fall out and disappear, the better."[17]

Under Marshall and his commander of ground forces in the United States, (then) Maj. Gen. Lesley J. McNair, a trusted World War I colleague, a major shake-up of the army was in fact being implemented. Marshall handpicked McNair to organize and train the U.S. Army for war. In 1940 it was thought that McNair might eventually command American forces in combat, but he was destined to remain in charge of the Army Ground Forces, the command he headed from its creation in early 1942 until his untimely (and needless) death in Normandy in July 1944. Other than the small military post named for him in Washington, D.C., McNair remains one of the least known but most influential American figures of World War II. Marshall once acclaimed him as "the brains of the Army," and as Marshall's official biographer notes, "In 1939 he had concluded that the short, wiry Scot was the type of single-minded driver he needed to reform the stuffy halls of Fort Leavenworth." The following year Marshall summoned McNair to Washington and put him in charge of training reserve and national guard units being called to active duty. McNair's philosophy was unmistakable: "[S]weat shed in training was preferable to blood shed on the battlefield."[18]

With Marshall's backing McNair began to evaluate—and by 1941 began to remove—the lazy, the incompetent, the overage, and those lacking the requisite leadership skills, including some senior officers who had influential political connections. Mark Clark's training skills were so impressive that he was tapped to become McNair's top assistant. In the summer of 1941 Clark was promoted from lieutenant colonel directly to brigadier general and was now senior to his friend Dwight Eisenhower. Working closely together, McNair and Clark made a formidable pair. Eisenhower knew McNair only by reputation, but recalled that George Van Horn Moseley "often told me that General McNair was *the* soldier of his time in the Army."[19]

On May 10, 1940, German armored forces launched a lightning blitzkrieg through the Ardennes Forest into Belgium and France, shattering the French army. Within a matter of days Paris fell, and the French government sued for an armistice. A jubilant Adolf Hitler danced a jig on the site of the German surrender and humiliation in the Forêt de Compiègne in 1918. The British Expeditionary Force was likewise overwhelmed and surrounded near the port city of Dunkirk. Most of the BEF escaped to England in a hastily organized operation by the Royal Navy, which the new prime minister, an apparent political has-been named Winston Churchill, called "the deliverance of Dunkirk." In truth it was the most humiliating defeat suffered by a British army since the disastrous siege of Gallipoli in 1916, for which many held Churchill responsible. Dunkirk was proof of Britain's unpreparedness to fight an all-out war with Germany. Britain braced for an anticipated German cross-Channel invasion, which never came. A homemade sign over a country pub signified the mood of the nation: "Save our beloved land from invasion, O God."[20]

Despite FDR's great empathy with Britain's plight, he remained hand-cuffed by the pervasive American isolationism of the 1930s. Indeed, by 1939, wrote historian Samuel Eliot Morison, "advocates of intervention on the side of England and France hardly dared to speak; leaders like President Roosevelt could only persuade Congress to vote for increased armaments by talking in terms of national defense."[21]

Although the United States still remained wrapped in its cocoon of complacency and isolationism, officers like Marshall knew better. The problem he faced in 1940 was not much different than that of 1917: poor organization, outmoded tactics, second-rate or nonexistent equipment, and too few professional soldiers. America must prepare for war, and part of that meant identifying and promoting the men who were best qualified to lead its army into battle.

As Marshall began an unprecedented revamping of the infrastructure of the U.S. Army, one of his first targets was to purge the chiefs of infantry, field and coast artillery, and the cavalry of their autocratic powers. Another was to begin streamlining an army riddled with elderly fossils who occupied key positions and had obstructed its modernization. He began the process of ruthlessly weeding out and retiring many aged officers. War was a young man's calling, and few over the age of fifty-five survived scrutiny. Injecting a youthful new image into an army so badly in need of overhaul meant that those over the age of fifty would not be tapped for high command positions. There were the inevitable exceptions, of course, one of whom was Dwight Eisenhower. Another was his friend George Patton, who had made a vivid impression on Marshall in France during World War I, but in the autumn of 1940 was already fifty-five years old. Both Eisenhower and Patton had many years earlier been identified by Marshall as two of the army's future leaders. However, as will be seen, any officer destined for high command had to pass muster with McNair or endure the remainder of his career in oblivion.

In September 1940 Patton, then commanding a brigade of the newly organized 2nd Armored Division, wrote that he anticipated being promoted to division commander in the near future and hoped to entice Eisenhower to Fort Benning. Would Eisenhower care to serve under him in the 2nd Armored? "I shall ask for you either as Chief of Staff which I should prefer or as a regimental commander; you can tell me which you want for no matter how we get together we will go PLACES. If you get a better offer in the meantime take it." Patton concluded with one of his typically outrageous statements that some historians have erroneously pointed to as evidence that he was an unbalanced warmonger. He told Eisenhower he hoped "we are all together in a long and BLOODY war."[22] While Eisenhower would not have made such a bald statement, there is no denying that he was just as anxious as Patton to test himself in battle. Both men understood perfectly that if the United States became a participant it would indeed be a long and bloody war.

Eisenhower described himself as "elated" by Patton's offer and replied at once that he was "flattered by your suggestion that I come to your outfit. It would be great to be in the tanks once more, and even better to be associated with you again. . . . I suppose it's too much to hope that I could have a regiment in your division. . . . *I think* I could do a damn good job of commanding a regiment. . . . Anyway, if there's a chance of that kind of an assignment, I'd be for it 100%."[23]

Privately, however, Eisenhower's ambition in 1940 never went beyond attaining a regimental command and the evidence is overwhelming that he had few expectations of attaining generalship, much less high command, in the coming war, and would have considered a regimental command under Patton the zenith of his military career. Historically Eisenhower understood that he was unlikely by virtue of his age ever to earn a promotion to general in peacetime, which made Patton's offer all the more attractive. As long as the United States remained neutral, he would likely never become a full colonel, much less a general. Thus his future remained as cloudy as it had been in 1935. Under the stifling army seniority promotion system, Eisenhower's chances of advancement to colonel would not come until 1950, when he would be sixty years old and facing mandatory retirement.[24]

Eisenhower not only took Patton's invitation to heart but immediately wrote to Mark Clark in Washington to solicit his support in securing the cooperation of the chief of infantry. In particular he fretted (with good reason) that he might be diverted to another staff assignment that would shut him out of a post with the armored force. "I have an ambition to command one of the next armored regiments to be formed," he wrote. "They will probably think me a conceited individual, but I see no objection to setting your sights high. Actually, of course, I will be delighted to serve in the Armored Corps in any capacity."[25]

But Eisenhower's dream was not to be realized. By late 1940 his services were being coveted by others. Gee Gerow, who was serving as the deputy director of the War Plans Division of the War Department, sent Eisenhower a terse cable that read: I NEED YOU IN WAR PLANS DIVISION. DO YOU SERIOUSLY OBJECT TO BEING DETAILED ON THE WAR DEPT. GENERAL STAFF AND ASSIGNED HERE. PLEASE REPLY IMMEDIATELY.

Eisenhower was horrified at the prospect of returning to staff duty in Washington or anywhere else. He was apprehensive that to have his troop assignment cut short would seriously deter if not permanently impede a future promotion to general. The irony was that Eisenhower had become the ultimate career bureaucrat he so disdained and was justifiably uneasy that he would be obliged to spend the war on yet another staff.

Eisenhower was not only in the autumn of his career but determined to prove himself an able troop commander before it was too late. The essence of a successful officer in the eyes of professional soldiers is how well one commands troops. Eisenhower clearly believed that "I've demonstrated an ability to 'command,' [and] I'm delighted to stay with troops for two reasons. (1) I like it. (2), I want to convince the most ritualistic-minded guy in the whole d—— Army that I get along with John Soldier."[26]

Gerow's request sent Eisenhower "into a tailspin. . . . I have never been so flattered in my life as by the inclusion, in your telegram of the word, 'need,' " he replied. When it suited him Eisenhower could be a master of indecision. An example was his response to Gerow, in which, torn between duty and his ardent desire to remain with troops, he explained his concern that a return to dreaded staff duty would result in his being rated as "*unfit for duty with troops.*" Neither accepting nor declining, he left the decision to his friend. "If you decide that I should come to the War Plans Division," he told Gerow, "all you have to do is have the orders issued without any further reference to me."[27]

He also again enlisted the good offices of Mark Clark to prevent a transfer to Washington. Eisenhower urged Clark to "see the Chief of Infantry and tell him to let me alone."[28] Gerow understood his friend's reluctance to leave his post and withdrew the request. Eisenhower had his desired reprieve. Others, however, both then and later, began requesting his services. Suddenly he had become a sought-after commodity, as various commanders or staffs unsuccessfully bade for his services, all of which were disapproved by the chief of infantry, thanks at least in part to Clark's intervention. The trouble was that in virtually every instance, except by Patton, Eisenhower was coveted as a staff officer, not as a commander.

But for a transitory case of the shingles, Eisenhower's health was as robust as it had ever been. Training troops had obviously reinvigorated him, without a recurrence of the physical ailments that had plagued him in Manila. Almost as if he were writing for posterity, Eisenhower found time to write lengthy, philosophical letters to old friends like Clark, Gerow, and Hughes. Nevertheless Mamie noticed the stress brought about by Gerow's cable and wrote to Nana and Pupah that "Ike is so busy these days he's cuckoo," adding that he was fearful of being reassigned to staff duty.[29]

Both Ike and Mamie loved Fort Lewis and its active social life, even though "Mamie doesn't think too highly of the Great Northwest but is so glad to be out of Manila that she takes most things . . . without too much concern."[30] Their brick quarters along officers' row were one of the most popular spots on post; "the place was full of people all the time," recalled Mamie. Eisenhower was frequently in the habit of bringing visitors home for lunch on as little as five minutes' notice, which kept Mamie hopping. Their home was also often the scene of the informal get-togethers that had characterized Club Eisenhower for nearly twenty-five years. Clambakes were the meal of choice until the week before the monthly payday, when everyone was usually broke and struggling to make ends meet.

Fort Lewis was the first place since Camp Meade that Mamie had lived on post as an army wife. She was repelled by the quaint class consciousness among many military wives, who took for granted that their husbands' military rank also conferred on them the status of Mrs. Colonel or Mrs. General. Mamie refused to play the rank game, even when Eisenhower rose to the highest positions in the army. Omar Bradley's wife, Mary Quayle Bradley, a pious woman who forbade smoking, drinking, or profanity in her presence, was one who succumbed to the lure of wearing her husband's stars.[31]

Visitors from Washington and elsewhere began making regular appearances at Fort Lewis to view training exercises. Some were friends or acquaintances of Eisenhower, whom he made a point of reminding of his great desire to continue serving with troops. His regiment spent considerable time in such exercises, where sleeplessness and discomfort were routine. Yet Eisenhower relished every minute of it, even bragging that he barely got two hours of sleep a night and was frequently caked with dirt and sweat. His new duties, he said, "fortified my conviction that I belonged with troops; with them I was always happy."[32] It was the sort of "grunt" soldiering that characterized the American infantry soldier, and after so many years away from it, Eisenhower realized what he had missed. His staff duties at a high level looked impressive on his résumé, but it was his love of soldiering that had driven Eisenhower to stay in the army through the lean interwar years.

The new commander of the 3rd Division appointed Eisenhower chief of staff in November 1940. "I'd been ducking Staff positions for some time, but finally the War Department failed to listen to my sob story. So again I'm looking down a pen instead of a gun."[33] By early 1941 Eisenhower had, by his own reckoning, held "a dozen different jobs since returning from Manila. Although being chief of staff made him the senior division staff officer and the commander's right-hand man, he had not lost his distaste for staff work, writing to one of his Philippine flying mentors, Hugh Parker, "I'm weary of these eternal staff details. I'd like to get a command of my own, even if just a squad."[34]

Eisenhower held his post until March 1941, when he was promoted to full colonel. Eisenhower deemed achieving the exalted rank of colonel cause for celebration. It is customary for a newly promoted officer to hold a "promotion party" for the officers of his unit, its true significance being that his friends and acquaintances eat, drink, and party at his expense. Eisenhower gladly did so and had barely pinned on his shiny new insignia when his friends and colleagues began to proclaim that before long he would be a general. Eisenhower preferred to savor the moment and muttered in mock anger to John, "Damn it, as soon as you get a promotion, they start talking about another one. Why can't they let a guy be happy with what he has? They take all the joy out of it."[35]

With the promotion came yet another transfer, this time to the same job with the IX Corps, also based at Fort Lewis and commanded by one of Patton's mentors, a prominent cavalry officer named Kenyon Joyce. His new job entailed carrying out his new superior's policies and directives. The G-3 was Lt. Col. Lucian K. Truscott, Jr., a career cavalry officer destined to become the architect of the Ranger force and one of the most outstanding American combat commanders of World War II. "The General is a perfectionist. Sloppy staff work is anathema to him," wrote Eisenhower in a staff memo. With one minor exception, in Colonel Eisenhower, Joyce had acquired an ideal chief of staff.[36] Eisenhower was so immersed in the demands of his new job that he was habitually careless of his personal appearance, and once had to be reminded by Gen. Joyce that brass polish and his belt buckle had never met. Eisenhower could not be bothered with what he deemed minutiae and promptly detailed an NCO to purchase eight new belts and replace them whenever one got dirty. Although Eisenhower's casual attitude toward his military dress was wholly inconsistent with his reputation as a strict disciplinarian, it did accurately reflect his disinterest in the spit and polish imposed by Patton and other officers who insisted that it was part and parcel of good morale and discipline.[37]

John Eisenhower actively considered applying for an appointment to West Point. In an attempt to dissuade him, his uncle Edgar offered to finance his education to become a lawyer if John would agree to join his law firm after graduation, with the unstated promise that he would be the heir apparent after Edgar retired. Privately Ike was appalled at the notion of his son becoming another faceless lawyer laboring for his brother in a profession for which he had scant respect. Eisenhower's lifelong rivalry with his older brother once again renewed his competitive juices, particularly when it came to his son's future career. Just as his father had never left any doubt that he earnestly hoped John would follow in his footsteps by attending West Point, Ed never bothered to conceal his scorn for the military life, dismissing as "professional killers" men like his brother who toiled for medals instead of the trappings of "real" success, affluence and prestige.

Despite Eisenhower's none-too-secret aspiration that his son follow in his footsteps, he insisted that the decision was entirely John's. As an army brat, John had grown up around military men and well understood the risks of a peacetime military career. It would, his father told John, be no different than it had been for him.[38] Armed with frank appraisals from his father and uncle, John declined Edgar's offer, bluntly remarking that "I could never work for you."[39] As much as he liked and respected Edgar, it was a choice he never regretted. Edgar, however, thought it a terrible career decision and a deplorable waste of a first-class mind.[40]

Ike and Milton began lobbying Kansas senator Arthur Capper to appoint John to West Point. However, like Ike's own case in 1910, Senator Capper would agree only to permit John to take the competitive exam in October 1940. To prepare himself, he was sent to a West Point "cram" school in Washington, D.C., after which he easily beat out the other applicants and was awarded a senatorial appointment. He would enter West Point in July 1941 as a member of the class of 1945.[41]

During Christmas 1940 John had clearly embraced his father's pessimism about the prospects of war. His gloomy observation that the singing of hymns proclaiming "Peace on Earth, Good Will to Men" brought an unexpected response. "When I frowned, the Old Man looked at me and murmured, 'Be glad for peace while you've still got it.' "[42]

In the autumn of 1940 Maj. Gen. Walter Krueger, one of the army's most highly regarded officers and the newly appointed commander of VIII Corps at Fort Sam Houston, Texas, required a new chief of staff. Well aware of Eisenhower's reputation as a staff officer, Krueger placed "Eisenhower" first of the three names on his preference list submitted to Washington. Although

Ike was not available for reassignment, Krueger remained committed to eventually obtaining his services. The following year Krueger was promoted to lieutenant general and given command of the Third Army, which was slated to be one of the two major maneuver elements of the forthcoming training exercises to be held in Louisiana in the summer of 1941.

In June 1941 Krueger wrote directly to his friend George Marshall to "urgently request" that his present chief of staff be replaced. "In my judgment, that position demands a younger man, one possessing broad vision, progressive ideas, a thorough grasp of the magnitude of the problem involved in handling an Army, and lots of initiative and resourcefulness. Lieutenant Colonel Dwight D. Eisenhower, Infantry, is such a man, and I urgently request that he be detailed" to Fort Sam Houston as the new Third Army chief of staff.[43] Marshall and the War Department approved Krueger's request and a telegram was sent to Fort Lewis directing Eisenhower to report to San Antonio at once.

24.

Third Army Chief of Staff

Why Dad got so much credit for the Third Army's performance . . . I do not understand.

July 1 continued to hold a special significance for the Eisenhowers. Their twenty-fifth wedding anniversary also marked a return to the place where they had begun married life in Ike's meager bachelor apartment in 1916. This time they moved into spacious field-grade quarters that Eisenhower described as "the size of a barn."[1] Once the resident silverfish and cockroaches had been fumigated, Mamie soon turned it into the latest revival of Club Eisenhower. With the grander quarters, however, came new responsibilities, such as tending the lawn and garden, which was too much of a strain on Mamie's health to manage alone. Eisenhower was far too busy to attend to such household details, even had he been so inclined. From the moment of his arrival, Eisenhower's new duties as chief of staff consumed him, and he was often obliged to excuse himself from gatherings at Club Eisenhower to return to work. Fourteen- to sixteen-hour days were the norm, and home was a place to eat and sleep. Eisenhower described it as "one of the busiest periods of my life," little knowing that his long days could be likened to the tip of a future iceberg. Nevertheless Eisenhower somehow managed to find time for an occasional letter of encouragement to plebe John Eisenhower.[2]

One aspect of Third Army operations that both Krueger and Eisenhower avoided was logistics, a common affliction of commanders unfamiliar with or frightened of the difficult and demanding business of keeping an army fully fed, gassed, armed, and maintained. Fortunately Third Army had a master magician/logistician in Lt. Col. LeRoy Lutes (later a lieutenant general), who consistently pulled rabbits from hats. In Third Army, logistics was the province of Lutes. "General Krueger didn't have a thing to do with logistics and neither did Ike. Ike said, 'You handle it.' And Krueger said, 'You handle it.' And I couldn't take a single question to them. They didn't want it. All they wanted to know was how I did it."[3]

For the first time in his career Eisenhower was authorized a striker (an enlisted aide). A help-wanted notice posted in the barracks brought forth a former New York City bellhop (at the Plaza Hotel) named Michael J. "Mickey" McKeogh, who thought that such duties plus a chance to earn extra money to help the colonel's wife were far preferable to whatever the army had in mind for him. Private First Class McKeogh quickly won Ike and Mamie's heart with his efficiency and devotion. The feeling was mutual. Mickey McKeogh regarded Colonel Eisenhower as "absolutely straight," mainly because "you always knew exactly where you stood with him." Nor was there a "trace of the master-servant attitude to irk Mickey's rugged Irish independence."[4]

Mickey had plenty to do to keep up with Mamie's insistence on neatness. The house usually reeked of cigarette smoke from the growing numbers of cigarettes Eisenhower smoked each day. Keeping a tidy house was made more difficult by his habit of leaving the newspaper wherever it fell and his proclivity for tossing his cigarette butts into the fireplace. Mickey McKeogh recalls that Mamie would admonish him, " 'Now, Ike, can't you stop being so messy?' But he never learned, not even when they lived in places that had artificial fireplaces."[5] Mamie never broke her husband of the habit until after the war, when he abruptly quit smoking.

Having a valet around their quarters produced its share of mirthful moments. Mickey would carefully button Eisenhower's clean shirts just as the army had taught him, which usually resulted in a stream of profanity-strewn language from Eisenhower, who did not want to be bothered unbuttoning them. To remove the source of irritation, Mamie got into the habit of undoing them, only to have Mickey return and rebutton them, thus perpetuating the daily litany of curses.[6]

Mickey McKeogh would remain with Eisenhower throughout World War II as the most faithful of his enlisted orderlies. Once, in North Africa, Eisenhower excused Mickey from accompanying him on a trip to the front. McKeogh refused, saying, "Sir, my mother wrote me that my job in this war was to take care of you. If General Eisenhower doesn't come back from this war, don't you dare come back."[7]

When Eisenhower assumed his new duties, one of the assistants he inherited was a jovial, fortyish San Antonio native, Ernest R. "Tex" Lee, who looked more like the former insurance and car salesman he was than an officer. Lieutenant Lee expected his tenure to be brief, given that his new boss was likely to assign someone he knew to the position. After grilling Lee on a variety of subjects over several days, Eisenhower retained him as his executive officer, a fancy title for what were mostly the duties of an office manager and gofer. Thus Mickey McKeogh and "Tex" Lee became the first and second members of what would become Eisenhower's loyal personal staff from 1942 to the end of World War II.[8]

Eisenhower's new boss, Walter Krueger, was highly regarded in the enlisted ranks as "a soldier's soldier." A Prussian-born émigré, Krueger was one of a number of officers of German extraction who would play important roles in the coming war. Among them were Albert C. Wedemeyer, Chester Nimitz, George Stratemeyer, Robert L. Eichelberger, Carl "Tooey" Spaatz, and Dwight Eisenhower. Krueger's career was a remarkable climb through the ranks from private soldier in 1898 to three-star general in 1941. In between he had served with distinction in the Spanish-American War, fought in the Philippine insurrection, participated in Pershing's punitive expedition in 1916, and held tank and infantry staff positions in the AEF during World War I.

He has been described as "one of the Army's best educated and most perceptive officers" and one of its ablest tacticians. While commanding the first of the newly organized divisions, Krueger proved so adept at the tactical employment of motorized vehicles that his soldiers referred to themselves as "Blitzkruegers."[9] His philosophy was straight to the point and a carbon copy of Patton's message to his men: "Weapons are no good unless there are guts at both sides of the bayonet."[10]

To emphasis his seriousness of purpose, junior officers with potential were sent to "Krueger Tech," a grueling six-week course at Camp Bullis, Texas, where they were prepared for higher leadership positions. "I know that it has been hard," he told the graduates. "If it had been humanly possible, I would have made it even harder." One graduate ended up in Australia, and on learning of Krueger's forthcoming assignment in 1943 to command an army under MacArthur, said, "Now I know why the Japs have given up Guadalcanal; they heard Krueger was coming."[11]

In superb physical condition at age sixty-two, Krueger had seemingly limitless stamina that often left younger men in his wake. Eisenhower described him as one of the few senior officers able to grasp the demands war would entail.[12] The self-effacing Krueger deliberately shunned the limelight, a trait that would soon play heavily in Eisenhower's favor. Krueger's stern countenance reinforced the perception of a no-nonsense disciplinarian who visibly frightened most of his soldiers. So much for perceptions: Krueger was actually held in high regard by his officers and enlisted men, and behind the mask of command he possessed a fine sense of humor. During the Louisiana maneuvers he was known by the informal code word "Meatsaw," which was flashed among Third Army units to indicate the general was nearby. One who did not get the word was an Italian-American enlisted man named Tony, who was found asleep while performing sentry duty at a road junction. "Gen. Krueger came by, waked him, and started angrily raking him over the coals. When Krueger paused for a breath, Tony, who spoke with a distinct Italian accent, replied, 'I no speaka English.' Krueger burst into laughter."[13] Once, while he was a regimental commander, his adjutant scribbled a note atop a stack of court-martial charges that "a crime wave" appeared to have broken out. Krueger laconically replied, "Captain Wheatley, I do not expect to get all of the virtues of mankind for thirty dollars a month." Krueger was notoriously hard on his staff, and the adjutant once commented, "I never served under an officer whom I disliked more, nor for whom I had greater admiration."[14]

His care for his men was legendary. Once, during a rainstorm in Leyte in 1945, Krueger summoned a shivering-wet sentry guarding his command tent and instructed him to towel off and change into one of *his* uniforms. When the rain stopped the sentry resumed his duties dressed in the uniform of a four-star general. When a subordinate asked why, Krueger replied, "Son, I've walked many an hour on sentry duty—wet and cold. I know how he felt out there."[15]

Even as he promoted him to lieutenant general in 1941, Marshall did so with reservations about Krueger's lack of combat experience and his competence to command a field army. Happily Marshall was proved wrong not only in the Louisiana maneuvers but in the Southwest Pacific under MacArthur.

Eisenhower and Krueger made an ideal pair. Eisenhower brought the vast staff experience Krueger needed and was undaunted by the challenge the forthcoming maneuvers presented. Experience and foresight were the traits Krueger sought, and in his new chief of staff he gained both. With little time left until the maneuvers, Eisenhower and Krueger began planning an orthodox but nevertheless aggressive strategy for Third Army. "Luckily I've spent most of my life in large headquarters, so am not overpowered by the mass of details," Eisenhower wrote to Moseley. He clearly had his hands full, given that Third Army was not only preparing for the Louisiana maneuvers but also for Third Army exercises to be held in eastern Texas and Louisiana beforehand. Eisenhower's self-assurance and background drew a never-ending stream of appeals for guidance from subordinates. "Everyone comes in here to discuss his troubles, and I'm often astonished how much better they seem to work after they have had a chance to recite their woes."[16]

Eisenhower dismissed warnings from "all the old-timers here, that we are going to a god-awful spot, to live with mud, malaria, mosquitoes and misery," which were made even more miserable by the remnants of a Gulf hurricane. "But I like to go to the field so I'm not much concerned about it."[17] Within a few weeks of assuming his duties, Krueger wrote to a friend in the War Department that Eisenhower "is going strong."[18]

Clark's glowing reputation as the army's best training expert resulted in his promotion to brigadier general in July 1941, and, while pleased at his friend's good fortune, Eisenhower was much too competitive not to have been envious. That he was now obliged to salute Clark and address him as "Sir" in public was privately unsettling. During the exercise preparations the two men were in daily contact. " 'Why haven't I been promoted?' Ike regularly wanted to know. 'It's in the works,' Clark replied just as regularly."[19] The answers were hardly satisfactory to an officer fearful of being surpassed by his contemporaries.

After Dunkirk, Britain endured one military debacle after another as the German army occupied Norway, Denmark, Greece, and Crete. The British homeland was under siege from a German naval blockade, and although the Royal Air Force had staved off invasion by winning the Battle of Britain, the outlook was still grim. In North Africa, Hitler's expeditionary force, Gen. Erwin Rommel's Afrika Korps, inflicted a series of stinging defeats upon the British Eighth Army. By the summer of 1941, Western Europe had become a Nazi-held dominion, while in the Far East, Hong Kong had fallen to Germany's Axis partner, Japan. In late June 1941, Hitler broke the Russo-German nonaggression treaty by invading Russia. More than three million German ground troops supported by three thousand tanks and two thousand aircraft swarmed over a front extending from the Black Sea to the Arctic, catching the Red Army flat-footed. Less visible but no less important was that the Allies were losing control of the Atlantic Ocean to German U-boats, which were feasting on Allied shipping faster than it could be replaced. Adm. Karl Dönitz's U-boats were exacting a mounting toll on convoys in the icy waters of the North Atlantic: Between September 1939 and the end of 1941, Allied shipping losses were an appalling 2,361 ships, totalling 8,545,606 tons.[20]

The situation in the Soviet Union was dire, and were it not for German unpreparedness for the winter of 1941–42, it would likely have fallen to Hitler's massive invasion force. If Hitler had read of Napoleon's campaigns, the war on the eastern front might have turned out differently. However, he made the same mistakes by starting his offensive too late and failing to prepare for the harsh Russian winter. The Red Army managed to hang on by the slenderest of threads before winter closed down the campaign until the spring of 1942.

By 1941 there was no doubt that the United States would be drawn into the war; the only question was when and under what conditions. Unfortunately, however, the United States had an army practically in name only. A worried McNair remarked, "We didn't know how soon war would come, but we knew it was coming . . . and we had to get together *something* of an Army pretty darn fast."[21] Correspondent Eric Sevareid described how Roosevelt was slowly "gathering together a reluctant, bewildered, and resentful army. No civil leaders dared call them 'soldiers'—as though there were something shameful in the word . . . few made so bold as to suggest that their job was to learn to kill."[22] Indeed, the process of assembling an army was as difficult and frustrating at McNair's level as it was at Eisenhower's. The first manpower draft in 1940 authorized the call-up of national guard and reserve units but initially mandated only one year of military service. Morale and discipline suffered accordingly. Disgruntled draftees coined an acronym, OHIO (Over the Hill in October [1941]), which became their graffiti of choice and was scrawled in latrines and elsewhere. The United States was, after all, still devoutly isolationist. One soldier called it "a goddamn mess," while another common complaint was "I want to get the hell out of this hole." After inspecting one division in September 1940, McNair observed with foreboding that it was a case of "the blind leading the blind."[23]

Nevertheless Marshall and McNair forged a more mobile, streamlined infantry division, created the armored division, and oversaw the introduction of improved new weapons. At the end of 1940 the army's strength was 620,000 men, and by June 30, 1941, it stood at 1,460,998. The time had come to test the U.S. Army's preparedness to fight on a modern battlefield.[24]

The year 1941 was thus monopolized by large-scale division-, corps-, and army-level war games held in Tennessee, Louisiana, and, in the autumn, the mountains of the Carolinas. Marshall billed the Louisiana maneuvers, to be held in the late summer of 1941, as "a combat college for troop leading" and a field laboratory "for the new armored, anti-tank, and air forces that had come of age since 1918."[25]

The Tennessee maneuvers were corps-level exercises.[26] With more of Europe and the Middle East falling to Nazi aggression, the forthcoming Louisiana maneuvers took on added importance and a heightened sense of urgency. Marshall's aim was unequivocal: "I want the mistakes [made] down in Louisiana, not over in Europe, and the only way to do this thing is to try it out, and if it doesn't work, find out what we need to make it work."[27] Marshall also wanted to draw the nation's and Congress's attention to its army's deplorable state of preparedness. The autumn exercise in Louisiana and East Texas would be the first where two armies battled each other. Under the overall control of McNair, using a scenario written by Mark Clark, the exercise pitted the 160,000 troops of Lt. Gen. Ben Lear's Second (Red) Army, whose mission was to invade Louisiana, against the 240,000 troops of Krueger's Third (Blue) Army. Twenty-seven divisions took part, and virtually the entire state of Louisiana became a gigantic maneuver area. In all 472,000 troops participated in various roles.

The Louisiana war games became one of the most watched and reported events of 1941. "War" between the Red and Blue forces kicked off at noon on September 15, with Lear's Red army attacking across the Red River and driving toward Shreveport with two corps, one of which was the I Armored Corps. Lear was a tough, spit-and-polish disciplinarian who was known more for his abrasive manner and his unpopularity with his troops than for his tactical brilliance. His plan was to use the mobility of his armored forces to outflank the Blue army, which was defending southern Louisiana. However, in Krueger and Eisenhower, Lear was up against worthy, imaginative opponents with clear ideas of how to defeat the invader. Despite heavy rains Krueger's airmen soon located the Red force armor (including Patton's 2nd

Armored Division) crossing the Red River. The Blue forces were able to bottle up Lear's tanks, and within a short time the Red forces were in desperate trouble. Patton's tanks attempted to pry open the flank for a breakout, but Krueger and Eisenhower were too quick, and the 2nd Armored suffered heavy losses in what soon became a rout. A disappointed Patton was unable to pay the fifty-dollar reward he had offered his men for the capture of "a certain s.o.b. called Eisenhower."[28] By the fourth day Lear's force was nearly surrounded and facing annihilation, when McNair mercifully ended the first phase.[29]

Although Third Army had "won" the first battle, Eisenhower was deeply troubled by the many failures of leadership that had emerged during phase one. The closer the United States came to war, the more passionate Eisenhower became on the subject of preparedness. Convinced that a war could not be won with inferior leadership, he continued to champion the weeding out of unfit officers who "have not the iron in their souls to perform the job . . . it is a hard thing to do, and in many cases it is too hard for some of the people in charge. But it is a job that must be done."[30]

During the maneuvers Eisenhower indulged his passion for inspecting mess facilities. In one Third Army maneuver unit, a young mess cook named Marty Snyder had devised a means of cooking on stoves mounted on the bed of a truck, thus enabling meals to be prepared in a timely fashion as the unit sped from place to place. Before long he received a visitor in the person of Eisenhower, who demanded to examine Snyder's makeshift mobile kitchen. Fully expecting a white-glove inspection, Snyder was surprised: "He was the first inspecting officer I had met who was interested in the food. And obviously he knew food." After he departed Snyder opined, "Now, there's the kind of man I'd like to work for." Before the war ended Snyder would get his wish.[31]

Among the horde of correspondents covering the maneuvers were Hanson Baldwin of the *New York Times* and Eric Sevareid of CBS, who was urged by reporter Robert Sherrod to look up a certain Colonel Eisenhower, who "makes more sense than any of the rest of them." The correspondents began converging on Eisenhower's tent for informal bull sessions, and as a gathering place where they could not only obtain straight talk but, just as important, relax and possibly even have a drink in an otherwise largely dry South. Sevareid would later recall "that many of his colleagues were at least as interested in personal strategies as in military ones . . . and in the case of at least one prominent analyst, how to obtain feminine solace."[32]

During the maneuvers Eisenhower discovered a previously unknown talent for public relations. The press liked his open, easygoing manner and his willingness to poke fun at himself and the army. Eisenhower's risqué side emerged in the company of other men, and he entertained them "with unprintable stories about the New Orleans whores with whom some of his troops had consorted."[33]

Eisenhower's reluctance to add procuring to his professional repertoire notwithstanding, all came away impressed by the balding colonel whose praises they extolled in newspaper columns across the United States, even as some misidentified him as "Lt. Col. D. D. Ersenbeing." Eisenhower did not mind a bit, pleased that at least the press had managed to get his initials right. Among those who wrote favorably about Eisenhower were syndicated columnists Robert S. Allen and Drew Pearson, whose "Washington Merry-Go-Round" column was read by millions. Praising Eisenhower's performance during the Louisiana maneuvers, they wrote that Colonel Eisenhower, "who conceived and directed the strategy that routed the Second Army has a steel-trap mind plus unusual physical vigor."[34]

When phase two began a week later, the roles of the two armies were reversed, with the I Armored Corps part of Krueger's attacking Blue force, whose mission was to capture Shreveport and defeat Lear's Red force defending the city. The original plan called for a Blue force frontal attack, but when Lear declined to do battle, Krueger elected to launch a bold flank attack with the I Armored Corps. It was spearheaded by Patton's 2nd Armored, which initiated a 350-mile end run to outflank the Red force. The journey took his tanks back into Texas, then north and later east, until he had gotten behind Lear's army and was poised to attack Shreveport from the rear. McNair again decided to end the final phase of the Louisiana maneuvers prematurely, after barely five days. With Patton's spearhead and the Blue force poised to deliver the coup de grâce to Lear, there seemed no reason to continue.[35]

Off the battlefield the primary battle being fought was by the infantry traditionalists, led by McNair, who argued that antitank weapons would render tanks useless on the battlefield. The outmoded concept that tanks were meant only to support advancing infantry proved to be a giant hurdle that was never quite overcome by the new breed of former cavalrymen who were convinced that tanks could play a vital offensive role and that the threat posed by antitank guns could be overcome through the development of new tactics of fire and maneuver. Moreover, the growing autonomy of the newly created armored force frightened the traditionalists until McNair promulgated the view that mobility was more important than firepower, a thesis that had already been proved wrong by the father of the German blitzkrieg, Gen. Heinz Guderian, and later by Erwin Rommel in North Africa.[36]

As Eisenhower had predicted, in the wake of the series of maneuvers in 1941 there ensued a ruthless, but necessary housecleaning, which, by year's end, resulted in the forcible retirement of hundreds of senior officers, one of whom was a two-star Missouri national guard division commander and the first cousin of Sen. Harry S. Truman. Thirty-one of the forty-two army corps and division commanders were either relieved or shunted aside to make way for a new generation of commanders that included Bradley, Allen, Gerow, Ridgway, Collins, Van Fleet, Simpson, and others whom Marshall had already identified. Twenty of twenty-seven division commanders were replaced in 1942. Only eleven (of forty-two) senior officers achieved higher command, among them Krueger and Lear.[37] Those who survived scrutiny were considered the nucleus of the rejuvenated army.

The 1941 maneuvers not only purged the overage and unfit but, just as important, also identified the army's most promising leaders, who would carry the burden of fighting during the coming war. Three names of star quality emerged from the maneuvers for very different reasons: Eisenhower for his role in devising Third Army strategy even as he grumbled that he would rather have been commanding a unit of Patton's tanks; Brig. Gen. Mark Clark, who wrote the maneuver scenario that earned him accolades as the army's preeminent planner; and George S. Patton, the epitome of the new breed of aggressive tank commanders whose name alone some said was worth an armored division. Time would reveal that the successes and failures of all three officers would soon be irretrievably linked during the coming war.

Eisenhower was credited with devising the strategy by which Krueger's Third Army bested Lear's Second. The praise given Eisenhower for the success of the Third Army has been exaggerated, however, in part retrospectively after his later rise to supreme command. Krueger and Eisenhower together had formulated a winning strategy that outsmarted that of the more conservative Lear. Eisenhower's contribution cannot be minimized, but as even his son later mused, "Why Dad got so much credit for the Third Army's performance . . . I do not understand, because he was not the commanding general. But Krueger had a tendency to take a back seat, and I guess Dad had more visibility. Dad was not one that tried to shove himself in front . . . but he received much of the credit anyway. It's a strange thing."[38]

Staff officers do not provide leadership, nor do they command; that responsibility belongs solely to the commander. A first-class staff will enhance a commander's ability to do his job, or it can ruin him. A general staff is not unlike the interior line of a football team: anonymous, generally underappreciated, hardworking officers who attend to the myriad, usually mindnumbing details of planning and execution, logistics, intelligence, and the thousand other areas that require attention. Nevertheless, Eisenhower's presence and his long experience served to add common sense and stability to the Third Army staff. However improbable the reasons, Eisenhower's performance was recognized by those who counted. He later proclaimed that the value of the experience gained during the Louisiana maneuvers was "incalculable." Less pleased at the acclaim given Eisenhower was Walter Krueger, who resented the credit going to his junior chief of staff for a plan he insisted he himself had conceived. Robert Eichelberger, a friend and classmate of Ike's at Fort Leavenworth in 1926, served as a corps commander under Krueger in the South Pacific. Eichelberger wrote that the two men were not quite the ideal match that has been portrayed. The lavish publicity accorded Eisenhower left lingering resentments in Krueger, who felt that his chief of staff was taking credit for (indeed, had stolen) his "brain-child"—that is, his handwritten operations order for the maneuvers—which, he told Eichelberger, Eisenhower had claimed to have originated as his own.[39] Whatever the truth, each man had an ax to grind with the other.

Despite the complaints of some congressmen that the army was wasting money conducting such exercises, the Louisiana maneuvers were, as its official historian concludes, "unprecedented in U.S. Army history and have never been duplicated in size or scope since." Under the tutelage of Marshall and McNair, "the Army was forced to make good two decades of virtual disarmament in two years' time." The result was that "the GHQ maneuvers of 1941 revealed both the penalties of military unpreparedness and the power of American resolve."[40]

Mark Clark conducted the critique of the Louisiana maneuvers. Near its end he was handed a telegram from the War Department containing the names of officers being nominated by Roosevelt for promotion to major general, and twenty or so from colonel to brigadier general. Clark scanned the list, read out their names, and then announced, "That's it." The group was dismissed and, as the fortunate selectees were surrounded and congratulated, Eisenhower, visibly deflated by the omission of his name from the list, had one foot out the door. That was when Clark banged his gavel and intoned, "I forgot one name—Dwight D. Eisenhower." Amid the throng of people Clark heard Eisenhower laugh and proclaim, "I'll get you for this, you son-ofabitch."[41]

Mamie later recalled it as the biggest thrill of their military married life. With Mamie and her parents present, Krueger pinned the single silver stars of a brigadier general on Eisenhower's shoulder tabs. Afterward the new general proudly accepted the salute during the first of many such parades that would be staged in his honor. Eisenhower had reached a goal he never expected to attain, "but the nicest part of all, I've quickly discovered," he wrote to a friend, "is to be assured by good friends that the War Department was not too d—— dumb in making the selection." A family friend, Aksel Nielsen, wrote from Denver to request that Eisenhower send him an autographed photo. Flattered, he wrote that "I am hurrying it off at once—it would be tragic to have you change your mind. Wouldn't you like three or four???"[42] To another he noted, "It was nice to be promoted, but it doesn't seem to make my work any easier." The only worrisome aspect was that Eisenhower had performed so well as Krueger's chief of staff that he feared having to serve out the war in a succession of staff jobs that would exclude him once again from obtaining a combat command.

Mamie's delight at Ike's promotion tapered off somewhat when he announced that their income would not change one iota. "I don't get a red cent with all this new glory," he wrote to another friend, "but she has to dole out to tailors some hundred and fifty bucks just to change over uniforms. She's been slightly punch drunk since learning all this."[43]

Four days after Eisenhower's promotion, McNair weighed in with his evaluations to Marshall of those he recommended for higher command. Almost as an afterthought, the last to appear on a list of seven unrated "others" named as potential division commanders was Eisenhower. McNair clearly felt no compelling need to rate any higher a career staff officer who had never commanded more than a battalion. Indeed, were it not for his glowing reputation gained during the maneuvers, it is arguable that Eisenhower's name would not have appeared at all, had it not been for Mark Clark's persistence in extolling his friend. (In 1989 Patton's son would tartly observe, "McNair's predictions were not too hot. Take notice of Ike at the bottom of the list—'an also-ran.' ")[44]

During Marshall's visit to observe the Carolina maneuvers in the autumn, he told Clark, "I wish you would give me a list of ten names of officers you know pretty well and whom you would recommend to be the head of the Operations Division" (of the War Department General Staff). Clark replied that there would only be one name on the list. "If you have to have ten names, I'll just put nine ditto marks below." The name: "Ike Eisenhower."[45]

The testing of the new army during the 1941 maneuvers had come none too soon. On Sunday, December 7, came a shocking news flash and the black headlines revealing the surprise Japanese attack that destroyed most of the U.S. Pacific fleet at Pearl Harbor in what was regarded, until September 11, 2001, as the blackest day in American history. Ordinarily it would have been a quiet Sunday in Washington and elsewhere, with only essential business being undertaken. In San Antonio, Eisenhower went to work in the morning over Mamie's protests, but by noon was exhausted and returned to his quarters, leaving orders that "under no circumstances" was he to be disturbed as he took a rare afternoon nap. Ike and Mamie were planning to visit West Point to spend Christmas with John, and he recalled dreaming of a two-week Christmas leave only days away. "But even dreams like this . . . could be shattered with impunity," he later wrote. Mamie heard the news flash on the radio. "I was absolutely stunned. It was unbelievable. . . . So I immediately went and wakened up my soldier."[46]

Third Army headquarters became a beehive of feverish activity as antiaircraft units were rushed to the West Coast to defend against what many thought was a possible Japanese invasion. At its center was Eisenhower, whose job was to hold everything together and coordinate the hourly directives from the War Department to shift units, provide security for Gulf Coast ports, and act on a rash of other urgent requirements.

In London, Winston Churchill assured U.S. ambassador John G. Winant that if Japan declared war on the United States, "We shall declare war on them within the hour." The prime minister then telephoned Roosevelt to reassure him of Britain's backing. Churchill fervently believed that the American tragedy at Pearl Harbor meant British salvation. "Britain would live," he announced with discernible relief in his voice; for the first time there was "no doubt about the end."[47]

On December 8, 1941, the Japanese mounted aerial attacks on Luzon that destroyed the greater part of the American B-17 bomber fleet parked on the ground at Clark Field. At a single stroke MacArthur's best defensive weapon was destroyed at the very outset, a tragic omen for what was to follow in the Philippines. Japanese aircraft also attacked Wake Island, Hong Kong, and Malaya. That same day the United States and Britain declared war on Japan. Germany and Italy reciprocated by issuing their own declarations of war on December 11, 1941. From the insularity of isolationism the United States was now irrevocably thrust into a two-ocean, global war that would swiftly test the nation's military training on the battlefield. On December 6, McNair had estimated the need for two hundred divisions merely to defeat the new Berlin-Rome axis, an estimate raised shortly thereafter to 334 divisions by the Joint Chiefs of Staff.[48]

The morning of December 12 Eisenhower's telephone rang, and a gruff voice on the other end said, "Is that you, Ike?" The caller was Col. Walter Bedell Smith, the secretary of the War Department General Staff, and his message was terse and unequivocal. "The Chief says for you to hop a plane and get up here right away. Tell your boss that formal orders will come through later."[49] Eisenhower's reaction was dismay. He had no idea of what lay ahead in Washington, but was certain it would mean his relegation to a dreaded staff job for the duration of the war. "Heavy-hearted, I telephoned my wife to pack a bag, and within the hour I was headed for the War Department."[50] Eisenhower later learned that Col. Charles W. Bundy, the officer whom he was to replace, had been killed in a plane crash in the Colorado Rockies the previous night. Bundy had been a senior War Plans Division planner for Pacific operations and needed to be replaced at once. For the second time in six months Eisenhower was urgently summoned to a new post on the basis of a telephone call and without benefit of formal orders.

25.

Marshall's Protégé

We've got to go to Europe and fight . . .

Eisenhower's first reaction—that he had been summoned to Washington for his expertise about the Philippines—was only partially correct, and when Mamie asked when they would see each other again, Eisenhower confidently replied, "I'll be back in a few days."[1] When she suggested that he might be kept in Washington, Eisenhower's brusque response was, "That would be just my luck to sit out this war too!"[2]

When he arrived in Washington on December 14, Eisenhower found the once-somnolent capital buzzing with activity. The sense of urgency brought about by Pearl Harbor was palpable. Eisenhower was met at Union Station by his brother Milton, who intended to take him to his home in Falls Church, Virginia. Instead, with Bedell Smith's words still ringing in his ears, Eisenhower had Milton take him straight to the War Department, which—until the new Pentagon building, then under construction, opened later in 1942—was located in the Old Munitions Building on Constitution Avenue. Eisenhower was immediately shown into Marshall's office, where, without preamble or small talk, the chief of staff got straight to the point, succinctly summarizing everything of relevance to the situation in the Pacific. The fleet and most of its repair facilities lay in ruins at Pearl Harbor, and the Philippines were under threat of invasion. Then Marshall demanded, "What should be our general course of action?" The chief of staff already knew the answer, but Eisenhower's first audience with Marshall was merely the start of a series of appraisals of an officer he believed had great potential. Eisenhower asked if he might be given a few hours to prepare a response. " 'All right,' Marshall snapped," dismissing him as curtly as he had greeted him, before "turning to the next document on his desk."[3] Eisenhower had just learned his first lesson about working for Marshall: The chief demanded results, and, at a stroke, he had been thrown from the frying pan into the fire. Whether or not he was aware of it at the time, what Eisenhower recommended would in large measure determine his immediate future.

His new boss was the chief of the War Plans Division, his friend Gee Gerow, who provided Eisenhower with a desk at which to prepare his response. As he began organizing his thoughts and scribbling notes and lists on a yellow pad headed by the words, "Steps to Be Taken," Eisenhower fully grasped that Marshall would not accept long oratory or flowery phrases. With Fox Conner's teachings firmly in mind, "I determined that my answer should be short, emphatic, and based on reasoning in which I honestly believed." There was, he understood only too well, no hope whatsoever of anything more than token reinforcement of the Philippines. Yet, some effort, no matter how futile, *had* to be made. When he returned to Marshall's office several hours later, Eisenhower succinctly laid out his recommendations, which included doing everything "humanly possible" to offer assistance by first establishing a secure base of operations in Australia by sea and air. The effort would be risky and costly, he warned, but, "The people of China, of the Philippines, of the Dutch East Indies will be watching us. They may excuse failure but they will not excuse abandonment." Marshall replied that he agreed with Eisenhower: "Do your best to save them." With that Eisenhower was dismissed and left to grapple with a problem that in his heart he knew "defied solution."[4] It was his first exposure to Marshall's methods, which could be defined as: "I want answers, not questions; explanations, not alibis."[5]

That Marshall had sent for Eisenhower was no surprise. Certainly Mark Clark, Gee Gerow, and others had been singing his praises for some time, among them a friend stationed in Manila, who had written in 1939 of Eisenhower, "He is 'going places' or I miss my guess."[6] Marshall did not need others to convince him that Eisenhower was special. What really counted was that he had long since formed a favorable impression. In 1942 hardly anyone in the U.S. Army had an intimate knowledge, much less an understanding, of industrial mobilization. One of the few exceptions was Eisenhower, thanks to his extensive investigation of the subject during his service in the War Department a decade earlier. This experience would not only prove to be of immense importance in the coming months but would greatly enhance his role as one of the most important figures on Marshall's staff.

Although he tried, Eisenhower never really understood Marshall. Few ever did. An intensely private man, Marshall was all business while in uniform, but off duty a great sense of humor often emerged. His passion was indulging his love of horses. Since he became chief of staff, Marshall's sole recreation was an early morning ride on the grounds of nearby Fort Myer, in which he found temporary liberation from the unending pressures of his position.

An example of the enigma that was Marshall was his particular soft spot for fighting officers who broke the mold of rigid military protocol—men such as Terry de la Mesa Allen, an unorthodox cavalry officer whose antics and perceived indiscipline infuriated conventional soldiers like Omar Bradley. Allen was a hell-raising, hard-drinking, but brilliant troop commander who became the only general to command two different divisions during World War II. Despite Allen's antics and disdain for authority, Marshall orchestrated his promotion from lieutenant colonel directly to brigadier general in 1942.[7]

Another of Marshall's favorites was Patton. Even when the mercurial Patton got himself into trouble, Marshall never lost sight of his leadership qualities and his great value to the army as a combat commander. "Marshall thought him an extraordinary character. 'He would say outrageous things and then look at you to see how it registered.' He would 'curse and then write a hymn.'"[8] Later, in England in 1944, after an especially troubling incident, Marshall quietly influenced a wavering Eisenhower to retain Patton for the most important battles of the war.

Marshall expected his subordinates "to be prompt and succinct. The unprepared would find themselves on the way to new posts; the long-winded he cut off. He insisted memoranda be terse. . . . His hardworking staff tended to hold him in awe, or fear, or both. Those who performed well . . . he marked for promotion."[9] One of Marshall's frequently heard exhortations was, "Gentlemen, don't fight the problem. Solve it!" In return Marshall never equivocated; if a decision was called for, he made it. After Eisenhower delivered his first briefing, assessing the Pacific problem, Marshall rather icily outlined what he demanded of his staff. "Eisenhower, the Department is filled with able men who analyze their problems but feel compelled to always bring them to me for final solution. I must have assistants who will solve their own problems and tell me later what they have done."[10]

Observing Marshall in action would serve Eisenhower well in the months and years ahead. On one occasion he was present when a senator telephoned the chief of staff to champion the promotion of an officer. Marshall's face visibly reddened with anger, and he interrupted to reply, "Senator, if you are interested in that man's promotion, the best thing you can do is never to mention his name to me. I will go out of my way to prevent the promotion of any man who seeks outside influence to gain it," and abruptly slammed down the phone without waiting for a response.[11] Eisenhower never forgot the lesson, which he would be obliged to put to use in a more diplomatic but nevertheless firm manner with men such as Churchill, as well as his own president.

Marshall and Eisenhower proved an excellent match. The new general regarded his boss as "a great soldier" and thought him "quick, tough, tireless, decisive and a real leader."[12] What particularly delighted Eisenhower was that the chief of staff left his trusted assistants to perform their jobs without interference and tolerated dissent in the belief that it enabled him to evaluate all sides of a problem. Eisenhower later recalled, "I resolved then and there, to do my work to the best of my ability and report to the General only situations of obvious necessity or when he personally sent for me."[13]

In Marshall's eyes the greatest sin one could commit was stupidity, real or perceived. Eisenhower likewise put up with neither fools nor the ineffectual and let them know it or replaced them. Marshall's impatience with incompetence was mirrored by Eisenhower, who derided the "petty jealousies" and "personal animosities" of career bureaucrats who placed self first. Eisenhower's impatience with those who were not team players or who impeded progress grew exponentially the longer he served in the War Department. Frustration and fatigue brought on by sixteen- to eighteen-hour days and too little sleep were a way of life in the War Department. Even under ideal conditions, preparing for a global war is a monumental undertaking. In 1942 such problems were magnified tenfold. Not surprisingly tempers grew famously short, and Eisenhower's was no exception. A telltale sign of an impending explosion of anger was a darkening of his ruddy complexion. Although he had a chauffeur to drive him back and forth in a staff car, some nights Eisenhower was so weary that he dreaded even the half-hour journey to Milton's home, only to have to return to his office early the following morning. Eisenhower could never recall having actually seen Milton's home during daylight. His only relaxation during these hectic months was the few moments he spent nightly with Milton and Helen Eisenhower's two children.[14]

Mamie had stopped off in Washington en route home from visiting John at West Point over Christmas, and their brief reunion came in time to welcome the new year. With help from the well-connected Harry Butcher, who seemed to know everyone of importance in Washington, the Eisenhowers leased a tiny apartment in the Wardman Tower, located not far from the War Department, and Mamie returned to San Antonio to undertake yet another move. This time was different; she would have been pleased if her husband spent the entire war in Washington. Her arrival in February 1942 did not alter Ike's frenetic schedule. They barely saw each other. "I feel like a football—kicked from place to place," Mamie wrote to her parents, but acknowledged, "Now that the break is made, I am glad to be here." To P. A. Hodgson, Eisenhower wrote, "You must have some inkling of the real pressure under which I am now working. The days are all too short. I rarely leave this rabid room in the daylight. We can never accept a social invitation, unless someone will invite Mamie to dinner and has me drop past later to pick her up."[15]

Assistant Secretary of War John J. McCloy was a World War I veteran disillusioned by his civilian role and convinced he could better serve his country as an officer in a field unit. Marshall had something else in mind, which provided the first clue of his future intentions regarding Eisenhower. "We're going to put a new man in charge of War Plans who may at some stage be destined for some pretty high command, and I'd like to have you go down and . . . give me a little impression of how you think it's being run, what you think of this new man." McCloy returned favorably impressed after meeting Eisenhower for the first time, and told Marshall that "that man Eisenhower makes more sense to me than any of the others down there."[16]

McCloy managed to work part-time under Eisenhower, a rather unusual arrangement, until Secretary Stimson learned of his deputy's deception and abruptly reined him in. "So that put an end to my espionage on General Eisenhower and my ambitions."[17] McCloy not only got to know Eisenhower well but later became a roving troubleshooter for Stimson and Marshall in the Mediterranean and in Northwest Europe in 1944–45. McCloy's interest in the employment of aerial observation and reconnaissance found a willing recipient in Eisenhower, who was well aware of its untapped potential. "He rather prided himself on the fact that he could fly one of those planes." McCloy also found Eisenhower "very sensitive to the fact that he had not gotten involved in combat in World War I."[18]

In December 1941 Winston Churchill and the British chiefs of staff arrived in Washington for three weeks of talks that constituted the Arcadia Conference, the first joint meeting of the two allies to formulate strategy and delineate Anglo-American command lines and relationships. They readily agreed that their first priority was the defeat of Germany and that operations in the Pacific would take a backseat. How and where Germany was to be defeated remained unresolved and the object of a controversy that would drag on well into 1943.

Eisenhower attended in the capacity of—as he described himself—one of the "unimportant" staff officers on the periphery of the conference. He was particularly anxious to observe firsthand the controversial British prime minister (and self-appointed minister of defense) about whom he had heard and read a great deal. It was also his first exposure to the new Combined Chiefs of Staff (CCOS), the term applied to the U.S. and British chiefs of staff operating as a single body to formulate strategic policy and issue command guidance to the Allied commanders in chief who would, in due course, be appointed to command the fighting units.

The British were represented by the chief of the air staff, the affable and astute Air Chief Marshal Sir Charles Portal; the First Lord of the Admiralty, Sir Dudley Pound; and Field Marshal Sir John Dill, whom Churchill had recently replaced as chief of the Imperial General Staff (CIGS). Dill's experience was put to good use as the British military representative in Washington where he became an effective link between the chiefs of staff and an intimate friend of Marshall. The U.S. military representatives were Marshall; the newly appointed chief of naval operations (CNO), Adm. Ernest J. King; the chief of the Army Air Corps, Gen. Henry H. "Hap" Arnold; and Adm. William Leahy, Roosevelt's personal military adviser and a former CNO. Missing was Marshall's counterpart, the newly appointed CIGS, Gen. (later Field Marshal Sir) Alan Brooke.

U.S. policy during World War II was unambiguous, asserting that direct military action take priority over political considerations. As American spokesman, Marshall advocated holding the line against Japan in the Pacific and for the primary emphasis to be the defeat of Nazi Germany. Eisenhower and his staff were crafting a plan for what was to be called Sledgehammer, an emergency cross-Channel invasion of northern France in 1942 to relieve the pressure on the Red Army by forcing Hitler to commit troops to the defense of the west.

Although Churchill himself had first conceived of a cross-Channel venture in the black days of 1940 after Dunkirk, the British thought Sledgehammer potentially disastrous and blocked its acceptance. As Marshall noted, "It appeared that the British staff and cabinet were unalterable in [their] refusal to touch SLEDGEHAMMER. . . . So we were at a complete stalemate. Churchill was rabid for Africa" and adamant that the Allies could not and should not mount a cross-Channel invasion in 1942.[19] Failure was unthinkable, argued Churchill, thus the operation must be deferred until the odds favored Allied success. British policy became acceptance of an eventual cross-Channel invasion, but opposition to any attempt to carry it out in 1942. As historian Martin Blumenson has written, "the British were averse to long-range planning and promises. They were unwilling to accept a fixed program of preparation. They preferred to be opportunistic, ready and able to take advantage of sudden and unexpected breaks."[20]

Marshall also faced the additional problem of attempting to dissuade Roosevelt from giving in to Churchill, who believed that Germany's Achilles' heel was what he termed the "soft underbelly" of Europe. Not only was a cross-Channel operation in 1942 impossible, but only in the Mediterranean, along the periphery of the Axis empire, did there exist an opportunity to defeat Axis forces and eliminate Italy from the war, thus "tightening the ring" and preparing for the day a full-scale cross-Channel invasion of France could be mounted in 1943. Glib and persuasive, Churchill's arguments found favor with Roosevelt. The British prime minister had a deeper motive: He was deeply distrustful of Stalin and undertook to introduce into American thinking a grand strategy that included curbing Russian hegemony and postwar territorial ambitions in Eastern Europe.

Marshall opposed Churchill on purely military grounds, arguing that it would be courting disaster to leave the Red Army facing the might of the Wehrmacht unaided; indeed, it would be one of history's worst blunders should eight million men be lost to Anglo-American inertia. Even if it failed, the Anglo-American response must be sufficiently confrontational to divert German reinforcements to France. Marshall also feared the consequences of becoming bogged down in military operations against the Axis in the Mediterranean, believing that the decisive battles of the war would be fought in Northwest Europe, *not* on the shores of the Mediterranean. Marshall freely admitted that Sledgehammer was "a desperate operation to save Russia" that he fully expected would fail.[21] Nevertheless Marshall believed that the operation would serve its purpose by drawing off German forces from Russia and by compelling the Luftwaffe to do battle with the RAF. The British not only disagreed but privately criticized what they deemed Marshall's political naïveté.[22]

As Marshall's chief planner, Eisenhower was deeply affected by Arcadia. Other than the conceptual Germany-first pledge, there was little else to cheer about. The two sides disagreed on the very first issue, the creation of a unified command to engage the Japanese in the Southwest Pacific. The British wanted the war run from both Washington and London, a two-headed bureaucracy, while FDR and Marshall strenuously advocated a single, unified commander. With the two sides unable to reach agreement, the matter was assigned to a joint study group, in which Eisenhower participated.

Eisenhower was actually caught at cross purposes. His first mandate from Marshall was to find the means—if not to aid the Philippines directly—to design a plan to create an Allied military presence in Australia to eventually fight Japan. However, the planning of Sledgehammer required that Eisenhower shift scarce assets from the Pacific to Europe.

Arcadia was notable for Churchill's rising popularity in the United States after a masterful speech to a joint session of Congress condemning Hitler and extolling the new alliance, ending with his famous V for victory sign, which brought thunderous applause from both houses and acclaim by the press. Although Churchill and FDR worked in apparent harmony, each was deeply suspicious of the other's vision of the postwar world. During the negotiations first lady Eleanor Roosevelt observed the two great orators huddled in the White House map room and was reminded of "two little boys playing soldier."[23] A dozen years later Eisenhower's own recollection of the interaction of the two war leaders was similar: Churchill, he wrote, evoked the "enjoyable feeling that he and our president were sitting on some rather Olympian platform with respect to the rest of the world and directing world affairs from that point of vantage."[24]

While FDR and Churchill toasted their "Common Cause," the workers at Eisenhower's staff level began marathon meetings to hammer out some means of stemming Japan's aggression in the Far East and resolving the command issue. Eisenhower was an active participant during this, his first but hardly memorable exposure to the British method of waging war. In January 1942 Eisenhower also resumed recording his thoughts and opinions in a diary, although, given his enormous workload, it was a wonder that he ever found the time. Mostly the diary was an outlet for his pet peeves and frustrations. Some entries were cryptic and a reflection of the pressures placed on his shoulders. Meetings and committees he found necessary evils he would have gladly abandoned for a field command. In fact, 1942 was a mere four days old when Eisenhower lamented, "I'd give anything to be back in the field."[25]

After a particularly numbing meeting on unity of command in the Southwest Pacific, Eisenhower scribbled disgustedly, "What an effort. Talk, talk, talk."[26] Within a short time he had also grown impatient with some of his colleagues. "There are lots of amateur strategists on the job, and prima donnas everywhere," he complained.[27]

"We were dealing with deficits, not strength, and our efforts to draw up a directive were almost as pitiful as our weakness in the region. We argued and fussed over minutia, each side trying to make sure that its own rights and prerogatives could not be damaged by the other." Still, "everyone tried to make the effort a useful one." In the end this first round of negotiations became moot when it proved impossible to provide the newly designated Allied supreme commander of U.S., British, Dutch, and Australian (ABDA) forces, Field Marshal Sir Archibald Wavell, with adequate reinforcements.[28]

Marshall's brusque managerial style thoroughly intimidated a number of otherwise competent officers. Rarely seen outside the confines of his office were Marshall's occasional monumental outbursts of temper. His intolerance of the slightest failure, his displeasure at anything less than perfection, and his general unwillingness to offer the slightest hint of praise all contributed to their fear of crossing Marshall. Once, angered by the contents of a staff paper, he hurled his briefcase, strewing its contents across the floor of his office.[29]

Gerow was among those who were either tongue-tied or unwilling to make decisions without the chief of staff's personal approval. Eisenhower was an exception and challenged Gerow: "Gee, you have to quit bothering the Chief with this stuff." Gerow admitted he was incapable of doing so. "I can't help it, Ike. These decisions are too important. He's got to make them himself." It was no coincidence that in February 1942 Gerow was promoted to major general and sent to command the 29th Infantry Division. Eisenhower could only envy his friend's good fortune. Marshall selected Eisenhower as Gerow's replacement. Eisenhower recorded his friend's parting words. "As Gee walked out, he said, 'Well, I got Pearl Harbor on the book, lost the Philippine Islands, Singapore, [and] Sumatra. Let's see what you can do.' "[30] Historian Geoffrey Perret has wryly pointed out, "It was bitterly ironic that having reached his level of incompetence, Gerow . . . [was rewarded with] a ticket straight into battle."[31]

Time magazine reported that in the "tall, bald" Eisenhower, who had made a name for himself during the Louisiana maneuvers, "Operations got a big operator."[32] Only later did Marshall reveal the most important reason why Eisenhower had replaced Gerow:

> When I brought him in to head the Operations Division after Pearl Harbor, I put him in the place of a good officer [Gerow] who had

been in that job two years. I felt he was growing stale from overwork, and I don't like to keep any man on a job so long that his ideas and forethoughts go no further than mine. When I find an officer isn't fresh, he doesn't add much to my fund of knowledge, and, worst of all, doesn't contribute to the ideas and enterprising push that are so essential to winning the war. General Eisenhower had a refreshing approach to problems. He was most helpful.[33]

Moreover, unlike those of his colleagues who were frightened of Marshall, Eisenhower relished working for a decisive boss who gave him the latitude to perform his duties as he saw fit.

As Marshall's chief planner, Eisenhower was now the unofficial architect of American strategy in 1942. More than one hundred officers reported to him. During the first half of 1942 Eisenhower resembled a juggler obliged to keep a large number of objects in the air at the same time. In replacing the taciturn Gerow, he brought a fresh sense of urgency to the task of developing U.S. war plans.[34] His success was affirmation of his organizational ability and clear thinking about the weighty issues he was faced with. Fortunately he and Marshall were bound by the same outlook and priorities in negotiations and meetings of the Roosevelt administration with the British. Yet the job was so demanding that by the spring of 1942 Marshall had already begun to regard Eisenhower as being as burned out as Gerow had been. "But he [too] began to work sixteen or eighteen hours a day and before he left, I was beginning to worry about him, just as I did his predecessor."[35]

Despite the taxing time spent in fulfilling his new duties, Eisenhower found time on Sunday mornings for geography lessons with "Hap" Arnold. "For two or three hours they'd pore over maps, trying to memorize the geography of the entire world in excruciating detail. There were scores of remote peninsulas, obscure mountains and far-flung islands that were to become militarily important in the years ahead. They intended to know them almost as well as if they'd walked over them."[36]

The OPD staff quickly learned that their new boss was a sterner taskmaster than his predecessor. Marshall demanded that his staff be more responsive to the overseas commanders and reminded them, "You gentlemen are not my staff officers. You are the representatives of those theater commanders and you'd better satisfy *them*." Eisenhower needed no persuading and instituted a rule that the word "no" was not within a staffer's purview. Anyone in OPD who objected to any plan of action had to submit an alternate solution. Another decree laid down tough guidelines for action officers responsible for what Eisenhower nicknamed Green Hornets. Any document sent to or from Marshall was placed in a green folder and given the highest priority. The officer "could not even leave the building until he produced a reply to the Green Hornet and drew its sting."[37] At times even Eisenhower had difficulty satisfying Marshall. One day he exited Marshall's office with a huge grin on his face saying, "Hot damn, I finally got one past the old man."[38]

Eisenhower and his staff worked furiously to present Marshall with plans for Sledgehammer, Bolero, Roundup, and many other proposed operations and options. Although initially skeptical of Sledgehammer, Eisenhower was quickly converted by Marshall's logic that *something* had to be done to aid the Soviet Union by engaging the Germans in 1942, even though he fully understood the possibly deadly nature of the operation.

Time was the principal enemy in contesting Germany, and Eisenhower had little patience for those who lacked his sense of urgency. "We must win in Europe," he declared. "It's going to be one h—— of a job, but, so what? We can't win by sitting on our fannies and giving our stuff in driblets all over the world, with no theater getting enough."[39]

Acutely aware of the necessity to curb his hot temper, Eisenhower tried hard but not always successfully to keep it under control. Most of his outbursts were confined to the privacy of his diary. Eisenhower compared his boss's disparate temperament with his own: "Marshall puzzles me a bit," he wrote. "I've never seen a man who apparently develops a higher pressure of anger when he encounters some piece of stupidity than does he. Yet the outburst is so fleeting, he returns so quickly to complete 'normalcy,' that I'm certain he does it for effect. At least he doesn't get angry in the sense I do—I blaze for an hour!"[40]

Eisenhower's diatribes were not aimed merely at MacArthur ("as big a baby as ever" who "still likes his boot lickers" and "is losing his nerve").[41] He blazed at virtually everyone around him; from the navy ("what a gang to work with") to Arnold's Army Air Forces and other staffers, no one was exempt from his increasing sharp invective, all of which was indicative of the tremendous stress under which Eisenhower functioned. Outwardly he seemed the same Ike of old; inside he seethed in large part in disillusionment over his inability to accomplish the impossible. Scant as it was, his only emotional outlet was to vent his anger in his diary.

Eisenhower's service in Washington was the most militant period of his career. The mood of the United States after Pearl Harbor was one of extreme anger, particularly in Washington, where a once-dovish Congress now insisted on retaliation against Japan. FDR's "day of infamy" speech had also had a galvanizing effect on the nation. No one reflected American sentiment more intensely than Dwight Eisenhower, whose hatred for what he termed the "Nazi beast" and the "low grade [Japanese] skunks" was limitless.

On December 22, 1941, the Japanese army invaded the island of Luzon at Lingayen Gulf and quickly marched on Manila. To prevent its wanton destruction, MacArthur declared Manila an open city on December 27, and the Philippine capital was occupied on January 2, 1942, as MacArthur's forces retreated to the Bataan Peninsula and the island fortress of Corregidor, which guarded the entrance to Manila Bay. MacArthur was ordered to Australia by PT boat and departed Corregidor on March 11, vowing, "I shall return," and was succeeded by Maj. Gen. Jonathan Wainwright. After more than three months of bitter fighting on Bataan, the gallant U.S.-Filipino force could hold out no longer and was compelled to surrender on April 9, 1942, with the loss of 75,000 men, 12,000 of them Americans. Its remnants under Wainwright were trapped on Corregidor but held out for another month before they too surrendered, "[w]ith broken heart[s] and head[s] bowed in sadness but not in shame," read Wainwright's final communiqué before he was led into captivity. Pearl Harbor, the loss of the Philippines, and the subsequent Bataan Death March (to imprisonment under unspeakable conditions) plunged a dagger into the heart of the American psyche.[42] Among those most deeply affected was Dwight Eisenhower.

The British colonial empire in the Far East was also being swept away by the Japanese, whose seizure of Burma, Hong Kong, and Malaya culminated in the greatest humiliation in the history of the British army—surpassing even Dunkirk—when Singapore fell in early 1942 and 85,000 troops of the British Tenth Army were lost.

Had it been even remotely possible, both Marshall and Eisenhower would have moved heaven and earth to reinforce MacArthur. The stark reality, however, was that the Philippines were some five thousand miles from Pearl Harbor, and as long as Japan controlled the air and sea-lanes in the Pacific, any attempt to send reinforcements, even if they had been available in sufficient numbers, would have been futile. What little Eisenhower could do did not even qualify as a Band-Aid, nor could it postpone the inevitable fall of the Philippines. A few navy submarines brought some urgently needed medical supplies to Corregidor in what was at best a token effort. MacArthur, railing that his urgent calls were falling on deaf ears, stepped up his demands for priority assistance. Even a lucrative cash offer from a ten-million-dollar fund Eisenhower sent to Australia for the purpose of hiring privateers to resupply the Philippines by running the Japanese blockade induced few takers.[43]

MacArthur bitterly asserted that he had been abandoned by Marshall and Eisenhower. Such was never the case, yet MacArthur's feelings were elementary. There are few more gut-wrenching emotions than those engendered by watching a military force left to its fate against a superior enemy force. The first printed allegation appeared in the summer of 1944, in which the author quoted MacArthur that "faceless staff officers" in Washington had lacked the courage to send reinforcements, which he maintained could have succeeded in running the Japanese blockade. MacArthur's barbs were an unambiguous reference to Eisenhower, who wrote to Marshall that it "practically gave me indigestion."[44]

Although Marshall was high on his list, MacArthur reserved his greatest malice for Eisenhower, whom he repeatedly accused of being a "traitor," not to his country but to MacArthur for having left his service. Again and again during the war, Eichelberger heard MacArthur speak disparagingly of "that traitor Eisenhower." Eichelberger was convinced that being a traitor to MacArthur "would have been considered by him to be the greater offense."[45]

Not only was Eisenhower acutely sensitive to the plight of MacArthur and Wainwright and openly distraught because so little could be done to resupply them, but his anguish was made more intense by his love for the Philippines and the cognizance that it was a disaster in the making whose outcome he was powerless to prevent. Mamie vividly recalled him restlessly pacing up and down their quarters at night, talking to himself. "Dear God, I don't have it. I don't have it to send."[46]

Eisenhower's attitude toward MacArthur was a curious mixture of scorn and compassion. From his first diary entry, on January 1, 1942, he both defended and criticized MacArthur. "I've been insisting [that the] Far East is critical, and no other sideshows should be undertaken until air and ground are in a satisfactory state."[47] Eisenhower was justifiably critical of the inexcusable loss of the preponderance of the U.S. B-17 bomber fleet in the Far East, blaming both MacArthur and his air chief, Maj. Gen. Louis H. Brereton. Clark Field was the only strategic target in the Philippines, but American failure to prepare adequately for Japanese air strikes if war came was compounded by MacArthur's refusal either to see Brereton or to issue orders during the early critical hours. Both proved calamitous. Two squadrons of B-17s were permitted to land and refuel at the same time on December 8, 1941, and were caught like sitting ducks by the Japanese air force. MacArthur publicly praised his air force for its valiant efforts, particularly the P-40 fighters, which were outnumbered and outgunned by the more versatile Japanese Zero. As for Brereton, MacArthur regarded his chief airman as a "bumbling nincompoop" and got rid of him in a hurry under the guise of a reassignment.[48] Brereton, an Annapolis graduate, was a pioneer airman with a World War I Distinguished Service Cross (DSC) and an impressive postwar career. In his case, however, past achievements were misleading indicators of his future performance. Historians have not been kind to Brereton, and properly so. He has been been characterized as "cocky, amusing, highly intelligent," but also "lazy," fond of "rich living, attractive women and partying till dawn."[49] Brereton's career was saved by his powerful benefactor and longtime friend "Hap" Arnold, who was astonished to learn that neat tidy rows of aircraft were lined up at Clark Field like pawns awaiting execution by the Japanese—who were equally astonished at their good fortune. Arnold blamed MacArthur but not Brereton. Instead of being demoted, retired, or shunted to a less demanding assignment, Brereton was sent by Arnold to the Middle

East to command the U.S. Ninth Air Force in Egypt. Ultimately Brereton would become a subordinate of Eisenhower in Northwest Europe in 1944. MacArthur's loss would not prove to be Eisenhower's gain.[50]

Many of Eisenhower's personal criticisms of MacArthur were capricious and patently unfair, and, as Geoffrey Perret correctly asserts, were the consequence of "arguments unfinished, anger unappeased, [and] resentments long suppressed."[51] They were also the reflections of a perpetually quick-tempered man whose feelings of frustration could be traced directly to his zeal to win the war of the bureaucrats.

Interservice rivalry had always existed in some form between the army and the navy. During World War II, a new equation was added with the creation of the U.S. Army Air Forces. Although technically a part of the army, the new air force boss, "Hap" Arnold, was given a seat on the unofficial U.S. Joint Chiefs of Staff headed by Marshall. Eisenhower's later insistence that Anglo-American cooperation was the golden rule of his command was not manifest in early 1942. After less than a month in Washington, Eisenhower noted, "What a job to work with allies. There's a lot of big talk and desk hammering around this place, but very few doers. They announce results in advance in a flashy way and make big impressions . . . and then the workers get the grief."[52]

During the negotiations for opening a lifeline to Australia, Eisenhower received his first real taste of the high-level infighting and the difficulty of dealing with another military service. With Marshall's mandate to take action foremost, Eisenhower found the "prolonged and earnest argument" interminable but necessary. His public face was amiable but all business. Only in his diary did he vent his true feelings. His greatest aversion was reserved for Adm. Ernie King, the bald, hard-bitten, outspoken new chief of naval operations. Eisenhower was accustomed to working with strong-willed, high-profile officers such as Pershing and MacArthur. King, however, was unlike anyone he had ever dealt with. An unabashed advocate of sea power, King was a veteran submariner, naval aviator, carrier commander, and a consummate professional who was "ruthless" and possessed of a "driving personality." The word "amiable" was never uttered of King, nevertheless, as one historian has observed, "FDR had not appointed Ernest J. King" commander in chief of the U.S. Fleet and later chief of naval operations "because he liked the man" but rather because he needed a "tough man to whip the Navy into shape," and no one in the navy was harder-nosed.[53] In fact, Marshall and King shared the singular trait of decisiveness. King's strengths outweighed his flaws, which included "other men's wives, alcohol, and intolerance." One of his daughters once noted that King was "the most even-tempered man in the Navy. He is always in a rage." Yet Roosevelt was proved right; King was the navy's leading strategist, whom the official naval historian, Samuel Eliot Morison, rated "the principal architect of victory" and "undoubtedly the best naval strategist and organizer in our history."[54]

Eisenhower's diary reveals both aversion and a grudging admiration for this "stubborn, arbitrary type, with not too much brains and a tendency toward bullying his juniors. But I think he wants to fight, which is vastly encouraging." Eisenhower may have been the only officer ever to question King's intelligence, a specious judgment made, like most of his remarks, under stress. Although he never warmed to the crusty admiral, there is no evidence that Eisenhower ever tangled directly with King, either in Washington or overseas. His harshest description of King was written in anger in March 1942, after a series of frustrating meetings, when he castigated the admiral for his perceived lack of cooperation. "One thing that might help win this war," he wrote, "is to get someone to shoot King. He's the antithesis of cooperation, a deliberately rude person, which means he's a mental bully."[55] Similar misunderstandings existed between the army and the airmen, each distrusting the other, and each failing to understand the problems and potential of the other service. Rude and crude as he was, Eisenhower respected fighting men, and in King the United States had a true warrior whose sole object was to punish Germany and Japan for their aggression. In his indignation Eisenhower simply tended to overlook King's strengths.

King had replaced Adm. Harold R. Stark ("a nice old lady," wrote Eisenhower), "but this fellow [King] is going to cause a blow-up sooner or later. I'll bet a cookie." After learning that King had returned unopened an important letter from Arnold because the envelope erroneously cited his rank as "Rear Admiral King," Eisenhower sarcastically observed, "that's the size of the man the navy has as its head. He ought to be a big help winning this war."[56] Eisenhower's wildly inaccurate impressions were not reciprocated, nor does his diary record a later meeting at which King pledged his cooperation after initially rejecting a request for assistance. "From that time on, I had a friend in the Navy," he said. As for Admiral King, he would demonstrate his high opinion of Eisenhower at Casablanca in January 1943.

On March 10, 1942, David Eisenhower died at the age of seventy-eight after being in failing health for nearly a year. A telegram from Roy Eisenhower several days earlier had warned of his impending passing, nevertheless, one of the more difficult travails Mamie faced during her marriage was calling Ike with the news. Whatever sentiments this impassive man possessed went to the grave with him. His son's diary for that sorrowful date recorded but a single line about the father he barely knew: "Father died this morning. Nothing I can do but send a wire." Eisenhower could certainly have taken a brief emergency leave to attend his father's funeral; the interchangeable cogs of the military are such that in his absence his capable deputies could have assumed his duties. However, faced with the depressing choice between what he believed was a question of duty or family, Eisenhower chose duty. He remained in Washington, rationalizing it as his obligation. "I have felt terribly. I should like so much to be with my mother these days. But we're at war. And war is not soft, it has no time to indulge even in the most sacred emotions. I loved my dad. I think my mother is the finest person I've ever known. She has been an inspiration for dad's life and a true helpmeet in every sense of the word. I'm quitting work now, 7:30 P.M. I haven't the heart to go on tonight."[57]

The day of David's funeral on March 12, Eisenhower shut himself in his office to meditate and pray for his father's eternal soul. His reactions seemed as much to reflect guilt at never having been close to David as they did the loss of a father. In the privacy of his diary he lauded David as a "quiet, modest" man. Although Eisenhower was "proud he was my father," he rued the fact that "it was always difficult to let him know the great depth of my affection for him." Underneath the entry Eisenhower wrote: "David J. Eisenhower, 1863–1942." As he had after Ikky's death, Eisenhower concealed whatever grief he felt behind his business-as-usual facade. It would undoubtedly have eased Eisenhower's growing burdens had he had the luxury of time to grieve, but public displays of affection or of sorrow were simply not the Eisenhower way. So instead his grief remained repressed in the name of duty.

A short time after David's death, Ike's younger brother, the jovial Roy Jacob Eisenhower, who, along with Arthur, was the only Eisenhower son to remain in Kansas, died suddenly, two months shy of his fiftieth birthday, in Junction City. After Roy's untimely death, hard on the heels of David's passing, Ida had never felt lonelier or more discouraged. She was near eighty years old and increasingly frail, and the spark that had lit her cheerful personality was close to being extinguished. Fortunately David had left her with sufficient savings to remain in her beloved family home for the remainder of her life. To assuage the loneliness, a longtime family friend named Naomi Engle moved into the Eisenhower home to become Ida's companion, her compensation paid by the surviving Eisenhower brothers. According to Kenneth Davis, Ida lived primarily in the past, with only her memories to block out her loneliness. With her only military son deeply involved in a war she abhorred and her other surviving sons scattered to the four winds, Ida felt that "nothing seems real any more. They're all so far away. About all I have to look at is their pictures."[58] It would be 1944 before she again saw her soldier son, Dwight.

26.

"I'm Going to Command the Whole Shebang."

[I] have the utmost confidence that through your efforts we
will eventually beat the hell out of those bastards

—PATTON

The major problem facing the Allies in 1942 was to agree on what they would do, and when and where they would do it. No plan had yet been drawn up by Eisenhower's directorate for the employment of assault landing craft for the coming conflicts in Europe and Japan. Although he would later be overruled, a stubborn Ernie King pursued a Pacific-first strategy that favored the navy.

Eisenhower's most difficult obstacle was the procurement of landing craft, without which no invasion could be carried out. One of the strangest circumstances of the war was that there were never sufficient numbers built to fulfill Allied requirements, thus making their lack the most serious logistical problem faced by the alliance. The arbitrator of the issue was King, who controlled with an iron hand the production and allocation of all U.S. landing craft. As the War Department's chief planner, Eisenhower was vexed by the issue and persisted in his arguments that there must be immediate resolution to a host of unanswered questions. He became part of a joint landing craft committee and noted in exasperation in early May 1942 that they were still embroiled, discussing "questions on which I begged the answers last February: (1) Who is responsible for building landing craft? (2) What types are they building? (3) Are they suitable for cross-Channel work? (4) Will the number of each type be sufficient, etc. How in hell can we win this war unless we can crack some heads?"[1]

The Philippines were not Eisenhower's only grave concern. The Middle East and Far East were crucial war zones. "I've been trying for some weeks to get some force in the Middle East and India. I want to help the British as much as possible, but avoiding use of our ground troops (except possibly one armored division [in the Middle East]). But I'm scared. We must save that region or run the risk of losing the war."[2]

In March 1942 Eisenhower and his staff produced what has been termed the Marshall memorandum, but it might also have been called the Eisenhower doctrine. It was a modification of Sledgehammer into a joint Anglo-American air-ground offensive to be launched in the late summer of 1942, culminating in Allied landings in France somewhere between Calais and Le Havre. It also proposed two other operations to be carried out separately: The first was code-named Bolero, a massive buildup of U.S. troops and equipment in the United Kingdom, followed by a full-scale cross-Channel invasion in the spring of 1943, Operation Roundup.

Marshall carefully studied the document. The strategy Eisenhower developed for pursuing Allied military efforts in 1942 was threefold: "hold open the line to England . . . keep Russia in the war as an active participant; [and] hold the India–Middle East buttress between Japs and Germans."[3] "All right," Marshall said. "It is persuasive to me." Roosevelt, perhaps heeding Stimson's advice that "the only way to get the initiative in this war is to take it," readily approved the plan.[4] As Marshall's official biographer notes, his almost casual "acceptance of the paper constituted his acknowledgement of a job well done." Said Eisenhower, "The nearest that he ever came to saying anything complimentary directly to my face was, 'You're not doing too badly so far.' "[5]

What followed the approval of Bolero gave Eisenhower his first taste of the problems he would have to deal with in the months ahead.

On May 5 came the further grim news of the fall of Corregidor. Eisenhower's bitter feelings toward MacArthur resurfaced. "Poor Wainwright! He did the fighting in the Philippine Islands, another got such glory as the public could find in the operation. . . . General MacArthur's tirades, to which T.J. [Davis] and I so often listened to in Manila, would now sound as silly to the public as they then did to us. But he's a hero. Yah."[6]

As he became an increasingly important cog in the War Department staff, Eisenhower had all but resigned himself to spending the war in another frustrating desk job. The fall of Tobruk to Rommel in June 1942 was the heaviest blow struck against the British in the Middle East, and it came during an official visit to Washington by Churchill. FDR offered whatever help the United States was capable of providing. Churchill readily accepted and asked that a number of the new Sherman tanks be sent at once to bolster the Eighth Army. Marshall countered with the offer of a fully equipped armored division. When Marshall asked Eisenhower whom he proposed to command the division, without hesitation Eisenhower replied, "Patton." Reminded that Patton was already commanding an armored corps and training new divisions for combat in North Africa at the Desert Training Center in Southern California, and unlikely to accept what amounted to a demotion, Eisenhower nonetheless asked for permission to offer his friend the assignment.

At Eisenhower's behest Marshall summoned Patton to Washington where, according to Eisenhower, he not only accepted but said, "When can we start? To get an outfit destined for immediate battle I'd sell my soul." Ordered to plan the deployment of a U.S. armored division to the Middle East to assist the British, Patton was reunited with Eisenhower for the first time in years. Patton's reaction was affirmation that their friendship was still strong after twenty-two years. "Of all the many talks I had in Washington, none gave me so much pleasure as that with you," he wrote Eisenhower a short time later. "There were two reasons for this. In the first place, you are about my oldest friend. In the second place, your self-assurance and to me, at least, demonstrated ability, gave me a great feeling of confidence for the future . . . and I have the utmost confidence that through your efforts we will eventually beat the hell out of those bastards—'You name them; I'll shoot them!' "[7] Eisenhower replied at once, "I don't have the slightest trouble naming the hellions I'd like to have you shoot; my problem is to figure out some way of getting you to the place you can do it."[8] In the spring of 1942 Patton wrote several prescient letters to his friend, the first of which proclaimed that Eisenhower would become "the 'Black Jack' [Pershing] of the dam[n] war."[9] A month later Patton, who fervently believed in destiny and reincarnation, wrote prophetically, "Sometimes I think your life and mine are under the protection of some supreme being or fate, because, after many years of parallel thought, we find ourselves in the positions we now occupy."[10]

Although the division was never deployed to Egypt, during one of their Washington conversations, Eisenhower remarked, "You see what's happened to our dream of 20 years ago, of going to war as a team. I'm slated to stick here to do a lot of heavy planning and operating on a global scale, but I wish you all the luck in the world in the field." Patton's reply would prove prescient: "Ike, don't give up. The basic truth of war is that the unexpected always happens. It will be a long war. We'll get together yet."[11]

Marshall and Eisenhower were a lot like a father and son whose relationship was not without its occasional tense moments. Eisenhower remembers only one occasion when Marshall ever called him Ike. "In the next two sentences, I'll bet he said 'Eisenhower' five times to make sure that I understood it was just a slip of the tongue."[12] Their first heated exchange took place in March 1942 and appeared to begin innocently enough, when Marshall said, "I want you to know that in this war the commanders are going to be promoted and not the staff officers." Marshall never did anything innocently, and after a few minutes to let this "real loaded brick" find its mark, he continued, "You are a good case. General [Kenyon] Joyce wanted you for a division command and the Army commander said you should have a corps command. . . . Eisenhower . . . you're not going to get any promotion. You are going to stay right here on this job and you'll probably never move."

Years of working for MacArthur had inured Eisenhower to standing up for himself, and he shot back, " 'General, I don't give a hoot about your promotions and the methods you use in making them. In two World Wars all I ever asked for was field duty. . . . I've been denied such a position. Now, you've brought me here to a job that I did not want and where I have no time to think of anything whatsoever except the demands upon me. I'll do my best to perform to your satisfaction but so far as I'm concerned you need give no thought about promotion for me—I simply don't care.

"I got up to start for the door. Already I was feeling sheepish over my outburst. Here I was, a subordinate, expressing personal feelings and in doing so was undoubtedly adding to the heavy burdens the Chief of Staff was carrying, whereas my real duty was to try to relieve him of some of them. His office was long and every step I took toward the door I felt more ashamed of myself. Finally, grasping the doorknob, I turned," in time to detect a semblance of a smile on Marshall's usually unemotional countenance. "Though I was chagrined with myself I managed a feeble grin," and left.[13]

Eisenhower's recollections of the incident years later had mellowed his true reaction at the time. Of course Eisenhower cared deeply—not particularly about high rank but simply about participating in the "shooting" side of the war as a division or corps commander rather than as an obscure desk jockey. It was ingrained in him that a true soldier marches toward the sound of the guns. Any chance of doing so meant being reassigned from the War Department. Now there seemed little chance. His aspirations apparently shattered, Eisenhower returned to his office in a towering rage, where he savagely deplored his plight in the privacy of his diary. The next day a calmer Eisenhower realized the futility of his outburst and wrote, "Yesterday I got very angry and filled a page with language that this morning I've 'expurgated.' Anger cannot win, it cannot even think clearly . . . for many years I've made it a religion never to indulge myself, but yesterday I failed."[14]

To a visiting West Point classmate Eisenhower let off steam. "My gang and I never get home. We sleep here and our food is sent in. They hit us with directives and queries late in the afternoon and we're expected to have a full set of plans at the White House by nine the next morning. I tell you, Buzz, it's awful. And then General Marshall called me in yesterday and told me I'd be in this job another year—and there'd be no promotion, either."[15]

A few days later, during a rare break for a brief visit to West Point, Eisenhower recounted the incident to John. At the time his father thought his fate had been sealed. "I think Dad was sort of apologizing to me," recalled John, "that he was going to be a brigadier for the rest of his life. Hell, that sounded pretty good to me." On reflection after the war, however, Eisenhower recognized his exchange with Marshall for what it actually was—"a great big test."[16]

Eisenhower was not the first and certainly not the last to misread Marshall.

Where others would have intimidated or fired a subordinate for such an outburst, Marshall was secretly impressed by those with the backbone to stand up to him and defend their position. Marshall had no use for yes-men, and his tiff with Eisenhower in no way deterred the chief of staff from carrying out his intention all along of promoting his outspoken subordinate to major general a short time later.

War Department policy in 1942 did not favor promotion of staff officers to high ranks. To obtain Eisenhower's promotion Marshall used the pretext that because the American observer group in London reported to Eisenhower, he was, in effect, a de facto commander, a rather unique definition of command but nevertheless sufficient for the chief of staff's purpose.

Much too preoccupied for much outward excitement, Eisenhower wrote on March 27, "The promotion is just as satisfactory as if a permanent one. I suppose one could call it the 'official' stamp of the War Department."[17] Naively, however, Eisenhower believed that the promotion "should assure that when I finally get back to troops, I'll get a division."

By the spring of 1942 Marshall had become increasingly concerned about the inertia of the U.S. observer group in London. Created in 1941 to liaise with the British, and after Pearl Harbor redesignated U.S. Army Forces in the British Isles, it was commanded by an air corps officer, Maj. Gen. James E. Chaney. Marshall returned from attending a conference in London in April 1942 disturbed by the fact that there seemed to be a complete lack of understanding of the mission of the United States in the United Kingdom. With Bolero and Roundup now approved, it was time for action, not apathy. Marshall summoned Eisenhower and instructed him to visit London and report back on the situation.

Eisenhower's journey required flying a tortuous, roundabout route via Montreal; Gander, Newfoundland; and Prestwick, Scotland, where he spent a day inspecting a fleet of various new amphibious landing craft and conferring with a British division commander. The following evening Eisenhower's party completed the final leg by train to London's Paddington Station. They arrived three hours late in a dense fog, where a half dozen staff cars awaited their arrival at one end of the platform. Each was driven by one of a group of civilian drivers engaged by Chaney's observer group to chauffeur members of his organization and visiting officers. Driving duties were randomly assigned by the motor pool, and one of the drivers that day was a pretty young Irishwoman named Kay Summersby, who was disappointed to be handed a dispatch to drive an obscure major general named Eisenhower. To be assigned an officer of high rank was considered a mark of prestige (and snobbery) among the drivers. Thanks to the foul weather, Kay and the other drivers had been waiting for nearly three days for the Americans to arrive, but the visitors suddenly all piled into U.S. ambassador John G. Winant's limousine, leaving five tired and angry drivers with empty vehicles to follow them to the American embassy in Grosvenor Square.

The last in line after returning to Grosvenor Square later that day, Summersby noticed two American generals walking away from the embassy. She rushed over and asked if one of them was General Eisenhower. When Eisenhower and Mark Clark introduced themselves, Kay announced that she was their assigned driver for the duration of their visit. They asked to be driven to their quarters in the nearby Claridge's Hotel. Upon their arrival, Eisenhower politely thanked her and requested that she present herself again at nine A.M. the following morning. Exhausted, steaming, and convinced that as a mere two-star, Eisenhower was just another flunky general of no importance, Kay drove away muttering to herself that she had driven them "exactly two blocks, after waiting three days for that trip."[18] It had been her first innocuous and unremarkable introduction to a man whose name would be notoriously—but wrongly—linked with hers throughout the remainder of both their lives.

Eisenhower was appalled to learn that Chaney's organization was befuddled and unclear about its mission. There was little sense of urgency, its members wore civilian clothes, kept conventional hours, and took weekends off. Out of touch with both the British and their own War Department, they seemed oblivious to the seriousness of Bolero and Roundup. Clearly something would have to be done at once to light a fire under Chaney and his officers.

During his whirlwind visit Eisenhower and Clark also met and conferred with everyone of consequence in the British military hierarchy. At the suggestion of the War Office, Eisenhower and Clark were sent to the south coast of England, where British and Canadian units were engaged in the most intensive training exercises held since Dunkirk. There they were briefed by the commanding general, a jaunty, diminutive British lieutenant general named Bernard Law Montgomery.

Eisenhower's first encounter with Montgomery began in anonymity and ended in disarray. Clark later described how the briefing took place in a small farmhouse, with a large map tacked to the wall, where they awaited the arrival of the general known simply as Monty. Montgomery, said Clark, seemed irked at having to take time from his other duties to brief two strange American generals. "He was very abrupt," and said, "I have been directed to take time from my busy life to brief you gentlemen."

As they were being briefed, "Ike took out a pack of cigarettes and . . . lit one." Sniffing the cigarette smoke, Montgomery instantly stopped his briefing to demand, "Who is smoking?" Eisenhower acknowledged, "I am, sir." None too gently Montgomery, whose aversion to cigarettes was well known throughout the British army, forcefully informed Eisenhower that he did not permit smoking in his presence. "So Ike stopped smoking, winked at me, and stumped the cigarette out."[19] Only Eisenhower's beet-red face betrayed his annoyance.

The first-ever meeting between the two men, neither of whom had any inkling of his future role, proved an inauspicious start to one of the most significant military relationships of World War II. Although Eisenhower tactfully wrote in his diary that "General Montgomery is a decisive type who appears to be extremely energetic and professionally able," he was angered beyond words and undoubtedly humiliated at being dressed down by this autocratic British officer. Eisenhower, who never forgot a slight, certainly never forgot the incident. Clark later wrote that Eisenhower had merely laughed it off. Kay Summersby, however, saw and heard Eisenhower's angry reaction to Montgomery as he and Clark discussed the day's events during the drive back to London. At one point she heard the words "that son of a bitch" uttered in the backseat. Eisenhower "was furious—really steaming mad. And he was still mad. It was my first exposure to the Eisenhower temper. . . . His face was flaming red, and the veins in his forehead looked like worms."[20]

During his whirlwind tour of meetings and visits, Eisenhower attended a high-level staff meeting where he was introduced to the chief of the Imperial General Staff, Gen. Sir Alan Brooke, a Royal Artillery officer and Marshall's counterpart as the head of the British Chiefs of Staff. Eisenhower's first formal encounter with Brooke was hardly more encouraging than had been the one with Montgomery. It was the start of an uneasy relationship with the brilliant but prickly Ulsterman, who had little use for Americans and sometimes made little secret of his disdain. Neither Marshall ("a pleasant and easy man to get on with" but "not a great man") nor Eisenhower ever fared well in Brooke's eyes. From the outset Brooke was suspicious of Eisenhower's lack of experience, regarding him as congenial but wholly lacking experience or competence to grasp grand strategy.[21]

Asked to express the U.S. position, Eisenhower stated that the first priority ought to be the naming of a commander. If Sledgehammer was to take place in 1942, the commander would of necessity have to be British. Whom would Eisenhower suggest for the job? inquired Brooke. Eisenhower named the junior member of the British Chiefs of Staff, Adm. Lord Louis "Dickie" Mountbatten, whom Churchill had appointed after Dunkirk to head up Combined Operations. Speaking of Mountbatten in the third person, Eisenhower stated he had heard that Mountbatten was "vigorous, intelligent and courageous . . . I assume he could do the job." Mountbatten's biographer notes, "A slightly embarrassed silence was broken by Brooke, who said: 'General, possibly you have not met Admiral Mountbatten. This is he, sitting directly across the table from you.' "[22]

Despite their uncomfortable introduction, the one British officer whom both Eisenhower and Clark established an immediate rapport with was Mountbatten, whom they found willing and eager to engage the Germans and to cooperate with his ally. All three shared a common belief in combined operations, particularly the necessity for an invasion of occupied Europe on a wide front under a single joint commander. An outspoken public hero, Mountbatten was a dynamic junior naval officer who had commanded a destroyer flotilla in the Mediterranean where his flagship, HMS *Kelly*, was sunk by the Germans off Crete in 1941, after which Churchill chose him to head up the training and planning preparations for the invasion of Europe. Mountbatten, however, was the odd man out on the BCOS and, although Brooke appreciated his unbounded enthusiasm, he regarded Mountbatten as something of a loose cannon whose ideas were to be reined in whenever possible. None of which prevented Mountbatten and Eisenhower from forming a lasting friendship.

Eisenhower returned to Washington in early June seriously troubled by what he had observed, and confirmed Marshall's perception, declaring, "It is necessary to get a punch behind the job or we'll never be ready by spring [1943], to attack [that is, a cross-Channel invasion]. We must get going!"[23]

Although he did not recommend Chaney's relief, his report to Marshall left no doubt that someone else was needed in a hurry. To establish an American military presence in Britain for Roundup, he recommended that a U.S. headquarters be established to coordinate and control the forthcoming buildup of American invasion troops in the British Isles. In response Marshall tasked him to draft a directive by which a commander of U.S. forces in Europe would function. When Eisenhower presented his draft to Marshall he was asked whom he recommended to replace Chaney. Eisenhower suggested Marshall's deputy, Maj. Gen. Joseph T. McNarney, a friend since West Point and another of the few who would openly challenge the chief of staff.[24] At no time did Eisenhower mention his own name as a candidate for any overseas post. McNair had also been consulted and recommended Vinegar Joe Stilwell, Patton, or Maj. Gen. Lloyd R. Fredendall. Marshall asked Clark for his opinion. Clark replied that he concurred in McNair's assessment, but when asked to consider a younger man for the job, replied, "Eisenhower."

Eisenhower had passed yet another of Marshall's challenges. Although the chief of staff had hinted "that it was possible I may go to England in command," no announcement had yet been made. If Eisenhower had any previous intimation that his days in the War Department were numbered, it was never reflected in anything he said or wrote. There is every evidence that, to the contrary, he indeed expected to spend the war as a staff officer. At a conference in Marshall's office about Torch on June 11 he probed Eisenhower: "In your opinion, are the plans as nearly complete as we can make them," and did Eisenhower approve of them? "Yessir," came the reply. This time Marshall was explicit: "That's lucky, because you're the man who is going to carry them out."[25] Eisenhower would assume command of all American forces in Britain. Asked whom he favored to take to England as his deputy, Eisenhower instantly replied, "Clark," to which Marshall drily observed, "It looks to me as if you boys got together."[26]

By virtue of his choice, Marshall "set Eisenhower on the road to the supreme command in Europe and, indirectly, on the way to the Presidency."[27] In a terse diary entry devoid of elation, Eisenhower penned matter-of-factly, "The chief of staff says I'm the guy."[28] The full import of his appointment had only begun to register. One of the few incidents in his life the prolific Eisenhower never revealed, even in private, was his reaction to Marshall's stunning declaration. Beneath that calm exterior was a profoundly intense man whose mind never seemed to rest. Hence a reasonable supposition is in order that his feelings undoubtedly consisted of a combination of pride, elation, awe, and apprehension. Pride and elation at having advanced so far, so fast, and having passed with flying colors the scrutiny of the army's sternest taskmaster. Awe at being handed a job whose dimensions had yet to be fully defined but that clearly was of enormous importance. And, finally, an instinctive gnawing feeling in the pit of the stomach, ill-defined, but consisting of fear of the consequences of failure coupled with a resolve to get the job done and justify the confidence Marshall had placed in him.

That evening Eisenhower was uncharacteristically blasé, a sure sign to Mamie that a revelation of some sort was forthcoming. During the meal Eisenhower said nothing, but over coffee and dessert he revealed that he was returning to London, this time for good. "What post are you going to have?" Mamie inquired. "I'm going to command the whole shebang," he replied.[29]

27.

The Architect of Cooperation

We're here to fight, not to be wined and dined.
—EISENHOWER

*Dealing with the enemy is a simple and
straightforward matter when contrasted
with securing close cooperation with an ally.*
—FOX CONNER

Before he left Washington, Eisenhower was briefly reunited with Manuel Quezon, who had fled the Philippines after the fall of Manila to establish a government-in-exile in the United States. Quezon offered his friend a lavish stipend of some one hundred thousand dollars for services rendered the Philippines during his four years there, which Eisenhower courteously rejected, telling Quezon that while it was legal for him to accept, it would likely be viewed unfavorably in Washington. Whether Eisenhower knew (as he should have known) or not, acceptance would have been in clear violation of a War Department regulation.[1]

Three days before his departure for England, Eisenhower's preparations were interrupted by a summons to attend a meeting with the British on a blistering, heat stroke–inducing day in Washington. Present were Marshall, Dill, Brooke, and Gen. Hastings Ismay, the prime minister's efficient and personable chief of staff and principal liaison with the Combined Chiefs of Staff. It was Eisenhower's first introduction to "Pug" Ismay, with whom he formed an exceptionally close friendship. The topic was again the thorny issue of strategy: What would be their first joint venture and where would it take place? Marshall and Eisenhower fought tooth and nail against the Northwest African venture that Secretary of War Stimson had nicknamed FDR's "secret baby."

On one point, however, there was complete agreement. Roosevelt and Churchill were meeting privately at Hyde Park, and both sides feared the worst—nor were they disappointed. Churchill used the occasion to bring his considerable charm and influence to bear on Roosevelt to approve Operation Gymnast, as the proposed invasion of Northwest Africa was then called. Then came the disclosure that the strategic bastion of Tobruk, in Libya, had fallen to the resourceful and audacious Afrika Korps led by Rommel, and thirty thousand British troops had surrendered in what Churchill lamented was a shameful capitulation. The increasingly precarious British position in North Africa gave even more leverage to Churchill's arguments in favor of a joint Mediterranean venture.

Prior to November 1942 the war in the Mediterranean was entirely British, and their grand strategy evolved from the ashes of Dunkirk. The German conquest of western Europe in May and June 1940 left Britain with only the RAF to fend off an invasion of the island nation. Long before there was any certainty of American involvement in the war, Britain's survival depended on postponing indefinitely a decisive engagement with the German army. Only in the Mediterranean was there any possibility of engaging the Axis on anything approaching a level playing field. It was the position of Churchill and his chiefs of staff that at least in this secondary theater British forces could be employed to harass the Axis and perhaps even win a major battlefield victory.[2]

Although formal approval of a joint Mediterranean venture did not come until July, Churchill was already preaching to a near convert. Roosevelt was determined to engage American forces somewhere in 1942, and Churchill's arguments in light of the disaster at Tobruk were tempting him away from Sledgehammer. When Eisenhower left for London there still had been no formal decision by the two allies, but everyone, Eisenhower included, saw the proverbial handwriting on the wall.

Eisenhower and Mark Clark called on Roosevelt at the White House and were formally introduced to Winston Churchill, an event Eisenhower termed no more than "an informal chat" with "no military significance." Despite the gloom surrounding the fall of Tobruk, Eisenhower detected no hint of pessimism in either man.[3] However, his and Clark's full exposure to the charms and manipulative ways of Churchill still lay ahead of them.

On the eve of his departure Eisenhower bade his good-byes to his staff, and was flattered when his secretary, Helen Dunbar, asked him to autograph a photograph of himself. Eisenhower's attempt to thank Marshall met with a mild rebuff: "Don't try to thank me. You go over and do a job and we'll have cause to thank you." His parting words to Eisenhower were vintage Marshall and straight to the point: "See what needs to be done, then do it. Tell me about it when you can."[4] With his chief's words ringing in his ears, Eisenhower prepared to face his greatest challenge.

Before he left Washington, Eisenhower jarred the navy with a highly unorthodox personal request to Ernie King. He asked that a certain Lt. Cdr. Harry C. Butcher, who had left his executive position at CBS to join the navy, be assigned as his "naval" aide. No army general had ever before requested a naval aide, and while there was no argument that one was needed, the navy would have preferred that a qualified regular officer be assigned to Eisenhower. Nevertheless Ernie King readily agreed. Eisenhower refrained from telling King the whole truth, that his sole reason for requesting Butcher was strictly personal. "I've got to have someone I can relax with," he said. "Someone I can trust absolutely. Someone who isn't subservient . . . [and] who'll talk back."[5] Indeed, "Butch" knew virtually nothing about naval matters and would have been ineffective as a staff adviser, but did ably fill the role of aide, companion, jack of all trades, and (his specialty) public relations man. Butcher once referred to himself by the British term for an aide—a "dog's body," a person "always under foot and easy to kick."[6] Eisenhower became almost overdependent on Butcher, so much so that his aide's periodic absences left him dejected and missing the man he routinely called "my pal."[7] Although Eisenhower once said he kept him around "just for laughs," Harry Butcher became an utterly indispensable member of his wartime staff. "I get back from the office to my quarters and I just want to curl up in a corner like a sick dog, but Butcher won't let me. Butcher's job is simple. It is to keep me sane." Thus began a quasi-professional association with his friend that was to last throughout the war, but that would become seriously strained in 1946 when Butcher published the private wartime diary he had kept for Eisenhower.

The night before his departure for England, Eisenhower was joined in his quarters by Butcher and Col. T. J. Davis, who would soon join him in London as his adjutant general. As Butcher and Davis said their farewells and wished Eisenhower good luck, he commented merely, "Now we go to work."[8]

Cadet John Eisenhower had just completed his plebe year and was given a weekend leave from West Point to visit his parents. For the first time during the war the family was briefly reunited before Eisenhower's departure for London, on June 23, 1942. Ike kept their talk lighthearted and mostly about West Point, the atmosphere "sober" but hardly "sad." As was his habit, he grilled John about his friends, his routines, and his "wife" (roommate). Even on the subject of West Point it seemed that father and son had little in common, including their respective views of the military academy.[9] From the tone of his father's reminiscences, it was clear to John, resplendent in his cadet uniform, that "Dad had perhaps developed an overly rosy picture of the place. He thought of it mostly in terms of athletics, pranks and fun," while his son thought of it more as drudgery than enjoyment. Mamie stayed largely in the background, preferring to leave the Eisenhower men to their small talk. All too quickly John had to return to West Point. Father and son parted formally outside the Eisenhower quarters, with John turning to face Ike, who stood on the front step, and received and returned "the snappy salute of one soldier to another. Poor old John's adam's apple was sure churning up & down as he turned the corner," Mamie wrote to her parents. The parting of father and son was no exception to Eisenhower's habitual disavowal of any public display of affection. It is striking that—even under such emotional circumstances—it never occurred to the elder Eisenhower that their leavetaking might have included an embrace for the son he adored and was uncertain of seeing again for the duration of the war.

Eisenhower dissuaded Mamie from accompanying him to Bolling Field. Instead, in the privacy of their quarters on the morning of June 23 he said his private good-byes to Mamie, who kept her emotions in check with the traditional stiff upper lip of a professional military wife. "He wanted it that way," she said. "But he asked me to stand under the flagpole at Fort Myer so that he could see me when the plane crossed [overhead]." As they finally parted Eisenhower reached out the window of the staff car idling at the curb and kissed her hand, saying, with his best grin, "Goodbye, Honey," and then he was gone.

Eisenhower left Washington without fanfare in the company of Mark Clark, Tex Lee, and Mickey McKeogh. There were no formal ceremonies at nearby Bolling Field as Eisenhower and Clark prepared to board an aircraft for the long journey to England. Ike left Clark alone to say his personal farewells to his wife, Maurine, and his son, Bill. As a visibly distraught Maurine Clark turned away toward a waiting automobile, however, "a figure came hurtling through the rain, out of the mist. It was Ike, trying to do just a little more to help me keep my chin up, kissing me once again and saying, 'Don't worry about Wayne, I'll take good care of him.' And then they were gone."[10] It was a rare gesture from a man rarely known for such acts.

Eisenhower's arrival in England on the evening of June 24, 1942, was equally devoid of publicity. His aircraft landed in West London at Northolt airfield, where Eisenhower was met by a small delegation headed by Admiral Mountbatten and the U.S. Army's chief logistician in the United Kingdom, Maj. Gen. John C. H. Lee. They were driven straight to Claridge's, conveniently only two blocks from Eisenhower's new headquarters.[11]

Eisenhower's departure from Washington had serious implications for Mamie, who was no longer authorized to remain in their quarters at Fort Myer. Nana and Pupah begged her to settle in Denver for the duration of the war, but Mamie demurred. By remaining in Washington she would be closer to Johnny, among friends, and able to receive news of her husband from other friends returning from overseas. Generals, by virtue of their rank, have certain privileges, but as a newly minted, unknown two-star, Eisenhower ran afoul of army regulations when he requested that the authorities permit Mamie to continue occupying Quarters #7. No way, they said. Instead, Mamie was given a mere seven days to clear out. Still indignant thirty years later, she never forgot how "I was ordered off the post. . . . They didn't care where I went [and] didn't give a darn about families. I never had a house that gave me such a headache."[12] For the third time in six months, Mamie moved the Eisenhower household, this time to a small apartment in the Wardman (later the Sheraton) Park Hotel, where she would stay for the remainder of the war, extremely lonely and very much on her own.

Eisenhower's appointment changed both their lives forever. The war and Ike's absence left Mamie habitually sleepless. By nature wary of the limelight, Mamie nevertheless found herself a greatly sought-after object of attention from the press. At times she became a virtual prisoner in her apartment as reporters discovered her whereabouts and eagerly vied to interview the wife of the new commanding general in Europe. Media intrusions into the Wardman Park only increased Mamie's sense of isolation. "The War Department," she said bitterly, "gave me *absolutely* nothing." Even when Ike became supreme commander, "I got nothing."[13] The lone exception was George Marshall, who unfailingly telephoned Mamie after each trip overseas to report on her husband's health and anything else he could reveal without compromising security.

For a press starved for human-interest stories, with mostly bad news to report from the battlefronts of the world, Eisenhower's appointment brought fresh opportunities. In Eisenhower they had the perfect vehicle: poor, small-town, midwestern-boy-made-good was the stuff of Jack Armstrong, and reporters arrived en masse in Abilene in search for stories about Ike and his boyhood. Everyone from Ida to his friends was interviewed, and stories—a great many of them embellished with fanciful anecdotes—began appearing in newspapers and magazines nationwide. As Stephen Ambrose points out, "If Eisenhower was not born in a log cabin, the shack in Denison, Texas, was close enough."[14]

Ida made great copy as well, but both she and Mamie were uncomfortable granting interviews about Ike and their private life, preferring (in vain) to not be photographed. Less exciting were the sparse accounts of Eisenhower's military career, which offered nothing dramatic compared to the dynamic experiences of the flamboyant Patton or MacArthur. His service in a series of staff jobs for more than twenty years was hardly headline material, thus Eisenhower was portrayed more simply as an all-American professional soldier, an attribute that would soon become a priceless asset.

When an equilibrium problem Mamie had first experienced in the Philippines worsened to the point where at times she could barely stand, her isolation was exacerbated by her inability even to drive the family automobile. The condition was serious and left her unable to carry out most routine daily activities without difficulty. Sometimes it became so bad she could only navigate by crawling on her hands and knees from one room to another. "I didn't dare try to walk."[15] Only later was it determined that Mamie suffered from an affliction of the inner ear called Ménière's disease, a condition then deemed incurable through surgery. Its effects were similar to those of being on the deck of a ship in heavy seas. She also suffered from chronic stomach pains, claustrophobia, and prolonged headaches, was unable to keep down solid food, and was perpetually tormented over her husband's safety, her fears heightened by a succession of bleak news reports from London and elsewhere on the radio. With too much time on her hands, Mamie would wander aimlessly around the apartment occasionally touching one of Ike's suits hanging in a closet and inhaling its lingering tobacco scent. In a short time she had lost nearly thirty pounds. Ruth Butcher, who lived across the hall, became increasingly worried about her friend. The only bright spots in her daily routine were the days when welcome airmail letters from Ike arrived, none of which revealed anything of his military activities. More than a quarter century of marriage had left Eisenhower acutely intuitive. "I find myself worrying about you a lot. Hope I'm not getting old maidish, but every once in a while I can begin to imagine a lot of things happening to you and then I get the cold chills."[16]

Malicious whispers circulated in Washington that Mamie had a drinking problem, which allegedly accounted for her apparent aloofness and perceived absence from public outings and social events. Her association with Ruth Butcher, who was known as a hard-drinking war "widow," added fuel to the gossip. Some wondered why Mamie did not participate in the volunteer war work performed by other officers' wives, never aware that, despite her health problems, Mamie had indeed performed numerous stints of volunteer work for the Army Relief Mission, the Army Women's Volunteer Services, the USO, and as a waitress at the Soldiers, Sailors and Marines Club on the Mall, all incognito, where no one but her closest friends even knew her name was Eisenhower. Once Mamie accidentally spilled gravy on the uniform of a soldier, eliciting an angry retort; another time, when a friend stopped in to visit her, she was publicly rebuked by the canteen supervisor for violating the ban on having guests while at work. An amused Mamie merely winked at her friend and went back to work.[17] So circumspect was Mamie that, with gasoline tightly rationed, whenever possible she avoided using taxis, afraid she would be thought extravagant and might somehow bring disgrace on her husband by riding when she could walk.

Only when her affliction worsened during her service at the Mall club was Mamie obliged to give up volunteer work. Either way she became a victim of spiteful women who envied her husband's position and thought she set a poor example for a senior officer's wife. Aware of the whispers, Mamie stoically refused to compromise her decision and remained out of the public eye even though it greatly increased her loneliness.[18] "It was three years completely out of my life . . . he didn't tell me a lot of things when he came home either. It would have frightened me, even afterward." Eventually Mamie's fears for Ike's safety were calmed by the same fatalism that spurred Patton: "that nothing was going to happen to him until God was through with what he had put him on this earth to do. . . . Ike had a great responsibility and it had come so unexpectedly in lots of ways. He (God) must have chosen this man for something."[19]

Eisenhower arrived in London at a crucial time during which the future direction of Allied strategy hinged on decisions made in the summer of 1942. He had been too busy with war planning to envision his present appointment. To the contrary, Marshall had given every indication of his indispensability as a staff officer, a fate to which he seemed resigned. His status as the senior American and heir apparent to supreme command thrust Eisenhower into a military and political minefield. Had World War II not erupted, Britain and the United States would never have become allies. The philosophical outlooks of the two nations were polar opposites, even without the inclusion of the strangest of all political bedfellows, the Soviet Union. Bringing together a Communist dictatorship more repressive than fascist Germany, a colonial power bent on retaining its empire, and the free world's bulwark of capitalism was hardly a prescription for a successful military alliance. As Stephen Ambrose points out, "Only Hitler could have brought them together, and only the threat of Nazi Germany could have held them together through four years of war. The Big Three mistrusted each other, but each of the partners knew it needed both of the others."[20] Into this morass of intrigue and self-interest stepped Dwight Eisenhower in June 1942, a man dedicated to defeating Germany by any means necessary, who lacked any interest in politics, petty or otherwise.

Eisenhower's new command was called the European Theater of Operations, U.S. Army (ETOUSA), with headquarters at No. 20 Grosvenor Square, in the heart of London's posh Mayfair district. Before long Grosvenor Square acquired the nickname "Eisenhowerplatz." Within hours of being again billeted in Claridge's, Eisenhower was uncomfortable and thought that his ornate VIP apartment with its nearly two-centuries-old Chinese wallpaper was overly pretentious and resembled "a funeral parlor." Not only did Eisenhower feel like he was "living in sin" in Claridge's, but he loathed being fussed over by an officious, elderly butler who made no effort to hide his disdain for his American client. For a man from Kansas with simple tastes, Claridge's was anathema. Within a short time he moved to a suite in the nearby Dorchester Hotel on Park Lane, but the move failed to soothe Eisenhower's restlessness.

Eisenhower quickly learned that his new position and increasing prominence destroyed any semblance of privacy in his life. Moving from obscurity to an object of intense interest, speculation, envy, and occasional criticism, Eisenhower had suddenly become a *very* public person. He was surrounded by guards, aides, secretaries, members of his personal and household staffs, and a constant daily stream of visitors that would last until the end of the war.[21] At times he felt like an orchestra conductor keeping everyone on the same sheet of music. Hardly a day passed without a series of meetings, and with good reason Eisenhower soon came to loathe the very sound of the word "conference."[22]

It did not take long for the engaging grin and outgoing public demeanor to personify Americans in the eyes of the British. By virtue of his position and charm, Eisenhower was soon in great demand. He was bombarded with social invitations from numerous British and American women hosting this or that soiree, dance, tea or dinner party, breakfast, or supper. The fact that there was no woman present in his life was not lost on some. An invitation from Lady Nancy Astor, the first American to sit as an MP in the House of Commons, to a dinner at which the playwright George Bernard Shaw was to be present, brought a tart response to Butcher: "To hell with it; I've work to do." His only solitude was in the late evening and during the few hours of sleep snatched after yet another grueling day. "I live in a goldfish bowl," he wrote in one of his first letters to Mamie from London, "and if it weren't for Butch and T.J. [Davis] I don't know what I'd do."[23] The demands "get me nuts at times. . . . In a place like this the C.G. [commanding general] . . . must be a bit of diplomat–lawyer–promoter–salesman–social hound–*liar* (at least to get out of social affairs)–mountebank–actor–Simon Legree–humanitarian–orator and incidentally (sometimes I think most damnably incidentally) a soldier!"[24]

Clark recalled with mirth Eisenhower's determination to avoid the social circuit. "We'd have dinner up in our rooms, and Ike would say to me day after day until I thought I would go crazy, 'Wayne, we must not go to any social functions at all over here in London. We must conduct ourselves in such a way that no body can criticize. The first officer that gets into a jam over here, I am going to put you in charge of it and you let him have it. Chop his head off.' "[25]

A short time later an incensed Eisenhower learned of an Anglo-American bar brawl and directed Clark to investigate the incident. "I want to make an example of them," he said. Two young recently arrived American aviators were in a pub when a slightly inebriated Briton challenged them. "You are not drinking our beer. Don't you like British beer?" To which one of the airmen replied, "You ought to pour it back in the horse." In the ensuing melee, chairs, tables, mirrors, and crockery met an untimely demise. Unable to share his chief's indignation, Clark duly summoned the frightened airmen, "two young officers, lieutenants, utterly magnificent kids. . . . It was just a typical British-American brawl." As they related their version, Clark could hardly keep a straight face. Later he announced their punishment. "You can never go back in that club again," he ordered. "Don't ever bring any more discredit on the uniform . . . it's over and I am proud of you. Go about your work." Some weeks later Eisenhower demanded to know the outcome, and Clark replied that he had thoroughly investigated the matter and had reprimanded the officers. When pressed, Clark admitted what he had done, adding that he had put the pub off-limits. "Damn your soul!" chided Eisenhower. "I am not having you investigate any more disorders."[26]

Americans and Britons have been described as two nations separated by a common language. Americans stationed in the United Kingdom during World War II, Eisenhower included, found themselves in an alien and austere world. Their hosts were a gritty, resolute race of people who lived in constant danger and deprivation that included shortages of every basic staple. Nylon stockings, for example, were unobtainable; instead young British lasses would draw a line up the back of their legs to simulate the seams. The streets of their cities and towns were blacked out at night against the inevitable Luftwaffe air raids, even as life went on in a semblance of normality ordered by Churchill, of whom one London cabbie noted, "That's what Winston wants. And *what Winston wants, Winston gets!*"[27] As American GIs began pouring into the United Kingdom in record numbers they were both welcomed and resented. Before long "Yanks" were jokingly referred to as "Overfed, overpaid, oversexed and over here!" American GIs, in turn, referred to the British as "underpaid, undersexed, and under Eisenhower."

One of Eisenhower's first acts was to make it clear to his new staff, many of them holdovers from the former observer group, that the fun and games were over. Henceforth everyone would work seven days a week—in uniform. "We're here to fight," he said, "not to be wined and dined." Eisenhower encouraged informality among his staff but demanded, as had Marshall, that they solve their own problems and not pass the buck to him to make every petty decision. Their mission, he said, was unambiguous: Win the war. All else would be forgiven. Eisenhower issued both a challenge and a warning. "Defeatism and pessimism will not be tolerated!" he said. "Any soldier who cannot rise above the recognized obstacles and bitter prospects in store for us has no recourse but to ask for release. Those who don't will go home anyway!"[28] Most got the message; those who didn't were sent home. All soon learned that their new commander, while a pleasant enough fellow, was tough as nails. Yet, despite his new rank and position, Eisenhower retained a strong measure of humility. Most officers have others answer their telephones and when they acknowledge a call state their rank and name; Ike would simply announce: "This is Eisenhower."[29]

When he assumed command of ETOUSA, Eisenhower moved quickly to bring in men he knew and trusted to fill key positions. "We've got to get some younger fellows over her to help us," he told Clark, who drew up a list of officers whom they requested Marshall send to London.[30] Among his appointments was his long-time friend T. J. Davis, now a brigadier general, as the adjutant general. Davis served Eisenhower as both confidant and senior staff officer through the war. Another officer recruited was Col. Alfred M. Gruenther, a brilliant staff officer and future commander in chief of NATO in the 1950s. His old and trusted friend Mark Clark took command of both II Corps (the first operational American combat force in the United Kingdom) and the planning for Operation Torch, the invasion of French North Africa, in the process relieving Eisenhower of a great burden. J. C. H. Lee (nicknamed "Jesus Christ Himself" for his imperious demeanor and sanctimonious Bible-thumping) was the top U.S. logistician in charge of ETOUSA's Services of Supply.

Eisenhower arrived in England determined to bring in his own chief of staff, even though there was nothing deficient in the existing occupant, Brig. Gen. Charles Bolte, other than that he represented the laissez-faire mentality of the Chaney regime.[31] Instinctively wary of anyone whom he did not personally know, Eisenhower was never comfortable unless surrounded by a circle of key officers he trusted. Topping his list to replace Bolte was the secretary of the War Department General Staff, Brig. Gen. Walter Bedell Smith, whom he urgently requested be released from his duties to become his new chief of staff. Despite repeated requests, however Marshall balked at losing an officer whose efficiency he prized. The scrimmaging for Smith's services persisted through mid-September before Marshall relented and sent him to London. Marshall had the same reasons for trying to retain Smith, who he regarded as his personal handyman, as Eisenhower did in requesting him. Forrest Pogue notes that Marshall required men like Beetle Smith, who "could hack a path through red tape and perform hatchet jobs when time and tradition and the dead hand of the past threatened to block progress."[32] In short, Smith had become indispensable to both Marshall and Eisenhower, who said of him, "They say there's no such thing as an indispensable man, but Beetle Smith comes very close to being one."[33] Believing that he would one day be named to command U.S. or Allied forces in Europe, Marshall eventually released Smith, reckoning it was only a matter of time until he regained his services.[34]

Eisenhower once remarked that every commander needs a son of a bitch to protect him and that the stone-faced Bedell Smith was *his*. Pug Ismay saw a good deal of Smith and came to regard him as a friend. His description of Smith was of a man who "had a face like a bulldog and many of the characteristics of that attractive breed" and was "a master at his profession," direct and businesslike, "with a quick temper which he was wont to vent on friend and foe alike."[35] Indeed, the first time they ever met, Churchill immediately but warily saw a great deal of himself in Smith and nicknamed him "Bulldog." Thereafter the two men related well to each other.

Smith not only ably filled the role of Eisenhower's "son of a bitch" but did so in the full knowledge that it was because "Ike always had to have . . . someone who'd do the dirty work for him. He always had to have someone else do the firing, or the reprimanding, or give any order which he knew people would find unpleasant."[36] Smith may not have relished his assigned role, but he carried it out with near perfection. Those closest to him, both British and American, never viewed Smith as a villain, and at least one, his British deputy for air matters, Air Marshal James M. Robb, believed that he was "never the dreadful 'Beetle' of Butcher's book."[37]

The grandson of a Prussian soldier, a former enlisted man ("mustang") who had risen through the ranks from national guard private to general, Smith was abrasive, more often than not extremely bad tempered, but intensely loyal to both Marshall and his new boss. Most regarded him as a martinet and avoided him like the plague, all the while praising him as a superb staff officer. Smith has been aptly described as "a specialist in psychological bullying."[38]

Those closest to Smith disagree whether his bad temper came from a painful duodenal ulcer or was merely his normal disposition. However, the other side of Beetle Smith was coldly efficient, decisive, and articulate. He was a chameleon, whose demeanor would vary from diplomatically suave to X-rated vulgarian in a flash. Although Eisenhower appreciated Smith's role of hatchet man, at times he attempted to mitigate his temperamental propensities. Some senior officers, weary of Smith's volatile temper, bypassed him and went directly to Eisenhower to request transfers elsewhere. Surprisingly Eisenhower sympathetically tolerated this breach of military protocol.

Nevertheless Eisenhower unreservedly entrusted Beetle with great responsibilities and often sent him to high-level meetings to represent him, calling him "a master of negotiation" with allies and enemies alike, and deeming his abilities "priceless." So greatly did Eisenhower trust Smith that he "informed Gen. Marshall that should any disabling accident befall me in the war, he should, after Bradley, select Bedell to take my place."

Although Smith and Eisenhower regarded each other as friends as well as colleagues, an early experiment in socializing after Smith's arrival in London failed, and thereafter the two went their separate ways off duty. Intensely private, Smith was a loner whom no one, Eisenhower included, could say they really knew. Only rarely did Smith ever lower his guard to reveal that underneath the veneer was a man Kay Summersby described as "a warm, friendly, and very likeable gentleman."[39] He generally kept to himself and engaged in his passion for fly-fishing during his free time. His efficient, long-suffering secretary, WAC captain Ruth Briggs, has described Smith thus: "He was terrifying. He would rattle off questions and orders with the speed of a machine gun. And the air would be blue with profanity."[40] Smith could be extremely insensitive. Once when Captain Briggs felt it necessary to interrupt a meeting he screamed, "Get the hell out of here," and then added, "You'll have to excuse her, gentlemen. She's an idiot." Eisenhower would later take note of Smith's "Prussian" qualities but praise him as "the perfect chief of staff," and a "godsend" who was like "a crutch to a one-legged man."[41] Despite Smith's utter tactlessness and his tendency to empire-build, Marshall often employed him as his chief troubleshooter, all the while occasionally assuming "that he knew the chief of staff's mind better than Marshall did.... In the end, Marshall tolerated Smith's imperiousness because he got things done."[42]

Eisenhower's first speech to a gathering of Americans and British took place on the Fourth of July at the dedication of an American Red Cross service club in London, the sort of public relations demand on Eisenhower's time that he viewed with impatience and would come to deplore as infringing on his actual duties. Butcher quickly noted that behind Eisenhower's good manners "the 'ladeda' of the occasion was getting under his skin . . . when he got up the red blood was rising up his neck." His brief remarks, while following Butcher's script, were delivered in a "soldierly and belligerent attitude," resulting in "a whacking ovation." Afterward, an elderly Englishwoman who had lost both her husband and son in the war told Butcher that Eisenhower's speech had assuaged her pain and "given her the first real confidence in the war. She had been waiting for toughness."[43] As time passed, Eisenhower grew to loathe the "political" demands placed on him, such as meeting and socializing with visiting royalty. Such events left him fuming with impatience. This was not what he believed to be the proper use of his time at such a critical period.[44]

As all successful commanders do, Eisenhower hid his anxieties from public view. Patton preached, as much to himself as to others: "Do not take counsel of your fears." It was an adage Eisenhower heeded. Nevertheless his first weeks in London as the senior American commander in Britain were a struggle to cope with the immense responsibilities suddenly thrust upon him.

The United States in 1942 was a democracy in everything but its racial policies. The officer corps of Eisenhower's era was strongly upper middle-class, overwhelmingly white Anglo-Saxon Protestant, conservative in its political views, and tainted by racial bias and institutional anti-Semitism. Officers did not necessarily dislike Jews or blacks, they simply found them different and therefore suspect. Eisenhower grew up barely knowing any Jews or blacks, except for Dirk Tyler, whom he fought but for whom he felt only pity. Although such terms are now unacceptable, the word "nigger" was an integral part of the contemporary vocabulary, and Eisenhower was no exception. The letters and diaries of many officers who attained high command in World War II contain frequent references to blacks and Jews. Their authors considered them routine vernacular of that era, and would have been surprised had they been informed that they were using racist epithets. The armed forces remained segregated until after World War II, when President Harry S. Truman ordered their integration.

The military profession was socially isolated from the outside world, encrusted in tradition, and extremely slow to adapt to or accept change. Many career officers were the second or third generation to attend West Point, appointments to which came from white Anglo-Saxon Protestant congressmen and senators. It was not until after World War II that the social base of the Regular Army broadened to include a larger percentage of officers with lower-middle-class and working-class backgrounds. The mental climate of the 1980s and 1990s, which produced a black chairman of the Joint Chiefs of Staff and many high-ranking black officers, was simply unthinkable in the early part of this century. Jews and blacks were viewed as outsiders, even those few who managed to gain entrance to West Point. In short, despite its isolation from the civilian population, the officer corps that led the United States during World War II represented the views of the society from which its members came, and that society was largely segregationist and anti-Semitic. Eisenhower never displayed any form of anti-Semitism, but was representative of his generation when it came to blacks, several of whom were used as servants on his personal staff.

Convinced by Butcher of the necessity to come to terms with the press, Eisenhower began holding periodic meetings with reporters soon after his arrival. Eisenhower had been in London only a few days when he was confronted by the problem of segregation in the armed forces. Although everyone knew the answer, Eisenhower was asked to justify the incompatibility of Americans fighting for democratic principles while black and white soldiers were segregated in separate units, the so-called separate-but-equal doctrine. His response to the London-based reporters was to point out that it was his responsibility to carry out national policy, not make it. When alerted that a reporter was about to file an unfavorable dispatch on the U.S. "color problem" in Britain, Eisenhower ordered the current rule on censorship on such stories lifted, regardless of whether or not they were complimentary. Butcher recorded his boss observing that it was "just as well [to] let the American public know what the problems are and our success or failure in meeting them."[45] This was in keeping with Eisenhower's insistence "that his policy was absolute equality of treatment, separate yes, but equal. . . . He could rally them against Adolf Hitler, but not against Jim Crow."[46]

In his relations with the press Eisenhower was forthright and extremely effective. In *The First Casualty* journalist Phillip Knightley wrote, "Public

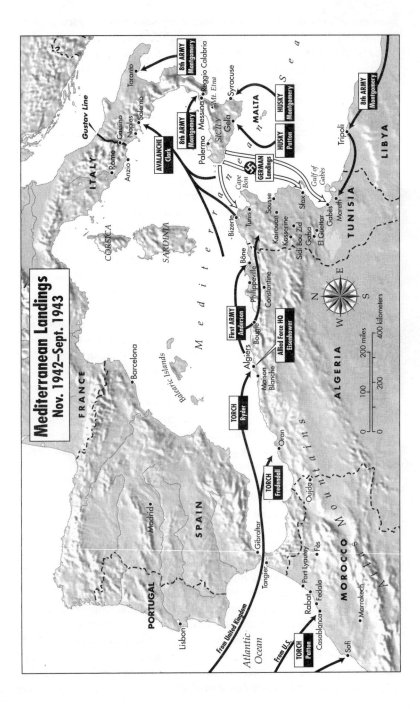

Mediterranean Landings
Nov. 1942–Sept. 1943

FRANCE

PORTUGAL

Lisbon •

SPAIN

Madrid •

Barcelona •

Balearic Islands

Mediterranean Sea

CORSICA

SARDINIA

ITALY

Rome •

Gustav Line

Cassino • Naples • Anzio

Salerno

AVALANCHE
Clark

8th ARMY
Montgomery

Taranto •

Reggio Calabria
Mt. Etna

8th ARMY
Montgomery

Palermo

SICILY

Messina

Syracuse

Gela

GERMAN
Landings

Cape Bon

Bizerte

Tunis •

Bône

MALTA

Tyrrhenian Sea

HUSKY
Montgomery

HUSKY
Patton

Gulf of Gabès

Sousse •

First ARMY
Anderson

Philippeville •

Constantine •

Kairouan •

Sidi bou Zid
Gafsa
El Guettar

Kasserine

Sfax •

Gabès •

Mareth

TUNISIA

LIBYA

Tripoli •

8th ARMY
Montgomery

Bougie •

Algiers •

Allied Force HQ
Eisenhower

Maison
Blanche

TORCH
Ryder

Oran •

ALGERIA

TORCH
Fredendall

Oujda •

Tangier •

Gibraltar

Fès •

Port Lyautey •

Rabat •

Fedala

MOROCCO

Marrakech •

Casablanca •

Safi •

TORCH
Patton

Atlantic Ocean

From United Kingdom

From U.S.

Atlas Mountains

N
W E
S

0   100   200 miles
0   200   400 kilometers

relations, of which war correspondents were considered a part, became another cog in the massive military machine the Americans constructed to defeat Hitler. The supreme commander, General Eisenhower, spelt it out very clearly. 'Public opinion wins war. I have always considered as quasi–staff officers, correspondents accredited to my headquarters.' "[47] After his first press conference in London, *The New York Times* wrote that Eisenhower gave "an excellent demonstration of being jovially outspoken without saying much of anything."[48] Still, when it came to handling the press, no one except Roosevelt was more adept than Eisenhower at effectively using the media to his best advantage.

One of Harry Butcher's first tasks after his arrival in London was to find simpler accommodations for his boss. "Ike and I," wrote Butcher to Milton, "are getting damned tired of looking at those four walls, and I expect he is getting 'tireder' of looking at me." Undoubtedly mindful of the British custom of country homes owned by the upper classes, Eisenhower directed Butcher to locate a "hideout" where he could escape the four walls of the Dorchester and the pressures of London even for brief periods. "I want to get the hell out of London," he complained.[49] Butcher located an ideal retreat called Telegraph Cottage, a quaint pseudo-Tudor country house situated in a woodland west of London near Kingston-upon-Thames, Surrey, only a forty-minute commute from Eisenhower's office. The rent was a princely thirty-two dollars per week, which included vegetables from its garden. Butcher was unaware until later that several hundred yards away the British had installed a dummy antiaircraft gun designed to draw German bombs, or that the surrounding area had been a dumping ground for ordnance jettisoned by the Luftwaffe during the Battle of Britain, which had left craters "big enough to swim in." As much for security reasons as privacy, great care was taken to avoid revealing that Eisenhower was its tenant.

Relaxation at Telegraph Cottage, however rare, consisted of marathon bridge games, banging golf balls, or tossing around a baseball. Another source of diversion was a new member of the unofficial Eisenhower "family," a dog named Telek.[50] Eisenhower had expressed a desire for a Scottie for his birthday. His rationale was simple: "You can't talk war to a dog, and I'd like to have someone or something to talk to, occasionally, that doesn't know what the word means! A dog is my only hope."[51]

When generals desire, staffs and aides provide. In this case, Bedell Smith, (who was not known for running errands for *anyone*, including Eisenhower) and Kay Summersby located several candidates.[52] One of Eisenhower's earliest "command" decisions was to select a black Scottie puppy who remained with his master for the rest of the war. Eisenhower named the animal Telek, after his country hideaway, and said the name was to remain a secret until the war ended. Telek was undisciplined, and one of his better-known bad habits was to drag unlit logs from the fireplace and scatter them all over the sitting room for his minders to pick up.

The following year Butcher acquired a mate for Telek named Caacie (pronounced *khaki*). Twenty-three puppies resulted, eight or nine of which were left in the care of an enlisted aide, Sgt. John A. Moaney, who served as a combination waiter and houseboy and would remain Eisenhower's personal valet until his death. Cocktail hour was "dog time," when the entire menage was released into the cottage to rush about, jump on Eisenhower's lap, lick his face, and leave the requisite puddles here and there for Moaney to clean up. John recalls, "Dad just loved it!"[53] Later, in the autumn of 1944, one of the more memorable "battles" of the war took place in France between Telek and Patton's bull terrier, Willie.

Eisenhower's simple tastes were reflected in his instructions to his mess sergeant, Marty Snyder, on how to prepare his favorite baked bean casserole. Otherwise it was a steady diet of steak, fried chicken, beef, pork or lamb chops, hominy grits, anything but "hifalutin gourmet stuff." Some of his tastes in food bordered on the bizarre but were throwbacks to his childhood: "raw onions in vinegar and mushrooms fried in butter with chopped bacon . . . [and] mush with chicken gravy." (Later, in France in 1944, Bing Crosby visited Eisenhower during a USO tour and, learning of his liking for hominy grits, broadcast an appeal on his radio program for listeners to send Eisenhower grits. "Very soon we began to get hominy grits," said McKeogh. "We got them in boxes and in cases; the whole place was piled up with hominy grits. We must have got a ton of the stuff and we had to give it to mess halls . . . the General said that was the last time he'd ever tell anybody in radio that he wanted anything.")[54] Mamie sent him "care" packages that included fresh supplies of his favorite packaged noodle soups, a new supply of Western dime novels, socks, toothbrushes, and toothpaste.

Ike's spirits were lifted when, by chance, he encountered his driver from his first trip to London, Kay Summersby, who was then driving for Maj. Gen. Carl "Tooey" Spaatz, the commander of the newly formed U.S. Eighth Air Force. Spaatz and future general Ira Eaker had been sent by Arnold to England as observers during the Battle of Britain in 1940. As effective, professional members of a tight-knit fraternity, both quickly cemented favorable relations and close friendships with the British fighter commanders. Arnold sent Spaatz back to England in the summer of 1942 to head the American strategic bombing effort, a gigantic undertaking that consumed Spaatz as deeply as it did Eisenhower. Once asked the secret to being a successful leader, Spaatz replied with a twinkle, "I drink good whiskey and I get other people to do my work."[55] His form of relaxation was poker, a game he played with fervor but mostly lost, which made him a sought-after participant. It was perhaps fortunate for Spaatz that he never played against that other well-known poker aficionado, Dwight Eisenhower.

Spaatz graduated from West Point a year ahead of Eisenhower and had been his file closer, marching behind him in parade formations. Although Eisenhower and Spaatz, a former infantry officer and pioneer airman, were already longtime friends, according to Spaatz, over the next five months the two established "a rather close personal relationship" during some fifty-five meetings to discuss and resolve a host of problems involving the air forces and their employment in support of Operation Torch.[56] Eisenhower would later say of Spaatz that he was the only officer with whom he served in World War II who never made a mistake.

However, Spaatz was dismayed when Eisenhower threatened to appropriate Kay Summersby away from him. "She's the only driver I've found who really knows London," he complained, to no avail. Nor was Summersby particularly enthused about giving up her job driving Spaatz, and the congeniality of air force life, in no small part because they afforded her ample free time for dalliances in London with her lover, Maj. Dick Arnold. Spaatz lost the battle to retain Summersby, who was transferred to No. 20 Grosvenor Square, where she became the newest member of Eisenhower's unofficial family.

An attractive and vivacious redhead, Mrs. Kathleen Summersby was a member of the Auxiliary Transport Corps (ATC), British civilians hired to drive Americans in Britain. Born Kathleen McCarthy-Morrogh in Ireland's County Cork to a "sheltered life" of privilege, she was one of four daughters of a retired cavalry officer who had spent most of his career in West Africa before returning home to marry a convent-educated young Englishwoman. "The only tragedy which could becloud life in those days was a sudden Irish thunderstorm—because it might spoil my lovely tennis party," she recalled.[57] Her parents separated when Kathleen was a teenager, and she moved to London with her mother. A model in London in 1939 for Worth's of Paris, Kay, as she was called, had held a variety of jobs, including bit roles in films. She was a self-described dilettante qualified to do little more than ride a horse and pour tea correctly. With the advent of war, Kay did what many proper young women of her social status did—join a group of volunteer drivers. Their lives changed dramatically with the coming of the blitz in 1940. Kay drove an ambulance in the Borough of Lambeth, a prime target of the Luftwaffe. The blitz was a horrific wake-up call, when death and destruction became as commonplace "as a cigarette."

Almost nothing is known of her marriage to a British army officer named Gordon Summersby. She claims only that she had tried and failed at marriage ("All play and no work turned out to be a very dull way of life"), not bothering to mention that her husband was serving with the British army in India and had filed for divorce because of her affair with a married U.S. Army officer, Richard Roberts Arnold, a 1932 graduate of West Point and a major in the Corps of Engineers, serving in the observer group. The two had met and fallen in love when Kay became a driver for Major Arnold. Their affair had commenced well before Eisenhower arrived in London. At the time she began driving for Eisenhower, Kay was still married to Major Summersby and seeing her American lover whenever circumstances permitted. According to Kay, Arnold's wife had agreed to a divorce so he could marry her, and she had eagerly accepted.

One of the persistent rumors that has dogged Eisenhower's reputation is the unproved but lingering allegation that he had a wartime affair with Kay Summersby. When, where, or how, one can reasonably ask, could Eisenhower and Kay Summersby have carried on an affair had they so chosen? Except when asleep, Eisenhower was constantly surrounded by a retinue of aides, friends, cooks, valets, drivers, WACs, visitors, hangers-on, and others from whom such a relationship could not possibly have been hidden. Eisenhower shared his suite in the Dorchester Hotel with Butcher, and Telegraph Cottage was simply not the place where one could carry on an affair, discreetly or otherwise. His friend Everett S. Hughes kept a detailed wartime diary in which he made disparaging references to the behavior of both in 1943, but he never actually claimed an affair occurred. In any case, Hughes was a notorious and unreliable gossip who carried on a long-running liaison of his own during the war.[58]

Eisenhower's letters to Mamie and hers to him formed the entire basis of their wartime relationship. Usually, but not always, their letters to each other helped make their separation bearable. Within a few weeks of his arrival in London, Eisenhower began acting like a typical father, grumbling petulantly that he had received only a single three-line letter from his son and demanding details from her. Within a short time four letters arrived from John. Although he had a hard time showing it, Eisenhower was inordinately proud of his son, and seemed perpetually disappointed when John failed to fulfill his ravenous yearning for letters.[59] On Mamie's forty-sixth birthday Eisenhower wrote of the "many happy hours and years you've given me. I am quite aware of the fact that I'm not always easy to live with—that frequently I'm irascible and even mean—and my gratitude is all the greater when I realize how often you've put up with me in spite of such traits. . . . Your love and our son have been my greatest gifts from life," hardly the words of someone alleged to have been smitten with his young chauffeur.[60]

Whether Eisenhower knew of it or not, Mamie received weekly letters from Mickey McKeogh reporting on his boss. Kay Summersby describes Mickey's role as Ike's "walking memo pad and his left hand, an impeccable and loyal orderly who did anything from shining shoes or brass to shopping. Above all, he shared his unfailing, bubbling Irish humor."[61] Butcher also took up a pen to write to those Eisenhower was too busy to write to, including Ike's younger brother Milton. "Our days are long . . . [and] the pressure on him has increased. . . . Sometimes I think he is on the busy end of a trans-Atlantic essay contest with dozens of essayists operating on the Washington end and only one super-draftsman here."[62]

Eisenhower continued his unhealthy smoking habit, which increased in direct proportion to the level of his responsibilities. From two to three packs a day, his nicotine habit later grew to as many as four packs of Camel cigarettes a day.[63] During his every waking hour Eisenhower was rarely without a cigarette in his hand or his mouth. He rationalized his habit, even when he knew it was contributing to his health problems, by noting, "It's the only bad habit I have."[64] Kay Summersby attempted, generally without success, to ration his consumption. One of Mickey McKeogh's unsavory jobs was to clean up after Eisenhower as he had at Fort Sam and Fort Myer. His boss had little use for ashtrays, usually knocking off the ashes by tapping them against whatever desk or chair was handy; "he believes that cigarette ashes are good for carpets," said Mickey with tongue in cheek. One of the benefits of Telegraph Cottage was the handy fireplace, where Eisenhower continued his habit of tossing his cigarette butts.

So pervasive was Eisenhower's addiction to nicotine that he began refusing invitations where British officers would be present because, by custom, smoking was not permitted until after the meal when the king was always formally toasted. After the first occasion, when Eisenhower had unwittingly violated the unwritten no-smoking protocol, he was discreetly reminded by U.S. ambassador Winant of his gaffe. A short time later, when Mountbatten invited him to a dinner where he was to meet a number of Mountbatten's staff, Eisenhower declined, and when pressed, admitted it was because he could not smoke. He finally agreed when Mountbatten assured him he would take care of the problem. Immediately on the guests being seated with their sherry in hand, Mountbatten leaped up and intoned the ritual "Gentlemen, the King!" then added, "[And] the President of the United States." Turning to his guest of honor, Mountbatten announced, "Now, General, smoke all you want."[65]

Those who worked for him realized the immense pressures he was under and the toll his new job was taking on his health. Within a short time Eisenhower began displaying increasing signs of fatigue, aggravated by his frequent night sessions with Churchill. Rather than causing him to fall asleep from fatigue, the pressure produced insomnia, progressive irritability, and bad temper. Nor was he taking proper care of himself. On one occasion his lunch consisted of peanuts and raisins and, of course, the customary cigarettes. The bursitis in his left shoulder that had pained him in the Philippines again flared up, to the point where he was compelled to seek medical attention. Concerned that the problem might be serious enough to affect his future, Eisenhower deliberately avoided the military doctors and instead had Butcher take him to a British clinic, where he was injected with novocaine and his ailing shoulder massaged by an osteopath. The condition, however, painfully persisted.[66]

When Col. Al Gruenther arrived for duty a short time later he was shocked how Eisenhower seemed to have aged ten years since he had last seen him during the Louisiana maneuvers. "He was not the cheerful man I remembered."

From the outset a single theme characterized Eisenhower's assumption of command: Allied unity. He took it upon himself to be the role model for the American presence in Britain, a role for which he was admirably suited by virtue of his experience and personality. Although he had very strong opinions of his own, Eisenhower's overriding theme was teamwork. The senior generals of both nations held very divergent views, only in Eisenhower was there a unitarian theme that the two allies would function as one.

Two of Eisenhower's warmest relationships were with Mountbatten and Pug Ismay. During his first trip to England in May 1942, Eisenhower and the blue-blooded Dickie Mountbatten had begun a lifelong friendship based on mutual admiration. In Mountbatten, Eisenhower had found a kindred spirit whose offensive-minded approach as head of Combined Operations was exactly what he sought. Eisenhower wasted no time in seeking out Ismay to discuss how best to cultivate good relations with the British. Ismay found him "tremendously alert" and self-assured, but with "no trace of conceit or pomposity. Frankness, sincerity and friendliness were written all over him . . . but he could be firm to the point of ruthlessness if the occasion demanded it." Nor did it take long for Ismay to experience the famous Eisenhower temper. "From the outset he regarded Anglo-American friendship almost as a religion." In strict confidence Ismay once related to Eisenhower that a senior American officer had an unfortunate tendency when under the influence of alcohol to boast that "his troops would show the British how to fight." Ismay expected Eisenhower merely to rebuke the officer. Instead Eisenhower "went white with rage" and barked to an aide for the officer to report to him early the following morning. " 'I'll make the son-of-a-bitch swim back to America,' he hissed." When Ismay protested he would not have informed Eisenhower had he known the officer would be so severely disciplined, Eisenhower turned his wrath on the British general. "If we are not going to be frank with each other, however delicate the topic," he said, "we will never win this war."[67]

Although either would have performed successfully as supreme commander, neither Brooke nor Marshall were possessed of dispositions that could have practiced cooperation as did Eisenhower. It was no longer, he said, a British war or an American war, it was an *Allied* war. In the weeks and months to come, in the midst of Allied squabbling that at times became bitter, Eisenhower remained the voice of reason and conciliation, to the point where some of his oldest and closest friends would view him as a turncoat.

28.

An Unlikely Friendship

If the disposal of all the Allied decorations were today placed by Providence
in my hands, my first act would be to award the Victoria Cross to
Winston Churchill. Not one of those who wear it deserves it more than he.
— GEN. DOUGLAS MACARTHUR

A British soldier once described Winston Spencer Churchill as "a pugnacious looking b[astard]." Others mistakenly regarded Churchill's plump figure as the affirmation of a jolly fat man. One historian has aptly described him as resembling a cherubic, jumbo-size baby with a cigar stuck in its mouth.[1] There are hardly sufficient adjectives in the English language to describe the British wartime prime minister, but a descriptive (and contradictory) few will suffice. Churchill was brilliant, pampered, petulant, romantic, pragmatic, courageous, egotistical, eccentric, possessed of enormous perseverance, opinionated beyond measure, and impossibly demanding; furthermore, he drank too much, suffered from depression (his "black dog"), "waddled rather than walked," and by *any* criterion ought to have been too old to carry the enormous burden of a prolonged war that threatened Britain's very existence.

His mood swings were legion and ranged from tears to jokes—on occasion at one and the same time. Eisenhower tells the tale of meetings during which "I've seen tears run over his chin." During one such encounter Eisenhower had just rejected as impossible something Churchill wanted done in Italy. "He painted a terrible picture if we didn't do it. . . : He said, 'If that should happen I should have to go to His Majesty and lay down the mantle of my high office.' And here were tears running down. But within ten seconds he was telling a joke. . . . The man could use pathos, humor, anecdote, history, anything to get his own way."[2]

Warts and all, Winston Churchill nevertheless represented the indomitable spirit and symbol of a defiant nation under siege. His oratory was stirring, and like FDR's, it galvanized an entire nation. In 1939 when Lord Halifax suggested that Britain make peace with Hitler, Churchill not only declined but instead vowed to rescue "mankind from the foulest and most soul-destroying tyranny which has ever darkened the stained pages of history." His defiance of "Corporal Hitler" (as he scornfully referred to the Nazi leader) was on full display throughout the war: from his "fight them on the beaches" to his "we shall fight on for ever and ever and ever." That alone would have been sufficient to impress Dwight Eisenhower, who had so long chafed to strike back at Germany. In the summer of 1942 the new alliance between Britain and the United States left Churchill under no illusions that his nation's generous ally would remain a bridesmaid for long. He did, however, employ his considerable powers of persuasion to maintain that illusion, even as he began to test the newly arrived American general who represented the U.S. military effort in the United Kingdom.

Winston Churchill was unlike anyone Eisenhower had ever met. Though he was a megalomaniac on a par with MacArthur, Churchill elicited a wholly contrary response from Eisenhower, whose aversion to big egos was built on a lifetime of experience with such men. With Churchill, Eisenhower found himself up against a powerful personality—with a penchant for the dramatic gesture—in whom were combined politician, statesman, warlord, and frustrated soldier who would much rather have been on the battlefield commanding troops: The latter he had in common with Eisenhower.

Soon after Eisenhower's arrival in England the prime minister got into the habit of inviting him to lunch once or twice a week at No. 10 Downing Street. On other, less auspicious occasions Eisenhower (and often Mark Clark) endured long nights with Churchill at Chequers, the stately Elizabethan country home of British prime ministers and a place during the war whose unheated rooms could have chilled the bones of the dead.[3] Its halls and rooms were decorated with the paintings of long-dead British noblemen and women, most of whose portraits, pointed out Churchill's naval aide, Cmdr. C. R. Thompson, "showed the royalty with dirty necks."[4] Eisenhower referred to Chequers none too fondly as "a damned icebox," and both he and Clark would come to dread overnight visits with Winston. On his first night at Chequers, Eisenhower slept in a bedroom that had once belonged to Oliver Cromwell, which felt as if its absence of warmth had survived the 284 years since his death in 1658. The following morning Eisenhower and Clark inspected an impressive honor guard of tall Coldsteam Guardsmen who provided security for Chequers. As they trooped its ranks, Churchill leaned out his bedroom window dressed only in his nightshirt and shouted, "Aren't they a fine body of men!"[5] Before another overnight ordeal at Chequers, Sergeant McKeogh forgot to pack his boss's pajamas. A butler lent Eisenhower one of Churchill's extra-large-size nightshirts. In the early morning hours he awakened from a vivid nightmare that someone was strangling him to discover that the culprit was the nightshirt. Until he saw the humor of it in the light of day, Eisenhower's only thought was how much he wanted "to get his hands on Mickey McKeogh."[6]

Eisenhower's years of working for and mingling with the high and mighty had prepared him well to deal with such a forceful and often high-handed character as Churchill. The one unwritten rule for anyone who dealt with Churchill, informally known as "the PM," was not to be intimidated. Though he was often exasperated and occasionally irked and exhausted by the prime minister's bulldoglike manner, Eisenhower never succumbed to his fulminations, an invariably fatal failing for those who did. Churchill not only liked Eisenhower personally but was secretly impressed by anyone who stood up to him. The tall, stately Mark Clark also became a favorite of the PM and was dubbed "the American Eagle."

Churchill and the other great military figures of World War II all shared a common desire to command great armies in battle. Despite his frontline service during World War I, Churchill was never destined for generalship. Nearly everyone aspires to be someone else, and in Churchill's case his goal was to have been a great battlefield general. Although he would later recognize his limitations, the general Churchill most wished to emulate was Gen. (later Field Marshal) Sir Harold Alexander. His envy of Alexander verged on hero worship, and he once said to Alexander, "I envy you the command of armies in the field."[7] Churchill's belief in his prowess as a military strategist led to many confrontations with his generals and with Eisenhower. Throughout the war his principal nemesis was Brooke, who did battle with the PM on virtually a daily basis, mostly trying to dissuade him from carrying out some of his more fanciful military ventures. And, as Eisenhower soon discovered, his conversations with Churchill were as often as not tests of will, particularly whenever the British leader was advocating one of his pet ideas for military action.

Eisenhower was careful never to be lulled into complacency when dealing with the wily Briton. Early on, Churchill's aim was to test his influence over the neophyte American commander. Eisenhower knew perfectly well that he was being thoroughly scrutinized by Churchill, and that it would be fatal to permit himself to be overpowered by the prime minister's aggressive personality and charm. In 1942 Eisenhower wrested no concessions from Churchill, who, for the time being, occupied the catbird seat in their relationship. It was not the type of mentor-pupil relationship Eisenhower had experienced with Fox Connor, MacArthur, or Marshall, but by winning over Churchill as a confirmed Eisenhowerphile, the alliance was strengthened immeasurably. In the process a warm and enduring friendship developed between the two men. Even during later stages of the war, when their roles were reversed, Churchill never stopped trying to win Eisenhower over to his point of view, and grudgingly but graciously the supreme commander would endure the PM's endless entreaties. Eisenhower later remarked that Churchill once announced, "All I want is compliance with my wishes, after reasonable discussion."[8] Although the two men would engage in numerous heated debates during the course of the war, neither ever lost his respect for or friendship with the other.

Their mutual love of history became a bond. Churchill was happiest when discussing history and its lessons, and in Eisenhower he found not only a worthy accomplice but one of the few who could match him. Once, while dining at Chequers, Churchill "remarked to Eisenhower that he had studied every campaign since the Punic Wars," leading Cmdr. Thompson to whisper to his neighbor, "And he's taken part in most of them!"[9]

Churchill's genuine fondness for Eisenhower was readily discernible in the PM's uncommon gestures of respect, such as invariably seating him to his right at dinner parties even though protocol dictated that the senior officer or politician present occupy that position of honor. That Eisenhower was typically junior to most of the officers present made no difference to Churchill, who himself relished flouting convention. Another example was his habit of personally walking Eisenhower to his staff car at the end of the evening, a gesture usually reserved for visiting royalty or statesmen.[10]

Churchill was the quintessential night owl and rarely retired to his bed until the wee hours of the morning. His usual evening attire was carpet slippers and a rather bizarre self-designed, one-piece "siren suit" that zipped up in the front and resembled a handyman's outfit (lacking only tools hanging from a belt). During the periods Eisenhower was based in London he too was subjected to the full Churchill treatment. All of Churchill's dinner guests at No. 10 were obliged to sit and squirm on the uncomfortable hardback dining-room chairs as their host pontificated for hours on end.

Such occasions became ordeals of physical endurance. Constantly reinvigorated by food and drink, Churchill presented a direct contrast to the fatigue on the faces of his captive audiences. Churchill's method of problem solving was "talking it out with anyone who would listen," a trait that would drive Eisenhower and others to distraction. Except socially with intimates, and on his own terms, Eisenhower despised small talk as much as he was averse to the PM's late night habits but, like others, stoically endured these weekly ordeals. Bedell Smith, also a frequent guest, was buoyed that senior British officers, such as Ismay and Brooke, were obliged to endure the ritual with the same pained expressions of resignation.[11] Brooke's private diary is filled with examples of Churchill's penchant for late-night meetings and the toll it took on himself and his colleagues. Whether it was an insignificant wager or an important strategic argument, Churchill used these marathon night sessions to physically wear down his opposition. Exhausted as they may have been on many occasions, Brooke and Eisenhower were themselves too stubborn to give in.

One could never anticipate the direction of Churchill's thinking, nor did he always accept unpleasant news gracefully, often subjecting the hapless messenger to a verbal roasting. Once, with Eisenhower present, he was briefed on British shipping capacity. "The picture was not bright, but it was as nothing to the dark annoyance on Winston's face . . . it was easy to see that some outburst was coming." The speaker had referred to British troops as "bodies," a common practice used to avoid having to spell out "officers, non-commissioned officers, and Other Ranks," and one of which Churchill was obviously aware. "How can you use such a disgusting word to describe His Majesty's fighting forces?" he erupted. "These men are not corpses. I will not have it. Stop it at once," he thundered.[12]

When spurned Churchill often became petulant, as he did one evening when, miffed that his generals had backed Eisenhower rather than him over an issue, took his theatrical displeasure out on his soup. "His chin [wasn't] very much above the soup plate. He crouched over the plate, almost had his nose in the soup, wielded the spoon rapidly. The soup disappeared to the accompaniment of loud gurglings," as Churchill deliberately ignored his table companions.

Temperamentally neither man could stand being bested by another. One night the two dueled each other on the subject of history, "each attempting to outdo the other in his knowledge. . . . Beetle said Ike ran rings around the Prime Minister, throwing dates and events around like AA fire in a London blitz."[13]

Like Churchill's, Eisenhower's single-mindedness was occasionally cause for concern, such as the day he decided to drive himself alone to Telegraph Cottage, "principally to prove to himself he could remember the route, but also to escape routine. That Eisenhower had no driver's license and was last seen weaving down the middle of the road was hardly reassuring; nevertheless he completed the trip unscathed. It was a measure of his restlessness that Eisenhower was inordinately proud of himself."[14]

In his wartime correspondence with Roosevelt, Churchill always referred to himself as the "Former Naval Person," a reference to his service as the First Lord of the Admiralty from 1911 to 1915, and again in 1939–40, when he first began exchanging letters and cables with Roosevelt. Yet, for all his oddities, Churchill had a clear vision of what it would take to win the war and for the uses and lessons of history, particularly that which he had personally experienced during World War I. Above all, he understood the nature of coalition warfare and, despite not always getting his way, was determined to make the coalition work, once telling Eisenhower that if he had any problem with any member of His Majesty's armed forces, he had merely to inform Churchill, who would personally see to it that the offender was removed or disciplined forthwith. Although Eisenhower never took up the offer, it was a reassuring sign of the prime minister's trust in the American general.

Eisenhower and Churchill shared a deep hatred of Hitler and his evil German empire. Privately during the war, Churchill looked forward to the day when he could display his contempt by urinating on Nazi soil, a fantasy brought to symbolic fruition on the Siegfried Line in 1945. Although Eisenhower was never known to have expressed such sentiments, his enmity ran no less deep. Together they would make a grand team.

29.

Sailing a Dangerous Sea

I don't know whether Eisenhower is a good general or not.
— EDWARD R. MURROW

By the summer of 1942, after more than six months of debate, the Allies had yet to agree on a strategy for the "how" of defeating Germany. With the exception of James H. "Jimmy" Doolittle's daring but largely symbolic bomber raid on Tokyo and the U.S. Navy's brilliant victory at Midway Island, there was little positive news to report in the United States in 1942. Eisenhower and what he represented were seen as the first visible signal of American intentions to engage the Axis powers.

Eisenhower's first priority in London was to persuade the British to mount Sledgehammer, but with talks stalled, an exasperated Roosevelt sent Marshall, Harry Hopkins, Ernie King, and a large entourage to London in mid-July with instructions to resolve Anglo-American differences and get the show on the road. The trouble was that Marshall, King, and Hopkins all had differing agendas. Hopkins represented Roosevelt, who, while committed to an eventual second front in Europe, was more concerned that the Allies act in 1942 and was thus already siding with Churchill's arguments for an Allied invasion of French North Africa.

The week before Marshall's arrival, Eisenhower and his staff toiled eighteen hours a day preparing for the most difficult negotiations the United States had yet engaged in with the British. Eisenhower called it a "blitz," and nearly wore out two stenographers drafting the American proposal for Marshall to negotiate with the British. He became so exhausted he fell asleep in his office and slept through a real blitz late one July night. After working without any sort of reprieve for a solid week, Eisenhower finally managed a relaxing night off—the highlight of which consisted of drinking noodle soup.[1]

The disparity in Allied strategic thinking could not have been greater. Realistically Sledgehammer's odds of success were about one in five, and both Marshall and Eisenhower realized it would probably fail but nevertheless deemed the risk necessary. "We should not forget," he wrote, "the prize we seek is to keep 8,000,000 Russians in the war." Anything less would make the Allies guilty of "one of the grossest military blunders of all history."[2] In the belief that Sledgehammer would do little to aid the Red Army and was far too risky, Brooke and Churchill led the opposition, with the CIGS noting in his diary that "Harry Hopkins is for operating in Africa, Marshall wants to operate in Europe, and King is determined to stick to the Pacific." Mountbatten best expressed the problems of Sledgehammer when he warned Churchill of its exceptional risks. There were sufficient landing craft then available for a mere four thousand men in the first wave. At best Mountbatten estimated only four to six divisions (all of them untested in combat) could have been landed against some twenty-five German divisions, which were capable of chewing up the invaders without transferring a single division from the eastern front. Even worse, another defeat in France would have doomed any chance of taking the pressure off the Red Army before 1943.[3]

Convinced that Sledgehammer was "dead off and without the slightest hope," the British successfully fended off what Brooke called American rigidity in favor of a hopeless plan.[4] Referring to Eisenhower, one of the British generals scoffed, "This man has dangerous ideas."[5] The British argued that Allied operations in the Mediterranean would not delay a cross-Channel assault beyond 1943, and would serve to "blood" inexperienced American combat forces against the Germans. Eisenhower and Marshall might as well have tried selling a certain bridge in Brooklyn rather than an operation that, without British backing and participation, was already doomed.[6]

Several other, even less palatable operations were put on the negotiating table, which led to Marshall's reluctant acceptance of Torch, the Anglo-American invasion of French North Africa, in the autumn of 1942. In return the British agreed to Roundup in 1943. To demonstrate their good faith, they also agreed to the appointment of an American to command the Allied expeditionary force. Although he would change his mind after the war, Eisenhower was convinced in the summer of 1942 that Torch was the "least harmful" option, but that the Allies had irretrievably blown a golden opportunity by failing to carry out Sledgehammer. In his diary he lamented that July 22, 1942, might well become "the blackest day in history."[7]

Churchill, however, relished Torch as a masterstroke that changed the entire course of Anglo-American grand strategy in favor of the British blueprint of "tightening the noose." The British gave up virtually nothing in return. Churchill would have been the first to concede that Roundup was inevitable, but now it would be carried out according to a *British* rather than an American timetable. As one writer has noted, "A picador strategy was precisely what the British wanted. They did not wish to engage the German army on the Continent until it had been profusely bled elsewhere."[8] Should Germany and Russia bleed each other to death, so much the better. What

Churchill anticipated and Marshall knew was inevitable was that once committed, the United States would never untangle itself from the Mediterranean. Churchill's military assistant Brig. Ian Jacob later observed in his diary that "the U.S. regarded the Mediterranean as a kind of dark hole into which one entered at one's own peril."[9]

Eisenhower did not participate in the final discussions leading to the demise of Sledgehammer. At their conclusion Marshall summoned Eisenhower to his suite in Claridge's. When Eisenhower arrived, the chief of staff was occupied in the bathroom, and their brief discussion took place through the door. In characteristic fashion Marshall announced that Eisenhower was being given the new title of deputy Allied commander in charge of planning for Torch, and that both he and Admiral King were backing his appointment to command the entire operation.[10]

Temporarily in limbo as the commander of American forces, pending the president's approval, Eisenhower reflected on Napoleon's remarks that a general must not permit himself to be impatient or distracted in any manner that would weaken or interfere with the execution of a major plan.[11]

When the Combined Chiefs of Staff met on July 25 and the subject of a commander for Torch was raised, the blunt-spoken Ernie King declared that the choice seemed obvious: "Well, you've got him right here," he pointed out. "Why not put it under Eisenhower?" As he would later ascertain, Eisenhower once again had reason to regret his earlier criticism of King, who had become one of his strongest supporters.[12]

Although the British concurred, for the time being it was not an endorsement of Eisenhower but merely an expedient means of placing someone in charge of planning for Torch. Eisenhower was Roosevelt and Marshall's clear choice to command Torch but, nevertheless, FDR did not officially affirm Eisenhower's appointment to Churchill until early August.[13] Eisenhower was all too aware that a significant reason an American was being chosen to command Torch was purely political. The ongoing hostility between Britain and France was certain to be intensified by the Torch landings. An American in command would enable the British to deflect French acrimony toward Eisenhower instead of themselves.

Eisenhower had made the significant leap from commander of a small, all-American unit to that of a supreme commander of an Allied air, ground, and naval expeditionary force. Yet there were already whispers concerning his lack of previous command and combat experience. Nevertheless Dwight D. Eisenhower, newly promoted to lieutenant general, was now officially named to command Torch.

A new command was created called Allied Force Headquarters (AFHQ), located in Norfolk House, in St. James's Square, London. One of Eisenhower's first acts was to ask Mark Clark to become his deputy supreme Allied commander and chief planner for Torch. A deputy's role is much like that of a vice president; each serves at the pleasure and direction of his superior. Clark's lofty ambitions included eventually commanding American ground forces when the invasion of France finally came about. However, accepting Eisenhower's request meant giving up command of II Corps and possibly any shot at a field command. Although he could have refused, Clark reluctantly agreed to play second banana to his friend, a role for which he was well suited but ill disposed.

There was no manual or precedent Eisenhower could consult on how to mold two disparate nationalities that generally distrusted each other into a single unified force. The limited American experience of coalitions during World War I was hardly a model on which to base the type of military alliance Eisenhower was determined to create. Quite the contrary model was Pershing's formidable but ultimately successful struggle to keep the AEF a single American entity during that war. Moreover, as British historian Sir Michael Howard points out, in 1942 "The British approached the alliance from the point of view that the Americans had everything to learn and the British were there to teach them. The Americans took the approach that if anyone had anything to teach them, it was not the British who had been beaten over and over again and were not a very good army."[14] Eisenhower compared the situation to a bulldog meeting a cat.

There was considerable controversy ahead over the specifics of Torch, but its overall objective of seizing Tunisia ahead of Axis forces was never in doubt. It was agreed that a British officer would command the Torch ground forces, which would advance into Tunisia from Algeria. A dour Scot, Lt. Gen. Kenneth A. N. Anderson, was appointed after the first choice, Gen. Sir Harold Alexander, was sent to Cairo to replace Gen. Sir Claude Auchinleck, whom Churchill had relieved as commander in chief, Middle East, and commander of the Eighth Army. Alexander was to have been replaced for Torch by Lt. Gen. Bernard Montgomery, but he too was removed from consideration when he was abruptly given command of the British Eighth Army after the death in an air crash of Auchinleck's successor, Lt. Gen. W. H. E. Gott.

In his new role Eisenhower was still a mystery, even to Americans. Edward R. Murrow of CBS, the dean of American correspondents in London, whose radio broadcasts during the blitz kept a nation spellbound, portrayed Eisenhower in one of his radio broadcasts as "just a combination of Kansas and Texas . . . a normal, middle-class American soldier. . . . But, when things go wrong, the big grin disappears and he becomes as bleak as a Kansas cornfield." Eisenhower listened to the broadcast and was amused by Murrow's observation that "I don't know whether Eisenhower is a good general or not."[15] At this early stage, neither did Eisenhower himself.

During the course of the war Churchill and Eisenhower engaged in numerous tests of will, with neither man the clear winner. What is indisputable is that without Churchill's backing, Eisenhower simply could not have been appointed the Allied supreme commander or survived for long in that position. Although Churchill was never particularly enthusiastic that an American would exercise overall command of Allied forces, the pragmatist in him recognized the inevitability of the occasion when the United States would assume the preponderance of fighting troops and could no longer be sub-ordinated to a British commander in chief. If an American was to be in command, Churchill wanted that person to be Dwight Eisenhower.

Eisenhower's exercise of command was perhaps best defined by Lt. Gen. Joseph M. Swing, who served under both MacArthur and his classmate. "Mac-Arthur could tell his staff what he wanted done. Ike had a big staff working for him, and they came up with plans and how to implement those things. Ike would approve or disapprove. Do you get the difference?"[16]

Eisenhower's critics would charge that his technique was devoid of orig-inal thinking and lacked the leadership expected of a commander, whereas MacArthur was a brilliant strategist who conceived the broad outlines of his strategy, then left his staff to work out the details. While it is true that Eisen-hower adopted a far different approach, what eventually made him so effective as an Allied commander was his success in assembling "a group of disputa-tious and quarrelsome generals from different countries into a winning team. That nearly everyone underestimated him was a major factor in his effective-ness."[17]

During his first months in London, British suspicions of Eisenhower had merit. His future success as an Allied commander had yet to be established, and uncertainty about him in the summer of 1942 was an open secret. Among the doubters was Brooke, who had little confidence in Eisenhower and regarded him as a novice in the art of war and ill suited to command an Allied force. After the war Brooke wrote of their first meeting after Eisenhower's arrival in London, "He certainly made no great impression on me . . . and if I had been told then of the future that lay in front of him I should have refused to believe it."[18]

Relations between the two men were always polite but rarely more than correct. Eisenhower in turn, thought the British general closed-minded. "Brooke was mercurial, and though he seemed familiar with some of the best military books on strategy and the conduct of war, he was, I thought, gov-erned more by pre-conception and rigid concepts rather than profound study of modern war. He was likeable; a good companion and a fine character but so far as I was concerned was preoccupied with his experiences of past wars rather than the realities of the present."[19] David Eisenhower writes, "Famous for a temper he fought to keep in check, Eisenhower met his match in the acerbic Brooke. They disagreed often, 'sharply and critically' in Eisenhower's words, though Eisenhower often conceded that Brooke was a 'brilliant sol-dier.' "[20]

Although he did not seek it, in the wake of Dunkirk, Brooke (nicknamed

"Colonel Shrapnel" by his underlings in the War Office) inherited the mantle of the conscience of the British army. "Men admired, feared, and liked him . . . a dark, incisive Irish eagle, the reluctant chairman of a council of war, frustrating, in selfless but far from patient services."[21]

The two men actually had more in common than either realized. Brooke's reflections were recorded in his wartime diary, and closely mirrored Eisenhower's own words to Mamie. Both longed deeply for peace and shared a common hatred of war and its futility. During the bleak days that marked the British evacuation from Dunkirk, Brooke saw himself in "some ghastly nightmare."[22] Brooke's "curtain was the mask of command. High rank, he believed, carried a heavy obligation. The lacerations must not show. His performance of public impregnability was precisely that: a performance, for others, just as Churchill performed the indomitable chauvinist-in-chief, complete with gesture and growl, and more props."[23]

Behind this emotionless exterior there existed a deeply compassionate professional soldier who served as a near-perfect complement (and foil) to Churchill. "To correlate the Prime Minister's prophetic vision with the realities of what was immediately practicable thus became Alan Brooke's task."[24] Brooke's love-hate relationship with Churchill was best summed up in a diary entry that read: "God knows where we should be without him, but God knows where we shall go with him!"[25]

Brooke was fond of quoting the epitome of a true soldier:

> The patience of a Saint in hardship;
> The tenacity of a bulldog in adversity;
> The courage of a lion when roused; and
> The chivalry of a Knight in all his dealings.[26]

What was not lacking in either man was a steely determination and commitment to bring about a successful conclusion to the war. Whatever Eisenhower lacked in experience—and it was a great deal—he more than made up for in resolve. His first challenge was Torch.

The fall of Tobruk was not the only disaster to befall the Allies in the summer of 1942. On August 19, 1942, an Anglo-Canadian force of six thousand men, five thousand of whom were Canadian soldiers, mounted an amphibious raid on the French port city of Dieppe, while overhead Allied airmen engaged the Luftwaffe in the most massive air battle ever fought. Conceived and planned by Mountbatten's Combined Operations to substantiate to the Russians that the Allies could successfully launch a cross-Channel operation with proper air cover, Dieppe was instead one of the deadliest military operations of the war. The Allies lost 106 planes, and during the four-hour battle the Canadians suffered 2,700 casualties, including more than 1,000 killed, before withdrawing empty-handed. The raid contributed virtually nothing to the war effort, ruined reputations, left a legacy of bitterness that has endured to this day, and is generally regarded as one of the blackest days in Canadian history. Worse, Dieppe failed to reassure anyone and certainly failed to intimidate the Germans or to cause Hitler to divert reinforcements from the eastern front. Quite the contrary, it revealed in stark terms to both sides the woeful Allied inability to mount a second front. Aside from the heavy losses, the other significant consequence of Dieppe was the demise of Marshall and Eisenhower's strategic blueprint: It buried all hope of Sledgehammer forever and cast grave doubts on the future of Roundup in 1943.

With Marshall and King's departure for Washington, Eisenhower and his staff were left to sort out the wreckage of what had been Sledgehammer. A new plan was created for Torch, which would evolve into a larger blueprint: a massive Allied pincer movement in North Africa combined with a westward offensive by the British Eighth Army to trap Rommel's Axis armies. Eisenhower's recommendations, endorsed by Marshall and King, were sent to FDR. Yet the months leading up to Torch were marked by almost constant wrangling. With the necessity to mount Torch and the virtual abandonment of Roundup, Eisenhower believed the Allies were "sailing a dangerous political sea and this particular sea is one in which military skill and ability can do little in charting a safe course." Ironically both Eisenhower and Patton referred to Torch in their private diaries as a "desperate" operation.[27]

In early August, Eisenhower learned that Patton would be part of his new command and wrote to Marshall, "I am delighted you fixed upon him as your choice for leading the American venture."[28] He had been hesitant to ask for Patton, who was still his senior in the Regular Army and was both pleased and reassured when Marshall anticipated his needs by ordering Patton to England to assist Eisenhower in planning Torch. At this early stage the operation was ambiguous and ill defined. Eisenhower believed it was "strategically unsound" because it impeded rather than enhanced the opening of a second front in Europe.[29] However, as has been suggested, if one of war's truisms is that "you don't always get to fight where you want to. Sometimes the important thing is just to have a fight," then Torch would become a prototypical example.[30]

Once in London, Patton telephoned his old friend. "Ike, Goddammit, I've just arrived in this blasted town. I'm holed up in Claridge's and don't know what to do with myself." Excited to hear his friend's voice, Eisenhower replied, "Georgie, oh, boy am I glad to hear your voice! Come right over and have some Godawful dehydrated chicken soup with me."[31] After a lighthearted reunion, Eisenhower asked what Patton thought of Torch. Patton replied that it was far too complicated and in need of major revision. "We both feel the operation is bad and is mostly political," wrote Patton. "However, we are told to do it and intend to succeed or die in the attempt . . . with a little luck, it can be done at a high price."[32]

It did not help that some on the British side perceived that Eisenhower was not wholeheartedly committed to Torch. One such doubter was Air Chief Marshal Sir John Slessor, a pioneer airman, who in 1942 was the assistant chief of the air staff. In his postwar memoir Slessor recalls Eisenhower's doubts: "I remember him saying on one occasion . . . that the whole thing was really crazy, though no doubt we should get away with it."[33]

Patton came away unimpressed with the American and British staff officers planning Torch, and during two conferences chaired by Eisenhower, thought the U.S. Navy planners were "certainly not on their toes." At this time Patton also recorded his first private criticism of his friend, who was, "not as rugged mentally as I thought; he vacillates and is not a realist."[34] Patton also mused that most American officers in London seemed too pro-British. "I am not, repeat not, Pro-British."[35] Despite a growing Anglophobia that eventually reached manic proportions, Patton rated Adm. Lord Louis Mountbatten and several of his senior staff officers "damn good fighting men."[36]

After a round-robin of meetings the plan began to jell in mid-August, however, it was late September before Eisenhower would even admit that Torch seemed workable, albeit still risky. "It still can be a very desperate venture if the enemy does everything he should and we make a few mistakes. I have a sure feeling we will win."[37] Eisenhower duly reported to Marshall his satisfaction with Patton, and quoted both Clark and Patton as saying: "We unanimously want to assure you that regardless of academic calculations as to [its] eventual success, we have no other thought except that of carrying out this operation through to the utmost of our abilities."[38]

During the remainder of the summer and into the autumn, the planning for Torch took place at an accelerated pace in both London and the United States. Marshall had promised to leave Eisenhower alone, but nevertheless kept up a steady flow of correspondence, both to assure himself that Eisenhower's needs were being met and to offer advice, which he did frequently for the duration of the war. Although he appreciated the chief of staff's concern, at times Marshall's advice irritated Eisenhower far more than he ever let on. Only rarely did Marshall speak forcefully about one of Eisenhower's decisions. In September, Marshall was openly appalled by Eisenhower's intention to appoint USAAF Maj. Gen. Walter H. Frank as the commander of the newly forming Twelfth Air Force in England instead of Jimmy Doolittle, who had become a national hero after leading the raid by B-25 bombers on Tokyo the previous April from the carrier *Hornet*. Marshall was even more disturbed by Eisenhower's intention to appoint an army two-star general, Russell P. Hartle, to command one of the invasion forces for Torch. Marshall had little confidence in Hartle and asked Eisenhower to consider either Clark or "practically anyone you name" from a list of eight corps commanders. Initially stubborn, Eisenhower eventually conceded to Marshall's advice. Frank was sent home, Doolittle was given the command of the Fifteenth Air Force in support of Torch, and Maj. Gen. Lloyd R. Fredendall, an officer whom Eisenhower did not know, was substituted for Hartle—a choice, seconded by Clark, that would prove extremely regrettable.[39]

Marshall's reassurances were also meant as advice for the new commander in chief, whose tentativeness and uncertainty were obvious to him from his correspondence and their face-to-face meetings in London. In June, Eisenhower had written to reassure his chief, "I shall try to apply your dictum— 'Persuade by accomplishment rather than by eloquence!' "[40] "When you disagree with my point of view," Marshall bluntly replied, "say so, without an apologetic approach; when you want something that you aren't getting, tell me and I will try to get it for you."[41]

For the first time Eisenhower had to mold British and Americans together into a single entity. Over and over Eisenhower pounded the theme that they were now allies and they had better get used to the idea. Nor would he permit Torch to be dragged into an Anglo-American bureaucratic mire awaiting approvals from London and Washington about matters he deemed his purview. "To Ike, the principle of unity of command is almost holy," wrote Butcher. Nevertheless, in the case of Anderson, when the British attempted to impose a tradition, begun in World War I, of permitting a commander to refer any order he received (and questioned) from a superior Allied commander of another nation to the War Office, Eisenhower politely but firmly intervened to effect a compromise: Any Allied commander who disagreed with an order must consult him first. Although this is usually cited as an example of Eisenhower's commitment to the alliance, it can also be argued that Eisenhower was too inexperienced and untested in 1942 to have won the right not to have his decisions second-guessed. Unfortunately this arrangement was a two-edged sword that also posed the additional dilemma that should one of Eisenhower's orders or directives be challenged or, even worse, overturned by the Combined Chiefs, his authority as supreme Allied commander would have been effectively destroyed, leaving him little choice but to resign.

At the time Eisenhower had more important problems to deal with. All too aware of U.S. bias against Torch, he warned his American subordinates that the last word on the subject had been spoken, and they were there to make it work. Success or failure would be the sole criterion for judging an officer's value. "The time has past for dillydallying," he said. Those who did not measure up would pay the price; for those who succeeded "there would be no limit to the representations I would make [to] the War Department in his behalf."[42] While the army and navy worked out their differences Eisenhower remained adamant that, with or without warships to protect the landing forces, Torch would proceed, even "if I have to go alone in a rowboat."[43]

The British preferred a series of landings as far east as Bône (now known as Annaba) to enable the Allies to quickly seize Tunis, thus depriving Hitler of the primary port required to reinforce his North African forces. Eisenhower concurred but was effectively overruled by his own chiefs of staff in Washington, who insisted on a landing at Casablanca to avoid the heavier commitment in the Mediterranean represented by landings near Tunisia. The U.S. chiefs were concerned that there be an Allied presence in Morocco to discourage Spain from entering the war on the side of Germany or from allowing its use as a springboard to bottle up the Strait of Gibraltar and attack the Allied rear in North Africa. This was the first and only time Eisenhower was overruled on an operational matter.

The clock continued to tick relentlessly without a resolution to the fundamental questions of what, when, and where. For the Torch planners, whose blueprints hinged on decisions not yet forthcoming, the lack of firm guidance was maddening. No one was more exasperated than Mark Clark, the general responsible for the operational planning. While the debates continued in London and Washington during the late summer of 1942, Clark assembled his key British and American planners and announced, "Some of you men are less confused than others about Torch. Let's all get equally confused."[44]

The requirement to invade Casablanca not only effectively eliminated Bône from consideration but ensured that there would be no early capture of Tunis. Although there was ample justification for the inclusion of Casablanca as one of three invasion sites, the price of failing to capture Tunis would change the entire complexion of the Allied venture into North Africa.

The Allied task was formidable: Land and seize nine important objectives along a nearly one-thousand-mile coastal front from the French Moroccan capital of Casablanca to Oran and Algiers. Once all three vital port cities were secured, the Allies were to thrust quickly into Tunisia to capture Bizerte and Tunis before the arrival of Axis forces. After considerable spilled ink and back-and-forth wrangling between London and Washington (with Eisenhower in the middle), it was finally agreed that three invasion forces would land simultaneously at Casablanca, Oran, and Algiers.

The situation in French North Africa was complex and beset with intrigue and a confusion of loyalties among the French military, some of whom were loyal to Marshal Henri Philippe Pétain's Vichy regime, while others supported the Allies. To complicate matters there was a legacy of French bitterness toward the British for the incident at Oran's main port of Mers-el-Kebir in July 1940, in which more than twelve hundred French sailors perished when the Royal Navy attacked the French fleet to keep it out of the hands of the

Germans. The reaction of the French to an Allied invasion of their North African colonies was uncertain, and fraught with the possibility that their forces might bitterly resist Torch.

The French situation not only vexed FDR and Churchill but deeply affected Eisenhower. To complicate matters the Allies had to deal with the formidable Brig. Gen. Charles de Gaulle, the tall, rebellious officer who had established the Free French government-in-exile in London and was the solitary voice of a dispirited nation whose Vichy government represented collaboration. A maverick within the French army, de Gaulle had a prickly personality and an imperious manner that rankled both Churchill and Roosevelt deeply, as did his relentless demands for inclusion in all decisions regarding the French. Although he represented a mere fraction of his nation, it was de Gaulle's fatherlike figure that represented the spirit of a free France. Although Churchill found him difficult and mistrusted him, the pragmatic Englishman ultimately became a great admirer and friend of the Frenchman, and once said, "De Gaulle, a great man? Why, he's selfish, he's arrogant, he thinks he's the center of the universe.... You're right—he's a great man!"[45]

Roosevelt was less charitable and utterly incapable of assessing de Gaulle's strong points. FDR so despised de Gaulle that he refused to deal with him. Eisenhower, however, did not have that luxury, and while the Frenchman was often a thorn in his side during the war, the two men developed a bond as soldiers that extended beyond the war to the time when each was president of his nation. Torch promised to exacerbate the problems between the Allies and the uncompromising de Gaulle. Thus it was Eisenhower who bore the brunt of the political dilemma that would soon pit de Gaulle against the Vichy French. As Churchill would say of de Gaulle, Eisenhower quickly learned that "the heaviest wartime cross he ever had to bear was ... the Cross of Lorraine."[46]

The French problem merely began with de Gaulle, from whom the Allies attempted unsuccessfully to keep Torch a secret. Eisenhower's most serious obstacle was that the Allies could not count on the Vichy forces in French North Africa to lay down their arms and join them. The last thing Eisenhower wanted was to fight a potential ally.

FDR's personal representative to the Vichy French in North Africa was a glib State Department career diplomat named Robert D. Murphy. As counsel general, Murphy was in contact with a sympathetic group of French officers headed by Maj. Gen. Charles Mast. In mid-September, Murphy was sent to London incognito, dressed in the uniform of an army lieutenant colonel to brief Eisenhower at Telegraph Cottage, away from prying eyes. Now, in a new ancillary role, Murphy was unceremoniously thrust on Eisenhower as a de facto political adviser. Murphy convinced a skeptical Eisenhower of Mast's assurances that the French would play ball under the right person. That individual, insisted Murphy, was not Charles de Gaulle, but Gen. Henri

Honoré Giraud, a distinguished sixty-three-year-old World War I hero who
Mast claimed would rally the French to himself and the Allies. A dignified,
respected, and gallant soldier, Giraud commanded the French Ninth Army
in 1940 and was captured and interned in Germany until April 1942, when
he escaped to the Unoccupied Zone of France. Although one of the few
senior French officers seemingly untainted by ties to the Vichy regime,
Giraud had nevertheless sworn an oath of loyalty to Pétain that he would do
nothing to embarrass Vichy. Politically de Gaulle was not an acceptable
option, thus Giraud was regarded by the Allies as their best (if only) choice.
"By all logic, Giraud seemed to be the man behind whom the French in
North Africa could rally," noted Eisenhower's son, John.[47] The problem with
Giraud would turn out to be his naïveté in the rough-and-tumble of French
politics, in which he was hopelessly outmatched, and the refusal of his colleagues to accept him.

In mid-October, Eisenhower dispatched Clark on a clandestine mission
to meet secretly near Algiers with Murphy and Mast and other French officers
in an attempt to rally them to the Allied side and avert unnecessary bloodshed
during the Torch landings. Clark was landed by a British submarine and met
the French at a remote seaside villa, at one point hiding in the wine cellar to
avoid detection by French police sent to investigate reports of suspicious
activities. Although the French were desirous of avoiding bloodshed, Clark
was precluded from revealing details of Torch and its date of launch, and the
negotiations proved inconclusive. Although Mast could not speak for every
French commander, Clark returned with a promise but no guarantee of
French cooperation. Clark left behind his uniform trousers, which were lost
in the heavy surf reboarding the submarine *Seraph*. The story of Clark's secret
mission later received enormous publicity in the United States, where his
relatives mirthfully referred to the event as "the day Wayne lost his pants."[48]

As the date for Torch approached and Clark's safe return from North
Africa remained uncertain, Eisenhower's nerves displayed visible evidence of
severe fraying. On October 20, for example, Butcher recorded that he was in
"a state of jitters," aggravated by concern over the lack of preparedness of the
invasion forces, to the point where he was unable to concentrate. With Clark's
return, and a message from Giraud approving the plan for him to take command of French North Africa, it seemed the Allies had indeed orchestrated a
major lifesaving compact with the French. Churchill pronounced himself well
satisfied, noting that "we'll back you up in whatever you do," words Eisenhower and Clark would have cause to recall when the French problem subsequently unraveled.[49]

At the end of October, Eisenhower and Clark paid an obligatory courtesy
call on King George VI at Buckingham Palace. Before wishing them "God-
speed," the king, with a straight face, indulged in his own brand of humor
by inquiring of Clark if he were not the fellow who got "stranded on the

beach without your trousers?"[50] The following day, in an attempt to deceive the French, it was widely reported on the front pages of American newspapers that Eisenhower was being recalled to Washington "for consultation." The deliberate leaking of news of her husband's alleged return home reached Mamie's ears. To her bitter disappointment, she finally learned weeks later from Ike that he would not be coming home; "in war plans are always subject to instant change," he wrote, without revealing it had all been a ruse.[51]

During several of his visits to the VIII Bomber Command (the forerunner to the Eighth Air Force) headquarters at High Wycombe, near Oxford, Eisenhower openly admired the uniform jacket worn by its commander, Maj. Gen. Ira C. Eaker. A short khaki jacket, it had been specially made for Eaker by a London tailor "after he noticed the sensible and good-looking battle jacket that was standard dress throughout the British armed forces," wrote James Parton, his wartime aide. Shortly before Eisenhower departed for Gibraltar, Eaker sent him the jacket along with a note. "I hope it fits. If so, please wear it for us. It will save your blouses and be much more comfortable when flying." Eisenhower loved it, wore it, and—although he has been credited with creating the famous "Eisenhower jacket" that soon became official wear in the U.S. Army—the inspiration if not the credit belongs to Ira Eaker.[52]

On Monday, November 2, Eisenhower and his entourage were scheduled to depart from an airfield in southern England, where six B-17 Flying Fortresses awaited their arrival to transport them to Gibraltar. Heavy fog and rain made flying impossible, and because of the threat of air raids, the authorities would not permit Eisenhower's train to remain in Bournemouth. The train was sent back to London. Two days later they returned again to Bournemouth, but the weather had not improved. Finally, on Thursday, November 5, increasingly distressed that the Torch landings were only three days off and he was still stuck in England, Eisenhower ordered their departure in dangerous weather conditions and near zero visibility. His pilot, Maj. Paul Tibbets (who later piloted the *Enola Gay*, which dropped the atomic bomb on Hiroshima on August 6, 1945), advised against flying, but Eisenhower was adamant. The weather be damned, he was going to Gibraltar. As his plane winged south over the Atlantic, it was with a sense of relief that Eisenhower was at last leaving the politically charged atmosphere of London and would no longer have to cope on an almost daily basis with Churchill and others with an agenda. Ahead lay ample uncertainty, but at least in his new role he would be more like a commander and less like a politician.

Seven hours later, after a harrowing trip that included three hours of low-altitude wave hopping, Eisenhower's plane arrived over the British airfield adjacent to the Rock, where congestion on the ground and vicious crosswinds forced his plane, the *Red Gremlin*, to circle for an hour before their precarious journey finally ended. The first non-British commander of one of the world's most famous symbols had arrived to oversee the Torch landings.

With Clark's mission to Algiers and Murphy's negotiations likewise indecisive in gaining the cooperation of the French commanders in North Africa, the Allies pinned their hopes on Giraud, who had been smuggled out of France and brought to Gibraltar by submarine on November 7 to meet with Eisenhower. At that juncture no one had any reason to doubt the French general's commitment. Nevertheless, the role Eisenhower had in mind for Giraud would be, by any description, that of an Allied-imposed puppet governor of French North Africa.

Then came a bombshell. Robert Murphy had planted the unfortunate notion, which he claimed emanated from the promise of General Mast, that Giraud would actually *replace* Eisenhower as supreme Allied commander after the landings. Murphy's intrigue proved costly. Attempts to recruit Giraud fell flat when the French general demanded Eisenhower's job. For seven hours the negotiations dragged on, with Eisenhower and Clark rotating like policemen interrogating an uncooperative suspect. After a four hour "struggle," a frustrated and disillusioned Eisenhower cabled Marshall, "He—so far—says 'Either I'm Allied C-in-C or I won't play!' . . . I'm weary."[53] Giraud turned out to be politically artless and with an inflated sense of his importance to the Allies, and was once described by Jean Monnet (the postwar architect of the European Economic Community) as "inflexible on military matters, hesitant on everything else."[54] The result was an impasse that no amount of vehement negotiations would change before D-Day.

But, worst of all, as Eisenhower would soon learn, "the overwhelming majority of the French were not and would not become involved in any act of resistance until German defeat seemed certain."[55] That included Giraud, whose unreasonable demands convinced Eisenhower that the Frenchman was deliberately posturing to avoid later blame for any French blood spilled in North Africa. Nevertheless Eisenhower respected Giraud as only one soldier can respect another. "Though dressed in civilian clothes, [Giraud] looked very much a soldier . . . erect, almost stiff in carriage, and abrupt in speech and mannerisms. He was a gallant, if bedraggled figure." Giraud seemed as disappointed as Eisenhower that there could be no immediate rapprochement. "General Giraud cannot accept a subordinate position . . . his countrymen would not understand and his honor as a soldier would be tarnished," he said, speaking in the third person. Eisenhower thought it was "pitiful, because he had left his whole family in France as potential hostages to German fury and had himself undergone great personal risks in order to join up with us."[56]

On the eve of the invasion, Robert Murphy made a last-ditch attempt to avert bloodshed by trying to enlist the support of Adm. Jean-François Darlan, the commander in chief of all Vichy French forces and Pétain's deputy, who was in Algiers visiting his ailing son. Darlan, however, procrastinated, and, with H hour not far off, the Allied commanders had no idea what resistance, if any, they would encounter on the beaches of French North Africa. "We are standing on the brink and must take the jump," Eisenhower wrote to Marshall the night before Torch, "whether the bottom contains a nice feather bed or a pile of brickbats!"[57] Patton was likewise edgy over the prospect of fighting the French in Morocco with a decidedly inferior invasion force. He had written to Eisenhower that if his own G-2's intelligence estimate proved correct, "we will have quite a fight." Eisenhower did not disagree and privately rated Torch's odds of success at a mere fifty-fifty.[58]

That the first vital campaign launched by the Allies required a primary reliance on chance was utterly bizarre and, notes Stephen Ambrose, "illustrated just how unprepared the United States had been for the war, and how poorly it had done in the eleven months since Hitler declared war."[59]

Ike's final note to Mamie before Torch cautioned only that he was in the Mediterranean area, where, "with a lot of luck, maybe I can do something here that will hurt the Axis—and that's what I live to do. . . . The Lord knows how long I'll be on this job."[60] In his pocket he carried six lucky coins, one for each of the Allied nations involved in Torch, which he constantly jangled and rubbed for good luck. As events unfolded, Eisenhower would need all the good luck he could muster.[61]

Part VI

A GENERAL'S EDUCATION: THE MEDITERRANEAN, 1942–1943

I have developed such a violent hatred of the Axis and all that it stands for, I sincerely hope the drubbing we give them will be one that will keep that crowd from wanting another war for the next two hundred years!

—DDE TO EDGAR EISENHOWER,
November 16, 1942

30.

"I Am Nothing but a Soldier."

I don't like to hear about Dwight being in this war . . .
[but] I know he'll do the right thing, even if war is wrong."
— IDA STOVER EISENHOWER

No untested commander seeking his first victory could have embarked on a more crucial initiation under more depressing circumstances than Eisenhower faced in his new command post, deep within the unfriendly confines of the dank, forbidding caves of the Rock of Gibraltar. Eisenhower found it the most depressing place he had ever been in. During the initial stages of Torch there was little for Eisenhower to do but await reports from the invasion commanders while listening to the "constant drip, drip, drip of surface water that faithfully but drearily ticked off the seconds of the interminable, almost unendurable wait which always occurs between completion of a military plan and the moment action begins."[1] Eisenhower had thus learned one of the first maxims of his new post: Once the cumbersome military machinery of the invasion had been set in motion, success or failure was in other hands; he could only await reports and pray all was well. It did not help that Torch was worse than most World War II operations in that communications between the invasion task forces and Gibraltar were unreliable.

While Eisenhower stewed inside the "Rock," on the morning of November 8, 1942, the three Allied invasion forces landed simultaneously at Casablanca, Oran, and Algiers. A U.S. force of 39,000 men commanded by Maj. Gen. Lloyd R. Fredendall sailed from Scotland and landed at Oran, while an Anglo-American force of 23,000 British and 10,000 U.S. troops of the 34th Infantry Division, commanded by Eisenhower's classmate Maj. Gen. Charles W. "Doc" Ryder met only scattered resistance and easily seized Algiers on D-Day with a minimum of losses on either side. Patton's Western Task Force sailed from the eastern United States to seize Casablanca, Safi, and Port Lyautey on the Atlantic side of French Morocco. In all, 117,000 troops were committed to Torch, 75 percent of them American.

To help pass the time, Eisenhower drew up the "Worries of a Commander," a brief list that focused on the lack of information and his troubles with the French. "We cannot find out anything," he complained.[2] Eisenhower and Mark Clark "sagely concluded that they would soon be lions or lice."[3]

As supreme commander what Eisenhower did least well was tolerate the interminable waiting. The first visible signs of the strain Torch had put on him had appeared in early November:

> Following upon many months of work and planning, conducted sometimes at almost hysterical intensity, a great Allied amphibious force had sailed from its ports to attack North Africa and my staff and I were condemned to days of almost complete passivity in the tunnels of Gibraltar as we awaited the outcome. During those anxious hours I first realized, I think, how inexorably and inescapably strain and tension wear away at the leaders' endurance, his judgment and his confidence.[4]

On November 9 Eisenhower killed yet more time by recording the "inconsequential thoughts of a commander during one of the interminable 'waiting periods.' " His jottings shed light on both his sense of history and his awe at finding himself in such an exalted position:

> War brings about strange, sometimes ridiculous situations. In my service I've often thought or dreamed of commands, battle commands of various types that I might one day hold . . . [the one] I now have could never, under any conditions, have entered my mind even fleetingly. *I have operational command of Gibraltar!!* The symbol of the solidity of the British Empire . . . An American is in charge, and I am he. . . . I simply *must* have a grandchild or I'll never have the fun of telling this when I'm fishing, gray-bearded, on the banks of a quiet bayou in the deep South.[5]

"What soldier," Eisenhower wrote, "ever took the trouble to contemplate the possibility of holding an *Allied* Command and, of all things, an Allied Command of ground, air, and naval forces? Usually we pity the soldiers of history that had to work with allies. But we don't now, and through months of work we've rather successfully integrated the forces of and the commands and staffs of British and American contingents."[6] Eisenhower's early joyful optimism was short-lived. Later the task of containing the internecine squabbling among the prima donnas on both sides of the alliance would sometimes lead to moments of near anguish.

Throughout the grueling days in Gibraltar and later in Algiers, when he managed to snatch brief moments for personal reflection, Eisenhower thought often of his mother and longed to be able to sit quietly with her and be reassured by her faith in God and what had been (until David and Roy's deaths) her serene, positive outlook on life.

Despite Eisenhower's lack of high command experience, many of his instincts would prove correct. From the outset he realized the absolute necessity for a commander to radiate confidence no matter how dire the circumstances or how pessimistic he might actually feel. "My mannerisms and speech in public would always reflect the cheerful certainty of victory—that any pessimism and discouragement that I might ever feel would be reserved for my pillow," he wrote.[7] Though it was a philosophy from which he never wavered, even during the darkest days of the war, little did Eisenhower know it would be put to the test almost immediately.

If he was still relatively unknown before the invasion, after the Torch landings were disclosed to the public, the name Eisenhower would never again dwell in obscurity. As blazing headlines in the London newspapers trumpeted the Allied invasion and featured Eisenhower's photograph, the Allied commander in chief read them in his underwear deep inside Gibraltar, while Tex Lee attempted to remove an ink spot from his uniform trousers. Both Eisenhower and Clark could now share claim to having lost their pants in the cause of advancing the war effort.

The Torch landings not only brought Eisenhower enormous publicity, but for the first time he had gained international stature. In the United States he symbolized an auspicious new phase of the war for the Allies. More than ever before, reporters scrambled to write stories about America's most prominent new military figure.[8]

In his letters to Mamie, Ike did his best to reassure her that he was in no danger but reminded her that war was a costly business. On November 8 he wrote, "We have got to steel ourselves to these things in war and just get down to earth and work as hard as we can so as to get the damn thing over quickly."[9] For her part Mamie merely said of her husband's role, "I always shudder when I think of it."

Among those captured in Algiers was Darlan, the Frenchman who, next to Pétain, was most closely identified with the detested Vichy regime. Darlan was the commander in chief of the French navy and held key positions in Vichy, including that of Pétain's designated successor. First and foremost an opportunist who sensed that the winds of war would shift to the Allies, Darlan still commanded the allegiance of most of the French officer corps, hence his potential value to Eisenhower and the Allies.

Eisenhower's euphoria at Torch's initial success was short-lived and replaced almost immediately by a myriad of unresolved problems. With the collapse of a deal with Giraud, it was left to Eisenhower to pick up the pieces any way he could. Inaction was not an option. Mindful of Churchill's admonition, "Kiss Darlan's stern if you have to, but get the French Navy," Eisenhower despatched Mark Clark on November 9 to spearhead the effort to win over the French. "I must have someone who can act for me without having to confer with me or get my opinions," he said of the only officer he trusted to carry out such a mission.[10]

Clark arrived in Algiers accompanied by Giraud, who was immediately spurned by his French colleagues, most of whom refused even to acknowledge his presence. To his dismay Clark learned that even had a deal been struck with Giraud, the French commanders would have refused to honor it. Darlan, however, commanded immense respect within the French navy, which the Allies both coveted and feared. As commander in chief of the Vichy armed forces, it was Darlan, not Giraud, who remained the only Frenchman with the prestige and authority to decree a cease-fire.

It was thus left to Clark and Robert Murphy to negotiate with Darlan, who, for two days, refused to issue a cease-fire order until threatened with house arrest by an exasperated Clark.

In order to find some means of stopping the shooting before the casualty lists got any longer, a quid pro quo that was more coercion and intimidation than diplomacy was concluded with Darlan on November 10. In return for arranging an immediate general cease-fire, Darlan would become the de facto military governor of North Africa in the name of Marshal Pétain, the aged hero of World War I and the figurehead leader of Vichy. When Darlan cabled his intentions to Vichy, the Germans reacted with fury by invading the Unoccupied Zone of France.

Darlan's cease-fire order ended hostilities in French North Africa. However, when the Germans moved to seize the fleet, the French naval commanders, unpredictable to the bitter end, spurned Darlan's orders and instead scuttled it in the harbor of Toulon rather than let it fall into either Allied or German hands, prompting de Gaulle to declare it a "pitiful and sterile suicide."[11]

Thus was born the so-called Darlan Deal (sometimes called the Clark-Darlan deal), which Eisenhower personally endorsed when he arrived in Algiers on November 13. With approval from the State Department in Washington, the Darlan deal became official three days later when the admiral was named high commissioner for North Africa.[12] Clark had fulfilled his mission and would count himself fortunate that he did not have to endure the brunt of the political fire storm that ensued.

Eisenhower's decision to embrace the controversial French admiral was almost immediately the subject of a torrent of criticism, much of it contrived hypocrisy emanating from Washington and London, where its disclosure left de Gaulle "incredulous" and defiant. "The U.S. can pay traitors but not with the honor of France," he declared.[13] Churchill proclaimed himself "disgusted" and said, "Darlan ought to be shot."

Robert Murphy later wrote that there was simply "no thought in the minds of American war planners that a 'Darlan Deal' would not be acceptable in Washington."[14] Politically, it wasn't and the ensuing uproar was aimed directly at Eisenhower for having instigated such an odious rapprochement. "These worthies acted as if they had never heard the name Darlan before and seemed astonished that General Eisenhower had taken such liberties in political matters."[15] Conveniently forgotten was the fact that Eisenhower had been expressly authorized by both Roosevelt and Churchill to use whatever means necessary to resolve the French problem. Indeed, Churchill had remarked that "If I could meet Darlan, much as I hate him, I would cheerfully crawl on my hands and knees for a mile if by doing so I could get him to bring that fleet of his into the circle of Allied forces."[16]

The Darlan Deal came too late to avert bitter resistance at Oran, where battles raged for two days before French forces there surrendered to Maj. Gen. Terry Allen's 1st Infantry Division. Eisenhower was particularly worried about Morocco, where Patton's Western Task Force met considerable resistance and was engaged in bitter fighting around Casablanca, Fedala, and Mahdia after the French elected to resist. Eisenhower's impatience was implicit in a blunt cable to Patton on November 10 that read: "Dear Georgie—Algiers has been ours for two days. Oran defenses crumbling rapidly. . . . The only tough nut left is in your hands. Crack it open quickly." Clearly anxious, Eisenhower cabled Bedell Smith, who had remained behind in London, "If he [Patton] captures Casablanca by noon tomorrow, I will recommend both him and Fredendall for third stars." Patton hardly needed reminding, and the same afternoon of November 10 the French resident-general, Auguste Noguès, capitulated after Patton threatened to launch an all-out assault on the city.

Communications between Patton and Gibraltar were faulty, leading Eisenhower to rebuke Patton for failing to keep him informed. However, as Patton, genuinely troubled for the first of many times by his new boss's displeasure, later pointed out, he had indeed faithfully kept Eisenhower abreast of events by means of several lengthy letters. "I regret you are mad with me over my failure to communicate," he wrote, "however, I cannot control interstellar space and our radio simply would not work."[17]

Eisenhower's sole inducement to deal with Darlan was practical, not political, and while others accused him of political naïveté, he viewed Darlan entirely from a soldier's perspective. "This guy can stop the fighting and nobody else can," said Eisenhower. Well aware of the volatility of the diverse segments of the Arab population of French North Africa, Eisenhower realized that things were to ready explode at any moment. The already impoverished region was suffering from such a grave shortage of basic staples that uprisings were a distinct possibility. Money bought nothing and was therefore virtually useless. "Many things done here that look queer," he wrote to Mamie, "are just to keep the Arabs from blazing up into revolt. We sit on a boiling kettle!!"[18] If anyone could keep the lid on, it was the French, with their long-established civil and military administration.

Eisenhower, however, "neither understood French politics nor appreciated the psychological effect of the 1940 debacle. He felt betrayed by any Frenchman not wholeheartedly at his service."[19] Eisenhower's disdain for the French, dating to his guidebook days in France in 1928, did nothing to prepare him, nor did he seem particularly interested in learning their side and what made them tick. On the day of the Torch landings, he was already venting his frustration with the French. "All of these Frogs have a single thought— 'ME,' " he railed to Bedell Smith. "It isn't this operation that's wearing me down—it's the petty intrigue and the necessity of dealing with little, selfish, conceited worms that call themselves men. Oh well—by the time this is over I'll probably be as crooked as any of them."[20] And this was but the beginning; for the remainder of the war Eisenhower would grapple with one problem after another concerning the French. Part of his maturing as a supreme commander was that he got a lot better at this than he demonstrated in 1942 and 1943.

Above all else, however, Eisenhower's embrace of Darlan had a significant military motive. Faced with the enormous logistical problems of moving an Allied force from Algeria, the quickest and surest means of seizing Tunisia ahead of the Germans was to land Allied troops at the two vital all-weather airfields controlled by French forces in Tunis and Bizerte. Through Darlan's authority Eisenhower had every reason to believe the Allies could expedite the capture of Tunisia without a prolonged and costly fight.

Eisenhower unwaveringly believed that if the political uproar resulting from the Darlan Deal meant replacing him, so be it. The price of saving lives at the cost of his job was simply a nonissue; Eisenhower was perfectly willing to have made that sacrifice. "I am nothing but a soldier," he said. "Anybody who steps into this position has got to realize he can be replaced very easily, and should be replaced if national prestige and politics require it."[21] To Eisenhower's credit, in response to the crocodile tears of outrage that ensued over his so-called deal with the devil, he calmly stuck to his guns, replying that the bargain would save lives. "I do not understand anything about diplomacy," he said.[22]

Like it or not, politics and diplomacy were essential, never-ending components of Eisenhower's job. Virtually every decision he made had political implications of some sort. Despite his uneven performance in North Africa as a military commander, Eisenhower's earlier experience served him well.

Whether briefing, pacifying, or simply schmoozing some visiting bigwig, he was at the center of an eternal minefield, knew it, but was not dissuaded from acting. The timing of Torch was a typical illustration: The landings occurred five days after the midterm congressional elections rather than before them, as FDR had urged Marshall as a visible affirmation of his strong leadership. When Torch was delayed for valid military reasons until after the election, Roosevelt accepted that it was Eisenhower and not the Democratic National Committee that was calling the shots. Nevertheless, just as headlines praising Eisenhower and Torch were elevating American morale on the home front, White House Press Secretary Steve Early was heard to lament, "Jesus Christ! Why couldn't the Army have done this just before [the] election!"[23]

Well aware that he was a potential sacrificial lamb, he preempted Churchill's reaction before the deal was struck, taking note of the fact that "I have too often listened to your sage advice to be completely handcuffed and blindfolded by all of the slickers with which this part of the world is so thickly populated."[24]

With only the newspapers to provide information, Mamie could have been forgiven for wondering how her husband could be the most celebrated and written-about man in the United States at one moment and labeled a fascist the next. It was a harsh lesson to both in the vagaries of public opinion. Eisenhower took a beating in both the British and American press and was uncomfortably aware that his reputation was suffering badly. In Britain came the first rumblings that he was, after all, only a Kansas hayseed, easily exploited by "the wily Fascist opportunists" in North Africa. As the criticism mounted, so too did Eisenhower's defensiveness. Privately he deeply resented the injustice of being blamed for doing his job. If nothing else the Darlan affair taught Eisenhower that one of the keys to surviving the exalted jungle he now inhabited was a near-limitless supply of nervous energy.

Eisenhower's fate was actually in FDR's hands, and the president was under a barrage of criticism, particularly from the liberal media. The editor of the liberal journal *The Nation*, Freda Kirchwey, charged that "[p]rostitutes are used; they are seldom loved," and that in backing Darlan, the United States had sold its political soul.[25] One of Roosevelt's options would have been to sack Eisenhower, an act for which there was ample precedent in American history. As Stephen Ambrose and Richard Immerman point out, "The politically sensitive Roosevelt must have been tempted to fire Eisenhower, repudiate the Darlan deal, put someone acceptable in Darlan's place, and make a fresh start. Churchill had fired a string of generals in Egypt and now looked like a genius," particularly after Montgomery had won a seminal victory over Rommel at El Alamein shortly before Torch. Roosevelt, however, chose instead to reaffirm his commitment to Eisenhower, although his endorsement of his neophyte commander was hardly ringing.[26]

Churchill found himself pressured by his foreign secretary, Anthony Eden, to repudiate the "deal," which one Briton had described as smelling "so much like Appeasement again." At one point the two men engaged in a shouting match that ended with Churchill attempting to dismiss the contretemps with the rejoinder that Darlan was "not as bad as de Gaulle anyway."[27] Although Churchill steadfastly refused to forswear Darlan, he did send a trusted aide named Harold Macmillan to Algiers as his personal representative in an effort to influence Eisenhower's future decisions.

Fortuitously Milton visited North Africa in his capacity as the head of the Office of War Information (OWI), and vigorously took up the defense of his embattled brother, who was "as excited as a bride" to see him.[28] Those who crossed Milton soon felt the lash of yet another Eisenhower tongue. Unless drastic action were taken at once, complained Milton to Robert Murphy, his brother's career might be "irreparably damaged." " 'Heads must roll, Murphy!' he exclaimed. 'Heads must roll!' " he said, referring to innuendos in various media that painted his brother as a Fascist. Well aware that he was little more than an Allied stooge, Darlan protested to Milton that he was "but a lemon which you intend to use and then toss aside."[29]

The troubled deal with Admiral Darlan is generally regarded as a blot on Eisenhower's record that was never quite erased, despite the obvious question of what other choices Eisenhower had under the circumstances. The contretemps certainly left Eisenhower wishing he could undertake the simpler task of commanding combat troops instead of fighting political battles. The reality was that, like it or not, Eisenhower was both a military commander and a politician in the swamp of intrigue in North Africa. Darlan and Gibraltar were symbolic of the role he loathed but was obliged to play, all the while longing to be shed of both.[30] His hope of a role as simply a soldier and commander rather than a politician was wishful thinking. Eisenhower later observed to Bedell Smith that with his priority now Tunisia, "When I can make a present of that place," then Churchill would be welcome to "kick me in the pants and put a politician here who is as big a crook as the chief local skunk."[31]

Historians have dismissed Torch as relatively unimportant because it took place against the French instead of the Germans, yet the three invasions might just as easily have turned out disastrously. The problems that plagued the Allied commanders during the landings ran the gamut from the wrong priorities for landing equipment, inadequate communications, and mechanical failures to the crucial absence of combat engineers, who were left stranded on troop transports. Training had been rushed and was generally inadequate. Most landing craft losses occurred in the heavy surf, and had the French resisted as fully as they were capable, Torch might well have miscarried. As a major operation of war, Torch was never considered a model of planning.

Lucian K. Truscott, Jr., who commanded the 3rd Division in the Mediterranean and, later the U.S. Fifth Army in Italy, called Torch "a hit and miss affair that would have spelled disaster against a well-armed enemy intent on resistance." Valuable lessons were learned, and the only post mortem that really counted was that, however flawed, Torch got the job done. Without doubt Eisenhower had good reason for having prayed for its success harder than he had ever prayed in his whole life.

31.

"The Dreariest Chapter in the History of Allied Collaboration"

*Had we struck out boldly and landed forces far to the east
. . . we would almost certainly have been successful.*
— MARK CLARK

For Dwight Eisenhower the learning experience in North Africa was a painfully dismal one of mistakes, uncertainty, and tentativeness. The Torch landings and the Darlan Deal were but the first of an endless string of problems he faced in North Africa. With the completion of Torch, his primary problem was Tunisia.

Tunisia and its two deep-water ports of Bizerte and Tunis were vital to future Allied operations in the Mediterranean. As long as Tunisia remained under Axis control, an invasion of Sicily, Sardinia, or the Italian mainland would have been next to impossible from Algeria. After neutralizing French North Africa, Allied intentions were to thrust quickly into Tunisia and capture Bizerte and Tunis before the Axis forces in North Africa could be reinforced. Then, while Montgomery's British Eighth Army pursued Rommel across Libya, Allied forces would drive east to Tripolitania and trap Panzer Armee Afrika.

The French still held airfields in both cities, and Eisenhower had intended to employ Darlan's influence to turn French troops in Tunisia against the Germans. Spurning Rommel's appeal that the Germans should abandon the place rather than needlessly sacrifice veteran troops, Hitler elected to stand and fight in North Africa. He created the Fifth Panzer Army under veteran panzer commander Gen. Hans-Jürgen von Arnim. While the Allies were preoccupied securing Algeria and Morocco, the Germans began pouring troops and matériel from bases in Sicily and Italy into North Africa through the port of Tunis, a key Allied objective that by mid-November was wholly out of reach. German dive-bombers began arriving at Bizerte airfield on November 9, as the French commander stood idly by in the absence of orders to close the runways and resist. In succeeding days

German paratroopers were air-landed, and the narrow window of time necessary to secure Bizerte airfield had closed. In truth, any notion of a quick seizure of ports or airfields in Tunisia was wishful thinking, as was a farfetched recommendation from the CCOS that Eisenhower employ his floating reserve to invade Sardinia.[1]

As he would be throughout the war, Eisenhower was continually being second-guessed. Irked at what he believed was meddling and naïveté on the part of the CCOS in an operation barely a week old, he was "unalterably opposed" to any attempt to reduce or break up his forces for other tasks than seizing Tunisia, venting to Bedell Smith, "For God's sake, let's get one job done at a time. . . . I am not crying wolf nor am I growing fearful of shadows." He refused to have his forces diverted elsewhere or to return to London for consultations. "I am disturbed by the apparently bland assumption that this job is finished. It would take only five minutes actually on the ground to convince anyone that nothing could be further from the truth."[2]

In war timing is everything, and the Darlan deal had taken too long to be realized. Moreover, the consequences of altering the Torch plan to include the Casablanca landings doomed any chance of an early seizure of Tunisia. Although Eisenhower did employ his floating reserve to land a British brigade at the small port of Bougie, some 125 miles east of Algiers, and, on November 13, a commando force at Bône, near the Tunisian border, neither operation solved the immediate problem.

Although Eisenhower evaded the issue in *Crusade in Europe*, Mark Clark candidly reflected on the mistakes of Torch in his postwar memoir. Uppermost, said Clark, was that the Allies permitted the threat posed by Spanish Morocco to cloud the more important issue of securing Tunisia before the Germans. "We had been unquestionably timid (although far less than Washington) in the scope of our original invasion of Africa. Had we struck out boldly and landed forces far to the east, even in Tunisia . . . we would almost certainly have been successful."[3]

Allied intentions were almost thwarted by the foresight of a wily new nemesis, Field Marshal Albert Kesselring. A former artilleryman in World War I, Kesselring was one of the first to grasp the enormous potential of airpower and transferred to the Luftwaffe during the interwar years. By 1942 Kesselring's steady performance of duty had earned him promotion to field marshal and command of all German forces in the Mediterranean. He brought to the position a keen understanding of both ground and air operations. The Allies would come to regard the shrewd and resourceful Kesselring highly for his defensive genius in what would have been, in other hands, impossible military situations. Kesselring never backed away from a fight he thought he could win, and his unfailing optimism (which his critics claimed was his most serious flaw) had earned him the nickname "Smiling Albert." Kesselring and Rommel, his rival, rarely agreed on anything. However, in the wake of the Torch landings it was Kesselring whose authority reigned supreme in the Mediterranean.

Kesselring saw the coming battle for Tunisia as one in which airpower would carry the day and had prepositioned some four hundred bombers and fighters at airfields in nearby Sicily and on Sardinia. For one of the few times at this point in the war the Luftwaffe held air superiority. Kesselring forcefully took control of Axis operations, determined to protect the Axis front in Tunisia during the reinforcement phase, while Rommel continued withdrawing his army across Libya and into Tunisia. A hastily assembled force of German infantry, airborne, and artillery units and Italian units deployed to block the Allied advance into Tunisia.[4]

Maj. Gen. Lloyd Fredendall commanded II Corps, the U.S. fighting element in Tunisia, while Patton's Western Task Force remained in Morocco in a training role and on quasi-occupation duty. Eisenhower appointed the British First Army commander, Lt. Gen. Kenneth Anderson, to command what was called the Eastern Task Force, under which fell all British, French, and American forces. Eisenhower's orders to Anderson were to move into Tunisia "with all possible speed" and seize Bizerte and Tunis.

The distance from Algiers to the Tunisian battle front was vast, and the roads were among the world's most primitive, often dating to Roman times. The only existing railroad ran along the Mediterranean coastline. Originally built by the French, it was antiquated and in deplorable condition. Overall the North African theater of operations encompassed nearly a million square miles of some of the bleakest, least hospitable terrain on earth. Resupply was to become the single most difficult problem facing the Allies during the Tunisian campaign and a familiar dilemma to Eisenhower throughout the war.

Weather and the five-hundred-mile supply line between Algeria and Tunisia were the primary reasons why the overoptimistic timetable for Torch turned into a shambles. To make matters worse, the Allies lacked sufficient vehicular transportation, in no small part because during the Torch planning, Eisenhower had been allotted an inadequate number of ships. Motor transport units and other vehicles were among those that had to be left behind in England. Once ashore, the Torch forces had almost no mobility. Like Casablanca this decision, however justified, had its price, and it was Eisenhower who bore its brunt.[5]

Mostly ignored by military historians for its lack of glamour, logistics is the bread and butter of war. A modern army cannot fight and win battles without adequate supplies of fuel and ammunition for its vehicles, tanks, and guns, all of which must be transported to the battlefield. The longer the distance from the source of those supplies to the front, the more difficult the problem. The functions of the quartermaster, the ordnance technician, and transportation corps troops are vital in any modern army. Rommel may have said it best when he observed, "The bravest men can do nothing without guns, the guns nothing without ammunition. The battle is fought and decided by the quartermasters before the shooting begins."[6] In Washington, notes Marshall's biographer Ed Cray, "Logistics governed Marshall's War Department. They determined global strategies. They set timetables for campaigns in the field. The clamor for supplies never ceased."[7] Military historian Martin van Creveld has astutely observed that failure to take logistics into account "has probably led to many more campaigns being ruined than ever were by enemy action."[8]

With Darlan's authority to facilitate the seizure of the Tunisian airfields no longer viable, by the time Anderson launched a two-pronged offensive into Tunisia in mid-November, the Germans already controlled Bizerte and Tunis. The race for Tunis was as much an attempt to beat the arrival of winter weather as that of German reinforcements. For nine out of twelve months each year North Africa is one of the most arid and desolate regions of the world. From December to March, however, torrential winter rains arrive with a suddenness and fury that turn the ground into mud with the consistency of tar. Airfields that were once grass became bogs into which vehicles and aircraft sank, sometimes irretrievably; roads became quagmires. Patton described Tunisia as "the coldest damn place I have ever seen . . . it is very hard on the men."[9]

From Eisenhower on down, no one had anticipated the extent of the mud and bad weather. The day after Eisenhower settled permanently in Algiers in late November, he received his first exposure to the pervasive winter elements. On a visit to Fredendall, his plane burst a tire landing near Oran. Butcher described the area around the airfield as "a blanket of sticky mud." Col. Lauris Norstad, a postwar four-star general, recalled that there seemed nothing but oceans of mud everywhere, making it "impossible to get anything clean, including yourself."[10] Soldiers cursed "General Mud" as often and as vehemently as they did their own generals.

Eisenhower's performance was an increasing cause for concern in London, where Brooke fretted that he was already demonstrating he was not up to the job:

> It must be remembered that Eisenhower had never even commanded a battalion in action. . . . No wonder he was at a loss as to what to do, and allowed himself to be absorbed in the political situation at the expense of the tactical. I had little confidence in his having the ability to handle the military situation confronting him, and he caused me great anxiety. . . . He learnt a lot during the war, but tactics, strategy and command were never his strong points.[11]

Eisenhower moved permanently from Gibraltar to Algiers on November 23, 1942, resolved to fashion a military coalition as strong as his own personal belief in the righteousness of the Allied cause. What he found in colonial Algiers was a hotbed of intrigue and corruption. Writing to Ismay, he noted, "I sensed every individual was suspicious of everyone else—every man was sure all others were crooks and liars." Eisenhower decided on a get-tough approach: "I immediately started a personal campaign to establish for myself a reputation for the most straightforward, brutal talk that could be imagined." Eisenhower's approach was merely another illustration of his practice of lulling others into the belief that he was "just a man too simple-minded to indulge in circumlocution."[12] Eisenhower's approach may have made him feel in control, but it had little discernible effect on those whom it was intended to impress. Psychological warfare raged behind the scenes even as a real war was being fought in Tunisia. While the Gaullists sniped at the Americans, the British, and their countrymen in Algeria with equal fervor, Joseph Goebbels's efficient German propaganda machine was busily planting rumors and making broadcasts designed to create unrest within the Allied side and make Eisenhower's life miserable.[13]

As the latest in a long line of uninvited guests to occupy their country, Eisenhower felt it "advisable to throw a little dog to impress the natives" and instructed Butcher to find him suitable accommodations befitting his position. Butcher rented a large villa in the hills overlooking the harbor of Algiers that was actually far less elegant than its stately facade. Kay Summersby, who arrived from England in late December, found it "ugly" and thought that "as usual, General Eisenhower had chosen a house more appropriate for a captain than for the Allied commander." Eisenhower himself reported to Mamie that it was rather gloomy and the "facilities" typically French, "and you know what that means."[14]

When it came to the trappings of high command, Eisenhower was enigmatic. A stickler for punctuality, he insisted on being ten minutes early for an appointment. His special aversion was keeping men in the field waiting for him, and whenever possible he avoided formal inspections that he knew meant troops standing around awaiting his arrival.[15] Lack of military discipline infuriated him, as did such small things as missing his daily bath or not having adequate hot water, or if his coffee was not up to snuff. Yet Eisenhower eschewed being babied, as subordinates are wont to do with high-ranking generals. There was no private toilet in his office, necessitating that he use one adjacent to an outer office. A major insisted on opening the door for him each time. Eisenhower grew increasingly annoyed and grumbled to Butcher that he wished the officer would stop. "Damn it, I always expect him to come in and unbutton my fly for me." When the practice continued, Eisenhower let his anger show, and it was clear that he had hurt the officer's feelings. Often, after rebuking an underling, Eisenhower would regret losing his temper. "Damn my hide," he would say to Mickey McKeogh, "now I've got to go back and apologize."[16]

Although he longed to share the hardships of his troops, Eisenhower was fond of creature comforts and amenities that even MacArthur spurned. However, a worried Marshall would soon detect signs of burnout and insist Eisenhower begin taking better care of himself. Butcher, who by now had perfected his real estate skills, was directed to find his boss another abode in more intimate surroundings. He located a small farmhouse some ten miles outside Algiers, which came equipped with a tennis court, stables, and a view of the Mediterranean. When he could spare the time, Eisenhower and Butcher resumed their long-standing practice of banging golf balls or tossing around a baseball. The AFHQ staff acquired several Arabian stallions for Eisenhower's use, which he and Kay Summersby were seen riding whenever he could escape from his military duties, thus fueling the AFHQ rumor mill that the two were having an affair.

Flown from England, Telek duly made his reappearance and nearly drove his handlers to distraction. Both Kay Summersby and Butcher regarded Telek as truly stupid. Most days Telek went to work with Eisenhower and slept under his desk. Never housebroken, the unruly, yapping black dog twice demonstrated its disdain for his master by peeing on Eisenhower's bed, once in Marshall's presence. If disciplinarian Ike was unduly bothered, he gave no outward indication; instead, in a rare moment of levity, he casually remarked to Sergeant McKeogh, "Mickey, when he does things like that, he's your dog." Both Marshall and Eisenhower began to laugh.[17]

After weeks of strain and coping with political intrigue, Eisenhower was impatient to escape Algiers to see for himself the situation at the front. On a miserably cold, rainy day in late November, accompanied by Mark Clark, Eisenhower set off to visit Anderson's First Army command post at Guelma, a village some sixty-five miles east of Constantine.

The journey was not without incident. The convoy was exceedingly vulnerable to air attack by the Luftwaffe. Security consisted of a handful of .50-caliber vehicular-mounted machine guns, as lookouts anxiously scanned the skies overhead for any sign of marauding enemy aircraft. In Tunisia, one particular long stretch of road was nicknamed "Messerschmitt Alley." One of the first rules for staying alive under aerial attack in Tunisia was as unambiguous as a fire alarm: Let common sense overrule one's courage when it came to the Luftwaffe, which wreaked havoc by pouncing on and strafing Allied convoys and any vehicle caught in the open. "If you see the plane in time," remarked Patton, "you stop the car and run like hell for 50 yds off the road and lay down. It seems most undignified but all do it." Those who did usually lived to see another sunrise. As Patton forthrightly admitted to his wife during his service in North Africa, combat frightened him just like everyone else. "I still get scared under fire," but "I dislike the strafing the most."[18]

Patton was indeed obliged to "run like hell" on more than one occasion. Before he left North Africa, Eisenhower experienced an aerial attack and the hazards of nighttime driving in blackout conditions, when his jeep was bumped and unceremoniously pushed into a ditch, bruising his back.

During his numerous trips to the front, Eisenhower felt an affinity for the vast, barren spaces of Algeria, likening them to the similar emptiness of the Kansas plains. However, throughout the grueling, nearly 350-tail-bruising-mile journey to Guelma, along ancient roads built for pack animals, not machines, Eisenhower was ailing with a nagging upper respiratory infection that he had developed in the dripping tunnels of the "Rock." His perpetual flulike colds tended to last for weeks at a time and were aggravated by his heavy smoking and his inability even to consider cutting back. Although well aware of the consequence of smoking, he once rationalized the habit to Mamie by noting, "It's the only bad [one] I have."[19] On those occasions when Butcher had the courage to suggest that perhaps his boss ought to try resting, he was generally met by a withering blast of the Eisenhower temper.

Eisenhower and his party arrived in Guelma to find no sign of Anderson, who had recently moved his headquarters and left no forwarding address. Apparently no one in AFHQ had thought to confirm Anderson's whereabouts beforehand.[20]

Eisenhower and Clark were offered sanctuary for the night in a local home while the rest of their party camped by the roadside. The following morning, purely by chance, Eisenhower finally located Anderson near the Tunisian border at a tiny town called Souk-Ahras.[21] In all, the journey had been in excess of four hundred miles. Though the experience was both humbling and frustrating, it was one that Eisenhower relished as essential (Clark patronizingly referred to it as a "Boy Scout" trip). The image of Eisenhower wandering rather aimlessly in the vast wasteland of eastern Algeria in search of his elusive subordinate was clearly not part of any job description of a supreme commander. Eisenhower wrote to Mamie that the trip "was a jinx from start to finish—but we had to go through with it."[22]

When they finally connected, Anderson's news was somber. Although Allied elements had staked out positions inside Tunisia by mid-November and actually outnumbered the Axis forces assembled by Kesselring, they were spread too thin and lacked sufficient artillery, armor, air support, and supplies to have successfully sustained an offensive to capture Bizerte and Tunis.

Anderson was by nature uncommunicative and habitually pessimistic. Eisenhower liked him personally, but although he put the British general in the best possible light, the truth was that Anderson inspired neither Eisenhower nor Montgomery, who once described the Scotsman as "a good plain cook." His confidence in Anderson, Eisenhower admitted to Marshall, was not terribly high. Despite his "will to win," Anderson "blows hot and cold, by turns," he wrote. The American ground commanders over whom he exercised operational control generally disliked his cold, imperious manner. Anderson would later be shunted into obscurity after his alleged mishandling of the First Army in Tunisia.

Fredendall, the inexperienced senior American field commander whose reputation was built on his success at training troops, proved to be no better. Foulmouthed, arrogant, and critical of everyone around him, Fredendall topped this list with a bad case of Anglophobia. He reserved his greatest hostility for the British in general and for Anderson in particular, whom he openly disdained. Fredendall had similar sentiments for the French and—as Eisenhower would soon learn to his utter dismay—turned out to be an atrocious and cowardly field commander.

It was the Luftwaffe, however, that truly thwarted Allied aims. The sudden surge of strength in Luftwaffe tactical aircraft aggressively disrupted and delayed the Allied advance in western Tunisia, on one of the few occasions during the war that the German airmen could claim exceptional success. The Luftwaffe operated virtually unimpeded from all-weather fields as close as five miles to the battlefield, while the closest all-weather Allied air base was at Bône, more than 120 miles from the front lines. From bases in the Mediterranean the Luftwaffe bombed Algiers and other cities with virtual impunity. The Algiers harbor was filled with sunken ships, infuriating Eisenhower, who was troubled by—but was powerless to curb—the effect the situation was having on both civilian and military morale.

Adding to Eisenhower's woes was a grave misunderstanding of the fundamentals of close air support of the ground forces among the Allied air commanders. Already trouble was brewing over the lack of Allied air support of its ground troops. The German airmen were more adept at shifting their aircraft to cope with conditions on the ground, and their pilots were aggressive and took full advantage of the open terrain to bomb and strafe Allied convoys and airfields. In later campaigns German troops would curse the absence of the Luftwaffe over the battlefield; in Tunisia it was Tommies and GIs who did the cursing. A British colonel had indignantly complained to Eisenhower during his first trip afield that the absence of Allied air support was resulting in the "murder" of British ground troops by the Luftwaffe.[23] Thereafter, whenever he visited the front, Eisenhower would hear an endlessly familiar lament: "Where is this bloody air force of ours? Why do we see nothing but Heinies?"[24]

The exceptional cooperation in the Western Desert between the Eighth Army and the Desert Air Force was an example that simply was not yet understood by the Allied airmen in Tunisia, most of whom were fresh from England or the United States. Discipline was lax, and the new commander of the U.S. Twelfth Air Force, Medal of Honor winner Jimmy Doolittle, at first seemed more interested in piloting a fighter than in taking a firm grip on his new command. Relations with the RAF were frosty, air defenses lacking or nonexistent, communications between air and ground equally defective—all evidence of Allied growing pains in North Africa. On more than one occasion Eisenhower summoned his air commanders and staff officers for informal pep talks and sometimes official exhortations for the airmen to get their act together. Once, when Doolittle began pouring out his troubles, an exasperated Eisenhower cut him off. "Those are your troubles—go and cure them. Don't you think I've a lot of troubles too?"—hardly the words of a general in firm control of his subordinates.[25] Moreover, as an RAF historian has written, "As the Allied air forces began their advance eastwards towards Tunis, one of the earliest lessons of the Desert war was distressfully relearned—this, too, was a 'war for aerodromes.' "[26] Unable "to bring order out of fumbling," during this latest dilemma Eisenhower admitted he urgently needed help, and in early December he summoned Tooey Spaatz from England to become his acting deputy commander in chief for air operations. Spaatz reorganized the air forces and gradually brought a measure of order into what had been chaos.[27]

Thus the battle for Tunisia became in equal measure a contest for domination of the air as well as control of the ground. On both counts the Allies failed in 1942. The initial Allied offensive in western Tunisia was doomed to failure for other reasons as well. Not only were Allied ground forces woefully meager and spread too thin, but their tactics had long since proved to be a dismal failure. First employed by the British Eighth Army in Libya, the concept of fighting entirely separate battles, independent of one another, by brigade-size formations of infantry, artillery and armor violated a fundamental principle of war, concentration of force, and was one of the primary reasons for their earlier setbacks in North Africa. When Montgomery took command of the Eighth Army, one of his first acts was to disband these formations. In late 1942 and early 1943, however, the inexperienced Allied commanders in Tunisia elected to use them, with equally disastrous results.[28]

Although it was clear by the end of November that the Allied effort would likely fail, Anderson persuaded Eisenhower to approve a final attempt in December to capture Tunis. On December 23 Eisenhower once again undertook a day-and-a-half-long bone-jarring journey to the front. There he made his first-ever acquaintance with the dreadful conditions under which his troops would have to fight. Eisenhower never traveled without his lucky coins in his pocket in a zipper case that included an allegedly miraculous medal sent to him by a little girl in Detroit, who said she had adopted him and prayed daily for his safety. Throughout the war the two exchanged letters, with Eisenhower referring to the child as "my little godmother." Whenever he left on an unanticipated trip Eisenhower would refuse to embark until Sergeant McKeogh fetched his lucky coins.[29]

During his forays to the front Eisenhower would stop to provide a lift to any Allied soldier he met along the way. He also habitually made small talk with soldiers, usually asking the name of their home state or town and, from long habit, how their chow was. Particularly anxious to meet GIs from Kansas, Eisenhower was disappointed that he never encountered one from his hometown. He tried particularly hard to act like an ordinary soldier, disdaining a helmet (which his field generals all routinely wore) on the grounds that he should never pose as a frontline soldier when he was, in reality, a rear-echelon soldier relatively immune from danger. The fact that the threat to his safety was as great as that of the troops he was visiting never seemed to enter Eisenhower's thinking. Whenever Sergeant McKeogh or an aide would suggest he don his helmet, Eisenhower barked an order to put "that damn thing" away.[30] He preferred being known by his trademark unadorned garrison cap, which he felt immediately identified him and his status to his troops. (In fact, Eisenhower saw it as a mark of his respect for his troops that he did *not* wear a helmet.) By 1943 Eisenhower had begun to wear what he called a "goop suit" to ward off the cold during his visits to the front. It consisted of long overalls that encased him nearly to his armpits, a heavy field coat, and a knitted hoodlike cap over his head that made him look a modern-day science-fiction character.

One of Eisenhower's other trademarks in the field was his dislike for any formality or special treatment. He was known to hold a quick conference in the rain under the wings of his aircraft, or to be briefed in makeshift huts or crude frontline command posts. He insisted on seeing his soldiers as they actually lived, rather than in a contrived situation fantasized by a subordinate eager to impress. Eisenhower's presence at the front always made his hosts fearful for his safety. Noted Butcher, "Every time he wants to get where the shooting is, every front-line officer tries to discourage him. Then if he insists, so much protection is thrown around him . . . too many lives are needlessly endangered. So most of the time he just growls at his job in this war."[31]

Eisenhower also displayed his well-known low tolerance whenever the combat soldiers were shortchanged. On one occasion the troops complained to him that they could not obtain chocolate bars or cigarettes although both were in plentiful supply. Given the excuse by the Services of Supply that there was simply no transportation available to move these items to the front, Eisenhower solved the problem by directing that until every frontline unit and forward airfield was supplied, there would be no further issues of these items to the supply troops. Almost magically the necessary transport was found.[32]

By early December Eisenhower could barely restrain his frustration or his feelings. Butcher likened his boss to "a caged tiger, snarling and clawing to get things done." His staff felt his wrath with increasing frequency, and his only solace was in the form of letters from his beloved Mamie. However, mail, like everything else in North Africa, was a hit-and-miss proposition. Letters tended to come in batches, and the in-between periods were the most trying. Eisenhower relied heavily on his wife's letters to sustain his sagging morale. "Sometimes I get to missing you so that I simply don't know what to do. . . . No one else in this world could ever fill your place with me. . . . I LOVE you! . . . Never forget that, because, except for my duty, which I try to perform creditably, it is the only thing to which I can cling with confidence."[33] In his final letter of 1942 he reminded Mamie, "I've never *been in love with anyone but you*! I never will."[34]

Eager for a professional assessment of the problems in Tunisia by someone he trusted, Eisenhower turned to his old friend Patton, whom he summoned to Algiers. Patton was sent to inspect the front and report back why Allied tank losses were so high. Patton drove 250 miles in an open scout car into Tunisia, arriving soaked and half frozen at Anderson's First Army headquarters. After he made the rounds of British and American units in the front lines, his somber report to Eisenhower offered little encouragement. The American Grant tank, with its puny 37-mm gun, was helpless in battle against the German Mark IV panzer; only the eventual arrival of the new Sherman tank would even the playing field somewhat.[35]

The two men usually talked late into the night during their infrequent informal meetings, in which Eisenhower could unburden himself to a friend who did not covet his job. Although—as a result of a series of admonishments and what Patton deemed gratuitous advice—Patton found that Eisenhower was becoming increasingly grating, he remained high on his list of friends. For his part, Eisenhower wrote in his diary, "Among the American commanders, Patton I think comes close to meeting every requirement made on a commander."[36]

The tension under which Eisenhower functioned was most visible during the dark days of December 1942. As his problems mounted, he was grimly determined to carry on in Tunisia and informed Marshall at the end of November, "My immediate aim is to keep pushing hard."[37] With the sinking of the French fleet, Darlan had conspicuously failed to become the unifying force Eisenhower had counted on, and the fallout from the Darlan deal was taking its toll. Within AFHQ, Eisenhower was being pestered with the petty problems of staff officers, whose concerns ought to have been deflected and solved by Bedell Smith, newly arrived from London but yet to take his trademark firm grip on the staff.[38] In discouraging moments Eisenhower was overheard to grumble publicly to all around him that anyone who wanted his job was welcome to it. Morale was already at a low ebb, and such remarks were inappropriate, even in jest. Butcher's diary entries became as testy as his boss's mood and included disdainful remarks about Bedell Smith, whom Butcher characterized as "a neurotic with an aching ulcer."

"This job gets back breaking at times," Eisenhower wrote to Mamie in early December. "I jump from high military strategy to the lowest form of intrigue—I don't know if I'm a rhinoserous [*sic*] . . . or a house fly. I envy my Scottie dog, he has no worries. . . . Still, the heck of it is—I wouldn't miss my chance to help lick the Hun, to the very limit of any capabilities I have." Eisenhower's hatred of the Germans sometimes also found its way into his letters to Mamie. "My one passion is to see him beaten to his knees." He cheered "the Russian fight [which] continues to stir me to the depths of my soul. . . . I hope they kill a million Huns—even more! And I wish we could be hammering at the d—— Germans this instant, just as hard and on as big a scale as the Russians."[39]

Christmas 1942 brought no joy. At Longstop Hill, overlooking the Gulf of Tunis, a French-American-British task force was severely mauled during a bloody, bitterly contested four-day battle in which German forces launched a powerful counterattack on Christmas Day. Although losses on both sides were high, Allied forces suffered their heaviest casualties so far. The once optimistic Eisenhower was glumly forced to conclude that the Tunisian campaign was dead in its tracks.

The battle for Longstop Hill was merely a microcosm of the problems the Allies faced in Tunisia. There were mistakes in both the planning and execution of the operation. Reconnaissance and air and artillery support were lacking. Allied troops and airmen were not lacking in courage, but their inexperience and the results of their first ventures in coalition warfare left no doubt that there would have to be considerable improvement before they would be a match for the veteran German troops in Tunisia.

Eisenhower had intended to spend Christmas at the front. While visiting GIs of the 1st Armored Division in a heavy rain, Eisenhower saw for himself that "General Mud" reigned supreme and—reluctantly—the futility of continuing an offensive against Tunis. If the four men he was observing were unable to remove a motorcycle from the mud at a nearby airfield, certainly nothing heavier could move or function until the rainy season ended. Still, Eisenhower envisioned methodically pushing forward yard by yard if necessary until Tunis fell. Had he remained in Algiers, he might well have ordered the impossible, but after he viewed the situation at firsthand, the grim reality that the war in Tunisia was in a winter hiatus was inescapable.

With no other options a dejected Eisenhower made a "bitter decision" to cancel further Allied offensive operations in Tunisia in 1942. Equally thorny was the refusal of the French commander, Gen. Alphonse Juin, to serve under Anderson's direct command. Juin, an experienced, highly competent officer who would ultimately emerge as France's finest battlefield commander of the war, would cooperate with Anderson, but he would not place his command under the Allied field commander. Deep in discussions with Juin, Eisenhower received a telephone call from Clark summoning him back to Algiers at once. Although speaking guardedly on an open phone line, Clark nevertheless managed to convey the message that Darlan had been shot. Christmas Eve and Christmas Day were spent retracing the route to Algiers.

Although exhausted, Eisenhower went immediately to his office, where he learned that Churchill's wish to be rid of Darlan had indeed come true. The complexities of the Darlan Deal had literally exploded on Christmas Eve, when the admiral was assassinated by a young French monarchist. "Rarely in recent history can a political assassination have been so unanimously condemned and so universally welcomed," noted one historian of the abrupt ending to the Darlan Deal.[40] At a stroke Darlan's death removed an enormous political embarrassment and liability from Eisenhower's shoulders—but not from his reputation.[41] It had political ramifications as far away as Moscow, where Stalin questioned whether the Darlan Deal had been an indication of Allied expediency. Might the West not one day make a similar unilateral deal with Germany behind his back? The French Resistance was similarly dismayed that the Allies would strike a deal with the odious Vichy regime.[42] Last, it left a sour taste of distrust in the mouth of Charles de Gaulle that the French leader appears never to have forgotten. Ultimately, however, the intense revulsion stirred by Darlan served to strengthen de Gaulle's claim to represent France.[43]

That night, away from the glare of having to present the impeccable image of a man in total control, Eisenhower's staff saw the toll the job was taking on both his health and his state of mind. Kay Summersby noted that "his face wore that familiar gray pall of exhaustion. He was in a dismal state of mind . . . only the inner circle was allowed to see how depressed he really was." With only a few short hours left on Christmas, Eisenhower took time to draft a handwritten condolence note to Darlan's widow, then announced it was time to forget the war for a few hours. "Even a general is allowed to celebrate Christmas," he said. At Bedell Smith's villa he was treated to a traditional Christmas dinner, courtesy of Patton, who had sent Smith two live turkeys he had "liberated." Eisenhower possessed a remarkable ability to bounce back from fatigue and for a few hours shut out the war. Soon he began to sing "God Rest Ye Merry, Gentlemen" as if he hadn't a care in the world.[44]

Eisenhower's mood soured, however, when Smith informed him of Roosevelt's intention to award him a Medal of Honor for the Torch landings. Eisenhower was appalled. While serving in the War Department, he had vehemently opposed a similar award to MacArthur. To award the medal for anything but heroism in combat would be to cheapen it, he said. He was a desk soldier and both unqualified and unworthy of the nation's highest decoration. Eisenhower's reply (through Smith) was harsh and unequivocal: "I don't want it and if it is awarded I won't wear it. I won't even keep it."[45] To his friend Robert Eichelberger he later related with ill-concealed scorn, "I knew a man who had received one for sitting in a hole in the ground and [I] refused to accept it."[46]

The following day, ailing and soon to be bedridden with the flu, Eisenhower dutifully attended a funeral service for Darlan in Algiers, where Giraud shed a tear at the dead admiral's bier, thus bringing to a close an episode of the war everyone longed to forget.

As 1942 drew to a close, the cold reality that virtually nothing had gone right since the Torch landings was producing a ripple effect in London and Washington. The disquiet spilled over into a cable from Churchill to Roosevelt: "I am most anxious about the military situation," he wrote on December 31. An equally blunt cable to Eisenhower the same day said, "I am deeply concerned about the unfavorable turn in Tunisia, and our staffs take an even more serious view."[47] Brooke and the other British chiefs were growing increasingly mistrustful that Eisenhower was too soft and inexperienced to be in command of a large multinational force. The "situation in North Africa is none too good," Brooke wrote in his diary, worried that Eisenhower was too preoccupied "with political matters connected with Darlan . . . [wasn't] paying enough attention to the Germans," and had failed to take firm control of the campaign—which, Brooke's biographer notes, "needed urgent leadership at and from the front."[48] A later entry was one of his most scathing of the war. "I am afraid that Eisenhower as a general is hopeless! He submerges himself in politics and neglects his military duties . . . he knows little if anything about military matters. I don't like the situation in Tunisia at all!"[49]

Ismay's fair-minded deputy, Ian Jacob, visited Eisenhower during December and came away with a similar opinion. An extremely able officer who would later become one of Eisenhower's greatest admirers, Jacob thought that Eisenhower's inexperience was glaringly evident and that he was "too easily swayed and diverted to become a great commander in chief."[50]

Brooke was right: The Tunisian campaign showed signs of unraveling virtually before it began. Eisenhower seems to have understood this while at the same time he was frustrated by his inability to alter a situation in which he was saddled with an inexperienced field commander—Anderson—who had no grasp of air operations and maintained acrimonious relations with the RAF commanders.[51] To make matters worse, field communications were dreadful, and Anderson's problems were compounded by logistical deficiencies that only a veteran and more versatile commander might have been capable of surmounting.

In the final analysis, responsibility for the Allied failure to secure Tunisia in 1942 rested not with Eisenhower but with Marshall and Ernie King, whose insistence on invading Casablanca traded the strategic advantage of landings in eastern Algeria for the security of Gibraltar. That, combined with the inability of the Allies to resolve the French dilemma, was more than Eisenhower or anyone else could reasonably have been expected to overcome.

Nevertheless Eisenhower was quick to rate his own performance as dismal. Writing to his friend and successor as head of OPD, Maj. Gen. Thomas T. Handy, Eisenhower was harshly critical of himself, noting that Allied military operations in North Africa "have violated every recognized principle of war, are in conflict with all operational and logistic methods laid down in textbooks and will be condemned, in their entirety, by all Leavenworth and War College classes for the next twenty-five years."[52] The worst, however, was yet to come.

32.

Four Stars

Our chief of course was General "Ike"
whom everyone at once did like.
Who gave wise counsel and, as well,
If need be, just a bit of hell.
—AFHQ OFFICE DITTY, 1943

These were trying times for Dwight Eisenhower. The disappointing, near-disastrous early stalemate in Tunisia obliged Eisenhower and the AFHQ planners to revise Allied strategy once the winter rains ended and offensive operations could be resumed in the early spring of 1943. For the most part the Torch forces had been hastily trained and were ill equipped to do battle with veteran German troops and superior equipment such as the Tiger tank.

Eisenhower found himself mired in Algiers, fighting the war of the paper shufflers, coping with the aftermath of the Darlan Deal, and incapable of overseeing the battle in Tunisia. By early 1943 he had become inured to the fact that exercising high command was nothing at all like what he had once romantically envisioned: generals of almost Promethean powers moving men and equipment at will, like chessmen, around the field of battle. "In my youthful days," he later said, "I used to read about commanders of armies and envied them what I supposed to be a great freedom in action and decision. What a notion! The demands upon me that must be met make me a slave rather than a master. Even my daily life is circumscribed with guards, aides, etc., etc., until sometimes I want nothing so much as complete seclusion."[1] Some months later Eisenhower observed, "My life is a mixture of politics and war. The latter is bad enough—but I've been trained for it! The former is straight and unadulterated venom! But I have to devote lots of my time, and much more of my good disposition, to it." At times the constant wrangling nature of running a coalition produced monumental headaches. "I've just talked and argued until I'm weary," he wrote after the negotiations leading to the surrender of Italy in September 1943.[2]

Eisenhower attempted to take "personal command" of the Tunisian campaign by establishing an advance headquarters in Constantine while at the same time administering AFHQ. To act in his absence he appointed Brig. Gen. Lucian Truscott, a fiery cavalry officer who had come to Marshall's attention during the interwar years. One of the army's finest polo players, Truscott was fiercely competitive, hard driving, a strict disciplinarian, and a flamboyant dresser, appearing in a uniform consisting of a red leather jacket, yellow cavalry scarf, and his "lucky" cavalry boots. Truscott, destined to become one of the most successful Allied battlefield commanders of World War II, was an ideal choice to act as Eisenhower's point man. Nevertheless, even with a surrogate, it was an impossible and implausible endeavor to oversee military operations from four hundred miles away in Algiers.

The campaign in Tunisia required a hands-on tactical commander. Eisenhower attempted to fulfill two responsibilities at the same time: supreme commander and field commander, each of which by itself was a demanding full-time job. The result was that he did neither particularly well. For all his intellectual brilliance, Eisenhower had never before commanded above battalion level, and never in combat. And, as good as Truscott was (and he was very good), there was simply no substitute for the authority of a commander permanently present.

Anderson was in many ways the victim of Eisenhower's inexperience as a battlefield commander. The result was that, as one biographer has charged, "From Algiers he was not able to exert a grip on the battle, but he also failed to forge an effective chain of a command."[3] At times field commanders were not at all certain who was commanding them.

The most serious of Eisenhower's proliferating command problems in Tunisia remained Lloyd Fredendall. In addition to undermining an already messy campaign with his anti-British and anti-French sentiments, the II Corps commander had the reprehensible habit of commanding from his secure command post well behind the lines. Increasingly troubled by Fredendall's poor performance, Eisenhower already had good reason to rue having written to Marshall after the capture of Oran, "I bless the day you urged Fredendall upon me." Instead of demanding that he mend his ways, Eisenhower merely sent Fredendall one of the most ineffectual letters he ever wrote, timidly noting his concern that "some of our generals . . . [are] staying too close to their command posts."[4] Eisenhower's restraint at a crucial time was a discouraging example that his philosophy of leadership by persuasion had failed.

Allied disarray was obvious even to those in the remotest frontline position. Soldiers possess a marvelous ability to reduce events to their simplest common denominator, and an American GI summed it all up with the observation that "Never were so few commanded by so many from so far away!"[5]

The lessons of war had yet to be learned. American troubles in Tunisia can be ascribed in part to an unjustified overconfidence. Patton's son-in-law,

Lt. Col. John K. Waters, who commanded a battalion of the 1st Armored Division, overheard some of his men bragging about how well they had done against the French and silenced them: "We did very well against the scrub team," he said. "Next week we hit the German troops . . . when we make a showing against *them*, you may congratulate yourselves."[6] One of Eisenhower's former aides, Maj. H. H. Arnold, Jr., serving in a frontline artillery unit, wrote that "it takes a helluva lot more" than basic training and a few maneuvers to make a combat soldier. "Too bad we can't train them right."[7] *New York Times* correspondent Drew Middleton encapsulated the extent of Waters's observation. Too many Americans involved in the capture of Algiers, he wrote, "viewed its capture as a sort of football game. . . . Many appeared to feel that . . . the season was over, and they would go home. They had been away from the United States for five weeks and they were acutely homesick."[8]

Yet, if anything was to sustain Eisenhower it was his unfailing commitment to the conception that the war would be won only by Americans and Britons fighting together. Despite his plethora of problems and the amounts of criticism directed at him personally, Eisenhower never swayed from an almost sacred commitment that the war would be won jointly. Even when besieged, Eisenhower was able to write to Tom Handy that "I am not British and I am not ambidextrous in attitude. But I have got a very wholesome regard for the terrific tasks facing the United Nations in this war, and I am not going to let national prejudice or any of its related evils prevent me from getting the best out of the means you fellows struggle so hard to make available to us."[9]

The Hotel St.-George, situated on a hill overlooking the sparkling city of Algiers, was requisitioned to house AFHQ. A once-elegant French hotel, with floors of mosaic tile that had long since seen their best days, it has been described as "a white, rambling building, decorated with hideous statues and paintings, the kind of hotel favored by elderly spinsters on Mediterranean tours."[10] When he was not traveling, Eisenhower spent up to eighteen hours at day in his office attempting to tame the beast that AFHQ had become. Whether in his villa or his corner office, Eisenhower always had a front-row view of the often spectacular German aerial attacks on Algiers merely by stepping onto the balcony outside. Invariably the long hours, nagging colds, too many cigarettes, and nights of sleeplessness when the Luftwaffe came calling took a toll on his health. He looked as tired as he felt.

After the move to Algiers, Mickey McKeogh was one of many who saw ample evidence of Eisenhower's frayed nerves. Repercussions from the Darlan mess and German air raids, some of them heavy, robbed him of sleep. Inconsequential things tended to bother him, such as a letter from a woman in Texas who wrote to chastise Eisenhower for his use of profanity and suggest that his energies would be put to better use in prayer. "The General was sort of annoyed by that, and hurt too. He said: 'Damn it, I don't curse. I just use some words as adjectives.' "[11]

Orchestrating the creation of an Anglo-American headquarters that functioned in complete harmony was one of Eisenhower's most pressing challenges. To demand the same from his field commanders required an example to be set in his own headquarters: Here expectations and reality clashed. Mark Clark was hardly alone among Americans who distrusted the British and made no bones about displaying it. When Clark was Fifth Army commander in Italy and, later, an army group commander, his Anglophobia led to strained relations, reflected in a frustrated entry in his diary: "I was about to agree with Napoleon's conclusions that it is better to fight Allies than to be one of them."

Patton, Clark, and others were mindful of America's World War I experience and Pershing's fight to keep the AEF independent of French command. What they harshly viewed as favoring the British and submerging his allegiance to the U.S. Army, Eisenhower saw quite differently. In the 1920s, Fox Conner had drummed into him that "[w]e cannot escape another great war. When we go into that war it will be in company with allies. Systems of single command will have to be worked out . . . we must . . . learn how to overcome nationalistic considerations in the conduct of campaigns."[12] Although he accepted that his actions sometimes gave the appearance of a sellout, Eisenhower remained unwavering throughout his tenure as supreme commander that winning came first. Nevertheless too much of his valuable time was spent in smoothing over hurt feelings and resentments on both sides, and in countering silly suggestions and gratuitous advice, such as the notion of invading Sardinia.

In retrospect Eisenhower would have functioned far more effectively had he delegated more authority. While his ferocious chief of staff kept the wolves from his door, a perusal of Eisenhower's wartime desk diaries reflects an inordinate amount of time spent in non-decision-making meetings and hosting visiting VIPs anxious to secure a photo opportunity.

For both allies, each other's varying methods of doing business took some getting used to. There were the usual misunderstandings and occasional bad blood between Yanks and Brits, which led to more than one American officer being sent home. The story is told of the American in AFHQ who made the mistake of calling his opposite number a *British* son of a bitch, causing Eisenhower to explode in anger and send the offender home, not for cursing but for the nationalistic distinction as to what sort of SOB he was.

Churchill's handpicked representative in North Africa was Harold Macmillan, a longtime friend and political ally, himself a future prime minister. Cast in a role similar to that of Robert Murphy vis-à-vis Ike, Macmillan was given the title of minister resident, as Churchill's personal representative (and chief snoop) in AFHQ. Unlike Murphy, who was actually assigned to AFHQ,

Macmillan's only allegiance was to Churchill. The afternoon of his arrival in Algiers, Macmillan was summoned to a glacial audience with Eisenhower, who bluntly demanded, "What have you come for? I have been told nothing of it. You are a Minister, but what sort of Minister are you?" Macmillan replied, "Well, General, I am not a diplomatic Minister; I am something worse," to which Eisenhower retorted, "There is nothing worse." When Macmillan explained that he was there "to relay the Prime Minister's feelings 'on anything that comes up,' " their conversation "began to languish." However, Eisenhower's initial suspicions of the British diplomat soon softened when Macmillan pointed out that his mother was from Indiana, which technically made him a "Hoosier."[13]

"I could soon see that the General was a man of rapidly changing moods. But it was also clear he was naturally open-hearted and generous." Eisenhower was still smarting over outpouring of criticism for the Darlan Deal, and "greatly resented" being "branded as a Vichy reactionary. I can't understand why these long-haired, starry-eyed guys keep gunning for me. I'm no reactionary. Christ on the Mountain! I'm as idealistic as Hell."[14]

Despite their rocky beginning, Macmillan departed from his first encounter with Ike encouraged that "in General Eisenhower as our leader . . . we were indeed fortunate. Even at this first meeting I sensed the inherent goodness and firmness of his character. If sometimes impetuous, he was always fair."[15] From cold cynicism to a lifelong friendship best describes relations between the two men.

No such feelings existed for Ike's deputy, Mark Clark, who was roundly disliked by the British element within AFHQ. Not surprisingly, the British blamed much of the inevitable early disarray within AFHQ on Clark, whom they regarded as a disruptive influence. It was inevitable that Clark, given carte blanche by Eisenhower to establish AFHQ in Algiers, would step on toes, many of them British. They disliked his imperious manner and believed (not always incorrectly) that he intrigued against them. He was also a hugely disruptive force for his habit of issuing direct and occasionally contradictory orders to the staff. Equally resented was that Clark seemed to go out of his way to terrify the American staff officers in the manner of Bedell Smith. Brig. Ian Jacob, who accompanied Churchill to Casablanca, noted in his diary that there was "a great deal of restless confusion" within AFHQ, and that Clark's anti-British bias was complemented by the fact that he "sows dissension between British and French" and was regarded as AFHQ's "evil genius."[16]

In fact Clark's tenure at AFHQ was stormy but brief. Although Eisenhower hated to lose his services, Clark was eager to prove his mettle commanding an army. In early January 1943 the U.S. Fifth Army was activated in Morocco and placed under Clark's command. Jacob recorded in his diary of Clark's departure that "it will not be only the British officers who will heave a sigh of relief."[17]

As the AFHQ staff soon learned, Bedell Smith was not always the only SOB in the headquarters. Eisenhower seemed to delight in the occasional "grand quarrels with my staff. Every once in a while Staff Officers get all confused in a bunch of charts and drawing lines on blank paper. I take a fiendish delight in ripping them to pieces and breaking up their little play-houses," he gleefully wrote to Tom Handy.[18]

Harold Macmillan epitomized the British inclination within AFHQ to patronize. While Macmillan certainly liked Eisenhower, he held most Americans in North Africa in utter contempt, and once instructed another Englishman, Richard Crossman, AFHQ director of psychological warfare and a minister in a postwar Labor Government, "We, my dear Crossman, are the Greeks in this American empire. You will find the Americans much as the Greeks found the Romans—great big, vulgar people, more vigorous than we are and also more idle, with more unspoiled virtues but also more corrupt. We must run A.F.H.Q. as the Greek slaves ran the operations of the Emperor Claudius."[19] There was an equal lack of charity within AFHQ toward de Gaulle, who acquired the code-name Ramrod. As Harold Macmillan would later write, "This nickname recalled the famous definition of a man who was alleged to have all the rigidity of a poker without its occasional warmth."[20]

Although Eisenhower refused to give in to the frustrations of coalition warfare, his patience and resolve were sorely tried in North Africa. As he gained experience and the confidence that went with success, he was better able to deal with the challenges thrown his way by Churchill and others in the chain of command. However, in early 1943 such problems were part of Eisenhower's daily agenda.

One of the anomalies of war is the void between command and staff. The ideal staff officer is one with sufficient command experience to understand a field commander's needs and problems, and to plan accordingly. In reality such is rarely the case. While AFHQ (and later SHAEF) was staffed by dedicated officers, too many lacked this requisite knowledge and understanding. Combined with Eisenhower's own inexperience, AFHQ got off to a rocky start. While it is a commander's duty to listen and act on the advice of his staff, that is only one aspect of decision making. Too often Eisenhower was unduly influenced by some of his staffers, whose pronouncements would have been challenged had he been better informed by having spent more time at the front conferring with his field commanders. At times Eisenhower was nearly overwhelmed dealing with diplomatic and administrative matters.

Although the initial size of AFHQ was modest enough, under Eisenhower it soon swelled to enormous proportions. Clark believed that Eisenhower should have had a lean and manageable headquarters, and argued in vain that its initial authorization of seven hundred was perhaps two to three times larger than needed, but he was overruled by Bedell Smith, who was primarily responsible for creating a bureaucratic behemoth. By January 1943 the American contingent alone numbered over fourteen hundred and while Smith was right to insist on a staff of sufficient size to both manage current operations and plan future ones, the end result was a monstrosity that Marshall seriously questioned and Eisenhower loyally defended, promising reductions in manning levels. Yet by May 1943, while he was professing to be "appalled by the number of headquarters seemingly required to run this sprawling theater," Eisenhower was also complaining that his staff officers were seriously overworked.[21] His so-called pruning resulted in an AFHQ staff that by the autumn of 1943 numbered 4,070, rivaling that of Admiral Mountbatten, whose staff when he was supreme commander in Southeast Asia numbered more than 4,100. Between them they vied over having created the largest military command bureaucracies in the history of warfare—until 1944 when both were surpassed in size by that even larger headquarters called Supreme Headquarters Allied Expeditionary Force (SHAEF).[22]

In January 1943 Roosevelt, Churchill, and the CCOS met at Casablanca, primarily—as Churchill reminded Roosevelt—"because we have no [suitable] plan for 1943." No plan existed beyond Torch, and, other than the still imprecise commitment to a cross-Channel invasion, the two allies had yet to agree even remotely on a common strategy to defeat Germany and Italy. Torch had been foisted on an unwilling Marshall by Churchill, and abetted by Roosevelt's unwillingness for the United States to sit on the sidelines until 1943. At Casablanca, Marshall's hopes for untangling the United States from the Mediterranean were solidly dashed.

Stalin pointedly declined to attend, but his absence was probably a blessing in that it gave the two Western Allies the opportunity to meet in secret to resolve the many questions left unanswered by Torch. Churchill, the master politician, understood that once "in for a penny" in the Mediterranean, the United States was indeed "in for a pound," proclaiming that once North Africa was secure we "must go forward to the attack on Italy, with the object of preparing the way for a very large-scale offensive on the underbelly of the Axis in 1943."[23]

Stalin's long shadow was nevertheless present during the deliberations of his two allies. Although the Red Army would soon win the most important victory of the war on the eastern front at Stalingrad, Stalin had badgered Churchill and Roosevelt during the second half of 1942 to open a second front in the West without delay, to further relieve the pressure on his hard-pressed armies.

In the autumn of 1942 Churchill was amenable to mounting the cross-

Channel invasion in the late summer of 1943, but when it became evident in December that the Tunisian campaign was in trouble, he began to insist on playing out the Mediterranean option. Thus, while again affirming the eventual necessity for the cross-Channel invasion, soon to be given the code-name Overlord,[24] the British leader sought to buy time for its planning and preparation by continuing to nibble away at Germany's "soft underbelly." The Allies had the Axis on the defensive in the Mediterranean and must not, he argued, surrender the initiative.[25]

Churchill and the British chiefs of staff arrived fully committed to the removal of Mussolini and the Italians from the war. For support, offshore was anchored a British ship filled with staffers prepared at a moment's notice to retrieve information or draft a position paper. An invasion of the island of Sicily following the Tunisian campaign, the British argued, was an obvious choice for the Allies to reinforce their success in the Mediterranean and, at the same time, gain a foothold in southern Europe. The deadlock centered on the timing of the cross-Channel invasion. Marshall adamantly asserted that "the Mediterranean was a blind alley to which American forces had only been committed because of the President's insistence that they should fight the Germans somewhere."[26] Marshall's demands for the transfer of Allied forces in North Africa to the United Kingdom were countered by Churchill's avowed goal of the "cleansing of North Africa to be followed by the capture of Sicily."[27]

There was also deadlock over the allocation of resources between Europe and the Pacific. In the end, the CCOS reached a compromise on Pacific operations that satisfied Admiral King and was what Churchill loftily proclaimed "the most complete strategic plan for a world-wide war that had ever been conceived."[28] One of its main provisions was the invasion of Sicily. The masterful compromise orchestrated by the British left their Mediterranean strategy fully intact, American hopes in tatters, and Marshall dismayed that he had lost an uneven fight to extricate the Allies from the Mediterranean. (The question of when and where to mount Operation Overlord would not be resolved until the Quebec Conference, held in August 1943.)

Eisenhower played virtually no role at Casablanca but noted, "I do not see how the 'big bosses' could have deviated very far from the general course of action they adopted."[29] He was neither included in the intense negotiating sessions nor consulted by the Combined Chiefs. Indeed, Eisenhower's office diaries, maintained by Butcher and Kay Summersby, reflect only one day, January 15, when Eisenhower actually met with the Chiefs, Roosevelt, and Churchill. For the remainder of the conference he remained in Algiers or visited units in the field. The "two emperors" (as Harold Macmillan referred to Roosevelt and Churchill) and the other high ranking participants indulged in "a curious mixture of holiday and business . . . you would see the field marshals and admirals going down to the beach for an hour to play with the pebbles and make sand-castles," before the debates and discussions resumed each night.[30]

Eisenhower's summons to Casablanca resulted in a memorable journey. His aircraft was a decrepit B-17 Flying Fortress that had seen better days, and was (charitably) described as "battle fatigued." Over the Atlas Mountains an engine malfunctioned and began spewing oil across the wing, its propeller bent and twisting wildly, and the pilot unable to feather it. Had the propeller detached itself from its bent shaft it might well have destroyed the aircraft. The pilot ordered everyone aboard to don a parachute and stand near the exits in the event of a bailout, which looked likely when another of the plane's four engines also failed. As Eisenhower and Butcher helped each other strap on their parachutes, one of Eisenhower's stars was torn off his shoulder. Butcher's hands trembled so badly he was unable to replace it. Eisenhower chided, "Haven't you ever fastened a star before?" Suddenly formal, Butcher replied, "Yes, sir, but never with a parachute on, sir." Eisenhower put the star in his pocket. Eisenhower admitted he debated taking his chances instead of jumping. The thought crossed his mind that his bad knee might well be incapable of withstanding the rigors of hiking out of the wild Atlas Mountains in winter. Either way, he thought he would likely perish. The pilot managed to keep the plane under control and glided the final leg of the journey into Casablanca, landing without incident. Eisenhower was met by Patton and taken at once into the city. The B-17, irreparable, was scrapped.[31]

Early that evening Roosevelt was in high spirits and asked to see Eisenhower alone in his quarters for a private conversation. Come what may, Eisenhower had decided that he owed the president absolute candor rather than the bull too often spoon-fed to political leaders, and if Roosevelt fired him, so be it. According to Roosevelt's close personal adviser, playwright (*Abe Lincoln in Illinois*) Robert E. Sherwood, Eisenhower told Roosevelt that "generals could make mistakes and be fired but governments could not. He was entirely ready to take the rap for whatever went wrong."[32] When Roosevelt pressed for a date when the Tunisian campaign would end, Eisenhower blurted out, "May 15 [1943]." In the event, Eisenhower's prediction would turn out to be "my most miraculous guess of the war."[33] It also reassured Eisenhower that in Roosevelt's eyes he had been reprieved.

Afterward the president remarked to Harry Hopkins, "Ike seems jittery," unaware of Eisenhower's brush with death a few hours earlier or that he had only just emerged from his sickbed after the latest chapter of his two-month-long battle with cold and flu—which he was no closer to winning than he was the campaign in Tunisia. His blood pressure had twice measured an unhealthily high reading, although his doctors dismissed it as not unusual for someone under his particular stress.[34]

During his one night at Casablanca, Eisenhower and Patton had a long private talk into the early morning hours. Eisenhower related to his friend that he thought "his throat [was] about to be cut." Patton urged him to take personal command in Tunisia.[35]

Before returning to Algiers, Eisenhower paid his respects to the president, who was still in bed. As he left, Eisenhower gave Roosevelt a crisp salute. Harold Macmillan was present and whispered to Robert Murphy, "Isn't he just like a Roman centurion!" However, as one biographer points out, while openly acknowledging Eisenhower's prowess as a conciliator in holding together a prickly coalition, "Macmillan's colleagues would have found it a suitable simile, for they considered Ike's military expertise was roughly on a par with [that of] a Roman centurion."[36]

One of Harry Butcher's unofficial duties was to act as his boss's eyes and ears—which often entailed being the purveyor of bad news. His many friends and contacts in high places led him to warn Eisenhower that he believed neither Roosevelt nor Churchill would hesitate to get rid of him should be fail.[37]

Most telling of all during his first months as a commander in chief was that Eisenhower was not his own man. His debt to Marshall was so huge that he was unable or unwilling to carve out his independence. Being a commander in name and actually *being* in command are vastly different. In 1942 and early 1943 Eisenhower rarely showed glimpses of having his hand firmly on the tiller. North Africa was hardly the place for the indoctrination of an inexperienced supreme commander, a serious issue with the British, who believed that war was no place for amateurs. In the half century since World War II, many American historians have pointed to the British position as a smug attitude of arrogance and superiority of a nation that had defeated the Spanish Armada and Napoleon. The inescapable conclusion, however, is that on the basis of Eisenhower's early performance in North Africa, they had every right to question the political decision that resulted in the appointment of an inexperienced American general to command the all-important first Allied effort against the Axis.

Thus another important decision taken at Casablanca had a major bearing on Eisenhower. Brooke's utter lack of confidence in Eisenhower as a commander prompted him to mastermind a second British triumph. The United States was cleverly outmaneuvered when Brooke orchestrated a committee system of commanders that placed experienced British officers in the positions of semi-independent commanders in chief for the Sicily operation, dubbed Operation Husky: Naval operations were placed under Admiral Cunningham, and the Allied air forces came under Air Chief Marshal Sir Arthur Tedder.

Although he had briefly considered moving Patton to Algiers to become his "Deputy Commander for Ground Forces," and utilizing "his great mental and physical energy in helping me through a critical period," the quid pro quo of Casablanca was American acceptance of a British suggestion (originated by Brooke and put to Roosevelt personally by Churchill) that Eisenhower ought to appoint Gen. Sir Harold R. L. G. Alexander his deputy.[38] Alexander, then in Cairo serving as commander in chief of British Middle East forces, was one of Britain's most experienced and acclaimed soldiers. His appointment to take command of the faltering ground campaign in Tunisia resulted in the creation of the Eighteenth Army Group, which consolidated all Allied forces under a single commander.

The plan to utilize Patton thus died when Marshall cabled Eisenhower, ALEXANDER WILL BE YOUR MAN WHEN BRITISH EIGHTH ARMY JOINS YOU AFTER [CAPTURING] TRIPOLI."[39] Eisenhower retained Patton in Morocco to plan the American component of the invasion of Sicily. Patton was pleased to be off the hook; he wanted nothing more than to lead troops in battle, not play second fiddle in AFHQ.

Brooke was particularly pleased over Alexander's appointment, which "could not help flattering and pleasing the Americans in so far that we were placing our senior and experienced commander to function under their commander who had no war experience. We were pushing Eisenhower up into the stratosphere and rarefied atmosphere of a Supreme Commander."[40]

Brooke's shrewd ploy effectively relegated Eisenhower to the position of a titular head of a committee, which exercised the real decision-making power. In practical terms it meant that all future operations in the Mediterranean would be British dominated. Should Eisenhower disagree and an impasse result, his resignation was not beyond the realm of possibility. In effect, Eisenhower commanded no one except rear area troops.

Eisenhower was on probation and knew full well the insecurity of his position, particularly as Alexander, who outranked him, would soon be commanding Allied ground forces. Nevertheless, "What weighed most heavily with Churchill and Roosevelt, aside from Marshall's persistent faith in Eisenhower," wrote Sherwood, "was the tremendous admiration and affection for him of the British officers who had served with him, most importantly Admiral Cunningham, a fighting sailor who was held in very high esteem by the two Naval Persons."[41]

Eisenhower readily embraced the new command arrangements, in particular the appointment of Alexander, whom he came to admire above all other British officers with whom he was associated during the war. However, Eisenhower had no intention of being anyone's patsy. About that time, for example, when he received an organizational directive from the Combined Chiefs that he believed impinged on his authority as supreme commander, Eisenhower exploded and drafted an extremely angry and intemperate reply that, in effect, told the Chiefs to mind their own business. It took all of Bedell Smith's powers of persuasion to get Eisenhower to moderate his answer.

Brooke's opinion of Eisenhower might have been more favorable had he ever experienced firsthand the depth of the fires that burned so deeply in the man in whom he had so little confidence. Eisenhower viewed his task as not merely an important and prestigious military assignment, but as a quest to vanquish by whatever means necessary a wicked empire he despised. It was no accident that his war memoir was later titled *Crusade in Europe*. To his mind, it was indeed nothing less than a great crusade against the greatest evil the world had ever known.

After Casablanca, Marshall visited Algiers to see for himself the problems facing Eisenhower. After inspecting rear-area service and supply units, Marshall came away so appalled at their sorry state of disorganization, poor training, and indiscipline that he instigated the relief of several senior officers as an object lesson that "drug store cowboys standing around" would not be tolerated. "The iron was not in their souls," he said of a mess so chaotic that Marshall feared a scandal would develop if it were not straightened out at once. "I found that Ike was almost in tears over the situation," and that Bedell Smith was too busy in Algiers establishing AFHQ to have done anything about the problem.[42]

Marshall was sufficiently concerned about Eisenhower, whose health and morale had taken a severe beating since Torch, that the chief of staff gave him an earful on the subject of command. After Eisenhower mentioned his uneasiness about a subordinate, "He turned to me to say slowly and emphatically, 'Eisenhower, there is one thing that you must understand clearly. Retention under your command of any American officer means to me that you are satisfied with his performance. Any man you deem unsatisfactory . . . you must re-assign . . . or send him home!' " Eisenhower was free to seek the services of or promotion of any individual he deemed worthy, for which Marshall would "pay attention to your recommendation only." Having reassured Eisenhower of his full backing, Marshall concluded with this word of warning: "This principle will apply to the letter, because I have no intention of ever giving you an alibi for failure on the excuse that I forced unsatisfactory subordinates [on you]. I hold you responsible."[43]

Marshall also counseled Eisenhower about letting himself be pushed around as a result of the committee system imposed upon him at Casablanca. "I believe that I have grasped your idea," he wrote a short time later, and "I will be constantly on my guard. . . ."[44]

On the basis of his visit it was clear to Marshall that Eisenhower was in over his head and not only needed all the help he could get, but that he was spending far too much time writing reports justifying his actions and attempting to deal with the Byzantine politics of French North Africa, and too little time commanding Torch. Marshall pointedly suggested that Eisenhower employ the services of a few officers he knew and trusted to act in the capacity of his eyes and ears. Eisenhower readily agreed and the sent the chief of staff a list of names in order of priority. Heading the list was the name of his West Point classmate, Maj. Gen. Omar N. Bradley. In late February, Marshall, true to his word proposed to send him Bradley. Delighted at the prospect of being reunited with his classmate, whom he had not seen since West Point, Eisenhower cabled Marshall that Bradley should arrive via the "first available air transport." Marshall's real intentions for Bradley's employment in North Africa were far different than Eisenhower's, however. "I wanted to use Bradley to straighten out this mess in the rear, but Ike sent Bradley up to the front, and then I sent [Maj.] Gen. [Harold R.] Bull but he too was sent up to the front."[45]

Before returning to Washington, Marshall, certain that Eisenhower would not heed him, took Butcher aside and in a fatherly way "ordered" him to take good care of his boss. "You must look after him. He is too valuable an officer to overwork himself. Make him relax," said Marshall, get him some exercise, and find a masseur to "do things that relax his mind and body. . . . He may think he has troubles so far, including Darlan, but he will have so many before this war is over that Darlan will be nothing."[46]

What Marshall saw was an Eisenhower who had visibly aged and gained weight since leaving London. He wryly acknowledged to Mamie that "at this rate I'll be something like the equivalent of 92 when I get back to the U.S. Maybe you'll have to meet me at the pier with crutches—or a litter."[47] Also cognizant of the toll his career had taken on Mamie, he wrote to P. A. Hodgson that he was proud of the manner in which she had borne the pressures of constant moves and his absence from her life. Beyond offering his praise and sympathy, he could only hope for the best and trust that their mutual friends would help fill the void.[48] Eisenhower wisely concluded that he was ruining his health, and began taking better care of himself and, in general, seemed more relaxed even as his troubles worsened.

Kay's frequent presence with Eisenhower had become the object of considerable gossip. By early 1943 Mamie was already hearing the name Kay Summersby all too regularly. Before long it had become a cross Mamie was obliged to bear. Photographs of her husband sometimes contained Kay in the background, and the very mention of her name became like an angry sore. Rumors about the two that began circulating in Washington increased even more Mamie's profound sense of isolation.

Then as now, Washington thrives on scandal and malicious gossip, the juicier the better. "Army cats of the worst sort, I know," wrote Eisenhower's postwar aide Kevin McCann, "surrounded her, each of them intent on sinking their teeth into . . . [Mamie's] heart."[49] While Mamie fully understood her husband's perpetual need for off-duty social diversion as a means of relieving the immense pressures placed on him, and had enough faith in their love to realize that it was unlikely there was a dalliance between the two, Mamie's pride and her lonely exile in Washington made Kay's growing presence in Ike's life, however innocent, all the more hurtful. Nor could she even acknowledge her critics, much less refute the gossip. As her granddaughter points out, "There is no doubt that she felt twinges of jealousy for *everyone* associated with Ike's 'official family.' But whatever her feelings, she kept her own counsel."[50]

Whenever Kay Summersby was mentioned in one of Mamie's letters, Ike was quick to pour cold water on any suggestion of impropriety. When *Life* magazine reported that Kay had been assigned to Eisenhower's HQ in Algiers, he felt obliged to acknowledge to Mamie the reasons for her presence and to deny anything untoward between them, pointing out that her principal motivation in serving in the Mediterranean was to be near to her lover, Dick Arnold, who was commanding an engineer battalion in Tunisia. "She is terribly in love with a young American Colonel and is to be married to him come June—assuming both are alive. I doubt *Life* told that. But I tell you only so that if anyone is banal and foolish enough to lift an eyebrow at an old duffer such as I am . . . you will know that I've no emotional involvements and will have none."[51]

Mamie was not gladdened by her husband's frankness and the long-distance debate continued, with Ike assuring her that Kay Summersby was nothing more than an important cog in his official life, and Mamie restraining her growing feelings of hurt. Throughout the remainder of the war both put a brave face on what had clearly become an area of dissent between them. Although Eisenhower's devotion to his family and his enormous emotional dependence on both Mamie and John were unquestioned, Kay Summersby remained a troubling presence.[52] While there is no evidence the two ever consummated a physical relationship, there was also no doubt that Eisenhower's attraction went beyond mere friendship.[53]

Kay became Eisenhower's regular driver not only in Algiers but on his trips to the front as well. The journey from Algiers to Constantine usually took eight hours. She found these occasions "sheer, unadulterated torture" and bluntly warned her VIP passenger, "If we're ever attacked, don't wait for me to open the door for you. It's every man for himself, then!"[54]

Whenever Eisenhower appeared in Constantine, Truscott became nervous for the safety of both and would breathe a sigh of relief when they departed for Algiers. On one occasion in February 1943, Eisenhower hastened to the front to assess the situation with Truscott in a convoy of open scout cars. He instructed Truscott to have his sedan and driver meet the convoy on the road to Constantine during the return trip, however, under the assumption that Eisenhower would not want his female driver placed at undue risk, Truscott issued instructions to leave Kay behind and have someone else drive the staff car forward. A visibly angry Eisenhower conveyed his displeasure to Truscott in no uncertain terms. "Miss Summersby was the only driver in whom General Eisenhower had complete confidence for black-out driving at night," wrote Truscott, the memory of his chief's displeasure still vivid years later.[55]

Eisenhower's responsibilities also included those of commanding general of all U.S. rear-area service, supply, and headquarters troops in North Africa, a task he delegated to his old friend Brig. Gen. (later Maj. Gen.) Everett S. Hughes, whom he summoned from England.[56] Since the 1920s Hughes had been one of Eisenhower's closest friends and confidants, and a regular social companion. Hughes, who agreed with the criticism that Eisenhower was too pro-British, kept a near-illegible diary filled with juicy tidbits of gossip and observations about his boss, Kay Summersby, Patton (also a close friend and West Point classmate), and others. What Eisenhower never knew was that most of what he unburdened himself of usually ended up in Hughes's diary, in what were often unflattering comments. Of relations between Eisenhower and the winsome Kay Summersby, Hughes wrote, "Discussed Kay [with Ike]. I don't know if Ike is alibi-ing or not. Says he wants to hold her hand, accompanies her to house, doesn't sleep with her. He doth protest too much, especially in view of the gal's reputation in London. . . . Maybe Kay will help Ike win the war."[57]

FDR delighted in gossip and, having met Kay in Algiers in 1943, was convinced she and Eisenhower were having an affair. "Roosevelt had come to the conclusion, he confided in [his daughter] Anna, that this attractive young British woman was sleeping with General Eisenhower!" What made the subject even more titillating was that Anna's brother, FDR, Jr., had fallen hard for Kay Summersby but nevertheless regarded her as unstable and "a bit of a psychopathic case."[58]

Since Torch it had become increasingly evident to Marshall that Eisenhower's job was being made more difficult by having to deal as a lieutenant general with British and French officers far senior to him. At Casablanca, Marshall sought to persuade Roosevelt to advance Eisenhower to four-star rank but ran into unexpected opposition when the president complained "that he would not promote Eisenhower until there was some damn good reason for doing it, that he was going to make it a rule that promotions should go to people who had done some fighting; that while Eisenhower had done a good job, he hadn't knocked the Germans out of Tunisia."[59]

While visiting Eisenhower in Algiers after Casablanca, Marshall revealed that he was recommending Ike's promotion to four-star general, itself an affirmation that his position as supreme commander was secure, at least for the moment. It took some persuasion by Marshall before Roosevelt agreed to submit his name, on February 11, 1943, to the Senate for promotion. Later that day the Senate ratified the president's nomination, thus making Eisenhower only the twelfth officer in U.S. history ever to attain four-star rank, joining such luminaries as Ulysses S. Grant, who had been the first.

In little more than sixteen months, Eisenhower had catapulted from obscure colonel to four-star general with the awesome responsibility of winning (or losing) the war in the Mediterranean. Eisenhower noted wryly that he was still only a permanent lieutenant colonel in the Regular Army, and a short time later was required to present himself for a physical examination to qualify him for promotion to (permanent) full colonel.

When a friend praised his rapid rise to four stars, Eisenhower responded that the way down was a lot faster. When asked what he would do in that event, Eisenhower drew a cartoon of a man sitting on a riverbank with a fishing pole. The news was announced on the BBC, but Eisenhower was unaware of his promotion until Butcher verified its authenticity and offered his hand in congratulations. Instead of showing his pleasure, Eisenhower erupted: "I'm made a full general, the tops in my profession, and I'm not told officially." Complaining that "maybe it isn't true," Eisenhower at last accepted the news when he was handed a teletype from Mamie that read: "Congratulations on your fourth star." At last "he believed it," wrote Butcher, "but was still grousing because he hadn't been informed officially." When the import of having attained such a lofty height sank in, Eisenhower assembled his entire household staff and promoted them one grade on the spot. That evening Ike, Butcher, and Everett Hughes celebrated with toasts while the new general sang the lyrics to his favorite song as "One Dozen Roses" played on the phonograph. "He sang all the words and let out all the stops. . . . Mamie's ears must have burned," noted Butcher.[60]

Although his staff toasted him, fair-weather "friends" he never knew he had suddenly emerged to congratulate him, ask for favors and autographed photos, and hint at promotions and assignments. The elation was soon tarnished when his wife appeared to take no further notice of his promotion, and his son ignored it entirely. When he had received no letter from Mamie after two weeks, Eisenhower plaintively wrote, "I am curious to learn how it struck you."[61] After receiving a letter from John that failed to mention his promotion he wrote, "You congratulated me, at least feebly, on being a Lieutenant General; but you paid not the slightest attention to the fact that I finally got my fourth star. I do not mind confessing that I really got a laugh out of it because I have had so many messages of congratulations that I suppose I just naturally expected you to fall in line with the rest." Lightheartedly he concealed his hurt feelings by rationalizing that "you are the only one that had the sense to see that it doesn't amount to a tinker's damn in the winning of this war—and that is all that concerns me."[62] None of which was true: What his wife and son thought mattered a very great deal. There was, however, no time to savor the honor.

33.

"Ikus Africanus"

Sometimes I get so impatient that I want to . . . grab a rifle myself and start fighting Germans.

In February 1943 the war in Tunisia resumed. Von Arnim's Fifth Panzer Army had attacked and captured the Faid Pass at the end of January, and all of the eastern passes leading to central and western Tunisia were under Axis control. With the winter rains nearly over, the Germans took the initiative to strike a powerful counterblow first. Local indications pointed to a tiny speck on the map called Sidi Bou Zid as the next target. However, on the basis of German communications intercepted by the Ultra code-breakers at Bletchley Park, near London, the AFHQ intelligence officer (G-2), Brig. E. E. Mockler-Ferryman, predicted that Rommel was incapable of moving the Afrika Korps into Tunisia and that von Arnim was preparing to attack farther north at Fondouk despite considerable visual evidence that tanks and troops were massing in and around the Faid Pass. Anderson responded by moving a brigade of the 1st Armored to Fondouk to backstop the British, thus further splitting the already fragmented U.S. II Corps.

Aware that their efforts had earned them a brief respite from the final confrontation with the Allies, Kesselring and Rommel discerned an opportunity to split the Allied front, destroy the inexperienced American corps defending southern Tunisia, and threaten the overextended Allied lines of communication from Algeria. The more conservative von Arnim preferred to limit his army to a series of spoiling attacks, leaving Rommel the responsibility for halting the advance of Montgomery's Eighth Army into Tunisia. Unable to reconcile the conflicting views of his quarrelsome generals, Kesselring permitted each to conduct separate offensives. Fifth Panzer Army would attack the fragmented French and American forces guarding the southern flank of the Allied front, while Rommel's Afrika Korps would hit at Gafsa and thrust northward.

Fredendall's corps was already thinly deployed across a large area and vulnerable to attack by superior Axis forces. Contrary to Eisenhower's orders, which called for a large mobile reserve to be deployed behind a reconnaissance and screening force, "American infantry had been lumped on isolated djebels [hills] along the line and mobile reserves were scattered in bits and pieces along the line," the very same unsound dispositions that had been the bane of the British Eighth Army. To make matters worse, the U.S. 1st Armored Division commander, Orlando Ward, was left with few troops to command after Fredendall fractured the chain of command by ordering one of his brigade commanders, Brig. Gen. Paul Robinett, to report directly to him. The stage was set for disaster, which was not long in coming.

Eisenhower's eagerness to resume the offensive in Tunisia grew with each passing day. The extent of his burning desire to win and his even deeper hatred of his enemy and all they stood for was rarely seen except by his intimates. "Sometimes I get so impatient," he wrote to Joseph McNarney, "that I want to run up to Medjez-el-Bab, grab a rifle myself and start fighting Germans."[1] Nor was Eisenhower even remotely satisfied with his status. He had come to North Africa to be a fighting commander, not a rear area desk jockey issuing orders from Algiers.

Eisenhower's dilemma was that neither he nor his Allied force in Tunisia was prepared to fight anyone. His problems multiplied because Fredendall remained in command of II Corps long after it was glaringly obvious that he was a liability and must be replaced. II Corps headquarters was located in an enormous underground bunker, honeycombed with tunnels, some sixty-five miles behind the front lines, near Tebessa. A battalion of combat engineers had spent valuable weeks constructing this grotesque monument to a spineless commander when their skills were urgently needed elsewhere. Fredendall exemplified the low British opinion of American leadership and fighting ability. He was, wrote a British combat general, "a prime specimen of the traditional over-ripe, over-bearing and explosive senior officer in whom the caricaturists have always delighted."[2]

Before Eisenhower visited the II Corps command post on February 13, he had been warned what to expect by Truscott. Nevertheless he was merely the latest appalled visitor to emerge from Fredendall's bunker, which was called a variety of snide nicknames, among them "Shangri-la, a million miles from nowhere."[3] The depressing evidence and Eisenhower's instincts all pointed to an immediate need to replace Fredendall. Eisenhower's inaction was in direct contrast to his bravado two weeks earlier when he had proclaimed to Tom Handy that he "would ruthlessly eliminate any man who violates my instructions and my convictions . . . in this theater."[4] He later gratuitously counseled Patton and Bradley that they must be tough and cold-bloodedly eliminate unfit officers. Failing to practice what he preached, a mere eleven days after his visit to Fredendall, Eisenhower wrote to Gee Gerow, then commanding the 29th Division in

Scotland, "You must be tough . . . [on] the lazy, the slothful, the indifferent or the complacent. Get rid of them. . . . For God's sake, don't keep anybody around that you say to yourself 'He may get by'—He won't. Throw him out."[5]

That night Eisenhower inspected U.S. troops of the 1st Armored Division at Sbeitla and Sidi Bou Zid. He arrived in a vile mood and nothing he observed reassured him. Poor deployment, inadequate communications, a muddled chain of command within the division, and a defensive line stretched dangerously thin were all harbingers of what was to follow.

Shortly after midnight, at Sidi Bou Zid, Eisenhower's spirits rose momentarily as he silently observed an infantry company commander address his men:

There was no outward stamp of piety on this officer but his words moved me as deeply as any I have ever heard. "Almighty God, as we prepare [for] . . . action from which some of us may not return, we humbly place our faith and trust in Thee. We do not pray for victory, nor even for our individual safety. But we pray for help that none of us may let a comrade down—that each of us may do his duty to himself, his comrades and his country, and so be worthy of our American heritage." I walked away with tears in my eyes, dropping into the sand.[6]

Eisenhower used the occasion to engage in his long-standing habit of seeking solitude. For a few brief moments he found surprisingly peaceful contemplation in the ominously quiet moonlit desert. In the distance was the Faid Pass, where there was no sign of enemy activity. Gen. Matthew B. Ridgway would later describe "the strange exhilaration that grips a man when he knows that somewhere out in the distance hostile eyes are watching."[7]

Eisenhower had barely returned from Sidi Bou Zid when two of von Arnim's veteran panzer divisions attacked from the Faid Pass and the passes to the south. American units were overwhelmed "one packet at a time," Eisenhower later wrote in his diary, his memories of the place still vivid.[8] Unable to contain Arnim's powerful forces or to reinforce in time, Sidi Bou Zid quickly turned into a first-class military disaster as the American positions were surrounded, attacked, and eventually overrun. A colonel reporting that the front had cracked and that GIs could be seen abandoning the battlefield was disbelieved and told that they were merely "shifting positions." The officer retorted, "I know panic when I see it." Five days later, from the vicinity of Gafsa, a German-Italian battle group of Rommel's Afrika Korps advanced with little opposition and attacked U.S. forces defending the Kasserine Pass, with equally grave consequences. The American commander had failed to fortify the commanding terrain of the hillsides (which were taken quickly) but instead had deployed his troops across the valley floor "as if to halt a herd of cattle."[9] American losses were more than six thousand killed and wounded and three thousand more missing, most of them captured. At the front the debacle was seen by many as far more than merely inexperienced troops failing against veteran soldiers. "To some of us, at least," wrote Brigadier General Robinett, "a better explanation might have been green commanders and obsolete equipment."[10]

The failures of American leadership began with Eisenhower himself, who continued to exhibit his uncertainties and inexperience of high command, manifested by a tendency to interfere on the battlefield and in his hesitation to redress the growing problems within II Corps. "Eisenhower's willingness to interfere in the affairs of his subordinates," observes Stephen Ambrose, "ill became a man who often waxed eloquent on the subject of the sanctity of unity of command and the chain of command; his violation of his own principles was a reflection of his lack of confidence in Fredendall, whom he was either unwilling or afraid to remove."[11]

Not only was the U.S. Army humiliated in its first major test of the war, but "To the American people the event was incredible. It shook the foundations of their faith, extinguished the glowing excitement that anticipated quick victory, and, worst of all, raised doubt that the righteous necessarily triumphed."[12] Headlines across the United States searched for answers and questioned if "our boys" were equal to the task. The British pointed to American inexperience and leadership at Kasserine as affirmation of the unpreparedness of the U.S. Army to fight a first-class foe. It also left American commanders with the problem of restoring the confidence of their British ally and the shattered morale of their troops. The outcome would have been worse but for damaging blunders by both Rommel and von Arnim, which cost the Germans a strategic success and resulted in their withdrawal after what would prove to be a Pyrrhic victory.

Eisenhower compounded his own problems by permitting the inter-Allied squabbling to persist. Sidi Bou Zid and Kasserine struck Eisenhower like a hammer blow, but not so the inept Fredendall, who refused to accept blame for Kasserine, placing it instead on Anderson and Ward, whose relief he demanded. Eisenhower ignored Fredendall's absurd assertions. Nevertheless what stung badly was that "at the crucial moment, when Rommel was at his most vulnerable, he had failed to galvanize his commanders, which allowed Rommel to get away. Kasserine was Eisenhower's first real battle; taking it all in, his performance was miserable. Only American firepower, and German shortages, had saved him from a humiliating defeat."[13] The only faintly positive postscript to this fiasco came from Rommel, who was not deceived by the poor American performance and believed that, once matured by combat, the U.S. Army would prove a formidable foe.[14]

After Kasserine, British Tommies derisively sang "How Green Was My Ally" and snidely alluded to the American as "our Italians."[15] In turn there was bitter resentment among American troops of the British, in part, thought Drew Middleton, because "[a]rmies never learn from other armies. They have to learn by themselves, and a lot of the tactics that we used were those the British had used disastrously two years earlier and discarded."[16] Butcher put it more bluntly: "The outstanding fact to me is that the proud and cocky Americans today stand humiliated by one of the greatest defeats in our history. . . . Fortunately, this is being followed by a determination to profit by our mistakes."[17]

An inescapable conclusion after Sidi Bou Zid and Kasserine was that, had the arguments of Marshall and Eisenhower for Sledgehammer prevailed in 1942, an even greater disaster would have occurred. Notes historian Charles B. MacDonald, "Americans could be grateful in the end for a Winston Churchill who saw that they got a tryout on the brown land of North Africa rather than a disastrous opening performance on the green shores of France."[18] Omar Bradley came to the same conclusion, agreeing with Brooke's assessment that had the battlefield education of the U.S. Army taken place in France, it would have "resulted in an unthinkable disaster."[19]

When Eisenhower returned to Algiers, Mickey McKeogh had never seen his boss more depressed. Occasionally Eisenhower liked to sit at the piano and bang out "Chopsticks." That night he sat glumly at the piano in his villa slowly picking out a tune that McKeogh recognized as "Taps." "I don't think I ever saw him lower."[20] Reporting to Marshall, Eisenhower emphasized the urgency of replacing lost and captured equipment and the need for a change of attitude. Kasserine, he said, had been a reality check; "all of our people from the very highest to the very lowest have learned that this is not a child's game . . . the troops are in good heart . . . they are [also] now mad and ready to fight."[21]

It is axiomatic that after a military debacle someone has to pay. In the wake of Sidi Bou Zid and Kasserine, Eisenhower—concluding that the inexperienced Mockler-Ferryman had unrealistically overrelied on Ultra without independent confirmation—sacked him.[22] Although Mockler-Ferryman clearly bore a measure of responsibility, he alone cannot be held accountable for the poor tactics, the sheer command disarray, or the unsound dispositions of the Allied force in Tunisia.

The assessments of what went wrong at Sidi Bou Zid and Kasserine were cruel object lessons to those (and they were many) who misunderstood the difficulty of defeating the German army on the battlefield. The warnings of Waters, Arnold, and others had come shockingly true. Yet as late as February 23 Eisenhower was still refusing to acknowledge that Fredendall had lost control of his command, and failed to act on the grounds that to relieve a commander in the midst of battle would be inappropriate.[23]

Instead, to help right a situation spinning out of control in Tunisia, Eisenhower summoned from Morocco Maj. Gen. Ernest N. Harmon, a tough, outspoken tank commander, who was training the 2nd Armored Division for the invasion of Sicily. When Harmon reported to Eisenhower on the afternoon of February 21, he had no idea why he was there but quickly discerned that "Ike's encouraging and magnetic grin was not much in evidence." Sketching out the problems in Tunisia, Eisenhower explained that Fredendall was demanding Ward's relief and appeared to have lost control of II Corps, but seemed uncertain what he wanted Harmon to do. Finally Harmon was told, "I was to take over command of either the II Corps or of the First Armored, whichever I thought necessary. To my astonishment I blurted out, 'Well, make up your mind, Ike, I can't do both.' " Eisenhower replied that he simply didn't know what had to be done. " 'I'm going to send you as deputy corps commander. Your first job is to do the best you can to help Fredendall restore the situation. Then you will report direct to me whether you should relieve Ward or Fredendall.' " Eisenhower's orders were, in effect, a carte blanche to help reverse the situation by any means necessary. Exhausted, Harmon and his aide repaired to a nearby hotel to snatch a few hours' sleep. At two o'clock the following morning they were awakened by Eisenhower and Butcher, who helped them dress. "Ike helped me lace up my combat boots," an amazed Harmon wrote.[24]

At 3:00 A.M. on February 22 Eisenhower, Butcher, and Harmon set out for Constantine, where Eisenhower was to be briefed on the Tunisian situation. At the wheel was Kay Summersby, who (said Harmon) was "fearless, and she handled an automobile over a bad highway better than any man in my whole division." Harmon found confusion in Fredendall's command post: Clearly demoralized, Fredendall willingly turned over the running of the battle to an astonished Harmon, and took to his bed in one of the most bizarre episodes in American military history.

The spectacle of a commander willingly turning over the conduct of a crucial battle to an outsider while still remaining in nominal command was as unprecedented as it was disgraceful. Fredendall was guilty of the worst sin a commander can commit: cowardice. Not only willing but seemingly eager to shed his responsibility, Fredendall remained in his bunker and took no active role in the rapidly deteriorating situation at the front, leaving Harmon as the de facto corps commander. Harmon's firm leadership was a key factor in stabilizing the U.S. front during the critical days after Rommel's breakthrough at the Kasserine Pass, convincing proof of the intangible but pivotal importance of strong leadership—a trait that Fredendall sorely lacked.

American and British troops weakened the German offensive at Thala, which was enough to convince Rommel to call off his offensive and withdraw.

Other than the havoc Rommel had wreaked on II Corps (and on the American psyche), the Axis offensive was ultimately inconsequential. When Harmon reported back to Fredendall after the battle, he again found him in bed, "showing some effects of several helpings of whiskey."

Harmon reported his findings to Eisenhower on March 1, and they were unequivocal. When Eisenhower asked him, "Well, what do you think of Fredendall?" Harmon bluntly replied, "He's no damned good. You ought to get rid of him." Eisenhower immediately offered the command of II Corps to Harmon, who refused, saying he could not accept the position after recommending the relief of its commander.[25]

Soon after Alexander arrived for duty as the new Allied ground commander, he too visited Fredendall and had found him "utterly shaken" and with "no ideas . . . to improve the situation." When asked his opinion by Eisenhower, Alexander replied diplomatically, "I'm sure you must have better men than that."[26] Privately, Alexander was shocked and disgusted.

After the candid assessments offered by Alexander, Harmon, Anderson, Truscott, and others, Eisenhower belatedly acted to relieve Fredendall on March 5, 1943.[27] Eisenhower asked Mark Clark to replace Fredendall and assume command of II Corps, but Clark refused, noting that he was already an army commander and that taking over a corps was tantamount to a demotion. Although he camouflaged his anger, Eisenhower was infuriated with his longtime friend, believing that Clark had put his own personal desires over duty, an unforgivable sin in Eisenhower's book. His indignation was still evident in June 1943, when, in a private assessment of Clark, he pointedly characterized his friend's refusal as "a bad mistake."[28]

However, something had to be done—and done fast—before the II Corps situation in Tunisia got entirely out of hand. The growing estrangement between Eisenhower and Clark triggered an immediate summons for Patton to help pull U.S. chestnuts from the fire. Along with the arrival of Omar Bradley, Eisenhower's decision to call on Patton, taken three weeks after it was clear that he had lost all confidence in Fredendall, may well have saved his job.

During a brief stopover at Maison Blanche airfield outside Algiers, Patton conferred for a half hour on the tarmac with both Eisenhower and Bedell Smith before flying on to Constantine to meet with Alexander. The flimsy "official" grounds for the changeover was "that it was primarily a tank show," which Patton was better equipped to direct. Patton thought that Eisenhower seemed obsessive as he hammered "that criticism of the British must stop. I fear he has sold his soul to the devil on 'Cooperation,' which I think means we are pulling the chestnuts for our noble allies," wrote Patton in his diary. The meeting was primarily a lecture by Eisenhower, who reversed the guidance he had given Fredendall by instructing Patton to control the battle from the corps command post. Harry Butcher witnessed the meeting and recorded that Patton, emotional and embittered over the capture of his son-in-law at Sidi Bou Zid, "damned the Germans so violently and emotionally that tears came to his eyes three times. . . . Now he has the opportunity to chase Rommel to his heart's content." Eisenhower also warned Patton about his reckless disregard for his own safety: "He doesn't need to prove his courage. General Ike wants him as a corps commander, not as a casualty."[29] Eisenhower also instructed Patton to be "cold-blooded" about getting rid of inefficient officers, which—given his failure to sack Fredendall earlier—was paradoxical.

When Patton arrived to assume command of II Corps on March 6, he was surprised to find Omar Bradley present in Fredendall's CP. Eisenhower had sent him to II Corps as his "personal observer" a week earlier, where he received an extremely hostile reception from Fredendall, who banished him to a dingy, windowless, filthy hotel nearby. Although flattered that Eisenhower had asked for him by name, Bradley disliked being assigned a duty that gave him no authority and no demonstrable role other than that of adviser. Bradley informed Patton that American problems in northwestern Africa were not limited to II Corps; there was a lack of urgency that went as high as Eisenhower, who was, he thought, strangely unconcerned about the outcome of the campaign. Bradley's ambiguous status quickly ended when Patton, unlike Fredendall, would not tolerate "one of Ike's goddamn spies" in his command, and easily persuaded Bedell Smith to assign Bradley to the position of deputy corps commander.

Alexander's first impression of his new command was, not surprisingly, dismay at the muddled command setup and the utter lack of cohesion on the battlefield. Although Anderson's problems were mostly Eisenhower's fault, Alexander was so unimpressed by the Scot that he would have relieved him had Lt. Gen. Oliver Leese, a corps commander in the Eighth Army, been available. What concerned Alexander more, however, was his perception of American fighting ability. To Brooke he wrote glumly that the U.S. Army in Tunisia was "soft, green and quite untrained. Is it surprising then that they lack the will to fight. . . . There is no doubt that they have little hatred for the Germans and Italians and show no eagerness to get in and kill them . . . unless we can do something about it, the American Army in the European theatre of operations will be quite useless and play no useful part whatsoever." Of more immediate concern to Alexander was the urgent need for a rapid improvement in their performance before the invasion of Sicily. "I have only the American 2d Corps. There are millions of them elsewhere who must be living in a fool's paradise. If this handful of Divisions here are their best, the value of the remainder may be imagined."[30] Alexander discreetly reported his findings to Eisenhower, noting that although American troops were inexperienced in battle, they should soon be the equal of any fighting soldiers in the world. Left unspoken was Alexander's real meaning: In his opinion the American fighting elements in Tunisia, as exemplified by Fredendall, were rank amateurs in the art of war.

Equally dismaying, the obvious problems of training and leadership made it evident that unless there was quick and decisive action, the possibility of strategic defeat loomed large. Of even greater harm was the impact of Kasserine on Anglo-American relations. The British viewed Kasserine as irrefutable evidence that American fighting ability was mostly bravado. Although Eisenhower attempted to put on a brave face in his communications to Marshall, the truth was that Kasserine and Sidi Bou Zid had left a bitter legacy. First impressions count, and it would take virtually the entire war to sway Alexander's poor opinion of American troops and their commanders.

Although he regarded Patton as a substantial improvement over Fredendall, Alexander remained skeptical of the future fighting ability of II Corps. In this he was soon proved mistaken, when II Corps flourished under Patton's whip hand. But the damage had been done, and even the significant American recovery came too late to change Alexander's mind. Nevertheless Alexander's presence was ample evidence of the need for a full-time land force commander and the futility of the half measures in effect before his arrival.

While Montgomery's Eighth Army hammered away at the Mareth Line (a prewar French defensive system in Southern Tunisia), Alexander launched the British First Army in a successful offensive against von Arnim's panzer army in northern Tunisia. Unwilling to entrust II Corps to a more meaningful mission, Alexander relegated Patton to a supporting role of attacking the Axis flank and drawing off Axis reserves that might otherwise interfere with Montgomery's offensive along the coastal plain toward Tunis, where Alexander intended to trap von Arnim's army between the British First and Eighth Armies.

Even with Patton and Bradley in subsidiary roles, the reversal of American fortunes during the final two months of the campaign was swift and dramatic. Although Patton's command of II Corps lasted a mere five weeks, it was sufficiently long for him to restore order and morale. Patton was exactly the right antidote to the inept Fredendall. "Patton pushed his men to fight and dress like the best soldiers in the world. Within days they knew they were led by a commander who would not let them fail."[31] In one of the outstanding leadership feats of the war, Patton and Bradley led II Corps to victory at El Guettar, and during the climactic battles of the campaign in the spring of 1943 the improvement in American performance was precisely what Rommel had predicted. By World War II standards El Guettar was a relatively minor engagement, but for the U.S. Army it was that one small but vital step in the maturation process that produces a battleworthy fighting force. In the process the reputations of Patton and Bradley as battlefield commanders soared. Still, American resentments lingered, based on a sense that many of their Anglo counterparts disdained them as "colonials" inexperienced in the higher art of war.

Since Kasserine, American commanders from Patton and Bradley on down had seethed with frustration over what they considered unfair British criticism, loose talk to war correspondents, and Eisenhower's order that there was to be no protesting of British leadership. Even the mild-mannered Bradley began to question the wisdom of Eisenhower's failure to restrain the British. When correspondents reported severe criticism of the U.S. 34th Division by a British corps commander who complained that they were "no good," the issue became yet another cause célèbre that further exacerbated Anglo-American discord at the top.[32] "No words can describe Patton's rage and fury at Ike," Bradley later wrote. Patton's purple prose in his diary reflected his frustration with Eisenhower. "God damn all British and all so-called Americans who have their legs pulled by them. I will bet that Ike does nothing about it. I would rather be commanded by an Arab. I think less than nothing of Arabs." A day later Patton was still seething that "Ike is more British than the British and is putty in their hands. Oh, God, for John J. Pershing."[33]

Bradley was no less irate, merely more circumspect in his private expressions. Patton's indignation was a microcosm of American disgust that, "after having spent thousands of casualties making a breakthrough, we are not allowed to exploit it. The excuse is that we might interfere with the Eighth Army. . . . It is an inspiring method of making war and shows rare qualities of leadership, and Ike falls for it."[34]

And while the observation—widely attributed to Clark—that "I was about to agree with Napoleon's conclusions that it is better to fight Allies than to be one of them" was excessively harsh, until the end of the war there were often rancorous differences of opinion between the two allies. The single most harmful factor that marred Anglo-American relations in both the Mediterranean and the European theater in 1944–45 remained the long-term damage done by the disastrous example of Fredendall's inept leadership of II Corps in Tunisia.

Bad feelings persisted, not only between the Allies but between the ground commanders and the air forces. American frustration at the paucity of close air support finally erupted in early April. Partly in frustration after the death of his aide at the hands of the Luftwaffe, Patton delivered a bombshell by appending a note to a routine situation report (sitrep) that read: "Total lack of air cover for our units has allowed German air force to operate almost at will." To emphasize the point, Patton took the unusual step of sending the sitrep over his personal signature.[35]

When it landed on the desk of the bullheaded commander of Allied tactical air forces in North Africa, Air Vice Marshal Arthur Coningham, the airman angrily retaliated by sending a provocative signal to every commander in the Mediterranean, sarcastically suggesting that the sitrep must be some-one's idea of an April Fool's Day joke, and that the real problem was that II Corps was not battleworthy.[36]

Coningham's message created an international incident. Eisenhower's chief airman, Air Chief Marshal Tedder, was handed a copy of the signal, thought it "ill-judged" and "dynamite" that "could well have led to a major crisis in Anglo-American relations." Moving quickly to defuse the situation, Tedder notified Eisenhower that he had ordered Coningham to cancel the signal and to apologize personally to Patton.

Eisenhower was so upset by this latest crisis that he nearly resigned. According to Tedder, Eisenhower actually drafted a cable to Marshall, saying that if he could not control his own subordinate commanders he had no business being the Allied commander in chief and "would ask to be relieved." Only timely intervention by Bedell Smith, who managed to convince his dis-traught boss that "the damage could be repaired," prevented Eisenhower from sending this ruinous cable to Marshall.[37]

Tedder and Spaatz did some hasty fence-mending by assuring Patton that Coningham would personally call on him to apologize. The Luftwaffe picked that precise moment to attack Patton's headquarters. Several Focke-Wulf 190 fighter-bombers strafed the street outside the building, firing their machine guns and dropping small bombs. "Tedder packed his pipe, looked up mis-chievously from the table and smiled. Tooey looked out the window . . . turned to Patton and shook his head. 'Now how in hell did you ever manage to stage that?'" Patton grinned and retorted, "I'll be damned if I know, but if I could find the sonsabitches who flew those planes I'd mail them each a medal."[38]

An epic showdown between two of the war's foremost prima donnas resulted in considerable shouting and finger-pointing before Coningham apologized. Patton demanded a cable "specifically retracting your remarks about the lack of battle-worthiness of our men," to be sent "to the same people to whom you sent the first message." Coningham's so-called apology was little more than a brief message that attempted to paint the incident as an error in transmission, a common ploy that Patton himself later used in Sicily.

Publicly, the contretemps had been resolved. Both Coningham and Patton swallowed their oversize egos to resolve what might easily have been the nastiest, most potentially damaging Anglo-American quarrel of the war, which could not have occurred at a more inopportune moment.

Yet, for all Eisenhower's talk of harmony and cooperation, the Anglo-American marriage was teetering on the brink of rebellion by the American ground commanders, who, like Patton and Clark, believed Eisenhower had sold them out to the British. Indeed, the souring relations between both par-ties threatened to poison the alliance at its most formative moment, and claim

Eisenhower as its best-known victim. Although heavy-handed, Patton's handling of the potentially explosive Coningham incident may have saved Eisenhower's job. At the very least, Patton converted the strong-willed Coningham into an uneasy ally in the war against their real enemy.

American success failed to impress Alexander, whose continued skepticism was reflected in his plan for the decisive battle of the Tunisian campaign, in which the British were to make the main effort, while II Corps was again relegated to a minor role of protecting the British flank. Eisenhower would not challenge Alexander's decision. Patton, however, did, wringing a grudging concession from Alexander that the role of II Corps be expanded. Even as he did so, Patton worried that his challenge of Alexander might bring about his relief by Eisenhower. However, an angry Marshall likewise challenged the insignificance of the U.S. role. The chief of staff bluntly cabled his dissatisfaction to Eisenhower that the menial tasks being given American troops on the battlefield were unacceptable.

The discontent was enough to deepen Eisenhower's mounting alarm over the U.S. role in Tunisia, and on April 14 he met with Alexander, Patton, and Bradley in an attempt to clear the air. The discussions were frank and centered on expanding the American troops' role to permit them to fight as a national entity. If he and Bradley were in full accord, as Eisenhower's diary suggests, their agreement was not shared by Patton, whose diary was a bitter diatribe of complaints that Eisenhower had never even mentioned his and Bradley's victory at El Guettar ("some leader"), and scorned Ike's "we are all allies" pitch. In a stunning turnabout, Eisenhower later criticized Patton for taking his orders about cooperation "so literally that they had been meek in acquiescing without argument to [Alexander's] orders from above." Having been sent two widely varying but well meaning sets of guidance by Eisenhower, Bradley and Patton both might have been forgiven for wondering precisely what it was their boss expected of them.

Bradley's postwar memoirs are scathingly critical of Eisenhower, and make clear his disgust with his superior's apparent favoritism toward the British. When Eisenhower wrote that as the new II Corps commander he must be "tough" and produce results, Bradley thought it so "patronizing" that he filed it without reply as "so much grist for the historians."[39]

Eisenhower, on the other hand, was thrilled to have Bradley. "He has been a godsend in every way," he wrote to Marshall.[40] Yet there is little evidence of warmth in what was primarily a professional relationship between the two West Point classmates. Since graduation Bradley's career had been unspectacular. Like Eisenhower, he had not served overseas during World War I. During the interwar years Bradley was among those who caught Marshall's eye at Fort Benning for his steady performance as an instructor in tactics and later as the head of the weapons department at the Infantry School. With

Marshall as his mentor, Bradley had by 1943 risen to the grade of major general and had briefly commanded a division stateside.

By Bradley's own admission he and Eisenhower had not been particularly close at West Point, had never served together since graduation, nor had their wives taken to each other during their brief encounters at class reunions or Army-Navy football games. Bradley was impressed by his classmate's warmth, maturity, and "first-class mind," but if Eisenhower thought he had a close friend in Bradley, he seems to have been mistaken. After the war they again had little to do with each other. After Eisenhower's death Bradley revealed, "I shared Patton's misgivings about Ike, though I was less harsh in my private judgments and never criticized him before others. Ike was too weak, much too prone to knuckle under to the British, often . . . at our expense." Bradley's harsh opinion of his superior extended to his generalship. He thought Eisenhower led an "extraordinarily charmed life," and had his position not been affirmed at Casablanca, thought he would have been sacked after Kasserine. Describing Eisenhower as a "political general of rare and valuable gifts . . . ," Bradley went on to say that "his African record clearly demonstrates [that] he did not know how to manage a battlefield."[41]

By mid-April Eisenhower decided that the situation in Tunisia was under control and that he could afford to send Patton back to Morocco to continue planning for Operation Husky, appointing Bradley to succeed him as II Corps commander. Patton not only favored Bradley but also recommended that Eisenhower designate II Corps the principal U.S. combat element for Sicily instead of another corps slated for the invasion, whose commander Patton did not know. "I've worked with you and have confidence in you," he told Bradley. Eisenhower agreed, and Maj. Gen. Ernest J. Dawley's VI Corps was shifted to Mark Clark's new Fifth Army.

For all his savage criticism of Eisenhower, Patton still esteemed him as a friend and found they had a great deal in common, including the need for toughness "to build and run an effective army." During one of their marathon nights of conversation in Algiers (on April 17), the two agreed that "utter ruthlessness, even to their best friends, was mandatory. Troops had a right to good leadership," with Patton observing that what the army required most was "bravery plus brains." A fascinated Harry Butcher observed this exchange and concluded that "both gave every exterior indication of toughness but actually were chicken-hearted underneath"—a reference to softheartedness, not cowardice. After receiving a congratulatory telegram from Marshall, Patton said, "I owe this to you, Ike." Eisenhower replied, "Like hell you do."[42]

Although Patton warmly praised Bradley in North Africa, the compliment was not returned. Bradley disliked Patton personally and professionally. The longer he served under Patton, the more Bradley came to detest him. Theirs was a relationship based in no small part on Bradley's jealousy, cloaked in the contempt of one rival for another. He loathed Patton's flamboyant style of command and was bewildered by his profanity and his erratic behavior. A teetotaling midwesterner from a frugal family background in which profanity and alcohol were forbidden, Bradley not only never understood the mercurial Patton but made no attempt to do so. Trained in the rigid doctrines of Fort Benning's Infantry School, Bradley was uncomfortable with men like Patton, who displayed independence and dash, instead preferring the company of more conservative infantrymen like himself, who thought in similar terms. Bradley recognized Patton's genius but regarded him as too obsessed with attainment of personal glory. In short, they were, as Martin Blumenson has written, World War II's "odd couple," and "their problem of accommodating their distinctly different styles and outlooks was a contributory cause of why the Allies faltered" during the latter stages of the Normandy campaign.[43] Beginning in North Africa and continuing to war's end, relations and problems between these two vastly different soldiers would both elate, enrage, and disenchant Eisenhower.

After Eisenhower suggested to Ernie Pyle that he ought to "go and discover Bradley," the famed war correspondent virtually canonized Bradley in his dispatches as the "G.I. General." Yet, just as Patton's private persona bore no relation to his public image, so did Bradley's, thanks to Pyle and New Yorker reporter A. J. Liebling. The latter wrote that, compared with Patton, Bradley "seemed a man of milk."[44] The public was fed the perception of a plain, soft-spoken general with whom the average civilian back home could readily identify. If truth is the first casualty of war, so it was with the image of Omar Bradley as a general of the masses, one that Bradley himself encouraged for the remainder of his life. The real Omar Bradley was rather narrow-minded and utterly intolerant of failure. Historian S. L. A. Marshall, no admirer of Patton, categorically asserts that Bradley "was played up by Ernie Pyle. . . . The GI's were not impressed with him. They scarcely knew him. He's not a flamboyant figure and he didn't get out much to the troops. And the idea that he was idolized by the average soldier is just rot."[45]

Rommel had been recalled to Germany by the time his Panzer Armee Afrika linked up with von Arnim's Fifth Panzer Army in early March 1943. This combined force was placed under the command of von Arnim and designated Army Group Afrika. Allied inexperience and miscalculations in North Africa were more than offset by the inconsistency of their adversary. With the air and sea-lanes firmly under their control and Ultra secretly providing advance information of their air and sea movements, Axis forces in Tunisia were slowly but surely strangled during the spring of 1943. The Luftwaffe in the Mediterranean was decimated, and Allied submarines and attack aircraft had a field day sinking Axis shipping. With their lifeline shut down and von Arnim's panzers starved of both fuel and ammunition, the end was inevitable. The final offensive in Tunisia saw II Corps play a key role in the entrapment and surrender of Army Group Afrika on May 8, 1943. While the British Eighth Army drove Arnim's army into the plain of Tunis like a herd of cattle, the U.S. II Corps was acquitting itself brilliantly, nowhere more so than on bloody Hill 609, a heavily defended major obstacle on the road to Bizerte, captured by Doc Ryder's 34th Division, which had been declared unfit a month earlier. When the U.S. 9th Division marched triumphantly into Bizerte on May 7, it marked the completion of a remarkable turnaround since the dismal days of February. The American GI had shown that he could fight with the best of them when properly led and supported.

The price was high. Allies losses in North Africa were more than 70,000 British, American, and French (including 10,290 killed, of whom 2,715 were American).[46] When the Tunisian campaign ended with the Allies in complete control of North Africa, it was also the turning point in the war, whereby they, not Hitler, would dictate the time and place of future engagements. Although Hitler dismissed the Axis effort in North Africa as a sideshow, the defeat of Army Group Afrika was the second disastrous setback of 1943 for Germany. Hitler's decision to fight for North Africa resulted in the loss of an entire army group of about 240,000 men, after von Arnim's army was ruthlessly abandoned and left to wither and die in the Allied trap after urgent appeals for food, fuel, and ammunition were ignored by Berlin. Germany could ill afford to lose more troops to a hopeless venture than had been lost at Stalingrad. "German generals bitterly called this strategic and avoidable debacle 'Tunisgrad.' "[47] As von Arnim was signaling that he and his army had fought to the bitter end, Alexander cabled Churchill, "Sir, it is my duty to report that the Tunisian campaign is over.... We are masters of the North African shores."[48] In his history of the war, Churchill wrote, "Henceforward ... the danger was not Destruction but Stalemate.... The hinge had turned."[49]

The Allied victory in Tunisia also marked the end of Eisenhower's apprenticeship in high command. The official U.S. historian wrote that the experience of Tunisia had prepared AFHQ (and, by extension, Eisenhower himself) for the future. "If the coalition, with the disappointments, frustrations, and recriminations inherent in such a union, could survive the initial and struggling phases, it seemed certain to remain effective as the war in the Mediterranean proceeded."[50]

A group of his West Point classmates stationed in the China-Burma-India (CBI) theater dubbed him "Ikus Africanus."[51] And, while the satisfactory end in Tunisia was widely acclaimed, Eisenhower's war in the Mediterranean was far from over.

34.

Monty and Alex

... the higher art of war is beyond him.
—MONTGOMERY, ON ALEXANDER

... he is unwise, I think, to take all the credit for
his great success as a commander entirely to himself.
—ALEXANDER, ON MONTGOMERY

As the war in the Mediterranean entered a new phase after Tunisia, Eisenhower found himself functioning as the only senior American officer in a sea of British admirals, generals, and airmen. Churchill's attitude toward Eisenhower suggested, wrote his son, John, "that he regarded Eisenhower as a sort of constitutional monarch, whose continuing position as Supreme Commander should be a cause for the Americans to be grateful" even though British commanders dominated every major level of command. It was all part of Churchill the master manipulator's shrewd attitude that kept the British in the driver's seat even though the chauffeur was an American. "If you treat Americans well," he said, "they always want to treat you better."[1] It may have been patronization at its worst, but it worked in the Mediterranean.

Eisenhower's relationships with his key subordinate commanders would spell the difference between success and failure. His most contentious relationship was destined to be with the man he had met and disliked at their first meeting the year before: Gen. Bernard Law Montgomery, now the commander of the famed British Eighth Army.

Like that of his adversary Erwin Rommel and his ally George S. Patton, Montgomery's reputation was exemplified by his forceful personality, a trait possessed by all successful battlefield commanders. The Tommies had a reassuring sense that their commanding general not only knew what he was doing but would look out for their welfare and—most important of all—their lives. Rommel, Patton, and Montgomery made such a deep impression on their men that they felt that all would be well as long as their commander led them. A British writer has described such men as follows: "Soldiers love a character, whether he happens to be their platoon commander, C.O., or commander-in-chief. Montgomery was a genuine character, a born exhibitionist with a sense of the dramatic and with tremendous confidence in himself."[2]

Fearless and occasionally foolhardy in his public and private utterances, Montgomery was thoroughly disliked by many of his contemporaries for the usual reasons: jealously and rivalry. However, right or wrong, Montgomery was scrupulously honest in his opinions, which, combined with his rasping personality, attracted legions of detractors, both during the war and since, especially some American historians, who have been unable or unwilling to judge him fairly. Yet, as was said of Adm. Ernie King's appointment by FDR, Montgomery was not picked for high command because he was pleasant or a gentleman. In fact, what separated Montgomery from his peers was that he was unafraid to be unpopular.[3] In short, neither Monty's personality nor his sexuality are the criteria by which he should have been judged—then or now.

He was a consummate professional soldier at a time when Britain was desperate for competent battlefield commanders, not chivalry. Indeed, one of the ills of the British army was that it was staffed with far too many "nice chaps." *No one* ever referred to Bernard Law Montgomery as a "nice chap."

Those who misjudged him on the basis of first impressions were soon disabused of their lapse, however. He exuded the air of authority characteristic of all great commanders.[4] Montgomery's most striking feature was his penetrating gray-blue eyes, which literally flashed with authority and determination. Montgomery's lack of physical presence was more than compensated for by the magnetism with which he dominated the British Eighth Army. Other than Brooke, whom he both respected and rather feared, no one intimidated Montgomery, not even Churchill, with whom he maintained a spirited professional relationship that was devoid of the warmth and intimacy the prime minister enjoyed with men like Eisenhower and Alexander. Thus, while Montgomery may have had Churchill's ear, he never seemed to have had his heart. Churchill once said of him that he was "indomitable in retreat; invincible in advance; insufferable in victory!"

Perhaps the most controversial of the Allied World War II battlefield generals, Montgomery became a lightning rod of controversy both for his perceived arrogance and, all too often, for simply being right. He was one of the few to recognize the strengths and weaknesses of the British army of World War II, which, as historian Sir Michael (Lord) Howard, a veteran of the desert war and holder of the Military Cross for valor, has observed, "was not very good."[5] During the interwar years its leadership had failed to develop a common doctrine of employment for the infantry, and its use of armor proved unimaginative and ineffective on the sands of the Libyan desert.

One historian has described the military differences between the United

States and Britain as unquestioned American experience and "institutional-ized amateurism that the British sometimes mistake for professionalism. The prewar British army was idea-resistant to a degree . . . and it had no George Marshall to weed out deadwood and nurture the gifted. The strategy of poking at the perimeter of Europe and hoping for the best was not sophisticated, it was merely the acceptance of the inability to do anything else."[6]

To the dismay of professionals like Brooke, the British army chain of command was rife with far too many "old boys," whose chief qualification for their rank and position was their social class rather than their proficiency as soldiers. The higher ranks of the British army were populated with senior officers Brooke wanted desperately to remove but could not, because there were no qualified men to replace them. As Noel (Lord) Annan notes, "The British officer between the wars was not the professional he is today. The Army provided him with a life in which hunting, shooting and playing games [were] almost considered to be part of his work. . . . He knew the points of a horse, not of a tank. He cared for his men, but his horizon rarely rose above the regimental mess."[7]

Moreover, too many of Britain's future generals had died as promising young officers during World War I, which had claimed the lives of a million men whose crosses filled the military cemeteries that proliferated in the war's aftermath. During the dark days in Britain after the humiliation of Dunkirk, Brooke lamented, "How poor we are in Army and Corps commanders. We ought to remove several but heaven knows where we shall find anything very much better."[8]

Like Patton and Eisenhower, an accomplished student of war, Montgom-ery spent the interwar years studying, writing, and preparing for the world war he too was convinced would one day occur. At first sight Montgomery neither inspired nor intimidated. Habitually dressed in a nondescript uniform of his own design, Montgomery's five-foot seven-inch frame, hawklike fea-tures, thinning hair, high-pitched voice, and—although he was born an Ul-sterman—English accent, all added to an impression far more reminiscent of a faceless civil servant than a general. Indeed, Omar Bradley's aide once described Montgomery, "with his corduroy trousers, his enormous loose-fitting gabardine coat and his beret," as resembling "a poorly tailored boh-emian painter."[9]

Like Eisenhower, Montgomery sprang from the relative obscurity of the middle ranks of the officer corps, and despite an impressive record during World War I, he too languished during the interwar years. In a tradition-filled army where being a "nice chap" was considered de rigueur, Montgom-ery wore his nonconformity as a badge of honor and refused to respect such constraints. New Zealand's Gen. Sir Bernard Freyberg, a holder of the Victoria Cross, who once called Montgomery a "little bastard," also proclaimed that "if Montgomery is a cad, it's a great pity that the British Army doesn't have a few more bounders."[10] Monty's character traits intensely annoyed the old guard of the British army, whose absurd class consciousness was exemplified by a remark by Field Marshal Lord Gort: "In dealing with him one must remember that he is not quite a gentleman."[11]

In the hidebound, elitist British army, Montgomery was the ultimate outsider, an antiauthoritarian black sheep in an exclusive old-boys' club where one's lineage and social standing counted for more than one's ability. His official biographer notes, "Monty's genius—as Rommel's—would be to see, instinctively and in a manner that had eluded the callous commanders of World War I, that great military leadership in a people's century *could* still be achieved, despite the mechanical, inhumane nature of 'total war.' "[12] Montgomery was the first British general openly to signal his rebellion and his disdain for membership in this exclusive club by his refusal to wear conventional military dress. What counted was only that his troops received his message loud and clear.

Possessed of a priceless asset in the same stubborn, bulldoglike traits as Churchill, Montgomery was rarely daunted—exactly what was needed in September 1942, when he assumed command of a beaten and dispirited Eighth Army, which had been pushed all over the Western Desert and humiliated by Rommel.

"The bad old days are over," he said. "A new era has dawned." Issuing perhaps his most famous order, Montgomery threw down the gauntlet by ordering all previous plans for retreat to be burned. "We will fight the enemy where we now stand; there will be no withdrawal and no surrender. If we cannot stay here alive, then let us stay here dead!" The impact was electric, his leadership unparalleled. His men willingly entrusted their lives to him. Consider this typical exchange between Monty and an infantry soldier: Asked what his most valuable possession was, he replied, "My rifle, Sir." "No, it isn't," said Monty. "It's your life, and I'm going to save it for you."[13]

It was his traits of outrageous behavior and showmanship that catapulted Montgomery to fame. Churchill had every reason to dislike Montgomery, who, like himself, was stubborn and opinionated, yet he not only condoned but encouraged individualism, which mirrored his own eccentric behavior. Once, when a critic complained that Montgomery was wearing unauthorized badges on his bush hat, Churchill retorted, "If I thought that badges would make my other generals as good as Monty I would order them all to wear badges."[14]

After the war Churchill took note of the acrimony directed at his former field marshal, much of it from within the British establishment, and said, "I know why you all hate him. Your are jealous: he is better than you are. Ask yourselves these questions. What is a general for? Answer: to win battles. Did he win them without much slaughter? Yes. So what are you grumbling about?"[15]

· · ·

The most significant difference between Eisenhower and Montgomery was what has been called Monty's fundamentalism. "Nothing would induce him to compromise between what he considered militarily sound and the politically desirable,"[16] whereas Eisenhower frequently sought compromise, if for no other reason than to meet the demands caused by having to answer to too many masters. What Montgomery saw as black and white was to Eisenhower multihued. Monty's candor and refusal to compromise—his unconcern with anything but what he deemed militarily sound—were both a strength and a source of friction with Eisenhower and others.

Montgomery liked Eisenhower personally, but regarded him professionally as "probably quite good on the political side . . . [but] he knows nothing whatever about how to make war or to fight battles; he should be kept away from all that business if we want to win this war."[17] In 1943 it is doubtful if Eisenhower fully appreciated Montgomery's matchless abilities as a military trainer, a trait he shared with Patton. Nor is it likely that he recognized that his affiliation with Montgomery was no more difficult than the Eighth Army commander's often contentious relationships with other British and Commonwealth officers. Thus the regrettable outcome of their early interchanges was that neither man ever really understood the other. Over time their differences would only intensify.

Historians of World War II have proved remarkably incapable of judging Montgomery on his merits. History records that most successful military commanders, from Alexander the Great to Napoleon, were ruthless bastards. Montgomery was merely the latest in this long line. He has been bashed and castigated with equal fervor by British and Americans unable to separate his professional virtues from his personal faults, of which there were indeed many. As biographer Nigel Hamilton writes, "The very virtues which gave his leadership its inspiring quality—absolute conviction, insistence on proper planning, ruthless professionalism—made him an infuriatingly opinionated and stubborn ally."[18] Historians Williamson Murray and Allan R. Millett have come the closest in recent years to an accurate assessment of the most controversial British soldier of the war. Describing him as "one of the great field commanders of World War II," they note, "He was not a nice person; dogged, conceited, vain, completely sure of his own abilities, and incapable of understanding other human beings, Montgomery also possessed the attributes of a great general . . . he was a first-class trainer; and he understood the mind and stomach of the common soldiers." Montgomery also understood better than any other that "He must fight his battles within the limitations imposed by the weaknesses of the forces under his command . . . he refused to fight the Germans in a war of mobility but instead forced them fight on his terms—with firepower and sheer numbers."[19]

. . .

From the outset Montgomery's relationship with Eisenhower was unpredictable. Both sprang from humble roots, but that was not enough for their relationship to ever have jelled. Fundamentally Eisenhower disliked Monty the person but respected him as a soldier. Typically, Montgomery found unique means of irritating Eisenhower. A case in point was the infamous B-17 incident. Montgomery was fond of betting small sums on practically anything. The unwary who visited his field headquarters invariably found their names in his betting book and their wallets open. Montgomery's best-known victim was Bedell Smith, who foolishly agreed to provide him with a B-17 Flying Fortress, complete with an American crew, if his Eighth Army captured Sfax by April 15, 1943. Sfax fell on April 10, and a joyful Montgomery cabled a mystified Eisenhower demanding immediate delivery in payment of Smith's bet, then sent a follow-up cable several hours later. Montgomery received not only his Flying Fortress but a blistering rebuke from Brooke, who had seen its negative impact on Anglo-American relations. Although Eisenhower never again brought up the matter after complaining to Brooke, the incident, which the CIGS described as "crass stupidity" in his diary, was the forerunner of future misunderstandings of a more serious nature.[20]

By contrast, the most admired of the British generals was Harold Alexander, who ranked as Eisenhower's favorite. Although many of the most illustrious names of World War II—Montgomery, Brooke, Auchinleck, Dill, Gort, and Alexander—had Ulster origins, it was Alexander alone who earned the distinction of becoming Churchill's favorite general, and won almost universal admiration and respect from the Americans. Even when they were angry with his blatant favoritism in Sicily, neither Patton nor Bradley lost their regard for the man best known as "Alex."

Why, then, did Eisenhower identify so closely with Alexander? Suddenly injected into the command of a British-dominated, class-conscious coalition, Eisenhower, a man from humble roots, found himself dealing with and bossing men who were the sons of aristocracy, of princes, earls, or barons. Eisenhower, the son of a working-class failure, was in awe of such men. It is no coincidence that the two men with whom Eisenhower maintained the closest, most intimate relations were the son of a prince (Mountbatten) and the son of an earl (Alexander), nor is it far-fetched to suggest that Eisenhower's compulsive need for comradeship invariably drew him to men like Mountbatten and Alexander. In his own way Eisenhower's behavior was consistent with that of a military monarch obliged to build bridges between British officers, many of whom scorned his inexperience, and American generals, not all of whom always found his exercise of command to their liking.

A professional soldier since the age of nineteen, Alexander had gained a well-deserved reputation for fearlessness in battle. In less than a year during World War I, he rose from platoon leader to battalion commander as one of the youngest lieutenant colonels in the army and—indisputably—the most highly regarded officer of his regiment, the Irish Guards. His success was based on his personal leadership on the battlefield rather than on brilliant planning, on personal example rather than on the execution of a well-thought-out strategy. Throughout his career Alexander had simply done what came naturally, with scant thought to the evolving role that an officer assumes as he ascends in rank. And, unlike Montgomery, Alexander personified what a successful British general was *supposed* to be.

In the Western Desert in 1942, Alex and Monty made an ideal pair. As Alexander's official biographer notes, "Montgomery was a General who must either be left unpinioned or his neck wrung."[21] Although Montgomery typically took full credit for his success in the desert, it was to Alexander's credit that he instinctively understood that giving his subordinate a long leash and letting him run was the best course of action. Although he privately resented it, Alexander was quite willing to cede the limelight to Monty: "Montgomery enjoyed adulation; Alexander was surprised and embarrassed by it."[22]

In retrospect Alexander's rise to fame and high command seemed inevitable, taking him from the sands of Dunkirk, where—as commander of the 1st Division of the British Expeditionary Force in 1940—he was the last Englishman to leave France, to Burma, the Middle East, and North Africa. The story is told that at Dunkirk, Alexander was building sand castles on the beach during the height of the German dive-bombing when an excited staff officer rushed up to report: "Our position is catastrophic," only to receive the reply "I'm sorry, I don't understand long words."[23]

Like Eisenhower, Alexander shunned the trappings of high command and seemed embarrassed when they were foisted on him. On one occasion he politely ordered the dismissal of a covey of motorcycle outriders, who were supposed to clear the road ahead for him, with the comment, "I have a marked objection to clearing my own troops off the road for me."[24] To his men Alex was a hero. His frequent and highly visible presence at the front sent a message to his troops that he too was prepared to share a common danger. "He not only commanded his men but represented them. He was one of them. . . . He came to inform and enquire and discuss, to encourage and to sympathize. One felt he was capable at any moment of changing places with a subaltern." Instead of a helmet Alexander deliberately wore his garrison gap with its prominent red band, which usually managed to draw enemy fire whenever he visited the front. *New York Times* correspondent C. L. Sulzberger once asked Alexander why, and learned that "he wanted the men to see that their commander went right up to the front line. He liked to advertise this fact with the red band—unlike our American theory under which officers wear helmets, both for safety and so that, at any distance, they are indistin-guishable from GIs."[25] Small wonder Eisenhower and Alexander liked and admired each other.

Still, the very traits that made Alexander a success were those that led to his greatest failing. His laid-back style of leadership by persuasion was designed to take advantage of his intuition for the art of the possible—for tactfully handling his subordinate generals in different ways, each designed to take advantage of that man's strengths and minimize his weaknesses. Yet this method had mixed results with strong-minded generals like Patton, Montgomery, and Clark, who were determined to prevail and often did so by taking advantage of his reluctance to impose his will.

The Americans with whom Alexander dealt universally liked him. But despite his outstanding record there were justifiably grave doubts about Alex-ander's ability to function as a high-level commander. His style of command was detached, lacking in the essentials of formulating command guidance, and often so vague in execution that his subordinate commanders were unclear as to his intentions. In short Alexander never fully grasped the reins of high command, and this deeply troubled his superiors. Maj. Gen. John P. Lucas—an American—may have said it best: "The last man who sees him will, I am afraid, get a 'yes.' "[26] Although Churchill "placed Alexander at the center of his Pantheon of heroes," a significant element of his appeal to Chur-chill lay in the fact that he was one of the few senior British officers who never challenged the prime minister, yet whose relations with Brooke, Tedder, Portal, and Montgomery were often adversarial.[27] Brooke privately questioned Alexander's fitness for high command during the Italian campaign, the sub-stance of which appeared after the war in Sir Arthur Bryant's two interna-tional bestsellers.

Alexander's biographer was equally candid. "He had great courage but not much daring . . . [he] depended on advice from very, very brilliant sub-ordinate generals who often disobeyed his orders, but brought it off! . . . He was an English country gentleman, almost uneducated, who never read a book or had any interest in the arts at all. . . . He had no politics. He wasn't inter-ested in the causes of war, or the cause of that particular war in which he was fighting."[28]

In short Alexander was an unfathomable enigma whose admirers ran the gamut from frontline soldiers, who loved him for his courage, to generals who served under him, and politicians, like Harold Macmillan, who consid-ered him "first class." Others, Brooke and Adm. Andrew Cunningham among them, saw an entirely different person, as did one of his best division com-manders, who wrote of him: "he is quite the least intelligent commander I have ever met in a high position. . . . I found that I could not talk to him for more than five minutes: whereas I can talk for hours to intelligent men.

Perhaps it is too harsh to say that he's bone from the neck up, but perhaps it isn't."[29]

Nor was Marshall among Alexander's admirers. Ever since Kasserine, Marshall had considered Alexander's attitude toward Americans patronizing. (In 1945 Churchill had to intervene to defuse a flare-up between the two.) The British attitude was disturbingly widespread and included King George VI, who once remarked to Marshall how good it was to have Eisenhower in nominal supreme command with Monty at his side.[30]

The line between leadership by persuasion and the abrogation of responsibility is thin, and even Eisenhower, who was in virtual awe of Alexander, occasionally discerned signs of his deficiencies as a commander. Before Operation Husky he observed in his diary his personal impressions of the senior Allied leaders. Of Alexander he observed that he suspected that "[a]t times he seems to alter his own plans and ideas merely to meet an objection or suggestion of a subordinate, so as to avoid direct command methods."[31]

The ultimate irony of Alexander's enormous popularity with Americans was that, in the end, he proved to be one of their biggest detractors over the course of the campaigns in North Africa, Sicily, and Italy.

Montgomery actually fared better. As Eisenhower said of him: "I personally think the only thing he needs is a strong immediate commander. . . . I have great confidence in him as a combat commander. . . . Like all other British officers, he has been most loyal—personally and officially—and has shown no disposition whatsoever to overstep the bounds imposed by allied unity of command."[32]

Other than the commonality of their Ulster origins and their nicknames, which brought instant recognition, Montgomery and Alexander could not have been more different: the patrician, aristocratic, but rather aloof Alex and the rebellious "colonial," whose practice of generalship was to banish anyone, regardless of his pedigree, if he failed to meet his exacting standards of leadership and ability. These two British generals would nevertheless, each in his own way, not only become essential players but also generate enormous problems for Eisenhower in the Allied campaigns in the Mediterranean and northwestern Europe.

35.

"What in Hell Does Eisenhower Command?"

Seldom in war has a major operation
been undertaken in such a fog of indecision,
confusion and conflicting plans.
— BRADLEY

I'm almost at my wit's end trying to solve
some of these knotty problems.
— EISENHOWER

Since Torch, Eisenhower had been swamped with letters from worried parents, schoolchildren, or those writing simply to offer their moral support. They came in every conceivable form, "written in everything from a sharecropper's scrawl to an executive's stiff but touching dictation." It was almost as if Eisenhower were a father figure to whom strangers confessed their most intimate feelings. Many requested autographed photos. He also received a flood of packages filled with everything from cigarettes, gloves, and socks to homemade fudge, cookies, and—once his pet likes had been publicized—pulp Westerns. Eisenhower had them sent to hospitals and rest centers and insisted that each and every letter and package be acknowledged, a task that required additional administrative manpower. One of Kay Summersby's jobs was answering mail and forging Ike's signature on letters and photos, a skill at which she became quite efficient.[1]

One of the messages was a brief telegram from MacArthur. Although he would never publicly admit it, Eisenhower craved recognition from his old chief for having risen from the position of MacArthur's principal "man Friday" to that of a successful supreme commander. Butcher later told David Eisenhower that victory in Tunisia had been "a supreme moment" for his grandfather, and that "he was afraid MacArthur would not notice."[2]

Eisenhower himself was ambivalent, his mind now focused on the forthcoming invasion of Sicily. "Ike's disposition does not permit relaxation. He scarcely ever has a feeling of self-satisfaction," wrote Butcher. His single concession was elation that he had accurately predicted the end of the campaign to Roosevelt and Marshall.[3]

Eisenhower's deep hatred of the Germans remained manifest by his refusal to meet with Arnim, who had been captured during the battle for Tunis. "Ike . . . does not trust his own reactions before a representative of the Prussian and Nazi regime."[4] To his new intelligence officer "Eisenhower snarled . . . 'the only German generals I'm interested in are the ones we haven't captured yet.' "[5] Patton was known for his bloodthirsty comments about killing his enemies, but although Eisenhower's were more private, it would sometimes have been difficult to tell them apart. "Nothing could please me quite as much as news of the killing of a lot of Japs!" Eisenhower wrote to a friend stationed in India.[6]

One of Eisenhower's burdens was the constant influx of generals and politicians for whom he was obliged to play the handmaiden. The pressures never let up. In one of his occasional letters to P. A. Hodgson, Eisenhower wrote, "When this war is over I am going to find the deepest hole there is in the United States, crawl in and pull it in after me. As an alternative, I am going to live on top of Pike's Peak or some other equally inaccessible place."[7]

Eisenhower rarely read his press clippings, but the famous temper erupted after reading a newspaper article critical of his mother's attendance at a Jehovah's Witness convention. Eisenhower's true feelings about the Jehovah's Witnesses boiled over in a fiery letter to his brother Arthur. He suggested that they were hypocrites for using his mother's presence to jump on

> the publicity bandwagon, even if that publicity is generated out of a circumstance which they publicly deplore . . . I doubt whether any of these people, with their academic or dogmatic hatred of war, detest it as much as I do. They probably have not seen bodies rotting on the ground and smelled the stench of decaying human flesh. They have not visited a field hospital crowded with the desperately wounded. But far above my hatred of war is the determination to smash every enemy of my country, especially Hitler and the Japs . . . my hatred of war will never equal my conviction that it is the duty of every one of us, civilian and soldier alike, to carry out the orders of our government. . . . Stephen Decatur told the whole story when he said, "Right or wrong, my country."[8]

Well-meaning people wrote to Eisenhower, sometimes via Marshall, with suggestions, some of them amusing. One, on learning that Eisenhower drank cold water with his meals, counseled that "many nations and armies have gone down to defeat on just such an insignificant point and we cannot afford to let a brilliant mind like Eisenhower's be hampered by his stomach."[9]

·   ·   ·

The notion that Eisenhower was an easy person to work for was largely a myth created by the press, which tended to portray him as a sort of Saint Patrick come to rid the world of the Axis. While he was often considerate of his staff, sometimes worrying unnecessarily about their personal welfare, working for Eisenhower was no picnic. His occasional short-tempered railings of frustration generally took place in private and were either aimed at or bounced off the ever-loyal Tex Lee, Commander Butcher, who "works like a dog to get a grin on my face," or other members of his personal staff. Whenever Eisenhower's normally sunny disposition turned into a black cloud, he would growl at his aides for the slightest indiscretion. In one of his periodic letters to Mamie, Butcher noted she ought to be glad "you are several thousand miles away where his growls don't bother."[10]

When Eisenhower erupted in public his tantrums were fearsome to behold, although he would usually later regret his lack of self-control. Incidents he deemed harmful to the smooth functioning of the Allied war machine drew special ire.

Most of his outbursts, however, were confined to the privacy of his diary, letters to Mamie, or remarks to Butcher, Hughes, Kay Summersby, or a handful of intimates, and were the only visible signs of the boiling cauldron behind the grin than few ever saw. Although Eisenhower went to great lengths to hide his emotions in public, they occasionally ran so deep that it was sometimes all he could do to control them—and his impatience.

Constantly surrounded by an entourage of aides and staff officers, Eisenhower had little opportunity for contemplation. The pressures of his duties and the incessant demands on his time were at times intolerable. Eisenhower longed for occasional solitude but seldom found time for such an indulgence. In May 1943, during the planning for Operation Husky, an important meeting was to take place one morning at Eisenhower's headquarters in Algiers, in which he knew he would be put on the spot by arguments from Churchill and a high-level British delegation. A West Point classmate, Col. Carl C. Bank, happened to be at AFHQ that day. With time on his hands, he

decided to take a walk and try to forget the looming combat assignment. I wandered down the Algerian streets toward the beach where American troops had made their initial landing. As I approached a deserted section of the beach I saw Ike seated on the wreckage of a small boat, facing out to sea. In his hand was a crusty, ripped canteen cover which had been half buried among the other military debris discarded on the sand. I stopped and watched Ike. He stared at the canteen cover for a long while, then looked out across the sea. Finally, he folded the cover carefully and placed it inside the boat, stood up, adjusted his cap firmly, and strode off toward his staff car which was parked up the beach.[11]

Reenergized, Eisenhower returned to the Hôtel St.-George. As he had at West Point, such private interludes enabled him to find an inner peace that somehow helped relieve the stress of his position.

As much as he detested being a desk-bound general, Eisenhower managed to lead by example, often small things few ever observed. Eisenhower's friend and classmate Joseph M. Swing, who later commanded the 11th Airborne Division in the Pacific, was a tough, hard-nosed paratrooper. Swing recalled learning a valuable lesson from Eisenhower in how to handle people. "Joe, I didn't learn how to command at Leavenworth or any other Army institution. And it isn't written in the book how to do it. But I've discovered you don't get far by just issuing orders. You've got to take into consideration the viewpoints of the nationalities concerned and try to solve problems through reasoning rather than by merely issuing commands."[12]

Among the many problems Eisenhower had to deal with in the spring and summer of 1943 was the endless labyrinth of French wartime politics that pitted de Gaulle and Giraud against each other for control of the Free French movement and the establishment of a provisional government, which de Gaulle was determined to head. Although an uneasy peace between the two had been brokered at Casablanca, the real issue had been the urgent need to bring about a common French front. De Gaulle's refusal to budge from his insistence that he and he alone should lead a Free French government nearly wrecked the conference before the Allies contrived a shotgun wedding of sorts, which signaled a unity more theoretical than real.[13]

De Gaulle had the full support of the fighting elements in Tunisia and was rapidly gaining support in Algiers as well. In June both parties met in Algiers and agreed to establish a joint French Committee of National Liberation (FNCL). However, within days of the FNCL compact, de Gaulle resigned, precipitating a crisis that Eisenhower believed threatened the success of Husky.

Like it or not, Eisenhower was immersed in the sinkhole of French politics. Fearful of possible civil war and the disruption of Husky, he found himself opposed to Roosevelt, who, not for the first time, permitted his abiding enmity toward de Gaulle to cloud reality and common sense. The president was determined to get rid of de Gaulle, a prospect Eisenhower found so appalling that he urged Marshall to dissuade Roosevelt from acting rashly at a critical time. Eisenhower needed de Gaulle's influence to keep the peace, and arranged a meeting between de Gaulle and Giraud. The three met at the Hôtel St.-George on June 19, with the hapless Giraud largely a spectator in a heavyweight contest. Eisenhower appealed to de Gaulle's sense of duty as a soldier to keep the status quo intact. Though the meeting changed no one's mind, it did establish a relationship of mutual respect between two proud soldiers, neither of whom had any inkling of their future roles on the world stage.

With only Roosevelt standing in his way, de Gaulle pressed for recognition of the FNCL as France's legitimate provisional government. Everyone else, from the more pragmatic Churchill to Eisenhower (and his two political advisers, Macmillan and Murphy), believed that recognition of the FNCL was in the best interest of the Allies, which of course meant that they supported de Gaulle. Eventually, after tortuous negotiations, Roosevelt was persuaded to recognize the FNCL, with de Gaulle as its undisputed head and Giraud in a largely figurehead role. It was an achievement for which Eisenhower deserved a measure of credit, for helping to bring it about and for steadfastly supporting it in the face of Roosevelt's intransigence. In a new role of general as diplomat, it was Eisenhower's first major triumph.[14]

The price of having a woman drive Eisenhower around North Africa along the narrow, crowded highways of Algeria and Tunisia were the inevitable whistles, catcalls, and lewd proposals. Kay was amused; Eisenhower was livid. But the biggest trouble with his fondness for Kay was that it was common knowledge, and their public appearances together merely fueled the rumors. Rude remarks about the two began appearing in Everett Hughes's gossipy diary, and before his death Bradley opined that he thought Eisenhower protested far too much over Kay Summersby in response to Mamie's searching questions about her husband's driver and her role in his life.[15]

In June, shortly before they were to have been married, Kay's intended, Col. Dick Arnold, was killed instantly in Tunisia, when another officer set off a trip wire during a mine-clearing operation. Eisenhower broke the news personally, and—if her alleged deathbed memoir is to be believed—held her in his arms and consoled her as she sobbed out her grief. Arnold's death left Kay Summersby devastated, which is not evident in *Past Forgetting*, in which she dismisses Arnold's death as the end of a wartime romance with a man she barely knew and had trouble even mourning.[16]

It was during the summer of 1943 that Kay Summersby claims they began a romance that included everything but sex. While it can legitimately be argued that Eisenhower's reputation was being protected by those who served him, all have vehemently denied that there was ever an affair between the two. Both Mickey McKeogh and Capt. Sue Sarafian Jehl,[17] Kay's wartime friend and roommate, vehemently rejected any notion of an affair. Of those in a position to know, the person closest to Kay Summersby was Anthea Gordon Saxe, an Englishwoman who was also a civilian driver in the Motor Transport Corps when they first met after Pearl Harbor. The two remained lifelong friends, and after Kay's death Saxe acted as the executor of her estate. Kay Summersby left no love letters from Eisenhower, and no evidence exists, beyond the fanciful allegations in a memoir she never lived to see published. Moreover, according to Saxe, Dick Arnold was no mere fling but a man with whom she was deeply in love. "After Dick died, she went into a deep depression. She felt dreadful. Everything was bleak and black." With Eisenhower's encouragement, she gradually overcame her grief, but "Richard

Arnold remained forever in her memory." To the end of her life, recounted Mrs. Saxe, Kay "never forgot Dick. To the day she died, she kept all the letters he ever wrote, all his pictures, everything."[18]

That Eisenhower was extremely fond of Kay Summersby and valued—even treasured—her company is beyond dispute, but it is improbable that this affinity ever developed into something deeper. Certainly Kay's presence was both reassuring and comforting to a man beset with endless problems and responsibilities. Nor did Eisenhower attempt to conceal his desire for her company, whether she was driving him, horseback riding with him, or relaxing in the informality of his quarters. Kay played the role of hostess, confidante, and adviser, the very ones Mamie herself would have filled had she been present. Eisenhower called her "Irish," and at times would scribble brief notes asking her to share tea or a meal, but never anything of an intimate nature.

By the summer of 1943, John Eisenhower notes, Mamie had begun "to realize that Dwight Eisenhower would no longer be her personal property."[19] Mamie's resentments were very real. Her frustration at being unable to share her husband's life translated into dislike and envy of any surrogate who was temporarily filling that void with the man around whom she had built her entire adult life. That it happened to be an intelligent, attractive woman merely added to Mamie's anguish—which she bore with stoicism; none of her friends had any inkling of her heartache.

Eisenhower was very much a creature of habit. He seemed to need a retinue of familiar faces with whom he was comfortable. Kay Summersby was by no means the only important person in his daily life. In their own way, Mickey McKeogh and Harry Butcher filled equally prominent roles.

Although she was well liked, Eisenhower's enlisted men occasionally found Kay's presence unsettling, particularly her habit of bossing them around. Mickey McKeogh described her as "nice, unmilitary, and very emotional," but at least once he complained to Eisenhower, who dismissed it with the comment, "Bear with her, she's not a well person." In Eisenhower's eyes there was little Kay could do wrong.[20]

After Dick Arnold's death, Mamie took note of gossip in Washington that his marital difficulties had "not been a pretty story." Whatever Arnold had done, Eisenhower replied, "here we considered him a valuable officer and a fine person." By now very much aware of Mamie's distress over Kay, he added, "Your letters often give me some hint of your loneliness, your bewilderment and your worries in carrying on your own part in this emergency. . . . Just please remember that no matter how short my notes I love you—I could never be in love with anyone else—and that you fill my thoughts and hopes for the future always. You never seem to comprehend how deeply I depend upon you and need you."[21]

Although Eisenhower would never have admitted it, his lonely job required considerable daily doses of the kind of reassurance that Mamie's quiet presence had been there to provide for him virtually all of his adult life. Men like Marshall and MacArthur may or may not have required such emotional support, but Eisenhower clearly did: "Like many another strong man with a weakness for which there is neither armor nor cure, he needed to see the sustaining reflection of himself that shines only in a woman's eyes," observes Geoffrey Perret.[22]

High command brings with it a constant and unwelcome accomplice. In perhaps the most revealing letter of the war, written at both the high and low points of his career, his promotion and the Sidi Bou Zid–Kasserine debacle, Eisenhower tried to explain to Mamie what his job meant:

> Loneliness is the inescapable lot of a man holding such a job. Subordinates can advise, urge, help, and pray—but only one man in his own mind and heart can decide, "Do we, or do we not?" The stakes are always high, and the penalties are expressed in terms of loss of life or major or minor disasters to the nation. No man can always be right. So the struggle is to do one's best, to keep the brain and conscience clear; never to be swayed by unworthy motives or inconsequential reasons, but . . . to do one's duty. It is not always easy.[23]

The invasion of Sicily was the most ambitious large-scale landing on a hostile shore ever attempted, and remains to this day the second largest amphibious operation in history, after the Normandy landings in June 1944. From the inception of Operation Husky as a strategic compromise at Casablanca, the planning that began in early February 1943 was plagued by interminable problems of organization and command at the very moment when the invasion commanders found themselves preoccupied with the faltering campaign in Tunisia. As the commander in chief of the ground forces, Alexander had the responsibility of developing the invasion plan. However, both he and Eisenhower became so involved with the problems in Tunisia that neither was able to give anything more than token attention to Husky, even though only a full-time commander could resolve a growing list of problems. From the outset the June timetable for the invasion decreed by Churchill and Roosevelt at Casablanca proved impossible to meet. Although five months seemed a sufficiently wide margin, the British official history notes that "brute facts were to show that it was narrow."[24]

The designated invasion commanders were Montgomery and Patton, whose I Armored Corps (located in Rabat, Morocco, and designated the Western Task Force) was the American invasion element. Only Montgomery, whose Eighth Army would form the (British) Eastern Task Force, had any early involvement or active interest in the planning of Husky.[25] To complicate matters, it was a nightmare to coordinate. Husky had to be planned in five separate locations: Washington, London, Algiers, Malta, and Tunisia.

The initial invasion plan called for a series of small amphibious landings, from D-Day to D+5, along the six-hundred-mile-coast of Sicily. When he first learned of it, Montgomery was horrified by the unwelcome reversion to the "penny-packet" tactics that had been so disastrously employed under his predecessor, Auchinleck, and in the early days of Tunisia by the Torch forces. Disparaging the entire Husky planning effort as "a hopeless mess" and "a dog's breakfast," with his typical candor, Montgomery repeatedly warned that unless a sensible plan were soon developed, the results would be calamitous.

The committee system imposed on Eisenhower by the British at Casablanca exacerbated the ever-widening divisions in what was an entirely British, internecine, and often acrimonious quarrel between the three force commanders.

After Tunisia, Allied operations in the Mediterranean were characterized by an unwillingness to assume any undue risk in military operations. Mounting evidence of Allied conservatism thoroughly displeased Churchill. After receiving a pessimistic signal from Eisenhower in April, which stated that the Husky planners feared failure if more than two German divisions were encountered in Sicily by the invaders, the prime minister scathingly replied that "these pusillanimous and defeatist doctrines . . . would make us the laughing stock of the world."[26]

Despite the conservative rhetoric, there is evidence that had he possessed the capability in May 1943, Eisenhower would have favored a quick, surprise strike against Sicily. However, with most of his combat troops either tied down in Tunisia or, in the case of the 45th Division, still in the United States, and lacking shipping, a bold operation was out of the question. "I am convinced that if I could undertake HUSKY today with only two divisions," he wrote to Marshall in mid-May, "I could gain a bridgehead and an advantage that would make the further conquest [of Sicily] a very simple affair."[27]

Instead, the planning impasse dragged on to the point that it took a calculated act of insubordination by Montgomery to bring about a compromise plan that everyone finally agreed on. In late April, frustrated by the inaction and deeply worried that the planning stalemate might not be broken in time for the invasion, Montgomery, at considerable risk to his reputation, deliberately precipitated a crisis by signaling Alexander that he intended to proceed on his own with planning for the employment of the entire Eighth Army in southeastern Sicily.

On May 2 Montgomery cornered Bedell Smith in the lavatory of AFHQ, where he outlined his proposed plan by blowing his breath on the mirror and insisted it be presented at once to Eisenhower. However ludicrous the setting, Montgomery's lavatory discussion with Smith actually broke the impasse. It was the only major operation of World War II in which a crucially important decision was orchestrated in an Algerian privy, adding yet another bizarre chapter to the story of the war in the Mediterranean.

Eisenhower had long favored a concentration of force in southeastern Sicily, thus Montgomery's plan was rapidly sold to the Allied chiefs, and although it did not endear him to his associates, there was general relief all around. Addressing his fellow commanders, Montgomery frankly admitted he could be a "tiresome person," but few quarreled with his logic. "I have seen so many mistakes made in this war, and so many disasters happen, that I am desperately anxious to try and see that we have no more."[28]

The newly approved invasion plan called for Eighth Army to land along a fifty-mile front in southeast Sicily, from Syracuse to the Pachino Peninsula. At the same time, along the south coast, Patton's forces would make their primary landings at Gela and Scoglitti, with the 1st and 45th Divisions of Bradley's II Corps; while to the west, at Licata, newly promoted Maj. Gen. Lucian Truscott's 3rd Division would land to protect the American left flank. The object of the assault landings was to seize an Allied bridgehead in southeastern Sicily and, in the process, capture the key ports of Syracuse, Licata, and the airfields near Gela, from which Tedder's airmen would operate in support of the advancing ground forces. D-Day was designated as July 10, 1943.

Historians have long quarreled over Eisenhower's leadership role, and whether he was little more than the chairman of a giant military board or if he possessed true strategic vision. Eisenhower's chief function in the Mediterranean, and later in northwestern Europe, was to weld and hold together the machinery of war, which he did admirably in Europe and less well in the Mediterranean, at least initially. Comparable commanders, such as MacArthur, were more definitive about what they intended, whereas Eisenhower was more detached, preferring to rule on the plans developed by his staff, which he then brokered into policy. Eisenhower's decisions were taken not from any grand scheme or plan such as MacArthur would have articulated but, as a good company man, from the depths of the staff bureaucracy at AFHQ and, later, SHAEF.

Husky was a classic example. Eisenhower's involvement was minimal and indecisive. His planners and his three commanders in chief all quarreled over the most fundamental aspect of the plan—where to invade Sicily—while Eisenhower remained passive. For virtually the entire spring of 1943 there was near-paralysis over Husky that Eisenhower failed to resolve until Montgomery did him the favor of initiating a solution. Interference in the operational spheres of his subordinates had to be avoided, but as the one man responsible for Husky, Eisenhower had an obligation to act to end the bickering. The resulting impotence, which left the specifics of the invasion dangling until early May, was Eisenhower's responsibility, one that he conspicuously failed to fulfill. Moreover, to have a major operation of war resolved on a lavatory mirror was never taught by Clausewitz or in any service school.

That Eisenhower was not master of his own house was evident when a group of visiting U.S. senators questioned his authority. "Cunningham commands the naval forces, Tedder commands the air forces, and Alexander commands the ground forces. What in hell does Eisenhower command?" they wondered.[29] Although the three British officers answered to Eisenhower, he actually commanded only U.S. rear area troops in North Africa, a responsibility which he delegated to Everett Hughes, who ran its day-to-day operations for him. At one point a frustrated Hughes scribbled in his diary, "God, I wish we could forget our egos for a while!"[30]

Yet Eisenhower was never quite the virgin lamb among the wolves that his critics have suggested. "I am not so incredibly naive," he confessed to his friend Tom Handy after Casablanca, "that I do not realize that Britishers instinctively approach every military problem from the viewpoint of the Empire." But "one of the constant sources of danger to us in this war is the temptation to regard as our first enemy the partner that must work with us in defeating the real enemy."[31] Boxed in by two cantankerous (Tedder and Cunningham) and one aloof (Alexander) British chiefs, Eisenhower was at a distinct disadvantage and knew it. Nevertheless, he refused then, just as he did later, to permit criticism, from whatever the source, to deter him.

Under Montgomery's plan, once the Gela airfields were captured, Patton's only mission would be to protect Eighth Army's left flank while the British made the main effort toward Messina. Although disappointed and disgusted at playing second fiddle to Montgomery and the British, Patton was uncharacteristically reticent. Privately he was furious at what he described as "war by committee" and thought Husky was yet another betrayal by Eisenhower of the U.S. Army. When Alexander anxiously inquired if he was satisfied with the new plan, Patton tersely replied, "General, I don't plan—I only obey orders."[32]

The three senior British commanders all despised Montgomery, whom Tedder once snidely referred to as "a little fellow of average ability who has had such a build-up that he thinks of himself as Napoleon." Despite the disappointing change of mission, Patton's opinion of Montgomery remained favorable. "Monty is a forceful, selfish man," he remarked, but "I think he is a far better leader than Alexander."[33] Back in Morocco, Patton finally vented his anger to his staff. "This is what you get when your Commander-in-Chief ceases to be an American and becomes an Ally."[34] More disturbing was that, as the date for the invasion grew near, there had yet to be any indication of what Alexander intended to do after the landings.

Therein lay the crux of Eisenhower's problems: He had to break bread with two generals of vastly different character and temperament, one whom he liked and admired, the other a man he would on occasion gladly have strangled.

May 20, 1943, was one of the most memorable days of Eisenhower's life. The Allies held a giant victory parade in Tunis, an impressive and majestic affair planned by Alexander and Anderson, in which thirty thousand troops participated. First came French spahis, described by Harold Macmillan as "magnificent with their white horses and red cloaks," followed by French regiments, Foreign Legionnaires, and colorfully garbed Algerian and Moroccan troops. After a token number of American GIs of Bradley's II Corps passed in review, next came the British. To the haunting strains of massed bagpipers, many of the most famous British regiments, 14,000 men in all, garbed in "desert-stained battle-kit," slow-marched past the reviewing stand to receive Eisenhower's salute. Among the British contingent of the reviewing party there were few dry eyes. As Macmillan later wrote, "At no subsequent time would British arms play so preponderant a role in the victory, nor did British prestige stand higher."[35]

According to Butcher, Eisenhower had requested a ceremony that both celebrated the Allied victory and commemorated those who sacrificed their lives. What he got instead was a victory celebration he "abhorred." Although the concept may not have appealed to him, Eisenhower's heart won over his head. Flanked by two Churchill tanks placed on either side of the reviewing stand, Eisenhower proudly accepted the salute of each unit as it passed. As a gesture of courtesy—and shrewd politics—a resplendent Giraud in full-dress uniform stood at his side. According to Macmillan, who was present that day behind Eisenhower, when Giraud effusively praised the British First Army, "All that old Ike could do was to say ecstatically to me and others (and repeat it the next day) that he had never believed it possible to dream of having an honor as to command an army like this."[36]

A number of senior British officers and civilians were included in the official reviewing party with Eisenhower, but Bradley and Patton were relegated to a minor reviewing stand occupied by French civilians and inconsequential military officers. Patton cloaked his distress in anger, declaring it "a goddamned waste of time," and Bradley was disgusted that it seemed "to give the British overwhelming credit for the victory in Tunisia. For Patton and me, the affair merely served to reinforce our belief that Ike was now so pro-British that he was blind to the slight he had paid to us and, by extension, the American troops who fought and died in Tunisia."[37]

On the flight back to Algiers, Eisenhower's B-17 passed over an enormous Allied convoy sailing to Alexandria—the first since the dark days of 1941 to undertake passage across the once-dangerous Mediterranean Sea. Macmillan turned to Eisenhower and said, "There, General, are the fruits of your victory." With tears in his eyes, a deeply moved Eisenhower replied, "Ours, you mean, ours—that we have all won together."[38]

For some months Patton had been deeply troubled by the effect that his criticism was having upon his twenty-four-year friendship with Eisenhower. After the victory parade he was more than ever perplexed by what he perceived to be Eisenhower's lack of control over his British subordinates, all the while feeling a sense of guilt over his complaints about his friend. Patton wrote in his diary of reminding Eisenhower of Grant's declaration at Vicksburg:

> "Don't let my personal reputation interfere with winning the war." I feel the same way. . . . He needs a few loyal and unselfish men around him, even if he is too weak a character to be worthy of us. . . . I owe him a lot and must stay in with him. . . . I know of no one except myself who could do any better than Ike, and God knows I don't want his job.

At a press conference the correspondents asked Eisenhower what had happened to Patton, who had officially "disappeared." He would only reply evasively, "I have had to pull General Patton out to plan a bigger operation, and at the moment he commands the I Armored Corps. Please lay off mentioning him."[39]

Before the invasion Eisenhower sent Maj. Gen. John Porter Lucas to Patton as his personal "eyes and ears." Lucas was highly rated, had extensive experience in a variety of command and staff jobs, and had been sent by Marshall to Eisenhower as an officer of "military stature, prestige and experience." Had the new "spy" in his headquarters been anyone but Johnny Lucas, Patton would have complained bitterly to Eisenhower. However, the two were longtime friends, and Patton trusted him implicitly. Lucas was diplomatic, sensible, and persuasive, and Patton frequently sought his advice, even to the point of employing him as a conduit to Eisenhower.

Bathrooms became an unofficial place of business whenever Winston Churchill came to call, whether he was at the White House—where a shocked FDR once had to conduct a conversation while the naked, cherubic prime minister attended to his ablutions—or in Algiers. At the end of May 1943, after the Trident conference in Washington, Churchill arrived in Algiers. His purpose was not only to present personally to Eisenhower his case for the invasion of Italy after Sicily, but also to thwart any American attempt to shut down Allied operations in the Mediterranean after Husky. At Trident, Churchill, Roosevelt, and the Combined Chiefs had failed to reach agreement on the strategic considerations left unresolved at Casablanca. The bone of contention remained the same: U.S. opposition to further Mediterranean operations and the British belief that the route to France lay through Sicily and Italy, which would force Germany to expend its dwindling military strength defending southern Europe. Brooke and Marshall clashed. When Marshall expressed reservations at having acceded too easily to Allied operations in the Mediterranean there was this exchange between the uneasy allies:

BROOKE:"What strategy would you have preferred?"
MARSHALL:"The cross-Channel attack. We should finish the war more quickly."

Marshall bluntly reiterated his disdain for Mediterranean operations, which he argued would act like a "suction pump" at the expense of the cross-Channel invasion, and would also needlessly prolong the war in the Pacific. He asserted the Allies were "now at the crossroads" and implicitly threatened to turn instead to the Pacific. The two sides compromised, with the British readily agreeing to Overlord in May 1944, but at the price of continued operations in the Mediterranean, which would be dictated by Eisenhower. For once the British were in some disarray, when Churchill repudiated policy over which Brooke had labored to obtain agreement. Calling it "tragic," Brooke lamented, "There are times when he drives me to desperation."[40]

Eisenhower was represented at Trident by Bedell Smith, and during his chief of staff's absence unknowingly found himself in trouble over a cable sent to Washington by his G-3 (operations officer) that would never have been sent had Smith been present. The cable appeared to be at odds with the Casablanca political decision that decreed a policy of unconditional surrender for Germany and Italy. Disgruntled at Roosevelt's failure to rein Marshall in, Churchill had taken potshots at Eisenhower for not moving faster to invade Sicily, ignoring the fact that an earlier invasion was impossible without sufficient landing craft, then unavailable. The AFHQ cable had suggested that the policy of unconditional surrender was misguided and would make the Allied task in Sicily more difficult and ought to be softened to "Peace with Honor," along with a guarantee of self-determination once Benito Mussolini and his fascist regime were deposed. Eisenhower received a rocket from the Combined Chiefs that expressed the president's displeasure in no uncertain terms. While not specifically a reprimand, it was a pointed reminder that Washington and London made policy, not Eisenhower. As if Ike needed convincing, the incident was proof of how valuable Smith was to the running of AFHQ.

Churchill's last-minute decision to decamp for Algiers has been dubbed the Algiers conference. Marshall, who confided to Stimson that he felt like "a piece of luggage useful as a trading point," had to postpone a trip to the southwestern Pacific to be present at Roosevelt's insistence to protect American interests.[41] Eisenhower greeted Churchill and his party at Maison Blanche airfield on May 28, intending to follow his earlier practice of riding with Marshall in order to be apprised of events before meeting with Churchill. The prime minister, however, ambushed Eisenhower by insisting on riding with him, whereupon he immediately began arguing for an Italian campaign, and to "dangle before him the mirage of strategic riches beyond."[42] Churchill had barely settled into Admiral Cunningham's villa before he met privately with Eisenhower for a second one-on-one session and yet another relentless hammering over Italy.

The following day, with Eisenhower hosting a meeting on the porch of his villa, the Allied leadership heard Ike's plans for Husky and discussed future strategy, all the while pointing him toward Italy like a retriever toward a downed duck. "I could not endure to see a great army stand idle when it might be engaged in striking Italy out of the war," he wrote.[43] Whether soaking in the bathtub, with pungent cigar smoke filling the air, at mealtimes, or in formal or informal meetings, Churchill was his usual argumentative, relentless self, cajoling and pleading his case with the fervor of a carnival barker peddling his wares. The CCOS had granted Eisenhower latitude in deciding military operations after Sicily, and Churchill was determined that the course lead to Italy. In a moment of overexuberance, Eisenhower suggested that an invasion of Europe might be "a drop in the bucket" and possibly "unnecessary." Moreover, he said, should Sicily "prove to be an easy proposition, we ought to go directly into Italy." Churchill responded that, of course, "both the British people and the British Army were anxious to fight across the Channel." Although Marshall's reaction has never been fully documented, given his extreme aversion to Mediterranean operations, Eisenhower's optimism probably made the chief of staff cringe. Determined to hold operations in Italy to a minimum, but unable to prevent the employment of Eisenhower's military force, which had grown to nearly one million men in the Mediterranean theater, Marshall kept largely silent, leaving Churchill with the false perception that he accepted the British position.[44]

The Algiers meetings ended with Churchill satisfied that, with post-Sicilian operations "in General Eisenhower's hands," no formal plan was needed, and assurances from Eisenhower that he proposed to exploit the success of Husky by continuing military operations across the Strait of Messina into southern Italy would suffice, and he would notify the Combined Chiefs in ample time for them to concur without the need for a delay.[45]

Churchill, like the guest who comes to dinner and then refuses to take the hint and leave, enjoyed Algiers so much he remained for eight days, later recalling, "I have no more pleasant memories of the war."[46] His host, who was left to worry constantly about the security of his VIP guest, lost more than his usual share of sleep. Even Butcher's ploy of parading around in his bathrobe, yawning openly and loudly, once waving a flashlight as a signal that was never taken, failed to move the oblivious Englishman to his bed at a civilized hour.[47] Sometimes war is hell.

36.

"Everything That Planning Should Not Be"

This is the roughest country in the world,
and everything favors the defensive.
— MAJ. GEN. JOHN P. LUCAS

During the Algiers talks Eisenhower explained his intention to capture the islands of Pantelleria and Lampedusa, the largest of a chain of windswept, barren atolls that lay approximately fifty miles off Tunisia and directly in the path of Allied convoys sailing for Sicily. Long regarded as an impregnable Italian Gibraltar, they had since 1937 been a forbidden zone established by Mussolini as a counterpart to the British island fortress of Malta. Of greater concern to Eisenhower was that Pantelleria had long been an Axis listening post, equipped with the radio direction finders that had proved so troublesome to Allied shipping and aircraft that, in Eisenhower's judgment, "left in enemy hands, they would be a serious menace." Equally important, Tedder coveted its excellent airfield as a base for aerial operations against Sicily. Eisenhower was itching for action, and his decision to invade the two islands was as much a reaction to recent stinging criticism from Marshall of "his lack of adaptability" as it was for military reasons. "I want to make the capture of Pantelleria a sort of laboratory to determine the effect of concentrated heavy bombing on defended coastline," he told Marshall.[1] The decision was met with outright resistance from Alexander (who feared failure and its effects on Allied morale) and skepticism from Tedder and Cunningham. Eisenhower refused to back off, and for one of the first times as supreme commander used his authority to press for the operation. A task force was established to plan an operation that was code-named Corkscrew.

Wars create odd situations: The planners of Corkscrew were assisted by Professor Solly Zuckerman, a renowned zoologist, recruited by Tedder as his scientific adviser. Zuckerman had turned himself into an expert in devising bombing policy and would later play a key role in developing the controversial bombing strategy in Normandy.

The invasion of Pantelleria called for massive aerial and naval bombardments, followed by an amphibious invasion by a brigade-size force of the British 1st Division.

In mid-May one of the greatest sideshows of the war commenced when the Allies launched a relentless aerial campaign that severed the island's communications with the outside world. It was also one of the greatest examples of overkill of the war; during the three-week aerial campaign, the Allied air forces pulverized Pantelleria with 6,400 tons of bombs during more than five thousand sorties, leaving the island covered by a pall of smoke.

Eisenhower's insatiable itch to become more involved in the war he was directing was fulfilled on June 8, when he and Admiral Cunningham undertook their own form of "personal reconnaissance" to observe firsthand the aerial and naval bombardment of Pantelleria aboard the Royal Navy cruiser HMS *Aurora*. Amid the smoke, smell, and boom of naval guns and the explosions of bombs, the *Aurora* sailed within point-blank range of the island. Eisenhower took immense satisfaction in at last being a part of a military operation, even if briefly. He may not have been pulling a trigger, but he felt as if he was doing something positive, with an element of danger thrown in for good measure. He watched with some merriment as Cunningham personally adjusted the naval gunfire from the *Aurora*. (To the intense annoyance of the prime minister, who suffered from the same affliction of exuberance, Eisenhower and Cunningham had firmly refused Churchill's entreaties to accompany them before he returned to London in early June. That the seas around the island were heavily mined was one of the many reasons why Churchill had been left in Algiers.)

Although it was garrisoned by twelve thousand Italian soldiers, Pantelleria was a paper tiger whose defenders were overage, ill trained, and eager to surrender. Awed by the destruction, Eisenhower exclaimed to Cunningham, "Andrew, why don't you and I get into a boat together and row ashore on our own. I think we can capture the island without any of these soldiers."[2] On June 11, 1943, the invasion commenced and was quickly over, when the defenders emerged waving white flags of surrender. Lampedusa likewise fell without losses. The lone British casualty was a soldier bitten by a mule.[3]

Adm. Andrew Browne Cunningham was a fighting admiral in the grand tradition of British seafaring warriors, known throughout the fleet simply as "ABC." Of his many relationships with British officers, Eisenhower forged perhaps the strongest with Cunningham, whom he regarded as "the Nelsonian type of admiral. . . . He thought always in terms of attack, never of defense. . . . He was a real sea-dog. . . . I had the utmost respect for his military judgment." Cunningham returned the compliment: "I liked him at once. He struck me as being completely sincere, straightforward and very modest. In those early days I had the impression that he was not very sure of himself; but who could wonder at that? . . . We soon became fast friends. . . . From the very beginning he set Anglo-American unity and friendship as his aim. . . . He left nothing undone to advance it."[4]

Eisenhower's great elation was reflected in an eyes-only cable to Marshall on June 11, in which he boasted over the success of Corkscrew "in the face of contrary advice," after predicting Pantelleria's surrender "before any infantry soldier goes ashore." Moreover, he noted, "today marks the completion of my twenty eighth year of commissioned service and I believe that I am now legally eligible for promotion to colonel [in the Regular Army]."[5]

In the month before Husky the Allied air forces subjected the Luftwaffe and the Italian air force to the same relentless treatment, forcing the evacuation of their bomber force to southern France and northern Italy. Although Tedder had attained a valuable airbase from which to strike Sicily, and his air forces had the upper hand, he was greatly disturbed that everyone from Eisenhower on down had overreacted to the easy capture of Pantelleria and Lampedusa. "Even Eisenhower has begun to say," he wrote to Portal, " 'can't we possibly do something like this for "Husky?" ' "[6] Some of the senior Allied airmen, including Corkscrew's principal advocates, Tooey Spaatz and Bomber Harris, used it as confirmation of their growing but ultimately delusional conviction that airpower alone could singlehandedly change the course of the war, if not end it entirely. It was a misguided concept that would, in 1944, produce the most controversial arguments of the war, in which Eisenhower became thoroughly entangled.

On the afternoon of July 8 at Maison Blanche, Eisenhower boarded his Flying Fortress for Malta, the focal point of the invasion. Alexander had previously relocated his headquarters to a tunnel in Malta, which he and Eisenhower shared. Although it was more than 100 degrees outside, it was so cold in the tunnel that the two generals had to wear overcoats to ward off the chilly dampness.[7] His quarters were in the same cold, damp, unwelcome tunnel, over a former British dungeon "used for centuries to confine prisoners guilty of traditional sailor sins—mutiny, drunkenness, sodomy."[8]

A massive Allied fleet was already at sea, proceeding under strict radio silence toward the coast of Sicily, when, on the afternoon of July 9, it was suddenly buffeted by Force 7 (more than forty mile per hour) winds, ominously rough seas, and rampant seasickness. That night Eisenhower met with Cunningham and Alexander amid an atmosphere of mounting anxiety. In a precursor to the Normandy landings the following year, Eisenhower had to decide at once whether or not to postpone Husky. Eisenhower had earlier that day observed the numerous Maltese windmills twirling furiously and was not encouraged. After meeting with Royal Navy meteorologists, who reported that the Mediterranean winds usually abated after dark, Eisenhower announced that Husky would proceed as scheduled: There would be no postponement. To Marshall, who had prodded him with a message asking if Husky was "on" or "off," Eisenhower replied, "The operation will proceed as scheduled."

No one, however, was confident. Near midnight Cunningham went to the cliffs overlooking the sea to catch a glimpse of the British gliders; Bradley was seasick aboard Adm. Alan R. Kirk's flagship, *Ancon;* Patton was on Adm. H. Kent Hewitt's flagship, *Monrovia,* where he prayed, then fell into a restless sleep. For some days as D-Day drew near, Eisenhower had been tense, "as if my stomach were a clenched fist." In a brief note to Mamie he said, "Everything that we could think of to do has been done. . . . The answer is in the lap of the gods!" Under such conditions, he said, "men do almost anything to keep them from going slightly mad. Walk, talk, try to work, smoke (all the time)—anything to push the minutes along to find out a result that one's own actions can no longer affect in the slightest degree. I stand it better than most, but there is no use denying that I feel the strain."[9] This night he rubbed his seven lucky coins and "offered up a silent prayer for the safety and success of all the troops under his command."[10] As he later wrote, "There was nothing we could do but pray, desperately."[11]

D-Day, July 10, 1943, began disastrously, when the British glider force that was to land near Syracuse ahead of the seaborne forces encountered not only dangerously high winds but smoke from the island and heavy flak, from both enemy and friendly guns, which mistakenly fired on the aerial armada. Casualties were heavy. Col. James M. Gavin's 505th Parachute Infantry Regiment of the 82nd Airborne fared little better when the winds and flak dissolved its neat aerial formations into a confused jumble. More than three thousand paratroopers, who were to have been dropped northeast of Gela, instead landed over a thousand-square-mile area of southeastern Sicily.

Coordination and cooperation between the air forces and the naval and ground forces were extremely poor, and became one of the bitterest inter-Allied problems. The air plan was so vague that the naval and ground commanders did not have the foggiest notion *how* the airmen intended to support their particular operation. During May and June they had raised these and other questions, but satisfactory answers were never forthcoming from the RAF and the U.S. Army Air Forces chiefs, who had grown increasingly independent—and reluctant to take orders from the army or navy.

Unlike the airborne and glider operations, the amphibious invasion was a great success. The Eighth Army landings were so successful that Montgomery ordered his two corps commanders to push inland and up the coast toward Catania without delay.

The most important of the three American landings took place at Gela, where the 1st Infantry Division landings occurred along the beaches opposite the Plain of Gela. For two days they fought off Axis counterattacks, by the

Hermann Göring Division and the Italian Livorno Division, to drive them back into the sea. By July 12 the two Allied armies were in control of firm bridgeheads—and in Sicily to stay.

A triumphant American stand at Gela on July 11 was marred by tragedy that night, when the aerial convoy ferrying the 504th Parachute Regiment of the 82nd Airborne was shot to pieces by panicked gunners of the Allied naval forces only minutes after an enemy aerial attack. "Friendly fire" killed sixty pilots and crewmen and eighty-one paratroopers. This tragic incident not only cost precious lives but nearly sounded the death knell for the future employment of airborne forces. Eisenhower ordered a halt to further operations pending a formal inquiry. Air, ground, and naval commanders all blamed one another, but Patton bore the brunt of Eisenhower's outrage in a bitter and depressing end to the most crucial day of the Sicily campaign.

Eisenhower sent Patton an angry cable demanding action against those responsible and implying that the fault lay within Patton's command. (It did not.) Eisenhower was still visibly irritated and in a foul mood when he visited Patton aboard the *Monrovia* on the morning of July 12. Eisenhower was so angry he tongue-lashed Patton unmercifully. "Ike spoke vigorously to Patton about the inadequacy of his reports of progress reaching headquarters at Malta," recorded Butcher. According to Lucas, who had personally checked the reports, Eisenhower's criticism was misplaced: "They seemed to me to be as complete as they could well be under the circumstances."[12] It hardly mattered to Eisenhower; someone had to bear the brunt of his wrath, and that someone was Patton.

Their unpleasant encounter illustrates the extent of the deterioration in their relationship. "Ike had stepped on him hard. There was an air of tenseness. I had a feeling that Ike was disappointed. He said previously that he would be happy if after about five days from D-Day, General Bradley were to take over because of his calm and matter-of-fact direction," noted Butcher.[13] Not once during his visit did Eisenhower ever compliment Patton on any aspect of Seventh Army operations, which had been brilliantly carried out. Moreover, his criticism of Patton's alleged reporting failures was indeed misplaced, for the chain of command was through Alexander's headquarters. What they did with Patton's reports was outside the control of the Seventh Army commander. As Lucas observed, "The C-in-C should have mentioned the fact that a most difficult military operation was being performed in a manner that reflected great credit on American arms."[14]

Butcher also wrote in his diary, "When we left General Patton I thought he was angry." Patton was indeed livid and thought that the incident merely represented a further example of Eisenhower's pro-British bias. The following day Patton received a cable from Eisenhower "cussing me out" for the loss of the paratroopers. "As far as I can see, if anyone is blamable, it must be myself . . . perhaps Ike is looking for an excuse to relieve me . . . if they want

434   A General's Education: The Mediterranean, 1942-1943

a goat, I am it."[15] Patton well understood the principle that in such instances a commander is always ultimately responsible. Still, he was deeply hurt by Eisenhower's tongue-lashing and cable. Although a formal investigation later concluded that no one was to blame, Patton remained frustrated that everyone's best efforts had failed to prevent a tragedy.

Eisenhower had traveled to Sicily aboard a British destroyer, HMS *Petard*. Before commencing the return trip after visiting Patton, the destroyer came under fire from German artillery ashore. His British hosts became very worried about their VIP guest, who preferred to watch the exchanges of gunfire from a vantage point on the deck. Urged to take cover belowdecks, Eisenhower wanted to balk at their polite concern for his safety. "They treat me like a bird in a gilded cage," he grumbled, mockingly noting he was "a valuable fellow," before turning serious, admitting he wanted no one hurt on his account, and meekly descending below.[16] Later, as the *Petard* approached the boundary between the U.S. and Canadian sectors, where there were visible signs of fighting, Eisenhower ordered the captain to stop the vessel so he could go ashore. From somewhere a DUKW amphibious landing craft appeared. Once ashore Eisenhower was the first to disembark on Sicilian soil. He located a startled British officer and announced, "Good morning. I am General Eisenhower. I want to talk to the senior Canadian officer on this beachhead." Told the nearest headquarters was inland, Eisenhower demanded, "I don't care if it's a second lieutenant, but I want to meet some Canadian officer. I have come to welcome Canada to the Allied command." Borrowing a jeep, Eisenhower literally wandered through narrow, bumpy lanes that passed for roads in search of an elusive Canadian officer, with no idea whether he was in harm's way. Eventually a sweating Eisenhower returned, his mission accomplished. "I kept thinking," wrote correspondent John Gunther, who accompanied him, "that this man might be a four-star general and all that, but what I would always remember about him was that he was such a splendid human being."[17]

Despite the generally feeble resistance of the Italians, the Germans had no intention of ceding Sicily without a fight. A German corps headquarters (the XIV Panzer Corps) was ordered to the island, as were elements of the elite 1st Parachute Division, which parachuted into the Plain of Catania to reinforce a beleaguered German battle group operating northwest of Augusta in an attempt to block the coastal highway to Messina.

During the night of July 13–14, Montgomery launched a night airborne and glider operation to seize a key bridge on the northern edge of the Plain of Catania. The target, Primosole Bridge, was not lightly held by the Italians as supposed, but by a regiment of the newly arrived veteran German paratroopers. After a savage five-day battle failed to dislodge the German airborne, Montgomery conceded failure and switched his main offensive effort inland in an attempt to circle the northern edge of the great Mount Etna massif to the coast below Messina. However, by splitting his army Montgomery unwittingly presented the opportunistic Germans with unexpected time to bolster their defenses and delay the British advance. The German corps commander, General der Panzertruppen Hans Valentin Hube, a battle-experienced tank officer who had lost an arm in Russia, was not intimidated in the slightest by the massive Allied force arrayed against him. His brilliant defense of Sicily was a classic example of the German genius for defensive operations personified by his superior, Albert Kesselring.

The battle for Sicily was characterized by the lack of direction from Alexander, who failed to develop either a strategic or tactical plan for its conquest. There was no master plan or even an agreed strategy among the three commanders, Alexander, Montgomery, and Patton—merely Alexander's notion that Patton would act as the shield in his left hand while Eighth Army served as the sword in his right. But, as one of Montgomery's senior staff officers has written, "the two armies were left largely to develop their operations in the manner which seemed most propitious in the prevailing circumstances." More important was the lack of any strategic objective, although Messina, the gateway between the island and mainland Italy, should have been the Allies' obvious objective. Whoever controlled Messina controlled Sicily. Alexander nevertheless elected to allow the land battle to develop before deciding the strategy his two armies would employ.

This lack of direction exploded soon after the Catania venture failed. Alexander's unwillingness to take control of the ground campaign at its most critical moment shattered all pretense of cohesiveness, and led to a situation whereby Montgomery and Patton dictated virtually conflicting and divisive courses of action for their respective armies and created an absurd and unnecessary personal rivalry.

The improved U.S. performance in Tunisia in the spring of 1943 had failed to alter Alexander's conviction that American fighting ability was still inferior to that of the British army, even though the U.S. force fighting in Sicily bore scant resemblance to the one that had been humiliated at Kasserine five months earlier. Alexander firmly believed that the troops of the Eighth Army were more experienced and reliable than any American troops, despite the fact that most of Montgomery's veteran formations were worn out from too many months of combat in North Africa. Thus Alexander was simply unwilling to entrust Seventh Army with anything more than a secondary role in Sicily.

As disgusted as Patton, Bradley, and others were at what they perceived as Eisenhower's pro-British bias, there were limits beyond which he would not tolerate British criticism. One was the British Broadcasting Corporation (BBC), the only source of news in English. Throughout the Sicilian campaign the BBC had consistently praised the exploits of Eighth Army and openly and blatantly demeaned the American contribution. Snide references and inaccurate reporting finally brought Eisenhower's temper to the boiling point when a report aired that Patton's army was eating grapes in western Sicily while the British did all the fighting. "Ike wrote a scorcher to the P.M." that was hand-carried to England by an AFHQ officer.[18] Eisenhower strongly criticized the BBC for undermining his efforts to create a unified Anglo-American community in the Mediterranean. The BBC made lame excuses but thereafter noticeably improved the tenor of its coverage.

Prior to D-Day Alexander never saw fit to provide even the vaguest guidance, nor did he anticipate the speed with which the two armies would secure such sizable bridgeheads. In the absence of direction his two strong-willed subordinates inevitably began to act independently of Alexander and each other. Montgomery found ready acceptance when he proposed what Alexander had envisioned all along but never articulated: that Eighth Army make the main effort to cut Sicily in half.

To do so meant cutting directly across the boundary between the two armies and directly across the route of the advancing U.S. 45th Division. Montgomery signaled that he wanted the troublesome boundary line moved. Alexander agreed and ordered Patton to hand over a disputed road to the Eighth Army, thus requiring Bradley to move the entire 45th Division back to the Gela beaches, and then north to new positions. It was the most contentious and militarily unsound decision of the campaign and, at a stroke, forfeited an opportunity to have encircled the entire German XIV Panzer Corps defending the island. Disgusted, Patton nevertheless complied without protest.

Bradley was thunderstruck. "My God," he told Patton, "you can't let him do that," believing Patton ought to have resisted Alexander's order.[19] Bradley correctly considered the decision to be the turning point of the campaign:

> We were ready to strike for Messina, the only real strategic prize on Sicily. Now Monty would deny us this role, relegating us (as in southern Tunisia) to the demeaning and inconsequential task of protecting the Eighth Army's rear and flank. Would George Patton sit still for such an outrageous decision? He would—and did. Like a lamb. . . . By all rights, he could have been expected to roar like a lion. My guess is that at that point, Patton sincerely believed Ike was "looking for an excuse" to relieve him.

Indeed, Patton was clearly still stunned over the airborne disaster and Eisenhower's stinging criticism, and Bradley's conclusion that he felt "certain that Patton believed that if he caused a ruckus on this day Ike would fire him," was undoubtedly correct.[20]

The earliest known photo of Dwight Eisenhower, age three. *Front:* baby Roy and Dwight. *Back:* Arthur and Edgar. *(Dwight D. Eisenhower Library)*

The Eisenhowers, 1902. *Front:* David, Milton, and Ida. *Back:* Dwight, Edgar, Arthur, Earl, and Roy. *(Dwight D. Eisenhower Library)*

As adults, the six Eisenhower sons rarely returned to Abilene. The only reunion of the entire family took place in 1926. On the porch, behind Ike, David, and Ida, are *(left to right)* Roy, Arthur, Earl, Edgar, and Milton. *(Dwight D. Eisenhower Library)*

As a young man, Eisenhower developed a passion for the outdoors. In this 1904 photo taken during a camping trip near Abilene, young Ike was clearly having the time of his life. *(Dwight D. Eisenhower Library)*

Eisenhower (*second from right, back row*) loved sports and was a member of the Abilene High School baseball team. *(Dwight D. Eisenhower Library)*

BELOW LEFT: Before reporting to West Point in 1911, Eisenhower stopped in Chicago to visit his best friend from Abilene, Ruby Norman, who took this photograph. *(Dwight D. Eisenhower Library)*

BELOW RIGHT: Summer camp in 1911. Although he was an indifferent cadet, Eisenhower (*second from right*) later came to venerate West Point. One of his first duties as a cadet was as a member of the color guard. *(Dwight D. Eisenhower Library)*

Cadet Dwight D. Eisenhower, West Point, 1915 *(Dwight D. Eisenhower Library)*

Ike and Mamie in the parlor of the Doud home in Denver on their wedding day, July 1, 1916 *(Dwight D. Eisenhower Library)*

Doud Dwight Eisenhower ("Ikky"), Gettysburg, 1918. His death in December 1921 from scarlet fever nearly broke Dwight Eisenhower's heart. *(Dwight D. Eisenhower Library)*

"We're Off to Frisco!" The 1919 Transcontinental Motor Convoy. (*Dwight D. Eisenhower Library*)

During World War I Eisenhower (here posing beside a Renault light tank at Camp Meade, Maryland) was a highly regarded lieutenant colonel, but by the summer of 1920 he had been demoted to his prewar grade of captain. (*Official U.S. Army photograph, Dwight D. Eisenhower Library*)

Eisenhower, T. J. Davis (*center*), and MacArthur during the infamous 1932 Bonus March in Washington, D.C. (*Official U.S. Army photograph, Dwight D. Eisenhower Library*)

ABOVE LEFT: John S. D. Eisenhower with his parents, Rock Creek Park, Washington, D.C., 1934 *(Dwight D. Eisenhower Library)*

ABOVE RIGHT: During the interwar years there was a backlash against military personnel. Those, like Eisenhower, who were stationed in Washington, D.C., rarely wore their uniforms. *(Dwight D. Eisenhower Library)*

Although he could barely afford to own one, Eisenhower loved automobiles. During the family's visit to Denver in 1938, he drove John Doud's 1912 electric automobile. The photo was taken by his son, John. *(Dwight D. Eisenhower Library)*

His head shaved bald, Eisenhower poses with the fledgling Philippine Air Force during a farewell review held in his honor in December 1939. *(Dwight D. Eisenhower Library)*

Despite her abhorrence of war, during World War II Ida Eisenhower posed for this photograph in front of her prized ebony piano, displaying a magazine featuring her celebrated soldier son. *(Dwight D. Eisenhower Library)*

During the 1941 Louisiana Maneuvers, Eisenhower's tent became a convivial gathering place for colleagues and correspondents. *(Dwight D. Eisenhower Library)*

LEFT: Air Chief Marshal Sir Arthur Tedder, Eisenhower's deputy in the Mediterranean and Northwest Europe *(Dwight D. Eisenhower Library)*

RIGHT: Eisenhower and General Henri Giraud in Algiers, May 1943 *(Official U.S. Army photograph, Dwight D. Eisenhower Library)*

The Allied team in the Mediterranean, Algiers, 1943. *Front row, left to right:* Eisenhower, Tedder, Alexander, and "ABC" Cunningham. *Back row:* Macmillan, Bedell Smith, and two unidentified British officers. *(Official U.S. Army photograph, Dwight D. Eisenhower Library)*

The Allied leadership discussing strategy in North Africa, 1943. *Standing, second row, left to right:* Sir Arthur Tedder, Andrew B. Cunningham, Harold Alexander, and Bernard Montgomery; *seated, left to right:* Anthony Eden, Alan Brooke, Winston Churchill, George C. Marshall, and Dwight Eisenhower. *(Official U.S. Army photograph, George C. Marshall Library)*

Eisenhower's visits to the front were a respite from the unrelenting problems and pressures presented each day at AFHQ and, later, at SHAEF. Here he enjoys a rare moment of quiet while lunching on a Tunisian hillside, 1943. *(Official U.S. Army photograph, George C. Marshall Library)*

When the Allies invaded Sicily in July 1943, it was the largest amphibious operation ever mounted. *(Official U.S. Army photograph, Dwight D. Eisenhower Library)*

RIGHT: Lt. Gen. Mark Clark *(Official U.S. Army photograph, National Archives)*

BELOW: Eisenhower and Montgomery looking across the Strait of Messina at the conclusion of the Sicily campaign *(Official U.S. Army photograph, Dwight D. Eisenhower Library)*

LEFT: Eisenhower and Lt. Gen. George S. Patton, Jr., Sicily, 1943 *(Official U.S. Army photograph, Dwight D. Eisenhower Library)*

Captain Harry C. Butcher,
USNR—naval aide, diarist,
and confidant

Lt. Col. James Gault,
Ike's British
aide-de-camp

Maj. Gen. Kenneth W. D.
Strong, the chief
intelligence officer

Eisenhower's inner circle at both AFHQ and SHAEF
(Dwight D. Eisenhower Library)

Lt. Gen. Walter Bedell Smith, the chief of staff

Ike and Monty confer during one of the first Overlord planning conferences in London, February 1944. *(Official U.S. Army photograph, Dwight D. Eisenhower Library)*

The two architects of British strategy, Churchill and Field Marshal Alan Brooke *(Dwight D. Eisenhower Library)*

Kay Summersby and Telek *(Dwight D. Eisenhower Library)*

Admiral Sir Bertram Ramsay and Air Chief Marshal Sir Arthur Tedder in Normandy shortly after the D-Day landings *(Official U.S. Army photograph, Dwight D. Eisenhower Library)*

LEFT: Eisenhower and Gen. Charles de Gaulle meet in Normandy, August 1944 *(Official U.S. Army photograph, Dwight D. Eisenhower Library)*

BELOW: Lt. Gen. Omar N. Bradley briefing Montgomery at his Tac HQ during the Normandy campaign *(Official U.S. Army photograph, National Archives)*

The first attempt to break out of the Cotentin peninsula in early July 1944 ended in a costly failure. The grim expression on Eisenhower's face as he met with the VII Corps commander, Maj. Gen. J. Lawton Collins (*left*), and Bradley on July 4 reflects his concern over the dangerous stalemate occurring in Normandy. (*Official U.S. Army photograph, National Archives*)

The unexpected success of Operation Cobra unleashed the U.S. First and Third Armies through the Avranches Gap to carry out the great pursuit and end the Normandy campaign. (*Official U.S. Army photograph, courtesy of the Patton Museum*)

As the Normandy campaign nears an end, Bradley and Eisenhower confer at the 12th Army Group Tac HQ, August 1944. (*Official U.S. Army photograph, Dwight D. Eisenhower Library*)

The most appalling sights Eisenhower viewed during the war were in the Falaise Gap—the remnants of what had once been the world's most modern army. *(Imperial War Museum)*

Eisenhower, Devers, Patton, and Patch meeting at an airfield in eastern France, March 1945 *(Official U.S. Army photograph, Dwight D. Eisenhower Library)*

Churchill and Eisenhower
meet at the Rhine, March 1945
(*Official U.S. Army photograph,
Dwight D. Eisenhower Library*)

LEFT: Bradley, Eisenhower, and
Patton, Bastogne, February 1945
(*Photo courtesy USMA Library*)

BELOW: Eisenhower and Bradley
visited the Remagen bridge
shortly after its dramatic capture
in March 1945. On the right is
the First Army commander, Lt.
Gen. Courtney H. Hodges.
(*Official U.S. Army photograph,
Dwight D. Eisenhower Library*)

A rare moment of elation, on May 8, 1945. Eisenhower is holding the two pens used in the signing of the instrument of unconditional surrender. *Left to right*: Russian general I. Susloparoff, F. E. Morgan, Bedell Smith, Butcher, and Tedder. *(Dwight D. Eisenhower Library)*

The high price of war: the Normandy American cemetery and memorial, Colleville-sur-Mer, (Calvados), France, where 9,387 servicemen and women are buried *(Courtesy American Battle Monuments Commission)*

Once the orders were issued, Canadian units encountered stiff resistance while the 45th Division stood helplessly by, unable to come to their aid even though their artillery was within one mile of the highway. What the better-positioned American infantry, with the advantage of close artillery support, could have accomplished with relative ease became a costly ordeal for the Canadians.

Alexander's unfortunate decision left a bitter legacy. It also granted the German commanders precious time to impart their defensive genius and dictate the timetable for the campaign. "Thereafter, Bradley and Patton assumed what Montgomery always practiced, that under weak leadership senior commanders should interpret their orders to suit themselves. In North West Europe it led to tacit conspiracy to ignore Eisenhower."[21]

On July 17 Patton, determined that there be no repeat of Tunisia, arrived unannounced at Alexander's headquarters in North Africa, seeking a more important role for his army. With the British advance stalled and in serious trouble on the Plain of Catania, and unable to crack the Etna Line (the principal German defenses), Alexander agreed to Patton's plan to employ II Corps to thrust to Sicily's northern coast, while the remainder of Seventh Army cleared western Sicily. In reality this was merely a clever ploy by Patton to maneuver Seventh Army into a position to capture Messina. Patton was correct in his belief that any further demeaning of the American fighting role in Sicily would be intolerable, and the only means of preventing it was by means of a great American victory, which in Sicily meant the capture of Messina.

Alexander could have struck a killing blow with Seventh Army where the Etna Line defenses were weakest and incomplete, thus tightening a noose from which the only escape was retreat or surrender. Instead the opportunity was squandered by the capture of Palermo and a secondary sweep into western Sicily, neither of which were of any strategic importance. Greeted by thousands of flag-waving, cheering Sicilians, Patton's army liberated Palermo on July 21. While the publicity focused on Palermo, Patton began a new offensive along the north coast and across north central Sicily with two infantry divisions. Their destination: Messina.

When the three Allied ground commanders finally met on July 25, Montgomery proposed that Seventh Army rather than his Eighth Army capture Messina. Patton now had the full backing of both Alexander and Montgomery to seize Messina and end the troublesome Sicily campaign. By early August the Germans, skillfully utilizing the mountainous terrain to maximum advantage, had carried out a succession of delaying actions. Although the German formations in Sicily had performed brilliantly, they now faced entrapment in the northeastern corner of the island and had to either evacuate Sicily or surrender. While the Germans' tactics made American progress a painful and costly experience, plans were implemented for an audacious mass evacuation across the Strait of Messina to the Italian boot, beginning in early August.

Ferry traffic in the strait was efficiently organized and performed flawlessly under the cover of heavy antiaircraft support as the Allied air forces made a half-hearted and largely futile effort to interdict the evacuation. The Germans fully expected catastrophic losses; instead they carried out a stunningly successful strategic withdrawal. By the time it ended, on the morning of August 17, 1943, they had extricated their entire force of nearly 55,000 troops and virtually every weapon and vehicle capable of being ferried to the mainland, all of which would be later employed in the defense of Italy.[22] The U.S. 3rd Division entered the smoking ruins of Messina that same morning, only to find that the last German soldier had long since departed.[23]

None of the words of praise and self-congratulation that followed could mask the hollowness of the victory in a campaign beset by military blunders, controversy, and indecision. The Allies needlessly prolonged it by fighting a frontal battle of attrition, with the result that a veteran German army corps that never exceeded sixty thousand men, devoid of air and naval support, managed to delay for thirty-eight days two Allied armies whose combined strength exceeded 480,000 troops—adding the final insult by carrying out one of the most successful strategic withdrawals in military history.[24]

Eisenhower played no role, made no important decisions, and had virtually no impact on Operation Husky. His three force commanders ran the show without a helmsman—with utterly predictable results. Montgomery's verdict was unsparing: "Alexander's plan for Sicily was idiotic," he said after the war.[25]

An after-action report prepared by the [British] War Office called Sicily a "chaotic and deplorable example of everything that planning should not be," and further evidence that the Allies had to improve in all aspects before attempting to invade France.[26]

Despite his rebuke from Eisenhower over the airborne incident, by mid-August 1943 Patton was being hailed as the conqueror of Sicily, and had appeared on the covers of both *Time* and *Newsweek*, and was clearly poised to assume even higher command and responsibility in the cross-Channel invasion of northwestern France, then planned for the late spring of 1944.

Visiting the wounded is one of the most traumatic but important duties of a commander. An emotional man, Patton was torn by the sight of badly wounded and dying men, some missing limbs, but nevertheless faithfully visited aid stations and field hospitals on a regular basis, which Bradley and Eisenhower rarely did. In early August, while visiting two different U.S. Army field hospitals, Patton slapped a soldier in each, believing they were malingering by feigning battle fatigue, and thereby dishonoring men actually wounded in battle.

The news of the slappings was quickly leaked to the American correspondents attached to Seventh Army. Four outraged correspondents, Demaree

Bess of the *Saturday Evening Post*, Merrill Mueller of NBC, Al Newman of *Newsweek*, and John Daly of CBS, made no attempt to file the story but took it upon themselves to complain personally to Eisenhower. Bess, Mueller, and Quentin Reynolds of *Collier's* flew to Algiers, and on August 19 presented a summary written by Bess to Bedell Smith. The Bess report noted that Patton had committed a court-martial offense by striking an enlisted man and ended, "I am making this report to General Eisenhower in the hope of getting conditions corrected before more damage has been done."[27]

Eisenhower was already aware that he had a potentially explosive problem on his hands, having been briefed two days earlier by his chief surgeon, Brig. Gen. Frederick A. Blessé. While shocked, Eisenhower did not immediately grasp the full implications of Patton's acts and merely remarked that he guessed it would be necessary to give Patton a "jacking up." This unwelcome news came the very day Patton had triumphantly entered Messina, officially ending the Sicily campaign. Eisenhower's spirits were high, and without further details he was inclined to believe that the report might be exaggerated. However, the more he reflected on it, the more Eisenhower realized the implications. He ordered Blessé to Sicily at once to investigate the incidents and also to carry a handwritten letter to Patton. "If this thing ever gets out, they'll be howling for Patton's scalp, and that will be the end of Georgie's service in this war. I simply cannot let that happen. Patton is *indispensable* to the war effort—one of the guarantors of our victory."[28]

The letter Eisenhower sent to Patton contained the strongest words of censure written to a senior American officer during World War II, and expressed shock and dismay over the allegations of misconduct. "I clearly understand that firm and drastic measures were at times necessary in order to secure the desired objectives. But this does not excuse brutality, abuse of the sick, nor exhibition of uncontrollable temper in front of subordinates." If the reports were true, lamented Eisenhower, then "I must so seriously question your good judgment and your self-discipline, as to raise serious doubt in my mind as to your future usefulness." Contrary to popular belief Eisenhower's letter did *not* require a personal apology to every soldier and unit in Seventh Army, only that "you make in the form of apology or otherwise such personal amends to the individuals concerned as may be within your power."[29]

The arrival of the three correspondents reinforced Eisenhower's awareness that he had a tiger by the tail. What they wanted was a deal: In return for killing the story they wanted Patton fired. Correspondent Reynolds summed up the strong anti-Patton bias within the press corps when he told Eisenhower that there were "at least 50,000 American soldiers on Sicily who would shoot Patton if they had the chance," a statement Eisenhower knew was utterly fatuous.[30]

Eisenhower had no intention of submitting to a blatant attempt by the reporters to get rid of Patton. Torn between loyalty to an old friend, the clear necessity that he must be disciplined, and the consequences of losing Patton altogether if the incidents became public, Eisenhower unhesitatingly decided that "Patton should be saved for service in the great battles still facing us in Europe, yet I had to devise ways and means to minimize the harm that would certainly come from his impulsive action and to assure myself that it was not repeated."[31] He summoned the three correspondents and turned up the Eisenhower charm full bore to make his case for Patton, explaining that he had written a sharp letter of reprimand, ordering him to apologize personally for his behavior.[32] While making it clear that there would be no censorship if they elected to ignore him, Eisenhower said he hoped they would see fit to keep the matter quiet in the interest of retaining a commander whose leadership he considered vital. More out of respect for Eisenhower than compassion for Patton, the correspondents entered into a gentleman's agreement not to publicize the story.

No sooner had General Blessé arrived with Eisenhower's letter of censure than a cable arrived from the Allied commander in chief, ordering Patton to meet Lucas at the Palermo airfield on the afternoon of August 20. Lucas would be carrying a personal message from Eisenhower, and he was to listen closely to what Lucas had to tell him.[33] Lucas's advice to Patton was "kindly but firm": Apologize to the soldiers he slapped; apologize personally to every division in Seventh Army, and promise never to repeat the act.[34] It was on Lucas's advice rather than Eisenhower's order that Patton made amends to his entire army.

Since World War II a great deal has been learned of the effects of combat on soldiers, but in Patton's time "shell shock" and "battle fatigue" were equated by many with malingering and cowardice. Despite the fact that in one of the two incidents, there was clearly neither malingering nor cowardice, Patton would never concede that all men are not created with equal tolerance to combat conditions. Privately, he insisted that "my motive was correct because one cannot permit skulking to exist. It is just like a communicable disease. I admit freely that my method was wrong and I shall make what amends I can. I regret the incident as I hate to make Ike mad when it is my earnest study to please him."[35]

Patton never understood that throughout the slapping affair Eisenhower had stood firmly behind him. While Patton was complaining that Eisenhower had not congratulated him on his great victory, Eisenhower agonized over whether he might yet have to send him home in disgrace. Butcher recorded that "Ike is deeply concerned and has scarcely slept for several nights, trying to figure out the wisest method of handling this dilemma. The United Nations have not developed another battle leader as successful as Patton, Ike thinks," yet he had to consider the very real possibility that he might be obliged to court-martial his old friend. "He's sweating it out."[36] Torn between loyalty and professional duty, Eisenhower had to make his primary consideration the best interests of the U.S. Army. Clearly that meant retaining Patton.

Had it been up to Bradley, who by this time had come to despise Patton as deeply as he did Montgomery, Patton would not have been let off so easily: "I would have relieved him instantly and would have had nothing more to do with him. . . . His whole concept of command was opposite to mine."[37] Patton did offer to resign; Eisenhower refused and merely replied, "You owe us some victories; pay off and the world will deem me a wise man."[38]

As Patton made the rounds of every Seventh Army unit, his "apology" generally took the form of an oblique reference of regret "for any occasions when I may have harshly criticized individuals."[39] His reception ranged from stony silence to bewilderment as to why Patton was even there in the first place. The reaction in most of the combat units was quiet indifference. In Patton's former division, the 2nd Armored, there was great enthusiasm and a tendency to discount rumors about Patton as untrue. A regiment of the 9th Division refused to let Patton even make his apology by cheering him. "It sounded like a football game . . . [steel pots] started flying through the air, coming down all over—raining steel helmets and the men just shouted 'Georgie, Georgie.' . . . Patton was standing there . . . big tears streaming down his face. . . . He was our hero. We were on his side. . . . We knew what he had done and why he had done it. . . . He never came back."[40]

Patton's most impassioned apology was reserved for his friend Dwight Eisenhower. In a lengthy letter Patton wrote, "I am at a loss to find words with which to express my chagrin and grief at having given you, a man to whom I owe everything and for whom I would gladly lay down my life, cause to be displeased with me."[41]

Although by the autumn of 1943 the incident was common knowledge to thousands, Eisenhower's gentleman's agreement with the press held until late November, when muckraking columnist Drew Pearson sensationalized the story to the American public on his weekly syndicated radio program. The result was a storm of criticism of Patton—a groundswell that might well have forced weaker men than Eisenhower, Marshall, and Stimson to sacrifice Patton on the altar of public opinion. Some congressmen and senators called for Patton's dismissal, but Marshall and Stimson refused to bow to the pressure, while overseas Eisenhower reaffirmed his decision to retain Patton for Overlord. Nevertheless, wrote Eisenhower to Patton, "I want you to know though that I think I took the right decision then and I stand by it. You don't need to be afraid of my weakening on the proposition in spite of the fact that, at the moment, I was more than a little annoyed with you."[42]

Of the many reckless acts committed by Patton during his lifetime, none was to prove more ruinous than his slapping two GIs in Sicily. Important decisions were about to be made, and his name would certainly have led the list of those being considered to command the American invasion force in the forthcoming cross-Channel invasion. Instead it took Eisenhower's intervention and the steadfastness of Marshall and Stimson merely to keep from losing Patton's services altogether. And while Eisenhower was adamant that Patton was essential to the defeat of Nazi Germany, he would no longer consider entrusting him with the command of all American ground forces. Eisenhower was willing to tolerate his eccentricities, but any post Patton held would have to be under whoever was appointed to the ground forces command. In September, Marshall announced that Omar Bradley had been selected to command the U.S. First Army, the designated American ground force for Overlord. A dispirited Patton was left in lonely exile in Sicily as his Seventh Army was gradually stripped away to meet Allied commitments in Italy and England.

Had Patton been a lesser general his career would have ended ignominiously after Sicily. That his superiors elected to retain him was best summarized by Assistant Secretary of War John J. McCloy, who told Eisenhower: "Lincoln's remark when they got after Grant comes to mind when I think of Patton—'I can't spare this man—he fights.' "[43]

37.

"A Grinding War of Attrition"

The Italian campaign was "a slogan[,] not a strategy."
—DAVID REYNOLDS

In 1943 one indication of a person's importance differed little from the present day. Movers and shakers appeared on the cover of Henry Luce's influential *Time* magazine. Eisenhower made his first appearance on September 13, 1943, in a cover story about his successes in Sicily and as Allied commander in chief. Full of praise, *Time* even quoted an admiring woman who gushed that Eisenhower was "the handsomest bald man she had ever met."[1]

Such was his popularity in the summer of 1943 that in July, when Eisenhower wrote to Mamie that "at least no crack-brain has yet started running me for political office," he had no idea that he was already being mentioned as a possible presidential candidate. Spearheaded by former subordinates at Camp Colt in 1918, a resolution was drafted urging Eisenhower's election as president for his "leadership qualities." With Marshall the heir apparent for Overlord, some in Washington, among them a Kansas senator, wrote to propose that he run. "A great many of our best people [in Kansas] told me they would like to see you become the Republican candidate for President [in 1944]." Eisenhower, who had never even voted in an election, politely replied that "for any soldier to turn his attention elsewhere would constitute a neglect of duty to his country." To his older brother Arthur he was far more candid. "I live by one doctrine: All of us have now one job to do, which is winning the war. I have been given a responsible post by the President and the War Department. For a soldier to turn from his war duty for any reason is to be guilty of treachery to his country and disloyalty to his superiors. Nothing could sway me from my purpose."[2]

By the early autumn of 1943 the war had begun to tilt in favor of the Allies. With decisive victories at Stalingrad and Kursk, the Red Army had gained the upper hand on the eastern front. Even so the Wehrmacht still posed a considerable threat, and Stalin, impatient to ease the burden of the

Red Army, continued to issue increasingly urgent demands that the Allies open a second front in the west. The inability of the two western allies to agree on a timetable for the cross-Channel invasion made Italy an attractive alternative to the British, who relentlessly insisted that Allied operations continue in the Mediterranean.

At Casablanca the Allies had "kept the question of what they were to do after Sicily hidden in a closet, an unwanted guest at a banquet of accord."[4] Later, with the invasion of Sicily heading toward culmination, try as Marshall might, there was little he could do to resist the next logical step—the invasion of Italy, where the Allies could establish air bases from which their air forces could aid the strategic bombing effort throughout Churchill's so-called soft underbelly of Europe. More importantly, by electing to carry the Mediterranean war into Italy, it was thought that the Allies would compel Hitler to maintain large numbers of troops there instead of in northwest France.

Although there have been periodic attempts at making a case for why the Allies could have made the cross-Channel invasion in 1943, all have floundered on the most critical point, namely that the Allies were simply not prepared militarily to successfully carry out such a momentous event that year. The problem in 1943 was not so much launching an invasion, but in sustaining it once an Allied force landed in France. The specialized amphibious landing craft used later were not available to carry out such an operation in 1942, and in insufficient numbers in 1943. Moreover, the unpredictable weather conditions alone would have precluded any cross-Channel venture after midsummer, and made resupply in the autumn and winter problematic if not impossible. The British had a more fundamental reason. The experiences of the Somme and Passchendaele were still fresh in the minds of a British leadership determined not to squander its army in fruitless causes. Moreover, the British army lacked both the size and perhaps the requisite morale to stand the heavy losses inevitable in a cross-Channel venture in 1942 or 1943.[5]

The Combined Chiefs met again in August 1943 in Quebec, and once again they clashed over the scope of future operations in the Mediterranean before finally agreeing that Overlord would take precedence, but that operations would continue into Italy. Seven divisions were to be transferred to the United Kingdom to prepare for the cross-Channel attack; thus Eisenhower would have to fight with considerably reduced forces and logistical support.

What was lacking both at Quebec or indeed at any time during the Italian campaign was a statement of Allied grand strategy. If the political goals were vague, even less clear were the aims of the forthcoming military operations. Each side viewed grand strategy "through different spectacles," wrote an American official historian. Churchill's Mediterranean strategy envisioned continued Allied operations into Italy, including an offensive that would carry them into its northern provinces so that the Allied air forces could be employed in a direct support role in Overlord operations.[6] Marshall did everything within his power to put the brakes on British zeal for a full-fledged campaign in Italy. The inevitable result was that the Allies launched their campaign in Italy divided along nationalistic and philosophical lines, and with only a short-term vision of what was to become a long-term problem.[7]

Thus, the advent of the Italian campaign came about more by inertia than by deliberate strategy. As Gen. Albert C. Wedemeyer has written, "North Africa led to Sicily . . . and Sicily led to the Italian boot." Militarily the forthcoming campaign would, said historian David Reynolds, become "a slogan[,] not a strategy."[8]

The invasion of Sicily hastened the downfall of the Italian dictator, Benito Mussolini, and his fascist government, both of which were deposed in late July 1943. King Victor Emmanuel III immediately appointed Field Marshal Pietro Badoglio, an officer as much a part of the problem as of the solution, to head a new Italian military government. Although Badoglio, "a barely fumigated Fascist," proclaimed the war would go on as before, within weeks the new Italian leader was already double-crossing his German ally by secretly negotiating an armistice with the Allies, all the while proclaiming his allegiance to Germany, leading Hitler angrily to proclaim his actions "the biggest impudence in history." While the new Italian government played both ends of a deadly game by extricating themselves from the Germans without severe repercussions and suing for peace with the Allies, it fell to Eisenhower to make it happen.

Secret negotiations took place in neutral Lisbon, Portugal, during August between the Allies and the new Badoglio government for the surrender of Italy. The Allied policy of unconditional surrender mandated at Casablanca did not originally include Italy, but the Combined Chiefs gave Eisenhower little latitude. The official Allied position was a demand for unconditional surrender before any concessions would even be discussed. Roosevelt was adamantly unwilling to let fascist Italy so easily off the hook; "we will have no truck with Fascism in any way, shape or manner," he told the nation in one of his famous "fireside chats," while privately admitting he would accept something less.[9] Churchill might well have taken a much softer stance had Foreign Secretary Anthony Eden not sold the British War Cabinet on the same hard-line approach. Eisenhower was more pragmatic, and had he been given the authority, would have extended an olive branch to the Italians. He tried a ploy to soften Allied terms by attempting to win approval for a draft ultimatum to the Italians that merely called for an armistice. It was rudely chopped to pieces by the Combined Chiefs, and when neither Churchill or Roosevelt would back him, Eisenhower's attempt at compromise was officially stillborn.

The Allies were represented by Bedell Smith and the AFHQ G-2, Kenneth

Strong. As his chief negotiator, Eisenhower praised Smith as "a master of negotiation," an ability that "in an Allied command . . . was priceless."[10] The Italian representative was an anti-Mussolini emissary, Gen. Giuseppe Castellano, who arrived with hopes of Italy switching sides and joining the Allies, but with no real authority to negotiate anything. The ominous German buildup in Italy made the new government correctly nervous that Hitler would retaliate before the Allies could land in sufficient numbers to protect their army and the Eternal City from retributions. To keep the Germans in the dark, there followed a series of secret negotiations and clandestine meetings using false names—enough to have filled a James Bond novel.

As the negotiations dragged on through August, the Italians accepted that they had virtually no bargaining position and no other options but, deeply concerned about what was certain to be a violent German reaction, pleaded that the announcement of the Italian surrender be withheld until the Allies could land and protect Rome. In July the Allies had bombed Rome's two huge marshaling yards, the hub of all rail movement between northern and southern Italy. Another raid in mid-August put even further pressure on the Italians. The Allies became convinced that surrender was feasible, but that some concession was necessary in order to spur completion of the deal and enlist Italian aid against the Germans.

Italian fears were well founded. Mussolini's fall led the Germans to hastily revive earlier contingency plans in the event of an Italian collapse. Sixteen German divisions began pouring into northern Italy under the guise of reinforcing Kesselring in the event of an Allied invasion, and Rommel was recalled from a special mission to Greece and given command of the newly formed Army Group B. "Overnight, Italy went from German ally to German-occupied country. Now it was about to become a battleground in a grinding war of attrition whose costs were justified by no defensible military or political purpose."[11]

Field Marshal Kesselring convinced Hitler that German strategy should be to defend south of Rome, along Italy's narrowest point. Such a defense offered the advantages of denying the Allies vital air bases in central and northern Italy and discouraging any attempt to invade the Balkans and threaten the crucial sources of raw materials used to fuel the German war machine. Kesselring realized he could not hold southern Italy indefinitely, but preferred defending there to doing so in the Apennines and the Po Valley of northern Italy. Unlike most of the other German theater commanders, Kesselring was permitted to conduct the Italian campaign according to his own dictates—something that was to make the Allies pay dearly for every foot of ground in Italy during the longest and bloodiest campaign fought by the Allies in the West during World War II.

·   ·   ·

Italy presented an entirely new set of challenges for Eisenhower, beginning with the decision to invade Italy at two different points in early September with Mark Clark's Fifth Army and Montgomery's Eighth Army. In effect Eisenhower was directed to fight a war in Italy with no identifiable or stated strategic goal, rapidly diminishing assets, and only the vaguest prior planning. Eisenhower was further handicapped by the requirement to use only assets already available to him, a great many of which were due to be sent to England by the end of 1943.

Clark favored and fought hard for an invasion in the Bay of Gaeta, north of Naples, a site that met all the necessary criteria for an amphibious landing but one. Clark was overruled by Tedder, who rejected Gaeta primarily on the basis that Naples represented the maximum range of his Sicily-based squadrons. Even at that distance, air cover would only amount to approximately twenty minutes over the battle front. Hence the Allied planners recommended that Fifth Army invade Italy along the Gulf of Salerno, approximately twenty miles south of Naples. Clark thought Salerno a poor choice because the mountains that encircled the beachhead strongly favored the defender, and appealed to Eisenhower for a change of venue. Although Eisenhower had learned from Torch and Husky to mistrust the optimism of his planners, with both Tedder and Cunningham strongly opposed to Gaeta, he refused to intervene. The committee system still ruled.[12]

Indeed, the boldness and quick-strike philosophy that Eisenhower had so favored in Tunisia and Sicily was entirely lacking over Salerno, despite an earlier recommendation of the Combined Chiefs in July for just such an operation at Gaeta that would simply outflank enemy forces in southern Italy. Marshall favored a quick strike to seize Naples, erroneously leading the British to conclude that he was now supporting their strategy for Italy. To the contrary, by carrying out such a strike, Marshall hoped to *minimize* operations in Italy. The Allies, he believed, were at the "crossroads" of the war, represented by a short, limited campaign in Italy and an all-out effort toward Overlord.[13] While not rejecting the idea outright, Eisenhower thought it "unlikely to succeed," and eventually opted for a far more conservative approach via Salerno and Calabria.[14]

The Allied planners were also worried about control of the Italian boot and the vital shipping lanes of the Strait of Messina. Eisenhower decided that a force was necessary in southern Italy to draw valuable German reserves away from Salerno, to allow for the Eighth Army invasion, called Operation Baytown. No consideration seems to have been given to the possibility that the Germans might refuse to do battle in southern Calabria.

The shortage of landing craft was to prove the single greatest impediment to Allied operations in the Mediterranean and northwestern Europe. There were never enough, and with priorities split between Europe and the Pacific, it became a constant struggle to obtain adequate craft with which to mount amphibious operations. More ominous in the Italian theater was the knowledge that, by early 1944, most of the Mediterranean-based shipping would be shifted to the United Kingdom for Overlord. The inadequacy of landing craft meant that Baytown must necessarily precede the Salerno landings. Once Montgomery gained a foothold in the toe of southern Calabria, the landing craft were to be committed to the Salerno landings a week later, on September 9.[15]

With the close proximity of Naples to Salerno, the architects of what was dubbed Operation Avalanche focused on the former, which the Allies urgently required for its excellent port facilities. The basic concept of the plan was that, once established ashore, Fifth Army would link up with Montgomery's Eighth Army, driving north through the Italian boot. Together they would capture Naples, then advance to Rome.

Salerno, however, was dangerously ill conceived. Clark's plan was less like an avalanche and more like a snowball, wrote Eisenhower biographer Geoffrey Perret. The inexperience of Clark and his planners was evident in a deeply flawed plan that called for landing a mere three-division force across a lengthy thirty-six-mile front, split by the River Sele, a formidable obstacle to mutual support that Patton correctly predicted would lead to a potentially disastrous German counterattack. "Clark had chosen to be strong nowhere and weak everywhere. The Germans might as well have done his planning."[16] Equally ill advised was Clark's decision to launch his landing craft from nearly seventeen miles at sea and to forgo a naval bombardment on the (unfounded) assumption that he would achieve tactical surprise. Despite strong representations from the navy that surprise was impossible, and "any officer with a pair of dividers could figure out that the Gulf of Salerno was the northernmost practicable landing place for the Allies," Clark insisted on proceeding against their advice.[17]

Clark's optimism about the chances of Allied success was not shared by Alexander, the designated commander of all ground operations in Italy. Following the pattern established in Sicily, Alexander elected not to redress the plan's serious shortcomings, even after declaring it "a dangerous gamble." In an inexplicable twist of logic, his misgivings over Salerno failed to dampen Alexander's conviction that the Allies would capture Rome by mid-October at the latest.

Among those who considered Baytown a wasteful and unnecessary operation was Montgomery, who complained to Brooke that the same lack of coordination and strategic goals that had characterized operations in Sicily now threatened the forthcoming campaign in Italy. The focus of his concern was Alexander, whom he esteemed as a friend but about whom he had few illusions when it came to masterminding a major operation of war. The end of the Sicily campaign only reinforced his apprehension about what lay ahead in Italy. "The trouble is there is no higher-up grip on this campaign. . . . It beats me how you can run a campaign . . . with each of the three Commanders of the three Services about 600 miles from each other." However unpleasant it seemed to his critics, there was considerable merit to Montgomery's criticism.[18]

Montgomery believed that a costly and laborious drive north through southern Italy was unnecessary. "Before we embark on major operations on the mainland of Europe we must have a master plan and know how we propose to develop these operations," he said. "I have not been told of any master plan and I must therefore assume that there was none."[19] His chief of staff, Maj. Gen. Francis "Freddie" de Guingand, asked the question no one seemed willing to address: "If AVALANCHE is a success, then we should reinforce that front for there is little point in laboriously fighting our way up Southern ITALY. It is better to leave the enemy to decay there or let him have the trouble of moving himself up from the foot to where we are concentrated."[20] Yet neither Eisenhower nor Alexander ever delineated who was going to do what, with what objective. Thus the Italian campaign was already adrift before it even began.[21]

There was little Montgomery could do to alter Allied thinking or persuade Eisenhower to cancel Baytown and use the threat of landings in Calabria as a means of tying down enemy forces that might otherwise imperil Fifth Army at Salerno. His uncompromising stand over Husky had all but worn out his welcome as an arbitrator of Allied policy. Consequently his complaints about the futility of Baytown were not only ignored but provided additional ammunition to those anxious to discredit him. Eisenhower was infuriated by the time it took Montgomery to launch Baytown. He wanted action, and complained, "I told General Alexander I believed we could do it in a rowboat. We sat there in Messina from 17 August until 3 September."[22]

Although the decisions made by the Allied high command during this period of the war in the Mediterranean reflected a lack of strategic goals for the Italian campaign, there was one example of uncharacteristic rashness and meddling by a senior staff officer who had no real concept of the consequences. Giant II was an operation by which Rome was to be seized by the U.S. 82nd Airborne Division. In theory it was a brilliant masterstroke; if put in practice, like Salerno, it was a recipe for potential disaster. Its most powerful advocate was Bedell Smith, who sold both Alexander and Eisenhower on its merits. The plan was to drop the division outside Rome, where it would link up with approximately four divisions of Italian troops and, together, seize Rome by a *coup de main,* assisted by the Roman citizenry, who, according to Smith, would "drop kettles, bricks, [and] hot water on the Germans in the streets of Rome."[23] The result, argued Smith, would have been a mandatory retreat to the north by German forces then in central and southern Italy. If ever an argument existed for a staff officer to stick to his own business, it was Smith's ludicrous assertion that this half-baked operation would intimidate Kesselring.

Among the opponents of Giant II was Clark, who would have lost his only strategic reserve for Avalanche, which he intended to employ in blocking positions along the Volturno River to prevent panzer reserves from rushing from the north to the aid of General Heinrich von Vietinghoff's Tenth Army at Salerno. An irate Clark told Eisenhower, "No! That's my division! . . . Taking away the Eighty-Second just as the fighting starts is like cutting off my left arm." Eisenhower refused to budge, and Clark was left with a vague assurance that he would get the division back as soon as Giant II was completed.

The commander of the 82nd Airborne, Maj. Gen. Matthew B. Ridgway, refused to commit his division on the assurance of AFHQ staff officers whom he distrusted. In declining to cancel Giant II, Alexander assured Ridgway that ground troops would fight their way to Rome to reinforce the 82nd Airborne within five days. Ridgway persisted, and with Eisenhower's consent the division artillery commander, Brig. Gen. Maxwell Taylor, undertook a secret mission to Rome. Taylor soon determined that Smith's claims were absurd. Not only was the Italian will to fight dubious, but the notion that two nearby veteran German panzer grenadier divisions would be deterred by a small U.S. airborne force without heavy supporting weapons or air support was sheer fantasy.[24]

Initially there was sufficient airlift capability only to move the equivalent of a reinforced regiment to Rome, and the situation not only bore scant relation to the claims of its proponents, but the Italians, fearful of German retaliation, backed out of their earlier commitment to support the operation. Only hours before the operation was to have commenced, Taylor urgently radioed AFHQ to abort Giant II. In Sicily sixty-two aircraft, engines running and loaded with paratroopers, awaited final instructions for takeoff to Rome, when Brig. Gen. Lyman Lemnitzer (a postwar army chief of staff and NATO supreme commander), sent personally by Eisenhower, arrived from North Africa barely in time to avert what would have been certain annihilation of major elements of the 82nd Airborne. For daring to oppose this foolish operation, Taylor and Ridgway became objects of censure from Smith and certain other members of the AFHQ staff. Taylor in particular was singled out for vilification by Smith, who branded him a coward. In his memoirs the gallant Ridgway put his career on the line. "And when the time comes that I must meet my Maker, the source of most humble pride to me will not be accomplishments in battle, but the fact that I was guided to make the decision to oppose this thing. . . . I deeply and sincerely believe that by taking the stand I took we saved the lives of thousands of brave men."[25]

On September 3, six days before the invasion of Salerno, Eisenhower flew to Sicily to witness the signing of a secret armistice agreement with the Italians at Alexander's headquarters in Cassible, Sicily. Signed by Smith and Castellano and sealed by toasts of whiskey, the document contained only deliberately vague references to unconditional surrender, which permitted the Italians to accept and sign what they believed to be a face-saving armistice. When it came to duplicity, nothing the Allies did in the name of diplomacy during World War II exceeded what happened next, when Smith suddenly produced another document that contained a list of demands headed by the words "The Italian Land, Sea and Air Forces hereby surrender unconditionally."[26] The Italians had been sandbagged, and there was nothing they could do about it. To prevent instant German retaliation there would be no public announcement until barely five hours before the Salerno landings, when Eisenhower would broadcast the surrender of Italy to the world at the same time that Badoglio made a similar announcement to the Italian nation. Unlike the Darlan deal, this decision was not made by Eisenhower, who had hoped in vain to keep politics out of what he believed ought to have been purely a military matter, but dictated by London and Washington. Personally Eisenhower was disgusted at its duplicity and thought its terms unduly harsh, describing it as "a crooked deal" that would probably remain secret for at least ten years after the war.

Eisenhower's disappointment at having to cancel Giant II turned to rage the morning of September 8, when he arrived at his forward headquarters at Amilcar, Tunisia, expecting to meet with Castellano. Instead he was handed Maxwell Taylor's message from Rome that Badoglio had backed out of his commitment to secure the Rome airfields and help defend the city with Italian troops. Badoglio's reason was that it seemed clear that the Allies would be unable to protect Rome from German reprisals. Nearly apoplectic with rage, Eisenhower began snapping pencils in half drafting an immediate reply to Badoglio that threatened dire consequences. News of the armistice would be broadcast as planned. "Today is X-day and I expect you to do your part. I do not accept your message," he said. When Castellano arrived a short time later, a scowling Eisenhower curtly read the Italian the message in the presence of Alexander and Cunningham.

An equal measure of Eisenhower's fury was reserved for his own chief of staff. When Badoglio's message of retraction arrived in Algiers, Smith not only duly sent it on to Eisenhower, but also to the Combined Chiefs, including with it "a message in Eisenhower's name advising on the cancellation of GIANT II. . . . When Smith's message arrived at Amilcar, Eisenhower displayed the temper he usually succeeded in concealing. He was furious that Smith had asked for a recommendation from the CCOS; he wanted no advice from Washington and London. (Smith's hide was saved only by the distance between Amilcar and Algiers.)"[27]

Other than this foolhardy moment, the AFHQ staff leaned toward conservatism, and, as Marshall later observed, with such a diverse staff there was bound to be a broad spectrum of points of view. With the exception of Churchill, the British tended to be the more conservative in planning military operations. Marshall thought that under such conditions, "by the time you watered down the plan it was a question if you would have an operation or not." Specifically he had Italy in mind.[28] It was the first but not the last time Marshall criticized Eisenhower's handling of the Italian campaign.

Badoglio lost his battle with the Allies to withhold the announcement of Italy's capitulation until after the invasion of Salerno, and on September 8 the BBC announced that "the Italian armed forces have accepted unconditional surrender." Over Radio Algiers came a similar proclamation from Eisenhower. To most members of the war-weary Italian army the news was greeted with a sense of relief. There were few true fascists left with a desire to continue fighting as an ally of Nazi Germany.

The invasion of Salerno on September 9, 1943, was the first of the bloodiest campaigns fought by the Western Allies during World War II, and was bitterly contested by elements of the German Tenth Army. Their relentless defense of the Salerno beachhead was typical of what the Allies encountered in each of their battles in the Mediterranean. The Germans fought tenaciously to retain their positions and counterattack; when that was impossible or militarily impractical, they fought delaying actions until they could establish new defenses elsewhere. In Sicily they had been outnumbered, outgunned, outmaneuvered, and unable to meet the Allied invaders on the beaches. At Salerno, however, despite Allied air superiority and an overwhelming preponderance of firepower, the Germans controlled the high ground and the exits from the invasion beaches and demonstrated that they had every intention of driving the Allies back into the sea.

Without the timely and often valiant support of the Allied fleet, Clark's force might not have survived. Time and again destroyers and gunboats braved the intense German fire to maneuver close to the shore to deliver counterbattery fire or to suppress a German counterattack. The Fifth Army beachhead was perilous because of a seven-mile gap between the British and U.S. corps, which would have to be closed before the Germans rolled up its flanks. By the third day (D+3) the situation had become so dire that the Allies were close to being driven back into the sea. American losses mounted with disturbing speed. Units were isolated from one another and chopped to pieces, communications were severed, and the battle became a struggle for survival, not conquest. With his reserves already committed and virtually nothing left with which to stop a determined German counterattack, Clark began making plans to evacuate the entire U.S. VI Corps and reland it in the British sector, a military operation of frightful difficulty.

The news from the beachhead hit AFHQ like a thunderclap appeared to be a disaster in the making visibly disturbed Eisenhowe openly questioned if his longtime friend had lost his nerve and wheth.. ne had erred in giving Clark command of the Fifth Army. Eisenhower was also heard to mutter that he would probably be "out" if the battle ended in disaster, and sent a pessimistic cable to the Combined Chiefs, noting that Salerno "will be a matter of touch and go for the next few days . . . we are in for some very tough fighting."[29] Butcher noted that Eisenhower thought that "Clark should show the spirit of a naval captain. If necessary, he should go down with his ship." Nevertheless Eisenhower was determined to "move heaven and earth" to save Fifth Army. Cunningham and Tedder lent their support by sending additional naval reinforcements to Salerno, and by increasing air support that included the use of B-17 strategic bombers to attack German positions. With commendable understatement Cunningham later wrote of the proposed evacuation that it "would have resulted in a reverse of the first magnitude—an Allied defeat which would have completely offset the Italian surrender, and have been hailed by the Germans as a smashing victory."[30]

There was one slender thread of hope, and Clark seized upon it. He ordered the 82nd Airborne Division to the rescue. Across the front came the order to "hold at all costs," until two regimental combat teams were parachuted into the beachhead on successive nights, in what was the most successful Allied airborne operation of the entire war. Their presence became a major factor in the outcome of the battle for Salerno.[31]

After numerous German counterattacks failed to push the Allies back into the sea, and with German equipment losses mounting and fatigue beginning to take a toll, Kesselring ordered Tenth Army to withdraw. By September 17 the Germans were on the move to the north, and when Naples fell to the Allies on October 1, 1943, the first phase of the Italian campaign was over. Churchill sent Eisenhower a telegram of congratulations that quoted the Duke of Wellington: " 'It was a damned close-run thing,' but your policy of running risks has been vindicated."[32]

Eisenhower liked to portray himself as more or less impervious to criticism. In truth he craved praise and was thin skinned when slighted or in self-defense. He had no sooner begun to bask in Churchill's praise than, twenty-four hours later, George Marshall "took the starch out of Ike" by means of a telegram, devoid of praise, that was a jolting reminder that there could be no resting on Allied laurels after Salerno. Ever anxious to dispose of the Italian campaign as quickly as possible, Marshall wanted to know if Eisenhower could hold the line below Naples and concentrate instead on an amphibious end run behind enemy lines to capture Rome. Eisenhower was shocked by Marshall's no-nonsense bluntness and the absence of even a simple gesture of congratulations. His pride was so deeply wounded by the intimation that he lacked aggressiveness and initiative that he ate neither breakfast nor lunch; "he is grieved," recorded the faithful Butcher, "to think that General Marshall does not give him credit for cracking the whip. . . . [It] caused him a great deal of mental anguish. . . . We have the paradox of the Prime Minister applauding Ike's willingness to take risks while General Marshall . . . criticize[s] him."[33]

On September 17 Eisenhower visited Clark's beachhead command post in a forest not far from where heavy fighting was still raging. The two generals sat under a tree and were so engrossed in conversation that when a German artillery shell whizzed overhead and exploded close by, they scarcely took note of men diving into nearby ditches. Eisenhower was amused by newspaper accounts that the two had been so green and therefore too dumb to realize they ought to have taken cover, recalling how, in North Africa, he and Clark had been obliged to dive ignominiously into numerous ditches virtually "every time we saw a plane in the air."[34]

The Allied admirals, airmen, and generals Eisenhower commanded in the Mediterranean were a fractious lot who did not always serve him well. The airmen were stubbornly determined to assert their autonomy as a military arm and balked at attempts to curb their pursuit of that goal. Sicily had exacerbated the problems of interservice rivalry, first exposed in Tunisia when Patton and Coningham had clashed over the proper role of close air support. Eisenhower's air chief, Sir Arthur Tedder, presided over the most independent-minded group of men ever assembled. Dubbed "Eisenhower's Flying Scot" by *Saturday Evening Post* correspondent Demaree Bess, Tedder was committed to creating a unified air command in the Mediterranean, and remained stubbornly independent when it came to air operations.[35]

Eisenhower's relations with ABC Cunningham were perhaps the most solid of all. "There will always live with me his answer when I asked him in the fall of 1943 to send the British fleet, carrying a division of soldiers, into Taranto Harbor, known to be filled with mines and treachery. 'Sir,' he said, 'His Majesty's Fleet is here to go wherever you may send it!' "[36] The aggressiveness lacking in the Royal Navy in Sicily was very much in evidence at Salerno, where the U.S. Navy and the Royal Navy not only saved the day but paid a stiff price in lost lives and warships.[37]

His ground commander in chief, Alexander, possessed every desirable trait that Eisenhower could have desired in a subordinate, save one. Alexander could have served as the poster boy for the ideal commander of a large multinational force. Unfortunately his laissez-faire style of command varied little from his performance throughout the war in the Mediterranean. At Salerno he failed to influence the outcome of the battle in any but a negative way. Alexander's most important responsibility was to ensure that Clark as invasion commander received the optimum support, but he failed to invest the beachhead with additional support at an earlier moment by committing the 82nd Airborne when and where their presence would have avoided the near disaster. Although Eighth Army's advance north from Calabria to reinforce Fifth Army at Salerno was impeded by mines and the fact that the retreating Germans had destroyed practically every bridge, Alexander failed to instill a sense of urgency in Montgomery, address the obvious problem of Clark's flawed invasion plan, or even so much as state publicly his opinion that he considered it faulty.

The mess at Salerno was entirely of Alexander's and Clark's own making and the solution was not for Montgomery to race to Fifth Army's rescue but for the two commanders to have made better use of the resources immediately available. Salerno was Mark Clark's baptism of fire as a commander, and it taught him the wrong lessons, one of which was that it would pay dividends to "follow Montgomery's advice not to take any notice of what Alexander told him to do because Alexander was a man of straw."[38]

Clark was constantly at war with his superiors over real and imagined slights to American prestige by the British. His lack of battlefield experience was painfully evident at Salerno, which marked him as a commander with a great deal to learn about high command. What some perceived as self-confidence and professionalism, others viewed as conceit and extreme arrogance, an image that was not enhanced at Salerno, where Clark would only permit his photograph to be taken from his "good [left] side" by an army photographer who always accompanied him.

As they had in North Africa, the British senior commanders continued to be critical of the American performance, believing that, Sicily notwithstanding, little had changed since Kasserine. The veteran British corps commander at Salerno, Lt. Gen. Richard McCreery, held Clark in utter contempt, and in return the Fifth Army commander scornfully referred to the British general as a "feather duster," a term he also used to describe Alexander. In a little-known interview with the official U.S. Army historians after the war, Alexander revealed that, with few exceptions, he did not rank the American generals under his command highly.[39]

Someone had to pay for the near disaster at Salerno, and it was the beachhead commander, Maj. Gen. Ernest J. Dawley, in whom neither Eisenhower nor Alexander had confidence. At Alexander's instigation, and prodded by Eisenhower, Clark relieved Dawley of his command.[40] In keeping with his ruthless policy of dealing harshly with failed commanders, Eisenhower swiftly reduced him to colonel and had him sent home. In a defense of his generalship in early 1944, Eisenhower's assertion that "we had a happy family" sugarcoated the difficulties of the coalition war fought in the Mediterranean under his aegis.[41] On several occasions in Italy, Lemnitzer, Alexander's American deputy chief of staff, thought his boss would relieve Clark. There was, in fact, ample justification for relieving him, as he had made every mistake in the book and then heaped the majority of the blame on Dawley, whose performance as beachhead commander was not nearly as inept as Clark portrayed it to Eisenhower. Thus, Dawley's relief was partly a face-saving gesture by the Allied high command, as he became the first of several senior field commanders who would pay a high price for a faulty plan.

Although Salerno ought to have reinforced Eisenhower's earlier reservations about his friend, he gave Clark the benefit of his doubts. Whatever his private misgivings, as a practical matter, with American prestige on the line, it would have been a public relations disaster had Eisenhower fired Clark. In a report to Marshall written after the battle, Eisenhower hedged, noting that Clark was "not so good as Bradley in winning, almost without effort, the complete confidence of everyone around him, including his British associates. He is not the equal of Patton in his refusal to see anything but victory . . . but he is carrying his full weight and, so far, has fully justified his selection for his present important post."[42] Left unspoken was Eisenhower's great debt to Clark.

Eisenhower's choice to replace Dawley was John P. Lucas (who would pay for another flawed plan in early 1944 at Anzio). All in all the ship of command was adrift but not sinking. What made Ike's job all the more difficult and frustrating during the dismal autumn of 1943 was his awareness that he was virtually helpless to alter course—short of mass firings that might have claimed him as a victim as well.

The newly appointed supreme commander in southeast Asia, Adm. Louis Mountbatten, hoped to emulate Eisenhower and wrote for advice. In his reply Eisenhower admitted that his role was somewhat analogous to that of a chairman of the board. However, this did not make him a mere figurehead. He had "very definite executive responsibilities," which had to be executed "firmly" and "wisely." On one point Eisenhower was adamant: "The British system of command has proved that it can work where only *British Empire forces* are involved." Ultimately, he warned Mountbatten, "your personality and good sense *must* make it work. Otherwise *Allied* action in any theater will be impossible."[43] What he did not reveal to Mountbatten was that the job was not all it was cracked up to be—something he would have to learn for himself. "In my youthful days I used to read about commanders of armies and envied them what I supposed to be great freedom in action and decision," he disclosed to Mamie in one of his increasingly frequent moments of frustration. "What a notion! The demands upon me that must be met make me a slave rather than a master."[44] Nevertheless, despite the difficulty of working with strong-willed men, there is little doubt that, under anyone other than Eisenhower, the problems facing the alliance might well have proved insoluble.

·   ·   ·

Harold Macmillan frequently dealt with Eisenhower, often one-on-one, and his assessment of the Allied commander in chief in the autumn of 1943 was a reflection of Eisenhower's unique ability to charm supporters and critics alike. "Although completely ignorant of Europe and wholly uneducated (in any normal sense of the word)," wrote Macmillan,

he has two great qualities which make him much easier to deal with than many superficially better-endowed American or British generals. First, he will always listen to and try to grasp the point of an argument. Second, he is absolutely fair-minded and, if he has prejudices, never allows them to sway his final judgment. Compared with the wooden heads and desiccated hearts of many British soldiers I see here, he is a jewel of broad-mindedness and wisdom.[45]

Writing to Mamie, Eisenhower wondered "whether anyone who has carried heavy responsibilities and has had to jump constantly from hither to thither to yon can really settle down and live a serene life. The eternal pound, pound, pound seems a burden, but when it once ceases it is possible that many of us will be nigh onto nervous wrecks, and wholly unfit for normal life."[46] To old friend Aksel Nielsen he had written that although he felt pretty good, "I must admit that sometimes I feel a thousand years old when I struggle to my bed at night."[47]

During the summer and early autumn of 1943 there were signs of tension in the letters Ike and Mamie wrote each other that went beyond the subject of Kay Summersby. When, for example, Mamie wrote to suggest that Tex Lee ought to be promoted, he swiftly rebuked her for venturing to tell him what to do. Disappointed when she failed to acknowledge his promotion to major general in the Regular Army, he sent Mamie a none-too-subtle reproof, saying, "I thought it rather curious that you didn't send me a teletype. . . . Maybe, to you, the incident did not constitute a significant personal honor—I thought it most unusual."[48]

His infrequent exchanges with John were more lighthearted. After receiving a letter from his father "full of parental advice," John wrote back that while he appreciated the counsel, "after reading what you said about an officer's appearance, I picked up the paper and saw a picture of you in the raunchiest dress [service] cap I ever saw," which would have been worth six demerits at West Point. Unwilling to be upstaged, Eisenhower immediately replied that several of John's grades were too low, later crowing to Mamie that he had "ragged" Johnny "because he had ribbed me a lot on the appearance of my cap in a picture."[49]

Salerno failed to dampen the Allied belief that Rome would fall within the next six weeks. This optimism was directly attributable to Ultra, which intercepted Nazi message traffic in mid-August indicating an intention to establish the main German defenses in the northern Apennines. When Hitler changed his mind and supported Kesselring's view that southern Italy should be defended, it was in the belief that Allied aims in Italy were Rome and the establishment of air bases from which to launch further operations into either southern France or the Balkans. By early October, Ultra had provided conclusive evidence that the Germans would defend south of Rome during the winter of 1943–44. This news relieved Alexander's anxiety that the Germans would fail to "cooperate" in the Allied strategy of tying down the maximum number of German divisions in Italy. Everything has its price, and this strategic decision meant that Kesselring's twenty-five divisions were fully capable of limited offensive action against the Allies.

At Quebec the CCOS had at long last determined that Overlord would occur in May 1944. Allied strategy centered on keeping the Wehrmacht in Italy fully committed, so that its veteran divisions could not be shifted to France to help repel the cross-Channel invasion. Although the primary Allied task in Italy was allegedly diversionary, there was considerable pressure on Alexander to act offensively and capture Rome. Churchill was emphatic that Rome must fall by the end of the year, warning Alexander that if its liberation were prolonged, "no one can measure the consequences."[50]

The Eternal City meant far more to the Allies than merely the capital city of their former enemy. Militarily Rome was of considerable strategic importance for its road and rail net and nearby airfields. The immense political and cultural significance of the Italian capital also made its capture of psychological value to the Allies. Moreover, the elimination of Rome from the Axis sphere of control would send a signal to Hitler and to the rest of the world that Berlin, which was being pounded into rubble by the round-the-clock combined bomber offensive of the RAF and USAAF, was next.

Though speed was of the essence before the Germans were able to strengthen their defenses between Naples and Rome, it was impossible to achieve. The mountainous terrain and the many rivers of central Italy were formidable obstacles—and Kesselring's greatest ally. Combined with freezing winters, mud and rain, and a poor road net, the terrain was the worst imaginable on which to fight a large-scale military campaign. The mountains could be negotiated only via mule train by sweating, weary soldiers, who had to take over the portage of guns, ammunition, and supplies when the trails became too steep even for the animals. The successful crossing of a mountain pass merely led to yet another series of identical obstacles. No less difficult were river-crossing operations, where the logistics were enormous, the execution demanding, and rapid exploitation essential. Italian rivers run mostly west or east, thus the old line about "one more river to cross" took on a grim reality throughout the campaign. In Italy the Allies were forced to overcome such obstacles during the most difficult time of year, when the wretched weather grounded the Allied air forces that Eisenhower regarded as being worth another ten divisions.[51]

As the weather worsened and the Allied advance slowed to a crawl, the capture of Rome in 1943 became an illusion to which the Allied commanders, from Eisenhower on down, continued to cling with increasing naïveté. As one biographer has noted, "Ike refused to admit that a stalemate was developing . . . [and] doggedly persisted with a strategy that made less sense every day."[52]

Eisenhower's initial enthusiasm soon waned as he became the first to recognize that the optimistic predictions about the capture of Rome were pie in the sky. The U.S. official history records that in early October 1943, Eisenhower's optimism suddenly "underwent a startling change." If the Germans elected to defend southern Italy, "there will be very hard and bitter fighting before we can hope to reach Rome," he informed the Combined Chiefs.[53]

After Salerno the Allies' main accomplishment was the Eighth Army's capture of the all-important Foggia airfield complex in late September, ushering in a new phase of the air war. For the first time the vital Romanian oil fields, and strategic targets within Germany, were vulnerable to attack by Allied bombers. Clark's Fifth Army was a spent force, unable to mount a serious pursuit operation, and the British Eighth Army was little better off. Most formations, particularly the veteran desert troops, were simply worn out from endless combat that, for most, dated to Alamein the previous year, and in poor shape to sustain an offensive under the conditions existing in Italy. Most of the senior American commanders, including Clark, believed the British to be overcautious on the battlefield. Few understood the magnitude of their growing manpower shortages, or that by the end of 1943 they faced a major crisis wherever they fought.

The Allies literally inched toward a winter stalemate along the Liri Valley, where Kesselring had established his defenses behind what was called the Gustav Line, a bulwark centered on the town of Cassino and on the heights above the town, which were dominated by the imposing Benedictine monastery of Monte Cassino. By November 1943 Eisenhower and Alexander had come to the conclusion that the stalemate over the advance to Rome could not be broken unless the Allies initiated an amphibious end run and drew away German troops manning the Gustav Line. An operation was planned to land a corps-size force of some sixty thousand U.S. and British troops behind enemy lines at Anzio and Nettuno, thirty-five miles southwest of Rome. Lack of confidence and the imminent withdrawal of landing craft left the fate of the Anzio landings uncertain until late December, when Churchill became involved and pressured the Combined Chiefs to delay their return to the United Kingdom.

The crux of the great dilemma facing Eisenhower and the Allies in Italy was one that plagued the Allies throughout the entire war: namely that the Germans usually failed to do what the Allies assumed they would. In Italy, Hitler and Kesselring determined the course of events. As Alexander later described it, "We had the initiative in operations but the Germans had the initiative in deciding whether we should achieve our object since they were free . . . to refuse to allow themselves to be contained in Italy. Had they decided to withdraw altogether, for instance, they could have defended the line of the Alps, or one of the strong river lines in northeastern Italy, with the minimum of forces and, instead of us containing them, they would be containing us."[54]

The term "Murphy's Law" had yet to be coined, but it certainly would have applied to Italy, where during twenty months the Allies fought one bloody battle after another for reasons no one ever fully understood. Allied strategy in Italy never seemed to be to win, but rather to drag out the war there for as long as possible and in so doing to keep Kesselring's army group from being dispersed to fight in France. Eisenhower was among the first to learn that the war in Italy bore scant resemblance to the precampaign ivory tower that dominated Allied conceptions. As one historian has written, "Few soldiers of World War II experienced the kind of deadening, soul-destroying fighting that characterized" World War I. "Most of those who did experience it fought in Italy."[55]

Despite the bloody nose at Salerno, Eisenhower and Alexander believed that Kesselring's army group would cede southern Italy and Rome to the Allies, carry out a fighting retreat into northern Italy, and defend the Apennines. Kesselring not only failed to play that hand but managed to convince Hitler that the best place to defend Italy was at Cassino. The soundness of Kesselring's judgment was borne out in the deadly and prolonged stalemate that not only kept the Allies pinned down from September 1943 to mid-May 1944 but extracted increasingly heavy casualties at a time when there were other options available to the Allied leadership. As the weather worsened in the autumn of 1943, the Italian campaign slipped deeper into bloody stalemate.

38.

"Who Will Command Overlord?"

I could not escape the feeling that both Marshall and I were like two pieces in a chess game, each compelled to await the pleasure of the players.

For almost all of 1943 one key decision had not been made: Who would command Overlord? The time had long since passed when this question should have been resolved. That it had not became the latest complication in the long-running soap opera of Allied decision making. Both Marshall and Brooke coveted the post of supreme commander for the cross-Channel invasion. Prior to Quebec it had been assumed that the supreme commander would be British, partly in return for Eisenhower's selection in the Mediterranean in 1942, but mainly because Overlord would be mounted from Britain and British forces would play a dominant role, at least initially. In July 1943 Churchill had told Brooke he wanted him to take the invasion command, only to change his mind at Quebec for the same reasons Roosevelt eventually did over Marshall. FDR's change of heart was induced by a warning from Secretary of War Stimson that "the shadows of Passchendaele and Dunkirk" would be obscured by the notion that the war could be won via the Mediterranean and the nonexistent "soft underbelly."[1]

Churchill thought he had sold FDR on Brooke, only to have the president later change his mind and insist that public opinion would demand an American commander. Churchill had reluctantly acceded, with a British officer to be named second in command. Marshall categorically refused either to lobby for the job or even to respond on the subject when asked by Roosevelt, replying that it was the president's decision, not his, and that "I would cheerfully go whatever way he wanted me to go."

Marshall's apparent future appointment was known even to the Germans. Joseph Goebbels unleashed propaganda proclaiming "that Marshall had been 'fired' and that Roosevelt himself was now assuming the job of Army Chief of Staff."[2]

In the autumn of 1943 Eisenhower was not under consideration, and indeed, had no intimation that the most important and prestigious post

462   A General's Education: The Mediterranean, 1942–1943

of the war would fall to anyone but George C. Marshall. He had learned through the grapevine it was likely he would be named to replace Marshall. When Navy Secretary Frank Knox arrived in Algiers on October 1, "he brought to me news that I was to be relieved as commander in the Mediterranean in order that General Marshall could have command in England." Knox's news left Eisenhower in no doubt his days in the Mediterranean were numbered.

On November 17 Eisenhower flew to Malta to meet with Churchill and the British chiefs of staff. At dinner, Churchill candidly discussed the Overlord command. The PM spoke of his acute embarrassment at having to tell Brooke he would not command Overlord, but pledged his full support to Marshall, pointing out that a British officer would naturally take control of Allied operations in the Mediterranean. Churchill's remarks were not good news for Eisenhower. Such a scenario effectively ruled out his remaining in command in the Mediterranean and, short of a demotion to army group commander under Marshall, which he would have welcomed, Eisenhower's return to Washington seemed inevitable. Privately Eisenhower viewed the prospect glumly and with mounting dismay; publicly he made no secret of his lack of enthusiasm for Marshall's job. To Butcher, Eisenhower made it plain that he was temperamentally unsuited to head the army, repeating his long-standing aversion to politicians and his impatience in dealing with them. Butcher did not disagree, opining that his boss would either make the best or worst chief of staff the army ever had. His reputation for forthrightness and refusal to play politics were positives; his lack of patience and diplomacy, detrimental qualities. Dismissing the very thought of it, Eisenhower grumbled, "They'll have to carry me up to Arlington [National Cemetery] in six months."[3]

The Western leaders were to meet for the first time with Stalin in late November for a conference of the "Big Three" at Tehran. After his meeting with Churchill and the British chiefs of staff, Eisenhower returned to Algiers, then traveled in Oran in time to greet Roosevelt, who arrived aboard the battleship USS *Iowa*. Roosevelt's entourage included Marshall, King, and Harry Hopkins. The president and Eisenhower flew in one of a convoy of five aircraft to El Aouina airfield near Tunis. As the president's plane taxied to a halt, Eisenhower's Cadillac, driven by Kay Summersby, pulled up alongside to receive Roosevelt. She was immediately accosted by a very angry Mike Reilly, Roosevelt's chief Secret Service bodyguard, who demanded, "You're not expecting to drive the President, are you, Lady?" Replying that she was General Eisenhower's driver and damned well expected to drive both men, Summersby was rudely informed, "No woman ever drives the President! . . . Certainly no Limey woman!" Tempers flared, and Reilly won the day when a sergeant was summoned to drive the Cadillac. Later the president found it amusing and asked if she would drive him and Eisenhower, who seemed nonplussed that his choice of presidential driver had caused such a tempest.[4]

The following day Eisenhower escorted Roosevelt to a battlefield near Tunis in a heavily armored column of half-tracks, armored cars, and weapons carriers that looked more like an armored division in assault mode than a sightseeing expedition. The only problem encountered was the troublesome, barking Telek, whom Eisenhower rather unwisely brought along, perched in the front seat next to Kay Summersby. At one point the dog took a flying leap straight for the president and would have landed on Roosevelt's crippled legs had not Eisenhower managed to catch him in midair.[5]

Their conversation turned from dogs to Eisenhower's recent battles; then the two discoursed at length about the famous battles fought on the ancient battlegrounds of the Punic Wars between the Romans and Carthaginians. According to Robert Sherwood, it was more than merely a Sunday drive. Eisenhower "did not realize at the time that he was being subjected to [a] most searching scrutiny and appraisal. . . . Roosevelt, in his casual, seemingly offhand manner, also talked about the future—particularly OVERLORD," and how strongly he felt that Marshall deserved a chance to secure his place in history. "It is probable that Eisenhower expressed to the President his total lack of enthusiasm for a career in the Pentagon building, but he was a soldier, and he would go where he was sent."[6] It was the only time Roosevelt ever spoke with Eisenhower before making his decision.

King and Marshall were billeted in Eisenhower's villa, nicknamed "Times Square," outside Tunis. During a rare moment of relaxation, King abruptly brought up the subject of who should command Overlord. King said, "The time has come for the President and Churchill to decide who the Overlord commander should be." Marshall sat silently as King "explained that Roosevelt wanted the supreme command for Marshall, then bluntly enumerated the reasons why he and the remainder of the JCS wanted Marshall to remain in Washington." Still, Marshall remained silent and "seemed embarrassed." Then King got to the point. "You, Eisenhower, are the proper man to become the supreme commander for the Allies in Europe." Butcher was present and recorded in his diary that "Ike was embarrassed, not only by the warmth of the Admiral's statement, but the spontaneity of his comment in Marshall's silent presence."[7] Eisenhower could not and did not respond to King, and Marshall would only repeat what he had said all along: "The President has to make his own decisions." When Eisenhower met with Roosevelt, the president's indecision was clear. "I just do not know what Marshall would like to do because he will not tell me; but of one thing I am sure, in military history it is only the names of field commanders that are remembered, not that of a Chief of Staff." Nevertheless Eisenhower emerged from this meeting convinced that Roosevelt intended to appoint Marshall. Other than on this lone occasion, Eisenhower's name was never mentioned for the post of supreme commander.[8]

Cairo was chosen as the venue where the Western leaders were to meet both before and after the Tehran conference. Eisenhower saw a good deal of both Roosevelt and Marshall in Tunis and Cairo. He arrived in Cairo on November 25 with a small group that included Kay Summersby. During what has been designated the first Cairo conference, Eisenhower excelled at one of the things he did best. He briefed the Combined Chiefs on the situation in the Mediterranean and his intention to capture key airfields in central Italy, followed by Rome and the Po Valley. The CCOS were impressed, and even the normally skeptical Brooke came away pleased by what he heard.

At a small ceremony the following evening, the president pinned the Legion of Merit medal on Eisenhower's breast. Marshall had arranged for a splendid Thanksgiving dinner with all the trimmings, after which Eisenhower admitted he hadn't even known what day it was. Eisenhower's exhaustion was plain to Marshall, who pulled him aside and declared, " 'Eisenhower, you've been working too hard and too long without respite.' . . . For one star-tled moment," Eisenhower noted, "I wondered whether he was about to relieve me." At Marshall's insistence he was directed to take several days off to relax and take in the sights of Egypt. Others could run the damn war for a few days without him, said Marshall, reminding Eisenhower, "If your sub-ordinates can't do it for you, you haven't organized them properly."[9] Eisen-hower gratefully accepted Marshall's "order" to take a brief vacation he would never have taken of his own volition.

Tedder placed his personal aircraft at Eisenhower's disposal and recom-mended the services of a British major who was a noted archaeologist in civilian life. Accompanied by a small party that included Kay Summersby, Eisenhower spent several days exploring the ancient burial grounds of the great pharaohs of Egypt, in the Valley of the Kings and nearby Luxor. Despite crushing heat, humidity, and swarms of mosquitoes, Eisenhower was briefly able to forget about the war and indulge his love of history amid surroundings that undoubtedly brought back memories of his father's fascination with Egyptology and the mysterious chart he had drawn during his bleak exile in Denison, Texas, more than a half century earlier. Their tour guide was aston-ished at the extent of Eisenhower's historical knowledge. "General Ike was as happy as a kid . . . a different person, tired but mentally refreshed by the sights," Summersby recorded.[10]

His brief Egyptian respite was one of Eisenhower's few opportunities to fantasize about a time when he was not at war. He wrote to Mamie that he envisioned "a little place far away from cities . . . and the two of us just getting brown in the sun (and possibly thick in the middle). A dozen cats and dogs, with a horse or two, maybe a place to fish (not too strenuously) and a field in which to shoot a few birds once in a while—I think that's roughly my idea of a good life."[11] (His postpresidential years at the Eisenhower farm in Gettysburg would actually come close to realizing the reverie born in Cairo in December 1943.)

Ernie King's endorsement notwithstanding, Eisenhower still had no reason to believe his return to Washington as chief of staff was any less imminent. He worried over what to do with Kay Summersby. Bringing her to Washington was out of the question. Everett Hughes noted that "Ike wants me to take Kay with car thrown in." Hughes (who loathed women drivers) was inclined to accept only because it meant inheriting his boss's coveted Cadillac limousine.

In the autumn of 1943 Churchill's disquiet over his inability to sway the U.S. chiefs of staff to the British point of view, and his increasing irritation with the flagging Italian campaign, led him to champion a British invasion of the German-held Greek island of Rhodes, the largest of the Dodecanese Islands, in the eastern Mediterranean. Churchill argued passionately that the boldness of such an operation would pay off by dragging Turkey into the war and setting the Balkans ablaze, thus enabling the Allies to threaten Germany via the "soft underbelly." The problem was more than a shortage of landing craft and the fact that such an operation violated the agreements reached at Quebec, which limited future Allied military operations in the Mediterranean. From the American viewpoint Churchill's enthusiasm for this scheme smacked of yet another excuse for evading or delaying Overlord. As the prime minister later admitted, the incident produced "the most acute difference I ever had with General Eisenhower," who successfully argued that Allied resources in the Mediterranean were not large enough to carry out operations in both Italy and the Aegean. "We must therefore choose between Rhodes and Rome . . . we must concentrate on the Italian campaign."[12] It also left Marshall more determined than ever that nothing detract from Overlord.[13]

The Rhodes venture was typically Churchillian: bold, imaginative, and opportunistic, "an immense but fleeting opportunity," he called it, arguing that "it was intolerable that the enemy, pressed on all fronts, could be allowed to continue to pick up cheap prizes in the Aegean."[14] It was also a prime example of Churchill's penchant for imposing his vast authority and intellect to overwhelm opposition and influence the outcome of events. As official British naval historian Stephen Roskill writes, Churchill's "hope of bringing Turkey into the war, which was the principal plank on which he rested his case, was an illusion; for the Turks could not have defended themselves as long as the Germans held Greece and most of the Aegean Islands."[15]

Although he agreed with its basic premise, Brooke despaired that Churchill's dogged pursuit of the invasion of Rhodes would upset the delicate balance of U.S.-British relations. "The Americans are already desperately suspicious of him," wrote Brooke, "and this will make matters worse."[16]

True to form, at Cairo, Churchill refused to temper his insistence on invading Rhodes. "It got hotter and hotter," recalled Marshall. Finally the chief of staff had had enough and exploded: "[N]ot one American soldier is going to die on that goddamned beach," he thundered to the horrified assemblage.[17]

During the previous eighteen months, Churchill had successfully persuaded Franklin Roosevelt that the Allies must attack attainable targets in the Mediterranean instead of impossible ones in France. This strategy had successfully driven Italy out of the war, and now was an opportune moment to seize a very important military and political objective that was certain to alter the course of the war in the Mediterranean. That prize was Rome, and by his forceful intervention, the prime minister had seen to it that his trusted lieutenant, Harold Alexander, would make it his number one priority.

"Mr. Churchill later told me he thought [my failure to agree with military operations in the eastern Mediterranean] was one of my major wartime mistakes," Eisenhower later said, noting that he did not agree with Churchill in 1943 or in hindsight. Their disagreement was a prime illustration, he said, of "the great differences that, from beginning to end, existed in [British and American] methods . . . of waging war."[18]

For nearly a year Stalin had been badgering his two allies to open a second front in Europe and to name its commander. At Tehran this issue was at the top of the Russian agenda. Of the military matters under discussion, "we the U.S.S.R. consider Overlord the most important and decisive," said Stalin, who challenged Churchill to reveal if the British actually believed in the cross-Channel invasion or were merely giving it lip service for his benefit. "Who will command Overlord?" he tersely demanded. "It has not been decided," replied Roosevelt to the skeptical Russian leader, who remained unconvinced that the cross-Channel operation would ever be realized without a commander.[19]

After Tehran, Roosevelt and the U.S. chiefs returned to Cairo for a second round of meetings. The decision as to who would command Overlord was Roosevelt's alone, and he could no longer put off confirming everyone's expectations that it would be Marshall. Roosevelt understood how badly Marshall wanted the command of Overlord, and had told Pershing that he wanted "George to be the Pershing of the Second World War and he cannot be that if we keep him here." Roosevelt was torn between rewarding Marshall for his faithful service and losing his services as chief of staff. Still indecisive, he sent Harry Hopkins to ascertain Marshall's preference. The chief of staff would only reiterate that he "would go along wholeheartedly with whatever decision the president made."[20]

On December 6, at Churchill's insistence, he and FDR visited one of the world's seven wonders: the Great Pyramids and the Sphinx. Almost casually Roosevelt raised the issue that had been hanging over the heads of the alliance for months. He simply could not afford to lose Marshall and proposed nominating Eisenhower to command Overlord. Was Eisenhower acceptable to the British? Churchill graciously replied that the British would warmly entrust their fortunes to Eisenhower.[21] "I feel I could not sleep at night with you out of the country," he candidly told Marshall. Roosevelt's close adviser Robert Sherwood thought it was one of the most difficult decisions the president ever made.[22]

Roosevelt arrived in Tunis on December 7, 1943, to inform Eisenhower. Earlier in December, Eisenhower had received a garbled message from Marshall that referred to his forthcoming change of assignment. Without specifics Eisenhower was not certain if it meant Washington or London. Roosevelt had barely been seated by his Secret Service bodyguards in Eisenhower's staff car when the president got straight to the point. "Well, Ike," he said, "you are going to command Overlord." Although the announcement had to have come as a surprise, the prolific Eisenhower has left little record of his feelings at this decisive moment. Matter-of-factly Eisenhower states he managed only to reply, "Mr. President, I realize such an appointment involved difficult decisions. I hope you will not be disappointed."[23]

By the time of Tehran, Eisenhower's role had evolved, crossing military lines into the realm of politics. For example, what was the Allied plan for the future occupation of Germany? Such decisions were more political than military, and Eisenhower was not afraid to ask such questions of Roosevelt. Indeed, as John Eisenhower relates, his father would converse with the president "on political subjects that Marshall wouldn't touch."[24] Later, as the war neared an end and Roosevelt's health declined precipitously in the months prior to his death, Eisenhower required answers in the form of guidance from the Combined Chiefs, which were not always forthcoming.

Good soldier that he was, Marshall concealed the most intense disappointment of his career behind a wall of stoicism that even his closest aide could not penetrate. In naming Marshall its "Man of the Year" for 1943, *Time* magazine said it best: "General Marshall has now attained the stature of a military statesman."[25] A short time later Marshall graciously sent Eisenhower a scrap of paper that became "one of my most cherished mementos of World War II." Addressed to Stalin, it read: "The immediate appointment of General Eisenhower to command of Overlord operation has been decided upon." It was signed by Roosevelt.[26]

While it is true that Roosevelt was loath to lose Marshall, he had another, equally compelling reason for appointing Ike. When his eldest son, James Roosevelt, asked the president why he had chosen Eisenhower over Marshall, he was told: "Eisenhower is the best politician among the military men. He is a natural leader who can convince other men to follow him, and this is what we need in his position more than any other quality."[27]

Churchill warmly embraced Eisenhower as the new supreme commander.

Doubtless it was not lost on Churchill that Eisenhower was a more preferable choice than Marshall, with whom he had clashed on more than one occasion. Not only was Marshall less tolerant of the PM's powers of persuasion and coercion, but he was not someone with whom Churchill would have had anything other than a businesslike relationship.

As Allied involvement in Italy deepened, Eisenhower became more and more concerned that his headquarters was too far out of touch based in North Africa, and he made plans to establish a small, advanced command post at the grand palace of Caserta, where Alexander had likewise established his army group headquarters. Yet after the announcement of his Overlord appointment, Eisenhower's interest in the Italian campaign had begun to wane, his thoughts turning to what lay ahead in England. Deciding a final visit to Italy to "get muddy for a week," as a sort of farewell tour of his command, would be appropriate, he and Smith left Algiers on December 18 to spend a week in Italy visiting British, American, and Italian frontline troops.[28]

Butcher acquired the stone hunting lodge of an Italian crown prince near Caserta, where Eisenhower could relax in splendid isolation. The place turned out to be the original "house from hell." Eisenhower had no sooner arrived for his first night in residence when a rat was discovered imperiously perched on the toilet seat of his bathroom. The two men decided a bit of target practice was in order, with Eisenhower remarking that "if he couldn't shoot a German the next best thing would be to shoot a rat." The light was poor, and Eisenhower growled that he could not see well enough without his glasses to hit the pest. With spectacles in place, his first shot missed; the second merely wounded the rat, which had leapt onto a pipe and was mercifully dispatched by an aide. For a man who prided himself on being a crack shot, the event was not Eisenhower's finest hour. Kay Summersby gleefully wrote in her memoir, "Let it be recorded for history that the Supreme Commander was a rotten shot."[29] Further surprises awaited. The day ended in a cold bedroom, where the fireplace also malfunctioned and lice abounded in the beds. "It's a tough war," Butcher wryly noted in his diary.[30]

The following morning Eisenhower and Smith left for their second round of visits to the front. A particularly grueling day left both men in a foul mood, after traveling of some seven hours in driving rain and fog. On their return Eisenhower invited Smith to dinner. Smith refused, and Eisenhower testily retorted that subordinates were not permitted to refuse such invitations from their superior officer. His own dander awakened, Smith said to hell with it— he would quit. "Eisenhower replied it would be fine with him, adding it could easily be arranged for Smith to remain behind in the Mediterranean. After this childish exchange . . . Smith apologized and Eisenhower said that all would be forgotten." Smith later added a postscript to a subordinate: "Never vacation with the boss."[31] "That Eisenhower could so completely lose his temper with Smith only illustrates how tired he was and how badly he needed a rest."[32]

On Eisenhower's final day in Italy, he and members of his personal staff were taken on a sightseeing tour of the Isle of Capri, part of which had been turned into a rest area for GIs and airmen. During his tour of the famous island, Eisenhower pointed to an elegant Italian villa and asked whose it was. "Yours, Sir," he was told. In reply to the same question about another, even more majestic villa nearby, Eisenhower was told it belonged to General Spaatz. Eisenhower's face reddened, and he angrily erupted, "Damn it, that's *not* my villa! And that's not General Spaatz's villa! None of those will belong to any general as long as I'm Boss around here. This is supposed to be a rest center—for combat men—not a playground for the Brass!" Spaatz was already in the doghouse when Eisenhower learned the previous day that Capri was being utilized strictly as a rest center for air corps officers. He fired off an angry cable ordering the practice to cease and Capri opened immediately to Allied soldiers and airmen of all ranks. What he learned back in Tunisia enraged Eisenhower even more: Spaatz and Clark had conspired to reserve Capri for air force officers, Sorrento for army officers, and nothing for their enlisted soldiers, who were left "the run of the back streets of Naples and the chance for five minutes with a cheap whore." Soldiers were impressed when word that Eisenhower had slapped down his brass hats quickly made the rounds of the ever-efficient military grapevine, but despite his anger, Eisenhower made no attempt to convey his displeasure to his friend Mark Clark.[33]

Before her husband's appointment was officially announced, Washington was abuzz with scuttlebutt. Mamie presciently concluded that Ike would not be returning home to replace Marshall. After examining a photograph appearing in a Washington newspaper, she remarked to John that Ike "looked like the cat who'd swallowed the canary."[34] Inexplicably Pupah wrote to Mamie that he hoped his son-in-law became neither chief of staff nor the Overlord supreme commander. Mr. Doud apparently believed Eisenhower had already earned his place in history and that neither command would help his reputation. Mamie refused to endorse her father's rationale or the Washington rumors that Marshall was a shoo-in for the Overlord post. "Don't believe all this stuff about Ike's coming home as Chief of Staff," she wrote, noting that it would be "a shame to pull him out now—when he's done so well."[35]

Cadet John Eisenhower was granted leave from West Point to spend Christmas with his mother in Washington. On Christmas Eve an announcement came over the radio that his father had been appointed supreme commander for Overlord. In short order "the halls leading to Mother's apartment were packed with reporters. She refused to see any of them. Finally, Christmas morning, someone discovered a lone young woman who had sat up all night in the hall. Mother relented," and the diligent reporter secured an exclusive interview.[36]

For John's father, Christmas 1943 was simply another working day. In the morning he flew from Naples to Carthage to meet with Churchill, Alexander, Tedder, and his designated successor in the Mediterranean, Gen. (later Field Marshal) Sir Henry Maitland Wilson, a six-foot seven-inch giant whose large ears, not his height, had earned him the nickname "Jumbo."

It was Churchill's lifelong fantasy to command a military operation, and in January 1944 he came as close as he ever would as a civilian to fulfilling his vision of himself as a battlefield commander. Churchill's long-standing obsession with capturing Rome led him to pressure the Allied military leadership to break the stalemate at the Gustav Line by initiating amphibious landings at Anzio, thirty-five miles southwest of the Italian capital. When Eisenhower pointed out the pitfalls of a relatively weak force on its own behind enemy lines and virtually helpless without a steady infusion of supplies, Churchill dismissed Eisenhower's fears. An exasperated Eisenhower pointed out the PM's habit of ignoring whatever was inconvenient. "Prime Minister, when you want to do something you dismiss logistics with a wave of your hand; when you dislike a proposal . . . you effectively discourage an unwary listener." With a twinkle in his eye, Churchill replied, "It does make a difference whether your heart is in a project, doesn't it?"[37] Nevertheless, the prime minister's failure to heed Eisenhower's warning would result in perhaps his greatest failure as Britain's wartime leader.

As the outgoing commander who would not be around to see the operation carried out, Eisenhower was reluctant to take a firmer stance than he did—a reluctance that the manipulative Churchill played to the hilt. Eisenhower's failure to do so turned out to be a decisive moment in the war in Italy. The British now held the reins of power in the Mediterranean, leaving the key decisions in the hands of British officers, all of whom were subject to the intrigues and enormous influence of Churchill. With Eisenhower's departure there was no one, other than Brooke, with sufficient power and prestige to stand up to the prime minister—certainly not Jumbo Wilson, who was regarded as putty in Churchill's hands.

With misgivings Eisenhower had agreed to postpone the return of the landing craft to England for Overlord. The Anzio landings took place on January 22, 1944, resulting in yet another Allied near disaster on a scale even larger than Salerno, and leading Churchill to criticize his generals and bemoan the fact that instead of landing a tiger, the Allies had "a stranded whale" on the beaches of Anzio-Nettuno. Within days the Anzio beachhead became a colossal liability for the Allies, who were obliged to rush reinforcements from the south to meet the threat of the massive German buildup.[38]

Shortly after after Casablanca, British Lt. Gen. Frederick E. Morgan was appointed to head a planning group to develop an invasion plan for the British chiefs. His role was soon expanded, and Morgan formed a small Anglo-American planning headquarters in London in March 1943, designated Chief of Staff to the Supreme Allied Commander, which became known simply as COSSAC. Nevertheless, what was to become the greatest military operation in history was, in 1943, essentially a rudderless ship, with no captain and nothing more than a vague destination. Without a supreme commander, Morgan essentially headed a committee attempting to carry out a mission without a decision maker. Morgan later recalled Brooke's words: "Well, there it is; it won't work, but you must bloody well make it."[39]

Mountbatten's Combined Operations first saw the potential of Normandy as an invasion site early in the war. An examination of the possible options had already quickly narrowed the options to Normandy and the Pas de Calais region of northern France. Some favored the Pas de Calais, mainly because it was the closest point to Britain, provided the most direct route of advance into Germany, and afforded maximum air cover from airfields in southern England. The problem was that it was such an obvious invasion site that the Germans had heavily reinforced its defenses and concentrated the bulk of their troops in France in this region. Moreover there were few adequate ports to accommodate the enormous flow of troops and matériel required for the postinvasion buildup.

Under tight time constraints, and instructed to plan the assault based only on *available* landing craft, Morgan and his staff decided that the site for the invasion should be Normandy. The initial plan called for three divisions to land along a thirty-mile front in the Caen sector. In one of the best examples of Anglo-American cooperation of the entire war, in less than three months COSSAC resolved what had been a chaotic mess of disparate planning by many different headquarters by producing a solution to the question of where and how a cross-Channel invasion could be launched.

Nevertheless, the plan was stalled in the absence of a supreme commander. Briefed on the Overlord plan in mid-October, Eisenhower found it so deficient that he wondered if he would even want to command its forces.[40] "I didn't have any idea at that time it would be my operation and I gave my views for whatever value our own lessons from the North African experience would be to the COSSAC planners."[41]

Limited to a three-division assault by the lack of amphibious landing craft, the COSSAC plan satisfied no one. Eisenhower, whose interest in Overlord was no longer abstract, realized that a monumental problem awaited resolution in London. During the coming months serious criticism ("wishful thinking" was among the kinder epithets) would be leveled at Morgan and his COSSAC organization for a plan that was never meant to be the final blueprint for Overlord.

Immediately after his appointment was announced, Eisenhower began drawing up a list of British and American commanders and staff officers he wanted to bring to England with him. Despite his earlier misgivings, at the top of his list was Alexander, primarily for his cool manner and ability to get along with subordinate commanders, British and American alike—qualities he sensed would be particularly valuable in the difficult campaign ahead. However, Brooke's private doubts about Alexander's abilities had grown steadily, and he began quietly to block his appointment. Brooke's feelings were rooted in the immutable belief that the gulf between field and supreme command was enormous and required a commander of great imagination to plan and coordinate the actions of the Allied naval, air, and ground forces. Alexander was better qualified to remain a field commander. "He will never have either the personality or the vision," Brooke wrote gloomily in his diary.[42] The irony was that Brooke's concerns mirrored Eisenhower's, with the difference that Eisenhower chose to ignore them in his quest to influence Alexander's appointment.

Still, Eisenhower's position was awkward, and while he badly wanted Alexander, he did not want to be perceived as interfering in what was solely a British matter. As tactfully as possible he began to champion Alexander to Churchill, pointing out that he was willing to place him in temporary command of all ground forces until such time as he personally took over command of all Allied forces in Europe after the invasion. Although the decision was Churchill's, it required the concurrence of the War Cabinet. Had the prime minister's health been better, he might have fought harder to persuade them to approve Alexander. With Churchill in North Africa, Brooke used his influence to lobby quietly for Montgomery. Aware that his cabinet favored Monty, and that Alexander's influence could be put to better use if he remained in Italy, where the PM had yet to renounce his aim of winning the war via the Balkans, Churchill elected not to dispute the matter. Brooke breathed a sigh of relief, and on Christmas Eve Montgomery received a cable from the War Office directing him to turn over command of the Eighth Army to Lt. Gen. Oliver Leese and return to London.

Montgomery's promotion made him both the commander of the British 21st Army Group in England, and the acting commander of all Allied ground troops until such time as a suitable bridgehead was established in France, when Eisenhower would assume command. Eisenhower kept his disappointment to himself.

Anxious to discuss the plan with Montgomery before each went his separate way, Eisenhower summoned him to Algiers to discuss Overlord on the afternoon of December 27. Both men agreed that the plan needed strengthening. Eisenhower instructed Montgomery to convey to the planners in London that the Overlord assault must be broadened, and that he was willing to pay the price of a month's delay if necessary to achieve the right balance. As Smith recalled, "We were all unanimous . . . the addition of divisions was accepted by acclamation."[43]

The official announcement that Eisenhower was the new Allied supreme commander set in motion a flurry of activity. As his staff was preparing to move to London, George Marshall had other plans for Eisenhower, who was ordered home by the chief of staff, allegedly for conferences but in reality to provide him with a brief respite before he tackled his greatest challenge. His ability to withstand the pressures had been remarkable, but as Marshall soon reminded him, even someone of Eisenhower's prodigious energies required an occasional break. It was a message only Marshall could have written. Offering no leeway for Eisenhower to vacillate, his unambiguous cable read:

> You will be under terrific strain from now on. I am interested that you are fully prepared to bear the strain and I am not interested in the usual rejoinder that you can take it. It is just as important that you be fresh mentally and you certainly will not be if you go straight from one great problem to another. Now come on home and see your wife and trust somebody else for twenty minutes in England.[44]

Although he would have no role in carrying it out, Eisenhower's final act before departing the Mediterranean was to detour to Marrakech to discuss the Anzio landings once again with Churchill, whose persistence knew no bounds. "He was full of the Anzio project and chided me gently and a bit humorously on my doubts . . . he said he hoped that the guarding of such reputation for success as I had established had not made me a cautious soldier." Not to be outdone, Eisenhower quickly replied that, historically, many generals confused rashness and boldness with success, Napoleon and Custer being prime examples.[45]

The next day, January 1, 1944, Eisenhower boarded an aircraft to return to the United States for the first time since June 1942. At his farewell press conference Eisenhower was asked when he thought the war would end. Without hesitation he replied, "I believe we will win the European war in 1944."[46]

Part VII

THE INVASION OF EUROPE, 1944

He made the battle, and the battle made him.

——TIME,
June 6, 1994

39.

Supreme Allied Commander

You will enter the continent of Europe and . . . undertake
operations aimed at the heart of Germany and the
destruction of her armed forces.
— COMBINED CHIEFS OF STAFF DIRECTIVE

Had Marshall not intervened to compel it, it is extremely doubtful that Eisenhower would have returned home of his own volition. As much as he missed Mamie, he had deeply mixed emotions about returning home. Eisenhower arranged for three convalescents to ride in his plane, stipulating that two of them must be bridge players so that he and Butcher would have a foursome. Also included were Telek's two offspring, both unruly pups adorned with Scotch-plaid collars and leashes. When he arrived in Washington shortly after midnight on the morning of January 2, 1944, Eisenhower awoke from a nap and was startled to see the city lit up below. "My instant reaction was, 'Has someone gone crazy?' " before he comprehended that he was no longer in a war zone under blackout conditions. From the time he landed, Eisenhower's visit was shrouded in extraordinary secrecy. For the duration of his visit Eisenhower traveled with his overcoat collar pulled up and his hat pulled low over what had become one of the world's best-known faces.

Eisenhower and Butcher were driven to the service entrance of the Wardman Park Hotel and, via the freight elevator, arrived for a long-anticipated reunion with their wives. Mamie was overjoyed to see her husband but less than enthralled at meeting Telek's offspring, neither of which, like their sire, was housebroken. "Our reception," wrote Butcher, "was somewhat jarred by the presence of the dogs." The pups immediately despoiled Mamie's prized Oriental carpets, later rendering similar homage to Ruth Butcher's carpets before being banished to new homes.[1]

The first thing Mamie noticed about her long-absent husband was that he was more restless than ever. Their grandson, David, would later write, "In private, Eisenhower seemed somber and hard to approach."[2] Although he had lost none of his trademark enthusiasm, he was visibly overweight and smoked incessantly, his fatigue-lined face making it obvious why Marshall had ordered him home for a rest. Their initial reunion was short-lived. Rest was not his immediate agenda; home barely a few short hours, Eisenhower suddenly left Mamie to meet with Marshall the following afternoon.

His personal escort was Marshall's right-hand man, Col. Frank McCarthy, whose task it was to ensure that no one knew of Eisenhower's presence in the United States. On the days he visited the newly opened eighth wonder of the world, the Pentagon building, on the shores of the Potomac in northern Virginia, Eisenhower employed a rarely used servant's staircase to meet an unmarked sedan, its curtains drawn shut, at the back door of the Wardman Park. "With the stars from his overseas cap removed and those on his shoulder covered by his overcoat collar, Ike then was driven to a private entrance to the Pentagon in a black sedan, by a soldier in a civilian chauffeur's uniform. No one but the office staff could see him as he entered."[3]

From the outset there was discernible tension between Mamie and Ike. Long separations affect a marriage in various ways. From necessity both parties tend to become independent and often return to each other almost like strangers. Expectations can sometimes exceed reality and require getting to know each other all over again. The Eisenhowers were no exception. The depth of their affection had not changed, but the circumstances of their long separation had transformed each in ways over which they had little control. "How difficult it was for men to come home and live in a home, and how hard it was for us to have a man around the house," said Mamie. He seemed far less tolerant of her attempts at small talk and her complaints about life in Washington without him. Since ascending to the high plateau of generalship, Eisenhower had developed the habit of abruptly announcing his departure. In his world time was something too precious to be wasted. And while such deportment was perfectly routine, in Mamie's narrow, prisonlike existence it was an irksome habit that—unintentionally—seemed to suggest disinterest.

Mamie, too, had changed and was more independent than she had been at any time during her twenty-seven years with Ike. She explained to an interviewer years later, recalling their first reunion in eighteen long months, "He'd made his own life running his house . . . and we [women] had made our own lives." With Ike's arrival suddenly imminent, "I was so afraid that he'd come home and find everything a mess. And Ike . . . wasn't beyond mess himself, but he certainly didn't want it around his house or me." Although Mamie thought "he was the same old Ike," she could also discern that "he was very keyed up." As had been his custom throughout their marriage, Eisenhower spoke very little to Mamie about his job and, as was her custom, she did not intrude.[4]

On his second day home Eisenhower was summoned to the White House for the first of what would be three meetings with Roosevelt, followed by a dinner that night for Ike and Mamie, hosted by Marshall and attended by a bevy of military brass and influential congressmen. Late that evening the Eisenhowers were driven to an obscure railway siding in rural Maryland for an overnight journey in a snowstorm aboard Marshall's private Pullman car to West Point to visit John, now a cadet sergeant in his third year. The rail car was shunted into a siding along the Hudson River in the town of Highland Falls, only a short distance from where Eisenhower had detrained in the summer of 1911.

John was summoned by the officer of the day and introduced to Col. McCarthy, who hustled the astonished cadet in a staff car to meet his parents. For a few hours behind drawn curtains, the Eisenhowers were reunited for the first time since the summer of 1942. John found his father both preoccupied and seemingly impatient to return to his new post in London. The signs, however slight, of tension between Mamie and his father were evident to their son. "His no-nonsense life of the past eighteen months had sharpened his manner somewhat," he said. "Mother at one time chastened him for his abruptness. He growled amicably, 'Hell, I'm going back to my theater where I can do what I want.' "⁵ Before the train chugged off into the night later that evening, Ike and Mamie hosted a dinner for John and five cadet friends, all sworn to secrecy.

John's class was being graduated a year early due to the war, but Ike's four stars carried no weight with the young man when his father failed to persuade him to apply for a commission in the field artillery, where he was less likely to be in harm's way. He did not want John in the front lines facing death and the possibility of capture, a risk he deemed unacceptable. John, however, was determined to be commissioned in the infantry and ultimately spurned the advice.

As much as Ike had missed Mamie, the last thing he wanted was to be in the United States when the immense problems of organizing a new headquarters, resolving thorny command issues, dealing with Churchill and de Gaulle, and restructuring the invasion plan all beckoned. He appears to have derived little enjoyment from his twelve days in the United States. Almost from the moment he landed in Washington, Eisenhower seemed consumed by the need to resume his war and champed at the bit to leave.

Lighter moments were in short supply. One such occasion was the morning when the doorbell rang and Mamie said, " 'Ike, that's the trash man, go let him in.' Ike padded down the hall in his pyjamas; he opened the door and this fellow's face turned gray. He's never seen a man in my apartment. He took the trash and Ike came back laughing like mad. He climbed into bed and said, 'Talk yourself out of that one!' I don't believe he'd lost his sense of humor."⁶ Thus Eisenhower's visit spurred rumors within the Wardman that Mamie had a secret lover she entertained in her apartment. The rumors were, of course, quite true, the only difference being that the lover in question was her husband.

Marshall thoughtfully shipped the two off to White Sulphur Springs, West Virginia, again hidden from public view in his private railway car, for what was intended to have been a week of genuine rest. A cottage had been set aside for them on the grounds of the Greenbrier Hotel, which had been turned into an army convalescent hospital.[7] Two issues hung like a pall over their time together: Overlord and Kay Summersby. The latter intruded when, once (possibly even twice) Eisenhower mistakenly called Mamie "Kay"—all but ruining their time together.[8] His excuse that Kay had been the only woman with whom he was in constant contact for the past eighteen months further overshadowed what ought to have been a cheerful occasion. In his first letter to Mamie after arriving in London, Eisenhower admitted that he had been glad to be home, "even though things did seem to be a bit upsetting! I guess it was just because we'd been separated so long, and before we could get really acquainted again, I was on my way."[9]

Eisenhower interrupted their vacation to fly to Kansas on January 8 for a brief family reunion with his mother, Milton, Arthur, and Mamie's parents. Mamie was forbidden to fly because of her inner-ear condition and remained in White Sulphur Springs. From the Fort Riley airfield, Eisenhower was driven to nearby Manhattan, hidden as usual behind the curtains of an anonymous vehicle, to the home of his brother Milton, who had left his job as head of OWI to become the president of Kansas State University in 1943. Eighty-two-year-old Ida arrived from Abilene, overjoyed to see her son. "Why, it's Dwight!" she exclaimed, tearfully kissing and hugging her son—the famous general she still called only by his given name. Although Ida had faltered considerably since David's death nearly two years earlier, Ike found her much like "her former self, bright and quick and laughing." As John had at West Point, those present found Eisenhower a changed, somewhat withdrawn man, "as though he were keeping a good deal of himself in reserve for emergency use."[10]

Before returning to London, Eisenhower was again summoned to the White House, arriving to find Roosevelt in bed with the flu. Discussing matters of grave importance with heads of state in bedrooms and bathrooms had become routine, and before getting down to business, Eisenhower asked the president to autograph a photo of himself for Kay Summersby, a matter he doubtless neglected to bother mentioning to Mamie. Eisenhower had expected to talk about Overlord, but their principal topic of discussion was postwar Germany and the problems presented by governing a conquered nation. Eisenhower ventured concern over dividing Germany into zones of occupation, indicating his distrust of the Russians and suggesting it would be a mistake. Roosevelt, however, appeared already to have made up his mind to do just that, and left Eisenhower in no doubt that such decisions were the province of politicians, not generals. Before Eisenhower departed, the president asked him how he liked the title of supreme commander and was told it contained "the ring of importance, something like 'Sultan.' " Eisenhower wished the president a speedy recovery and took his leave. "I never saw him again."[11]

Mamie had hoarded her time with Ike as if it were gold, and the third and final presidential summons left her fuming. "I was so provoked to think that Mr. Roosevelt, *knowing* that I hadn't seen this man in so long, would demand that he come to the White House and spend a whole evening when I thought that time belonged to me."[12] Before he left to return to the war, in what must have been one of the most painful moments of her life, Mamie said to him, "Don't come back again till it's over, Ike—I can't stand losing you again." He did not.[13]

Eisenhower landed in Prestwick, Scotland, at midnight on January 15, where he was met by his new British military aide, Lt. Col. James Gault. A member of the Scots Guards, and an investment banker in civilian life, Gault had become close friends with Eisenhower in London in 1942. He had arranged for Eisenhower's private railway car, code-named Bayonet, to take his party to London, where they arrived in fog so thick the small greeting party appeared ghostlike. Present to drive him was Kay Summersby. To no one's surprise, she had returned to London to become a member of Eisenhower's personal staff and resume her membership in the supreme commander's inner circle. There was no ceremony and no public announcement of his arrival. Eisenhower's new London abode, which Gault had secured for him, was a comfortable town house off Berkeley Square in Mayfair, called Hays Lodge, within walking distance of his office at No. 28 Grosvenor Square.[14]

As he had in 1942, Eisenhower again wore two hats: commander of all U.S. forces in the ETO and supreme allied commander. Although the primary headquarters of SHAEF was a mile away at Norfolk House, in St. James's Square, Eisenhower chose to keep his office in Grosvenor Square, although for security reasons an office was also established at an alternate location at No. 47 after photographs of No. 28 appeared in the press.

The London to which Eisenhower returned in 1944 was a far different place than he had left in November 1942. The city teemed with more military personnel than ever and was still being frequently bombed by the Luftwaffe. The real difference was the air of expectation that hung over the nation. "The spirit was one of hope, high courage, extraordinary endeavor, and above all, expectation. Only a few men [meeting in the war room] under the pavements of Westminster really knew what was afoot." Under the cloak of secrecy was "a mood that was both fearful and carefree . . . as it was in the flight lines during the Battle of Britain."[15]

In the ensuing months Hitler would unleash a new weapon of terror launched from sites in Holland, the V-1 (and later V-2) rockets packed with high explosives that exploded indiscriminately, usually killing civilians. Churchill had a private air raid shelter several blocks away, equipped with its own bedrooms, which he set aside for Eisenhower's personal use. Eisenhower declined to use it or another shelter close by that Butcher had found for him on the grounds that his soldiers did not have such a luxury, therefore, it was his responsibility to share the same danger.[16] Sudden death from the skies was simply the least of his worries.

When he returned to England in January 1944, Eisenhower brought a renewed determination that both parties in the alliance had to put aside their differences if the war was to be won. One of Eisenhower's first acts was to staff his new SHAEF headquarters with senior officers he knew and trusted. Without apology, he raided AFHQ, ruthlessly stripping it of virtually all its senior officers and key personnel and assigning them to new positions in London. Tedder, T. J. Davis, Bedell Smith (for whom Eisenhower had to battle Churchill, who wanted him retained in the Mediterranean to keep the iron in Jumbo Wilson's spine), Strong, and a number of other key AFHQ staffers all filled high positions in Eisenhower's new headquarters. Jumbo Wilson howled in protest, but to no avail.

Eisenhower also required a great many new faces as he attempted to assemble the best commanders and staff officers available to him. The task of acquiring these officers fell largely to Smith, recently promoted to the three-star rank of lieutenant general. Smith and Brooke clashed over British officers in AFHQ, whom Smith tactlessly demanded be transferred to SHAEF. Smith won as Brooke fumed. Even so, unlike Montgomery—who obtained nearly everyone he wanted—Eisenhower had to fight a long series of bureaucratic battles to fill the U.S. command positions.[17] Not all of Smith and Eisenhower's choices were inspired. An example was the SHAEF G-3, Maj. Gen. Harold R. "Pinky" Bull, a humorless, unimaginative bureaucrat who was disliked with equal intensity by the Americans and the British.

At the highest level there was a dangerously provincial belief that only those who had served in the Mediterranean had the requisite experience and knowledge. In a gesture designed to provide Eisenhower with men who had successful amphibious experience, Marshall sent Maj. Gen. J. Lawton "Lightning Joe" Collins and Maj. Gen. Charles H. "Pete" Corlett to England. Collins and Corlett were the only two veterans of the Pacific war to occupy a high position on the Eisenhower team. Unfortunately neither Bradley nor Eisenhower had the slightest interest in learning from these men, whose advice was all but ignored in a prevailing atmosphere of "anything that had happened in the Pacific was strictly bush league stuff" in the ETO. Corlett later wrote that his suggestions pertaining to amphibious operations were routinely ignored by Bradley and others. "I felt like an expert according to the naval definition: 'a son-of-a-bitch from out of town.' "[18] Their indifference did no credit to either Eisenhower or Bradley, particularly when, for example, Corlett's warnings that fire support and ammunition allocations were being seriously underestimated went unheeded and subsequently proved tragically correct.[19]

Joe Collins, a postwar army chief of staff, was an aggressive, gung-ho infantryman. Another Marshall protégé and a friend of Eisenhower's from West Point (class of 1917), Collins, who acquired the nickname "Lightning Joe" as the highly successful commander of the 25th Division on Guadalcanal, has been accurately described as an officer who "harbored something of the ruthless intolerance of a Philip H. Sheridan toward leaders less impatient than himself for success."[20] Notorious for firing division and regimental commanders, Collins found himself in good company with Bradley, who was even more intolerant of failure.

Eisenhower was ruthless in accepting only men he knew and trusted in the ETO. Those who crossed him also paid, among them Lt. Gen. Jacob L. Devers, his replacement in England as commander of U.S. forces when Ike moved to North Africa. A West Pointer and member of Patton's class of 1909 who had drawn Marshall's attention for being the type of hard-charging, can-do officer favored by the chief of staff, Devers had run afoul of Eisenhower in the summer of 1943 when he had, with Marshall's concurrence, blocked the temporary transfer of four medium bomber groups from Britain to North Africa. According to Bedell Smith's biographer, "This angered Eisenhower, who thereafter bore ill feelings toward Devers," who once said of him that he was ".22 caliber."[21]

Retribution was not long in coming. The two had never served together, and Devers was not part of Eisenhower's circle of close friends, which made him an outsider, and therefore expendable. With Eisenhower's appointment, Devers was sent packing to the Mediterranean to become Jumbo Wilson's deputy, and Marshall's personal choice to protect American interests in what had become an exclusively British-controlled theater of war. Later, as 6th Army Group commander in Europe, Devers would be studiously ignored by Eisenhower. On those occasions when the two men had direct contact, there was "none of the warmth of the Supreme Commander's dealings with his friends in [Omar Bradley's] 12th Army Group," notes Russell F. Weigley. "Instead there was a too-ready willingness to adopt an accusatory tone at the least hint of anything's going wrong."[22] The most uncharitable toward Jake Devers was Bradley, who scathingly described him as "overly garrulous (saying little of importance), egotistical, shallow, intolerant, not very smart, and much too inclined to rush off half cocked."[23]

Another choice that would turn out to be controversial was his appointment of Lt. Gen. John C. H. Lee to be his deputy commander of U.S. forces and chief Overlord logistician. Lee, who was variously referred to as "Court House," "Jesus Christ," or "Jesus Christ Himself," was an officer who valued his creature comforts. Eisenhower inherited Lee and declined to get rid of him despite the frequent urging of Bedell Smith, advice he was later to rue when Lee and his entire organization moved into Paris after its liberation in August 1944 and took over the city's finest hotels for their personal use. As Smith bluntly said of him, "Lee was a stuffed shirt. He didn't know much about supply organization . . . [and] was one of the crosses we had to bear."[24] Although Eisenhower acted tough with Patton, he was entirely too soft on those, like Lee, who flouted the system for their own benefit. Lee, a born-again Christian who saw no conflict between his piousness and living lavishly, was perhaps the most blatant example of one who violated the unwritten law that an officer should endure the same hardships as his men. Patton was not alone in wholeheartedly endorsing another's description of Lee as "a pompous little son-of-a-bitch only interested in self-advertisement." Lee, who was the only general known to have worn his stars on both the front and the rear of his helmet, had his own, personal, lavishly outfitted train and lived far better than his boss.[25]

There was an urgent need for a single headquarters to control all ground operations during the early phase of the forthcoming campaign. Eisenhower was adamant that there would be no separate headquarters created between him and his field commanders. Bradley was destined to eventually command an American army group, but in early 1944 his First Army headquarters was barely operational. Thus, with Eisenhower's blessing, Montgomery now carried the additional title of temporary commander of all Allied ground forces for the invasion. Eisenhower's decision was for Montgomery to retain command of the ground forces until such time as Patton's U.S. Third Army could be landed and the U.S. army group made operational under Bradley. With no firm date predictable, the timing of the changeover was left undecided.[26]

Like Eisenhower, Montgomery only trusted officers he knew personally and who had proved their mettle in battle. He ruthlessly purged the existing 21st Army Group staff and, headed by his able and genial chief of staff, Freddie de Guingand, replaced them with key members of his Eighth Army staff, all of whom were what Montgomery termed "proper chaps" who knew and understood his methods, giving rise to the observation soon circulating in London that "the Gentlemen are out and the Players are in."[27] The only difference between the ruthlessness of Eisenhower and Smith and that of Montgomery was the criticism leveled at the latter for what was deemed yet another example of his alleged egotism and contempt for others. In truth, the original British staff lacked combat experience, and the time for niceties had long since passed. In Montgomery, Churchill no longer had to complain, "Why can't I get someone who wants to fight?"[28]

To command the British invasion army Montgomery orchestrated the appointment of an infantry officer, Lt. Gen. Miles Dempsey, one of the original "Monty men," who had commandeded an Eighth Army corps during the Sicily campaign. A resolute professional soldier and one of the least-known senior British commanders of the war, Dempsey was blessed with a photographic memory and a unique ability to read maps. An ardent student of war who had studied the European battlefields firsthand during the interwar years, Dempsey would leave his staff dazzled by his ability to remember everything on a map and thus to visualize a battlefield even though he had never actually seen it.

The other two key players at the top of the Allied team were the commander in chief of Allied naval forces, Adm. Sir Bertram Ramsay, and Air Chief Marshal Sir Trafford Leigh-Mallory, the former commander of RAF Fighter Command and a hero of the Battle of Britain, who was appointed to command the Allied Expeditionary Air Force. Ramsay was an experienced naval officer who understood amphibious operations. Brought out of retirement to mastermind the naval evacuation of Dunkirk in 1940, he then became Adm. Andrew Cunningham's chief naval planner for Torch. A quality choice to head the Allied naval effort, Ramsay has been praised as "[q]uiet, brilliant, intelligent, determined and easy to get on with"—the antithesis of Leigh-Mallory, a controversial airman with many enemies, who would prove a thorn in Eisenhower's side from the outset.[29] Although Leigh-Mallory was a successful RAF commander of unquestioned courage, in his present role he was indecisive and pessimistic, was universally detested and distrusted, even by other British as well as American airmen and was widely regarded as a poor choice for the post of air commander in chief.

Although Tedder became a close adviser and supporter of Eisenhower, as deputy supreme commander he held what amounted to an essentially meaningless title, one scarcely more than that of a minister without portfolio. Tedder, a man of principle and one of the pioneer airmen of the RAF, was routinely ignored by Churchill, with whom he maintained frosty relations. Early in the war, when he served in the Ministry of Air Production, Tedder had strongly opposed its chief, Lord Beaverbrook, in aircraft matters and been exiled in 1941 to North Africa, where his reputation soared as air commander in chief, Middle East. Although he did not oppose Eisenhower's request for Tedder as his deputy, Churchill nevertheless failed to utilize him in any meaningful way in his role as the senior British officer in SHAEF, and declined to include him in his weekly meetings with Eisenhower and Bedell Smith. The normally feisty Tedder accepted his diminished role and, rather than challenge Churchill, confined his role primarily to that of Eisenhower's adviser. Even then, however, Tedder was not fully employed, thanks to the jealousy of Bedell Smith, who—according to Tedder's wartime aide—did his level best to exclude him from the high councils of SHAEF by preventing "any link being established to Gen. Eisenhower."[30]

While Leigh-Mallory's indecisiveness was enough to have given Eisenhower pause, he needed men who could fight, and in Bertram Ramsay he had an able veteran naval commander and fighter. Nor was it merely friendship but that same need for fighting commanders that led Eisenhower to stick out his neck to salvage the career of George S. Patton, who had been in lonely exile in Sicily since the slapping incidents, his future hanging by the slender thread of Eisenhower's promise of a future role. When Eisenhower returned to Washington, Patton's future was still unresolved. Although Eisenhower seems already to have settled on him to command an army, he and Marshall nevertheless debated Patton's fate. Marshall raised the question of perhaps letting Patton command Anvil, the proposed invasion of southern France. Although he too was loath to lose Patton, Marshall played devil's advocate and questioned Patton's suitability for an Overlord command. Eisenhower "assured the chief of staff that the volatile, offensive-minded Patton would always serve under the more even-handed Bradley."[31]

Eisenhower placed his personal stamp of approval on every division commander or higher. His criterion was unambiguous: No officer was selected whom he did not know personally. "Eisenhower's lieutenants," a term coined by historian Russell F. Weigley in his superb account of the war in Europe, was an apt description. Numerous West Point classmates, along with veterans of the North African and Italian campaigns, were among those tapped to fill the roster of jobs.

When Omar Bradley assumed command of First Army, the three corps commanders slated to lead the D-Day landings were already assigned and in place. Eisenhower's closest friend, Gee Gerow, commanded V Corps, destined for the most important of the five invasion sectors—the landings on a critical stretch of Normandy beach, code-named Omaha. Another friend and classmate of both men was Maj. Gen. Roscoe B. Woodruff, who commanded VII Corps, which was to assault the Utah sector, secure the Carentan Peninsula, and eventually capture the port of Cherbourg. Maj. Gen. Willis D. Crittenberger, an aggressive tank officer, commanded XIX Corps. Like so many other former cavalry officers, however, Crittenberger simply did not fit the profile of the Fort Benning–trained infantryman. Cut loose, he was quickly claimed by Devers for a corps command in Italy.

Neither Gerow nor Woodruff had commanded a large formation in combat or participated in an amphibious landing. Both men were question marks for such important command positions. Woodruff, the first captain of the class of 1915 and a friend of both Eisenhower and Bradley, was shuffled to briefly command another corps, then again replaced by the incoming Corlett. Ultimately Woodruff was sent back to the United States, deeply embittered by the experience, but he later proved his mettle as a division commander in the Pacific. Collins was given command of VII Corps and a key role in the D-Day landings.

Although Gerow later justified his selection, at the time there were few valid reasons for his retention, particularly given Corlett's amphibious experience in the Pacific. Between Eisenhower's affinity for an old friend and Bradley's intense dislike of Corlett, the inexperienced Gerow retained command of V Corps.[32] With Gerow the glass was always seemed to be half empty; he expressed the same pessimism over the fate of the Omaha landings as he had previously in the War Department. Gerow insisted he was merely being realistic, but Eisenhower felt it necessary to remind his friend that "the greatest firepower ever assembled on the face of the earth" would be supporting him. Gerow remained unconvinced.[33]

To complete the nucleus of corps commanders, Eisenhower selected Troy Middleton, who had commanded the 45th Division in the Mediterranean and was so highly regarded by Eisenhower that he insisted on his assignment despite Middleton's knee problems, which had landed him in Walter Reed Army Hospital. "I don't give a damn about his knees," Eisenhower is reputed to have said. "I want his head and his heart. And I'll take him into battle on a litter if we have to."[34] Middleton commanded VIII Corps, which would follow Collins's corps into the Cotentin Peninsula.

Perhaps the most worrisome aspect of the planning period was that someone would violate the strict security blanket that had been cast over the date and location of Overlord. Two such incidents might have compromised the operation. The first involved a friend and West Point classmate, Army Air Forces Maj. Gen. Henry J. F. Miller, commander of the Ninth Air Force Service Command. In the presence of British civilians in the dining room of Claridge's, Miller, his tongue loosened by liquor, was clearly overheard complaining about supply problems that he said would be resolved by mid-June, by which time the invasion would have taken place. When informed of Miller's unforgivable and potentially fateful indiscretion, Eisenhower was distraught. Ultimately unmoved by his friend's pleas of innocence, he demoted him to colonel and sent him home in disgrace. A speedy retirement followed. A second incident a short time later involving a drunken naval officer left Eisenhower boiling. "I get so angry ... that I could cheerfully shoot the offender myself," he told Marshall. "This following so closely on the Miller case is almost enough to give one the shakes."[35]

One thing that had not changed was Eisenhower's sensitivity to criticism—a skin thin enough to produce a strongly worded reply to a letter from a lone British detractor who had written to complain that his appointment ought to have gone to Monty or Alexander. Eisenhower's assertions that he ignored what was written about him were likewise not credible in February 1944, after remarks began to appear in British newspapers alleging that he

was more of a figurehead than an actual leader. Obviously smarting over being
so cavalierly dismissed, Eisenhower penned a vigorous defense of his generalship in his diary. British columnists, he wrote,

> try to show that my contributions in the Mediterranean were admin-
> istrative accomplishments and "friendliness" in welding an Allied
> team. They dislike to believe that I had anything particularly to do
> with campaigns. They don't use the words "initiative" and "boldness"
> in talking of me, but often do in speaking of Alex and Monty.
>
> The truth is that the bold British commanders in the Mediterra-
> nean were Admiral Sir Andrew Cunningham and Tedder. I had per-
> emptorily to order the holding of the forward American airfields in
> the bitter days of January 1943. I had to order the integration of an
> American corps and its use on the battlelines. . . . I had to order the
> attack on Pantelleria . . . the British ground commanders . . . wanted
> to put all our ground forces into the toe of Italy [*sic*]. They didn't like
> Salerno, but after days I got them to accept.

His final rationalization of what had essentially been an unhappy experience
in Tunisia, Sicily, and Italy was, "We had a happy family. . . . But it wearies
me to be thought of as timid, when I've had to do things that were so risky
as to be almost crazy. Oh hum."[36]

Patton arrived in England in late January and went straight to London to
meet Eisenhower, who greeted him with the news that he was to command
the Third Army, which was still in the United States and would shortly begin
arriving in the United Kingdom. Eisenhower also left the mercurial Patton in
no doubt where he stood by giving him "a severe bawling out" for his impulsive behavior. Butcher would later observe that Patton was "a master of flattery" who was able to turn any difference of opinion with Eisenhower "into
a deferential acquiescence to the view of the Supreme Commander. . . .'Ike,
as you are now the most powerful man in the world, it is foolish to contest
your views.' . . . Ike glumly and noncommittally passes off such flattery."
Knowing it would get back to Eisenhower, Patton told Butcher a few days
later that Ike was "on the threshold of becoming 'the greatest general of all
time—including Napoleon.' "[37] Several months later Patton was delighted
when someone related that Gen. Albert Wedemeyer had been overheard
stoutly defending him in a heated conversation with Eisenhower: "Hell, get
on to yourself, Ike; you didn't make him, he made you."[38]

Detailed by Eisenhower to give Patton the "sixty-four-dollar tour" of the
city, Kay Summersby thought he was the "most glamorous, dramatic general
I'd ever met." Unlike other generals she had chauffeured, Patton rode in the

front seat, "his ramrod back never once unbent, never touched the seat." He was appalled by the magnitude of the bombing damage to London. " 'Those sonsabitches,' he would mutter, 'those sonsabitches.' Then, he'd turn to me. 'I'm sorry, Miss Summersby. Excuse me, please.' " Kay admitted she had been around Americans long enough to learn how to curse and had once yelled "Goddamn!" in the office. When Patton inquired from whom she had learned such language, Kay replied that it had been Dwight D. Eisenhower.[39]

Although Patton sincerely liked Kay Summersby, he was not alone in being uneasy whenever she was present with Eisenhower, and would clam up immediately, once saying, "I *do* have secrets from her." Many were appalled at Eisenhower's habit of sometimes including Kay in top-level meetings, where highly classified information was discussed. Although she had no security clearance, Eisenhower was undaunted, proclaiming, "We have no secrets from Kay."[40]

Apparently oblivious to the inevitable gossip, Eisenhower also thought nothing of routinely including her during visits to subordinate commands. One such occasion occurred in August 1944, when the entire 82nd Airborne Division passed smartly in review for Eisenhower. Invited to tea at Ridgway's quarters after the review, Eisenhower included Kay, prompting James M. Gavin (then a brigadier general) to note that in military protocol "Chauffeurs do not normally join their generals for tea"—or similar official functions, for that matter. Those who met Kay Summersby found her attractive and vivacious; that she was a sight for sore eyes did not alter the fact that her presence regularly raised eyebrows wherever Eisenhower went. Curious, Gavin asked a veteran war correspondent if it was merely gossip. The correspondent, John "Beaver" Thompson of the *Chicago Tribune,* replied, "Well, I have never before seen a chauffeur get out of a car and kiss the General good morning when he comes from his office."[41] Bradley merely thought Eisenhower foolish, and his aide Chester "Chet" Hansen shrugged it off with the observation, "If they were sleeping together it was their business."[42] If Eisenhower was ever aware of the gossip surrounding an obvious appearance of impropriety, he neither acknowledged it nor took steps to mitigate it, despite blunt warnings from Jimmy Gault that it was unwise and would lead to assumptions that she was more than merely his driver. As Gault predicted, the rumors that had begun in Algiers inevitably resurfaced in London. True beyond doubt was that, Mamie's disfavor notwithstanding, Kay Summersby had become such an indispensable part of Dwight Eisenhower's military life that he was oblivious to any and all adverse reactions to her presence, however inappropriate it was at times.

Although planning was moving ahead at full speed, it was not until February 12, 1944, that Eisenhower received a formal directive from the CCOS on which he was to plan and carry out the final destruction of Nazi Germany. There was still considerable debate about strategy and other unresolved matters, but Eisenhower's stated mission was unequivocal: "You will enter the continent of Europe and, in conjunction with the other United Nations, undertake operations aimed at the heart of Germany and the destruction of her armed forces."[43]

In early March the greater part of the SHAEF staff was moved to Bushy Park, the former headquarters of the Eighth Air Force, in a southeastern London suburb near Kingston-on-Thames and Hampton Court Palace. Code-named Widewing by the air force, Eisenhower's new headquarters was little more than a collection of Quonset huts, tents, and hastily erected temporary buildings in an ancient royal forest. Eisenhower longed for the nostalgic times he had spent at nearby Telegraph Cottage and the comfort factor it engendered. By coincidence Tedder and his new wife were about to move into Telegraph Cottage, but were persuaded to move into a more stately mansion intended for Eisenhower.

Eisenhower may have been overjoyed to be back in the rather crude but intimate surroundings of Telegraph Cottage, but SHAEF's move to Bushy Park was far less successful. Because of the necessity of keeping key planning staffers in London, there was an inevitable duplication of effort at both Norfolk House and Bushy Park. The move, orchestrated by Beetle Smith, infuriated Leigh-Mallory, who had wanted his headquarters and SHAEF's located nearer each other. Although Smith admitted that moving to Bushy Park was a mistake ("My God, I've married the wrong woman!"), Eisenhower was so adamant ("even if he has to become established in 'Widewing' alone," wrote Butcher) that the move would probably have occurred in any event.

Eisenhower's office was in a nondescript corner building with a tin roof, bright fluorescent lights, cracking linoleum, and paint peeling from its walls. There was no heat, and the narrow rug on the floor failed to deter a numbing chill from seeping through the concrete floor. Everyone wore two pairs of socks in a largely futile effort to stay warm. According to Kay Summersby, Eisenhower "suffered acutely from the cold" and developed a cold that "lasted for months." Virtually every time he returned from his frequent visits to Allied units, his voice would be so hoarse that the headquarters nurse would be "popping into and out of the office all day long, spraying his throat, taking his temperature and scolding him" (to no avail) that he ought to be home in bed.[44]

Shortly before moving to Bushy Park in early March, Patton paid Eisenhower a visit. The two dined alone that night, and Patton was struck by Eisenhower's loneliness: "He is drinking too much but is terribly lonely. I really feel sorry for him."[45] Visitors to his office would sometimes find Eisenhower putting an imaginary golf ball to help relieve the stress.[46]

The obscure, insecure officer who had arrived in London unheralded in the summer of 1942 bore scant resemblance to the general who took command of SHAEF in January 1944. Confident and poised, Eisenhower arrived in London determined to put his personal imprint on Overlord. His name was now known to all, and when Churchill publicly announced his appointment in Parliament, the MPs cheered. (By contrast, when Bedell Smith's name was announced there was dead silence.) Those who knew Eisenhower and had worked with him in the Mediterranean were aware of the subtle changes in his performance. Those meeting him for the first time in 1944 encountered a man supremely confident. Among the newcomers was Eisenhower's chief meteorologist, RAF Group Capt. J. M. Stagg, a Scotsman on whom the fate of Overlord would hinge in a few short months. Stagg saw a far different man than Mamie had only a few weeks earlier. "With a broad smile . . . he looked in first-class mental and physical condition. He spoke quietly and naturally. . . ."[47]

There was ample reason for Eisenhower's demeanor. No commander in military history faced a more daunting task than the one he did in 1944. Not only was he charged with welding together the largest force ever assembled for an amphibious invasion, but it had to work the first time: There would be no second chances.

40.

"A Monument to the Imagination of British and American Planners"

The history of warfare knows no other like undertaking.
—STALIN

The plan was simple in conception yet breathtaking in scope.
—ALAN A. MICHIE

The most bedeviling aspect of Allied operations during the war was the perpetual shortage of landing craft. There were never enough to meet operational needs, and the problem had grown so acute that to meet the requirements of the revised Overlord plan the Allies virtually had to strip the Mediterranean theater of its precious cache of LSTs (Landing Ship Tank). Given the incredible industrial war-making capability of the United States, why should this have been so? The short answer lies in the fact that in 1943 the Allied planners had yet to determine where and on what scale the cross-Channel invasion would take place. Their inability to determine requirements in time to produce and deliver the vessels, intense competition with other types of warships being built in U.S. shipyards already stretched to capacity, and the less-than-enthusiastic backing of the program by Ernie King and the navy, which predicted dire consequences to the naval construction program, all led to insufficient numbers of landing craft in 1944.[1] The bitter truth, wrote the official historian of the invasion, was that "[d]uring the first years of the war the majority of the naval leaders resisted the development of landing craft as a foolhardy gamble with an untried weapon and a waste of resources," a philosophy to which even Roosevelt subscribed.[2] When the British warned the United States in early 1943 that they could not produce enough landing craft to meet the needs of a cross-Channel operation in 1944, they were disbelieved and bitterly resisted by the U.S. Navy. Small wonder that Churchill made his now-famous remark that "the destinies of two great empires seemed to be tied up in some god-damned things called LSTs."

Eisenhower had learned early the difficulties posed by the constraint shortage of landing craft, once remarking to Butcher that when he was buried, "his coffin should be in the shape of a landing craft, as they are practically killing him with worry."[3] As historian Eric Larrabee points out, the landing craft contretemps was one of the sorriest sagas of World War II, "from which few emerge with much credit."[4]

As the senior Allied ground commander, Montgomery assumed full responsibility for the invasion plan and for the development of the strategy to be employed during the battle for Normandy. Throughout January 1944 Morgan's original invasion plan was drastically revised by Montgomery's team of planners. With the backing of both Eisenhower and Bradley, Montgomery began orchestrating significant changes. At Eisenhower's first Overlord briefing, held on the morning of January 21, Montgomery outlined his proposed solutions, which would make it far more difficult for the German defenders to concentrate their forces to defeat the invasion before the Allies could establish a beachhead and then strike inland. Vital to the long-term success was securing the major port of Cherbourg, which was destined to become the logistic lifeline between Britain and France. The inadequacy of the COSSAC plan would impede both the capture of Cherbourg and the establishment of a secure bridgehead that could withstand the German counterattacks that Rommel would certainly launch to push the Allied invaders back into the sea.

Though the price of adding assault divisions was an approximate one-month delay in mounting Overlord, postponing the invasion until late May, it was one Eisenhower was more than willing to pay in order to obtain a strengthened invasion force. As finally approved by the Combined Chiefs of Staff, the assault was to be organized under the control of one British and one American army. The invasion sector was widened from thirty to fifty miles, and two additional divisions were added to the D-Day assault force. The area from Bayeux eastward to the river Orne was British, and from Bayeux westward, American. The U.S. sector was to extend as far as the Cotentin Peninsula, where the 4th Infantry Division would land on Utah Beach in the Carentan Estuary, protected by the 82nd and 101st Airborne Divisions, which were to land and seize key points along the Cotentin around midnight before the invasion proper, which would take place the following morning. While the 82nd and 101st held the critical approaches to Cherbourg, a British airborne division would be employed to carry out a similar mission to secure the approaches to Caen. With heavy air and naval gunfire support, the infantry would seize the Caen-Bayeux beachhead, thus enabling follow-up armored brigades to land and quickly push inland. To accommodate the weather forecasts, Eisenhower was given flexibility over the final date.

.   .   .

Prior to Rommel's appointment by Hitler in mid-January 1944 as commander of Army Group B, with responsibility for preparing Germany's defenses against a second front in the West, the much ballyhooed Festung Europa (Fortress Europe) was, except for the Pas de Calais, a sham. Rommel was in charge of an area from Holland to Brittany, and he responded to the challenge in the manner that had made him a legend in North Africa, by initiating an all-out effort to plug the gaps evident in Normandy. He tirelessly prodded Berlin for more troops, supplies, and construction equipment. Although he had no particular suspicion that Normandy was to be the Allied target, Rommel gave the sector from Caen to the Cotentin Peninsula special attention. He began to enclose possible landing sites in rings of steel and concrete. Mines were emplaced along the beaches, along with metal spikes and other obstacles below the low-tide line. Potential airborne landing zones inland were similarly studded with metal stakes topped with deadly antipersonnel mines (called *Rommelspargel*—Rommel's asparagus). By the time the final Overlord planning measures were initiated in early 1944, Rommel had greatly strengthened the German defenses of Normandy.

Once the Allies were ashore, their strategy was to concentrate in the initial stages of the operation on quickly gaining control of the main centers of road communication, followed by deep thrusts by armored formations between and beyond these points to gain and control terrain for the establishment of tactical airfields, and to provide blocking positions that would thwart certain German attempts to counterattack and destroy the beachhead. The keys to success in Normandy were the seizure of Caen, and of the equally important Caen-Falaise Plain to its southeast by the British Second Army. The American assault force consisted of Bradley's First Army, whose mission was to capture Cherbourg as quickly as possible, then to mount an offensive to secure the dry ground south of St.-Lô and Périers, from which First Army would advance toward Paris, while Patton's Third Army would land and secure Brittany and its potentially valuable ports.

During April and May 1944 the Allies finalized the most massive and complex military plan ever conceived. The magnitude of the problems that had to be grappled with and solved within a short period of time dwarfed any other single event in recorded history. The planning involved every single military element: air, sea, and ground forces of many nationalities—U.S., British, Canadian, Polish, and Free French. The logistical details alone were staggering in their magnitude and complexity. The navy had to plan not only the sealift of 156,000 troops but to choreograph the employment of nearly seven thousand Allied naval vessels, fifteen of which were hospital ships, and 195,700 naval and merchant marine personnel in the waters off Normandy on D-Day. Eight thousand doctors supplied with 600,000 doses of penicillin,

100,000 pounds of sulfa, and 800,000 pints of plasma had been assembled to treat the wounded.[5] The British War Office was producing 170 million maps covering all aspects of the invasion and subsequent operations. In all, nearly two million soldiers, sailors, and airmen would be involved in carrying out Operation Overlord.

It was, writes Max Hastings, "the greatest organizational achievement of the Second World War, a feat of staff work that has dazzled history, a monument to the imagination of British and American planners and logisticians which may never be surpassed in war."[6] And it was not without controversy.

Eisenhower's memories of the problems and mistakes made in the Mediterranean was like a barely healed wound he was determined not to permit to be reopened in Overlord. The most important lesson that had been learned the hard way in the Mediterranean was at the top of his list: the tortuous command setup that had left him frustrated and nearly powerless. Salerno in particular still deeply rankled Eisenhower, who arrived in London adamant that something be done to control the Allied air forces.

Backed by Tedder, Eisenhower demanded and eventually gained operational control of both the tactical and strategic air forces. He pointedly noted in *Crusade in Europe* that "when a battle needs the last ounce of available force, the commander must not be in the position of depending upon request and negotiation to get it. . . . I stated unequivocally that so long as I was in command I would accept no other solution."[7] How Eisenhower finally gained that control was an exasperating venture through the minefields of military infighting.

By mid-1943 it had become clear that the air war could not be won so long as Luftwaffe fighters were able to knock Allied strategic bombers from the air in droves. In June 1943 the Combined Chiefs of Staff issued a directive called Pointblank, ordering a massive strategic bombing offensive against German industrial targets. One of its principal aims was the destruction of the Luftwaffe fighter arm through pinpoint bombing of aviation factories by Lt. Gen. Ira Eaker's Eighth Air Force. The concept of pinpoint bombing was a myth, however. "More USAAF bombs landed in fields and killed cows than hit German factories."[8] In early 1944 not only were Hermann Göring's airplane factories still actively in business, but German fighter production had actually increased, as had Allied bomber losses. Hap Arnold replaced Eaker, charging Spaatz with responsibility for destroying the Luftwaffe.

Air Chief Marshal Sir Arthur "Bomber" Harris, the autocratic boss of the RAF's Bomber Command, and his American counterpart, Tooey Spaatz, were zealous in their conviction that an around-the-clock strategic bombing effort would bring Germany to its knees without the necessity for a major ground campaign in Europe.[9] With Churchill's enthusiastic backing, for nearly two years Harris had been on a personal crusade to do precisely that. He initiated relentless night attacks against industrial targets in

Germany, Italy, and the Balkans, coupled with the systematic area bombing of high-density population centers such as Berlin, Hamburg, Nuremberg, and, later, Dresden. Hamburg was relentlessly destroyed in late July and early August 1943 by Bomber Command, which left the city a charnel house. The cost in lives and aircraft was astronomical, with 96 of 795 RAF bombers lost in a single night raid on Nuremberg on March 30, 1944. The expectation that an RAF or USAAF bomber crew would survive to complete the required number of combat missions to complete their tour of duty had decreased to a frighteningly low percentage. The men of Bomber Command none too affectionately referred to their commander as "Butcher Harris."

By the time Eisenhower assumed command of SHAEF in January 1944 it was already clear that Pointblank had failed and that—unless reined in—the air barons would continue pursuing their own agenda at the expense of Overlord. The Allied airmen had always been an independent-minded group of men with a belief in airpower that verged on the fanatical. The key players—Harris, Spaatz, Arnold, and Brereton (now commander of the Ninth Air Force)—all subscribed to the almost sacrosanct big-bang tenet that the war could be won on the basis of airpower alone. In November 1943 Spaatz had confidently predicted that by the spring of 1944, when round-the-clock bombing operations could take place from both England and Italy, "Germany will give up within three months."[10]

The only air plan that existed for Overlord in January 1944 vaguely proposed minimal measures for air support during a two-to-three-week period before D-Day in order to knock out coastal defenses and soften the way for the invasion force. When first briefed on air operations in January 1944, Eisenhower and Spaatz were shocked by Leigh-Mallory's prediction that it was still uncertain if the Allies would even gain air superiority before Overlord was launched.

Professor Solly Zuckerman, the scientist whom Tedder had brought back to England specifically to help devise bombing policy for Overlord, was horrified at the inadequacy of the original air plan, and its failure to consider how the air forces could possibly provide the necessary support in the (likely) event of bad weather. Nor had a great deal of consideration been given to the fact that targeting only Normandy would easily have alerted the Germans that it was to be the site of the Allied landings. A Bombing Committee, representing all players in the air war, convened under the auspices of Leigh-Mallory's AEAF and began drafting alternative proposals that called for a wide-ranging, systematic bombing campaign to knock out not simply the entire French railway transportation system but that throughout northwestern Europe. Thus was unveiled what has been called the Transportation Plan, a scheme that quickly exploded to become one of the most controversial strategies of the war and the focus of rancorous debate.

The gravest danger surrounded not the D-Day landings themselves but German reinforcements sped to Normandy to seal off the Allied beachhead with greater numbers of forces than the Allies could insert across the English Channel. "Eisenhower and Tedder were rapidly persuaded that Zuckerman's plan represented the most promising means of wrecking the German army's communications with Normandy."[11] The essence of the Transportation Plan was a massive strategic bombing campaign to destroy the French rail network, bridges, and choke points to paralyze Normandy, making it impossible to reinforce after D-Day while at the same time providing the Germans with no indication of where the invasion would occur.

The bomber chiefs, backed by most in the Air Ministry as well as Churchill's personal Rasputin, Professor F. W. Lindemann (later Lord Cherwell), arose as one in fierce and formidable opposition, proclaiming that such operations would be a gross misuse of the strategic air forces. Harris gained Churchill's attention by refusing to offer an endorsement that the Transportation Plan would not produce high civilian casualties. Neither Spaatz nor Harris would renounce their wildly inaccurate "private conviction that Overlord was a vast, gratuitous, strategic misjudgment, when Germany was already tottering on the edge of collapse from bombing."[12] An escalating war of words between the airmen and Churchill on the one side, and Eisenhower, Tedder, Zuckerman, and Air Chief Marshal Sir Charles Portal (chief of the air staff) on the other, turned the Transportation Plan into an intra-Allied free-for-all.[13] More than thirty years later Zuckerman would write of still being "utterly amazed by the nonsensical arguments about the plan."[14]

Two points on which Eisenhower refused to back down, Anvil and control of the air forces, brought him into direct conflict with Churchill, who, along with the members of his War Cabinet, despised the plan for what historian Weigley rightly defines as its "implicit inhumanity."[15] It took until the end of March for a compromise to be brokered that effectively cut Leigh-Mallory from the air chain of command when Eisenhower agreed to appoint Tedder to control air operations as his designated "executive." Haggling over the date on which Tedder would actually take control further delayed matters. The only certainty was that Leigh-Mallory had lost most of his autonomy and would now fall under Tedder's direction. What perplexed Eisenhower was the extent of British loathing for Leigh-Mallory, the airman approved for his post by the same men who were determined to keep him from exercising any control over the strategic bombers.

Believing (with good reason) that, as a fighter commander, Leigh-Mallory was ill suited to control bomber operations, Spaatz made it clear to Eisenhower that while he would—however reluctantly—accept SHAEF control, he could not work under the authority of the AEAF commander. With Harris in the background damning Leigh-Mallory to Churchill and insisting that he should not be given control of the strategic bombers, the circle was complete.

Eisenhower was not only in the middle of a monumental intramural war but no closer to resolving his problems. "Just when Ike thinks he has the problem of air command solved," wrote Butcher on March 3, "as he put it today, 'someone else's feelings get hurt and I have another problem to solve.'"

By early April, shortly before the plan was to have been implemented, it had yet to be approved. Outside SHAEF almost no one liked the Transportation Plan. Its formidable critics included Churchill, Eden, the majority of the War Cabinet, Harris, Spaatz, Doolittle (who had assumed command of the Eighth Air Force from Eaker), the Joint Intelligence Committee, the Ministry of Economic Warfare, and a host of other critics in the Air Ministry.[16]

On April 5 it was debated before the Prime Minister's Defence Committee. If the plan was adopted, an animated Churchill—his anger turned up several degrees by arguments over the accuracy of a prediction of 80,000–160,000 casualties—charged it would inevitably result in the "cold-blooded butchering" of French civilians. Brooke also opposed the plan for the same reason, although he admitted after the war that he had made a mistake in not backing Tedder.[17] During the most heated confrontation yet, a testy Winston Churchill, when informed that Montgomery was insisting on bombing, exploded in fury. "Who is Montgomery that he can *insist*," he complained, then turned his wrath on Tedder. Having decided that if the plan was rejected he would resign his post as Eisenhower's deputy, Tedder wondered if he would soon be a civilian growing tomatoes.[18]

Both Tedder and Eisenhower stubbornly insisted that, risky or not, the Transportation Plan was vital. Eisenhower disputed the British casualty figures as "grossly overestimated. The French people are slaves. Only a successful OVERLORD can free them," he wrote to Churchill.[19] He also wrote to Roosevelt and Marshall, "I have stuck to my guns because there is no other way in which this tremendous air force can help us, during the preparatory phase, to get ashore and and stay there."[20] As for the French, when queried about the possibility of heavy losses, Maj. Gen. Pierre Koenig, the commander of Free French forces in the United Kingdom, replied, "This is war and it is to be expected that people will be killed. . . . We would take twice the anticipated loss to be rid of the Germans."[21] The normally stubborn de Gaulle also signed on, effectively undermining Churchill's arguments against the bombing.

Spaatz and Harris not only fought hard to avoid implementing the Transportation Plan, but they clashed with each other as well. Harris's single-minded obsession that destroying Germany's cities would end the war was in direct opposition to American beliefs that precision bombing of German industrial infrastructure was the correct approach. The infighting within the ranks of the air forces was as bitter as their joint opposition to SHAEF control of their bombing operations and to the Transportation Plan, which a senior air marshal in the Air Ministry decried as "a national disaster."

Spaatz argued that the Overlord bombing violated the Pointblank directive and countered with what was called the Oil Plan, a scheme for the systematic destruction of Germany's synthetic petroleum capacity, which he said would win the war. Spaatz's Oil Plan was also designed to steal the limelight from Harris. "He was haunted by fear that Bomber Command might somehow win the laurels while his Fortresses were reduced to running a bomb shuttle for Eisenhower," while Harris would be permitted to "go on bombing Germany and will be given a chance of defeating her before the invasion, while I am put under Leigh-Mallory's command."[22]

Eisenhower, firmly backed by Tedder, refused to allow the Transportation Plan to be held hostage by the warring airmen with their own agendas. Not for the first time, thoughts of resignation crossed his mind. He had long since wearied of dealing with "a lot of prima donnas," and although the notion of an actual resignation only weeks before the most critical operation of the war was unthinkable, Eisenhower seemed fully prepared to use the mere *threat* of resignation to gain control of the airmen. "By God," he declared to Tedder, "you tell that bunch that if they can't get together and stop quarreling like children, I will tell the Prime Minister to get someone else to run this damn war! I'll quit."[23]

Eventually he turned to Marshall, recommending that "a word be adopted that leaves no doubt in anybody's mind of my authority and responsibility for controlling air operations . . . during the critical period of Overlord." Eisenhower was so frustrated by the infighting and its consequent lack of a favorable decision that he wrote in his diary that if the matter of the Transportation Plan and the control of the air barons was not approved, "I am going to take drastic action and inform the combined chiefs of staff that unless the matter is settled at once I will request relief from this command."[24]

On April 19 Spaatz and Eisenhower, two men who greatly respected each other, had a furious confrontation over a decision by Tedder that the bombing of V-1 launch sites would take priority over German industrial targets and the carrying out of his mandate to destroy the Luftwaffe, a policy that Spaatz argued was self-defeating. At one point Spaatz was thought to have threatened resignation. When tempers cooled Spaatz and Tedder reached a compromise, but the incident was a prime example of the passions that drove the debates over air operations before Overlord.[25]

Throughout April the debate raged, estimates were revised, targets altered, and the plan limped forward when Churchill and his committee endorsed provisional approval for the bombing on a week-to-week basis. In early May the plan was grudgingly approved. Nonetheless Churchill never lost his distaste for the scheme, and his demands for repeated consultations were a perpetual source of irritation for Tedder and Eisenhower. Churchill complained to a sympathetic War Cabinet that he had failed to understand "that our use of air power before 'Overlord' would assume so cruel and remorseless a form." Clearly "a great slaughter would inevitably result" unless Roosevelt intervened to stop it. FDR pointedly refused to interfere or to imperil Overlord, a strong endorsement of Eisenhower.[26] It was, noted an official British historian, one of the few examples of War Cabinet involvement in a strategic military decision. While Eisenhower had the necessary authority to proceed without their approval, the issue was so incendiary that prudence dictated it be resolved by means of compromise.[27]

On April 7, Good Friday, Montgomery assembled the senior Allied generals, admirals, and airmen at St. Paul's School (which he had attended as a boy) in the London borough of Hammersmith, for a dry run of the Overlord plan. Both Eisenhower and Churchill attended at least one of the sessions to hear Montgomery brief the plan, how he envisioned Rommel would defend Normandy, and how Allied strategy would unfold once the assault forces had established a beachhead.

On May 15, in the presence of King George VI, Churchill and Eisenhower and the Allied commanders assembled at St. Paul's on an exceptionally cold spring day for the final Overlord briefing. In a setting that would be repeated on a smaller scale in an icy room in Verdun later that year, the participants huddled in their overcoats to ward off the chill. It may have been the most notable gathering of Allied military leaders and senior officers ever brought together in one place. Churchill arrived, the ever-present cigar in hand, wearing a black frock coat. When King George VI arrived, everyone stood as Churchill bowed in respect but kept his cigar in hand. There was no applause or ceremony, and before Eisenhower arose to deliver the opening remarks an air of expectation gripped the room.

The king, Churchill, Eisenhower, Field Marshal Jan Smuts, the prime minister of South Africa and a onetime general in the British army, and the British chiefs of staff all sat in armchairs in front of a stage on which resided a giant relief map of Normandy and northern France. Bradley, Patton, Dempsey, Hodges, Simpson, Lt. Gen. Henry D. G. Crerar (the Canadian army commander); the naval and air task force commanders; the Canadian, American, and British corps commanders; and a bevy of other senior officers from SHAEF and Whitehall, including the members of the War Cabinet, sat on hard wooden benches rising in tiers to the rear of the crescent-shaped room. In one of the few accounts ever written of the event one participant noted, "It was a curious experience to see so great and vital a secret, written so large and revealed to so large a company."

An American admiral later recalled how "[i]t seemed to most of us that the proper meshing of so many gears would need nothing less than divine guidance. . . . All in that room were aware of the gravity of the elements to be dealt with." Eisenhower's speech lasted barely ten minutes, but in that time he managed to capture his audience. "It has been said that his smile was worth twenty divisions. That day it was worth more." Eisenhower showed a confidence he had not possessed during Torch; "the mists of doubt dissolved. When he had finished the tension was gone. Not often has one man been called upon to accept so great a burden of responsibility. But here was one at peace with his soul."[28] Possibly the only person present that day who was unmoved was Brooke, who wrote in his diary that Eisenhower was "just a co-ordinator, a good mixer, a champion of inter-Allied co-operation, and in those respects few can hold a candle to him."[29] After the war an unrepentant Brooke wrote that, in hindsight, he would "repeat every word" of his opinion. "Charming," a "good co-ordinator. But no real commander. . . . Ike might have been a showman calling on various actors to perform their various turns, but he was not the commander of the show."[30] Eisenhower never reciprocated Brooke's hostility, magnanimously calling his chief critic "honest," but an irate Ismay wrote his friend Ike that the so-called wartime partnership in genius was "ninety-five percent of Winston, five percent of Brooke."[31]

Eisenhower was followed by the three commanders in chief, who each briefed their portion of the Overlord plan. The focal briefing was Montgomery's, a presentation that was clear, confident, and made a positive impression, despite frequent interruptions from Churchill, whose questions seemed designed mainly to show off his knowledge of strategy and tactics. Even his critics admitted it was a bravura performance, a brilliant and simple summary of what lay ahead. "*We* have the initiative," he said, "we must rely on the violence of our assault, our great weight of supporting fire from the sea and the air, simplicity and robust mentality." His briefing has been described in these terms: "Montgomery's demeanor was very quiet and deliberate. He was not at all showy and seemed cautious, for he made no attempt to minimize the difficulties of the task. One thing he made clear, and that was his opinion that he had the measure of Rommel. He could be described as confident but certainly not complacent."[32] Pug Ismay remembered that "Montgomery was quite first-class. . . . 'This is a perfectly normal operation which is certain of success. If anyone has any doubts in his mind, let him stay behind.' I think he must have been reading Henry V before Agincourt: 'He that hath no stomach for this fight, / Let him depart.' "[33]

Montgomery spoke at length about Rommel as "an energetic and determined commander; he has made a world of difference since he took over. He is best at the spoiling attack; his forte is disruption. . . . He will do his level best to 'Dunkirk' us." However, while the Allies should respect Rommel, they need not fear him, said Montgomery, if the Allies stormed ashore "seeing red" and "imbued with infectious optimism, and offensive eagerness. Nothing must stop them. If we send them into battle in this way—then we shall succeed."[34]

The day ended with brief remarks from the king and Smuts, who was in a gloomy mood and depressed by the size of the task ahead. When Churchill's turn came, he rose and, gripping his lapels firmly in his hands, said: "I am hardening to this enterprise. I repeat, I am *now* hardening toward this enterprise." Churchill's turn of phrase unhappily conveyed a misleading impression to Eisenhower and other Americans present that he had previously been against Overlord. Failing to understand that Churchill's statement was mainly one of semantics, Eisenhower took the PM's remarks as a signal that only now was he becoming a believer. Privately Eisenhower was dismayed by what was actually intended as a fighting speech: "I then realized for the first time that Mr. Churchill hadn't believed in it all along and had had no faith that it would succeed. It was quite a shocking discovery. Sir Alan Brooke had been extremely pessimistic at all times about our prospect of fighting through the bocage [small fields ringed by earthen banks topped with dense shrubbery] country and I believe the PM reflected Sir Alan's tactical views."[35]

Churchill's speech ended on a note of clairvoyance: "Let us not expect all to go according to plan," he told the commanders. "Flexibility of mind will be one of the decisive factors." Still smarting over the near disaster at Anzio, he concluded with a warning that "[w]e must not have another Anzio . . . risks must be taken."[36]

Eisenhower closed a long day by lightheartedly remarking to the assembled commanders, "In half an hour Hitler will have missed his one and only chance of destroying with a single well-aimed bomb the entire high command of the Allied forces."[37]

As he had demonstrated by repeated attempts to sell his "soft underbelly" strategy, Churchill was not an easy convert to the notion of Overlord or that it would succeed. Although Eisenhower was misled by Churchill's phraseology, the PM was now firmly behind Overlord even though fully aware of the horrendous consequences of failure. A few days earlier he had lunched privately with Eisenhower and, with tears in his eyes, told the supreme commander, "I am in this thing with you to the end, and if it fails we will go down together."[38]

Although it was Churchill who first articulated the need for a cross-Channel invasion in the dark days after Dunkirk, he also wavered when it came to the actual event, employing instead fanciful but impossible visions of winning the war via what was never truly a "soft underbelly." Both Eisenhower and Bedell Smith insisted that the prime minister had grave doubts, which he freely expressed in private. In his unpublished recollections Eisenhower wrote:

> In spite of his own spirit of combativeness it was only slowly that he could develop any genuine enthusiasm for Overlord. Time and time again he would express his forebodings, not in an argumentative tone but quietly as an inescapable doubt that we were wise in carrying the

ground battle to Nazi Europe. At times he spoke of visions of beaches choked with the bodies of the flower of British and American youth and of the tides running red with their blood.[39]

At one point during the preparations for Overlord, Churchill told Eisenhower, "My dear General, if by the time the snow flies you can have restored her liberty to our beautiful Paris, I shall proclaim to the world that this has been the best conceived and most remarkably successful military operation of all history."[40]

Another problem that plagued Eisenhower was a controversial plan to invade southern France in support of Overlord. An invasion along the Riviera was deemed essential by those who saw a pressing need to divert German attention and troops from Normandy during the critical days immediately after the D-Day landings. The result, code-named Anvil (redesignated later in 1944 as Dragoon), eventually became the most hotly debated Allied operation of the war.

The primary problem created by expanding the invasion remained landing craft. Anvil was conceived to coincide with the D-Day landings, and—although mainly diversionary to draw German attention and reinforcements from Normandy—it was also intended to open the port of Marseilles. Eisenhower, strongly backed by Roosevelt and Marshall, was adamant that Anvil was essential; however, as the months passed Churchill (supported by the British chiefs of staff) became increasingly hostile to an operation that would cripple his "soft-underbelly" strategy. Arguing that Anvil was unnecessary, would necessitate employing forces urgently needed in Italy, and so weaken the Allies that the current stalemate might never be broken, Churchill attacked Anvil with relentless fervor.

The twin aggravations of Anvil and landing craft surfaced at about the same time in early February as the Anzio beachhead came under a massive German counterattack that nearly rolled the Allies back into the sea, but for the last-ditch heroics of the soldiers in the front lines, led by Truscott and Harmon. Lucas became the scapegoat for having failed to carry out an impossible mission and was replaced by Truscott as VI Corps commander. Worse, the stalemate threatened Anvil and required the retention of precious landing craft in Italy. "We can't close our eyes to that, no matter how much we shout 'principle and agreements,'" Eisenhower penned in his diary. "It looks like Anvil is doomed. I hate this in spite of my recognition . . . that Italian fighting will be some compensation for a strong Anvil."[41]

The Anvil question was never far from the forefront of Churchill's agenda, and his arguments were merely the opening shots in a war of words between Eisenhower and the stubborn British prime minister, to whom the word "no" was a challenge rather than a conclusion. The Anvil debate pitted Marshall and Eisenhower against Churchill and Brooke in a battle of the heavyweights that occupied center stage for the next eight months. Of the many contentious issues separating the two allies, only the transportation plan generated as much passion as this one, which led to some of the most acrimonious exchanges of the war between Roosevelt and Churchill. For Eisenhower the Anvil controversy grew to become the most trying aspect of his relations with Churchill. Although the debate was billed as a military quarrel over strategy, it was actually a political clash of wills between Roosevelt and Churchill, with Eisenhower the pawn caught in the middle.[42]

With his unerring instinct for the jugular, Churchill used the mess at Anzio as justification for canceling Anvil. The uncertain situation in Italy led Eisenhower to conclude that the operation would either have to be postponed or scrapped entirely. As the battle raged at the political and Joint Chiefs level, Eisenhower was content just to keep Anvil alive. At the end of February a formal compromise was approved by the chiefs and ratified by FDR and Churchill: "The Italian battle fronts are to have overriding priority . . . but Anvil is to be planned with hope of launching it shortly after Overlord. . . . As this action largely meets Ike's wishes, he is satisfied."[43] Although agreeing to postponement to insure adequate landing craft for Overlord, Eisenhower would not countenance the cancellation of Anvil.

In that regard Eisenhower proved as stubborn as Churchill. Among his reasons was his conviction that Anvil would do more than merely draw off German reserves and protect the southern flank of the Allied armies. He was not at all optimistic over the usefulness of the Brittany ports, which he believed the Germans would destroy rather than allow to fall into Allied hands. Having experienced firsthand the growth of Churchill's fixation about the "soft underbelly" in recent months, Eisenhower seems to have had a more practical reason to employ Anvil as a useful quid pro quo against Churchill and Brooke—to ensure Overlord did not lose emphasis to Italy.[44]

Churchill and Brooke were not Eisenhower's only bêtes noires during the Overlord planning, however. It was a measure of Eisenhower's growing on-the-job maturity that he rejected advice from Marshall and Hap Arnold that the planned airborne operations in Normandy were far too conservative.

The size of Overlord alone was daunting, but even more difficult was the Allied planners' task of deceiving Hitler and his generals as to the site of the invasion. Keeping Overlord's date and destination secret was a challenge like no other. During the months leading up to D-Day the Allies executed the most massive and successful hoax in the history of warfare. In February 1944 SHAEF brought to fruition the most daring deception operation of the war, originally the brainchild of the COSSAC staff.[45] Assigned the innocuous code-name Fortitude South, it was designed to persuade Hitler and the German commanders in the West that the Normandy landings were merely a feint, and that the main Allied invasion was to be launched against the Pas de Calais by six divisions, with a massive force of fifty divisions to follow.[46]

Patton's appointment as Third Army commander was deliberately kept secret. Publicly the Germans were permitted to learn that he was to command a fictitious First U.S. Army Group (FUSAG), created to convince the Germans that the Allies were planning to invade the Pas de Calais. FUSAG's principal forces were real: the First Canadian Army and Patton's own Third Army, both of which were destined to play follow-up roles in the Normandy campaign. Whenever he visited Third Army units Patton would remind them, "You have not seen me. Remember, I am not here!"[47]

The architects of Fortitude South played to the inherent German bias toward the Pas de Calais, and their belief that the Allies would invade there in order to eliminate the V-1 and V-2 rocket sites, from which the Germans would unleash a terror campaign against England starting in June. In doing so they fulfilled the most essential requirement of any successful deception operation: that there be sufficient elements of truth to reinforce an already existing belief. Moreover, the Germans had an exaggerated sense of the effect these weapons were having on the British populace. The result was, as the British official history records, the creation of "the most complex and successful deception operation in the entire history of war."[48]

Patton's presence in England completed the deception. The German high command's regard for him as the most able Allied battlefield commander made Patton the most likely candidate to command the invasion force, a deception buttressed by the deliberate public acknowledgment that he was in England. Only the fact that he was commanding the Third Army was kept secret. By April 1944, the secret decrypts of German message traffic clearly showed that the Germans were convinced that Patton would lead the Allied invasion.

While the real Overlord force was assembling and training all over the United Kingdom, nonexistent troop units were created in East Anglia. Cleverly designed dummy troop concentrations were emplaced in eastern England, using wooden and rubber replicas of tanks, guns, boats, vehicles, fuel depots, hospitals, ammunition dumps, and troop cantonments, many of which were created by the wizards at the famed Shepperton (film) Studios, near London. Double agents actually working for Allied intelligence sent Berlin information corroborating the presence of a large invasion force in East Anglia.[49] A signal network established solely for the purpose of transmitting a steady stream of phony around-the-clock message traffic created the illusion of at least six divisions training in East Anglia. False reports to Berlin by British agents posing as German spies (who had been captured and were interned) also convinced the Germans that the Allied target was indeed the Pas de Calais. By the spring of 1944 there was clear evidence that the Germans had taken the poisoned bait.[50]

Fortitude was part of a larger cover plan called Bodyguard, whose aim was not only to deceive the Germans over the invasion site but to continue the deception after the landings. Within days of his arrival in London, Eisenhower was briefed on Bodyguard and Fortitude and scribbled on his copy, "I like all this." However, much as he wanted to believe in its lofty aims, as a practical matter he was deeply skeptical that the German General Staff, which comprised that country's best and brightest officers, could possibly be outfoxed by even this clever tissue of lies and trickery. It seemed to be such a formidable task that Eisenhower noted that he would be satisfied if Fortitude managed to tie down one or two German divisions for even a couple of days.[51]

In April 1944 Patton's propensity for saying the wrong thing resulted in another crisis for Eisenhower, landing Patton in yet more trouble, of such magnitude that it again threatened to remove him from the war only weeks before the unleashing of its most decisive campaign. What later became known as the "Knutsford Incident" began innocuously enough, when Patton was invited to deliver a few remarks on the evening of April 25, at the opening of a service club run by local British volunteers for American GIs in Knutsford.

In the wake of the slapping incidents, it appears that many American newspaper editors were eagerly awaiting another Patton faux pas. His remarks—apparently suggesting Anglo-American domination of the postwar world—made terrific copy, and editors across the nation made the most of it. *The Washington Post* editorialized, "General Patton has progressed from simple assaults on individuals to collective assault on entire nationalities," while a prominent Republican congressman, Karl Mundt of South Dakota, complained on the floor of the House of Representatives that Patton had managed to slap "the face of every one of the United Nations, except Great Britain." There were also howls of protest over Patton's references to welcoming his enemies into hell, and "English dames" and "American dames," which the *Post* found "neither gracious nor amusing. . . . Whatever his merits as a strategist or tactician he has revealed glaring defects as a leader of men."[52]

This latest example of a Patton indiscretion could not have come at a worse moment for him personally and the U.S. Army professionally. As required by law, Marshall had recently submitted to the Senate a list of officers' promotions for approval. With the latest uproar over Patton, the list was in sufficient peril that Marshall wrote, "I fear the harm has already been fatal to the confirmation of the permanent list."[53]

Once again the question was what to do about Patton. Marshall left Patton's fate entirely in Eisenhower's hands, noting, "Patton is the only available Army Commander for his present assignment who has had actual experience fighting Rommel and in extensive landing operations followed by a rapid campaign of exploitation."

With a multitude of problems consuming his time, absolutely the last thing Eisenhower needed was another Patton incident. Exasperated beyond measure at having to deal for the second time in less than a year with a major indiscretion by his friend and subordinate, Eisenhower was angry and on the verge of sacking him. "I'm just about fed up," he told Bradley. "If I have to apologize publicly for George one more time, I'm going to have to let him go, valuable as he is. I'm getting sick and tired of having to protect him."[54]

Eisenhower was especially irritated because "I had made a particular point of directing George to avoid press conferences and statements. He had a genius for explosive statements that rarely failed to startle his hearers. He had so long practiced the habit of attempting with fantastic pronouncements to astound his friends and associates that it had become second nature with him." The most recent warning had come less than three weeks earlier, when Eisenhower had warned him about talking too much, then backed off, saying, "Go ahead but watch yourself."[55]

After Patton was widely quoted in the British press, Bedell Smith telephoned Patton and in Eisenhower's name verbally ordered him never again to talk in public without first submitting in writing his proposed remarks to the supreme commander for his personal censorship. Patton blamed British influence for his troubles and complained bitterly that "Benedict Arnold was a piker compared with them," including "Ike and Beedle . . . damn all reporters and gutless men."[56]

Eisenhower formally rebuked Patton by letter, warning that the incident was "still filled with drastic potentialities regarding yourself. . . . I have warned you time and again against your impulsiveness . . . and have flatly instructed you to say nothing that could possibly be misinterpreted. . . . You first came into my command at my own insistence because I believed in your fighting qualities and your ability to lead troops in battle." However, wrote Eisenhower, more in exasperation than anger, "I am thoroughly weary of your failure to control your tongue and have begun to doubt your all-around judgment. . . . My decision in the present case will not become final until I have heard from the War Department. . . . I want to tell you officially and definitely that if you are again guilty of any indiscretion in speech or action. . . . I will relieve you instantly from command."[57]

Everett Hughes, who had followed his boss from Algiers to London, told Patton that Eisenhower had drafted a cable to Marshall stating that he had no further use for Patton's services but then said, "Oh, hell," and tore it up. But in fact Eisenhower had *not* torn up the cable, which was sent to Marshall on April 30, saying, "I have sent for Patton to allow him opportunity to present his case personally to me. On all of the evidence now available I will relieve him from command and send him home unless some new and unforeseen information should be developed in the case."[58]

The morning of May 1, 1944, an anxious and contrite Patton reported to Eisenhower in utter uncertainty but aware that he faced being relieved of command of the Third Army. Eisenhower deliberately kept him waiting for a considerable period of time outside his office. Patton's version is that he was at once reassured by Eisenhower's cordial manner and that he was asked to sit down. Eisenhower began the conversation with: "George, you have gotten yourself into a very serious fix." Before he could continue Patton interrupted to state, "I want to say that your job is more important than mine, so if in trying to save me you are hurting yourself, throw me out."

Eisenhower did not mince words; he had even consulted Churchill, who had dismissed Knutsford as a tempest in a teapot. Patton insisted that if reduced to colonel he would demand the right to command an assault regiment, but Eisenhower said that he might need Patton's services to command an army at a later date and was not considering his reduction. Though he might yet be obliged to send him home, he had still to make up his mind. Patton left crestfallen, his future more uncertain than ever. "I feel like death, but I am not out yet. If they will let me fight, I will."[59] Calling the incident the "unkindest cut of all," Patton wrote to his wife, "If I survive the next couple of days it will be O.K. . . . But still I get in a cold sweat when the phone rings."[60]

In Eisenhower's very different version of their meeting, Patton remained silently at attention throughout, while Eisenhower explained to Patton that he had become a liability, and that it was now questionable if he ought to be retained in command of the Third Army. Patton promised to be

> a model of discretion and in a gesture of almost little-boy contriteness, he put his head on my shoulder. . . . This caused his helmet to fall off— a gleaming helmet I sometimes thought he wore in bed. As it rolled across the room I had the rather odd feeling that I was in the middle of a ridiculous situation . . . his helmet bounced across the floor into a corner. I prayed that no one would come in and see the scene. . . . Without apology and without embarrassment, he walked over, picked up his helmet, adjusted it, and said: "Sir, could I now go back to my headquarters?"[61]

Marshall again reaffirmed that Patton's future lay in Eisenhower's hands, cabling on May 2, "The decision is exclusively yours. My view, and it is merely that, is that you should not weaken your hand for OVERLORD. If you think that PATTON's removal does weaken your prospect, you should continue him in command. . . . Consider only OVERLORD and your own heavy burden of responsibility for its success."[62]

Two days later Eisenhower sent Patton an eyes-only cable: "I am once more taking the responsibility of retaining you in command in spite of damaging repercussions resulting from a personal indiscretion. I do this solely because of my faith in you as a battle leader and from no other motives."[63] What also seems plain is that Marshall was indirectly responsible for saving Patton. The evidence suggests that Eisenhower was not only prepared but felt obliged to relieve Patton until he received the chief of staff's cable of May 2. Marshall took Eisenhower off the hook and cleverly implied that he thought Patton ought to be retained for Overlord. Any other allusion would have meant the immediate and undoubtedly irrevocable death of Patton's career. As Eisenhower explained to Marshall on May 4, to relieve Patton would be enormously counterproductive, and "because your telegram leaves the decision exclusively in my hands, to be decided solely upon my convictions as to the effect upon OVERLORD, I have decided to retain him in command."[64]

Eisenhower's public relations officer, Col. Justus "Jock" Lawrence, was sent to Patton to deliver the following message: "Sir, the Supreme Commander has directed me to inform you that there are to be no more public statements *by you or any of your staff* until further notice from him personally." Patton laughed and replied, "Come on, Jock, what did Ike *really* say?" Somewhat reluctantly Lawrence answered, "*He said that you were not to open your goddamned mouth again publicly until he said you could!*" Patton erupted in gales of laughter.[65]

Given the choice, Omar Bradley would have rid himself of Patton. "I fully concurred in Ike's decision to send Patton home. I, too, was fed up." It was Patton's good fortune that despite Eisenhower's request for Truscott's transfer to England, he was unavailable, having only recently succeeded Lucas in command of the VI Corps at Anzio. Had Truscott been transferred, it is more than likely that Eisenhower would have carried out the relief of Patton.[66]

In April, Eisenhower established his advance command post on England's south coast, at Admiral Ramsay's naval headquarters, Southwick House, a palatial Georgian country mansion in a parkland some six miles north of the city of Portsmouth. Not long before the move Eisenhower decided to have a all-American Sunday afternoon lawn party at Telegraph Cottage for Churchill. A bevy of VIPs, which also included Tedder and Montgomery, speared their own frankfurters from a boiling kettle. It took Churchill several tries, but he drew cheers when he finally succeeded. Afterward, Churchill presented cigars to the enlisted men and with a straight face, thanked them "for a delicacy fit for a king."[67]

Even on nights when he managed only a few hours sleep, Eisenhower invariably arose before his staff. At Southwick, before and after the invasion, Snyder would usually arrive to begin preparing breakfast only to find Eisenhower in the kitchen cooking his own meal of eggs or pancakes. "This was relaxation for him but I knew he was the kind of man who was busy concentrating on his problems even when he appeared idle, so after exchanging greetings I would let him alone."[68] Until dissuaded by Snyder, Eisenhower would insist on washing his own dishes. Cooking became a diversion that did not always make points with his personal staff, particularly his penchant for fried foods. An early precursor of Julia Child, Eisenhower liked having an audience to whom he would describe his every action. The scary part came when he added dollops of chili powder, leading Butcher to complain that when it came to eating Eisenhower's chicken, "There's not enough beer in England to put out that kind of fire."[69]

The Allied buildup throughout the United Kingdom continued on an unprecedented scale. Southern England became a virtual armed camp as training for Overlord continued at a frantic pace. Amphibious training exercises took place in Scotland and off the south coast of England. It has often been facetiously said that it was a miracle that England did not sink under the incredible weight of the incalculable items of war matériel that clogged every available space from the Sussex coast in the south to northern England, the West Country, the Midlands, and as far north as Scotland. Ships, tanks, vehicles of every size and shape, artillery pieces, airplanes (fighters, bombers, and even light aircraft)—whatever was not stacked in fields or any available open space was stored in warehouses containing millions of tons of supplies, all poised in some fashion to support the invasion and the subsequent campaign. In the history of warfare there has never been a more massive buildup of war matériel or a logistical effort of such staggering magnitude as that undertaken before D-Day.[70]

Within the United Kingdom were thirty-nine armored, infantry, and airborne divisions (with many more to come) and, excluding the strategic bomber force, 11,000 tactical combat aircraft. In ports along the coast of England the 6,939 vessels that would comprise the invasion fleet were being assembled.[71] It was essential that there be some means of resupply until Cherbourg was captured and made operational. A Royal Navy officer had proposed the novel idea of building artificial harbors, observing that "if we can't capture a port we must take one with us."[72] Two giant floating artificial harbors called Mulberries had been devised and were secretly under construction, each of them to be towed across the Channel and emplaced off the Normandy beaches to enable the Allied logisticians to resupply the invading force. When it came to ingenuity, the British proved masters of improvisation. A brilliant British tank officer named Maj. Gen. Sir Percy C. S. "Hobo" Hobart (a previously retired officer who had enlisted and was serving as a corporal in the British Home Guard until saved by Churchill) was placed in command of an armored division that employed a number of vehicles specifically designed to overcome problems such as the clearing of mines and obstacles both during and after the invasion. Nicknamed "Hobart's funnies," these ingenious and practical inventions were foolishly scorned by American commanders, primarily Bradley, whose closed-mindedness to anything British ultimately resulted in need-less casualties both on D-Day on Omaha Beach and later during the deadly battle for the hedgerows.

The evolution of Overlord planning also resulted in the introduction of an entirely new vocabulary of strange-sounding military acronyms and terms: Gooseberries (ships to be sunk to form a breakwater for each Mulberry); Whales (floating piers connecting to the shore); Phoenixes (huge concrete caissons to be towed across the Channel, then filled with water and sunk to form protected anchorages); and PLUTO (Pipeline Under the Ocean), an undersea pipeline from England to France as a means of supplying fuel.

In March, Eisenhower escorted Churchill on an inspection visit to Maj. Gen. Maxwell Taylor's 101st Airborne Division, where he was to witness a regimental airdrop and a division review, and to tour a static display of weap-ons used by the airborne. The prime minister stopped by an 81-mm mortar manned by two corporals. "This 81," Eisenhower explained to Churchill, "using this new ammo has a range of about 3,000 yards." One of the weapon's guardians spoke up and said, "Excuse me, sir, it's 3,250 yards." Churchill was amused, and the supreme Allied commander countered with mock severity: "Look, soldier, you wouldn't make a liar out of me in front of the prime minister for 250 yards, would you?" Thereafter the corporal became a celeb-rity as "the one who keeps Eisenhower on the ball."

Using the same custom as Montgomery, Churchill climbed up on a jeep and asked the men to gather around him. He said, "I stand before you, a man with no unrealized ambitions except to see the Axis wiped off the face of the earth." The paratroopers cheered.[73] In Winchester, Eisenhower and Churchill were mobbed by admiring crowds and were obliged to dismount to acknowl-edge their enthusiasm.

Eisenhower was a great hit with British troops, just as Montgomery proved to be with Americans. Using the informal style that proved so suc-cessful with his own troops, Montgomery made a point of visiting them with the message that "General Eisenhower is the captain of the team and I am proud to serve under him." When Monty visited the U.S. 2nd Armored Divi-sion he made everyone remove their helmets. "He paused and gazed slowly, in silence, round the great mass of men. At last he said: 'All right, put them back on. Now next time I see you, I shall know you.' It was brilliant stage-management."[74]

Whatever their later quarrels, Montgomery's admiration for Eisenhower was unequivocal. On the evening of June 2 Eisenhower traveled to Montgom-ery's nearby command post for dinner. In his diary that night an upbeat Montgomery wrote, "EISENHOWER is just the right man for the job . . . he is a really 'big' man and is in every way an Allied Commander—holding the balance between Allied contingents. I like him immensely; he has a generous and lovable character and I would trust him to the last gasp."[75]

41.

"O.K., We'll Go."

*The first 24 hours of the invasion will be decisive . . .
the fate of Germany depends on the outcome . . . for
the Allies, as well as Germany, it will be the longest day.*
—FIELD MARSHAL ERWIN ROMMEL

After months of intensive planning and preparation, D-Day was set for June 5, 1944, and with the German supreme command still convinced that Patton was to lead the invasion against the Pas de Calais, the many complex pieces of the Overlord plan displayed every sign of cohesion.[1] Now that Eisenhower had at last overcome the intense opposition to the Transportation Plan, involving months of stalling, argument, and bad blood, Allied air might was unleashed. Between them the RAF and USAAF bombed the French railway system into a vast "railway desert" of smashed rail lines, bridges, depots, and equipment, while Leigh-Mallory's tactical aircraft shot up anything that moved. Convoys and trains were mercilessly shot to pieces, generating some of the most spectacular combat film footage of World War II. By mid-May the German Transport Ministry attested to the success of Allied bombing by noting that "the raids carried out in recent weeks [in Belgium and northern France] have caused systematic breakdown of all main lines . . . large-scale strategic movement of German troops by rail is practically impossible," and the wide-scale destruction had caused "critical dislocation of traffic."[2] Spaatz's greatest success came in carrying out his mandate to destroy the Luftwaffe, which by D-Day could barely muster a paltry one hundred sorties against the Allies in Normandy. "The achievement of air supremacy over France and the invasion area and of air superiority over Germany before D-Day was the decisive contribution of Spaatz and USSTAF to Overlord," and was, wrote Spaatz's biographer, "a turning point in the air war" that "ranked with the defensive victory of the RAF in the Battle of Britain."[3]

Success came at a terrible price. With historical focus on the D-Day landings and the fight for a beachhead in Normandy, images of landing craft swarming ashore under heavy enemy fire have become the most acclaimed

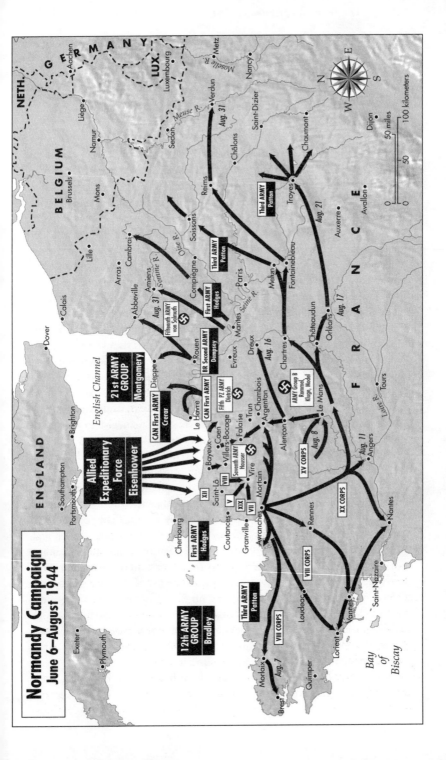

Normandy Campaign
June 6–August 1944

and remembered aspect of the war in Europe. The most devastating losses, however, were incurred by the valiant Allied air crews. Between April 1 and June 5, 1944, the Allies lost two thousand aircraft and twelve thousand air crew killed in action in pre-D-Day operations. By the time the Normandy campaign officially ended in August 1944, twenty-eight thousand air crew had been lost in air operations over France.

In the weeks leading up to D-Day Eisenhower traveled to Scotland, Northern Ireland, and all over England on inspection visits to British, American, and Canadian combat units; naval vessels; staging areas; hospitals; air bases; supply depots and logistical units; a Polish division; a graduating class at Sandhurst; the dedication of a B-17 bomber nicknamed "General Ike" in his honor; and mock invasion exercises, and took his first flight in a new fighter aircraft, all sandwiched around briefings, meetings, and the tiring, obligatory sessions with Churchill, whom he occasionally accompanied on similar trips. Though the foul weather contributed to his perpetual cold, away from his desk and among his men, Eisenhower was in his element. His usual mode of travel was aboard his personal railway carriage or by air or car, with Kay Summersby at the wheel. His handlers had the difficult task of keeping him on schedule to adhere to his mandate that troops should never be kept standing around awaiting his arrival. Inevitably delays occurred and the Eisenhower temper would erupt at being late or being hounded by reporters anxious to record his remarks. It was as if their presence infringed on his special relationship with his troops. Although he gave numerous informal pep talks when visiting large troop formations, Eisenhower managed to convey his message without repeating himself. Almost effortlessly he seemed to possess a magic touch when dealing with soldiers. No matter what they did in civilian life, Eisenhower seemed able to ask an appropriate question or produce a suitable comment that established an immediate bond. His only disappointment was in never encountering anyone from Abilene.[4]

During these trying days Eisenhower's only tenuous connection to his private world was his letters to Mamie. But even this was not always enough. Mamie's comprehension of the extent of her husband's grave responsibilities during their long-distance marriage was sometimes utterly bereft of forbearance. Deeply immersed as he was in the problems of the final, hectic days before D-Day, absolutely the last thing on Eisenhower's mind was remembering Mother's Day—a failure that landed him squarely in the doghouse with Mamie, who complained that he had failed to acknowledge the occasion. He quietly took the blame, saying, "I was just stupid about it," but tactfully reminded Mamie that "you shouldn't hold me guilty of negligence merely because I may be forgetful. God knows I am busy; and I do try to write to you often. . . . Please don't get annoyed with me. I depend on you and your letters so much, and I'm living only to come back when this terrible thing is over."[5]

What he needed least of all during this grueling period was a nagging wife who displayed scant empathy and an even smaller grasp of reality.

Of the amphibious exercises witnessed by Eisenhower, the most controversial occurred on the night of April 27–28 off a stretch of the Devonshire coast near Slapton Sands that resembled the beaches of Normandy. Code-named Tiger, the exercise was a dress rehearsal for the landings on Utah Beach by troops of the U.S. 4th Infantry Division and the 1st Engineer Special Brigade. Suddenly a flotilla of eight LSTs was attacked by nine German motor torpedo boats (called E-boats, *Schnellboote*) based in Cherbourg.[6] Painted an ominous black, the E-boats had found the Channel prime nighttime hunting grounds, and during earlier engagements had sunk eighteen ships off South Dorset and Devon. Such operations to seek out enemy shipping were routine, as they were that night when they encountered the Tiger flotilla in Lyme Bay.

Like foxes loose in a chicken coop, the marauding German boats succeeding in sinking two LSTs and heavily damaging another with their torpedoes, killing an estimated 191 sailors and 441 American troops,[7] most of them combat engineers, some of whom drowned due to a lack of training in the proper use of their life preservers, which were strapped around their waists instead of being worn. Ironically the loss of life off Slapton Sands was twenty times greater than the actual D-Day losses on Utah Beach. Tiger was an example of poor planning, indecision, a lack of protection for the vulnerable landing craft, missed rendezvous, faulty equipment, poor communications, and an absence of rescue vessels, all of which contributed to a Murphy's Law disaster. One of the E-boats was seen scanning the waters with a searchlight, and—most troubling of all—some American officers at sea that night had knowledge of Neptune, the code-name for the assault phase of the Normandy landings. Not all the dead could be accounted for.[8] SHAEF sweated out the awful possibility of detection and carefully watched Ultra to determine if the Germans were making any changes in their defenses that would indicate knowledge of Allied intentions. Within a week Hitler ordered that Normandy be closely watched and fresh defenses prepared, none of which, it turned out, had resulted from the Tiger debacle.[9] The VIPs assembled aboard an LCI (Landing Craft Infantry) to witness the exercise—Eisenhower, Tedder, and Bradley—were deeply concerned over the clear absence of coordination between the army and navy. Butcher probably spoke for Eisenhower when he professed, "I came away from the exercise depressed."

To further protect Neptune, Eisenhower directed that a veil of secrecy be thrown over Tiger to avoid any further damage from exposure. That secrecy was lifted in July when a SHAEF press release revealed what had occurred off

Slapton Sands. Nearly forty years later the actions of several well-meaning but misguided individuals led to a rash of media coverage, most of which suggested that there had been a cover-up of the tragedy. In fact not only was there no cover-up by Eisenhower or anyone else, but accounts of Tiger appeared in numerous postwar publications, including the official histories of the army and navy. Unfortunately the tragedy of the most deadly training accident of World War II was eventually tarnished by an unseemly feeding frenzy in both the print and television media in Britain and the United States, most of which inaccurately alleged a cover-up and indifference on the part of the U.S. Army to the fate of the dead.[10]

The final days of May were marked by clashes and jitters. Leigh-Mallory had concluded that with intelligence reporting a new German division in the Cherbourg region, the proposed airborne operations in the Cotentin would be an utter disaster. At a commanders' conference on May 27, he warned Eisenhower of his misgivings that both the 82nd and 101st Airborne Divisions faced annihilation and urged cancellation of the airborne landings, leading Bradley flatly to refuse to carry out the assault landings on Utah Beach without the airborne shield. Since Leigh-Mallory was Ike's chief air commander and adviser, his misgivings were not only deeply worrisome but could not be ignored. Bradley and Montgomery both argued that Leigh-Mallory's appalling prediction notwithstanding, the possible consequences of cancellation were equally, if not even more, dire. On May 29 Eisenhower affirmed that the airborne operations would proceed as planned.

The following day Leigh-Mallory visited Eisenhower to protest once again "the futile slaughter" of two first-class divisions. "It would be difficult to conceive of a more soul-racking problem," Eisenhower later wrote. Although he said nothing directly to his chief airman, he was frustrated that Leigh-Mallory had waited until the last minute to muddy the waters. However, if his air chief's prediction was to prove correct, "the attack on Utah Beach was probably hopeless, and this meant that the whole operation suddenly acquired a degree of risk, even foolhardiness, that presaged a gigantic failure, possibly Allied defeat in Europe." Instructing Leigh-Mallory to convey his misgivings in writing in order to protect him in the event he overruled him, Eisenhower promised an answer in several hours and retreated to his quarters to mull over his decision alone. Finding himself between the proverbial rock and a hard place, whichever way he decided portended disaster. In the end Eisenhower refused to be swayed and decided that, Leigh-Mallory's misgivings notwithstanding, the Utah landings simply could not be abandoned. He telephoned Leigh-Mallory that the airborne landings would proceed as scheduled, a decision as difficult as the one he would make a short time later. The airborne commanders were infuriated that Leigh-Mallory had doubted their capabilities and would have left them behind, but relieved that Eisenhower believed in their mission.[11]

Cast in a role that would keep his Third Army in England until summoned to Normandy at an unspecified date after the invasion, Patton was becoming restless in the role of bridesmaid. Shortly before D-Day word reached Eisenhower that Patton was grumbling about not playing a role in the forthcoming invasion. Once again Eisenhower employed the good offices of John J. McCloy to rein Patton in. "You go down and tell Georgie," he directed McCloy, "I'm going to get him in where he's going to have all the fighting he wants, but in the meantime you . . . tell him to keep his God damn mouth shut!" McCloy duly repeated Eisenhower's order word for word to Patton. Ever the actor, Patton puffed himself to his full height and complained, "You're taking a good deal of responsibility to come here on the eve of battle and destroy a man's confidence." McCloy retorted, "Listen, George, if I thought I could destroy your confidence by anything I might say, I would ask General Eisenhower to remove you," whereupon Patton immediately stopped emoting.[12]

The Fateful Days: Thursday, June 1, 1944

The weather in May 1944 was exceptional—and deceptive. Admiral Ramsay wrote in his diary on May 29, "Summer is here and it is boiling hot!" However, as an experienced sailor Ramsay knew better than to trust this as an especially good harbinger for D-Day.[13] At the end of May it was not the condition of the sea but rather the cloud cover over the Channel and Normandy that was of primary concern. There was only a three-day window in early June on which the operation could commence. The moonlight required by the three airborne divisions that were to be landed by parachute and glider the night before the invasion to secure the vital flanks, and the low tides necessary to carry out the landings and the demolition of Rommel's underwater obstacles in the forty minutes after first light, would only be present during the three-day period from June 5 to June 7. Any delay due to inclement weather meant postponement for a minimum of another two weeks—a possibly fatal delay that might threaten the Allied foothold if the notoriously bad Channel weather prevented resupply through Cherbourg and over the beaches before a breakout.

Every element of the Overlord plan could be controlled except the volatile weather. With Group Captain Stagg as the chief meteorologist and spokesman, Eisenhower's team consisted of experts from the Admiralty, the air forces, and the U.S. and British weather services. What Stagg and colleagues saw on their charts that day and were receiving from signals from the United States was portentous. Weather aircraft flying over Newfoundland and ships at sea were gathering weather data for the SHAEF meteorologists, and what they began reporting noted the first major change in the previous weeks of clear weather. The combination of a high-pressure system moving southward from Iceland was resulting in the formation of several deep depressions in the mid-Atlantic. The problem, other than growing uncertainty, was that the members of Stagg's team were unable to agree among themselves as to the extent of the change of weather or what the impact would be on the invasion on June 5. Stagg reported their disagreement to the SHAEF G-3, Pinky Bull, who said, "For Heaven's sake, Stagg, get it sorted out by tomorrow morning before you come to the Supreme Commander's conference. General Eisenhower is a very worried man." In the coming days Bull's stipulation must have served to remind Stagg of how General Morgan had wished him well before his departure for Southwick, with the admonition, "May all your depressions be nice little ones: but remember, we'll string you up from the nearest lamp post if you don't read the omens right."

Friday, June 2, 1944

The countdown began on June 2, when Eisenhower first moved from Bushy Park to Southwick House, where an unpretentious, concealed trailer he dubbed "my circus wagon" would be his home for the next several weeks. As was his custom, Eisenhower eschewed more spacious quarters in Southwick House in favor of a Spartan existence in a mobile home devoid of heat except for the tiny bedroom, whose only adornments were a jumbled pile of Western novels and photos of Mamie and of John in his cadet uniform. His staff worked and lived in nearby tents. Beginning that day Eisenhower and his chief adviser would convene at least twice daily for weather briefings in the library—a large, rather plain room with dark oak bookcases, easy chairs, and sofas, its windows hidden behind heavy blackout drapes. With his typical disdain for any special treatment, one day he returned to find that a camouflage battalion had rigged netting over the entire SHAEF command post. Eisenhower was furious, demanding to know how many man-hours had been wasted, until he was assured by Butcher that it had been valuable training for the unit. "All right, as long as it was only practice. I don't want any time wasted making a fuss over me."[14]

The weather that day provided no hint of what was to come. At the morning briefing the SHAEF weathermen had already wrangled for hours over the Atlantic depressions and their probable impact on D-Day. Other than note that the present good weather would begin changing over the weekend with increasing winds and clouds, the Friday-morning briefing offered no assessment of its impact on D-Day, nor was one demanded by Eisenhower or the other participants. The weathermen had bought themselves nearly twelve hours to refine their own conclusions. The wrangling continued until shortly before the evening briefing, and still there was no consensus. As Stagg would later write, "Had it not been fraught with such potential tragedy, the whole business was ridiculous. In less than half-an-hour I was expected to present to General Eisenhower an 'agreed' forecast for the next five days . . . [when] no two of the expert participants . . . could agree on the likely weather even for the next 24 hours." Like it or not, it was now up to Stagg what to report. What made his task all the more difficult was that he had been warned by Britain's premier meteorologist that predicting the weather in the Channel for even a one- or two-day period was virtually impossible.

The second briefing convened at 9:30 P.M. that evening, again attended by all the key players and senior staff officers. "Well, Stagg, what have you for us this time?" said Eisenhower. Although Stagg was inwardly uneasy, this time there could be no equivocation. What he had to report was troubling. The chief meteorologist disclosed that a series of depressions moving in from the west would make the weather in the Channel for the next three or four days "potentially full of menace" in the form of completely overcast skies and winds of up to Force 4 or 5, and a cloud cover ranging from as high as five hundred feet to as low as zero. The seriousness of the occasion could be read in their faces and in the almost deathly silence. Eisenhower ruled that there would be no change of plan that day and authorized the navy to proceed with all necessary preliminary operations.

Saturday, June 3, 1944

Eisenhower's extensive diary entry for June 3, 1944, reveals little of a personal nature with the exception of this cryptic comment: "Probably no one who does not have to bear the specific and direct responsibility of making the final decision as to what to do can understand the intensity of these burdens." Kay Summersby recorded in her new diary only that her boss was "very depressed."[15] Eisenhower ate little and slept even less. Although he enjoyed watching movies on the rare occasions when time permitted, Eisenhower imposed an inviolable rule that no film be shown to him that otherwise deprived or delayed GIs from seeing it. That night, when he learned that if he was to see a film it would conflict with its showing to the men and women working in Southwick, Eisenhower "turned on me and gave me a good cussing out," noted Butcher. "I knew then he really had the pre-D-Day jitters."[16]

On June 3 Churchill and Field Marshal Jan Smuts were inspecting British troops along the south coast, and that evening the PM unexpectedly visited Eisenhower, primarily to "pour the heat on Ike" for refusing to countenance his participation in D-Day, and to take one last crack at persuading the supreme commander to change his mind. Eisenhower, though sympathetic, refused, and Churchill left as "peevish" as he had arrived. The visit was hardly welcome; "last night," wrote Butcher, "the P.M.'s caravan of cars and dashing cyclists swirled in behind. Filled their gas tanks and diminished our small supply of Scotch like the devil," before departing as abruptly as they had arrived.[17]

At the evening briefing, in an attempt to lighten the atmosphere, one admiral cracked, "[T]here goes six feet two of Stagg and six feet one of gloom." Stagg's face reflected no encouragement. Eisenhower sat motionless throughout his presentation. Without preamble Stagg delivered the bad news: "Gentlemen, the fears my colleagues and I had yesterday . . . have been confirmed," he said. His latest forecast offered little but wind, waves, and clouds lasting until at least June 5. Eisenhower questioned his three invasion commanders one by one. "Could the Navy manage it? Ramsay thought not. The assault might go ashore all right, but if the weather worsened there could be no adequate build-up." Leigh-Mallory replied that his air crews would not be able to see what they were attacking. Of the three, only Montgomery thought the invasion should proceed. "I'm ready," he told Eisenhower, raising eyebrows among some for what they deemed Monty's reckless response.[18] Before Stagg was dismissed and the star-studded jury convened to consider its verdict, Eisenhower's final question was if there was unanimity among the weathermen on what had been presented. For the first time Stagg could reply, "Yes, Sir."

Eisenhower had no choice except to provisionally postpone the invasion for twenty-four hours. The armada waited in grim anticipation of some glimmer of hope from the weather gods. Some of the troops crowded aboard landing craft like cattle were already seasick from the heavy tides without ever having embarked from their harbors and ports. A short time later Bull emerged to announce, "The Supreme Commander has made a provisional decision to hold up the operation on a day-to-day basis. Some of the forces will sail tonight but General Eisenhower and his commanders will meet again at 4:15 A.M. tomorrow [Sunday] morning to hear what you have to say." At that time Eisenhower would have to decide the fate of Overlord. As Stagg left the building for another sleepless night of grappling with the latest weather data, Tedder, who was known for his puckish sense of humor, was lighting his trademark pipe on the steps outside; with a smile he said, "Pleasant dreams, Stagg."[19]

Sunday, June 4, 1944

Some naval forces had to be recalled, and there was a measure of disarray and some loss of life when several landing craft overturned in the rough seas. At the 4:15 A.M. meeting Stagg reported no change. As if to confirm the prediction, Admiral Ramsay noted that the weather outside was then virtually windless and clear. Stagg assured him the predicted bad weather would arrive within four to five hours. "In that case, gentlemen, it looks to me as if we must confirm the provisional decision we took at the last meeting," said Eisenhower. "Compared with the enemy's forces ours are not overwhelmingly strong: we need every help our air superiority can give us. If the air cannot operate we must postpone. Are there any dissentient votes?" None were offered. Overlord was officially on hold. After the meeting broke up, the meteorologists met to assess the latest weather reports before snatching a few hours' sleep. As Stagg headed to his tent, there was no hint of what was to come shortly; "a peaceful dawn glow was already showing . . . with little cloud."

As predicted, a full-blown gale not only rendered any hope of launching the invasion the morning of June 5 unthinkable, it now threatened to wreck the entire invasion timetable.

While the armada literally trod water, the participants had become virtual prisoners in their encampments and aboard naval vessels, final briefings postponed and sealed instructions revealing their target unopened.

A mood of pessimism prevailed among many senior Allied commanders that in spite of the detailed preparations and training, things might still go wrong on the beaches of Normandy. The atmosphere was not lightened by updates from Allied intelligence that Rommel had strengthened the Normandy front by several new divisions, with more possibly on the way.

During the day the winds rose. Eisenhower spent most of June 4 either alone in his trailer or outside pacing aimlessly, his hands deep in his pockets, kicking small stones much as he had as a boy in Abilene, a lighted cigarette continually in his hand as he scanned the skies seeking some sign, *any* indication that the weather might change for the better. During one of his strolls he recognized NBC's Merrill "Red" Mueller and beckoned to him. "Let's take a walk, Red." As a newsman, Mueller instinctively wanted to ask questions of the supreme commander. But not this day; it would not have been appropriate, even for a seasoned reporter. "Ike seemed completely preoccupied with his own thoughts. . . . It was almost as if he had forgotten I was with him," Mueller later told Cornelius Ryan. When they parted company it seemed to Mueller that Eisenhower was "bowed down with worry . . . as though each of the four stars on either shoulder weighed a ton."[20]

Charles de Gaulle arrived from Algiers that morning "to uphold the interests of France" and for the first time learned of the invasion.[21] Indignant that Eisenhower would be the controlling authority in liberated France, rather than his French Committee of National Liberation, de Gaulle was chilly during his talks that day with Churchill. That afternoon Churchill escorted de Gaulle to Southwick, "where he was most ceremoniously received. Ike and Bedell Smith," said Churchill, "vied with one another in their courtesy." Eisenhower spent twenty minutes in the map tent describing to the Frenchman the Allied invasion plan. Eisenhower's earlier experiences with the prickly de Gaulle did not dissuade him from an appreciation of his military wisdom. Flattered when Eisenhower asked him for his opinion, de Gaulle replied, "I will only tell you that if I were you, I should not delay."[22]

The problem began when Eisenhower informed de Gaulle with "evident embarrassment," that "General, on the day of the landings, I will broadcast a proclamation to the French population, and I would like you to do the same." De Gaulle later wrote that Eisenhower expressed a willingness "to alter it at your suggestion," but the version of his defense chief of staff, Gen. Emile Béthouart, differed: Eisenhower said that his proclamation had been approved by his government "and he could make no alterations." De Gaulle angrily asked how Eisenhower dared to presume this. Handed a copy of Eisenhower's proposed remarks, de Gaulle found them unacceptable, particularly the phrase in which he "urged the French nation to 'carry out his orders.' . . . [H]e appeared to be taking charge of our country even though he was merely an Allied general entitled to command troops, but not in the least qualified to intervene in the country's government."[23] De Gaulle left insisting that he would submit proposed changes. After de Gaulle spurned an offer of dinner, Churchill and his party returned to London "in an agony of uncertainty" over the fate of the invasion.[24]

At the late-evening briefing "Eisenhower presided over one of the most important councils of war in military history."[25] The sounds of rain and the wind howling in rage outside could distinctly be heard by the assembled generals, admirals, and air marshals. Eisenhower's trademark smile was missing, replaced by a unmistakable air of solemnity. As was their custom, the commanders were seated informally on couches and chairs, most with cups of coffee.

Although the weather was vile, Stagg reported to the tense commanders there was a *glimmer* of hope for June 6: While the weather would remain poor, visibility would improve and the winds decrease barely enough to risk launching the invasion. "A cheer went up. You never heard middle-aged men cheer like that!" recalled Strong.[26]

Stagg was closely questioned by Tedder, who demanded to know: "What will the weather be on D-Day in the Channel and over the French coast?" For perhaps two minutes there was total silence while Stagg pondered Tedder's question. Finally Stagg replied, "To answer that question would make me a guesser, not a meteorologist."[27] Others peppered the meteorologist with questions. Ramsay asked about the condition of the sea and the expected wind velocity, while Leigh-Mallory was principally concerned about the extent of the expected cloud cover. Eisenhower wanted to know how many hours of decent weather could be counted on for the invasion and when they would end.

This was arguably the most important weather prediction in history: A mistaken forecast for D-Day could turn the entire tide of the war in Europe against the Allies. After consulting with each of the invasion commanders, Eisenhower swiftly learned that time had run out. Then and there, he had to make a decision for or against. Ramsay announced, "[I]f Overlord is to proceed on Tuesday [June 6], I must issue provisional warning to my forces within the next half-hour." Eisenhower went around the room to poll his chief advisers one by one. Leigh-Mallory remained troubled, calling it "chancy," and for once Tedder agreed with him. Doable, but nevertheless risky. Pacing the floor, Eisenhower turned to Montgomery and asked, "Do you see any reason why we should not go on Tuesday?" The little British general replied emphatically and without hesitation, "No. I would say—*Go!*"

There was some further discussion of other issues and then, as usual, the staff officers left the room, none of them certain of Eisenhower's final decision. He was obliged to weigh not only the decision itself but its longer-term impact. There was utter silence in the room, the only sounds to be heard were the wind and rain pounding Southwick House. Beetle Smith, a man rarely emotional about anything, was awed by "the loneliness and isolation of a commander at a time when such a momentous decision has to be taken, with full knowledge that failure or success rests on his judgment alone. He sat there quietly, not getting up to pace with quick strides as he often does. He was tense, weighing every consideration of weather as he had been briefed to do during the dry runs since April, and weighing them with those other imponderables."[28]

In preparation for this very eventuality Eisenhower and his weather team had practiced at his Monday meetings for some weeks. Eisenhower would select a hypothetical D-Day and the weathermen would make what proved to be accurate predictions. Group Captain Stagg was one of the many unsung heroes of D-Day—a man whom Eisenhower could trust implicitly, "a scientist to his bones with all of the scientist's refined capacity to pass unimpassioned judgment on the evidence, a man of sharp mind and soft speech, detached, resolute, courageous. In these trial forecasts Eisenhower had learned that the man whose opinion and nerve he could trust in the hour of decision was Stagg."[29]

Although Ike later agonized over what he had wrought, it seemed clear what his decision must be. As with Stagg earlier, he recognized that the time for equivocation was long past. In retrospect it may appear to have been almost casually made, but it was in fact a decision he had long since prepared himself to make. His heart and his head told him that he must trust Stagg and his weather forecast. The invasion must go ahead. It was a very slender thread on which to base the fate of the war, but it was all Eisenhower had, and he embraced it. "Finally he looked up, and the tension was gone from his face."[30]

Still pondering, Eisenhower said, "The question is, just how long can you hang this operation on the end of a limb and let it hang there?"[31] Despite the presence of men accustomed to making life-and-death decisions, it was as if Eisenhower's query were merely rhetorical. No one in the room responded; it was equally clear to them that the time for discussion had passed and that the matter rested solely with Eisenhower.

"I am quite positive we must give the order," he said. "I don't like it but there it is. . . . I don't see how we can do anything else." With that low-key pronouncement, the invasion of Normandy would take place the morning of June 6, based on the most important weather forecast in history. As Montgomery's official biographer has noted, "It was Eisenhower's moment of trial—and he responded with what can only be called greatness."[32] Someone noted that the mantelpiece clock had just registered 9:45 P.M. Within seconds the room emptied as men scrambled to set the invasion in motion.

Yet the decision to go was still only conditional on a last minute weather update the following morning.

All but spent, Eisenhower was the last to emerge and remarked to Stagg, who was waiting outside the library, "Well, Stagg, we're putting it on again: for heaven's sake hold the weather to what you told us and don't bring any more bad news." As Eisenhower emerged from Southwick House there was not the slightest hint of improving weather to come; to the contrary, the blasting wind, rain, and muddy ground seemed to be mocking his decision. Nor could Eisenhower have been uplifted by Kay Summersby's remark: "If all goes right, dozens of people will claim the credit. But if it goes wrong, you'll be the only one to blame."[33]

As if Eisenhower and Admirals Ramsay and Cunningham did not confront enough problems, in the critical week before D-Day they had to contend with Churchill's insistence on viewing the invasion from a British warship, the cruiser HMS *Belfast*. Exasperated, Eisenhower forcefully told the prime minister that he would not sanction his presence in harm's way. Not to be outdone by a mere general, Churchill insisted that as minister of defense he had a duty to take part, insisting he would circumvent Eisenhower's authority by going as a crew member; "it is not part of your responsibilities, my dear General," he said, "to determine the exact composition of any ship's company in His Majesty's Fleet." Eisenhower could only concede his helplessness to stop Churchill, even as he "forcefully pointed out that he was adding to my personal burdens in this thwarting of my instructions." King George VI learned of the prime minister's intentions and put a stop to it. In a letter hand-delivered from Buckingham Palace, the king pointed out that of course he would never presume to interfere in the affairs of his government's principal minister. However, should Churchill carry out his intentions, the king would likewise feel obliged to witness the invasion as the (titular) head of Britain's armed forces. "Mr. Churchill gave in ... bitterly disappointed and not a little resentful."[34] In his post-war memoirs Churchill described his disappointment and abiding defiance in terms that left no doubt that he had "deferred to the Crown, not to Eisenhower."[35]

In an example of the kettle calling the pot black, Eisenhower himself had not only been thinking along similar lines but, until dissuaded by his horrified staff, had planned to watch the landings and possibly go ashore to visit with his troops. If he was killed, he said, Tedder would do the job, pending Marshall's arrival to replace him. The notion of Eisenhower on any Normandy beach on D-Day is chilling. At heart Eisenhower was still an infantry soldier whose training had ingrained in him the spirit of sharing the same hardships as his men.

Monday, June 5, 1944

At what turned out to be their final meeting, the Allied commanders in chief reconvened at 4:15 A.M. on June 5 for another weather update. The atmosphere was again palpably somber and even more tense than at earlier meetings, at which there had been informal small talk between the participants. As he entered the room Beetle Smith detected "the ghost of a smile on the tired face of Group Captain Stagg."[36] Stagg reported no substantial change, and he cautioned against any tilt toward a more optimistic forecast. Stagg's prediction of the D-Day weather and beyond brought smiles all around, instead of the grim expressions that had only moments before permeated the room.

According to Strong, "Eisenhower got up from his chair and walked slowly up and down the room. . . . His head was slightly sunk on his chest, his hands clasped behind his back. From time to time he stopped in his stride, turned his head quickly and jerkily in the direction of one of those present, and fired a rapid question at him . . . then resumed his walk. Montgomery showed some signs of his impatience, as if to say that had he had to make the decision it would have been made long ago." Leigh-Mallory had his usual gloomy countenance, and Strong thought it was the face of a brave man having to confront his fears that many brave men would soon have to be needlessly sacrificed. Eisenhower retreated to a sofa, on which, most recalled, he sat for some five minutes to ponder his decision. Eisenhower thought it was only forty-five seconds: "Five minutes under such conditions would seem like a year."[37]

There was still time for another postponement. Whatever Eisenhower decided would stand. Stagg noted that the tension evaporated and that Eisenhower's face now wore a broad smile. "Well, Stagg, if this forecast comes off, I promise you we'll have a celebration when the time comes." After a brief discussion Eisenhower reaffirmed his decision to launch Overlord: "O.K., we'll go," he said. The invasion was now unalterable.[38] A signal—which read "Halcyon plus 5 finally and definitely confirmed," code for June 6, 1944— was quickly sent to the Combined Chiefs of Staff.

Having made the most important decision of the war, Eisenhower was now incapable of either reversing it or altering in any way the outcome of the invasion, which was now in other hands. For the time being his immediate role was all but irrelevant. "That's the most terrible thing for a senior commander. He has done all that he can do."[39]

On June 5 the limelight shone briefly on the capture of Rome. Newspaper headlines trumpeted the fall of the Eternal City to Mark Clark's Fifth Army. There was considerable irony in the date. From the time of Salerno, Mark Clark had been obsessed with being the triumphant liberator of Rome; the following day the world's focus on its liberation would all but disappear with the launch of Overlord.

With nothing more to be done at Southwick, on the morning of June 5 Eisenhower inspected British assault troops embarking aboard landing craft at nearby Portsmouth, who greeted him with cries of "Good old Ike!" The day dragged on interminably. When he discerned the sun peeking briefly through the clouds his spirits rose.

In early May the SHAEF staff drafted an order of the day to be given each member of the AEF. Eisenhower made numerous changes and placed his personal imprint on a one-page document that could conveniently be carried in everyone's wallet or breast pocket. The words were quintessential Eisenhower, a heartfelt statement of his personal beliefs. Shortly before D-Day he recorded the same words as a proclamation to be broadcast to the world on the day of the invasion.

> *Soldiers, Sailors and Airmen of the Allied Expeditionary Forces!*
>
> You are about to embark on the great crusade, toward which we have striven these many months. The eyes of the world are upon you. The hopes and prayers of liberty-loving people everywhere march with you. In company with our brave Allies and brothers-in-arms on other Fronts you will bring about the destruction of the German war machine, the elimination of Nazi tyranny over oppressed peoples of Europe, and security for ourselves in a free world.
>
> Your task will not be an easy one. Your enemy is well trained, well equipped and battle-hardened. He will fight savagely. . . .
>
> I have full confidence in your courage, devotion to duty and skill in battle. We will accept nothing less than full victory!
>
> Good luck! And let us all beseech the blessing of Almighty God upon this great and noble undertaking.[40]

Little of the spirit of Eisenhower's inspiring message was evident on June 5, 1944. An indication of Eisenhower's state of mind can be inferred from a far different document he scribbled that afternoon, tucked in his wallet, and carried unremembered until July, when he gave it to Butcher. It read: "Our landings in the Cherbourg-Havre area have failed to gain a satisfactory foothold and I have withdrawn the troops. My decision to attack at this time and place was based upon the best information available. The troops, the air, and the Navy did all that bravery and devotion to duty could do. If any blame or fault attaches to the attempt it is mine alone.—June 5."[41]

Eisenhower's smoking had increased incrementally as D-Day grew closer. Calm on the outside, inside he was seething with the gravity of the invasion. His health again deteriorated from a plethora of ailments that included headaches, recurring throat infections exacerbated by his heavy smoking, a mild eye infection, insomnia, and high blood pressure.[42] "Ike looks worn and tired," wrote Butcher on May 12. "The strain is telling on him. He looks older than at any time since I have been with him but fortunately he has the happy faculty of bouncing back after a night's sleep, or a ride on a horse or some exercise." On rare occasions when he was in London, Eisenhower stole an hour or so for a ride in Richmond Park, but as Kay Summersby noted, he had "far less social life than the most lowly member of his staff."[43]

In public Eisenhower continued to exude confidence. In private, however, he was a seething bundle of nervous energy. "Ike could not have been more anxiety ridden," noted Kay Summersby. As D-Day neared his smoking had increased to four packs a day and he was rarely seen without a cigarette in his hand. On this day he drank one pot of coffee after another and was once heard to mutter, "I hope to God I know what I'm doing." For once Eisenhower would have sympathized with Douglas MacArthur, who had once observed, "A general's life is loneliness."[44]

June 5 was a supreme test of his generalship and his ability to keep his nerve under the most trying circumstance he would ever face as a commander. There would be other crises ahead, but none approached the magnitude of D-Day. Mamie once asked him how in the world he ever had the nerve to do what he did. He replied simply, "I had to. If I let anybody, any of my commanders, think that maybe things weren't going to work out, that I was afraid, they'd be afraid too. I didn't dare. I had to have the confidence. I had to make *them* believe that everything was going to work."[45]

At midday on June 5 Churchill assembled his chiefs of staff for lunch. Brooke found him in a "very highly-strung condition," but was astonished at Churchill's "over-optimistic" mood "as regards prospects of the cross-Channel invasion." Admiral Cunningham recorded that the prime minister was "very worked up about Overlord and really in almost a hysterical state. He really is an incorrigible optimist."[46] It was all an act, befitting a leader in a time of crisis. Churchill was actually beset by doubt. The night of June 5 was easily the most nerve-racking of the war. As Eisenhower smoked his way through pack after pack of cigarettes, Churchill was still on edge, all his long-standing fears of a bloodbath rushing back in a nightmarish vision. Before retiring for a sleepless night, he somberly said to Clementine, "Do you realize that by the time you wake up in the morning twenty thousand men may have been killed?"[47]

Brooke's own sense of gloom on the eve of D-Day was reflected in his diary: "I am very uneasy about the whole operation. At the best it will fall so very short of the expectation of the bulk of the people, namely all those who know nothing about its difficulties. At the worst it may well be the most ghastly disaster of the whole war. I wish to God it were safely over."[48]

Only Montgomery, Ramsay, and Franklin Roosevelt displayed no outward signs of strain. Monty's principal military assistant remembered him as "supremely confident" that all would turn out well. As was his custom, Montgomery was in bed by his usual hour of approximately nine-thirty. One of the most important events in military history would not deprive Monty of his sleep.

Admiral Ramsay had been stalwart in backing Eisenhower, but once the decision was taken he too knew that matters were in other hands. When asked by Montgomery what he intended to do, he replied, "There is wireless silence and we can expect no signals. I am therefore going to bed." When he arose Ramsay wrote in his diary, "I am under no delusion as to the risks involved. . . . We shall require all the help that God can give us and I cannot believe that this will not be forthcoming."[49]

FDR too remained calm, in large part, thought Eleanor Roosevelt, "because he'd learned from polio that if there was nothing you could do about a situation, then you'd better try to put it out of your mind and go on with your work at hand."[50]

That evening Eisenhower made his spur-of-the-moment, emotional visit to the 101st Airborne Division in Newbury, Wiltshire, before returning to Southwick to wait out the night.

Other than the sounds of friendly aircraft, all over Britain the night of June 5, 1944, was unusually calm. For once there were no Luftwaffe raids or the mournful wailing of air raid sirens, simply a peaceful stillness rarely heard in a nation that had been at war for more than four years. In England's lush West Country a young boy named John Keegan stood awestruck in the garden of his home as the sky suddenly filled with the roar of airplanes. "It seemed as if every aircraft in the world was in flight, as wave followed upon wave without intermission."[51] Had they been merged together nine planes wide, the aerial train ferrying the three Allied airborne divisions to Normandy on June 5 would have extended two hundred miles in length.

.   .   .

Across the English Channel, at the headquarters of Army Group B, at Château La Roche Guyon, situated in a tiny hamlet on the river Seine, forty miles west of Paris, there was also tension and anticipation that the invasion would not be long in coming. The bad weather that had so dogged Eisenhower also served to mislead the Germans. Neither Field Marshal Gerd von Rundstedt (the commander in chief, OB West) nor Rommel believed the Allies would mount an invasion in such inclement weather, which their forecasters had predicted would be as high as Force 7 in the Cherbourg sector and Force 6 in the Pas de Calais. In Paris, at OB West, Stagg's counterpart, the chief German meteorologist, a major named Lettau, advised his superiors that any invasion after June 4 was unlikely due to the bad weather.[52] Rundstedt notified Berlin, "As yet, there is no immediate prospect of the invasion." Gen. Walter Warlimont, the deputy chief of operations for the Oberkommando der Wehrmacht (OKW—the German armed forces high command), later wrote that Berlin "had not the slightest idea that the decisive event of the war was upon them."[53]

The German weather forecast for June 6 concluded: "Invasion possible, but not probable." Rommel used the bad weather to return to Germany for his wife, Lucie's, birthday on June 6 and, he hoped, to see Hitler, to whom he intended to make a personal plea for greater priority for his army group. When he departed by automobile for his home in Swabia, near Ulm, early on June 4, Rommel was confident that nothing untoward would occur in his absence.

For months the BBC had been broadcasting innocuous nightly coded messages to the French underground. June 5 was no different, with the exception of one particular message from *"Chanson d'automne,"* a poem by Paul Verlaine: *"Blessent mon coeur d'une langueur monotone"*—"Pierce my heart with monotonous languor," the signal that invasion was imminent. The intelligence officer of the German Fifteenth Army, headquartered in the Pas de Calais, knew exactly what the message meant, but his warnings were ignored by both his commanding general and by von Rundstedt, who dismissed the BBC announcement as a red herring. "Does anyone think the enemy is stupid enough to announce his arrival over the radio," exclaimed one German officer.

Rommel's chief naval adviser, and later a respected postwar military historian, Vice Adm. Friedrich Ruge, marveled that Eisenhower made such an important decision without recourse to higher authority, noting that no one in the German chain of command would have dared. It was, Ruge believed, "one of the truly great decisions in military history."[54]

42.

"I Thank the Gods of War We Went When We Did."

The sons of bitches. They didn't even let us have the
newspaper headlines for the fall of Rome for one day.

— MARK CLARK

At the first light of dawn the phones in the SHAEF advance command post at Southwick were ominously silent until 6:40 A.M., ten minutes after the Utah landings commenced, when the quiet was shattered by the first phone to ring in the tent where a bleary-eyed Butcher lay on a cot staring at the roof. Butcher picked up the phone; on the other end was Leigh-Mallory calling to report personally to Eisenhower that the airborne and glider landings had gone well, with minimal losses of aircraft and gliders. On June 7 Eisenhower received a gracious letter of apology from Leigh-Mallory for having doubted the success of the airborne operations in the Cotentin. "I am more thankful than I can say that my misgivings . . . were unfounded," he wrote. "May I congratulate you on the wisdom of your choice."[1]

Only minutes before Butcher answered the phone at SHAEF, Field Marshal Erwin Rommel was summoned to the telephone by the family maid at his home in Herrlingen to learn from his chief of staff, Lt. Gen. Hans Speidel, that the Allies had invaded. Stunned by the news, Rommel made plans to return immediately to Normandy.[2]

In an Allied POW camp in nearby Austria a group of American airmen learned of the invasion via a clandestine homemade wireless set before the German dictator or the German public, which remained in ignorance of Eisenhower's announcement.[3]

The disarray within the German chain of command served Eisenhower well. As Chester Wilmot has pointed out in his landmark study of the campaign, "Since the summer of 1942 the Germans had been preparing to meet and defeat an invasion across the Channel, and yet the arrival of D-Day found them with no clear and agreed plan of command or campaign."[4] The morning of June 6, Adolf Hitler was asleep at the Berghof, his Bavarian retreat in Berchtesgaden, unaware of what was transpiring in Normandy. As each fresh report from Army Group B and OB West brought increasingly unfavorable news, no one dared wake the habitually late-rising Hitler until nearly noon. The time lost by failing to wake the Führer was critical. When he learned of the airborne landings, von Rundstedt immediately ordered two veteran panzer divisions being held in reserve (Panzer Lehr and the 12th SS) to the Caen sector, but because OKW retained control over their employment von Rundstedt elected to request formal permission. Fearful of Hitler's wrath, OKW refused and the only two formations that might have made a difference on June 6 sat uselessly until 4:00 P.M. that afternoon, when Hitler ordered their commitment. It was too little, too late.[5] How much of a difference they could have made is open to debate, however. Only had they moved at night would either division have escaped decimation by Allied aircraft.

Hitler's response to the landings was pure bravado: "The news couldn't be better.... Now we have them where we can destroy them."[6] Rommel's repeated warnings that to defeat an invasion of Normandy required the presence of the panzer reserves at the front, under his direct control for immediate commitment, had been spurned. Hitler's visceral distrust of his generals and his unwillingness to entrust Rommel with the panzer reserves guaranteed that Rommel's prediction would come true. The penalty incurred by Hitler's unwillingness was paid on June 6.

When Sergeant McKeogh poked his head into Eisenhower's trailer at about 7:15 in the morning, he found him awake reading a Western novel, his ashtray—which had been empty four hours earlier—filled with cigarette butts. McKeogh's first reaction was, "He hasn't had any sleep. His face was drawn and tired, and he had only a half smile."[7] A short time later Eisenhower and Butcher stood outside, "enjoying the beautiful, oh, what a beautiful day. A GI came grinding along with the morning papers from Portsmouth, with headlines of the fall of Rome.... Ike said, 'Good morning, *good* morning,' to the GI, most cheerfully indeed."[8] It was as if an enormous burden had been lifted from his broad shoulders, and while the situation on the beaches had yet to unfold, at least the dire predictions of the fate of the airborne had proven inaccurate.

In Rome, Mark Clark was informed by his aide of the Normandy landings. Up to that moment he had been euphoric over the Fifth Army's liberation of the Eternal City; his men, he said, had performed magnificently and deserved recognition. Clark's terse reaction to the news was that the invasion had stolen their moment of glory. "The sons-of-bitches. They didn't even let us have the newspaper headlines for the fall of Rome for one day."[9]

Reports from Normandy were slow to trickle in on June 6, and Eisenhower's initial elation was little more than a reprieve, as he anxiously awaited news from the five beachheads: Sword, Juno, and Gold in the British and Canadian sectors, and Omaha and Utah in the American. Chesterfield cigarettes filled his ashtray to overflowing, and he consumed endless cups of black coffee. Time seemed to stand still. From the adjoining room in his quarters he could overhear Jimmy Gault attempting to put together a coherent situation report from the navy over a scrambler phone. Eisenhower fidgeted, all the while attempting to glean from Gault's end of the conversation what was occurring. "God, this must be bad, it's so long," Eisenhower lamented. There had been some naval losses but nothing to indicate trouble ashore. Shortly after 9:30 A.M. Eisenhower authorized SHAEF to issue a brief communiqué that read, "Under the command of General Eisenhower, Allied naval forces, supported by strong air forces, began landing Allied armies this morning on the northern coast of France."

The effect of the announcement was stunning. In Britain the BBC interrupted its normal broadcasts to air the news. The British seemed to breathe a collective national sigh of relief. Workers in war plants stopped and sang "God Save the King," and everywhere people flocked to churches to pray. American military men were accosted on the streets by strangers who wanted to shake their hand. The architect of the Overlord plan, Lt. Gen. Frederick Morgan, heard the announcement on his car radio en route to Southwick.[10]

In the United States, June 6 was one of the most extraordinary days in American history, and an unofficial national day of prayer. Across the nation word of the landings spread like wildfire through the night and early morning. Church bells tolled, stores closed, Broadway shows and sporting events were called off as Americans in record numbers flocked to churches.[11] Roosevelt called the invasion of Normandy on June 6, 1944, "a mighty endeavor to preserve . . . our civilization and to set free a suffering humanity."[12] That night FDR went on national radio to deliver a prayer for "our sons, pride of our Nation," asking God to "[g]ive strength to their arms, stoutness to their hearts, steadfastness in their faith . . . in our united crusade."[13]

On June 6, 1944, France was entering its 1,453rd day of German occupation. For the people of the onetime realm of William the Conqueror, deliverance was at hand. The invasion of Normandy had actually begun late on the night of June 5 and the early morning hours of June 6, when massive airborne landings took place near Caen and in the western sector in the Carentan Peninsula. The British 6th Airborne Division assaulted both sides of the Orne River and the Orne Canal sector, north of the ancient city of Caen, by parachute and glider landings. Their mission was to secure intact the vital Pegasus Bridge, the only bridge over both the river and the canal between Caen and the sea, and to take out German communications centers and strong points that menaced the nearby landings on Sword Beach by the British 3rd Division.

At dawn elite commandos of Lord Lovat's 1st Commando Brigade landed on the extreme left flank of the British sector, to knock out the German artillery batteries and the garrison at Ouistreham, link up with the 6th Airborne Division, and protect the left flank of the beachhead until the British and Canadian assault troops were established ashore on three separate invasion beaches.

At the same time the U.S. 82nd and 101st Airborne Divisions were parachuted into the Carentan Estuary to secure the terrain and support the landings on Utah Beach by the U.S. VII Corps. In the darkness the paratroopers landed over a wide area and were unable to link up with their units. Nevertheless, operating in small groups, they severely disrupted German attempts to interfere with the Utah landings.

Between 3:00 and 5:00 A.M. on the morning of June 6 more than one thousand British aircraft dumped more than five thousand tons of bombs on the German coastal defenses in the British landing sector. As soon as this preliminary bombing had ceased, the guns of the Allied fleet opened fire across the Normandy front.

At 7:00 A.M. Lt. Gen. Miles Dempsey's British Second Army was disgorged from a flotilla of landing craft, most of which were adorned with homemade decorations, such as the LCT (Landing Craft Tank) whose bridge sported crossed lavatory brushes and a bucket under which was inscribed "*Semper in Excreta.*"[14] Three divisions and three armored brigades of the British I Corps landed on Sword, Juno, and Gold Beaches in the Caen sector, set to seize Caen and anchor the Allied left flank by preventing the Germans from reinforcing from the west.

Within two and a half hours thirty thousand men, three hundred guns, and seven hundred armored vehicles came ashore. Although the Canadian 3rd Division took more than two hours to crush German resistance in the Juno sector and open exits before they could begin moving inland, overall the British landings went exceptionally well.

In the U.S. sector Omaha and Utah Beaches had been subjected to the same bombardment by air and naval forces. The VII Corps assault of Utah beach began at 6:30 A.M. and was spearheaded by the 4th Infantry Division, which achieved total surprise and the least opposition and fewest casualties of any Allied assault unit. The division quickly moved inland and seized its D-Day objectives.

The landings on Omaha Beach by the veteran 1st Infantry Division and a regiment of the 29th Infantry Division of Gee Gerow's V Corps ran into heavy resistance from the German 352nd Division, which, despite Ultra, had managed to escape the attention of Allied intelligence when it moved into the Omaha sector three months earlier. From the steep bluffs overlooking Omaha Beach the Germans poured a hail of artillery, mortar, and automatic weapons fire, inflicting heavy casualties on the confused and badly exposed troops.

Heavy seas swamped many of the landing craft, resulting in most of the armor failing to get ashore, along with the demolition engineers, whose task it was to clear obstacles from the beach. For the first six hours the invaders held only a few yards of beach, which remained under intense enemy fire. It soon became evident to the American commanders that to remain where they were was suicidal, and they rallied their men to attack or die. One commander exposed himself to enemy fire by striding up and down the beach to rally his troops, while another led an attack against German machine-gun positions, declaring that "two kinds of people are staying on this beach, the dead and those about to die. Now let's get the hell out of here." Eventually American leadership and exceptional acts of gallantry by terrified men of all ranks saved the day.

Nevertheless, throughout June 6 the situation on Omaha remained so perilous that Omar Bradley seriously considered evacuating the beachhead and switching the follow-up units to the British sector or to Utah Beach. Later calling it a "nightmare," Bradley said that the brave men who fought there must never be forgotten: "Every man who set foot on Omaha beach that day was a hero." U.S. casualties on D-Day in the Omaha sector alone numbered over more than 2,000 killed, wounded, or missing. Stark evidence of the brutality of the battle were the corpses littering the beach and bobbing like corks in the sea until recovered by the graves registration crews.

On that momentous day more than 130,000 Allied ground and 23,000 airborne troops were landed in Normandy. In spite of the unexpected setbacks at Omaha, where the toehold around the beaches was still slender but gradually improving, the invasion was a stunning success. The awful bloodletting notwithstanding, the landings went remarkably well. Neither Churchill's nightmarish vision of the English Channel running red with the blood of corpses nor Leigh-Mallory's dire predictions about the fate of the airborne and glider landings had come true. More significant, the Germans had failed to mount a single serious counterattack, particularly on Omaha Beach. The fact was that the Allies had won the battle of the beaches, and among the German commanders only Rommel realized its profound implications.

On June 5 and 6 the Allied air forces flew 14,674 sorties in support of the landings. Total Allied losses on D-Day have never been precisely established, but they appear to have exceeded 10,000, with American losses of 6,577 the highest: 1,465 killed, 3,184 wounded, and 1,928 missing in action, including 2,499 killed, wounded, or missing in the two U.S. airborne divisions. British and Canadian losses were approximately three thousand.

What made D-Day and the first days of the Normandy campaign significant was that it was a soldier's battle, not a general's. From the sketchy reports, Eisenhower knew little of actual events in Normandy, and other than his trips to the war room at Southwick House and a visit to Montgomery's nearby headquarters, June 6 passed with agonizing slowness. Mickey McKeogh called it "the soberest day" he had ever had in his years of service to

Eisenhower. "Nobody made any of the silly little jokes we usually made. . . . We just waited."[15] Eisenhower chafed at the inaction, doomed to listen and powerless to make decisions. "I could see from his questions," noted Butcher, that "he wished he were running the 21st Army Group so he could do something about it himself, but from where he sits he just can't step in."[16] What kept Eisenhower going was the knowledge that the next day he would have a chance to see for himself the situation in Normandy.

On June 6 Eisenhower's proclamation was broadcast to the French, but as the day wore on, suspense grew over what de Gaulle would say in his broadcast that was to air over the BBC at 6:00 P.M. that evening. Only the night before de Gaulle had declined to broadcast, later changing his mind. When Eisenhower learned of the French general's stance, his anger got the better of him. "To hell with him," he told Smith; they would find someone else, which was, of course, an utterly fatuous comment.[17] There was no one else with whom to deal, as Eisenhower knew perfectly well. In the end Charles de Gaulle spoke and was at his most eloquent—and devious—best, delivering a brief but artfully crafted speech that managed to override what Eisenhower had previously said in his.[18]

On the morning of June 7, accompanied by Admiral Ramsay, Eisenhower boarded the mine-laying vessel HMS *Aurora* for the trip to Normandy, where he conferred at sea off Omaha Beach with Bradley, Rear Adm. Alan G. Kirk, the U.S. Navy task force commander, and Rear Adm. John L. Hall, who commanded the Omaha assault force. It was an awe-inspiring sight: LSTs and ships of every description were anchored or plying the Channel, most awaiting their turn for landing space on the crowded sandy beaches where they disgorged a torrent of troops and equipment. As fast as one vessel unloaded, another was waiting to take its place. The beaches were piled with supplies of every description, barrage balloons kept silent watch overhead, and the giant Phoenix components of the two artificial harbors were being slowly towed across the Channel to be anchored in place off Omaha and Arromanches, all under the watchful eye of Allied warships acting like sheepdogs guarding their flock. The flashes and puffs of smoke from the big guns of cruisers and battleships meant that shells were being hurled inland against unseen targets, bringing with them a hail of death that led Rommel to seek Hitler's permission to move his defenders out of their deadly range.

Ashore on Omaha Beach, almost as far as the eye could see, were troops, most trudging up its steep slopes and inland toward combat, while others organized the chaos into a semblance of order. Never before or since has there been such a sight, and Eisenhower could not help being astonished at the magnitude of what he had unleashed.

Eisenhower was joined by Montgomery, who was establishing his tactical headquarters ashore that day. At one point both Ramsay and Eisenhower prodded the *Aurora*'s skipper to maneuver his ship closer to shore so they could better observe what was happening—too close, it turned out, when the ship ran aground on a sandbar at what Eisenhower later said was a terrific speed, damaging its propeller; "the boat just shook to pieces. All of us fell on our faces." Eisenhower and Ramsay were shifted to another Royal Navy ship for the return trip to Portsmouth. Although Ramsay explained that he was certain the captain (who was "wallowing in despair") would be reprimanded rather than court-martialed ("most good naval officers have a reprimand or two on their records," he said), Eisenhower later wrote a letter to the First Sea Lord, ABC Cunningham, stating that he shared responsibility for the mishap and appealing for leniency. Still near exhaustion, Eisenhower awoke the following morning after having had his first decent night's sleep in some time. It was rough going in Normandy, but the Allies were there to stay, he told McKeogh.

Eisenhower held his first press conference on June 8, an occasion at which he seemed visibly ill at ease. "He seemed tired and almost listless," recorded Butcher. In his off-the-record briefing, Eisenhower somberly recounted the events of the past forty-eight hours, noting that the situation was still "hazardous" and that they should not mislead their readers by embellishing their stories with overoptimism. Continued good weather was vital, and he suggested, "You fellows pray for it too."[19] Overall it was not one of Eisenhower's better performances. The day itself was significant. British troops captured Bayeux, the first French city to be liberated by the Allies.

On June 9, Mamie received a telegram from Eisenhower, in which, with tongue in cheek and no small understatement, he had written, DUE TO PREVIOUS ENGAGEMENT IT WAS IMPOSSIBLE TO BE WITH YOU AND JOHN MONDAY [Eisenhower had forgotten that West Point's graduation was on June 6, not Monday, June 5] BUT I THOUGHT OF YOU. . . . TIME HAS NOT PERMITTED LETTER WRITING RECENTLY AND PROBABLY WILL NOT FOR A WHILE BUT I KNOW YOU UNDERSTAND. He also wrote a brief note to Mamie that he hoped wasn't too incoherent. He preferred to focus not on himself but his troops: "Anyway, we've started," he reported. Everything humanly possible was being done. "The soldiers, sailors, and airmen are indescribable in their elan, courage, determination and fortitude. They inspire me."[20]

For the German army in France D-Day was calamitous. Coupled with the German conviction that conditions were simply too awful for the Allies to try, the invasion had succeeded in large part because of the weather rather than in spite of it. Of the many German mistakes that day, the greatest seems to have been Rommel's unfortunate absence in Germany. His forceful personality on the spot on June 6 would surely have spurred a quicker response, but whether it would have substantially altered the course of events is problematical. When he hurriedly returned that night after an all-day dash by automobile from Germany, all he could do was attempt to stitch together his defenses across the breadth of the Normandy front. Despite the enormity of the invasion, both Hitler and OKW continued to be misled by Fortitude into believing that this was only an Allied feint to draw off their vital reserves. For perhaps the only time ever, Rommel, von Rundstedt, and Hitler were in mutual agreement about Allied intentions.

With deadly naval gunfire from Allied warships inflicting steadily debilitating casualties on Army Group B, there was little Rommel could do to launch a decisive counterattack to throw the British Second Army back into the sea. Unless he could establish a defensive line behind the natural barriers of the Orne and Odon Rivers, and out of range of the Allied guns, a counterattack was impossible. Despite strong personal pleas by both Rommel and von Rundstedt when they met with him in a bunker near Soissons on June 17, Hitler issued "fight to the death" orders, forbidding any retreat or withdrawal. At the Berghof that night Hitler commented that "Rommel had lost his nerve and become a pessimist."[21]

Caught between Hitler's fanaticism and the might of the Allied navy, Rommel nevertheless could not allow Montgomery simply to have his way at Caen. If the British were able to break through onto the Caen-Falaise Plain, where their armor could be unleashed, Normandy would be lost. Hitler had approved the release of panzer reinforcements from the eastern front, but these would take many days to arrive even under the best of conditions. Twenty-four-hour Allied harassment from the air made travel to Normandy a deadly undertaking.

Like a boxer with one arm tied behind his back, Rommel did the only thing he could by "roping off" the most vulnerable areas of his front and instantly committing his reserves when attacked. As Max Hastings put it, "[T]he only sane strategic course open to the Germans was precisely that which Hitler's madness would not allow—a progressive, carefully ordered retirement forcing the Allies to fight hard for every gain."[22] The measures adopted by the veteran German field commanders evolved from their precarious situation, which virtually ruled out the set-piece battle that was impossible without air support from the Luftwaffe. Outgunned, outmanned, and often outflanked, harassed day and night, short of virtually every logistic necessity of war, Army Group B nevertheless fought a remarkable delaying action, tenaciously counterattacking even though vastly outnumbered, and with only a shred of air support from the largely absent Luftwaffe.

What ensued was not a conventional land battle but a campaign that rapidly evolved into a series of vicious, small-unit actions, a classic confrontation at close quarters with no holds barred, in which—as in most wars—the dirty business of winning battles fell to the frontline infantryman. Despite their many problems, the Germans in Normandy benefited immeasurably from the close, confined terrain, which gave the defender an advantage. Most of the Normandy battlefield was dominated by bocage—thousands of small fields ringed by earthen banks and dense shrubbery—which usually made it impossible to see beyond a single field at a time.

The first few days following the landings were an enormous letdown for Eisenhower. Unable to set foot on French soil until June 12, he felt isolated from the battle raging there. Kay Summersby described him as depressed and chafing at his sense of helplessness, "as if he had run out of steam." Despite the generally encouraging situation reports, Eisenhower never seemed satisfied, as if he were grasping at straws and that the receipt of yet one more SITREP would finally provide assurance that all would be well. "He would sit there and smoke and worry," noted Summersby. "Every time the telephone rang, he would grab it."[23]

He awoke on June 10 "in a snit," as Butcher politely put it, his mood darkened by a meeting with Churchill, who badgered him about the restrictions on his visiting Normandy. On June 12 Eisenhower played host to a stellar cast of Washington VIPs, aides, and cameramen. Marshall, King, and Arnold had ostensibly come to London to meet with the British chiefs and to be on hand should the landings fail, but as Marshall's biographer notes, their presence "was born as much of the American chiefs' desire to see just what the labors of two and a half years had wrought," and they were as anxious as Eisenhower to see the battlefront for themselves.[24] They disembarked from the U.S. destroyer *Thompson* onto the American Mulberry off Omaha Beach and, after conferring with Bradley, the group was driven to the shattered crossroads town of Isigny, on the neck of the Carentan Peninsula. Wherever his convoy went Eisenhower was cheered by GIs who recognized him with unmilitary waves, shouts of "There's Ike" or "The old man himself," and even an occasional salute.[25] Later a PT boat sped them to Utah Beach. Although their sea journey that day was without incident, it was not without danger: Ten U-boats known to be stalking prey in the waters of the Channel were themselves being hunted before they could inflict serious damage on the Allied fleet.

During the homeward journey Marshall drew Eisenhower aside and began to talk of a postwar role for his protégé as army chief of staff, noting that he was still a young man. "Why do you think we have been pushing you? When the war is over I expect you have ten years of hard work ahead of you." Eisenhower could not have found Marshall's words reassuring. Chief of staff was never a post he had coveted, and—having already endured nearly two years in the cauldron of Allied high command, and exhausted by it— Eisenhower merely replied, "General, I hope then to have a long rest."[26] A few months shy of his fifty-fourth birthday, Eisenhower could be forgiven for feeling considerably older.

.   .   .

On June 6, 1944, 2nd Lt. John S. D. Eisenhower graduated from West Point a year early, still somewhat uneasy over his decision to follow in his father's footsteps. Yet it was wartime, and—as much to please his father as to defy his wishes—John was commissioned in the infantry. Mamie, who traveled to West Point for the occasion with Ruth Butcher, had no idea it was D-Day until awakened that morning in the Hotel Thayer by a telephone call from a New York reporter inquiring what she thought of the invasion. Never comfortable in the limelight or around high-ranking brass, John was dismayed that on a day meant to honor his entire class, he and Mamie had become the center of attention as a horde of reporters converged on them for photographs and possible quotes (which were not forthcoming).

Mamie brought with her a cable for her son from his famous father. While filled with obvious pride, it read more like an officer's code of conduct than heartfelt recognition from a father to his son on one of the most important days of his life.

> Second Lieutenant John S. D. Eisenhower, U.S. Army. I hope you know how happy I am that both you and I are now officers in the great U.S. Army. I am especially proud of the fact that in all the years since your birth you have never once deliberately given your mother or me any cause for anxiety or worry and you are now entering upon your chosen career splendidly equipped by character and training to meets its exacting demands. I am completely confident in your readiness and ability to perform any appropriate duty and to be a real leader of any men that may be assigned to your command. I know that your actions will be characterized by firmness based upon knowledge and leadership based upon human understanding.
>
>   My sincere congratulations together with the assurance that although you will be following your own individual path through life you will always have the enthusiastic support, love and admiration of your mother and me.—Devotedly, Dad.[27]

John fumed when the superintendent placed him and Mamie in his personal automobile for the short ride to the barracks to collect his gear. Still, in such instances newly commissioned second lieutenants, even if their name is Eisenhower, do not say no to a two-star general who insists that they ride in his automobile. Like his father, John Eisenhower shunned the limelight, and on this seminal day he wanted nothing more than to be just another member of his graduating class. It was his first experience of what it would henceforth be like to bear the name of the most famous soldier in the United States.

Though Mamie Eisenhower endured June 6 as if in a dream, the knowledge that she would one day be grilled by Ike for every detail of their son's graduation day helped to keep her focused. The worst moment came when she learned that John would not, as she had expected, be spending his graduation leave with her in Washington. Unlike other cadets, he would spend his month of graduation leave in Europe, thanks to Marshall, who had responded to Ike's personal request to have his son with him.[28] "The reality of the news was a shock. I had two of them—my husband and my son, all I had in the world. Ike was in it; Johnny was heading right toward it."[29] That night young Eisenhower bade his mother farewell and was secretly driven to New York where he boarded the liner *Queen Mary* for a weeklong voyage to Scotland.

John was met by Lt. Col. Tex Lee and accorded VIP treatment aboard his father's personal train. Their first reunion in two years took place at Southwick on June 13, where Eisenhower was in the middle of a one-sided telephone conversation with J. C. H. Lee, colorfully warning the logistician that if he cared to keep his job, it behooved him to get over to Normandy and straighten out the supply situation at once.[30]

The day before John's arrival the Germans had launched the first V-1 pilotless aircraft attacks in what became in the summer of 1944 a wave of random terror, with London and other cities, such as Brighton, their principal targets. Quaintly called doodlebugs or buzz bombs by most Britons, many of these deadly missiles struck within a short distance of the most famous London landmarks. Once again fear permeated the British populace as civilian morale plummeted. No one was spared.[31] During the first eighty days 8,000 V-1s were launched against Britain, 2,300 of which struck in and around London. Shortly after John arrived, a devastating attack occurred when one struck on Sunday, June 18, exploding inside the Guards chapel, filled with worshipers, killing eighty officers and members of their families. Finding some means of countering the buzz bombs became the single overriding priority of Churchill and his government. The V-1 attacks had a greater effect on British morale than had the blitz, not only for the sense of helplessness they created, but because the Londoners were war weary and thought their ordeal from the air had ended. Nearly a million and half Britons were evacuated to the countryside in scenes reminiscent of the darkest days of 1940. As the attacks worsened, the pressure would increase on Eisenhower to finish off the German army in Normandy.

Most of the V-1s were shot down or impacted harmlessly in rural areas, but enough got through to cause a massive, high-priority, and largely futile effort to destroy the missile launch sites in Holland. By September, however, the Germans had perfected a more sophisticated, longer-range weapon, the V-2, which was fired from sites in occupied Belgium. Soaring to heights of sixty thousand feet, the V-2s were neither detectable nor subject to interception, as were the V-1s. They traveled at a rate of 2,200 miles per hour before descending faster than the speed of sound to strike without warning and with lethal efficiency.

During the weeks before he moved permanently to Normandy, some nights when Eisenhower stayed over at Telegraph Cottage he actually spent on cots crammed into a nearby bomb shelter, much to his disgust. Sometimes Eisenhower was obliged to make multiple trips to the shelter, where he cursed the Germans with colorful profanity and admitted that whenever he heard a rocket nearby he would pray, "Oh Lord, keep that engine going."[32]

The sometimes awkward father-son relationship took on a new shape in June 1944. "How I look forward to seeing Johnny. It will be odd to see him as an *officer of the Army*! I'll burst with pride." Only hours before his arrival Eisenhower proclaimed himself "really as excited as a bride—but luckily I have so much to do I haven't time to get nervous!"[33] John immediately noticed his father's strain; his abrupt demeanor was a departure from his normal behavior, and his eagerness to wring every last drop of information from whoever was briefing him on Normandy betrayed his desire to escape his passive role.

Despite their affection for each other, "there existed a certain military wall between us," said John. "I was not only his son; I was a young lieutenant who needed on occasion to be straightened out . . . having been brought up in a more relaxed Army than the one Dad had joined thirty years earlier, I think sometimes he considered me a sign that West Point had gone to hell."[34] Yet as Kay Summersby noted on observing the two, "[E]ven an idiot could see he [John] adored his father."[35] Freshly indoctrinated in military protocol by West Point and eager to please, John was determined never to embarrass himself in the presence of his demanding father. One evening, as father and son strolled together outside Telegraph Cottage, John innocently inquired about saluting when the two of them were together. Should he salute an officer senior to him first, and then the officer he saluted would in turn salute his father? "John, there isn't an officer in this theater who doesn't rank above you and below me," he replied in obvious annoyance, indicating that the subject was closed but neither satisfying nor mollifying the son, who felt he was being patronized.[36]

Eisenhower seemed incapable of going beyond the formality of a superior-subordinate relationship with his son, even in the privacy of Telegraph Cottage. No matter the endeavor, Eisenhower seemed compelled to criticize his son, from his bridge skills to his disapproval their first night together when John spoke of spending an uncomfortable last night at West Point on the bare springs of his bunk after turning in his mattress and equipment in anticipation of a hasty departure on graduation day. When asked by Kay Summersby why he had grimaced, Eisenhower replied that while thousands of soldiers were sleeping in foxholes under combat conditions in Normandy, "my son complains about a restless night" at West Point. "I think he should toughen up." On other occasions when John ventured opinions of a military nature, his father would interject, "Oh, for God's sake!"[37]

Nevertheless, their brief reunion was a tonic for Eisenhower, who was inordinately proud of his son but, much like his own father, simply incapable of unbending during their all-too-brief times together. "What a God send [*sic*] he has been for me," he wrote to Mamie. John badly wanted assignment to an infantry unit fighting in France but first had to complete basic training at Fort Benning. The reality was that neither Eisenhower nor the army could permit John to be placed in harm's way or to face capture. Although Eisenhower would have liked to have his son by his side for the remainder of the war as an aide, he realized it would result in justifiable allegations of nepotism, and inevitably harm John's military career.[38]

John and Tedder accompanied Eisenhower to Normandy on June 15 for an inspection of the front and to tour the liberated town of Bayeux. He traveled in an open jeep and was recognized and cheered by GIs. Some waved, others grinned, and a few yelled out, "Hi, Ike." According to John, his father "would wave and yell back to them with a broad grin."[39] Wherever he went Eisenhower fired endless questions at ordinary GIs and their NCOs and officers. Most were innocuous ("Where are you from, soldier?" "What would you do if . . . ," or "What is the range of your weapon?"), and others phrased as wisecracks, but all of them were designed not only to make his troops feel at ease in his presence but also as a means of testing their morale and readiness.[40] Although John was not permitted to listen in on his father's conversation with Montgomery he was able to observe the two men relate to each other. He noticed that despite their military differences, Eisenhower habitually treated Montgomery "with every courtesy, even deference," but saw no evidence that this deference was reciprocated.

No longer a mere symbol, de Gaulle had consolidated his hold over the Free French movement despite attempts by Roosevelt and Churchill to force him to play the role scripted for him by the United States and Britain. Over Churchill's strenuous objections, de Gaulle was at last permitted, on June 14, to visit French soil for the first time since 1940. With no intention of being bound by Roosevelt's mandate that Eisenhower was to be in charge of civil authority in liberated France, de Gaulle was mindful that Eisenhower had made a "secret pledge at their last meeting in Algiers that 'whatever apparent attitudes are imposed upon me, I will recognize no other French power in France than your own in the political sphere.' "[41] De Gaulle's relations with every Allied leader save Eisenhower were stormy. Both men were soldiers first, and it was this bond that drew the two together. Although Eisenhower and de Gaulle would repeatedly clash over issues both military and political in the coming months, neither man ever let momentary pique stand in the way of a relationship based on mutual respect and a bond only soldiers possessed—or could understand.

In Bayeux, de Gaulle dismissed the Vichy prefect and calmly installed his own man, a career civil servant named François Coulet, as his personal representative of the Provisional Government of the French Republic. Early on de Gaulle had astutely recognized that the restrictions placed in his path by the Allies would come to naught. Roosevelt badly misjudged that others would emerge to supersede the perception that de Gaulle was the savior of France. Henry Stimson got it right, however, writing in his diary, "He has become the symbol of deliverance to the French people." Within a matter of days de Gaulle's de facto civil administration seized control of the liberated cities and towns of Normandy and replaced its officials with men who answered to the new regime. "Recognized or not, the provisional government of General de Gaulle had arrived in France and was firmly in control."[42] Within a matter of weeks his Provisional Government of France was recognized by every other provisional government of occupied Europe.

Eisenhower learned of de Gaulle's activities the following day from one of Montgomery's aides during an inspection trip to Second Army. From the back seat of their jeep, John was able to observe his father's neck turn a shade of red that matched his anger. "I could see the Old Man's blood pressure rise," after he learned of de Gaulle's remarks to the people of Bayeux.[43] Yet there was an enormous difference between Eisenhower's perception that de Gaulle had suggested that, with the aid of the Allies, he was liberating France, and what he actually said. Eisenhower could hardly have objected had he heard de Gaulle say, "We shall fight beside the Allies, with the Allies, as an ally. And the victory we shall win will be the victory of liberty and the victory of France."[44] "Absorbed in the overriding task of running the battle, Eisenhower simply paid no attention at all to Roosevelt's restrictive instructions about supervising civil affairs in France."[45]

At the end of June, John Eisenhower returned to the United States aboard his father's personal B-17. Mamie was on the tarmac to meet him. In addition to her son, among the passengers was Kay Summersby, who, thanks to Eisenhower's generosity, was making her first trip to the United States carrying papers she hoped would result in a commission as a Woman's Army Corps (WAC) officer, and to track down Dick Arnold's mother.

The unexpected appearance of Eisenhower's alleged paramour set the Washington gossipmongers loose with sharpened claws and fresh rumors. Everett Hughes's wife, Kate, thought Kay "was on the make" and gleefully passed along fodder for his diary. Another general's wife reported that Mamie was unimpressed with the woman so close to her husband. Kay recounts in her 1948 memoir that the two women met for drinks at Mamie's apartment, and that Mrs. Eisenhower's "cordially" enabled her to have a wonderful time in Washington. Her account, posthumously, paints an entirely different picture: that she had been invited solely at John's insistence and was decidedly uncomfortable meeting Mamie and her friends, who had gathered for the occasion. It was also her first awareness that she and Ike were the object of venomous gossip. "No wonder the women at that little cocktail party had been eyeing me so closely. Wherever I went I began to feel as if I were on display."[46] Within the social hierarchy in the closed society of military wives, had she not been Eisenhower's alleged lover, Kay Summersby would barely have rated notice.

Through no fault of her own, Kay did not endear herself to Mamie when John insisted on taking her on a whirlwind tour of New York City. Mamie had expected him to remain in Washington with her and, annoyed and hurt, the two had words. Although Mamie kept her opinions about Kay Summersby to herself, granddaughter Susan believes she never succumbed to the lurid gossip that Ike and Kay were sleeping together. "It is inconceivable that Ike would have sent his 'lover' to the United States in the care of his son."[47] What defies rational explanation is why Eisenhower, knowing full well that Kay Summersby was an extremely sore subject with Mamie, and that the two were the object of far more than merely passing gossip, would send her to the United States in the first place, except in naive innocence.

The month of June was a marathon to land reinforcements and build up the vast stores of supplies, fuel, and ammunition. Already the delays had slowed the pace and, without Cherbourg, threatened to worsen. The buildup of troops and supplies was seriously affected when, on June 19, one of the most severe storms in forty years lashed Normandy. Nearly eight hundred ships were either beached or lost, and the American Mulberry artificial harbor off Omaha Beach was destroyed and never replaced. What has been called the "Great Storm" virtually shut down the war for three days and destroyed more shipping than the Germans had during the entire campaign. Losses in material amounted to more than 140,000 tons. When Eisenhower landed on Omaha Beach on June 24, he found it strewn with the carcasses of ships lying on their sides in the sand like beached whales, victims of nature's unforgiving fury.

The effects on manpower were equally dire. Before the storm the British Second Army was already two brigades behind schedule, and the numbers increased to three divisions by the time the storm finally abated on June 22. It also delayed the arrival of the U.S. VIII Corps. "I thank the gods of war that we went when we did," Eisenhower wrote to Stagg in appreciation that he had not postponed D-Day until the next available full-moon date, June 19.[48] Churchill lamented to Eisenhower, "They have no right to give us weather like this." John Eisenhower witnessed the exchange and remembers thinking, "[I]t seems that Churchill and General George Patton had an attitude in common. Dedicated to their respective missions, each seemed to feel that the Almighty had an obligation—a personal obligation—to render all necessary assistance to their accomplishments." By contrast John thought his father, who did not share the notion that God owed him anything, more hardheaded than either Churchill or Patton.[49]

During his two-week stay, John Eisenhower saw his father in virtually every conceivable range of emotion, from anger and elation to outright pessimism. Only when the British captured Caen and Bradley took Cherbourg would he "really feel we're here to stay."[50] After a long and vicious fight during which the 4th Division sustained six thousand casualties, Cherbourg surrendered to Collins's VII Corps on June 26. Its garrison had virtually destroyed the port, leaving it a tangled mess that took several months to become functional again. Even then, Cherbourg was barely able to supply 50 percent of the tonnage required by First Army and Patton's Third Army.

Everyone around him noticed that Eisenhower seemed edgy and "considerably less than exuberant these days. He didn't even seem to get a kick out of the fall of Cherbourg," recorded Butcher.[51] He was under increasing pressure from his deputy, Air Chief Marshal Tedder, and others to replace Montgomery as the ground commander in chief. Rumblings of discontent were heard in both London and Washington, and when, on June 27, Everett Hughes brought word of yet another delay, this time by Bradley, who delayed his offensive to clear the Cotentin, Eisenhower was heard to lament, "Sometimes I wish I had George Patton here."[52]

While Eisenhower worried over his battlefield problems, Patton chafed with impatience in England anxiously awaiting the summons to battle and a chance to redeem himself for his disastrous conduct in Sicily. Incredibly the Germans were still taking the Fortitude bait, with most of the German Fifteenth Army still awaiting Patton to lead the main invasion into the Pas de Calais. Patton had only the vaguest notion of what was transpiring in Normandy. "Apparently things are not going well and one gets the impression that people are satisfied to be holding on, rather than advancing."[53]

Patton's perceptions were correct. The campaign in Normandy was clearly in trouble, and the controversy over who was to blame and what to do about it would soon reach the boiling point. Patton composed a paper he had Everett Hughes slip into Eisenhower's reading file, proposing to land a corps of one armored and two infantry divisions at Morlaix, on the north coast of Brittany.

> We can make a rear attack on the Germans confronting the First U.S. Army, and then driving on to the line Alençon-Argentan, and thereafter on Evreux and Chartres, depending on circumstances, we will really pull a coup. On the other hand, if we play safe and keep on attacking with articulated lines driving to the south, we will die of old age before we finish.[54]

43.

The Battle for Normandy

*We were stuck. Something dreadful seemed to have
happened in terms of the overall plan. Things were going very awry.*

—CPL. BILL PRESTON

By the end of June the two sides were locked in a protracted, bitter stalemate around the vital city of Caen, which became the litmus test of the Normandy campaign. The strategy devised by Montgomery for securing the left flank had been thwarted by the fanatical resistance of the enemy, who held the city and the Caen-Falaise Plain to the south, which Tedder required for the establishment of Allied tactical airfields. Repeated attempts to capture the Norman capital through enveloping attacks, including the bloodiest battle yet, the fight for Hill 112 along the Odon River Valley during an offensive code-named Epsom, produced not only heavy losses but mounting criticism that Montgomery had lost control of the campaign. A golden opportunity to have encircled the city from the west shortly after D-Day was botched by one of Monty's veteran desert divisions, the famed 7th Armored, the "Desert Rats," which he had personally hand-picked for an important role in Normandy.

First Army was fighting a debilitating battle in the bocage, hedgerow by hedgerow. Until Cherbourg was captured in late June, Bradley had been unable to expand the American sector or carry out his intended breakout toward St-Lô. "By July 10, we faced a real danger of a World War I–type stalemate," Bradley admitted.[1]

Criticism of Montgomery's handling of the ground campaign continued. While American airmen were cracking jokes to their army counterparts about another Anzio, Tedder and Coningham were actively plotting Montgomery's relief.[2] As the controversy heightened, Montgomery insisted even more obstinately that he was merely adhering to a master plan to draw the bulk of the German forces and their panzers to the Caen front, and away from Bradley's sector. However, what Montgomery's concept of the battle for Normandy *never* included was a protracted battle of attrition for Caen. Later he sought to deflect criticism of his generalship by suggesting that his enemies at SHAEF took advantage of the controversy to discredit him. One British officer remarked, "It became the mark of a good British SHAEF officer to express dismay at the behavior of Montgomery."[3] The outrage and frustration of the air commanders and many American officers still rankled long after the war. They were among many who failed to understand the reasons for the delay at Caen, and suspected that U.S. forces were being used as a sacrificial lamb while the British dallied in the east. A 1981 account by controversial historian David Irving dubbed the entire campaign in northwest Europe *The War Between the Generals* and suggested that the Allied brass were more interested in preserving their reputations than in defeating the Germans.[4]

Although Patton's proposed end run into southern Normandy was an excellent example of his boldness and ability to think ahead, Eisenhower carefully considered but eventually rejected it, on the grounds that it was too dangerous and too much of a sideshow. The plan was actually neither, and, in fact, foreshadowed precisely what occurred in August.[5] Neither Eisenhower nor Bradley, unschooled in the freewheeling ways of the cavalry and tank men, was rarely open to such risks. Yet it was precisely for such reasons that Eisenhower had left Patton in command of Third Army.

By early July, Third Army began deploying to Normandy in strict secrecy to preserve the fiction that Patton was still in England, soon to lead his army group in the "real" invasion across the Pas de Calais. The bulk of the German Fifteenth Army remained in northern France fruitlessly awaiting the main invasion by Patton's fictitious First U.S. Army Group. For nearly a month Patton's presence in Normandy was a closely guarded secret that kept alive the great deception.

For some time Bradley had been preparing his first attempt to break out from the Cotentin Peninsula, but the storm delayed the arrival of Troy Middleton's VIII Corps and the operation was postponed until early July. Anxious to be on hand for the event, Eisenhower flew to Normandy on July 1 for a four-day sojourn at Bradley's First Army HQ. He brought only a bedroll, a single aide, and his orderly. Mickey McKeogh neglected to pack his toilet kit, and Eisenhower had to borrow one from Bradley's aide. Insisting that "I want nothing but a slit trench with a piece of canvas over it," Eisenhower threatened he would not stay at First Army should Bradley make available his trailer. He was billeted in an ordinary tent and slept in red pajama bottoms, no top, shaved and bathed in cold water like everyone else, and ate C-rations topped off with a bottle of French champagne that had been "liberated" by a member of Bradley's staff. In short, it was exactly what Eisenhower relished: no special treatment and the illusion of roughing it.[6]

Omar Bradley's daily routine centered around the large maps that covered the walls of his mobile office. Much like Montgomery, who abhorred distractions, Bradley would spend hour upon hour by himself studying the terrain and using his trademark colored crayons to plot his next moves.

Whenever Eisenhower visited (seventeen times during the campaign), the two men would discourse endlessly over tactics. At one of the most critical moments of the war it might have seemed incongruous to an outsider that its three prime architects were a British general whose uniform consisted of a civilian turtleneck sweater and corduroy pants, and "two balding middle-aged men with reading glasses perched at the end of their noses" isolated in a cramped trailer in a Norman wood.[7]

That Eisenhower was little more than a spectator to the great drama being played out around him frustrated him beyond measure. He now pinned his hopes of breaking the stalemate on Bradley's First Army offensive, which was launched on July 3 but almost immediately ground to a halt far short of its objectives in the dense bocage north of St-Lô. Despite Montgomery's later claims of pinning the German panzer divisions to his front, two of them had already slipped away to reinforce the German left flank and participate in a series of counterattacks against First Army. Bradley's offensive breakout of the Cotentin had opened the day before but soon bogged down. During the month of July, First Army advanced less than ten miles.[8]

In all the vast pre-D-Day planning, seemingly no one had taken note of the deadly terrain through which the Allies would have to fight once a bridge-head was secured and the land battle in Normandy began in earnest. Consequently the fighting in the bocage came as a complete shock. Bradley's initial attempts to clear the Cotentin resulted in some forty thousand American casualties, and exacerbated his own frustration at his inability to devise some way out of the Cotentin. The dirty, bloody business of advancing one hedge-row at a time was inexorably grinding down the soldiers of both sides, so much so that "a German corps commander called the struggle [in July 1944] nothing less than 'a monstrous bloodbath.' "[9]

"We were flabbergasted by the *bocage*," said Maj. Gen. (later Lt. Gen.) Elwood "Pete" Quesada, commander of IX Tactical Air Command (the American tactical air force supporting Bradley's First Army). "Our infantry had become paralyzed. It has never been adequately described how immobilized they were by the sound of small-arms fire among the hedges."[10]

Despite his intense study of maps, Bradley was high on the list of those who had failed to detect or even anticipate the serious problems the bocage would pose. His response was to begin sacking subordinate division and regimental commanders, but whatever their lapses in leadership, the stalemate had less to do with failure and far more to do with the weather, the bocage, and the fanatical resistance by German troops, who were fighting less for Adolf Hitler than in the hope, however futile, of survival.

Montgomery's troubles cracking Caen, combined with Bradley's problems in the Cotentin, which Eisenhower viewed firsthand, should have convinced him that there was good reason for the stalemate and that a breakout was not merely a question of constantly remaining on the offensive until something positive occurred.

The war of words for and against Montgomery was largely British, spearheaded by the air barons, Tedder and Coningham, both of whom carried long-standing grudges dating from North Africa and what each considered insufficient credit for their role in Eighth Army's victories over Rommel. Behind the scenes Tedder intrigued in a concerted effort to persuade Eisenhower to sack Monty.

Despite the setbacks and the increasing criticism, Montgomery held firm to his original concept that once a bridgehead was established across the entire Allied front, Bradley's army was to expand its front beyond the bocage and swing to their left so that a concerted drive could be mounted to push the German army toward the Seine. Successful accomplishment of this required the British Second Army to secure the Caen-Falaise Plain and then act as a hinge while the Allied door slammed shut to pin the Germans against the Seine. Neither of these conditions existed in early July, and therein lay the crux of the problem.

On July 4 the one millionth Allied soldier arrived in Normandy, where the U.S. First Army marked Independence Day with a thousand-gun salute as each artillery piece fired a single round at noon sharp. There was little else to celebrate. As the official army historian has written, American troops had to fight their way through a "flooded pastoral region of ten thousand little fields enclosed by hedgerows." It was terrain "made for ambush . . . from field to field, from hedgerow to hedgerow, measuring the progress of their advance in yards," across the rich Normandy soil polluted by the sickening smell of unburied corpses.[11]

Although Montgomery had become the focus for everything that had gone wrong since D-Day, it was unrealistic of Eisenhower and the host of Monty-bashers to have expected an easy ride to Caen. For, as two British historians— one of them a veteran senior commander who fought in Normandy—have pointed out, "In retrospect, the Allies surprisingly underestimated the tactical grasp of the Germans. It should have been apparent that if they were strengthening the beach defenses, they would do the same to Caen. Yet nearly everyone connected with the invasion planning assumed that Caen would be taken on D-Day or very shortly afterwards."[12] It was an assumption based on the same underestimation of German tenacity that plagued Allied thinking throughout the war.

Eisenhower's itch to fly had never abated, and on July 4 it overwhelmed his common sense when he could not resist the lure of risking his life. When he learned that Pete Quesada intended to fly one of the newly introduced P-51

Mustang fighter aircraft, Eisenhower, with what Quesada described as "boyish enthusiasm," inveigled an invitation to accompany him. The P-51, which became the workhorse of the U.S. tactical air forces, was a single-seat fighter with a seventy-gallon fuel tank jury-rigged in the compartment behind the pilot to give it additional range. One of the P-51s at a newly constructed forward airfield had a seat installed instead of the fuel tank. Bradley looked on disapprovingly as Eisenhower responded brusquely as he was literally being crammed into the back of the P-51, "All right, Brad, I'm not going to fly to Berlin."

"So we stuffed General Eisenhower in that seat and conducted a mission off of a very, very crude airstrip that was still under construction . . . the mat had just been laid, its full length had not been extended, you had to touch down within a few feet of the end," to avoid skidding off the end of the runway.

For between thirty and forty-five minutes Eisenhower left his cares behind as he and Quesada flew over German-held territory, sometimes as deep as fifty miles, escorted by three fighters. Eisenhower convinced no one that it was simply another day's business, maintaining that its purpose was to better understand the hedgerow terrain, but the reality was as much the irresistible lure of danger and a fleeting opportunity to recapture the exhilaration he had not known since the Philippines. According to Quesada, "He enjoyed the hell out of it." The possibilities for misfortune eventually made Quesada apprehensive enough to turn back, even though he secretly nurtured hopes of getting into a dogfight with the Luftwaffe. "I had the Supreme Commander stuffed behind me in a single-engine airplane with no parachute over enemy territory," and no way to get him out in the event of an emergency. Eisenhower later described the flying over occupied France to Jimmy Gault as "a peaceful scene," and had he gotten his way he would have had Quesada fly at an even faster speed.

The landing was itself an adventure, requiring a precision touchdown at the very end of the unfinished runway. As Quesada slowed the aircraft, the unsettled pierced-steel planking rippled in front of its wheels, creating a bumpy and potentially dangerous ending to Eisenhower's July 4 adventure. Eisenhower's secret was exposed when they were met by Bradley and an entourage of war correspondents and newsreel cameramen. Emerging from the P-51, the two "grinned like sheepish schoolboys caught in a watermelon patch," said Bradley. Eisenhower remarked that "General Marshall would give me hell," and to head off Marshall's certain admonition, he wrote to the chief of staff the next day that the flight had been "pure business." The escapade did indeed irk Marshall, as well as earning Eisenhower a front-page headline in the *New York Times*, EISENHOWER FLIES OVER NAZI LINES. The accompanying article noted that "he was often in danger" and "in exposed positions most of the time." He hastened to reassure Mamie that "I'm most careful."[13]

Truth be told, Eisenhower didn't give a damn what anyone thought; he had loved every minute of his escapade.

The euphoria quickly wore off when Eisenhower returned to England on July 5 deeply concerned over the divisiveness of the feud between the air barons and Montgomery, and "smouldering over the whole business" in Normandy.[14] British and Canadian casualty rates were skyrocketing, and numbered 24,698 killed, wounded, and missing on the last day of June. American casualties in the deadly bocage were rising at an equally alarming rate.[15]

Heavy bombers were employed in direct support of the ground forces to blast a gap in the German lines that would enable Second Army to finally capture Caen.[16] During the night and early morning hours of July 7–8, 450 British heavy bombers dropped six thousand tons of bombs that reduced what was left of Caen to smoking rubble. The value of the bombing was questionable, and the rubble it created was responsible for holding up the advance of the infantry, which, in the two days of hard fighting that followed, was able to secure only the northern half of Caen. Stiff resistance from the remnants of Caen's defenders, who had established new blocking positions on the south bank of the Orne River, temporarily prevented any further advance.

While Montgomery had unquestionably improved his position, the mere possession of the northern half of Caen was hopeless as a hinge for support of future operations on either flank. Adding to Montgomery's problems, Bradley's offensive was stalled in the mud and bocage of western Normandy with time the critical factor, it was essential that the Allied commanders develop and execute a concerted plan for a breakout that would snap Rommel's "roping-off" policy once and for all.

Under the best of circumstances Churchill was never a patient man, and by July 1944 he was beside himself, not only over the stagnating drive against Caen, but also the invasion of southern France, Operation Anvil/Dragoon, which he repeatedly badgered Eisenhower to cancel. The British case hinged on their Mediterranean strategy, and the conviction that too much had already been invested in the Italian campaign to rob it of the potential to end the war in Italy at the very moment when the Germans were in disarray after the fall of Rome. A series of harshly worded cables flew between London and Washington as Churchill argued doggedly but ultimately in vain against pulling troops from Italy, where, he insisted, victory was at hand. On June 28 Churchill issued a plea to Roosevelt that no troops or landing craft be pulled from Italy. "Let us resolve not to wreck one great campaign for the sake of another. Both can be won." The Italian campaign, he said, offered "dazzling possibilities," whereas the landings in southern France would "relieve Hitler of all his anxieties in the Po [River] basin" and serve no useful purpose in aiding Eisenhower's forces in northern France.

Uppermost in Churchill's mind were the political benefits he foresaw from a successful thrust through Trieste and the Ljubljana gap to seize Vienna before the Russians arrived. What Churchill never accepted was that keeping Alexander's army group intact would not have overcome the problems encountered during the deadly Allied advance into northern Italy during the summer of 1944, which cost thirty-four thousand casualties. How such a military operation might actually have been carried out through the exceedingly difficult terrain of the Apennines and the even more daunting Yugoslavian mountains, all the while overcoming German resistance, was simply not part of Churchill's logic.

Eisenhower, whose virtues as a pragmatist had been honed by nearly two years of high command, would have no part of an offensive through "that gap whose name I can't even pronounce." Time and again he refused to scrap Anvil, despite a chorus of pleas in the days and weeks before the operation, which was scheduled for mid-August. Eisenhower had already compromised by backing away from his earlier insistence on simultaneous landings in both Normandy and the Riviera, and he was determined not to give in to Churchill a second time.

Eisenhower believed the Allies in France required additional ports, particularly Marseilles, and that Anvil would serve to protect the right flank of the Allied armies during their broad advance toward Germany. The American response was firm in its insistence that the invasion of the Riviera proceed as scheduled. At the behest of Marshall and the U.S. chiefs of staff, Roosevelt replied on July 2, "We are still convinced that the right course of action is to launch 'Anvil' at the earliest possible date," ending with a reminder that "[a] straight line is the shortest distance between two points," a clear message to the British that the road to Berlin ran through France and western Europe, not Italy and the Balkans.

Eisenhower's insistence on retaining Anvil included the expectation that the operation would draw off German reserves and protect the southern flank of his armies, once they broke free from the Normandy bridgehead. Nor was he optimistic over the usefulness of the Brittany ports, which he correctly believed the Germans would destroy before they could be captured. Eisenhower's distrust of Churchill's Balkan strategy may have caused him to realize that the only way of guaranteeing the priority of Overlord was to exercise his authority as the Allied commander in chief by affirming Anvil, thus ensuring that operations in France did not lose emphasis to Italy.

Although the Riviera landings ranked high on Eisenhower's litany of problems, Normandy remained center stage. Tiring of what he believed was Montgomery's inaction, Eisenhower is thought to have complained directly to Churchill in an effort to "persuade Monty to get on his bicycle and start moving."[17] In an unpublished postwar manuscript Eisenhower denied initiating the dialogue and claimed it was Churchill who first came to him to express his "unhappiness" and "fear that we were descending into a bitter 'trench-warfare' situation similar to that of World War I" or Anzio. Less plausible is Eisenhower's recollection that "I told him I had personally never paid any attention to predictions that envisioned specific geographical gains at specific times."[18] Quite the contrary, everyone, including Eisenhower, Tedder, and the majority of the airmen, had been seduced by Montgomery's May 15 presentation, which focused so strongly on the capture of Caen. Monty had made what they believed amounted to an unfulfilled promise.

Churchill's strong feelings about Montgomery and Caen led to open and hostile criticism of the British general at a stormy chiefs-of-staff meeting the night of July 6. An angry Brooke noted in his diary that, during an intense encounter between the prime minister and his CIGS, Churchill "began to abuse Monty because operations were not going faster, and apparently Eisenhower had said he was over-cautious. I flared up and asked him if he could not trust his generals for five minutes instead of continuously abusing them and belittling them." Churchill, said Brooke, "was infuriated, and throughout the evening kept shoving his chin out, looking at me and fuming at the accusation that he ran down his generals."[19]

Communications between Eisenhower and Montgomery mostly consisted of frequent exchanges of letters and cables. Eisenhower's were attempts to exhort the British general to greater action. The supreme commander's obvious unease in Monty's presence, though it may account for his reluctance to engage in face-to-face meetings, did little to promote either understanding or harmony between the two men or their respective headquarters. Between June 6 and August 27 they met only nine times, with Montgomery's chief of staff, the affable Maj. Gen. Freddie de Guingand, generally acting as Montgomery's go-between with Eisenhower and SHAEF.[20] This suited Eisenhower, who was far more comfortable with de Guingand, with whom he had formed a close friendship.

The crisis of confidence seemed to grow in direct proportion to the length of time Caen remained in German hands. Americans and British may be two peoples linked by a common language, but when it came to military doctrine they could have not been farther apart. American doctrine, evolved from the time of the Civil War, could best be described as the brute-force method employed by Ulysses S. Grant, and had all the subtlety of a sledgehammer: Mass a more powerful army than your enemy and overwhelm him with what in today's sports parlance would be called smash-mouth tactics. Eisenhower, Marshall, Bradley, and other career infantrymen schooled at Fort Leavenworth were wedded to the unyielding principle of applying constant pressure across an entire front. Inaction was simply anathema to Eisenhower, who, as an unabashed "advocate of the direct approach, put his faith in the sheer smashing power of great armies."[21]

The British experience of such tactics during World War I was reflected in the corpses of a million of its sons, nearly half of whom were buried beneath rows of white crosses in the fields of Flanders and other sites whose names symbolized slaughter, marked only by Rudyard Kipling's sorrowful words, "A Soldier of the Great War Known unto God."[22] Their ghastly losses had never been forgotten. Patton had seen death firsthand commanding tanks during World War I, but the inexperience of Eisenhower and Bradley left them unappreciative of the British experience. The younger British officers of that war who became the leaders of World War II were haunted by the appalling specter of wasted lives. High among them was Montgomery, who had served at the sharp end, nearly died from battle wounds, and believed with every fiber of his being that to engage in bullheaded tactics was as foolish as it was futile. In the summer of 1944 he had even stronger reasons. British manpower resources were dwindling so rapidly that by early July he was obliged to begin disbanding entire formations, including the 59th Division, for lack of infantry replacements.[23] The British "indirect approach," espoused by military theorist Basil Liddell Hart, was to unbalance the enemy by forcing him to attack and commit his reserves, then strike hard at his most vulnerable point.

The enormous disparity between the two diametrically opposed doctrines of war was too deep to ever be resolved, and Montgomery's postwar observation that "when it came to the conduct of war," he and Eisenhower were "poles apart," could not have been more accurately stated.[24] On a practical level it resulted in misunderstanding, bad feelings, and controversy.

Bedell Smith has described an ever-restless Eisenhower "up and down the line like a football coach, exhorting everyone to aggressive action," an analogy Montgomery would later scorn in his memoirs, saying that attacking all the time was the wrong way to run a war.[25]

The doubts already felt by Churchill and Eisenhower spread like a disease to Bradley's headquarters, where there was growing disbelief and disgust over Montgomery's alleged inaction and his claims to be adhering to a master plan. A number of senior officers there were appalled by what was perceived as British impotence at American expense. A good deal of their anger was directed at Eisenhower, who they felt should have been exercising tighter control over Montgomery.

A similar reaction was exhibited at the highest levels of the War Department. After touring Normandy in mid-July, Secretary of War Henry Stimson returned to Washington openly troubled and questioning why the ground armies had made so little progress despite virtual air supremacy. Stimson summoned Marshall and the other top War Department brass and "laid it right on the line," said Assistant Secretary for Air Robert A. Lovett. "He recommended very bluntly that General Eisenhower be told to get his advance headquarters into France at once and let the American armies know that he is the Commander-in-Chief."[26]

An equally unhappy Marshall bluntly informed Eisenhower that it was time for him to take personal charge of the ground campaign. "Marshall was nettled first of all by reports that the Press was talking of Montgomery's victories . . . when the troops in most cases were American. . . . There was considerable grousing by American commanders on Ike's tendency to be too easy on Montgomery."[27] However, in fairness to Montgomery, isolated as he was at his battle headquarters, there is no evidence that he actively courted the attention he was getting in the press. Moreover, as the Allied ground force commander, it was natural that press reports should credit him with the Allied success as well as blame him for the stagnation into which the campaign was falling.

The American press had become increasingly hostile in its Normandy coverage and had begun asking the same questions as Stimson. Lovett wrote to Spaatz that the subject was a "burning one." War Department unrest was focused less on Montgomery than Eisenhower, who was faulted for failing to exercise a stronger grip on the campaign.

Roosevelt too "began complaining to Marshall that Montgomery was hogging all the credit and that the sooner Ike moved across the Channel and took over personal command, the better for public (and Anglo-American) relations."[28] The contretemps in Washington notwithstanding, Eisenhower declined to be pressured into modifying his original plan not to replace Montgomery before Third Army was committed and Bradley elevated to the command of the 12th Army Group.

SHAEF headquarters had swelled to such an enormous size and become so cumbersome that any early move to Normandy would prove a major logistical and communications problem. Nor had plans been laid to create a small tactical headquarters from which Eisenhower might have directed the campaign. Nevertheless, because he spent so much time commuting from Portsmouth to Normandy, in early July Eisenhower established a small advance command post in Normandy from which he could operate during the time he spent there.

Although the Germans could take considerable comfort from their superb defense, their losses continued to mount in both men and matériel, for which there were few if any replacements. Most grievous of all, they lost their inspirational commander: Rommel was gravely wounded on July 17 when his staff car was strafed by British fighters. Although he survived, the Desert Fox had fought his final battle and was replaced by Field Marshal Günther von Kluge.

On July 20, an event occurring in East Prussia might have altered the course of the war, had Col. Count Claus von Stauffenberg's powerful bomb, planted in a briefcase placed under the table of Hitler's war conference room at the Wolfsschanze ("Wolf's Lair"), in Rastenburg, actually killed the Führer, who instead miraculously escaped with only superficial wounds and burst eardrums. The assassination plot failed only because, moments before the briefcase exploded, an officer sitting at the heavy oak table innocently pushed it away from his feet, and from where Hitler was standing, to the far side of the table support, which deflected the blast.

Although Eisenhower as yet knew nothing of either event, July 20 was also one of his most frustrating days of the war. Pressured from all sides to act in a manner he deemed precipitous, he was criticized in the American press as little more than a figurehead, pressed by Tedder to sack Monty, subjected to Churchill's grumblings, and the recipient of Marshall's expression of concern. To his credit Eisenhower refused either to seek Montgomery's relief (virtually unthinkable for political reasons) or to assume control of SHAEF ground forces in Normandy until what he judged an appropriate time. Yet around his personal staff Eisenhower was incapable of hiding his frustration or the storm brewing inside him. Barred by bad weather from flying to France on July 19, Eisenhower was "blue as indigo over Monty's slowdown." When the weather held up his flight the following day, he was unable to conceal his emotions. "Ike is standing around, crunching the cinders with his heel impatiently," saying that "he's got to get across, if he has to swim." Eisenhower neither swam nor flew that day, returning instead to spend another day in isolation at Southwick. Between the situation on the ground and the unseemly quarreling generated by Tedder and Coningham, "Ike is like a blind dog in a meat house—he can smell it, but he can't find it," wrote Butcher.[29] "The slowness of the battle, the desire to be more active in it himself, his inward but generally unspoken criticisms of Monty for being so cautious: all pump up his system."[30]

His frayed nerves were evident. Far worse was that anger and frustration combined to raise his blood pressure to dangerous levels. Butcher persuaded him to see the SHAEF chief medical officer, Maj. Gen. Albert C. Kenner, who ordered him to slow down, prescribed "slow down medication," and carefully concealed the fact that Eisenhower was under his care or taking medicine for stress.[31]

Over lunch with Churchill on July 26, Eisenhower raised the problems in Normandy, and later that afternoon Brooke recorded, "I was sent for by Winston" after Eisenhower "had again run down Montgomery and described his stickiness." Churchill arranged for Brooke to dine with Eisenhower, Bedell Smith, and himself the following night in an effort to smooth the troubled waters. "It did a lot of good. I have offered to go over with Ike if necessary to assist him in handling Monty," wrote Brooke. "My God what psychological complications war leads to!!!" Brooke was justifiably irked that the press had it wrong by suggesting that the British were doing nothing while the U.S.

Army was bearing the brunt of the war in Normandy and suffering the majority of the casualties:

> There is no doubt that Ike is all out to do all he can to maintain the best of relations between British and Americans, but it is equally clear that Ike knows nothing about strategy and is *quite* unsuited to the position of Supreme Commander as far as any of the strategy of the war is concerned! . . . I am tired to death with and by humanity and all its pettiness. Will we ever learn to "love our Allies as ourselves"??!! I doubt it!

Anged and frustrated by misunderstandings and bickering, Brooke could not be blamed for lamenting that " 'national' spectacles pervert the perspective of the strategic landscape."[32]

With the British stalled at Caen, the British Second Army commander, Miles Dempsey, proposed a daring plan to break the impasse. Operation Goodwood (named after the famed British race course) was designed to employ heavy bombers to blast open a gap in the front lines, followed by a massive tank attack to shred the entire German flank and drive clear to Falaise. Bomber Harris readily agreed to support the operation, and everyone from Eisenhower on down applauded what seemed at least a full-blooded effort to break the Normandy stalemate.

Early on the morning of July 18 three waves of British bombers carried out one of the most awesome air attacks ever launched against ground troops. During the next two hours they pulverized the battlefield, creating a cauldron of smoke, dust, and destruction then unprecedented in the history of ground combat. Before the day ended more than 4,500 Allied tactical and strategic aircraft had been in action against the Germans east of the Orne River. The Bomber Command attack was followed up by the massed artillery fire of three corps, supported by naval gunfire, which together hurled nearly a quarter of a million rounds onto the Goodwood battlefield. Tiger tanks were literally buried and others flung upside down as if they were no more than playing cards instead of fifty-eight-ton behemoths. Some of the survivors were dazed and demoralized, while others were crazed from the incessant bombing and shelling, describing the experience as a vision of hell.

The British expected that the sheer weight of their assault would overwhelm the Germans, but despite the fact that the attacking armor had been positioned at night the Germans had detected this shift and were expecting a major attack. Under the direction of Gen. Heinrich Eberbach, the Germans had prepared their strongest defensive positions in Normandy to counter this new threat. The massive bombardment failed to knock out all the antitank guns and panzers situated in and around key hamlets covering the British avenues of approach. The Germans held the high ground along Bourguébus Ridge, from which they could control the battlefield and block the access necessary for a breakthrough to the Caen-Falaise Plain beyond. What proved decisive was the great depth of the German defenses, which included artillery positioned out of harm's way behind the ridge, and a battery of four 88-mm guns that survived unscathed. Under heavy fire the British advance stalled on the slopes of Bourguébus Ridge. By the time reinforcements arrived, the British had lost the initiative, which they never regained. Despite considerable territorial gains, Second Army had been unable to exploit the bombing and drive into the plains leading to Falaise. British tank losses numbered nearly two hundred, and infantry losses were uncomfortably high. Even worse, Goodwood had raised false hopes at SHAEF and in Whitehall and convinced both Eisenhower and Montgomery's critics that he had again failed to win a decisive battle. What hardly anyone realized was that the British had fought "the best formations in the German Army to exhaustion," kept them from even considering a counteroffensive, and tied down fourteen divisions (six of them first-rate panzer divisions)—no mean feat.[33]

Bradley's detestation of Montgomery left him loath ever to admit anything positive about the British general. Yet, although nominally subordinate to him, Montgomery treated Bradley as an equal well before he became an army group commander. On July 10 Montgomery, Dempsey, and Bradley met to discuss present and future operations. Bradley had by now at last recognized the futility of attacking on a broad front in the Cotentin and was already formulating an operation to spring First Army from the shackles of the bocage. Montgomery offered both his support and a diplomatic suggestion: "Take all the time you need, Brad"; then he went on to say, "If I were you I think I should concentrate my forces a little more," noting on the map with two fingers together what he meant.[34] Although he would never acknowledge that Montgomery ever did anything positive to assist him, it was hardly a coincidence that Bradley would soon refine the idea into an offensive he called Cobra, which would irrevocably alter the course of the stalemated Normandy campaign and unleash Eisenhower's secret weapon—George S. Patton and his Third Army.

44.

"Dear Ike, To-day I spat in the Seine."

Make peace, you idiots!
—FIELD MARSHAL GERD VON RUNDSTEDT

When Omar Bradley unleashed Operation Cobra on July 25, 1944, neither he nor Dwight Eisenhower had any reason to believe it would turn a dangerous stalemate into a spectacularly successful end to a troubling campaign, and alter the course of the war in northwestern Europe.

On the afternoon of July 20, at about the time Stauffenberg was attempting to kill Hitler, Eisenhower arrived in Normandy to confer with Bradley and Montgomery. At Bradley's field headquarters he damned the weather that was keeping his aircraft grounded. "When I die," he complained to Bradley, "they can hold my body for a rainy day and bury me during a thunderstorm, for this weather will be the death of me yet." And Bradley, who rarely swore, lamented, "Goddammit, I'm going to have to court-martial the chaplain if we have very much more weather like this."[1] Before departing, Eisenhower chatted with a group of soldiers who were milling around to talk with him, but earlier, when asked to pose for photographers shaking hands with Bradley, gruffly replied, "I'll stand here for your pix but I will not pose."[2] According to Bradley's aide Chet Hansen, the weather was "so misty you could not see the end of the runway. Weather would not have permitted anyone but the Theater Commander to fly in such soup. I told him Marshall would not approve of his flying in weather like this. He laughed," thumbed his nose at both the weather and Marshall, and promptly took off for London to spend the night at Telegraph Cottage.[3]

Postponed from July 19 because of the continued inclement weather, Cobra, strikingly similar to Goodwood, was an offensive intended merely to spring First Army from the confines of the bocage and permit the commitment of Patton's Third Army. Using the highway connecting Saint-Lô with the town of Périers as a starting line, Bradley planned to employ American bombers and fighter-bombers to blast open gaps that the massed forces of

Collins's VII Corps would then exploit. Once the carpet bombing opened a gap of some three and a half miles, Bradley intended to utilize two infantry divisions to hold open the shoulders of the bulge while two armored divisions blitzed through toward Avranches and a motorized division drove on Coutances. Quesada, Bradley, and Eisenhower all endorsed the operation; privately Spaatz "grumbled bitterly about using [aircraft] 'to plow up the ground' and claimed all that was preventing a breakout from Normandy was a lack of guts by American ground troops."[4]

Anxiously chafing to fulfill the destiny he had predicted for himself years before was Patton. Depending on the outcome of Cobra, Patton's Third Army was Bradley's strategic reserve, available to exploit whatever success the operation might bring. During the planning phase the American hope was for a breakthrough, not a breakout. The popular conception is that Cobra was a brilliant masterstroke designed to achieve spectacular results. In reality Bradley was increasingly desperate to find a suitable means of breaking the German defenses, thus enabling First and Third Armies to operate in terrain far more favorable to exploitation than the bocage, where it was an impossibility. In the end Bradley got both, but at the time no one was thinking in such bold terms.

On the morning of July 25, in a virtual repeat of the Goodwood bombardment, wave after wave of U.S. Ninth Air Force fighter-bombers attacked the target area, followed immediately by fifteen hundred heavies of the Eighth Air Force, which disgorged some 3,400 tons of bombs. However, unlike Goodwood, which began with great promise and ended unsatisfactorily, Cobra opened disastrously but ultimately resulted in one of the greatest American triumphs of the war. Some bombs fell short of their intended targets and instead struck the 30th Division and a unit of the 9th Division, killing 111 and wounding 490. Among the dead was the highest-ranking officer killed in northwestern Europe—Lt. Gen. Lesley J. McNair, commander of army ground forces, who, despite warnings, had gone to the front to observe the bombing. Bradley's reaction was an anguished, "Oh, Christ. Not another short drop?" Eisenhower, who reported to Marshall that he had "warned him time and again about unnecessary risk," was "visibly depressed" on learning of McNair's death. Unable to conceal his frustration, he told Marshall, "I get so weary looking for even one minute of sun that I am thinking of living in a dark room where I will know nothing at all about outside conditions."[5] His pronouncement in the heat of the moment that he would never again permit heavy bombers to be utilized in a direct support role was neither the last such use of bombers nor had the bombing been the failure Eisenhower and Bradley supposed. Bradley blamed the air force generals for their "duplicity" by allegedly violating an agreement for their aircraft to carry out the bombing parallel to the Saint-Lô–Périers road, when in fact there was at best a clear misunderstanding (and at worst an outright lie by Bradley) between the army and the air force that the bombing could only meet Bradley's demands if carried out *perpendicular* to the highway. If there was any duplicity, it lay in Bradley's distorted and blatant postwar attempt to make the air force scapegoats for the tragedy when he had insisted the frontline troops be placed only twelve hundred yards from the bombing zone instead of the three thousand mandated by the airmen.[6] Cobra was a shocking example of Bradley's unwillingness to trust the warnings of the airmen.

No one comprehended at the end of the first day of Cobra that what appeared to be continued stiff resistance was in fact a brittle facade, which soon cracked under renewed pressure by Lightning Joe Collins's spearheads. Third Army was to have become operational on August 1, but when German resistance suddenly began to collapse, Bradley recognized that with this sudden turn of fortune it was time to turn Patton loose to spearhead a breakout into Brittany and the plains of southern Normandy, where the mobility of his armored divisions could be exploited.[7] Although Bradley privately admitted he did not want Patton serving under his command, he was soon to have ample reason to be pleased with Patton's presence in Normandy.

By July 29 the front had dissolved as four armored divisions thrusting south made spectacular gains that threatened complete dismemberment of the German left flank in Normandy. Quesada's aircraft attacked anything that moved, demonstrating for the first time in the war that American air and ground forces could work effectively together. After the war von Rundstedt would call the bombing the most effective use of airpower he had ever seen.[8] One of the hardest-hit German units defending along the edge of the target area was the Panzer Lehr Division. "It was hell," said its veteran commander, who later recounted how his division was all but blown to pieces. Although the Germans defending the Cotentin were pounded by U.S. tactical aircraft, constantly hammered by artillery and relentlessly attacked on the ground, in retreat they somehow managed to fight with their usual tenacity. After one particularly savage encounter between the 2nd Armored Division and an SS panzer force, an American officer described the carnage as "the most Godless sight I have ever witnessed on any battlefield."[9] Von Kluge reported to Berlin: "It's a madhouse here. . . . You can't imagine what it's like."

By July 30 American spearheads had driven to Avranches, the gateway to Brittany and southern Normandy, which "in the summer of 1944 was deemed a prize beyond compare." When this last barrier fell, for the first time since June 6 the German defenses had not only been bent but broken by the Allied attack. Now, with the full weight of two American corps descending on Avranches like a torrent, the moment was at hand to capture the Brittany ports and crush the remnants of the shattered German Seventh Army.

What von Kluge described as "one hell of a mess" became more like a nightmare when the Third Army was unleashed. Field Marshal von Rundstedt, the aged commander in chief west, whose advice was routinely ignored by Hitler and the OKW, when asked by Berlin what ought to be done, bluntly replied: "Make peace, you idiots! What else can you do?"[10]

On August 1 Patton's Third Army officially became operational; Omar Bradley became the commander of the newly activated U.S. 12th Army Group, and was succeeded as First Army commander by another infantryman, Lt. Gen. Courtney Hicks Hodges, a longtime friend from his Fort Benning days. A dignified, soft-spoken Georgian who had entered West Point with Patton in 1904 but had flunked out, Hodges had entered the army as a private soldier, earned a commission, and ascended through the ranks to three-star general. Deeply imbued in the ways of the infantry, Hodges was cautious, tactically unimaginative, and "seemed more worrier than warrior.... When Hodges took over the First Army, the new broom swept nothing."[11] Although both Bradley and Eisenhower heaped praise on Hodges in their postwar memoirs, Russell Weigley notes that "critical associates thought him the reverse of a strong military commander, but instead the model of a rumpled, assertive, small-town banker."[12]

The stunning success of Cobra irrevocably altered the entire Allied concept of a deliberate advance to the Seine. Neither the breakout nor the subsequent pursuit operations across the plains of southern Normandy were ever part of the Allied blueprint for the campaign.[13] What had begun with only modest aspirations had turned into a deep exploitation that suddenly threatened to encircle the German army in Normandy. Within days two American armies swept eastward in the open, rolling country south of the bocage.

Patton was the first to grasp the immense possibilities and was determined to take full advantage of the opportunity to employ the great mobility of his army. "What emerged was a concept quite different from that which had governed operations in the Cotentin," wrote the official army historian:

> Patton saw his immediate objectives far in advance of the front, for his intent was to slash forward and exploit not only the mobility and striking power of his armored divisions but also the German disorganization.... There seemed little point in slowly reducing Brittany by carefully planned and thoroughly supervised operations unraveled in successive phases.[14]

Bradley's gravest concern about Patton was that he would act too aggressively. Ignoring Patton's oft-repeated remark that in pursuit operations his flanks would take care of themselves, Bradley was more cautious and ordered a division diverted to shield First and Third Armies from a possible German reaction. In reality, as Weigley notes, Patton "was not so heedless in such matters as Bradley feared." Independently Patton had given the 5th Armored Division nearly identical orders. With more forces than he required to clear

Brittany, Patton and Bradley both recognized that they had an offensive force capable of accomplishing far more than merely acting as a shield.[15]

There now came a milestone of the kind for which generals are given stars: to decide whether the original Allied master plan to seize Brittany was still more important than taking advantage of the sudden opportunity to drive to the Seine across the unprotected underbelly of Normandy. It was a mission tailor-made for Patton and his Third Army. Time was of the essence.

During these crucial days neither Patton nor Montgomery was in a position to challenge decisions made by Bradley that were firmly endorsed by Eisenhower. Montgomery's image was badly tarnished after Goodwood, which he had deliberately oversold in order to obtain the cooperation of the air chiefs. He was also in Churchill's doghouse—in part through no fault of his own—when the prime minister mistakenly thought a cable sent by Eisenhower forbidding him to visit the front had been sent by Montgomery.[16]

Conversely, Bradley's prestige was growing after Cobra. He found himself "the object of flattery from his fellow Americans, who rarely ceased to remind him of his preeminent place in the campaign. He was, after all, the senior American troop commander on the Continent," notes Martin Blumenson. "He had won his spurs by his victories, he was about to step up to army group, where he would be Montgomery's organizational equal. . . ."[17]

The Germans resisted tenaciously in Brittany, especially when American units attacked the fortress of Brest, which proved an even tougher nut to crack than Cherbourg. As the First and Third Armies poured through the funnel at Avranches, Bradley was not convinced that the German army in Normandy was beaten and, wisely, as it turned out, "was determined to embark on no reckless adventures south-eastwards unless he was certain of holding the Avranches 'elbow' in their rear."[18]

Nevertheless, historian Max Hastings is correct when he criticizes Bradley's lack of imagination in failing to alter the Overlord plan to seize Brittany more quickly, to take advantage of the open door to the east. Even Montgomery envisioned only a single corps being diverted to Brittany, not the two that were employed there.

Patton was convinced he was attacking in entirely the wrong direction when the path to the east was wide open for exploitation. Although he concluded that operations in Brittany could be minimized while the remainder of Third Army drove toward the Seine through the Orléans gap, he felt unable to act aggressively, as he undoubtedly would have had his and Bradley's roles been reversed. His strained relations with Eisenhower and Bradley's unmistakable disdain for his former commander left Patton insecure in his relations with his superiors, and less inclined to challenge either.

It took nearly three critical days for the Allied leadership to scrap its abruptly outmoded master plan to take advantage of Cobra's success. Not until August 3 did Bradley make one of the most important strategic decisions of the war, which, as the U.S. official history records, altered the entire course of the campaign. Patton was ordered to leave VIII Corps to secure Brittany, while the other three corps of Third Army turned eastward to drive toward the Seine. Montgomery immediately concurred, for he too saw that the spectacular success of Cobra had radically changed the entire conception of how operations would be likely to develop. "The main business lies to the east," he told Brooke. Thus, with Eisenhower's blessing, the original Allied strategy of Overlord was scrapped.

Eisenhower's role varied little from what it had been since D-Day. He was a supreme commander who did not control the ground war, and thus temporarily filled the role of a boss whose employees answered to him in name only. As the acting ground commander in chief, Montgomery was responsible for the conduct of the campaign in Normandy, but in reality he never assumed a true command role in his relations with Omar Bradley. The two generals coordinated their actions with each other but otherwise each fought his own battles in his own way. For all practical purposes Bradley was virtually autonomous, and Eisenhower's role was even further reduced to that of an engrossed observer. It was a role he intensely disliked but believed he should do nothing to alter until the timing was right.

Montgomery's affinity for Eisenhower had not changed, but his respect for Eisenhower's generalship was rapidly diminishing. His diary for July 29 reflected:

I went over to see Bradley at First U.S. Army HQ. Eisenhower was there, and we had a talk. Ike is not an easy person to have listening in when you are having a conference with your subordinates; he cannot stop "butting in" and talking—always at the top of his voice!! He is so keen that you cannot be angry with him; but he is a nuisance. I like him very much but I could never live in the same house with him; he cannot talk calmly and quietly.[19]

The great success of Cobra failed to calm Eisenhower. On August 2 he seemed exultant; "[W]e are to hell and gone in Brittany and slicing 'em up in Normandy." Two days later Butcher found him "impatient, repeat impatient, and I mean impatient."[20] Part of his restlessness was his role on the sidelines as little more than a glorified spectator; another was directed at Patton's offensive into Brittany, which he mistakenly believed "will fall like a ripe apple."

The capture of Brest had been intended to relieve the logistical problem of resupplying what by the end of the Normandy campaign was more than two million Allied troops. Yet its vast distance from the front posed problems of its own. Before D-Day the SHAEF planners had decided that the Brittany ports were vital, and the Normandy campaign had been mapped out with deliberation so that the logisticians could keep pace with the advancing armies. The whole concept had fallen victim to Cobra, but only after Brest fell in September did they conclude that the port was simply too far away to be of much use. Ultimately Brittany became a monument to the notion that in war campaigns rarely evolve as planned.

On August 7 Eisenhower moved into his advanced command post in a Norman apple orchard approximately twelve miles southwest of Bayeux, near the village of Tournières. Known by its code-name, Shellburst, it was surrounded by hedgerows and was the usual crude arrangement Eisenhower favored, consisting of tents and a few trailers. His office was in a tent with a board floor and was utterly lacking in privacy. Nearby were slit trenches in the event of an air attack. "There are few secrets that can be kept by General Ike," noted Butcher, "for his voice can be heard for rods around as he dictates or telephones." Butcher soon christened the place "Grand Central Station in the Apple Orchard."

During his trips around the Normandy countryside in the company of Bradley or some other general, Eisenhower would typically stop by the side of the road for a quiet picnic lunch. Although Eisenhower was now based in Normandy he could not escape from Churchill, who arrived on August 8 to reopen the debate in yet another last-ditch effort to persuade Eisenhower to cancel the Riviera landings and, he said, reap far greater rewards by leaving Alexander's divisions intact for operations in northern Italy and Yugoslavia. Ultimately, Eisenhower's refusal to cancel Anvil/Dragoon proved to be enormously important. The great port of Marseilles would not only be captured undamaged but become a logistical bonanza. The destruction wrought by the Transportation Plan did not include the French railway system in the Rhone Valley, which was left largely undamaged and instantly became a primary means of resupplying Eisenhower's armies during the autumn and winter of 1944–45.[21]

In early August, Eisenhower's unending "war" with Winston Churchill over the Riviera landings reached a crescendo. Although the date for the landings was barely more than a week off, Eisenhower still had a major fight on his hands with Churchill, who arrived at Shellburst for discussions on August 7. All was calm at lunch as the prime minister delighted in feeding milk to Eisenhower's resident pet, a black kitten named Shaef. But the discussion under the canvas tent turned serious when Churchill employed American battle tactics in an attempt to wear Eisenhower down. The arguments raged for some six hours. The more Churchill cajoled and pleaded, the more strongly Eisenhower resisted. Noted Butcher, "Ike said no, continued saying no all afternoon, and ended saying no in every form of the English language at his command. . . . Ike's position was that sound strategy called for making the Germans fight on as many fronts as possible. . . . he was practically limp when the PM departed," with the last words on the subject yet to be heard. Exhausted but unbowed Eisenhower felt secure in the knowledge that he had the full backing of Marshall, King, and Arnold, and—most important of all— Roosevelt. "I will not repeat not under any conditions agree . . . to a cancellation of Dragoon," he stubbornly informed Marshall.[22]

Eisenhower was nevertheless obliged to endure a fresh Churchill harangue at No. 10 Downing Street the following day, August 9, when an impassioned PM declared that the Americans, who now fully dominated the war in Europe, were "bullying" the British and, having become "a big, strong and dominating partner," were failing to listen to the strategic ideas of their ally. Therefore "he might have to go to the Monarch and 'lay down the mantle of [his] high office.' "[23] Eisenhower, who for more than two years had experienced every variation of Churchill's wiles, refused to budge. If Eisenhower seemed cold and unmoved to Churchill, he was, in fact, deeply troubled by their August 9 meeting. Two days later he wrote to Churchill to note "the depth of my distress" and to reaffirm that "I do not for one moment believe that there is any desire on the part of any responsible person in the American war machine to disregard British views, or cold-bloodedly to leave Britain holding an empty bag in any of our joint undertakings."[24]

Eisenhower's words may have reassured the prime minister about their strong personal relationship, but nothing could mask the fact that Britain was now irreversibly the junior partner in the alliance it had once dominated. Their differences notwithstanding, the great debate between the irresistible force and the immovable object was at last mercifully ended. When Ismay came to dinner the day of the Dragoon landings, Eisenhower could look back on his draining experience with Churchill with humor, much like "two admiring sons discussing a cantankerous yet adorable father."[25]

At his first press conference at Shellburst, held the morning of August 15, Eisenhower revealed for the first time that Patton was in France commanding the Third Army. The duplicity of Fortitude had exceeded everyone's wildest dreams of success, and Patton's presence could no longer be concealed. Eisenhower also "vehemently castigated those who think they can measure the end of the war 'in a matter of weeks.' " It proved to be a warning hardly anyone would heed. The very success enjoyed by U.S. forces, given enormous publicity by the American press, led Stimson and Marshall to exhort Eisenhower at once to assume full command of the ground forces from Montgomery. Again refusing to be stampeded into acting precipitously, Eisenhower declined to alter his original timetable of assuming command when the Allies reached the Seine.

.   .   .

August 15 was another landmark day of the war. A great fleet of 2,000 Allied warships and landing craft, carrying 151,000 American, British, Canadian, and French soldiers, appeared off the coast of the French Riviera, the largest such force ever to sail the Mediterranean. The sands of Nice, Saint-Tropez, Cannes, and the other plush resorts lining the Riviera, once noted for expensive yachts and amenities fit for royalty, became the landing sites for what has been called "the other D-Day." Pristine beaches where scantily clad women once swam had been fortified with pillboxes, gun emplacements, mines, booby-traps, and underwater obstacles.

Unable to influence Eisenhower or the United States to cripple or cancel Dragoon, Churchill elected to witness what he had been denied in June in Normandy. Churchill was still asleep when the landings commenced, but later, from the deck of the destroyer HMS *Kimberley*, on the morning of August 14, the PM, his trademark cigar stub firmly clamped in his mouth, was recognized by American GIs on nearby landing craft, who cheered, "Winnie! Winnie!" They had no idea that if Churchill had had his way, none of them would have been there that day. Unyielding to the end, he continued to insist that, on strategic questions, "Eisenhower's operations [in Normandy] have been a diversion for this landing instead of the other way round." Had he gotten his way, said Churchill, the August landings would have taken place at Saint-Nazaire. As for Operation Dragoon, "One of my reasons for making public my visit was to associate myself with this well-conducted but irrelevant and unrelated operation," he wrote dismissively to Clementine.[26]

The bulk of the landing force consisted of Lucian Truscott's U.S. VI Corps and its veteran divisions of the Anzio beachhead, (the primary element of Lt. Gen. Alexander M. Patch's U.S. Seventh Army) and a French army commanded by Gen. Jean-Marie de Lattre de Tassigny. The landings were preceded by days of Allied bombing raids on Toulon and other military targets in southern France. The enormous naval bombardment was accompanied by airborne and glider landings that suffered heavy losses from both enemy action and misplaced drops. With minor exceptions the amphibious landings were unhindered, and the defenders, mostly Poles conscripted from German POW camps to serve as frontline cannon fodder, were either killed or surrendered after token resistance. Churchill found the landings boring and retired to his cabin to read a novel. Eisenhower was merely relieved that Dragoon had been successfully carried out.

Within a short time Patch's army and de Lattre's French First Army were driving up the Rhone Valley against only token opposition. Patch's troops liberated Grenoble on August 23, the same day French forces captured Marseilles and its great port. By September 12 the Dragoon force had linked up with Patton's Third Army near Dijon to form the third of Eisenhower's army groups: the 6th, commanded by Lt. Gen. Jake Devers. Although Eisenhower went out of his way to explain to Marshall that "I have nothing in the world against General Devers," the truth was that Jake Devers would never become a member of Club Eisenhower nor would his advice as 6th Army Group commander ever carry the weight of friends like Bradley.[27]

The first week of August was the most decisive period of the Normandy campaign: Not only were the Allies poised to deliver a killing blow, but it was the week when Hitler personally sealed the fate of his forces in Normandy by committing an astonishing miscalculation. As First and Third Armies advanced east, Hitler arbitrarily ordered a powerful armored counterstroke against Avranches, which he believed would cut off and isolate all American forces that had advanced beyond the town. Over strenuous protests that he had nothing resembling the forces required and that failure inevitably meant catastrophe, von Kluge was ordered by Hitler to attack the First Army at Mortain.

The German attack on August 6–7 was repulsed by the heroic stand of the U.S. 30th Division at Hill 317, which the VII Corps commander, J. Lawton Collins, called "one of the outstanding small-unit actions of World War II."[28] It was also Bradley's finest hour as a commander. Instead of splitting the U.S. First and Third Armies, Hitler's blunder left the German Seventh Army and elements of the Fifth Panzer Army exposed and in grave jeopardy of encirclement. Hitler's response was to sack von Kluge and order his recall to Germany. Known to have had prior knowledge of the July 20 plot, von Kluge committed suicide by the side of a road near Metz rather than face one of Hitler's so-called People's Courts and likely death by hanging. He was replaced by the officer known as "Hitler's fireman," Field Marshal Walther Model, a commander known for his prowess at rescuing the German army on the eastern front from impossible situations. This time, however, even Model could not pull the rabbit from his hat. The situation was already too far out of hand by the time he arrived.

Montgomery opened two major offensives in early August: a drive to capture Falaise by Lieutenant General Crerar's Canadian First Army, and another farther west by Dempsey's British Second Army. Together the two armies would pivot to their left and drive east while the U.S. First and Third Armies thrust across the open southern flank and trapped Army Group B in a double envelopment along the river Seine. This was the so-called long envelopment.

However, as Patton sped east across southern Normandy, and First Army checked the German counterthrust, Mortain suddenly changed the thinking of Bradley and Eisenhower. Maj. Gen. Wade Haislip's XV Corps was spearheading the Third Army drive east and was already outside Le Mans. The failure of the Mortain attack had left the Germans trapped in a pocket from which the only escape was to retreat eastward before the open neck closed between Argentan in the south and Falaise in the north. Bradley reasoned that if he could quickly swing XV Corps behind the Germans in the direction of Alençon and Argentan, in what he termed a "short [left] hook," the Allies might be able to trap and annihilate all German forces inside in the jaws of a pocket between the Canadians advancing toward Falaise and Haislip's corps.

An exultant Bradley briefed visiting Secretary of the Treasury Henry Morgenthau that he had "an opportunity that comes to a commander not more than once in a century. . . . We're about to destroy an entire hostile army. . . . We'll go all the way from here to the German border."[29] Eisenhower enthusiastically endorsed Bradley's change of plan, which would later spawn one of the greatest controversies of the war, the one centering on the misnamed Falaise pocket.

Although Montgomery was confident of his ability to close the pocket, by August 9, the Canadians were barely halfway to Falaise, and their advance had met with deadly opposition and become a bloodbath. Like the earlier protracted battles for Caen, renewed attacks to punch through to Falaise were unsuccessful. By August 13 Haislip was less than twenty-five miles south of the Canadians. Patton foresaw that the Canadians could not close the gap quickly, and on the night of August 12, he directed XV Corps to capture Argentan and then push slowly north toward Falaise. When Bradley learned of Patton's intentions he made the most controversial decision of the campaign by ordering Haislip to halt at Argentan.

Although Allied aircraft were wreaking severe damage on the retreating Germans, Bradley would not relent, fearing that Patton's forces might be caught in the middle of a certain and very determined German attempt to break free of the trap. He later defended his decision by arguing that he was fearful of a deadly collision with the Canadians, and "much preferred a solid shoulder at Argentan to the possibility of a broken neck at Falaise. The decision to stop Patton was mine alone; it never went beyond my CP."[30]

On August 14 Hitler reluctantly accepted the urgent necessity for withdrawal before his forces inside the pocket were annihilated. Two more days elapsed before the Germans began organizing their withdrawal to the east in a desperate bid to escape the Allied trap. When the Canadians finally captured Falaise late on August 16, after one of the most bitter series of battles fought in Normandy, there was still a fifteen-mile gap between the U.S. and Canadian armies.

Two strategic options were open to the Allied ground commanders: the so-called short hook (Bradley's original intention), and the long envelopment to the east envisioned by both Montgomery and Patton. Although Montgomery was committed to closing the pocket, he appears to have viewed the problem in broader terms of reference; that is, to prevent the Germans from escaping en masse if the gap continued to remain open, which looked more and more certain with each passing day. This meant deploying a suitably strong blocking force along the Seine to prevent a German escape across the river, something that could be accomplished only by dint of a long envelopment by Bradley. The choice had existed since August 8, and it represented Montgomery's preferred strategy.

However, with both Bradley and Eisenhower favoring the short hook, Montgomery was in an awkward position. Refusal would have created yet another storm of controversy and pressures from above he could ill afford in the wake of Goodwood. He therefore left the decision to Bradley. However, there was no assurance that Bradley or Montgomery could close the trap and destroy the German army inside. And, without a blocking force somewhere to the east, preferably at the Seine, the undertaking was little better than a colossal gamble. Finally, with intelligence revealing that the Germans had already begun to break out to the east and safety, Bradley elected (with Patton's blessing) to send two of Haislip's divisions on a dash to the east to establish blocking positions along the Seine. At the same time, with German resistance collapsing everywhere, the Canadian army and Dempsey's British Second Army began a similar drive to block the Seine.

As Third Army swept relentlessly toward the Seine, liberating growing numbers of French cities and towns in rapid succession, the distinction between Patton and Hodges became plain. "Hodges's First Army was more than twice the size of Patton's and had far more armor in it, but it was Patton who came to symbolize the ultimate in pursuit."[31] Philosophically the two could not have been more different: Patton the dashing cavalryman, Hodges the dour, unimaginative infantryman whose thinking and training did not extend to future battles or taking risks. Yet, both Eisenhower and Bradley, with their natural infantryman's parochialism for one of their own, would later praise Hodges as superior to Patton.[32]

By August 14 it was clear that the Argentan-Falaise pocket would never be closed in time. Although Montgomery made a determined effort to capture Falaise and close the original pocket, he was already advancing his own options by exhorting Crerar to seal it farther east, where he hoped to block the only remaining corridor of escape still left open, a narrow valley between the farming villages of Trun and Chambois.

The Polish 1st Armored Division, attached to the Canadian First Army, and elements of a Canadian corps were sent toward Trun and Chambois to establish blocking positions. In so doing Montgomery signaled his growing belief that the pocket could still be plugged at those villages. "These are great days," he wrote to the secretary of state for war, Sir James Grigg. "We have the great bulk of the German forces partially surrounded; some will of course escape, but I do not see how they can stand and fight seriously again this side of the Seine."[33]

A Polish armored brigade occupied the commanding high ground east of

Chambois, called Mount Ormel. They discovered the valley below filled with thousands of soldiers, most on foot, desperate to escape before the trap closed. Aware through daily radio contact of the slaughter of their countrymen in the Warsaw ghetto, the Poles on Mount Ormel thirsted for revenge. Although they were surrounded for three days and all contact with the Canadians was lost, they nevertheless inflicted a terrible toll on their enemy before being rescued by a Canadian tank force just as their food, water, and ammunition ran out. The battle for Mount Ormel was the among the least known and most ferocious in a campaign where savagery was an everyday occurrence. The valley between the villages of Trun and Chambois became a wasteland of dead Germans and burned, broken, and smashed equipment, earning it the grisly designation of the *chemin du couloir de la mort*, the corridor of death.[34]

On August 19 U.S. and Canadian troops slammed shut the final escape route between Trun and Chambois. Those Germans who had escaped were bombed, strafed, and harassed unmercifully as they attempted to find sanctuary east of the Seine. The vestiges of what had once been the German Seventh Army and the Fifth Panzer Army took very little with them. In one instance a column of some three thousand vehicles was destroyed. Of the nearly eighty thousand Germans thought to have been originally trapped in the two pockets, at least ten thousand perished and an estimated fifty thousand were taken prisoner. Most formations simply disappeared, as German troops fled individually and in small groups toward the Seine. Of the fifty divisions in action in June, only ten could still be described as fighting units.[35]

While the fighting raged inside the pocket, Patton's *corps de chasse* sliced across southern Normandy against little opposition. Le Mans, Orleans, Chartres, and Dreux all fell to the Third Army, while to the north First Army began a series of drives also aimed at blocking the Seine. An ebullient Patton's self-confidence soared during this period, which he called "a damned fine war!" Third Army had moved so quickly since August 1 that his command post had to be relocated farther forward virtually every night, leading to an ongoing joke about one-night stands. A delighted Henry L. Stimson euphorically observed that Patton had "set his tanks to run around in France 'like bedbugs in a Georgetown kitchen.' "[36] On August 26 Eisenhower received a cable from Patton that read: "Dear Ike, To-day I spat in the Seine."[37]

Hitler's blunder at Mortain and Bradley's decision to envelop and entrap German forces at Argentan-Falaise marked the end of the Normandy campaign, and resulted in one of the most crushing and decisive victories ever attained by the Allies during World War II. Other than mopping-up operations, four Allied armies were in hot pursuit of the survivors. For a brief time France was virtually undefended all the way to the western wall of the German Reich.

The scope of the German defeat, starkly visible around Trun, St-Lambert, and Chambois, was one of the most appalling scenes of the war. The area was littered with unburied dead, thousands of dead horses and cattle, and smashed and burning vehicles. The totality of the German defeat is evident in the grisly photographs of the death and destruction wrought by the Allies, and in the tormented faces of the survivors. The powerful stench of death reached hundreds of feet in the air to sicken the pilots of Allied spotter planes.[38] "If every civilian in the world could smell this stink, then maybe we wouldn't have any more wars," said a British graves registration NCO.[39] A British account, aptly titled *The Killing Ground*, described how "[i]n the hot August sun . . . there was no dignity of death. In the worst bombarded areas fragments of bodies festooned the trees. . . . Some roads were impassable due to the congestion caused by burnt-out trucks, dead horses, smashed tanks and destruction on a scale which the Western Allies had never seen."[40] German disarray was typified by the example of one British corps, which took prisoners from thirteen different divisions southeast of Falaise.

Eisenhower was horrified and described it as unquestionably one of the greatest killing grounds of the war. "Forty-eight hours after the closing of the gap I was conducted through it on foot, to encounter scenes that could be described only by Dante. It was literally possible to walk for hundreds of yards at a time, stepping on nothing but dead and decaying flesh."[41] Montgomery called the carnage around Trun "almost unbelievable."[42]

The German generals who fought there were in no doubt as to the extent of their crushing defeat and who was responsible. Shortly before committing suicide, von Kluge wrote to Hitler in a last-ditch attempt to convince the Führer of the futility of further resistance by the Germans in the west. His plea fell upon deaf ears; instead von Kluge's suicide served to convince Hitler not only of his complicity in the plot on his life, but that he was a defeatist who would have sooner surrendered than fight on.[43] Yet even the most ardent Nazi commanders expressed German rage and frustration over their humiliating defeat. Kurt Meyer, the fanatical commander of the 12th SS Panzer Division, called Hitler's decisions "crass folly," and one of his favorites, SS Gen. Josef "Sepp" Dietrich, declared: "There was only one person to blame for this stupid, impossible operation. That madman Adolf Hitler."[44]

Although the Normandy campaign ended on a note of triumph for the Allies, it also marked the beginning of the worst quarrels and greatest controversies of the war in Europe. Montgomery would repeatedly clash with Eisenhower over Allied command and strategy east of the Seine; Patton would rage at Eisenhower for denying him supplies, ammunition, and precious fuel for his vehicles, believing he could have won the war in 1944; and what had been merely disapprobation and resentment of Montgomery by Bradley would erupt into an irreparable spilt during the German counteroffensive in the Ardennes in December.

45.

Triumph and Controversy

In war . . . things happen differently from what
we expected, and look differently when near
from what they did at a distance.
— CLAUSEWITZ

The eighty-day Normandy campaign can be said to have officially ended on August 25, 1944, the day that four Allied armies established themselves along the Seine. This date also marked the liberation of Paris after more than four years of German occupation. What was for the world a great day was for Eisenhower a stomach-churning experience. Once again it brought him into conflict with Charles de Gaulle.

With the collapse of the German army the road to Paris was wide open to Bradley's two armies. Paris and what to do about it became one of Eisenhower's primary headaches. His intention was to bypass the city, which he deemed of no military value. Notes Geoffrey Perret, "He didn't need it, didn't want it, and whatever he did, he couldn't be drawn into fighting a street battle."[1] Moreover, should Eisenhower become entangled in Paris, it would inevitably commit him to feeding its near-starving population of two million and draining other precious commodities, such as gasoline, that he could not spare to keep the city resupplied. Already the supply line from Cherbourg to the Seine was 250 miles long. Any diversions to Paris might well impede the Allied advance to the wide-open German border and perhaps change the course of the war. In short, Eisenhower found himself on the horns of a new dilemma that promised few benefits and a multitude of problems, including the possible destruction of the city in a prolonged fight with the German garrison. The obvious answer lay in finding some means of persuading the Germans to surrender the city.

Paris became a precursor to Berlin. Eisenhower's insistence that politics and war did not mix was a throwback to his West Point days. He had fought Churchill and Roosevelt over this issue, and, as de Gaulle's biographer notes, "[H]is successes as supreme commander had rested on his

refusal to countenance for political considerations or pressures any altera-
tion or adjustment in his *military* plans."[2] In Eisenhower's world nothing
was that simple or straightforward. Soon he began receiving disturbing
intelligence that the Germans would fight if he bypassed the city, but that if
he elected to capture it, Paris would fall easily. Then events within the City
of Light dictated Eisenhower's next move.

At first Bradley thought the Germans would fight for the city, and Hitler
demanded it be held at all costs. "History," he said, "showed that the loss of
Paris meant the loss of all France." Hitler's "never or only as a heap of rubble
must Paris fall into Allied hands" edict to the city's new occupation commander, Gen. Dietrich von Choltitz, seemed to confirm German intentions
not to surrender the city.[3] A Prussian with a ruthless reputation and a track
record to match, Choltitz might well have carried out his orders had he not
personally been summoned before Hitler after the July 20 assassination
attempt and found him drooling, drugged, and in Choltitz's opinion, a raving
lunatic. The experience convinced him that Germany had lost the war, and
that wantonly destroying Paris would be barbaric: The threats to do so were
a bluff. Although ordered by OKW to destroy each of the city's seventy-odd
bridges, its factories, and every major Paris landmark (including the Eiffel
Tower, Nôtre-Dame cathedral, and the Arc de Triomphe), Choltitz insisted
to his captors that he had "taken no great steps to do so."

The partisan forces of the Resistance (French Forces of the Interior, or
FFI) were a tangled web of conflicting loyalties and political allegiances held
together only by a common aim to rid France of the Germans. Led by Gen.
Pierre Koenig, the FFI was nominally under the wing of SHAEF, and the
London-based Koenig reported to Eisenhower, with whom he had established
cordial relations. Although well aware of Koenig's loyalty to de Gaulle, Eisenhower trusted him. With full-scale street fighting under way on August 20
against the Germans, Choltitz responded by cutting off all power and food
supplies. Choltitz's bluff was taken very seriously, and it therefore seemed
inevitable that he would not hesitate to issue an order to destroy the city.
Swedish consul general Raoul Nordling intervened to broker a cease-fire and
attempted to persuade Choltitz to surrender Paris.

Through Nordling, Choltitz indicated that he was amenable to surrendering Paris to the Allies. He did not, said Choltitz, wish to be remembered
as "the man who destroyed Paris." His refusal to surrender to the FFI included
a justifiable fear that he would be executed. He would, however, surrender
the city to the Allies and openly abetted Nordling's attempts to broker a
surrender. A courier from the Paris Resistance turned up at Patton's forward
CP near Chartres with what he said was "a mission to General Eisenhower."
After hearing their story Patton sent the party to Bradley, who agreed that
Paris could no longer be ignored.

The liberation of Paris posed differing dilemmas for both Eisenhower and de Gaulle. The latter was deeply concerned about separate, known plots by the Vichyite and communist factions to seize control of the city. Eisenhower had already wisely decided that Maj. Gen. Jacques Philippe Leclerc's French 2nd Armored Division would spearhead the liberation of Paris. However, de Gaulle's arrival in France from Algiers on August 20 turned up the heat on Eisenhower. The insurrection in Paris was already under way when the two men met later that day in Eisenhower's tent at Shellburst. Eisenhower recalled the Frenchman's warning: "He made no bones about it; he said there was a serious menace from the Communists in the city, and that if we delayed moving in we would risk finding a disastrous political situation, one that might be disruptive to the Allied war effort."[4] De Gaulle was insistent that the Allies take immediate steps to liberate Paris. Specifically he wanted Eisenhower to send Leclerc's division into Paris at once, noting that he thought any German resistance would melt under a move against the city. De Gaulle followed up his demands the following day with a letter in which he politely but firmly threatened to order Leclerc to take Paris should Eisenhower fail to do so, pointing out that Leclerc would be expected to carry out orders from his own government.[5] As if to prod Eisenhower to action, the BBC broadcast a report on August 23 that the city had already fallen.[6] Bradley agreed with de Gaulle, noting his concurrence with his intelligence officer's assessment that "we can and must walk in."[7] After conferring with Koenig, Eisenhower reluctantly came to the same conclusion, scribbling a note to Bedell Smith in the margin of de Gaulle's letter: "It looks as if we'd be compelled to go into Paris."[8]

The sight of French troops led to an excess of celebration and too little progress, as they were showered along the way with wine and joyous exultation. An angry Bradley had seen enough. "To hell with prestige," he said to his chief of staff, "tell the 4th [Division] to slam on in and take the liberation." Leclerc instantly got the message; "his troopers mounted their tanks and burned up their treads on the brick roads" to Paris.[9]

Leclerc's spearheads entered Paris on August 24, and early the following afternoon Choltitz was captured and signed a surrender document even as heavy street fighting raged throughout the city. Hitler raged and demanded of Col. Gen. Alfred Jodl, his chief of staff, "Is Paris burning?" Upon learning it was not, he ordered V-2 rockets and German artillery turned on the city. General Speidel ignored the order.

De Gaulle arrived on the afternoon of August 25 and promptly went to the Arc de Triomphe and placed a wreath in the shape of the Cross of Lorraine on the tomb of France's unknown soldier of World War I. The eternal flame was relit for the first time since the dark days of 1940. Eisenhower had authorized the transfer of the French 2nd Armored Division from Third Army to First Army, where it was attached to Gerow's V Corps. The following day Leclerc's division paraded down the Champs-Élysées, angering Gerow, who wanted the division committed to combat, but was helpless to pry them from Paris. Eisenhower agreed to leave the division in the city for the time being in order to provide de Gaulle with a show of strength and the means to enforce it. "I have given you Leclerc; surely I can have him back for a moment, can't I?" de Gaulle is reputed to have said.[10]

Paris was free, and shortly de Gaulle would be in control of France's new provisional government. Eisenhower deliberately stayed away in order not to steal the limelight from de Gaulle and the French in their hour of triumph. Believing he would not attract much attention on a Sunday morning, Eisenhower arrived in Paris on August 27, a picture-perfect day, his first visit to the city since 1929. With Kay Summersby at the wheel, his armored Cadillac passed through French villages festooned with American, British, and French flags, and on his face was what Mickey McKeogh called his "happy smile." Everywhere Eisenhower was showered with cheers, flowers, and the V-for-victory symbol made famous by Churchill.

In Paris they were met at the Porte d'Orléans by General Koenig and escorted to de Gaulle's headquarters. Bradley was present, and Montgomery had been invited to attend but declined, saying he was too busy pushing his armies to the Seine. Eisenhower found de Gaulle deeply concerned over how to feed the huge population of Paris. That Eisenhower decided to call on de Gaulle was a gesture of tribute from one soldier to another, in full knowledge that he was openly defying the wishes of Roosevelt, who had as yet refused to accept the reality that Charles de Gaulle would head the new Free French government. "I did this very deliberately," said Eisenhower, "as a kind of de facto recognition of him as the provisional President of France. He was very grateful—he never forgot that," and "looked upon it as . . . a very definite recognition of his high political position and his place. That was of course what he wanted and what Roosevelt had never given him."[11]

At the Arc de Triomphe, the two generals paid their ceremonial respects to the unknown soldier. The Champs-Elysées, where for four years only the sound of German jackboots was heard, was filled with thousands of Parisians. The swastikas that had hung from the Arc de Triomphe had been replaced by an enormous tricolor. A great roar went up as Eisenhower was instantly recognized. "*Eisenhower! Eisenhower!*" they chanted in unison as military police attempted to clear a path through the cheering crowd. A very large Frenchman managed to collar Eisenhower and plant wet kisses on each of his cheeks. "The crowd squealed in delight," recalled Bradley, "as Ike reddened and fought free." Bradley fled to his jeep, which roared off, leaving his superior to fend for himself. Nevertheless, Bradley did not escape the kisses of a Frenchwoman, who left his cheeks smeared with lipstick. When he was kidded about it by his aide he laughingly replied, "Better than the one General Eisenhower got."[12] As Eisenhower's Cadillac, its four stars gleaming in the bright sunlight and small British, French, and American flags flapping from the radiator cap, moved along the Champs-Elysées in low gear, people shouted his name and attempted to reach through the open windows to touch or kiss him. Eisenhower was touched and could not resist giving them the full measure of his famous grin.[13] He was the symbol of the Allies, and they adored him. (Curiously, although it was one of the most moving events of his life, Eisenhower barely mentioned in his wartime memoirs his visit to Paris on that memorable day.)

In additional to logistical help, de Gaulle asked Eisenhower to provide a show of American force in the form of two U.S. divisions as a means of reassuring the Parisians and establishing his own authority over a nervous city. With Bradley's concurrence, Eisenhower authorized two divisions headed east toward Lorraine to pass directly through Paris instead of around its outskirts. As they marched through Paris, Eisenhower said, they would do so in a ceremonial victory march. Would General de Gaulle care to review them? While Eisenhower declined to be present out of respect for de Gaulle, and to avoid offending British sensibilities, Bradley would be present on the reviewing platform to exemplify American unity with France. The 28th Division, followed by some units of the 5th Armored, marched victoriously through the liberated capital, and before the day ended, were engaged in pitched battles with the Germans east of Paris.

Paris may have been free, but Parisians were hungry and lacked precious coal and oil for cooking. With barely twenty-four hours worth of food on hand, Eisenhower had no choice but to earmark material for a resupply effort that faced the same problem beginning to plague his armies: a growing shortage of fuel and transport. The U.S. official historian notes, "More than a month and a half after the liberation of Paris, French relief was still a consequential Allied military responsibility."[14]

As for the liberation itself, it "was as much a Franco-American conflict as an Allied-German struggle. The French secured almost all they wanted by convincing a reluctant, but in the end, amenable, Allied command to do their bidding. The restoration of French dignity, implicit in the liberation, had come about largely through French efforts sustained by Allied complaisance."[15]

Strong anti-British feelings, similar resentments (which even the relief supplies failed to dissipate) that the presence of American troops had stolen some of the limelight from the French, and the Byzantine politics of the liberation were all reasons why Eisenhower would have preferred to distance himself as far as possible from the French. Some of the British press sniffed that the Americans seemed to possess an inordinate love of parades, eventually retracting their stories when it was learned there were no British troops anywhere near Paris that could have participated. For Eisenhower it was merely the latest reminder that pleasing allies was a thankless task, and the liberation of Paris just another example of the untidiness and unpredictability of war.

•   •   •

During the eighty days of the Normandy campaign more than 600,000 combatants on both sides were killed or wounded, the bulk of them German—an estimated 200,000 killed or wounded and another 200,000 captured.[16] The legacy of the final battle for Normandy was not the triumph of a liberated Paris, but bitterness and controversy that the Allies had somehow squandered an opportunity of epic proportions. Montgomery has generally emerged as the culprit for supposedly failing to spur his advance to a faster pace to close the gap before the remnants of what had once been Rommel's Army Group B could escape across the Seine. The result has been unfounded charges and countercharges, all designed to support a particular point of view. The truth was far more complex.

The Battle of the Falaise Gap (a term not coined until after the war) was arguably a significant event. The fact that an unknown number of Germans did manage to elude the Allied trap resulted in postwar accounts, written for their sensational value rather than for historical accuracy, alleging a great Allied blunder. While the exact figures will never be conclusively established, the official U.S. history points out that even before the Germans began their retreat, some nonessential personnel and equipment had been moved toward the Seine. "Later estimates of the total number of Germans escaping varied between 20,000 and 40,000 men, but combat troops formed by far the smaller portion of these troops. The average combat strength of divisions was no more than a few hundred men."[17]

All but ignored by those who have charged the Allied high command with various sins was not only the documented losses but what the Germans themselves had to say about the final battle of the Normandy campaign. U.S. official historian Martin Blumenson revealed that very little matériel was saved, and that only "seven armored divisions managed to get the infinitesimal total of 1,300 men, 24 tanks and 60 artillery pieces of varying caliber across the Seine. The German remnants east of the Seine, lacking armament, equipment, even demolitions to destroy bridges behind them, could do nothing more than retreat toward Germany."[18]

Gen. Hans Speidel, Rommel's chief of staff, supported this assessment, noting that "there were barely a hundred tanks left out of six panzer divisions." Field Marshal Walther Model reported: "Five decimated divisions returned to Germany. The remains of 11 infantry divisions allowed us to regroup 4 units, each with a handful of field guns and other minor equipment. All that remained of eleven armored divisions when replenished with personnel and matériel amounted to eleven regiments, each with 5 or 6 tanks and a few artillery batteries." Other German veterans delivered similar assessments.

Whatever failure there may have been to close the noose sooner had as much to do with German will to survive as with the lapses in Allied generalship. What is routinely overlooked is that Germans in both pockets (first between Argentan and Falaise, and later between Trun and Chambois), even in disarray, comprised an extremely dangerous and tenacious fighting force that was struggling for its very survival. The Polish and Canadian experience during the murderous battles around Trun, Saint-Lambert, Chambois, and on Mount Ormel offers stark counterpoint to the accusation that failing to close the two pockets, and thereby crushing all German forces within, was even possible, much less a great missed opportunity. The overflowing POW camps and the thousands of corpses strewing the landscape of death told an entirely different tale.[19]

The furor over Montgomery's alleged failure to carry out his intended strategy in Normandy has obscured a basic truth that warfare is not an exact science, and battles and campaigns rarely evolve as they are projected on paper. A great deal of the criticism leveled at Montgomery was provoked by his ill-conceived, single-minded assertion, both at the time and after the war, that "I never once had cause or reason to alter my master plan," while contradictorily admitting, "It had been my intention to secure the high ground between Caen and Falaise as early as possible . . . and when I found it could not be in accordance with the original plan without suffering unjustified casualties, I did not proceed with that venture. This was not popular with the Air Command."[20]

What got Montgomery into trouble in Normandy was that he instilled false hopes in the minds of Churchill, Eisenhower, and the other senior commanders that he would capture Caen on D-Day. It apparently never dawned on Montgomery that his promise would be used as a wedge by his enemies in an attempt to rid themselves of the general they detested. If there was a single, consistent Allied failure in Normandy that distinguished the campaign, it was that Eisenhower and Bradley, and to some extent Montgomery himself, disregarded Napoleon's principle that battles are fought to destroy the enemy, not to capture terrain, an omission that was to manifest itself again in August. As one historian points out, "All three senior commanders failed to grasp that the most important strategic objective of the campaign was the elimination of German forces in Normandy."[21]

Patton wrongly believed that Montgomery was his rival for the headlines and the glory. Montgomery, in fact, exercised command of the Allied ground armies "with exquisite discretion and tact, never interfering with Bradley's tactical arrangements and tacitly supporting his prudent directives," noted one of Patton's biographers, Ladislas Farago. "But at the same time he did nothing to restrain Patton and, in fact, gave him a free hand even when and where Bradley sought to stop him or slow him down." Montgomery also made it clear in his frequent praise of Patton to Brooke that he was pleased with the performance of Third Army and that of its commander.[22]

There is considerable merit to the suggestion that had Patton commanded

12th Army Group—as indeed he would have had he not so significantly self-destructed his career in Sicily—the events of August 1944 would have been very different. Martin Blumenson has concluded that "their problem of accommodating their distinctly different styles and outlooks was a contributory cause of why the Allies [later] faltered."[23]

The specious arguments that have proliferated since the war have generally focused on the wrong aspect of the battles—Bradley's original decision to attempt to trap the remnants of the abortive Mortain counter-offensive in the so-called Argentan-Falaise pocket. Blumenson's lucidly argued, scathing indictment of Bradley's indecisive generalship at the end of the Normandy campaign notes that he vacillated repeatedly over what he wanted to do, and then botched what decisions he did make. But, worst of all, Bradley elected to halt Third Army at the Seine and at Dreux, Chartres, and Orleans

> and thereby slowed the tempo of achievement. He permitted Patton to gain a bridgehead over the Seine at Mantes, then forbade him to reap the benefits of the action, nullifying Patton's wish to fashion a potent pincer. Finally, he let Patton charge off toward Germany even though the main work lay west of the Seine.

Bradley's generalship was "troubled by doubt. He made instant decisions, then second-guessed himself. . . . He initiated potentially brilliant maneuvers, then aborted them because he lacked confidence in his ability to see them through to completion."[24]

Behind his mild-mannered facade, Bradley bore grudges longer and with far more vehemence than Patton. He never forgave Montgomery for trespassing across his boundary line in Sicily, and made no effort in Normandy to find common ground in such situations as existed in August 1944.

As he had been since the D-Day landings, Eisenhower was more spectator than active participant in these events. As Bradley's chief cheerleader, his major contributions were to endorse his subordinate's decisions throughout and to spend as much time as possible with his friend. With the end of the Normandy campaign clearly in sight, however, Eisenhower was mere days from assuming a hands-on role with the Allied ground forces for the remainder of the war.

After the war Montgomery observed that "the battle of the Falaise pocket never should have taken place and was not meant to take place"—that is, that the short envelopment was not his idea and did not fit in with his concept of the battle.[25] In September 1944, when Patton was asked by a war correspondent if the Falaise encirclement had been part of the original Overlord master plan or an improvisation, he replied: "Improvisation by General Bradley. I thought we were going east and he told me to move north."[26] Patton's death in December 1945 not only excluded him from participation in the postwar controversies but meant that he never knew that he and Montgomery had been in agreement over the manner in which the Normandy campaign ought to have concluded.

Although Montgomery still nominally commanded all Allied ground forces, the crucial decisions that took place in August 1944 were solely Omar Bradley's. He created the Falaise gap, and ultimately he failed to close it. Patton was little more than a spectator during these final days of the Normandy campaign. Moreover, as Patton himself learned, his problems in northwestern Europe proved to be less with Montgomery than with Eisenhower and Bradley. As had been the case in Sicily, what Patton never grasped about Montgomery was that he had far greater worries in Normandy managing a difficult campaign than upstaging Patton. When Third Army succeeded beyond expectations, no one was more pleased than Montgomery, who later cited the breakout as proof that his master plan had worked to perfection—that while he had kept the Germans busy around Caen, Bradley and Patton had finally been able to unleash the potent power of two American armies.

Montgomery's critics, who were wedded to the estimated dates placed on the phase lines, could not have it both ways by criticizing the failure of Second Army to capture Caen until D+33 while failing to acknowledge that the Allies reached the Seine well before the projected date of D+90.

The postwar battle lines were generally drawn in accordance wih nationality, with one exception—Bedell Smith, the only senior American general to defend Montgomery. "I am no Montgomery lover," he wrote to Eisenhower in 1948, "but I give him his full due and believe that for certain types of operations he is without an equal. The Battle of Normandy is such an operation."[27]

SHAEF Forward had barely been established at Shellburst than, at the end of August, it was decided to move again, this time to a new site at the village of Jullouville, near Granville, a seaside resort town north of Mont St-Michel, on the southern neck of the Cotentin Peninsula. Eisenhower, seemingly bored spending too much time in one place and ever anxious to move on, was like a Gypsy. The primary reason for selecting this obscure location was that the forward elements of both the Allied naval and air forces were already present. The decision to move—and its timing—could not have been worse. SHAEF was located in temporary huts and tents, and while this may have satisfied Eisenhower's and Smith's desire that the staff "rough it," the front was already hundreds of miles to the east and northeast and growing more distant with each passing day. The problem with the various relocations of SHAEF was communications, a vast and intricate challenge to move and reestablish. The blame for the fiasco that divided SHAEF into three disparate parts—Bushy Park, Portsmouth, and now SHAEF Forward, at Granville, an out-of-the-way and inaccessible place—belongs to Bedell Smith, who had consigned his boss to virtual exile where the most important factor, communications, was utterly lacking. In short, SHAEF was ill prepared to assume responsibility for either tactical, administrative, or civil affairs in France, Belgium, or Holland. There was ample time between the decision to move to the Granville area and the events unfolding after Cobra for Smith or Eisenhower to have seriously questioned why SHAEF was being relocated farther *away* from the war than it had been beforehand. The move crippled what little command and control existed within SHAEF in France. Thus, at one of the crucial moments of the war, SHAEF became so far removed from the fighting front that it might as well have been on the moon.[28]

As the Allies entered this new phase of the war, Eisenhower wrote to Marshall on the eve of the Quebec conference that "as signs of victory appear in the air, I note little instances that seem to indicate that Allies cannot hang together so effectively in prosperity as they can in adversity. Any backward step in the progress we have made along that line would be a pity."[29] The move to Jullouville/Granville was just such a step, and within the SHAEF records, was correctly described as "completely unworkable."[30] Within days of SHAEF's establishment a decision was made to move it again, this time to the royal Paris suburb of Versailles. Before the move could be carried out, however, Eisenhower spent three of the most critical weeks of the war in virtual exile.

Part VIII

CRISIS IN COMMAND:
NORMANDY TO THE ELBE, 1944–1945

It became obvious to me in the autumn of 1944 . . .
[that] we were going to "muck it up." I reckon we did.

—MONTGOMERY, *MEMOIRS*

I planned to crush the enemy on the broadest possible
front. . . . No political directive was ever given to me
to stop at the Elbe or to go on to Berlin and Prague.

—EISENHOWER

46.

"A Tactician's Hell and a Quartermaster's Purgatory"

In hardly any respect were the Allies prepared to take advantage of the great opportunity offered them to destroy the German forces before winter.

—SHAEF OFFICIAL HISTORIAN

The end of the Normandy campaign signaled a new phase of the war, which appeared to be a case of two adversaries heading in opposite directions. When the Normandy campaign ended there were forty-nine Allied divisions on the Continent, 3.5 million tons of supplies in France, and SHAEF had become a military Goliath comprising 2,168,307 men and 460,745 vehicles, with more troops and supplies arriving daily.[1]

By early September, as Bradley's and Montgomery's armies swept eastward hot on the heels of the remnants of Army Group B, and Devers's 6th Army Group advanced up the Rhone Valley, all signs pointed to an early victory, perhaps by the end of 1944. Twenty-first Army Group crossed into Belgium on September 2 and liberated Brussels two days later, while the First and Third Armies were moving with sometimes dizzying speed to the east. In the three-week period between August 18 and September 11 the Allies had captured most of northern and southeastern France and the greater part of Belgium and Luxembourg and were poised to enter Holland. Patton's Third Army had captured Verdun and had advanced to within eighty miles of the German border and the Saar.

The stunning German defeat in Normandy may have been the most visible sign of how favorably the war had turned in favor of the Allies, but it was by no means Hitler's only problem. In the west, German losses in three months of fighting were three hundred thousand killed, wounded, or missing. As Hitler's recent biographer Ian Kershaw points out, "Between June and September the Wehrmacht lost on all fronts well over a million men. . . . The losses of tanks, guns, planes, and other armaments were incalculable. . . . The war at sea had also by this time been definitively lost by Germany."[2] To anyone but the intransigent Adolf Hitler, Germany's days were plainly numbered. With the Luftwaffe all but finished as a fighting force and the Nazi empire shrinking daily, the German commanders who had to conduct the actual fighting viewed continuation of the war as pointless. Rommel, Rundstedt, Kluge, and before long even Model—that most ardent of Nazis and a staunch defender of Hitler—would accept that the war had been lost. Rommel would soon die by his own hand; Rundstedt had been replaced at OB West by Model, and others of Hitler's ablest commanders were either dead or captured. When Model insisted that twenty-five infantry and six panzer divisions were required to hold the west, Hitler replaced him and barely three weeks after relieving him brought back von Rundstedt as the latest of the revolving-door commanders.[3]

Though on the face of it the Allies were clearly in the driver's seat, at the end of August 1944 an unhealthy aura of overoptimism and self-deception swept through the ranks of the Allied high command. The crushing triumph in Normandy, followed by Allied gains of as much as fifty miles a day north of the Seine, created the illusion that the war was virtually over except for the final mopping up. The so-called victory disease swept unchecked through SHAEF, leaving in its wake myopically preconceived perceptions that failed to take into account the earlier lessons of the war. The euphoria was magnified by reports of spectacular advances by the Red Army in the Ukraine and in Poland and East Prussia. *Daily Mail* correspondent Alexander Clifford, who accompanied Dempsey's British Second Army, recorded the sense of sheer delirium: "This mad chase is getting crazier hour by hour. . . . You can't digest it in the least as you go along. It is so big and so swift that you almost feel it is out of control. . . . Our columns just press on and on and on. . . . The atmosphere is heady and intoxicating."[4]

Indeed, to be anything but an optimist at this juncture was to risk being admonished. Within Bradley's headquarters there existed the same intoxication: "Everything we talk about now is qualified by the phrase 'if the war lasts that long,' " noted his aide Chet Hansen. Studying his wall maps, Bradley concluded that "his next CP would be in Metz, the one thereafter for an army of occupation in Weisbaden [*sic*]."[5]

How could it not be so with the German army in complete disarray and the Allies gobbling up territory at such a rate? German losses—900,000 on the eastern front and as many as another 450,000 in the west—were staggering, and the idea that Germany might win the war was seeming hopeless. Their quality and inexperience notwithstanding, what was overlooked was the fact that there still remained some 3.4 million troops in the German army, of which well over a million had yet to be committed to the western front and the defense of the Reich.[6] But even these numbers are misleading: In early September 1944 the Allies could easily have penetrated Germany's borders.

They were prevented by what has been aptly described as "the tyranny of supply." The Allies had long since outstripped their lines of supply.

A rosy intelligence estimate issued by the SHAEF G-2, Maj. Gen. Kenneth W. D. Strong, in late August, was typical: "The August battles have done it and the enemy in the West has had it," it proclaimed. "Two and a half months of bitter fighting have brought the end of war in Europe within sight, almost within reach. The strength of the German Armies in the West has been shattered." A week later SHAEF declared that the German army in the west was "no longer a cohesive force but a number of fugitive battle groups, disorganized and even demoralized."[7]

On September 4 Eisenhower sounded one of the very few notes of caution to emanate from SHAEF. Writing to Marshall he noted, "We have advanced so rapidly that further movement in large parts of the front even against very weak opposition is almost impossible."[8] At a press conference held in London on August 15 he had "vehemently castigated those who think they can measure the end of the war 'in a matter of weeks.' Hitler and his gang have nothing to lose by enforcing prosecution of the war," he warned the correspondents.[9] Despite his accurate warnings and disregarding his own pronouncements, Eisenhower too fell victim to the prevailing optimism. Russell Weigley notes that as late as September 15, Eisenhower was "euphoric about the prospects for an imminent ending of the war. On that date he issued a circular letter to his army group and air and naval commanders, based on the assumptions that the Allied armies were about to close up to the Rhine," stating that "it was time to plan the final offensive" to capture the prize objective in Germany, Berlin.[10]

Later SHAEF official pronouncements were foolishly at odds with Eisenhower's stated position. Among those who should have known better were Bedell Smith, who authorized a public quotation from an interview in which he said, "Militarily, the war is won"; and the deputy SHAEF intelligence officer, Brig. Gen. T. J. Betts, who replied, "We'll go right through it," when questioned about the Siegfried Line.[11]

Eisenhower's public and private comments notwithstanding, he accepted that an early end to the war was not only possible but probable. How that end was to be attained formed the crux of the great debate that tore through the upper ranks of the Allied leadership in August and September 1944. Although Eisenhower had prudently warned Marshall on August 24 that his armies did not have sufficient supplies "to do *everything* that we should like to do," by mid-September he was already disregarding his own dictum, yet another casualty of what Stephen Ambrose has labeled the " 'victory disease', a malady which caused the patient to believe anything was possible."[12] This extended to Washington, where the War Production Board rashly canceled some military contracts in the mistaken notion the war in Europe was all but over. Even Marshall expected an end to the war not later than early November 1944, and was already discussing the redeployment of troops to the Pacific.

Until disillusioned by dwindling supplies and the dreadful weather that plagued Lorraine in the autumn and winter, Patton was so confident in the early days of September that he predicted, "Give me 400,000 gallons of gasoline and I'll put you in Germany in two days."[13] However, his shrewd intelligence officer, Col. Oscar Koch, was never taken in by the fanciful predictions emanating from on high. "It is clear," he wrote on August 28, "that the fixed determination of the Nazis is to wage a last-ditch struggle in the field at all costs ... the German armies will continue to fight until destroyed or captured."[14]

Only Churchill seems not to have been taken in by the razzle-dazzle, warning that the future remained uncertain. "It is at least as likely that Hitler will be fighting on the 1st January [1945] as that he will collapse before then. If he does collapse before then, the reasons will be political rather than purely military."[15]

The great Allied victory was a triumph for everyone except the logisticians, for whom it proved to be their worst nightmare. A German general once remarked that the blitzkrieg was paradise for the tactician and hell for the quartermaster, but it was Ernie Pyle who described the events of August and September 1944 as "a tactician's hell and a quartermaster's purgatory."[16]

The original Allied blueprint for fighting the war in Europe was predicated on an orderly German retreat across Normandy and a solid defense of the Seine River line, not the rout that occurred in August as a result of Cobra. There were, in fact, sufficient stocks of virtually all classes of supply already positioned in France to fill at least 90 to 95 percent of the fuel and supply needs of the forward armies. The dilemma was that they were positioned too far away in the Normandy supply dumps. Thus, the shortages facing the Allies at the end of August 1944 were not of fuel or ammunition, but of transportation.

The logistical pinch was felt immediately. The Normandy supply dumps were now more than three hundred miles from the front lines, and with the transportation system in western France all but destroyed by the pre-D-Day aerial campaign to isolate the Normandy battlefield, it could not be restored overnight. Faced with the immense task of attempting to keep up with supply lines that were being stretched to the breaking point by four Allied armies dashing across France and Belgium, the supply system faced collapse. For example, on D+100 (September 14, 1944), the Allies had advanced to where the logisticians thought they would reach only in May 1945.[17] No one ever forecast a breakout or mobile war on the scale of the one the Allies engaged in during August 1944. Each mile the Allies advanced closer to Germany became a larger headache for the logisticians. The ultimate irony of post-Normandy pursuit operations was that they were carried out *against* the advice of the logisticians.[18]

By the time the Allied armies had advanced beyond the Seine, logistics had become the dominant factor.[19] The logisticians tried but were hopelessly unable to keep pace with the great Allied broom that was now sweeping across France and into Belgium. Eisenhower had become a victim of his own success.

This fortuitous turn of events did not include the luxury of a pause at the Seine to allow the Allied armies to regroup, advance their logistical bases farther forward, and make plans to resume offensive operations toward Germany. With the German army in the west in full retreat now was the time for pursuit, not consolidation. SHAEF, however, had failed to propose plans for dealing with success on such an epic scale.

By the end of the Normandy campaign the Allies were supporting more than two million soldiers on the Continent, including thirty-eight divisions, with more units arriving every day. A World War II combat division required an average of seven hundred tons of supplies *per day* during periods of sustained combat. As the Allied spearheads—all of which possessed the same insatiable appetite for supplies, which were either being landed across the Normandy beaches or through the port of Cherbourg—extended farther northeast and east with each passing day, Eisenhower's logistical problems multiplied to frightening proportions. They ranged from ammunition shortages to the grossly inadequate port and transportation capabilities, later capped by a growing shortage of replacements. Pursuit operations, such as the one mounted by the Allies in late August and early September 1944, are only as effective as their logistical tail, and that tail no longer wagged the dog.

To have sustained the fighting units committed in early September required at least one million gallons of fuel per day. The official SHAEF historian bluntly defines the problem existing at the end of August 1944. "In hardly any respect were the Allies prepared to take advantage of the great opportunity offered them to destroy the German forces before winter . . . virtually the whole intricate military machine was geared to a slower rate of advance. . . . Unfortunately, the period of the great opportunity lasted for only a few weeks and there was not sufficient time, however vast the effort, to make the necessary readjustments in the logistical machinery which would insure speedy victory."[20]

For a very brief time the German army was tantalizingly close to complete collapse; the backdoor to Germany was wide open, but the Allies were unable to take advantage. Had that advantage been exploitable, Eisenhower might well have won his 1943 wager with Montgomery that the war would end before Christmas 1944.[21]

There were actually two competing plans for the campaign fought in northwestern Europe, the tactical plan and the far more conservative logistical plan, which was based on an advance to the Seine with adequate time given for regrouping and consolidation to permit the logisticians to move forward sufficient supplies before any advance to the German border commenced.

In July a SHAEF logistical study revealed the impossibility of sustaining rapid Allied advances east of the Seine. As Russell Weigley notes, "Every informed Allied officer had foreseen the fuel crisis." In the end, however, "risking the logistical crisis was a price the field commanders decided was worth paying for the chance of hastening the end of the war."[22]

The task of any logistician is traditionally thankless, and the essential traits of those who succeed are great initiative, a "can-do" personality, and a willingness to improvise, traits Eisenhower's chief logistician, Lt. Gen. J. C. H. Lee lacked in abundance.[23] Although he had several capable subordinates, Lee's narrow-mindedness, pessimistic outlook, conventional peacetime quartermaster's mentality, and unwillingness to use every means at his disposal to improvise the logistic system to the needs of the combat armies ill served the Allied cause. Among his inexcusable transgressions was rewarding his friends for past favors and punishing his enemies by providing or withholding supplies. In September 1944 his most egregious sin was transporting thousands of tons of prefabricated housing to keep COMZ officers warm during the coming winter, while declining to ship and preposition vital winter clothing for U.S. troops on the grounds that it would probably never be needed.[24] Had Lee had his way, the timetable would have included delaying the liberation of Paris until late October and supplying a maximum of four divisions for operations beyond the Seine, for he seemed more interested in winning the race with SHAEF to claim the best hotels and facilities in Paris, and in indulging his mania for creature comforts. In early September, before Eisenhower knew of it or could stop it, Lee—in a striking case of noblesse oblige in reverse, moved his inflated COMZ headquarters to Paris, filling virtually every hotel with its eight thousand officers and twenty-one thousand enlisted men, in the process preempting precious fuel and transportation that was desperately needed at the front. The French rightly complained that the Germans had made fewer demands than did the U.S. Army, and a French magazine mocked SHAEF as the Societé des Hôteliers Américains en France, enraging Eisenhower.[25]

After the war Lee lamely complained to the official SHAEF historian that "[t]he rear echelon have their morale problems too."[26] Lee's flimsy rationale was that "we occupied only buildings that had been used by the Germans. Thus we deprived the French of no space that they had been recently using."[27] Smith renewed his advice to fire Lee, but Eisenhower demurred. The best Smith could do was to draft a scorching letter for Eisenhower's signature that called Lee's actions "extremely unwise" and ordered him to remove all non-essential personnel from Paris at once.[28]

Eisenhower's rebuke was little more than a token slap of Lee's wrist. Smith was never able to persuade him to take stronger action against his chief logistician, primarily because Lee had the support of both Marshall and the powerful chief of the Services of Supply, Lt. Gen. Brehon Somervell.[29] Had others crossed Eisenhower in such flagrant fashion, they would have been summarily dismissed. Presented with successive options to fire Lee, Eisenhower never could.[30]

In a stopgap effort to keep the forward armies resupplied, the Red Ball Express—in which six thousand trucks ferried supplies along a dedicated one-way highway system around the clock from the rear-area depots to the rapidly expanding front—was created on August 25. Its object was to deliver 82,000 tons of supplies between August 25 and September 2 (it actually dispensed 89,000 tons). Although mythologized as the savior of the front, it could provide only a small fraction of the supplies required. It took such a heavy toll in trucks and drivers that it could not have been sustained indefinitely. The Red Ball "represented a calculated gamble that the war would end before the trucks broke down . . . [but] consumed 300,000 gallons of precious fuel every day—nearly as much as a field army." The Red Ball continued in a modified form until the pursuit ended, a heroic but ultimately futile effort to keep the wheels from coming off the great Allied war machine, which had become a casualty of its own spectacular triumph.[31] To make matters worse, at a crucial moment fourteen hundred newly introduced three-ton British trucks broke down almost immediately with cracked piston rings, leaving the British 21st Army Group without crucial transportation and dependent on U.S. assistance.[32] SHAEF's logistical arm was plainly in need of reorganization, and its failure to reform itself was "the gravest shortcoming of the planning phase and the pre-invasion period." One of the champions of reform was Everett S. Hughes, but his exhortations to Eisenhower to implement change brought only an angry outburst that led Hughes to note in his diary, "The man is crazy. He won't issue orders that stick. He will pound the desk and shout." Not without reason, Hughes believed that Eisenhower was simply not prepared to cross the powerful Somervell.[33]

Both Marshall and Somervell were concerned about COMZ, but neither was prepared to see Lee sacked. To have done so would have called attention to the mounting deficiencies of COMZ and sent a clear signal that the U.S. house was not in order. The chief of staff received an earful of complaints when he toured the U.S. armies in early October. Hodges, Collins, Corlett, and others aired their frustrations over COMZ and the chronic shortages of fuel and ammunition.[34]

Under-Secretary of War Robert Patterson, who also visited in October, returned to Washington disturbed by what he had seen. Eisenhower's logisticians seemed merely to be "limping along from crisis to crisis, rent by dissention and jealousy, split down the middle between competing Allied and American jurisdictions."[35] Patterson recommended three able officers as possible replacements for Lee, all of whom were close and respected colleagues of Eisenhower: Henry Aurand; LeRoy Lutes, Ike's chief logistician during the Louisiana maneuvers; and Lucius D. Clay, "an old and dear friend whose ability he prized highly."[36] All three were sent to COMZ and did commendable jobs attempting to clean up the mess, which included rampant black market activity. However, the two most promising replacements for Lee, Lutes and Clay, remained in limbo when neither Marshall nor Somervell indicated to Eisenhower that he was free to replace Lee, who retained command of COMZ through the end of the war.

Eisenhower, Bradley, and others of their military generation evinced little interest in logistics or its problems, except as it affected their operational status. As Bedell Smith's biographer, D. K. R. Crosswell, points out, "Clausewitz had only contempt for commanders who allowed themselves to be dominated by logisticians. The work of logisticians existed 'in about the same relationship to combat as the craft of the swordsmith to the art of fencing.' . . . Eisenhower approached the Clausewitzian ideal [and] illustrated all the standard prejudices of line officers against the central role played by supply, admin and technical services in modern war. Aside from the bromides Eisenhower offers in his memoirs about the centrality of logistics in the conduct of modern war, there is scant evidence that enlightened view informed his actions as supreme commander."[37]

Although Lee controlled COMZ with an iron hand, SHAEF directed the allocation of its precious logistical assets. Eisenhower washed his hands of such problems and delegated responsibility to Bedell Smith, who in turn wielded his considerable power as "a means of directing operations at the front." Concerned, for example, that Patton's exuberance might get him into trouble, Smith saw to it that Third Army received just enough supplies to get it to Metz. Similarly, notes Crosswell, "When SHAEF wanted to build a fire under Montgomery in Belgium, Smith used logistics as a lever. He never saw the problem from the logisticians' point of view nor would he admit the system itself contained flaws."[38] At times Lee bore the brunt of problems that were properly Smith's responsibility. Thus, between Lee and Smith, COMZ was further politicized by those who misused it to their own ends.

Logistics and communications are the vital supporting cast of waging successful war; to lack for either is to court failure. Yet just as the Allies had scored their greatest victory, Eisenhower's hands were tied by both. His logisticians determined how far his armies could advance, and his signals officers, who controlled the flow of communications into and out of SHAEF, determined how well and how fast he could communicate with his subordinates. During the first three critical weeks of September 1944, when SHAEF was located in Granville, communications were dangerously ineffective and periodically nonexistent. The system, installed by COMZ, was chronically unreliable. There were no telephone links or radiophone capability between SHAEF and its subordinate commands. Eisenhower could communicate only by telegraph or by letter; in effect he was often incommunicado, a serious problem for any commander but a potentially fatal flaw for one exercising supreme command. Signals from the field typically took twenty-four hours to reach Eisenhower, and another full day was usually lost before his replies were received. By contrast Hitler was in virtually instantaneous communication with OB West. An example of how seriously flawed communications to and from Granville were was Eisenhower's "Most Immediate" signal of September 5, sent to Montgomery in response his proposed single-thrust strategy, which did not reach Brussels for some thirty-six hours. Even then several paragraphs were missing and were not received by 21st Army Group for yet another two days.[39]

A headquarters that is uninformed and unable to communicate cannot exercise command and control over operations, and is essentially useless. It was no way to run a war and was yet another affirmation of Montgomery's contention that SHAEF was ill-equipped to manage the land battle. On at least one occasion communications between SHAEF and 12th Army Group broke down completely, leaving Bradley out of touch with Eisenhower. By themselves the twin problems of logistics and communications would have been sufficient to hold Eisenhower's focus, but beginning in September 1944 his strongest battles would be with his own generals.

47.

Which Way to Germany?

God deliver us from our friends. We can handle the enemy.

—PATTON

In mid-August, Eisenhower announced his intention to assume command of the Allied land forces on September 1. In the spring of 1944, while most were concentrating on the D-Day invasion, a small group of SHAEF planners had for many weeks been busy analyzing Eisenhower's mandate "to undertake operations aimed at the heart of GERMANY and the destruction of her armed forces." On May 3 they presented Eisenhower with alternative courses of action after Normandy to attain that goal. These included the capture of the Ruhr in order to cripple Germany's war-making capability, and the capture of Berlin. The four options presented for an advance to the Ruhr were all variations of a broad Allied advance both north and south of the rugged Ardennes Forest. Eisenhower rejected Berlin as a military objective and began to study his two options for seizing the Ruhr by either a frontal assault or an envelopment. On May 27 Eisenhower affirmed the broad-front strategy recommended by his planners. This is the only known document that spelled out SHAEF's post-Normandy strategy. A key factor in the long-running historical arguments is that, although the document was approved by Eisenhower, there is no evidence to support a contention that it or its contents was ever sent to Montgomery and Bradley, or that they even knew of its existence.[1]

For Eisenhower, the student of history, the solution was self-evident. Military commanders dream of the double envelopment, of surrounding an objective on two sides by pincer movement and crushing it between their combined weight as had been intended at Falaise. When he studied the map of Europe in 1944, Eisenhower was drawn by his knowledge of history to one of his boyhood heroes, Hannibal, the Carthaginian general whose masterful defeat of the Romans at Cannae in 216 B.C. is considered one of the classic battles of all time. With the Ardennes as an impediment that of necessity had to be bypassed, Eisenhower envisioned a Hannibal-like Cannae by means of a double envelopment of the Ruhr. A force under Montgomery's 21st Army

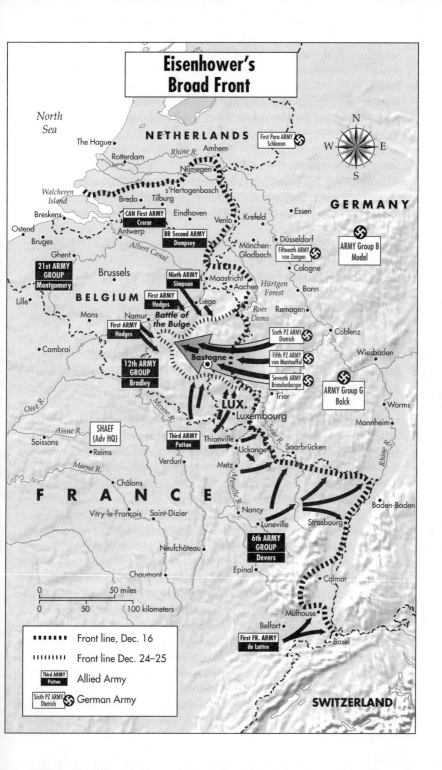

Eisenhower's Broad Front

North Sea

NETHERLANDS

The Hague

Rotterdam

Rhine R.

Amhem

First Para ARMY
Schlemm

Walcheren Island

Breda · Tilburg

s'Hertogenbosch

GERMANY

Breskens

Ostend

CAN First ARMY
Crerar

Eindhoven

Venlo · Krefeld

· Essen

Bruges

Ghent ·

Antwerp

BR Second ARMY
Dempsey

Mönchen-Gladbach

· Düsseldorf

ARMY Group B
Model

Albert Canal

Fifteenth ARMY
von Zangen

· Cologne

21st ARMY
GROUP
Montgomery

Brussels

Ninth ARMY
Simpson

Maastricht · Aachen

Hürtgen Forest

· Bonn

BELGIUM

First ARMY
Hodges

· Liège

Roer Dams

Remagen

Lille ·

Mons ·

Namur

Battle of the Bulge

Sixth PZ ARMY
Dietrich

· Coblenz

First ARMY
Hodges

Bastogne

Fifth PZ ARMY
von Manteuffel

· Wiesbaden

· Cambrai

12th ARMY
GROUP
Bradley

Meuse R.

Seventh ARMY
Brandenberger

· Trier

ARMY Group G
Balck

· Worms

Oise R.

SHAEF
(Adv HQ)

LUX.
· Luxembourg

Saar R.

· Mannheim

Aisne R.

· Soissons

· Reims

Third ARMY
Patton

Thionville

Uckange · Saarbrücken

Rhine R.

Marne R.

Verdun ·

· Metz

Moselle R.

F R A N C E

· Châlons

· Nancy

· Baden-Baden

Vitry-le-François · Saint-Dizier

· Lunéville

Strasbourg

· Neufchâteau

6th ARMY
GROUP
Devers

· Chaumont

Epinal ·

· Colmar

| 0 | | 50 miles |
| 0 | 50 | 100 kilometers |

Mulhouse

Belfort ·

First FR. ARMY
de Lattre

· Basel

SWITZERLAND

Front line, Dec. 16

Front line Dec. 24–25

Third ARMY
Patton   Allied Army

Sixth PZ ARMY
Dietrich   German Army

Group would advance north of the Ardennes to strike the Ruhr, while a second force consisting of Bradley's 12th Army Group advanced south of the Ardennes through Lorraine and swung north to Cologne to complete the double envelopment. The scheme bore a more than passing likeness to the plan of another general Eisenhower had studied at length: Ulysses S. Grant and his 1864 strategy for defeating the Confederacy.[2]

Both Montgomery and Bradley began to weigh in with plans of their own that would guarantee them a key role in the post-Normandy battles. Each lobbied hard to win Eisenhower's approval. Although aware that his days as Allied ground commander were numbered, Montgomery not only argued against changing the command setup at this late date but pressed ahead to influence future Allied strategy. The sudden collapse of German resistance in mid-August gave rise to a proposal for what he called a single "full-blooded" thrust toward the Ruhr, with his and Bradley's army group marching abreast. This force of some forty divisions "would be so strong that it need fear nothing."[3]

Montgomery was also convinced, not without justification, that Eisenhower and SHAEF were ill prepared for the task of running the ground war. "The whole command set up was fundamentally wrong. There was no one who could give his complete and undivided attention to the day to day direction of the land battle as a whole," he told Chester Wilmot after the war. Eisenhower

> had not the experience, the knowledge, the organization, or the time.
> He should have been devoting himself to questions of overall strategy,
> to political problems, and to problems of inter-Allied relations and
> military government. . . . Instead he insisted on trying to run the land
> battle himself. Here he was out of his depth and in trying to do this
> he neglected his real job on the highest level.[4]

As the Normandy campaign had progressed, Montgomery found Eisenhower's presence more distraction than help. Montgomery conducted meetings in a brisk and businesslike manner, but when Eisenhower was present Monty was critical of what he believed tended to be too much conversation and too little substance. Montgomery cited one such instance when Eisenhower visited him on August 13. Afterward he wrote to Brooke that "Ike is apt to get very excited and to talk wildly—at the top of his voice!!! He is now over here, which is a very great pity. His ignorance as to how to run a war is absolute and complete; he has all the popular cries, but nothing else. He is such a decent chap that it is difficult to be angry with him for long. One thing I am firm about; he is never [to be] allowed to attend a meeting between me and my Army commanders and Bradley!" Eisenhower, he thought, was simply too theatrical at a time when there was still heavy fighting ahead. He believed that Ike was far too mercurial: First there was his ill-concealed impatience with Montgomery over the progress and strategy of the campaign, and now excessive exuberance when the war was far from won. Notes Montgomery's official biographer, "It was vital, Monty felt, to keep a 'grip' on the battle—and not allow over-excitement to masquerade as military judgment."[5]

Although Montgomery's and Bradley's meetings were cordial, there was growing ill will on Bradley's part. Montgomery met privately with Bradley on August 17 and left believing that he had secured his approval for his plan—a claim Bradley vigorously disputed in his postwar memoir. Describing it as deceitful, Bradley maintained that he never wavered in his support of a two-thrust strategy.[6] Also, realizing that he stood little chance of winning over Eisenhower at any meeting involving members of the SHAEF staff, Montgomery arranged to have Eisenhower visit his field headquarters at Condé-sur-Noireau on August 23. Eisenhower was accompanied by Bedell Smith, whom Montgomery managed to exclude from the meeting. While Smith seethed in a nearby orchard with his friend and British counterpart, Freddie de Guingand, Montgomery made his case to Eisenhower: Either he or Bradley should control the ground war, and with the growing insufficiency of supplies, the war could not be won in 1944 unless priority was given his proposed offensive—which, he argued, must also include the U.S. First Army on his right flank. Eisenhower agreed to give priority of resupply to Dempsey's British Second Army and, "no matter what the command arrangements," he "would see to it that Montgomery retained 'operational coordination' over the northern flank of the Allied advance."[7]

On September 5 Eisenhower cabled Montgomery to reaffirm his intention to advance on a broad front, pointing out that with the destruction of the bulk of the German army in the west, "We must immediately exploit our success by promptly breaching the Siegfried Line, crossing the Rhine on a wide front and seizing the Saar and the Ruhr. This I intend to do with all possible speed . . . [which] will give us a stranglehold on two of Germany's main industrial areas and likely destroy her capacity to wage war." He would give priority to the Ruhr, including the allocation of the precious logistical resources.[8]

In a private office memorandum written that same day, Eisenhower summarized his position, stating, "I see no reason to change this [broad-front advance] conception," and criticizing Montgomery for "his usual caution." Eisenhower's conclusions would soon prove dangerously incorrect:

> For some days it has been obvious that our military forces can advance almost at will, subject only to the requirement for maintenance. . . . The defeat of the German armies is complete, and the only thing now needed to realize the whole conception is speed. Our rapidity of movement will depend upon maintenance, in which we are now stretched

to the limit. . . . I now deem it important, while supporting the advance on eastward through Belgium, to get Patton moving once again so that we may be fully prepared to carry out the original conception for the final stage of the campaign, that is, the broad front.[9]

Montgomery was horrified by Eisenhower's intended strategy, believing he was fully capable of ending the war by thrusting clear to Berlin, provided he was allocated the necessary resources. Nor was Montgomery a victim of the "victory disease." His official biographer notes: "If he bombarded Eisenhower with signals daily more urgent in their appeal for a meeting, for concentrated strategy, for priority to be given to one thrust and for all resources to be thrown behind it, it was because he did *not* consider the war all but won."[10]

From mid-August until the end of the war, disagreements would proliferate over precisely what Eisenhower's armies ought to be doing and where. In September 1944 they revolved around a single issue: "Which way to Germany?"

Eisenhower believed that both strategically and logistically Montgomery's narrow-front strategy was impractical and would shut down all other transportation and virtually immobilize the preponderance of American forces east of Paris simply to support 21st Army Group. Butcher noted in his diary in mid-August that "Ike intends to hustle all his forces up against the Rhine, including those coming in from southern France. He will build up maintenance and reserves as rapidly as possible and then put on one sustained and unremitting advance against the long-coveted heart of the enemy country— the Ruhr industrial area."[11]

Eisenhower's penchant for compromise and consensus led him to approve some of Montgomery's recommendations. "What Eisenhower was unconsciously counting on was a repetition of November 1918, when the Germans signed the armistice while their armies were still well west of the border. Eisenhower had chosen the safe, cautious route."[12] Priority of resupply was allocated to 21st Army Group, primarily to enable the British and Canadian armies to capture Antwerp and, equally important, the deadly Crossbow V-weapon sites from which the more sophisticated V-2 rockets, which struck without warning, were now being launched. Eisenhower also approved the temporary attachment of Hodges's First Army to Montgomery, to the fury of Bradley, who failed to change his friend's mind.[13]

The distinctive and disparate personalities, philosophical dissimilarities, and differing styles of leadership separating Eisenhower and Montgomery from each other now escalated to far more serious proportions. Montgomery believed, with some justification, that SHAEF was simply not up to the task of running the war from Granville, and that the campaign required a full-time commander who would not be distracted by competing priorities that had little or no immediate tactical importance. To make his point that a single ground commander was vital, Montgomery even offered to serve under Bradley, never really perceiving Bradley's total disdain for him. Another misconception is that Montgomery's sole motivation was to retain the power and prestige of being the Allied ground force commander. Some historians have charged that his offer to serve under Bradley was specious; it was not. Montgomery lacked the guile to make false promises. For all his vanity and at times insufferable insistence on pursuing his own ideas, Montgomery, like Eisenhower, was heartily sick of war and eager to end it quickly. Given the precedent of the independence of the army group commanders, little would have changed with Bradley in command. Eisenhower thus rejected the offer for the same reason he had earlier rebuffed keeping Montgomery: public opinion. The British public, he believed, would not stand for a junior American general in command of a British field marshal and his army group.[14]

Eisenhower's decision to assume command of the ground war unleashed a tide of emotion. It was greeted by the British press as a national slap in the face, which was only partly assuaged when Churchill announced Montgomery's promotion to field marshal on September 1, the official date Eisenhower assumed command of Allied ground forces. Although the decision had plainly been scripted months in advance, it nevertheless came as "an appalling shock" to Montgomery, whose promotion seemed to mollify the British public but did little to mitigate the disappointment over what he regarded as nothing less than a demotion. In the War Office a young aide to the vice chief of the Imperial General Staff reacted bitterly, by calling Ike, "Colonel Eisenhower of the Operations Division of the US War Department, who had never seen a shot fired in his life."[15]

Eisenhower was in a classic no-win quandary. The American press also criticized him, but for *not* taking command and restoring American prestige, which they maintained was being stolen by Montgomery and the British. At one point Eisenhower apparently considered leaving the present command arrangements intact. According to one of Bradley's senior plans officers, Col. C. H. Bonesteel III, about the time of Cobra, Eisenhower seemed disinclined to alter the command structure then in place. Present in Bradley's trailer one evening when Eisenhower turned up, Bonesteel remained as a spectator. "Ike was sold on the British view of [a] single command at the time. . . . One of the few times I've seen Bradley angry." Bradley protested, horrified that Montgomery might remain in command of the ground forces.[16]

If Eisenhower was indecisive over the command issue during and after Cobra, a telegram from Marshall on August 19 settled matters. American correspondents were filing increasingly critical stories about Eisenhower that were receiving prominent space in *The New York Times* and other high-profile newspapers across the United States. Through a censor's mistake it had been made public that Bradley was now coequal with Montgomery. Why were British commanders still running the war in Europe? And why hadn't Eisenhower assumed control of the ground war? Marshall's implications were obvious, and—not for the first time—his prompting stiffened Ike's resolve. Eisenhower later revealed the extent of his irritation over the deluge of advice and criticism coming from both sides of the Atlantic, recalling that "I expressed a bit of resentment when I wrote to him, 'It seems that great victories are not enough; *how* you gain them is more important to some people.' "[17]

Many American officers somewhat cynically viewed Montgomery's promotion as an unmerited concession by Churchill. Patton raged, "The Field Marshal thing made us sick, that is Bradley and me." Ever the diplomat, Eisenhower smoothed troubled waters at a Whitehall press conference in which he described Montgomery as a "great and personal friend . . . anyone who misinterpreted the transition of command as a demotion for General Montgomery simply did not look the facts in the face. . . . Montgomery is one of the great leaders of this or any other war."[18] Montgomery's promotion was both a reward for his past successes and also an attempt to keep British prestige from slipping any further into the backwash of American supremacy.

With Eisenhower's assumption of command on September 1, Montgomery's relationship with him took a downward turn. From the time Eisenhower assumed command of SHAEF in January 1944, Montgomery felt he had had the supreme commander's full backing, not only for the major changes to the Overlord plan but for his role as commander in chief of Allied ground forces. The fact that his was merely a temporary role neither lessened its significance in Montgomery's view nor deterred him from acting as a full-fledged, permanent Allied commander would have done. Yet with the role there remained an ambiguity that did not exist with either the air or naval commanders in chief, whose authority was unmistakable. Nevertheless Montgomery felt himself well supported and was grateful to Eisenhower for his efforts—much like those of Alexander in 1942 before and after Alamein—to shield him from Churchill's meddling while he grappled with the problems of fighting the war. Although he clearly understood and accepted that there must be political direction of war, once political issues had been articulated, Montgomery believed, the field commander must be given license to run the battle without interference or the annoyance of ensuring, for example, that a visiting Churchill received his four o'clock whiskey on time (and similar distractions, inevitably part of a visit by the PM).

With the change of command the former honeymoonlike atmosphere between the two men unraveled completely. To the point of obsession, Montgomery suffered from an inability to see others' points of view or to accept that his beliefs were not always shared. He became overwrought in his refusal to accept the reality that Eisenhower intended to take his job. His refusal to attend the ceremonies in Paris was a symbolic gesture of his inability to swallow the bitter pill that Eisenhower would shortly be superseding him. Instead of accepting what Eisenhower constantly preached—that he and everyone else were members of an *allied* team, Montgomery could not find it in himself to accept Eisenhower's way of warfare or his authority. The times had changed, but Montgomery had not changed with them, hence his insistence that the present lines of command remain intact. What made the changeover so bitter was Montgomery's conviction that Eisenhower was too inexperienced and organizationally ill prepared to assume the mantle of land force commander.

Eisenhower's problems were not limited to Montgomery. With Third Army soon crippled by a lack of fuel and ammunition, Bradley and Patton aligned themselves against both Montgomery and Eisenhower, whom they believed had sold out the U.S. Army to the British. Once, when a convoy of rations arrived, Patton raged to a sympathetic Bradley that he would "shoot the next man who brings me food. Give us gasoline; we can eat our belts."[19] To correspondent Cornelius Ryan, Patton declared that there were only 5,000 to 10,000 "Nazi bastards" blocking the advance of Third Army. "Now, if Ike stops holding Monty's hand and gives me the supplies, I'll go through the Siegfried line like shit through a goose."[20]

Eisenhower was not unresponsive, and had there been sufficient supplies forward to increase Third Army's allocations, he would undoubtedly have turned Patton loose in Lorraine. As it was, on September 5 Eisenhower gave Bradley and Patton fresh hope by allocating 250,000 gallons of fuel to Third Army and an additional 1.4 million gallons over the three-day period that followed, before the fuel tap was all but turned off and Third Army ground to a halt along the Moselle River, a tantalizing seventy-odd miles from the then-unmanned Siegfried Line.

Still, Eisenhower's broad-front decision sent a discernible chill through Patton and his Third Army staff and seemed confirmation of Ike's pro-British bias. Convinced that winning the war was being squandered on the altar of Allied cooperation, Patton frequently lamented that they were fighting two enemies, the Germans and SHAEF. When the criticism reached Eisenhower's ears, he sent Butcher to Third Army to investigate claims that junior officers were repeating the story. Patton denied it, and Butcher, who genuinely liked Patton, attempted to defuse the situation with Eisenhower.

The decisions made at this critical moment of the war occurred in the "unforgiving minute" of history, as Patton called it, in which, once a decision was taken, it could not be easily reversed. "No one realizes the terrible value of the 'unforgiving minute' except me," he seethed in frustration.[21]

During the second half of August, Bradley and Montgomery took turns bying Eisenhower to accept their plan. Eisenhower's personal relationship with Bradley did not prevent the latter from aggressively entering the fray. His partisan views and his hostility toward Montgomery would at times overwhelm Bradley's common sense and help fuel Eisenhower's feelings against the British general. Bradley's reputation had grown immensely since Cobra, and with his increased stature came what he believed should be commensurate clout as an army group commander. Bradley, by his own definition, was "flying high" and in no mood to be relegated to the second string at the expense of his nemesis, Montgomery. Bradley's newfound celebrity status was evident when Tedder arrived one day at his command van, "stomped up to the front, kneeled on the leather seat in front of the rail and said, 'May I have communion please.' "[22]

Bradley proposed his own plan—a thrust across central and southern France through the Frankfurt gap and into the heart of the Third Reich by both First and Third Armies. Third Army would advance into Lorraine and breach the Siegfried Line in the Saar while First Army advanced on an axis to the north—both of them routes Bradley argued were the most direct ones into the Reich.

Eisenhower was beset on all sides by unhappy commanders scrapping for an equal share of the logistical pie. Montgomery's seemingly endless demands for priority were mirrored by Bradley and Patton, who conspired to milk the supply system for all it was worth. Caught in the middle was Eisenhower, whose authority was challenged repeatedly. For once Bradley set aside his dislike of Patton and willingly supported his efforts to keep Third Army on the move. Bedell Smith thought it was Eisenhower's own fault. "The trouble with Ike," he said, was that "instead of giving direct and clear orders, [he] dresses them up in polite language and that is why our senior American commanders take advantage." Nor was Eisenhower's handling of Montgomery any more effective. "He lacked the firmness of will to deal with Monty as he should," thus leaving ajar the door for further arguments.[23]

As for Patton, he was victimized by neither Eisenhower nor Montgomery, but by the broad-front strategy and a logistics system geared for the snail's pace of the Normandy bocage, and incapable of keeping pace with the rapid, mobile warfare that Cobra had wrought.

Eisenhower's grandson, David, argues that "the thrust of Eisenhower's position was military," and that he believed the Germans, while disorganized, were far from beaten. Moreover, Montgomery's single-thrust plan would actually have made the German defense of the homeland easier by permitting them to concentrate their opposition on the single-thrust advance. "Thus, Montgomery's talk of defeating the German army and driving to Berlin with forty Allied divisions was 'fantastic'—Eisenhower would not ever consider it."[24]

Eisenhower's assertion that his decisions were made solely for military reasons was not completely valid. Stephen Ambrose notes:

> No matter how brilliant or logical Montgomery's plan for an advance to the Ruhr was (and a good case can be made that it was both), and no matter what Montgomery's personality was, under no circumstances would Eisenhower agree to give all the glory to the British, any more than he would agree to give it to American forces. But as things stood Eisenhower could not make his decisions solely on military grounds. He could not halt Patton in his tracks, relegate Bradley to a minor administrative role, and in effect tell Marshall that the great army he had raised in the United States was not needed in Europe.[25]

Although Eisenhower may well have convinced himself that his broad-front decision was primarily military, the political aspects simply could not have been ignored. From the time he took command of Torch, his role—indeed the very basis of his success—had been unity in a war that would be won by the Allies, not by British or Americans acting singularly. Thus, from Eisenhower's perspective, the controversy was no more than a tempest in a teapot.

Yet Montgomery's single most compelling argument was one that left Eisenhower in a quandary that defied resolution: "If we attempt a compromise solution," he wrote to the supreme commander on September 4, "and split our maintenance resources so that neither thrust is full-blooded, we will prolong the war."[26] He cabled his concerns to Brooke on September 7: "I am not (repeat not) happy about [the] general strategic plan for further conduct of operations but I do not (repeat not) see how I can do anything more in the matter and must now do the best I can to carry out the orders of the Supreme Commander."[27]

His memories still bitter after the war, Montgomery said that Eisenhower's method "was to talk to everyone and then try to work out a compromise solution which would please everyone. He had no plan of his own. . . . Eisenhower held conferences to collect ideas; I held conferences to issue orders."[28] Patton likewise later labeled Eisenhower's attempts to satisfy everyone by compromise the "momentous error of the war."[29] Another major point that further muddied the waters was Montgomery's contention that his offensive encompass forty divisions, a figure wildly beyond the capacity of the logisticians to have supported without the port of Antwerp.[30] The most reasonable figure was only twelve divisions, which, in turn, might have justified Eisenhower's scornful description of a "pencil-like" thrust. The great argument has focused on whether or not the war would have been shortened had his single-thrust strategy prevailed. On this point historians still disagree, as did the logisticians in 1944.

Not only were the SHAEF logisticians "not cast in the heroic mould," but, as Martin van Creveld concludes in his landmark study of logistics, even though—on paper—it appeared that such a thrust by twelve divisions could have reached the Ruhr, "[i]t is not at all certain that, even if strategic developments could have been foreseen in time, the supply apparatus could have adapted itself with sufficient speed or displayed the necessary determination. Given the excessive conservatism and even pusillanimity that characterized the logistic planning for 'Overlord'... there is good reason to believe that this would not have been the case."[31] Although it did not influence Eisenhower to change his mind, his own staff report on Montgomery's plan concluded, "This operation is logistically practicable but only by ruthless subordination of all considerations other than the support of the main effort."[32]

Eisenhower questioned if Montgomery, given the necessary resources, could have carried out a systematic, aggressive offensive into the Ruhr. He concluded that Montgomery could not. A year earlier, at the end of the Tunisian campaign, he had sent a scathing private assessment to Marshall in which he described the British general as "very conceited... [and] so proud of his success to date that he will never willingly make a single move until he is absolutely certain of success—in other words, until he has concentrated enough resources that anybody could practically guarantee the outcome."[33] All of which was precisely the thrust of Montgomery's arguments.

August and September saw a return of Eisenhower's health troubles. On August 10 he inspected both the 82nd and 101st Airborne Divisions, which had returned from Normandy to England, delivering speeches and presenting decorations. Sometime on that day he wrenched his left knee, an injury that would plague him for the remainder of the war. In a near repeat of his experience at West Point, this knee injury was followed by a much more serious aggravation three weeks later. On September 2 his personal pilot, Maj. Larry Hansen, flew the supreme commander in his B-25 to Chartres to confer with Bradley and Patton, who found him

> very pontifical and [he] quoted Clausewitz to us.... He kept on talking about the future great battle of Germany, while we assured him that the Germans have nothing left to fight with if we push on now. If we wait, there *will* be a great battle of Germany.... Ike is all for caution because he has never been at the front and has no feel of actual fighting. Bradley, Hodges and I are all for a prompt advance.[34]

When Patton pleaded that he would stake his reputation on breaching "that goddamned Siegfried Line" if only he were given the necessary supplies, Eisenhower replied, "Careful, George. That reputation of yours hasn't been worth very much." To which, Patton replied with a grin, "That reputation is pretty good now."[35]

Eisenhower's B-25 had no sooner taken off on the return trip than the right engine caught fire and Hansen hastily returned to Chartres, where he ordered Eisenhower and the crew to abandon the aircraft in the middle of the runway. Although the weather was worsening, Eisenhower was in no mood to be dissuaded from returning to Granville. He was flown to an airfield at Pontoroson, near Mont St. Michel, in Bradley's plane, flown by Hansen's copilot, Capt. Richard Underwood, and would normally have flown on to an airfield at Granville. However, with the weather deteriorating by the minute, Underwood elected to fly Eisenhower in an L-5 light observation aircraft across the bay to Granville. Visibility was now so poor that Underwood could not locate the airfield, and with the aircraft nearly out of fuel, it was either crash or make an emergency landing on a beach. Fortunately Underwood selected a beach that was no longer mined and managed a landing without incident. To help save the aircraft from being swamped by the sea, Eisenhower was helping to push it to higher ground through the thick wet sand when he slipped and badly twisted his right knee, his so-called good knee.

By now the staff at Granville were extremely worried for Eisenhower's safety. They knew he had left Chartres, but when by late afternoon there was no indication of his whereabouts, calls were made to various airfields in an attempt to locate him. However, as Kay Summersby wryly noted, "the great Allied army had no trace of its own Supreme Commander."[36]

After securing the L-5, Eisenhower and Captain Underwood had to walk nearly a mile to a road in order to hitch a ride to Granville. A sergeant driving a jeep stopped to pick up what he assumed were simply two stray Americans in need of a ride. When the sergeant saw who his passenger was, "he almost drove off the highway."[37] Eisenhower, who had spent only a single day in Granville, went to bed, grimacing in considerable pain. The SHAEF chief surgeon, Albert Kenner, was summoned from England, diagnosed an acute joint injury, and ordered Eisenhower to rest the knee in bed. Eisenhower complied—briefly—before ignoring the pain and resuming his travels using a light removable cast fashioned by the doctors. Whenever he was not traveling, they insisted Eisenhower rest his knee. Some days the pain was so bad he had no other choice. That he rested at all was a measure of the seriousness of the injury.

The storm brewing between Eisenhower and Montgomery came to a head on September 10 during a tense face-off. Montgomery had insisted on a meeting, and in keeping with his custom that the senior officer should visit his subordinates, Eisenhower readily agreed. His knee was still too stiff and painful to permit any but basic movement, and the two met aboard Eisenhower's aircraft parked on the tarmac at Brussels airport. Also present were Tedder and Maj. Gen. Miles Graham, the chief logistician of 21st Army Group and the only other officer present after Eisenhower unaccountably permitted his own G-4, Lt. Gen. Sir Humfrey Gale, to be banished from the aircraft at Montgomery's insistence.

The meeting began innocently enough, until Montgomery pulled from his pocket the signals exchanged between them for the past week. The new field marshal wasted no time launching into perhaps the most intemperate and foolish outburst of his career. In language fit for a drill instructor addressing recruits, Montgomery testily condemned everything about Eisenhower's plan, detailing why it would not work. Of Eisenhower's recent signals he exclaimed, "They're balls, sheer balls, rubbish!" Perhaps only Eisenhower would have the forbearance to sit in stony silence while a subordinate verbally assaulted him. When Montgomery at last paused for breath, Eisenhower put his hand on Montgomery's knee and gently said, "Steady, Monty! You can't speak to me like that. I'm your boss." For one of the few times in his career, Montgomery muttered, "I'm sorry, Ike," and the meeting concluded in less acrimonious fashion, but with neither man giving in to the other. The broadfront advance to the Rhine would continue, declared Eisenhower.[38]

Eisenhower's refusal to back Montgomery's single-thrust plan was based not only on philosophical differences but on intelligence estimates that the Germans were simply too weak to hold the Siegfried Line or to stop an Allied advance on *both* the Ruhr and the Saar "without the unpalatable necessity of ordering either Patton or Montgomery to stop."[39]

Eisenhower was troubled by the rancorous September 10 meeting and privately questioned Montgomery's loyalty. He derided Monty's plan as a "mere pencil-like thrust" inconsistent with his concept that the war would be fought and won by Allies advancing on a broad front. Smith, as usual, was more blunt; the narrow-front strategy was "the most fantastic bit of balderdash ever proposed by a competent general."[40]

When Admiral Ramsay visited Eisenhower the following evening at Granville, he found the supreme commander in bed in his pajamas and not only in considerable physical distress but still smarting over his meeting with Montgomery. Ramsay recorded in his diary, "He is clearly worried and the cause is undisputably Monty who is behaving badly. [Ike d]oes not trust his loyalty and probably with good reason. He has never let himself go like this before."[41]

Like Churchill, Montgomery had failed to discern that to attempt to run roughshod over Eisenhower was a waste of time that did more harm than good, or that behind the calm exterior that permitted the British field marshal free rein was the unforgiving side of Eisenhower, who never forgot slights or criticism of his decisions. Montgomery's pride and his belief in the correctness of his plan left him equally unapologetic. "I'm trying to fight a war, and I can't help it," he told his aide.[42] Two proud men, both of whom believed in the validity of their cause, was a prescription for an impasse.

Lost in the great debates over strategy in the more than half century since then is not who was right or wrong, but the fact that the argument over a broad or narrow front was not a clash of personalities. Their true disagreement and the real issue was a conflict of ideologies over the best way to win the war. Montgomery never intrigued behind Eisenhower's back to get his way, nor was he disloyal. Again and again he candidly (and often too forcefully) voiced his concerns and advice to Eisenhower personally or in writing. Equally remarkable was that Churchill chose not to interject himself into the strategic debate during one of the most crucial periods of the war. "It probably owed something to his awareness of diminished British leverage," suggests historian David Reynolds. "In any case, Churchill's attention at this time was devoted to southeastern Europe."[43]

The great void between their differing beliefs was never more evident than when, in rejecting Montgomery, Eisenhower said, "The American public would never stand for it; and public opinion wins wars." To which Montgomery asserted, "Victories win wars. Give people victory and they won't care who won it."[44] Both were right but, in the end, the scheme stood no chance in the climate of coalition warfare nurtured by Eisenhower. Not only the months of controversy but the intrusion of nationalism and outside pressures into the equation brought a certain inevitability to Eisenhower's decisions. Chester Wilmot has made a case for the British point of view, and it is as compelling as it was politically impossible. As supreme commander Eisenhower "had shown himself to be the military statesman rather than the generalissimo . . . except for one brief period early in the Tunisian Campaign, he had never attempted to exercise direct operational control over his armies." Instead Eisenhower had done what he did best, establishing the conditions under which his field commanders carried out his strategic guidance. Eisenhower commanded by consensus and compromise and made the Allied team work by dint of his ability to accommodate multinational interests. "When he could gather his commanders and advisors around a conference table, he had a remarkable capacity for distilling the counsel of many minds into a single solution, but when his commanders were scattered over France he was open to persuasion by the last strong man to whom he talked."[45]

Eisenhower's voluminous responsibilities were an equally effective argument for retaining a ground commander. The demands on his time and the myriad of problems dumped on his desk for resolution on any given day was staggering. The problems and challenges were endless, but there were only a finite number of hours available to Eisenhower in which to address them.

Although civil affairs, administrative matters, and stroking visiting political and military egos all had varying priorities, they often had no direct bearing on the day-to-day problems and responsibilities of a ground-force commander. Moreover, without a small operational field headquarters of the sort Marshall would have established, the cumbersome organization of SHAEF simply did not lend itself to managing the battlefield or making decisions in a timely manner. It was not that the SHAEF staff did not recognize the fact that it was incapable of fulfilling Eisenhower's command needs, a point his G-3, Pinky Bull, has made. SHAEF Forward, he said, "must be cut to small, mobile elements and have only those personnel required to handle matters that cannot be delayed twenty-four hours."[46]

As historians Graham and Bidwell point out:

> Throughout September Eisenhower conducted operational affairs by telegrams, fleeting visits and inconvenient "conferences," repeating the error that had cost French commanders the battle in 1940. Like them, he was out of touch, not just physically with his commanders, but with the "feel" of operations. Consequently, he easily misunderstood the meaning of their written and even their verbal communications.[47]

The war of words over the choices by which the war might have been won in 1944 was, in the end, all but irrelevant. Not only was it politically impossible to have permitted the British to win the war by means of the narrow front, but there is ample evidence to question if such a drive could have been logistically sustained beyond the Ruhr. Thus, as a British historian has noted, "There was, therefore, no real alternative to Eisenhower's broad front advance."[48] The final word on the matter belonged to Eisenhower. Rejecting Montgomery's narrow-front strategy, he said, "Such an attempt would have played into the hands of the enemy," and would have resulted in an "inescapable defeat" for the Allies.[49] Equally telling is his grandson's blunt assessment: "Often overlooked is the fact that Eisenhower never considered the single-thrust idea—only ways to derail it."[50]

What was evident but unappreciated by Eisenhower and other key players in the Allied high command in the aftermath of Normandy was the example of earlier campaigns. The German army had repeatedly been shown to be at its most dangerous whenever its back was to the wall or the odds against its survival the highest. North Africa, Sicily, Salerno, Anzio, Cassino, and now Normandy were all examples of tenaciously fought battles and campaigns that were soon to be repeated in Holland, Lorraine, and in the forests of the Ardennes and the Hürtgen. Place-names that would shortly become prominent on the Allied battle maps: Arnhem, Aachen, Metz, the Reichswald, Elsenborn Ridge, Bastogne, and Saint-Vith would provide stark illustrations that the war was far from over.

Montgomery's argument that forty divisions was no mere "pencil-like thrust" but a force so powerful it would sweep away all German opposition had not only fallen on Eisenhower's unsympathetic ears but would perish permanently at the Dutch town of Arnhem, in the wake of Operation Market-Garden, the great, ill-fated Allied airborne operation launched on September 17, 1944.

48.

"Coins Burning Holes in SHAEF's Pocket"

I not only approved Market-Garden, I insisted upon it. We needed a bridgehead over the Rhine.

In September 1944 the Allies planned a massive airborne operation in Holland to gain a bridgehead over the greatest obstacle to an advance on the Ruhr, the mighty Rhine River. By outflanking the heavily defended fortifications dating from World War I along the German border called the West Wall, the Allies would have had an unimpeded clear shot into the Ruhr. Moreover, once across the Rhine, Montgomery was convinced that Eisenhower would be obliged to give logistical priority to his single-thrust concept. Breaching the Rhine had important psychological implications as well. An Allied advance into the heart of the Reich in 1944 would have sent a clear signal that for Germany to continue the war would be futile.[1]

During their contentious meeting in Brussels on September 10, Eisenhower had given Montgomery a green light to mount a major airborne operation in Holland. Speed was of the essence to prevent a German reaction, and on that basis it was quickly approved for the following Sunday, September 17.

The operation was to be carried out by the newly created First Allied Airborne Army (FAAA), commanded by Lt. Gen. Lewis Brereton, the high-living air commander whom Arnold had sent first to the Middle East and later to England to head the Ninth Air Force.[2] Brereton's relations with Bradley were frosty, and when he was replaced by Hoyt Vandenberg in August 1944 there was quiet celebration in the 12th Army Group. Bradley regarded the hedonistic Brereton as "marginally competent" and more interested "in living in the biggest French chateau."[3] Unwanted or ineffective commanders protected by a high-ranking mentor are often shuffled into new jobs. As a protégé of Hap Arnold, Lewis Brereton—and his career—was repeatedly protected. However, when the First Allied Airborne Army was created, Brereton seemed a logical choice to head it. As a junior staff officer under aviation pioneer Billy Mitchell during World War I, Brereton had helped devise Mitchell's trailblazing plan to air-transport an infantry division behind German lines.[4]

Whereas Brereton's qualifications were debatable on the basis of his World War I experience, his deputy, Lt. Gen. F. A. M. "Boy" Browning, was considered a pioneer in the evolution of British airborne operations. A qualified glider pilot who had briefly been the initial commander of the 1st Airborne Division when it was formed in 1942, Browning was also the commander of the British airborne corps. On paper Browning had brilliant qualifications; in reality he lacked battle experience.

Marshall was a longtime advocate of airborne operations and emphatically on record favoring the creation of an Allied airborne army, as was Arnold, who pressed unrelentingly for a role for the vast USAAF troop-carrier fleet, which had reluctantly been created by the airmen to support airborne and glider operations but was currently sitting idle in England. Both exhorted Eisenhower to employ his airborne forces. From the time of the airborne fiascoes in Sicily in July 1943, Eisenhower had sent out mixed signals about the usefulness of airborne operations. At one point he had written to Marshall that he "did not believe in the airborne division," only to reverse himself after a thorough investigation by a joint Anglo-American board of officers. "I think you will agree that, considering the magnitude of the operation, the inexperience of personnel, and the unfavorable weather conditions encountered [in Sicily], the results were most promising for the future effectiveness of this powerful arm of opportunity."[5] Although Eisenhower had given an inspiring speech to the 101st Airborne Division and the crews of the USAAF Troop Carrier Command on August 10, declaring that "one of the great futures of our success" lay in airborne operations, it is not clear that he was ever completely sold on the worth of the airborne.

By the summer of 1944 Eisenhower had little choice except to embrace the airborne concept thrust upon him by the creation of the First Allied Airborne Army, which became the Allied strategic reserve, a versatile force to be employed when and where Eisenhower and SHAEF decided. Once the decision was made to create such an organization, the pressure immediately mounted to find some means of using it. During preliminary discussions with Brereton on July 17, the airman found Eisenhower in a particularly aggressive mood and demanding "imagination and daring."

"He does not leave anything to the imagination. He never does," noted Brereton, who promised results. "I told General Eisenhower if he wanted plans with daring and imagination he would get them, but that I did not think his staff or the ground commanders would like it."[6] Nevertheless, Brereton was eager to carry out Eisenhower's mandate by committing his new command to a major operation of genuine consequence.[7]

On September 4 Eisenhower laid the groundwork for the Arnhem operation by directing Brereton to "operate in support of the Northern Group of Armies [i.e., Montgomery] up to and including the crossing of the Rhine."[8] In a private memorandum written the next day, he noted that in conjunction with the broad-front advance, "we should use our airborne forces to seize crossings over the Rhine and be in a position to thrust deep into the Ruhr and threaten Berlin."[9]

The First Allied Airborne Army brought under a single command three American airborne divisions, one British airborne division, and an independent Polish airborne brigade plus various RAF and USAAF troop carrier formations. Although based in England, the FAAA was equally smitten with the "victory disease," and "the euphoria which existed across the Channel and in the Airborne Corps . . . that the war was nearly over," said Maj. Gen. R. E. Urquhart, who commanded the British 1st Airborne Division.[10] In his diary Brereton noted, "Airborne troops are the most modern expression of warfare," and to add emphasis he framed a prescient 1784 quote by Benjamin Franklin that "ten thousand men descending from the clouds . . . [would] do an infinite deal of mischief before a force could be brought together to repel them."[11]

Numerous plans (some ill conceived by an untried and inexperienced staff) to employ an airborne force had to be abandoned as the Normandy campaign turned into a rout and Allied troops overran proposed targets before airborne operations could be mounted. Eighteen such plans had already been created and scrapped, some because of intramural rivalries within the airborne army.

Before it was abandoned, Browning and Brereton expressed sharp differences of opinion over a proposed operation around Aachen and Maastricht in support of Hodges's First Army. Browning was adamant that the new airborne force be used exclusively in support of Montgomery, and tendered his resignation (later withdrawn) when it appeared he would not get his way. "This in turn put pressure on Montgomery: use them or lose them."[12] With each passing day the pressures increased to employ the air and ground forces immobilized in England. Thus, as an official U.S. historian notes, "The paratroopers and glidermen resting and training in England became in effect coins burning holes in SHAEF's pocket."[13]

It was in an atmosphere of eagerness on the part of the new airborne force to initiate a valid mission, and with Montgomery's burning determination to keep alive his single-thrust concept, that the most ill-conceived major operation of World War II was created. Code-named Market-Garden, it was a daring plan to open the way to the heartland of the German Ruhr by means of airborne landings in Holland by the 82nd and 101st Airborne Divisions, to seize the rivers and canal crossings around Eindhoven, the bridges across the river Waal at Nijmegen, and the Maas at Grave; and by the

British 1st Airborne Division to capture and hold the vital bridge over the Rhine at Arnhem. In reserve was the Polish 1st Independent Parachute Brigade, which was to reinforce the British at Arnhem.

To relieve the airborne landings, they were to be followed by a ground thrust by Dempsey's British Second Army from the Belgian-Netherlands border area. The airborne operation by the First Allied Airborne Army was code-named Market. The ground operation by which a British corps was to thrust north along the narrow sixty-five-mile corridor from Eindhoven to Nijmegen opened by the airborne was code-named Garden. Once in control of the Arnhem bridge, the remainder of the Second Army was to turn the German flank and rapidly assault the Ruhr. By means of this surprise assault through the so-called back door to Germany, Montgomery hoped to hasten the collapse of the Third Reich and end the war in 1944.

Although the concept of Market-Garden was straightforward enough, its execution would prove disastrously complex. Its success hinged on the slender thread that the airborne would seize the various bridges while British ground forces of Lt. Gen. Sir Brian Horrocks's XXX Corps fought their way along a single highway to rapidly relieve the lightly armed airborne troops at each of the bridges.

From the outset Market-Garden was a prescription for trouble that was plagued by mistakes, oversights, false assumptions, and outright arrogance. Neither Brereton nor Browning were inclined to heed advice from their more experienced subordinate airborne troop commanders: Maj. Gen. Matthew B. Ridgway, the U.S. airborne corps commander, Maj. Gen. Maxwell Taylor (101st Airborne), S. F. Sosabowski, the Polish airborne commander, and Brig. Gen. James M. Gavin, the new commander of the 82nd Airborne. The commander of the British 1st Airborne Division, Maj. Gen. Roy Urquhart, was an infantry officer only recently assigned to the airborne arm. Arnhem would be his first airborne operation, and he was thus without the experience or the influence to overcome Browning and Brereton, both of whom seized upon Market-Garden as the answer to their preoccupation to mount a significant and aggressive airborne operation. "I told my staff," said Brereton, "that General Eisenhower wants the airborne army used in mass. He believes that if it is used that way the effect on the morale of the Germans would be devastating."[14]

In Market-Garden, Brereton had the ideal operation to meet Eisenhower's wishes. With the scent of victory in everyone's mind, caution and pessimism were unacceptable. The last thing either Brereton or Browning would countenance was a reason, no matter how valid, to scrap or even modify the operation. What made matters even more tragic was that Browning himself had grave concerns about Arnhem when he first learned of the proposed plan, but did nothing about them.

The decision to launch the operation was made despite accurate and timely intelligence from the Dutch underground indicating that two German divisions of the II SS Panzer Corps were bivouacked near Arnhem. The intelligence officer on Browning's staff who reported the presence of these divisions, which were refitting after Normandy, was Maj. Brian Urquhart, a future deputy UN Secretary General and no relation to the 1st Airborne Division commander. Urquhart was soundly rebuffed when he tried to warn Browning. When Urquhart then produced aerial photographs taken by the RAF that clearly depicted German tanks near Arnhem, Browning dismissed his warnings as those of a "nervous child suffering from a nightmare," and ordered him on sick leave for "nervous strain and exhaustion."[15]

Yet disaster could still have been averted. Shortly before the operation the British Ultra code-breakers at Bletchley Park intercepted and decrypted a number of German signals that reliably revealed the presence of not only the 9th and 10th SS Panzer Divisions, but an assault gun regiment and the headquarters of Field Marshal Model's Army Group B in and around Arnhem.[16] Whether or not 21st Army Group knew of Major Brian Urquhart's warnings and the compelling aerial reconnaissance photos is unclear, but what is certain is that Montgomery's G-2 failed to take either the intelligence or its implications seriously.

Unlike Browning and others, when Bedell Smith learned of the reported presence of two panzer divisions near Arnhem, he took the matter gravely enough to recommend strongly that not one but two airborne divisions be employed at Arnhem to counter the threat. With Eisenhower's permission, Smith personally voiced his concerns to Montgomery, who "ridiculed the idea and waved my objections airily aside."[17] Others were likewise concerned but went unheard. SHAEF intelligence correctly identified the two panzer divisions and warned that they likely had been reequipped with new tanks.[18] Miles Dempsey, who, among the British ground commanders, understood airborne operations better than his counterparts did, was sufficiently concerned that he recommended an airborne drop be made near Wesel, which would have enabled First Army to help block a counterattack. Dempsey's proposal was never seriously considered nor his concerns addressed.

Although Maj. Gen. Roy Urquhart was inexperienced, he knew enough to warn his superiors that the British landing zones were too far away (four to nine miles) from Arnhem bridge and would therefore forfeit the vital element of surprise necessary to carry out a coup de main.[19] Moreover, the decision to lift his division into Arnhem over a three-day period seriously impaired Urquhart's ability to carry out his assigned mission, yet his appeal for two lifts on D-Day was rejected when the air commanders refused to drop the paratroopers or land the glider troops closer to the bridge, in the mistaken belief that German ack-ack ringing Arnhem made the operation too dangerous for their aircraft. The combined effect of both decisions was to cripple the chances of Market's success before the first aircraft ever left the ground. It was in this highly charged atmosphere that the planning for Market went full steam ahead, as if its pitfalls were of little or no consequence.

Browning received other warnings from both Sosabowski and the experienced British airborne commander in Sicily and Normandy, Maj. Gen. R. N. Gale (whose 6th Airborne Division was not involved but who was consulted by Browning) that the drop zones at Arnhem were ill conceived and potentially disastrous. Browning not only disregarded but actually concealed their advice.[20]

Market-Garden was a disaster waiting to happen. Its key players were like the three blind mice: Montgomery and Brereton had little experience of airborne operations, while Browning's experience was at the staff level. Anyone familiar with airborne operations would never have permitted the 1st Airborne Division to be landed at sites so far from their objective. All three were utterly blinded by their eagerness to make something happen, and, as with Mark Clark's decision to launch the fateful Rapido River crossings in Italy in January 1944, the Market-Garden commanders and their staffs attempted to mold their plan to fit a flawed premise. Montgomery's staff was opposed to the plan, as was his own chief of staff. Unfortunately, Freddie de Guingand, who had appeared headed for a breakdown from overwork, had been sent by Montgomery to England for a rest and medical care. De Guingand was sufficiently worried about Market-Garden to telephone a warning to Montgomery from his sick bed, only to be told that "he was too far from the scene of action and was out of touch," yet another telling harbinger of trouble ahead that went unheeded.[21]

Complicating the planning and decision-making process was SHAEF's ill-chosen location in Granville, so far away that Eisenhower's staff was largely ignorant of the details of Market-Garden. With SHAEF in Granville, Montgomery's HQ near Brussels, Dempsey's elsewhere in Belgium, and the airborne army based in England, the principal organizations never met to coordinate and resolve Market-Garden's obvious flaws or question its contradictions. Montgomery, whose reputation and success were based on meticulous planning, was caught up in the politics of the broad-front strategy and, in a shocking lack of critical analysis, never viewed the dual operation as he should have. Instead, he approved Market-Garden more from a sense of despair, frustration, and pressure to overrun and put out of commission Hitler's V-weapon sites in Holland than from a solid military foundation. No one in the Allied chain of command ever asked the crucial question: Even if we capture Arnhem and the bridge, what then? How will the Germans react, and what forces can we muster to sustain an offensive into the Ruhr?

On Sunday, September 17, 1944, the Allies mounted the largest airborne and glider operation of the war. A massive aerial armada of more than 1,545 troop carriers and 478 gliders literally blackened the skies over England and Holland throughout the day. In all more than five thousand aircraft would participate in the airborne and glider landings. Over Arnhem and Nijmegen parachutes and gliders floated from the sky in an operation so mammoth that a second wave of the 1st Airborne Division had to be postponed until the next day—yet another crucial mistake, this one by Brereton, who seemed to think that flying two lifts in one day was too much for his pilots, when it had been accomplished during Dragoon without incident.

Although the landings initially went well, Boy Browning's failure to heed the warnings from the Dutch underground would soon exact a terrible price. Units of the spearhead brigade were obliged to march long distances on foot toward Arnhem bridge. Only one unit actually reached the bridge, Lt. Col. John Frost's 2nd Parachute Battalion. The remainder of the division was soon pinned down in and around Arnhem by the veteran German panzer troops whose presence Browning had disregarded. At this crucial moment not only did the British radios fail, making the growing dilemma of the British airborne even more acute, but the following day bad weather in England grounded Brereton's aircraft. With no reinforcements or resupply of his lightly armed airborne, Urquhart found his worst fears coming true.

Congestion and savage German resistance along the narrow road to Nijmegen and Arnhem soon earned it the nickname "Hell's Highway" and delayed the British ground advance by crucial hours. The Germans also recovered a copy of the Market-Garden plan from the corpse of an American officer who should not have been carrying it into combat. Thus forewarned, their commanders anticipated and eventually thwarted each Allied maneuver. Although XXX Corps linked up with the 101st Airborne at Eindhoven on September 18, the U.S. 82nd and British 1st Airborne Divisions remained engaged in savage battles for survival.

On the afternoon of September 20 two assault elements of the 82nd Airborne stormed across the Waal in rubber rafts directly into heavy German fire and seized the northern end of the Nijmegen railway bridge. Despite their heroics, the British failed to exploit the 82nd Airborne's hard-fought triumph by thrusting through the disrupted German defenses and relieving the besieged force at Arnhem bridge.[22]

At Arnhem, Frost's battalion controlled the northern approaches to Arnhem bridge and very quickly was permanently cut off from the rest of the division, which itself had become heavily engaged in Arnhem.

Frost's intrepid paratroopers held Arnhem bridge for four days before being overwhelmed and compelled to surrender. An attempt by the Polish airborne to reach the bridge compounded the tragedy when the Germans attacked the landing zone and sunk a ferry that was to have taken them across the river. Browning had backed the incompetent commander of the Anglo-Polish force sent to reinforce Arnhem, Maj. Gen. G. I. Thomas. Nicknamed by his own troops "Butcher" Thomas, he insisted on an assault crossing of the Rhine into the teeth of the German defenses despite Sosabowski's warnings that it would be suicidal and could be carried out without opposition further downstream.

By September 25 the operation had failed, and a decision was made to attempt to save what remained of the British 1st Airborne Division. Under the cover of darkness 2,400 Polish and British paratroopers and glider pilots managed to cross the Rhine to the safety of the south bank in small rubber boats. Of the ten thousand men who had landed at Arnhem on September 17, fourteen hundred had been killed and more than six thousand were prisoners of the Germans. The gallant 1st Airborne had ceased to exist as a fighting unit.

What had begun with high optimism turned into a military disaster. Although the heroic stand of Frost's battalion at Arnhem bridge is widely considered one of the legendary episodes of World War II, Market-Garden was an abject failure that has been mythologized by that eccentric British practice of turning military disasters such as Dunkirk into glorious occasions. Churchill, with his romanticized view of war, bought into the hyperbole, calling Arnhem "a decided victory. . . . I have not been affected by any feeling of disappointment over this and am glad our commanders are capable of running this kind of risk."[23] Neither the brave British paratroopers nor the Poles who fought to save them would ever have conceded that Arnhem was anything but a tragedy.

Montgomery's later claim that 90 percent of its objectives had been attained was meaningless. The Allies had failed to establish a bridgehead north of the Rhine, without which Montgomery's narrow front had died ingloriously.

Although Montgomery described himself as "bitterly disappointed" by Arnhem, and admitted mistakes were made for which he bore responsibility, "I remain *Market-Garden*'s unrepentant advocate," he proclaimed in his memoirs, noting that "[i]n my—prejudiced—view, if the operation had been properly backed from its inception . . . it would have succeeded *in spite of* my mistakes."[24] Eisenhower was similarly unapologetic when he declared after the publication of Cornelius Ryan's best-selling account, *A Bridge Too Far*, "I not only *approved* Market-Garden, I insisted upon it. We needed a *bridgehead* over the Rhine. If that could be accomplished I was quite willing to wait on all other operations. What this action proved," said Eisenhower, "was that the idea of 'one full-blooded thrust' to Berlin was silly."[25]

Neither ever acknowledged that Market-Garden needn't have been a failure. Nor perhaps did Eisenhower recall a particularly testy letter he had written to Marshall on March 10, 1944, questioning the premise of airborne operations deep behind enemy lines such as he and Arnold were pressing with

618   Crisis in Command: Normandy to the Elbe, 1944–1945

vigor before Overlord. Eisenhower's letter to Marshall tartly suggested that the chief of staff should inform Arnold, "The fact is that against a German defense, [airborne] fingers do not stab out rapidly and join up in the heart of enemy held territory unless there is present a solid tactical power and overwhelming strength." The merits of Eisenhower's argument before Normandy had changed little in the succeeding six months and fit Market-Garden to a T.[26]

In *Crusade in Europe*, Eisenhower barely mentions Market-Garden, dismissing it with the observation that it would "unquestionably have been successful except for the intervention of bad weather."[27] In the postwar years, after the two generals traded criticism in their memoirs and their falling out was irrevocable, Eisenhower thrust the entire blame on Monty. "My staff opposed it," he wrote to Ismay in 1960, "but because he was the commander in the field, I approved."[28]

Market-Garden was an embarrassment that did neither credit. Responsibility for the failure of Market-Garden began with Eisenhower and extended to Montgomery, Brereton, Browning, and, on the ground side, Dempsey and Horrocks, neither of whom heeded Montgomery's edict that the Second Army/XXX Corps drive to Arnhem must be "rapid and violent, without regard to what is happening on the flanks." Neither general galvanized their tank units while there was still time to have seized and held Arnhem bridge.

The most ludicrous postmortem was Brereton's preliminary after-action report, sent to Eisenhower in early October, which proclaimed, "Despite the failure of the 2d Army to get through to Arnhem and establish a permanent bridgehead over the Neder Rijn, Operation MARKET was a brilliant success."[29] It took until 1960 for Eisenhower to admit privately that Market-Garden had "miserably failed."

It is axiomatic that military debacles require scapegoats, and Arnhem was no exception. The ire of the British commanders fell upon the one officer to whom they ought to have listened. Instead they compounded the tragedy of Arnhem by pointing the finger of responsibility at Sosabowski, who was unjustly relieved of his command at Browning's instigation. In fact Sosabowski, an experienced and highly competent officer, was removed because he had become an embarrassment to Browning's own ineptitude. Had Sosabowski's counsel been heeded the battle might have been won, even at the eleventh hour. "It was," writes a recent historian of Arnhem, "a shameful act by the British commanders."[30] Like Browning, Montgomery, despite his postwar admissions, outrageously made the Poles the scapegoat. In a scathing letter to Brooke he characterized them as gutless. "I do not want this bde [brigade] here again," he said, and suggested they be sent to join their comrades in Italy.[31] To this day, the unfortunate stain upon the honor of these brave men has yet to be officially erased.

Montgomery's bluster failed to conceal his anguish. His once high standing as the D-Day ground commander had evolved into the perception of a whining, "arrogant, opinionated and self-serving 'Brit.' "[32] That the triumphant Allied leadership, which had carried out the greatest victory of the war, should have turned so sour so fast was as destructive as it was disheartening. The spotlight may have been on Montgomery, but it was never off Eisenhower, who bore the brunt of the barbs and the criticism leveled by the principal players at him and at one another. At the height of his frustration after Arnhem, Montgomery told Brooke that Eisenhower was "quite useless," and when Montgomery later attempted to shift the entire blame onto Eisenhower, his official biographer declared, "It was in truth his own doing," and "nothing less than foolhardy." Moreover, notes Nigel Hamilton, the failure at Arnhem carried with it a greater "penalty of incalculable significance to the Allied campaign in the west: Antwerp."[33] Other than his first few months in North Africa, not even Overlord compared in intensity to the test of Eisenhower's will that occurred in the autumn and early winter of 1944.

SHAEF's brief tenure at Granville came to a merciful end when it was moved to the Trianon Palace Hotel in Versailles on September 20. Eisenhower refused the many fancy villas offered for his use, settling instead for a rather modest but elegant house in the Paris suburb of Saint-Germain, formerly occupied by German Field Marshal von Rundstedt before his sudden impetus to seek other accommodations. When asked if there wasn't a certain symbolism involved, Eisenhower replied, "We can't expect to liberate Europe just by taking over enemy generals' homes. We've got to liberate a lot of European minds from their distorted human values."[34]

Determined to be closer to his army group commanders, Eisenhower also established a small forward headquarters consisting of tents and trailers similar to Shellburst near the Champagne city of Reims. Not surprisingly, Eisenhower intensely disliked his new quarters in Saint-Germain and, still enamored of living rough, preferred living in Reims in a trailer recently presented to him by Tooey Spaatz. His staff was grateful that Rundstedt's quarters were available to entertain the crush of visiting dignitaries and straphangers who passed through SHAEF in the autumn of 1944.

Although rare in the case of a foreign national, with Eisenhower's full backing, Kay Summersby was granted a commission as a second lieutenant in the U.S. Army Women's Army Corps (WAC) in November. With it came a new title of secretary, although she remained his principal driver. Eisenhower's office was situated in a gloomy, cavernous room in an annex of the Trianon Palace Hotel that was livened only by a perpetually blazing log fire that more often than not turned the room uncomfortably hot. Half the office had been partitioned off for Kay Summersby's desk, which, she said, "gave me shameless opportunity to hear as much as a whisper. . . . I thoroughly enjoyed the luxury of eavesdropper on conversations in the Throne Room." The arrangement also enabled her to determine at once which Eisenhower was present for duty and to gauge by his mood whether or not he could be interrupted.[35]

Like Omar Bradley, Eisenhower spent hours studying while chain-smoking one cigarette after another, overflowing his ashtrays and leaving the air heavy with the acrid smell of cigarette smoke. After ordering that front-line troops be given double cigarette rations and severely reducing those of rear-area troops, Eisenhower insisted he be treated no differently, and began to roll his own cigarettes when his ration ran out. He never learned that Kay Summersby was providing him with a portion of her own ration to make up for the cutbacks.[36]

Telek had free run of the office. With his usual disdain, the Scottie sometimes exercised his "supreme command" of the supreme commander by deciding to plop himself onto the battle maps during a staff briefing. Eisenhower would issue an order: "What the hell are you doing there, you little devil? Get off." Telek would routinely disobey his master. On one occasion when Telek was summarily banished he took the division symbol for the 101st Airborne with him. When no one could find it, Kay Summersby finally located it, stuck to Telek, and retrieved it so the war could go on.[37]

With all eyes directed toward the breaching of the German border and on Market-Garden, there occurred one of the great blunders of the war. The importance of a bridgehead across the Rhine notwithstanding, the greatest Allied priority in September 1944 was the capture and opening of Antwerp, one of the world's largest deepwater ports. Along with Marseilles, the Normandy ports continued to bear the brunt of resupplying three army groups deployed across an enormous area running from eastern France to the Low Countries. With the Normandy beaches and ports ever more distant from the front lines, barring a sudden German collapse and surrender, no matter what strategy the Allies employed the opening of Antwerp had become vital. The logisticians expected Antwerp to enable the Allies to funnel 15,000 tons of supplies per day by December, and 22,500 per day by March 1945.[38]

Brussels was liberated on September 3 by the British Second Army, and Antwerp the following day. Unaccountably the British spearheads failed to secure the vital crossings over the Albert Canal leading to Antwerp's access routes to the sea, and just as inexplicably, neither Montgomery nor Dempsey ordered the capture of the vital Scheldt Estuary, which remained in German hands, thus preventing the opening of the port. By the time attempts were made to seize the Albert Canal crossings, the Germans had blown up all its bridges.

Alone among the combatants only the Germans recognized and acted with urgency to keep Antwerp from being utilized by the Allies. Although everyone from the Combined Chiefs of Staff to Eisenhower and Montgomery had previously identified the importance of the sixty-mile Scheldt Estuary, its capture was virtually ignored until late September, when a fresh controversy erupted with the realization that, with the priority of effort and attention diverted to Market-Garden, the future of Antwerp had yet to be resolved. The British official historian chides both Eisenhower and Montgomery with failing to pay sufficient attention to "the *immediate* importance of the Scheldt."[39]

The consequences were disastrous. Not only did most of the German Fifteenth Army escape, but the Germans were able to reinforce Antwerp's approaches—Walcheren and North Beveland Islands and the South Beveland Peninsula—with some eighty thousand troops ferried across the Scheldt. Some of the bloodiest fighting of the war took place in these Dutch marshlands until well into November, as the Canadian First Army fought to clear the estuary against German formations heeding Hitler's mandate to fight to the bitter end to prevent the port of Antwerp from becoming an Allied staging area for the final battles for Germany.

"Only casualty figures could adequately bespeak the bitterness of a fight waged under appalling conditions of cold, rain, mud, and flood," wrote an official U.S. historian. Of the thirteen thousand Allied casualties, more than six thousand were Canadian, while German losses in POWs alone exceeded forty thousand, or nearly half the force defending the Scheldt.[40] Antwerp, with its great capacity to resupply the ravenous Allied armies, remained useless until the first Allied convoy finally docked on November 28.

While the fight for the Scheldt played out, competition for a slice of the logistical pie heightened. Patton raged at Montgomery for the loss of supplies and fuel to the British, seemingly never grasping that his destiny was actually in the hands of Eisenhower and the logisticians. Nor did Patton know that Eisenhower felt a strong aversion to having to halt his friend, and, when Antwerp was captured on September 4 (before the British blunder was recognized), he specifically noted the importance of getting Patton on the move again.

Whenever Third Army seemed about to run out of gasoline, Patton would intervene to cajole and bargain in an effort to persuade Bradley to keep him going. However, by September 12 Bradley had begun applying the brakes, warning Patton that with the launching of Market-Garden on September 17, Third Army might well be stuck west of the Moselle indefinitely without ammunition or fuel. "Don't stop us now, Brad," Patton pleaded. "I'll make a deal with you. If I don't secure a couple of good bridgeheads east of the Moselle by the night of the 14th, I'll shut up and assume the mournful role of defender."[41] Bradley granted him two days. And so it went: Whenever the final cutoff of his fuel and ammunition seemed imminent, Patton would introduce some new scheme, until the day the taps were finally shut off and even Bradley could not get them turned back on. As late as mid-September, Bradley continued to articulate orders for an advance by 12th Army Group to the Rhine and the securing of a bridgehead between Mannheim and Cologne, all of which came to naught when Eisenhower decreed that the priority of supply would go to Montgomery and to First Army (temporarily under British control), whose drive on the British right flank was to protect the British drive into Arnhem.

Eisenhower's only concession was to permit Third Army to establish itself astride the Moselle, a decision justified on defensive grounds: that Third Army's presence would help anchor the Allied right flank. As Eisenhower put it, Patton would have forty-eight hours "to become so heavily involved I might reconsider."[42] When the supply situation grew even more desperate, Patton would continue to "edge" eastward in limited operations until Third Army simply sputtered to a halt.[43] "Books will some day be written," he informed Beatrice, "on that 'pause which did not refresh' any one but the Germans."[44] Eventually all Patton could do was to order his troops to move as far as they could, then get out of their vehicles and walk. Third Army's plight was actually no different from that of First Army, which had been forced to halt many of its vehicles to conserve precious fuel supplies and likewise advance on foot. Bradley repeatedly challenged and cajoled Eisenhower on behalf of Patton and Hodges, to little avail.

The misunderstandings, aura of confusion, and the erosion of confidence that existed between Eisenhower and Montgomery reached a new low in early October when, his frustration at the boiling point, Eisenhower cabled Montgomery citing a navy report that the Canadians lacked ammunition and therefore might not be able to resume attacking in the Scheldt until November 1. Complaining that "we are now squarely up against a situation which has been anticipated for months . . . of all our operations on our entire front from Switzerland to the Channel I consider Antwerp of first importance," Eisenhower prodded Montgomery by bluntly stating, "I believe the operation to clear up the entrance requires your personal attention."[45]

Furious, Montgomery replied, implying that Eisenhower did not know what he was talking about. The "wild statements" by the navy were erroneous, he said; there was ample ammunition available. "The facts are the Canadian Army attack began two days ago," and that "operations *are* receiving my personal attention. . . . You can rely on me to do every single thing possible to get ANTWERP opened for shipping as soon as possible."[46] The U.S. official historian notes that Montgomery also reminded Eisenhower that, at a conference held in Versailles on September 22, the supreme commander had cited the main priority of current operations as the Ruhr and "only the day before had declared that the first mission of both army groups was gaining the Rhine north of Bonn."[47] What Montgomery neglected to note, however, was that at this conference his army group had been directed "to open Antwerp as a matter of urgency."[48]

Although Eisenhower backed down the following day with a pseudo-apology, he also asserted that "nothing I may ever say or write with regard to future plans in our advance eastward is meant to indicate any lessening of the need for Antwerp, which I have always held as vital, and which has grown more pressing as we enter the bad weather period."[49]

Their differences might not have boiled over had not Montgomery, "in growing resentment, ... launched his own V2 rocket at SHAEF."[50] Writing to Bedell Smith on October 10, Montgomery pointedly blamed Eisenhower for the serious command disarray that existed whereby the Allied ground forces had "been separated on a national basis and not on a geographical basis." A proven system of command, he said, had been abandoned in favor of one in which two commanders (himself and Bradley) had been given the same mission (the Ruhr). Leaving no doubt that in his view the Allied ship of command was rudderless, Montgomery noted that while compromise was "suitable in political life, when the answer to most problems is a compromise between conflicting interests ... in battle very direct and quick action is required; a compromise will never produce good results and may often produce very bad results; delays are dangerous and may lead to the initiative passing to the enemy." If the Allies were to succeed, Eisenhower must actually run the battle personally or appoint himself or Bradley to command and coordinate the capture of the Ruhr.[51]

Naively Montgomery not only asked Smith to show his notes to Eisenhower but actually believed they would be favorably received. Eisenhower exploded. His lengthy reply, drafted by one of his senior British staff officers, was a curt warning that he would tolerate no further challenges to his authority from Montgomery. Antwerp was still "the real issue now at hand." Compared with the "woeful state" of supply within SHAEF, "you are rich!" Antwerp was not an issue of command. Eisenhower's emphasis on Antwerp stemmed in no small part from pressure from both Marshall and Brooke that they "seriously considered giving me a flat order that until the capture of Antwerp and its approaches was fully assured, this operation should take precedence over others."[52]

As for the command issue, Eisenhower said, in hopes that

> we may continue to operate in the same close and friendly association ... that has characterized our work in the past, I will again state ... my conceptions of logical command arrangements for the future. If, having read these, you feel that you must class them as "unsatisfactory," then indeed we have an issue that must be settled soon. ... I am quite well aware of the powers and limitations of an Allied Command, and if you, as the senior Commander in this Theater of one of the great Allies, feel that my conceptions and directions are such as to endanger the success of operations, it is our duty

to refer the matter to higher authority for any action they may choose to take, however drastic.[53]

Montgomery's "Dear Ike" reply was immediate and unequivocal: "You will hear no more on the subject of command from me. I have given my views and you have given your answer. That ends the matter and I and all of us up here will weigh in one hundred per cent to what you want. . . . I have given ANTWERP top priority in all operations in 21 Army Group. . . . Your very devoted and loyal subordinate, MONTY."[54] Although a crisis had been averted, it was not the last Eisenhower would hear on the subject from Montgomery.

Eisenhower's approval of Market-Garden at the expense of Antwerp was a calculated risk that the war might be won without the latter. And while he was willing to take that risk, Eisenhower did not later seem willing to acknowledge the culpability that went with it. As the editors of his papers have pointedly noted, "Although throughout this period Eisenhower emphasized the importance of opening Antwerp, in fact his decision in favor of Market-Garden meant a postponement of operations against the Scheldt Estuary and Walcheren Island. Still, Tedder is correct in reporting that he and Eisenhower had insisted from September 10 on 'that without Antwerp we could not get to Berlin.' "[55] Neither, it seems, made that point to Montgomery.

Montgomery's official biographer notes that it was "incredible that Monty should have allowed himself to be enticed by the idea of a unilateral British drive into Germany to the exclusion of the vital need to secure quickly the Channel ports, open Antwerp and ensure the capture of the German forces corseted between Second [British] Army and the sea." Montgomery candidly admitted that it was "a bad mistake on my part—I underestimated the difficulties of opening up the approaches to Antwerp. . . . I reckoned the Canadian Army could do it *while* we were going for the Ruhr. I was wrong."[56] In this respect Montgomery was unique: His was the only open admission of failure by a senior Allied commander.

What ultimately ensured there would be no victory in 1944 stems from the very makeup of the Anglo-American coalition. Had the United States allied itself with a smaller and weaker coalition partner, Eisenhower might have felt justified in a single-thrust military operation in the autumn of 1944, but so long as Winston Churchill led Britain, such a decision was unimaginable. The beneficiary of the Allied blunders of September 1944 was Adolf Hitler and his beleaguered but as yet unbeaten armies.

49.

The Autumn Stalemate

The whole business is a first class example of the futile doctrine of everybody attacking everywhere with no reserves anywhere. —MONTGOMERY

Within the space of a single month the euphoria and promise of late August and early September had given way to an equally dismal reality in the autumn of 1944 that the war would not end that year. Brooke's biographer has described Allied operations in the wake of Market-Garden as "a 'push' in all Army Group sectors, a punch in none," and Montgomery wrote, "After Normandy our strategy became unstitched. There was no plan; and we moved by disconnected jerks. . . . We did not advance to the Rhine on a *broad* front; we advanced to the Rhine on several fronts, which were uncoordinated."[1] The broad front had turned into the stalled front. The official SHAEF historian notes, "So far as the debate between proponents of the single thrust to the north or south of the Ardennes was concerned, the result at Arnhem settled nothing."[2]

Eisenhower's belief as supreme commander that the war could only be won by the two allies working together merely reinforced the case for the broad front. Such tactics might well have worked in the autumn of 1944 had the Allies not lost the initiative after Normandy. Thus crippled, the broad front was by now devoid of reserves and reduced to a futile search for "tactical rewards, even when no strategic ones were attainable."[3]

No longer were predictions when the war would end casually bandied about. Casualties rose, the air forces were grounded more and more frequently by the increasingly bad weather, and the mounting logistical and personnel problems promised only a winter stalemate on the borders of Germany. Advances were measured in yards, if at all, and hardship abounded. From the Saar to Aachen, a series of bloody battles collectively called the Siegfried Line campaign accomplished relatively little except to raise the casualty count.

Eisenhower wrote gloomily to Mamie to downplay the optimism of an early end to the war: "You can be certain this war is not 'won' for the man that is shivering, suffering and dying up on the Siegfried Line. . . . My whole time and thought is tied up in winning the bloody mess."[4]

. If ever there was evidence of the terrible price extracted by war, it was in the autumn and early winter of 1944–45. Death and destruction were the only constants in a mounting war of attrition that proved nothing more than that men can kill one another by a variety of savage means. Soldiers of both sides endured a miserable existence in mud, rain, record floods, freezing snow, thick ground fogs, and the gnawing, bone-deep, damp cold that is the signature characteristic of European weather in late autumn and early winter. "Instead of hedgerows, the Allies encountered pillboxes, dense forests, canals, urban snares, and defended villages."[5] Eisenhower described it as "the dirtiest kind of infantry slugging."[6]

The German West Wall consisted not only of the renowned Siegfried Line guarding the Saar, but a series of fortifications running from Switzerland to a point north of Aachen. Unlike France's easily penetrated Maginot Line, Hitler's West Wall was a serious obstacle consisting of interlocking pillboxes and "dragon's teeth" and other tank obstacles, all of which made maximum use of the rough terrain.[7]

The saga of Third Army epitomized the problems faced by the Allies. During the month of August, Patton's spearheads had advanced nearly four hundred miles to the banks of the Moselle River, but during the three and one-half months from September to mid-December, Third Army advanced less than twenty-five miles and suffered enormous casualties during a prolonged and questionable siege of the ancient fortress city of Metz. First Army fared little better, suffering more than 47,000 casualties during the three months between September and December.[8] Like their counterparts in Italy, Allied troops had to cope not only with rotten weather, but the natural river barriers that both protected the Reich and enabled the Germans to delay their advance. The Rhine, Waal, and Maas Rivers in Holland, and in France the Seine, Meuse, and Moselle Rivers were all difficult obstacles, as was the deadly Roer River and its dams inside the German border near Aachen.

On every front there was bloodletting: Along the Scheldt the Canadians were still battling the stubborn German defenders of Beveland Island; Patton was incurring the highest casualties of the war attempting to capture Metz, and in October, at Aachen, American infantrymen fought ferocious street battles before the city fell. The victors' "prize" was heaps of rubble in what remained of what had once been the seat of Charlemagne. Attempts to crack the West Wall and gain access to the heartland met with failure across the entire Allied front, from the Roer River in the north to the Moselle in the south. Metz held out throughout October against the siege warfare that Patton detested, turning the Lorraine campaign into yet another series of bloody infantry battles that Bradley described as "a ghastly war of attrition."[9]

Advancing through the Rhone Valley from the Riviera, Devers's 6th Army Group had better luck in cracking the Belfort Gap in the southern Vosges mountains, driving as far as the west bank of the Rhine before its offensive stalled. Despite their success, the German Nineteenth Army still controlled an extensive bridgehead from Colmar in the north to Mulhouse in the south, dubbed the Colmar pocket.

The most brutal battle of all was fought in the frigid, dense Hürtgen Forest, which lay astride the route to the Roer dams, which the Germans threatened to demolish and flood if the Allies attempted to penetrate the West Wall through that sector. In a series of misguided engagements often compared to the worst battles of World War I, the First Army commander, Lt. Gen. Courtney Hodges, flung one division after another into the bloody cauldron of the Hürtgen in November 1944. Heavily defended by the Germans, the forest became a deathtrap that consumed men at a shocking rate in a series of futile and costly frontal attacks that gained nothing. "It was misery unrelieved . . . Passchendaele with tree bursts, Ernest Hemingway called it."[10]

Before it was finally captured, eight American divisions were bloodied in the Hürtgen, where by mid-December the butcher's bill had produced 24,000 Americans killed, wounded, or captured and "another 5,000 victims of trench foot, respiratory diseases, and combat fatigue."[11] Overall, during the battles along the Roer River during the autumn of 1944, the U.S. First and Ninth Armies suffered 57,000 combat losses and 70,000 more to the ravages of the elements. When they ended the Germans remained in control of the vital Roer dams, and the Allies were left with a hollow victory in what was undoubtedly the most ineptly fought series of battles of the war in the west. Its architects, Bradley and Hodges, were effusively praised by Eisenhower in March 1945. When he called Hodges "the spearhead and the scintillating star" of the great Allied advances into Germany and Bradley "the greatest battle-line commander I have met in this war," he was clearly ignoring or had forgotten the Hürtgen. Others never did.[12]

The grimness of such warfare eventually drove veteran war correspondent Ernie Pyle to seek a respite from what he described as "a revulsion of the mind and an exhaustion of the spirit."[13] The toll on Eisenhower had begun to tell as well. "God, how wearying and wearing it all gets," he wrote to Mamie in late October.[14] To a *New York Times* correspondent Eisenhower described the autumn war as "like climbing the last and hardest ascent of a mountain in a thick fog. You can't see where the top is and you won't until you suddenly . . . begin to go down the other side."[15]

As Patton's casualty count mounted in Lorraine, his disposition, which had grown as grim as the weather, boiled over one night in late October: "How long, O Lord, how long? We roll across France in less time than it takes Monty to say 'Regroup' and here we are stuck in the mud of Lorraine. Why? Because somewhere up the line some so-and-so who never heard a shot fired in anger or missed a meal believes in higher priorities for pianos and ping-pong sets than for ammunition and gas."[16]

No less disillusioned and exhausted was Montgomery, who, at one point, "in his heart of hearts sensed the coming misfortunes" and vowed to continue "hammering at it—until I go mad," in a futile effort to persuade Eisenhower to change his mind.[17] In late October he returned to England for a brief rest, but mostly he remained silently in Brussels and "sulked," recorded an aide.[18]

Montgomery refused to back away from his oft-stated insistence that there should be a separate commander to run the land battle. The subject became so irksome to Eisenhower that Brooke was obliged to rein in Monty, who "still goes on harping over the system of command in France and the fact that the war is being prolonged."[19] Brooke bluntly asked if Montgomery had "considered whether you are likely to be very acceptable in American eyes for this Command?"[20]

Eisenhower's problems seemed to multiply with the worsening of the weather. Supply shortages were still crippling. In early October, Bradley, not for the first time, complained that ammunition shortages were seriously impairing First Army's attempts to penetrate the German border and drive to the Rhine, which might well require postponement. In response Eisenhower "did nothing to hasten the supply of ammunition [to First Army] beyond having his staff write a note to Lee," note Graham and Bidwell.[21]

COMZ was plagued by black-market activities, much of it involving well-organized criminal gangs, despite Eisenhower's efforts to curb the profiteers, some of whom had managed to utilize U.S. aircraft to ship stolen goods to England. The last straw occurred when the liquor cabinet in his own forward command post was ransacked by daring thieves. His frequent tirades aimed at COMZ failures had little visible impact on "Jesus Christ Himself" Lee, who appeared unfazed by his superior's displeasure.

Incidents of rape, murder, and looting were on the increase, as were the AWOL and desertion rates. Each day brought fresh problems and challenges, ranging from venereal disease, pressure from the French and Belgians to close down all brothels, supply shortages, trench foot, a growing shortfall of U.S. replacement personnel, reviewing court-martial sentences, determining what to do with captured liquor, establishing the basis for allocating cigarettes, planning the occupation of Germany, and a multitude of civil affairs questions pertaining to the liberated countries until their governments could be restored.

One day, when touring a rear-area GI hospital in Normandy, Eisenhower became enraged after learning that many of its patients were there from self-inflicted wounds. Although he did not overreact as Patton had in Sicily by slapping the offenders, the sight of soldiers he deemed cowards was deeply offensive. As reports of looting and other crimes became more frequent throughout the ETO, Eisenhower decreed harsh measures to put a stop to such acts, even suggesting that public hanging for rape might be in order.[22]

During the autumn and winter stalemate there were increasing signs of plummeting morale, manifested by a rapidly rising desertion rate so serious that Eisenhower, in his capacity as commander of all U.S. forces in the ETO, became the first since Lincoln in the Civil War in 1864 to order an American soldier executed for desertion. (Desertion in wartime was an offense punishable by death under the Articles of War.) During the campaigns in the ETO in 1944–45, a total of forty-nine GIs were court-martialed for desertion and sentenced to death. One of them was Pvt. Eddie D. Slovik of the 28th Division, who, in late 1944, was court-martialed and condemned to death by firing squad. The case came before Eisenhower for automatic review and approval or disapproval of the sentence. The SHAEF judge advocate general (JAG) recommended the sentence be carried out, and Eisenhower concurred, believing that doing so would set an example for other would-be deserters in the ETO.[23]

In the Slovik case, however, the death penalty was imposed on a soldier who had committed no violent act and whose intent to desert was questionable. Eddie Slovik became a cause célèbre when journalist William Bradford Huie published *The Execution of Private Slovik* in 1954. When Eisenhower was interviewed in 1963 by historian Bruce Catton, his recollection of the event bore the hallmarks of a faulty memory. Claiming he had sent his judge advocate general to offer Slovik an olive branch if he would express remorse and return to his unit, Eisenhower described Slovik as "one of these guardhouse lawyers who refused to believe that he'd ever be executed." Eisenhower asserted that he had instructed his JAG to say, "If you will go back and serve in your company honorably until this war is over, you'll get an honorable discharge and not the death sentence. And he said, 'Baloney,' and so he was executed."[24]

Slovik had actually written Eisenhower a heartfelt personal plea to spare his life, and would willingly have complied with an offer to return to duty. It has not been established if Eisenhower ever saw Slovik's letter, but what is clear is that no one from SHAEF was ever sent to the 28th Division before Slovik's execution on January 31, 1945, in the courtyard of a villa in the town of Ste-Marie-aux-Mines, deep in the Vosges Mountains of Alsace.

Eisenhower was unmoved by bad apples within the ranks of American soldiers, whom he felt deserved their punishments. He viewed his approval of Slovik's execution as simply an unpleasant but necessary part of his job. What further tainted the Slovik execution was that, as a so-called object lesson, it not only failed miserably to act as a deterrent but was not even well publicized within the 28th Division.[25]

. . .

Eisenhower's problems did not end there. Ammunition was consumed at a far greater rate than had been anticipated or planned for by the War Department. An example was the policy of the U.S. Ninth Army commander, Lt. Gen. William H. Simpson, one of the least known but most admired and effective field commanders in the army. Simpson had a straightforward, iron-clad rule in the Ninth Army: "Never send an infantryman to do a job that an artillery shell can do for him."[26] Though such tactics were not the only reason for the high rate of expenditure, Simpson's policy was not atypical.

Frontline units in the ETO had since June 6 been decimated by combat and noncombat losses that had all but drained dry the replacement pool. The problem that had plagued the British since late 1943 was now seriously affecting American combat units. Eisenhower's broad-front strategy was predicated on winning the war with a strength of approximately ninety divisions (sixty-one of them American) but when both battle and nonbattle casualties rose dramatically in the post-Normandy period and the replacement system could not fill his needs, Eisenhower was left with a serious deficiency. Within Bradley's 12th Army Group there was a shortfall of more than thirty thousand, of which nineteen thousand were infantry. Although Marshall was committed to keeping Eisenhower's American divisions at full strength through replacements sent from the United States, army planners in Washington had underestimated the numbers and the attrition rate in the ETO. Shortages of riflemen, which began mounting as early as July 1944, eventually reached thirty thousand men. To fill the ranks of his depleted infantry divisions, Eisenhower, in his other role as commander of U.S. forces in the ETO, permitted the reassignment of noncombatants and rear-echelon troops to combat duty. Support units were stripped to the bone, and some desk officers who had once professed a desire to see combat duty scrambled to convince their superiors that the paperwork they shuffled was suddenly critically important.[27] The casualty rate among both trained and untrained replacements was staggering. During some of the bitter winter battles, many replacements joined units already in the front lines and became casualties before anyone had time even to learn their names.

As autumn lapsed into winter and the notoriously bad European weather worsened, Eisenhower found road travel increasingly difficult and time consuming. One day he spent three hours waiting until his Cadillac could be pulled from a ditch. While visiting troops of the 29th Division on a soggy hillside, Eisenhower slipped and fell flat on his back, covered in sticky mud. "From the shout of laughter that went up I am quite sure that no other meeting I had with soldiers during the war was a greater success. . . . Even the men who rushed forward to help pick me out of the mire could scarcely do so for laughing."[28] Despite the urging of his staff to abandon the stress of such trips, Eisenhower refused, even though his ailing knee was a painful reminder of the folly of pushing airplanes through sand. Pain and fatigue notwithstanding, Eisenhower remained determined to meet and mingle with the men fighting his war and to ensure that everything possible was being done for their comfort and welfare.

The proximity of Kay Summersby continued to fuel gossip and speculation. When Churchill and Brooke arrived at the SHAEF advance command post near Reims, Kay sat at the head of the table next to the prime minister at lunch. "I was interested to see that Kay his chauffeur, had been promoted to hostess. . . . In so doing Ike produced a lot of undesirable gossip that did him no good," remarked Brooke.[29]

On Thanksgiving Eve and Day, Eisenhower visited his friend Wade Haislip's field headquarters for a conference with Haislip, Devers, and Patch. Haislip greeted Eisenhower with, "For God's sake, sir. I was just on my way down to tell you not to come. Please go on. We don't want you [here]." Not far away German and American tanks and artillery began trading heavy fire. Deeply concerned that their commander in chief was in danger, his hosts attempted to hustle him back to the safer confines of SHAEF, but Eisenhower would have none of it. "Listen, if you think a little Kraut armor is going to deprive me of Thanksgiving dinner, you're quite mistaken."[30]

Even his dog went to war. Whenever Eisenhower traveled by automobile he was generally driven by Kay Summersby, who often brought Telek. In mid-November, Eisenhower visited Third Army in Nancy. During lunch Patton's bull terrier, Willie, who looked ferocious but was something of a coward, was banished. Telek was under the table between the two generals when suddenly war broke out beneath their feet. Willie had wandered back in and, finding Telek occupying *his* place of honor, precipitated a noisy brawl. As Summersby later recounted, "Patton let loose with every curse in his celebrated vocabulary. It was classic, that tirade. . . . I was terrified for Telek. It took four generals, the Theater's top brass, to separate Willie and Telek. And even then they had to throw water on the fighters." Patton apologized profusely, but Eisenhower insisted, "This is Willie's home. We should lock up Telek." Shaking his head, Patton replied, "No Sir! Telek outranks Willie, so Telek stays right here. Willie is confined to quarters, under arrest. That's Army protocol." However, unable to contain his elation, Patton could not resist needling his friend: "But my Willie was chewing bejesus out of your Gawdamned little Scottie—rank or no rank!"[31]

Later Eisenhower was escorted to a suite in Nancy's finest hotel as Patton's guest. To ward off the cold, someone lit a fire in the fireplace, which no one noticed was fake and had no chimney. Clouds of smoke and flames soon filled the room. A chagrined Patton arrived in the wake of the Nancy fire department to find mayhem and the wry comment from Eisenhower: "Nice place you've got here, Georgie." It was a very grouchy Eisenhower who decamped for less hazardous environs the following morning. Spending time with Patton, he decided, was just too unrestful.[32]

Mamie Eisenhower's burdens did not ease. When John completed his infantry training he was assigned to the 71st Division, then based at Fort Benning. Although the division was not due to deploy to Europe until January 1945, Mamie angrily lashed out at Ike in a letter in which she complained that their son was being put in harm's way and that he was doing nothing to stop it. Mamie, who had always been overprotective of John, seemed unwilling or unable to grasp that she was but one of millions of mothers whose sons faced daily peril and that her husband simply could not interfere. His patience taxed once too often, Ike replied with the most explosive letter he wrote to his wife during the war—a combination rebuke and plea for understanding. "It always depresses me," he wrote,

> when you talk about "dirty tricks" I've played and what a beating you've taken apparently because of me. You've always put your own interpretation on every act, look, or word of mine. Don't forget I take a beating every day. . . . I constantly receive letters from bereaved mothers, sisters, and wives, and from others [who] are begging me to send their men home, or at least outside the battle zone, to a place of comparative safety. So far as John is concerned, we can do nothing but pray. If I interfered even slightly or indirectly he would be so resentful for the remainder of his life that neither I (nor you, if he thought you had anything to do with it) could be comfortable with him . . . please try to see me in something besides a despicable light and at least let me be *certain* of my welcome home when this mess is finished. . . . I do know that when you blow off steam you don't really think of me as such a black hearted creature as your language implies. I'd rather you didn't mention any of this mess again.[33]

Given their lifelong rivalry, Eisenhower was quite used to his brother Edgar's blunt manner and sharp tongue. Nevertheless he could not have been pleased with a tart letter from his brother accusing him and all professional soldiers of liking war. His favorite term for Regular Army men was "professional killers." The often fierce interaction of opinions between Dwight and Edgar had always had a somewhat rough edge, even when in jest, and this exchange between two extremely strong-willed men was not unusual, except for its timing, which was not calculated to raise Ike's morale.

He fired back immediately, chastising Edgar for getting it all wrong, and reiterating his own long-standing disgust with war:

Unquestionably any soldier would agree with almost any cynical philosophy you might care to develop respecting the progress of a civilization that allows itself to get plunged into a world war every quarter of a century. The mistake that people like yourself make is in assuming that the soldier—and I mean the professional—likes it. . . . The average soldier hates it, probably a lot more than you do.[34]

It was not to be the last time these two fundamentally different men would disagree: Edgar, the elder, his outlook defined by his boyhood poverty, who made his fortune in the law; and Dwight, the younger, idealistic brother who, despite his own deep aversion to his hardscrabble boyhood, had taken a different path. Although proud of Ike's stature and achievements, Edgar had never concealed his disdain for his brother's career choice, and of the five surviving Eisenhower brothers, Edgar always seemed to have the most difficulty accepting Dwight's fame.

After promising that Eisenhower "would hear no more" from him on the subject of command, Montgomery reopened the festering wound in late November by demanding a meeting and noting with his usual bluntness that the Allies had "failed" and "we have suffered a strategic reverse." He was troubled by recent visits to the U.S. First and Ninth Armies. In Simpson's Ninth Army "the general picture is one of tired, cold and wet troops operating over country which is a sea of mud." Overall, "the whole business is a first class example of the futile doctrine of everybody attacking everywhere with no reserves anywhere," he wrote to Brooke, a missive his biographer calls "perhaps his most pungent and deeply felt criticism of American tactics in World War II."[35]

At Montgomery's request Eisenhower arrived at his tactical headquarters in Holland on the afternoon of November 28 for what turned out to be a three-hour conference. Montgomery pointed to the large operations map that covered the wall of his trailer and—in terms as undiplomatic as those he had used in Brussels in September—proclaimed that Eisenhower's latest directive, issued on October 28 with the aim of mounting an advance to the Rhine, had failed. "The Allies," he said, "had suffered a strategic reverse" when the Germans refused to be drawn into battle anywhere west of the Rhine. Again pointing to the map, Montgomery noted that with the 21st and 12th Army Groups divided by the dense Ardennes forest, it was essential for both army groups to operate north of the Ardennes under a single ground commander. Once again Montgomery offered to serve under Bradley if Eisenhower so decided. The meeting concluded with Montgomery mistakenly believing that Eisenhower had agreed with him and would again place Bradley under his operational control. He had not. When Eisenhower departed the following morning Montgomery thought him "worried and ill at ease."[36]

Two days later Montgomery wrote "to confirm the main points that we agreed on." The letter reopened the debate by asserting that, with an offensive to establish a bridgehead east of the Rhine unlikely until the following spring, "We now require a new plan," which would "get away from the doctrine of attacking in so many places that nowhere are we strong enough to get decisive results. And this time *we must not fail.*" Given Eisenhower's insistence on a broad-front advance, it made sense, said Montgomery, to empower a single commander on each front to run the battle. Moreover, he insisted that he and Bradley had actually made a "good team" but that nothing had gone well "since you separated us," a none-too-subtle reference to Eisenhower's decision to take command himself.[37]

"Monty's letter made Ike hot under the collar," penned Butcher. On December 1, Eisenhower bluntly rebutted Montgomery's arguments. Not only had Eisenhower not changed his mind, but he was reassured by an appreciation prepared by his intelligence chief, Kenneth Strong, which noted that the Allies were winning the war of attrition. Strong concluded that German units were being written off at such an accelerated pace (twenty divisions per month) that defending the Reich would soon become impossible, and that Allied strategy should continue to be one of constant attack. Buoyed by Strong's optimism, Eisenhower declined to reduce operations by Devers and Patton south of the Ardennes "as long as they are cleaning up our right flank." It would become important "later on," he asserted, "to have two strings to our bow. Don't forget that you were very wise in making a provision for this at Mareth, and it paid off."[38]

A meeting between Montgomery, Bradley, and Eisenhower was scheduled for December 7 at Maastricht, at which Montgomery insisted that only their respective chiefs of staff should be present but "must not speak." Eisenhower flatly rejecting silencing Smith. "I will not by any means insult him by telling him that he should remain mute." He concluded, "I beg of you not to continue to look upon past performances of this great fighting force as a failure merely because we have not achieved all that we could have hoped."[39]

The afternoon before the Maastricht conference Eisenhower arrived at 12th Army Group headquarters in Luxembourg City and went straight to Bradley's office, where he "slumped down into the large couch in front of the map and the two of them talked there, conversing quietly . . . Ike with his face heavily wrinkled" in a frown, "his neck stuck deeply into the fur collar of the flying jacket he wears."[40] With the arrival of Tedder, the three men reviewed what would occur the following day. It was almost as if they were gearing up for battle, not with the enemy but with Montgomery.

The next day a suspicious Bradley rejected Montgomery's plan for a concentrated two-army-group offensive against the Ruhr, and Eisenhower would agree only to launching "an all-out offensive north of Ardennes early in 1945."[41] Having been given virtual carte blanche to advance when and where he chose, Bradley, who had thought he "would stand pathetically alone" at the conference, emerged the clear victor and returned to Luxembourg in "high spirits," recorded his aide. A more sobering note was sounded by Pinky Bull, the SHAEF G-3, who glumly observed, "I don't know what he [Bradley] has to be happy about."[42]

That Bradley would get his way is clear from the historical record. In a memorandum of his notes withheld from publication during his lifetime, Bradley wrote that Montgomery had not only made a poor impression with his arguments for a single commander of all ground forces, but that "I told General Eisenhower that, of course, if he put the Twelfth Army Group under Marshal Montgomery, he would of necessity have to relieve me of command, because it would be an indication that I have failed as a separate Army Group Commander."[43] Thus, as Montgomery's official biographer points out, "faced with Bradley's threat, Eisenhower had had no option but to give in to Bradley's strategy."[44]

After the meeting broke up, a dismayed Montgomery wrote to Brooke that it had been "dreadful" and had "produced no good results," continuing:

> Eisenhower has obviously been "got at" by the American generals; he reversed his opinion on all major decisions which he had agreed when he visited me. . . . Eisenhower and Bradley have their eyes firmly on FRANKFURT. . . . We shall split our resources, and our strength, and we shall fail. . . . I think now that if we want the war to end within any reasonable period you will have to get Eisenhower's hand taken off the land battle. I regret to say that in my opinion he just doesn't know what he is doing.[45]

What even Montgomery had finally come to understand was that this was an American-dominated war and that he was virtually powerless to influence its outcome.

Until the weather permitted an all-out offensive the Allies would continue their World War I approach to wearing down and writing off the German army. Perhaps sensing a negative reaction from Brooke and the British chiefs of staff, Eisenhower cabled Churchill that he and Tedder would be in London early the following week and would like to update them on SHAEF's situation and current plans. Brooke's diary recorded that the meeting took place in Churchill's map room, on December 12 where,

> Ike explained his plan which contemplates a double advance into Germany, north of [the] Rhine and by Frankfurt. I disagreed flatly with

> it and accused Ike of violating principles of concentration of force, which had resulted in his present failures. . . . Ike also *quite* incapable of understanding real strategy. To make it worse Tedder talks nothing but nonsense in support of Ike. . . . Amongst other things discovered that Ike now does not hope to cross the Rhine before May!!! [1945]

The meeting left Brooke so disheartened that, not for the first time, he "seriously" considered resigning. "I feel I have utterly failed."[46]

Whether or not Eisenhower's motive and "political dexterity" to avert certain criticism from the British chiefs of staff by appealing directly to Churchill was "awesome," as Montgomery's official biographer has described it, Eisenhower's decision to brief the prime minister was clearly designed to win the support of "the one man in Whitehall who did not have the heart or professional military stature to say no."[47]

Despite Brooke's impassioned arguments, Eisenhower had clearly prevailed. The following day Churchill weakly explained to Brooke that he felt obliged to support Eisenhower, "as he was one American against five of us with only Tedder to support him. And also as he was his guest. I think he felt I had been rather rough on Ike." Brooke managed to alarm Churchill sufficiently that he convened a meeting of the War Cabinet the evening of December 13. Although the "date of May [1945] for crossing of the Rhine had a profound effect on the Cabinet," noted Brooke, there was little the British could do to influence the course of events in Europe.[48] For perhaps the first time Brooke had to admit that it was Dwight Eisenhower whose actions and decisions would determine the outcome of the war.

50.

"There Will Be Only Cheerful Faces at This Conference Table."

Your great hour has arrived. . . . We gamble everything!
—FIELD MARSHAL GERD VON RUNDSTEDT

By October, and continuing throughout the autumn of 1944, the various Allied intelligence staffs were aware that the Germans had assembled the Sixth Panzer Army in the area east of Aachen. However, the positioning of its divisions was misinterpreted by Allied intelligence as preparation for defending the Reich against what SHAEF defined as "a final showdown before the winter," rather than as the preparation for a massive counteroffensive. The lone exception was the astute Third Army G-2, Col. Oscar Koch, who was not deceived by the German buildup opposite the Ardennes.[1] Even as Patton's Third Army staff was planning a major new offensive, to commence on December 19, to crack the Siegfried Line and drive to the Rhine, Eisenhower had already made up his mind, "regardless of the results" of the forthcoming offensive, to transfer divisions from Third Army to the northern armies to support a breaching of the Rhine and the main assault into the heartland of the Reich.[2] While Koch closely noted signs of further German buildup, Third Army was also planning measures to counter any potential threat in the Ardennes so that, as Patton told his staff, "We'll be in a position to meet whatever happens."[3]

By mid-December there was something of a lull in the bloodletting, brought about largely by the weather. In the rugged, heavily forested Ardennes, with its poor road net, Bradley had taken what he later described as "a calculated risk" by lightly defending what had traditionally been a major German invasion route. On the thinly held front lines were only two newly arrived, untested American infantry divisions and two battered veteran divisions of Troy Middleton's VIII Corps in the process of absorbing replacements. In such vile weather it was deemed unlikely that the Germans could mount a serious threat. Moreover, despite Germany's historical pattern of initiating counteroffensives when things looked darkest, it was assumed by the Allied high command that there was simply no way the Germans could secretly pull off such an operation in the Ardennes. As early as November 25 Patton had disagreed, noting that "First Army is making a terrible mistake in leaving VIII Corps static, it is highly probable that the Germans are building up east of them."[4]

The dispersal of American units in the Ardennes was a direct result of Eisenhower's broad-front strategy, which had been reduced to, as one historian has noted, "the premise that 'more is better'—that is, more tanks, more bullets, more beans, more fuel, and above all more men. 'More men' was Eisenhower's principal worry on 16 December 1944, not the threat of a German attack."[5] Indeed, the existing situation in the Ardennes, concludes Russell Weigley, revealed a fundamental and damaging flaw: "It was not that the broad-front strategy was wrong; the more basic trouble was that the Anglo-American alliance had not given Eisenhower enough troops to carry it out safely. . . . There were not enough Anglo-American divisions, or enough replacements for casualties in the existing divisions. Eisenhower could not create a reserve unless he abandoned the broad-front strategy."

Moreover, notes Weigley, "the events unfolding in the Ardennes on December 16 indicated that the ninety-division gamble had gone sour. The American army in Europe fought on too narrow a margin of physical superiority for the favored American broad-front strategy to be anything but a risky gamble."[6] Eisenhower would later accept—and fully deserve—responsibility for the dispositions of his armies, which permitted the Germans to mount their counteroffensive. Yet there was another basic reason why the Allies were about to be caught with their pants down: "Everyone at SHAEF was thinking offensively, about what they could do to the enemy, and never about what the enemy might do to them."[7]

The German counteroffensive in the Ardennes would turn out to be the latest example of the principle learned and relearned the hard way by the Allies during World War II: Expect the unexpected. From North Africa to Arnhem and the Ardennes, the German army could be counted on never to panic and always to fight back tenaciously with whatever reserves could be mustered. Thus it should not have come as the surprise it did that, with Allied operations at a standstill and the Third Reich on the verge of invasion from both east and west, Adolf Hitler elected to gamble the fate of Germany on a last-ditch attempt to salvage the war by a sudden, lightning thrust through the Ardennes.

The twin keys to a German success were surprise and speed: splitting the Allied front and driving across the Meuse before the Allies could react. Hitler's intent was nothing less than the destruction of all Allied forces north of a line running from Bastogne to Antwerp. Seeking to repeat the success of the 1940 invasion of western Europe, which had worked to near perfection, Hitler believed that once across the river Meuse and into the Belgian lowlands beyond the Ardennes, his armies could drive clear to Antwerp and, with this vital port in German hands, compel the Allies to sue for peace.

To accomplish this Herculean task, Hitler assembled in great secrecy a massive force of three armies, consisting of twenty-eight divisions, twelve of them panzer, to launch the first and only German counteroffensive of the war in northwestern Europe.[8]

However, Hitler's senior commanders responsible for carrying out his orders had severe misgivings. When they first heard of the plan in late October 1944, both the reinstated commander in chief west, Field Marshal Gerd von Rundstedt, and the commander of German ground forces (Army Group B), Field Marshal Walther Model, opposed Hitler's Ardennes counteroffensive. Model, who had earned the Führer's trust, was typically blunt: "This plan hasn't got a damned leg to stand on." Both commanders believed that to seize Antwerp was a hopelessly unrealistic goal and attempted to persuade Hitler to scale down its scope. Their advice was ignored, even though Hitler himself understood the extent of his gamble. The alternative was worse: the certain loss of the war and the destruction of Germany in a rear-guard action against the powerful vise of the Russian and Allied armies.

Nevertheless, in early December both Model and his two panzer army commanders, Waffen SS general "Sepp" Dietrich and General der Panzertruppen Hasso von Manteuffel, spoke forcefully at a conference with Hitler, urging that the plan be reconsidered. Hitler once again adamantly refused, and under the cover of the bitter winter weather, more than fourteen hundred tanks, two thousand guns, and twenty divisions were quietly moved forward into the thick forests of the Schnee Eifel on the eastern fringes of the Ardennes to await the signal to attack.

At SHAEF, Saturday, December 16, 1944, began on a promising note for Eisenhower. He was presented the Polish Medal of Honor at a ceremony and learned that Roosevelt had nominated him for the exalted five-star rank of general of the army. Noted Butcher in his diary, "The man who always cautioned his family not to expect him to be promoted has risen from lieutenant colonel to five-star general in three years, three months, and sixteen days."[9] Eisenhower seemed elated. "God, I just want to see the first time I sign my name as General of the Army," he said when congratulated by Bradley's aide, Chet Hansen.[10]

Also on December 16, his faithful orderly, Mickey McKeogh, was married to a WAC driver named Pearlie Hargreaves, whom he had met in North Africa. With Eisenhower's blessing the two were married in the ancient chapel of King Louis XIV on a bitterly cold afternoon. Except for Eisenhower, whose only defense against the cold was his uniform blouse, the guests sat huddled in heavy overcoats during the ceremony in the freezing cold chapel. Afterward Eisenhower turned over his quarters for a reception for the newlyweds. The beaming bride earned a kiss from the supreme commander, who presented the couple with a one-hundred-dollar war bond.

Bradley arrived later that afternoon to discuss the growing replacement crisis and briefly joined Eisenhower at the reception. The two generals then attended an early-evening meeting in the SHAEF war room with Bedell Smith, Spaatz, Tedder, and Kenneth Strong, the SHAEF G-2. The meeting had barely begun when Strong was summoned by his deputy, Brig. Gen. Tom Betts, who appeared at the door, his usual calm demeanor visibly missing. When Strong returned it was to reveal that fragmentary reports revealed that a series of powerful German attacks had commenced in the eastern Ardennes at dawn against the weakest link in the Allied front, a thinly dispersed cavalry group and the newly arrived, unblooded 106th Division, which had been put there by Bradley primarily to keep them out of harm's way. Although what SHAEF knew at this point was sketchy, Strong suggested that the attack more than likely posed a serious threat to First Army.

The German buildup in the sparsely populated Schnee Eifel had, with the exception of the Third Army's Koch, deceived intelligence officers up and down the Allied chain of command. Despite a steady influx of timely information from Ultra and other reliable sources, the German attack in the Ardennes revealed serious lapses in Allied intelligence, whose G-2s had, at the very least, been provided sufficient evidence of the German buildup to discern that something major was afoot in the Ardennes. In mid-November SHAEF had concluded that the Germans were preparing to defend against an offensive that they believed the Allies would launch around Aachen, aimed at Cologne and the Ruhr. That judgment never varied despite fresh evidence of a German buildup to the south. Lulled by deception measures worthy of Fortitude, the Allies, from Eisenhower on down, were convinced that German intentions were purely defensive.[11] The Allies seemed wedded to the belief that it was Rundstedt who was making the military decisions in the west in December 1944, failing to grasp that they were not the "rational, 'traditional' decisions of von Rundstedt but . . . those of Hitler. The Allied High Command," wrote French historian Jacques Nobécourt, "was indulging in wishful thinking."[12]

Eisenhower was ill served by Strong and his intelligence staff, who were reluctant to submit intelligence estimates of a negative nature. A British intelligence officer in the SHAEF G-2, Noel Annan, observed that their intelligence appreciations

> were tuned to justify Eisenhower's policy to attack all along the line. This policy required intelligence to report the German army as being incapable of mounting an offensive. Strong was later to say that intelligence officers were regarded as defeatist if they did not believe the end of the war was in sight. . . . The most spectacular blunder of the interpreters of intelligence was our failure to forecast the German offensive in the Ardennes.[13]

In early December, Strong had warned only of a possible disruptive German spoiling attack somewhere in the Ardennes during a period of bad weather. Bedell Smith took the threat seriously and had sent Strong to personally warn Bradley, who dismissed the forecast with the observation that he had already made provisions to reinforce the Ardennes. The danger, he said, was exaggerated: "Let them come."[14]

Despite the news on December 16, Bradley again dismissed the reports as merely localized attacks designed to hamper forthcoming offensives by his First and Third Armies. Eisenhower was not misled and at once emphatically disagreed, declaring, "That's no spoiling attack."[15] At the instant when decisions were crucial, it was Eisenhower, not Bradley, who took the initiative to act without hesitation even though the situation was chaotic and ill defined. While German intentions were still unclear at this early stage, from the time of the first reports by Strong, Eisenhower was convinced that the German attack was a serious attempt to split the Allied front, and reacted accordingly. Why else, he reasoned, would they even bother attacking in an area that led nowhere and contained no tangible objectives?

This was the first occasion since he had assumed command of Allied ground forces that Eisenhower was able to influence the outcome of a battle. Other than to approve it, he had played no role in Market-Garden. Since then he had been beset by the day-to-day problems brought about by the weather and the breakdown of his broad-front strategy. Now, when it mattered most, he was at the center of a seminal battle whose outcome would determine the final course of the war.

On December 16, facing a dilemma that was a direct result of the broad-front strategy, Eisenhower had no theater reserve to commit to the battle. The only two units available were the veteran but lightly armed U.S. airborne divisions, the 82nd and 101st, both still refitting near Reims from the savage fighting in Holland in September. Neither was adequately equipped for sustained ground combat. Eisenhower's other dilemma was the same old problem that had plagued SHAEF from the time of its relocation to France: communications. It had taken until early evening on December 16 to learn even fragmentary details of the German attack. To make informed decisions, a commander must have knowledge of the situation he faces. On this day Eisenhower had neither knowledge nor the other vital ingredient, timely intelligence. By early afternoon on December 16, the First Army G-2 already had a captured copy of Rundstedt's order of the day, which "confirmed that an all-out offensive was under way," notes the official First Army historian. Yet the First Army staff still could not agree (or would not accept the evidence) that it was a major offensive, and by as late as December 18, "First Army headquarters had little idea of the status of the battle."[16]

As the two generals weighed the initial Allied reaction, Bradley remained noncommittal, while Eisenhower made a decision to alert the 82nd and 101st

Airborne for urgent deployment to the Ardennes as a stopgap measure. Although unwilling to be seen as interfering personally in the conduct of Bradley's command of his army group, Eisenhower did press Bradley to move quickly to reinforce the Ardennes, pointedly suggesting, "I think you'd better send Middleton some help." There were two obvious options in the form of two uncommitted U.S. armored divisions, the newly arrived 10th Armored in Third Army, and the 7th Armored, then located north of the penetration, in the Ninth Army sector. Bradley was openly apprehensive at the prospect of issuing orders he knew Patton would loudly and heatedly dispute, but Eisenhower was in no mood for Patton's histrionics and snapped, "Tell him that Ike is running this damn war."[17] Bradley's inertia and Eisenhower's proactive stance was the first inkling of what would shortly become an open rift between the two friends.

It was early evening when Patton was summoned to the telephone and ordered by Bradley to commit the 10th Armored immediately. The division was to report to Troy Middleton at the crossroads market town of Bastogne, which the VIII Corps commander had already identified as a vital choke point.

The decision to shift forces into the Ardennes made, Eisenhower and Bradley attended a second reception for the newlyweds. Before returning to the war room to spend a sleepless night awaiting fresh developments, they played five rubbers of bridge with Everett Hughes and another, and drank a bottle of champagne and the best part of a bottle of Scotch whiskey to celebrate Eisenhower's promotion.

Bradley remained sufficiently unconcerned that he did not return to his headquarters in Luxembourg until the afternoon of December 17. Just how inaccurate he had been in his assessment was grimly evident during the first two days of the battle. Seventeen German divisions had already been identified, with more to come. From all sections of the Ardennes the news was dismal. The so-called spoiling attack had turned into a torrent as the Germans pressed their attacks with surprising vigor—and success. As the initial penetration deepened, it soon became an enormous "bulge" on the map, hence the nickname given the battle.

On December 17 and 18 Eisenhower and his staff developed the broad outlines of the Allied response. These were to contain and delay the German counteroffensive until a plan of action could be worked out and implemented to defeat it. Eisenhower ordered the two airborne divisions to the Ardennes by truck in a race against time, and summoned Matthew B. Ridgway's XVIII Airborne Corps HQ from England. The decision where the airborne would be sent Eisenhower left to his staff to determine. Eisenhower's most powerful weapon, the Allied air forces, remained grounded as the bad weather made any aerial response impossible.

The road net in the Ardennes is sparse, and two sites were vital to stopping the German spearheads: Saint-Vith and Bastogne, where the main east-west roads converged, both of which the German armored columns had to pass through to attain bridgeheads over the river Meuse and before gaining access to the plains of Belgium beyond. Three men played key roles: Bedell Smith, Strong, and the deputy G-3, Maj. Gen. J. F. M "Jock" Whiteley, who was one of Eisenhower's most trusted staff officers and generally regarded as the ablest British general in SHAEF.[18] Although officially he was the deputy G-3, Smith also employed Whiteley in an unofficial capacity as his deputy chief of staff.

When the three generals closely examined a map of the Ardennes spread out on the floor, it seemed evident that the German attack was aimed at splitting the British and U.S. army groups. It was equally clear that a grave risk existed unless the shoulders of the penetration held firm in the northern and southern Ardennes, and the German advance was confined to the corridor in between, where it could be controlled and eventually defeated. Using a captured German sword, they indicated potential choke points, searching for places critical for the Germans to capture. The point of the sword barely wavered before settling on Bastogne, one of the few towns where the road net in the Ardennes converged.

After Smith was assured that reinforcements could reach Bastogne by road, it was quickly decided to employ the 101st Airborne Division.[19] After a race against the clock, the 101st arrived in Bastogne in the nick of time to join an element of the 10th Armored and several other units just as the Germans began attacking the town, which was soon surrounded and under siege. In the days that followed the 101st would fight the bitterest battles in its distinguished history. The acting commander of the 101st, Brig. Gen. Anthony C. McAuliffe, soon attained immortality when he rejected a German demand to surrender with a single word: "Nuts!" Thereafter Bastogne would come to symbolize one of the finest hours of the U.S. Army.

Back in his headquarters in Luxembourg, Bradley glumly studied his operations map and muttered, "Pardon my French . . . but where in hell has this son of a bitch gotten all his strength?"[20] On December 18 Bradley summoned Patton to Luxembourg, where he displayed on the map the depth of the German penetrations, which were far more serious than Patton had previously thought. Asked what Third Army could do, Patton replied he would have two divisions on the move the next day, and a third in twenty-four hours, if necessary. Although disappointed that his Third Army offensive in the Saar was canceled, Patton shrugged it off with the observation, "What the hell, we'll still be killing Krauts," grinning when Bradley assured him they would "hit this bastard hard."[21] Later that evening Bradley telephoned Patton and directed him to report to Verdun the following morning to meet with Eisenhower and the other SHAEF commanders to determine the Allied response.

On December 19, 1944, Eisenhower, Tedder, Bradley, Devers, Patton, Bedell Smith, and a handful of key SHAEF staff officers converged on Verdun, the scene of the bloodiest battle in history in 1916. Before departing for Verdun, Patton briefed his staff and two of his corps commanders at Third Army headquarters in Nancy, explaining that Third Army would be called on to come to the relief of First Army; how and where would be decided at Verdun.

The meeting site was a dismal second-floor room of a French stone barracks—"a huge heavy structure set in quadrangle form in a sea of mud." Very little warmth emanated from a potbellied stove, and most attendees kept their coats on to ward off the pervasive chill. Other than a table and chairs, the room was bare save for the easels on which would eventually repose Kenneth Strong's situation maps. Accompanied by Tedder, Eisenhower arrived at 11:00 A.M. in his armor-plated Cadillac, escorted by military police jeeps with machine guns, "looking grave, almost ashen." His mood was soon brightened by the presence of Bradley, who awaited him upstairs, and Patton, his stern war face firmly in place, who arrived a short time later, followed by Devers. As always during periods of crisis, Eisenhower's chief weapon of motivation to defuse tense situations was optimism. However, the cheerfulness he exuded at Verdun seemed forced, and the usual Eisenhower smile could not hide the grimness and the aura of crisis that was present in the room.

Montgomery was absent and had sent de Guingand to represent him. Most thought Monty's absence a calculated insult to both Eisenhower and themselves, but David Eisenhower has suggested a more plausible reason: "that the British did not want to complicate matters" over what was primarily an American battle. Eisenhower's impatience was apparent when Strong and Pinky Bull arrived a few minutes late. "Well," snapped Eisenhower, "I knew my staff would get here; it was only a question of when."[22]

The atmosphere remained tense despite Eisenhower's fragile attempt at levity when he opened by announcing, "The present situation is to be regarded as one of opportunity for us and not of disaster. There will be only cheerful faces at this conference table." Patton immediately chimed in, "Hell, let's have the guts to let the sons of bitches go all the way to Paris. Then we'll really cut 'em up and chew 'em up." The room erupted in laughter, much of it forced. Eisenhower replied, "George, that's fine. But the enemy must never be allowed to cross the Meuse."

The commanders quickly agreed to stop offensive action in all Allied sectors and concentrate on blunting the German drive. Eisenhower's strategy was to draw a stop line at the Meuse, beyond which there would be no further retreat. Once the German attacks were contained, the Allies would counterattack. Eisenhower said, "George, I want you to command this move—under Brad's supervision of course—making a strong counterattack with at least six divisions. When can you start?"[23] Patton replied, "As soon as you're through with me." "When can you attack?" Eisenhower asked. "The morning of December 21, with three divisions," Patton replied instantly.

Forty-eight hours! Eisenhower was not amused, wrongly assuming that

Patton had once again picked a very inopportune moment to act boastful. "Don't be fatuous, George," he retorted in obvious disbelief. "If you try to go that early, you won't have all three divisions ready and you'll go piecemeal. You will start on the twenty-second, and I want your initial blow to be a strong one! I'd even settle for the twenty-third if it takes that long to get three full divisions."

Patton, however, was not being flippant. Where others at Verdun came with only vague ideas and without specific plans, Patton, a lifelong student of war, had devised three plans beforehand, each tailored to meet any contingency that Eisenhower and Bradley might direct. "This was the sublime moment of his career," wrote Martin Blumenson. After more than thirty-four years, it was as if destiny had groomed him for this single, defining instant in which the fate of the war rested on the right decisions being made and carried out by the men in that dingy room. While near panic existed elsewhere, there was in the Third Army a belief that there existed a magnificent opportunity to strike a killing blow. While others debated or waffled, Patton had understood the problem facing the Allies, had created a plan to counterattack the Germans and occupy Bastogne, which—although not yet surrounded—was clearly soon to be besieged. By contrast, Bradley, whose army group had been attacked, "mostly observed" throughout the two-hour conference, "saying little, offering nothing." Even he realized that the only principal players were Eisenhower and Patton.[24]

Opinions vary, but certainly the reaction of some present that day was skepticism of yet another smug prediction by Patton that was quite out of place in this somber setting. Strong noted, "There was some laughter, especially from British officers, when Patton answered 'Forty-eight hours.' "[25] Patton's aide, Lt. Col. Charles R. Codman, witnessed "a stir, a shuffling of feet, as those present straightened up in their chairs. In some faces skepticism. But through the room the current of excitement leaped like a flame." John Eisenhower wrote, "Witnesses to the occasion testify to the electric effect of this exchange. The prospect of relieving three divisions from the line, turning them north, and [moving them] over icy roads to Arlon to prepare for a major counterattack in less than seventy-two hours was astonishing, even to a group accustomed to flexibility in their military operations."

"It meant a 90-degree turn that would pose logistical nightmares—getting divisions on new roads and making sure supplies reached them from dumps established in quite a different context, for quite a different situation. Altogether it was an operation only a master could think of executing," notes Blumenson. Moreover, only a commander with exceptional confidence in his subordinate commanders and in the professional skill of his fighting divisions could dare risk such a venture. Patton not only never hesitated but embraced the opportunity to turn a potential military debacle into a triumph.

Cigar in hand, Patton illustrated his intentions on the map. Pointing to the obvious "bulge" in the Saint-Vith–Bastogne sector and speaking directly to Bradley, he said, "Brad, the Kraut's stuck his head in a meatgrinder." Turning his fist in a grinding motion, he continued, "[a]nd this time I've got hold of the handle." He then replied to the inevitable questions with specific, well-rehearsed answers. "Patton would have liked to have seen the Germans drive some forty or fifty miles, then chop them off and destroy them, but he recognized that he would never muster support for that kind of daring."[26] Codman recorded, "Within an hour everything had been thrashed out—the divisions to be employed, objectives, new Army boundaries, the amount of our own front to be taken over by [Devers's] Sixth Army Group, and other matters—and virtually all of them settled on General Patton's terms." Two of Patton's three corps were to be extricated for a counterattack into the Ardennes, with Patch's Seventh Army to take control of most of the Third Army sector in the Saar.[27] Bradley later acknowledged that this was a "greatly matured Patton," and that the Third Army staff had pulled off "a brilliant effort." It was perhaps the most remarkable hour of Patton's military career.

If ever there was justification for Eisenhower to have saved Patton's career, it was now, and before they parted, Eisenhower remarked, "Funny thing, George, every time I get a new star I get attacked." Patton shot back affably to remind his friend, "And every time you get attacked, Ike, I pull you out" (a reference to the debacle in Tunisia at Kasserine Pass, the time when Eisenhower attained his fourth star).[28]

Those who visited First Army HQ, at Chaudfontaine, returned disturbed by the chaotic conditions and the lack of leadership they encountered. The previous command post at Spa had been so hastily abandoned in utter panic that top-secret maps were found still pinned to the walls, along with classified documents strewn on desks; even unopened Christmas presents had been left behind.[29] After the war, tales abounded that Hodges played no role in the crucial first two days of the battle. What has been established, notes the official historian, is that "the First Army commander was incapacitated for at least two days and that [his chief of staff, Maj. Gen. William B.] Kean, in effect, operated as the commander of the First Army." Kean later stated that Hodges had been "confined to his bed, barely conscious with viral pneumonia," an account disputed by another member of the staff who reported that his commander "was sitting with his arms folded on his desk, his head in his arms."[30] Although the official historian records the various reasons for First Army's failure to predict the German counteroffensive, Bedell Smith trod where official historians are not permitted: "First Army had a very bad staff," he said, and "Hodges [was] the weakest commander we had."[31]

It was left to Gerow to exercise the initiative lacking from First Army by deploying his V Corps to confine the penetration by defending the key terrain of Elsenborn Ridge along the northern shoulder, in what became one of the outstanding defensive actions of the war.

Montgomery was greatly disturbed by the state of paralysis in First Army and by the seriousness of the situation in the north and conveyed his misgivings to the visiting Jock Whiteley, who maintained close contacts with 21st Army Group through his close friend Freddie de Guingand. Although occasionally one of the field marshal's sternest critics, Whiteley nevertheless returned to SHAEF the night of December 19 convinced that Montgomery must be given immediate command of the northern sector before it was too late. Placing a telephone call to Montgomery, Whiteley said, "If Ike asked you to take over First Army, when could you do it?" Montgomery replied he could do so the following morning. Whiteley made it clear that nothing had yet been decided. Montgomery not only did not press the matter but exerted no pressure in favor of the idea.[32]

Whiteley found an ally in Strong, who was receiving a steady stream of reports that led him to conclude independently that it was "absolutely essential to inform Bedell Smith about my growing doubts whether the Allies were matching up to the situation," and his belief that Bradley did not appreciate the severity of First Army's dilemma.

At about midnight the two generals awakened Bedell Smith and explained the urgency of an immediate decision. Smith, a grouch even under ideal conditions, exploded at the two staff officers, calling them "sons of bitches" and "limey bastards" and complaining, "Whenever there is any real trouble, the British do not appear to trust the Americans to handle it efficiently." Their recommendation, said Smith, was "completely unacceptable." Although Strong and Whiteley were two of SHAEF's most loyal and senior staff officers, Smith, still in a fury, exclaimed, " 'You are no longer acceptable to Eisenhower as staff officers!' and told them to consider themselves fired."[33]

Although both thought they were finished at SHAEF, Smith had actually taken their recommendations very seriously. Realizing that placing Montgomery in command in the north might well be a necessity, he telephoned Bradley to discuss a possible shift in command of First Army. Two versions of that conversation exist: Smith's is that Bradley said that "it was the logical thing to do." In *A Soldier's Story*, however, Bradley recounts that Smith said, "Ike thinks it may be a good idea to turn over to Monty your two armies on the north and let him run that side of the Bulge from the 21st Army Group. It may save us a great deal of trouble." According to Bradley, he questioned if such a changeover was at all necessary, claiming it was Smith who had then described it as the "logical thing to do."[34] In his later memoir, *A General's Life*, Bradley lashed out at Smith and Whiteley, avowing to have been "completely dumbfounded—and shocked" by Smith's phone call, which, he said, had "an Alice-in-Wonderland air." Bradley's conclusion was a marvel of obfuscation in which he said, "I made one of my biggest mistakes of the war . . . instead of standing up to Smith, telling him that SHAEF was losing its head, that I had things under control, and reassuring him that Hodges was performing magnificently under the circumstances," Bradley lamely questioned the necessity of a changeover and "knuckled under."[35]

After Smith's morning staff conference on December 20, he informed both Strong and Whiteley that he would put their proposal to Eisenhower as his own recommendation, and as an American. During Eisenhower's morning staff conference, Ike telephoned Bradley and emphatically stated, "Where is the line you can hold the best and the cheapest? I don't care how far back it is."[36] Bradley was in no position to supply Eisenhower with answers. What had convinced Smith that a changeover was vital was that 12th Army Group had lost communications with First Army for more than forty-eight hours. Moreover, Bradley had no idea whatsoever if Hodges had the situation under control, which—as has been conclusively shown—he did not during the crucial first days of the battle. The truth was that Bradley himself had nothing under control and was in no position to influence the outcome of the battle from his headquarters in Luxembourg. Smith called it "an open-and-shut case."

At this point Smith raised the question of a reorganization of command in the Ardennes. Eisenhower accepted Smith's recommendation to split the Ardennes front in two until the situation could be brought under control, with Montgomery to be given temporary operational command of all Allied forces (principally the U.S. First and Ninth Armies) in the northern half of the Bulge, and Bradley to command only the southern flank (Third Army). Later that day Smith apologized to Strong and Whiteley: "What made me really mad," he said, "was that I knew you were right. But my American feelings got the better of me."[37]

Both Smith and Eisenhower would have preferred to leave Bradley in command. However, the reality of the situation that existed on the morning of December 20 dictated that the shift of command was necessary, and Eisenhower immediately communicated his decision to Bradley by telephone. During the confrontation between the two, Strong could hear the other end of the conversation. Bradley was loudly and angrily protesting, "By God, Ike, I cannot be responsible to the American people if you do this. I resign." Eisenhower pointed out that it was he, not Bradley, who was responsible, then curtly noted, "Your resignation therefore means absolutely nothing." Bradley's protests continued vehemently until Eisenhower felt compelled to end the matter with, "Well, Brad, those are my orders."[38] Once off the phone, Bradley reacted with uncharacteristic cold fury, pacing back and forth while cursing Montgomery, startling even Chester Hansen, who was unused "to see[ing] Bradley like this."[39]

Moreover, had Bradley seized the initiative to visit Hodges during the first days of the battle and taken charge, as he should have, Eisenhower might well have decided against shifting command to Montgomery. In short, despite his complaints, Bradley needed to look no farther than himself to determine the reasons for Eisenhower's decision. His intransigence in failing to move his headquarters away from Luxembourg on the grounds that it would create panic did not mean he had to remain there in isolation.[40]

For the rest of his life Bradley bitterly (and erroneously) blamed Montgomery for inciting the order, and refused to admit that there was ample justification for SHAEF's (and later Montgomery's) loss of confidence in the exhausted, taciturn Hodges, who lacked Patton's flair "at a time when we needed Pattonesque bravado." It was a bad beginning to the attempt to reverse a battle brought about by the abysmal failure of Allied intelligence and Bradley's uncharacteristic unwillingness to exercise leadership when it was most needed.[41]

51.

"If I Can Keep the Team Together, Anything's Worth It."

We can still lose this war.
—PATTON

The German counteroffensive included an attempt by Waffen-SS Lt. Col. Otto Skorzeny, who had daringly rescued Mussolini from captivity the previous year, to infiltrate a commando brigade dressed in American uniforms behind Allied lines to seize the bridges across the Meuse. Although Skorzeny's mission in the Ardennes was a dismal failure, a captured German officer revealed that one of the unit's objectives was to assassinate Eisenhower and other senior Allied officers. The report created unprecedented alarm at SHAEF headquarters in Versailles. Eisenhower scoffed at the threat to his life, but Smith disagreed and instituted Draconian security measures.[1] Mickey McKeogh described "the Security boys" as "scared . . . really scared." SHAEF HQ became a virtual fortress, surrounded by barbed wire and tanks and a large guard force. Except for Eisenhower himself, the staff became jumpy and the slightest disruption, such as a car backfiring, brought a flood of phone calls to Eisenhower's office seeking reassurance that he had not been attacked.

Eisenhower was guarded wherever he went by armed, trigger-happy military police and, at the insistence of his staff and security detail, was reluctantly persuaded to move from his remote Saint Germain-en-Laye villa to a new location nearer his headquarters, grumbling that he was only doing it so they would "forget about this damned business and get back to the war." Lt. Col. Baldwin Smith, a security officer who vaguely resembled Eisenhower, assumed his place in the villa and was driven back and forth to the supreme commander's office each day wearing his five-star overcoat.

To his intense annoyance, Eisenhower became a virtual prisoner, his quarters and his office surrounded by guards, his windows securely locked, politely but firmly ordered by his minders not to expose himself lest he become a sniper's target. Eisenhower vented his feelings in colorful language unfit for publication in family newspapers, and after several days stormed out of his office and announced, "Hell's fire, I'm going out for a walk. If anyone wants to shoot me, he can go right ahead. I've got to get out." Different routes were utilized to chauffeur him back and forth in secrecy and anonymity. A week later Eisenhower moved permanently into a large villa, once occupied by Field Marshal Pétain, on the grounds of the Trianon Palace, which was soon dubbed "Hotel Eisenhower." Eisenhower loathed the place and longed for the peace and quiet of his former hideaway at Telegraph Cottage. The assassination scare lasted about ten days, but for some time thereafter, Eisenhower's "double" continued his twice-daily drive to and from Saint Germain-en-Laye.

A measure of the nervousness at SHAEF occurred outside Bedell Smith's walled villa one night when gunfire erupted in what sounded like a pitched battle against an intruder. Smith himself joined in, charging into the night in his pajamas, wildly firing his carbine. The next morning the "intruder" turned up dead, a stray cat.[2]

Mamie was at Fort Benning, Georgia, visiting John over the Christmas holidays. Her host, the post commander, who had no knowledge of the German attack in the Ardennes, received an unexpected telephone call from a reporter inquiring if she would comment "on reports that her husband had been shot." Issuing a gruff "No comment," the general instructed an aide to "[s]ee to it that Mrs. Eisenhower doesn't listen to the radio."[3] For Mamie, who later admitted she had spent most of the war worrying incessantly about her husband's safety (and now her son's), the incident served as an epiphany: the realization that nothing was going to happen to Ike "until God was through with what he had put him on this earth to do.... He must have chosen this man for something."[4] Yet Mamie remained clueless that it was impossible for Ike to write to her on a regular basis. "It always distresses me," he wrote on January 7, 1945, "when I get a message from you indicating anxiety or impatience because I have failed to write. Please, please understand that I do go through periods when I simply cannot sit down and write a note.... These are trying days."

Eisenhower's relationship with Beetle Smith, which Thomas Betts described as "the pepper and the fire," took on a new dimension during the autumn battles. Not only had it sharpened in the months since D-Day but Smith's hold on SHAEF was stronger than ever, even as his health failed and his notoriously bad temper grew shorter. And while Smith was grateful that Eisenhower delegated him a free hand to run SHAEF almost as his own personal fiefdom, some things cannot be delegated. Thus, as the strategic debates raged during the second half of the campaign in northwestern Europe, Smith used his influence to press the supreme commander to take a more proactive role.[5]

. . .

Montgomery's first decision in his new role as commander of the northern sector was to visit First Army to meet with Hodges and Simpson in order to assess for himself what needed to be done. He deliberately flew British pennants on the hood of his staff car, which was surrounded by motorcycle outriders. An aide to Hodges described his arrival as like "Christ come to cleanse the temple," a remark that Bradley would later gleefully repeat in his memoirs. Monty's object, however, was simply to restore confidence in an organization that was bereft of morale. Flying the British flag was his means of demonstrating that no one had anything to fear.

Although Montgomery's need to exude confidence in the presence of Hodges and Simpson made him appear imperious to his new American subordinates, his demeanor was no different than with his British subordinates. The line between confidence and arrogance is thin, and his no-nonsense, take-charge approach to generalship was certainly open to misinterpretation. Montgomery's intentions, however, were clear enough. Foremost it was to restore the flagging morale that existed at First Army. Hodges was not without resolve, but what he and Simpson lacked was guidance from Bradley. Thus it was clear to Montgomery that his first task was to provide the necessary leadership to stabilize the front and halt the German attack. What is equally clear is that Montgomery's air of confidence (his version of Eisenhower's "There will be only cheerful faces" remark at Verdun) was misinterpreted as censure.[6]

Montgomery found Hodges in a state of near exhaustion and had he been British, would have relieved him of command; as it was he tactfully suggested to Bedell Smith that it might be necessary to relieve Hodges. Smith did not disagree but said if it was necessary, SHAEF would do it. Montgomery suggested waiting twenty-four hours before any decision was made. The following day de Guingand telephoned Smith and said, "Hodges is not the man I would pick, but he is much better [today]." Eisenhower later confirmed that he would have agreed to Hodges's relief when he wrote to Monty on December 22: "I know you realize that Hodges is the quiet, reticent type and does not appear as aggressive as he really is. Unless he becomes exhausted he will always wage a good fight. However, you will of course keep in touch with your important subordinates and inform me instantly if any change needs to be made on [the] United States side."[7]

The First Army staff, already resentful of the change of command, is alleged to have been less than pleased to be under British command. Such resentments—and many seem to be of postwar creation—were not evident to James Gavin, the 82nd Airborne commander, when he dined with Hodges and his staff several days later: "The staff spoke of Montgomery with amusement and respect. They obviously liked him and respected his professionalism." For his part Gavin was impressed with Montgomery as a soldier. "I took a liking to him that has not diminished with the years."[8]

With the exception of Patton, Montgomery was the only senior commander regularly to visit his troops at the Ardennes front. Montgomery's presence and his decisions to reassign responsibilities and realign units of both First and Ninth Armies were precisely the fitting remedy. For American commanders to cede ground was considered sinful, however, after visiting Saint-Vith and determining that if the 7th Armored remained it would be annihilated, Montgomery decreed that further defense of the town was futile and, with Hodges's concurrence, ordered what was left of the division to withdraw to new positions on December 22. The 7th Armored's brilliantly orchestrated defense of Saint-Vith against near-impossible odds had stemmed the advance of Manteuffel's Fifth Panzer Army until December 23, when the last elements evacuated the shattered town. The defense of Saint-Vith was a key factor in the German failure in the Ardennes. The official U.S Army historian wrote that Montgomery's decision reflected his "ability to honor the fighting man which had endeared him to the hearts of the Desert Rats [of the British 7th Armored Division] in North Africa: 'They can come back with all honor. They come back to the more secure positions. They put up a wonderful show.' "[9] The defenders of Saint-Vith were unambiguous about their feelings toward the field marshal. "Montgomery saved the 7th Armored Division," said Robert Hasbrouck.[10]

On December 23 Eisenhower issued his first Order of the Day since D-Day, in which he exhorted everyone to fight back and turn the enemy's "great gamble into his worst defeat. So I call upon every man, of all the Allies, to rise now to new heights of courage, of resolution, and of effort. Let everyone hold before him a single thought—to destroy the enemy on the ground, in the air, everywhere—destroy him."[11] Those who knew Eisenhower intimately could discern the message as yet another indicator of just how deeply he detested his foe. Undoubtedly the brutal massacre of 350 American troops and 100 Belgian civilians at Malmédy and 12 other places by SS troops of Lt. Col. Joachim Peiper's Kampfgruppe Peiper contributed to Eisenhower's barely restrained outrage.[12]

On December 23 and 24 the skies cleared, permitting the Allied air forces to fly for the first time in days and to strike back at the Germans and, more important, to airdrop desperately needed supplies into beleaguered Bastogne. Help came on the ground the afternoon of December 26 with the arrival of units of the 4th Armored Division, but Bastogne still remained under siege on three sides. Although Bastogne had held, the Battle of the Bulge was far from over, and the bloodiest battles of the winter war in the Ardennes were yet to come.

Only hours earlier Eisenhower obviously still entertained doubts that Patton's thrust from the south would succeed in breaking through to Bastogne. Even as the 4th Armored was fighting its way into the town, Eisenhower's edginess was evident when, at his morning staff conference on December 26, he erupted: "I have just been set back thoroughly on my heels by this failure of the attack from the south to join up with the 101st." Given how little SHAEF actually knew and the length of time it took to receive and analyze intelligence before it reached Eisenhower, it was clear that the information he possessed was already obsolete.[13] Shortly before his death, Eisenhower would write glowingly of his onetime friend and how, during the struggle to advance and relieve Bastogne, Patton would telephone almost daily and say, "General, I apologize for my slowness. This snow is God-awful. I'm sorry." Ike would ask, "George, are you still fighting?" And when Patton replied that he was, Eisenhower would simply say, "All right then, that's all I've asked of you. Just keep at it."[14]

The near-panic at SHAEF not only kept Eisenhower penned up like a POW against his will but seriously curtailed his practice of visiting his commanders at the front. From his return to Versailles from Verdun on December 19, until January 27, 1945, Eisenhower left his headquarters only once, on December 28, when he journeyed to Hasselt, Belgium, to meet with Montgomery.[15] Eisenhower had become increasingly impatient for Montgomery to launch his counterattack in the north. Montgomery, however, had no intention of initiating an attack until he was convinced that the tide had been stemmed, the front reorganized, and a reserve created for First Army. Informed at his morning staff conference on December 27 that a counterattack was under consideration, Eisenhower, in a rare outburst, exclaimed, "Praise God from Whom all blessings flow!"[16]

Eisenhower's made his journey to Belgium by train. Although he and Montgomery were originally scheduled to meet in Brussels, the ice and fog were so bad that the field marshal could not travel by road. Instead the two met in the Hasselt railway station. The elaborate security measures, which included troops manning machine guns on the platform, thoroughly annoyed the supreme commander, who found the attention understandable but nevertheless an embarrassment. Pointing out to the officer in charge that for a German assassination team to know he would be in that railway station at that precise moment would be nothing short of miraculous, Eisenhower suggested his men remain inside the train. Apparently more scared of his superiors than of Eisenhower, the officer ignored the supreme commander's wishes and kept his men deployed outside, weapons at the ready.[17]

While Ike and Monty debated in private, in the next car de Guingand, Brig. Bill Williams, and other staff officers huddled half-frozen with blankets over their heads to ward off the cold. At one point Eisenhower came in and asked, "Where is Frankfurt?" a statement his critics subsequently misinterpreted as evidence of his ignorance. In fact, what Eisenhower clearly meant was that he needed a map of Germany that included Frankfurt.[18]

Montgomery reiterated that he was not convinced that the Germans were finished launching a major attack in the north. Eisenhower agreed that a delay to reorganize and strengthen the northern sector was the right move, but decreed that if the Germans did not attack by January 3, 1945, Montgomery was to launch his own attack with First Army. Their meeting might have ended satisfactorily had Montgomery not once again revived the issue of command when the Allies again resumed the offensive into Germany. "E. and Monty had a long talk," Kay Summersby's diary recorded. "Monty wouldn't let his C/S [de Guingand] be present. Monty still tries to convince E. that there should be one commander. From all accounts he was not very cooperative."[19] Each left apparently misunderstanding what the other had said or would do. When Eisenhower emerged he was rubbing his head and said merely, "Monty, as usual." According to Williams, Eisenhower was not angry, "just vexed at having to explain the same thing so many times," noting also that the remarks were not said with bitterness but rather with resignation.[20]

When Montgomery cabled Brooke that he had wrested agreement from Eisenhower that he would have full authority over Bradley's army group for the northern thrust into Germany, Brooke sensed trouble. "Monty has had another interview with Ike. I do not like the account of it. It looks to me as if Monty with his usual lack of tact has been rubbing into Ike the results of not having listened to Monty's advice!! Too much of 'I told you so' to assist in producing the required friendly relations between the two. . . . He [Eisenhower] is a hopeless commander."[21]

Eisenhower returned tight-lipped to Versailles, where he and Smith were overheard discussing how much they thought Montgomery had changed since the Allied team had first been formed in the Mediterranean. With Montgomery everything was a negotiation, but, other than his personal rebuke to the field marshal on September 10 in Brussels, Eisenhower attempted to hold the coalition together by avoiding conflict whenever possible through a combination of carrot dangling and compromise as long as it was within the spectrum of his broad-front strategy. Eisenhower's critics on both sides of the debate have deemed it a poor way to run a war, but when Kay Summersby remarked at his great patience with his troublesome subordinate, Eisenhower merely replied, "If I can keep the team together, anything's worth it."[22]

The months of acrimony between Eisenhower and Montgomery came to the boiling point on December 30, 1944, when Brooke's worst fears were nearly realized. The Anglo-American coalition almost came permanently unglued when Eisenhower received a letter from Montgomery that he deemed the final straw in his relations with his troublesome subordinate. At the height of what many consider Monty's finest hour, he naively forced a showdown with Eisenhower that—had the supreme commander elected to pursue it—would almost certainly have resulted in his relief from command.

Once again Montgomery argued that if plans to resume the offensive were to be successful, there must be a single commander (himself) with complete control in the north over both army groups. Otherwise the Allies would again fail. Although it was merely the latest example of Monty being Monty, to Eisenhower the letter smacked of an insubordination he was no longer willing to tolerate.

Reports by his field liaison officers reflected an increasing disquiet at SHAEF over the headlines in the British press, which suggested, in the usual ostentatious Fleet Street custom, that Montgomery was the savior sent to rescue the U.S. generals in the Ardennes from disaster. "The rumblings in the [British] press have now grown to a roar of demand that there be a British deputy commander for all of General Ike's ground forces," Butcher wrote. "The implication is clearly given that General Ike, much as he is respected, has undertaken too much of a task himself." When Marshall learned of the British criticism he cabled his support: "You are doing a grand job and go on and give them hell."[23]

De Guingand sensed trouble was brewing for his boss and immediately telephoned Bedell Smith to determine its extent and what could be done to defuse it. What Smith told him was so alarming that, at great personal risk, de Guingand flew from Brussels to Paris through thick fog and blizzard conditions to make a personal last-minute appeal to save Monty's job. De Guingand entered Eisenhower's dimly lit office, where he found the supreme commander "really tired and worried." With Tedder, Gault, and Smith looking on, calmly but firmly Eisenhower explained

> how serious matters were. . . . Bradley's position had become intolerable, and that there was every chance that he would lose the confidence of his troops. . . . Eisenhower went on to say that he was tired of the whole business, and had come to the conclusion that it was now a matter for the Combined Chiefs of Staff to make a decision. It was quite obvious that with Montgomery still pressing for a Land Force Commander it was impossible for the two of them to carry on working in harness together.

When Eisenhower handed de Guingand a copy of the signal he intended to send to Marshall, "I was stunned by what I read. In very direct language it made it crystal-clear that a crisis of the first magnitude was indeed here," and either Eisenhower or Montgomery would have to go.[24]

Montgomery seemed incapable of grasping that the political ramifications of the Anglo-American alliance, American public opinion, and, ultimately, Roosevelt, made it impossible for a British general to command the final battles of World War II. "Thus we were brought to that dreadful day when the Alliance was very near cracked asunder," observed one of Monty's early biographers, historian Ronald Lewin; "the day when Montgomery was really within a pen-stroke of being removed by Eisenhower, the consequences of which I dread to think."[25]

"I was absolutely shattered," said de Guingand, who employed every ounce of his considerable charm to convince Eisenhower, Tedder, and Smith that the problem could be defused if only they would give him time to sort the matter out with Montgomery, who, he assured them, had no idea that his actions had caused such a crisis. "I virtually went down on my bended knees and asked him whether he wouldn't hold it up . . . give me 24 hours, and then Beetle Smith magnificently came to my support and I eventually persuaded Eisenhower to give me that 24 hours."[26]

By the time de Guingand returned to Brussels late the following afternoon, time was again running out. Casting aside his usual tact for bluntness, he said to Montgomery, "I've just come from SHAEF and seen Ike, and it's on the cards that you might have to go." Montgomery's initial reaction was disbelief. "Well, who will take my place? Who?" Only when informed that Eisenhower would nominate Alexander did it dawn on a somber Montgomery that he had indeed pushed matters too far with Eisenhower. Montgomery "looked completely nonplussed—I don't think I had ever seen him so deflated. It was as if a cloak of loneliness had descended upon him. His reply was, 'What shall I do, Freddie?' " De Guingand had drafted a signal to Eisenhower, which Montgomery approved without dissent. "Dear Ike," it read,

> have seen Freddie and understand you are greatly worried by many considerations in these very difficult days. I have given you my frank views because I have felt you like this. I am sure there are many factors which have a bearing quite beyond anything I realize. Whatever your decision may be you can rely on me one hundred per cent to make it work, and I know Brad will do the same. Very distressed that my letter may have upset you and I would ask you to tear it up. Your very devoted subordinate, Monty.[27]

Eisenhower relented and withdrew his cable, but the lingering resentments against Montgomery would explode again after an infamous press conference on January 7, 1945. The irony of this latest nearly fatal crisis in Allied relations was that on the day he received Montgomery's letter, Eisenhower had been prepared to grant a measure of the field marshal's demands. His unpublished outline plan to tidy up the mess in the Ardennes was another compromise and, notes John Eisenhower, "an attempt to blend personal and military considerations . . . [and] it gave Montgomery the one thing he wanted—detailed emergency coordination along army group boundaries—while denying him the main thing he had been campaigning for—operational control of both his own and Bradley's army groups."[28]

Eisenhower replied with a handwritten letter of his own, which was

intended to bury the hatchet once and for all. Pointing out that he was demonstrating his faith and confidence in his subordinate by placing U.S. First
Army under his command, he wrote, "You know how greatly I've appreciated
and depended upon your frank and friendly counsel, but in your latest letter
you disturb me by predictions of 'failure' unless your exact opinions in the
matter of giving you command over Bradley are met in detail. I assure you
that in this matter I can go no further." Eisenhower ended his letter with a
none-too-subtle warning that he was tired of Monty's demands.

> I know your loyalty as a soldier and your readiness to devote yourself
> to assigned tasks. For my part I would deplore the development of
> such an unbridgeable group of convictions between us that we would
> have to present our differences to the Combined Chiefs of Staff. The
> confusion and debate that would follow would certainly damage the
> goodwill and devotion to a common cause that have made this Allied
> Force unique in history. As ever, your friend, Ike.[29]

By the end of December, Hitler's strategic aim of splitting the Allied front in
half was clearly doomed to failure, and Germany's ultimate defeat had become
only a matter of time. Nevertheless considerable heavy fighting lay ahead
before the Battle of the Bulge could be called over. As the fighting raged
around Bastogne, Patton observed in his diary on January 4, "We can still
lose this war. The Germans are colder and hungrier than we are, but they
fight better."[30]

The forecast by Hitler's generals that the German counteroffensive was
doomed to failure was proved right by the heroic American stands at Saint-
Vith and Bastogne. Although the encircled 101st Airborne ("Battered Bastards
of Bastogne") and McAuliffe's famous reply of "Nuts!" when the Germans
demanded his surrender have become the focus of the story of the Bulge,
Bastogne would have fallen had it not been for the stalwart defense of Saint-
Vith by Combat Command B of the 7th Armored Division. For eight critical
days the 7th Armored and an ad hoc collection of hastily assembled troops
from the 28th and 106th Divisions successfully averted disaster. The stubborn
defense of Saint-Vith and the 1st, 2nd, and 99th Infantry Divisions' equally
valiant defense of Elsenborn Ridge frustrated the German advance long
enough to permit the Allied commanders to rush reinforcements and plug
the gaps. Gavin's 82nd Airborne Division also fought tenaciously, contributing mightily to the ultimate German failure by denying Manteuffel's Fifth
Panzer Army the rapid breakthrough that was the key to the success of the
counteroffensive. Manteuffel well understood that failing to break Saint-Vith
meant the Fifth Panzer Army offensive would never reach the Meuse, and
recommended to Rundstedt that it be canceled. And yet, how close it was!

The Germans never knew that "the biggest filling station in Europe," located in the Ardennes, near Stavelot, contained 2.5 million gallons of fuel, enough to have kept Sepp Dietrich's fuel-starved panzers on the move and perhaps have changed the outcome of this deadly campaign.[31] The only unit to advance near to the Meuse was the 2nd Panzer Division, which ran headlong into Ernie Harmon's 2nd Armored Division, which all but annihilated this vaunted German unit in a pitched battle.

"The real victory in the Ardennes belonged to the American soldier," wrote historian Charles B. MacDonald, "for he provided time to enable his commanders—for all their intelligence failure—to bring their mobility and their airpower into play . . . the American soldier stopped everything the German Army threw at him,"[32] a sentiment that Eisenhower would whole-heartedly have endorsed.

The Bulge reflected the best and worst of Eisenhower's leadership style. His commitment to a unified SHAEF and to the broad front never wavered, even when under the twin and increasingly strong pressures from Montgomery and Bradley. Devers, who was never in favor with Eisenhower, played a minor supporting role and, rather than attempt to influence Eisenhower, tended to stay out of his way. Eisenhower disliked face-to-face meetings with Devers as much as those with Montgomery and on at least one occasion sent Pinky Bull to convey his orders to 6th Army Group.

After his capture at the end of the war, Rundstedt heaped praise on Patton; "[H]e is your best," said the field marshal.[33] Everett Hughes reported to Patton that Eisenhower had said, "Do you know, Everett, George is really a very great soldier, and I must get Marshall to do something for him before the war is over."[34] Patton remained embittered that Eisenhower would never compliment him to his face. He wanted the approval and praise of his oldest friend, more than anything. Few things were to disappoint him more deeply. Eisenhower genuinely appreciated Patton's accomplishments but seemed incapable of or uninterested in praising the one friend and associate who would have thrived on his words.[35]

Omar Bradley's role in the Battle of the Bulge was primarily irrelevant. Not only did Bradley and his staff have no discernible appreciation of the situation in First Army, but it was Patton and Third Army that planned and carried out the initial counterattacks in the Ardennes. Both Hodges and Bradley, notes J. D. Morelock, "possessed an incredibly poor appreciation of the true tactical situation," as evinced by the fact that until Gerow did so on his own initiative, no action had been taken to halt a V Corps offensive against the Roer River dams.[36] Bradley not only remained cooped up in Luxembourg but, unlike Montgomery, had all insignia identifying him as a general officer removed from his vehicles as a security precaution. "Frequent visits to forward units and subordinate commanders had been such a hallmark of Bradley's battle leadership up to this point that it is nearly inconceivable that he proposed to Ike that he command the toughest battle to be faced in the war solely by radio and telephone."[37] Moreover, at no time during the thirty-three-day battle did Bradley ever meet with either Hodges or Simpson; instead he sulked and took potshots at Monty, who accomplished what he had failed to do.[38]

Controversy once again swirled around Montgomery, who was either revered or condemned for his role in the Bulge. Most of it was second-guessing. And, while both Ridgway (XVIII Airborne Corps) and J. Lawton Collins (VII Corps) would have preferred an earlier American counterattack, the hard-nosed Collins defended Montgomery's generalship, calling it "probably the most effective Allied cooperation of the war. For the Army's part of this success Monty deserves much credit. . . . Eisenhower was right, in my judgment, in placing Montgomery temporarily in command of all troops on the north side."[39]

All sorts of other silly charges were leveled, including the assertion that Montgomery had compelled Eisenhower to appoint him to command the U.S. forces in the northern sector and, once in command, had mishandled them by not counterattacking soon enough to satisfy his critics. Another is that he contemplated a withdrawal behind the Meuse and that by failing to rush British troops into the breach, Montgomery left the U.S. Army to bear the brunt of the battle—and the casualties. Neither charge has ever had merit. An objective account of the Bulge by Robert Merriam, an American combat historian present during the fight for Saint-Vith, puts some badly needed perspective on the controversy. As Merriam points out, "National spirit, which we have in abundance, sometimes blinds us to good sense and understanding. . . . To criticize Montgomery for not counterattacking in the midst of the hell swirling around him is only to indicate ignorance of the situation." Moreover, "the brutal criticism of Montgomery's tactics does not square up with the facts . . . many of the mistakes he is charged with were not of his making."[40]

Lost in the controversy over the timing of Monty's counterattack is what would have been the high cost of failure had he acted too soon. According to the First Army official historian, "One of the main reasons for the field marshal's reluctance to take the offensive was a serious lack of infantry, especially riflemen." First Army lost more than 41,000 men in the second half of December but received only 15,295 replacements. "On 23 December Montgomery warned that the V Corps' four divisions were short 7,000 men, mostly infantrymen. . . . Before First Army could attack, it would have to replace heavy losses in equipment as well."[41]

Unfortunately the crisis in Anglo-American relations would only worsen in the days ahead. Bradley's childish behavior and Monty's ham-handedness would both ensure that Eisenhower had yet more problems with which to cope in 1945.

Not until mid January 1945 could the bloody Battle of the Bulge be declared won when three American divisions broke the back of the siege and erased the final German salient, dooming some fifteen thousand of Hitler's best troops to capture. As the crisis in the Ardennes faded, for the first time in weeks Eisenhower seemed more relaxed. Kay Summersby saw tangible evidence of it the evening of January 17, when Ike invited Spaatz to his quarters for a movie and instructed him to bring his guitar with him. "The two of them let off the past month's accumulated steam by booming out a medley of slightly off-key but boisterous West Point songs."[42]

In its aftermath, Eisenhower was asked if he had been frightened by the German counteroffensive. "Well, not at the time," he said, then added with a grin, "But I was scared stiff three weeks later when I got around to reading the newspaper accounts."[43]

52.

The Invasion of Germany

Optimism is a mania for saying things are well when one is in hell.

—VOLTAIRE

The year 1945 began on a tragic note when, on January 2, Eisenhower lost a close friend: Adm. Sir Bertram Ramsay was killed when his aircraft crashed on takeoff from an airfield outside Paris. "His is a desperate loss," mourned Brooke; and an equally distraught Eisenhower wrote to Mamie that "war is a truly brutal business!"[1] The death of Bertie Ramsay was the second misfortune to befall the Allied team. The AEAF, which had from the outset been the unwanted stepchild of the Allies, caught between SHAEF and the American and British air barons, was disbanded after Normandy. In November 1944 Leigh-Mallory was en route to a new assignment as Mountbatten's air commander in Southeast Asia when his plane disappeared in the French Alps and was not found until the spring of 1945.

The battles that raged for six weeks in the frozen hell of the Ardennes were among the bitterest and bloodiest of any fought in the west. "The Ardennes offensive was a rude awakening. The surprise lay not so much in the resurgence of German power as in the revelation of Allied weakness."[2] The Battle of the Bulge was disastrous for Germany in many ways: Hitler's only strategic reserve had been all but destroyed, and with it his last hope of defending the Reich for long. Irreplaceable losses in men and equipment were staggering: The German high command could only estimate losses of more than 80,000 men (12,642 killed, 38,600 wounded, and another 30,582 missing).

Eisenhower never attempted to deflect blame and publicly accepted full responsibility for the Bulge. "The fighting in the autumn followed the pattern [that is, the broad front] I had personally prescribed. . . . This plan gave the German opportunity to launch his attack against a weak portion of our lines. If giving him that chance is to be condemned by historians, their condemnation should be directed at me alone."[3]

The year was barely a week old when, on January 7, Montgomery again

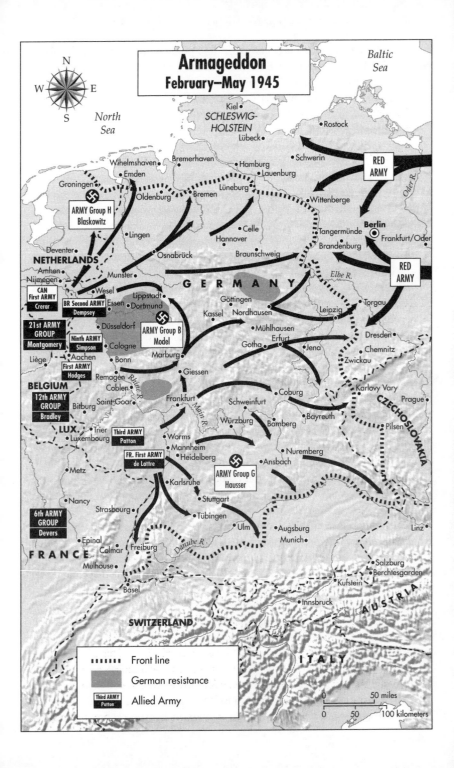

Armageddon
February–May 1945

Baltic Sea

North Sea

Kiel
SCHLESWIG-
HOLSTEIN
Lübeck
Rostock

Wihelmshaven
Emden
Bremerhaven
Hamburg
Lauenburg
Schwerin

RED ARMY

Groningen
Oldenburg
Bremen
Lüneburg
Wittenberge

ARMY Group H
Blaskowitz

Deventer
Lingen
Celle
Hannover
Tangermünde
Brandenburg

Berlin
Frankfurt/Oder

NETHERLANDS
Arnhem
Nijmegen
Munster
Osnabrück
Braunschweig

G E R M A N Y

Elbe R.

Oder R.

RED ARMY

CAN First ARMY
Crerar

Wesel
Lippstadt
Essen
Dortmund
Göttingen
Nordhausen
Leipzig
Torgau

BR Second ARMY
Dempsey

Kassel

Dresden

21st ARMY GROUP
Montgomery

Ninth ARMY
Simpson

Düsseldorf
Cologne
Bonn
Mühlhausen
Gotha
Erfurt
Jena
Chemnitz
Zwickau

ARMY Group B
Model

Liège
Aachen

First ARMY
Hodges

Marburg

Karlovy Vary
Prague

BELGIUM

Remagen
Coblenz
Giessen
Coburg

CZECHOSLOVAKIA

12th ARMY GROUP
Bradley

Bitburg
Saint-Goar
Frankfurt
Schweinfurt
Bamberg
Bayreuth
Pilsen

LUX.
Trier
Luxembourg

Rhine R.
Main R.

Würzburg

Third ARMY
Patton

Worms
Mannheim
Heidelberg
Nuremberg

Metz

FR. First ARMY
de Lattre

Karlsruhe

ARMY Group G
Hausser

Ansbach

Nancy
Strasbourg
Stuttgart

Linz

6th ARMY GROUP
Devers

Epinal
Colmar
Tübingen
Ulm
Augsburg
Munich

FRANCE

Mulhouse
Freiburg

Danube R.

Salzburg
Berchtesgaden

Basel
Kufstein

SWITZERLAND

Innsbruck

AUSTRIA

ITALY

.... Front line

▨ German resistance

Third ARMY
Patton Allied Army

0   50 miles
0   50   100 kilometers

became the focus of controversy, this time publicly, when his penchant for irritating his American ally reached its zenith. He appeared at a press conference for what he sincerely intended to be an antidote to the chorus of anti-American and anti-Eisenhower criticisms that had been appearing for weeks in the British press. Instead it turned into a fiasco that further inflamed Bradley's already sensitive feelings. However, in a case of good intentions gone badly awry, it was Montgomery's choice of words and the manner in which he uttered them that opened fresh wounds. Instead of smoothing troubled waters, what came across to the correspondents was arrogance and the impression in several passages of his speech that it was Montgomery and the British army that had saved the day in the Ardennes. Or, as his chief of staff has said, it was Montgomery's " 'what a good boy am I' attitude" that outraged and dismayed so many.[4] Bradley, who was still smarting over having been compelled by Eisenhower to cede control of First Army to the field marshal, was infuriated. Monty's G-2, Brig. Bill Williams, described it as "*disastrous*," and the *Daily Express* correspondent Alan Moorehead later exclaimed, "Oh, God, why didn't you stop him? It was so awful."[5] At a stroke Montgomery had turned possibly his finest hour as a military commander into an unmitigated disaster. He later candidly admitted in his memoirs that it was "probably a mistake to have held this conference at all."[6]

Montgomery's words were broadcast over the BBC, and several days later a German propagandist broke into a BBC broadcast channel and, in the guise of being a genuine announcer, mocked American generalship in the Ardennes. Embarrassed, the British press chief, Minister of Information Brendan Bracken, tried to smooth over the matter, but the damage had been done.[7] Churchill attempted to redress the damage in a speech to the House of Commons noting that "what was done to meet von Rundstedt's counterstroke was resolute, wise, and militarily correct. . . . Let no one lend themselves to the shouting of mischief makers when issues of this momentous consequence are being successfully decided by the sword."

Although Eisenhower would rather have simply ignored Montgomery's latest outburst, the press conference left in its wake a profusion of anger, hurt feelings, and yet another predicament in his ongoing battle with his prima donna subordinates—this time, how to pacify Bradley. On the one hand there was the relentless British pressure to push the issue of a land-force commander, and Bradley's threats to resign if he was obliged to serve under Monty; on the other there was Marshall, who made it clear that he would not stand for anyone coming between Eisenhower and his three army group commanders.[8]

Eisenhower's problems did not end with Montgomery and Bradley, however. When the Germans attacked in the Ardennes, the Allied southern flank was left exposed, particularly Strasbourg, which had been liberated in late

November by Jacques Leclerc's armored division, a feat that—second only to the liberation of Paris—had stirred French pride. On December 26 Eisenhower ordered the French First Army commander, General de Lattre de Tassigny, to pull back and consolidate his forces in the shadow of the Vosges Mountains to form a cohesive defensive line in the south. Eisenhower's order reached the French at the worst possible moment, only days after de Gaulle had made a triumphal visit to the city. The new French leader had no intention of relinquishing the Alsatian capital to the Germans, and cabled Eisenhower stating unequivocally that he would not let Strasbourg "fall into enemy hands again. Whatever happens the French will defend Strasbourg."[9]

The situation turned critical when the Germans launched heavy counterattacks in the Colmar pocket. Devers believed that these seriously threatened his ability to hold Strasbourg. A decision whether to hold the city or regroup was urgently required.

De Gaulle sent telegrams to Churchill and Roosevelt questioning Eisenhower's decision and the "extremely serious consequences which would result for France." While Roosevelt refused to intervene, Churchill for once agreed with de Gaulle that the evacuation of Strasbourg would not only result in severe German reprisals but seriously weaken the new French provisional government. Churchill and Brooke hastened to Paris the morning of January 3 for the express purpose of mediating a solution by persuading Eisenhower to reverse his order.[10]

The stage was set for a showdown of epic proportions between Eisenhower and de Gaulle, who arrived accompanied by General Juin, his chief of staff.[11] Their meeting in the SHAEF war room was turbulent. At one point Eisenhower thought it was "degenerating into a complete break." According to Eisenhower's recollection, Churchill sat silently throughout, an interested spectator offering no comment, but Kay Summersby's diary suggests otherwise. "It was quite a conference," she noted. "The P.M. was magnificent, de Gaulle got heated to say the least of it but in the end everyone parted on good terms."[12] Militarily de Gaulle agreed that although Eisenhower's decision had merit, there were other, more serious consequences. A withdrawal from Strasbourg would be "a national disaster. For Alsace is sacred ground."

Once again Eisenhower was on the horns of a dilemma. As David Eisenhower notes, "Strasbourg could not be held without U.S. military support, and exposing U.S. forces to risks in Alsace would not pass unnoticed by a War Department and Cabinet already prone to question whether Eisenhower was too greatly influenced by intransigent local demands and thus unable to to control the situation in Europe."[13] Eisenhower compromised, convinced that there were military grounds to do so, and telephoned Devers canceling the withdrawal. Churchill approvingly proclaimed, "You have done the right and proper thing," and in a private conversation with de Gaulle said, "Eisenhower was not always aware of the political consequences of his decisions, yet for all that he was an excellent supreme commander and he had a heart—as he had just shown."[14]

While Eisenhower and Churchill were meeting with de Gaulle, Brooke and Strong were locked in a furious encounter. Brooke ridiculed Bradley's plans to pinch off the German advance and rather contemptuously dismissed SHAEF's proposed actions, calling them "hogwash," arguing (wrongly) that the Germans had nothing further to gain in the Ardennes and would withdraw of their own volition. They adjourned to Eisenhower's office to study maps of the Bastogne sector. Accompanied by Churchill, Eisenhower returned to find Brooke, Strong, and others closely studying his maps, each man utilizing a pointer to make his case. It was obvious that there was a serious disagreement raging, and that Eisenhower had walked into its midst. Strong was mortified, describing it as "a rather painful occasion, as the British visitors so obviously displayed their lack of confidence in Eisenhower. Whenever Brooke and Eisenhower met one sensed there was some barrier between them."[15] For Eisenhower it was merely the latest example of the growing, and now openly blatant, British distrust of his leadership since assuming command of the land battle from Montgomery. Whereas the criticism had previously been more subtle, it now bordered on open contempt. Ever the optimist, Eisenhower insisted to Marshall that the dissension was "largely froth," and that the "fundamental soundness of this organization and readiness of all components to carry out my orders have been remarkable from the beginning."[16] Churchill's report to Roosevelt was a glowing endorsement of Eisenhower:

> CIGS and I have passed the last two days with Eisenhower and Montgomery and they both feel the battle very heavy but are confident of success. I hope you understand that, in case any troubles should arise in the press, His Majesty's Government have complete confidence in General Eisenhower and feel acutely any attacks made on him. He and Montgomery are very closely knit and also Bradley and Patton, and it would be disaster which broke up this combination which has, in nineteen forty-four, yielded us results beyond the dreams of military avarice. . . . I have a feeling this is a time for an intense new impulse, both of friendship and exertion, to be drawn from our bosoms and to the last scrap of our resources.[17]

Churchill's peace offering to FDR notwithstanding, British skepticism about Eisenhower reached a new low during Churchill and Brooke's visit, when, for the first time, Alexander's name surfaced as a possible replacement for Tedder as the deputy supreme commander.[18] Aware of Eisenhower's rapport with Alexander, Churchill cleverly used the occasion to put forth an ill-conceived plan to replace Tedder. Not only would such a move displace Tedder, but Churchill believed that Alexander's mere presence at SHAEF would invariably lead him to the de facto role of ground commander in chief sought by Brooke and Churchill.

Eisenhower seemed ready to accede, and drafted a letter of acceptance. Although Smith held Tedder in low regard ("He was lazy [and] wanted authority without responsibility"), he was nevertheless strongly opposed to replacing the British airman. To help make his case, Smith sent for the highly respected Jock Whiteley, who joined him in vehemently advising Eisenhower against proceeding. With both men unable to completely dissuade the supreme commander, a compromise was reached: A letter was sent to Marshall laying out the fact that Eisenhower would indeed accept a new deputy. "It would be helpful," he said, hinting that only Alexander met his criteria of "a man of fine personality, respected by all and willing to serve as *my deputy* and not repeat not under independent charter from my superiors." What was surprising was Eisenhower's scant vote of confidence in Tedder, whom he seemed more than willing to dump. "In spite of my personal and official admiration for Tedder he is not repeat not in position to help me by visits and conferences with troop commanders," Eisenhower told Marshall.[19]

As painful as his relations with Brooke and Montgomery were, next to the perpetual shortage of landing craft, Eisenhower ranked his problems with the French as having caused "more trouble in this war than any other single factor."[20] He might well have added the name of Omar Bradley. His problems with Bradley escalated visibly during the Bulge, and by early 1945 had become downright contentious, none more so than an acid exchange witnessed by Kenneth Strong.

Bradley's smoldering resentment over the humiliation of losing command of two armies to Montgomery burst into flames on January 31, when Eisenhower informed him that Simpson's Ninth Army would remain under Montgomery's operational control. Enraged, Bradley announced that he would never again serve under Montgomery and would ask to be sent home if ordered to do so, as "I will have lost the confidence of my command." Strong, the only British officer present, felt as if he had intruded on a family quarrel. Stunned by Bradley's outburst, Eisenhower replied, "I thought you were the one person I could count on for doing anything I asked you to."

"You can, Ike," said Bradley. "I've enjoyed every bit of my service with you. But this is one thing I cannot take." Strong describes Bradley as accepting the situation after putting his friend in an "awkward dilemma," a polite description for a disagreement more contentious than any Eisenhower ever had with Montgomery.[21]

Historian Charles B. MacDonald, a rifle company commander who fought in the Bulge, has scoffed at Bradley's contention that his service under Montgomery would "forfeit the confidence of my command." What did it matter to an American GI in a foxhole, "[f]ighting for his life in the harsh cold and snow of Ardennes, who commanded him at the top? Who was this Montgomery? Who was Bradley? ... A front-line soldier was immensely well informed if he knew the name of his company commander."[22]

Bradley was rewarded for his disloyalty with a promotion to four-star general after Eisenhower attempted to soften the blow by convincing Marshall that a failure to promote Bradley would be seen as evidence of an American failure in the Ardennes. Although Eisenhower went out of his way to mend fences with his colleague during a brief respite on the French Riviera in March 1945, Bradley never quite forgave him and went to his grave convinced that his friend had humiliated and betrayed him.

The inescapable fact was that some decisions made at this stage of the war were judged by its senior commanders in terms of nationalism and prestige rather than on military merit. Rampant suspicion replaced common sense, and actions and decisions were tied to sensibilities, by none more so than Bradley, who saw sinister motives behind anything Montgomery did during the Bulge, and blamed Eisenhower for having creating the situation.

Not only Bradley but his 12th Army Group staff had become contentious in the weeks since the shift of command in the Ardennes. Eisenhower once complained that "12th Army Group was getting as difficult to work with as 21st Army Group." One of the few senior American officers who maintained cordial relations with the British was Simpson, whose Ninth Army had fallen under British operational control. The soft-spoken, self-effacing Simpson was considered as unflappable as he was competent. Amid the squabbles large and small that plagued Eisenhower's relations with Bradley and Montgomery, Simpson stood out. Of all the American generals, no one was ever heard to say a bad word about Simpson. An appreciative Eisenhower wrote Simpson a note of thanks in March 1945. "I have been particularly grateful to note that your relationships with our British friends, including your seniors, your associates, and your subordinates, have been based on mutual respect and friendly cooperation."[23]

Eisenhower remained under substantial pressure from Montgomery and Bradley, neither of whom was prepared to sacrifice the priority of his operations to the other. The other army group commander, Jake Devers, the veteran artilleryman, was a virtual pariah who had no influence with either the senior SHAEF staff or Bedell Smith, who had become an increasingly key player on whom Eisenhower relied heavily, or with Eisenhower himself. Devers had made an enemy of Smith in the clashes over the staffing of SHAEF in early 1944, and little had changed by 1945. On November 23, 1944, Devers recorded in his diary, "Had a long talk with [Maj. Gen. H. R.] Bull in which I tried to impress him with the fact that we belong to SHAEF, that we are not just a piece on the end; that we are just as important as 12th Army Group; and that we had not asked for any help except when we thought it was vitally necessary; that we wanted him to understand when we asked for something, we really needed it."[24]

There is little doubt that Devers's message fell on deaf ears—if not Bull's, certainly SHAEF's. Within SHAEF, Devers was criticized for allegedly failing to have taken a firm enough grip on the campaign in Alsace and for not being sufficiently aggressive. Smith once noted, his voice dripping with sarcasm, that there was little confidence "in our friend Jakey," and Eisenhower was at one point overheard discussing replacing him with the Seventh Army commander, Alexander "Sandy" Patch.[25]

Eisenhower's disdain for Devers did not go unnoticed by Marshall. On taking the supreme command in January 1944, Eisenhower recommended that Devers be sent to the Mediterranean as Field Marshal Jumbo Wilson's deputy. An official U.S. historian later wrote:

At the time, Marshall felt that Eisenhower was trying to ship out his potential rivals for the post of Supreme Allied Commander, and he was disturbed that Eisenhower rejected Devers for any high command position in the invading forces. Nevertheless, Marshall approved the transfer, feeling that Eisenhower would be more at ease with generals who had served under him during the recent campaigns in the Mediterranean. . . . Eisenhower may have been unpleasantly surprised in July 1944 when he learned that Marshall intended to appoint Devers [to the command of 6th Army Group].[26]

Eisenhower's low opinion of Devers is confirmed in a list he prepared ranking his officers in order of their perceived merit. He ranked Devers a lowly twenty-fourth of thirty-eight senior officers in the ETO. Eisenhower did add a caveat that he was uncertain where Devers should be ranked, noting that "he had not, so far, produced among the seniors of the American organization here that feeling of trust and confidence that is so necessary to continued success."[27] Notes the official historians, "Devers was still not part of the team."[28]

Devers believed that Eisenhower placed undue precedence on the capture of territory over the destruction of the enemy. He felt strongly that the Allied mission was "not cracking the line or pushing the enemy back to line or river but the destruction of the enemy itself that counts . . . we must capture the German army or what exists of it and take our minds off terrain."[29]

Nor was Devers shy about expressing his views, some of which are thought to have gotten back to Eisenhower. None was personal, but earlier criticism of the supreme commander's operational strategies had stung and hardly endeared Devers to Eisenhower. And, although he had long since demonstrated an ability to withstand withering criticism from a variety of sources, when it came to Jake Devers, Eisenhower seemed particularly thin-skinned. Their relationship seems to have been exacerbated by Eisenhower's belief that Devers possessed political influence with Marshall. Thus, as the official historians note, "Although Eisenhower may have overrated Devers' political influence within the upper echelons of the American high command, the persistent differences between the Supreme Commander and Field Marshal Montgomery may have made Eisenhower even less forgiving of Devers' independent attitudes."[30]

What is more certain is that Eisenhower's low regard for Devers was based too much on personal dislike and too little on his effective performance as 6th Army Group commander. He second-guessed several of Devers's decisions during the Alsatian campaign, and in the employment of the French and Patch's Seventh Army during the period of the battle for the Colmar pocket, even blaming him for its existence. Had Devers not been an outsider and an unwelcome protégé of Marshall whose mere presence in the Allied lineup led to criticism of virtually everything he ever did, Eisenhower's attitude might have been quite different. From the outset, his criticism of his subordinate often verged on the irrational: "a too-ready willingness [by Eisenhower] to adopt an accusatory tone at the least hint of anything's going wrong," notes Russell Weigley.[31] Although neither Smith nor Eisenhower would willingly have admitted it, their behavior toward Devers was in no small part retaliation for his having opposed them in 1943 and 1944.

Devers never received much credit for his command of the 6th Army Group despite the fact that he did a highly creditable job in a position that had no real precedent. Possibly his biggest failing was believing the illusion presented by Bedell Smith that he supported Devers. "I think he was impressed with the way we operate," Devers wrote when Smith visited Patch's Seventh Army on January 5. Despite being stripped of his assets and replacements, Devers loyally carried out his orders. "You can kill a willing horse by overdoing what you require of him," Devers wrote in his diary. "I feel that SHAEF has given me too much front and taken away too many of my troops. . . . However, we shall loyally carry out our orders and, I believe, hold our own, no matter what the cost."[32]

Whereas Bradley's army group staff numbered some twelve hundred, Devers employed a smaller headquarters consisting of some six hundred officers and men, and commanded his armies with a loose rein, permitting his commanders to plan their own operations. Devers spent the majority of his time visiting his commanders and units down to division level. By contrast Bradley "engaged in intricate, detailed planning and dealt with in most cases only his army commanders," maintaining very tight control over them, although he had less success doing so with Patton.[33]

• • •

The tug-of-war between SHAEF and its subordinate headquarters followed a pattern in which bitching and second-guessing were occupational hazards. Typically each headquarters thought it knew best and often resented orders and interference (real or imagined) from above. The extent of the divisiveness was never more evident than Bradley's angry response the day Jock Whiteley telephoned him while he was visiting Third Army, to inform him that the new theater reserve being constituted by SHAEF would necessitate the removal of several of Bradley's divisions and their transfer to Devers. Bradley exploded. Patton, who had never seen Bradley lose his temper, observed with fascination as his superior raged, "If you feel that way about it, then as far as I am concerned, you can take any goddamned division or corps in the 12th Army Group, do with them as you see fit, and those of us that you leave behind will sit on our ass until hell freezes. I trust that you do not think I am angry, but I want to impress on you that I am goddam well incensed." Virtually every officer in the room stood up and applauded. Patton could be clearly heard on the other end of the telephone thundering, "Tell them to go to hell and all three of us will resign. I will lead the procession." A frustrated Whiteley handed the telephone to Bull, and the tirade on the other end resumed as Bradley lambasted the SHAEF G-3.[34] SHAEF relented.

Although he would always stoutly defend SHAEF, even Bedell Smith eventually became exasperated by the politics and the constant need for consensus and to placate competing personalities at various levels. "We never do anything bold. There are at least seventeen people to be dealt with so [we] must compromise, and compromise is never bold," he once proclaimed at a staff conference.[35] Because of Smith's instinct for plain speaking and direct action, Eisenhower's modus operandi often drove him to distraction. Although he understood Eisenhower's motives, Smith thought that Eisenhower's insistence on compromise had an adverse impact and was clearly at the root of the difficulty in achieving any semblance of boldness. Sometimes, he felt, orders needed to be issued irrespective of the negative impact on someone's psyche.

It took Allied forces until the end of January to restore the lost ground, and, as Eisenhower contemplated the forthcoming invasion of Germany, the lingering arguments from the previous year resumed. Hitler misread the Allied will to continue on the offensive after the furious battles in the Ardennes, believing he would be given a respite that would enable him to reinforce the crumbling eastern front. Eisenhower, however, had no intention of easing up and was determined to pursue the advantage by attacking across the same broad front he had created the previous August.

In the east, with nearly four million troops, 9,800 tanks, and 40,000 artillery pieces, the Red Army unleashed a massive offensive on January 12 across four fronts, aimed at the heart of Nazi Germany. By early February Marshal

Georgi Zhukov's 1st Belorussian Front had slashed its way to the Oder at a point where the river ran to within fifty miles of Berlin. Eisenhower's armies were finally in control of what had once been the great "bulge" in the Ardennes and were still regrouping to launch the final offensive in the west. Eisenhower welcomed the great Soviet offensive: "How I hope this new Russian offensive keeps right on going into the heart of Germany . . . its initial success must be a shock to the d—— Germans."[36]

The arguments and debates after Normandy were merely a prelude to the nastiness of 1945, during which the contentiousness over the direction of the final campaigns of the war reached its zenith. Eisenhower was beset from two sides by British and American generals with opinions contrary to those of the supreme commander. Montgomery and the British chiefs of staff continued to support a powerful offensive in the north to capture the Ruhr and breach the Rhine. It was, said Eisenhower, like "trying to arrange the blankets smoothly over several prima donnas in the same bed."[37]

While the generals fought over whose strategy would prevail, Brooke and the British chiefs of staff, horrified at the notion of fighting major battles west of the Rhine, raised the stakes by pressuring Eisenhower to agree to Montgomery's proposed "single, full blooded thrust" toward Berlin. They roundly condemned Eisenhower's strategy as akin to what someone sarcastically coined "Have a go, Joe," an expression commonly uttered by London prostitutes seeking business from American GIs.[38] To end this unseemly brawl, Marshall finally threatened the British by insinuating that Eisenhower would ask to be relieved as supreme commander unless they accepted his broad-front strategy.

The invasion of Germany was a deadly business. When the Allies resumed their advance in the wake of the Battle of the Bulge, the war may have been lost and their cause ultimately hopeless, but the German army fought tenaciously in the early months of 1945. To align the Allied front for the final assault, certain preliminary attacks were necessary to seize the Roer dams and eliminate the German pockets around Colmar and in the Saar, along the Moselle and Saar Rivers near Trier. Eisenhower ceded priority of effort to the British and beefed up the U.S. Ninth Army, which remained attached to Montgomery's 21st Army Group.

The Roer dams were blown up and flooded the area, over which an offensive into the Reichswald and the heart of the Siegfried Line cost six thousand British casualties. On the Germans' part it was the same old scenario: Create every possible obstacle, fight stubbornly, and only give ground when it could no longer be held. On both sides the casualty rates rose alarmingly: In six weeks the German army lost an estimated one-third of its total remaining strength defending the area west of the Rhine. Unmoved that his nation was bleeding to death, Hitler decreed that his soldiers fight on until they too died. But his generals understood the limits of what could be asked of a soldier, and eventually even the fanatical Model disobeyed the Führer. The cost to the Germans of the Allied broad-front thrust to the Rhine was 250,000 in POWs alone.

However, the Allies also paid a high price. Tanks functioned poorly in the Eifel, where the Third Army was attacking and, as in Lorraine, the fighting devolved into yet another series of bloody infantry battles fought by cold, weary GIs. "How human beings could endure this continuous fighting at sub-zero temperatures is still beyond my comprehension," Patton marveled.

Capturing the Ruhr was a blunder instigated by Bradley that was contrary to Eisenhower's stated goal that Berlin was the "main prize." It was wholly unnecessary to have fought these battles, with their consequent casualties, against a battered German army group in the Ruhr that would have no bearing on the outcome of the war, and that ought to have been easily contained by a handful of American divisions. Instead, notes Russell Weigley, "in the face of strategic logic, Bradley persuaded Eisenhower to divert from the drive toward Berlin a huge slice of the American armies—eventually eighteen divisions . . . forces best positioned to strike toward Berlin—and to turn these divisions into the urban jungle of the Ruhr, a battleground long shunned in SHAEF planning, to grapple head on with German armies whose strategic significance was in fact essentially nil."[39]

Thus Eisenhower had indeed wavered from his strategy whereby his armies would continue their advance across a broad front to the Rhine. To breach the great obstacle of the Rhine, Eisenhower's strategy was to unfold in three phases, during which the Allied armies would spread into Germany and engulf the Third Reich like the tentacles of an octopus. While Montgomery made plans for Operation Plunder, a massive airborne and amphibious operation in the Ruhr to breach the lowlands of the Rhine in Holland with the Canadian First and British Second Armies, and the Ruhr with Simpson's U.S. Ninth Army, Bradley was to clear the Eifel and drive to the Moselle with the Seventh and Third Armies. Once across the Rhine, the armies of Hodges and Simpson would encircle the Ruhr and crush Model's Army Group B in the jaws of a huge Allied pincer: Eisenhower's Cannae. Third Army and Devers's 6th Group would advance toward Czechoslovakia, Austria, and the Elbe River, where Eisenhower intended to halt the Allied advance and link up with the Red Army, which was busily overpowering everything in its path during its relentless advance from the east. Capturing the Ruhr may have seemed like a brilliant masterstroke, but in the end it was a wasteful quest for useless real estate.

Despite Hitler's failure in the Ardennes, any doubts that there would be an easy resolution to the war were erased when, in early February, the Big

Three met at the Crimean resort city of Yalta and reiterated their long-standing but ill-conceived demand to accept only unconditional surrender. In what was later termed a sellout to Stalin, Churchill and a seriously ailing Roosevelt agreed on the division of Germany, including the establishment of four zones of occupation (French, American, British, and Russian) when the war ended. In return for a Russian commitment to join the war against Japan, Churchill and Roosevelt agreed to the realignment of the borders of eastern Europe. In the aftermath of the war, Stalin's assurances of free elections in the liberated nations of eastern Europe proved hollow, as they were cut off by what Churchill later called an Iron Curtain of Soviet domination. Until then the war would continue until the Allied armies and the Red Army met somewhere in a crushed Nazi Germany. Although victory in Europe was mere weeks off, in the aftermath of Yalta, Soviet betrayal of the accords was also imminent. Britain's foreign secretary, Anthony Eden, foretold the future when he exclaimed in dismay, "My God, what a mess Europe is in! What a mess!"[40]

The Big Three communiqué issued after Yalta, which spelled out that postwar Germany was to be dismembered, merely reinforced Hitler's intention to fight to the bitter end rather than surrender.[41]

The U.S. and British chiefs of staff met at Malta in late January, prior to Yalta, to map out grand strategy for the remainder of the war. The near fiasco in the Ardennes had left the British more skeptical than ever that Eisenhower did not have a firm hand on the tiller of command of SHAEF. Well aware that Eisenhower would be under fire from Churchill and the British chiefs at Malta for the perceived flaws in his plan for the final campaign in Germany, Marshall cabled Eisenhower to meet with him beforehand at a château near Marseilles. For the first time in the war Marshall entertained a degree of doubt "about the man he had chosen almost three years before to be supreme commander"—uncertain that perhaps Eisenhower had lost control of SHAEF. The cloud that hung over Eisenhower was, Marshall felt, only resolvable by a face-to-face meeting with his protégé in which he could assess for himself the degree to which Eisenhower had fallen.[42]

Secretary of War Henry Stimson also questioned Eisenhower's resolve, noting in his diary that he agreed with Marshall that Eisenhower had been giving away too much to the British in an effort to peacefully reconcile the strategic and command debates. "I myself have been worried lest he lose sight of the necessity of supporting sufficiently our national views where they were at variance with the British. That was the reason why I favored the appointment of Marshall for this European command . . . but with Marshall's vigorous interposition at this conference he seems to have readjusted the balance and given [Eisenhower] a healthy boost."[43]

Marshall was particularly disturbed by Eisenhower's apparent willingness to accept Alexander and pointed out that conceding to the British over Alexander was tantamount to the field marshal filling the ex officio role of ground commander, which Eisenhower and Washington had so strongly resisted. Even worse, with Alexander in place, "you would have great difficulty in offsetting the direct influence of the P.M.," Marshall warned.[44] Thus, when Eisenhower signaled that he was amenable to Alexander, Marshall decided Eisenhower's backbone needed stiffening.

The man Marshall encountered bore scant resemblance to the confident leader he had seen on earlier occasions. Sheer fatigue from months of endless crises both on the battlefields and in the boardrooms of Whitehall had left Eisenhower worn out, with his usual confidence badly shaken. At Marshall's suggestion Eisenhower sent Bedell Smith to Malta to represent himself and SHAEF. Marshall took on the role of Eisenhower's protector, vowing that he would resign before permitting the British to impose a ground commander on him.

The Malta meeting, which centered on the single issue of how to successfully prosecute the final campaign of the war, turned into an unseemly quarrel that renewed the long-standing and fundamental differences between the American and British chiefs of staff. Although Eisenhower was not present, Malta became, in effect, a critique of him and his leadership of the coalition, with powerful opponents arrayed along national lines. Brooke and the British chiefs arrived with a proposal that was nothing less than a formalized revival of the single-thrust argument, and the appointment of a land force commander, that had been raging for months.

Eisenhower's plan to advance methodically to the Rhine, establish bridgeheads east of the river, and then continue a broad-front advance into the heart of Germany was rejected by Brooke, who argued not only that the Germans were beaten but that unless the advance was speeded up, the Russians, who were already astride the German-Polish border, and whose relentless advance on Berlin was now virtually unstoppable, would surely capture the German capital ahead of the Allies. The answer, said Brooke, was a thrust by Montgomery with some thirty-five to forty divisions through the Ruhr to Berlin.

By the second CCOS meeting on January 31, "the British delegation hardly bothered to disguise its lack of faith in Eisenhower's judgment—not to mention his good faith. Eisenhower was not strong enough for the job, Brooke insisted. A deputy commander was the implicit solution."[45]

Although "the British put great pressure on him," recalled Marshall, Smith forcefully presented Eisenhower's plan to advance all elements of SHAEF to the line of the Rhine River, and stoutly defended it when Brooke criticized the scheme for being too methodical and permitting the Red Army to fill the void if the Allied advance stalled short of the German capital. Ian Jacob's biographer has noted that "usually a very diplomatic operator took a very strong line, making it clear that any support given to Montgomery's plea would result in the resignation of Eisenhower."[46] Marshall backed Smith and privately excoriated Montgomery, who he believed was fueling the British position by his repeated demands upon Eisenhower that he command the ground forces.

The British chiefs refused to endorse what Brooke described as Eisenhower's "awful appreciation which points to no decisive action."[47] Although the official minutes reveal not the slightest hint of discord, Robert E. Sherwood has described the January 31 meeting as producing "the most violent disagreements and disputes of the war," in which "the arguments reached such a point that Marshall, ordinarily one of the most restrained and soft-spoken of men, announced that if the British plan were approved by the Prime Minister and President he would recommend to Eisenhower that he had no choice but to ask to be relieved of command. The issue was settled in Eisenhower's favor."[48] Marshall later described it as "a terrible meeting."[49]

On the evening of January 31, Smith sought out Brooke in his quarters. The subject was Eisenhower, whom Brooke had continued to criticize. The evidence points to a showdown between two stubborn men with no love for each other. Brooke's complaints that Eisenhower seemed unable to control his subordinates, combined with his demand that Eisenhower be given a directive to supply additional resources to Montgomery, provoked a strong reaction from Smith, who angrily retorted, "Goddamn it! Let's have it out here and now." Were Eisenhower to agree, Smith noted, "this would be a vote of no confidence in Ike and if he felt that way he should suggest that the [Joint] Chiefs of Staff relieve him. He [Brooke] then spoke of Ike as a good chairman of the board and disavowed any intention of getting rid of him." Neither man ever recorded their conversation in full. Brooke's diary barely mentions the meeting, except to note that Smith seemed to appreciate "the dangers of Ike's strategy,"[50] and that he thought their talk did some good.

It did not, and the following morning, February 1, the subject of Eisenhower flared up again at the CCOS meeting. The arguments grew so heated that Marshall excused Smith from the room and insisted on a closed session with only the principals present and no minutes kept. Brooke refused to accept Marshall's "quite unacceptable appreciation and plan" and agreed only "to take note of it." Ernie King later remarked that "neither side would give an inch, so the matter had to be carried over until FDR arrived in Malta." Roosevelt effectively ended the debate when he approved Eisenhower's plans, and Churchill quickly fell into line.[51] "I noted that Brooke was rather glum after Roosevelt and Churchill agreed to what Eisenhower wanted done," noted King.[52] Although there would be further scattered shots fired across Eisenhower's bow by Brooke before the war ended, the contentious Malta meetings marked the end of effective British opposition to Eisenhower. Marshall and the U.S. chiefs had, however crudely, checkmated their British colleagues and laid down the law that the United States would have its way.

The scheme to replace Tedder with Alexander had not quite died, however. On the night of February 2 the issue was raised yet again at a meeting between Roosevelt, Churchill, Brooke, and Marshall. This time a swap of jobs between the two was discussed, which Roosevelt and Marshall indicated a willingness to accept some six weeks later, to avoid any suggestion that Alexander was being brought in to prop Eisenhower up.[53] Although the plan was never pursued and eventually faded away, Eisenhower was incensed when he learned from Pinky Bull (who had accompanied Bedell Smith to Malta) of Marshall's about-face several days later. It had all the earmarks of the sort of backroom dealing that Eisenhower detested, and left him with a sense that he had been betrayed.

When he visited Bradley on February 12, in considerable pain from his bad knee and his morale at perhaps its lowest ebb since the darkest days in Tunisia, Eisenhower was both angry and hurt that Marshall had not only broken his promise but had failed to inform him about what had transpired. He had already changed his mind about accepting Alexander, acknowledging that it was a bad idea. Not only would it be construed as tacit acceptance that American leadership in the Ardennes had been found wanting, but the British press would have a field day.

Eisenhower was convinced that Montgomery had schemed to further Alexander's appointment, and that a confrontation was unavoidable. Unable to fly to Holland in the bad weather the following day, Eisenhower, with Chet Hansen as his escort, was driven in Bradley's Cadillac to meet Montgomery at his former command post at Zonhoven. As Eisenhower strode, scowling, into Monty's CP, his famous temper was at the boiling point. "I have never seen a man as angry as he was at that time," said Hansen. "He was furious. He was going to have a showdown . . . he walked in and started talking to Monty—no affability at all."[54]

Neither man ever alluded to a showdown, and Hansen toned down his description of their meeting in his diary to merely "some slight table thumping." Eisenhower might not have been so agitated had he known that his assumption was misdirected. Montgomery had not been involved in the Malta machinations and by this time had likewise concluded that Alexander's appointment would only ignite fresh controversy when the present command structure seemed more satisfactory. In his diary that evening Montgomery wrote that Eisenhower complained that Churchill had criticized him for failing to visit him often enough. "This hurt him a good deal and [he] went on to say he was always being bullied by Marshall and the U.S. Chiefs of Staff for being too British, or by the P.M. and the British Chiefs of Staff for being too American. . . . I am sorry this was said at Malta; it got to Ike very quickly, and was no doubt attributed to me; he is such an awfully decent chap that I hate to see him upset." In what became a routine convergence of views, Monty wrote that when he told Eisenhower that "I was very well satisfied with the present system about command, he became a different man; he drove away beaming all over his face."[55]

No doubt Eisenhower was relieved that for once Montgomery had become his ally instead of his nemesis. Two days later Eisenhower sent a cleverly worded letter to Brooke about Alexander. Noting that "any change in our working team is to be deplored," Eisenhower did not outright refuse Alexander, but implied that if Churchill carried out the Malta decision, there would not only be no change in the present command setup—that is, no ground commander—but Alexander might find his new duties "of less influence than he should properly have." Moreover, should the British press misinterpret Alexander's presence as signaling a new ground headquarters, "I would find it immediately necessary to make a formal announcement setting forth the facts."[56]

The letter was a bombshell, and it detonated when Brooke informed Churchill that Eisenhower proposed "to employ Alex in the back areas if he comes to him as a Deputy!"[57] With Montgomery in favor of leaving the Allied command unchanged and Brooke satisfied that Eisenhower finally seemed to be fulfilling the plan outlined by Bedell Smith at Malta, the British chiefs of staff took no action. Only Churchill was miffed and, when he personally replied to Eisenhower, refused to admit defeat and deferred any further action until the two could meet in person. He noted that transferring Alexander would merely be "a waste of Field Marshal Alexander's military gifts and experience."

Eisenhower emerged the clear victor in this latest skirmish with a thoroughly displeased Churchill. However, as Kay Summersby noted in her diary, the prime minister would "get over it."[58] Indeed, Churchill understood only too well that the pupil had long since learned how to beat the master at his own game. "It was," observed Bradley, "the most emphatic demonstration yet that Ike had taken full command of the war on the Continent."[59]

53.

All Roads Lead to Berlin

The things I saw beggar description.

When it came to war-weariness Eisenhower mirrored his friend Patton, who had aged visibly during the course of the war. As *Time* magazine's "Man of the Year" for 1944, his portrait on the cover vividly captured a tired Eisenhower at the end of a year of incredible pressures and responsibilities. The bags under his eyes and the absence of even a semblance of the traditional Eisenhower smile conveyed a sense that here was a man living on the sharp edge of stress and fatigue. "I know you lead a nomadic and sometimes almost miserable existence," he later wrote to Mamie in an effort to convey some sense of what she and others in the United States could not even imagine, "but I think that those of us that are bearing real responsibility in this war will find it difficult ever to be restful—[or] serene, again."[1]

In early February, Eisenhower's bad leg began acting up, and his physician ordered him to bed for thirty-six hours, one of the rare medical directives he ever followed to the letter. For a brief period SHAEF business was conducted from a phone installed at his bedside. A growth was also removed from his back, and he joked that the procedure left him "in stitches."[2] On a less droll note, Eisenhower complained there was not one single part of his body that did not pain him. His mood, said Kay Summersby, was "truly vile."[3]

Publicly Eisenhower appeared his normal, effusive self. At a February 24 press conference, his first since the previous November, he gave a world-class performance. The correspondents "were struck by Ike's appearance of fitness," during a deft performance that included questions about Montgomery. Roosevelt's visiting presidential press secretary, Steve Early, observed that "Ike is a master, though for my taste he smiles too much and says too little. Sometimes, when he chooses he uses a great many words to say nothing at all." Such was the case with questions about Montgomery, when Eisenhower managed to spend nearly five minutes saying "absolutely nothing[,] but the boys and girls of the press acted as if they had heard Einstein explain relativity." Nevertheless Early called it "the most magnificent performance of any man at a press conference that I have ever seen."[4]

So much for Eisenhower's public face. His old friend Everett Hughes was not alone in noticing his friend's increasing testiness in early 1945. "Ike shouts and rants. . . . He acted like a crazy man," said Hughes.[5] Everyone around him detected disturbing signs of his obvious distress. He was irritable, increasingly bad-tempered, and given to acerbic outbursts over trivial matters; his usual smile replaced by the grim countenance of a man devoid not only of his sense of humor but his fundamental compassion toward those closest to him. Chief among Eisenhower's worries was his belief that Marshall was unhappy with his performance in the Ardennes and, according to Hughes, the issue of Kay and Mamie, which simply refused to go away. For months his relationship with Kay had been the butt of gossip in London, Paris, and elsewhere. It was common knowledge among war correspondents that something was going on between them. Cynical jokes and scuttlebutt were particularly rife in the Paris bureau of the GI newspaper, *Stars and Stripes*. One tale that circulated described them spending an illicit weekend in a château owned by an affluent Frenchman. And so it went—endless gossip fueled by titillating speculation that Eisenhower was taking advantage of his position to have "a better deal than the rest of us," as one GI staffer complained.[6] Despite the widespread belief that the two were too close *not* to be sleeping together, there is simply no evidence of anything more than a nurturing friendship. Unfortunately, Eisenhower fostered the perception of an affair by naively showcasing Kay at times when she ought properly to have been relegated to the background. Whether or not Eisenhower knew of the gossip, he certainly knew of Mamie's unhappiness. "Ike was on the defensive," observed Hughes.[7]

Finally Beetle Smith confronted Eisenhower and bluntly declared that if he did not slow down his frantic pace he could expect a nervous breakdown. When Eisenhower angrily remonstrated, Smith bore in. "Look at you. You've got bags under your eyes. Your blood pressure's higher than it's ever been, and you can hardly walk across the room." Eisenhower reluctantly agreed and secretly took a brief five-day leave in Cannes with Smith, Kay, and several other staffers. When Bradley arrived for a conference on March 18, he was shocked by Eisenhower's run-down condition. "He looked terrible—exhausted."[8] Eisenhower never left the luxurious villa owned by a rich American and placed at his disposal. For the first two days, except for lunch, he took to his bed and slept around the clock. His weariness was so complete, both mentally and physically, that he had entered a zombielike state where body and mind simply refuse to function properly. Even a game of bridge seemed too much effort when Kay Summersby suggested it. "I can't keep my mind on cards," he said. "All I want to do is sit here and not think."[9] After the second day Kay pronounced her boss "somewhat human" and chafing at his enforced solitude. By the time he returned to the war on March 23, Eisenhower looked and felt considerably better.

In late February, Eisenhower moved his headquarters from Versailles to a French technical training school for young boys, a large, nondescript red-brick building in Reims.[10] The location of SHAEF's new forward HQ was astride a main convoy route, and the noise was deafening as trucks roared by at all hours only a few yards from Eisenhower's office, until they were mercifully diverted. "Ike loved it. The proximity of Versailles to Paris had made him nervous"; his staff loathed the place. From a huge office in the Trianon Palace Hotel, Eisenhower now occupied a minute, unpretentious office. His quarters in a nearby château were equally plain and merely the latest examples of Eisenhower's penchant for an unadorned lifestyle.[11]

Eisenhower spent as little time as possible in his new headquarters, preferring instead a round of daily visits to the front. Now that the Allies were in Germany, Eisenhower expressed his total lack of sympathy for the devastation wrought on German cities, once noting to Summersby that "they're all in ruins, just like Aachen. Maybe they'll make up for places like Coventry, London, Rotterdam and St. Lô!"[12]

By March 1945 the largest Allied force ever assembled, consisting of nearly four million U.S., British, and Canadian troops of three army groups, seven field armies, twenty-one corps, and seventy-three divisions, was poised to launch the final offensive that would finish off Nazi Germany and end the war. By VE day these numbers would grow to 4.5 million and ninety-one divisions.

On March 7 the obscure Ludendorff railway bridge across the Rhine at Remagen was captured intact by a reconnaissance force of the 9th Armored Division (assigned to Hodges's First Army), even as a German demolition crew was attempting to blow it up. Taking advantage of this extraordinary stroke of luck, the commander, Brig. Gen. William M. Hoge, never hesitated, and his troops swarmed across the river and established a bridgehead east of the Rhine.

The incident at the Remagen bridge was typical of the lack of connection between SHAEF and its subordinate elements. When word of its capture was telephoned to 12th Army Group on the evening of March 7, the SHAEF G-3, Pinky Bull, was meeting with Bradley over a SHAEF directive to detach three of his divisions and a large number of supporting units to Devers to reinforce a 6th Army Group offensive in the Saar. Calling the order "larcenous," the two were engaged in a shouting match, with Bull complaining, "By gosh, but you people are difficult to get along with, and I might add that you are getting more difficult every day."

During their argument Hodges telephoned Bradley about the Remagen bridge. "Hot dog, Courtney," exulted Bradley, ordering Hodges to "shove everything you can across it" before the Germans reacted. Bull's reaction was to basically enjoy the moment, because "you're not going anywhere down there at Remagen. It just doesn't fit in with *the* plan. Ike's heart is in your sector, but right now his mind is up north." Chester Hansen noted that Bull "hotly resents this infringement on his plan." As Bradley and his staff hammered at the stupidity of giving away the enormous advantage of Remagen, Bull stubbornly refused to concede.

Angry and astonished, Bradley retorted, "What in hell do you want us to do, pull back and blow it up?" When Bull refused to answer, Bradley placed a call to Eisenhower, who was hosting the U.S. airborne commanders at dinner when he was summoned to the telephone. As his guests listened raptly from the next room to Eisenhower's end of the conversation, they heard, "Brad, that's wonderful. Sure, get right across with everything you've got. It's the best break we've had." There was a pause while Bradley explained Bull's reluctance; then Eisenhower said, "To hell with the planners."

With Eisenhower's formal blessing, Bradley exploited Remagen, although he would gladly have strangled Bull, who seemed more concerned about "the plan" than he was in winning the war.[13] In the end, however, it was Bull who won the argument. Eisenhower's continued insistence on a broad-front approach and priority of effort given to Montgomery resulted in a lost opportunity to have established a larger bridgehead east of the Rhine. The area east of this sector of the Rhine is extremely rugged terrain, and without a further infusion of combat power the initial small American force of some five divisions (which soon grew to nine) was contained until nearly the end of March in the Remagen bridgehead. Contained or not, the Remagen bridge was one of the great sagas of the war and an example of inspired leadership.

The furious German counterattacks left sectors of the river to the south relatively unprotected. As Montgomery was preparing for his massive breaching operation in the north, both Bradley and Patton were determined to take advantage of the opportunity to beat Monty across the Rhine. Indeed, the final battles of the war were as much about prestige as any fought by the Allies. The rift between Montgomery and the American commanders in the wake of his abysmal press conference left Bradley and Patton determined to prevent 21st Army Group from reaping the victory headlines. Bradley admitted his political naïveté and that of the other Americans, who thought only in terms of military objectives. Yet the unsophisticated Bradley had quickly learned how to play Montgomery's game, and in the process had made himself nearly as unpopular at SHAEF as the British field marshal.

The tug-of-war continued unabated. When, in early February, just as Patton correctly sensed the time was ripe to attack and keep attacking, he was shocked when, on February 10, Bradley telephoned to report that Eisenhower was transferring divisions to Simpson's Ninth Army. Third Army was to go on the defensive. Patton replied that he was the oldest serving general in both age and combat experience and he was goddamned if he would do so—he would resign first. Bradley replied that Patton owed too much to his troops to even consider such an act. After being prodded Eisenhower permitted

Bradley "to assume a posture of 'aggressive defense.' . . . I chose to view it as an order to 'keep moving' toward the Rhine with a low profile."[14]

By early March, Patton had sensed a fresh opportunity to break loose from the confining terrain of the Palatinate, in which Third Army had been fighting. Instead of advancing shoulder to shoulder with 6th Army Group in the south, Patton persuaded Bradley, who in turn persuaded Eisenhower, to permit a new offensive whereby Third Army would exploit its success by sweeping south from Trier to envelop the remaining German units defending the Siegfried Line in conjunction with an attack by Patch's Seventh Army. Patton unleashed the 4th Armored Division in a successful dash to the Rhine, north of Coblenz, which the division reached on March 7, having thrust some fifty-five miles in less than forty-eight-hours. "On March 19 alone Third Army overran more than 950 square miles of territory. Coblenz was captured, and two more cities along the Rhine were within reach: Patton's tanks were just ten miles from Mainz, six miles from Worms."[15] The day the 4th Armored broke through to the Rhine, Tedder noted the fresh arrow on the situation map and observed, "There goes Patton with another of his Phallic symbols."[16]

Visualizing a Rhine crossing "as a glorious opportunity to score off Montgomery and steal some of the limelight from Hodges, whose Remagen coup had temporarily snatched the headlines for First Army," Patton had ordered his engineers forward and had collected large quantities of bridging material in anticipation of just such an opportunity.[17] On the night of March 22 the first elements of Third Army crossed the Rhine at Nierstein, about the same time as an infantry unit fought its way across farther south at Oppenheim. Having scored a coup at Montgomery's expense, on the night of March 23 Patton telephoned his boss to plead, "Brad, for God's sake tell the world we're across. . . . I want the world to know Third Army made it before Monty."[18]

Eisenhower and Patton shared a mutual contempt for the Germans. The War Department had found Patton's daily situation reports often too profane and wanted them toned down into less colorful language. His initial report of Third Army's Rhine crossing was a model of proper military language, but under his signature was this handwritten postscript: "I peed in the Rhine today."[19]

On the night of March 23 Montgomery launched Operation Plunder, his long-awaited blitzlike offensive that included a parachute and glider operation by two airborne divisions. More than two thousand guns had been assembled to fire on targets that were also plastered by hundreds of RAF bombers. It was the largest military operation since D-Day, involving nearly a million troops, and has been criticized as the most overrated of the war. Among a bevy of war correspondents and spectators to the event were Churchill, Brooke, and Eisenhower, who arrived at Simpson's headquarters to view the night crossings by Ninth Army. As Simpson and Eisenhower strolled along the west bank of the Rhine, they encountered a group of infantrymen from the U.S. 30th Division. Eisenhower began putting the usual questions to the GIs. One GI, when asked how he felt, replied, "General, I'm awful nervous. I was wounded two months ago and just [got] back from the hospital yesterday. I don't feel so good."

Eisenhower put the young man at ease by assuring him they made a good pair, and that he too was nervous but there was really nothing to worry about. All the necessary ingredients were in place to give the Germans a good licking. "Maybe if we just walk along together . . . we'll be good for each other." Obviously relieved by Eisenhower's words, the GI said: "Oh, I meant I *was* nervous. I'm not anymore."[20] Neither the anxious GI nor Eisenhower slept that night.

On March 25 Eisenhower met with Montgomery, Brooke, and Churchill. It was during this visit that one of the most highly debated incidents of the war occurred, when Eisenhower and Brooke made their famous stroll into controversy. According to Eisenhower, the CIGS said, "Thank God, Ike, you stuck by your plan. You were completely right, and I am sorry if my fear of dispersed efforts added to your burdens. The German is now licked."[21]

Brooke disputed Eisenhower's version, insisting he had clearly been misquoted. "I am quite certain that I never said to him, 'You were completely right,' as I am still convinced that he was 'completely wrong,' as proved by the temporary defeat inflicted on him by Rundstedt's counter stroke, which considerably retarded the defeat of Germany."[22]

Churchill was ebullient as he and Eisenhower viewed the massive display of Allied might along the Rhine. "My dear General, the German is whipped," he exulted. "We've got him. He is all through."[23]

With the Rhine now breached at numerous points, and both the First and Third Armies also securing bridgeheads east of the river, the end was near for the German armed forces defending their homeland. As the Red Army continued its relentless push west toward Berlin, some three hundred thousand troops of Model's Army Group B were trapped in the rapidly closing Ruhr pocket. Like an unstoppable tide the Allied armies swept ever deeper into the heart of Germany, in what Associated Press correspondent Hal Boyle described as "the greatest armored joyride in history."[24]

By mid-April the Ruhr was enveloped and split in two, and even the loyal Model conceded defeat and ordered Army Group B dissolved rather than carry out Hitler's scorched-earth decree before committing suicide as a matter of honor. Rundstedt was again dismissed by Hitler and Kesselring summoned from Italy in a futile attempt to restore the situation in the Ruhr. From far and wide German soldiers anxious to escape the wrath of the Red Army sought any American they chanced upon to surrender. One GI arrived at a temporary stockade like the Pied Piper; he had started out with sixty-eight German POWs and arrived with some twelve hundred in tow.[25] A swelling tide of German survivors of the fighting against the Red Army choked Hitler's famed autobahns, frantically making their way west to escape the advancing Russians in order to surrender to the Allies.[26]

No one was more ebullient over the progress of his army than George S. Patton. When John Eisenhower's unit deployed to Germany in early April, he spent a night with his father before moving on to Frankfurt, then the temporary site of Third Army HQ. Patton was in his element and told both John and visiting financier Bernard Baruch, "I've been told to hold up and let the rest of them catch up with me. But I'm advancing fifteen miles a day anyhow." Pointing at John "with mock severity," Patton said, "Don't tell your Daddy!"[27]

Eisenhower was sometimes known for his strange pronouncements, but one of the most singular occurred in mid-March when, during a visit to Third Army, he told Patton's staff, "The trouble with you people in Third Army is that you don't appreciate your own greatness. You're not cocky enough. Let the world know what you are doing, otherwise the American soldier will not be appreciated at his full value." Eisenhower also told Patton, "George, you are not only a good General, you are a *lucky* General, and, as you will remember, in a General, Napoleon prized luck above skill." Patton replied laughingly, "Well, that is the first compliment you have paid me since we served together."[28] Later, when his chief of staff, Brig. Gen. Hobart R. "Hap" Gay, wondered why Eisenhower had made his remark about Third Army, Patton replied, "That's easy. Before long, Ike will be running for President. The Third Army represents a lot of votes." When those present began to smile, Patton continued, "You think I'm joking? I'm not. Just wait and see."[29]

Although he failed to express his feelings adequately, Eisenhower was grateful to Patton, and in early April recommended to Marshall that Patton and Hodges be promoted immediately to four-star general. Within a matter of days both men received their promotions. Although there would be a permanent falling out between Patton and Eisenhower less than six months later, Patton was immensely grateful for the recognition and later informed John Eisenhower with considerable emotion "that he owed all his success to Dad."[30]

When the concentration camps were liberated much of the world learned for the first time of the gruesome atrocities perpetrated by the Nazis. Belsen, Buchenwald, Dachau, and other place-names became synonymous with the worst evils ever perpetrated. In April, Third Army liberated the Merkers industrial salt mine, where the XII Corps commander, Maj. Gen. Manton S. Eddy, discovered the entire German gold bullion reserve hidden inside a vast cavern situated some two thousand feet deep in the ground. Patton ordered a total embargo on the story until it could be confirmed. "His fury knew no bounds" when a SHAEF censor permitted a leak of the story to pass unchallenged. Although the officer was assigned to SHAEF, Patton ordered him from the Third Army sector forthwith. When Eddy informed Patton that he still did not know for certain what lay inside a sealed vault, Patton exploded: "Goddamnit it, Eddy. You blow open that fuckin' vault and see what's in it."[31]

Eisenhower and Bradley arrived to inspect this incredible cache, and as the generals began the long descent in an ancient elevator held by a single, none-too-secure cable in the pitch black shaft, Patton quipped, "If that clothesline should part, promotions in the United States Army would be considerably stimulated." From the inky blackness an unamused Eisenhower said, "O.K., George, that's enough. No more cracks until we are above ground again." All marveled at the sight of more than 4,500 twenty-five-pound gold bars, worth an estimated $57,600,000, and millions more in currency. There were also hundreds of paintings, and the few Patton examined he thought worth $2.50, and best suited for saloons. An interpreter noted that the three billion Reichsmarks were badly needed to meet the army payroll. Bradley retorted that he doubted the Wehrmacht would be meeting many more payrolls. There were also thousands of gold and silver fillings, eyeglasses, and other items stolen from the corpses of those murdered in the concentration camps, a visible legacy of Hitler's loathsome Final Solution.[32]

The gallows humor of that morning was replaced in the afternoon by disgust and horror when the generals visited the Ohrdruf-Nord concentration camp, near Gotha, just liberated by the 4th Armored. In an effort to ensure that no one would ever testify to their crimes, the SS guards had murdered everyone before fleeing. Bodies were piled everywhere, along with macabre evidence of torture and butchery. Some had been set ablaze in huge funeral pyres. The stench was indescribable. It was evil incarnate, and it left Bradley speechless. Patton disappeared briefly and vomited against the side of a building. He refused to enter one room containing the corpses of naked men starved to death. The generals had seen war in all its brutal forms, but none had ever seen anything so utterly evil. Eisenhower was appalled, calling the atrocities "beyond the American mind to comprehend." Every American unit not in the front lines was to see Ohrdruf, he ordered. "We are told the American soldier does not know what he is fighting for. Now, at least, he will know what he is fighting *against*."[33] To a nearby GI, Eisenhower exclaimed, "Still having trouble hating them?"[34] That night Mickey McKeogh had never seen his boss so furious; his face was "black," and "[he] looked sick . . . and very angry."[35] After dinner Eisenhower, still pale and shaken, accepted the drink Patton poured for him. What he had viewed that day was beyond his ability to comprehend. "I can't understand the mentality that would compel these German people to do a thing like that," he declared.[36] After the mayor of Gotha and his wife hanged themselves after being compelled to view Ohrdruf, Eisenhower remarked, "Maybe there is hope after all."[37]

The following day, April 13, 1945, Eisenhower visited the infamous

Buchenwald concentration camp. "I never dreamed that such cruelty, bestiality, and savagery could really exist in this world! It was horrible," he confided to Mamie, sparing her the gory details of images that defy explanation.[38] As the diplomat Robert Murphy later wrote, "The inmates liberated by our forces were skeletons . . . many of the captives were professional soldiers . . . and they pulled their wasted bodies into gallant salutes as Eisenhower, Patton and their staffs passed them. It was enough to make strong men weep—and some American officers did so unabashedly."[39] Writing to Marshall the same day Eisenhower painted some of the horror he had witnessed in the camps. "The things I saw beggar description," he said, suggesting that Marshall come to Germany to see for himself. "I made the visit deliberately, in order to be in a position to give firsthand evidence of these things if ever, in the future, there develops a tendency to charge these allegations merely to 'propaganda.' "[40]

After dinner on the night of his traumatic visit to Ohrdruf on April 12, Eisenhower, a man long accustomed to living in a fishbowl of controversy, lit the fuse for the most debated decision of his tenure as supreme commander.

54.

Armageddon

How glad I'll be when it's all over. Whew!

The battle maps of Germany, filled with arrows, strings, and the tiny symbols used by the generals and their staffs to assess the current status of operations, covered large walls, while others were barely large enough to cover the hood of a jeep or staff car. But all had in common a forest of arrows depicting the movement of Allied forces eastward and the relentless advance of the Red Army toward the west. To the uninitiated, such maps may have seemed chaotic but, notes historian Charles B. MacDonald, it was an illusion, and "in reality from each of the columns strings led, as from puppet to puppeteer, to General Eisenhower's supreme command."[1] Whether pointing east or west, the arrows were all aimed at one key location on the map: Berlin.

On the evening of his shocking visit to the Merkers mine and Ohrdruf, Eisenhower revealed privately to Patton that he was soon to halt the First and Ninth Armies at the Elbe River to await the arrival of the Red Army. Third Army would be given a new mission to drive southeast toward Czechoslovakia. "From a tactical point of view, it is highly inadvisable for the American Army to take Berlin and I hope political influence won't cause me to take the city," he said. "It has no tactical or strategic value and would place upon the American forces the burden of caring for thousands and thousands of Germans, displaced persons and Allied prisoners of war."

Patton's reaction was incredulity. "Ike, I don't see how you figure that out. We had better take Berlin, and quick—and on to the Oder!" Later on, in the presence of his chief of staff, Patton reiterated the need to drive on to Berlin, arguing that it could certainly be done in forty-eight hours by Ninth Army. Eisenhower wondered aloud, "Well, who would want it?" Patton did not reply at once, but placed both hands on his friend's shoulders and said, "I think history will answer that question for you."[2]

Bradley admitted that he was sorely tempted by the lure of his troops capturing the greatest political prize of the war but realized it was simply not militarily feasible. A strong dose of reality set in when he calculated the cost, and noted that to have sent Montgomery on a mission to capture Berlin would have necessitated detaching a U.S. army-size force to guard his flank and correspondingly thwart the defeat of the German army on the 12th Army Group front. "As soldiers we looked naively on the British inclination to complicate the war with political foresight and nonmilitary objectives."[3]

Among those dismayed by Eisenhower's decision was Simpson, who when ordered by Bradley to halt his Ninth Army at the Elbe, replied, "Where the hell did you get this?" Told, "From Ike," Simpson obeyed his orders but was convinced it was a terrible mistake, and that his army could have advanced to Berlin. The U.S. official historian agrees: "The American armies, the Ninth in particular, could have continued their offensive some fifty more miles at least to the fringe of Berlin. The decision of the Supreme Allied Commander and nothing else halted the Americans at the Elbe and the Mulde [Rivers]."[4]

As Patton prepared for bed after his conversation with Eisenhower later that fateful April 12, he tuned to the BBC to obtain the correct time, and learned of Roosevelt's sudden death in Warm Springs, Georgia. Patton immediately awakened Eisenhower and Bradley, who was also spending the night at Third Army. In their bathrobes the three generals somberly contemplated Roosevelt's loss and its impact until two A.M. the following morning. All agreed that FDR would be sorely missed at a critical moment of history.[5] No one knew much about their new commander in chief, Harry S. Truman, who would turn out to have little use for either Eisenhower or Patton. Truman's fellow Missourian, Omar Bradley, thought that "[f]rom our distance, Truman did not appear at all qualified to fill Roosevelt's large shoes."[6] Eisenhower would later recall, "We went to bed depressed and sad."[7]

With the Russians already astride the Oder, a mere thirty miles east of the German capital, the question of Berlin was of paramount importance. Eisenhower's concern over a collision with the Russians was high, and on March 19 a Russian observer and unofficial liaison, Gen. Ivan Susloparoff, arrived at SHAEF. To Susloparoff, Eisenhower conveyed his deepening concern regarding the impending linkup and coordination problems with the Red Army, but the Russian had scant knowledge of the Red Army situation along the Oder, and had no authorization from his Soviet masters to reveal what little he did know.

On March 28 Eisenhower, without reference to the Combined Chiefs, felt compelled to take the unusual step of sending a cable directly to Stalin, to whom he laid out his plans for the final weeks of the war and asked if the Soviet leader could "tell me your intentions, and let me know how far the proposed operations outlined in this message conform to your probable action."[8]

. . .

At the time of his decision the four occupation zones of Germany had already been decided on. At Quebec in September 1944, the United States and Britain approved some of the provisions—first drawn up in early 1944 by the European Advisory Commission (EAC), based on British suggestions—rejected certain others, and, notes Warren Kimball, "allowed still others to apply by failing to act. But, either way, by 1945 the Big Three had set the parameters for much of the German settlement from presumably temporary occupation zones to the frontiers between the Germans and other European states."[9] At Yalta the Soviet Union ratified the Anglo-American recommendations, which included the division of Berlin into four separate sectors, each to be administered by one of the four Allied powers (which for purposes of the occupation included France). Thus when controversy flared over Berlin, Eisenhower's decision had already become a moot point. The real problem was not Berlin but the occupation zones of Germany that left the German capital a virtual island deep in the Soviet sector, a fact about which Eisenhower could do nothing.

While the Western Allies wrung their collective hands over the fate of postwar Poland, which the Yalta agreements failed to protect adequately, Berlin had already slipped through the cracks. Roosevelt thought the Soviets ought to be given a fair chance to implement the Yalta accords, and was loath to challenge Stalin over Berlin. And when Churchill raised the issue of an Allied race for Berlin, he was rebuffed. FDR had been urged by Marshall not to interfere with Eisenhower and wholeheartedly rejected any attempt to compromise Eisenhower's authority. The question of Berlin was not one in which Eisenhower was operating in some sort of vacuum. To the contrary, with the Red Army nearly at its gates, Marshall and the U.S. chiefs saw little value in making the city an objective. Moreover, with the war against Japan as yet far from won, the United States was anxious to end the fighting in Europe and begin deploying troops home, and to the Pacific.

The United States also had cause for concern over Churchill's impossible Balkan notion of sending Alexander's armies through the so-called Ljubljana Gap and into the plains of the Danube and Vienna, a scheme scarcely more than a Churchillian fantasy. Thus such British proposals targeting Berlin and the Ljubljana Gap received short shrift from the United States at this stage of the war.

At the time Berlin was already under siege by a score of Russian divisions, and an estimated 2,200 big guns would pound the city into rubble during the operation. "The fact that the Soviets were so close to Berlin, in such strength," said Eisenhower, "would seem to give pause to those armchair strategists who say, 'Of course, the Western Allies could have captured Berlin without any trouble.' "[10] The cost, he noted, would have been high, including the diversion of forces sent to free Denmark and Austria.

On this issue the differences between Britain and the United States were as deep as they were fundamental. Britain was anxious to carve out a postwar role for what was left of its fragmented colonial empire, whereas the intentions of the United States were to see the war ended victoriously, and to bring home its fighting men promptly, before too many more lost their lives, which, in the case of Berlin, Eisenhower was convinced would be needless.

From the time of Eisenhower's original directive from the Combined Chiefs of Staff in February 1944, Berlin had been the key objective that had permeated Allied thinking and planning. Certainly it was foremost in Eisenhower's mind when he took command of the Allied ground forces in September 1944. "Clearly, Berlin is the main prize," he wrote to Montgomery, "and the prize in defense of which the enemy is likely to concentrate the bulk of his forces. There is no doubt whatsoever, in my mind, that we should concentrate all our energies and resources on a rapid thrust to Berlin."[11]

Roosevelt first articulated his position on the postwar occupation of Germany in November 1943, while en route to the conferences in Cairo and Teheran, on the battleship USS *Iowa*. FDR not only viewed Berlin as a key Allied objective but fully expected that "[t]here would definitely be a race for Berlin. We may have to put United States Divisions into Berlin as soon as possible."[12] On a *National Geographic* map he drew in pencil his view of the proposed zones of occupation. On Roosevelt's sketch Berlin was incorporated into the U.S. zone.

Inexplicably the president's wishes vanished almost immediately into the vortex of a nasty bureaucratic clash between the War and State Departments over the occupation of Germany. The map actually disappeared into a desk drawer in the Operations Division of the War Department and was never acted on. "The shelving of the Roosevelt plan by his own military advisors," wrote Cornelius Ryan, "was just one of a series of strange and costly blunders and errors of judgment that occurred among American officials in the days following the *Iowa* meeting."[13] The turf wars in Washington and months of wrangling within the EAC itself between Britain and the United States and with the USSR ultimately resulted, in the final version ratified at Yalta, in the placement of Berlin in the Russian zone—with no provision for U.S.-British access to the city. Although Roosevelt had doubts about Stalin's postwar aims, his optimism, articulated at Quebec in September 1944, won out. He could "manage Stalin," and the United States, he said, "could get along with Russia" and indeed must do so in the postwar world, a position also taken by Churchill, who in his heart had serious misgivings.[14] FDR did not contest the final EAC proposals. It was one of the most fateful political decisions of World War II. Within six weeks of signing the Yalta agreements, Stalin had already broken one of its provisions.[15]

Bound by the Big Three protocols, Eisenhower had by the end of March 1945 come to regard Berlin as "no longer a particularly important objective," at best a diversion. Certainly, however, a precedent existed for unilateral action as supreme commander. Decisions ranging from Darlan to Normandy and the broad front had been made, and Eisenhower deemed Berlin as simply yet another problem requiring action. Less certain is the extent to which Eisenhower anticipated the buzz saw of controversy, criticism, and dissension his Berlin decision would produce. His grandson suggests that for Eisenhower to have acted aggressively over Berlin would likely have fractured British and Armerican cooperation with the USSR and "probably destroyed the emerging settlement of World War II."[16]

Nor was Eisenhower in any mood to be dissuaded at this critical juncture of the war. He complained to Marshall that the British had opposed virtually everything he did as supreme commander, from Anvil to the advance to the Rhine. And now came their latest proposal: that Montgomery advance across the plains of northern Germany, whose wet conditions, he argued, were unsuitable terrain at that time of year. "I submit that these things are studied daily and hourly by me and my advisors and that we are animated by one single thought which is the early winning of this war."[17]

Notes John Eisenhower, "Dad felt seriously that he'd been given a military objective: to defeat the armed forces of Germany. All of our military doctrine from the days at West Point emphasizes that the object of military operations is the enemy's armed forces, *not* cities ... in the last days of the war, [Dad] was going to fight a *military* rather than a *political* war, unless told other-wise. ... This was paramount in his thinking. That doesn't mean to say he wasn't suspicious of the Russians. He had been suspicious of them from as far back as the days at O.P.D. [Operations Division, War Department] in 1942 when a couple of them had come there, and they were so arrogant that he said, 'My God, what are these people? What are they about?' "[18]

Eisenhower formalized his views in a letter to the Combined Chiefs of Staff on April 7. "I regard it as militarily unsound," he wrote,

> at this stage of the proceedings to make Berlin a major objective, particularly in view of the fact that it is only 35 miles from the Russian lines. I am the first to admit that a war is waged in pursuance of political aims and if the Combined Chiefs of Staff should decide that the Allied effort to take Berlin outweighs purely military considerations in this theater, I would cheerfully readjust my plans and my thinking so as to carry out such an operation.[19]

Eisenhower's intentions remained to capture Berlin "only if feasible and practicable," and he did suggest to Montgomery, "Naturally, if I get an opportunity to capture Berlin cheaply, I will take it."[20] Otherwise Eisenhower's intentions were to continue implementing his present plan, which included a broad-front advance into the heart of Germany, establishing the Allied left flank on the Baltic Sea around Lübeck, and to disrupt any German effort to establish a national redoubt in the Bavarian Alps.

Eisenhower retained bitter memories from his experience in North Africa over Darlan, and knew better than to invade a political sphere without directions from above. However, in the case of Berlin, Eisenhower's decision had the enthusiastic backing of Marshall, who likewise wanted no part of the German capital, and despite strong remonstrations from both Churchill and his military chiefs that Eisenhower had committed a political gaffe and exceeded his authority, the U.S. chiefs gave the supreme commander their full backing to run the war his way.[21]

If the United States and Britain (collectively or individually) had developed a strategy to deal with the Russians, it was never communicated to Eisenhower. Thus, when the Combined Chiefs failed to take up the question of Berlin or instruct him what action he should take regarding the city, Eisenhower felt free to continue operating under his original broadly worded mandate to "enter the continent of Europe, and in conjunction with the other United Nations, undertake operations aimed at the heart of Germany and the destruction of her armed forces." With Roosevelt's health failing badly, there was a power vacuum in Washington that, in military matters, was filled by Marshall. In Eisenhower's mind the lack of response from the chiefs constituted tacit acceptance of his present intentions. He would therefore continue to direct the final weeks of the war on a strictly military basis.

Although Churchill protested that Allied failure to take Berlin would "raise grave and formidable difficulties in the future," Roosevelt endorsed Eisenhower's decision to halt at the Elbe. The final humiliation for the British was that with Leipzig and the Elbe the principal Allied objectives instead of Berlin, Montgomery not only lost Ninth Army, which was given back to Bradley, but he was now placed in the unaccustomed role of supporting Bradley's advance.[22]

Churchill and Eisenhower exchanged spirited telegrams over Berlin, but the prime minister's entreaties that the city was too important to ignore ("the supreme signal of defeat to the German people") fell on unresponsive ears. When the prime minister expressed dismay that His Majesty's forces would be relegated "to an unexpectedly restricted sphere," Eisenhower retorted that he was "disturbed, if not hurt, that you should suggest any thought on my part to 'relegate His Majesty's forces. . . . Nothing is further from my mind and I think my record of over two and a half years commanding the Allied forces should eliminate any such idea." Exasperated, Churchill exclaimed to Brooke, "There is only one thing worse than fighting with allies, and that is fighting without them!" To Roosevelt he expressed his disappointment over Eisenhower's telegram to Stalin, but assured FDR that he and Ike remained on good terms with each other, as characterized by Churchill's rare use of a Latin quotation: *Amantium irae amoris integratio est,* which evoked smiles when someone in the War Department translated the phrase and sent it to Eisenhower: "Lovers' quarrels are a part of love."[23]

Churchill cabled Roosevelt that he wished to place on record "the complete confidence felt by His Majesty's Government in General Eisenhower, our pleasure that our armies are serving under his command and our admiration of the great and shining qualities of character and personality which he has proved himself to possess." Nevertheless, it was simply not in Churchill's nature to concede defeat, and he renewed his argument over Berlin to Roosevelt, "as the truest friends and comrades that ever fought side by side as allies. . . . I say quite frankly that Berlin remains of high strategic importance." The following day he cabled Eisenhower, "I deem it highly important that we should shake hands with the Russians as far east as possible."[24] Churchill's entreaties failed to sway Roosevelt or to alter Eisenhower's intention to halt at the Elbe.

Any attempt by the United States and Britain to capture Berlin might have brought about open conflict not only with the Red Army, but certainly with the city's German defenders, and the resulting bloodbath of Allied casualties would have all but ruined Eisenhower's reputation. What remains indisputable is that Eisenhower's hands were already tied by the Big Three agreement over the division of occupied Germany, and had the British or Americans captured Berlin, most of the territory taken west of the city would have had to be ceded right back to the Russians. "Why should we endanger the life of a single American or Briton to capture areas we soon will be handing over to the Russians?" Eisenhower would remark more than once at SHAEF staff meetings.[25]

While most of the postwar controversy was second-guessing, hindsight also serves to raise the obvious question of why there was no policy in place regarding Berlin and the Russians other than the zones of occupation formally agreed to at Yalta. Robert Murphy believes that Eisenhower had been so deeply affected by the scenes at Buchenwald and Ohrdruf that his "hatred for Nazism intensified his determination to have no conflict with Russia about Germany."[26]

Eisenhower nevertheless remained apprehensive about the meeting of Russian and Allied forces: "You know the Russians have been arrogant, and I just don't know what our future is going to be with them. I've got to send Patton down into Austria to take as much of Austria as possible. But I sure wish I had more of my divisions concentrated up here on the First Army front, ready to meet these people when they come in, on the Elbe and Mulde Rivers."[27]

In the early morning hours of April 17 the Russians launched their final offensive along the Oder, which led to the capture of Berlin. Twenty-two divisions backed by massive artillery and rocket fire rained some half million

rounds on the Germans, who, in one of their final paroxysms of defensive
fury, managed to slow but not stop the vast numbers of tanks and infantry
arrayed against them. On both sides it was butchery rivaling the Somme or
Verdun.

Shortly before noon on April 25, two separate patrols of the U.S. 69th
Division made contact with the Red Army at the Elbe, and in one of the most
epic moments of the war the eastern and western fronts were joined. After
the war Bedell Smith had mixed emotions over Eisenhower's decision. "The
line of the Elbe," he said,

> was decided on as a primarily military tactical matter. We frankly
> wanted water between us and the Russians. . . . We needed a definite
> line of demarcation. The Elbe was the most convenient one. Berlin
> had ceased to have military value. The political heart of Germany was
> Berlin, the industrial one the Ruhr. The latter had ceased to beat, while
> the former was about to stop. . . . Churchill bitterly opposed our stop-
> ping and . . . I have often thought . . . it would have been better to
> follow him. But the American people wouldn't have put up with it.
> They would have hanged us to a lamp post. We leaned over backward
> to give them a proper deal, and it was a mistake.[28]

The Berlin controversy spawned various wildly erroneous scenarios,
including that Eisenhower made some sort of "deal" to keep Allied forces out
of Berlin. Smith has emphatically stated, "Nothing could be further from the
truth. There was no political consideration involved and there was no agreement on this score with the Russians."[29]

Eisenhower rarely defended himself publicly, but in the postwar years the
debates and criticism over his Berlin decision did lead to a testy defense of
his decision during the 1952 presidential election campaign: "None of his
critics, he noted bitingly, had offered 'to go out and choose the ten thousand
mothers' whose sons would have been killed capturing 'a worthless objective.' "[30]

Eisenhower's numbers were, in fact, very conservative, and when Eisenhower asked Bradley for his estimate of what it would cost in casualties to
take Berlin, was told to expect at least one hundred thousand. Given the
ferocious street-by-street fighting between the Red Army and the last Nazi
holdouts, Bradley's estimate also appears to have been conservative. In mid-
April the Red Army began a three-week siege of Berlin. Russian losses were
staggering. During the siege, between April 16 and May 8, 1945, German
troops responded to Hitler's order to fight to the death by inflicting a staggering 361,367 casualties on the Red Army before Berlin was reduced to
smoking rubble.[31]

The final word on Berlin is summed up by Marshall's official biographer, who points out that "[t]he crux of the argument lies in the charge that Marshall and Eisenhower failed to think politically. . . . It was not the failure by the military leaders to think of political consequences but their refusal to make political decisions that their critics apparently deplore. On that point the position of Marshall and Eisenhower was in the soundest tradition of the Republic."[32]

Eisenhower's Berlin decision was closely tied to one of the war's great fantasies: the so-called but mythical National Redoubt in the mountains of southern Bavaria and northern Austria, where Hitler and a group of Nazi leaders were thought to have planned to retreat and conduct a last-ditch fight to the death. The myth had its origins in September 1944 when the Office of Strategic Services (OSS) element operating in Bern, Switzerland, headed by Allen Dulles, reported that Nazi leaders were preparing to make their final stand in the Bavarian Alps centered on Hitler's Eagle's Nest at Berchtesgaden. This was followed by a report issued by the OSS HQ in Washington that not only asserted German intentions but stated that the Redoubt was all but a reality. However, the OSS predictions were at odds with intelligence reports emanating from SHAEF and—with one exception—its subordinate armies. "Most Allied intelligence officers discounted the likelihood of any formidable, self-contained fortress in the Alps," noted an official U.S. historian.[33] The British official history concluded that "the very name 'National Redoubt' seems to have been introduced by the Allies, who borrowed it from the Swiss."[34]

Although the fiction ought to have died, it could no longer be ignored when its three strongest proponents became Eisenhower, Bedell Smith, and Bradley, all of whom grew obsessed with the notion that Hitler was planning a final stand in a National Redoubt, which might well prolong the war for a lengthy period of months, perhaps more than a year.

The theory was fueled at SHAEF by Smith, who believed that the Germans could muster between 100 and 150 divisions. This utterly preposterous notion was arrived at despite the fact that there was almost nothing of substance in SHAEF's own intelligence estimates to encourage such a conclusion, particularly one so wildly inaccurate. Kenneth Strong headed the skeptics and would allow only for the possibility that Hitler *might* leave a core of Nazis in the Alps to one day restore Nazism to Germany. Smith and Eisenhower may have been misled initially by the SHAEF intelligence summary of March 11, 1945, which reported various signs of preparations in the area thought to be the redoubt, along with "considerable numbers of SS and specially chosen units" withdrawing into Austria.[35]

The value of intelligence as a commander's coin of the realm cannot be overemphasized. However, intelligence is only as useful as it is current, and by early April SHAEF's intelligence summaries were increasingly discounting the possibility of such organized resistance. By mid-March it was clear that resistance was crumbling so fast that even the hard-core Nazis no longer believed they could avoid defeat.[36] Moreover, any lingering doubts about the existence and threat of a National Redoubt ought to have been satisfied by a report issued by the SHAEF Joint Intelligence Committee on April 10, which stated unequivocally, "There is no evidence to show that the strategy of the German High Command is being conducted with a view to occupying eventually the so-called National Redoubt." Moreover, "the area is not one which could support large forces for any length of time even if, as is improbable, large quantities of supplies have been dumped [there]."[37]

"The plot," notes Smith's biographer, "might more properly have been found in the cheap spy novels Eisenhower and Smith liked to read than in the councils of the Allied high command."[38] At a press conference on April 21 Smith admitted,

> This so-called "national redoubt" is something we don't know a whole lot about. We do know that the Germans have, as they could, shifted men and matériel and supplies down there. . . . Just what we will find down there we don't know. We are beginning to think it will be a lot more than we expect. . . . Our target now, if we are going to bring this war to an end and bring it to an end in a hell of a hurry, is this national redoubt and we are organizing our strength in that direction. . . . We may find that when we have cut the head from the snake the tail won't wiggle very long.[39]

Smith not only completely misjudged the issue, but even when it was clear that the Russians were in Berlin, he refused to alter his view that a quick victory was still not probable.[40] There can be little doubt that Smith's miscalculations played into Eisenhower's concerns about the National Redoubt. "The evidence was clear," an unrepentant Eisenhower wrote after the war, "that the Nazi intended to make the attempt and I decided to give him no opportunity to carry it out."[41]

Eisenhower had the full endorsement of Bradley, who was likewise convinced of the existence of a National Redoubt, which, he said, was "too ominous a threat to be ignored and in consequence it shaped our tactical thinking during the closing weeks of the war." Bradley, wrote Chester Hansen in his diary, "is convinced that we shall have to fight the Germans in the mountain wilderness of southern Germany and there destroy the core of his SS units which are determined to carry on the battle." Bradley predicted there might be twenty SS divisions, "supplied through a system of underground factories and supported by aircraft from underground hangers [*sic*]" from which "he could presumably have held out for a year."[42] No one seems to have questioned where these divisions might have come from, particularly in view of the fact that Model's forces in the Ruhr had been thoroughly bottled up and then surrendered. In *A Soldier's Story* Bradley ruefully admitted that it had existed "largely in the imaginations of a few fanatic Nazis." Only after a senior German general in a position to have known surrendered to Ninth Army did it finally become clear, at least to Bradley, that they had been chasing a ghost. "I am astonished we could have believed it as innocently as we did."[43]

Not until a week before his death did Hitler issue a rather broadly worded directive outlining the creation of a "last bulwark of fanatical resistance" in the Alps, which came far too late in the war to have been established. The British official historian was unable to discern "any clear intention" on the part of Hitler

> to make a "last-ditch" stand in the Alps or anywhere else in particular unless it were in Berlin. . . . Indeed, the greater the threat to Berlin, the more tenaciously did Hitler cling to the idea of holding out there at all costs . . . for Hitler the notion of a "redoubt" was no more than a momentary idea. . . . An examination of the contemporary German evidence available to us [in 1968] shows quite conclusively that the so-called "National Redoubt" never existed outside the imaginations of the combatants.[44]

The final irony was that in the last days of the Third Reich, when Joseph Goebbels learned of the Allied delusion over the Redoubt, his propaganda machine scored one of its greatest coups by effectively playing on Allied suppositions in much the same way that the Germans had been hoaxed before D-Day by Fortitude.[45]

The myth of the National Redoubt might have been merely incidental and a lesson in leaping to false conclusions had it not been for its profound effect on Eisenhower's strategic thinking. As Russell Weigley points out, despite evidence to the contrary, "Eisenhower and Bradley had already moved their armies as though the threat of the Redoubt merited a high strategic priority, higher than Berlin."[46]

The decision to turn de Lattre's French First Army, Hodges's First Army, and Patton's Third Army south toward Switzerland, Bavaria, and Austria came at a time when Montgomery's army group was thinly spread. With Ninth Army committed to securing and guarding the Elbe, there was no American force available to provide support to carry out his mission of capturing northern Germany, securing the Baltic ports, and liberating Denmark.

Eisenhower's controversial decisions regarding Berlin and the National Redoubt notwithstanding, during the month of April 1945 the death knell of the Third Reich sounded as the rampaging Allied armies began mopping up pockets of resistance from the central plains to the Alps, capturing tens of thousands of prisoners and drawing the noose ever tighter.

With his nation in ruins and his armies destroyed, Hitler designated the head of the German navy, Grossadmiral Karl Dönitz, to carry on the fight as his successor, then committed suicide on the night of April 30. His corpse and that of his mistress, Eva Braun, were burned on a funeral pyre outside his Berlin bunker in a scene that would have done justice to Wagner's *Götterdämmerung*. To the bitter end the German madman who had unleashed the worst conflagration in history entertained fantastical delusions that somehow he could still snatch victory from the jaws of defeat.

By May 1, 1945, both the U.S. First and Ninth Armies were astride the Mulde and Elbe Rivers, where they halted as ordered, while to the south the Seventh Army was advancing deep into Bavaria and Austria. To the north Montgomery's troops were nearing Hamburg and Lübeck. Patton's Third Army had driven into Austria and Czechoslovakia, but—in yet another controversial decision by Eisenhower—his troops were forbidden to enter the capital of Prague. At Churchill's instigation the British chiefs of staff exhorted the U.S. Joint Chiefs to compel Eisenhower to liberate Prague and Czechoslovakia before the arrival of the Red Army. The State Department, agreeing that Czechoslovakia was a political prize that should be denied the Russians, urged Truman's concurrence. Truman consulted Marshall, who passed the request back to Eisenhower, who replied that he thought that the Red Army would liberate Prague before Patton could get there, and thus elected to halt Third Army at the prewar border near Pilsen (now Plzeň). Marshall supported his decision. "Personally and aside from all logistic, tactical or strategical implications, I would be loath to hazard American lives for purely political purposes."[47]

However, Third Army, which had captured Nuremberg, advanced to the Danube, and been astride the Czech border for several weeks, was primed to advance into both Czechoslovakia and Austria. Patton had begged for permission to push on but had been firmly restrained by a stop line beyond which Third Army was not to advance without permission. Bradley thought that Prague could have been liberated within twenty-four hours. On May 4 Eisenhower finally authorized Third Army to cross the Czech border, but there was to be no advance beyond Pilsen. That same day units of the U.S. Seventh Army and the U.S. Fifth Army driving north from Italy made contact at Austria's Brenner Pass.

Bradley believed that Patton might ignore the new stop line, and on May 6 excitedly telephoned to reaffirm Eisenhower's order. "You hear me, George, goddamnit, *halt!*" Reluctantly Patton complied. This decision brought about the repercussions Churchill had correctly feared. An uprising by the Czech Resistance against the SS in Prague was ruthlessly suppressed, while Third

Army sat idle, a mere forty miles away, but under orders not to intervene. Although conceding that Eisenhower's reasons for halting at Pilsen were sound, Patton wrote shortly before his death, "I was very much chagrined, because I felt, and I still feel, that we should have gone on the Moldau River and, if the Russians didn't like it, let them go to hell."[48]

John Eisenhower had arrived in France in command of a rifle platoon of the 71st Division in early February, but on his arrival was immediately transferred. Both Bradley and Patton "offered to take me as their aides. I was given no choice in the matter and I was embarrassed." Although John would willingly have continued to serve in his division, Bradley was taking no chances of getting the son of the supreme commander killed or captured. John spent several days with his father in Versailles before reporting to Bradley, who sent him to England for duty with a special new signal intelligence unit being formed, and out of harm's way for a time.[49]

Mamie was upset at not hearing from John and let Ike know about it. He sympathized but pointed out that he knew barely any more than she did and could not help:

> I can't find anything concerning him myself except in a round about way by telephoning to people who may have seen him "day before yesterday."
>
> But I keep remembering that he is a man now with his own problems. . . . It is exceedingly hard for him to realize how important he is to us. But it is difficult to be philosophical. . . . It would be a tremendous help to me (but the ruination of his career) if he could stay right here all the time. God—how I hate to let him go whenever he comes to see me.[50]

In other respects Mamie, lonely and rather isolated within the confines of her own world, seemed perpetually incapable of fathoming the circumstances under which her husband functioned any better than she had when he first left for London in June 1942. His exasperation at her often scolding letters was evident right up to the end of the war. But, for the first time, Eisenhower permitted himself to think about bringing Mamie to Europe when the war ended and he became the U.S. occupation commander.

In Italy the German commander, Gen. Heinrich von Vietinghoff, defied Hitler's orders to fight to the bitter end, and at noon on May 2, 1945, unconditionally surrendered all German forces to the Allies. With Hitler dead, Grossadmiral Dönitz viewed further hostilities as useless and on May 3 sent his best negotiator, General Admiral Hans-Georg von Friedeburg, a former aide to Hitler and then commander in chief of the German navy, to lead a small German delegation to Montgomery's headquarters on Lüneburg Heath. With typical bluntness the field marshal barked, "Who are these men? What do they want?" Friedeburg replied that he brought an offer to surrender all German forces in northern Germany. The German aim was to avoid, at all costs, surrendering to the Russians, and to stall for time in order for as many Germans as possible to escape to the west to avoid certain Red Army retribution, which had already been unleashed in an orgy of mass killings, rapes, and plundering.[51]

Unsympathetic to Friedeburg's attempt to buy time, Montgomery replied that "the Germans should have thought of all these things before they began the war, and particularly before they attacked the Russians in June 1941." Montgomery refused to accept any conditions other than unconditional surrender, making it clear that "[i]f you refuse, I shall go on with the battle." With no bargaining chips left to play, Dönitz instructed Friedeburg to surrender all forces in northern Germany, Denmark, and Holland the following day. At 6:30 P.M., May 4, 1945, Friedeburg signed his name to the "Instrument of Surrender," which was accepted by Montgomery in the name of the supreme commander, its terms to take effect at 8:00 A.M. on May 5.[52]

At Reims, Eisenhower anxiously awaited a telephone call from Montgomery, but when it had not come by 6:55 P.M., he decided to return to his quarters. Kay Summersby encouraged him to wait another five minutes; "The call may come," she said. And, at precisely 7:00 P.M., it did. The conversation was brief. "Fine. Fine. That's fine, Monty," he was heard to say, as Summersby and Butcher eavesdropped. "Ike told Monty if the Germans had authority of Doenitz [sic] to stop all the fighting, to send them to Rheims."[53] A short time later Bedell Smith notified Eisenhower that the German delegation was being flown to Reims the following morning.

Friedeburg and another officer arrived at supreme headquarters at 5:00 P.M. on the afternoon of May 5 and were escorted to Bedell Smith's office, where a map of Allied dispositions was deliberately left lying where the Germans would see it. On the map Smith and Strong had placed two large imaginary arrows, one pointing east and the other west, each intended to represent advances by the Red Army and the British and American armies to crush the remaining elements of the German army. Friedeburg did not fall for the ruse, but as they had at Lüneburg Heath, his attempts to prolong the surrender negotiations by bargaining for time by surrendering to the Western Allies while continuing to fight against the Russians fell on deaf ears. Eisenhower at once refused, and after hours of discussion Smith and Strong managed to convince the German that he had no chips left with which to bargain and would be well advised to persuade Dönitz to accept unconditional surrender without further delay.

Dönitz's biographer notes that the admiral "was not prepared to sign his eastern armies into slavery," and "sent Jodl to try his hand."[54] The following day Gen. Alfred Jodl, the chief of staff under Keitel, the head of the OKW, arrived with the intention of persuading Eisenhower to change his mind. As he had done with Castellano in the Mediterranean, Smith deliberately made Jodl cool his heels before having him ushered into his office. It became clear immediately that Jodl's primary aim was to stall for twenty-four hours and then surrender Germany to the Western Allies but not the Russians. With Strong interpreting, Smith, his stern, icy war face in full glower, invited Jodl to present his case, which the German did with the same consummate skill that had elevated him to a key position in the highest echelon of the Third Reich. "He told us quite frankly and with deep conviction that we would soon find ourselves fighting Russia," and that the German soldiers and civilians in the western sector would aid the Allies.[55]

The former Bavarian artillery officer was not the first but merely the latest to realize that he had met the immovable object in the hard-nosed Bedell Smith. Eisenhower directed Smith and Strong to inform Jodl that the Germans must either accept Allied terms by midnight and surrender to the Big Three or negotiations would cease. The war would continue, the front lines would be sealed, and no German soldier or civilian would be permitted to surrender in the west: Take it or leave it! Smith coldly and forcefully reminded Jodl the war was lost and that he had exactly one half hour to decide. Jodl, who was strongly opposed to unconditional surrender, still balked. With time running out, Strong suggested that Smith appeal to the German officer as one soldier to another. With a straight face Smith delivered a long speech that Strong said showed "a fine understanding of [the] German mentality."[56]

Despite his opposition to the terms, Jodl reported to Dönitz that they had no choice. At 1:30 A.M. on the morning of May 7, Jodl received a message reading: "Grossadmiral Dönitz gives full authority for signing terms as communicated."[57]

Lt. Gen. Frederick Morgan, the original architect of Overlord, found the scene in the SHAEF war room, which had once served as a recreation room for students to play chess and table tennis, slightly surreal. Jammed together with barely room to breathe were the press and a phalanx of floodlights and cameras to record the historic moment. "The effect of make-believe was, if anything, heightened by the arrival in the room of the German uniforms." Present to formalize Germany's death warrant were Jodl and Admiral von Friedeburg.

At 2:41 A.M., May 7, 1945, Jodl signed the documents of the "Act of Military Surrender." The only sounds came from the photographers jockeying for the best location. Missing from the room was the man who had orchestrated the events leading to this historic moment. Eisenhower, in what Robert Murphy has described as "a very personal decision," evinced his disdain for his enemy by declining even to be present at the surrender ceremony. When von Arnim surrendered Axis forces in Tunisia in May 1943, Eisenhower had said, "I won't shake hands with a Nazi!" Since then nothing had changed except that viewing evidence of Nazi atrocities had deepened his hatred of the evil Jodl represented.[58]

Eisenhower delegated to Bedell Smith the task of signing the surrender documents on behalf of the AEF. Susloparoff, the Russian general, signed for the Soviet Union, and a French general signed as an official witness on behalf of France. The Russian's participation may have cost him his life. On returning to Moscow he is thought to have been "reprimanded" for his participation. "According to Smith, all future enquiries about Susloparoff's fate would be met with embarrassed silence."[59]

Under its terms the German surrender was to take effect at one minute before midnight on May 8, 1945. "The strange thing," wrote Smith, "was the lack of emotion that was shown when the surrender was signed. The Germans—Jodl and Admiral von Friedeburg—were militarily correct in their stone-like expressions. But I do not remember any of the Allied officers around the table displayed elation.... It was a moment of solemn gratitude."[60]

While the surrender ceremony was taking place Eisenhower paced back and forth in his office. Kay Summersby described the atmosphere as "electric with his impatience; at the same time I thought it rather lonely and pathetic."[61]

Afterward the German delegation was summoned to the supreme commander's office, where, with Strong as escort and interpreter, a stone-faced Eisenhower, with Tedder on his right, stood rigidly behind his desk, looking more military than Summersby had ever seen him. Coldly, his voice brittle, Eisenhower curtly said, "Do you understand the terms of the document of surrender you have just signed?" When Jodl replied, *"Ja, ja,"* Eisenhower declared that he would be held officially and personally accountable should there be any violation of its terms. "That is all," said Eisenhower, signaling that the interview was at an end. Jodl made a slight bow and saluted as Eisenhower "stared silently, in dismissal." As Jodl did a precise military about-face to leave the room—and a date with the hangman after being tried and convicted of war crimes at Nuremberg—from his nearby place under Eisenhower's desk Telek growled his displeasure at the back of the retreating German.[62]

Only after the Germans had departed did Eisenhower finally unbend and relax. As a horde of photographers were admitted to his office and scrambled to record the scene, Eisenhower gathered Smith, Strong, Summersby, and Tedder around him. Although he was exhausted, Dwight Eisenhower's famous grin reappeared at a historic moment, as he signaled a V for victory by holding aloft the two gold pens with which the German surrender documents had been signed. Eisenhower telephoned Bradley with the news; in turn Bradley roused Patton from sleep to state, "Ike just called me, George. The Germans have surrendered."

Eisenhower and Tedder repaired to the war room to face the cameras for a newsreel recording. Eisenhower spoke off the cuff, and partway through was interrupted by Butcher, who thought his use of the word "armistice" was inappropriate. "Growling and scowling at me," Eisenhower did a second take in which he substituted the word "surrender." As Tedder and Butcher were returning to Eisenhower's office, "Tedder poked me in the ribs and said with a twinkle in his eyes that General Ike could make the best speech in the world and I should mind my own damned business."[63]

Eisenhower proclaimed that the special occasion merited champagne, and everyone decamped to his quarters where, for the next two hours, there was surprisingly little gaiety, joking, or even a sense of pride. Instead there was a rather somber realization of the significance of the day. Few words were said. "Everyone simply seemed weary, indescribably weary," remembered Kay Summersby. "There was a dull bitterness about it. Everyone was very, very tired."[64]

Before he fell into bed exhausted at 5:00 A.M. Eisenhower performed one final duty. During their many nights together Eisenhower and Butcher had joked about what language the supreme commander would use to inform the Combined Chiefs when the day finally came that Germany surrendered, quips such as "We have met the enemy and they is ours" were mentioned. As a soldier Eisenhower understood that it was not his place to announce the end of the war in Europe; that was a function reserved for the heads of state, who would make the formal announcement.

Beetle Smith recounts that in the afterglow of the surrender ceremony, "the staff prepared various drafts of a victory message appropriate to the historic event. I tried one myself and, like all my associates, groped for resounding phrases as fitting accolades to the Great Crusade.... General Eisenhower rejected them all, with thanks, but without other comment, and wrote his own."[65]

Eisenhower often wrote long-winded missives, but on this occasion he dispatched the briefest cable of his tenure as supreme commander to the Combined Chiefs of Staff. Utterly devoid of self-congratulation, it was as unpretentious as the man himself. Only a single sentence long, it read simply: "The mission of this Allied Force was fulfilled at 0241, local time, May 7th, 1945. //signed// Eisenhower."[66]

A witness to this historic event, CBS correspondent Charles Collingwood, called it "the best news the world ever had."[67] On May 8, 1945, the war in Europe officially ended.[68] The headline in the GI newspaper, *Stars and Stripes*, on V-E day was equally brief: "VICTORY."[69]

Epilogue

Dwight Eisenhower once said, "I hate war as only a soldier who has lived it can, only as one who has seen its brutality, its futility, its stupidity." Ike was not a sentimental man, nor was he known for public displays of emotion. Yet, on the occasion of the twentieth anniversary of D-Day, his words, uttered as he sat on a wall of the American military cemetery situated on the bluffs overlooking Omaha Beach, came straight from his heart and evoked his still painful remembrance of the haunting days of June 1944:

> These men came here—British and our allies, and Americans—to storm these beaches for one purpose only, not to gain anything for ourselves, not to fulfill any ambitions that America had for conquest, but just to preserve freedom. . . . Many thousands of men have died for such ideals as these . . . but these young boys . . . were cut off in their prime. . . . I devoutly hope that we will never again have to see such scenes as these. I think and hope, and pray, that humanity will have learned . . . we must find some way . . . to gain an eternal peace for this world.[1]

Whether in war or peace, Eisenhower always insisted there were no such things as indispensable men. One night at dinner aboard the liner *Queen Elizabeth* during his nostalgic return to the scene of his greatest triumph, Eisenhower pulled a well-worn clipping from his wallet and read it to his dinner companions. It ended with these words:

> The moral of this quaint example
> Is to do just the best that you can.
> Be proud of yourself, but remember,
> There is no indispensable man.[2]

Dwight Eisenhower may not have thought of himself as indispensable, but history has a way of recording its own verdict. Although he achieved ever-lasting distinction as the thirty-fourth president of the United States, Dwight David Eisenhower would have been elated merely to be remembered as a good soldier.

Notes

ABBREVIATIONS AND CODE NAMES

AEAF	Allied Expeditionary Air Forces (air element of SHAEF)
AEF	Allied Expeditionary Force
AFHQ	Allied Force Headquarters
Anvil	Original code name for the invasion of southern France, August 1944
Avalanche	Code name for the Allied invasion of Salerno, Italy, September 9, 1943
BCOS	British Chief of Staff
CCOS	Combined Chiefs of Staff [collectively the U.S. and British Chiefs of Staff]
CIGS	Chief of the Imperial General Staff
CGSS	U.S. Army Command and General Staff School, Ft. Leavenworth, Kansas
CMH	Center of Military History, U.S. Army, Washington, D.C.
Cobra	Code name for the breakout of the Normandy lodgment by U.S. First Army, July 1944
COMZ	Communications Zone
COSSAC	Chief of Staff to the Supreme Allied Commander (the Allied planning staff formed in 1943 to plan Operation Overlord)
DDE	Dwight David Eisenhower
Dragoon	Revised code name for the Allied invasion of southern France, Aug. 1944
EL	Dwight D. Eisenhower Library, Abilene, Kansas
ENHS	Eisenhower National Historic Site, Gettysburg, Pennsylvania
EP	*The Papers of Dwight D. Eisenhower: The War Years, vols. 1–5; Occupation, vol. 6.; The Chief of Staff, vols. 7–9*
ETO	European Theater of Operations
ETOUSA	European Theater of Operations, U.S. Army
Fortitude	Code name for the Normandy deception operations
FUSAG	Patton's fictional First U.S. Army Group
Garden	Code name for the ground operation to seize bridgeheads over the Rhine at Arnhem
GCM	Gen. George C. Marshall
GCML	George C. Marshall Library, Lexington, Virginia
GSP	Gen. George S. Patton, Jr.
Goodwood	Code name for the attempted British breakout operation at Caen, July 18, 1944
Husky	Code name for the Allied invasion of Sicily, July 11, 1943
IWM	Imperial War Museum, London

JSDE	John S. D. Eisenhower
LC	Library of Congress
LHC	Liddell Hart Center for Military Archives, King's College, London
Market	Code name for the Allied airborne operation, Holland, September 17, 1944
MDE	Mamie Doud Eisenhower
MHQ	*The Quarterly Journal of Military History*
NA	National Archives, Washington, D.C.
NA II	National Archives II, College Park, Maryland
NYT	*New York Times*
OCMH	Office of the Chief, Military History, U.S. Army
ONB	Gen. Omar Nelson Bradley
OPD	Operations Division, War Department (prior to March 1942 called the War Plans Division [WPD])
Overlord	Allied invasion of Normandy, June 6, 1944
Pre-Pres Papers	Dwight D. Eisenhower Library
Pres Papers	Dwight D. Eisenhower Library
Post-Pres Papers	Dwight D. Eisenhower Library
Post-Pres Papers, A-WR series	Dwight D. Eisenhower Library, Augusta–Walter Reed series
PP-LC	George S. Patton Papers, Manuscript Division, Library of Congress, Washington, D.C.
RAF	Royal Air Force
SHAEF	Supreme Headquarters, Allied Expeditionary Force
Sledgehammer	A never-implemented Allied contingency plan for an emergency invasion of France in the autumn of 1942
Torch	Allied invasion of French North Africa, Nov. 8, 1942
ULTRA	Collective name for the secret British code-breaking operation that intercepted and decrypted German message traffic
USAMHI	U.S. Army Military History Institute, Carlisle Barracks, Pennsylvania
USMA	United States Military Academy, West Point, New York
VMI	Virginia Military Institute, Lexington, Virginia

PROLOGUE: "AN ASTONISHING MAN"

1. Kay Summersby Morgan, *Past Forgetting* (New York, 1976), 215.
2. Stephen E. Ambrose, *D-Day: June 6, 1944* (New York, 1994), chap. 10, passim.
3. Kay Summersby, *Eisenhower Was My Boss* (New York, 1948), 145–47, and Dwight D. Eisenhower, *Crusade in Europe* (New York, London, 1948), 277.
4. Cornelius Ryan, *The Longest Day* (New York, 1959), 102.
5. Summersby, *Eisenhower Was My Boss*, 146–47.
6. John S. D. Eisenhower, *Agent of Destiny: The Life and Times of General Winfield Scott* (New York, 1997), xiii.
7. Dwight D. Eisenhower, *At Ease: Stories I Tell to Friends* (New York, 1967), 250. Hereafter cited as DDE, *At Ease*.
8. Peter Lyon, *Eisenhower: Portrait of the Hero* (Boston, 1974), 33.
9. Henry B. Jameson, *Heroes by the Dozen* (Abilene, Kans., 1961), 156.
10. Ibid.
11. Eric Larrabee, *Commander in Chief* (New York, 1987), 412.
12. Martha Byrd, *Chennault* (Tuscaloosa, Ala., 1987), ix.

1. "SAY EISENHAUER FOR IRONCUTTER."

1. Steve Neal, *The Eisenhowers* (Lawrence, Kans., 1984), 3.
2. John R. Hertzler, "The 1879 Brethren in Christ Migration from Southeastern Pennsylvania to Dickinson County, Kansas," *Pennsylvania Mennonite Heritage* (Jan. 1980). The transition from the spelling of "Eisenhauer" to "Eisenhower" probably took place during the first half of the nineteenth century. The family genealogy cites numerous Eisenhowers by the time of the Civil War.
3. Despite what previous writers have stated, they did not call themselves River Brethren because they baptized their children in rivers, but rather as a reminder that their origins were along the mighty Susquehanna. Less than two percent of the River Brethren were baptized in rivers.
4. Neal, *The Eisenhowers*, 7. Of the fourteen children born to Jacob and his wife Rebecca Matter Eisenhower, only six survived to adulthood.
5. Francis Trevelyan Miller, *Eisenhower: Man and Soldier* (Philadelphia, 1944), 40.
6. The Homestead Act was clearly a major factor in the decision by the River Brethren to settle in Kansas. (Hertzler, "The 1879 Brethren in Christ Migration.")
7. Robert W. Richmond, *Kansas: A Land of Contrasts* (Arlington Heights, Ill., 1974), chap. 8. The Chisholm Trail derived its name from the trading post of Jesse Chisholm along the Little Arkansas River at the site of what is now the city of Wichita.
8. Samuel Carter III, *Cowboy Capital of the World: The Saga of Dodge City* (Garden City, 1973), 10.
9. The first settler in Abilene was an Illinois pioneer named Timothy Hersey, an Indian scout and expert surveyor. When Hersey arrived in July 1857, he had to shoot his way through a herd of buffalo grazing on the lush grasslands. His decision to found a town along Mud Creek was based in part on Indian lore, which held that the area would never be hit by a tornado, a prophecy that, despite several near misses, has remained true to this day.
10. It is a common misconception that all cowhands squandered their hard-earned wages in the pursuit of pleasure. To the contrary, as Robert Richmond notes in *Kansas: A Land of Contrasts* (126), many were "sober, sensible men who stayed out of trouble."
11. Abilene lumberman Theophilus Little quoted in 1871 in ibid., 202–3; and Harry Sinclair Drago, *Wild. Woolly & Wicked* (New York, 1960), 47.
12. The *Abilene Chronicle* is now called the *Abilene Reflector-Chronicle*. The Texans preferred gunfights to fisticuffs, which they derided "as something reserved for teamsters, bullwhackers, and soldiers." (Drago, *Wild, Woolly & Wicked*, 48.) As one Abilene citizen recalled, "When you heard one or two shots, you waited breathlessly for a third. A third shot meant a death on Texas Street." (Quoted in Dee Brown, *The American West* [New York, 1994], 57.)
13. Francis Trevelvan Miller, *Eisenhower: Man and Soldier* (Philadephia, 1944), 42. "Wild Bill" Hickok may have been a dazzling gunfighter but on one occasion he mistakenly killed one of his own deputies during one of Abilene's most notorious shoot-outs over a rivalry for the favors of a local dance hall queen. (Brown, *The American West*, 203.)
14. Walter Prescott Webb, *The Great Plains* (New York, 1931), 223.
15. McCoy was a superb entrepreneur, and to lure potential buyers from Chicago, he filled a train with wild buffalo and adorned it with colorful posters that advertised "the wonderful cattle bargains at Abilene." Once in Chicago the buffalo were put on public display at the Union Stock Yard. "McCoy's clever stunt worked like magic. Chicago buyers came back on a special excursion train, the market revived, and the 1868 cattle season closed successfully." (See Brown, *The American West*, 55.)
16. Quoted in ibid., 203.
17. Carter, *Cowboy Capital of the World*, 12–14.
18. "Abilene—Land of Boom and Bust, 1883–1895," monograph by J. Earl Endacott, Box

4, Endacott Papers, EL; and DDE, *At Ease*, 66. At one time an area of Abilene was fancifully plotted in the belief that the state capital was to be moved there from Topeka. Earl Endacott settled in Abilene in 1923 and became one of the most knowledgeable scholars of the town and the Eisenhowers. He later served as the first executive director of the Eisenhower Foundation, an adjunct organization of the Eisenhower Presidential Library.

19. DDE, *At Ease*, 65.

20. Quoted in Jameson, *Heroes by the Dozen*, 11.

2. THE PROMISED LAND

1. Endacott manuscripts, Box 4, Endacott Papers, EL. The River Brethren brought with them fifteen freight car–loads of personal property and farm equipment, and an estimated half-million dollars in cash. In anticipation of their arrival they had been preceded by an advance party, who had constructed a elongated, shedlike building alongside the Union Pacific tracks in Abilene. Dubbed "Emigrant House," it was a haven that temporarily housed newly arrived families and their household goods, and was typical of the virtuous manner in which the River Brethren took care of their own. A second River Brethren party arrived from Pennsylvania in 1879 and established a separate community northeast of Abilene.

2. At their organizational meeting held in a grove of trees near Jacob Eisenhower's farm, the River Brethren who founded the creamery were discussing a name when they noticed a milk cow with a bell around her neck drinking from the spring, hence the name Belle Springs. (See Abram Forney oral history, EL. Forney was a boyhood friend of Dwight Eisenhower who worked at the Belle Springs Creamery until World War I.)

3. Endacott manuscripts, Box 4, Endacott Papers, EL. In its first full year of operation in 1887 the Belle Springs Creamery produced 167,450 pounds of butter, and within two years that figure had increased to 225,708. (See Hertzler, "The 1879 Brethren in Christ Migration.")

4. David Jacob Eisenhower was the fifth son of Jacob Eisenhower. His first four sons, John, Jacob, Samuel, and Peter, all died before the age of nine.

5. Stephen E. Ambrose and Richard H. Immerman, *Milton S. Eisenhower* (Baltimore, 1983), 11.

6. Lyon, *Eisenhower*, 34. Lane University was founded in 1865 and named in honor of its supposedly biggest donor, the state's first U.S. senator, a man of questionable reputation named Jim Lane, whose suicide in 1866 deprived the university of its promised one thousand dollar endowment. (See William Christian Hoad, "Recollections of a Kansas Town," *Michigan Quarterly Review*, Dec. 16, 1939.)

7. During its forty-year existence Lane struggled financially and by 1910 was forced to merge with Campbell University, another United Brethren–sponsored school in Holton, Kansas. The school later merged with Kansas City College, which closed after the stock market crash of 1929.

8. Paxton Link, *The Book of Links* (n.p., 1951), 373–74.

9. Jerry Bergman, "Steeped in Religion: Pres. Eisenhower and the Influence of the Jehovah's Witnesses," *Kansas History* (autumn 1998). A record of Ida's memorizations is still said to exist at the Lutheran Church in Mount Sidney, Virginia.

10. Link, *The Book of Links*, chap. 18, passim. As a child Ida considered herself a tomboy who played the same tough games as her brothers, including horseback-riding stunts. "I was tough and wiry and could gallop bareback as heedlessly as any of my brothers over those wooded hills," she later recalled. (Quoted in Kunigunde Duncan, *Earning the Right to Do Fancywork* [Lawrence, Kans., 1957], 5.) Some accounts state that the

Reverend William Stover lived near Topeka; however, the *Lecompton Monitor* article of Sept. 24, 1885, states that the Stovers were from Lecompton.

11. Merle Miller, *Ike the Soldier* (New York, 1987), 53.

12. Letter of Fred O. Bartlett in Kansas History Collection, Watson Library, University of Kansas, Lawrence (italics in original). Copy in David & Ida Eisenhower Folder, Vertical Files, EL.

13. Nettie Stover Jackson oral history, EL.

14. *Lecompton Monitor* (Sept. 24, 1885), copy in Vertical Files, EL. Some accounts inaccurately state that the ceremony took place in the chapel of Lane University, among them Kenneth S. Davis, Dwight D. Eisenhower; *Soldier of Democracy* (New York, 1945), 32. Hereafter referred to as *Soldier of Democracy*.

15. Quoted in Miller, *Ike the Soldier*, 78, and Rev. Ray I. Witter oral history, EL. Witter was the son of one of David's sisters, and a cousin of Dwight Eisenhower.

16. Nettie Stover Jackson oral history, EL.

17. Letter, John E. Long to Earl Endacott, Mar. 6, 1970, Endacott Papers, EL. Long was a childhood friend of Dwight Eisenhower, and he notes that his own mother was the first to discard the use of the River Brethren cap.

18. Thomas Branigar, "No Villains, No Heroes," *Kansas History* (Autumn 1990). Dwight Eisenhower's scathing criticism of Milton Good is in DDE, *At Ease,* 31.

19. DDE, *At Ease,* ibid.

20. Ibid., 71–72, and *Hope Herald,* April 4, 1887.

21. Quoted in Branigar, "No Villains, No Heroes."

22. As early as December 1887 the *Hope Dispatch* reported that David Eisenhower was planning an extended trip "south" to secure a new location for the business. And in July 1888 David's travels to Kansas City and St. Joseph, Missouri, for the same reason were duly reported by the *Hope Dispatch.*

23. Davis, *Soldier of Democracy,* 38.

24. DDE annotations in Davis, *Soldier of Democracy,* typed version, Box 21, Pre-Pres Papers, EL.

25. Quoted in Henry B. Jameson, *They Still Call Him Ike* (New York, 1972), 44. Jameson was a former war correspondent and the editor and publisher of the *Abilene Reflector-Chronicle* after World War II.

26. Branigar, "No Villains, No Heroes." After David quit the business in October 1888, Abe Eisenhower became the store's new owner and renamed it "A. L. Eisenhower & Co."

27. There is no evidence that David Eisenhower was ever in Tyler, Texas. Dwight Eisenhower's official biography, released in 1942, after he was named commander of Allied forces in North Africa, mistakenly reflected his birthplace as Tyler. The *Fort Worth Star-Telegram* investigated and confirmed a tip in 1942 that Eisenhower was actually born in Denison. (See Jack Maguire, *Katy's Baby: The Story of Denison, Texas* [Austin, 1991], 85.)

28. Maguire, *Katy's Baby,* 57. During Denison's banner years as many as forty-three trains passed through the town each day.

29. Davis, *Soldier of Democracy,* 41.

30. John S. D. Eisenhower oral history, EL.

31. Lyon, *Eisenhower,* 35.

32. John McCallum, *Six Roads from Abilene: Some Personal Recollections of Edgar Eisenhower* (Seattle, 1960), 19–20.

33. Ibid., 20.

34. None of the Eisenhower sons had birth certificates, and the only records kept were entries in the family Bible.

35. A USMA questionnaire, titled "Instructions," completed at the time he entered West

Point in 1911, reflects his full name as "Dwight David Eisenhower, place of birth: Denison, Texas." Copy in USMA Archives. One of Eisenhower's biographers, Merle Miller (*Ike the Soldier*, 61), was among many misled by earlier incorrect references to Tyler. The proposition that Eisenhower never knew his place of birth had no factual basis, however.

36. McCallum, *Six Roads from Abilene.*
37. Davis, *Soldier of Democracy*, 43.
38. With the exception of Tom Branigar's article, "No Villains, No Heroes," and Geoffrey Perret's recent biography, those who have written about the Eisenhowers have inaccurately recorded the date of the family's move from Denison to Abilene as 1891. The records of the Belle Springs Creamery have been preserved and clearly reflect that David J. Eisenhower began work there on March 11, 1892. (See Paul D. Hoffman, *Chronicle of the Belle Springs Creamery Company* [Abilene, 1975], 7–8.)
    The source of the funds David Eisenhower required to relocate his family to Abilene was probably his brother-in-law, Christian O. Musser. Abram Forney believed that five dollars per month was deducted from David's salary at the Belle Springs Creamery as repayment for monies advanced for the Eisenhowers' relocation from Denison to Abilene, however, the original contract between the creamery and David Eisenhower makes no mention of anything other than 12 percent being withheld until the end of the year, when it was paid. (See chap. 4 and Forney oral history, EL.)
39. Lyon, *Eisenhower*, 39.

3. "A GOOD PLACE FOR BOYS TO GROW INTO MEN"

1. Quoted in Francis Trevelyan Miller, *Eisenhower: Man and Soldier*, 61.
2. Ibid.
3. Rev. Ray I. Witter oral history, EL.
4. McCallum, *Six Roads from Abilene*, 69, and Milton S. Eisenhower oral history, EL.
5. Davis, *Soldier of Democracy*, 72.
6. DDE, *At Ease*, 2.
7. *Overview* (Eisenhower Foundation Newsletter) 9, no. 2 (Fall 1983).
8. See article by Dick Taylor, "Tom 'Bear River' Smith," University of Kansas Web site, "Kansas Collection."
9. Stephen E. Ambrose, *Eisenhower: Soldier, General of the Army, President-Elect: 1890–1952* (New York, 1983), 35.
10. Eisenhower's description of Bob Davis is in *At Ease*, 88–89.
11. Endacott, "Abilene—Land of Boom and Bust, 1883–1895."
12. John E. Long oral history, EL.
13. Abram Forney oral history, EL.
14. Musser recollections. The creamery remained the most phenomenally successful business venture in Abilene. In 1908, for example, its annual butter production hit an all-time high of nearly three million pounds.
15. Records of the Belle Springs Creamery, EL, and Dickinson County Historical Society, Abilene.
16. DDE, *At Ease*, 29.
17. Ibid., 30.
18. Quoted in Summersby Morgan, *Past Forgetting*, 68.
19. Lyon, *Eisenhower*, 39, fn. After World War II the nonprofit Eisenhower Foundation was established, and in 1947 the family home was first opened to the public. Later a museum and presidential library were added, along with a chapel, where Eisenhower, Mamie, and their first son, Doud Dwight are buried.
20. Draft of article about the family by Earl Eisenhower, probably for publication in the *American Weekly* magazine. Earl Eisenhower Papers, EL. The first Abilene house where

the Eisenhowers resided from 1892 to 1898 was originally owned by Jacob Eisenhower, who had deeded it to David in 1890, two years *before* the family moved from Denison to Abilene. Why David and Ida continued to live in misery in Texas rather than take advantage of Jacob's generosity will forever remain inexplicable, but it is more than likely due to David's pride and stubborn nature.

Jacob had also owned what became the permanent Eisenhower home on Southeast Fourth Street before deeding it to Abraham in 1894. In 1898 Abe deeded the home not to David Eisenhower but to Ida. In 1907 Ida turned the property over to her husband for $1.00. One of Abraham's conditions for deeding the house to Ida was that Jacob be permitted to live there until his death, which suggests a serious lack of confidence in David Eisenhower. In 1902 David sold the Second Street house for an undisclosed sum. (Endacott, Box 4, "Official Records of Eisenhower Properties," EL, which are based on Dickinson County records.)

21. Transcript, "Young Mr. Eisenhower," CBS television news special, interview by Harry Reasoner, Sept. 13, 1966, GCML.

22. R. Alton Lee, *Dwight D. Eisenhower: Soldier and Statesman* (Chicago, 1981), 9; and DDE, *At Ease*, chap. 5.

23. McCallum, *Six Roads from Abilene*, 63.

24. Ibid., 64.

25. Related by Milton Eisenhower in JSDE oral history. Feeding six growing boys with enormous appetites was a feat. Dwight's favorite meal consisted of an old Pennsylvania Dutch recipe called fried mush, which consisted of ground bits of pork or ham hocks and other ingredients that were fried, then topped with brown sugar or maple syrup. In today's health-conscious age, this old-time recipe, extremely high in fat, calories, and cholesterol, would no doubt be considered appalling. However, for the Eisenhower brothers, such a meal was considered heavenly.

26. McCallum, *Six Roads from Abilene*, 59.

27. Bela Kornitzer, *The Great American Heritage* (New York, 1955), 55. The date may have been Sept. 5, 1947, when he attended a dinner in Chicago in honor of his longtime friend and colleague, Gen. Thomas T. Handy.

28. McCallum, *Six Roads from Abilene*, 45, and Miller, *Ike the Soldier*, 92–93.

29. Nettie Stover Jackson oral history, EL.

30. "Mother Eisenhower Talks About Her Most Famous Son." *Better Homes & Gardens*, June 1943.

31. Davis, *Soldier of Democracy*, 38, and Kornitzer, "The Story of Ike and His Four Brothers." When one store mistakenly sent him a bill, David paid it but never again traded with the firm. "I don't believe Dad ever bought a thing on time except his house," recalled Milton. Throughout their own lives, each of the six Eisenhower sons believed that their father's abhorrence of debt was the result of his (alleged) ruinous business experience in Hope.

32. Thomas Branigar's assessment of David Eisenhower's muddled business venture and his behavior between 1886 and 1899 is: "The responsibility for Milton [Good]'s tarnished reputation undoubtedly lies with David Eisenhower who appears to have been more vindictive than historians have realized. Numerous events confirm his violent temper, and the [E. A.] Gehrig incident demonstrates that he was capable of circulating malicious rumors about persons with whom he disagreed. . . . The younger generation" [of Eisenhowers], writes Branigar, "could only repeat what they had been told by their elders." Throughout his dealings with Milton Good, there was a touch of self-righteousness about David's behavior that would surface from time to time whenever he believed he had been wronged. "Unfortunately for the Good family, the fame of one Eisenhower offspring dictated that only the Eisenhowers' story was made public." (Branigar, "No Villains, No Heroes.")

33. David Eisenhower could also speak and write Greek.

34. Neal, *The Eisenhowers*, 48. Earl remembers how his father would sit forlornly on the front porch and "make friends with every little girl that came by." It is an example of how society has changed that one hundred years later David Eisenhower's motives might have been seriously misconstrued.

35. Davis, *Soldier of Democracy*, 35–36, and DDE, *At Ease*, 85. Eisenhower was later troubled whenever he saw any of his grandchildren playing with an object that might result in an eye injury.

36. DDE to Earl Eisenhower, April 10, 1944, in Alfred D. Chandler, Jr., ed., *The Papers of Dwight David Eisenhower* (Baltimore, 1970), vol. 3, 1816 (hereafter cited as EP and volume and page).

37. Kornitzer, *The Great American Heritage*, 49.

38. In December 1896 David's own temper finally got him into considerable trouble. In a fit of anger, he severely spanked a neighboring child for some transgression. The boy's parents filed a complaint with the police; David was arrested for assault and battery and released only after paying a fine.

39. Geoffrey Perret, *Eisenhower* (New York, 1999), 11.

40. "A Personal Appraisal of the Eisenhower Family," Box 4, Endacott Papers, EL.

41. McCallum, *Six Roads from Abilene*, 26.

42. Once, after Arthur accidentally struck Edgar's foot with a pickax as they were digging a cistern, Edgar was more concerned that his twenty-five-cent socks were ruined than he was by the gash in his foot. (Ibid., 35.)

43. Both quotes from DDE, *At Ease*, 69–70.

44. Bergman, "Steeped in Religion."

45. The Jehovah's Witnesses were founded in Pittsburgh, Pennsylvania, in 1870 by Charles Taze Russell, the son of religious-minded Presbyterian parents. According to their history, *Jehovah's Witnesses: Proclaimers of God's Kingdom* (Brooklyn, 1993), 120, "Jehovah's Witnesses have not set out to introduce new doctrines, a new way of worship, a new religion. Instead, their modern-day history reflects conscientious effort to teach what is found in the Bible. . . . Instead of developing beliefs that reflect the permissive trends of the modern world, they have sought to conform ever more closely to the Biblical teachings and practices of first-century Christianity."

Biographer Merle Miller incorrectly identifies several key facts about the Jehovah's Witnesses. The sect originated in 1870, not 1885. The Abilene sect that converted the Eisenhowers were then called Bible Students, not "Russellites," a none-too-complimentary term coined by the clergy of other religions. Another myth is Miller's assertion that David was fired from the Belle Springs Creamery in 1916 after attending a Jehovah's Witness convention in Washington, D.C. Not only had David long since lost interest, but the authoritative history of the Witnesses reflects no such events held in 1916 anywhere in the United States. Moreover, Witness conventions did not occur with regularity until the 1920s. Edgar Eisenhower's memoir makes no mention of their parents' affiliation with the Witnesses. (See Miller, *Ike the Soldier*, 67; *Jehovah's Witnesses*, 42, 63, 150, 156, and 719, and records in the Dickinson County Historical Society, Abilene.)

46. McCallum, *Six Roads from Abilene*, 21.

47. Quoted in Kornitzer, *The Great American Heritage*, 53.

48. Bergman, "Steeped in Religion."

49. Ibid. Subsequent publicity in the media usually referred to the Eisenhowers as "River Brethren, a Mennonite sect." Milton asked the biographer of the Eisenhower brothers, Bela Kornitzer, to remove a reference in his manuscript to the Jehovah's Witnesses. Kornitzer complied.

50. Ibid.

51. Richard L. Tobin, "Dwight D. Eisenhower: 'What I Have Learned,'" *SR*, Sept. 10, 1966.

52. DDE, *At Ease*, 62–63. During Eisenhower's presidency, his brother Milton dedicated a monument in Jacob's memory in front of his former home in Elizabethville, Pennsylvania. Eisenhower's reverence for his antecedents was on display whenever he returned to Abilene after his boyhood home had become a public museum. He was fond of pointing out to visitors the significance of everything in the house. During one such visit Eisenhower learned that one of the heirlooms preserved in the house, an afghan quilt made by his great-grandfather, Frederick, was missing from its customary spot on the living room couch. Curiosity turned to fierce anger when he learned that Edgar had somehow inveigled the Eisenhower Foundation into removing the quilt and sending it to him, even though the family's contract with the Eisenhower Foundation specified that everything in the home was to be left as it originally existed. "Get the damn thing back," he demanded, "this is where it belongs." Several weeks later the quilt was quietly returned, where it remains to this day. Neither brother ever publicly commented on what occurred between them but it seems to have exacerbated their lifelong, frequently testy rivalry. (Miller, *Ike the Soldier*, 74–75. The source of the quote was J. Earl Endacott, the director of the Eisenhower Foundation.)
53. Quoted in Kornitzer, *The Great American Heritage*, 49. Edgar ascribes the quotation to David. See also McCallum, *Six Roads from Abilene*, 30.
54. DDE, *At Ease*, 36–37.
55. "Young Mr. Eisenhower."
56. Ibid.
57. Miller, *Ike the Soldier*, 51. Milton later thought that the worst punishment they could receive were the few occasions when Ida would say: " 'I'll tell your father about this when he gets home.' Because now you had two punishments." (Milton Eisenhower oral history, EL.)
58. DDE, *At Ease*, 37, 77.
59. Nettie Stover Jackson oral history, EL.
60. DDE, *At Ease*, 32.
61. Quentin Reynolds, "The Eisenhowers of Kansas," *Collier's*, Dec. 18, 1948, and JSDE oral history, EL. Ida had only two known aversions: lawyers and cats.
62. DDE, *At Ease*, 33.
63. Quoted in Kornitzer, *The Great American Heritage*, 76–77.
64. DDE, *At Ease*, 34.
65. Letter, JSDE to the author, Mar. 11, 1999.
66. Ibid.
67. Lyon, *Eisenhower*, 40.
68. DDE, *At Ease*, 35, and Kornitzer, *The Great American Heritage*, 48.
69. McCallum, *Six Roads from Abilene*, 77, and DDE, *At Ease*, 85–86.

4. A YOUNG MAN'S EDUCATION

1. DDE, *At Ease*, 81, 94.
2. Ibid., 99.
3. Lee, *Dwight D. Eisenhower: Soldier and Statesman*, 13; letter, Robert R. Bolton to Kevin McCann, n.d., Vertical File, EL; and Lelia Grace Picking oral history, EL. Miss Picking was also a member of the River Brethren.
4. Quoted in Richard Rhodes, "Ike: An Artist in Iron," *Harper's Magazine*, July 1970.
5. DDE, *At Ease*, 95.
6. Miller, *Ike the Soldier*, 64–65, and article from Ventura, California, newspaper, 1962 (exact date unknown; copy in "School Chums" folder, Vertical File, EL.)
7. It is an interesting contrast that his future friend, George S. Patton, who grew up in

rural Los Angeles and was renowned for his iron-handed image, actually had a relatively tranquil childhood virtually free of fisticuffs. (See Carlo D'Este, *Patton: A Genius for War* [New York, 1995], chap. 3.)

8. John E. Long letters, Box 4, Endacott Papers, EL.

9. Lyon, *Eisenhower*, 40.

10. McCallum, *Six Roads from Abilene*, 81.

11. DDE, *At Ease*, 94. Edgar remembers the fight occurring when Dwight was fifteen, which would have been in 1905. (McCallum, *Six Roads from Abilene*, 81.) Other accounts substantiate that the date was 1903.

12. Ibid.

13. Davis, *Soldier of Democracy*, 76–78, and DDE, *At Ease*, 94. *Soldier of Democracy* is an example of the attempt by early Eisenhower biographers to embellish even the most trivial incident into a heroic event. In the Davis version, "both faces were bleeding pulps. The show had become . . . an epic of brutal courage." What had started out as a typical after-school boyhood fight was further described as "one of character" and its continuance as "a spiritual achievement." A 1962 newspaper account further magnified the tale into a two-and-a-half-hour battle. A schoolmate, Wilbur Jeffcoat, witnessed the fight and confirms Eisenhower's version. "They both got tired they just had to quit." ("School Chums" folder, Vertical File, EL.)

14. During his high school years the entire faculty of Abilene High consisted of five teachers and the principal, who also taught.

15. Lelia Grace Picking oral history, EL.

16. Davis, *Soldier of Democracy*, 80.

17. Brig. Gen. Thomas W. Mattingly, M.D., "A Compilation of the General Health Status of Dwight D. Eisenhower," Box 20, Mattingly Papers, EL. Davis's account breathlessly recounts, "And the miracle came! . . . Life was flickering, flickering out in labored breaths hour after hour, until . . . the fever began to subside. The blackness faded. After a while Dwight awoke . . . he was alive and whole." (*Soldier of Democracy*, 80.)

18. Dr. William E. Litterer of Falmouth, Massachusetts, concurs in Dr. Mattingly's diagnosis. He believes that the infection probably resulted from either a streptococcus or staphylococcus bacterium that infected the lymph channels, which "bathe the tissues of the body with plasma derived from the blood. Clinically there would be redness, warmth, swelling, pain . . . and a red streak ascending up the leg (not black)." Dr. Litterer assesses Eisenhower's risk of death at "slightly worse than 50-50." (Correspondence and consultation, May 2001.)

19. DDE, *At Ease*, 97, and Eisenhower high school record, Box 4, Endacott Papers, EL.

20. Edgar Eisenhower oral history, EL; McCallum, *Six Roads from Abilene*, 74; and DDE, *At Ease*, 96–97.

21. Interview of Suzanne Conklin Sexton, May 2, 2001. Dr. Conklin died in 1946 and undoubtedly would have given Kenneth Davis a more accurate and balanced account of the episode had he been interviewed.

22. Francis Trevelyan Miller, *Eisenhower: Man and Soldier*, 61.

23. "Young Mr. Eisenhower."

24. Miller, *Ike the Soldier*, 123.

25. Davis, *Soldier of Democracy*, 85.

26. Charles M. Harger, "The Eisenhower I Know . . . ," *American Magazine*, Nov. 1951. His daughter, Lois Bradshaw Harger, was the salutorian of the class of 1909 and an associate editor of the *Helianthus*.

27. DDE, *At Ease*, 95. There is no indication that Eisenhower was ever punished by the superintendent, W. A. Stacey, for misconduct in school.

28. Lelia Grace Picking oral history, quoting a classmate, Mrs. C. D. Wetzel (née Winifred Williams), EL.

29. Eisenhower high school record, Box 4, Endacott Papers, EL.

30. Ivan Fitzwater oral history, EL.
31. Francis Trevelyan Miller, *Eisenhower: Man and Soldier*, chap. 8, passim.
32. Alice Gentry, quoted in "Old Textbooks Bear Scribblings of Ike Eisenhower, Schoolboy," *Kansas City Star*, July 24, 1958. Algebra was taught during the first two years. DDE averaged 88 in his repeat of his freshman year and 90 in his sophomore year. Miss Gentry managed to conceal just how badly "the big boys terrified me."
33. DDE academic record, Abilene High School; article, "Old Textbooks Bear Scribblings of Ike Eisenhower, Schoolboy," *Kansas City Star*, July 24, 1958, Vertical File, EL, and DDE, *At Ease*, 100. In 1962 Wilbur Jeffcoat, who sat next to Eisenhower in the eighth grade, recalled that "he was a studious kid, not a bad boy either. But he was as ordinary as the rest of us."
34. DDE, *At Ease*, 100.
35. Letter, John E. Long to Earl Endacott, Apr. 5, 1966, Box 4, Endacott Papers, EL.
36. James C. Humes, *Confessions of a White House Ghostwriter* (Washington, D.C., 1997), 39.
37. DDE, *At Ease*, 43. During his sophomore through senior years the curriculum included ancient history, English history, and American history.
38. See DDE, *At Ease*, chap. 3, passim.
39. Letter, DDE to Lester Schreyer, Nov. 30, 1963, Post-Pres Papers, EL.
40. Ironically, in nearby Independence, Missouri, another young man, by the name of Harry S. Truman, had developed a similar passion for history during his youth. Many of Truman's heroes were also those of Patton and Eisenhower. Like Eisenhower (who was six years younger), Truman read voraciously. "Reading history," he said, "to me, was far more than a romantic adventure. It was solid instruction and wise teaching." (Quoted in David McCullough, *Truman* [New York, 1992], 58.)
41. Howard Funk and Orin Snider oral histories, EL. There were rarely more than two footballs on hand, a new one bought each year and one from the previous year, which was used for practice. They tended to get used so often that they became larger than normal. A touchdown was worth five points, one for the extra point, and two for a drop-kick field goal, the only kind employed at that time.
42. Orin Snider, the football coach, recalls that an athletic association existed prior to 1908 but had probably been dormant prior to being revived in 1908. (Snider oral history, EL.)
43. Miller, *Ike the Soldier*, 103.
44. *Helianthus '09*, copy in Vertical File, EL. Eisenhower also played tackle and halfback with equal skill when called upon.
45. Ambrose, *Eisenhower*, 33. In 1946 Eisenhower wrote to a friend about the incident, noting that the "rest of the team was a bit ashamed." (Letter, DDE to Lucy Eldridge, Jan. 17, 1946, Box 38, Pre-Pres Papers, EL.)
46. Quoted in the *Abilene Daily Reflector-Chronicle*, May 24, 1909, and DDE, *At Ease*, 101.
47. DDE, *At Ease*, 79. Eisenhower was one of nine boys in a graduating class of thirty-one—at the time, the largest ever to graduate from Abilene High School.
48. *Helianthus '09*.
49. Lelia Grace Picking oral history, EL.
50. DDE, *At Ease*, 103.

5. FROM ABILENE TO WEST POINT

1. Ambrose and Immerman, *Milton S. Eisenhower*, 16.
2. Quoted in Harger, "The Eisenhower I Knew."
3. Although not yet eighteen in 1917 when the United States entered World War I, Milton was also so anxious to leave Abilene that he announced his intention to Charlie

- Harger's daughter to lie about his age and enlist in the U.S. Army. Harger talked Milton out of this idea by hiring him as a full-time reporter for his newspaper. (Ambrose and Immerman, *Milton S. Eisenhower,* 26–27.)

4. McCallum, *Six Roads from Abilene,* 92–93, and Miller, *Ike the Soldier,* 110. Miller correctly suggests that Chris Musser disliked his brother-in-law David Eisenhower but was extremely fond of Edgar, whom he regarded more like the son he never had. Edgar, who had his heart set on becoming a successful lawyer, had no interest in medicine.

5. Davis, *Soldier of Democracy,* 106.

6. "Young Mr. Eisenhower."

7. DDE, *At Ease,* 97–98.

8. Letter, Swede Hazlett to DDE, 23 May 1944, Box 17, Pre-Pres Papers, EL.

9. Eisenhower's memory failed him when he wrote in *At Ease* that he earned $90 per month. In 1910 he earned $45 per month from January through March, $55 in April and May, $53 in June, and $60 from October through December. (Source: Hoffman, *Chronicle of the Belle Springs Creamery,* 13.) In 1910 the average annual wage for all industrial jobs in the United States was $600 per year, which meant that Eisenhower's pay had he remained at the creamery ($720) would have exceeded the norm by 20 percent. (Source: Scott Derks, ed., *The Value of a Dollar, 1860–1989* [Detroit, 1994], data for 1910.)

10. DDE, *At Ease,* 103–4, and McCallum, *Six Roads from Abilene,* 93. During the time he worked at the creamery one of Eisenhower's household duties was to carry an empty gallon can to the creamery and return home with it filled with buttermilk. On one occasion he went headfirst to retrieve a bolt that had fallen into a narrow, water-filled ice can, which he could all too easily have been stuck in.

11. McCallum, *Six Roads from Abilene,* 93.

12. Memo by aide Robert L. Schulz, Aug. 3, 1961, Ann Whitman File, Pres-Papers, EL.

13. Francis Trevelyan Miller, *Eisenhower: Man and Soldier,* 78–79.

14. John F. "Six" McDonnell oral history, EL.

15. Francis Trevelyan Miller, *Eisenhower: Man and Soldier,* 81.

16. So too did Eisenhower scholar Robert H. Ferrell, who wrote an article titled "Eisenhower Was a Democrat," *Kansas History,* Autumn 1990.

17. On November 18, 1909, Howe reprinted the entire speech in the *Dickinson County News,* along with a photograph of Eisenhower.

18. Ferrell, "Eisenhower Was a Democrat." In 1952, when he was quite elderly, Charlie Harger, a staunch Republican, asserted that the speech was "strictly nonpartisan." However, it seems improbable that Harger would have attended a Democratic Party function. He probably read the text that Howe printed in the *Dickinson County News.* When Eisenhower ran for president in 1952, someone unearthed the 1909 speech, sparking a brief controversy that had no effect on the campaign.

19. Miller, *Ike the Soldier,* 107.

20. Robert Griffith, ed., *Ike's Letters to a Friend, 1941–1958* (Lawrence, Kans., 1984), 3.

21. Joseph L. Bristow was a native of nearby Salina and is described as "a prominent Kansas newspaper publisher and editor"; he was U.S. senator from 1909 to 1915. Bristow was also the first Kansas senator to be elected by popular vote instead of the state legislature. (See Daniel D. Holt and James W. Leyerzapf, eds., *Eisenhower: The Prewar Diaries and Papers, 1905–1941* [Baltimore, 1998], 8 [hereafter cited as *Eisenhower: The Prewar Diaries*], and Miller, *Ike the Soldier,* 113.

22. Joseph L. Bristow Papers, Kansas State Historical Society archives, Topeka. It is also reprinted in Holt and Leyerzapf, *Eisenhower: The Prewar Diaries,* 8.

23. Eisenhower's letter to Bristow contained two serious flaws, the first of which was that he had neglected even to learn the senator's first name, and had addressed it only to "Senator Bristow." Whether deliberately or through outright and uncharacteristic

carelessness, Eisenhower also misstated his own age. His next birthday, a few months hence in 1910, would be his *twentieth*, not his nineteenth.

24. DDE to Bristow, Sept. 3, 1910, Bristow Papers, Kansas State Historical Society archives.
25. "Memoirs of Ike," in letter, Swede Hazlett to DDE, May 23, 1944, Box 17, Pre-Pres Papers.
26. Letter, Bristow to DDE, Oct. 24, 1910, Bristow Papers; Holt and Leyerzapf, *Eisenhower: The Prewar Diaries*, 9, and Ambrose, *Eisenhower*, 40.
27. Francis Trevelyan Miller, *Eisenhower: Man and Soldier*, 82.
28. Davis, *Soldier of Democracy*, 114.
29. Orin Snider coached the Abilene team but on this occasion was the referee. He intervened to pull away the actual culprit who had a Salina player by the throat and was choking him. (Snider oral history, EL, and Davis, *Soldier of Democracy*, 115–16.)
30. Eisenhower's memory was faulty when he wrote in *At Ease* that he had only gotten into West Point after the principal nominee failed the physical. Neither failed, and the alternate, George Pulsifer, also entered West Point in June 1911 with an "at-large" appointment, and graduated in 1915.
31. Letter, John E. Long to Earl Endacott, Mar. 21, 1966, Box 4, Endacott Papers, and Long oral history, EL. The onetime Abilene home of Dr. Hazlett is presently a bed-and-breakfast inn in which the author has resided during research at the Eisenhower Library.
32. "Young Mr. Eisenhower."
33. Bergman, "Steeped in Religion."
34. Milton S. Eisenhower oral history, EL.

6. THE LONG GRAY LINE

1. DDE, *At Ease*, 3–4.
2. Quoted in Jeffrey Simpson, *Officers and Gentlemen* (Tarrytown, N.Y., 1982), 17.
3. Ibid., 25, and USMA, *Register of Graduates*, passim.
4. Simpson, *Officers and Gentlemen*, 132.
5. Lyon, *Eisenhower*, 44.
6. "MacArthur," PBS documentary, 1999.
7. "Eisenhower's West Point," unpublished account by Joseph C. Haw, USMA, 1915, CU#5377, USMA Archives.
8. Ibid.
9. DDE, *In Review* (New York, 1969), 12–13.
10. DDE, *At Ease*, 5.
11. Ibid., 4–5.
12. DDE, *In Review*, 13.
13. Haw, "Eisenhower's West Point." For another excellent account of life at West Point, see "The West Point Letters of Roscoe Barnett Woodruff, USMA, 1915," USMA Archives.
14. Ibid.
15. Thomas Fleming, "West Point in Review," *American Heritage*, Apr. 1988.
16. "Young Mr. Eisenhower."
17. Quoted in Edward M. Coffman, " 'My room mate . . . is Dwight Eisenhower,' " *American Heritage*, Apr. 1973.
18. P. A. Hodgson, quoted in "From Plebe to President," *Collier's*, June 10, 1955.
19. "Young Mr. Eisenhower," and DDE, *At Ease*, 12.
20. DDE, *In Review*, 13–14. There is no record of any demerits issued.
21. "From Plebe to President."
22. "Extracts from Records of Cadet Dwight D. Eisenhower, USMA, 1915," Vertical File, USMA Archives.

23. Davis, *Soldier of Democracy*, 133.
24. DDE, *At Ease*, 12.
25. "Young Mr. Eisenhower."
26. Ibid.
27. "From Plebe to President."
28. The recollections of Charles Herrick, Class of 1915, USMA Archives. During summer camp Eisenhower and his friends often arranged to have a cache of food left beside the Hudson River at the bottom of a steep cliff by a local grocer. It could be retrieved only at great physical risk and a heavy disciplinary penalty if caught. Neither Eisenhower nor his friends were deterred. (See also Edward Ziegler, "Ike: The Man Behind the Soldier," *Reader's Digest*, Mar. 1991.)
29. Alexander M. "Babe" Weyand, "The Athletic Cadet Eisenhower," *Assembly*, Spring 1968.
30. Recollections of a classmate, DDE Vertical Files, USMA Archives.
31. P. A. Hodgson, quoted in Weyand, "The Athletic Cadet Eisenhower."
32. Marty Maher, *Bringing Up the Brass* (New York, 1951), 177.
33. Weyand, "The Athletic Cadet Eisenhower."
34. DDE, *At Ease*, 15, and *In Review*, 14.
35. Davis, *Soldier of Democracy*, 139.
36. "Young Mr. Eisenhower."
37. Weyand, "The Athletic Cadet Eisenhower." Brig. Gen. Thomas W. Mattingly, M.D., a U.S. Army Medical Corps physician and one of Eisenhower's doctors during his presidency, has conducted the most extensive study ever undertaken of the lifelong health problems of Eisenhower. Of the knee injury incurred at West Point, he writes: "his knee injury was in retrospect, an injury to the internal structures of the joint . . . which normally support and stabilize a normal joint. Without surgical repair of these injured structures such as has been developed in recent years, the injury left him with a weak and unstable knee . . . which was susceptible to further problems by even minor trauma." (See "A Compilation of the General Health Status of Dwight D. Eisenhower," Box 1, Mattingly Papers.)
38. Haw, "Eisenhower's West Point."
39. Ibid.
40. Letter, P. A. Hodgson to family, Sept. 21, 1913, Hodgson Papers, EL.
41. Quoted in John Gunther, *Eisenhower* (New York, 1952), 34.
42. Michael R. Beschloss, *Eisenhower: A Centennial Life* (New York, 1990), 20.
43. Letter, Eisenhower to Ruby Norman, Nov. 22, 1913, Ruby Norman Lucier Papers, EL.
44. Letter, P. A. Hodgson to parents, Mar. 16, 1913, Hodgson Papers, EL.
45. Letter, Eisenhower to Ruby Norman, Nov. 30, 1913, Ruby Norman Lucier Papers, EL.
46. Robert H. Ferrell, *Ill-Advised: Presidential Health and Public Trust* (Columbia, Mo., 1992), 55.

7. "POPULAR BUT UNDISTINGUISHED"

1. Haw, "Eisenhower's West Point."
2. Weyand, "The Athletic Cadet Eisenhower."
3. Quoted in Fleming, *West Point*, 290.
4. Dwight D. Eisenhower, *In Review*, 17.
5. Quoted in Rick Atkinson, *The Long Gray Line* (New York, 1991), 79.
6. Circa spring 1912, Hodgson Papers, EL.
7. DDE, "Yearly Standing," Class of 1915, USMA Archives.
8. DDE, *At Ease*, 18.
9. Harger, "The Eisenhower I Knew."
10. Needless wearing of his uniform proved costly the day he returned home to find Ida

attempting without success to remove a long stovepipe for cleaning. Unable to free the pipe himself, Eisenhower gave it "a big jerk." Both Eisenhower and the pipe came crashing down, covering his immaculate white uniform with black soot. "You never saw such a mess in your life," he laughingly recalled.

11. Davis, *Soldier of Democracy*, 141–42. As Merle Miller points out, Eisenhower never challenged Davis's account of their brief meeting in 1913 as he did many other events and incidents recounted in that biography. (See Box 21, Pre-Pres Papers, for DDE's notations concerning the Davis book.)

12. DDE, *At Ease*, 22. This incident had the hallmarks of an anxiety attack.

13. Davis, *Soldier of Democracy*, 142–43. Afterward Tyler was teased unmercifully until Eisenhower made amends by intervening to order that enough was enough. Thereafter Tyler was said to have reverted to the "nice guy" status he had once held.

14. "From Plebe to President." See also Miller, *Ike the Soldier*, 47.

15. "Young Mr. Eisenhower."

16. "From Plebe to President."

17. Haw, "Eisenhower's West Point."

18. Letter, P. A. Hodgson to his mother, Oct. 6, 1913, Hodgson Papers, EL.

19. "From Plebe to President."

20. Ibid.

21. All quotes are contained in DDE's letter to Col. J. Franklin Bell, Feb. 14, 1967, Box 20, Post-Pres Papers, Secretary's Series, EL. See also DDE, *At Ease*, 20, and Form D, Class of 1915, "Yearly Standing," USMA Archives. Eisenhower's class standing in mathematics at the end of the year was ninety-seventh, by far his lowest score and no coincidence.

22. Coffman, " 'My room mate . . . is Dwight Eisenhower.' "

23. The Gordon R. Young Papers, USAMHI. For the most part Eisenhower's letters were rarely dated, however, Mrs. Young preserved several of his envelopes, which indicate that most were written during February and March 1915. Until her husband donated her letters to USAMHI, Dorothy's brief relationship with Cadet Eisenhower was unknown. Eisenhower himself never mentioned her, and no other correspondence is known to exist.

24. Letters, DDE to Dorothy Mills, Feb. 23 and Mar. 26, 1915.

25. Ibid., Mar. 26, 1915.

26. S. D. Eisenhower, *Strictly Personal* (New York, 1974), 9.

27. Davis, *Soldier of Democracy*, 130–31. When Eisenhower annotated Davis's book, he wrote, "A Solomon sits in judgment." Not surprisingly, another cadet who relished the solitude of exploring West Point by himself was George S. Patton.

28. Letter, P. A. Hodgson to his parents, Mar. 3, 1912, Hodgson Papers, EL.

29. Few of Eisenhower's letters written to his family or friends from West Point survive except those to Ruby Norman, which she had the foresight to preserve. Letter, DDE to Ruby Norman, Nov. 5, 1913, Ruby Norman Lucier Papers, EL.

30. Beschloss, *Eisenhower: A Centennial Life*, 21.

31. Letter, DDE to Miss Brush, Dec. 1, 1914, Box 9, Pre-Pres Papers. There is no known reply from the young lady.

32. Omar N. Bradley and Clay Blair, *A General's Life* (New York, 1983), 34. Bradley was later promoted to cadet lieutenant but remained in his beloved F Company.

33. Davis, *Soldier of Democracy*, 134, and 1915 *Howitzer*.

34. Staff paper, undated, USMA Archives.

35. Correspondence between Col. Herman Beukema and DDE, 1946, Pre-Pres Papers.

36. DDE, *At Ease*, 25, "Young Mr. Eisenhower," and Box 4, DDE Personnel File, 1910–73, EL.

37. "DDE Medical Records, 1910–45," Box 2, Howard McCrum Snyder Papers, EL. (Snyder was Eisenhower's chief physician during his years as president.)

38. D'Este, *Patton*, 149.
39. DDE to Ruby Norman Lucier, Nov. 24, 1913, in Holt and Leyerzapf, *Eisenhower: The Prewar Diaries*, 11.
40. 1915 *Howitzer* entry, and DDE, *At Ease*, 80.
41. Francis Trevelyan Miller, *Eisenhower*, 149–50, and 1915 USMA efficiency report, Box 4, DDE Personnel File, EL.
42. "Young Mr. Eisenhower."
43. Ambrose, *Eisenhower,* 45.
44. Haw, "Eisenhower's West Point."
45. Gen. Mark W. Clark, quoted in Miller, *Ike the Soldier*, 14.

8. "1915—THE SUMMER DWIGHT CAME BACK FROM WEST POINT"

1. Bergman, "Steeped in Religion."
2. Letter, JSDE to Frank X. Tolbert, July 1963, copy in EL. The "instructions" Eisenhower completed in June 1911 are in the USMA Archives. Under the block asking for prior military service, Eisenhower also sloppily entered "United State [*sic*] Military Academy." The two forms completed on Sept. 1, 1915, are in Box 22, Misc. File, Pre-Pres Papers, EL.
3. "The Ike I Remember and Other Stories," Box 4, Endacott Papers, EL.
4. Six McDonnell oral history, EL.
5. Jameson, *They Still Call Him Ike*, 34.
6. Miller, *Ike the Soldier*, 125, and the papers and diary of Gladys Harding Brooks, copies furnished the author by historian Cole Kingseed (Col., U.S. Army, Ret.), who obtained them from Brooks's son. Colonel Kingseed has written an illuminating essay about their romance titled "Ike and Gladys Harding—The Summer of 1915," DDE Vertical File, USMA Archives. Mrs. Brooks specified that the diary and letters were not be opened to researchers until after the deaths of Eisenhower and Mamie, and "*after my death!*" All letters quoted are courtesy of Colonel Kingseed. See also the Gladys Harding Brooks Papers, EL.
7. D'Este, *Patton*, 102.
8. Davis, *Soldier of Democracy*, 155–56, and DDE's annotations of Davis's book, Box 21, Misc. File, Pre-Pres Papers.
9. Miller, *Ike the Soldier*, quoting Gladys Harding's son, Robert Brooks, 125.
10. Letter, DDE to Gladys Harding, written in Sept. 1915.
11. Six McDonnell oral history, EL.
12. *Washington Post*, Oct. 16, 1953, and J. Earl Endacott, quoted in Six McDonnell oral history, EL.
13. Miller, *Ike the Soldier*, quoting Ruby Norman's daughter, 123.
14. DDE to the War Dept. Adj. Gen., Aug. 9, 1915, copy in Holt and Leyerzapf, *Eisenhower: The Prewar Diaries*, 10.
15. DDE, *At Ease*, 111.
16. Ibid., 112.

9. MISS MAMIE DOUD

1. Richard Rhodes, "Ike: An Artist in Iron," *Harper's*, July 1970.
2. DDE to Ruby Norman, Jan. 17, 1916, Ruby Norman Lucier Papers, EL.
3. Rhodes, "Ike: An Artist in Iron."
4. Rosalind Massow, "Mamie and Ike Talk About 50 Years of Marriage," *Parade*, June 26, 1966.
5. Miller, *Ike the Soldier*, 64.
6. Ibid., 65.

7. Samuel P. Huntington, *The Soldier and the State* (Cambridge, Mass., 1957), chap. 9, passim.

8. "Young Mr. Eisenhower."

9. Ambrose, *Eisenhower*, 56.

10. DDE to Col. George W. Helms, June 14, 1943, Box 51, Pre-Pres Papers, EL.

11. Russell F. Weigley, *History of the United States Army* (New York, 1967), 561.

12. Ibid., 328, 334. Attempts at consolidation and modernization by secretaries of war and chiefs of staff dating to 1880 had failed to overcome congressional pork-barrel self-interest in keeping the so-called hitching-post forts for the purpose of allocating funds to their constituencies, where, in turn, they would earn votes for reelection.

13. DDE, *At Ease*, 115–17.

14. JSDE quoted in Susan Eisenhower, *Mrs. Ike* (New York, 1996), 129.

15. DDE, *At Ease*, 92.

16. Undated letter, Gladys Harding Brooks Papers, copy furnished by Cole Kingseed.

17. Susan Eisenhower, *Mrs. Ike*, chap. 1, passim.

18. Ibid.

19. Susan Eisenhower, *Mrs. Ike*, 33–34, and DDE, *In Review*, 19.

20. MDE, quoted in the *Denver Post*, July 2, 1958.

21. MDE, quoted in Susan Eisenhower, *Mrs. Ike*, 34.

22. Dorothy Brandon, *Mamie Doud Eisenhower* (New York, 1954), 51.

23. Susan Eisenhower, *Mrs. Ike*, 33–35.

24. Brandon, *Mamie Doud Eisenhower*, 52. "Mike" was the Doud family prankster, a free spirit who eloped with her boyfriend and once, during Prohibition, refilled Pupah's supply of illegal gin with water. (JSDE, *Strictly Personal*, 13–14.)

25. Susan Eisenhower, *Mrs. Ike*, 46–47, and notes of MDE interview by Maud Hart Lovelace, Delos W. Lovelace Papers, EL.

26. JSDE, quoted in Susan Eisenhower, *Mrs. Ike*, 43.

27. MDE, "My Memories of Ike," *Reader's Digest*, Feb. 1970.

28. DDE to Ruby Norman, Jan. 17, 1916, Ruby Norman Lucier Papers, EL.

29. Ibid.

30. D'Este, *Patton*, 166, and Richard O'Connor, *Black Jack Pershing* (Garden City, N.Y., 1961), 123.

31. O'Connor, *Black Jack Pershing*, chap. 6, passim, and Weigley, *History of the United States Army*, 351. Aviation's potential for aerial reconnaissance and intelligence was eventually recognized by the War Department and Congress, which raised the appropriation from $300,000 to $800,000. Compared to the Germans, who had spent a whopping $28 million on aviation between 1908 and 1913, the United States had spent less than 2 percent of that figure.

32. Miller, *Ike the Soldier*, 130–31. Quotes are attributed to Mary Jane Stineman, daughter of Ruby Norman.

33. See Mattingly, "A Compilation of the General Health Status of Dwight D. Eisenhower," and Ferrell, *Ill-Advised*, chap. 3.

34. Letter, Susan Eisenhower to the author, July 12, 1999.

35. MDE, "My Memories of Ike."

36. Susan Eisenhower, *Mrs. Ike*, 42.

37. MDE oral history, and Maud Hart Lovelace interview, Delos W. Lovelace Papers, EL.

38. Susan Eisenhower, *Mrs. Ike*, chap. 3, passim.

39. JSDE, quoted in ibid., 43.

40. Ibid. 42.

41. One of the apocryphal tales about the Eisenhowers alleges that during their first visit to Abilene, Ike left Mamie alone with his parents while he went off to play poker with his friends. After he failed to return, she telephoned to insist that he do so at once. Eisenhower refused, annoyed at being nagged, and said that he was losing and on

principle never left a poker game while behind. When he finally did return in the early morning hours after he had won a comfortable sum, a furious argument ensued. Biographer Kenneth Davis claims it was the worst quarrel the two ever had but that each emerged from it with a better understanding of the other's feelings. There was indeed such an incident, but it occurred some years later. Unfortunately, once erroneously recounted the story was repeated by numerous biographers. The newlyweds are said to have remained for three days in Abilene, during which time the poker incident allegedly took place. However, Eisenhower was given only a ten-day leave, most of which had already been consumed by his lengthy journey to Denver, the wedding and short honeymoon, and the thirty-hour train trip to Abilene. Both have cited the fact that they were in Abilene for only a matter of hours. (Davis, *Soldier of Democracy*, 166, Ambrose, *Eisenhower*, 59. DDE's annotations of Davis's book, Box 21, Pre-Pres Papers, DDE, *At Ease*, 123, and MDE oral history, EL.)

10. ROSES HAVE THORNS

1. Susan Eisenhower, *Mrs. Ike*, 45.
2. Ibid.
3. Davis, *Soldier of Democracy*, 167.
4. Quotes from MDE interview by Maud Hart Lovelace, Delos W. Lovelace Papers, EL.
5. Brandon, *Mamie Doud Eisenhower*, 48.
6. "It is a sign of the kind of woman she was and of the role then expected of middle-class women that she made this transformation with determination, commitment and cheer," wrote Jonathan Yardley in the *Washington Post*. "Portrait of a Lady," review of *Mrs. Ike*, Nov. 17, 1996.
7. MDE oral history.
8. Miller, *Ike the Soldier*, 166.
9. MDE interview by Maud Hart Lovelace, Delos W. Lovelace Papers, EL.
10. Julie Nixon Eisenhower, "Mamie," *Ladies' Home Journal*, June 1977.
11. Quoted in Martin M. Teasley, "Ike Was Her Career," *Prologue* (Summer 1987).
12. Brandon, *Mamie Doud Eisenhower*, 48.
13. Lester and Irene David, *Ike & Mamie* (New York, 1981), 95. One day shortly after they were married, Mamie erupted over some trifling matter and slapped Ike's hand, breaking the amethyst stone in his class ring. "He looked at it sadly for a moment, then said very quietly: 'Young lady, for that fit of temper, you will buy me a new amethyst with your own money.' And I did—although parting with those dollars almost killed me." (MDE, "My Memories of Ike.")
14. Susan Eisenhower, *Mrs. Ike*, 131.
15. Ferrell, *Ill-Advised*, 54–55, and Mattingly, "A Compilation of the General Health Status of Dwight Eisenhower," EL.
16. DDE Medical Records, 1910–45, Box 2, Howard McCrum Snyder Papers, EL.
17. DDE, *At Ease*, 124–25. In 1917, while Eisenhower was away, an intruder attempted to break in through a screen. Mamie's screams aroused the neighbors. She sat up all that night with the lights blazing but, despite the temptation, was never even able to handle the weapon. (Brandon, *Mamie Doud Eisenhower*, 76.)
18. Miller, *Ike the Soldier*, 151.
19. Maj. Gen. John B. Wogan, quoted in "From Plebe to President."
20. Herbert Molloy Mason, Jr., *The Great Pursuit* (Garden City, N.Y., 1961), 38–40.
21. Vernon L. Williams, "Lieutenant George S. Patton, Jr., and the American Army: On the Texas Frontier in Mexico, 1915–16," *Military History of Texas and the Southwest* 17 (1982).
22. Ibid.
23. Susan Eisenhower, *Mrs. Ike*, 47.

24. In June 1946 Eisenhower was at West Point to attend the graduation ceremony when he encountered one of his former NCOs, Sgt. Tom Blazina, whose son was in the graduating class. Blazina accorded Eisenhower the ultimate compliment when he related that after serving under him in 1916 he had vowed, "If I ever had a boy, he would go to West Point and be an officer like you." The younger Blazina became an Air Force test pilot. (Quoted in Kirkpatrick Cobb, *Ike's Old Sarge* [Dallas, 1964], 145.)

25. DDE, *At Ease*, 119, and DDE to Ruby Norman, Jan. 16, 1916, Ruby Norman Lucier Papers, EL.

26. Cobb, *Ike's Old Sarge*, 29, 31.

27. British casualties at Gallipoli were 41,000 killed and missing and 78,500 wounded. The French lost 9,000 killed and 13,000 wounded and together the British and French sustained another 100,000 nonbattle losses due to sickness. The Turks lost 66,000 killed and 152,000 wounded. See Brigadier Peter Young, ed., *A Dictionary of Battles (1816– 1976)* (New York, 1977), 358.

28. Two British lieutenant colonels serving in the front lines were a future prime minister named Winston Churchill, and a field marshal in the next world war, Lt. Col. Bernard Law Montgomery, who was severely wounded in the chest during the First Battle of Ypres in 1914, in which he won the Distinguished Service Order (DSO).

29. James W. Rainey, "The Questionable Training of the AEF in World War I," *Parameters* (Winter 1992–93).

30. Weigley, *History of the United States Army*, 353.

31. *Army Times*, eds., *The Yanks Are Coming* (New York, 1960), 59, Edward M. Coffman, *The War to End All Wars* (Madison, Wis., 1986), 40, and Laurence Stallings, *The Doughboys* (New York, 1963), 25.

32. Coffman, *The War to End All Wars*, 37.

33. By April 1917 the Regular Army consisted of 5,800 officers and 133,000 men, while the national guard numbered 3,200 officers and 67,000 men. (Rainey, "The Questionable Training of the AEF in World War I.")

34. Coffman, *The War to End All Wars*, chap. 2, passim.

35. David, *Ike & Mamie*, 68.

36. Brandon, *Mamie Doud Eisenhower*, 74.

37. DDE, *At Ease*, 129–30.

38. Ibid., chap. 10, passim. Mamie never really caught on to driving. "She finally gave it up completely by the early 1930s and was driven ever since." (David, *Ike & Mamie*, 70.)

39. Brandon, *Mamie Doud Eisenhower*, 74.

40. DDE, *At Ease*, 130–31. To add insult to injury, Eisenhower later received yet another demand for payment. Fortunately Mamie had kept the cancelled check in the family account book as proof the debt had been paid.

41. Ibid., 131.

42. Box 4, DDE Personnel Files, 1910–73, EL. A similar efficiency report on a present-day U.S. Army officer would not only be regarded as poor but a career killer.

43. Susan Eisenhower, *Mrs. Ike*, 51.

44. Ibid. Susan Eisenhower notes that the better-known spelling of the child's nickname as "Icky" is incorrect, and that it was always spelled "Ikky" in correspondence by both Eisenhower and Mamie. Several examples of this spelling exist.

45. DDE to MDE, Sept. 25, 1917, James S. Copley Library, La Jolla, Calif.

46. Ibid.

47. Eisenhower's efficiency report for his service at Fort Oglethorpe was hardly a ringing endorsement of his brief tenure there. He was rated "Average" in job performance and in six specific categories (two steps below the highest possible rating). His rating officer called him "a capable and industrious young officer. Will improve with service."

In response to an entry in which the rating officer is asked if he would "Especially desire to have him" [in his command], the answer was "No." (Officer Efficiency Reports, Box 4, DDE Personnel File, 1910–73, EL.)

48. MDE interview with Maud Hart Lovelace, Delos W. Lovelace Papers, EL.
49. DDE, *At Ease*, 132–33.
50. Ibid., 133.

11. "I . . . WILL MAKE UP FOR THIS."

1. Lt. Edward C. Thayer to his mother, Jan. 1918, Pres Papers, Ann Whitman Diary Series, EL.
2. Coffman, *The War to End All Wars*, 57.
3. Col. John E. Harris, quoted in "From Plebe to President."
4. F. Mitchell, *Tank Warfare: The Story of the Tanks in the Great War* (London, 1933), 4–5.
5. So named for the German crown prince who had derisively been nicknamed "Little Willie" by British troops. The "Little Willie" prototype tank proved impractical and eventually evolved into the first operational models, which were called "Big Willies." (Ibid., 8–9.)
6. To preserve what was now becoming a prized secret from the Germans, the responsibility for the development and production of the land cruiser was given to a small group called the Executive Supply Committee. The cover name given this group was "Tank Supply Committee," and soon what had previously been called by the names "land cruiser," "landship," and "caterpillar machine-gun destroyer" became shortened to "tank." J. F. C. Fuller asserts that this was the first use of the word "tank." (See Fuller, *Tanks in the Great War, 1914–1918* [London, 1920], 29.)
7. The French developed their own version of the tank, which was designed as an infantry personnel carrier but, after observing the success of the British, they redesigned their machines to become a direct-fire weapon to support the advancing infantry. The lightly armored but far more mobile French Renaults were employed for the first time in the spring of 1917. The Renault light tanks of 1918 contained none of today's high-tech instruments for communication between tanks or between members of the crew. Since it had no lights inside, the crews became proficient by learning to operate the tank and its guns blindfolded. The commander could signal instructions to his driver only by means of a series of kicks. (Dale E. Wilson, *Treat 'Em Rough!: The Birth of American Armor, 1917–20* [Novato, Calif., 1990], 2–3.)
8. Mitchell, *Tank Warfare*, 34.
9. Ibid., 10. The Mark VI was a prototype heavy tank of 27–30 tons, which was never produced.
10. Dale E. Wilson, *Treat 'Em Rough!*, 31, 62.
11. Ibid., 62.
12. DDE, *At Ease*, 137.
13. Ibid., 135.
14. Wilson, *Treat 'Em Rough!*, 60.
15. DDE, *At Ease*, 137.
16. Named in honor of Samuel Colt, the facility was first known as Camp U.S. Troops, Gettysburg, before the name change, when it became the primary Tank Corps training center.
17. Eisenhower might have been promoted sooner had the bureaucracy not intervened. Welborn had failed to indicate to the War Department that the Camp Colt CO's slot should be that of a major. When the oversight was discovered, Eisenhower was quickly promoted. (Wilson, *Treat 'Em Rough!*, 66–67.)
18. Francis Trevelyan Miller, *Eisenhower*, 163–64.

19. DDE, *At Ease*, 143–44. The congressman seems to have had better luck elsewhere, and the officer was allowed to return to active duty.

20. Perret, *Eisenhower*, 71.

21. Poem in Box 1, Kevin McCann Papers, 1918–1981, EL.

22. DDE, *At Ease*, 144–45.

23. Wilson, *Treat 'Em Rough!*, 65. Eisenhower gave the owner a final chance to cooperate, but warned that if he served even a single drink to one of his soldiers, "I'll put you out of business."

24. Quoted in Wilson, *Treat 'Em Rough!*, 64.

25. "Order of Battle of the U.S. 'Zone of the Interior' Land Forces in the World War (1917–1919)," copy in USAMHI.

26. John B. Shinn files, Pre-Pres Papers, EL.

27. Reproduced in *Treat 'Em Rough!* (the Camp Colt newsletter), Sept. 10, 1918, copy in W. Louis Schlesinger file, Pre-Pres Papers.

28. Brandon, *Mamie Doud Eisenhower*, chaps. 4 and 5, passim.

29. MDE oral history, EL, and Susan Eisenhower, *Mrs. Ike*, 54.

30. Brandon, *Mamie Doud Eisenhower*, 97–99.

31. Data are from Gina Kolata's landmark study, *Flu: The Story of the Great Influenza Pandemic of 1918 and the Search for the Virus That Caused It* (New York, 1999), chap. 1, passim. Its name, "Spanish flu," is a reference to San Sebastián, where it was first detected in the winter of 1918. Kolata notes that the precise numbers of people stricken can never be known but that, "when it was over, humanity had been struck by a disease that killed more people in a few months' time than any other illness in the history of the world." Twenty-five percent of the world's population was stricken, 28 percent in the United States. The proper definition of the 1918 virus was a pandemic, an epidemic that spreads over a very large geographic region. As a basis for comparison, AIDS has killed approximately 22 million people worldwide since 1981.

32. DDE, *At Ease*, chap. 10, passim, Miller, *Ike the Soldier*, 172–73, and Wilson, *Treat 'Em Rough!*, 68–69. Eisenhower was not certain if Ikky was given Dr. Scott's "medication." There were 350 cases of Spanish flu diagnosed at Camp Colt, and the death rate for those who contracted it was 47 percent. Another 106 were taken ill with pneumonia. Coffmen, *The War to End All Wars*, 84, 363, and DDE, *At Ease*, 150.

33. Susan Eisenhower, *Mrs. Ike*, 17.

34. Ibid., chap. 4, passim. Buster had developed a severe kidney infection that led to blindness and a painful death. Mamie traveled from Harrisburg to Chicago on November 10, and from Chicago to Denver on November 11, 1918. In Chicago and elsewhere there were wild but premature celebrations of the armistice. John Eisenhower believes the Douds never recovered from the blow of losing two of their four daughters. (*Strictly Personal*, 11–12.)

35. Quoted in Wilson, *Treat 'Em Rough!*, 70.

36. Quoted in Ambrose, *Eisenhower*, 65, and Col. (in 1918, Lt.) Norman Randolph to DDE, June 20, 1945, Box 97, Pre-Pres Papers, EL.

37. Bradley, *A General's Life*, 44–45.

38. DDE, *At Ease*, 152.

39. "From Plebe to President."

40. Wilson, *Treat 'Em Rough!*, 69.

41. Efficiency report, dated July 26, 1919, Box 4, DDE Personnel File, 1910–73, EL.

42. DDE, *At Ease*, chap. 10, passim.

12. "A JOURNEY THROUGH DARKEST AMERICA"

1. D'Este, *Patton*, 210–11.

2. MDE oral history, EL.

3. Ibid.
4. Vaughn Smartt, "1919: The Interstate Expedition," *Constructor* (Aug. 1973).
5. Martin Blumenson, *The Patton Papers*, vol. 1 (Boston, 1972), 655–56.
6. Quoted in *Overview* (the official newsletter of the Eisenhower Foundation, Abilene, Kansas) 10, no. 3 (Fall 1984).
7. Ibid. The expedition was commanded by an infantry officer, Lt. Col. Charles W. McClure.
8. John E. Wickman, "Ike and 'The Great Truck Train'—1919," *Kansas History* (Autumn 1990).
9. Harry Carlton DeMars, quoted in the *Riverton* (Wyoming) *Ranger*, May 21, 1976.
10. Wickman, "Ike and 'The Great Truck Train'—1919."
11. Ibid.
12. DDE, *At Ease*, chap. 11, passim. Even in old age, Eisenhower clearly had not lost his love of such shenanigans. In *At Ease* he devoted nearly six pages to detailed descriptions of the pranks he and Brett had perpetrated.
13. Recollections of M/Sgt. Harry Carlton DeMars, 20th century collection, USAMHI.
14. *Overview* (Fall 1984).
15. Quoted by Stephen E. Ambrose in "Divided Highways: The Interstates and the Transformation of American Life," PBS documentary, 1999.

13. A FRIENDSHIP FORGED

1. Miller, *Ike the Soldier*, 182.
2. Ibid., 183.
3. Piers Brendon, *Ike: His Life and Times* (New York, 1986), 49. The only other thing they shared in common was that each was losing his hair at an alarming rate, a competition that Eisenhower would win hands down.
4. DDE, *At Ease*, 169.
5. JSDE, quoted in Miller, *Ike the Soldier*, 186.
6. MDE oral history, EL, and Julie Nixon Eisenhower, *Special People* (New York, 1977), 199–200.
7. DDE to "Nana" Doud, Nov. 16, 1919, in Susan Eisenhower, *Mrs. Ike*, 61.
8. D'Este, *Patton*, 286.
9. Eight hundred dollars in 1919 would have equated to more than twenty-three thousand dollars in 1989. (*The Value of a Dollar*, 2.)
10. MDE oral history.
11. Brendon, *Ike*, 49, and D'Este, *Patton*, 291.
12. D'Este, *Patton*, 291.
13. Susan Eisenhower, *Mrs. Ike*, 64.
14. D'Este, *Patton*, 865, n. 19.
15. "The U.S. Army Between World Wars I and II," Association of the U.S. Army Background Brief, no. 28, Mar. 1992. A further seven thousand troops served in the Philippine Scouts.
16. Ibid.
17. Robert Leckie, *Delivered from Evil* (New York, 1987), 11.
18. D. Clayton James, *The Years of MacArthur, 1880–1941*, vol. 1 (Boston, 1970), 261.
19. Weigley, *History of the United States Army*, 396.
20. Miller, *Ike the Soldier*, 589.
21. Patton became so discouraged that he wrote to his sister, Nita, "We are like people in a boat floating down the beautiful river of fictitious prosperity and thinking that the moaning of the none too distant waterfall—which is going to engulf us—is but the song of the wind in the trees. We disregard the lessons of History . . . and we go on

regardless of the VITAL necessity of trained patriotism—HIRING an army." (D'Este, *Patton*, 301.)

22. George F. Hofmann, "The Demise of the U.S. Tank Corps and Medium Tank Development Program," *Military Affairs*, Feb. 1973. Patton's friend Maj. Gen. Charles P. Summerall, the wartime commanding general of the 1st Division, also spoke in favor of retaining an independent tank arm.

23. Ibid. An Infantry Tank School was established at Camp Meade, and one of its early graduates was Eisenhower.

24. Only Pershing, the army's highest-ranking officer, was untouched by the reductions. The army system of promotions resulted in most officers holding two separate ranks. Regular officers held what was known as a temporary active-duty grade, usually one or two ranks higher than their permanent grade. Permanent grades were established by Congress, while the temporary grades were those needed to fill the requirements of the army during any particular year. During World War I, for example, Eisenhower held the temporary grade of lieutenant colonel and the permanent grade of captain. Thus, when Congress ordered massive personnel reductions after World War I, officers like Eisenhower, who were retained, reverted to their permanent ranks.

25. DDE, *At Ease*, 170.

26. Ibid., 171.

27. Ibid., 173.

28. Because of the dearth of material being written in the aftermath of World War I, some articles written for the *Cavalry Journal* also appeared in the *Infantry Journal*. An example was Patton's 1920 article, "Tanks in Future Wars."

29. Eisenhower, "A Tank Discussion," *Infantry Journal* 17 (Nov. 1920). While Eisenhower's article articulated an important vision for the tank, his lack of combat experience was reflected in a recommendation that the future organization of an army infantry division include an extra company of tanks that would replace the existing machine-gun battalion. Eisenhower's recommendation would have removed one of the key weapons in the arsenal of a division in combat, and it is doubtful if any of his compatriots would have supported his proposition. Patton's article appeared in *Infantry Journal* 17 (May 1920).

30. DDE, *At Ease*, 173.

31. Lucian K. Truscott, *The Twilight of the U.S. Cavalry* (Manhattan, Kans., 1990), 156–57. As late as 1938, when the clouds of World War II were already visible, the chief of cavalry, Maj. Gen. John K. Herr, expressed sorrow that so many of his officers were transferring to mechanized units. He blamed the General Staff for deliberately attempting to destroy the cavalry, and refused to recognize that armor would ever replace the current missions performed by the cavalry. Herr, a gallant and highly regarded officer, was proof that during the interwar years outdated beliefs would die hard.

32. DDE, *At Ease*, 173.

33. Unpublished assessments of World War II personalities, Box 7, Post-Pres Papers, A–WR series, EL.

34. DDE, *At Ease*, 173–74.

35. Miller, *Ike the Soldier*, 186, and DDE, *At Ease*, 173.

36. Dale E. Wilson, "Patton, Eisenhower and the Birth of American Armor," paper presented to the Society for Military History, May 1993.

37. Roger H. Nye, *The Patton Mind* (Garden City Park, N.Y., 1993), 50–51, and DDE, *At Ease*, 176–77. Eisenhower's decision was prompted by an incident in which an officer who had no poker sense suffered heavy losses and was obliged to pay his debt with one of his wife's precious fifty dollar savings bonds. The next night Eisenhower and two friends deliberately lost fifty dollars, a task made far more difficult by the man's incompetence.

38. Dwight D. Eisenhower, *Crusade in Europe* (London, 1948), 47.
39. Stephen E. Ambrose, "A Fateful Friendship," *American Heritage*, Apr. 1969.
40. Most of Eisenhower's correspondence with Patton during the interwar years disappeared when one of his steamer trunks was lost en route from the Philippines to the United States in 1939. The handful of letters from Patton that survive in the Eisenhower Library are dated after 1939.
41. "Tanks with Infantry," copy in USAMHI archives, also quoted in Hofmann, "The Demise of the U.S. Tank Corps and Medium Tank Development Program." This document is erroneously thought to have been written while Eisenhower was a student at the Command and General Staff School, Fort Leavenworth, in 1925–26. However, the matter is cleared up in Holt and Leyerzapf, *Eisenhower: The Prewar Diaries*, 42, n. 1. On the basis of extensive research, the authors believe it was instead written at Camp Meade in 1920 or 1921.
42. D'Este, *Patton*, 299, and Blumenson, *The Patton Papers*, vol. 1, 716–17. Few of the old army cavalrymen had succumbed to the lure of the iron horse, and with its demise only a matter of time, these men remained adamant that one of the most elite arms of the U.S. Army be kept alive. Moreover, peacetime offered a return to the nostalgic days of polo, mounted drill, and the routine of a simpler, romantic life prized by cavalrymen everywhere.
43. Ambrose, *Eisenhower*, 71–72.
44. The best description of Ikky's illness and death is in Susan Eisenhower, *Mrs. Ike*, chap. 5.
45. Susan Eisenhower, quoted in *Mamie Eisenhower*, 48.
46. Mamie Eisenhower, "The Ike I Remember," interview with Barbara Walters, reproduced in *Ladies' Home Journal*, Apr. 1974, and Susan Eisenhower, *Mrs. Ike*, 67. Mamie's memory seems to have been faulty when she told Barbara Walters that she had "held Ike's hand until he was completely gone." In her lengthy oral history taped for the Eisenhower Library, Mamie pointedly omitted any mention of Ikky's death. She did, however, speak of it to her daughter-in-law, Barbara Thompson Eisenhower, shortly before her own death in November 1979.
47. Letter, DDE to Louis Marx, Jan. 27, 1948, Pre-Pres Papers, EL.
48. Mamie wrote to her parents that she was "nervous and restless." Only her husband knew how close to the edge she actually was. See MDE to her parents, Jan. 31, 1921, Box 1, Barbara Thompson Eisenhower Papers, EL, and Susan Eisenhower, *Mrs. Ike*, 74.
49. Brandon, *Mamie Doud Eisenhower*, 122.
50. Susan Eisenhower, *Mrs. Ike*, 73–4.
51. DDE, *At Ease*, 181. In 1952 Eisenhower confessed in a letter to his mother-in-law that his inability to talk about Ikky's death stemmed in part from his belief that the bereaved should be granted "privacy of heart and mind." (See Susan Eisenhower's remarks in *Mamie Eisenhower* [Gettysburg, Pa., 1998], 51, the published version of a centennial seminar about MDE held at the Eisenhower National Historic Site in November 1996.)
52. DDE, *At Ease*, 181–82. Ike and Mamie believed the most likely source of Ikky's illness to have been the Eisenhowers' maid, whom they had hired a short time before. (See Susan Eisenhower, *Mrs. Ike*, 68–69.)
53. Miller, *Ike the Soldier*, 193.
54. Julie Nixon Eisenhower, *Special People*, 198–99.

14. "THE MAN WHO MADE EISENHOWER"

1. "Memorandum for the Adjutant General," Dec. 14, 1921, Box 22, Pre-Pres Papers, EL. The wording of the memo was the substance of what clearly amounted to a letter

of reprimand. It did not advance Eisenhower's defense that he was a West Pointer and therefore held to a higher standard and, in fact, it made what he had done all the more inexcusable in the opinion of the IG. "Your admitted ignorance of the law," wrote the assistant chief of staff of the army, "is to your discredit, and your failure to take ordinary precautions to obtain from proper authority a decision as [to] the validity of your claims, is, in an officer of your grade, likewise to your discredit. . . . A copy of this letter will be filed in your [official] record." (The complete record of the Inspector General investigation of Eisenhower is in National Archives II, RG 159, Box 605, Correspondence 1917–34, Office of the [Army] Inspector General. Portions are also in Box 22, Pre-Pres Papers, Misc. Files, EL.)

2. None of Eisenhower's efficiency reports from 1921–22 reflects any mention of the IG investigation or his subsequent reprimand.

3. Charles H. Brown, "Fox Conner: A General's General," *Journal of Mississippi History* (Aug. 1987). Brown's article was based on a 1964 interview with Eisenhower.

4. Quoted in Michael E. Bigelow, "Brigadier General Fox Conner and the American Expeditionary Forces" (master's thesis, Temple University, 1984, copy in GCML.

5. DDE, quoted in Brown, "Fox Conner."

6. Ambrose, *Eisenhower*, 73, and Blumenson, *The Patton Papers*, vol. 1, passim. Patton had reverted to the cavalry and had been assigned to Fort Myer, Virginia, since September 1920 and could not have introduced Eisenhower to Conner at Camp Meade in 1921. Eisenhower himself later wrote in *At Ease* that Conner invited him to become his executive officer in Panama shortly after their first meeting. Conner, however, was not transferred from Washington to Panama until November 1921, and the offer could only have come a short time earlier.

7. D'Este, *Patton*, 294.

8. Fox Conner's wife, Virginia, credits Patton with recommending Eisenhower to accompany him to Panama. There is, however, no independent corroboration of this fact, and Mrs. Conner's version remains suspect. (See Virginia Conner, *What Father Forbad* [Philadelphia, 1951], 109.)

9. MDE oral history, EL.

10. Ibid.

11. Ibid.

12. Julie Nixon Eisenhower, *Special People*, 200.

13. Susan Eisenhower, *Mrs. Ike*, 77.

14. Virginia Conner, *What Father Forbad*, 120.

15. Virginia Conner, quoted in David, *Ike & Mamie*, 90.

16. Lyon, *Eisenhower*, 58–59.

17. Clarence G. Lasby, *Eisenhower's Heart Attack* (Lawrence, Kans., 1997), 37.

18. DDE, *At Ease*, 185.

19. F. Douglas Mehle, "Sponsorship," *Army* (Mar. 1978).

20. Cole Kingseed, "Mentoring General Ike," *Military Review* (Oct. 1990).

21. Virginia Conner, *What Father Forbad*, 120.

22. Kingseed, "Mentoring General Ike."

23. Box 4, DDE personnel records, 1910–78, EL.

24. Brown, "Fox Conner."

25. DDE, *At Ease*, chap. 13, passim. Interestingly, as biographer Merle Miller points out, Eisenhower spent more time in *At Ease* discussing his training and exploits in Panama with Blackie than he did describing the major individuals in his life. (Miller, *Ike the Soldier*, 211.)

26. Brown, "Fox Conner."

27. Ibid.

28. MDE oral history, EL.

29. Susan Eisenhower, quoted in *Mamie Eisenhower*, 51.

30. Susan Eisenhower, *Mrs. Ike*, 80. Katherine Herrick remained in the employ of the Eisenhowers for four years.
31. Virginia Conner, *What Father Forbad*, 120–21.
32. Susan Eisenhower, *Mrs. Ike*, 83.
33. MDE, quoted by Susan Eisenhower, in *Mamie Eisenhower*, 52.
34. Susan Eisenhower, *Mrs. Ike*, 83, *Mamie Eisenhower*, 52.
35. See Mattingly, DDE health compilation, Box 1, Mattingly Papers, EL, and "DDE Medical Records, 1910–1945," PO Box 2, Snyder Papers, EL. The real reason Eisenhower preferred surgery seems to have been the knowledge that a close friend had died from acute appendicitis. One of several apocryphal tales of DDE and his famous appendix operation appeared in Demaree Best, "The Army's Favorite General," *Saturday Evening Post*, Oct. 3, 1942.
36. David, *Ike & Mamie*, 86, and JSDE, *Strictly Personal*, passim.
37. JSDE, *Strictly Personal*, 1.
38. Quoted in Miller, *Ike the Soldier*, 216.
39. Ibid.
40. Bradford G. Chynoweth, *Bellamy Park* (Hicksville, N.Y., 1975), 100.
41. Letter, Chynoweth to Col. George S. Pappas, Oct. 24, 1987, Chynoweth Papers, USAMHI. Chynoweth and the other two battalion commanders were placed in a no-win position by Connor, who insisted on dictating the terms of a sentence for anyone convicted by court-martial. Predictably, Chynoweth refused to bow. "I told Ike openly that while I wanted to back the C.G. I would not relinquish my duty to vote . . . according to my conscience."
42. Dwight D. Eisenhower, *Mandate for Change* (Garden City, N.Y., 1963), 440–42.
43. Miller, *Ike the Soldier*, 224, based on Miller's interview with Fox Conner's son, who also noted his father's observation that the chief, Maj. Gen. John L. Hines, was frequently intoxicated when he showed up for work.
44. Frank Van Riper, "The Man Who Made Eisenhower," *Sunday News* (n.p.), Apr. 13, 1969, copy in DDE Vertical File, EL.

15. "A WATERSHED IN MY LIFE"

1. Letter, Third Corps to the Adjutant General, War Dept., July 25, 1924, Records of the Adjutant General's Office, RG 407; and RG 98, "Army Schools, 1917–1925," Box 9, National Archives.
2. Endorsement to letter of July 25, 1924, dated Aug. 1, 1924. (Copies also in Box 22, Pre-Pres Papers, Misc. Files, EL.)
3. *Baltimore Evening Sun*, Nov. 10, 1924.
4. Efficiency report (Sept. 27 to Dec. 15, 1924), Box 4, DDE personnel records, 1910–1978, EL.
5. Quoted in Mark C. Bender, *Watershed at Leavenworth: Dwight D. Eisenhower and the Command and General Staff School* (Leavenworth, Kans., 1990, CGSC monograph), 37.
6. Letter, Chief of Infantry to the Adjutant General, War Department, Jan. 30, 1925, National Archives, copy furnished the author by archivist Timothy K. Nenninger.
7. There is no known record of any such note or letter in DDE's personnel records or elsewhere.
8. Patton, "Notes on the Command & General Staff School Course," Box 59, Patton Papers, LC.
9. The first school established at Fort Leavenworth was the School of Application for Infantry and Cavalry (1881), later the U.S. Infantry and Cavalry School (1886). At the turn of the century Secretary of War Elihu Root established four schools for junior officers, two of which were the School of the Line (formerly the Infantry and Cavalry

School) and the General Staff School, to train staff officers. When the Army War College in Washington, D.C., took over the functions of the latter, what emerged was the Command General Staff School, whose mission was "to train officers in the use of combined arms in the division and corps and the command and staff functions for division and corps as they related to tactics and logistics." (See Jonathan M. House, "The Fort and the New School, 1881–1916," passim, in John W. Partin, ed., *A Brief History of Fort Leavenworth, 1827–1983* [Leavenworth, Kans., 1983].)

10. A notable exception was Pershing, who failed to receive an appointment in 1889, at a time when the prestige of the school had yet to be fully established, and before it became a college for future staff officers.

11. The curriculum covered a wide variety of subjects, ranging from tactics and logistics to every aspect of operations at the division, corps, and army level. (Sources about Fort Leavenworth and the curriculum are: Timothy K. Nenninger, *The Leavenworth Schools and the Old Army* [Westport, Conn., 1978], Boyd L. Dastrup, *The U.S. Army Command and General Staff College: A Centennial History* [Fort Leavenworth, Kans., 1982], Elvid Hunt, *History of Fort Leavenworth, 1827–1937* [Fort Leavenworth, Kans., 1937], and Partin, *A Brief History of Fort Leavenworth*.)

12. Chynoweth, *Bellamy Park*, 121.

13. Ibid.

14. A rare exception was one of Eisenhower's classmates, an iconoclastic cavalryman named Terry de la Mesa Allen, who later commanded the 1st Infantry Division in North Africa and Sicily in 1942–43, and the 104th Division in Northwest Europe in 1944–45. The fun-loving Allen managed to start off on the wrong foot the very first day by cutting class to keep a tennis date with a senior officer's attractive blond daughter. Not surprisingly the commandant, General King, called him the "most indifferent student ever enrolled there." (Carlo D'Este, *Bitter Victory: The Battle for Sicily, 1943* [New York, 1988], 269.)

15. Ambrose, *Eisenhower*, 80.

16. MDE oral history, EL. The bed was later the only item from Abilene in the Eisenhowers' retirement home in Gettysburg.

17. JSDE, *Strictly Personal*, 1–2.

18. DDE, *At Ease*, 203.

19. Patton asked Eisenhower to return the notes, which were an inch thick, and later wrote in the margin of the title page, "Prepared by Major G. S. Patton, Jr., GSC (Cav), Honor Graduate, C&GS, 1924. Every user of these notes has graduated from the Command and General Staff School in either the honor or Distinguished Group— G.S.P., Jr." (Nye, *The Patton Mind*, 61, and Box 59, Patton Papers, LC.)

20. The most useful account of Eisenhower's year at Leavenworth is in Bender, *Watershed at Leavenworth*.

21. Nenninger, *The Leavenworth Schools and the Old Army*, 105, and Ed Cray, *General of the Army: George C. Marshall, Soldier and Statesman* (New York, 1990), 36. Marshall attended the School of the Line and finished first in a one-year course of instruction. Those in the top half then attended a year at the Staff College. By the time Eisenhower attended in 1925–26, the two schools had evolved into the Command and General Staff School.

22. Quoted in Bender, *Watershed at Leavenworth*, 49–50.

23. Susan Eisenhower, *Mrs. Ike*, 89.

24. Bender, *Watershed at Leavenworth*, 44.

25. Lt. Gen. John T. Leonard, oral history, EL, and letter, Brig. Gen. Edgar T. Collins to DDE, Aug. 26, 1927, Pre-Pres Papers, EL. Previous biographies assert that the other competitor whom he barely beat out was his close friend Gee Gerow, who was said to have finished a mere two-tenths of a point behind Eisenhower. Although Gerow was an honor graduate, he actually finished 11th in a graduating class of 245 students.

The number two graduate was Maj. Charles M. Busbee, a 1915 West Point classmate, whose score of 92.85 was .23 points behind Eisenhower's.

Eisenhower scored 93.08 out of a possible 100. Gerow's score was 91.37. In *At Ease* Eisenhower modestly mentions only that he and Gerow attained "high marks." The mistaken attribution of Gerow as number two likely comes from Eisenhower, whose memory was faulty in this instance. (Bender, *Watershed at Leavenworth*, 52–53.)

26. Quoted in Brandon, *Mamie Doud Eisenhower*, 15, 158.
27. Quoted in Bender, *Watershed at Leavenworth*, 55.
28. Neal, *The Eisenhowers*, 28, and McCullough, *Truman*, 72–73.
29. Quoted in Lyon, *Eisenhower*, 65, fn.
30. GSP to DDE, July 9, 1926, Box 91, Pre-Pres Papers. Patton's letter is frequently quoted by, among others, Ambrose in *Eisenhower*, 82, and Bender, *Watershed at Leavenworth*, 47.
31. Bender, *Watershed at Leavenworth*, 47. The notebook clearly seems to have helped but, as he would during World War II, Patton tended to underestimate the brilliance of Dwight Eisenhower.
32. GSP to DDE, July 9, 1926, Box 91, Pre-Pres Papers, EL, and Ambrose, *Eisenhower*, 82.
33. "A Young Graduate," "The Leavenworth Course," *Infantry Journal*, June 1927. Although the article was published written anonymously, the author was clearly Eisenhower. Research by such Leavenworth scholars as Tim Nenninger and Mark Bender overwhelmingly establishes DDE as the author. Moreover, the writing itself is pure Eisenhower. He never revealed that he was the author or why he chose to remain unnamed. See also letter, Timothy K. Nenninger to Richard M. Swain, July 18, 1989, copy in EL.
34. Cray, *General of the Army*, 37.
35. Lyon, *Eisenhower*, 63.
36. Nenninger, *The Leavenworth Schools and the Old Army*, 106.

16. FORT BENNING, WASHINGTON, AND FRANCE, 1926–29

1. McCallum, *Six Roads from Abilene*, 114.
2. Accounts vary wildly about who did what to whom: (*1*) that David said that at age sixty-three he could still best any of his sons (Miller, *Ike the Soldier*, 232); (*2*) that Dwight issued the challenge but hoped to avoid embarrassing his father when he beat him—which Kenneth Davis says he did (*Soldier of Democracy*, 218); (*3*) that David, not Dwight, won or drew the match; and (*4*) DDE states the match never took place, while Milton recalls such a match but at a different time and outcome. (Miller, *Ike the Soldier*, 232, and Box 21, DDE, Pre-Pres Papers, Misc. File.)
3. Kornitzer, *The Great American Heritage*, 49, and McCallum, *Six Roads from Abilene*, 83.
4. Miller, *Ike the Soldier*, 232.
5. Davis, *Soldier of Democracy*, 215.
6. Susan Eisenhower, *Mrs. Ike*, 90. Several years later Mike and her husband took John into the Colorado countryside without informing anyone of their whereabouts. When seven-year-old John was found missing, the family panicked and thought he had been kidnapped.
7. After World War II the U.S. Army War College moved to its present location in Carlisle, Pa.
8. Efficiency report, Aug. 1926 to Jan. 1927, Box 4, DDE Personnel File, 1910–1973, EL.
9. Milton too became proficient at making his own well-aged whiskey in his basement, thus earning himself "a reputation for making the best homemade bourbon in

Washington.... Once again," Milton's biographers wrote, "their Abilene background served the Eisenhowers well." (Ambrose and Immerman, *Milton S. Eisenhower*, 48.)

10. Ibid., 40.
11. Neal, *The Eisenhowers*, 76.
12. Ibid., 74.
13. Interview of Milton S. Eisenhower by Stephen Ambrose, in *Eisenhower*, 83.
14. Ambrose and Immerman, *Milton S. Eisenhower*, 40. David Eisenhower rarely wrote letters, but he did send Helen a note of welcome rather plaintively hoping she and Milton would visit them in Abilene after their marriage. "I am sure," he wrote, "we shall love you very much for your own self and also as one of the family. I am sure this invitation needs no repetition and you will come." (David J. Eisenhower to Helen Eakin, May 6, 1927, Box 4, Milton Eisenhower Papers, 1938–1973, EL.)
15. Ambrose, *Eisenhower*, 83, and Davis, *Soldier of Democracy*, 241.
16. Perret, *Eisenhower*, 117.
17. Ambrose and Immerman, *Milton S. Eisenhower*, 48.
18. JSDE, *Strictly Personal*, 11.
19. Brandon, *Mamie Doud Eisenhower*, 141.
20. JSDE, *Strictly Personal*, 9.
21. Ibid., 8.
22. Ibid., 10–11.
23. Ibid., 11–12.
24. Frank E. Vandiver, *Black Jack: The Life and Times of John J. Pershing*, vol. II (College Station, Tex., 1977), 1062.
25. Forrest C. Pogue, *George C. Marshall: Education of a General, 1880–1939* (New York, 1963), 219. (Dr. Pogue was Marshall's official biographer.)
26. See also D'Este, *Patton*, chap. 20, passim.
27. The American Battle Monuments Commission was established by law in 1923 as an independent agency of the executive branch and remains so today.
28. "Pershing and the ABMC," unpublished essay by Roger Cirillo, former ABMC historian.
29. When Eisenhower reported for duty with the ABMC, the problem he encountered was that there was no viable plan for the future, and no one really knew what to do with the material collected. Eventually it became the grist for an official history and the published battlefield guidebooks. The original intent, however, was merely to mark the battlefields. Grave registration and cemeteries were then the responsibility of the quartermaster general. After the war a series of makeshift, unsanctioned memorials began appearing in and around various battlefields. Pershing resolved that suitable memorials be established and maintained by the U.S. government in perpetuity. In time the mission of the ABMC evolved into one of maintaining all American overseas cemeteries and memorials.
30. Lyon, *Eisenhower*, 63–64. As is frequently the case with government publications, Eisenhower's name as the author is missing.
31. D'Este, *Patton*, 272–73.
32. DDE efficiency report, Jan. through June 1927. The endorsement was by a different chief of infantry than Eisenhower perceived had been biased against him in the early 1920s. A superior rating from the ABMC was qualified by a rating of only "above average" by the chief of infantry's executive officer for his part-time duties as detachment commander. However, given the tendency during the prewar years to render efficiency reports based on real rather than inflated, career-enhancing ratings, Eisenhower's report in 1927 was not deemed adverse, nor did it deter his selection to attend the War College.

33. DDE quoted in Neal, *The Eisenhowers*, 72–73.
34. Benjamin F. Cooling, "Dwight D. Eisenhower at the Army War College, 1927–1928," *Parameters* 5, no. 1 (1975). (Eisenhower's paper is in the Pre-Pres Papers, EL.)
35. Quoted in ibid.
36. Memo, W. D. Connor to DDE, May 5, 1928, Connor folder, Box 23, Pre-Pres Papers, and DDE efficiency report, Dec. 1927 to June 1928.
37. MDE oral history. Eisenhower disingenuously wrote that the choice between duty in the War Department or a year in France with the ABMC made his decision easy. (*At Ease*, 205.)
38. Ibid. Eisenhower biographer Geoffrey Perret points out that had Eisenhower accepted the War Department job he would probably have been miserable serving under an unpopular chief of staff, Charles P. Summerall, "a small-minded, mean-spirited and vindictive man" who was "a mental bully and a reactionary." Summerall was a patron of the school of military thought propounded by Britain's Field Marshal Sir Douglas Haig: that battles were won by means of massive frontal assaults by infantry who were scarcely more than cannon fodder. (Perret, *Eisenhower*, 100–01.)
39. "Three Years with Eisenhower, Reminiscences," Box 7, Harry C. Butcher Papers, EL. Butcher's personal reminiscences of his long friendship with Eisenhower are related in this unpublished manuscript. The tale of Eisenhower's attempts to learn French was related to Butcher in 1943.
40. Miller, *Ike the Soldier*, 241, and DDE, *At Ease*, 206.
41. Brandon, *Mamie Doud Eisenhower*, 167. They also occasionally attended Paris theater performances. Eisenhower's phenomenal memory, however, did not extend to remembering much about what he had seen. He once commented that they had seen "the show that has 'Old Man River' in it—whatever that is." (Susan Eisenhower, *Mrs. Ike*, 98.)
42. MDE oral history, EL.
43. D. L. Kimball, *I Remember Mamie* (Fayette, Iowa, 1981), 83.
44. Brandon, *Mamie Doud Eisenhower*, 165–66.
45. George A. "Bo" Horkan, Jr., interview by the Eisenhower National Historic Site, Gettysburg, Pa.
46. JSDE, *Strictly Personal*, 3–4.
48. Eisenhower had experienced abdominal pain and nausea twice in 1927 and in April 1929. Mamie likewise experienced periodic stomach distress—a condition both are thought to have acquired in Panama. (See Mattingly, "Compilation of the General Health Status of Dwight D. Eisenhower," and Susan Eisenhower, *Mrs. Ike*, 99.)
48. Eisenhower-Gruber travel diary, Aug. 28, 1929–Sept. 5, 1929 (written by both Gruber and DDE, they titled it the "Gruber-Eisenhower Expedition"), Box 1, William R. Gruber Papers, EL.
49. DDE, *At Ease*, 206. Eisenhower's recollections of his year in France mellowed in the fullness of time. As NATO supreme commander after World War II, he insisted that two of his personal staff take the afternoon off to see Paris. One of his favorite haunts in 1928–29 had been the Musée Grévin, a Parisian equivalent of Madame Tussaud's Wax Museum in London. Extolling its virtues, Eisenhower sent them on their way. Afterward one of the officers remarked: "Do you *really* suppose this was the most exciting spot he could find when he was still in his thirties?"
50. Chief of Staff Diary, Box 22, Pre-Pres Papers, EL, hereafter referred to as COS Diary. This document was penned periodically by DDE during his War Department service. In it he recorded his thoughts, observations, and personal evaluations of those for whom he worked or knew.
51. Copies in the Thomas North Papers, EL.
52. DDE efficiency reports: July 1, 1928–June 30, 1929 and July 1, 1929–Nov. 8, 1929. The latter was not submitted until August 9, 1930. Eisenhower should have had an

endorsing officer (usually by his superior's superior) add his comments, but for unknown reasons Price was his only rater. By contrast, Pershing had lavishly praised his service in August 1927 in a letter to the chief of infantry in "appreciation of the splendid service which he had rendered since being with us . . . he has shown superior ability not only in visualizing his work as a whole but in executing its many details in an efficient and timely manner."

53. In 1938 the army published *American Armies and Battlefields in Europe*, a greatly expanded version of the original booklet written by Eisenhower in 1927. The acknowledgments pointedly omit Eisenhower's name despite the fact that his pioneering work at the ABMC made it possible. Full credit went to his nemesis, Xenophon Price, who was still the commission secretary and under whose personal supervision the book has been prepared." (The book was reprinted in 1992 by CMH.)

54. Susan Eisenhower, *Mrs. Ike*, 107.

17. "NOTHING SHORT OF A GENIUS"

1. Pershing was the only American officer ever accorded the five-star rank of General of the Armies. After World War II, Eisenhower, Marshall, Bradley, MacArthur, and "Hap Arnold were all promoted to five-star General of the Army. Five-star rank has since been abolished.

2. Quoted in Cray, *General of the Army*, 110, and Kingseed, "Mentoring General Ike." Marshall would later be astonished to learn how highly Fox Connor thought of him. "Fox Connor never hinted to me that I made such an impression on him." (Quoted in DDE, "Churchill-Marshall," unpublished memoir, Aug. 24, 1967, Box 8, Post-Pres Papers [Augusta–Walter Reed Series], EL.)

3. Oral history interview with DDE, July 13, 1967, by Raymond Henle, director, Herbert Hoover Presidential Library, West Branch, Iowa.

4. Cray, *General of the Army*, 54.

5. Ibid., 56.

6. Harold E. Raugh, "Pershing and Marshall: A Study in Mentorship," unpublished research paper, n.d., GCML.

7. Pogue, *George C. Marshall: Education of a General*, 153, and Vandiver, *Black Jack*, vol. 2, 798, 800.

8. Larry I. Bland and Sharon R. Ritenour, eds., *The Papers of George Catlett Marshall*, vol. 1, *The Soldierly Spirit: December 1880–June 1939* (Baltimore, 1981), 144.

9. Raugh, quoting James G. Harbord, *The American Army in France, 1917–1919* (Boston, 1936), 430.

10. Cray, *General of the Army*, 85.

11. Pogue, *George C. Marshall: Education of a General*, 208.

12. Vandiver, *Black Jack*, vol. 2, 1064.

13. Cray, *General of the Army*, 105, and Geoffrey Perret, *A Country Made by War* (New York, 1989), 354.

14. Speech by General of the Army Omar N. Bradley to the Association of the U.S. Army, 1964, DDE vertical files, USMA archives.

15. Pogue, *George C. Marshall: Education of a General*, 248.

16. Ibid., 347.

17. Gen. John J. Pershing, *My Experiences in the World War* (New York, 1931), and DDE, *At Ease*, 208–09.

18. Vandiver, *Black Jack*, vol. 2, 1084.

18. THE INDISPENSABLE STAFF OFFICER

1. James, *The Years of MacArthur*, vol. 1, 674, n. 17.
2. Efficiency report, Nov. 9, 1929–June 30, 1930, Box 4, DDE personnel records, 1910–1978, EL.
3. Holt and Leyerzapf, *Eisenhower: The Prewar Diaries*, 232, n. 6.
4. D'Este, *Patton*, 345.
5. Letter, Moseley to DDE, Feb. 18, 1933, Box 4, DDE Personnel Records, EL. Eisenhower, wrote Moseley, possessed "one of those exceptional minds which enables you to assemble and to analyze a set of facts, always drawing sound conclusions and, equally important, you have the ability to express those conclusions in clear and convincing form. Many officers can take the first two steps of a problem, but few have your ability of expression." A disappointed Eisenhower wrote that "much of the kick will be gone because I'm particularly keen about working with Gen. *M*." (COS Diary, Dec. 11, 1930.)
6. Perret, *Eisenhower*, 106.
7. Robert A. Miller, "The United States Army During the 1930s" (Ph.D. diss., Princeton University, 1973).
8. Ibid.
9. One member, Rep. Fiorello La Guardia of New York, summed up their quandary by observing "The subject of equalizing the burdens of war and minimizing the profits of war is about the easiest of any to make a speech on, but probably the most difficult to work out in details." (Rep. Fiorello La Guardia, quoted in Eisenhower, "War Policies," *Cavalry Journal* [Nov.–Dec. 1931].)
10. Robert Montgomery was recommended by Bernard Baruch and warmly endorsed by Eisenhower, whose recommendations had already begun to carry considerable weight.
11. Lyon, *Eisenhower*, 67. Charles P. Summerall (USMA, 1892) was a friend and mentor of George S. Patton.
12. Ambrose, *Eisenhower*, 91.
13. COS Diary, May 18, 1931.
14. Undated DDE oral history interview by Raymond Henle, July 13, 1967, Hoover oral history program, Herbert Hoover Presidential Library, copy in EL.
15. Weigley, *History of the United States Army*, 402.
16. James, *The Years of MacArthur*, vol. 1, 384.
17. Geoffrey Perret, *Old Soldiers Never Die* (New York, 1996), 159. Eisenhower never admitted in *At Ease* that Moseley was anything more than a misunderstood, patriotic American.
18. COS Diary, circa 1932.
19. Eisenhower, "War Policies," *Cavalry Journal*.
20. COS Diary. See also Holt and Leyerzapf, *Eisenhower: The Prewar Diaries*, 100–01, n. 3. Frederick H. Payne served as assistant secretary of war from April 29, 1930, to April 6, 1933.
21. Brandon, *Mamie Doud Eisenhower*, 171.
22. COS Diary, Mar. 28 and Apr. 27, 1931.
23. Once, after coaching an afternoon football game, "Milton asked Ike how his knee was, which it developed later was a stock question all members of the family and close friends put to him. Ike allowed it still wasn't any better but, fortunately, it wasn't worse. Showing the soldier football players of the team he coached how to block and kick hurt at times . . . [however], he'd passed the stage when he worried that he might not pass his physical and have to quit the Army." ("My Three Years with Eisenhower," Box 7, Harry C. Butcher Papers, EL.)
24. Neal, *The Eisenhowers*, 78.
25. MDE oral history, EL. During his guayule trip Eisenhower was appalled that he had

spent five dollars for dinner and drinks in Juarez, Mexico. "Most expensive bust I've been on this trip. . . . Won't do that again," he vowed. (Guayule diary, Apr. 18, 1930, Box 22, Pre-Pres Papers, EL.)

26. MDE oral history, EL.
27. Ibid.
28. DDE to MDE, July 1, 1931, Pre-Pres Papers, Box 23, Misc. Files, EL.
29. MDE to the Douds, Nov. 16, 1934, Box 2, Barbara Thompson Eisenhower Papers, EL.
30. George Horkan oral history interview, ENHS. On another occasion, when young Horkan had attained a new rank in the Boy Scouts, "Major Eisenhower came up with a huge smile and said, 'I believe I have the honor to shake the hand of a second class scout' . . . and he really made me feel like I'd done something."
31. JSDE, *Strictly Personal*, 16.
32. Susan Eisenhower, *Mrs. Ike*, 115–16.
33. A friend who once visited the Eisenhowers remembered how Ike said to his son who was then about five, " 'John, this is a classmate of mine. Can you tell me his name?' John, who was seeing me for the first time, studied me closely for a few moments. 'Boye,' he said triumphantly. Ike laughed at my bewilderment, then said proudly: 'Fritz, this boy has gone over the [1915] yearbook with me so many times that he knows the names that go with the pictures as well as I do.' " (Brig. Gen. Frederic W. Boye, quoted in "From Plebe to President.")
34. JSDE, *Strictly Personal*, 7–8. At John's behest these men became his "blood brothers" by carrying out a ceremonial mixing of blood from a finger. From then on they addressed him as "Blood Brother John."
35. Ibid., 8.
36. JSDE, *Strictly Personal*, 8–9. See also D'Este, *Patton*, chap. 24, passim.
37. Neal, *The Eisenhowers*, 74–75.
38. David, *Ike & Mamie*, 113, fn.
39. Ibid. Butcher relates the story of Eisenhower's inquisitiveness. At dinner one night in the Butcher apartment, Ike was shown a tear-gas fountain pen. "I had never tried it but Ike immediately wanted to see how it worked. Closing behind us the French doors to the small sunroom so the gas wouldn't escape, Ike pressed the button. . . . Soon I had tears in my eyes, as did Ike, but he wasn't satisfied. I came out but Ike stayed. In a minute or two he emerged, happy as a boy but crying like a baby. Our wives also had tears in their eyes, as much from laughter as from the escaping gas, but Ike was satisfied." ("Reminiscence," Box 7, Butcher Papers, EL.)
40. Davis, *Soldier of Democracy*, 239–40, and Perret, *Eisenhower*, 116–17.
41. COS Diary, June 17, 1931. Eisenhower also proudly sent a copy to the Douds, admitting, "I think Mamie had a cheap frame put on the original simply to preserve it."
42. COS Diary, June 15, 1932. The complete text of Eisenhower's ratings is in Holt and Leyerzapf, *Eisenhower: The Prewar Diaries*, 224–33.
43. Robert Goldston, *The Road Between the Wars, 1918–1945* (New York, 1978), chap. 9 and 189–90.
44. Dwight D. Eisenhower, *Crusade in Europe* (New York/London, 1948), 447.
45. JSDE oral history, EL.
46. COS Diary, Feb. 28, 1933. Eisenhower scorned as "dirty liars!" those ("and there will be plenty") whom he expected to jump onto the recovery train after it had left the station.
47. Susan Eisenhower, *Mrs. Ike*, 42. According to Kenneth Davis, both Dwight and Milton backed Edgar during their contentious debate. However, there remained a whiff of disapproval for brother Earl when Eisenhower complained in his diary that he and Mamie had not heard from him regarding a later visit to Washington. "He will probably drop in some day and very casually remark that he is here . . . a telegram will antedate his arrival by an hour or two."

48. COS Diary, Oct. 29, 1933.
49. Although there were occasional instances of officers selected for higher rank skipping a grade in wartime, there is no known example in modern times of an officer being promoted three grades, in this case from major to brigadier (one-star) general. Before Payne left office on March 4, 1933, he too wrote to congratulate Eisenhower for his performance of duty. (Letter, Payne to the Adjutant General, Mar. 3, 1933, DDE Personnel Files, EL.)
50. COS Diary, Jan. 30, 1932.
51. Ibid., Feb. 15, 1932.
52. Letter, DDE to John S. Doud, Jan. 1932, MDE Papers, EL. See Holt and Leyerzapf, *Eisenhower: The Prewar Diaries*, 212–13, for a complete copy of DDE's letter and additional explanation of its origin.
53. Quoted in David Eisenhower, *Eisenhower: At War, 1943–1945* (London, 1986), 57.

19. "SHAME! SHAME!"

1. An excellent description of the Bonus March and Patton's role in the affair is Lucian K. Truscott's *The Twilight of the U.S. Cavalry* (Lawrence, Kans., 1989), chap. 5.
2. Accounts of the actual size of the Bonus Army vary and are largely dependent on the time frame cited. Initially there were an estimated sixteen to seventeen thousand protesters in Washington before Congress passed the compromise bill authorizing loans to the marchers for transportation home. Some six thousand accepted the offer. The army's official report concluded that on July 28 a maximum of ten to twelve thousand remained in Washington. (See Holt and Leyerzapf, *Eisenhower: The Pre-War Diaries*, 234, the Bonus March File, Pre-Pres Papers, and James, *The Years of MacArthur*, vol. 1, 392.)
3. James, *The Years of MacArthur*, vol. 1, 386–87.
4. Geoffrey Perret, "MacArthur and the Marchers," *MHQ (Military History Quarterly)* (Winter, 1996).
5. COS Diary.
6. Gene Smith, *The Shattered Dream* (New York, 1970), 157–58.
7. Henle interview with DDE, Herbert Hoover Presidential Library.
8. Susan Eisenhower, *Mrs. Ike*, 119, 121, and letter, MDE to the Douds, July 30, 1932, Box 1, Barbara Thompson Eisenhower Papers, EL. Susan Eisenhower points to the Bonus March as an example of her grandfather's penchant for not sharing any details of his army duties with Mamie. ". . . the separation, between work and home was very much in place even during such dramatic times." Mamie's letter to her parents is a good illustration of how Eisenhower's military duties were a closed book he never shared with her. (*Mrs. Ike*, 122, fn.)
9. Smith, *The Shattered Dream*, 161.
10. Perret, "MacArthur and the Marchers."
11. James, *The Years of MacArthur*, vol. 1, 401.
12. Eisenhower may have been wrong about Wright being the bearer of Hoover's order. According to James, Wright delivered a message sometime that afternoon or early evening directly to MacArthur. Wright conveyed to MacArthur that army G-2 (Intelligence) had reliable information that the marchers in Hooverville were armed and intend to fire on his troops if they crossed the Anacostia Bridge. (James, *The Years of MacArthur*, vol. 1, 402.)
13. Henle interview with DDE.
14. Brendon, *Ike*, 63, and Smith, *The Shattered Dream*, 158. MacArthur's belief that this was the start of a Communist uprising throughout the country had absolutely no basis. Although no record of the incident appears anywhere in Patton's personal papers, one account notes that he was hit by a brick that knocked him into the mud

during the melee on the night of July 28. (Smith, *The Shattered Dream*, 164, and Matthew Josephson, *Infidel in the Temple* [New York, 1967], 99–100.)

15. Perret, "MacArthur and the Marchers," Lyon, *Eisenhower*, 73, and transcript of Mac-Arthur's press conference on July 28, 1932, Bonus March File, Box 129, Pre-Pres Papers, EL.
16. Brendon, *Ike*, 63.
17. Unidentified newspaper correspondent quoted in Truscott, *The Twilight of the U.S. Cavalry*, 130.
18. After-action report from the army chief of staff to the secretary of war, Aug. 15, 1932, Bonus March File, Box 129, Pre-Pres Papers, EL.
19. DDE, *At Ease*, 217.
20. Brendon, *Ike*, 63.
21. COS Diary, Aug. 10, 1932.
22. DDE interview with Henle. His bland recollection of the event both in *At Ease* and the Henle interview was hardly a condemnation of either the Bonus March or Mac-Arthur.
23. Perret, *Eisenhower*, 113.
24. COS Diary, Apr. 26, 1934.
25. Eisenhower diary, Dec. 12, 1954, Pres Papers, Ann C. Whitman Diary File, EL.
26. Ambrose, *Eisenhower*, 98.
27. Despite his pitiless stance against the bonus marchers, there was a less visible, more compassionate side to MacArthur. As Geoffrey Perret writes, "A year after the clash on the streets of Washington, a shabby, dejected figure asked to see the army chief of staff. . . . The man was ushered in, and MacArthur recognized him at once. It was Walter Waters. He had come, he said, to ask if MacArthur would help him find work. Before the day was out, MacArthur had gotten him a job as a government clerk—which Waters held for the rest of his life." (Perret, "MacArthur and the Marchers.")

20. TOILING FOR MACARTHUR

1. Arthur MacArthur's Medal of Honor was not awarded until 1889, and then only as the result of intensive lobbying for the medal on his part. (See Perret, *Old Soldiers Never Die*, chaps. 1 and 2, passim.)
2. Perret, *Old Soldiers Never Die*, 154.
3. Quoted in Geoffrey Perret, "My Search for Douglas MacArthur," *American Heritage*, Mar. 1996.
4. James, *The Years of MacArthur*, vol. 1, vii.
5. Lyon, *Eisenhower*, 71, based on his interview with DDE in 1967.
6. Ibid.
7. Joshena M. Ingersoll, *Golden Years in the Philippines* (Palo Alto, Calif., 1971), 192.
8. Perret, *Old Soldiers Never Die*, 194.
9. Ambrose, *Eisenhower*, 93.
10. Gen. Harold K. Johnson interview with D. Clayton James, July 7, 1971, MacArthur Archives.
11. Huntington, *The Soldier and the State*, 367–70, and T. Harry Williams, "The MACS and the IKES," *American Mercury*, Oct. 1952.
12. COS Diary, Mar. 15, 1933.
13. DDE, *At Ease*, 223.
14. Miller, *Ike the Soldier*, 259.
15. Lyon, *Eisenhower*, 77.
16. Perret, *Eisenhower*, 120.
17. Lyon, *Eisenhower*, 71.
18. Perret, *Eisenhower*, 110.

19. William Manchester, *American Caesar* (New York, 1978), 180.
20. MacArthur to DDE, Oct. 12, 1932, Pre-Pres Papers, EL.
21. Second endorsement to DDE efficiency report, July 1931–June 1932.
22. MacArthur gave Eisenhower the title "senior aide"; however, his efficiency reports merely described him as "on duty in Office of Chief of Staff."
23. Perret, *Eisenhower*. 108.
24. Letter, Eisenhower to Capt. John C. Whitaker, May 31, 1934, Box 124, Pre-Pres Papers, EL.
25. JSDE quoted in Holt and Leyerzapf, *Eisenhower: The Prewar Diaries*, xxvii.
26. DDE medical records for 1934, Box 2, Snyder Papers, EL.
27. DDE to Moseley, Sept. 24, 1934, Pre-Pres Papers.
28. In 1967 Eisenhower reflected on America's unpreparedness for both World War II and Korea. "Everybody wants peace. We like to shove under the rug the unpleasant prospects. The reason that we, in times of peace, have always been unready to meet emergencies is because we don't like to think of such possibilities." The mission of the military is precisely the opposite, but during the interwar period, "they said, 'Oh, there are going to be no more wars.' People have been saying that back to the time of . . . Greece." (Henle interview with DDE.)
29. Letter, DDE to John Conklin (the 1915 class representative), Sept. 21, 1934, Box 27, Pre-Pres Papers. It was customary for a friend or classmate to write an obituary, which was published in an annual West Point alumni report. Such tributes now appear in the alumni magazine, *Assembly*. Eisenhower's tribute was never published.
30. Susan Eisenhower, *Mrs. Ike*, 134.
31. Ibid., chap. 9, passim.
32. The actual decision-making power was vested in the Department of Labor, and the army was relegated to the role of administrator. The CCC planted millions of trees and stocked waterways with literally billions of fish, as well as constructing a myriad of other facilities.
33. Robert E. Sherwood, *The White House Papers of Harry Hopkins*, vol. 1, Sept. 1939 to Jan. 1942 (London, 1948).
34. Daniel D. Holt, "An Unlikely Partnership and Service: Dwight D. Eisenhower, Mark Clark, and the Philippines," *Kansas History* (Autumn 1990).
35. Robert H. Ferrell, ed., *The Eisenhower Diaries* (New York, 1981), 6.
36. For a full assessment of MacArthur's turbulent Washington years, see Perret, *Old Soldiers Never Die*, and James, *The Years of MacArthur*, vol. 1.
37. JSDE, *Strictly Personal*, 21.
38. MDE to the Douds, June 25, 1935, Box 2, Barbara Thompson Eisenhower Papers, EL.
39. Susan Eisenhower, "Mamie Eisenhower," lecture presented at an Eisenhower seminar, Nov. 1996, ENHS.
40. Unpublished memoir of Lt. Gen. Robert L. Eichelberger, Eichelberger Papers, USAMHI. Eichelberger tried to reassure Mamie as to how highly MacArthur valued her husband.
41. Quoted by Susan Eisenhower in "Mamie Eisenhower," 55.

21. MISSION IMPOSSIBLE

1. James, *The Years of MacArthur*, vol. 1, 493.
2. A full account of the incident is in ibid., chap. 17, passim.
3. Letter, Bonner F. Fellers to L. A. Davison, Dec. 21, 1967, RG-44, Box 1, Folder 15, MacArthur Archives, Norfolk, Va. Fellers, one of MacArthur's closest confidants, rose from the duties of liaison officer to brigadier general on MacArthur's staff in Australia during World War II.
4. Ferrell, *The Eisenhower Diaries*, 7.

5. MacArthur's remark was thought to have been made on the occasion of Eisenhower's election as president in 1952. MacArthur prefaced his tart comment with: "He'll make a fine president."

6. Eliot A. Cohen, "The Strategy of Innocence? The United States, 1920–1945," in Williamson Murray, ed., *The Making of Strategy* (New York, 1994), 462.

7. Ibid., 442.

8. Brian McAllister Linn, *Guardians of Empire: The U.S. Army in the Pacific, 1902–1940* (Chapel Hill, N.C., 1997), 226–27, 230–31. To have implemented Plan Orange by dispatching the fleet to the Philippines at the first sign of trouble would have been "literally an act of madness," concluded Embrick, who later became the chief of war plans in the War Department, where "he continued to argue for a withdrawal from the indefensible Philippine position."

9. With the exception of two torpedo boats, there were to be no naval or air forces that might otherwise be construed as offensive in nature and thus unnecessarily provoke Japan.

10. Jim Marshall, "Spearhead of Our Defense," *Collier's*, Sept. 5, 1936.

11. Unpublished memoir of Lt. Gen. Robert L. Eichelberger, Eichelberger Papers, USAMHI.

12. MacArthur's conception for the new Philippine army was purely defensive and based upon the Swiss system of citizen soldiers called to serve the state in time of national peril and defend the Philippine homeland from invasion. Given the terrain and conditions in the Philippines, the notion of using as a model a small, independent, mountainous nation with natural defenses, a strong economy, and an existing professional militia that rivaled some of the regular armies of other nations was improbable.

13. James, *The Years of MacArthur*, vol. 1, 501, and DDE Philippine diary, first entries, Nov. 1935–May 29, 1936, Box 24, Misc. File, Pre-Pres Papers, EL.

14. Holt and Leyerzapf, *Eisenhower: The Prewar Diaries*, 285.

15. Perret, *Eisenhower*, 123. Some of his classmates rated Jimmy Ord the brightest light in the class of 1915, "who added more sparkle and gaiety to our cadet days than any other member of the Corps." (Tribute to Ord by classmate C. H. Tenney, "USMA Class of 1915 Bios," USMA Archives.)

16. By 1941 the more modest goals recommended by Eisenhower and Ord, of a small cadre of professional soldiers numbering about eight thousand backed by ten reserve divisions, were a reality. The object was to train an estimated forty thousand Filipino reservists annually, with a goal of a ten-division reserve force by 1946. Although by 1941 the entire Philippine defense force did consist of the planned numbers, the army was woefully undertrained and equipped. The only professional soldiers were the eight thousand–strong Philippine Scouts, who were incorporated in 1941 into the U.S. Army's Philippine Division, commanded by Maj. Gen. Jonathan Wainwright. (See Perret, *Eisenhower*, 125, and I.C.B. Dear, ed., *The Oxford Companion to World War II* [Oxford, 1995], 877–78.)

17. MacArthur's salary was the equivalent of $122,735 per month in 1989 dollars. (*The Value of a Dollar*, 2.)

18. DDE oral history interview with D. Clayton James, Aug. 29, 1967, EL, and James, *The Years of MacArthur*, vol. 1, 506.

19. DDE Philippine diary, Feb. 15, 1936.

20. Lyon, *Eisenhower*, 81, quoted from his interview with DDE in Aug. 1967.

21. DDE Philippine diary, Oct. 8, 1937.

22. JSDE, in Holt and Leyerzapf, *Eisenhower: The Prewar Diaries*, xxvii.

23. Letter, DDE to JSDE, Mar. 2, 1967, Box 20, Post-Pres Papers, EL.

24. Maj. Gen. John E. Hull, interview with D. Clayton James, June 23, 1971, MacArthur Archives.

25. DDE Philippine diary, May 29, 1936, second entry. Another issue that divided the two

men was MacArthur's confident prediction that Kansan Alf Landon would win the 1936 presidential election and oust his adversary, FDR. When Davis and Eisenhower advised MacArthur that Landon would be lucky even to carry his home state, "we came in for a terrible bawling out over a most ridiculous affair. . . . We couldn't understand the reason for his almost hysterical condemnation of our stupidity until he suddenly let drop that he had gone out and urged Q[uezon] to shape his plans for going to the United States on the theory that Landon will be elected." Both Eisenhower and Ord were chastised as " 'fearful and small-minded people who were afraid to express judgments that are obvious from the evidence at hand.' Oh hell." (DDE Philippine diary, Sept. 26, 1936.)

26. Cables, MacArthur to Maj. Gen. William D. Connor, Sept. 15, 1936, and to the War Department, Jan. 4 and 5, 1937, Box 117, Pre-Pres Papers, EL.

27. Letter, DDE to Col. G. A. Lincoln, Sept 6, 1967, Box 20, Post-Pres Papers, EL.

28. Letter, DDE to Col. Joseph Sullivan, Oct. 7, 1941, Box 112, Pre-Pres Papers, EL.

29. Although her affection for Gerow never flagged, Mamie was indignant when she learned that he had remarried while they were in Manila. Mamie never warmed to Gerow's second wife, who in her eyes was a pale imitation of Katie Gerow. (Susan Eisenhower, *Mrs. Ike*, 153.)

30. Susan Eisenhower, *Mrs. Ike*, 136–37.

31. Ibid., and letters, MDE to the Douds, Feb. 13, 1936, and March 31, 1936, Box 2, Barbara Thompson Eisenhower Papers, EL.

32. Susan Eisenhower, *Mrs. Ike*, 137–38.

33. Over the years Eisenhower's hair loss had continued unabated, and when it came to their progressive baldness, Eisenhower and his friend Patton willingly tried *any* remedy (no matter how silly) touted to reverse the decline. While attending the Command and General Staff School in 1924–25, Patton was summoned before an academic board for allegedly employing an unauthorized study aid after a classmate "noticed Patton studying under a strange blue light and reported him. Upon questioning, an embarrassed Patton ruefully admitted he bought the light because it supposedly restored his hair. He stopped using the light—he went on getting bald." (Partin, *A Brief History of Fort Leavenworth*, 52.)

34. Perret, *Eisenhower*, 127–28, and Susan Eisenhower, *Mrs. Ike*, 142–44.

35. JSDE, *Strictly Personal*, 22–3, and Brandon, *Mamie Doud Eisenhower*, 196.

36. Susan Eisenhower, "Mamie Eisenhower." Ike and Mamie escaped serious injury when a major earthquake struck Luzon in 1937. Its force propelled a large, very heavy armoire across the Eisenhowers' bed. Ike and Mamie were at a party at the time of the earthquake, or the consequences might well have been serious. "I sat up all night with my clothes on," she wrote the Douds. "The darn things scare me pink." (MDE oral history, EL.)

37. MDE oral history, EL.

38. Susan Eisenhower, *Mrs. Ike*, 147, and Alden Hatch, *Red Carpet for Mamie* (New York, 1954), 164.

39. Brandon, *Mamie Doud Eisenhower*, 187–88.

40. Ken Caulkins, "Ike the Pilot," *Boeing Magazine*, Jan. 1954.

41. "Fledgling at Fifty," unpublished memoir of Eisenhower's first flight at the controls of an aircraft, Pre-Pres Papers, EL. The memoir is thought to have been written in July 1939, after Eisenhower obtained his private pilot's license. Inasmuch as his account was written before he had soloed in May, the event probably took place in early 1937.

42. Brig. Gen. William L. Lee oral history, EL.

43. Gen. Hugh Parker oral history, EL.

44. Jerry Lee, "Get Going, Ike," article about DDE's flying in the Philippines in an unidentified postwar aviation journal, copy in the Vertical File, EL.

45. Brandon, *Mamie Doud Eisenhower*, 189–90, Susan Eisenhower, *Mrs. Ike*, 145–46, and Hatch, *Red Carpet for Mamie*, 164–65.
46. Letter, MDE to the Douds, Easter, 1938, Box 2, Barbara Thompson Eisenhower Papers, EL.
47. DDE Philippine diary, July 31, 1937.
48. DDE, *At Ease*, 226.
49. MDE to the Douds, April 4, 1938, Box 2, Barbara Thompson Eisenhower Papers, EL. Mamie also wrote, "I told him he would have to do what he wanted, as I didn't want any comebacks like the France detail. You know how he blamed me for that."
50. Eisenhower medical records, 1910–45, Box 2, Snyder Papers, EL. According to Dr. Snyder's notes in 1949 after Eisenhower suffered a similar attack, his patient's condition "was undoubtedly due to ileitis."
51. Lee oral history interview, EL, and DDE, *At Ease*, 227–28.
52. DDE and Quezon quoted in C. H. Tenney's tribute to Ord, USMA Archives.
53. Perret, *Old Soldiers Never Die*, 194–95. Another of MacArthur's idiosyncrasies was his refusal, dating to the collapse of his first marriage a decade earlier, to dance with anyone, including his new wife, Jean. When the occasion demanded it, MacArthur solved the problem by designating Eisenhower, Ord, or T. J. Davis to do the honors in his stead.
54. Manchester, *American Caesar*, 202–03. In January 1942, shortly after the Japanese invasion of the Philippines, MacArthur cabled the War Department that in the event of his death, Sutherland would succeed him. Eisenhower's reaction was, "He picked Sutherland, showing that he still likes his bootlickers." (DDE War Department diary, Jan. 23, 1942, Box 26, Pre-Pres Papers, EL.)
55. Perret, *Old Soldiers Never Die*, 288.
56. DDE Philippine diary, June 13, 1938.
57. JSDE, in Holt and Leyerzapf, *Eisenhower: The Prewar Diaries*, xxvii.
58. JSDE, *Strictly Personal*, 25, and Susan Eisenhower, *Mrs. Ike*, 154–55.
59. DDE Philippine diary, Summer/Autumn 1938, passim.

22. "I'M A SOLDIER. I'M GOING HOME."

1. JSDE oral history, EL.
2. MDE oral history, EL.
3. DDE to Mark W. Clark, Sept. 23, 1939, Mark Wayne Clark Collection, the Citadel Archives, South Carolina.
4. Eichelberger unpublished memoir, USAMHI.
5. Ferrell, *Ill-Advised*, 56.
6. Martin Blumenson, *Mark Clark* (New York, 1984), 17.
7. Holt, "An Unlikely Partnership and Service."
8. DDE to Gen. Malin Craig, Aug. 3, 1939, Pre-Pres Papers, EL.
9. DDE Philippine diary, July 20, 1939, EL. Eisenhower indicated in his diary that he too had written Ulio to solicit his assistance.
10. DDE interview with D. Clayton James, Aug. 29, 1967, MacArthur Archives (copy in EL), and DDE, *At Ease*, 231.
11. Gen. Lucius D. Clay, quoted in Jean Edward Smith, *Lucius D. Clay* (New York, 1990), 80–81.
12. James, *The Years of MacArthur*, vol. 1, 365. Quezon thought so highly of Eisenhower that before he left the Philippines, Quezon's secretary, Jorge Vargas, asked Eisenhower to send the president his own personal observations and recommendations after his four years in the Philippines. The report was not completed in time but was completed during the voyage home in December 1939. It contained a candid (but typically dip-

lomatic) twenty-page assessment of every aspect of the Philippines from personnel to defense.

13. DDE, *Crusade in Europe*, 8.
14. Ambrose, *Eisenhower*, 109.
15. Eichelberger unpublished memoir, USAMHI.
16. James, *The Years of MacArthur*, vol. 1, 564.
17. DDE to Col. Norman Randolph, Oct. 6, 1941, Box 94, Pre-Pres Papers, EL.
18. Susan Eisenhower, *Mrs. Ike*, 159, MDE to the Douds, Dec. 15, 1939, Box 2, Barbara Thompson Eisenhower Papers, EL, and DDE to Hugh A. Parker, addendum to letter of Feb. 8, 1941, Misc. Manuscripts, EL.

23. "THIS WORK IS FUN!"

Unless otherwise cited, all correspondence and diary entries are from Eisenhower's Pre-Pres Papers in the EL.

1. Gen. John J. Pershing, quoted in Weigley, *History of the United States Army*, 422.
2. Miller, "The United States Army During the 1930s."
3. Thomas Parrish, *Roosevelt and Marshall* (New York, 1989), 519. Marshall's standing with the president was enhanced by the support of FDR's powerful adviser Harry Hopkins, who also greatly admired him.
4. Ibid., 114, and Christopher R. Gabel, *The U.S. Army GHQ Maneuvers of 1941* (Washington, D.C., 1991), 8. With fewer than 190,000 men in 1939, the Regular Army was well below its authorized strength of 210,000. Moreover, 45,300 of the 176,000 enlisted men were stationed overseas.
5. Parrish, *Roosevelt and Marshall*, 114.
6. DDE to Hugh A. Parker, addendum to letter of Feb. 8, 1941, Misc. Manuscripts, EL. The Fourth Army's area of responsibility extended from the West Coast as far east as Minnesota.
7. DDE Philippine diary, Jan. 25, 1940.
8. Having worn civilian attire for so many years in Washington and Manila, Eisenhower was obliged to purchase new uniforms at heavy personal expense he deeply resented. "It grinds my soul to put out the money," he complained, "but there is no way out unless I retire. Guess I'm hardly ready to do that." Nevertheless the prospect of purchasing a complete new military wardrobe elicited an "Ouch!!" (DDE Philippine diary, Jan. 25, 1940.)
9. Eisenhower, *At Ease*, 236.
10. Until it was recently closed, many of the makeshift wooden structures created to last through World War II were still in use at Fort Ord, California.
11. Maurine Clark, *Captain's Bride, General's Lady* (New York, 1956), 71–72.
12. Blumenson, *Mark Clark*, 44.
13. Miller, *Ike the Soldier*, 310. The two met again in 1943 in North Africa. Eisenhower was then a lieutenant general, and Barr had advanced to the grade of major. Eisenhower immediately recognized his former lieutenant and as the two shook hands, the new Allied commander in chief inquired, "Barr, how did you get promoted so rapidly?" (Miller, 312.)
14. Letter, DDE to Lt. Col. Omar N. Bradley, July 1, 1940.
15. DDE, *Crusade in Europe*, 10.
16. Miller, *Ike the Soldier*, 310.
17. Letter, DDE to Everett S. Hughes, Nov. 26, 1940.
18. Forrest C. Pogue, *George C. Marshall: Ordeal and Hope, 1939–1942* (New York, 1966), 82–83.

19. Letter, DDE to Mark Clark, Sept. 17, 1940.
20. Quoted in Eric Sevareid, *Not So Wild a Dream* (New York, 1969), 482.
21. Samuel Eliot Morison, *American Contributions to the Strategy of World War II* (London, 1958), 11.
22. D'Este, *Patton*, 390. Such comments were typical of Patton's propensity to say things for their shock value to old friends like Eisenhower.
23. Letter, DDE to George S. Patton, Sept. 17, 1940. Patton became the 2nd Armored Division commander on April 11, 1941. He again wrote to Eisenhower on November 1, 1940, "If I were you, I would apply for a transfer to the Armored Corps NOW. There will be at least one vacant shortly. . . . If you have any pull, use it for there will be 10 new generals in this Corps pretty damn soon."
24. Ambrose, *Eisenhower*, 119.
25. Letter, DDE to Mark W. Clark, Oct. 31, 1940. The same day Eisenhower wrote a similar letter to T. J. Davis in which he related Patton's offer. "My ambition is to go, eventually, to the armored outfit . . . as one of his regimental commanders. That would be a swell job, and I only hope the War Department won't consider me too junior in rank to get a regiment." (Letter, DDE to T. J. Davis, Oct. 31, 1940. See also DDE, *At Ease*, 237, and Holt and Leyerzapf, *Eisenhower: The Prewar Diaries*, 491–92.)
26. Letter, DDE to Everett S. Hughes, Nov. 26, 1940.
27. Letter, DDE to Leonard T. Gerow, Nov. 18, 1940, quoted in Holt and Leyerzapf, *Eisenhower: The Prewar Diaries*, 505. Eisenhower ended his letter with, "If war starts, I expect to see you raise the roof to get a command, and *I go along!*"
28. Holt, "An Unlikely Partnership and Service." Eisenhower attempted to repay the favor by recommending Clark as one of the "finest officers in our Army. . . . When you get a chance, get hold of him." Unbeknownst to Eisenhower, Clark was already earmarked for higher rank and more important duties.
29. Letter, MDE to the Douds, Nov. 27, 1940, Box 3, Barbara Thompson Eisenhower Papers, EL.
30. DDE to Hugh A. Parker, addendum to letter of Feb. 8, 1941, Misc. Manuscripts, EL.
31. Susan Eisenhower, *Mrs. Ike*, 164. Tales of army wives abusing their husbands' rank and authority would fill a separate volume. Mark Clark had one such encounter at Fort Lewis when an Army Day display was proclaimed hideous by an officious colonel's wife. "I won't have it!" she said. Clark refused to dismantle the display unless ordered by the colonel himself. The colonel declined to do so. (Maurine Clark, *Captain's Bride, General's Lady*, 80–81.)
32. DDE, *At Ease*, 237.
33. DDE to Hugh A. Parker, addendum to letter of Feb. 8, 1941, Misc. Manuscripts, EL.
34. Ibid.
35. Davis, *Soldier of Democracy*, 263.
36. DDE, "Notes for Colonel Charles H. Corlett," June 1941, Pre-Pres Papers.
37. Miller, *Ike the Soldier*, 320–21. Later in 1941, Eisenhower's newly hired striker, Mickey McKeogh, may have been the only person to assert that his boss, when dressed in his pinks, blouse, and riding boots was "the best dressed soldier in the world," an opinion that would have drawn few converts.
38. DDE, *At Ease*, 240.
39. JSDE, *Strictly Personal*, 28.
40. McCallum, *Six Roads from Abilene*, 111. Although Eisenhower had prevailed in their skirmish with Edgar over John's future, he was destined never to win his perennial war with his elder brother. Ike simply could not resist the temptation to compete with Edgar on the golf course, an uneven playing field where he routinely failed to prevail over his more experienced older brother. A drubbing in *anything* by Edgar was bad enough; however, to be humiliated at a pastime that, until his presidency, was more

hobby than sport whetted his competitive juices to keep trying—and failing. Even when he was fifty, Eisenhower's love-hate relationship with his elder brother remained as fresh as it had been during their youth in Abilene.

41. JSDE, *Strictly Personal*, 32.
42. Ibid., 33.
43. Letter, Lt. Gen. Walter Krueger to Marshall, June 11, 1941, Marshall Papers, GCML.

24. THIRD ARMY CHIEF OF STAFF

1. Letter, DDE to P. A. Hodgson, Nov. 4, 1941, Box 52, Pre-Pres Papers, EL.
2. Letter, DDE to JSDE, Aug. 5, 1941. His letters included questions such as "the name of your wife (roommate)," and "How's your weight?" as well as advice not to eat rich foods.
3. Lt. Gen. LeRoy Lutes oral history, EL.
4. Davis, *Soldier of Democracy*, 266–67, and Susan Eisenhower, *Mrs. Ike*, 169–70.
5. David, *Ike & Mamie*, 104.
6. Brandon, *Mamie Doud Eisenhower*, 207.
7. DDE, *Crusade in Europe*, 148.
8. Davis, *Soldier of Democracy*, 267–68.
9. Gabel, *The GHQ Maneuvers*, 67.
10. Letter, R. W. MacGregor to Krueger, Aug. 31, 1964, Box 40, Krueger Papers, USMA Archives.
11. "General Walter Krueger," Box 40, Krueger Papers,
12. DDE, *Crusade in Europe*, 13.
13. "Turner Catledge Discusses Gen. Douglas MacArthur," interview with D. Clayton James, Mar. 25, 1971, RG 49, Box 1, MacArthur Archives.
14. Letter, Lt. Col. Edwin T. Wheatley to Walter Krueger, Jr., Aug. 21, 1967, Box 3, Krueger Papers.
15. Anonymous description of Krueger's military career, written in 1945, Box 40, Krueger Papers. This document is based on the observations of and input from war correspondents and subordinates.
16. Letter, DDE to George Van Horn Moseley, Aug. 28, 1941, Box 84, Pre-Pres Papers, EL.
17. Letter, DDE to Leonard T. Gerow, Aug. 5, 1941, Box 46, Pre-Pres Papers, EL.
18. Letter, Krueger to Maj. Gen. William S. Bryden, Aug. 2, 1941, Box 3, Krueger Papers, USMA Archives.
19. Perret, *Eisenhower*, 141.
20. Extracted from the *Times Atlas of the Second World War* (New York, 1989). With Britain solely dependent on resupply by sea, German naval strategy was to force her surrender by sinking at least 750,000 tons of shipping each month for a year, thus threatening the sixty million tons of imports a year the British required for survival.
21. Gen. Lesley J. McNair, quoted in Gabel, *The GHQ Maneuvers*, 8.
22. Sevareid, *Not So Wild a Dream*, 201.
23. Pogue, *Marshall: Ordeal and Hope*, 154–55, and Gen. Lesley J. McNair, quoted in Weigley, *History of the United States Army*, 428.
24. Gabel, *The GHQ Maneuvers*, chap. 1, passim.
25. Ibid., 5.
26. A similar exercise was held in Texas in June 1941 by Krueger's Third Army.
27. Pogue, *Marshall: Ordeal and Hope*, 89, and Gabel, *The GHQ Maneuvers*, 64.
28. Brendon, *Ike*, 74.
29. Donald E. Houston, *Hell on Wheels: The 2d Armored Division* (San Rafael, Calif., 1977), chap. 5, passim, and Geoffrey Perret, *There's a War to Be Won* (New York, 1991), 43–44.

30. Letter, DDE to Gerow, Sept. 25, 1941.
31. Marty Snyder, *My Friend Ike* (New York, 1956), 28–31.
32. Thaddeus Holt, "Relax—It's Only a Maneuver," *MHQ* (Winter 1992).
33. Lyon, *Eisenhower*, 86.
34. Drew Pearson and Robert S. Allen, *Washington Merry-Go-Round*, 194, quoted in Davis, *Soldier of Democracy*, 272.
35. See Gabel, *The GHQ Maneuvers*, 111.
36. Russell F. Weigley, *Eisenhower's Lieutenants* (Bloomington, Ind., 1981), 17–19.
37. Gabel, *The GHQ Maneuvers*, 187. Krueger's retention was affirmation that age was not itself necessarily a detriment to keeping competent officers.
38. JSDE oral history, EL.
39. Quoted in the Eichelberger Papers, USAMHI.
40. Gabel, *The GHQ Maneuvers*, 194.
41. Blumenson, *Mark Clark*, 53–54, Perret, *Eisenhower*, 143, and Richard M. Ketchum, *The Borrowed Years, 1938–1941: America on the Way to War* (New York, 1989), 650. McNair had played a similar trick on Clark when he was promoted to brigadier general.
42. Letter, DDE to Aksel Nielsen, Oct. 31, 1941, EL.
43. Letters, DDE to James O. Curtis, Oct. 2, 1941, letter, DDE to Edgar Eisenhower and his wife, Oct. 7, 1941, and DDE to Col. Joseph Sullivan, Oct. 7, 1941, Pre-Pres Papers, EL.
44. McNair memo to GCM, "Higher Commanders," Oct. 7, 1941, and letter, Maj. Gen. George S. Patton to Col. Roger H. Nye, Box 3, Patton Papers, USMA. McNair rated Patton the second best of five armored division commanders, with the caveat that "division [command] is probably his ceiling."
45. Mark Clark, *Calculated Risk* (London, 1956), 21.
46. DDE, *Crusade in Europe*, 16, and MDE oral history, EL. There are several other minor variations on this event, in addition to Mamie's recollection. One is that Tex Lee called, awakening Eisenhower when the telephone on his bedside table rang; another, that an aide came to his quarters with the news.
47. Churchill quoted in Ketchum, *The Borrowed Years, 1938–1941*, 770–71.
48. Weigley, *Eisenhower's Lieutenants*, 12. An indicator of American unpreparedness was that the Italian dictator, Benito Mussolini, scorned the United States as a second-rate power whose industrial capacity was nothing more than a journalistic hoax, and whose military importance was so negligible that its involvement in the war would be of little consequence.
49. DDE, *Crusade in Europe*, 17.
50. Ibid.

25. MARSHALL'S PROTÉGÉ

1. MDE oral history, EL. Eisenhower had been due to address a graduating class of Air Corps lieutenants at nearby Kelly Field that same day. His speech emphasized the duties of a newly commissioned officer, particularly his "high and almost divine duty" to take care of his enlisted men. Eisenhower called it "a challenge to his talents, his patriotism, his very soul." The speech was not delivered by Eisenhower's last-minute replacement who conveyed his own remarks to the new officers. (Holt and Leyerzapf, *Eisenhower: The Prewar Diaries*, 563–65.)
2. Quoted in Hatch, *Red Carpet for Mamie*, 179.
3. Cray, *General of the Army*, 264–65.
4. DDE quotes are from *Crusade in Europe*, 25.
5. DDE manuscript, "Churchill and Marshall," Box 8, Post-Pres Papers, A-WR series, EL.

6. Maj. Ben F. Caffey, quoted in Pogue, *George C. Marshall: Ordeal and Hope*, 337.
7. Ibid., 407.
8. Parrish, *Roosevelt and Marshall*, 117.
9. Cray, *General of the Army*, 150–51.
10. Pogue, *George C. Marshall: Ordeal and Hope*, 337.
11. DDE, "Churchill and Marshall."
12. Cray, *General of the Army*, 330.
13. Eisenhower's address at a ceremony dedicating the George C. Marshall Library at Marshall's alma mater, the Virginia Military Institute, May 23, 1964, copy in GCML.
14. Neal, *The Eisenhowers*, 119, and Michael J. McKeogh and Richard Lockridge, *Sgt. Mickey and General Ike* (New York, 1946), 21. Milton and Helen did their best to make Ike's stay with them comfortable. There was always a hot drink and a snack awaiting him nightly. Eisenhower's greatest pleasure was to awaken his niece and nephew and simply chat for a few moments before they inevitably fell asleep. (Ambrose and Immerman, *Milton S. Eisenhower*, 66.)
15. Letter, DDE to P. A. Hodgson, Mar. 29, 1942, Eisenhower File, USMA Archives.
16. Kevin McCann, quoting John J. McCloy, McCann oral history, EL. McCloy was equally impressed by Eisenhower's writing ability, noting that he possessed clarity of expression to "a very marked degree." McCloy's other confidential reports to Marshall were equally positive. (John J. McCloy oral history, EL.)
17. McCloy oral history, EL.
18. McCann oral history, EL.
19. "George C. Marshall Interviews and Reminiscences for Forrest C. Pogue," George C. Marshall Foundation (Lexington, Va., 1986), 545.
20. Martin Blumenson, "Difficult Birth of a Grand Alliance," *Army*, Dec. 1992.
21. "Marshall Interviews," 545.
22. Marshall noted in his postwar interviews with Forrest Pogue, "Our embarrassment was that we didn't have many troops in England to help with the operation. So it involved a great deal of British troops and matériel. . . . The criticism of SLEDGE-HAMMER is that we had so little and that it could virtually have been destroyed."
23. Warren F. Kimball, *Forged in War* (New York, 1997), 13, and Doris Kearns Goodwin, *No Ordinary Time* (New York, 1994), 310–12. Privately Eleanor Roosevelt never warmed to Churchill and once wrote prophetically that "he's lovable and emotional and very human but I don't want him to write the peace or carry it out." Eleanor was not alone; correspondent Martha Gellhorn remarked how Churchill usually managed to get Roosevelt "steamed up in his boy's book of adventure (Goodwin, 310)."
24. DDE War Department diary, Jan. 6, 1953, Box 22, Misc. File, Pre-Pres Papers, EL.
25. Ibid., Jan. 4, 1942.
26. Ibid., Jan. 2, 1942.
27. Ibid., Jan. 4, 1942. The entry for Jan. 20, 1942, for example, was simply, "One hell of a day."
28. ABDA was created in November 1941 and lasted until February 1942, when Wavell returned to his post in India as commander in chief of British forces.
29. Unpublished biography of Maj. Gen. Orlando Ward by Russell Gugeler, Ward Papers, USAMHI. Ward, a 1915 West Point classmate of Eisenhower, was the War Department secretary of the general staff (SGS) in 1939–41 and in that capacity spent as much time with Marshall as anyone in the War Department. Ward handpicked Lieutenant Colonels Bedell Smith and Bradley, who were assigned to the War Department as assistant SGSs.
30. DDE War Department diary, Feb. 16, 1942, EL.
31. Perret, *Eisenhower*, 148.
32. *Time*, Apr. 13, 1942.

33. The World War II diary of Capt. Harry C. Butcher, USNR, Jan. 26, 1943, EL. Hereafter referred to as Butcher diary. The diary is in the Pre-Pres Papers, Boxes 165-70.

34. Shortly after Eisenhower took charge of WPD it was renamed the Operations Division (OPD).

35. Butcher diary, Jan. 26, 1943, EL.

36. Geoffrey Perret, *Winged Victory: The Army Air Forces in World War II* (New York, 1993), 137.

37. Perret, *Eisenhower*, 156, and oral histories of Brig. Gen. Thomas W. Betts and Col. James Stack, EL.

38. Col. H. Merrill Pasco (a member of Marshall's staff), quoted in documentary film, *George Marshall and the American Century*, 1993.

39. DDE War Department diary, Jan. 27, 1942. Sledgehammer was eventually modified into a plan to seize and hold a bridgehead in the Cotentin Peninsula around the important port of Cherbourg until Roundup could be mounted in 1943.

40. DDE War Department diary, Mar. 21, 1942, EL.

41. Ibid., passim.

42. Some seven thousand American and Filipino soldiers perished from a variety of ailments, wounds, and from Japanese executions of anyone unable to keep up during the horrific death march.

43. Ambrose, *Eisenhower*, 137–38. Three of the six vessels that tried actually succeeded in reaching the Philippines. None tried a second time.

44. Ibid., 138, and DDE to GCM, Sept. 25, 1944, Pre-Pres Papers. The book Eisenhower referred to was Frazier Hunt's *MacArthur and the War Against Japan* (New York, 1944). Eisenhower has denied the existence of an anti-MacArthur clique in the War Department. "This was an illusion either of General MacArthur or of his staff. I never heard General Marshall disparage MacArthur," he said. "In fact, Marshall initiated the move for a Congressional Medal of Honor for MacArthur in 1942. I saw little grounds for awarding this highest medal to him and told Marshall so. . . . But Marshall went ahead in the belief that we should do something and that MacArthur already held all the other medals the Army could give." (DDE interview with D. Clayton James, Aug. 29, 1967, MacArthur Archives.)

45. Eichelberger memoir, and letter to Samuel Milner, Mar. 8, 1954, Eichelberger Papers, USAMHI.

46. MDE oral history, EL.

47. Neal, *The Eisenhowers*, 120. Eisenhower was referring to proposed Anglo-American operations then under consideration for later in 1942.

48. Perret, *Old Soldiers Never Die*, 249–54.

49. Perret, *Winged Victory*, 176–77. Brereton's professed memoirs, *The Brereton Diaries* (New York, 1946), were among the first to be published after the war. Among its misleading contents was a section dealing with the Philippines actually written *after* the war, based on a nonexistent diary. As a defense of Brereton's reputation, the book was a great success; however, as a historical document *The Brereton Diaries* is unreliable and self-serving.

50. On September 18, 1942, Marshall sent Brereton a de facto reprimand in the form of a bluntly worded letter asserting that "your relations with your secretary have given rise to facetious and derogatory gossip in India and in Egypt" and should cease forthwith. (See Larry I. Bland, ed., *The Papers of George Catlett Marshall*, vol. 3, *The Right Man for the Job, Dec. 7, 1941–May 31, 1943* [Baltimore, 1991], 357.)

51. Perret, *Eisenhower*, 153.

52. DDE War Department diary, Jan. 24, 1942, EL.

53. William L. O'Neill, *A Democracy at War* (New York, 1993), 143.

54. Quoted in Dear, *The Oxford Companion to World War II*, 650–51. This compendium is by far the best single-volume reference work on World War II.

55. DDE War Department diary, Mar. 10, 1942, EL.
56. Ibid., Mar. 14, 1942.
57. Ibid., Mar. 11, 1942.
58. Davis, *Soldier of Democracy*, 306–07. Roy Jacob Eisenhower was born on August 9, 1892, and died on June 17, 1942. There is no indication in any biography of Eisenhower (or in his papers) of his reaction to Roy's death. Even Kenneth Davis, who conducted extensive interviews with members of the Eisenhower family and their friends shortly afterward, sheds no light on the subject.

26. "I'M GOING TO COMMAND THE WHOLE SHEBANG"

1. DDE War Department diary, May 6, 1942, EL.
2. Ibid., Mar. 28, 1942, EL.
3. Ibid., Mar. 10, 1942, EL.
4. James MacGregor Burns, *Roosevelt: The Soldier of Freedom* (New York, 1970), 229.
5. Forrest C. Pogue interview with DDE, Pogue interviews, USAMHI, and Pogue, *George C. Marshall: Ordeal and Hope*, 338.
6. DDE War Department diary, May 6, 1942, EL.
7. GSP to DDE, Feb. 20, 1942, Patton folder, Box 91, Pre-Pres Papers, EL.
8. DDE to Patton, Feb. 25, 1942, ibid.
9. GSP to DDE, Apr. 4, 1942, Patton file, CMH.
10. Ibid., May 1, 1942, Box 91, Pre-Pres Papers, EL.
11. DDE, unpublished assessments of World War II personalities, Box 7, Post-Pres Papers, A-WR series, EL.
12. Pogue interview with DDE, Pogue interviews, USAMHI
13. "Churchill and Marshall," Aug. 24, 1967, Box 8, Post-Pres Papers, A-WR Series, EL.
14. DDE War Department diary, Mar. 21, 1942, EL.
15. Brig. Gen. Charles M. Busbee, quoted in "From Plebe to President."
16. Pogue interview with DDE, Pogue interviews, and JSDE oral history, EL. Eisenhower wrote to John in 1967 that "he was not in the least concerned with Marshall's power to promote him," but admitted that it "was scarcely a proper way for a new Brigadier General to address the Army Chief of Staff." (Letter, DDE to JSDE, Mar. 2, 1967, Box 20, Post-Pres Papers.)
17. DDE War Department diary, Mar. 28, 1942, EL. Eisenhower's permanent rank in the Regular Army remained lieutenant colonel.
18. Summersby, *Eisenhower Was My Boss*, 1–3.
19. Gen. Mark W. Clark oral history interview, Clark Papers, USAMHI.
20. Summersby Morgan, *Past Forgetting*, 20–21.
21. Stephen E. Ambrose, *The Supreme Commander: The War Years of General Dwight D. Eisenhower* (London, 1971), 46.
22. Philip Ziegler, *Mountbatten* (New York, 1985), 180–81.
23. DDE War Department diary, June 4, 1942, EL. DDE is also quoted in Ray S. Cline, *The U.S. Army in World War II: The War Department, Washington Command Post: The Operations Division* (Washington, D.C., 1951), 163.
24. Those who dared to tangle with Marshall usually left feeling that they would soon be fired. He placed the hard-nosed Joe McNarney in charge of reorganizing and streamlining the War Department. During their first meeting to discuss the plan, Marshall "suggested some change his subordinate disapproved. McNarney blurted out, 'Jesus, man, you can't do that!'" McNarney believed he had gone too far and would pay the price, only to be reassured by Marshall's executive officer, "Don't worry. He likes for people to speak up."
25. Hatch, *General Ike*, 113.
26. Quoted in Blumenson, *Mark Clark*, 58.

27. Pogue, *George C. Marshall: Ordeal and Hope,* 337.
28. DDE War Department diary, June 11, 1942, EL. Eisenhower's description of his appointment in *At Ease* is just as brief and even less revealing: "General Marshall sent me to London . . . and the desk job in Washington was behind." (250.)
29. Hatch, *Red Carpet for Mamie,* 180–81.

27. THE ARCHITECT OF COOPERATION

Unless otherwise noted, all quotes by Eisenhower in this and succeeding chapters are from the Harry C. Butcher Diary, which is in Boxes 165–70, Butcher diary series, Pre-Pres Papers, EL. Copies of most of Eisenhower's wartime letters to Mamie are in Box 1, JSDE Papers, EL.

1. Quezon's offer was worth $162,100 in 1989 dollars. Its illegality did not prevent Mac-Arthur from accepting a payment of $500,000 in March 1942, nor did it stop Richard Sutherland, who was paid $75,000, or other of MacArthur's senior staff officers, who received lesser sums from the Philippine government. However questionable these payments, they were nevertheless legal under the terms by which MacArthur went to the Philippines in 1935. For a full explanation see Perret, *Old Soldiers Never Die,* 271–72.
2. Michael Howard, *The Mediterranean Strategy in the Second World War* (London, 1968), 7–9. This book comprises essays that were the Lees-Knowles Lectures delivered at Trinity College, Cambridge, in 1966.
3. DDE, *Crusade in Europe,* 58.
4. DDE unpublished manuscript, copy furnished the author by JSDE.
5. Davis, *Soldier of Democracy,* 302–03.
6. Butcher diary, July 24, 1942.
7. DDE to MDE, Mar. 12, 1943. When Butcher was away in the United States in March, 1943, Eisenhower lamented, "I miss Butch all the time. He is a fine, loyal friend."
8. "Three Years with Eisenhower" Box 7, Butcher Papers.
9. JSDE, *Strictly Personal,* 47.
10. Maurine Clark, *Captain's Bride, General's Lady,* 97, and MDE oral history, EL.
11. Alfred D. Chandler, Jr., ed. *The Papers of Dwight David Eisenhower: The War Years* (Baltimore: 1970), vol. 5, 74–75, hereafter referred to as *EP.*
12. MDE oral history, EL.
13. Ibid.
14. Ambrose, *Eisenhower,* 174. Doubtless Eisenhower would have been less than thrilled by the title of an August 29, 1942, profile in the *Christian Science Monitor:* "Little Ike Makes Good." The worst intrusion was by a Chicago reporter who managed to photograph a letter from Ida to her son in the Eisenhower home, which was published along with several others he had obtained without anyone's permission. Such acts are common in the current age of anything-goes ethics, but in the 1940s it was a major breach of press etiquette. (Davis, *Soldier of Democracy,* 311.)
15. MDE oral history, EL, and Susan Eisenhower, *Mrs. Ike,* 196–99.
16. DDE to MDE, Aug. 28, 1942. Eisenhower had also received an earlier note from Bedell Smith that Mamie was ailing.
17. David, *Ike & Mamie,* 219. Mamie's work at the USO was from 11:00 A.M. to 1:00 A.M. She would wait on a deserted street for a taxi to take her home to an empty apartment. With her instability worsening, Mamie later wondered "how in the world I ever did it." (MDE oral history.)
18. Susan Eisenhower, *Mrs. Ike,* 196–99.
19. MDE oral history, EL.
20. Stephen E. Ambrose, *Rise to Globalism,* (New York, 1980), 44.

21. A day-by-day list of visitors and meetings from June 23, 1942 to V-E day, 1945, makes up 116 pages of *EP*, vol. 5.

22. DDE to MDE, Oct. 13, 1942.

23. Butcher was pleased that a friend, George E. Allen, was in London when they arrived. Allen, a wealthy and successful businessman (and a Democrat), became a close friend of Eisenhower. Allen later sold Eisenhower his retirement farm at Gettysburg in 1950. A lifelong crony, the amiable Allen was a good bridge partner and one of those whose presence helped make Eisenhower's scant free time tranquil. Allen, said Butcher, was "a good tonic for Ike."

24. DDE to MDE, Aug. 26, 1942.

25. Gen. Mark W. Clark oral history, Clark Papers, USAMHI.

26. Ibid.

27. "Some Personal Memoirs of Justus "Jock" Lawrence," GCML. Col. Lawrence was chief public relations officer, ETO, and a former Hollywood publicist for film mogul Samuel Goldwyn.

28. Quoted in Davis, *Soldier of Democracy*, 323.

29. Lt. Col. Ernest R. "Tex" Lee, quoted in Davis, *Soldier of Democracy*, 268.

30. Blumenson, *Mark Clark*, 62.

31. Eisenhower was so put off by the social demands on his time and the pressures of his new job that for a time he contemplated moving his headquarters some fifty miles outside London. Reality intervened when General Bolte reminded him that it would take hours to drive to London under wartime conditions. Moreover, it was quite obvious that both Eisenhower and his HQ plainly needed to be near the British military ministries and No. 10 Downing Street. "You can't even drive 20 miles an hour in the blackout," Bolte pointed out. "You'll be so far away, you won't count. Well, he didn't like it and got red in the face . . . but we stayed at Grosvenor Square." (Gen. Charles L. Bolte oral history, EL.)

32. Pogue, *George C. Marshall: Ordeal and Hope*, 408.

33. Arthur Nevins oral history, EL.

34. D. K. R. Crosswell, *The Chief of Staff* (Westport, Conn., 1991), 105.

35. *The Memoirs of Lord Ismay* (London, 1960), 262.

36. Crosswell, *The Chief of Staff*, 297.

37. Monograph by Air Marshal Sir James Robb, "Higher Direction of War," Robb Papers, EL.

38. Dominick Graham and Shelford Bidwell, *Coalitions, Politicians and Generals* (New York, 1993), 258.

39. Summersby, *Eisenhower Was My Boss*, 50.

40. William P. Snyder, "Walter Bedell Smith," *Military Affairs* [now *Journal of Military History*] (Jan. 1984).

41. Ambrose, *Eisenhower*, 187–88.

42. Crosswell, *The Chief of Staff*, 98. If turnaround is fair play, Smith's enemies would have been delighted by the incident one dark night in January 1943 when the MP guarding his villa, suspicious that he might be an enemy paratrooper, challenged Smith, made him place his ID card on the ground, step back ten paces, and then lie flat on his belly until properly identified. Smith refused to admit the incident ever occurred. (Butcher diary, Jan. 27, 1943.)

43. Eisenhower could not avoid attending Ambassador Winant's Fourth of July reception later that day, which he was given to believe would be a small event. Instead he was thrust into the receiving line and obliged to shake hands with all 2,630 attendees. His staff thought it was "a hell of a way to fight a war."

44. Kay Summersby recounts numerous examples of the nonmilitary demands placed on Eisenhower in *Eisenhower Was My Boss*, passim.

45. Butcher diary, Aug. 15, 1942.

46. Joseph E. Persico, *Edward R. Murrow* (New York, 1988), 199.
47. Phillip Knightley, *The First Casualty* (London, 1982), 299.
48. Davis, *Soldier of Democracy*, 310.
49. Perret, *Eisenhower*, 164.
50. Butcher recorded that Eisenhower summoned him into his office, where, with a grin "as wide as a slice of watermelon," he said, "I'm going to get a dog." With tongue in cheek Butcher noted that he "rather thought I was fulfilling that mission as a 'dog's body.'" (Butcher diary, Oct. 8, 1942.)
51. DDE to MDE, Oct. 13, 1942.
52. Summersby, *Eisenhower Was My Boss*, 30–32. Among those "consulted" by Eisenhower over his acquisition of a dog were Ismay and Adm. Sir Bertram Ramsay, the able architect of the Dunkirk evacuation in 1940. It can be legitimately argued that Eisenhower spent an inordinate amount of his valuable time pondering the acquisition of a pet dog. By the time Telek had been acquired for Eisenhower, his pedigree had already been registered with London's exclusive Kennel Club, as later were the offspring of Telek's three litters sired during the war. A semiofficial "201" dog file was maintained on Telek and his offspring by Kay Summersby. Copies are in the "Pedigree, dog" file, Box 153, Pre-Pres Papers, EL.
53. JSDE oral history interview, Eisenhower National Historic Site.
54. McKeogh, *Sgt. Mickey and General Ike*, 34–35.
55. Spaatz, quoted in Edgar F. Puryear, *American Generalship* (Novato, Calif., 2000), 269.
56. Richard G. Davis, *Carl A. Spaatz and the Air War in Europe* (Washington, D.C., 1993), 93. Hereafter cited as Davis, *Spaatz*.
57. Summersby, *Eisenhower Was My Boss*, 6–7.
58. Diary of Maj. Gen. Everett S. Hughes, microfilm copy, USAMHI library. The original is in the Manuscript Division, Library of Congress.
59. DDE to MDE, Aug. 9, 1942. See also letter of Aug. 16, 1942. John's class standing in the autumn of 1942 was also a source of pride. To Mamie he wrote, "Please send him my love and say I'm for him, *flat* out!" (Oct. 13, 1942.)
60. Ibid., Oct. 30, 1942.
61. Summersby, *Eisenhower Was My Boss*, 18.
62. Harry Butcher to Milton S. Eisenhower, Sep. 1, 1942, Box 14, Milton Eisenhower Papers, EL.
63. Ferrell, *Ill-Advised*, 57.
64. DDE to MDE, Feb. 11, 1943.
65. DDE, *At Ease*, 281–82. After learning that smoking was never permitted in the dining rooms of the service clubs in London, Eisenhower routinely avoided accepting invitations. Although the two incidents were not related, Eisenhower quietly reined in Winant a short time later after learning that the ambassador had cabled Washington without his knowledge to propose that he head a committee to be created to choose strategic bombing targets. (Butcher diary, July 29, 1942.)
66. Mattingly, "A Compilation of the General Health Status of Dwight D. Eisenhower," EL., and Butcher diary, passim.
67. *The Memoirs of Lord Ismay*, 258–59.

28. AN UNLIKELY FRIENDSHIP

1. Perret, *Eisenhower*, 167.
2. Quoted in transcript of Eisenhower's conversation with Alistair Cooke, "General Eisenhower on the Military Churchill" (1967, ABC television), Eisenhower General File, GCML.
3. During his first three months in London, Eisenhower met with Churchill on ten occasions, several of them "overnights" at Chequers. Harry Hopkins found Chequers

so bone-chillingly cold that he hated the place "more than the devil hates holy water," and wore an overcoat in an attempt to keep warm. (Butcher diary, Sept. 21, 1942.)
4. Ibid.
5. Clark, *Calculated Risk*, 33.
6. McKeogh, *Sgt. Mickey and General Ike*, 44.
7. Lord Moran, *Winston Churchill: The Struggle for Survival, 1940–1965* (London, 1968), 191.
8. "General Eisenhower on the Military Churchill."
9. Gerald Pawle, *The War and Colonel Warden* (London, 1963), 307–08. Churchill overheard Thompson's remark and groused, "I'm not as old as all that."
10. Summersby, *Eisenhower Was My Boss*, 20.
11. Bedell Smith to GCM, July 1942, quoted in Miller, *Ike the Soldier*, 383.
12. "General Eisenhower on the Military Churchill."
13. Butcher diary, Oct. 21, 1942.
14. Ibid., Oct. 24, 1942.

29. SAILING A DANGEROUS SEA

Eisenhower's World War II letters and telegrams to Marshall are in the Subject Series, Pre-Pres Papers, EL, and are noted herein only by date.

1. Butcher diary, July 23, 1942.
2. DDE memoranda for Marshall and King, Butcher diary, July 19, 1942, and *EP*, vol. 1, 392–95. The original version is quoted in the text. However, as Butcher notes, in the final draft that was sent to Roosevelt, "some of Ike's pungent language was toned down."
3. Mountbatten, Thames Television interview, "The World at War, 1939–1945," transcript in IWM.
4. Diary of Field Marshal Lord Alanbrooke, July 15 and 17, 1942, hereafter referred to as the Alanbrooke diary, which is deposited in the Liddell Hart Center for Military Archives, King's College, London. After the war, Brooke was invested with the title of Field Marshal the Viscount Alanbrooke.
5. Gen. Charles Bolte oral history, EL, and Perret, *Eisenhower*, 168.
6. Historians have argued for more than a half century regarding Churchill's motives in North Africa, with some insisting it was primarily an aversion to a second front and its likely butcher's bill. Others, such as Sir Michael Howard, have made a strong case for the Mediterranean. Historian Colin Baxter writes that "Michael Howard argued that Churchill's advocacy of the North African campaign, rather than displaying an obsession with 'sideshows,' was more an indication of his eagerness to grapple with the Germans on land at the only place then available that Britain had a real chance of success." (Colin Baxter, "Winston Churchill: Military Strategist?" *Military Affairs*, Feb. 1983.)
7. Peter Andrews, "A Place to Be Lousy In," *American Heritage*, Dec. 1991. In 1960, Eisenhower wrote to Lord Ismay, "Many of our people, *looking backward*, still believe that we would have been better off had we undertaken the operation in late 1942 in view of the fact that Hitler was so busy on the Eastern Front. *I do not share this view* and have often publicly stated I think that the alternative, TORCH, provided us with many later advantages, not the least of which was the training opportunity, through which both sides learned how Allied commands could and would work effectively." (Letter, DDE to Lord Ismay, Dec. 3, 1960, Box 19, A-WR series, Pres Papers, EL.)
8. Ibid.
9. Operation "Symbol," the unpublished diary of Brigadier Sir Ian Jacob. Extracts furnished the author by the late Sir Ian Jacob.

10. Cray, *General of the Army,* 334.
11. Butcher diary, July 23, 1942.
12. DDE, *At Ease,* 252.
13. Cable, FDR to Churchill, Aug. 6, 1942, in Warren F. Kimball, ed., *Churchill and Roosevelt: The Complete Correspondence,* vol. 1 (London, 1984), 552–54. On July 31 Churchill wrote to Roosevelt indicating he thought Marshall would eventually be designated supreme commander and until that time Eisenhower would act as interim commander.
14. Sir Michael Howard, quoted in *Eisenhower,* a PBS documentary film produced for the series *The American Experience.*
15. Persico, *Edward R. Murrow,* 198. Murrow told Butcher he thought the bravest people in London were the prostitutes who "stayed on the streets in the heaviest [air] raids."
16. Lt. Gen. Joseph M. Swing interview with D. Clayton James, Aug. 26, 1971, MacArthur Archives.
17. Williamson Murray and Allan R. Millett, *A War to Be Won* (Cambridge, 2000), 301.
18. Alanbrooke, "Notes of My Life," July 2, 1942, Alanbrooke Papers, King's College, London.
19. DDE's reflections of the Arcadia Conference, Box 8, Post-Pres Papers, A-WR Series, EL.
20. David Eisenhower, *Eisenhower: At War, 1943–1945,* 66.
21. "Statesman and Soldier," *The Economist,* Feb. 23, 1957, quoted in Alex Danchev and Daniel Todman, eds., *War Diaries, 1939–1945: Field Marshal Lord Alanbrooke* (London, 2001), xv.
22. Alanbrooke, "Notes on My Life."
23. Danchev and Todman, *War Diaries, 1939–1945: Field Marshal Lord Alanbrooke,* xvii.
24. Sir Arthur Bryant in the prologue to David Fraser, *Alanbrooke* (London/New York, 1982), 20.
25. Alanbrooke diary, Dec. 4, 1941.
26. Fraser, *Alanbrooke,* 514.
27. DDE diary, Sept. 2, 1942, and World War II diary of Gen. George S. Patton, Jr., Sept. 24, 1942, Box 3, PP-LC, hereafter referred to as Patton diary.
28. Quoted in Pogue, *George C. Marshall: Ordeal and Hope,* 404. Whether Marshall picked Patton, whose assignment was approved by Eisenhower, or vice versa, is a moot point. Both officers wanted Patton for a command role in Torch.
29. Brendon, *Ike,* 86.
30. Andrews, "A Place to Be Lousy In."
31. Ladislas Farago, *Patton: Ordeal and Triumph* (New York, 1963), 84.
32. Patton diary, Aug. 9, 1942.
33. Sir John Slessor, *The Central Blue* (London, 1956), 401.
34. Quoted in D'Este, *Patton,* 419.
35. Patton diary, Aug. 11, 1942.
36. Lucian K. Truscott, *Command Missions* (New York, 1954), 59.
37. DDE diary, Sept. 24, 1942.
38. Patton and Clark quoted in letter, DDE to GCM, Aug. 17, 1942, in Joseph P. Hobbs, *Dear General: Eisenhower's Wartime Letters to Marshall* (Baltimore, 1971), 34.
39. Letter, GCM to DDE, Sept. 26, 1942, in Bland, ed., *The Marshall Papers.* vol. 3, 367.
40. DDE to GCM, June 26, 1944.
41. Bland, *The Marshall Papers,* vol. 3, 368.
42. DDE diary, Sep. 15, 1942.
43. Butcher diary, Aug. 11, 1942.
44. Clark, *Calculated Risk,* 52.
45. François Kersaudy, *Churchill and De Gaulle* (London, 1981), 210.
46. Ibid., 426.

47. JSDE, *Allies* (Garden City, N.Y., 1982), 134.

48. Blumenson, *Mark Clark,* 110.

49. Kersaudy, *Churchill and De Gaulle,* 216.

50. Clark, *Calculated Risk,* 88.

51. DDE to MDE, Nov. 24, 1942.

52. James Parton, *"Air Force Spoken Here": General Ira Eaker and the Command of the Air,* (Bethesda, Md., 1986), 195. Parton was present when Eisenhower visited Eaker and expressed his liking for the "Eaker jacket."

53. Cable, DDE to GCM, Nov. 7, 1942, *EP* vol. 2, 668.

54. Don Cook, *Charles de Gaulle* (New York, 1983), 157.

55. Perret, *Eisenhower,* 173.

56. DDE, *Crusade in Europe,* 111–12. To Giraud's credit, his primary desire was that the Allies invade France to expel the German invaders. Part of his insistence on being appointed supreme Allied commander was to this end.

57. DDE to GCM, Nov. 7, 1942, in Hobbs, *Dear General,* 59.

58. Perret, *There's a War to Be Won,* 137.

59. Ambrose, *Eisenhower,* 200.

60. DDE to MDE, Nov. 6, 1942.

61. Perret, *Eisenhower,* 177.

30. "I AM NOTHING BUT A SOLDIER."

1. DDE, *Crusade in Europe,* 106.

2. Butcher diary, Nov. 8, 1942.

3. Brendon, *Ike,* 91.

4. DDE unpublished ms., Box 11, Pre-Pres Papers, EL.

5. Butcher diary, Nov. 9, 1942.

6. Ibid.

7. Ibid.

8. While his brother Dwight was gaining fame (and notoriety) in North Africa, Milton Eisenhower was overseeing one of the most disgraceful episodes in American history. Roosevelt had picked him after Pearl Harbor as the first administrator of a new agency called the War Relocation Authority (WRA). The WRA was responsible for interning some 120,000 Japanese Americans (Nisei and Sansei) in squalid camps in California and the Rocky Mountain states. Most were loyal American citizens rounded up and interned for the duration of the war in a odious U.S. version of the infamous concentration camps of Nazi Germany, merely for being of Japanese descent and therefore of suspect loyalty. Milton's administration of the internment program was the single blot on his otherwise distinguished career of public service. (Ambrose and Immerman, *Milton S. Eisenhower,* 67, and chap. 4, passim, and Burns, *Roosevelt: The Soldier of Freedom,* 266–68.)

9. DDE to MDE, Nov. 8, 1942.

10. Blumenson, *Mark Clark,* 92.

11. Neal, *The Eisenhowers,* 134. French losses included sixteen submarines, three battleships, seven cruisers, and sixty-two other vessels in an unparalleled act of self-destruction. De Gaulle had correctly predicted that the French navy would "never" rally to Darlan; "the Fleet's one ambition is to sink yours," he told an infuriated Lady Churchill. (John Charmley, *Churchill: The End of Glory* [New York, 1993], 516.)

12. Roosevelt's contempt for the French was reflected in a sarcastic remark that Darlan, Giraud, and de Gaulle were all prima donnas and that his solution to the governance of French North African problem was quite elementary: "Put all three of them in one

room alone, and then give the government of the occupied territory to the man who comes out." (Kersaudy, *Churchill and De Gaulle*, 221.)

Eisenhower's arrival in Algiers on November 13 caused a quite different stir, when the plane (called the "Rambling Wreck") carrying Eisenhower and Adm. Andrew Cunningham encountered bad weather en route and ran short of fuel. Visibility at the airfield where he was to land was reduced to less than forty feet. His staff frantically attempted to divert the pilot to another airfield, but the pilot made a perfect landing in the dark with his fuel tanks nearly empty. A grateful Eisenhower sent the pilot a letter of commendation, noting, "My staff is mad as hell at me. They accused me of disobeying orders, but the fact is we never received them." Nor would it have made a difference, with the plane too low on fuel to have been diverted. (From an Associated Press report in the *New York Times*, Nov. 15, 1942.)

13. Charles de Gaulle, *The Complete War Memoirs* (New York, 1954), 134.
14. JSDE, *Allies*, 137.
15. Ambrose and Immerman, *Milton S. Eisenhower*, 69
16. DDE, *Crusade in Europe*, 116.
17. Patton to DDE, Nov. 15, 1942, Box 24, PP-LC.
18. DDE to MDE, Nov. 27, 1942.
19. Crosswell, *The Chief of Staff*, 132.
20. DDE to Bedell Smith, Nov. 8, 1942, *EP*, vol. 2, 677.
21. JSDE oral history, EL.
22. Kersaudy, *Churchill and De Gaulle*, 221.
23. Kimball, *Forged in War*, 172, and Goodwin, *No Ordinary Time*, 389.
24. Cable, DDE to WSC, Nov. 14, 1942.
25. Burns, *Roosevelt: The Soldier of Freedom*, 295.
26. Ambrose and Immerman, *Milton S. Eisenhower*, 70. "I have accepted General Eisenhower's political arrangements for the time being," said FDR, in an attempt to defuse the storm of public criticism by issuing a statement, noting also that the Darlan deal was "only a temporary expedient."
27. Charmley, *Churchill: The End of Glory*, 516. The appeasement quote is attributed to Sir Oliver Harvey.
28. DDE to MDE, Dec. 10, 1942.
29. Ambrose and Immerman, *Milton S. Eisenhower*, 70, and Robert Murphy, *Diplomat Among Warriors* (Garden City, N.Y., 1964), 150–51.
30. Eisenhower's postwar version of the affair has subsequently been proved incorrect. On October 17, 1942, Butcher recorded in his diary, "Darlan expected in Algiers within a week," thus suggesting it was known well in advance that he would be there. Moreover, in the same entry, Butcher also records Robert Murphy stating that "Darlan apparently wants to play ball." In *Crusade in Europe*, Eisenhower maintains that "Darlan's presence was purely accidental." (116.)
31. Miller, *Ike the Soldier*, 432.

31. "THE DREARIEST CHAPTER IN THE HISTORY OF ALLIED COLLABORATION"

1. An invasion of Sardinia, concluded Eisenhower's planners, could have been mounted only in March 1943 at the earliest, and would have required a huge naval force of four battleships, ten cruisers, and seven aircraft carriers; three infantry and one armored division; plus hundreds more supporting ships, aircraft, and ground units. (*EP*, 764–66, vol. 2.)
2. Cable, DDE to Walter Bedell Smith, Nov. 12, 1942, Pre-Pres Papers, EL.
3. Clark, *Calculated Risk*, 127.

4. By the end of November 1942, a German provisional force in Tunisia had grown to approximately 25,000, supported by some seventy panzers, of which twenty were the new Tiger model, mounting an 88-mm gun that had a deadly impact against British and American vehicles and their more lightly armored tanks.

5. DDE to Maj. Gen. Thomas T. Handy, Dec. 7, 1942, Box 54, Pre-Pres Papers, EL.

6. B. H. Liddell Hart, ed., *The Rommel Papers* (New York, 1953), 328. Logistical problems for Torch were compounded by the fact that many of the supplies sent to England to support the operation were scattered in numerous British warehouses to make them less vulnerable to German air raids. As a result many became "lost" in a disorganized supply system. It became at times difficult if not impossible to determine what was stored where and in what quantity. The problem was straightened out, but not until well after Torch. (See George C. Marshall interview by Howard McGaw Smyth, et al., part 1, July 25, 1949, USAMHI.)

7. Cray, *General of the Army*, 374.

8. Martin van Creveld, *Supplying War* (New York, 1977), 2.

9. D'Este, *Patton*, 464.

10. Gen. Lauris Norstad oral history, EL.

11. Alanbrooke Papers, "Notes on My Life," Nov. 24, 1942.

12. DDE to Ismay, Dec. 16, 1942, *EP*, vol. 2, 846.

13. An illuminating account of the propaganda wars is Wallace Carroll's *Persuade or Perish* (Boston, 1948).

14. DDE to MDE, Dec. 9, 1942.

15. McKeogh, *Sgt. Mickey and General Ike*, 58–59.

16. Ibid., 74.

17. Summersby Morgan, *Past Forgetting*, 131, and Summersby, *Eisenhower Was My Boss*, 51. Butcher once stepped into one of Telek's frequent puddles getting out of bed, leading to the observation "This war is hell." (Butcher diary, Dec. 12, 1942.)

18. Patton to Beatrice Ayer Patton, Mar. 25, 1943, PP-LC. Although Eisenhower would later be driven in an armored Cadillac staff car, his first trip to the front was in a Daimler shipped from England for his use. The vehicle, which his staff despised, was sent to Casablanca for use by FDR in Jan. 1943.

19. DDE to MDE, Feb. 11, 1943. Upon his return to Algiers, exhausted, aching, and utterly miserable, Eisenhower readily agreed to be confined to bed for twenty-four hours by a dispensary physician who prescribed paregoric, a usual remedy for this type of ailment. (Mattingly, "A Compilation of the General Health Status of Dwight D. Eisenhower," EL.)

20. Accounts of the abortive search for Gen. Anderson are in the Butcher diary, and McKeogh, *Sgt. Mickey and General Ike*, chap. 4.

21. Butcher diary, Nov. 29–30, 1942.

22. DDE to MDE, circa Dec. 3, 1942.

23. Butcher diary, Nov. 30, 1942.

24. DDE, *Crusade in Europe*, 134.

25. Butcher diary, Dec. 4, 1942.

26. John Terraine, *The Right of the Line: The Royal Air Force in the European War, 1939–1945* (London, 1985), 391.

27. For a full description of Spaatz's role and the problems of air operations in North Africa, see Davis, *Spaatz*, chaps. 4–6, passim.

28. See C. E. Lucas Phillips, *Alamein* (London, 1962), 50–52.

29. McKeogh, *Sgt. Mickey and General Ike*, 85.

30. Ibid., 76. By contrast, Patton rigidly enforced a rule that everyone in his command wear a helmet at all times. Violators were routinely fined twenty-five dollars.

31. Butcher diary, Apr. 17, 1943.

32. DDE, *Crusade in Europe*, 354.

33. DDE to MDE, Dec. 30, 1942.

34. Ibid., Dec. 31, 1942.

35. Miller, *Ike the Soldier,* 440–41. The Grant's armament was simply no match for the 75-mm guns of the Mark IV. The arrival of the Tiger tank rendered the Grant little better than a popgun.

36. DDE diary, Dec. 10, 1942.

37. DDE to GCM, Nov. 30, 1942, quoted in George F. Howe, *Northwest Africa: Seizing the Initiative in the West* (Washington, D.C., 1957), 309.

38. Norman Gelb, *Desperate Venture: The Story of Operation Torch, the Allied Invasion of North Africa* (New York, 1992), 277.

39. Quotes are from letters, DDE to MDE, Dec. 5, 1942, and Nov. 27, 1942. Eisenhower also aired his frustrations to P. A. Hodgson: "I think sometimes that I am a cross between a one-time soldier, a pseudo-statesman, a jack-legged politician and a crooked diplomat. I walk a soapy tight-rope in a rain storm with a blasting furnace on one side and a pack of ravenous tigers on the other.... In spite of all this, I must admit that the whole thing is intriguing and interesting, and is forever presenting new challenges that still have the power to make me come up charging." Letter, DDE to P. A. Hodgson, Dec. 4, 1942, Hodgson file, USMA Archives.

40. Kersaudy, *Churchill and De Gaulle,* 231. The British reaction to Darlan's death was so overly ebullient that the State Department finally requested that they "please calm down their gloating." (Gelb, *Desperate Venture,* 280.)

41. To the present day the assassination of Darlan remains shrouded in secrecy. The assassin was tried by a military court, sentenced to death, and speedily executed. Suspicion has pointed to de Gaulle's Free French as the architects. Cook, *Charles de Gaulle,* 168.)

42. Ambrose, *Eisenhower,* 210.

43. Other persistent but unproved suspicions remain to this day that Darlan's assassination was either plotted by William J. ("Wild Bill") Donovan's Office of Strategic Services (OSS) or the British Special Operations Executive (SOE) as a means of removing an embarrassment. For a brief discussion of the circumstances surrounding Darlan's death, see Gelb, *Desperate Venture,* chap. 17, passim. In the aftermath of Darlan's death, Giraud (whom Darlan once accurately described as "a political infant") was appointed the high commissioner and commander in chief of all French forces in North Africa, in accordance with the deal previously struck by Eisenhower at Gibraltar. Giraud may not have been favored by all of the other senior French officers, but he was at least an untainted patriot with none of Darlan's political baggage.

44. Summersby Morgan, *Past Forgetting,* 109–10.

45. Perret, *Eisenhower,* 187; Ann Whitman diary, Jan. 15, 1958; "Memo for Jim Hagerty," June 10, 1958, James C. Hagerty Papers, EL; and DDE interview with D. Clayton James, Aug. 29, 1967, MacArthur Archives. Eisenhower reiterated to Col. James V. Collier that he had opposed awarding the medal to MacArthur and told Marshall, "I would refuse to accept it—and thought that all men in high command and headquarters jobs should be excluded from that honor." (Collier interview with James, Aug. 30, 1971, MacArthur Archives.)

46. Eichelberger memoir, Eichelberger Papers, USAMHI.

47. Cable, Churchill to DDE, Dec. 31, 1942, quoted in Martin Gilbert, *Winston S. Churchill, Road to Victory: 1941–1945* (London, 1986), 286.

48. Alanbrooke diary, Dec. 7, 1942, and Fraser, *Alanbrooke,* 305.

49. Ibid., Dec. 28, 1942.

50. Diary of Lt. Gen. Sir Ian Jacob, Dec. 30, 1942, quoted in Charles Richardson, *From Churchill's Secret Circle to the BBC* (London, 1991), 150.

51. Davis, *Spaatz,* 171.

52. DDE to Maj. Gen. Thomas T. Handy, Dec. 7, 1942, Box 54, Pre-Pres Papers, EL.

32. FOUR STARS

1. DDE to MDE, May 27, 1943.
2. Ibid., Sept. 27 and Oct. 2, 1943. In retirement after two terms as president, Eisenhower seriously contemplated writing a book titled "The Great Exception," in which he intended to demonstrate that historically most military coalitions failed, but that the Allied alliance of World War II was an exception. Although by 1967 Eisenhower had written some one hundred pages in draft about his wartime relationships with Marshall and Winston Churchill, he never got around to completing it, in part because John Eisenhower was writing a book about the same subject. (See JSDE, *Allies*, xviiii–xx, and letter, DDE to JSDE, July 27, 1967, Box 20, Post-Pres Papers, Secretary's Series, EL.)
3. Brendon, *Ike*, 99.
4. DDE to GCM, Nov. 11, 1942, ibid., 690, and DDE to Lloyd Fredendall, *EP*, vol. 2, 939–41.
5. Paul M. Robinett, *Armor Command* (Washington, D.C., 1959), 190.
6. Lt. Col. John K. Waters, quoted in Peter Andrews, "A Place to Be Lousy In," *American Heritage*, Dec. 1991. Waters was one of the many Americans captured at Sidi Bou Said in February 1943.
7. Quoted in DDE to GCM, Apr. 5, 1943, *EP*, vol. 2, 1071.
8. Drew Middleton, *Our Share of Night* (New York, 1946), 168–69.
9. DDE to Thomas T. Handy, Jan. 28, 1943, *EP*, vol. 2, 928.
10. Middleton, *Our Share of Night*, 191.
11. McKeogh, *Sgt. Mickey and General Ike*, 51. Eisenhower's use of profanity had already been well publicized in the press. Another curious phenomenon was Eisenhower's insatiable hunger for Western pulp novels, which Mickey asked Mamie to keep supplying. "It was sort of funny," McKeogh later wrote, "considering the amount of shooting we were getting most nights, that he still wanted stories full of six-shooters and bar-room brawls, but he did."
12. DDE, *Crusade in Europe*, 22.
13. Harold Macmillan, *The Blast of War, 1939–1945* (London, 1967), 220–21.
14. Ibid., 221.
15. Ibid., 222.
16. Jacob diary, Dec. 30, 1942.
17. Ibid.
18. DDE to Thomas T. Handy, Jan. 28, 1943, *EP*, vol. 2, 929.
19. Alistair Horne, *Macmillan*, vol. 1 (London, 1990), 160. As the two men became friends, Horne writes, "Macmillan came to enjoy Eisenhower's forthright soldier's vocabulary." This quote originally appeared in Nigel Fisher, *Harold Macmillan* (New York, 1982), 100–01.
20. Quoted in Horne, *Macmillan*, 153.
21. Cable, DDE to GCM, May 25, 1943, *EP*, vol. 2, 1154–55.
22. Crosswell, *The Chief of Staff*, 140.
23. Quoted in Gilbert, *Road to Victory*, 253.
24. Overlord was the best known of the many code names given military operations in World War II. As he had with Torch, Churchill personally selected "Overlord" from a list of some nine thousand potential code names provided him in his capacity as the minister of defence. The list was maintained by a group known as the Inter-Services Security Board, which operated under the jurisdiction of the Joint Intelligence Committee. (Martin Gilbert, *Winston S. Churchill*, vol. 6, *Finest Hour, 1939–1941* [London, 1983], 966. In *Road to Victory* Gilbert does not indicate why Churchill selected the code name Overlord.)

25. For a full account of Churchill's Mediterranean strategy, see Gilbert's *Road to Victory*, passim.

26. Fraser, *Alanbrooke*, 314. Fraser's biography presents one the best accounts of the Casablanca Conference.

27. Jacob diary. With uncharacteristic patience Churchill remained in the background and refrained from imposing himself on the negotiations of the Combined Chiefs of Staff.

28. Arthur Bryant, *The Turn of the Tide* (London, 1957), 559. The U.S. chiefs insisted (and got) a 70/30 percent split of landing craft assets, instead of the nearly 100 percent originally demanded by the British for European operations.

29. DDE to Thomas T. Handy, Jan. 28, 1943, *EP*, vol. 2, 927–28.

30. Harold Macmillan, *War Diaries* (London, 1984), 8–9.

31. JSDE, *Allies*, 229–30; DDE, *Crusade in Europe*, 150; Perret, *Eisenhower*, 192–93; Butcher diary, Jan. 17, 1943, and Macmillan, *The Blast of War*, 240. In his diary Macmillan wrote that three of the plane's four engines failed (*War Diaries*, 7). Macmillan had hitched a ride to Casablanca with Eisenhower. General Ira Eaker (the commander of the Eighth Air Force in the U.K.), loaned his aircraft to Eisenhower to return to Algiers the following day. Eaker was present at Casablanca to help Arnold bolster his case to Churchill for continuation of American daylight bombing, which the prime minister thought too costly and wanted to shut down. (Davis, *Spaatz*, 161–63.)

32. Robert E. Sherwood, *Roosevelt and Hopkins*, vol. 2 (New York, 1948), 677.

33. DDE, *Crusade in Europe*, 152.

34. Butcher diary, Jan. 12, 1943.

35. Patton diary, Jan. 15 and 16, 1943, PP-LC.

36. Murphy, *Diplomat Among Warriors*, 166, and Brendon, *Ike*, 101.

37. Butcher diary, Jan. 20, 1943.

38. Quoted in Pogue, *George C. Marshall: Organizer of Victory*, 182.

39. Quoted in Lyon, *Eisenhower*, 201.

40. Alanbrooke, "Notes on My Life," Alanbrooke Papers.

41. Sherwood, *Roosevelt and Hopkins*, vol. 2, 677.

42. Marshall interviews with a group of U.S. Army official historians, Part 1, July 25, 1949, OCMH Collection, USAMHI.

43. DDE, Churchill-Marshall memoir.

44. DDE to GCM, Feb. 8, 1943.

45. Marshall interviews, Part I.

46. Butcher diary, Jan. 26, 1943.

47. DDE to MDE, April 6, 1943.

48. DDE to P. A. Hodgson, March 29, 1943, Box 52, Pre-Pres Papers, EL.

49. Kevin McCann, quoted in Susan Eisenhower, *Mrs. Ike*, 204–05.

50. Ibid., 206.

51. DDE to MDE, Mar. 2, 1943.

52. Occasionally Eisenhower's affection for John manifested itself in the form of extreme disappointment when the young man failed to write as often as he would have wished.

53. Kay Summersby gave Eisenhower peace of mind no one else—including Mamie, had she been present—was capable of providing. As for the widely held belief of an affair between Ike and Kay, Sgt. Mickey McKeogh scoffed at the notion. "I put him to bed every night and I woke him every morning. He was in bed by himself and he was still in bed by himself when I awoke him." Mickey McKeogh, quoted in *Eisenhower* documentary.

54. Summersby, *Eisenhower Was My Boss*, 64.

55. Truscott, *Command Missions*, 170. Whenever Eisenhower flew to the front the air force laid on fighter escorts. Knowing how badly such aircraft were needed for what

he deemed more important missions, Eisenhower would sometimes insist on returning to Algiers by road. (See, for example, Butcher diary, Feb. 15, 1943.)

56. The official title of Eisenhower's other command in North Africa was North African Theater of Operations U.S. Army (NATOUSA), formed in February 1943.

57. Diary of Maj. Gen. Everett S. Hughes.

58. Goodwin, *No Ordinary Time*, 480.

59. Admiral Ernest J. King, notes for Jan. 22, 1943, Papers of Fleet Admiral Ernest J. King, LC.

60. Butcher diary, Feb. 15, 1943. Marshall had personally telephoned Mamie about Ike's promotion. Butcher has the date Eisenhower learned of his promotion via the BBC wrong. His diary entry for February 15 indicates the date was February 10; however, Eisenhower's promotion was not approved by the Senate until February 11. The date it was announced on the BBC was either late on February 11 or on February 12. Ike's promotion brought Mamie a deluge of mail (all of which she answered personally), even greater demands from the press for interviews, but no assistance, official or unofficial, from the army. As before, she was left on her own to cope as best she could. (Susan Eisenhower, *Mrs. Ike*, 200–02.)

61. DDE to MDE, Feb. 26, 1943.

62. Quoted in DDE, *Letters to Mamie* (Garden City, N.Y., 1978), 111.

33. "IKUS AFRICANUS"

1. DDE to Lt. Gen. Joseph T. McNarney, Jan. 19, 1943, *EP*, vol. 2, 914.

2. H. Essame, *Patton the Commander* (London, 1974), 67; and Martin Blumenson and James L. Stokesbury, *Masters of the Art of Command* (Boston, 1975), "Command at Kasserine," passim.

3. Miller, *Ike the Soldier*, 472.

4. DDE to Thomas T. Handy, Jan. 28, 1943, *EP*, vol. 2, 928.

5. DDE to Leonard T. Gerow, Feb. 24, 1943, ibid, 986–87.

6. Quoted from a letter written by DDE to a small California newspaper on Oct. 15, 1952, Box 1, Post-Pres Papers, Convertible File, 1945–69, EL.

7. *Soldier: The Memoirs of Matthew B. Ridgway* (New York, 1956), 166.

8. DDE diary, Feb. 25, 1943, and Ambrose, *Eisenhower*, 228.

9. Omar N. Bradley, *A Soldier's Story* (New York, 1951), 27.

10. Robinett, *Armor Command*, 198.

11. Ambrose, *Eisenhower*, 228.

12. Martin Blumenson, *Kasserine Pass* (Boston, 1966), 3–4.

13. Ambrose, *Eisenhower*, 231.

14. Liddell Hart, *The Rommel Papers*, 407. Rommel had been recalled to Germany by the time his Panzer Armee Afrika linked up with von Arnim's Fifth Panzer Army. This combined force was placed under the command of von Arnim and designated Army Group Afrika.

15. Brendon, *Ike*, 103.

16. Drew Middleton quoted in part 13 of *The World at War* television series, Thames Television, London.

17. Butcher diary, Feb. 23, 1943.

18. Charles B. MacDonald, *The Mighty Endeavor* (New York, 1969), 129. There was no lack of willingness to fight, nor were U.S. forces caught napping. To the contrary, an attack was expected and they were on the alert. Sidi Bou Said and Kasserine Pass were lost as the result of military dispositions that no force could have withstood.

19. Bradley, *A General's Life*, 159.

20. McKeogh, *Sgt. Mickey and General Ike*, 73.

21. DDE to GCM, Feb. 24, 1943, *EP*, vol. 2, 984–85.
22. For a full account of the incident see Ralph Bennett, *Ultra and Mediterranean Strategy* (New York, 1989), chap. 8, passim.
23. Eisenhower wrote to Fredendall on Feb. 23, 1943, "I have every confidence that under your inspiring leadership current advances of the enemy will be stopped in place." (*EP*, vol 2, 980.) What Fredendall had done to inspire that "confidence" will forever remain a mystery.
24. Harmon was not the only recipient of Eisenhower's sartorial largess. Gen. Vernon Walters, who frequently served as President Eisenhower's top-level interpreter/translator, once found himself ordered on short notice to accompany the president to a white-tie dinner for French president Charles de Gaulle. His only wing collar was in the laundry, and Walters was in a dilemma until Eisenhower, dressed in white tie and tails, bailed him out by fabricating a suitable replacement from one of his own smaller collars, using a nail file, a trick he had learned as a young officer. As Walters later recalled in awe, "I marveled that the man who had ordered the invasion of Europe and launched a thousand ships and eleven thousand aircraft on D-Day could find time to worry about the problems of a lieutenant colonel . . . with a missing wing collar." (Vernon A. Walters, *Silent Missions* [Garden City, N.Y., 1978], 291–92.)
25. Harmon's account is in "Personal Memoirs of Maj. Gen. E. N. Harmon," most of which later formed the basis of his published account *Combat Commander* (Englewood Cliffs, N.J., 1970), 111–21. Harmon was even more outspoken to Patton, calling Fredendall a moral and physical coward. In a postwar interview with the U.S. Army historian George F. Howe, Harmon also scathingly condemned Fredendall as "a son-of-a-bitch" unfit for command. (Patton diary, March 2, 1943, and Howe interview of Maj. Gen. Ernest N. Harmon, Sept. 15, 1952, USAMHI. The unpublished Harmon memoir was furnished to the author by Norwich University trustee Robert Johnson.)
26. Nigel Nicolson, *Alex: The Life of Field Marshal Alexander of Tunis* (London, 1973), 212.
27. In late February, Bedell Smith escorted Eisenhower's newly arrived observer Omar Bradley to the II Corps command post and, as Bradley describes it, they found both Fredendall and his staff "rapidly, if not obscenely, anti-British and especially anti-Anderson." Smith thought Fredendall either "incompetent or crazy or both" and urged Eisenhower to relieve him at once. Bradley, *A General's Life*, 135, and Crosswell, *The Chief of Staff*, 162. Neither Bradley nor Eisenhower ever forgot the abhorrent specter of Fredendall's command post. Once, in France in 1944, Bradley's staff situated his CP in a narrow canyon. Bradley thought it showed a lack of courage and ordered it moved to an open space. Soon after, Eisenhower arrived and said, "Thank God, you are out here in the open, Brad. The way some generals hide their command posts you would think they were afraid of getting hit. . . . This is fine!" (Bradley, quoted in "From Plebe to President.")

It has been suggested that Eisenhower failed to sack Fredendall earlier because he was Marshall's man, but if Eisenhower thought that, he was wrong. "I didn't know Fredendall very well," Marshall later revealed to his official biographer. "It infuriated me when I found he was foul-mouthed. No man for [an] Allied job."

To avoid further bad press, Fredendall's removal was misrepresented (not entirely successfully) to appear as if he were merely returning home for reassignment in order to take advantage of his troop-training skills. He was given a hero's welcome, the command of a training army, and a dreadfully undeserved promotion to lieutenant general. (Pogue interviews with Marshall, GCML.) Fredendall actually owed his promotions to McNair. Fredendall, said Clark, "had a rather noteworthy name in those days." Fredendall's loyal aide bitterly blamed his general's relief on Eisenhower and Clark's jealousy because he outranked both in permanent grade. (Mark Clark oral history, USAMHI, and James R. Webb Papers, EL.)

28. DDE diary, June 11, 1943.

29. Butcher diary, Mar. 7, 1943.

30. Alexander to Brooke, Apr. 3, 1943, Alanbrooke Papers. To the end of the war Alexander was never able to overcome his innate distrust of the American soldier. Eisenhower was forced to admit to Marshall that his troops often looked like "an armed mob." (Lee Kennett, *G.I.: The American Soldier in World War II* [New York, 1987], 82.)

31. "Tunisia," U.S. Army Center of Military History pamphlet, 1993.

32. The British blamed the 34th Division for failing to carry out a mission while attached to one of their corps. The assessment was wholly unwarranted after the corps commander, Lt. Gen. J. T. Crocker, had decreed the tactics to be used by the 34th Division commander, Maj. Gen. Charles W. "Doc" Ryder, who had a better plan that he was not permitted to carry out. Ryder was a classmate of Eisenhower's at West Point.

33. Patton diary, Apr. 11 and 12, 1943.

34. Ibid., Apr. 7, 1943.

35. Martin Blumenson, *The Patton Papers*, vol. 2 (Boston, 1974), 206.

36. Air Vice-Marshal Arthur Coningham commanded the Northwest African Tactical Air Force, and in that role was the Allied tactical air commander. A New Zealander with a Patton-like tendency to put his foot in his mouth, Coningham was a pioneer aviator who was proud of the nickname "Maori," which eventually became simply "Mary." In World War I he won the DSO, MC, and DFC as a pilot in the Royal Flying Corps, and in 1925 set a long-distance record by leading a flight from Cairo to Nigeria, which inspired the opening of the African air routes. Coningham was a decisive commander and a brilliant strategist who was quick to grasp a situation and react with sound judgment. Unfortunately, not long after assuming command of the Desert Air Force, in support of the Eighth Army, the strong-willed Coningham clashed with Montgomery over what the airman believed was a deliberate denial of credit for the feats of the RAF. It was one of the bitterest quarrels of the war. (See Carlo D'Este, *Bitter Victory: The Battle for Sicily, 1943* [New York/London], passim, and Vincent Orange, *Coningham* [London, 1990], 146–50.)

37. Lord Tedder, *With Prejudice* (London, 1966), 411, Ambrose, *Eisenhower*, 232, Orange, *Coningham*, 149, Bradley, *A General's Life*, 148, and Crosswell, *The Chief of Staff*, 163. The document itself was not retained within the AFHQ records. Inasmuch as it was never sent, its retention would have been unusual.

38. Patton diary, Apr. 3, 1943, Gen. Lawerence S. Kuter, "Goddammit, Georgie!" *Air Force*, Feb. 1973, Tedder, *With Prejudice*, 411, and Bradley, *A General's Life*, 63–64. The actual incident is well portrayed in the film *Patton*.

39. Bradley, *A General's Life*, 154.

40. DDE to GCM, Mar. 11, 1943, *EP* vol. 2, 1024.

41. Bradley, *A General's Life*, 130, 151. After the publication of *A General's Life* (completed by coauthor Clay Blair after Bradley's death), there was some criticism that the overall tone of the book was uncharacteristically harsh. Acutely aware of his dilemma, Blair not only had a number of distinguished military historians read the manuscript but armed with thousands of pages of Bradley's transcribed words, believed that what he wrote was not only accurate and verifiable but would have met with Bradley's approval had he lived.

42. Butcher diary, April 17, 1943.

43. Martin Blumenson, "Bradley-Patton: World War II's 'Odd Couple,'" *Army*, Dec. 1985.

44. Butcher diary, May 8, 1943, and A. J. Liebling, *Liebling Abroad* (New York, 1981), 313–14.

45. S. L. A. Marshall oral history, Marshall Papers, USAMHI. Historians Murray and Millett similarly concluded, "Only hacks among American journalists called Omar Bradley a soldier's general." (Murray and Millett, *A War to Be Won*, 418.)

46. MacDonald, *The Mighty Endeavor*, 129.
47. Gen. Siegfried Westphal, quoted in Perret, *Eisenhower*, 211.
48. Quoted in Nicolson, *Alex*, 229.
49. Winston S. Churchill, *The Hinge of Fate* (Boston, 1950), 831.
50. Howe, *Northwest Africa*, 675.
51. DDE to Brig. Gen. Benjamin G. Ferris, May 21, 1943, *EP*, vol. 2, 1149.

34. MONTY AND ALEX

1. JSDE, *Allies*, 304.
2. John Laffin, *Links of Leadership* (London, 1970), 257.
3. A point made to the author by Col. Douglas MacGregor (USA), April 2001.
4. A fuller portrait of Montgomery is in chap. 4 of the author's *Bitter Victory: The Battle for Sicily, 1943*.
5. Sir Michael Howard, quoted in "Scholarship on World War II: Present and Future," *Journal of Military History*, July 1991.
6. Larrabee, *Commander in Chief*, 498.
7. Noel Annan, *Changing Enemies* (Ithaca, N.Y., 1997), 55.
8. Bryant, *Turn of the Tide*, 239.
9. Diary of Lt. Col. Chester B. Hansen, July 20, 1944, USAMHI.
10. Quoted in Colin F. Baxter, *Field Marshal Bernard Law Montgomery, 1887–1976: A Selected Bibliography* (Westport, Conn., 1999), 5.
11. Patton diary, May 5, 1943.
12. Nigel Hamilton, *The Full Monty: Montgomery of Alamein, 1887–1942* (London, 2001), 559.
13. Quoted by Alistair Home in *The Times*, Sept. 19, 2001.
14. Shelford Bidwell, "Monty, Master of the Battlefield or Most Overrated General?" *RUSI Journal*, June 1984.
15. Quoted in Alistair Horne, "In Defense of Montgomery," in Robert Cowley, ed., *No End Save Victory* (New York, 2001), 493.
16. Graham and Bidwell, *Coalitions, Politicians and Generals*, 193.
17. Letter, Montgomery to Brooke, Apr. 4, 1943, Montgomery Papers, IWM. In the view of his chief of staff, Francis de Guingand, "They got on well," despite Montgomery's verdict that Eisenhower was a "good chap; no soldier!" (Quoted in Gen. Sir Charles Richardson, *Flashback* [London, 1985], 55.)
18. Nigel Hamilton, *Monty: Master of the Battlefield, 1942–1944* (London, 1983), xxv.
19. Murray and Millett, *A War to Be Won*, 270.
20. Alanbrooke diary, June 3, 1943.
21. Nicolson, *Alex*, 196.
22. Ibid, 199.
23. Charles J. Rolo, "General Sir Harold Alexander," *Britain*, July 1943.
24. Nicolson, *Alex*, 280.
25. C. L. Sulzberger, *A Long Row of Candles* (New York, 1969), 230.
26. Lucas diary, Aug. 1, 1943.
27. John Colville, *The Churchillians* (London, 1981), 152.
28. Nigel Nicolson, quoted in Hamilton, *Monty: Master of the Battlefield*, 472.
29. Quoted by Canadian historian William J. McAndrew in the *Toronto Globe and Mail*, Aug. 30, 1986.
30. Marshall interviews, and D'Este, *Fatal Decision*, 476, n. 53.
31. DDE diary, June 11, 1943. In early May, Everett S. Hughes recorded in his diary this remark: "Ike says Alex isn't as good as he thinks he is." (Hughes diary, May 1, 1943.)
32. Ibid, June 11, 1943.

35. "WHAT IN HELL DOES EISENHOWER COMMAND?"

1. Summersby, *Eisenhower Was My Boss*, 74–76.
2. David Eisenhower, *Eisenhower: At War*, 199.
3. Butcher diary, May 13, 1943.
4. Ibid., May 13, 1943.
5. JSDE, *Allies*, 288.
6. DDE to Brig. Gen. Benjamin G. Ferris, May 21, 1943, *EP*, vol. 2, 1149.
7. DDE to P. A. Hodgson, Sept. 30, 1943, DDE Vertical Files, USMA Archives. Shortly after the campaign in Tunisia ended, Eisenhower established a new advance head-quarters outside Tunis at Amilcar. His staff located a large villa called La Maison Blanche, "the White House," which, as usual, Eisenhower thought was too grand. It was used mainly as a mess and the temporary residence of visiting VIPs, from King George VI to Roosevelt and Churchill.
8. DDE to Arthur Eisenhower, May 18, 1943, *EP*, vol. 2, 1148–49.
9. Butcher diary, May 13, 1943, and *EP*, vol. 2, 1131, n. 3.
10. Butcher to MDE, June 14, 1943, Box 2, Butcher Papers, EL. Among the trivia Butcher related to Mamie were such things as how her husband stepped in one of Telek's numerous puddles one dark night in slippers with holes chewed by said dog.
11. Quoted in "From Plebe to President."
12. Ibid.
13. Kimball, *Forged in War*, chap. 6, passim, and Cook, *Charles de Gaulle*, chap. 10.
14. Macmillan, *The Blast of War*, chaps. 13 and 14, Kersaudy, *Churchill and De Gaulle*, chap. 12, and Ambrose, *Eisenhower*, chap. 13.
15. Bradley, *A General's Life*, 133.
16. Summersby Morgan, *Past Forgetting*, 132–34. The Butcher diary also describes Kay Summersby's grief over Arnold's death.
17. Sue Sarafian Jehl oral history, EL.
18. Anthea Gordon Saxe, quoted in David, *Ike & Mamie*, chap. 5, passim. The authors were the only ones to have interviewed Anthea Saxe, who settled in the United States after World War II with her American husband.
19. DDE, *Letters to Mamie*, 122.
20. David Eisenhower, *Eisenhower: At War*, 198.
21. DDE to MDE, June 12, 1943.
22. Perret, *Eisenhower*, 216.
23. DDE to MDE, Feb. 15, 1943.
24. C. J. C. Molony, *The Mediterranean and Middle East*, vol. 5 (London, 1973), 6.
25. The Canadian 1st Division and the U.S. 45th Division were being staged directly from Britain and the United States, respectively. London and Washington thus became two of five separate centers of planning. The inevitable result was considerable confusion, compounded by the fact that Cunningham, Tedder, and Alexander each eventually established their operational headquarters in separate locations.
26. Churchill also observed, "What Stalin would think of this when he has 185 German divisions on his front, I cannot imagine." (A full account of both the planning and the Sicily campaign is in D'Este, *Bitter Victory: The Battle for Sicily, 1943*.)
27. DDE to GCM, May 13, 1943.
28. "Remarks Made at Conference in Algiers on 2 May 1943 by Gen. Montgomery," copy in Butcher diary.
29. Ambrose, *Eisenhower*, 246.
30. Everett S. Hughes diary.
31. DDE to Lt. Gen. Thomas T. Handy, Jan. 28, 1943, *EP*, vol. 2, 928.
32. Quoted in Farago, *Patton: Ordeal and Triumph*, 273.
33. Patton diary, May 7, 1943.

34. Farago, *Patton: Ordeal and Triumph*, 273.
35. Macmillan, *The Blast of War*, 324–25, and Horne, *Macmillan*, 183. A fuller account of the Allied victory parade is in Macmillan's *War Diaries*, 87–93.
36. Butcher diary, May 25, 1943, and Macmillan, *The Blast of War*, 324–25. The bickering French complicated matters when Gen. Jacques Leclerc's French troops refused to march with the Giraudist French contingent. Anderson solved the problem by having Leclerc's troops march with the Eighth Army.
37. Bradley, *A Soldier's Story*, 109, and *A General's Life*, 170; Patton, "Description of Victory Parade," Box 13, PP-LC; Miller, *Ike the Soldier*, 505; and Farago, *Patton: Ordeal and Triumph*, 256.
38. Macmillan, *The Blast of War*, 325.
39. Both quotes in Patton diary, May 8, 1943.
40. Alanbrooke diary, May 24, 1943.
41. The diaries of Henry L. Stimson, Yale University microfilm copy, May 25, 1943.
42. Perret, *Eisenhower*, 221.
43. Churchill, *The Hinge of Fate*, 826.
44. Cray, *General of the Army*, 400–01.
45. Gilbert, *Road to Victory*, 424.
46. Churchill, quoted in ibid., 421.
47. Butcher diary, May 30, 1943. All had long since learned that there was no way to take the measure of the irrepressible Winston Churchill, whose breakfast one morning while in Algiers consisted of a bottle of white wine, soda water, and ice.

36. "EVERYTHING THAT PLANNING SHOULD NOT BE"

1. DDE to GCM, May 13, 1943, *EP*, vol. 2, 1130.
2. Quoted in Maj. Gen. Sir Kenneth Strong, *Intelligence at the Top* (London, 1968), 97.
3. Stephen E. Ambrose, *The Supreme Commander* (London, 1971), 215. Churchill made a wager with Eisenhower that there were no more than three thousand Italians on Pantelleria, promising to pay an Italian sou [*sic*] for every soldier captured above that number. Delighted when the figure reached some eleven thousand POWs, Churchill paid off the debt, which amounted to the grand sum of approximately $1.60, with the remark that at that rate he would gladly buy all the Italians Eisenhower cared to capture. (DDE, *At Ease*, 265.)
4. Eisenhower and Cunningham quoted in Oliver Warner, *Cunningham of Hyndhope* (London, 1967), 184–85.
5. Cable, DDE to GCM, June 11, 1943, *EP*, vol. 2, 1185–86.
6. Letter, Tedder to Portal, June 14, 1943, quoted in *With Prejudice*, 443. Tedder was right. Spaatz's biographer writes that, despite its intensity, "the air bombardment probably provided a face-saving excuse for an action the garrison would have taken in any case. A more resolute defending force, despite the damage inflicted by Allied air power, would certainly have made the landing a far bloodier affair." (Davis, *Spaatz*, 239.)
7. Nicolson, *Alex*, 236.
8. Perret, *Eisenhower*, 225.
9. DDE to MDE, July 9, 1943.
10. Butcher diary, July 6, 1943, and Albert N. Garland and Howard McGaw Smyth, *Sicily and the Surrender of Italy* (Washington, D.C., 1965 [the official U.S. Army history]), 109.
11. DDE, *Crusade in Europe*, 190.
12. Butcher diary, July 13, 1943, and diary of Maj. Gen. John P. Lucas, USAMHI.
13. Butcher diary, ibid. Patton noted that Eisenhower seemed disinterested in his situation briefing and more interesting in nit-picking the alleged inadequacy of his reports. Patton was also criticized for being "too prompt in my replies and [I] should hesitate

more, the way he does before replying," an apparent reference to the Coningham incident. "I think he means well, but it is most upsetting to get only piddling criticism when one knows one has done a good job." (Patton diary, July 12, 1943.)

14. Lucas diary. Prior to the invasion Alexander's command, once called 18th Army Group, had been redesignated 15th Army Group.

15. Patton diary, July 13, 1943, Box 3, PP-LC.

16. John Gunther, *Eisenhower: The Man and the Symbol* (New York, 1951), 154. Gunther was present with Eisenhower during his trip to Sicily on July 12, 1943.

17. Ibid., 155–57.

18. Everett S. Hughes diary, Aug. 6, 1943.

19. Bradley, *A General's Life*, 188–89.

20. Both quotes in ibid.

21. Graham and Bidwell, *Coalitions, Politicians and Generals*, 219. Lt. Gen. Oliver Leese, one of Montgomery's corps commanders, later conceded that it was "an unfortunate decision. We were still inclined to remember the slow American progress in the early stages in Tunisia, and I for one certainly did not realize the immense development in experience and technique which they had made in the last weeks of the North African campaign. I have a feeling now that if they [the 45th Division] could have driven straight up this road, we might have had a chance to end this frustrating campaign sooner." (D'Este, *Bitter Victory*, 332–33.)

22. The German XIV Panzer Corps successfully evacuated 9,789 vehicles, 51 tanks, 163 artillery weapons, and some 40,000 tons of precious supplies.

23. Returning from Messina on August 17, Patton's chief of staff, Brig. Gen. Hobart R. Gay, encountered Bedell Smith cowering in a ditch from artillery fire of what was actually a nearby battery of U.S. 155-mm guns. When he arrived a short time later, "I have never seen Patton so completely abashed—ashamed of an American," wrote Gay. "Smith thought it was [incoming] enemy shells . . . and jumped from the car into the ditch in one leap, and refused to leave it, even when . . . told it was quite safe," Patton recorded in his diary. With a mixture of disgust and compassion, Patton coaxed Smith into his command vehicle and drove away. Other than the various private diary entries of Gay, Patton, and an aide, the incident was never publicized nor is it likely that Eisenhower even knew of it. (See D'Este, *Bitter Victory*, fn, 519.)

24. A full account of the German evacuation and its consequences is in *Bitter Victory*, chap. 30. Mockler-Ferryman's replacement as AFHQ G-2 was Brig. Kenneth Strong, a British career intelligence officer in whom Eisenhower placed great confidence. Strong, however, initially proved as inept as his predecessor. Despite strong evidence of Axis intentions, until their evacuation of Sicily was actually completed, Strong denied an evacuation was even taking place. His predictions ran counter to those of the Seventh Army G-2, Col. Oscar Koch, and Montgomery's intelligence officer, Brig. Edgar Williams, both of whom accurately predicted the evacuation. (*Bitter Victory*, chap. 31, passim.)

25. Montgomery interview with Samuel Eliot Morison, circa 1957, Morison Papers, Naval Historical Center, Washington, D.C.

26. Quoted in Hugh Pond, *Sicily* (London, 1962), 220. German battle losses in Sicily totaled an estimated five thousand killed. Allied battle losses totaled 22,293. Those killed in action were almost equally split between American and British/Canadians (2,783 U.S. killed, and 2,376 Royal Navy and Eighth Army.) Nonbattle losses on both sides from accidents and illness were considerably higher.

27. Demaree Bess report, Aug. 19, 1943, Box 91, Pre-Pres Papers, EL.

28. D'Este, *Bitter Victory*, 487.

29. DDE to Patton, Aug. 17, 1943, *EP*, vol. 2, 1340–41.

30. Garland and Smyth, *Sicily and the Surrender of Italy*, 427, Farago, *Patton: Ordeal and Triumph*, 335, and Butcher diary, Aug. 20, 1943.

31. DDE, *Crusade in Europe*, 199. Bedell Smith successfully implored the press pool in Algiers to keep mum about the affair.
32. The reprimand was unofficial and thus never became a part of Patton's official 201 personnel file.
33. Lucas enjoyed the full confidence of both generals and was the ideal officer to convey Eisenhower's extreme concern to Patton. He was also ordered to investigate the incidents from the soldiers' point of view. Eisenhower later sent two colonels from the NATOUSA inspector general's office to investigate the incidents, and a medical officer who submitted an eyes-only report directly to Eisenhower.
34. Lucas diary, entries of Aug. 20–21, 1943.
35. Patton diary, Aug. 20, 1943.
36. Butcher diary, Aug. 21, 1943.
37. Bradley Commentaries, USAMHI.
38. DDE, *Crusade in Europe*, 247.
39. Quoted in Blumenson, *The Patton Papers*, vol. 2, 338.
40. Gen. Theodore J. Conway oral history, USAMHI.
41. Quoted in DDE, *Crusade in Europe*, 201.
42. DDE to GSP, Dec. 1, 1943, Box 14, PP-LC.
43. Quoted in memorandum, John J. McCloy to DDE, Dec. 13, 1943, Box 75, Pre-Pres Papers, EL.

37. "A GRINDING WAR OF ATTRITION"

1. *Time*, Sept. 13, 1943.
2. DDE to MDE, July 24, 1943, Neal, *The Eisenhowers*, 46, and letter, DDE to Arthur B. Eisenhower, Oct. 20, 1943, *EP*, vol. 3, 1518–19.
3. Butcher diary, Oct. 28, 1943.
4. MacDonald, *The Mighty Endeavor*, 133.
5. Passionate arguments have raged on both sides of this question. In *1943: The Victory That Never Was* (New York, 1980), British author John Grigg asserts that Overlord could and should have taken place that year, before the Germans reinforced Normandy. Lt. Gen. James M. Gavin is among those who have disputed Grigg and others for failing to understand that American combat units in 1943 were simply incapable of fighting a first-class enemy like the Germans on the continent of Europe. In my conversations with General Gavin in the years prior to his death, he was adamant that U.S. combat experiences in the Mediterranean in 1943 and early 1944 were vital ingredients to the success later obtained in Normandy in the summer of 1944.
6. Maurice Matloff, *Strategic Planning for Coalition Warfare, 1943–1944* (Washington, D.C., 1959), 162.
7. Matloff has also written, "Although the basic decision of 'Europe First' held throughout the war, the question of how it was to be interpreted and applied arose early in the conflict and remained almost to the end." (Ibid., 9.)
8. David Reynolds, quoted in Kimball, *Forged in War*, 259.
9. David M. Kennedy, *Freedom from Fear* (New York, 1999), 595.
10. DDE unpublished memo, "Associates," dated July 5, 1967, Box 7, Post-Pres Papers, A-WR Series, EL.
11. Kennedy, *Freedom from Fear*, 596.
12. As Clark later explained, "I was forced to go in there because the Airman [Tedder] says I won't support you north—I can't. The Navy [Cunningham] says I won't support you north because your transports are too unprotected. . . . There was no one man to say, 'You'll do it!' " (meaning Eisenhower). Quoted in Hamilton, *Monty: Master of the Battlefield*, 406.
13. Matloff, *Strategic Planning for Coalition Warfare, 1943–1944*, 162.

14. Cable, DDE to Combined Chiefs of Staff, July 18, 1943, *EP*, vol. 2, 1261–62.
15. The shortage of landing craft exerted an enormous influence on the Salerno invasion plan, reducing the scope of the landings to three divisions (two British and one American), and small U.S. Ranger and British Commando forces.
16. Perret, *Eisenhower*, 236.
17. Samuel Eliot Morison, *Sicily-Salerno-Anzio* (Boston, 1954), 249.
18. Diary of Gen. Sir Bernard Montgomery, Aug. 7, 1943. Copies of the diary were furnished the author by Montgomery's official biographer, Nigel Hamilton. Montgomery's papers are presently in the IWM, London. Despite pleas from the British chiefs of staff, Allied problems in Sicily were directly attributable to the failure of Alexander, Tedder, and Cunningham to establish a joint headquarters in North Africa or Malta—a violation of the most important maxim of combined operations. With each of the Allied commanders based in a different location, the consequent lack of coordination and consultation was utterly predictable.
19. Ibid.
20. War Diary, Eighth Army, Minutes of Planning Conference, Aug. 10, 1943, PRO (WO 169/8494).
21. Marshall, for example, believed that Allied operations in Italy should have been limited to securing airfields around Foggia and tying down as many German troops as possible without undertaking an advance into northern Italy. He deplored the pressures by Churchill and the British chiefs of staff to advance deeper into Italy. (Marshall interviews, part 1.)
22. DDE interview, Feb. 16, 1949, OCMH file, USAMHI.
23. Interview of Lt. Gen. Walter Bedell Smith by official U.S. Army historian Howard McGaw Smyth, May 13, 1947, OCMH Collection, USAMHI.
24. Bedell Smith's case for Giant II was built largely around the fact that, in September 1943, the Germans were thought to have had a mere two battalions of combat troops based near Rome who might have intervened against an Allied raid. To the contrary, highly reliable signal intelligence (SIGINT) had by Aug. 28 disclosed that the 2nd Parachute and the 3rd Panzer Grenadier Divisions were known to be in the Rome area. Had either Bedell Smith or the other principal advocate of Giant II, the AFHQ G-2, Brig. Kenneth Strong, bothered to analyze their own intelligence they ought to have immediately determined that Rome could not have been held against what would certainly have been a rapid and violent German reaction. Details of these German dispositions were included in Strong's own AFHQ Weekly Intelligence Summary no. 53, published on Aug. 30, 1943. (See F. H. Hinsley et al., *British Intelligence in the Second World War*, part 1, vol. 3 [London, 1984], 108, and AFHQ Papers, PRO [WO 204/967]).
25. Ridgway, *Soldier*, 82. Bedell Smith interview, May 13, 1947, by Howard McGaw Smyth, USAMHI. The incident caused some of Ridgway's officers to revise their high opinions of Eisenhower. One senior officer said, "That was the first time I went against Ike. He wouldn't call if off merely because of loss of life. Hell, it wasn't *his* goddamned life. It was somebody else's." (Clay Blair, *Ridgway's Paratroopers* [New York, 1985], 168, contains a full account of this episode, as does Hamilton, *Monty: Master of the Battlefield*, part 4, chap. 2, and Crosswell, *The Chief of Staff*, chap. 10.
26. Perret, *Eisenhower*, 235.
27. JSDE, *Allies*, 353.
28. Marshall interviews.
29. Butcher diary, Sept. 16, 1943.
30. Admiral of the Fleet Viscount Cunningham, *A Sailor's Odyssey* (London, 1951), 570.
31. Proponents of Giant II never admitted that, had the operation gone ahead as planned and the 82nd Airborne committed in and around Rome, Salerno might well have been lost.

32. Butcher diary, Sept. 23, 1943.
33. Ibid.
34. DDE, *At Ease,* 267.
35. Demaree Bess, "Eisenhower's Flying Scot," *Saturday Evening Post,* Feb. 26, 1944.
36. DDE, *Crusade in Europe,* 99–100.
37. Of the 2,149 killed in action at Salerno, 296 were U.S. Navy and 83 Royal Navy. See Morison, *Sicily-Salerno-Anzio,* 313.
38. Dominick Graham and Shelford Bidwell, *Tug of War: The Battle for Italy, 1943–45* (London/New York), 99.
39. Diary of Gen. Mark W. Clark, Nov. 22, 1943, the Citadel Archives, Charleston, S.C., and the Alexander interviews, OCMH Collection, USAMHI. British embarrassment was evident when the official history (Molony, *The Mediterranean and Middle East,* vol. 5), failed (whether deliberately or inadvertently) to include any mention of the Salerno mutiny.
40. Alexander interviews, OCMH Collection, USAMHI, given to several official U.S. Army historians in Ottawa in 1949 during Alexander's tenure as the governor-general of Canada. Eisenhower would have relieved Dawley even earlier and when briefed on the problems at Salerno exclaimed, "Well, God Damn, why in the hell doesn't he [Clark] relieve Dawley?" (Gen. Lyman L. Lemnitzer, interview by Sidney T. Mathews, Jan. 16, 1948, OCMH Collection, USAMHI.)
41. DDE diary, Feb. 7, 1944.
42. DDE to GCM, Sept. 20, 1943, *EP,* vol. 3, 1440.
43. DDE to Adm. Lord Louis Mountbatten, Sept. 14, 1943, ibid., 1423.
44. DDE to MDE, May 27, 1943.
45. Macmillan, *War Diaries,* 259–60.
46. DDE to MDE, Dec. 2, 1943.
47. DDE to Aksel Nielsen, Sept. 6, 1943.
48. DDE to MDE, July 24 and Sept. 8, 1943.
49. DDE, *Letters to Mamie,* 144–45, 150.
50. Gilbert, *Road to Victory,* 483.
51. Brendon, *Ike,* 122.
52. Ibid.
53. Martin Blumenson, *Salerno to Cassino* (Washington, D.C., 1969), 180. As he would throughout the war, Eisenhower tended to rely too heavily on the pronouncements of Strong, the AFHQ intelligence officer. Strong failed to grasp that the Germans would only withdraw when forced to do so. Both "paid too little regard to field conditions and too much to the current indulgence in what one staff officer called 'the annual "collapse of Germany" predictions' which were greeted with derision and cynicism in the field." (Graham and Bidwell, *Tug of War,* 127.)
54. Alexander dispatch, published as a supplement to the *London Gazette,* June 12, 1950.
55. James L. Stokesbury, *A Short History of World War II* (New York, 1980), 299.

38. "WHO WILL COMMAND OVERLORD?"

1. David Eisenhower, *Eisenhower: At War,* 21–22, and Stimson and Bundy, *On Active Service,* 436–38.
2. JSDE, *Allies,* 372.
3. Butcher diary, Oct. 5, 1943, and Perret, *Eisenhower,* 242–43.
4. Summersby, *Eisenhower Was My Boss,* 87–89.
5. Ibid., 93.
6. Sherwood, *Roosevelt and Hopkins,* 770.
7. Thomas B. Buell, *Master of Sea Power: A Biography of Fleet Admiral Ernest J. King* (Boston, 1980), 404–05, and Butcher diary, Nov. 23, 1943.

8. DDE manuscript, "Churchill and Marshall," Box 8, Post-Pres Papers, A-WR series, EL. Marshall learned only later that King and Arnold had gone directly to Roosevelt to oppose his transfer. (Marshall interviews, Nov. 15, 1956.)

9. DDE, *At Ease*, 266.

10. Summersby, *Eisenhower Was My Boss*, 102–03. Kay Summersby was among those accompanying Eisenhower during his travels. The only negative aspect of an otherwise fascinating experience were the swarms of mosquitoes and heat intense enough to bake bread, none of which deterred Eisenhower in the slightest.

11. DDE to MDE, Dec. 2, 1943.

12. Quoted in Gilbert, *Road to Victory*, 526.

13. In recent years numerous British accounts and memoirs have stressed that Churchill and Brooke were indeed committed to Operation Overlord. An equal number of American participants were of the opposite view. In an unpublished memoir, Eisenhower described how Brooke privately expressed deep misgivings about the cross-Channel venture and spoke favorably of a "thrust and peck" strategy of hammering Axis flanks to the benefit of the Red Army, whose responsibility, he said, should be the destruction of Hitler's land forces. Brooke later insisted that Eisenhower had obviously misunderstood him.

14. Gilbert, *Road to Victory*, 523.

15. Stephen Roskill, *Churchill and the Admirals* (London, 1977), 222.

16. Alanbrooke diary, Oct. 8, 1943.

17. Marshall interviews. According to Marshall, Churchill was so shocked by Marshall's outburst that Ismay "had to stay up with him all night."

18. DDE manuscript, "Churchill and Marshall," Box 8, Post-Pres Papers, A-WR series, EL.

19. Sherwood, *Roosevelt and Hopkins*, 788. Gilbert, *Road to Victory*, chap. 34, passim, contains an account from Churchill's perspective.

20. Marshall, quoted in Sherwood, *Roosevelt and Hopkins*, 803.

21. DDE, *Crusade in Europe*, 227.

22. Burns, *Roosevelt: The Soldier of Freedom*, 415.

23. DDE, *Crusade in Europe*, 229. Underneath Roosevelt's note Marshall had thoughtfully written, "Dear Eisenhower, I thought you might like to have this as a memento."

24. JSDE oral history interview, EL.

25. Quoted in Cray, *General of the Army*, 438. Marshall's aide and executive secretary, Col. Frank McCarthy, saw no reaction on the part of his boss to the most disappointing professional news of his career. "He was really a duty-bound man," he told biographer Ed Cray.

26. DDE, *Crusade in Europe*, 229, and various other accounts in which this message has been reproduced.

27. FDR, quoted in James Roosevelt (with Bill Libby), *My Parents: A Differing View* (Chicago, 1976), 176.

28. Crosswell, *The Chief of Staff*, 202.

29. McKeogh, *Sgt. Mickey and General Ike*, 95, Butcher diary, Dec. 20, 1943, and Summersby, *Eisenhower Was My Boss*, 109.

30. Ambrose, *The Supreme Commander*, 317, and Butcher diary, Dec. 20, 1943.

31. Crosswell, *The Chief of Staff*, 202.

32. Ambrose, *The Supreme Commander*, 318.

33. DDE to Lt. Gen. Carl A. Spaatz, Dec. 23, 1943, *EP*, vol. 3, 1611, Ambrose, *The Supreme Commander*, 321, Perret, *Eisenhower*, 249, and DDE to Mark Clark, Dec. 27, 1943, *EP*, vol. 3, 1624. Eisenhower mildly said to Clark that "such an arrangement does not suit me at all. . . . I object to it." Like the armed forces, U.S. rest centers were also segregated. When Spaatz learned that black officers were being excluded from Capri, he

ordered a separate rest area built for combat pilots. However, facilities for black enlisted men and noncombat officers and enlisted men were not operational until May 1944. (Davis, *Spaatz*, 259–60.)

34. Quoted in Susan Eisenhower, *Mrs. Ike*, 214.
35. MDE to the Douds, Nov. 16, 1943, Box 4, Barbara Thompson Eisenhower Papers, EL.
36. JSDE, *Strictly Personal*, 50–51.
37. DDE manuscript, "Churchill and Marshall."
38. Churchill's role and culpability in the Anzio campaign is in chap. 6 of the author's *Fatal Decision*.
39. Quoted in Carlo D'Este, *Decision in Normandy* (New York/London, 1983), 32.
40. Perret, *Eisenhower*, 243.
41. DDE interview with S. L. A. Marshall, June 3, 1946, USAMHI. Eisenhower's later statement, "My God, if I were going to do it I would want ten or twelve divisions" (to establish a beachhead on the shores of France), was a reaction to his earlier misgivings.
42. Alanbrooke diary. Brooke was not alone; the new first sea lord, Eisenhower's friend and ardent supporter Admiral Andrew Cunningham, likewise thought that Alexander was "totally unfitted for the job." A fuller account appears in *Decision in Normandy*, chap. 4.
43. Walter Bedell Smith interview with Dr. Forrest C. Pogue, May 9, 1947, OCMH file, USAMHI.
44. GCM to DDE, Dec. 29, 1943. For some time Marshall had been urging Eisenhower to return home, to no avail, as each time Eisenhower would decline.
45. Winston S. Churchill, *Closing the Ring* (Boston, 1951), 426, and DDE manuscript, "Churchill and Marshall," Box 8, Post-Pres Papers, A-WR series, EL.
46. Butcher diary, Dec. 28, 1943. Afterward Butcher said he thought Eisenhower's pronouncement "would add to the over-optimism at home." Eisenhower added a qualification: "The only thing needed for us to win the European war in 1944 is for every man and woman, all the way from the front line to remotest hamlet of our two countries, to do his or her full duty." Butcher was right. The New York *Daily News* editorialized that Eisenhower had given rise to false hopes that would be "a convenient loophole through which a 'talking general' could slide if he did not deliver the goods in 1944." (Butcher diary, Jan. 23, 1944.)

39. SUPREME ALLIED COMMANDER

1. Butcher diary, Jan. 16, 1944. Butcher's homecoming could not have been without its uncomfortable moments. While overseas he had met a Red Cross woman with whom he began a long affair. After the war he divorced Ruth Butcher to marry his lover. Theirs was a solid marriage that lasted until Butcher's death in 1985.
2. David Eisenhower, *Eisenhower: At War*, 56.
3. Butcher diary, Jan. 16, 1944.
4. MDE oral history.
5. JSDE, *Strictly Personal*, 51.
6. MDE oral history, EL. Mamie remained defensive on this subject even though she knew Ike was only jesting. "I never allowed a man to come into my apartment if there wasn't another woman or somebody there. I was going to have nothing started of any kind. I never went out with even his best friend during the war."
7. David, *Ike & Mamie*, 120.
8. Summersby Morgan, *Past Forgetting*, 201–02. While the Kay Summersby Morgan version is suspect for having embellished her relationship with Eisenhower, the claim that Eisenhower had indiscreetly uttered Kay's name to Mamie does not appear to be in dispute, nor are her descriptions of life in AFHQ and SHAEF.

9. DDE to MDE, Jan. 20, 1944.
10. Davis, *Soldier of Democracy*, 456–57. With the exception of Davis, most accounts have Edgar and his wife present from Tacoma, Washington, which is doubtful given the short notice of Eisenhower's visit and the extreme difficulty of wartime travel for unofficial reasons such as this. For Arthur it would have been a brief journey from nearby Kansas City.
11. DDE, *Crusade in Europe*, 240.
12. David Eisenhower, *Eisenhower: At War*, 62–63, and MDE oral history, EL.
13. Beschloss, *Eisenhower*, 61.
14. David Eisenhower, *Eisenhower: At War*, 65.
15. Anthony Cave Brown, *Bodyguard of Lies* (London, 1976), 409–10.
16. McKeogh, *Sgt. Mickey and General Ike*, 102–03.
17. Eisenhower again filled a dual role, this time as commander of all U.S. forces in the ETO.
18. Charles H. Corlett, *Cowboy Pete* (Santa Fe, 1974), 88.
19. Murray and Millett, *A War to Be Won*, 419.
20. Russell F. Weigley, *Eisenhower's Lieutenants* (Bloomington, Ind., 1981), 99.
21. Crosswell, *The Chief of Staff*, 178, and Patton diary, Feb. 12, 1944.
22. Weigley, *Eisenhower's Lieutenants*, 551.
23. Bradley, *A General's Life*, 210. Devers fared little better with Marshall. By early 1944 he was deemed by the chief of staff to have been overambitious and thus suspect. (Pogue interviews, Nov. 13, 1956.) Only Albert Wedemeyer seems to have had an unbiased opinion of Devers. In the summer of 1943 he submitted a series of personal, confidential evaluations of the top American personnel to Marshall. Of Devers he wrote, "a happy selection [as CG, ETO]. He is rapidly winning the respect and confidence of the British, and all the Americans are uniformly pleased with the manner in which they receive decisions and sound directions." (Keith E. Eiler, ed., *Wedemeyer on War and Peace* [Stanford, Calif., 1987], 62.)
24. Interview of Lt. Gen. Walter Bedell Smith by Forrest C. Pogue, 1947, USAMHI. Lee routinely bypassed Smith and went directly to Eisenhower on matters others would have been skewered for by the SHAEF chief of staff.
25. Patton diary, Aug. 7, 1944, and Weigley, *Eisenhower's Lieutenants*, 84.
26. Having completed its mission, Morgan's COSSAC staff would shortly cease to exist.
27. D'Este, *Decision in Normandy*, 58.
28. Before January 1944, 21st Army Group was headed by Gen. Sir Bernard Paget, commander of British Home Forces, a fine soldier but considered too defense-minded for the Overlord command. (Quote from Paget interview with Dr. Forrest C. Pogue, OCMH Collection, USAMHI.)
29. Samuel Eliot Morison, *The Invasion of France and Germany, 1944–1945* (Boston, 1968), 24.
30. Pogue interview with Wing Commander Leslie Scarman, Feb. 25, 1947. Later Lord Scarman and a distinguished jurist, he was Tedder's aide during the war. According to Scarman, Tedder's full services were never employed in SHAEF although there were times when he was able "to break through his disadvantageous position to Gen. Eisenhower personally."
31. Cray, *General of the Army*, 444.
32. Bradley tried hard but failed to get Lucian Truscott released from Italy. Had he been successful, it is probable that he would have been given command of V Corps over Gerow. (Bradley, *A General's Life*, 233.)
33. Butcher diary, April 28, 1944.
34. Weigley, *Eisenhower's Lieutenants*, 121–22. Middleton was youngest colonel in the AEF during World War I and prior to 1940 had retired after a distinguished thirty-seven-

year career. In praise rare for Marshall, he cited Middleton as "the outstanding infantry regimental commander on the battlefield in France."

35. DDE to Henry J. F. Miller, May 5, 1944, and GCM, May 6, 1944, *EP*, vol. 3, 1848–50.
36. Both quotes in DDE diary, Feb. 7, 1944.
37. Butcher diary, Jan. 27 and Feb. 11, 1944. Patton's Jan. 26, 1944, diary entry notes that at dinner the same evening, "Ike very nasty and show-offish," which he blamed on the presence of Kay Summersby.
38. Patton diary, April 5, 1944.
39. D'Este, *Patton*, 567.
40. Miller, *Ike the Soldier*, 639.
41. Quoted in James M. Gavin, *On to Berlin* (New York, 1978), 142.
42. Miller, *Ike the Soldier*, 639.
43. Report by the Supreme Commander to the Combined Chiefs of Staff, 1946, reprinted in 1994 by the Center of Military History, U.S. Army.
44. Summersby Morgan, *Past Forgetting*, 206–07.
45. Patton diary, March 1, 1944.
46. Alan A. Michie, *The Invasion of Europe: The Story Behind D-Day* (New York, 1964), 94.
47. J. M. Stagg, *Forecast for Overlord* (London, 1971), 17.

40. "A MONUMENT TO THE IMAGINATION OF BRITISH AND AMERICAN PLANNERS"

1. The best explanation of the landing craft dilemma is in Gordon A. Harrison, *Cross-Channel Attack* (Washington, D.C., 1951), chap. 11, passim.
2. Ibid, 60–61, and Larrabee, *Commander in Chief*, 444.
3. Butcher diary, March 7, 1943.
4. Larrabee, *Commander in Chief*, 444.
5. Ambrose, *The Supreme Commander*, 413.
6. Max Hastings, *Overlord: D-Day, June 6, 1944* (New York, 1984), 34.
7. DDE, *Crusade in Europe*, 244.
8. Perret, *Eisenhower*, 265.
9. For a full account see Max Hastings, *Bomber Command* (London, 1979).
10. Butcher diary, Nov. 23, 1943.
11. Hastings, *Bomber Command*, 326–27.
12. Ibid., 327.
13. Portal, who was well respected and a sitting member of the Combined Chiefs of Staff, initially sided against the Transportation Plan but was eventually persuaded of its necessity. His word carried considerable weight.
14. Solly Zuckerman, *From Apes to Warlords* (London, 1978), 236.
15. Weigley, *Eisenhower's Lieutenants*, 62.
16. Zuckerman, *From Apes to Warlords*, chaps. 12 and 13, passim, and John J. Sullivan, *Overlord's Eagles* (Jefferson, N.C., 1997), 73, and chap. 7, passim.
17. Arthur Bryant, *Triumph in the West* (London, 1959), 182. Foreign Secretary Anthony Eden was also firmly opposed to the plan and did his best to emasculate it on grounds that it would have a detrimental effect on Britain's postwar relations with France. (Anthony Eden, *The Reckoning* [Boston, 1965], 522–25.)
18. Zuckerman, *From Apes to Warlords*, 251.
19. DDE to Churchill, April 5, 1944, *EP*, vol. 3, 1809–10. Eisenhower also bluntly reminded Churchill, "We must never forget that one of the fundamental factors leading to the decision for undertaking OVERLORD was the conviction that our overpowering air force would make feasible an operation which might otherwise be considered extremely hazardous, if not foolhardy."

20. Forrest C. Pogue, *The Supreme Command* (Washington, D.C., 1954), 131.
21. Ibid., 132.
22. Hastings, *Bomber Command*, 328–29.
23. Perret, *Eisenhower*, 267.
24. DDE diary, March 22, 1944.
25. Davis, *Spaatz*, 390–93.
26. Gilbert, *Road to Victory*, 739. "Terrible things are being done," Churchill wrote to Anthony Eden in late May. To Tedder he complained that the best targets had not been chosen and that "you [the RAF] are piling up an awful load of hatred." (Ibid., 784.)
27. See John Ehrman, *Grand Strategy*, vol. 5 (London, 1956), 298–304.
28. Rear Adm. Morton L. Devo, quoted in Morison, *The Invasion of France and Germany*, 69–70. Leigh-Mallory recorded in his diary that Eisenhower delivered a crisp speech in which he noted that they were assembled to hear the force commanders each brief their plan. "I would emphasize but one thing, that I consider it to be the duty of anyone who sees a flaw in the plan not to hesitate to say so. I have no sympathy with anyone, whatever his station, who will not brook criticism. We are here to get the best possible results and you must make a really co-operative effort." (Air Chief Marshal Sir Trafford Leigh-Mallory, "Impressions of the Meeting Held at St. Paul's School on May 15, 1944, PRO [AIR 37/784].)
29. Alanbrooke diary, May 15, 1944.
30. Alanbrooke, "Notes on My Life."
31. Brendon, *Ike*, 139, quoting Ismay letter to DDE, Dec. 30, 1960, Post-Pres Papers, A-WR series, EL.
32. Leigh-Mallory, "Impressions."
33. The Papers of General the Lord Ismay, the Liddell Hart Center for Military Archives, King's College, London.
34. Address given by Gen. Montgomery to the General Officers of the Four Field Armies on 15 May 1944, Pre-Pres Papers, EL.
35. Eisenhower interview with S. L. A. Marshall, June 3, 1946. Churchill used virtually the same language in a telegram to Roosevelt on April 1. "I harden for it [Overlord] the nearer I get to it." Eisenhower, he said, "is a very large man." (Churchill to FDR, in Warren F. Kimball, ed., *Churchill and Roosevelt: The Complete Correspondence*, vol. 3 [Princeton, N.J., 1984], 74.)
36. Allied Expeditionary Air Force (AEAF) Historical Record, PRO (AIR 37/1057).
37. Ibid.
38. Quoted in Butcher diary, May 9, 1944.
39. DDE manuscript, "Churchill and Marshall," Box 8, Post-Pres Papers, A-WR series, EL.
40. Ibid.
41. DDE diary, Feb. 7, 1944.
42. Kimball, *Forged in War*, 259–60. Roosevelt's suspicions of British imperialism mirrored American public opinion, reflected findings that in a June 1942 poll that had seen 56 percent of Americans believing the British were "oppressors," and that Churchill's arguments that "British imperialism has spread and is spreading democracy more widely than any other system of government since the beginning of time" fell "on deaf ears." (David Fromkin, *In the Time of the Americans* [New York, 1995], 562.)
43. Butcher diary, Feb. 26, 1944.
44. Eisenhower interview with S. L. A. Marshall, June 3, 1946, USAMHI.
45. F. H. Hinsley, *British Intelligence in the Second World War*, vol. 3, part 2 (London, 1988), 47.
46. There were actually two deception operations. Fortitude North was a simulated threat to Scandinavia by both Anglo-American forces and the Red Army; and Fortitude

South, the Pas de Calais operation. The original deception plan was drawn up by Lt. Gen. Sir Frederick E. Morgan's COSSAC planning staff in Sept. 1943. The initial invasion force against Normandy was inadequate in both size and scope, and it was considered essential that some means be found to ease the pressure on the invasion force both before and after Operation Overlord by pinning down as many German forces as possible in the Pas de Calais. Eventually COSSAC's deception plan evolved into Fortitude in 1944.

47. D'Este, *Patton*, 577.
48. Michael Howard, *British Intelligence in the Second World War*, vol. V, *Strategic Deception* (London, 1990), 105.
49. Daniel Wyatt, article on Operation Fortitude in *World War II* magazine, May 1994.
50. Before the invasion of Sicily, Hitler and the German high command were similarly hoaxed by a British deception operation as old as the Trojan horse: the notorious "man who never was." In April 1943 a corpse purporting to be that of a Royal Marine officer washed ashore in southern Spain, where an Abwehr agent was known to be operating. Chained to his wrist was a briefcase containing highly sensitive documents revealing that Sicily was merely a ruse to deflect Axis forces from the real Allied target, which was the Balkans. The corpse and its authentic documents were clever plants designed to hoodwink the Germans into believing that the British *wanted* the Germans to believe the target in the Mediterranean was Sicily—"so *that* obviously can't be the real target." Operation Mincemeat had an immediate impact, including the diversion of a panzer division shifted a thousand miles away from southern France, on a wild-goose chase to the Peloponnesus. (A full account is in D'Este, *Bitter Victory*, chap. 9.)
51. Brown, *Bodyguard of Lies*, 436–37.
52. GCM to DDE, Apr. 29, 1944, SHAEF Papers, NA II. The editorial also recommended the disapproval of a permanent promotion list of Regular Army officers then in the U.S. Senate for action. Patton offered to authorize having his name withdrawn from the list in order not to jeopardize the promotions of others.
53. Ibid. Patton's exact words have been the subject of some debate but as Eisenhower reported to Marshall, he apparently said, "Since it seems to be the destiny of America, Great Britain and Russia to rule the world, the better we know each other the better off we will be."
54. Quoted in Bradley, *A Soldier's Story*, 231.
55. Patton diary, Apr. 7, 1944.
56. Ibid., Apr. 27, 1944.
57. DDE to GSP, Apr. 29, 1944, *EP*, vol. 3, 1839–40.
58. DDE to GCM, Apr. 30, 1944, ibid., 1840–41.
59. Patton diary, May 1, 1944.
60. GSP to Beatrice Patton, May 2, 1944, Box 14, PP-LC.
61. Eisenhower, *At Ease*, 270–71. A slightly different version is in the unpublished memoir of Col. Justus "Jock" Lawrence (GCML), according to which, Eisenhower told him that when Patton "started to cry all over again . . . I could no longer stand it. This was too much for me! I stretched out on the couch in my office and burst into laughter, which I now regret for it was, in retrospect, cruel. General Patton stood at strict attention, not even looking at me lying on the couch, laughing." After Patton departed, "I had to tell someone, so I called in Beetle [Smith] and told him what had happened. It is probably the only time in the all the years of my long experience with Smith that I saw Beetle really lose himself in laughter!"
62. Cable, GCM to DDE, May 2, 1944. Marshall, who seems to have been pointing Eisenhower toward giving Patton yet another chance, noted that none of the editorials in the United States, however caustic, had actually called for his relief from command.
63. Cable, DDE to GSP, May 3, 1944, *EP*, vol 3, 1846–47. Eisenhower indicated that what principally saved Patton was the fact that he had resisted making a speech well before

the meeting, and had spoken in the (mistaken) belief that his remarks were off the record.

64. DDE to GCM, May 3, 1944, ibid., *EP*, vol. 3, 1846.

65. "Some Personal Memoirs of Col. Justus 'Jock' Lawrence," GCML.

66. Bradley, *A General's Life*, 222, and DDE to GCM, Apr. 30, 1944, SHAEF Papers. According to Bradley's collaborator, Clay Blair, Bradley was considerably miffed to learn that Eisenhower had not consulted him in reaching his decision to retain Patton. Bradley attributed Eisenhower's decision partly to the fact that there was no hope of getting Truscott from Italy, and that Churchill had dismissed Knutsford as trifling.

67. Marty Snyder, *My Friend Ike* (New York, 1956), 53–54. Unable to locate any hot dogs, Eisenhower's personal cook, Marty Snyder, turned in desperation to the navy, hoping to arrange a swap of favors. Given ten dozen (four dozen more than he asked for), a grateful Snyder asked what the navy wanted in return. No charge, replied the navy mess steward: "We're glad to get rid of 'em."

68. Ibid., 57.

69. Summersby Morgan, *Past Forgetting*, 210.

70. By D-Day, Eisenhower's U.S. and British logisticians had built housing for 1.2 million troops, 20 million square feet of covered storage, and another 44 million square feet of open storage; enough hospital beds to accommodate 124,000 patients; 270 miles of railroads, and 163 separate airfields. Between November 1943 and May 1944, 8,923,369 tons of military supplies were delivered to the United Kingdom from the United States. (*Logistics in World War II: Final Report of the Army Service Forces* [Washington, D.C., 1993], 160, and Roland G. Ruppenthal, *Logistical Support of the Armies*, vol. 1 [Washington, D.C., 1953], 237.)

71. Allied strength included twenty American, fourteen British, three Canadian, one Free French, and one (Free) Polish divisions; 5,000 thousand fighter aircraft; 2,300 transport aircraft, and 2,600 gliders.

72. Morison, *The Invasion of France and Germany*, 25. The author of the idea was Commodore John Hughes-Hallett. Churchill immediately embraced it, minuting Mountbatten, "Piers for use on beaches. They *must* float up and down with the tide. . . . Let me have the best solution worked out. Don't argue the matter. The difficulties will argue for themselves."

73. Barney Oldfield, *Never a Shot in Anger* (New York, 1956), 44–46. Colonel Oldfield was a public relations officer on the SHAEF staff.

74. Hastings, *Overlord*, 69.

75. Montgomery diary, June 2, 1944, Montgomery Papers, IWM. Montgomery also had praise for Bedell Smith: "I am very fond of him too; he is a very delightful person and a really high class staff officer." Montgomery was one of the few—possibly the only one—who ever referred to Smith as "delightful."

41. "O.K., WE'LL GO."

1. Various factors had combined to require changing the date of D-Day from late May to the first full-moon period in June.

2. "Report of Recent Attacks on Railways," issued by the German Transport Ministry, May 15, 1944, cited in L. F. Ellis, *Victory in the West*, vol. 1 (London, 1962), 111. At the end of May 1944 the Germans were able to operate only twenty trains per day in France. No bridge over the Seine below Paris was intact, and the SNCF (the French national railway) was operating at barely 10 percent of capacity. The road system was in equally bad shape.

3. Davis, *Spaatz*, 413, 414. Arguments continued after the war over the Transportation Plan, with its proponents convinced it made a significant contribution and its critics

claiming it was unnecessary. "The outstanding factor both before and during the invasion was the overwhelming air superiority of the enemy," wrote the historical staff of the Luftwaffe. (Ellis, *Victory in the West*, vol. 1, 110.) Once the decisions about the Transportation Plan were made, Bomber Harris proved surprisingly cooperative. Zuckerman wrote in his journal, "The amazing thing is that Harris, who was even more resistant than the Americans to the idea of AEAF domination, has in fact thrown himself wholeheartedly into the battle, has improved his bombing performance enormously, and has contributed more to the dislocation of enemy communications than any of the rest." (Journal of Prof. Solly Zuckerman, July 9, 1944, Zuckerman Papers, University of East Anglia.)

4. Ambrose, *Eisenhower*, 294.

5. DDE to MDE, May 21, 1944.

6. Powered by 6,000-horsepower Daimler-Benz diesel engines and capable of speeds of up to forty knots, each E-boat mounted two torpedos and one or more deck guns. (Nigel Lewis, *Exercise Tiger* [New York, 1990], 52.)

7. Morison, *The Invasion of France and Germany*, 66. Despite variations in the total number of killed in various official and unofficial accounts, what is certain is that more than seven hundred men were lost during Operation Tiger.

8. Harrison, *Cross-Channel Attack*, 270, and Ambrose, *D-Day*, 139, 292.

9. Cave Brown, *Bodyguard of Lies*, chap. 9, passim. German actions in the wake of Tiger, notes Cave Brown, indicates that "unknown to SHAEF . . . the Germans had obtained a significant hint of Neptune's destination through their ingenious penetration of the wireless communications of the Allied forces." (550.)

10. Charles B. MacDonald, "Slapton Sands: The Cover-Up That Never Was," *Army*, June 1988. MacDonald, a World War II combat infantryman and former U.S. Army official historian, was recalled from retirement to investigate Tiger, including an absurd allegation by an elderly British woman that the bodies of the victims had been thrown into a mass grave at Slapton Sands and forgotten. MacDonald's investigation and article effectively demolished the notions of the conspiracy theorists. The most malicious and specious coverage was by a Washington, D.C., television station, which alleged that Eisenhower authorized a massive cover-up of the event. The most honest investigation of Tiger is in Nigel Lewis, *Exercise Tiger*.

11. Blair, *Ridgway's Paratroopers*, 247, and Gavin, *On to Berlin*, 93–94.

12. Walter Isaacson and Evan Thomas, *The Wise Men* (New York, 1986), 196, and John J. McCloy oral history, EL.

13. W. S. Chalmers, *Full Cycle: The Biography of Sir Bertram Home Ramsay* (London, 1959), 216, and the diary of Adm. Sir Bertram Ramsay, May 29, 1944.

14. Michie, *The Invasion of Europe*, 120–21.

15. Kay Summersby diary, June 2, 1944, Box 140, Pre-Pres Papers, EL. The diary covers the period from June 1, 1944, to April 30, 1945 and offers not the slightest hint of intimacy between the two. Rather it is a series of periodic, brief remarks about what Eisenhower was doing, whom he saw, and occasionally what he thought or said.

16. Butcher diary, June 3, 1944. Eisenhower's abhorrence of any form of public displays of affection led even to his refusal to watch kissing scenes in a film. "He could never survive the kissing scenes," remembers John. "If there was a movie that had too much of that, he would leave." (JSDE oral history interview, ENHS.) Mickey McKeogh points out that during the war Eisenhower's cinematic tastes were similar. "He didn't like tear jerkers or pictures with too much love in them. Of course, he realized that some love is necessary in any story, but he didn't like it rubbed in too hard." (McKeogh, *Sgt. Mickey and General Ike*, 54–55.)

17. Ibid., June 4, 1944, writing of events of the previous day, June 3.

18. Maj. Gen. Sir Francis de Guingand, *Operation Victory* (London, 1947), 372–73.

19. Stagg, *Forecast for Overlord*, 99.
20. NBC's Red Mueller was one of four "pool" reporters permitted access to SHAEF's advance headquarters at Southwick Park. (Ryan, *The Longest Day*, 61.)
21. Cook, *Charles de Gaulle*, 210.
22. Kersaudy, *Churchill and De Gaulle*, 344.
23. Ibid., quoting from de Gaulle's memoirs, and Cook, *Charles de Gaulle*, 213.
24. Ismay, *Memoirs*, 357.
25. Crosswell, *The Chief of Staff*, 243.
26. Maj. Gen. Sir Kenneth Strong, quoted in Ambrose, *D-Day*, 187.
27. Tedder's account is quoted in Butcher's diary, June 5, 1944.
28. Walter Bedell Smith, *Eisenhower's Six Great Decisions* (New York, 1956), 55.
29. Chester Wilmot, *The Struggle for Europe* (London, 1952), 237.
30. Smith, *Eisenhower's Six Great Decisions*, 55.
31. Quote based on the notes and account of Air Vice Marshal J. M. Robb, in Harrison, *Cross-Channel Attack*, 274.
32. Hamilton, *Monty: Master of the Battlefield*, 605.
33. Summersby, *Eisenhower Was My Boss*, 145.
34. Pawle, *The War and Colonel Warden*, 301, and DDE, *Crusade in Europe*, 276.
35. David Eisenhower, *Eisenhower: At War*, 243, and Churchill, *Closing the Ring*, 622–24.
36. Smith, *Eisenhower's Six Great Decisions*, 53.
37. Ambrose, *D-Day*, 189.
38. There are numerous versions of Eisenhower's exact words, none of which the official historian, Forrest C. Pogue, could ever verify. Stephen Ambrose states that when he interviewed him in 1967, Eisenhower was certain that he had said, "O.K., let's go." (Ambrose, *The Supreme Commander*, fn., 417.) Chester Wilmot used "O.K., we'll go," based on his interview of Rear Admiral G. E. Creasy, Ramsay's chief of staff, and the written account of Air Marshal J. M. Robb. Eisenhower himself used the phrase in 1964 to *New York Times* reporter Herbert Mitgang, and thought that his decision had taken only about thirty seconds. ("D-Day plus 20 Years," *Look*, June 1964.)

    Alan Michie, another of the four pool reporters permitted at Southwick, immediately began to reconstruct Eisenhower's decision. "From Admiral Ramsay I extracted the hour-by-hour story of the meetings," wrote Michie. Ramsay insisted Eisenhower did not use the phrase "O.K., we'll go," but thought it was "O.K., let 'er rip," which Michie says Eisenhower agreed was what he had said. (Michie, *The Invasion of Europe*, 196.) Whatever the semantics, the intent was unambiguous and the fact was that it was uttered at the briefing held at 4:15 A.M., June 5, 1944, when Eisenhower merely affirmed his earlier decision to launch the invasion.
39. Ambrose, *D-Day*, 189.
40. The text of Eisenhower's June 6 proclamation appears in numerous publications, including *EP* vol. 3, 1913, and Pogue, *The Supreme Command*, 545.
41. Butcher diary, July 11, 1944. Eisenhower also revealed that he had written similar notes for every previous amphibious invasion but had secretly torn them up afterward. In none other, however, were the consequences of failure as daunting as in Overlord.
42. Mattingly, "A Compilation of the General Health Status of Dwight D. Eisenhower," EL.
43. Summersby, *Eisenhower Was My Boss*, 137.
44. Quoted in Perret, *Old Soldiers Never Die*, 192. Although MacArthur's remark was made in another context, its application to Eisenhower was certainly apt.
45. MDE oral history, EL.
46. Alanbrooke diary, June 5, 1944, and diary, Admiral of the Fleet Sir Andrew Cunningham, June 5, 1944, British Library.
47. Pawle, *The War and Colonel Warden*, 302.

48. Alanbrooke diary, June 5, 1944.

49. Chalmers, *Full Cycle,* 220, and Ramsay diary, June 5, 1944.

50. Goodwin, *No Ordinary Time,* 507–08.

51. John Keegan, *Six Armies in Normandy* (New York, 1982), 15.

52. Butcher diary, Aug. 17, 1944. After he was captured in August 1944, Maj. Lettau and Stagg met to discuss their respective roles. The German meteorologist was anxious to know how the Allies pulled off the invasion in light of the forecasts. Stagg noted that the Germans "had failed to grasp the significance of a 'weather front' which passed through the Channel early on June 5, with relatively good weather following it."

53. Brown, *Bodyguard of Lies,* 638, and Walter Warlimont, *Inside Hitler's Headquarters, 1939–1945* (Novato, Calif., reprint of 1964 British edition), 422.

54. Admiral Friedrich Ruge, quoted in David Eisenhower, *Eisenhower: At War,* 251. The account of Eisenhower's historic decision is based upon a compendium of sources: Stagg, *Forecast for Overlord,* Tedder, *With Prejudice,* Strong, *Intelligence at the Top,* Ambrose; *D-Day* and *The Supreme Commander,* Blair, *Ridgway's Paratroopers,* de Guingand, *Operation Victory,* Wilmot, *The Struggle for Europe,* Eisenhower, *Crusade in Europe,* Hamilton, *Monty: Master of the Battlefield,* Pogue, *The Supreme Command,* Brendon, *Ike,* Pawle, *The War and Colonel Warden,* Harrison, *Cross-Channel Attack,* Ryan, *The Longest Day,* Bedell Smith, *Eisenhower's Six Great Decisions,* David Eisenhower, *Eisenhower: At War,* Summersby, *Eisenhower Was My Boss,* and Summersby Morgan, *Past Forgetting,* Summersby diary, Butcher diary, J. M. Robb account, and Eisenhower's diary.

42. "I THANK THE GODS OF WAR WE WENT WHEN WE DID."

1. Leigh-Mallory to DDE, June 7, 1944, Box 71, Pre-Pres Papers. In July, Eisenhower would write to Sir Charles Portal, chief of the air staff, "I entertained some doubts as to the qualifications of Air Chief Marshal Leigh-Mallory. . . . In justice to him, I want to tell you now that I've liked the way he operated and cooperated. . . . I am extremely happy to have him." (DDE to Air Chief Marshal Sir Charles Portal, July 22, 1944, *EP,* vol. 2, 2025.)

2. There is a unresolved question about the timing of Speidel's telephone call to Rommel's home, which may have been as late as 10:30 A.M., June 6. Most accounts, however, still cite the call at approximately 6:30 A.M.

3. Ryan, *The Longest Day,* 258.

4. Wilmot, *The Struggle for Europe,* 307.

5. The only other significant decision Hitler could have made was to immediately release infantry units from the Fifteenth Army in the Pas de Calais to reinforce the Normandy front. Thanks to Fortitude, Hitler not only refused to do so on June 6 but at any time during the campaign. However, even had Hitler acted aggressively, the Fifteenth Army reserves lacked mobility and were simply too far away from Normandy to have made an immediate difference.

6. David Irving, *Hitler's War, 1942–1945* (London, 1977), 639.

7. McKeogh, *Sgt. Mickey and General Ike,* 116.

8. Butcher diary, June 6, 1944.

9. Walters, *Silent Missions,* 97. Walters, whose distinguished postwar career included service as UN ambassador and director of central intelligence, was the longest serving of Clark's World War II aides. After the war, Clark's daughter made the observation "Daddy always says that the only way to get things done in the headquarters is to grind down the aides." Walters replied, "[T]here is one thing you can say for your father; he is a man who lives by his principles." (109–10.)

10. Ryan, *The Longest Day,* 254–56.

11. Ambrose, *D-Day,* 492–93.

12. Roosevelt, quoted in "Normandy," U.S. Army campaign pamphlet, U.S. Army Center of Military History, 1994.

13. Goodwin, *No Ordinary Time,* 510.

14. Paul Lund and Harry Ludlum, *The War of the Landing Craft* (London, 1976), 146.

15. McKeogh, *Sgt. Mickey and General Ike,* 117.

16. Butcher diary, June 6, 1944.

17. Ambrose, *The Supreme Commander,* 386.

18. Cook, *Charles de Gaulle,* 217.

19. Butcher diary, June 8, 1944.

20. Telegram and letter, DDE to MDE, June 9, 1944.

21. Ian Kershaw, *Hitler: 1936–1945, Nemesis* (New York, 2000), 643.

22. Hastings, *Overlord,* 177.

23. Summersby Morgan, *Past Forgetting,* 222.

24. Cray, *General of the Army,* 458.

25. David Eisenhower, *Eisenhower: At War,* 298.

26. Butcher diary, June 13, 1944.

27. Cable, DDE to MDE and JSDE, May 24, 1944, *EP,* vol. 3, 1886–87.

28. Susan Eisenhower, *Mrs. Ike,* 221, and JSDE, *Strictly Personal,* 54. John Eisenhower graduated in the top third of the class of 1944: 137th of its 473 graduates. (Source: USMA *Register of Graduates.*)

29. David, *Ike & Mamie,* 123.

30. JSDE, *Strictly Personal,* 54.

31. The area around SHAEF Main at Bushy Park was hit frequently. On July 1, when Eisenhower was in Normandy, a V-1 struck within two hundred yards of his office, wounding five and blowing out panes of glass and part of the roof.

32. Perret, *Eisenhower,* 293, and Annan, *Changing Enemies,* 115.

33. DDE to MDE, June 9 and 13, 1944.

34. JSDE, *Strictly Personal,* 55.

35. Summersby, *Eisenhower Was My Boss,* 155.

36. JSDE, *Strictly Personal,* 63.

37. Summersby Morgan, *Past Forgetting,* 224–25.

38. Perret, *Eisenhower,* 292.

39. JSDE commentary in DDE, *Letters to Mamie,* 188.

40. JSDE describes one such occasion in *Strictly Personal,* 72–73.

41. Cook, *Charles de Gaulle,* 223.

42. Ibid., 228.

43. JSDE, *Strictly Personal,* 61–62.

44. De Gaulle, quoted in Cook, *Charles de Gaulle,* 225.

45. Don Cook, " 'Send Him Back to Algiers—in Chains if Necessary,' " *MHQ,* spring 1994.

46. Everett S. Hughes diary, July 15, 1944; David Irving, *The War Between the Generals* (New York, 1981), 192, Summersby, *Eisenhower Was My Boss,* 155–57, and Summersby Morgan, *Past Forgetting,* 229–30.

47. Susan Eisenhower, *Mrs. Ike,* 223.

48. Stagg, *Forecast for Overlord,* 126.

49. JSDE, *Strictly Personal,* 67.

50. Ibid., 68.

51. Butcher diary, June 27, 1944.

52. Everett S. Hughes diary, quoted in Hastings, *Overlord,* 166.

53. In late June Patton and Eisenhower inspected troop units in the West Country and Cornwall preparing to deploy to Normandy. Patton thought Eisenhower's habit of gathering them around (as Montgomery did) quite clever. "He talks very familiarly

to them . . . usually exhorting them to fight well, 'So that we can end this war and I can go home and go fishing.' " Patton remarked in his diary that Eisenhower relied too much on the use of the word "I," which he thought was the "style of an office seeker rather than that of a soldier. . . . I try to arouse fighting emotion—he tries [to get] votes—for what?" (GSP diary, June 26, 1944.)

54. D'Este, *Patton*, 612.

43. THE BATTLE FOR NORMANDY

1. Bradley, *A General's Life*, 272.
2. The blatant attempts by Tedder and Coningham to discredit Montgomery managed to draw him closer to the other outcast of the Allied hierarchy, Trafford Leigh-Mallory, of whom he wrote to his friend and confidant at the War Office, Maj. Gen. Frank Simpson (director of military operations), "We must definitely keep Leigh-Mallory as Air Commander-in-Chief. He is the only man who is out to help us with the land battle and has no jealous reactions." Unfortunately, notes air historian Richard Davis, "In the eyes of most of the top Allied airmen, Montgomery's support could only have been the kiss of death." (Richard Lamb, *Montgomery in Europe, 1943–45* [London, 1983], 126–27, citing Montgomery's letter to Simpson, and Davis, *Spaatz*, 468.)
3. Annan, *Changing Enemies*, 115.
4. Irving, *The War Between the Generals*.
5. Blumenson, *The Patton Papers*, vol. 2, 470.
6. Bradley, *A General's Life*, 267, and DDE to Bradley, July 1, 1944, *EP*, vol. 3, 1968.
7. Perret, *Eisenhower*, 295.
8. Ambrose, *The Supreme Commander*, 433.
9. Quoted in Martin Blumenson, *The Battle of the Generals* (New York, 1994), 121.
10. Hastings, *Overlord*, 245–46.
11. Martin Blumenson, *Breakout and Pursuit* (Washington, D.C., 1961), 46–47.
12. Eversley Belfield and H. Essame, *The Battle for Normandy* (London, 1975), 104.
13. Gen. Elwood P. Quesada oral history interview, EL, Thomas A. Hughes, *Over Lord: General Pete Quesada and the Triumph of American Tactical Air Power in World War II* (New York, 1995), 173–74, Bradley, *A Soldier's Story*, 325, Perret, *Eisenhower*, 295, entry by Lt. Col. James Gault in Butcher diary, July 5, 1944, *New York Times*, July 6, 1944, JSDE, *Letters to Mamie*, n. 2, 194–95, DDE to GCM, July 5, 1944, *EP*, vol. 3, 1972, and DDE to MDE, July 11, 1944.
14. Butcher diary, July 5, 1944.
15. Ellis, *Victory in the West*, vol. 1, 307.
16. The only time Eisenhower attended one of the daily Air Commanders' Conferences at Leigh-Mallory's HQ was on July 7, 1944, when he was present, presumably to provide his personal support in the event the bomber barons opposed Montgomery's request for saturation bombing. With no opposition and little debate the request was approved. (AEAF Historical Record, July 1944, PRO [AIR 37/1057].)
17. Ambrose, *The Supreme Commander*, 435.
18. DDE unpublished manuscript, "Churchill-Marshall."
19. Alanbrooke diary, July 6, 1944.
20. DDE chronology, June 6–Aug. 27, 1944, *EP*, vol. 5, passim. By contrast, Eisenhower met with Bradley seventeen times and de Guingand twelve.
21. Ambrose, *The Supreme Commander*, 426.
22. John Keegan, *The First World War* (New York, 1999), 421–22.
23. A detailed discussion of British manpower resources is in the author's *Decision in Normandy*, chap. 15, "The Manpower Dilemma."
24. Montgomery of Alamein, *Memoirs* (London, 1958), 262.
25. Smith, *Eisenhower's Six Great Decisions*, 75, and Montgomery, *Memoirs*, ibid.

26. Letter, Robert A. Lovett to Lt. Gen. Carl A. Spaatz, July 25, 1944, Spaatz Papers, LC.
27. Dr. Forrest C. Pogue, letter to the author, Oct. 21, 1980.
28. Leonard Mosley, *Marshall* (New York, 1982), 285.
29. Butcher diary, July 20, 1944.
30. Ibid., July 19, 1944.
31. Crosswell, *The Chief of Staff*, 249.
32. Alanbrooke diary, July 26 and 27, 1944.
33. Murray and Millett, *A War to Be Won*, 428.
34. "Notes on conversation with General [Sir Miles] Dempsey," by Chester Wilmot, n.d., Liddell Hart Papers, King's College, London.

44. "DEAR IKE, TO-DAY I SPAT IN THE SEINE."

1. Hansen diary, July 20 and 23, 1944.
2. Ibid.
3. Ibid., and DDE, "Chronology," entry for July 20, 1944, *EP*, vol. 5, 161.
4. Spaatz, quoted in Perret, *Winged Victory*, 310.
5. Bradley, *A Soldier's Story*, 349, DDE to GCM, July 26, 1944, *EP*, vol. 3, 2030, and Butcher diary, July 26, 1944. McNair's death was kept secret, and his funeral was attended only by Patton, Bradley, and three others. "No band. A sad ending and useless sacrifice," wrote Patton in his diary on July 26.
6. Bradley, *A Soldier's Story*, 348, Perret, *Winged Victory*, 310–11, Blumenson, *Breakout and Pursuit*, 220–21, and Davis, *Spaatz*, chap. 13, passim. The air force generals wisely insisted on a 3,000-yard safety zone between the forward troops and the target area. Bradley demanded the bombs be placed closer and only reluctantly did they agree to reduce the separation, first to 1,500 yards, "which still did not satisfy him [Bradley]. In the end he agreed to withdraw the troops only 1,200 yards." (*Spaatz*, 465.) At one point, Bradley had first asked that his troops be emplaced a dangerously close eight hundred yards before being dissuaded. (Sullivan, *Overlord's Eagles*, 173.)
7. Maj. Gen. Troy Middleton's VIII Corps was then under First Army operational control, but to take advantage of Cobra's apparent success, Bradley elected to place the corps under Patton's operational control prior to Aug. 1. (Blumenson, *Breakout and Pursuit*, 37, and chap. 2, passim.)
8. Wesley F. Craven and James L. Cate, eds., *The Army Air Forces in World War II*, vol. 3, *Argument to V-E Day, Jan. 1944 to May 1945* (Chicago, 1951), 236.
9. Weigley, *Eisenhower's Lieutenants*, 160.
10. D'Este, *Patton*, 625.
11. Perret, *There's a War to Be Won*, 345.
12. Weigley, *Eisenhower's Lieutenants*, 85.
13. D'Este, *Decision in Normandy*, chap. 6.
14. Blumenson, *Breakout and Pursuit*, 349.
15. Ibid.
16. Pawle, *The War and Colonel Warden*, 308. According to Commander Thompson, there was a heated telephone conversation between Eisenhower and Churchill before the matter was smoothed over and Montgomery taken off the hook.
17. Blumenson, *The Battle of the Generals*, 147.
18. Hastings, *Overlord*, 280.
19. Montgomery diary, July 29, 1944.
20. Butcher diary, Aug. 4, 1944.
21. Murray and Millett, *A War to Be Won*, 443.
22. DDE to GCM, Aug. 5, 1944, *EP*, vol. 4, 2055–56. It hardly mattered that only the previous day, before visiting Eisenhower, and a mere eleven days before the landings, Churchill attempted to alter Anvil/Dragoon by sending a telegram to the U.S. chiefs

of staff proposing a last-minute shift of the operation from the Riviera to Brittany, whose ports were still in German hands. The German garrison at Brest, the most important of the Brittany ports, held out until September 19, and Lorient and Saint-Nazaire were not captured until May 1945. The folly of attempting to shift a large-scale operation, beyond the reach of air cover and its base of operations, to German-held Brittany was apparently lost on the prime minister, whose proposal was opposed by Eisenhower and rejected by Roosevelt. With only a week left before the date of the landings, Churchill appeared finally to have caved in, cabling the president, "I pray God that you may be right." Churchill's true feelings over Anvil/Dragoon were contained in an angry memo to Ismay in July 1944. "The Americans must understand that we have been ill treated and are furious. Do not let any smoothings cover up this fact . . . if we take everything lying down there will be no end to what will be put upon us." (John Ehrman, *Grand Strategy*, vol. 5 [London, 1956], 362–67.)

23. Butcher diary, Aug. 11, 1944, and Pogue, *The Supreme Command*, 225.
24. DDE to Churchill, Aug. 11, 1944, *EP*, vol. 4, 2065.
25. Butcher diary, Aug. 15, 1944.
26. Winston S. Churchill to Clementine Churchill, Aug. 17, 1944, quoted in Gilbert, *Road to Victory*, 899.
27. DDE to GCM, July 12, 1944, *EP*, vol. 3, 2000.
28. The 2nd Battalion, 120th Infantry Regiment (30th Division) defended Hill 317, and nearly three hundred were killed or wounded. The unit was awarded a presidential unit citation, and each of the four company commanders received the Distinguished Service Cross for valor.
29. Bradley, *A Soldier's Story*, 375–76.
30. Ibid., 377.
31. Perret, *There's a War to Be Won*, 366.
32. Bradley, *A Soldier's Story*, 226, and Butcher diary, April 1, 1945.
33. Quoted in D'Este, *Decision in Normandy*, 449.
34. In 1984 the author and his wife were escorted into the infamous corridor of death by a veteran of the Polish 1st Armored Division who survived the battle of Mount Ormel, Z. L. Mieczkowski. Despite the passage of forty years, there was still clear evidence of war in the form of discarded helmets and other accoutrements. The place still retained an eerie presence and a stale aura of death. What Eisenhower saw during his battlefield tour is unimaginable.
35. D'Este, *Decision in Normandy*, 430–32. In the U.S. sector of the battlefield were found 220 tanks, 160 self-propelled guns, more than 700 artillery pieces, and 5,000 vehicles. British figures were equally staggering: 187 armored vehicles and self-propelled artillery pieces, 157 armored cars, 1,800 trucks, 669 civilian cars, and 252 other pieces of ordnance—a combined total of more than 9,000 vehicles. The once formidable 12th SS Panzer Division was a typical example. Its commander, SS Gen. Kurt Meyer, escaped and later reckoned he had lost 80 percent of his tanks, 70 percent of his reconnaissance vehicles and personnel carriers, 60 percent of his artillery, and 50 percent of his other vehicles.
36. Stimson and Bundy, *On Active Service in Peace and War*, 659–60.
37. Belfield and Essame, *The Battle for Normandy*, 219.
38. James Lucas and James Barker, *The Killing Ground* (London, 1981), 160.
39. Belfield and Essame, *The Battle for Normandy*, 218.
40. Lucas and Barker, *The Killing Ground*, 158.
41. DDE, *Crusade in Europe*, 306.
42. Quoted in D'Este, *Decision in Normandy*, 431, n. 4.
43. Kershaw, *Hitler*, 721–22.
44. Quoted in Eddy Florentin, *The Battle of the Falaise Gap* (New York, 1967), 340.

45. TRIUMPH AND CONTROVERSY

1. Perret, *Eisenhower*, 305.
2. Cook, *Charles de Gaulle*, 238.
3. British Enigma decrypt of Hitler's message of Aug. 23, 1944, to Gen. Dietrich von Choltitz, quoted in Hinsley, *British Intelligence in the Second World War*, vol. 3, part II (London, 1988), 371–72.
4. Cook, *Charles de Gaulle*, 238.
5. Ibid.
6. I. C. B. Dear and M. R. D. Foot, eds., *The Oxford Companion to World War II* (Oxford/ New York, 1995), 414.
7. Blumenson, *Breakout and Pursuit*, 603.
8. DDE to Bedell Smith, Aug. 22, 1944, *EP*, vol. 4, 2089–90.
9. Bradley, *A Soldier's Story*, 392.
10. Blumenson, *Breakout and Pursuit*, 620.
11. Cook, *Charles de Gaulle*, 251. Grateful as he may have been on August 24, de Gaulle managed to overlook Eisenhower's generosity in his memoirs.
12. Hansen diary, incidental comments, Aug. 1944.
13. Summersby, *Eisenhower Was My Boss*, 177.
14. Blumenson, *Breakout and Pursuit*, 627.
15. Ibid., 628.
16. For a breakdown of the figures, see D'Este, *Decision in Normandy*, Appendix B.
17. Blumenson, *Breakout and Pursuit*, 555–56. A case in point was the elite 12th SS Panzer Division, which at one time numbered more than ten thousand men, but was estimated to have had fewer than a hundred left.
18. Detailed examinations of the Falaise controversy are in D'Este, *Decision in Normandy*, chaps. 25 and 26, and in the author's "Falaise: The Trap Not Sprung," *MHQ*, Spring 1994.
19. Martin Blumenson, "General Bradley's Decision at Argentan," in Kent Roberts Greenfield, ed., *Command Decisions* (Washington, D.C., 1960), 417.
20. Montgomery, *Memoirs*, 254–55.
21. Cole C. Kingseed, "When the Allies Forfeited a Golden Opportunity," *Army*, March 1994.
22. Farago, *Patton: Ordeal and Triumph*, 492–93.
23. Blumenson, "Bradley-Patton: World War II's 'Odd Couple.'"
24. Blumenson, *The Battle of the Generals*, 273–74.
25. D'Este, *Decision in Normandy*, 447. The historian of the 21st Army Group wrote in 1954 that Montgomery originally envisioned "the rolling up of the German left flank [at Caen]—not [the] right. . . . He did not envisage—and could never have envisaged—the double envelopment battle that resulted in the dissolution of the German armies in Normandy."
26. Blumenson, *The Patton Papers*, vol. 2, 542.
27. Walter Bedell Smith to DDE, Apr. 1, 1948, Smith Papers, EL, and Crosswell, *The Chief of Staff*, 251.
28. While at Shellburst, Eisenhower had expressed a wish for a cow to provide fresh milk, and in Granville his wish came true when the locals presented SHAEF with one. None of his staff knew how to milk the cow, until Eisenhower unexpectedly turned up, sat down, and proceeded to demonstrate the right technique. "You city slickers have a lot to learn," he said with a laugh. (Snyder, *My Friend Ike*, 65.)
29. DDE to GCM, Aug. 31, 1944, *EP*, vol. 4, 2208.
30. *After the Battle* magazine, no. 84, 1994.

46. "A TACTICIAN'S HELL AND A QUARTERMASTER'S PURGATORY"

1. Charles B. MacDonald, *The Siegfried Line Campaign* (Washington, D.C., 1963), 5. In SHAEF reserve in the UK was the First Allied Airborne Army, consisting of two U.S. and two British airborne divisions, a Polish airborne brigade, and a British air-transportable infantry division. See chap. 48.)
2. Kershaw, *Hitler 1936–1945*, 717.
3. Model was replaced in part because of the extreme difficulty of simultaneously commanding both OB West and Army Group B.
4. Alexander Clifford, "Clifford Says: This Is Victory, Not War," *Daily Mail*, Sept. 2, 1944, quoted in G. E. Patrick Murray, *Eisenhower vs. Montgomery: The Continuing Debate* (Westport, Conn., 1996), 141.
5. Hansen diary, Sept. 2 and 5, 1944.
6. Leckie, *Delivered from Evil*, 767–68.
7. SHAEF intelligence estimates, quoted in Pogue, *The Supreme Command*, 244–45. Another high-level misjudgment occurred when the Joint Intelligence Committee in Whitehall loftily proclaimed that "organized resistance under the control of the German High Command is unlikely to continued beyond December 1, 1944, and . . . it may end even sooner." U.S. "post-exchange officials actually distributed a memorandum saying that they were arranging to return Christmas presents—already in the mail—to the United States." (Gavin, *On to Berlin*, 140–41.)
8. DDE to GCM, Sept. 4, 1944, *EP*, vol. 4, 2118.
9. Butcher diary, Aug. 15, 1944, and *New York Times*, Aug. 16, 1944.
10. Weigley, *Eisenhower's Lieutenants*, 347.
11. Both quotes in Butcher diary, Sept. 7, 1944.
12. DDE to GCM, Aug. 24, 1944, *EP*, vol. 4, 2092, and Ambrose, *The Supreme Commander*, 510.
13. Quoted in Lt. Col. George Dyer, *XII Corps: Spearhead of Patton's Third Army* (privately published, 1947), 196.
14. Third U.S. Army Intelligence Estimate no. 9, Aug. 28, 1944, quoted in Pogue, *The Supreme Command*, 245.
15. Prime Minister's Personal Minute, Sept. 8, 1944, quoted in Gilbert, *Road to Victory*, 943.
16. Quoted in Ruppenthal, *Logistical Support of the Armies*, vol. 1, 489.
17. Perret, *There's a War to Be Won*, 369, and Ruppenthal, *Logistical Support of the Armies*, vol. 1, 488.
18. Van Creveld, *Supplying War*, 215, aptly describes the campaign in northwestern Europe as the "war of the accountants."
19. A point that has been conclusively reiterated in the 1993 PBS eight-part documentary on the history of oil, "The Prize."
20. Pogue, *The Supreme Command*, 260. For an excellent analysis of the logistical situation after Normandy see *EP*, vol. 5, 39–48.
21. The following entry appeared in Montgomery's "betting book" on Oct. 11, 1943: "General Eisenhower bets war with Germany will end before Xmas 1944—local time. Amount: £5. //s// B. L. Montgomery, Gen. Eighth Army." Montgomery's betting book is in the Montgomery collection, IWM.
22. Weigley, *Eisenhower's Lieutenants*, 268.
23. Patton said of his onetime classmate: "Someone described him [Lee] very aptly the other day as 'a pompous little son-of-a-bitch only interested in self-advertisement.' I have seldom seen a man less suited for his job." (Patton diary, Aug. 7, 1944.) A scathing but fair assessment of Lee is in Graham and Bidwell, *Coalitions, Politicians and Generals*, chap. 15.

24. Perret, *There's a War to Be Won*, 372, and Jean Edward Smith, *Lucius D. Clay* (New York, 1990), 181. The litany of COMZ blunders under Lee's aegis is far too long to chronicle here. For a full account see Perret's "Running on Empty," chap. 20, ibid.

25. Larrabee, *Commander in Chief*, 473.

26. Lt. Gen. J. C. H. Lee interview with Forrest C. Pogue, Mar. 21, 1947, OCMH Collection, USAMHI.

27. "The Service Reminiscences of Lt. Gen. John C. H. Lee," Lee Papers, USAMHI. Lee's lengthy memoir was written in "we," "us," and "our" format, as if he were royalty. What might otherwise have been a useful historical document consists of only a handful of largely self-serving pages devoted to his tenure as COMZ commander.

28. DDE to J. C. H. Lee, Sept. 16, 1944, *EP*, vol. 4, 2153–54.

29. Lee was also six years senior to Eisenhower in the Regular Army, another factor that seems to have influenced Eisenhower's decision to retain him.

30. "I got Eisenhower prepared two or three times to fire him," said Smith, "but something would come up. Somervell and Marshall would intervene. . . . We couldn't relieve him over a bunch of little things. So we kept him on," despite the fact that there were two able replacements who would have done a better job, said Smith, who "simply threw up his hands and began dealing directly with Lee's subordinates."

   Lee's most harmful mistake was actually committed long before D-Day. In the summer of 1943 the Overlord logistical planners had calculated that 240 Transportation Corps truck companies would be required to support U.S. forces in Europe after the invasion. Lee reduced the number to 100 before eventually approving a total of 160 companies, a 33 percent reduction. Though SHAEF studies branded the COMZ estimates of transportation requirements as "unreliable" and "worthless," nothing was done to address the problem.

   One of Bedell Smith's two choices to replace Lee was Lucius Clay. What saved Lee was his past record of outstanding service under Harry Hopkins in the Works Progress Administration during the 1930s, and Eisenhower's gratitude for Lee's excellent performance during Overlord. Pogue interview of Lt. Gen. W. B. Smith, May 13, 1947, Smith, *Lucius D. Clay*, 181, and Ruppenthal, *Logistical Support of the Armies*, vol. 1, 553, 556.

31. Christopher C. Gabel, *The Lorraine Campaign*, U.S. Army monograph, 1985. Severe overloading added to the wear and tear that created a tire shortage, thus displacing thousands of vehicles from service, and into a maintenance system likewise incapable of keeping pace. Added to the already formidable Allied problems was the drain imposed on the overburdened transport system by the necessity to help supply Paris. The French railway system, which had been systematically pulverized during the pre-Overlord bombing campaign, had yet to be restored.

32. Perret, *There's a War to Be Won*, 371. This breakdown at a crucial time required the immobilization of three newly arrived U.S. combat divisions (the 26th, 95th, and 104th), and their vehicles were commandeered to support the British advance.

33. Crosswell, *The Chief of Staff*, 268–69, and Everett S. Hughes diary, July 19–20, 1944.

34. Graham and Bidwell, *Coalitions, Politicians and Generals*, chap. 15.

35. Smith, *Lucius D. Clay*, 180–81.

36. Ibid., 182.

37. Letter, D. K. R. Crosswell to the author, July 24, 2001.

38. Crosswell, *The Chief of Staff*, 269–70, and Pogue interview with Smith, May 13, 1947.

39. Wilmot, *The Struggle for Europe*, 537.

47. WHICH WAY TO GERMANY?

1. SHAEF G-3 planning document, "Post Neptune Courses of Action After Capture of Lodgement Area," May 3, 1944, PRO (WO 219/2506). Record Group WO219 is the official records of SHAEF. A similar set of records is in NA II. From time to time specious postwar arguments have surfaced to the effect that there was no broad-front plan until Eisenhower "discovered" it after the Normandy campaign. The evidence that such a plan for the post-Normandy period existed is beyond dispute. It is equally clear that it was used solely within SHAEF. Moreover, there was no distribution of what was merely a planning document signed by three British staff officers, one of whom was its primary architect, Brig. Kenneth McLean, one of the original COSSAC planners.

2. Perret, *Eisenhower*, 311.

3. Montgomery, *Memoirs*, 266.

4. "Allied Strategy After the Fall of Paris," Chester Wilmot interview of Montgomery, Mar. 23, 1949, Chester Wilmot Collection, Liddell Hart Papers.

5. Montgomery to Brooke, circa Aug. 14, 1944, Montgomery Papers, and Hamilton, *Monty: Master of the Battlefield*, 791.

6. Bradley, *A General's Life*, 312–13.

7. David Eisenhower, *Eisenhower: At War*, 422.

8. DDE to Montgomery, Sept. 5, 1944, *EP*, vol. 4, 2120.

9. DDE Office Memorandum, Sept. 5, 1944, ibid., 2121.

10. Nigel Hamilton, *Monty: The Field Marshal, 1944–1976* (London, 1986), 34.

11. Butcher diary, Aug. 14, 1944.

12. Ambrose, *The Supreme Commander,* 530.

13. Bradley did win a concession when, at Smith's behest, Eisenhower altered the status of First Army from that of operational control by Montgomery to attachment to his 21st Army Group—meaning that Bradley retained overall command and control.

14. Wilmot, *The Struggle for Europe*, 518.

15. Alistair Horne, with David Montgomery, *Monty: The Lonely Leader, 1944–1945* (New York, 1994), 271.

16. Interview of Col. C. H. Bonesteel by Forrest C. Pogue, June 18, 1947, Pogue interviews, USAMHI.

17. DDE, "Churchill-Marshall," Box 8, Post-Pres Papers, A-WR series, EL. Eisenhower's dilemma of being besieged by "insistent advice," recalled Lincoln's response during the Civil War to those who claimed that their particular advice was "God's will." Of his own circumstance Eisenhower wrote, "Lincoln's reply—which was one of wonder as to the confidence in which others quoted God's will while he, who so earnestly sought it, was left in the dark—has always been to me a classic expression of common sense. He had to follow his own convictions. I was in the same fix."

18. Butcher diary, Aug. 31, 1944.

19. Alden Hatch, *George Patton: General in Spurs* (New York, 1950), 184.

20. Cornelius Ryan, *A Bridge Too Far* (London, 1974), 7n.

21. Patton diary, Aug. 30, 1944.

22. Hansen diary, Aug. 28, 1944.

23. Smith interview with Pogue, May 8, 1947.

24. David Eisenhower, *Eisenhower: At War*, 422–23.

25. Ambrose, quoted in Baxter, *Bernard Law Montgomery*, 95.

26. Telegram, Montgomery to Eisenhower, Sept. 4, 1944, Montgomery Papers; also 21st Army Group papers, PRO (WO 205 series).

27. Cable, Montgomery to Brooke, Sept. 7, 1944, Montgomery Papers.

28. Chester Wilmot interview of Montgomery, Mar. 23, 1949, Chester Wilmot collection, LHC.

29. George S. Patton, *War As I Knew It* (New York, 1980 edition), 116.

30. At the time Eisenhower had only thirty-eight divisions at his disposal.

31. Van Creveld, *Supplying War*, 230.

32. Quote citing SHAEF Historical Section document 768/2, in Cabinet Office Historical Section document. (PRO [CAB 106/1106].)

33. DDE to GCM, May 28, 1943. Eisenhower's assessment of Montgomery's willingness to take risks was dead wrong. He mistook Monty's prudent generalship—which made needless sacrifices even more disastrous in the midst of steadily declining British manpower reserves in the summer of 1944—for overcaution.

34. Quoted in Blumenson, *The Patton Papers*, vol. 2, 537.

35. Leckie, *Delivered from Evil*, 766.

36. Summersby, *Eisenhower Was My Boss*, 180.

37. The account of Eisenhower's flight on Sept. 2, 1944, is in Hansen, *What It Was Like Flying for "Ike,"* 38–39.

38. Wilmot, *The Struggle for Europe*, 544, and the observations of Maj. Gen. Sir Miles A. P. Graham in an interview with Chester Wilmot, Jan. 19, 1949, Liddell Hart Papers. De Guingand later wrote that the great debate over the post-Normandy strategy was "the only major issue over which I did not agree with my Chief. I have always held the contrary view, and . . . Eisenhower was right when in August he decided that he could not concentrate sufficient administrative [that is, logistical] resources to allow one strong thrust deep into Germany north of the Rhine with the hope of decisive success." (De Guingand, *Operation Victory*, 411–13.) In a note to the vice chief of the Imperial General Staff, Gen. Sir Archibald Nye, Montgomery wrote, "The U.S. Troops on my right have no resistance in front of them but they cannot get on because they have no petrol!! The whole show is lamentable. . . . I shall go on hammering at it myself—until I go mad." (Montgomery to Nye, Sept. 10, 1944, Alanbrooke Papers.)

39. Wilmot, *The Struggle for Europe*, 546.

40. Smith interview with Pogue, May 9, 1947, USAMHI.

41. Ramsay diary, Sept. 11, 1944.

42. Hamilton, *Monty: The Field Marshal*, 35.

43. David Reynolds, "The Erosion of British Influence," in Charles F. Brower IV, ed., *World War II in Europe: The Final Year* (New York, 1998), 49.

44. Quoted in Baxter, *Field Marshal Bernard Law Montgomery*, 91.

45. Wilmot, *The Struggle for Europe*, 519.

46. H. R. Bull Papers, EL.

47. Graham and Bidwell, *Coalitions, Politicians and Generals*, 264.

48. John Ellis, *Brute Force: Allied Strategy and Tactics in the Second World War* (London, 1990), 420.

49. Eisenhower, quoted in Daniel Yergin, *The Prize* (New York, 1991), 388.

50. David Eisenhower, *Eisenhower: At War*, 422.

48. "COINS BURNING HOLES IN SHAEF'S POCKET"

1. Martin Blumenson, *Patton: The Man Behind the Legend* (New York, 1985), 241.

2. The Ninth (U.S.) Air Force was the American component of Leigh-Mallory's AEAF, the other was the British Second Tactical Air Force commanded by Montgomery's nemesis, Air Marshal Arthur Coningham.

3. Quoted in Hughes, *Over Lord*, 232. A veteran of the British 1st Airborne Division and Operation Market-Garden has written, "Brereton was a general whose fellow-countrymen seem to have had even less to say in his favor than had his allies." (Geoffrey Powell, *The Devil's Birthday: The Bridges to Arnhem, 1944* [New York, 1984], 234.)

4. Powell, *The Devil's Birthday*, 12.

5. In the wake of the ill-fated airborne operations in Sicily in July 1943, Eisenhower had suspended future airborne operations pending a review by a joint Anglo-American board, which submitted a detailed, commonsense report that ultimately saved them from being shelved as too risky. Eisenhower seemed convinced that a combination of factors contributed to the problems in Sicily and wrote to Marshall that, overall, "the results were most promising for the future effectiveness of this powerful arm of opportunity." (Cable, DDE to Marshall, July 29, 1943, *EP*, vol. 2, 1303.)

6. *The Brereton Diaries* (July 17, 1944), 308–09.

7. In addition to the 82nd and 101st Airborne, the third U.S. airborne division was the 17th, newly arrived from the U.S. Brereton's command also included the British 52nd (Lowland) Division, a nonairborne unit trained but never employed in mountain operations. The 52nd was deemed "air transportable" by troop carrier aircraft.

8. Supreme Commander's directive, Sept. 4, 1944, quoted in Wilmot, *The Struggle for Europe*, 542.

9. DDE Office Memorandum, Sept. 5, 1944, *EP*, vol. 4, 2121.

10. Hamilton, *Monty: The Field Marshal*, 66.

11. *The Brereton Diaries* (Aug. 8, 1944), 330.

12. Perret, *Winged Victory*, 322. Bradley had part of Brereton's troop carriers under his control to ferry gasoline and supplies during the logistical crisis, and was reluctant to give them up for an airborne operation that favored Montgomery.

13. MacDonald, *The Siegfried Line Campaign*, 119.

14. *The Brereton Diaries* (Aug. 17, 1944), 336.

15. Martin Middlebrook, *Arnhem 1944* (London, 1944), 66.

16. Hinsley, *British Intelligence in the Second World War*, vol. 3, part 2, 382–87, includes a detailed analysis of what Allied intelligence knew and when they knew it.

17. Bedell Smith quoted in MacDonald, *The Siegfried Line Campaign*, 122.

18. SHAEF Weekly Intelligence Summary no. 26, for the week ending Sept. 16, 1944, cited in MacDonald, *The Siegfried Line Campaign*, 122.

19. In 1983 General Urquhart admitted that "we became callous. . . . We had approached the state of mind when we weren't thinking as hard about the risks as we possibly had done earlier." (Quoted in Hamilton, *Monty: The Field Marshal*, 66.)

20. See Hinsley, *British Intelligence in the Second World War*, vol. 3, part 2, 382–87.

21. Gen. Sir Charles Richardson, *Send for Freddie* (London, 1987), 165.

22. During conversations in the early 1980s with Lt. Gen. James M. Gavin, the division commander of the 82nd Airborne during Market-Garden, it became clear that he had never forgiven the British Guards Armored Division for failing to take advantage of the price paid in blood by his paratroopers to seize the Nijmegen railway bridge. The road to Arnhem was wide open, yet the British tanks stopped and failed to resume their attacks until the following day. By then it was too late.

23. Churchill to Field Marshal Jan Smuts, Oct. 9, 1944, quoted in Winston S. Churchill, *Triumph and Tragedy* (Boston, 1953), 200.

24. Montgomery, *Memoirs*, 297–98.

25. Eisenhower is quoted in *EP*, vol. 4, 2135, n. 5.

26. Ibid., vol. 3, 1767. Eisenhower's misgivings about the employment of the Allied airborne force are outlined in a series of exchanges with Marshall and Arnold in early 1944. See also *The Marshall Papers*, vol. 4 (Baltimore, 1996), 282–85.

27. DDE, *Crusade in Europe*, 349.

28. DDE to Lord Ismay, Dec. 3, 1960, Box 19, Post-Pres Papers, A-WR series, EL.

29. Letter and report of the First Allied Airborne Army, with cover letter from Brereton to Eisenhower, Oct. 7, 1944, Box 14, Pre-Pres Papers, EL.

30. Middlebrook, *Arnhem 1944*, 448.

31. Lamb, *Montgomery in Europe*, 251.

32. Hamilton, *Monty: The Field Marshal*, 102.
33. Ibid., 89–90.
34. Quoted in Snyder, *My Friend Ike*, 66–67.
35. Summersby, *Eisenhower Was My Boss*, 184.
36. Ibid., 187.
37. Air Marshal J. M. Robb, "The Higher Direction of War," unpublished monograph, Robb Papers, EL. Robb was one of two British deputy chiefs of staff for air. Another dog story that no one found funny concerned FDR's son, Elliot, an air corps colonel who had obtained not one but two seats for his dog aboard an aircraft, bumping two wounded soldiers returning home. When the incident was revealed at a SHAEF staff briefing, there was a strained silence until Eisenhower said, "This is the first time in this war I've gotten so sick in the stomach." (Quoted in Robb.)
38. Murray, *Eisenhower vs. Montgomery*, 147. The SHAEF estimates were close: Antwerp, ten thousand tons per day the first week of operation, nineteen thousand per day the second week, and overall an average of eighteen thousand tons per day.
39. L. F. Ellis, *Victory in the West*, vol. 2 (London, 1968), 97.
40. MacDonald, *The Siegfried Line Campaign*, 229.
41. Quoted in Anthony Kemp, *The Unknown Battle: Metz, 1944* (New York, 1985), 83.
42. David Eisenhower, *Eisenhower: At War*, 466.
43. Kemp, *The Unknown Battle*, 83–84.
44. GSP to Beatrice Patton, Sept. 10, 1944, Box 15, PP-LC.
45. DDE to Montgomery, Oct. 9, 1944, *EP*, vol. 4, 2215.
46. Montgomery to DDE, Oct. 9, 1944, Montgomery Papers, IWM. Both Cherbourg and Arromanches were battered by high winds on October 8, further straining the already overstretched Allied supply system. Within 21st Army Group, Eisenhower's cable was seen as yet one more visible example that the supreme commander was out of touch with the situation at the front.
47. MacDonald, *The Siegfried Line Campaign*, 214.
48. Minutes of SAC Special Meeting held at SHAEF Forward, Sept. 22, 1944, PRO (WO 219/588). At this meeting de Guingand represented Montgomery.
49. DDE to Montgomery, Oct. 10, 1944, *EP*, vol. 4, 2216–17.
50. Hamilton, *Monty: The Field Marshal*, 110.
51. Montgomery to Bedell Smith, "Notes on High Command in Western Europe, Holland," dated Oct. 10, 1944, Montgomery Papers.
52. DDE to Montgomery, Oct. 13, 1944, *EP*, vol. 4, 2223–24. The author was Maj. Gen. J. F. M. Whiteley, the SHAEF deputy G-3. Marshall was also visiting the ETO and was a guest of Eisenhower at this time. No doubt his strong views about Montgomery played a part in Eisenhower's stern reply.
53. Ibid., 2222.
54. Montgomery to DDE, Oct. 14, 1944, Montgomery Papers.
55. DDE to GCM, Oct. 26, 1944, *EP*, vol. 4, 2135, n. 5.
56. Montgomery, *Memoirs*, 297.

49. THE AUTUMN STALEMATE

1. Fraser, *Alanbrooke*, 455, and Montgomery, *Memoirs*, 286.
2. Pogue, *The Supreme Command*, 288. The broad front might not have come as a surprise had the British commanders studied American military history. The American philosophy of waging war had been nourished in the western United States by the cavalry arm, with its emphasis on mobility during the settlement of the West in the second half of the nineteenth century. The Civil War tactics of Ulysses S. Grant (later refined by John J. Pershing during World War I) were harbingers of the European style of war, which would dominate war in both the nineteenth and the first half of

the twentieth centuries: head-on confrontation on the battlefield by large forces that would drag the United States—however reluctantly—away from its professed traditions of mobility. The lesson drawn from World War I, notes Russell Weigley, was that "victory in large-scale war depends on a strategy of direct confrontation with the enemy's main forces to destroy them."

Headed by Eisenhower, the U.S. World War II generals were trained in the Leavenworth philosophy of war, which modeled itself on Grant and Pershing. The only men who refused to buy into the doctrine of massive confrontation were the cavalrymen like Patton, who stuck to the heretical notion during the interwar years that mobility was the key to fighting and winning future wars. Although Eisenhower understood the latter, he was wedded to the former. Notes Weigley, "The same line of strategic thought led in World War II to the American insistence on direct cross-Channel assault—and to the deadlocks of Normandy and the West Wall." (Weigley, *Eisenhower's Lieutenants*, 728–29.)

3. Graham and Bidwell, *Coalitions, Politicians and Generals*, 287. Eisenhower's critics allege his futile pursuit of the broad front was little more than a delusion that there was a military strategy where none actually existed.
4. DDE to MDE, Sept. 23, 1944.
5. MacDonald, *The Siegfried Line Campaign*, 617.
6. DDE, *Crusade in Europe*, 363.
7. MacDonald, *The Mighty Endeavor*, 333–34.
8. Michael D. Doubler, *Closing with the Enemy* (Lawrence, Kans., 1994), 140.
9. Bradley, *A General's Life*, 343.
10. MacDonald, *The Mighty Endeavor*, 355.
11. Ibid., 355–56.
12. DDE to GCM, Mar. 30, 1945, *EP*, vol. 4, 2564. Without mentioning either Bradley or Hodges by name, Lt. Gen. James M. Gavin pointedly noted that senior American officers "frequently lacked the firsthand knowledge of the conditions under which the troops were being compelled to fight. They had fought the battle on maps. And battles are not won on maps." (Gavin, *On to Berlin*, 268, fn.)
13. Ernie Pyle, quoted in Stephen E. Ambrose, *Citizen Soldiers* (New York, 1997), 153.
14. DDE to MDE, Oct. 23, 1944.
15. Quoted in Miller, *Ike the Soldier*, 747–48.
16. D'Este, *Patton*, 667.
17. Hamilton, *Monty: The Field Marshal*, 71.
18. Ibid., 124.
19. Alanbrooke diary, Nov. 9, 1944.
20. Fraser, *Alanbrooke*, 455. Against Brooke's advice, Montgomery's combination of pique and anguish led to a fresh proposal, which the CIGS rejected as impractical and instructed him not to approach Eisenhower with it.
21. Graham and Bidwell, *Coalitions, Politicians and Generals*, 255.
22. Summersby, *Eisenhower Was My Boss*, 188–89.
23. After D-Day 443 GIs were tried and sentenced to death for various capital crimes such as rape and murder. Of the 443, 245 were Caucasian and 198 were African American. The sentences were carried out in ninety-five cases; the ninety-fifth GI to be executed was Pvt. Eddie Slovik.
24. Transcript of Eisenhower television interview on NBC with Bruce Catton, Box 5, Post-Pres Papers, Speeches Series, EL. The British army executed more than three hundred British and Commonwealth soldiers for desertion during World War I but abolished the death penalty in 1929.
25. Perret, *Eisenhower*, 333–34), and William Bradford Huie, *The Execution of Private Slovik* (New York, 1954), passim. The GIs executed in the ETO are buried in graves marked only by numbers at a secret location in eastern France. Only the remains of

Eddie Slovik were eventually returned to the United States for reburial. To this day critics of the death penalty cite the Slovik case as an example of a miscarriage of justice. It was Slovik's hard luck, points out Geoffrey Perret, that his case was sent to Eisenhower for review during the Battle of the Bulge, when he was otherwise preoccupied.

26. Gen. William H. Simpson, quoted in Mosley, *Marshall: Organizer of Victory*, 326.
27. Pogue, *The Supreme Command*, 306 and 541, Ellis, *Victory in the West*, vol. 2, appendix 4, and Summersby, *Eisenhower Was My Boss*, 209–10.
28. DDE, *Crusade in Europe*, 352.
29. Alanbrooke, "Notes on My Life," Nov. 14, 1944.
30. Hansen diary USAMHI, and "From Plebe to President."
31. Summersby, *Eisenhower Was My Boss*, 197–98.
32. Ibid.
33. DDE to MDE, Nov. 12, 1944.
34. DDE to Edgar Eisenhower, *EP*, vol. 4, 2289–90.
35. Montgomery to Brooke, telegram M-344, Nov. 23, 1944, in Hamilton, *Monty: The Field Marshal*, 154.
36. Montgomery to Brooke, Nov. 29, 1944, quoted in ibid., 156.
37. Montgomery to DDE, Nov. 30, 1944, quoted in Bryant, *Triumph in the West*, 344–55.
38. Butcher diary, Dec. 13, 1944, and DDE to Montgomery, Dec. 1, 1944, *EP*, vol. 4, 2323–25. Eisenhower's reference to the battle for the Mareth Line in Tunisia in early 1943 was a reminder that when his main effort was blunted, Monty had reinforced a diversionary flank attack and achieved a successful breakthrough.
39. Ibid.
40. Hansen diary, Dec. 6, 1944.
41. Pogue, *The Supreme Command*, 317.
42. Hansen diary, Dec. 9, 1944.
43. Bradley, Memorandum for Record, Dec. 13, 1944, quoted in Hamilton, *Monty: The Field Marshal*, 163.
44. Ibid.
45. Montgomery to Brooke, Dec. 7, 1944, Montgomery Papers.
46. Alanbrooke diary, Dec. 12 and 13, 1944.
47. Hamilton, *Monty: The Field Marshal*, 169–70.
48. Alanbrooke diary, Dec. 12 and 13, 1944.

50. "THERE WILL BE ONLY CHEERFUL FACES AT THIS CONFERENCE TABLE."

1. Weigley, *Eisenhower's Lieutenants*, 458. For a fuller description of Koch's and Third Army's role during the period preceding the Bulge, see D'Este, *Patton*, chap. 43.
2. Hugh M. Cole, *The Ardennes: Battle of the Bulge* (Washington, D.C., 1965), 485–86.
3. Oscar W. Koch, *G-2: Intelligence for Patton* (Philadelphia, 1971), 86–87.
4. D'Este, *Patton*, 676.
5. J. D. Morelock, *Generals of the Ardennes* (Washington, D.C., 1994), 58.
6. Weigley, *Eisenhower's Lieutenants*, 464.
7. Ambrose, *Eisenhower*, 365.
8. Hitler named the counteroffensive Operation Watch am Rhein ("Watch on the Rhine"), which was later changed to "Autumn Mist."
9. Butcher diary, Dec. 16, 1944.
10. Hansen diary, Dec. 16, 1944.
11. Postwar alibis later included an alleged lack of Ultra intercepts, an excuse thoroughly debunked when its existence was revealed in the late 1970s. For a detailed analysis of the intelligence picture, see Hinsley, *British Intelligence in the Second World War*, vol.

3, part 2, chap. 52, and Ralph Bennett, *Ultra in the West* (London, 1979), the first analysis of the role of Ultra during the campaign in northwest Europe.

12. Jacques Nobécourt, *Hitler's Last Gamble* (New York, 1967), 140.

13. Annan, *Changing Enemies*, 117. Annan's account of the intelligence side of the Battle of the Bulge is a damning indictment of a major Allied failure. Of the Bulge, Annan writes, "Those dead and wounded are the measure of our failure." (Chap. 6, 123.)

14. Pogue, *The Supreme Command*, 365 n. 20, and Strong, *Intelligence at the Top*, 159.

15. Harold C. Deutsch, "Commanding Generals and the Uses of Intelligence," *Intelligence and National Security*, July 1988.

16. David W. Hogan, Jr., *A Command Post for War: First Army Headquarters in Europe, 1943–1945* (Washington, D.C., 2000), 209 and 215.

17. Weigley, *Eisenhower's Lieutenants*, 458, and JSDE, *The Bitter Woods* (New York, 1969), 215.

18. Maj. Gen. J. F. M. "Jock" Whiteley was one of the British army's most experienced and accomplished staff officers. When the war came in 1939 he was serving in the operations directorate of the War Office before being sent to the Middle East as the Ops/Plans officer in GHQ, Middle East, in Cairo under Wavell and Auchinleck. Before his assignment to AFHQ, where he served as Eisenhower's deputy chief of staff, Whiteley was the chief of staff of the Eighth Army under Lt. Gen. Neil Ritchie.

19. Crosswell, *The Chief of Staff*, 283–84. In the aftermath of the triumphant defense, "numerous officers stepped forward to claim the credit for picking the city," notes historian J. D. Morelock. "Troy Middleton dismissed most of the posturing by saying that 'you didn't need to be a genius to know that Bastogne was a key location in the Ardennes. All you had to do was look at a map.' " (Unpublished monograph by J. D. Morelock, "Darkest of Times: A Critical Analysis of Bradley's Leadership in the Battle of the Bulge.")

20. Hansen diary, Dec. 18, 1944.

21. Bradley, *A Soldier's Story*, 469.

22. Principal sources for this account of the Verdun meeting are: Weigley, *Eisenhower's Lieutenants*, 499–501, Patton, *War As I Knew It*, 190–92, Charles B. MacDonald, *A Time for Trumpets* (New York, 1985), 420–21, Nobécourt, *Hitler's Last Gamble*, 219–22, Bradley, *A Soldier's Story*,470–73 and *A General's Life*, 358–59, DDE, *Crusade in Europe*, 389–92, Blumenson, *The Patton Papers*, vol. 2, 599–601, Miller, *Ike the Soldier*, 727–28, Ambrose, *The Supreme Commander*, 558–59, JSDE, *The Bitter Woods*, 256–57, David Eisenhower, *Eisenhower: At War*, 566–69, Charles Codman, *Drive* (Boston, 1957), 231–33, Strong, *Intelligence at the Top*, 161–63, the diary of Lt. Gen. Jacob L. Devers, Patton diary, Dec. 19, 1944, and his letter of Dec. 21 to Beatrice Patton.

23. Patton noted sarcastically in his diary, "The fact that three of these [six] divisions exist only on paper did not even enter his head," a reference to Middleton's three divisions badly battered in the Hürtgen and unfit for further combat.

24. Montgomery's official biographer has written, "What stunned Eisenhower was not the speed with which Patton reoriented his divisions, but the alacrity with which . . . Patton abandoned his planned Saar offensive. Eisenhower was bewildered. Was this the same commander who had railed against Monty's call for concentration of the main Allied land forces since August, and had made it a matter of American honor that his Saar offensive not be closed down?" (Nigel Hamilton, *Monty: The Battles of Field Marshal Montgomery* [New York, 1994], 481.)

25. Strong, *Intelligence at the Top*, 163.

26. MacDonald, *A Time for Trumpets*, 421.

27. The unhappiest participant at the Verdun conference was Lt. Gen. Jake Devers. Taking over much of Third Army's sector meant that Seventh Army would have to cease offensive operations at a time when Devers believed that 6th Army Group was being

called on to bail out 12th Army Group "just as we are about to crack the Siegfried Line." Although he understood fully the necessity for his new role, Devers's views were never made public until the publication of the official history in 1993. It was, he said, a "tragedy" because SHAEF had "not seen fit to reinforce success on this flank." Devers was also privately critical of Montgomery and Patton, whom he thought guilty of "wild and inaccurate statements." (Sources: Devers diary, Dec. 19, 1944, Jeffrey J. Clarke and Robert Ross Smith, *Riviera to the Rhine* [Washington, D.C., 1993], 491, and Michael A. Markey, "Quartermaster to Victory," *Army*, Aug. 1994.)

28. At Camp Meade, Maryland, in 1919 or 1920, Patton had predicted, "Ike, you will be the Lee of the next war, and I will be your Jackson." Whether or not Eisenhower qualified as Robert E. Lee, Patton was about to assert a definite resemblance to Stonewall Jackson. Third Army was poised to pull off one of the most remarkable feats of any combat army in history, "a maneuver that would make Stonewall Jackson's peregrinations in the valley campaign in Virginia and Gallieni's shift of troops in taxicabs to save Paris from the Kaiser look pale by comparison." (MacDonald, *A Time for Trumpets*, 421.)

29. Morelock, *Generals of the Ardennes,* chap. 2, passim, and "Darkest of Times." When James M. Gavin, the 82nd Airborne commander, met with Hodges, Kean, and the First Army G-3 on the morning of Dec. 18, the situation was still so unclear that Gavin left having learned only that there was German armor to the southeast. (Hogan, *A Command Post for War*, 215.)

30. Hogan, *A Command Post for War*, 212.

31. Ibid., chap. 7, passim, and Pogue interview of Bedell Smith, May 8, 1947. Given First Army's abysmal handling of the deadly battles in the Hürtgen Forest, Smith's harsh judgments are not exaggerated.

   Strong's deputy, Tom Betts, also visited First Army at its new headquarters at Chaudfontaine and brought back similar disturbing reports. "I found the place a terrible mess," he said. "They just didn't know what was going on. As far as fighting a war was concerned the First Army . . . seemed to have no plan at all for meeting this attack. And I couldn't see any orders going forth." Betts reported to Strong and Smith to whom he took the unprecedented step of recommending the relief of Hodges.

   The First Army G-2, Colonel B. A. "Monk" Dickson, who allegedly identified the coming offensive, was an opportunist whose intelligence estimates were replete with equivocations and identifications of phantom units actually still on the eastern front—one moment seeming to stop just short of predicting an attack, only to hint at an imminent German collapse. The best intelligence work in First Army G-2 was being accomplished by the Ultra officer, Adolf G. Rosengarten, who predicted the offensive but was ultimately ignored by Dickson, who "went off to Paris on leave on 15 December—scarcely the act of a man who knows that the army he serves is about to take the brunt of a panzer assault." (See Lewin, *Ultra Goes to War*, 356, and Brig. Gen. Thomas J. Betts oral history, EL.)

32. Interview of Maj. Gen. J. F. M. Whiteley by Forrest C. Pogue, Dec. 18, 1946.

33. Perret, *Eisenhower*, 330, Crosswell, *The Chief of Staff,* 285, Strong, *Intelligence at the Top*, 164–66, and Smith interview

34. Smith interview, and Bradley, *A Soldier's Story*, 476.

35. Bradley, *A General's Life*, 363–64.

36. Air Marshal Robb, "Notes of Meeting Held in Supreme Commander's Office, Dec. 20, 1944."

37. Strong, *Intelligence at the Top*, 166.

38. Bradley, *A General's Life*, 363, Ambrose, *Eisenhower*, 368, and Crosswell, *The Chief of Staff,* 284–87. Ambrose's description of the telephone conversation is based on an interview of Strong.

39. Hansen diary.

40. Without their own on the spot evaluations the 12th Army Group was of little help to First Army. The fact that the two staffs held each other in contempt was equally unhelpful. In particular, the respective G-2s, First Army's Dickson and 12th Army Group's Edwin Sibert, never saw eye to eye on intelligence matters.

41. Bradley's behavior in the aftermath of Eisenhower's decision, which he deemed a loss of confidence in his leadership, was ample justification for the supreme commander's order to shift First Army to Montgomery. Bradley's insistence that he could control the battle by telephone from Luxembourg was probably the last straw, for Eisenhower still retained vivid memories of Fredendall and his bunker in Tunisia.

51. "IF I CAN KEEP THE TEAM TOGETHER, ANYTHING'S WORTH IT."

1. In his postwar memoir Bradley charged that both Eisenhower and SHAEF had demonstrated "an acute case of the shakes." (*A Soldier's Story*, 475.)

2. Murphy, *Diplomat Among Warriors*, 239. Murphy witnessed the "battle" as a guest of Smith. In another incident four French officers were shot dead when they failed to halt after a sentry ordered them to.

3. JSDE, *The Bitter Woods*, 33.

4. MDE oral history, EL.

5. Betts oral history, EL, Smith interview, and Crosswell, *The Chief of Staff*, 299.

6. Wilmot, *The Struggle for Europe*, 662.

7. DDE to Montgomery, Dec. 22, 1944, *EP*, vol. 4, 2369.

8. Gavin, *On To Berlin*, 244 and 184.

9. Cole, *The Ardennes*, 413.

10. Morelock, "Darkest of Times." Brig. Gen. Bruce C. Clarke, who organized the defense of Saint-Vith, was equally impressed with Montgomery. "From Hasbrouck, Clarke later learned what Montgomery's attitude was: the 7th Armored mission was to delay the Germans three days. They had delayed them now a full working week, accomplishing the mission beyond the call of duty. These troops would be needed later. They should be pulled out immediately." (William D. Ellis and Thomas J. Cunningham, Jr., *Clarke of St. Vith* [Cleveland, Ohio, 1974], 128.)

11. Eisenhower's Order of the Day is reproduced in Butcher's diary, Dec. 23, 1944, and numerous other sources.

12. DDE's ringing sentiment could well apply to the United States in the wake of the terrorist attacks of Sept. 11, 2001.

13. Diary of Air Vice Marshal Sir Charles Robb, Robb Papers, EL.

14. "Patton" in unpublished evaluations of World War II associates, Box 7, Post-Pres Papers, A-WR series.

15. *EP*, vol. 5, chronology, Dec. 19, 1944, to Jan. 27, 1945, 176–80.

16. JSDE, *The Bitter Woods*, 379. Eisenhower's remarks reflected a consensus among his senior SHAEF staff officers and key advisers (primarily Smith, Strong, Whiteley, and Robb) that, while Montgomery had done a remarkable job restoring the situation in the northern sector of the Bulge, his reputation for overcaution might well result in a missed opportunity to strike a killing blow against the Germans in the north. (Pogue, *The Supreme Command*, 385–86.)

17. DDE, *Crusade in Europe*, 399.

18. Pogue interview with Brig. E. T. Williams, who witnessed the incident and was quite clear that Eisenhower merely wanted his maps.

19. Summersby diary, Dec. 29, 1944, EL.

20. Pogue interview with Brig. E. T. Williams, May 30–31, 1947, OCMH file, USAMHI.

21. Alanbrooke diary, Dec. 30, 1944. Brooke had in fact already warned Montgomery the day before about watching his words, writing after the shift of command in the Ardennes, "Events and enemy action have forced on Eisenhower the setting up of a

more satisfactory system of command. I feel it is most important that you should not even in the slightest degree appear to rub this undoubted fact in to anyone at SHAEF or elsewhere." (Cable, Brooke to Montgomery, Dec. 21, 1944.)

22. Sources: McKeogh, *Sgt. Mickey and General Ike*, 154–57, Summersby, *Eisenhower Was My Boss*, 202–08, Butcher diary, passim, and Summersby diary, Dec. 21, 23, and 24 1944, EL.

23. Butcher diary, Jan. 1, 1945.

24. Francis de Guingand, *Generals at War* (London, 1964), 108–09. Eisenhower's draft cable was apparently destroyed, and no copy has ever been located.

25. Ronald Lewin, "World War II: A Tangled Web," lecture given at the Royal United Services Institute for Defense Studies, London, *RUSI Journal*, Dec. 1982.

26. De Guingand interview, "The World at War, 1939–1945," Thames Television series, IWM film archives.

27. Cable, Montgomery to DDE, Dec. 31, 1944, Montgomery Papers.

28. JSDE, *The Bitter Woods*, 381.

29. DDE to Montgomery, Dec. 31, 1944, Pre-Pres Papers.

30. Patton diary, Jan. 4, 1945.

31. Yergin, *The Prize*, 347–48.

32. MacDonald, *A Time for Trumpets*, 618.

33. Quoted in Frederick Ayer, *Before the Colors Fade* (Boston, 1964), 181.

34. Everett S. Hughes diary, Jan. 18, 1945.

35. "But this was the kind of war that he [Patton] disliked," wrote Eisenhower shortly before his death. "Throughout the European campaigns [I] used him, whenever and wherever possible, in situations of great fluidity. In this kind of advance he has had no modern equal." (DDE, "Patton" in unpublished evaluations of World War II associates, Box 7, Post-Pres Papers, A-WR series, EL.)

36. Morelock, "Darkest of Times."

37. Ibid.

38. In his two memoirs Bradley criticized SHAEF, Eisenhower, and Montgomery.

39. J. Lawton Collins, *Lightning Joe* (Baton Rouge, La, 1979), 195.

40. Robert E. Merriam, *Dark December* (New York, 1947; reprinted in 1978 as *The Battle of the Bulge*), 179–80. Merriam points out that Montgomery sent the British XXX Corps into blocking positions on the Meuse rather than injecting them into First Army, "where they would have wasted precious days adjusting to American ways. . . . The question of using British forces east of the Meuse was discussed and rejected because to move them there would have entailed their crossing communication lines of both First and Ninth Armies, and the resulting tangle would have been chaotic." (178.)

41. Hogan, *A Command Post for War*, 225.

42. Summersby, *Eisenhower Was My Boss*, 214.

43. Davis, *Soldier of Democracy*, 524.

52. THE INVASION OF GERMANY

1. Alanbrooke diary, Jan. 2, 1945, and DDE to MDE, Jan. 3, 1945. With the new year, a deluge of letters and boxes of candy, books, cigarettes, and assorted gifts of every description began arriving at SHAEF for Eisenhower from all parts of the globe, much as they had in the Mediterranean in 1943. Eisenhower ordered them sent to the military hospitals.

2. Nobécourt, *Hitler's Last Gamble*, 17.

3. DDE, *Crusade in Europe*, 373.

4. De Guingand, *Operation Victory*, 434.

5. Quoted in Hamilton, *Monty: The Field Marshal*, 303.

6. Montgomery, *Memoirs*, 314.

7. Pogue, *The Supreme Command*, 388.

8. Pogue, *Marshall: Organizer of Victory*, 510. In a candid postwar interview with Cornelius Ryan, Eisenhower finally unburdened himself: "Monty got so damn personal to make sure that the Americans—and me, in particular—had no credit, that I just stopped communicating with him. . . . I was just not interested in keeping up communications with a man that just can't tell the truth." (Ryan, *A Bridge Too Far*, 82, fn.)

9. Cook, *Charles De Gaulle*, 268.

10. Gilbert, *Road to Victory*, 1139–40, Brooke diary, Jan. 3, 1945, and Crosswell, *The Chief of Staff*, 292.

11. On the afternoon of Jan. 2 Smith and Juin had engaged in an angry confrontation in which the French formally threatened to withdraw from SHAEF and fight alone if necessary should Eisenhower's order stand. So passionate was their exchange that Smith later said that if Juin had been an American he would have "socked him in the jaw."

12. "Churchill-Marshall," Box 8, Post-Pre Papers, A-WR series, EL., and Summersby diary, Jan. 3, 1945.

13. DDE, *Crusade in Europe*, 402, and David Eisenhower, *Eisenhower: At War*, 604.

14. Ibid., Alan Brooke diary, Jan. 3, 1945, and Cook, *Charles De Gaulle*, 269.

15. Strong, *Intelligence at the Top*, 170, and David Eisenhower, *Eisenhower: At War*, 605.

16. DDE to GCM, Feb. 20, 1945.

17. Churchill to Roosevelt, Jan. 7, 1945, quoted in Kimball, *Churchill & Roosevelt*, vol. 3, 498–99.

18. Tedder's role in SHAEF was never clear. He acted as a sort of minister without portfolio, admired by many, distrusted by others. Eisenhower never really gave Tedder a function other than that of adviser and roving ambassador for SHAEF.

19. Smith interview, May 8, 1947, and DDE to GCM, Jan. 10, 1945.

20. DDE to GCM, Feb. 20, 1945.

21. Bradley, *A Soldier's Story*, 487–88, and Strong, *Intelligence at the Top*, 171.

22. MacDonald, *A Time for Trumpets*, 614.

23. DDE to Lt. Gen. W. H. Simpson, Mar. 26, 1945. See also Morelock, *Generals of the Ardennes*, 178.

24. Diary of Lt. Gen. Jacob L. Devers, Nov. 23, 1944, OCMH Special Collections. The following day, during a meeting with Eisenhower, Devers challenged a decision to send two divisions to assist Patton's Third Army at a time when 6th Army Group was in a position to cross the Rhine in Alsace. Devers pointed out that Patton's front was too wide and, rather than transfer two divisions, the problem could be solved by shortening the Third Army front and widening Devers's front. Eisenhower compromised, which Devers believed to be a mistake. The points Devers made were sound military strategy, but being right earned him no credit with Eisenhower, who was angered at being challenged by a subordinate he so thoroughly distrusted. (For an evaluation of the Devers-Eisenhower relationship see Clarke and Smith, *Riviera to the Rhine*, 576–77.)

25. Crosswell, *The Chief of Staff*, 306.

26. Clarke and Smith, *Riviera to the Rhine*, 574.

27. Eisenhower memo, dated Feb. 1, 1945, copy in Butcher diary. Eisenhower's top-ten picks were Bradley and Spaatz (tied for first), Smith, Patton, Clark, Truscott, Doolittle, Gerow, Collins, and Patch.

28. Clarke and Smith, *Riviera to the Rhine*, 575.

29. Devers diary, Sept. 11–12, 1944.

30. Clarke and Smith, *Riviera to the Rhine*, 577.

31. Weigley, *Eisenhower's Lieutenants*, 551 and 580.

32. Devers diary, Jan. 5, 1945, and Dec. 30, 1944.

33. MacDonald, *The Mighty Endeavor*, 408.
34. Diary of Lt. Gen. Hobart R. Gay, Jan. 24, 1945, NA II, and Patton diary, Jan. 24, 1945. The third person referred to was Courtney Hodges.
35. Crosswell, *The Chief of Staff*, 306.
36. DDE to MDE, Jan. 18, 1945.
37. Quoted in Franklin M. Davis, Jr., *Across the Rhine* (Alexandria, Va., 1980), 22.
38. Ibid., 23.
39. Weigley, *Eisenhower's Lieutenants*, 678.
40. Anthony Eden, Mar. 1, 1945, quoted by Harold Nicolson in Gilbert, *Road to Victory*, 1238.
41. Kershaw, *Hitler, 1936–1945*, 778.
42. Cray, *General of the Army*, 499.
43. Diary of Henry L. Stimson, Feb. 9, 1945, Sterling Memorial Library, Yale University.
44. Cray, *General of the Army*, 499.
45. Ibid., 502.
46. Richardson, *From Churchill's Secret Circle to the BBC*, 197.
47. Alanbrooke diary, Jan. 31, 1945.
48. Robert E. Sherwood, *The White House Papers of Harry L. Hopkins*, vol. 2 (London, 1949), 840–41.
49. Pogue interview with Marshall, Nov. 19, 1956. In hindsight, Marshall also sympathized with the great pressures placed on the British chiefs not only by Churchill but by the British media, which influenced public opinion in favor of Montgomery—at Eisenhower's expense. With the postwar role of Britain in a war-ravaged Europe unsettled, Marshall also understood that the British were at a severe disadvantage at this stage of the war in any negotiations with the U.S. chiefs of staff. Malta was such an example: The British chiefs had no chance of winning their arguments.
50. Alanbrooke diary, Jan. 31, 1945, and "Notes on My Life," Crosswell, *The Chief of Staff*, 310, Smith interview, May 8, 1947, and Pogue interviews with Marshall, Nov. 19, 1956, and Feb. 4, 1957.
51. Alanbrooke diary, Feb. 1, 1945, and Buell, *Master of Sea Power*, 454–55.
52. Buell, *Master of Sea Power*, 456.
53. Alanbrooke diary, Feb. 2, 1945.
54. Chester Hansen, quoted in Bradley, *A General's Life*, 397. Bradley's collaborator, Clay Blair, points out in a footnote on page 703 that the chronology in *EP*, vol. 5, citing Bradley's presence, is incorrect. Bradley did not accompany Eisenhower to the meeting with Montgomery.
55. Quoted in Hamilton, *Monty: The Field Marshal*, 379.
56. DDE to Brooke, Feb. 16, 1945, *EP*, vol. 5, 2480–81.
57. Alanbrooke diary, Feb. 20, 1945.
58. David Eisenhower, *Eisenhower: At War*, 687, and Summersby diary, Feb. 24, 1945.
59. Bradley, *A General's Life*, 399.

53. ALL ROADS LEAD TO BERLIN

1. DDE to MDE, April 28, 1945.
2. Summersby, *Eisenhower Was My Boss*, 221.
3. Summersby Morgan, *Past Forgetting*, 248.
4. Butcher and Steve Early, Butcher diary, Feb. 26, 1945.
5. Diary of Everett S. Hughes, Mar. 4, 1945.
6. David, *Ike & Mamie*, 128. Coauthor Lester David was managing editor of the Paris edition of *Stars and Stripes*. When Kay Summersby was promoted to first lieutenant, she officially and proudly became the "first female five-star aide in American military annals."

Notes to Pages 680–685

7. Memo in Hughes diary, Mar. 4, 1945.
8. Eisenhower insisted that Bradley also take some time off with him in Cannes. Bradley arrived a day after Eisenhower and spent two days. (Bradley, *A General's Life*, 410.)
9. Summersby Morgan, *Past Forgetting*, 250.
10. The Collège Moderne et Technique des Garçons, built in 1931 to atrain boys aged nine to nineteen, was selected for its size. The building once held up to fifteen hundred students, but even this large space was insufficient to house the entire SHAEF staff. By the end of the war SHAEF Forward had nearly doubled in size to twelve hundred officers and four thousand enlisted men. (Pogue, *The Supreme Command*, 419–20.)
11. Summersby, *Eisenhower Was My Boss*, 224, and Summersby Morgan, *Past Forgetting*, 248.
12. Summersby, *Eisenhower Was My Boss*, 224.
13. Hansen diary, Mar. 7, 1945, Butcher diary, Mar. 11, 1945, and Bradley, *A Soldier's Story*, 511–13. After the war Bull wrote several letters to Eisenhower in a effort to explain that Bradley had misinterpreted his words. See H. R. Bull folder, Box 14, Pre-Pres Papers.
14. Bradley, *A General's Life*, 392.
15. Davis, *Across the Rhine*, 77.
16. Patton diary, Mar. 13, 1945.
17. Alexander McKee, *The Race for the Rhine Bridges* (London, 1971), 213.
18. Quoted in Bradley, *A General's Life*, 412. A liaison officer at Bradley's headquarters remarked, "Without benefit of aerial bombardment, ground smoke, artillery preparation or airborne assistance" Third Army had successfully breached the Rhine. (George Forty, *Patton's Third Army at War* [New York, 1978], 160.)
19. Butcher diary, Feb. 26, 1945. Patton and Churchill seem to have had at least one trait in common. At the end of his visit to observe Operation Plunder, the prime minister wandered off by himself to the banks of the Rhine, where he solemnly relieved himself in the river, his second such symbolic gesture of contempt for Hitler. From a distance Brooke "felt certain that on his face was that same boyish grin of contentment that I had seen at the Siegfried Line [on March 3, during a visit to Simpson's Ninth Army"]. (Alanbrooke, "Notes on My Life," Mar. 3 and 26, 1945.)
20. John Toland, *The Last 100 Days* (New York, 1965), 267.
21. DDE, *Crusade in Europe*, 407. Eisenhower repeated his version to Ismay in 1958; letter of Jan. 25, Box 19, Pres. Papers, Ann Whitman File, EL.
22. Alanbrooke, "Notes on My Life," Mar. 25, 1945.
23. Churchill quoted in MacDonald, *The Mighty Endeavor*, 449.
24. Quoted in David Eisenhower, *Eisenhower: At War*, 754.
25. MacDonald, *The Mighty Endeavor*, 473.
26. Charles B. MacDonald, *The Last Offensive* (Washington, D.C., 1973), 370–71.
27. JSDE, *Strictly Personal*, 84. John Eisenhower also noted that " 'telling Daddy' would never have occurred to me; I had my own business to do." As Lieutenant Eisenhower was going about his duties, he received a summons to report to First Army HQ at Marburg, where his father was visiting and wanted to see him. Hitching a ride on a light aircraft, he rushed to Marburg. His astonished father demanded to know, "Well, what the hell are *you* doing here?" Told he had been ordered to report to him, Eisenhower moaned, "Good God. All I said was that my son must be somewhere in the vicinity." A staff officer overly anxious to please the boss had misinterpreted Eisenhower's statement as a command. (86.)
28. Codman, *Drive*, 264.
29. Toland, *The Last 100 Days*, 237.
30. JSDE, *Strictly Personal*, 99. The promotions were speedily processed after the chief of staff cabled him on April 7 that he wanted Hodges and Patton promoted to four-star

general and several corps commanders to three-star rank. (DDE to GCM, April 9, 1945, EP, IV, 2595–96.)

31. Ladislas Farago, *The Last Days of Patton* (New York, 1981), 47. Patton caught the full measure of Eisenhower's wrath for what he described to Marshall as one of his "latest crackpot actions," and for his unauthorized censorship of the Hammelburg raid behind German lines, an attempt by a 4th Armored Division task force to liberate the POW camp at Hammelburg where his son-in-law, Lt. Col. John K. Waters, was being held. The task force was nearly annihilated in what became the most controversial act by Patton during the war. According to Butcher, Eisenhower took "Patton's hide off." (Butcher diary, April 18, 1945. For an account of the Hammelburg raid and Patton's role see D'Este, *Patton*, chap. 44.)

32. Ibid., 46.

33. Codman, *Drive*, 281–82, Patton diary, Apr. 11, 1945, and Butcher diary, April 18, 1945.

34. Toland, *The Last 100 Days*, 371.

35. McKeogh, *Sgt. Mickey and General Ike*, 164–65.

36. Toland, *The Last 100 Days*, 371.

37. DDE quoted in J. Robert Moskin, *Mr. Truman's War* (New York, 1996), 56. A 4th Armored Division combat commander ordered Ohrdruf's civilian officials (who predictably disclaimed any knowledge of what had occurred in the grisly concentration camp in their midst) to attend a memorial service for the victims and to view the corpses in the enormous open-pit crematorium.

38. DDE to MDE, Apr. 15, 1945.

39. Murphy, *Diplomat Among Warriors*, 255.

40. DDE to GCM, Apr. 15, 1945.

54. ARMAGEDDON

1. MacDonald, *The Mighty Endeavor*, 465.

2. Hobart R. Gay diary, Apr. 12, 1945, NAII, and Toland, *The Last 100 Days*, 371. On the question of Berlin and Czechoslovakia, Montgomery and Patton found themselves in agreement. In his memoirs the field marshal wrote, "The Americans could not understand that it was of little avail to win the war strategically if we lost it politically. . . . It became obvious to me in the autumn of 1944 . . . [that] we were going to 'muck it up.' I reckon we did." Montgomery believed Third Army ought to have been permitted to liberate Czechoslovakia, and never understood why it was halted on its western frontier in late April. (Montgomery, *Memoirs*, 332.)

3. Bradley, *A Soldier's Story*, 535–36.

4. MacDonald, *The Last Offensive*, 406.

5. Patton diary, April 12, 1945, and Toland, *The Last 100 Days*, 377. On the afternoon of April 12, 1945, the author, then not quite nine years old, was in an Oakland, California, cinema when the film was suddenly stopped and the manager appeared and announced Roosevelt's death to the stunned patrons. The silence that followed was broken only by the sounds that swept across the audience of people openly weeping.

6. Bradley, *A General's Life*, 429.

7. DDE, *Crusade in Europe*, 447.

8. DDE to Maj. Gen. John R. Deane, Mar. 28, 1945, *EP*, vol. 4, 2551. Deane headed the U.S. military mission to Moscow and acted as Eisenhower's intermediary in his communication with Stalin. Despite British fury that Eisenhower had exceeded his authority as supreme commander by communicating directly with Stalin, it was pointed out that Eisenhower wrote to Stalin in his capacity as the head of the Russian armed forces, not as head of state.

9. Kimball, *Forged in War*, 312.

10. DDE, "Churchill-Marshall," Box 8, Post-Pres Papers, A-WR series, EL.

11. DDE to Montgomery, Sept. 15, 1944, *EP*, vol. 4, 2148. On Sept. 24, 1944, the SHAEF G-3 proclaimed, "Our main object must be the early capture of Berlin, the most important objective in Germany." (Memorandum, "Advance into Germany After Occupation of the Ruhr," dated Sept. 24, 1944, Box 77, RG 331, NA II.)

12. Roosevelt, quoted in Maurice Matloff, "Wilmot Revisited: Myth and Reality in the Anglo-American Strategy for the Second Front," in Theodore A. Wilson, ed., *D Day 1944* (Lawrence, Kans., 1944), 18.

13. Cornelius Ryan, *The Last Battle* (New York, 1966), 149.

14. Gilbert, *Road to Victory*, 1235.

15. Ryan, *The Last Battle*, chap. 3. Ryan presents a very useful account of the tortured tale of the EAC and the creation of the postwar zones of occupation.

16. David Eisenhower, *Eisenhower: At War*, 731. There is implied criticism in David Eisenhower's observation that his grandfather never fully explained his decision in *Crusade in Europe*. By the time he had begun his political career he was "devoted to defending his wartime decisions which 'hewed strictly to Roosevelt's political desires,' as historian Forrest Pogue later put it." (*Eisenhower: At War*, 732, and Pogue, *George C. Marshall: Organizer of Victory*, 578.)

17. DDE to GCM, Mar. 30, 1945, *EP*, vol. 4, 2561.

18. JSDE oral history, EL.

19. DDE to GCM, Apr. 7, 1945, *EP* vol. 4, 2592.

20. DDE to Montgomery, Apr. 8, 1945, ibid., 2594.

21. Official SHAEF historian Forrest Pogue writes, "It is not clear whether the matter was ever presented to Mr. Roosevelt, who was then in Warm Springs, Georgia, where he was to die in less than a week." Pogue believes that Roosevelt "would probably not have agreed with the U.S. chiefs had they taken the opposite view." (*The Supreme Command*, 445.)

22. DDE to Montgomery, *EP*, vol. 4, 2552. The order read: "The mission of your army group will be to protect Bradley's northern [left] flank."

23. Alanbrooke diary, April 3, 1945, DDE to WSC, Apr. 1, 1945, *EP*, vol. 4, 2573, and Pogue, *The Supreme Command*, 443–44.

24. Churchill to Roosevelt, Apr. 1, 1945, in Kimball, *Churchill & Roosevelt*, vol. 3, 603–04, and Churchill to Eisenhower, Apr. 2, 1945, in Bryant, *Triumph in the West*, 444.

25. Murphy, *Diplomat Among Warriors*, 254.

26. Ibid., 255.

27. JSDE oral history, EL.

28. Smith interview, May 8, 1947. Smith's statement was made at a time when the Iron Curtain had dropped over eastern Europe and the Cold War was revealing the speciousness of Russian promises made in 1945 over, for example, Poland.

29. Smith, *Eisenhower's Six Great Decisions*, 185.

30. Perret, *Eisenhower*, 639, n. 36, and *New York Herald Tribune*, June 16, 1952.

31. Murray and Millett, *A War to Be Won*, 482. These incredible numbers amounted to 10 percent of the total troops on the three Russian fronts commanded by Zhukov, Konev, and Rokossovsky. Nor was Berlin the only city to extract a bloody toll for its capture. The siege of Breslau, for example, cost an estimated sixty thousand Russian casualties. John Eisenhower spoke for his father years later when he suggested that it would have been suicidal "to send 15,000 men dashing down the Autobahn to Berlin to be chewed up by 2 million Russians coming in from 30 miles away with 2,200 guns. . . . That is what Dad would have considered militarily foolish." (JSDE oral history, EL. See also John Keegan's essay "Berlin," in Cowley, ed., *No End Save Victory*, 565–79.)

32. Pogue, *George C. Marshall: Organizer of Victory, 1943–1945*, 577–78.

33. MacDonald, *The Last Offensive*, 407. The exception that muddied the waters was a Seventh Army G-2 document issued on Mar. 25, 1945, "Study of the German National

Redoubt," which proclaimed that there was solid evidence of Hitler's intentions to establish the National Redoubt. What made the report so enigmatic was that Col. William W. Quinn, the G-2, "whose lines to sources inside Germany were probably the best of any of the field army G-2s, believed many of the reports of active preparation were fanciful." (Weigley, *Eisenhower's Lieutenants*, 701.)

34. Ellis, *Victory in the West*, vol. 2, appendix 10
35. Ibid., 302–04.
36. Pogue, *The Supreme Command*, 448.
37. "The National Redoubt," report issued by the SHAEF Joint Intelligence Committee (JIC), April 10, 1945. See Weigley, *Eisenhower's Lieutenants*, 703, and NA II, RG 331, Box 114.
38. Crosswell, *The Chief of Staff*, 319.
39. Transcript of Smith press conference, Apr. 21, 1945, Butcher diary, Apr. 21, 1945. Smith cautioned the correspondents that his discussion of the National Redoubt "must be kept very secret." An example of Smith's sometimes skewed ideas occurred over the captured Nazi gold horde at Merkers. "Smith could not understand why Robert Murphy was so horrified at Smith's suggestion that part of the captured German gold horde be distributed among the American generals chiefly responsible for defeating Germany. 'Can't some of us quietly arrange some of our own bonuses?' he had asked." (Smith, *Lucius D. Clay*, 215.)
40. Crosswell, *The Chief of Staff*, 320.
41. DDE, *Crusade in Europe*, 438.
42. Bradley, *A Soldier's Story*, 536, and Hansen diary, March 9 and Apr. 7, 1945.
43. Ibid. Lt. Gen. Kurt Ditmar was a radio commentator who was familiarly known as the "voice of the Wehrmacht." Ditmar scoffed at the Allied intelligence reports and revealed that he had only heard of the so-called redoubt after reading about it in a Swiss newspaper in January 1945. (537.)
44. Ellis, *Victory in the West*, vol. 2, appendix 10.
45. "Since late 1944, Nazi agents had been diligently selling the myth of the Redoubt, to curiously eager buyers. At the end of April, Bradley had told visiting Congressmen that the war might go on for another year." (Weigley, *Eisenhower's Lieutenants*, 716.)
46. Ibid., 703.
47. GCM to DDE, quoted in Martin Gilbert, *The Day the War Ended* (New York, 1995), 41.
48. Patton, *War As I Knew It*, 309. The presence of Third Army reconnaissance units in the vicinity of Prague may have ignited the rumor that American liberation of the city was imminent.
49. JSDE, *Strictly Personal*, 78, 81, 83. The unit to which John Eisenhower was sent was modeled on the so-called British phantom units, which fed timely operational information collected from frontline units directly to army headquarters, thus providing the army commander with current information on what was occurring on his particular front.
50. DDE to MDE, Apr. 4 and 9, 1945.
51. In early 1945 Stalin had sent this bloodthirsty message: "Soldiers of the Red Army! Kill the Germans! Kill all Germans! Kill! Kill! Kill!" (Quoted in Christopher Duffy, *Red Storm on the Reich* [New York, 1991], 274.)
52. Montgomery, *Memoirs*, 335, and Toland, *The Last 100 Days*, 558. When Montgomery's Canadian aide, Lt. Col. Trumbull Warren, whispered to Monty's British aide, Lt. Col. Christopher C. "Kit" Dawnay, that the chief was putting on an excellent act, Dawnay hissed, "Shut up, you S.O.B., he has been rehearsing this all his life." (Hamilton, *Monty: The Field Marshal*, 502.)
53. Butcher diary, May 4, 1945.
54. Peter Padfield, *Dönitz: The Last Führer* (London, 1984), 423.

55. Strong, *Intelligence at the Top*, 203.
56. Ibid., 204.
57. Padfield. *Dönitz*, 422.
58. Murphy, *Diplomat Among Warriors*, 240 and 255.
59. David Eisenhower, *Eisenhower: At War*, 803.
60. Smith, *Eisenhower's Six Great Decisions*, 210–11. Correspondent Charles Collingwood's radio broadcast described the scene: "The air is tense, tense, tense . . . Jodl's face is like a death mask, drawn, unnatural looking, and with every muscle in it clenched." (Quoted in S. H. Murray, "Surrender at Reims," *The Retired Officer Magazine*, May 1995.)
61. Summersby, *Eisenhower Was My Boss*, 242.
62. Smith, *Eisenhower's Six Great Decisions*, 211, Strong, *Intelligence at the Top*, 207, Butcher diary, May 7, 1945, and Summersby, *Eisenhower Was My Boss*, 242–34. Eisenhower's British aide, Lt. Col. James Gault, slept through the surrender ceremony and blamed Butcher, for whom he had a strong antipathy.
63. Butcher diary, May 7, 1945.
64. Summersby, *Eisenhower Was My Boss*, 243–44, and Summersby Morgan, *Past Forgetting*, 254.
65. Smith, *Eisenhower's Six Great Decisions*, 229.
66. Eisenhower signed and presented a copy of the historic cable to Kay Summersby. After her death it was auctioned by Sotheby's where it was expected to command a price in excess of $25,000.
67. Charles Collingwood, quoted in David Eisenhower, *Eisenhower: At War*, 802.
68. The timing of the surrender caused a political brouhaha outside Eisenhower's province. Originally Eisenhower planned that the official announcement would be made at 6:00 P.M., London time, May 7, 1945. However, Stalin refused to accept the German and Allied signatures made at Reims and demanded that a formal surrender be signed in Berlin on May 8. After frenzied negotiations and a multitude of cables and telephone calls, the Big Three finally agreed and at 2330 hours (11:30 P.M.), May 8, the surrender documents were signed, and the war in Europe officially ended.

The day after the German surrender, Eisenhower invited some twenty-five British and American officers—those with whom he had been the closest during the war—to lunch at his quarters. One was Lucius Clay, recently appointed deputy occupation commander. "It started off as a great victory celebration. By the time the lunch was over and everybody began to tell everybody goodbye, all of a sudden this group of generals recognized they no longer had a job. The companionship of months and days was gone. And it was almost like having attended your own funeral, really. By the time we left everybody was sad, and General Eisenhower was saying goodbye with tears in his eyes. It was a sad occasion . . . [and] a terrible letdown." (Smith, *Lucius D. Clay*, 237.)
69. *Stars and Stripes*, May 8, 1945. V-E day, when the war in Europe formally ended, was Eisenhower's 450th day as the Allied supreme commander. Although Roosevelt announced on December 24, 1943, that Eisenhower would become the supreme Allied commander, he did not formally assume the post until February 13, 1944. See Pogue, *The Supreme Command*, chap. 1.

EPILOGUE

1. Eisenhower, quoted in CBS Reports, "Eisenhower and D-Day," 1964 television program.
2. Mitgang, "D-Day Plus 20 Years." Mitgang accompanied Eisenhower on his 1964 trip to England and France.

Sources and Selected Bibliography

UNPUBLISHED SOURCES

The principal source of information about Dwight Eisenhower and his military career are the Eisenhower Papers in the Dwight D. Eisenhower Presidential Library, Abilene, Kansas. The Pre-Presidential Papers, 1916–1952 consist of over 138 linear feet and are the principal source of material by and about Eisenhower. Other important collections include: the diary and papers of Harry C. Butcher, the Eisenhower Vertical Files, and the papers of J. Earl Endacott, Barbara Thompson Eisenhower, Mamie Doud Eisenhower, John S. D. Eisenhower, Milton S. Eisenhower, William R. Gruber, Edward E. Hazlett, Paul A. Hodgson, William Lecel Lee, John W. Leonard, Delos W. Lovelace, Ruby Norman Lucier, Thomas W. Mattingly, Kevin McCann, Walter Bedell Smith, Howard McCrum Synder, and James R. Webb, as well as oral histories of Eisenhower, his family, friends, and associates, and various official documents, miscellaneous papers, and photographs. Other sources include the following:

Center of Military History, U.S. Army, Washington, D.C.

Published and unpublished articles and papers about Eisenhower. Various monographs and official histories about World War II published by CMH.

Citadel Archives, Charleston, South Carolina

The papers of Gen. Mark W. Clark.

Combined Arms Research Library, U.S. Army Command and General Staff College, Fort Leavenworth, Kansas

Various monographs and secondary sources (World Wars I and II).

Eisenhower National Historic Site, Gettysburg, Pennsylvania

Interviews: David Eisenhower, John S. D. Eisenhower, Mamie Eisenhower, Kevin McCann, and Arthur Nevins.

The Imperial War Museum, London

Various published and unpublished articles, letters, photographs, and papers in the Dept. of Printed Books, Dept. of Documents, and Dept. of Photographs. Oral history transcripts from the Thames Television series *The World at War, 1939–1945*.

Kansas State Historical Society

Papers of Sen. Joseph W. Bristow.

Kreitzberg Library, Norwich University, Northfield, Vermont

The papers of Maj. Gen. Ernest N. Harmon.

Liddell Hart Centre for Military Archives, King's College, London

The papers of Sir Basil Liddell Hart; the papers and diary of Field Marshal Lord Alan-brooke, and the papers of Lord Ismay.

Manuscript Division, Library of Congress, Washington, D.C.

The papers of Gen. George S. Patton, Jr.; the diary and papers of Maj. Gen. Everett S. Hughes; the papers of General of the Armies John J. Pershing; the papers of General Carl A. Spaatz, and the papers of General James H. Doolittle.

The MacArthur Memorial, Norfolk, Virginia

The Papers of Gen. Douglas MacArthur, D. Clayton James; Bonner Fellers; and Lt. Gen. Robert L. Eichelberger; and various oral histories conducted by D. Clayton James: Lt. Gen. Edward M. Almond; Lt. Gen. Clovis E. Byers; Brig Gen. Bradford G. Chynoweth; Col. James V. Collier; Gen Clyde D. Eddleman; Brig. Gen. Bonner F. Fellers; Gen. Thomas T. Handy; Maj. Gen. John E. Hull; Gen. Harold K, Johnson; Lt. Gen. Joseph M. Swing; Gen. Albert C. Wedemeyer, and Maj. Gen. Courtney Whitney.

George C. Marshall Research Library, Virginia Military Institute, Lexington, Virginia

The papers of General of the Army George C. Marshall; the diary and papers of Gen. Lucian K. Truscott, Jr.; the papers of Lt. Gen. Thomas T. Handy Papers; George F. Howe collection; the papers of Brig. Gen. Frank McCarthy; the papers of Brig. Gen. Paul M. Robinett; the memoirs of Justus 'Jock' Lawrence of miscellaneous magazine and newspaper articles and television interviews.

S.L.A. Marshall Military History Collection, University of Texas at El Paso

"Eisenhower as a Field General," unpublished essay by S. L. A. Marshall

National Archives, Washington, D.C.

Secretary of War Files, RG 107 and RG 159: Correspondence 1917–34, Office of the [Army] Inspector General.

National Archives II, College Park, Maryland

Diary of Lt. Gen. Hobart R. Gay; Records of Allied Force Headquarters (AFHQ) and SHAEF.

Public Record Office, Kew, London

The personal papers of Field Marshal Earl Alexander of Tunis (WO 214); the Churchill Papers (PREM 3); Allied Force Headquarters (AFHQ) papers (WO 204); SHAEF papers (WO 219); 21st Army Group papers (WO 205); correspondence of Air Marshal Sir Arthur Coningham, Tunisian campaign; Cabinet Office Historical Section essay on post-Normandy strategy; various campaign and historical files, Mediterranean and northwest Europe.

Sterling Library, Yale University, New Haven, Connecticut

The papers of Secretary of War Henry L. Stimson (microfilm).

Still Photo Branch, National Archives II, College Park, Maryland

World War II photographs.

United States Military Academy, West Point, New York

Gen. George S. Patton, Jr., collection; the papers of General of the Army Omar N. Bradley; Col. B. A. Dickson collection; various miscellaneous collections, histories, and registers of the Corps of Cadets, USMA; and the papers of the Class of 1915.

U.S. Army Military History Institute (USAMHI), Carlisle Barracks, Pennsylvania

The papers of General of the Army Omar N. Bradley, including the papers and diary of Lt. Col. Chester B. Hansen; the diary and papers of Maj. Gen. John P. Lucas; the papers of Maj. Gen. Terry de la Mesa Allen; Brig. Gen. Bradford G. Chynoweth; Raymond H. Croll; Harry C. Demars; Lt. Gen. Robert L. Eichelberger; Lt. Gen. Hobart R. Gay; Lt. Gen. John E. Hull; Maj. Gen. Kenyon Joyce; Brig. Gen. Oscar Koch; S. L. A. Marshall; Maj. Gen. Orlando W. Ward; Gen. A. C. Wedemeyer; and Gordon R. Young and Dorothy Mills Young. Miscellaneous: "Service Reminiscences of Lt. Gen. John C. H. Lee"; "Vignettes of Military History." Also: the OCMH collections, "World War II, the Supreme Command," the Pogue interviews.

Oral histories: Gen. Lucius D. Clay, Gen. Theodore J. Conway, Gen. Paul D. Harkins, Gen. Alfred M. Gruenther, Gen. Ben Harrell, Gen. James H. Polk, Gen. John K. Waters, Lt. Gen. Hobart R. Gay, S. L. A. Marshall, Lt. Gen. Elwood R. Quesada, and Gen. A. C. Wedemeyer.

Library: David Irving microfilm collection, including extracts from the papers and diary of Maj. Gen. Everett S. Hughes; "Essays in Some Dimensions of Military History."

Library, U.S. Naval War College, Newport, Rhode Island

Monograph: "From Algiers to Anzio," the unpublished diary and recollections of Maj. Gen. John P. Lucas.

Miscellaneous Sources

"Operation Symbol," Lt. Gen. Sir Ian Jacob's unpublished personal diary of the Casablanca Conference.

PUBLISHED SOURCES

Books

Alexander of Tunis, Field Marshal Earl. *The Alexander Memoirs, 1940–1945.* New York: McGraw-Hill, 1962.

Allen, Robert S. *Lucky Forward.* New York: Vanguard Press, 1964.

Ambrose, Stephen E. *Eisenhower and Berlin, 1945: The Decision to Halt at the Elbe.* New York: W. W. Norton, 1967.

———. *The Supreme Commander.* London: Cassell, 1970.

———. *Eisenhower: Soldier, General of the Army, President-Elect, 1890–1952.* New York: Simon & Schuster, 1983.

———. *D-Day.* New York: Simon & Schuster, 1994.

Ambrose, Stephen E., and Richard H. Immerman. *Milton S. Eisenhower: Educational Statesman.* Baltimore: Johns Hopkins University Press, 1983.

Annan, Noel. *Changing Enemies.* Ithaca: Cornell University Press, 1995.

Arnold, Henry H. *Global Missions.* New York: Harper and Bros., 1949.

Atkinson, Rick. *The Long Gray Line.* New York: Pocket Books, 1991.

Baxter, Colin F. *The War in North Africa, 1940–1943: A Selected Bibliography.* Westport, Conn.: Greenwood Press, 1996.

———. *Field Marshal Bernard Law Montgomery, 1887–1976: A Selected Bibliography.* Westport, Conn.: Greenwood Press, 1999.

Belfield, Eversley, and H. Essame. *The Battle for Normandy.* London: B.T. Batsford, 1965.

Bender, Mark C. *Watershed at Leavenworth; Dwight D. Eisenhower and the Command and General Staff School.* Fort Leavenworth, Kans.: CGSC, 1990.

Bennett, Ralph. *Ultra in the West.* London: Hutchinson, 1979.

———. *Ultra and the Mediterranean Strategy.* New York: William Morrow, 1989.

Beschloss, Michael R. *Eisenhower: A Centennial Life.* New York: HarperCollins, 1990.

Blair, Clay. *Ridgway's Paratroopers.* New York: Dial Press, 1985.

Bland, Larry I., and Sharon Ritenour Stevens, eds. *The Papers of George Catlett Marshall.* Vol. 1, *"The Soldierly Spirit," December 1880–June 1939.* Baltimore: Johns Hopkins University Press, 1981.

———. Vol. 2, *"We Cannot Delay," July 1, 1939–December 6, 1941.* Baltimore: Johns Hopkins University Press, 1986.

———. Vol. 3, *"The Right Man for the Job," December 7, 1941–May 31, 1943.* Baltimore: Johns Hopkins University Press, 1991.

———. Vol. 4, *"Aggressive and Determined Leadership," June 1, 1943–December 31, 1944.* Baltimore: Johns Hopkins University Press, 1996.

Blumenson, Martin. *Breakout and Pursuit.* Washington, D.C.: U.S. Government Printing Office, 1961.

———. *Kasserine Pass.* Boston: Houghton Mifflin, 1967.

———. *The Patton Papers, 1885–1940.* Boston: Houghton Mifflin, 1972.

———. *The Patton Papers, 1940–1945.* Boston: Houghton Mifflin, 1974.

———. *Patton: The Man Behind the Legend.* New York: Morrow, 1985.

———. *The Battle of the Generals.* New York: Morrow, 1994.

Blumenson, Martin, and James L. Stokesbury. *Masters of the Art of Command.* Boston: Houghton Mifflin, 1975.

Bradley, Omar N. *A Soldier's Story.* New York: Henry Holt, 1951.

Bradley, Omar N., with Clay Blair. *A General's Life.* New York: Simon & Schuster, 1983.

Brandon, Dorothy Barrett. *Mamie Doud Eisenhower: A Portrait of a First Lady.* New York: Charles Scribner's Sons, 1954.

Brereton, Lewis H. *The Brereton Diaries.* New York: Morrow, 1946.

Brower, Charles F. IV, ed. *World War II in Europe: The Final Year*. New York: St. Martin's Press, 1998.

Brown, Anthony Cave. *Bodyguard of Lies*. London: W. H. Allen, 1976.

Brown, Dee. *The American West*. New York: Charles Scribner's Sons, 1994.

Bryant, Arthur. *The Turn of the Tide*. London: Collins, 1957.

————. *Triumph in the West*. London: Collins, 1959.

Burns, James MacGregor. *Roosevelt: The Soldier of Freedom*. New York: Harcourt Brace, 1970.

Butcher, Harry C. *My Three Years with Eisenhower*. New York: Simon & Schuster, 1946.

Carroll, Wallace. *Persuade or Perish*. Boston: Houghton Mifflin, 1948.

Carter, Samuel III. *Cowboy Capital of the World*. Garden City, N.Y.: Doubleday, 1973.

CGSC. *A Military History of the United States Army Command and General Staff School, 1881–1963*, Fort Leavenworth, Kans.: CGSC, n.d.

Chalmers, W. S. *Full Cycle: The Biography of Admiral Sir Bertram Home Ramsay*. London: Hodder and Stoughton, 1959.

Chandler, Alfred D., ed. *The Papers of Dwight David Eisenhower: The War Years*. Vols I–V. Baltimore: Johns Hopkins University Press, 1970.

Chandler, Alfred D., and Louis Galambos, eds. *The Papers of Dwight David Eisenhower*. Vol VI, *Occupation, 1945*. Baltimore: Johns Hopkins University Press, 1978.

Charmley, John. *Churchill: The End of Glory*. San Diego: Harvest Books, 1994.

Chynoweth, Bradford Grethen. *Bellamy Park*. Hicksville, N.Y.: Exposition Press, 1975.

Churchill, Winston S. *The Second World War*. Vol. 3, *The Grand Alliance*. Boston: Houghton Mifflin, 1950.

————. Vol. 5, *Closing the Ring*. Boston: Houghton Mifflin, 1951.

————. Vol. 6, *Triumph and Tragedy*. Boston: Houghton Mifflin, 1951.

Clark, Mark. *Calculated Risk*. New York: Harper & Row, 1951.

Clark, Maurine. *Captain's Bride, General's Lady*. New York: McGraw-Hill, 1956.

Clarke, Jeffrey J. and Robert Ross Smith. *Riviera to the Rhine*. Washington, D.C.: Center of Military History, 1993.

Cline, Ray S. *United States Army in World War II: The War Department. Washington Command Post: The Operations Division*. Washington, D.C.: Center of Military History, 1990.

Codman, Charles R. *Drive*. Boston: Little, Brown, 1957.

Coffman, Edward M. *The War to End All Wars: The American Military Experience in World War I*. New York: Oxford University Press, 1968.

Cole, Hugh M. *The Lorraine Campaign*. Washington, D.C.: U.S. Government Printing Office, 1950.

————. *The Ardennes, Battle of the Bulge*. Washington, D.C.: U.S. Government Printing Office, 1965.

Collins, J. Lawton. *Lightning Joe*. Baton Rouge: Louisiana State University Press, 1979.

Colville, John. *The Fringes of Power*. London: Hodder & Stoughton, 1985.

Conner Virginia. *What Father Forbad*. Philadelphia: Dorrance & Co., 1951.

Cook, Don. *Charles De Gaulle*. New York: Putnam, 1983.

Cowley, Robert, ed. *No End Save Victory*. New York: Putnam, 2001.

Cray, Ed. *General of the Army: George C. Marshall, Soldier and Statesman*. New York: Touchstone Books, 1990.

Cronkite, Walter. *A Reporter's Life*. New York: Knopf, 1996.

Crosswell, D. K. R. *The Chief of Staff: The Military Career of General Walter Bedell Smith*. Westport, Conn.: Greenwood Press, 1991.

Cunningham, Admiral of the Fleet Viscount. *A Sailor's Odyssey*. London: Hutchinson, 1951.

Danchev, Alex, and Daniel Todman, eds. *War Diaries, 1941–1945: Field Marshal Lord Alanbrooke*. London: Weidenfeld & Nicolson, 2001.

Daniels, Roger. *The Bonus March*. Westport, Conn.: Greenwood Press, 1971.

Dastrup, Boyd L. *The US Army Command and General Staff College: A Centennial History*. Leavenworth and Manhattan, Kans.: J. H. Johnston and Sunflower University Press, 1982.

David, Lester, and Irene David. *Ike & Mamie: The Story of the General and His Lady*. New York: Putnam, 1981.

Davis, Franklin M. *Across the Rhine*. Alexandria, Va.: Time-Life Books, 1980.

Davis, Kenneth S. *Dwight D. Eisenhower: Soldier of Democracy*. New York: Konecky & Konecky, reprint of 1945 edition.

Davis, Richard G. *Carl A. Spaatz and the Air War in Europe*. Washington, D.C.: Center for Air Force History, 1993.

de Guingand, Francis. *Operation Victory*. London: Hodder & Stoughton, 1947.

———. *Generals at War*. London: Hodder & Stoughton, 1964.

Depuy, Trevor N. *Hitler's Last Gamble*. New York: HarperCollins, 1994.

D'Este, Carlo. *Decision in Normandy*. New York: E. P. Dutton, 1988.

———. *Bitter Victory: The Battle for Sicily, 1943*. New York: E. P. Dutton, 1988.

———. *Fatal Decision: Anzio and the Battle for Rome*. New York: HarperCollins, 1991.

———. *Patton: A Genius for War*. New York: HarperCollins, 1995.

Drago, Harry Sinclair. *Wild, Woolly and Wicked*. New York: Clarkson N. Potter, 1960.

Duncan, Kunigunde. *Earning the Right to Do Fancywork: An Informal Biography of Mrs. Ida Eisenhower*. Lawrence: Univ of Kansas Press, 1957.

Eisenhower, David. *Eisenhower: At War, 1943–1945*. London: Collins, 1986.

Eisenhower, Dwight D. *Crusade in Europe*. London: Heinemann, 1948.

———. *At Ease: Stories I Tell My Friends*. Garden City, N.Y.: Doubleday, 1967.

———. *In Review: Pictures I've Kept*. Garden City, N.Y.: Doubleday, 1969.

———. *Letters to Mamie*. Garden City, N.Y.: Doubleday, 1978.

Eisenhower, Edgar Newton with John McCallum. *Six Roads from Abilene: Some Personal Recollections of Edgar Eisenhower*. Seattle: Wood & Reber, 1960.

Eisenhower, John S. D. *The Bitter Woods*. New York: Putnam, 1969.

———. *Strictly Personal*. Garden City, N.Y.: Doubleday, 1974.

———. *Allies: Pearl Harbor to D-Day*. Garden City, N.Y.: Doubleday, 1982.

Eisenhower, Susan. *Mrs. Ike*. New York: Farrar, Straus and Giroux, 1996.

Ellis, John. *Brute Force*. London: Andre Deutsch, 1990.

Ellis, L. F. *Victory in the West*. Vol. 1. London: Her Majesty's Stationery Office, 1962, and vol. 2, 1968.

Farago, Ladislas. *Patton: Ordeal and Triumph*. New York: Ivan Obolensky, 1963.

Ferrell, Robert H., *Ill-Advised*. Columbia: University of Missouri Press, 1992.

———. ed. *The Eisenhower Diaries*. New York: W. W. Norton, 1981.

Fisher, Nigel. *Harold Macmillan*. New York: St. Martin's Press, 1982.

Fleming, Thomas J. *West Point: The Men and Times of the United States Military Academy*. New York: Morrow, 1969.

Fraser, David. *Alanbrooke*. London: Collins, 1982.

Fromkin, David. *In the Time of the Americans*. New York: Knopf, 1995.

Gabel, Christopher R. *The U.S. Army GHQ Maneuvers of 1941*. Washington, D.C.: Center of Military History, U.S. Army, 1991.

Galambos, Louis, ed. *The Papers of Dwight David Eisenhower: The Chief of Staff*, vols. VI–IX. Baltimore: Johns Hopkins University Press, 1978.

Garland, Albert N., and Howard McGaw Smyth. *Sicily and the Surrender of Italy*. Washington, D.C.: U.S. Government Printing Office, 1965.

Gavin, James M. *On to Berlin*. New York: Viking Press, 1978.

Gelb, Norman. *Desperate Venture: The Story of Operation Torch, the Allied Invasion of North Africa*. New York: Morrow, 1992.

Gilbert, Martin. *Road to Victory: Winston S. Churchill, 1941–1945*. London: Heinemann, 1986.

———. *Churchill*. New York: Henry Holt, 1991.

———. *The Day the War Ended*. New York: Henry Holt, 1995.

Goodwin, Doris Kearns. *No Ordinary Time: Franklin and Eleanor Roosevelt: The Home Front in World War II*. New York: Simon & Schuster, 1994.

Graham, Dominick and Shelford Bidwell. *Tug of War: The Battle for Italy, 1943–45*. New York: St. Martin's Press, 1986.

———. *Coalitions, Politicians and Generals*. London: Brassey's, 1993.

Greenfield, Kent Roberts, ed. *Command Decisions*. Washington, D.C.: Center of Military History, U.S. Army, 1990 reprint.

Griffith, Robert, ed. *Ike's Letters to a Friend: 1941–1958*. Lawrence: Regent's Press of Kansas, 1984.

Gunther, John. *D-Day*. New York: Harper and Bros., 1943.

Hamilton, Nigel. *Monty: Master of the Battlefield, 1942–1944*. London: Hamish Hamilton, 1983.

———. *Monty: The Field Marshal, 1944–1976*. London: Hamish Hamilton, 1986.

———. *Monty: The Battles of Field Marshal Bernard Montgomery*. New York: Random House, 1994.

———. *The Fully Monty: Montgomery of Alamein, 1887–1942*. London: Penguin, 2001.

Hansen, Laurence J. *What It Was Like Flying for "Ike."* W. Largo, Florida: Aero-Medical Consultants, Inc. 1983.

Harmon, Ernest N. *Combat Commander*. Englewood Cliffs, N.J.: Prentice-Hall, 1970.

Harrison, Gordon A. *Cross-Channel Attack*. Washington, D.C.: Office of the Chief of Military History, 1951.

Hatch, Alden. *Red Carpet for Mamie*. New York: Henry Holt, 1954.

Hastings, Max. *Bomber Command*. London: Pan Books, 1981.

———. *Overlord: D-Day and the Battle for Normandy, 1944*. New York: Simon & Schuster, 1984.

Hinsley, F. H. *British Intelligence in the Second World War*, vol. III, part I. London: Her Majesty's Stationery Office, 1984.

———. *British Intelligence in the Second World War*, vol. III, part II. London: Her Majesty's Stationery Office, 1988.

Hobbs, Joseph P. *Dear General: Eisenhower's Wartime Letters to Marshall*. Baltimore: Johns Hopkins Press, 1971.

Hoffman, Paul D. *Chronicle of the Belle Springs Creamery Company*. Abilene, Kans.: Abilene Printing Co., 1975.

Hogan, David W., Jr. *A Command Post at War: First Army Headquarters in Europe, 1944–1945*. Washington, D.C.: Center of Military History, U.S. Army, 2000.

Holt, Daniel D., and James Leyerzapf, eds. *Eisenhower: The Prewar Diaries and Selected Papers, 1905–1941*. Baltimore: Johns Hopkins University Press, 1998.

Horne, Alistair. *Macmillan, 1894–1956*. London: Macmillan, 1988.

Horne, Alistair, with David Montgomery. *Monty: The Lonely Leader, 1944–1945*. New York: HarperCollins, 1994.

Howe, George F. *Northwest Africa: Seizing the Initiative in the West*. Washington, D.C.: U.S. Government Printing Office, 1957.

Howze, Hamilton H. *A Cavalryman's Story*. Washington, D.C.: Smithsonian Institution Press, 1996.

Huie, William Bradford. *The Execution of Private Slovik*. New York: Delacorte Press, 1954.

Humes, James C., *Confessions of a White House Ghostwriter*. Washington, D.C.: Regenery Publishing, 1997.

Hunt, Elvid. *History of Fort Leavenworth, 1827–1937*. Fort Leavenworth, Kans.: Command and General Staff School Press, 1937.

Huntington, Samuel P. *The Soldier and the State: The Theory and Politics of Civil-Military Relations*. Cambridge, Mass.: Harvard University Press, 1957.

Irving, David. *The War Between the Generals*. New York: Congdon & Lattès, 1981.

Ismay, Hastings Lionel. *The Memoirs of General the Lord Ismay*. London: Heinemann, 1960.

James, D. Clayton. *The Years of MacArthur*. Vol. 1, *1880–1941*. Boston: Houghton Mifflin, 1970.

Jameson, Henry B. *Heroes by the Dozen*. Abilene: Shadinger-Wilson Printers, 1961.

———. *They Still Call Him Ike*. New York: Vantage Press, 1972.

Josephson, Matthew. *Infidel in the Temple*. New York: Knopf, 1967.

Keegan, John. *Six Armies in Normandy*. New York: Viking, 1982.

Kennedy, David. *Freedom from Fear*. New York: Oxford University Press, 1999.

Kersaudy, François. *Churchill and De Gaulle*. London: Collins, 1981.

Kershaw, Ian. *Hitler: 1936–1945, Nemesis*. New York: W. W. Norton, 2000.

Kimball, Warren F. *Churchill and Roosevelt: The Complete Correspondence*. 3 vols. Princeton, N.J.: Princeton University Press, 1984.

———. *Forged in War: Roosevelt, Churchill, and the Second World War*. New York: Morrow, 1997.

Kingston-McCloughry, Air Vice-Marshal E. J. *The Direction of War*. New York: Frederick A. Praeger, 1955.

Kornitzer, Bela. *The Great American Heritage: The Story of the Five Eisenhower Brothers*. New York: Farrar, Straus and Cudahy, 1955.

Lamb, Richard. *Montgomery in Europe, 1943–45*. London: Buchan & Enright, 1983.

Larrabee, Eric. *Commander in Chief*. New York: Harper & Row, 1987.

Lasby, Clarence G. *Eisenhower's Heart Attack*. Lawrence: Univ Press of Kansas, 1997.

Laurie, Clayton D., and Ronald H. Cole. *The Role of Federal Military Forces in Domestic Disorders, 1877–1945*. Washington, D.C.: Center of Military History, 1997.

Leary, William M., ed. *MacArthur and the American Century*. Lincoln: University of Nebraska Press, 2001.

Lee, R. Alton. *Dwight D. Eisenhower: Soldier and Statesman*. Chicago: Nelson-Hall, 1981.

Lewis, Nigel. *Exercise Tiger*. New York: Prentice Hall Press, 1990.

Liddell Hart, B. H., ed. *The Rommel Papers*. New York: Harcourt, Brace, 1953.

Link, Paxton. *The Link Family*. Privately printed, 1951.

Linn, Brian McAllister. *Guardians of Empire: The U.S. Army in the Pacific, 1902–1940*. Greensboro: University of North Carolina Press.

Lisio, Donald J. *The President and Protest: Hoover, Conspiracy, and the Bonus Riot*. Columbia: University of Missouri Press, 1974.

Lyon, Peter. *Eisenhower: Portrait of the Hero*. Boston: Little, Brown, 1974.

MacDonald, Charles B. *The Siegfried Line Campaign*. Washington, D.C.: Office of the Chief of Military History, 1963.

———. *The Mighty Endeavor*. New York: Oxford University Press, 1969.

———. *A Time for Trumpets: The Untold Story of the Battle of the Bulge*. New York: Morrow, 1985.

Macmillan, Harold. *The Blast of War*. London: Macmillan, 1967.

———. *War Diaries*. London: Macmillan, 1984.

Magenheimer, Heinz. *Hitler's War: Germany's Key Strategic Decisions, 1940–1945*, London: Cassell, 2000.

Maguire, Jack. *Katy's Baby: The Story of Denison, Texas*. Austin: Nortex Press, 1991.

Maher, Marty. *Bringing Up the Brass*. New York: David McKay, 1951.

Manchester, William. *American Caesar*. New York: Dell, 1979.

McCallum, John. *Six Roads from Abilene: Some Personal Recollections of Edgar Eisenhower.* Seattle: Wood & Reber, 1960.

McCann, Kevin. *Man from Abilene: Dwight David Eisenhower—a Story of Leadership.* Garden City, N.Y.: Doubleday, 1952.

McCullough, David. *Truman.* New York: Simon & Schuster, 1992.

McKee, Alexander. *The Race for the Rhine Bridges.* London: Pan Books, 1974.

McKeogh, Michael J., and Richard Lockridge. *Sgt. Mickey and General Ike.* New York: Putnam, 1946.

Merriam, Robert E. *The Battle of the Bulge.* New York: Ballantine Books, 1978.

Michie, Alan A. *The Invasion of Europe: The Story Behind D-Day.* New York: Dodd, Mead & Co., 1964.

Middleton, Drew. *Our Share of the Night: A Personal Narrative of the War Years.* New York: Viking Press, 1946.

A Military History of the US Army Command & General Staff College, 1881–1963. Fort Leavenworth, Kans.: CGSC.

Miller, Francis Trevelyan. *Eisenhower: Man and Soldier.* Philadelphia: John C. Winston Co., 1944.

Miller, Merle. *Plain Speaking: An Oral Biography of Harry S. Truman.* New York: Berkeley Publishing, 1974.

———. *Ike the Soldier: As They Knew Him.* New York: Putnam, 1986.

Montgomery, Field Marshal Viscount. *Memoirs.* London: Collins, 1958.

Moran, Lord. *Winston Churchill: The Struggle for Survival, 1940–1965.* London, Sphere Books, 1968.

Morelock, J. D. *Generals of the Ardennes: American Leadership in the Battle of the Bulge.* Washington, D.C.: National Defense University Press, 1994.

Morgan, Frederick. *Overture to Overlord.* London: Hodder & Stoughton, 1950.

Morgan, Kay Summersby. *Past Forgetting.* New York: Simon & Schuster, 1976.

Morison, Samuel Eliot. *Operations in North African Waters, October 1942–June 1943.* Boston: Little, Brown, 1947.

———. *Sicily-Salerno-Anzio.* Boston: Little, Brown, 1954.

———. *The Invasion of France and Germany, 1944–1945.* Boston: Little, Brown, 1968.

Mosley, Leonard. *Marshall.* London: Methuen, 1982.

Murphy, Robert D. *Diplomat Among Warriors.* Garden City, N.Y.: Doubleday, 1964.

Murray, G. E. Patrick. *Eisenhower Versus Montgomery: The Continuing Debate.* Westport, Conn: Praeger, 1996.

Murray, Williamson and Alan R. Millett. *A War to Be Won.* Cambridge: Belknap Press of Harvard University Press, 2000.

Neal, Steve. *The Eisenhowers.* Lawrence: University Press of Kansas, 1984.

Nenninger, Timothy. *The Leavenworth Schools and the Old Army.* Westport, Conn.: Greenwood Press, 1978.

Nicholson, Nigel. *Alex: The Life of Field Marshal Earl Alexander of Tunis.* London: Weidenfeld & Nicolson, 1973.

Oldfield, Colonel Barney. *Never a Shot in Anger.* New York: Duell, Sloane & Pearce, 1956.

Orange, Vincent. *Coningham.* London: Methuen, 1990.

Parrish, Thomas. *Roosevelt and Marshall: Partners in Politics and War.* New York: Morrow, 1989.

Parton, James. *"Air Force Spoken Here": General Ira Eaker and the Command of the Air.* Bethesda, Md.: Adler & Adler, 1986.

Patton, George S., Jr. *War As I Knew It.* New York: Bantam, 1980.

Pawle, Gerald. *The War and Colonel Warden.* London: George G. Harrap & Co., 1963.

Perret, Geoffrey. *There's a War to Be Won.* New York: Random House, 1991.

———. *Winged Victory: The Army Air Forces in World War II.* New York: Random House, 1993.

————. *Old Soldiers Never Die*. New York: Random House, 1996.

————. *Eisenhower*. New York: Random House, 1999.

Pogue, Forrest C. *The Supreme Command*. Washington, D.C.: Office of the Chief of Military History, 1954.

————. *George C. Marshall: Education of a General, 1880–1939*. New York: Viking Press, 1963.

————. *George C. Marshall: Ordeal and Hope, 1939–1942*. New York: Viking Press, 1966.

————. *George C. Marshall: Organizer of Victory, 1943–1945*. New York: Viking Press, 1973.

Powell, Geoffrey. *The Devil's Birthday: The Bridges to Arnhem, 1944*. New York: Franklin Watts, 1984.

Register of Graduates and Former Cadets of the United States Military Academy, 1802–1990. West Point, N.Y.: USMA, 1990.

Report by the Supreme Commander to the Combined Chiefs of Staff on the Operations in Europe of the Allied Expeditionary Force, 6 June 1944 to 8 May 1945. Washington, D.C.: Center of Military History, 1994.

Richardson, Charles. *Send for Freddie*. London: William Kimber, 1987.

————. *From Churchill's Secret Circle to the BBC: The Biography of Lieutenant General Sir Ian Jacob*. London: Brassey's, 1991.

Richardson, Fannie Belle Taylor. "Eisenhower Lineage and Reference, 1691–Sept. 3, 1957." Unpublished ms. Greenwood, Indiana.

Ridgway, Matthew B. *Soldier*. New York: Harper and Bros., 1956.

Rostow, W. W. *Pre-Invasion Bombing Strategy: General Eisenhower's Decision of March 25, 1944*. Austin: University of Texas Press, 1981.

Ruppenthal, Roland G. *Logistical Support of the Armies*, vol. I. Washington, D.C.: Office of the Chief of Military History, 1953.

Ryan, Cornelius. *A Bridge Too Far*. London: Coronet Books, 1974.

————. *The Longest Day*. New York: Touchstone Books, 1994.

Sainsbury, Keith. *The North African Landings, 1942*. Newark: University of Delaware Press, 1979.

Schoenbrun, David. *America Inside Out*. New York: McGraw-Hill, 1984.

Sevareid, Eric. *Not So Wild a Dream*. New York: Knopf, 1969.

Sherwood, Robert E. *The White House Papers of Harry L. Hopkins*. 2 vols. London: Eyre & Spottiswoode, 1949.

Smith, Gene. *The Shattered Dream*. New York: Morrow, 1970.

Smith, Jean Edward. *Lucius D. Clay: An American Life*. New York: Henry Holt, 1990.

Smith, Walter Bedell. *Eisenhower's Six Great Decisions: Europe, 1944–1945*. New York: Longmans, Green, 1956.

Snyder, Marty, and Glenn D. Kittler. *My Friend Ike*. New York: Fell, 1956.

Stagg, J. M. *Forecast for Overlord*. London: Ian Allan, 1971.

Stimson, Henry, and McGeorge Bundy. *On Active Service*. New York: Harper & Bros., 1948.

Stoler, Mark. *George C. Marshall: Soldier-Statesman of the American Century*. Boston: Twayne Publishers, 1989.

Strong, Kenneth. *Intelligence at the Top*. London: Cassell, 1968.

Sullivan, John J. *Overlord's Eagles*. Jefferson, N.C.: McFarland & Co, 1997.

Summersby, Kay. *Eisenhower Was My Boss*. New York: Prentice Hall, 1948.

Tedder, Lord. *With Prejudice*. London: Cassell, 1966.

Toland, John. *The Last 100 Days*. New York: Random House, 1967.

Truscott, Lucian K. *Command Missions*. New York: E. P. Dutton, 1954.

————. *The Twilight of the U.S. Cavalry*. Manhattan: University Press of Kansas, 1990.

Van Creveld, Martin. *Supplying War*. Cambridge: Cambridge University Press, 1977.

Vandiver, Frank E. *Black Jack: The Life and Times of John J. Pershing.* Vols. I and II. College Station: Texas A&M University Press, 1977.

Verckler, Stewart, P. *Cowtown Abilene: The Story of Abilene, Kansas, 1867–1875.* Privately printed, 1967.

Walters, Vernon. *Silent Missions.* Garden City, N.Y.: Doubleday, 1978.

Watson, Mark Skinner. *Chief of Staff: Prewar Plans and Preparations.* Washington, D.C.: Center of Military History, 1991.

Wedemeyer, Albert C. *Wedemeyer Reports!* New York: Henry Holt and Co., 1958.

Weigley, Russell F. *History of the United States Army.* New York: Macmillan, 1967.

———. *Eisenhower's Lieutenants.* Bloomington: Indiana University Press, 1981.

Weinberg, Gerhard L. *A World at Arms.* New York: Cambridge University Press, 1994.

Wilmot, Chester. *The Struggle for Europe.* New York: Harper & Row, 1952.

Wilson, Dale E. *Treat 'Em Rough!: The Birth of American Armor, 1917–20.* Novato, Calif.: Presidio Press, 1990.

Wilson, Theodore A., ed. *D Day 1944.* Lawrence: University Press of Kansas, 1994.

Yergin, Daniel. *The Prize.* New York: Simon & Schuster, 1991.

Zuckerman, Solly. *From Apes to Warlords.* London: Hamish Hamilton, 1978.

Articles

Ambrose, Stephen E. "A Fateful Friendship." *American Heritage,* April 1969.

———. "Interviewing Ike." *American History Illustrated,* October 1970.

———. "The Bulge." *MHQ,* spring 1989.

———. "Eisenhower's Legacy." *Military Review,* October 1990.

"APOA'er Eisenhower Did Good Job Flying Cub Liaison Plane During War." *The A.O.P.A. 'Pilot' Magazine,* May 1958.

A Young Graduate [pseud. for Eisenhower]. "The Leavenworth Course." *Infantry Journal,* June 1927.

Baldwin, Hanson W. "The Greatest Martial Drama in History." *Army,* June 1980.

Baxter, Colin F. "Winston Churchill: Military Strategist?" *Military Affairs,* February 1983.

Bergman, Jerry. "Steeped in Religion: President Eisenhower and the Influence of the Jehovah's Witnesses." *Kansas History,* autumn 1998.

Berlin, Robert. H. "Dwight David Eisenhower and the Duties of Generalship." *Military Review,* October 1990.

Bess, Demaree. "Army's Favorite General." *Saturday Evening Post,* October 3, 1942.

———. "He United an Invasion Army." *Saturday Evening Post,* August 7, 1943.

Betson, William R. "Sidi Bou Zid: A Case History of Failure." *Armor,* November–December. 1982.

Bigelow, Michael E. "Kasserine Pass." *Military Review,* February 1993.

Blumenson, Martin. "The Most Overrated General of World War II." *Armor,* May-June 1952.

———. "Eisenhower: Great Commander or Chairman of the Board?" *Army,* June 1966.

———. "Patton and Montgomery: Alike or Different?" *Army,* June 1972.

———. "Bradley-Patton: World War II's 'Odd Couple.' " *Army,* December 1985.

———. "America's World War II Leaders in Europe: Some Thoughts." *Parameters,* December 1989.

———. "Eisenhower Then and Now: Fireside Reflections." *Parameters,* summer 1991.

———. "Disaster at Kasserine Pass." *Army,* February 1993.

———. "Essence of Command: Competence, Iron Soul." *Army,* March 1993.

———. "Ike and His Indispensable Lieutenants." *Army,* June 1980.

———. "The Problem of Berlin." *Army,* August 1998.

Branigar, Thomas. "No Villains, No Heroes: The David Eisenhower–Milton Good Controversy." *Kansas History,* autumn 1990.

Brown, Charles H. "Fox Conner: A General's General." *Journal of Mississippi History*, August 1987.

Cadden, Vivian. "Mamie Eisenhower Talks About Fifty Years of Marriage." *McCall's*, September 1966.

Calkins, Ken. "Ike the Pilot." *Boeing Magazine*, January 1954.

Coffman, Edward M. " 'My Roommate . . . is Dwight Eisenhower . . .' " *American Heritage*, April 1973.

Cohen, Eliot A. "Churchill and His Generals." *MHQ*, autumn 1996.

"Command and General Staff School." *Cavalry Journal*, vol. 25, 1926.

Cooling, Benjamin Franklin. "Dwight D. Eisenhower at the Army War College, 1927–1928." *Parameters*, vol. 5, no. 1, 1975.

Daniell, Raymond. "He Is Our Eisen and This Is Our Hour." *Life*, November 9, 1942.

———. "Hell, I Can't. I've Got a Date in Berlin." *New York Times Magazine*, November 15, 1942.

D'Este, Carlo. "Falaise: The Trap Not Sprung." *MHQ*, spring 1994.

———. "The Slaps Heard Round the World." *MHQ*, winter 1996.

———. "Patton's Finest Hour." *MHQ*, spring 2001.

Deutsch, Harold C. "Clients of Ultra: American Captains." *Parameters*, summer 1985.

Dodd, Gladys. "The Early Career of Abraham L. Eisenhower, Pioneer Preacher. *Kansas Historical Quarterly*, autumn 1963.

"Dwight D. Eisenhower." *Time*, January 1, 1945.

———. "War Policies." *Cavalry Journal*, November–December 1931.

———. "What I Have Learned." *SR*, September 10, 1966.

"Eisenhower and Sports." *Overview*, spring 1984.

"Eisenhower at West Point." *Assembly*, November 1990.

Eisenhower, Dwight D. "A Tank Discussion." *Infantry Journal*, November 1920.

Eisenhower, Earl. "I Grew Up with Ike." *American Weekly*, circa 1954.

Eisenhower, Mamie. "My Memories of Ike." *Reader's Digest*, February 1970.

———. "The Ike I Remember." Interview by Barbara Walters, *Ladies Home Journal*, April 1974.

Ferrell, Robert H. "Eisenhower Was a Democrat." *Kansas History*, autumn 1990.

Fleming, Thomas. "West Point in Review." *American Heritage*, April 1988.

"From Plebe to President." *Colliers*, June 10, 1955.

Funk, Arthur L. "Eisenhower, Giraud, and the Command of 'TORCH.' " *Military Affairs*, October 1971.

———. "Churchill, Eisenhower, and the French Resistance." *Military Affairs*, February 1981.

Greene, Douglas. "Ike: The Human Side." *American Legion Magazine*, May 1983.

Gunther, John. "With Eisenhower in Sicily." *Colliers*, September 25, 1943.

Hall, George M. "The Faces of Leadership." *Army*, June 1989.

Harger, C. M. "Abilene's Ike." *New York Times Magazine*, November 22, 1942.

Hatch, Alden, "Red Carpet for Mamie." *Ladies Home Journal*, date unknown, 1954.

Hertzler, J. R. "The 1879 Brethren in Christ Migration from Southeastern Pennsylvania to Dickinson County, Kansas." *Pennsylvania Mennonite Journal*, January 1980.

Holt, Daniel D. "An Unlikely Partnership and Service: Dwight Eisenhower, Mark Clark, and the Philippines." *Kansas History*, autumn 1990.

Horne, Alistair, and David Montgomery. "Monty and Ike, '44–'45: The Last Stages." *RUSI Journal*, August 1995.

Johnson, Falk S. "The Battle of the Bulge Foreshadowed." *Military Review*, December 1994–January 1995.

Kingseed, Cole C. "Mentoring General Ike." *Military Review*, October 1990.

———. " 'Ike' Takes Charge." *Military Review*, June 1991.

———. "Eisenhower's Prewar Anonymity: Myth or Reality?" *Parameters*, autumn 1991.

———. "Victory in Europe." *Military Review*, May–June 1995.

———. "The Juggler and the Supreme Commander." *Military Review*, November–December 1996.

Kirkpatrick, Charles E. "Joint Planning for Operation Torch." *Parameters*, summer 1991.

Kluckhorn, F. L. "With Eisenhower at Headquarters." *New York Times Magazine*, January 10, 1943.

Kornitzer, Bela. "The Story of Ike and His 4 Brothers." *U.S. News & World Report*, July 1, 1955.

Kuter, Gen. Lawrence S. "Goddammit, Georgie." *Air Force Magazine*, February 1973.

Liddell Hart, B. H. "Generalship in the Second World War." *Listener*, September 3, 1964.

Lisio, Donald J. "A Blunder Becomes Catastrophic: Hoover, the Legion, and the Bonus Army." *Wisconsin Magazine of History*, autumn 1967.

Madden, Robert W. "The Making of a General of the Army." *Army*, December 1990.

Marshall, Jim. "Spearhead of Our Defense." *Colliers*, September 5, 1936.

Martin, Lawrence A. "The Battle of the Bulge in Retrospect." *Military Review*, December 1994–January 1995.

Massengill, Lawrence. "A Corridor to Nowhere." *Military Review*, September 1994.

Massow, Rosalind. "Mamie and Ike Talk About 50 Years of Marriage." *Parade*, June 26, 1966.

McCarthy, Dan B. "Ike's Stearman Time and the Streetcar . . ." *Air Line Pilot*, July 1976.

McNeil, I. H. "Lessons of the Inter-War Period." *British Army Review*, April 1994.

Mehle, F. Douglas. "Sponsorship." *Army*, March 1978.

Middleton, Drew. "Eisenhower Plans Minutely, Then Strikes." *New York Times Magazine*, July, 25, 1943.

Mitgang, Herbert. "D-Day Plus 20 Years." *Look*, June 1964.

Morrow, Lance. "George C. Marshall: The Last Great American?" *Smithsonian*, August 1997.

Morton, Louis. "The Philippine Army, 1935–39, Eisenhower's Memorandum to Quezon." *Military Affairs*, summer 1948.

———. "Gen. George C. Marshall and the Army Staff." *Military Review*, August 1994.

Murray, G. Patrick. "The Louisiana Maneuvers: Practice for War." *Louisiana History*, vol. 13, 1972.

Murray, S. H. "Surrender in Reims." *Retired Officer Magazine*, May 1995.

Neal, Steve. "We Were Right to Like Ike." *American Heritage*, December 1985.

Nenninger, Timothy K. "Leavenworth and Its critics: The U.S. Army Command and General Staff School, 1920–1940." *Journal of Military History*, April 1994.

Newman, A. S. "Many Athletes Become Fine Soldiers." *Army*, March 1978.

"The 1919 Transcontinental Motor Convoy." *Overview*, fall 1984.

Painton, F. C. "How Eisenhower Does His Job." *Reader's Digest*, November 1943.

Parshall, Gerald. "The Strategist of War: The Father Figure: Dwight Eisenhower." *U.S. News & World Report*, March 16, 1998.

———. "The Strategists of War: The Straight Shooter: George Marshall." *U.S. News & World Report*, March 16, 1998.

Perret, Geoffrey. "MacArthur and the Marchers." *MHQ*, winter 1996.

Peterson, Elmer T. "Mother Eisenhower Talks About Her Most Famous Son," *Better Homes and Gardens*, June 21, 1943.

Pickett, William B. "Eisenhower as a Student of Clausewitz." *Military Review*, July 1985.

Pollack, Jack Harrison, "What D-Day Means to Ike." *Parade*, June 5, 1960.

Raugh, Harold E., Jr. "Pershing and Marshall: A Study in Mentorship." *Army*, June 1987.

Reynolds, Quentin. "Eisenhower of Kansas." *Colliers*, December 18, 1948.

Rhodes, Richard. "Ike: An Artist in Iron." *Harper's*, July 1970.

Shearer, Lloyd. "Kay Summersby, Eisenhower's Aide—a Woman Who Can't Make Up Her Mind." *Parade*, February 10, 1974.

———. "Kay Summersby and Dwight Eisenhower—the True Story of Their Friendship." *Parade*, January 2, 1977.

———. "Butch and Ike—Different Roads." *Parade*, 1985.

Smartt, Vaughn. "1919: The Interstate Expedition." *Constructor*, vol. LV, no. 8, August 1973.

Snyder, William P. "Walter Bedell Smith: Eisenhower's Chief of Staff." *Military Affairs*, January 1984.

Sullivan, John J. "The Botched Air Support of Operation Cobra." *Parameters*, March 1988.

"Supreme Headquarters." *After the Battle*, no. 84, 1994.

Tonkin, R. G. "I Grew Up with Eisenhower." *Saturday Evening Post*, May 3, 1952.

Villamor, Jesus A. "He Knew How to Take It." *American Legion Magazine*, September 16, 1960.

Vivian, James F., and Jean H. Vivian. "The Bonus March of 1932: The Role of Gen. George Van Horn Moseley." *Wisconsin Magazine of History*, autumn 1967.

Wade, Gary H. "World War II Division Commanders." *Military Review*, March 1986.

Weaver, John D. "Bonus March." *American Heritage*, June 1963.

Weigley, Russell F. "From the Normandy Beaches to Falaise-Argentan Pocket." *Military Review*, September 1990.

Weyand, Alexander M. "The Athletic Cadet Eisenhower." *Assembly*, spring 1968.

Wickman, John E. "Ike and 'the Great Truck Train'—1919." *Kansas History*, autumn 1990.

Williams, T. Harry. The 'Macs' and the 'Ikes': America's Two Military Traditions." *American Mercury*, October 1952.

Winton, Harold R. "The Battle of the Bulge." *Military Review*, December 1994–January 1995.

Woolley, William J. "Patton and the Concept of Mechanized Warfare." *Parameters*, autumn 1986.

Monographs

Berlin, Dr. Robert H. *U.S. Army World War II Corps Commanders: A Composite Biography*. Fort Leavenworth, Kans.: Combat Studies Institute, 1989.

Dodd, Gladys. *The Religious Background of the Eisenhower Family*. N.p., n.d.

Gabel, Christopher R. *The Lorraine Campaign: An Overview, September–December 1994*. Fort Leavenworth, Kans.: Combat Studies Institute, 1985.

General Eisenhower on the Military Churchill: A Conversation with Alistair Cooke. Script of ABC television documentary, George C. Marshall Library, 1967.

Partin, John W., ed. *A Brief History of Fort Leavenworth, 1827–1983*. Fort Leavenworth, Kans.: Combat Studies Institute, 1983.

Dissertations

Miller, Robert A. "The United States Army During the 1930's." Princeton University Ph.D., thesis, April 1973.

Acknowledgments

I owe an immense debt of gratitude to the staff of the Eisenhower Library, Abilene, Kansas. Director Dan Holt and assistant director Martin M. Teasley were instrumental in facilitating my research. Archivists Thomas Branigar and James W. Leyerzapf shared their encyclopedic knowledge, answered countless questions, and made my research immeasurably more rewarding. The indefatigable Tom Branigar also does volunteer work at the Dickinson County Historical Society, where he also assisted with my research about Abilene and the Eisenhowers. My thanks also to Kim Barbieri and Stacy Mueli, the director's secretary, librarian Dwight Strandberg, and audiovisual archivist Kathleen A. Struss for assistance with the photographs.

I am deeply indebted to John S. D. Eisenhower, who has not only lent his support to the writing of this book but graciously offered his incomparable perceptions and insights and filled in many blanks in the life of his father. Both John and his wife, Joanne, went out of their way to make me feel welcome in their home. My sincere thanks to Susan Eisenhower, who assisted with questions regarding her grandmother Mamie Doud Eisenhower.

Special thanks to the Mashpee (Massachusetts) Public Library, where director Helene Defoe and librarian Gerda Sano cheerfully and efficiently handled my numerous requests for interlibrary loans, photocopies, and hard-to-find books. Thanks also to Jill Erickson and Kathy Mortenson, reference librarians, and Toni Robertson, head of the Inter-Library Loan Department, Falmouth Public Library, Falmouth, Massachusetts, for their advice and assistance. Over the years they have all played a very special part in each of my books.

The archives and special collections of the United States Military Academy, West Point, New York are a particularly rich source of material on Eisenhower. My thanks to Suzanne Christoff, Susan Lintelmann, Judith Sibley, and Alan Aimone, assistant librarian for special collections.

The library and archives of the U.S. Army Military History Institute, Carlisle Barracks, Pennsylvania, are a rich and valued source of military history. I am once again greatly appreciative of the wonderful support rendered by MHI's dedicated staff: archivist-historian Dr. Richard J. Sommers; the wizard of the archives, David A. Keough; my friend and now retired chief librarian, John J. Slonaker; Louise Arnold-Friend; and the entire staff of the USAMHI. Thanks to all of you.

Once again, historian Roger Cirillo, my close friend and colleague, generously shared his extraordinary knowledge of military history and World War II. Roger also read and commented on portions of the manuscript. My debt of gratitude is beyond measure. Thanks also to Dr. Daun Van Ee, who kindly read and critiqued the opening chapters; my friend the historian and biographer Geoffrey Perret has been both a source of encouragement and assistance. My longtime friend Nigel Hamilton also read and offered enlightened advice on portions of the manuscript. Col. Cole Kingseed, USA, Ret., kindly provided a copy of his essay on Eisenhower and Gladys Dodd and their 1915 correspondence.

Historian David W. Hogan, Jr., U.S. Army Center of Military History, answered numerous questions and provided useful insights of the Battle of the Bulge. Thanks also to my friend and personal physician, Dr. William E. Litterer, for medical advice; and to Steve Jones for his assistance with Jake Devers. I am particularly grateful to Bedell Smith's biographer D. K. R. Crosswell, for his unique perspective of SHAEF and for sharing his knowledge of Eisenhower and Smith with me.

Thanks also to: Tim Nenninger and Mitchell Yokelson at National Archives II; the librarian and staff of the Kreitzberg Library, Norwich University, Northfield, Vermont; the staff of the Boston Public Library; James C. Roach and Carol Hegeman of the Eisenhower National Historic Site, Gettysburg; Donna Hunt, Texas Parks and Wildlife Department, Eisenhower Birthplace, Denison, Texas; James W. Zobel, archivist, MacArthur Memorial Archives, Norfolk, Virginia; Thomas F. Burdett, curator, S. L. A. Marshall Military History Collection, University of Texas at El Paso; and the staff of the George C. Marshall Research Library, Lexington, Virginia, and the Marshall Foundation: president Albert J. Beveridge III, library director Thomas E. Camden and his fine staff, Larry I. Bland, editor of the Marshall Papers, and, at VMI, my friend Dr. Bruce Vandervort, editor, *The Journal of Military History*.

Also: Colin F. Baxter, David Bennett, George Colburn, Anthony Colvin, Dr. Clayton Laurie, Dr. Jeffrey Clarke, Terry Hammond, the late Lt. Gen. Sir Ian Jacob, Steve Jones, David McCullough, G. Patrick Murray, Paul J. Pugliese, who did a superb job drawing the maps, Richard F. Reidy, Suzanne Conklin Sexton, and Barbara Sonnenmoser, Reference Librarian, Combined Arms Library, Command & General Staff College, Fort Leavenworth, Kansas.

At Henry Holt and Company, my sincere thanks to editor Jack Macrae, who first suggested I write this book, and his talented assistant, Katy Hope. My copy editor Susan H. Llewellyn has once again worked her magic during our third collaboration. No author could be better served than to have the best in the business in his corner. Special thanks to my friend and agent, Michael Congdon, for his enlightened advice and wise counsel. My wife, Shirley Ann, has been a tower of strength and a loving presence. As always, any mistakes of fact or interpretation in *Eisenhower* are my sole responsibility.

Index

Entries in *italics* refer to maps.

British ommand disputes, after Bulge, 662–71, 674–78
broad front stalls in autumn, 625–36
broad vs. narrow front and single comm and debates with Montgomery, 594–98, 601–9, 623–24, 662–64
command and strategy debate at Maastricht conference, 633–36
command dispute with Montgomery resolved, 677–78
crimes by armed forces during, 628–29
German assassination attempt on, 650–51
logistics problems, 630–31
Malta disputes and near resignation, 674–78
Market-Garden and, 611–19, 624
moves headquarters to Versailles, 619–20
Strasbourg and de Gaulle, 664–66
press, 416–17, 487–88, 599–600, 679
in Britain WW II, 320–22
Darlan Deal criticized by, 357
Louisiana war games and, 278–79
Mamie and, 312
Montgomery and Bulge, 656, 664
Normandy campaign and, 555–56, 566
Patton and, 506–7, 438–41
Tiger debacle training accident, 516
promotions
Clark's to brigadier general, 275–76
lack of in 1930s, 203–4
Marshall says he won't get, 301–3
to captain, 119
to brigadier general, 281–82
to first lieutenant, 112
to full colonel, 269–70
to general, 4 star, 389–90
to general, 5 star, 639
to lieutenant colonel, 240
to major, 150–51
to major general in Regular Army, 457
to major general, Marshall and, 303
to temporary lieutenant colonel, 128
to temporary major, 128
relationships
with Alexander, 406, 411, 413, 414
with Baruch, 215
with Bradley, 402–3, 642
with Brooke, 338–39, 684
with Butcher, 212–13
with Churchill, 309, 328–33, 337–38, 427–28, 467–68, 565–66, 693–94
with Clark, 251–53
with Cunningham, 430–31
with de Gaulle, 344, 521–22, 542–43, 576–77, 664–66
with FDR, 427, 462–63, 467
with Gerow, 98
with Ismay, 327
with Hodgson, 64
with King, 296–97
with MacArthur, stormy, 225–33, 238–40,

246, 251, 253–55
with Mountbatten, 327
with Parks, 131
relationship with Marshall, 285–87, 301–303, 304–5, 309, 341–42, 386–87, 406, 410–11, 414, 511, 553–54, 599–601, 605–7, 622–24, 655–58, 677–78
first meeting, 198–202
second encounter, 261–62
relationship with Patton, 400, 402–3, 488–91, 631–32
advance into Germany and, 685
Bulge and, 645–46, 654, 659
deteriorates in Sicilian campaign, 433–34
friendship begun in Tank Corps, 145–55
friendship renewed in Washington, 212
Ike and Patton compared, 81
incident on eve of D-Day and, 506–9
philosophical differences over tactics, 182–83
slapping incident and, 438–42
relationship with Kay Summersby, 323–25, 365, 387–89, 419–21, 480, 489, 544, 631, 680
first meets, 303–4
loneliness in North Africa, 419–21
romances
dating in high school, 42–43
dating in West Point, 77–78, 79
with Gladys Harding, 85–90, 97–98
Sicilian campaign (Husky)
British officers and, 406–14
Corkscrew and, 429–31
directs Husky, 431–38
disembarks on Sicilian soil, 434
Egypt vacation ordered by Marshall, 464–65
French and planning of Husky, 417–19
Husky planned, in North Africa, 421–28
Italian campaign and, 445–60, 468–69
Italian surrender and, 445–46
popularity of, increases, 443
staff and entourage in, 417–18
Tunisian victory and, 415–16
speeches and memos
first, to Young Men's Democratic Club, 54
4th of July in London, 319
to troops, begun at Camp Colt, 132
writing for Payne and Hurley, 208–9
writing for Quezon, 239
War Department between wars
assists MacArthur, 216, 217–24, 226–33
assists Moseley, 203–6
assists Payne, 208–9, 210–11
assists War Policies Commission, 1930, 205–8
Bonus March and, 218–24
with MacArthur during first FDR administration, 214–17
on MacArthur, 224
mobilization work, 204–6, 209, 228, 285

Panama tour strains marriage, 164–67, 170–71, 173–74
Pearl Harbor and, 282
personality and influence of, 111–12
Philippines and, 232–33, 241–43, 248, 255
pistol and, 113
reunited with Ike before Overlord, 477–81
rides in tank, 134
smoking, 103
in Washington between wars, 188, 209–12, 217, 221
in Washington during WW II, 287, 295, 307, 310–14, 323, 346, 417
Eisenhower, Milton (brother), 14, 58, 86, 191, 213, 216, 270, 284, 287, 322, 325–26, 358, 480
birth of, 31
bond with Ike, 51, 187–88, 210
childhood of, 23, 29–34, 43
Mamie and, 105
marriage to Helen, 187–88
personality of, 36, 51
Eisenhower, Paul (brother), birth and death of, 30, 33
Eisenhower, Rebecca (grandmother), 21
Eisenhower, Rev. Jacob (grandfather), 10–11, 14–15, 17, 19, 21, 22, 30, 34
Eisenhower, Roy (brother), 22–23, 30–31, 36, 297
death of, 298
Eisenhower, Susan (granddaughter), 109, 115, 544
Eisenhower Brothers store, 19, 20
Eisenhower Center (childhood home), 28
Eisenhower Presidential Library (Abilene), 19
El Alamein battle of, 357
Elbe River, 673, 699
Allied forces halted at, 688–95
El Guettar victory, 399, 402
Elsenborn Ridge, 608, 658
Embrick, Stanley D., 236
Endacott, Earl, 89
Engle, Naomi, 298
"Enlisted Reserve for the Regular Army, An" (War College paper), 192
Enola Gay (airplane), 346
Ethiopia, invasion of, 235
Etna Line, 437
European Advisory Commission (EAC), 690, 691
Execution of Private Slovik, The (Huie), 629

Faid Pass, 391, 393
Falaise Gap, Battle of, 568–71, 578–81
Farago, Ladislas, 579
Far East, 299
Farnsworth, Maj. Gen. Charles S., 152, 154, 176
Fedala fighting, 355
Federal Emergency Relief Administration (FERA), 230
Ferrell, Robert H., 71, 112, 235, 251
First Casualty, The (Knightley), 320–22

First Allied Airborne Army (FAAA), 610–12, 613
First U.S. Army Group (FUSAG, fictitious), 505, 547
Fitzgerald, F. Scott, 124
"Fledgling at Fifty" (reminiscence), 244
Foggia airfield, capture, 459
Fort Benning
Ike at, 137–38, 185–86
Marshall and, 200–201
Patton at, 263
Fort Douaumont (France), 195
Fortitude South (deception operation), 504–6, 537, 545, 566
Fort Leavenworth, Army Service School, 122, 124. *See also* Command and General Staff School
Fort Lewis, 260–65, 268–70
Fort Oglethorpe, 121–22, 124
Fort Ord (Camp Ord), 262
Fort Sam Houston, 94–98, 217
Mexican revolution and, 115–16
provost marshal at, 113
France. *See also* Vichy government
Allied plans to invade (*see also* cross-Channel invasion; Overlord; Sledgehammer), 289
Battle of Tunisia and, 360
Britain vs., 336, 343–44
Darlan Deal infuriates, 354–55
D-Day and, 512, 529, 535
de Gaulle and Mediterranean campaign, 417–19
Germany invades, 263, 265
North African invasion and, 343–45, 347–48
Ike and, 356
Ike spends year in after WW I, 192–96
Riviera landings, 567–68 (*See also* Anvil/Dragoon)
WW I and, 116, 117, 125, 132
WW II declares war on Germany, 250
Frank, Maj. Gen. Walter H., 341, 342
Frankfurt gap, 602
Franz Ferdinand, Archduke of Austria, 116
Fredendall, Maj. Gen. Lloyd R., 306, 342, 351, 355, 362–63, 367, 376, 391–400
Frederick the Great, 168
Free French movement, 418, 498, 542, 576
French First Army, 567
French 2nd Armored Division, 575
French Committee of National Liberation (FNCL), 418–19, 521
French North Africa, 360. *See also* North African campaign *and specific colonies*
French Resistance, 372, 529, 574
Freyberg, Gen. Sir Bernard, 408–9
Friedeburg, Adm. Hans-Georg von, 700–3
Frost, Lt. Col. John, 616–17
Fuller, 152, 155
Funston, Maj. Gen. Frederick, 97, 104

Gaeta, Bay of, 447
Gale, Lt. Gen. Sir Humfrey, 606

About the Author

CARLO D'ESTE, a retired U.S. Army lieutenant colonel and a distinguished military historian, is the author of four highly praised books on World War II and a biography of General George S. Patton.